1 MONTH OF
FREE
READING

at
www.ForgottenBooks.com

By purchasing this book you are eligible for one month membership to ForgottenBooks.com, giving you unlimited access to our entire collection of over 1,000,000 titles via our web site and mobile apps.

To claim your free month visit:
www.forgottenbooks.com/free650329

ISBN 978-0-483-33604-9
PIBN 10650329

This book is a reproduction of an important historical work. Forgotten Books uses
state-of-the-art technology to digitally reconstruct the work, preserving the original format
whilst repairing imperfections present in the aged copy. In rare cases, an imperfection in
the original, such as a blemish or missing page, may be replicated in our edition. We do,
however, repair the vast majority of imperfections successfully; any imperfections that
remain are intentionally left to preserve the state of such historical works.

THE

EDINBURGH REVIEW,

OR

CRITICAL JOURNAL,

FOR

APRIL AND JULY, 1842.

JUDEX DAMNATUR CUM NOCENS ABSOLVITUR.

PUBLIUS SYRIUS.

VOLUME LXXV.

AMERICAN EDITION.

NEW YORK:

PUBLISHED BY JOSEPH MASON,

102 BROADWAY, BETWEEN WALL AND PINE STREETS.

1842.

EDINBURGH REVIEW,

OR

CRITICAL JOURNAL

FOR

APRIL AND JULY, 1842.

VOLUME LXXV.

AMERICAN EDITION.

NEW YORK:
PUBLISHED BY JOSEPH MASON.

INDEX TO VOL. LXXV.

THE

EDINBURGH REVIEW.

No. CLI.

FOR APRIL, 1842.

ART. I.—*Die Deutschen Voelker Persoenlich betrachtet.*—(*The German Nations considered as Individuals.* 2 vols. 8vo. Tubingen: 1841.

THE local nature of the work which we have prefixed to this article, has led the writer into details comparatively uninteresting to a British public; but the subject which he has partially treated is one of great and advancing interest. We agree with him, that the great and permanent bodies which now constitute nations, have assumed, in their mutual relations, an individual character; and that while, under the influence of their increasing intercourse, the mere external peculiarities of the inhabitants of different countries are becoming obliterated, peculiarities in the public conduct of those countries are becoming more marked. The manners of an Englishman and a Frenchman differed much more in the seventeenth century than they do at present. But the conduct of the two countries as nations, their behaviour towards each other, and towards other independent communities, was then much more governed by similar causes than it is now. In fact, until within a very short period, the conduct of a nation, as a nation, depended principally on the accident of the character of the king, or of the minister. A succession of warlike kings made Denmark a military power; a succession of quiet half-witted sovereigns reduced her to political nullity. Under Richelieu, France

was intriguing and ambitious; under Fleury, she was careless and pacific. But now, that in almost every country the people interfere in public affairs, often direct them, and almost always influence them, the conduct of a nation must always be affected, and often is governed, by the general disposition of the millions who constitute it: it becomes a permanent reflection of the national character, and is tinged with all the peculiarities with which climate, race, religion, institutions, and past history, have coloured that character. In former times, the conduct of a nation could be best predicted by considering the feelings and habits of the individuals who presided over its councils. The principal elements of such a calculation are now drawn from the character of the people itself. Our ancestors at one time feared the ambition of Louis, and at another relied on the courage of Frederic. *We* dread the ambition of France, and rely on the prudence of Prussia.

The most remarkable exceptions to this rule are to be found in Russia and Austria. The conduct of each of these empires has often appeared to depend on the peculiarities of an individual. The death of Alexander, and the succession of Nicholas, altered the whole tone of Russian politics—they are still affected by the personal dislike of Nicholas to Louis Philippe; and the prudent and pacific behaviour of Austria is mainly attributable to the wisdom of Metternich. But this is accounted for when we recollect, that Russia and Austria are the empires least affected by the popular voice. In both of them, as far as foreign relations are concerned, the people are nothing—the government is everything. On the other hand, in the three great countries which enjoy the most popular institutions—the British Empire, France, and the United States of America—the character of the government for the time being has, under ordinary circumstances, little influence on the public conduct of the nation. A vain, or a rash, or a litigious, or a procrastinating minister, may indeed bring either of them into difficulty; but if the nation do not share his faults, he will be driven from power, and a successor appointed for the express purpose of retracing his steps. Of course, we do not mean to affirm that the public conduct of any of these communities is uninfluenced by the personal qualities of the statesmen for the time being in power; especially if those qualities are, as was lately the case in France, and perhaps in the United States, an exaggeration of the national peculiarities; but we affirm that those qualities, though not positively, are comparatively unimportant. In short, that whereas formerly the character of the minister determined the conduct of the nation, now the character of the nation determines the conduct of the minister.

For the purpose both of estimating the future prospects of the civilized world, and of deciding what ought to be the course of our own policy, it is therefore important to consider what are the characteristics by which these three great powers are distinguished in their public conduct towards other civilized states; in order that we may ascertain the chances of peace, and the means by which it may be promoted—and the chances of war, and the means by which it may be averted. We use the words 'public conduct,' because it is only as respects their public conduct that nations can be treated as persons. The enterprises of individuals, unsanctioned by their government, do not commit the nation. It is the duty, of course, of every government to do all that it can to prevent any of its subjects from injuring those of other governments in person or in property; but its public character is not affected by aggressions, though made by its own subjects, if it do not directly or indirectly sanction them, either by conniving while they are planned and executed, or by allowing the perpetrators to remain unpunished. In fact, for the purposes of this discussion, we identify nations with their governments. It is possible that if the opinion of the people of England could have been taken, it would have been found unfavourable to our treatment of Denmark in

1807, and again in 1813. It is possible, nay, it is probable, that the majority of the people of France may have disapproved of the invasions of Spain by Napoleon and by Louis; and that they may now disapprove of the intrigues with which their diplomacy is harassing her. But a nation, when considered as an individual, must be judged by her acts; and her act is what is done in her name, and by her authority. We should be grieved, indeed, if the majority of educated Englishmen, or the majority of educated Frenchmen, could act as their respective governments have acted. We use the words 'towards other civilized states,' first, because that part only of the public conduct of a nation affects the practical questions which we are considering; and secondly, because unhappily such is public morality, that the mode in which a nation treats barbarians, or even semi-barbarians, is no evidence of the mode in which it would be likely to treat a civilized community. In estimating the public character of France, therefore, we do not advert to her relations with the African tribes; and in estimating that of America, we do not allude to her treatment of the Indians. In estimating that of England, we shut our eyes to all that she has done in Hindostan or Cabul.

The qualities which principally mark the conduct of a nation, in its intercourse with other civilized nations, are pride, vanity—using that word to signify the desire of admiration—ambition, fear, resentment, sympathy, and justice; and the influence of these motives depends partly on the degree in which they are felt, and partly on the causes from which they originate. Different nations may be equally vain, but one may desire to be admired for her power, another for her civilisation, and a third for her integrity; and others are to be found who, like Austria, seem utterly careless as to the opinions of foreigners. Again, two nations may be both timid; but one may fear the evils of defeat, the other the evils of victory. One, surrounded by more powerful neighbours, may be in constant dread of invasion; the other may feel that her comparative force secures her from attack, but that a war, though it be successful, will ruin her finances. Under such circumstances, timidity would lead the former to contract alliances, in order to secure herself from aggression; the other to avoid them, in order to lessen the chances of being dragged by her treaties into a contest.

We now proceed to consider in detail the public character of the three great nations which we have mentioned, beginning with France.

The circumstances under which France has been placed, have been, in most respects, eminently unfavourable. Until the Revolution, the French people had no influence on the policy of their country. It was dependent sometimes on the will of a king, sometimes on the intrigues of a court, and sometimes on the caprice of a mistress. A dispute between Louis XIV. and Louvois, about a window, occasioned the devastation of the Palatinate. A well-timed visit by Horace Walpole to Fleury, rendered France for twenty years the ally of England. It was the casting voice of Madame de Maintenon that decided whether France should violate or respect the treaty which excluded the Bourbons from the Spanish succession. At length the power which the crown had abused for centuries, passed to the demagogues, whose influence depended on their popularity, and whose popularity could be maintained only by satisfying the desires, or flattering the prejudices, of the new sovereign—the people. From their hands it was extorted by a soldier more intent on conquest, and more unscrupulous as to the means of obtaining it, than any of the public enemies with whom Europe has had to struggle since the times of Attila. The great object of Napoleon was to seduce the people, by gratifying the passions which are strongest amongst uneducated politicians—vanity and ambition. His talents, his habits, and his inclination, led him to offer military glory to the one, an extension of territory to the other. Never were these intoxicating bribes so profusely supplied. Of course, for this purpose all treaties, all engagements, all faith, and all law, public and private, were to be disregarded. On no other condition could the empire of the French be stretched from the Vistula to the Guadalquivir. It was his business, therefore, while he inflamed and perverted their ambition, to stifle their feelings of morality and justice. In both attempts he was equally successful. His boast, that millions joined in his views, was, unhappily for those millions, well founded. The misfortunes of the latter portion of his career, though not quite so mischievous to the national character as his earlier successes, still helped to deteriorate it. He taught the French to submit to defeat. He taught them to welcome humiliation;—to receive with acclamation sovereigns twice forced on them by foreigners. The degradation of the early period of the Restoration, was followed by still more corrupting successes. The government of the Bourbons has wanted only power to teach lessons as demoralizing as those of the Empire. The invasion of Spain, in 1822, was as fraudu-lent, as unjust, and as rapacious as that of 1808. The only difference was, that Napoleon endeavoured to render Spain a dependency of France, under his brother; and Louis to throw her bound under the feet of 'a descendant of Henry the Fourth.' In fact, of the two pieces of injustice, monstrous as they both were, the last was the more oppressive; for Napoleon came as a reformer—his success might have regenerated Spain. The Duke of Angoulême was the restorer of tyranny.

We will now consider the national character which has grown up under such influences. If the picture be unfavourable, no one will be surprised when he reflects on the education which the nation has received.

Among the most striking qualities of France is her pride. One of her most acute and most philosophical statesmen has proclaimed from the tribune, that pride, nourished by the victories and triumphs of more than two hundred years of war, is now 'the only remaining link that keeps her in a social state.[*] We should differ from M. de Tocqueville with great diffidence, whatever the subject were, and as to the character of his own country we yield implicitly to his authority. But though military pride be the absorbing sentiment, not merely the ruling but the despotic passion of France, her glories in war are not the only objects on which she dwells with complacency. She is proud also of her power, of her influence, and of her civilisation. Her power is formidable, but it is probably not superior to that of Russia; it certainly is inferior to that of Germany when Germany can be combined. She believes it to be a match for all Europe. Her influence is considerable; but she believes that all the nations between her frontier and the Rhine are anxious to be incorporated in her dominions. It is fortunate for France, as well as for Europe, that she has had no opportunity of ascertaining the truth of this opinion. Her civilisation is great: she believes that it is unrivalled. She is certainly eminent in war, in literature, and in the fine arts; but in education, in morality, in wealth, in the ordinary arts of life—in short, in all that contributes to the welfare of the mass of the people, the bulk of the population of France is far inferior to that of Holland, of Belgium, of Switzerland, of Great Britain, and of the greater part of Germany.

In the midst, however, of this overweening self-estimation, she seems always beset by doubts as to the reality of the grounds on

---

* Speech of M. de Tocqueville in the Chamber of Deputies, 30th Nov. 1840.

which it is founded. Proud as she is of her glory and of her power, she cannot forget that at sea she has been unsuccessful for centuries, and that on land her defeats have been as signal as her victories. She cannot but perceive, that while all Europe is advancing, her own population is almost stationary; her agriculture declining, and her commerce bearing every year a less proportion to that of her neighbours: that while Belgium, Germany, and England, are becoming intersected by a network of canals and railroads, her own internal communications almost resemble those of Spain. She is restlessly anxious, therefore, to support her claims by the suffrage of her neighbours, and in constant fear that the verdict may be against her. She is as vain as sensitive to the sentiments of others, as if, like Russia, she were struggling to emerge from barbarism. All her conduct has reference, not so much to its effects on her own happiness, as to the opinions of the world around her. To induce her to make railroads, she is told that her national honour requires them.* To induce her to continue the fortification of Paris, she is told that London and Vienna will illuminate if she abandon it. With an inconsistency, not uncommon where vanity is the prevailing passion, she, at the same time, believes herself to be the object of general admiration, and is always watching to detect and punish an insult. She quarrels with her old allies the Swiss, obstructs their commerce, and threatens their independence, because the Diet has complained, as she thinks, too bluntly, that she has sent a spy with a fabricated passport into their territory. She conquers Algiers, because the Dey has been rude to her consul. She threatens all Europe, arms half a million of men, and is inclined to arm half a million more, because she has received, according to her own account, not an injury, or even an insult, but an act of discourtesy. She has all the arrogance of a giant, and all the susceptibility of a dwarf.

Another prominent part of her character is her ambition. She desires not happiness, but power; and aims at increasing that power, not by the improvement of her own resources, but by appropriating those of others. She still clings to the barbarous doctrine of the middle ages, that a nation becomes great, not by the growth of its own population, the increase of its own capital, and the improvement of its agriculture and manufactures, but either by seizing the territory and incorporating the subjects of its neighbours, or by

obtaining a preponderating influence over their councils. As far as she can, she proposes to extend herself by conquest; and where that is impossible, she strives, by treaties, by intermarriages, by promoting dissensions between states, and factions, party spirit, and civil war in each separate community, to create occasions for her interference, and the means of establishing or confirming her influence.

We lament to add, that she is checked by no feeling of justice, of faith, or of public morality. She does not even pay to virtue the homage of hypocrisy. She avows that a solemn treaty of peace is a truce to be broken by her as soon as it suits what she supposes to be her interest. She proclaims the right of every nation to manage its own affairs; and invades Spain, because the Spaniards have required a constitution from their despot. She fears that her influence may decline in Italy, and to restore it, seizes, in profound peace, on Ancona. She wishes for another island in the Mediterranean, and proposes to rob Spain of Majorca. She guarantees the integrity of the Ottoman Empire, and threatens war if she is not allowed to dismember it.

All these aggressive propensities she supports by fearless daring. 'La France,' said Chateaubriand, 'est un soldat.' She has the virtues as well as the vices of that unsocial profession. No nation is so little deterred by the dread of war; none supports its actual presence with more intrepidity. In every other civilized country the preservation of peace is held the great duty of a statesman: in France, M. Thiers could say, that he trusted he should not be considered very culpable for having occasioned the probability of war. In what other country could a statesman have declared, that, rather than that the Eastern Question should be settled without French intervention, or that France should be supposed to be unprepared for war, or that, on a matter which she had agreed to arrange in concert with other powers, she should be required to acquiesce in the unanimous decision of all the other parties to the agreement—rather than accept any one of these alternatives, he would plunge into a thousand wars? Yet such were the words of de Tocqueville. In fact, France thinks that she has nothing to fear from war. All her best colonies she surrendered long ago; and it is no slight set-off against the expense of a contest, that it would set her free from Algiers. Her continental territory is too compact, and her population is too homogeneous, for partition, and her own laws, in a great measure, exclude her from commerce.

---

* See the able Report of M. de Beaumont, No. 168.—1840.

On the other hand, she fancies that she has much to gain. She is anxious to extend her territory to the limits which, because she thinks them convenient, she calls natural. She burns to wipe from her arms the disgrace which she thinks was inflicted on them by the calamitous termination of the imperial wars. And, above all, she is anxious to punish those whose resistance occasioned those wars to terminate in her defeat, and to weaken those whose power overbalances her own.

And yet the boldness with which she meets danger is joined to a remarkable tendency to fear it where none exists. With the largest army, the strongest fortifications, the most compact frontier, and the most warlike population in Europe, she is as apprehensive of being attacked, invaded, and overrun, as if she possessed only the scattered and assailable territory of Prussia or Austria. She is spirited; but her spirit is like that of a high fed horse, always looking for something to start at, and heedless of the real danger into which it rushes to escape an imaginary one.

This constant state of anxiety and apprehension, so strange in a brave, powerful, and proud nation, may appear to be in part explicable by her vivid recollection of the calamities of 1814 and 1815; yet, while this restless fear of attack is peculiar, among the great nations, to France, there is not a country on the continent that has not been forced, during the present century, to conclude an unsuccessful war by a disgraceful peace. There is scarcely a capital that has not been occupied by an enemy. If the mere recollection of former misfortunes necessarily inspired a dread of their recurrence, every nation on the continent would share the fears of France.

We believe the real causes of the constant anxiety of France to be two. First, the consciousness of her own plans, and a tendency to believe that other nations are as rapacious and as unscrupulous as herself. She knows that nothing but despair of success prevents her from seizing on Belgium, on Rhenish Prussia, on the Bavarian Palatinate, on Switzerland, on Savoy; in short, on every territory which it would suit her convenience to usurp, and she naturally imputes corresponding feelings to her neighbours.

And secondly, she knows that she is an object of fear and of dislike to every people and to every sovereign around her. She knows that the despotic monarchs hate the freedom, such as it is, of her institutions—her trial by jury, her constitutional rights, her open debates, her licentious press; and above all, the example of an elected king. She may suppose them willing to follow the precedent of her own conduct towards Spain, and to occupy her territory in order to enable Henry V. to give to his subjects institutions which they cannot hold except from him.* She knows that both sovereigns and people regard her as a hostile camp, threatening them with the evils of war, and inflicting upon them those of an armed peace. They impute to her the stoppage of public works, the absorption of capital, the commercial disturbance, the pressure of taxation and military service, and the financial derangements which are the necessary consequences of that unsettled state. In believing that they would gladly see her weakened, France is right. But in fearing that, while she leaves them unattacked, they will attack her; in believing that there is a possibility of her being the object of an aggressive war, she is grossly deceived. There is not a country in Europe, except France, mad enough to engage voluntarily in war. In many of them, and among them are England and Austria, the public income is annually deficient; and those which have avoided a deficit, find their present expenditure pressing hard on their revenues. Again, there is not a single great country which could rely in time of war on the zealous co-operation of its whole population; or indeed which would not dread to find a portion of them among its enemies. Russia is vulnerable in Poland; Prussia in her Rhenish provinces; Sweden in Norway; England in Ireland, in Canada, and in Hindostan; and Austria consists of four nations, accidentally united under one head, but with scarcely more coherence than that which existed between England and Hanover. Can it be supposed that governments in such a situation, financial and political, would voluntarily incur the certain evils, and the uncertain but not less formidable risks, of war?

Among the qualities on which France prides herself is her sympathy. It was to be expected that a nation so susceptible of impressions would take a lively interest in the fortunes of her neighbours. And such an interest she certainly does take; but, with the exception of the first American war—and even there more is to be attributed to her hatred of England than to her sympathy with America—we do not recollect a case in which her sympathy has led her to make any sacrifice for the benefit of those on whose side her feelings were engaged. She has al-

---

* See the Speech of Louis XVIII., 28th January, 1823.

ways expressed a strong interest in the welfare of Poland. In 1806, and again in 1812, she might have restored Poland to nationality and independence. She half promised that she would do so; but, on consideration, she doubted whether she herself should be a gainer, and she refused. Another of her *protégés* has been Spain. For the greater part of the last century the two nations were in the closest alliance. The friendship of Spain has been rewarded during the present century by a succession of injuries and insults, such as one nation scarcely ever endured from another.

We shall conclude our view of the character of France, by some remarks on the mode in which she is influenced by resentment. In all generous natures—we might almost say, among all well-instructed persons,—resentment is felt only where there is a feeling of injustice. None but a child, and an ill-educated child, beats the ground on which it has fallen. Only the lowest criminal reviles the judge, for merely pronouncing the sentence of the law. A generous man admires the courage and skill that are opposed to him. He puts himself, from time to time, into the place of his adversary, and sympathizes with qualities which he hopes that, under similar circumstances, he would himself exhibit. And even a man deficient in generosity and virtue, though he may pursue his schemes of aggrandisement or avarice without regard to the rights of others—though he may be careless of the misery which their prosecution occasions—seldom retains, unless he be thoroughly uneducated, deliberate resentment against those who have offered to him what he feels to be a legitimate resistance. He may be an unfair judge as to the resistance which is legitimate. He may be indifferent to the suffering which he inflicts in order to crush or to intimidate his opponent; but, unless he can persuade himself that he has been unfairly treated, his anger ceases with the contest. Now, as individuals, Frenchmen are generous; in the Peninsular war the French troops treated the English, not only without animosity, but with as much forbearance and even kindness as was consistent with their hostile relation. But these qualities vanish when France feels and acts as a nation. She seems to consider all opposition to her wishes as an insult, and all actual resistance, whether just or unjust, as a crime; and she transmits an inheritance of hatred from one generation to another. Who would have supposed that in 1840, Waterloo and even Aboukir were unforgiven?

We now proceed to America. The char-

acteristic in which she most resembles France is pride. It is, however, less excessive and better directed. The pride of America dwells principally on her institutions, on the general wealth and intelligence of her population, on her rapid rise, and above all, on her vast prospects. These are more legitimate sources of self-esteem than most of those dwelt on by France; and America errs much less than France in her estimate of her own superiority. We certainly see much to disapprove in the institutions of America; we fear that they were better fitted to her earlier than to her present condition; and we fear that these defects are becoming more dangerous every day: but still, with the exception of our own, we know of no great country whose institutions we prefer; and we doubt whether there is one of our readers who would not rather be an Anglo-American, than a Frenchman, a Spaniard, an Austrian, a Russian, or even a Prussian.

Again, we may think that she boasts too much of the happiness and intelligence of her people. We may taunt her with her three millions of slaves, and with the mobs of her towns, and the ruffians of her borders. But no great community must be judged by its least fortunate portions. Ireland is not a sample of the British islands, nor Connaught of Ireland. And, after making all the deductions from the general average prosperity which are required by the vices and miseries of a comparatively small portion, we must admit, that the fourteen millions of Anglo-Americans form a community enjoying more comfort and more intelligence than any other equally numerous population. The rapidity of growth on which America dwells with so much complacency, is a statistical fact supported by unquestionable evidence. The reasonableness of her anticipations of further and proportionate advance, is of course a fair subject of controversy. If her numerous States, differing as they do in many respects as to their institutions, their feelings, and their interests, should preserve their union; if neither war, nor faction, nor resistance to taxation, should destroy their credit, and arrest the improvement of their vast but imperfectly subdued territories—if slavery be gradually extinguished, or confined within limits much narrower than those over which it now extends—if all these contingencies turn out in her favour, the progress of America may be as rapid and as great as she anticipates. Those who are now living may see her possessing a hundred millions of people, irresistible in her own hemisphere, and a match for all that could be opposed to her in ours. But has she a right to assume, as she uniformly does, that all these chances *will* turn out in her favour? Is not a contrary supposition possible as to all, and probable as to some? And to what extent, in the event of any one or more of these chances turning against her, is her progress likely to be stopped or retarded? These are questions which it would require a volume to discuss; we suggest them as indicating the grounds on which we think that America is open to the reproof, that she over-estimates her future prospects, bright and even dazzling as those prospects certainly are.

The vanity of America is notorious; and yet, subject to one exception, we doubt whether it much influences her conduct as a nation. She is so much accustomed to self-adulation, that she does not value the moderate applause which is to be obtained from other nations; and she has so perfect a reliance on her own wisdom and virtue, that their disapprobation excites her pity for their ignorance. Few of her public acts can be traced to her desire to obtain the admiration of foreigners, or to avoid their censure. But to this general statement there is, as has been remarked, one exception. There is a nation by whom America is anxious to be esteemed—or, to speak more correctly, to be admired and feared—and that is England. She takes the opinion of England from sources utterly undeserving of credit. She reads what is read by none of the well-instructed classes in England—the trash of the Ultra-Tory newspapers; believes that a hired editor speaks the opinions of a party in the state instead of those of a party in the shareholders of a Journal; and then fancies that she is undervalued in England—that we do not appreciate her power, that we are careless of her friendship, and almost indifferent to her hostility. And she thinks that by assuming a bold, or even a threatening tone towards England, she will obtain our respect, and perhaps alarm our prudence. These views are wrong from beginning to end. England thinks highly of America. She disapproves, indeed, of many of her institutions, and so do the most intelligent portion of the Americans. A highly-accomplished candidate for the Presidency comes forward as the proposer of wide organic changes.* England admires her energy, her perseverance, her courage, her skill—in short, she admires a character naturally, we may say necessarily, in many respects resembling her own. There is no country with whom she is so de-

sirous to keep on good terms, and certainly none with whom she would so much dread a war. And with ample reason. No two countries are so useful to one another in peace, or could do one another so much mischief in war; with the additional misfortune, that all the damage the one inflicted on the other would recoil on herself. On the other hand, England is naturally intolerant of all faults which differ from her own. She is so little accustomed to swagger or to bully, that she views such exhibitions from others with a mixture of surprise and disapprobation. What America means for spirit, England sometimes considers rudeness or rusticity. When America thinks that she must be admired for the courage with which she vindicates her rights, England wonders that she should think it worth her while to quarrel about trifles. If America cared less about the opinion of England, or did not look for it in the columns of newspapers, or knew better how our respect is to be obtained—if she knew that the virtues which we most prize are equity, integrity, and moderation, she would have avoided some of her disputes with us, and diminished the length and the danger of some others.

Compared with most other nations, America is not ambitious. She desires, indeed, to increase her power, but rather by the increase of her wealth and the spread of her population over the vast wilderness of which she is the undisputed owner, than by the extension of her influence or the enlargement of her territory. We have already stated, that we do not consider as parts of the public conduct of a nation the unauthorised enterprises of a portion of the community. The invasion of Texas, the attacks on the Canadian frontier, and, generally speaking, the encroachments from Maine on the disputed territory, were acts of this kind. They were private speculations for the purpose of individual gain. That they were not more effectually repressed by the American government is a proof of its weakness, and shows deep-seated defects in her institutions; but it is no proof of ambition.

In fact, if America were as ambitious as France, she would by this time, unless previously dismembered by an unsuccessful war, have reduced the greater part of the western hemisphere to direct dependence on her power, or to subservience to her influence. What resistance could Uraguay, or Colombia, or Buenos Ayres, or Peru, or Chili, or even Mexico or Brazil, have opposed to her arms, or, if she pre-

* See General Scott's Address, 1841.

ferred that weapon, to her intrigues? How easy, again, would it have been for her, if she had so thought fit, to mix in European politics—to require, for instance, to be heard on the Eastern Question, and to urge her pretensions by hinting the value of her maritime co-operation? That she has resisted these temptations, is fortunate for her immediate happiness and for her eventual greatness. It has enabled her to employ, as the elements of future wealth and power, resources which other nations have wasted in armaments and demonstrations. Yet if the American people had been deeply infected by the madness of ambition, no good sense on the part of their rulers would have been able to restrain them.

But though America is less ambitious of territorial aggrandizement than most other great nations, she is much more so than in her peculiar situation is wise. In reality, all such ambition on her part is folly. Her present territory is too large; the dispersion, not the concentration of her population, is her great obstacle and her great danger. And yet it was with difficulty, and only in obedience to the religious feelings of the northern abolitionists, that she abstained from adding Texas to the Union. By a mixture of violence, intimidation, and bribery, she half purchased and half extorted Florida from Spain. We doubt whether, if Canada were to offer herself, she would be refused. We doubt whether, if Canada were to throw off her connection with England, America would willingly allow her to exist as an independent republic. The ambition of America, though not great *positively*, is, relatively to her real interests, excessive.

The public conduct of America is little influenced by fear, perhaps not enough to give her prudence. She has twice maintained a war against the most powerful nation in the world. At the time of her first war, her population and her wealth were less than one-fifth of their present amount—at the time of her second war, they were less than one-half; and she came out of the first war with triumph, and out of the second without defeat. It is natural that now, with her resources doubled, she should believe herself invincible. She does not recollect—few nations do recollect such lessons—that in both these wars there were periods of extreme peril. Nor does she sufficiently bear in mind that her increase in population, while it has increased her power, has

materially increased her dangers. The vast states constituting the Union, most of them as large, and many of them as populous, as the average of an European kingdom, do not submit readily to the central authority, even in peace. From year to year the north, the south, and the west are becoming more dissimilar in their feelings, in their occupations, and in what they believe to be their interests. It is true that war might consolidate them. But is it not equally true, and is it not much more probable, that war might separate them? Again, her revenue is deficient. The last act of Congress was an expedient which seldom succeeds even in effecting its immediate objects, and which, whether it so succeed or not, always inflicts great and permanent evils on the community which is forced to adopt it—a general increase of import duties. Where would a war budget be found for a country reduced to such an extremity in peace? In fact, America has nothing to gain by war, and everything to lose. Her last war gave her as much glory by land and by sea as she can wish for; and the extension of her territory would, as we have already remarked, be an evil. All the results of the most successful war would be to throw her twenty-five years back. But the effects of a prolonged and calamitous contest are not to be told, perhaps not all to be foreseen. ΕΥΡΗΣΕΙ ΤΑ ΣΑΘΡΑ ΤΩΝ ΕΚΕΙΝΗΣ ΠΡΑΓΜΑΤΩΝ ΑΥΤΟΣ Ο ΠΟΛΕΜΟΣ. The south would lose her market, the north her commerce, the currency would fall to assignats; neither the federal union, nor even the freedom of many of the states, would be secure. All this, of course, is seen on that side of the water even more clearly than on this. And we have no doubt that, if the destinies of America were ruled by the same classes as those which govern in England, her prudence would be equal to our own. But, unfortunately, the suffrage, and, to a great extent, the real government of the Union, is vested in classes comparatively uneducated; and likely, on every occasion, to miscalculate the danger of a struggle, or the worth of a dispute. Party spirit and misrepresentation, acting on electors ill fitted to estimate the merits of international questions, might return a House of Assembly pledged to measures as ruinous to themselves as to their neighbours.

The public morality of America, considering how low is the general standard of public morality, deserves comparative praise. We have already remarked her comparative exemption from the great cause of national immorality—ambition. She is wise enough to make few treaties, and honest enough to keep them. Perhaps the least defensible part of her conduct is her behaviour towards Spain—a country which, after having in her day of power systematically disregarded justice and even mercy, seems now destined, by what may appear to be a just retribution, to suffer wrongs almost equal to those which she formerly inflicted. The occupation of Pensacola and St. Augustine, its avowal by President Monroe, and its sanction by Congress, are precedents which America would gladly obliterate. Her great moral fault is her litigiousness. She is always ready to stand on her extreme rights, and to refuse to allow a legal claim to be equitably arranged. We shall show, in a future portion of this article, that it is to this defect in the American public character, and to a defect of an opposite kind in our own, that the unhappy disputes between the two countries are principally owing. We are inclined to ascribe this quality, as well as her want of prudence, to the defect in her institutions which we have already pointed out—the preponderating influence of the comparatively uneducated portion of the people. The great cause of litigiousness is an inability to compare the certain costs of the contest with the value of the chance of obtaining the disputed object. In proportion only as a man is educated, is he able to enter into this calculation, and willing to act according to its results. Sir Walter Scott has well represented his shrewd and amiable, but uncultivated Dandie Dinmont, as willing to peril in a suit for a few acres of barren moor, ten times or twenty times their value. Precisely similar was the conduct of America in rejecting the award of the King of the Netherlands on the boundary Question. She could not pretend that there was any loss of honour in complying with the decision of a tribunal which she had joined in selecting; and every intelligent American must know, that the commercial loss occasioned during one year by the insecurity which the dispute occasioned, is worth twice as much as the difference between the value of the territory which she claims, and that which the award gave to her.

America has little sympathy. To use the words of one of her most distinguished statesmen,—'She contemplates the wars that drench Europe in blood, as a calm, if not a cold and indifferent spectator.'[*] She pays, of course, more attention to the affairs of her own hemisphere; but so far, and so far only, as they directly affect her own immediate interest. It is difficult to blame or even to regret the indifference of America, when we recollect what have been the effects of what is called national sympathy. When a nation wishes to weaken a rival, or to dismember and seize the territory, or to subjugate the councils, of a neighbour, the pretext is always a generous sympathy with some enemy of the rival, or with some party, or perhaps some province or dependency of the neighbour. Sympathy with Mehemet Ali and Egypt was the pretext of France when she wished to partition Turkey; sympathy with Ferdinand and with the noble Spanish nation, a prey to a knot of conspirators, was her pretext for destroying Spanish liberty in 1822. It was out of sympathy that Prussia, Russia, and Austria first protected one portion of the Polish nation against another, and then appropriated the whole. Sympathy sometimes for an oppressed people, sometimes for an injured ally, sometimes for an excluded successor, has gradually attracted the English dominion from the Ganges to the Tigris, and from Cape Comorin to Thibet. Perhaps America may be too apathetic. It seems to us probable—though from our imperfect knowledge we speak with great diffidence—that if she had interposed her advice and her mediation, she might have been able to diminish the anarchy and war which have laid waste almost every state between her frontier and Cape Horn; and we cannot but think, that if she had felt more for the sufferings of Africa, she would have given more co-operation to our efforts to prevent her flag from covering the slave-trade. But we repeat that, with respect to a passion so liable to excess, we ought to deal very leniently with what we may consider a deficiency.

In regard to the angry passions, America is certainly irritable. She is apt to take offence where no insult was intended; and to consider herself injured when the treatment which she applies to third parties is adopted towards herself. It is possible that this sensitiveness may be connected with her national growth, and with the change which every year makes in her relative position. Between thirty

---

[*] See Mr. Clay's Speech on the Emancipation of South America, March 24, 1818.

and forty years ago, the period at which most of those who are now her principal statesmen received their political education, America was weak, and was supposed to be much weaker than she really was; and she was treated as weak powers always have been treated, and always will be treated, until the tone of public morality has been materially improved. In the fierce struggle between France and England, her rights were disregarded by both parties. Now that she is one of the great empires of the world, with only one civilized nation superior to her in territory, and only four superior to her in population, she ought to feel how improbable it is that any other power will wantonly offend her. She ought to exhibit, and we trust that she will exhibit, the magnanimous candour and forbearance of conscious strength. But though America is irritable, she does not bear malice—a defeat does not rankle in her mind as a subject of revenge at the distance of half a century.

The last nation whose character we have to consider, is England—using the word England as a concise appellation for the nation inhabiting the British islands. We shall endeavour to perform the task fairly, though aware of the great difficulty of preserving real impartiality on the subject, and of the danger, perhaps we might say the certainty, that the portrait, if it be really impartial, will be unpopular. England has always been accused of pride. That she estimates herself very highly is obvious; and she would be a strange exception in the history of nations, if she did not in some respects overrate both her positive and her relative advantages. She is proud of her power, of her wealth, of her glory in arms, of her institutions, and of her civilisation. In the two first points we do not believe that she is guilty of exaggeration. Indeed, both her power and her wealth are generally estimated more highly by foreign statesmen than by her own. Her military and naval triumphs she may probably overrate; but not dangerously to herself or offensively to her neighbours. Nor can she be said to be too proud of her institutions, when we see that, with the exception of monarchy, there is not one in which large portions of the community do not demand fundamental changes. Her civilisation she does over-estimate. She is not sufficient-

ly aware of the misery and degradation of numerous classes of her inhabitants. She is only beginning to find how far she is behind-hand in architecture, in painting, in sculpture; in short, in almost all the fine arts. She does not know how inferior her education is to that of many parts of America and of Continental Europe. She does not see how much they have advanced while she has remained stationary, or proceeded more slowly. Still less does she perceive the evil, or the unchristian spirit, of the intolerance which separates her numerous religious sects. But with all these errors—and they are very great—we are inclined to think that she approaches more nearly to correct self-estimation than either of the two nations to which we have compared her.

Pride has generally been supposed to be inconsistent with vanity. It is certain that the same person seldom exhibits both on the same subject. To be the object of admiration is pleasing, partly in itself, and partly as an evidence of the possession of certain qualities; and, in both cases, the pleasure depends greatly on our estimate of the admirer. As all estimation is relative, the higher we place ourselves the lower we must place all others, and the lower must be our value for their opinion. It follows that a person who thinks very highly of himself is generally careless of the opinions of others; he does not want their evidence, and he considers them as his inferiors. England, therefore, believing herself to be clearly the first nation in the world, is naturally indifferent to the testimony of others to a truth which she holds to be obvious.

One important consequence is, that the foreign affairs of England seldom attract the attention of the nation. All that the people require from the minister is, that he keep them at peace. He need not fear of being accused at home of wanting spirit or wanting enterprise; they do not require him to feed the national vanity by restless endeavours to extend the influence and exhibit the superiority of the country. They demand no premature expositions of the progress of his negotiations. The policy of England is thus exempted from many misdirecting influences. She is not, like France, always acting a part. There is no danger of her wasting millions, merely to show to Europe that she has millions to waste. What she does, she does because she thinks it right and expedient; not because it will create a certain impression abroad, or even at home. This is a great advantage. It gives to the policy of England a consistency which is one of its most remarkable, and one of its most useful characteristics. But, like most advantages, it has its corresponding inconveniences.

With the exception of the Germanic and Swiss Diets, and the American Congress, which possess limited powers, and a mere local jurisdiction, there is no court to which independent states can appeal. Two checks only exist which can prevent one nation from pursuing, to the injury of the rights and of the welfare of another, the course which, after calculating all its risks, she thinks it would be for her own interest to adopt. These are—her respect for public opinion, and her sense of justice. It is obvious, that in proportion to a nation's value for the opinion of others, will be the force of the former check. It is true, that in the defective state of public morality, to which we have often referred, this check is always weak, and often inoperative. It is even true, that where the vanity of a nation is thoroughly ill-placed, that very vanity may misdirect her conduct. She may covet admiration for her spirit or her power, at the expense of her virtue. The feeling of France is an example; but this is an extreme case. Bad as nations are, they generally desire to be thought generous, or at least equitable. Such is the desire of England, so far as she feels any solicitude as to her character abroad. In proportion, therefore, to the slightness of that solicitude, is the slightness of one of the two checks to her misconduct.

The same state of feeling has a tendency to weaken the other check—her sense of justice. A candid man engaged in a dispute, though he may feel certain, as he considers each individual point, that he is right, seldom ventures to act on his own unaided judgment. He is aware that it is fallible, that it must be biassed by his interests and his prejudices, and that it is improbable that he has given due weight to all the reasoning of his opponent. If the matter is serious, therefore, he asks the advice of his friends. If it be likely to lead to a lawsuit, which is almost equivalent to a war among nations, he takes the opinion of counsel. As far as he can, he avoids being judge in his own cause. A man who neglects these precautions is arrogant; for it must be recollected that arrogance does not imply intentional injustice. Indeed, an arrogant man generally believes himself to be a model of impartiality and forbearance; and the more firmly he believes this, the more probable it is that he is mistaken—the more sure he is that he must always be right, the more likely it is that he will frequently be wrong. Now a nation is much more exposed to this danger than an individual. She has no friends to consult, no tribunal to resort to. There is one mode, and one mode only, by which she can correct the necessary partiality of her own views of her own conduct; and that is, by ascertaining the impression which it produces on third parties._ If she neglect this corrective, and if her force should be such as generally to enable her to carry her designs into execution, it is scarcely possible that her pride should not sometimes degenerate into arrogance, and her arrogance impel her to injustice.

From these accusations we cannot declare England free. Those who examine her conduct and her correspondence during the last fifty years, will find cases in which she has assumed a tone which she would not have endured if used towards herself; cases in which she has stretched the right of a belligerent to the utmost verge of the letter of that harsh law, and far beyond its spirit; cases in which she has disregarded the letter of international law, where it interferes with what she deems, very justly, a great and laudable object of her own; and cases where she has set at defiance both the letter and spirit of that law, because it suited her own convenience to do so. The more serious part of this charge will be considered when we treat of her character as a belligerent; but her endeavours to suppress the African slave trade afford a useful illustration of the degree to which she has sometimes allowed the end to justify the means.

During the eight years which have elapsed between the prohibition of that trade by England and the United States, and the general peace, and especially in the latter part of that period, its suppression was easy. England was entitled as a belligerent to visit and search the vessels of every country; and in fact scarcely a flag ever appeared in the African seas unless it were English, or flying by the permission of England. But it was believed, and subsequent events have fully justified the belief, that the feelings of

England with respect to the slave-trade would meet with weak sympathy in the rest of Europe ; that as soon as peace rendered the ocean again the common property of all mankind, it would again be used for the purposes of the slave-trade ; and that the vacancy occasioned by the secession of England and America from the trade would be instantly filled up, and much more than filled up. To prevent this, England inserted in her first treaty of peace with France, a treaty, signed only a few weeks after the entry of the Allies into Paris, an engagement on the part of France to endeavour to induce all other Christian powers to discontinue the trade, and a positive promise that France herself would terminate it within five years. She obtained from America an agreement to use her best endeavours to procure its general abolition. She obtained from the powers constituting the Congress of Vienna, a declaration that the trade is repugnant to public morality, and ought to be abolished ; ‘ but not without a just regard to the interest, the habits, and the prejudices of their subjects.’ And her definitive treaty with France, that of Nov. 1815, contained a recital that each of the contracting powers had, in their respective dominions, prohibited without restriction, their colonies and subjects from taking any part whatever in the traffic. These were vague stipulations, and the proposal of the Duke of Wellington, that they should be enforced by a maritime police, authorized to ascertain acts of slave-trading by visitation and search, was rejected.

In fact, with the exception of England and the Netherlands, few of the European nations possessing colonies appear to have been in earnest. They were ready to denounce the trade as inhuman; but they would take no active measures to suppress it, or even give any cordial support to such measures when taken by England. The recital in the French treaty was a positive falsehood. France had not, at the date of the treaty, prohibited her subjects from taking part in the traffic. She did not legislate on the subject until the year 1817, and even then the prohibition was partial. It prohibited the importation of slaves into the French colonies, but left her subjects at liberty to prosecute the carrier slave-trade to any extent which they might think proper. England, in the mean time, acted as if the Duke of Wellington’s proposal, instead of having been decidedly rejected, had been conceded. She authorised her cruisers

to seize *all vessels* prosecuting the African slave trade.* In obedience to these instructions, a British cruiser, on the 11th of March, 1816, attempted to visit a French vessel apparently engaged in the slave trade, was resisted, attacked her, captured her after an action in which twenty men were killed and wounded on the British side alone, sent her into Sierra Leone, and obtained her condemnation in the provincial Court of Admiralty. The French owners appealed to the High Court of Admiralty, then presided over by Sir William Scott. We extract a portion of the reasoning on which he reversed the decision of the Inferior Court, and decreed restitution of the ship :—‘ It is said that every nation has a right to enforce its own laws, and so it has, so far as it does not interfere with the rights of others : it has no right to visit or search the apparent vessels of other countries on the high seas, in order to institute an inquiry whether they are not in truth British vessels violating British laws. No such right has ever been claimed, nor can it be exercised without oppressing and harassing the lawful navigation of other countries ; for the right of search, when it exists, is universal, and will extend to the vessels of other countries, whether employed in slave-trading or in any other act. It is no objection to say that British ships may thus elude the obligations of British law. If even the question were reduced to this, that all British ships should fraudulently escape, or all foreign ships be injuriously harassed, Great Britain could not claim to embrace the latter alternative—You have no right to prevent a suspected injustice to another, by committing an actual injustice of your own. It is said, if this be not permitted, it will be extremely difficult to suppress the traffic. It will be so ; but the difficulty of the attainment will not legalise measures otherwise illegal. To press forward to a great principle by breaking through every other great principle that stands in the way—to force the liberation of Africa by trampling on the independence of Europe ; in short, to procure an eminent good by means that are unlawful, is as little consonant to private morality as to public justice. A nation is not justified in assuming rights that do not be·

---

* See the instructions given to the British cruiser *Caroline*, dated the 28th January, 1816. Published in the Appendix to the case of the *Louis*.—2. Dodson’s Admiralty Reports.

long to her merely, because she means to apply them to a laudable purpose ; nor in setting up a moral crusade of converting other nations by acts of unlawful force."*

The arguments òf Sir William Scott proved that England was required, by expediency, and even by justice, either to abandon her attempts to suppress the foreign slave trade, or to obtain the acquiescence of foreign nations in her treatment of their subjects. A few months after, in 1817, she purchased from Spain, at the price of £400,000, a treaty by which a right of visitation and search was given to the government vessels of each country, to be exercised in the merchant vessels of the other, ' when suspected, upon reasonable grounds, of having slaves on board, acquired by an illicit traffic.' Earnest endeavours were made to obtain a similar concession, if concession it could be called, from France. But when the Duke of Wellington made thè proposal at the Congress of Verona, the answer of France was more than a mere negative. She not merely rejected the proposal, but added, that ' if ever it should be adopted, it would have the most disastrous consequences: the national character of the two people, French and English, forbids it.' In the mean time the French slave-trade was flourishing. It was weakly repressed by the government ; and, we regret to add, that it was viewed by the people with little disapprobation. It appeared to them a means of acquiring and improving the great objects proposed to their ambition by Napoleon—ships, colonies, and commerce. They believed it to have been one of the foundations of the commercial prosperity of England, and ascribed her efforts for its suppression to her national jealousy. The English cruisers, sometimes from mistake, and sometimes from an indignation with which it is impossible to avoid sympathising, continued from time to time to interrupt it. One of the most remarkable instances was that of three French vessels, the *Vigilante,* the *Betsey,* and the *Ursule,* which were discovered in the river Bonny laden with more than nine hundred slaves, attacked by the boats of an English squadron, captured after a severe action, the slaves liberated, and the ships carried as prizes into . Portsmouth and Plymouth.

The Revolution of 1830, however, pro-

duced one of those periods of excitement during which France desires to be admired for something better than power and military glory. She was anxious for the approbation and for the support of England, and the result was the Convention of 1831, giving a mutual right of visitation and search. From that time the flag of France has disappeared from the slave-trade; and the change has been effected without any of the disastrous consequences predicted by the Government of the Restoration. Scarcely a complaint has been made by any merchant belonging to either nation of any improper proceeding under the treaty.

At length Portugal was the only European state with which no satisfactory arrangement had been made. In 1815, she had undertaken immediately to confine the slave-trade to the supply of slaves to her own possessions in the Brazils, and eventually to abolish it entirely ; and she agreed to permit a right of visitation and search north of the Line. For this treaty England paid to her L.600,000. The Brazils separated from her, and prohibited the trade. We required Portugal to fulfil the treaty, to prohibit her subjects from engaging in the slave-trade, and to make the prohibition effectual by conceding to us a more extended right to visit and search slave-trading vessels bearing her flag, and to send them to an admiralty court, constituted of Portuguese and English judges, for adjudication. She refused ; and the natural consequence was, that the trade was carried on to an enormous extent, both by Portuguese vessels and by vessels assuming her flag.

The determined refusal of Portugal to fulfil her engagement was a lawful cause of war, since, in the present state of the world, war is the only sanction by which nations having no common superior can compel adherence to treaties. Instead, however, of proceeding to this extremity, England pursued a course harsher than even war in appearance, principally from its unusualness ; but which had the effect of producing all the result that war could have effected, and of effecting it without the previous suffering. The 2d. and 3d. Victoria, cap. 73, was passed, which after reciting that her Majesty had been pleased to issue orders to her cruisers to capture Portuguese vessels engaged in the slave-trade, enacts, that it shall be lawful to detain, seize, and capture every such vessel, and to bring the same for adjudication into any British court of admiralty, as if

---

* The *Louis.*—2. Dodson, 210.

the vessel were British; and that it shall be lawful for any British admiralty court to condemn such vessel: That every such vessel shall be liable to seizure, detention, and condemnation, if there be found in her equipment more water-casks, mess-tubs, matting, or provisions than might probably be wanted for the use of the crew; or certain other articles—such as shackles, handcuffs, or planks for a slave-deck, which are used only in slave-trading; And lastly, that such vessel shall be taken into her Majesty's service, or broken up.

In the mean time, England had made treaties for the suppression of the slave-trade, giving mutual right of visitation and search with all the states of the western hemisphere except the United States; or, as we have usually termed that government in this article, America. .

Our readers are probably aware, that all questions connected with the right of visitation and search, or with slavery, are sore subjects in America. The Northern States, forming the seafaring portion of the Union, suffered so severely from the conduct of both the belligerents during the war, that they associate with the idea of a right of search, that of insolence and oppression; and they have professed doctrines relating to it which are repudiated by England, and are not those of the existing law of nations, but which they do not wish either to retract or to press. On the other hand, the Southern States, though caring less about maritime law, are anxious to stifle every discussion having a reference, however remote, to slavery. They know that the Northern States are opposed to that institution on political, on moral, and on religious grounds, and that they urge their opposition with the uncompromising, we had almost said, the unscrupulous vehemence, which is peculiar to a religious question. Yet the inhabitants of the South believe slavery to be essential to their existence. They believe that its abolition would devote the Whites to massacre, and even the Blacks to destruction, by civil war, intemperance, and famine. Knowing that discussion with their northern brethren only widens the breach and exasperates the disputants, they strive to keep the whole subject of slavery, and everything connected with it, out of sight; and, though they are opposed to the African slave-trade, their sense of its enormity is weakened by their familiarity with their own internal slave-trade between state and state, and by their recollection of the period when they or their fathers were dealers in imported negroes.

When we add to the difficulties occasioned by this state of feeling, the litigious, irritable, and suspicious character of America, we cannot wonder at the ill success of our attempts to obtain her full co-operation in the suppression of the trade. At first, indeed, the business appeared to be easy. It was not necessary, as it has been in France, to educate the public mind, and to convince the people that an immoral trade ought to be abandoned, even if it were a profitable one. We had not to complain of the inefficacy of her laws, or the corruption or unwillingness of her tribunals. America preceded us in the abolition of the trade, and enforced that abolition in her own courts as honestly as we did. In the addresses presented to the Crown by both Houses of Parliament in 1821, earnestly entreating his Majesty to renew his efforts to obtain the co-operation of France, the conduct of America is referred to as a model to ourselves, and as a ground for exulting in our common origin. But as we gradually deprived the slave-traders of the use of other flags, they endeavoured to usurp that of America. America did not think fit to incur the expense of maintaining a maritime police for their detection. We had the police, and requested to be allowed to employ it. And then began the discussions as to visitation and search, which still remain unconcluded. In 1821, a committee of the House of Representatives reported, that a mutual right of search was indispensable to the abolition of the trade. But the President, Mr. Monroe, refused to admit any negotiation on the subject. In 1822, a committee of the Senate concurred in the opinion which had been expressed by the House of Representatives, and earnestly recommended its being acted upon. 'Not doubting,' to use their own words, 'that the people of America have the intelligence to distinguish between the right of searching a vessel on the high seas in time of war, claimed by some belligerents, and the mutual, restricted, and peaceful concession by treaty suggested by your committee, and which is demanded in the name of suffering humanity.' The President either doubted the intelligence attributed by the Committee to his countrymen, or wanted that intelligence himself; for he continued his opposition to the opinion and recommendation of both branches of the Legislature. In 1824, however, his scruples had been overcome. A treaty-giving to the armed vessels of each country a right to board and examine vessels bearing the flag of the other, on suspicion of their being engaged in the slave-trade, and to send them, if the suspicion appeared to be well founded, to their native tribunals for adjudication, was signed by the plenipotentiaries of England and America. But, in the mean time, the Senate had changed its mind, or, in the intricacies of American politics, thought it convenient to differ from the executive. It refused to ratify the treaty. And thus the matter stands. Each branch of the Legislature has separately accepted the measure, but only when it was refused by the other.

In the mean time, the British cruisers appear to have acted pretty much as they would have done, if the right of visitation and search, instead of having been refused, had been conceded. They felt that, if a vessel by merely hoisting American colours protected herself from inquiry, no slaver would sail without a stock of such flags, and all the declarations and laws of Europe and America against slave-trading, would become waste paper. When a vessel under suspicious circumstances displayed the American flag, they visited her for the purpose of ascertaining whether she were entitled to bear it. If she proved to be a slave-trader, and could show no plausible claim to be considered an American, they dealt with her according to her real character. But if there were any grounds for believing her to be American, they sometimes dismissed her, and sometimes carried her across the Atlantic, to be proceeded against in the American courts.

The conduct of the American government was marked by the indecision and inconsistency which belongs to all men who have assumed a principle which they are ashamed to abandon, and yet are ashamed to push to its legitimate consequences. Whenever a lawful American trader was visited and searched by a British cruiser, they complained that their flag had been violated. They announced 'their determination, that the flag of the United States should be the safeguard of all those who sail under it.* That they would never consent to their vessels being boarded or searched, however qualified or restricted the right might be,† or under whatever pretence done; especially as the United States have not the means of carrying out a maritime police and *surveillance;* * and that these continued violations of the flag of the United States, under whatever colour or pretence, cannot be longer permitted.'† In this view of the case, the offence against America was the boarding of a vessel which thought fit to display her flag; and that offence was complete, that flag was violated, whether the vessel bearing American colours were or were not a slave-trader, or were or were not an American. America, however, never whispered a complaint against our capturing Spanish or French vessels, though sailing under American colours. She made no complaint, indeed, of our having captured and sent into her ports American vessels, or vessels supposed to be American, when found actually engaged in slave-trading. Instead of doing so, she requested the captors to remain at New York in order to give evidence. Her naval officers even entered into agreements with ours as to the mode in which our cruisers should deal with vessels bearing her flag. We subjoin a convention for that purpose, which may now be in force in the African seas:—

'Commander William Tucker, of her Britannic Majesty's sloop "Wolverine," and senior officer west coast of Africa, and Lieutenant John S. Paine, commanding the United States' schooner "Grampus," in order to carry into execution as far as possible the orders and views of their respective governments respecting the suppression of the slave trade, *hereby request each other, and agree to detain all vessels under American colours, found to be fully equipped for, and engaged in, the slave trade;* that, if found to be American property, they shall be handed over to the United States' schooner "Grampus," or any other American cruiser; and if found to be Spanish, Portuguese, Brazilian, or English property, to any of her Britannic Majesty's cruisers employed on the west coast of Africa for the suppression of the slave-trade, so far as their respective treaties and laws will permit.

'Signed and exchanged at Sierra Leone, this 11th day of March, 1840.

(Signed)   'WILLIAM TUCKER,
'Commander of her Britannic Majesty's ship "Wolverine,"
       and Senior Officer west coast of Africa.

(Signed) 'JOHN S. PAINE, Lieutenant,
'Commanding the U. S. schooner "Grampus."'‡

---

* See Mr. Stevenson's Letter, February 5, 1840, Class 8, Farther Series, p. 40.
† Mr. Stevenson's Letter of the 17th February, 1840, ibid. p. 44.

* Mr. Stevenson's Letter of the 13th November, 1840, Class D, p. 93.
† Mr. Stevenson's Letter of the 13th November, 1840, Class D, p. 85.
‡ Slave-Trade Correspondence, 1840, Class D. p. 76.

In this unsatisfactory, we may say absurd state, the question rests. In practice America allows that we may visit and search vessels bearing her flag; but in theory she forbids it. When, in compliance with the practice, we search and detect a slaver bearing her flag, she makes no remonstrance; but if the vessel searched turn out to be a fair trader—a fact which nothing but the search itself can ascertain—she complains of that search as a national offence. And thus, between the refusal of America to adopt principles of equity, and that of England to abide by those of law, the embers of a national quarrel have been lighted, which it will require all the wisdom and temper of Lord Aberdeen, Lord Ashburton, Mr. Webster, and Mr. Everett, to extinguish.

If it were not for the human suffering that would ensue, the easiest mode of getting out of the difficulty would be for us to admit the force of her arguments, and to direct our cruisers to abstain from violating the American flag—that is, to abstain from visiting any vessel that should display it. Of course, it would be immediately hoisted by every vessel—French, English, Spanish, or Portuguese—that thought fit to engage in this most lucrative of traffics. America admits that 'she has not the means of carrying out a maritime police and *surveillance.*' The African seas would swarm with slavers; every one bearing the American flag, and every one assured by that flag of impunity. The execration of mankind, and, not least, that of the people of the United States, would show to the American government the necessity of abandoning a position, in which her only companion, out of the whole civilized world, is Portugal.

As a really practicable solution, we venture to suggest that England should direct her cruisers to visit no vessel showing the American flag, unless convinced that she assumes it fraudulently; and that America should accept, as a sufficient excuse where an American vessel has been visited, a declaration on the part of the visiting-officer, that he visited her in the belief that she was *not* American. However sensitive American honour may be, it can scarcely be wounded by an involuntary mistake.

One consequence would be, that America would be obliged to increase the force which she maintains in the African seas. It is now so trifling—consisting, we believe, of a single schooner—that it is utterly inadequate to carrying her own laws against her own subjects into execution; and while the American minister in London was declaring, that under no pretext whatsoever should an American vessel be searched or even visited, the American commander at Sierra Leone was requesting the British commander to detain all vessels under the American flag equipped for the slave-trade!

And we trust that a further and far more beneficial consequence would be, that she would join with England in a really earnest endeavour to destroy the slave markets of Brazil, Cuba, and Porto-Rico. We agree with Mr. Forsyth and Sir Fowell Buxton in believing, that while those markets exist little good is effected by capturing slavers on the African coast. The influence of America in those countries far exceeds that of any other nation. That it has not been exerted for the purpose of suppressing the slave-trade is, as we have already remarked, a stain on the American character.

If the conduct of Portugal, France, America, and England, on the subject of the slave-trade, were submitted to the judgment of an impartial spectator, he must visit that of Portugal with unqualified disapprobation. He would probably treat the earlier conduct of France with nearly equal censure, and admit her behaviour in 1831 to be an imperfect atonement. He would lament that America should have allowed her party squabbles, her jealousy, and her litigiousness, to destroy her sense of humanity, her sympathy for Africa, and her respect for the example and for the public opinion of Europe. He would admire the self-devotion with which England has encountered offence, misrepresentation, expenditure of treasure and of life, and even the chances of war, in the hope of preventing evils with which she is acquainted only by report, and of civilizing, or at least improving, nations of which she scarcely knows the names. He might doubt whether the means adopted were wise. He might know, indeed, that their failure has been most complete and most calamitous; but he could not deny their generosity. We fear, however, that he must admit that the censure passed by Sir William Scott on her conduct, at its first beginning, has been in some measure deserved during its subsequent progress; and that, in her eagerness to liberate Africa, she has not always respected the independence of Europe.

England has often been considered ambitious. We admit that in India she has been so; and we believe that such was the inevitable result of her position. A civilized and powerful government, surrounded by semi-barbarous powers, too ignorant to be restrained by fear, and too faithless to be bound by treaty, is always forced by their aggressions to resist, to subdue, to reduce to vassalage, and finally to dismember and absorb them. But we have already expressed our intention to avoid this portion of the conduct of the nations whom we are endeavouring to characterize; since, in their treatment of barbarians, all nations act pretty nearly alike. Our business with England is not as an Asiatic, but as an European power; and as an European power we believe her to be eminently free from ambition. She feels, of course, the wish for power which is instinctive in every human being, and therefore in every human community; but she desires it only as a consequence of her prosperity. She knows that her prosperity depends on the extension of her commerce, not of her territory or dependencies. She knows, by bitter experience, that all her acquisitions in India, in America, and in the West Indies, have tended only to render her poorer and more vulnerable; that they have tended to increase her expenditure and to diminish her income – the first, by the enormous advances necessary for their government and protection; the second, by the mischievous preferences given by her to their productions. She knows that Canada and the West Indies alone cost her three millions a-year in establishments; and more than three times that amount, when the public and the private loss is added, in differential duties. Consistently with this view, she rejected Sicily, and she would now reject Syria. For more than a century she had the power of incorporating Hanover; but she always cherished the hope of throwing it off, and eagerly embraced the opportunity when it came.

The difference between the policy of England and France is marked by their respective treatment of Algiers. They each had a quarrel with Algiers: they each subdued it with the ease with which, in the present state of the arts of war, a civilized power subdues a barbarous one; but England never proposed to retain it. An English minister would have been thought mad if he had seriously suggested such a proceeding. She merely required the Dey to release all Christian prisoners, and to abstain from piracy on any Christian vessels; and then left the country in the degree of independence in which she found it. France deposed the Dey, confiscated his treasures towards payment of the expenses of the war, seized his territory, in violation of an express engagement with England; and now, principally because she thinks she has been dared to do it, is striving to convert it into a province of France.

England is equally free from the other form of ambition—anxiety to increase and extend her influence. She desires no imperial or royal alliances. She does not harass her neighbours by intrigues, and labour to keep them torn by factions in order that they may be weak, and weak in order that they may be subservient. She knows that her own welfare is intimately connected with the welfare of her customers She knows, that in proportion to the wealth and the population of a country is its power of consuming her commodities, and of furnishing her with equivalents. She knows that the increase of wealth and population is best promoted by liberal institutions, and by internal and external tranquillity; and she is anxious, therefore, for her own sake, to see those blessings spread over the whole world. The extension of freedom and the preservation of peace are the sole objects of her foreign policy. Her motive may be selfish, but the result is as beneficial as if she were prompted by the purest cosmopolitan philanthropy.

With respect to fear, England approaches the mean between timidity and rashness. So far as she errs, it is on the side of rashness; and her rashness often arises from the carelessness as to the opinions of others, which we have already mentioned as one of her marked characteristics. She sometimes treats other nations in a mode which, if she had taken the trouble previously to ascertain their feelings, she would have found likely to be highly offensive; and she still more frequently neglects to appease by slight concessions an angry irrational antagonist. She feels sure that she is in the right, and rashly assumes that her opponent cannot be mad enough to urge an absurd complaint, or an absurd pretension to extremities. But she is far less rash than either America or France. For this there are several reasons. Like America, she has nothing to gain by a contest, and everything to lose; she wants no glory—she would reject any increase of territory.

The most successful war would merely leave her with an increased debt, an increased half-pay, and a diminished commerce. An unsuccessful war might lead her to national bankruptcy and revolution. She is aware that her power renders her an object of universal jealousy. From the nature of that power, and from the element on which it is most displayed, it is kept constantly before the eyes, not only of her neighbours, but of all mankind. The power of Russia and of France—the two nations that most nearly rival her, is known principally by report Their vast armies lie concealed within their own frontiers, and must be visited before their force can be ascertained. The power of England is seen on every sea—her vessels of war show themselves in every port. Again, France and Russia are immediately formidable only to the countries which adjoin them. The frontier of England adjoins that of every nation that possesses a sea-coast and a ship; her blows are felt in the first week of hostilities. A power so widely diffused, and capable of such instantaneous exertion, is necessarily an object of dread; and we doubt whether there is a nation in Europe—even among those which profit most by the mode in which it is employed—that would not rejoice to see it diminished; and, if a war gave them an opportunity, would not join to reduce it. Another circumstance, which would materially increase the danger of England in war, is the doctrine which she has maintained as to the rights of Belligerents against Neutrals. The right which she has been accustomed to claim, of seizing an enemy's property in a friend's vessel, has indeed been assumed by every nation when it believed that it could gain by so doing. It is admitted by every modern jurist to be a part of the law of nations, so far as nations can be said to have a law; but it is one which no philosopher can approve, and no neutral can willingly submit to. A war would force England to relinquish or to enforce it. To give it up at such a period, would be a loss and a degradation; to enforce it, might throw all the maritime powers on the side of her enemy.

Under the influence of these considerations, England is prudent; but if it be difficult to get her into a war, it is still more difficult to get her out of one. When once she is engaged, nothing but success or absolute inability to continue the strife will induce her to relinquish it. Neither England nor her enemy can hope that the contest will be short, unless it end, like the Syrian matter, by her immediate triumph. No early defeats, no failures, will break her spirit, unless they should be such as actually to destroy her strength. She will continue the fight with dogged determination, gradually accommodating her habits to it, and throwing always as much as possible of the burden on posterity, until the chances turn in her favour, or pure exhaustion forces her to yield. Such was the history of the last two great wars in which she has been engaged—the first American war, and the Revolutionary war. She continued the former for years after all probability of success was at an end, merely because she could not bear to acknowledge herself beaten. The latter she fought on from 1793 to 1812, (for what was called the peace of Amiens was a mere armed truce),—while ally after ally was conquered or had deserted her, while every year seemed only to increase her own debt and the power of her enemy,—in the firm expectation, though it is difficult to say on what ground, unless it were the personal character of Napoleon, that at length the tide would turn; and turn at length it did, but in consequence of events which she certainly had no right to anticipate. It is obvious that this pertinacity materially increases the dangers and prolongs the evils of war, both to England and to her enemy. The statesman, whether English or foreign, who engages her in hostility with a first-rate power—and no other would venture to cope with her—opens a historical period, of which neither the duration nor the event can be predicted.

The angry feelings of England are not so easily roused as those of America or France. She has not the touchiness of the one, or irritable suspiciousness of the other; but her merits in these respects are comparative, not positive. Indeed, such are the defects of every national character, that a critic has little to do except to apportion blame in different degrees The pride of England, and the tendency which we have already remarked to rely on her own view of every case, without enlightening herself by the opinion of others, often persuade her that she is insulted or injured, when an impartial bystander can see little ground for her complaint. The late case of McLeod affords an example. If America had attempted to inflict any punishment on McLeod, or even to detain him after the termination of his trial, whatever the verdict were, England would have been aggrieved, and would have righted herself, whatever the risk or the sacrifice   But she was not aggrieved by the conduct of America in making the matter the subject of a solemn judicial inquiry.   The slowness with which the inquiry proceeded was very painful to the accused ; the successful opposition of the local authorities to the view taken by the Federal Government, showed great defects in the institutions of America.   But McLeod voluntarily subjected himself to the influence of those institutions.   When he voluntarily entered the territory of New York, he knew, or must be held to have known, what were its laws, and he tacitly engaged to be govern- ed by them.   England has always refused to deviate from her laws on the requisition of a foreign power ; she ought not to have com- plained that America followed her example. And yet the general opinion in England was, and perhaps still is, that the trial of McLeod was an injury to be resented and redressed.

But if the resentment of England, like that of every other powerful nation, is too easily roused, it is placable and generous.   She readily admits terms of reconciliation.   She does not trample on a beaten enemy.   She does not brood vindictively over the events of a contest that has ended.   She does just- ice to the virtues of an opponent.   When Marshal Soult visited London, he was known only as a formidable enemy.   He had shown no peculiar courtesy or forbearance, and he was even suspected—though we firmly be- lieve the suspicion to have been unfounded— of having forced on a battle after he knew that the war had virtually terminated.   It might have been expected that he would be received with cold civility.   That he imme- diately became the idol of the multitude— that on the very day of the coronation he divided with the Queen their admiration and their applause—is one of the strongest proofs that could be given of the sympathy of a people with the courage and talent of an ad- versary.   It may be said, however, that Marshal Soult had been beaten, and that his reception would have been different if he had defeated us.   As neither the defeats of Eng- land, nor her visiters have been numerous, we are unable to find a case in point.   But no one, we think, will doubt what would be the result if General Jackson were now to land on our shores ;—the man who with un- disciplined militia, and in the midst of a slave population, ventured to resist the veterans of our Peninsular campaigns, who defeated them, and perhaps prevented us from partitioning his country, would be received by his old enemies with a popularity as great as that of Soult.

It might be supposed that a nation so in- tent as England on her domestic affairs, and so indifferent to the sympathy of others, would care little about the welfare of those around her.   The inference, however, would be erroneous.   No nation feels a livelier con- cern in the fortunes of her neighbours ; and her sympathy has operated at least as fre- quently to the injury of her own interests, as to their advancement.   Sympathy on the part of one portion of her population with the sufferings of the royal family and aristo- cracy of France, and on the part of another portion with the efforts of the French people to obtain free institutions, absorbed public attention throughout the British Islands— broke up and recomposed parties—severed long-established political friendships—invad- ed even the tranquillity of private life, and materially promoted the war, which, while it raised the glory and augmented the appa- rent power of England, inflicted on her inju- ries which will never be completely repair- ed.   Sympathy for Greece, rebelling against the oppression of Turkey, led to the ' un- toward,' we may say the unjustifiable, event of Navarino ;—led England to aid a rival against an ally, and to help in breaking down a power whom she has ever since been vainly endeavouring to protect and to invigorate. Sympathy for Africa has led England into a vast expenditure of money and of life, and into a complication of diplomacy, dictation, and interference, which has roused the hos- tility of the whole maritime world, and has induced nations which cannot appreciate, or even comprehend her motives, to ascribe to some unintelligible plan of aggrandizement, conduct which arises from disinterested be- nevolence.   If England had looked on the happiness or misery of others with the selfish indifference of America, many a bright page would have been wanting in her history, but much would have been added to her prosperity and to her power.

In considering the influence of pride on the conduct of England, we made some in- cidental remarks on her justice.   We pro- ceed now to give a more detailed view of that part of her character.   The subject is so extensive that it will be convenient to subdivide it—to treat separately her conduct in war and in peace ; and to subdivide the former branch into the consideration of her behaviour towards her enemies, towards her allies, and towards her neutrals.

In her treatment of enemies, the conduct of England has been, in some respects, better than that of most of her contemporaries ; but, we regret to say, that it has seldom risen above that low standard, and sometimes has even fallen below it.

Among the rights of war, the most undefined are the right to confiscate the property of individuals; the right to inflict damage which does not really weaken the enemy; the right to treat certain forms of resistance as crimes; and the right to partition a conquered country, and to dispose of its inhabitants without their consent.

With respect to the first of these rights, the rule differs at sea and on land. It is admitted—though on no principle that would not equally apply on land—that at sea the private property of an enemy may be seized. England has always acted upon this principle to its fullest extent, and so, indeed, has every nation when it had the power. Equity, perhaps, would require—if there were room for equity in such a matter—that some warning should be given; and that merchants who had undertaken voyages in peace, should not unexpectedly find themselves entangled in the risks of war. No such indulgence, however, is afforded; and England is not peculiarly responsible for this injustice. But England is responsible for the extension which she gives to an unjust principle. She is responsible for the pertinacity with which she exercises the right, which some other nations have ceased to enforce—of confiscating in her own ports vessels which, when they arrived, were friends, and which a war has subsequently converted into enemies. She is responsible for the habit, when vessels have visited her ports in the full confidence of peace, of preventing their escape if she have a serious dispute with their government; and of detaining them, pending the dispute, for the purpose of confiscation if the dispute terminate in war. The *droits* of the Admiralty have been dearly purchased.

We are glad to turn to her conduct on land; for there she has generally acted with justice, and even with forbearance. She does not support her armies by plunder or by requisition. She endeavours to restrain them from all wanton devastation. Her treatment of the inhabitants of an invaded country has generally been less oppressive than would have been warranted by the laws of war. Of course, her behaviour has not been unvaried. The Duke of Wellington's threat—'If I have farther reason to complain of Bidarry, or any other villages, I will act towards them as the French did in the villages of Spain and Portugal; I will totally destroy them, and hang up all the people belonging to them that I can find;'[*] and his

subsequent statement of the execution of this threat,—'Pour moi, je fais pendre tous ceux qui font le métier de partisans, et je fais brûler leurs maisons,'[*]—are scarcely justifiable, even by the example which he quotes from France. The burning of Buffalo in 1814, was defended as the best means of preventing a repetition of the excesses committed by the Americans in Upper Canada. But no such excuse can be pleaded for the wholesale plunder of merchandize at Alexandria, or for the destruction of the public buildings of Washington.

Subject, however, to a few exceptions, we repeat, that on land England, as a belligerent, has been forbearing. Her conduct after victory has been of a mixed character. She has almost always been disinterested. She has sometimes, as in the case of France at the conclusion of the last war, been generous, and she has never been vindictive. But she has not always sufficiently respected the feelings, or even the rights of the inhabitants, of the countries whose fate has been placed in her hands by her military superiority. As an example, we will state shortly her treatment of Norway. In the beginning of the year 1812, Denmark, Sweden, Russia, and France, were united in war against England. In the course of that year, Russia quarrelled with France, and it became essential to her to obtain the neutrality, and, if possible, the aid of Sweden. But only four years before, by the assistance of France, she had robbed Sweden of Finland. She did not choose to restore it, and as a substitute offered to give her Norway, then, and for centuries before, a part of the territories of Denmark, with whom Russia, who made the offer, and Sweden to whom it was made, were allied. Sweden accepted the proposal, and England, now turned into the ally of Sweden and Russia, agreed to assist in carrying it into execution. Denmark, of course, refused her assent, and Sweden and Russia declared war against her. As soon as the defeat of France left the Swedish troops at liberty, they overran the continental dominions of Denmark, and forced the King to sign a treaty transferring Norway to Sweden. But Norway objected. She had been at variance with Sweden for centuries; her population was much smaller, her civilisation was more advanced, and she refused to become an appendage to a nation which she hated and despised. Relinquished by Denmark, she asserted her independence, took the present king of Denmark for her sovereign, and proclaimed herself at peace with all the world,

---

* Letter to Marshal Beresford, 28th January, 1814.—Despatches, Vol. XI., p. 483.

* Letter to the Mayor of Hagetman, 21st March, 1814.—Ibid., 601.

but ready to resist to the utmost any attempts to change her destiny without her consent. She might have been able to repel force, but she could not support famine. England blockaded her coast and starved her into compliance.

As a belligerent ally, the conduct of England has been exemplary. When she has made an engagement, no dangers or sacrifices to be incurred by its performance, no advantage to be obtained by its violation, will tempt her to break or to evade it. Where there has been a balance of conflicting duties, she has sacrificed to fidelity motives which may appear to have been still more important. Her blockade of Norway was an instance. England certainly ought not to have been a party to the iniquitous compact by which Russia and Sweden agreed to rob and dismember her enemy, but their ally; or, at least, she ought to have made it a condition, that the consent of Norway should be obtained. But having signed the treaty, she felt bound by it, and carried it into effect, in defiance of the just complaints of Norway, and in opposition, as we believe, to her own interest. The conduct of Austria and Bavaria, in directing against France, the instant her fortunes changed, the very armies which were in the field as her allies, was eminently beneficial to Europe, and perhaps, therefore, justifiable; but it would not have been adopted by England. The behaviour of the other European powers, during the late war, was a foil that showed this portion of the English character in high relief. While one continental alliance after another was dissolved by fear, or selfishness, or treachery, until the word 'coalition' seemed almost to mean disunion, the honour of England remained, not only without stain, but without suspicion. She imposed no selfish conditions —she evaded no stipulations—she made no separate treaties—she accepted no indemnities at the expense of her friends—she did not join her enemies to plunder and crush her allies. We have already remarked, that in general the conduct of the best nation is far inferior to that of an average individual; but on this point the best man could not do more than copy the example of England.

We earnestly wish that we could bestow a portion of this praise on her conduct towards neutrals. We wish that we could exempt it from severe censure. Two sacred duties are imposed on belligerents. One is, to force no nation to break her neutrality; the other, to inflict on neutrals no further inconveniences than those to which they are subjected by the existing law of nations. The violation of these principles has a ten-

dency to render every war universal; and, consequently, to render war the ordinary state of mankind, and peace only an armed truce. It has a tendency to sap the weak foundations of international law—to destroy the independence of all the feebler states, by rendering power necessary to security—and to force the civilized world to arrange itself in the form least favourable to moral and intellectual improvement, as the subjects of a few great military sovereignties. Both these rules have been broken through by England. An instance of her violation of the first rule may be taken from her behaviour to Denmark in 1807.

Until that year Denmark had preserved a strict neutrality. When the subjugation of Prussia, and the alliance of Russia, made the influence of France preponderate in the north of Germany, England, who still retained the alliance of Sweden, felt, that if she could obtain that of Denmark, a powerful barrier might be opposed to the progress of France; and she also felt, that if France could seize that alliance, Sweden could not resist, and the whole north of Europe would become hostile. It was known that mere solicitation on either side would not induce Denmark to take part in the war; but it was believed that France would not confine herself to solicitation. Napoleon, in his answer to the Hamburg deputies, had spoken with disapprobation of the commerce between Denmark and England, and had added. ' That little prince had better take care of himself.' Murat had hinted to Sweden, that if she would join France she should be rewarded with Norway, and a French force was collected near the frontier of Holstein. On these grounds, assisted by the usual tenour of French policy, England believed that France would take an opportunity, probably as soon as winter had closed the Sound, of entering the German possessions of Denmark, and of endeavouring to occupy Zealand and get possession of her fleet. Denmark herself seems to have participated in these fears; for she collected an army in Holstein for the apparent purpose of opposing, or, at least, deterring that of France. But she was little aware from whence her neutrality was really menaced; so little, that when her merchants confidentially inquired of the Danish government whether it might be advisable to remove their vessels from the English ports, they were answered, that there was not the slightest ground for apprehension. Suddenly an English fleet, carrying an English army, appeared before Copenhagen, and proclaimed, ' That it was impossible for Denmark, though it desired to be neutral, to preserve its neutrality: That the king of England had there-fore judged it expedient to desire the temporary deposit of the Danish ships of the line in one of his Majesty's ports.'* An envoy was sent to make this proposal to the Crown Prince, and 'If Denmark was really prepared to resist the demands of France, and to maintain her independence, his Majesty proffered his co-operation for her defence—naval, military, and pecuniary aid, the guarantee of her European territories, and the security and extension of her colonial possessions.'†

Such a proposal, so enforced, was repelled with indignation. But the British power was overwhelming. Copenhagen surrendered after a short bombardment, and her fleet, consisting of sixteen ships of the line, most of them old and unserviceable, and some frigates and sloops, was carried to England. The neutrality of Denmark was effectually destroyed The instant our troops quitted Zealand she threw herself into the arms of France, and continued, during the remainder of the war, one of our bitterest enemies. The defence of England rested on the supposed designs of France, and the supposed inability of Denmark to resist them. We do not doubt the truth of either of these suppositions; but it is obvious that, if they formed a valid excuse, there would be an end to the neutrality of the weaker powers. If an expected violation of the rights of neutrality by one state justified an actual violation by another, belligerents would run a race of injustice, of which the most unscrupulous would reap the profit, and the neutral would be the victim. It may be added, that this great crime was also a great *fault.* It had not the poor merit of immediate expediency. The three evils which England apprehended, if she allowed France to violate the neutrality of Denmark, instead of doing so herself, were, first, the exclusion of England from communication with the Danish shores; secondly, the closing of the Sound against her commerce and navigation, so far as Denmark could close it; and thirdly, that France might direct against her the maritime force of Denmark.‡ She attacked Denmark for the purpose of preventing these consequences. Her attack succeeded, and immediately produced them every one. She was instantly excluded from all communication with the Danish territory; the Sound swarmed with Danish privateers and gun-boats, almost before her squadron carrying off the Danish fleet had passed through it; and though she carried off the

fleet, she left behind the sailors, and men, not ships, were what France wanted. France could not man her existing navy. To the extent of the whole maritime population of Denmark, England, by converting them into active and determined enemies, supplied that want. The results of this most atrocious proceeding are an illustration of what we believe to be a truth, nearly as general among nations as among individuals—that injustice is folly.

We proceed to show the conduct of England towards the nations which she allowed to remain neutral. The maritime rights of a belligerent against neutrals are four:—

1. The right to prohibit neutral vessels from entering or attempting to enter a blockaded port—that is to say, a port so closely watched by a belligerent squadron as to make entrance without their permission difficult.

2. The right to prevent neutrals from supplying the enemy with certain commodities—such as military and naval stores, and other warlike provisions, which are termed ' contraband of war.'

3. The right to seize and confiscate an enemy's property found on board a neutral vessel.

4. As necessarily incidental to these rights, the right to board neutral vessels, and to examine their cargoes and papers, in order to ascertain the nature and the ownership of the cargo, and the object of the voyage.

The right of a neutral against a belligerent is, that, subject to the rights of war, her vessels on the high seas are to be treated as they are to be treated in peace—that is to say, as invested with all the privileges and all the independence of the country to which they belong.

During the portion of the war which preceded the peace of Amiens, France set all law at defiance She decreed that all vessels containing any commodities of English origin should be confiscated, and that neutral sailors found on board English vessels should be put to death. Her cruisers carried on a system of almost indiscriminate piracy; her prize courts were as iniquitous as her captors; and, in as far as her power extended, she preyed on the commerce of the whole world. Under the Consular government these decrees were repealed; but in a few years the system was resumed, though in a form somewhat different. By the decree of Berlin of the 21st November, 1806, the British islands were declared in a state of blockade, and the whole world was prohibited from holding intercourse with them. England answered by an Order in Council of the 7th January, 1807, by which she prohibited all

* British Proclamation, 16th August, 1807.
† British Declaration, September 25, 1807.
‡ Ibid.

neutral vessels, on pain of confiscation of ship and cargo, from trading from one port to another, each such port being in the possession, or under the control, of France or of her allies; and by another Order of the 11th November, 1807, which declared that all the ports of France, and of her allies, or of any other country at war with England, or from which the British flag was excluded, should be subject to the same restrictions as if the same were actually blockaded; that all trade in the produce or manufactures of such country should be unlawful; and that every vessel trading with any such country, and all her cargo, should be confiscated, unless she had previously visited a British port, or were on her way to a British port. And France replied by a decree of the 17th December, 1807, which declared that every vessel, of whatever nation, which had visited an English port, or a port occupied by English troops, should be lawful prize. England and France thus assumed each to apply to vessels trading with the dominions of the other, or with the dominions of the allies of the other, the punishment that is lawfully inflicted on those who break through a real blockade. As far as the two greatest powers in the world could effect it, neutral trade was annihilated. France, as far as she was able, confiscated vessels if they visited a British port, and England if they did not do so.

England's excuse was retaliation; but it was a retaliation directed, not against France, but against those whom France was oppressing. The vessels which she confiscated under her Orders in Council were not French vessels, but vessels belonging to nations with whom England was at peace.

Still, however, in this rivalry of oppression she had the miserable plea that she followed the example of her enemy. She was guilty of another violation of the law of nations for which she had not this shadow of an excuse. The crown of England is entitled by the law of the country to the services in war of all her sailors. But of course this right, like all other municipal rights, is incapable of exercise within the dominions of another state, except by the permission of that state. Subject to the rights of war, a vessel on the high seas is invested, as we have already remarked, with all the privileges and all the independence of the country to which it belongs. The rights of war entitled England to search neutral vessels, in order to ascertain the nature and ownership of their cargoes. In the execution of this duty her officers often found Englishmen among their crews. If the vessels had been English it would have been lawful to impress such men, to deprive their vessels of their services, and to force them into the royal navy. England thought fit to act thus, although the vessels were foreign. She thought fit to import her own laws into a floating portion of the territories of an independent nation; and to enforce them as if the high seas were really a part of her dominions. This would have been a most oppressive exercise of superior force, even if she could have been sure that the men whom she so impressed were English. There was no difference between her taking Englishmen out of an American or a Danish vessel, and her sending a pressgang into Elsinore or New York to seize all the English sailors whom it could detect on the quays. But there is another maritime nation with the same origin, the same habits, and the same language. It was impossible that when the British officer passed in review an American crew, and selected those whom he believed to be English, he should always escape error; it was impossible that an American should not sometimes be taken for an Englishman—and the mistake, if made, was generally irremediable. The man might be carried off to a distant climate, and years might elapse before he could prove, if he ever could prove his citizenship. America remonstrated, threatened, obtained no redress, and at length had recourse to arms. The war terminated with the general peace; and, with the exception of the mutual injuries which it inflicted, and the traces which still remain of those injuries, left all things as it found them. We trust that the time is not distant when England will voluntarily relinquish this monstrous pretension. She must feel that she would not submit to it herself; that if France and America were at war, she would not permit a midshipman from an American frigate cruising in the Channel, to muster the crews of her merchantmen, and to seize and carry into military servitude all those whom he thought fit to consider American citizens. Rights which she would not allow to others she cannot in justice, or even in prudence, endeavour to maintain for herself. *Now*, in time of peace, she may disavow them with dignity: if she should be engaged in war, she will be forced either to abandon them on apparent compulsion, or to rouse the hostility, and, what must be formidable even to England, the well-grounded hostility, of every neutral, by enforcing them.

In peace England is never intentionally unjust; and this is no slight comparative merit. We have already remarked that her pride, her confidence in her own wisdom and justice, and her neglect of the opinion of other nations, must have a tendency somewhat to warp her notions of what is right; and to lead her to take what a German would call a 'one-sided' view of disputed questions. But her motives are not sordid or ambitious. She never sins against her own conscience. She sometimes believes that she has rights which an impartial judge would not concede to her; and she often adheres more obstinately than is wise—more obstinately than she would do if she listened to the opinions of others—to the claims which she thinks she possesses in equity, if not at law. But we must add, that if she sometimes demands that a compact be interpreted according rather to the spirit than to the letter, to the substance than to the form, she readily acquiesces in such a demand from others; and if she can be convinced that there is a fair doubt, she gives to her opponent its full benefit.

Her conduct with respect to what has been called the 'Russo-Dutch Loan' is an instance. By a treaty, dated the 15th May, 1815, England and Holland agreed to pay to Russia in equal moieties, by instalments, the principal and interest of fifty millions of florins;—' It being understood,' added the treaty, ' that the said payments, on the part of the King of the Netherlands and the King of Great Britain, shall cease and determine, should the possession and sovereignty (which God forbid) of the Belgic provinces at any time pass, or be severed from the dominions of the King of the Netherlands, previous to the complete liquidation of the same.' In 1831, while a large portion of the debt remained unpaid, the event contemplated by the treaty seemed to have happened. Holland, consequently, discontinued her payment, and it rested with England to decide whether she should continue hers. The feeling between the nations was anything but amicable. Russia was engaged against Poland in a war to which all our sympathies were opposed; and was suspected, with reason, of designs and practices inconsistent with her professions of friendship, and injurious to our interests and to our tranquillity. There never was a period at which we less wished to court or to strengthen her. It seemed doubtful even whether the two countries would continue at peace. According to the words of the treaty, England was clearly released. The possession and sovereignty of the Belgic provinces had passed, and were severed from the dominions of the King of the Netherlands. England, however, felt that there was a doubt. It might be contended that the severance contemplated by the treaty, as the deter-

mination of her engagement, was a severance by external force, not, as had occurred, one by internal dissension; and it might be argued that one of the objects of the stipulation in question, was to bind Russia to use her utmost endeavours to preserve the connection between Belgium and Holland, and that Russia had performed that duty. We own that we do not acquiesce in this reasoning, nor was it held conclusive by England. We have little doubt that, if the question could have been submitted to a legal tribunal, judgment would have been given against Russia. But as the decision rested with England, she thought it became her to decide against herself. She has continued her payments as if no severance between Holland and Belgium had occurred.

We shall close our view of the three great nations whom we have compared, by some remarks on the degree in which the character of each seems to deteriorate or improve. During the present century the influence of the people on the public conduct of America, France, and England has been constantly incresing. In each of these countries the forms of government have become more and more liberal, and public affairs have excited among the people more and more attention. During that period, almost every state composing the American Union has approached nearer to a pure democracy. France has acquired a representative system; and the constituency on which it is founded, narrow as it is, has been progressively enlarged. The Government has been more and more under the influence of the Chamber, and the Chamber under that of the electors. Napoleon was more independent of public opinion than Louis, Louis than Charles, and Charles than Louis Philippe. In England the growth of the towns, and of the commercial and manufacturing interests, has enabled them to measure their strength with the aristocracy—to effect a revolution which, though tranquil, has been real —and to conquer an influence which, though its progress is irregular, and from time to time apparently checked, must ultimately predominate. Under such circumstances, the public conduct of a state becomes a better and better index of the character of its population.

We regret to say that the character of America seems to deteriorate. She appears to us to become more captious, more litigious, more rash, and, we fear, even more ambitious, as her power advances. And when we consider the probable magnitude of that power at no distant period, the possibility that she will abuse it is a source of alarm, both for her own sake and for that of Europe. As far, however, as European interests are concerned, it must be recollected, that every abuse of her power by America has a tendency to check its growth; and that, if ambition were to seduce her into prolonged war, or to an extension of territory much exceeding what-are now her acknowledged limits, the probable result would be, that she would be dissolved into independent, and rival, and frequently hostile states, less beneficial to mankind than if she had remained one pacific empire, but certainly much less formidable.

In the public character of France we see little change. Her ambition, her thirst for admiration, her indifference to the means by which it is to be obtained —perhaps we might say her desire to be admired rather for her courage than for her forbearance, rather for her power than for her justice—her want of faith and of candour—the unreasonableness of her resentment, and the fierceness of her hate—have been as conspicuous during the last few years as during any portion of her history.

England is still very different from what we could wish her to be; but she is improving. Her feelings have been more decidedly pacific—her sympathy in the welfare of other nations has been stronger— her resentment less readily aroused, and more easily appeased—and her whole conduct has been more disinterested and more prudent, during the last twenty-five years, than during any other period of equal length for a hundred years past. We trust that an extension and improvement of education, commensurate with the increased influence which the body of the people are acquiring over her Councils, will improve her good dispositions; that the reform in her Tariff, which the public voice demands, and must obtain, will direct her commerce towards the more civilized portion of her European neighbours: that increased intercourse will produce more community of feeling and opinion; above all, we trust that she will escape the great corruptor—war; that she will have no victories to inflame her passion for military glory—no defeats to

make her timid—and no disgraces to wipe out.

With respect to her conduct towards the two nations with which we have compared her, we hope that when any differences arise between her and America— and differences must constantly start up where there are so many thousand miles of contiguous frontier—she will instantly endeavour to have them referred to arbitration. It is scarcely possible that states, so litigious as America and so self-confident as England, should ever convince one another, or agree as to a basis of compromise;—even supposing, what never will be the case with respect to England, that each government had leisure and patience to understand the matter in dispute. A controversy attempted to be carried on direct between Downing Street and Washington, lingers on from year to year—sometimes apparently forgotten, and sometimes apparently on the brink of adjustment—but with a constant tendency in each party, at every renewal of the discussion, to become more acrimonious and more obstinate. With respect to France, we hope much from the Commercial Treaty, of which even the details have long been arranged—which each Government has long been anxious to sign—which is demanded by the departments—and delayed only in fear of the Journalists of Paris. Commerce, manufactures, and the desire for individual advancement, may, in time, direct to peaceful pursuits the restless ambition and vanity which now seek to be gratified by participating in the general glory of the nation. But while we desire to have with France as much of commercial intercourse as is possible, we desire to have as little as is possible of diplomatic intercourse.

It is with deep regret that we express our conviction, that until this change in the habits of thinking and feeling in France shall have taken place, (an event of which we see no present indication,) any durable alliance between the two countries is impossible. They may not, we trust that they will not, be at war; but their peace will not be the peace of friends. If the present hostility of France to England had arisen merely from the recollection of past defeats, it would wear out as those defeats receded more and more into the obscurity of history. If it had arisen from our disapprobation of her interference against the liberties of Spain, or of her colonization of Algiers, or from the Syrian dispute, the only matters in which for the last quarter of a century we have opposed her, it would have subsided when those questions had been disposed of. Her hostility springs from far deeper sources. Sixty years ago, towards the close of the American war, France was the most powerful kingdom in the world. Her population amounted to twenty-six millions, while that of the British islands did not exceed thirteen or fourteen; that of Austria and of European Russia about twenty-five each; and that of Prussia seven or eight. She had flourishing colonies, a fleet which could cope with that of England, and a population superior in wealth and industry to that of almost every other portion of the continent except the Netherlands. On her southern and south-eastern frontiers were Spain, Savoy, and Switzerland, all under her influence; then the territories of petty German states; and then to the north the Austrian Netherlands, the weak dependencies of a distant empire. Now Spain, Savoy, and Switzerland, have thrown off her control. Belgium, in close alliance with England, is on her north, and the grand duchy of Luxemberg, Rhenish Prussia, Rhenish Bavaria, and Baden—all connected by the powerful Germanic confederation—close her in on her remaining frontier. Her military marine, no longer supported by an extensive commerce, has ceased to be formidable. Algiers is the substitute for almost all her colonies; the wealth and industry of her people are scarcely equal to those of the inhabitants of many of the nations round her; and while her population has reached only thirty-four millions, that of the British islands amounts to twenty-seven millions, that of Austria to thirty-seven, that of Prussia to fourteen, and that of Russia in Europe to fifty. France looks at the change with a mixture of grief and terror.

> Æstuat ingens
> Imo in corde pudor, mixtoque insania luctu,
> •᾽ • • • et conscia virtus.

She fears, that if her neighbours outstrip her in the next half century as much as they have done in the last, she will sink to a secondary power. To a bystander, the remedy appears to be obvious. If she would cease to waste the resources of her subjects by a grinding taxation, for the purpose of maintaining armies and fleets of no use but to keep up the enmity of

Europe; if she would cease to throw, annually, thousands of men and millions of money into the vortex of Algiers; if she would modify the barbarous Tariff which excludes her from foreign commerce; if she would abolish the restrictions and monopolies which fetter and diminish her internal production, consumption, and exchange; in short, if she would liberally and honestly cultivate the arts of peace—there is no nation whose rivalry she need fear. With her territory, her soil, and her climate, she might in half a century possess a prosperous population of fifty millions. But the selfish shortsighted interests of large classes, and the vanity, impatience, and ignorance of all, seem to render such measures as these, for the present, impracticable. Self-condemned, therefore, to slow progress herself, she wishes to impede the progress of others. Since she cannot overtake them, she wishes to drag them back. Of all her rivals, England is the most powerful, and therefore the most detested. She believes, and we admit the justice of the opinion, that England would be seriously injured by a war. And hence her earnest desire to involve her in one—a desire which must last as long as its causes continue: that is to say, as long as England remains powerful, and France envious and ambitious. It is true, that France cannot be engaged in a serious war without overthrowing her present dynasty and her present constitution. They have no roots to withstand a storm. And this is the principal security for peace. But we doubt much whether the attachment of France to such a dynasty, and to such a constitution, would restrain her if a plausible pretext for war should arise. And the more numerous are the matters in which France and England have to act in common, the more numerous their points of political contact, the more numerous will be the occasions for a rupture.

We will venture to go further, and to suggest a doubt whether the variety and activity of our general diplomacy, since the termination of the war, may not have been somewhat excessive. Without adopting the opinion of one of our shrewdest statesmen, that the best thing for our foreign affairs would be, to lock up the Foreign Office for three or four years, and hide the key; we may wish that that Office were less easily accessible. It is possible that a plausible pretext might be brought forward for every case of our interference; but in how many of these cases were there not plausible grounds for remaining quiet? Up to the present time, interference has been the rule, and abstinence from it the exception. We are inclined to wish the rule and the exception to change places. It is not necessary, indeed it would not be prudent, for England to announce beforehand what are the precise points which she would consider cases for remonstrance, or cases for war. What we wish is, that it should be felt that she seeks to avoid *all* interference; that when she does interfere, it is for a great object, and one in which others are interested as well as herself; and that, in such a cause, she will put forth her whole force.

How much expense, how much anxiety, how much danger, and how much enmity, has America escaped by her system of non-interference? What is the circumstance which has allowed her to adopt that wise and fortunate system? Chiefly her belief that she is protected by the Atlantic from serious attack. But the sea which separates America from Europe, separates England from the Continent. We are nearly as difficult of access as she is. Experience, indeed, might lead to the belief that Washington is more exposed than London. It is supposed that our constant exertions are necessary in order to keep the Balance of Power. Is it difficult, however, to believe that this Balance may not be preserved by the mutual fears and mutual exertions of the great continental monarchies, with less action on the part of England. Germany now knows her own power; France is beginning to appreciate the power of Germany; Russia is an object of jealousy to both. It is certain that our intermeddling may not have tended as often to disturb the equipoise as to adjust it? We must add, that the indifference of the British public to foreign affairs, and the secrecy in which our negotiations are enveloped, greatly useful as these circumstances are in many respects, sometimes add to the dangers to which all diplomacy is exposed. The publicity of all the acts, and of all the correspondence of the American Government, and the co-operation of the Senate in treaties, have their peculiar evils and dangers; but they have at least one advantage. The country knows where it is. It cannot be surprised into an engagement or a war. It cannot be suddenly informed that, during a period of apparent inactivity, the national faith and the

national honour have been pledged to promises, demands, and threats, which the national opinion would have refused to sanction. But in England, alliances, guarantees, and all the other expedients of diplomacy, may be concocting in Downing Street, while the Bank Parlour and the Royal Exchange enjoy a fancied security; and the nation may be awakened from its dream of safety only by the presentation of Papers and the demand for a Vote of Credit.

———

Art. II.—1. *Mémoire sur la Variation de la Temperature dans les Alpes de la Suisse.* Par M. Venetz, (Denkschriften der Allgemeinen Schweitzerischen Gesellschaft. Band I. 2te Abtheilung.) Read 1821. Published 1833.
2. *Naturhistorische Alpenreise.* Von F. J. Hugi. 8vo. Solothurn: 1830.
3. *Notice sur la Cause probable du Transport des Blocs Erratiques de la Suisse.* Par M. J. Charpentier. 8vo. pp. 20. Paris: 1835. (Extrait du Tome VIII. des Annales des Mines.)
4. *Discours prononcé à l'ouverture des séances de la Societé Helvetique des Sciences Naturelles à Neufchatel, le 24 Juillet,* 1837. Par L. Agassiz. 8vo. pp. 32. 1837.
5. *Etudes sur les Glaciers.* Par L. Agassiz. 8vo. With folio Atlas of Plates. Neufchatel: 1840.
6. *Theorie des Glaciers de la Savoie.* Par M. le Chanoine Rendu. 8vo. Chambérry: 1840.
7. *Essai sur les Glaciers et sur le Terrain Erratique du Bassin du Rhone.* Par Jean de Charpentier. 8vo Lausanne: 1841.
8. *Etudes Géologiques dans les Alpes.* Par M. L. A. Necker. Tome I. 8vo. Paris: 1841.

Geology, as a science, is subject to Revolutions similar to those of which it treats. Alternations of opinion are as frequent as those of strata; and a change comes, from time to time, over the spirit of the cosmogonal dream, as one or another agent or mode of action seems best to fit the explanation of a certain large class of phenomena. At one time all in geology is turmoil, earthquake, and conflagration; at another, the speculator sees in the evidences of past change nothing but proofs of the long continuance of the existing comparatively peaceable state of things. For a series of years, whilst 'Plutonism' was on the ascendant, all was to be accounted for by the latent or developed action of heat : at another time, water, or an 'universal menstruum' bathed the surfaces of our valleys and mountains, producing by its changing condition not only all the chemical, but nearly all the mechanical changes which the earth's surface has undergone.

A soberer spirit of philosophising has united the two apparently inconsistent doctrines of geological change, and ascribes to fire and water their respective shares in the manipulations—if we may use the phrase—which reduced the external crust of a once chaotic sphere to a condition fit for the existence and mainte. nance of varied organic bodies. But amidst the prevalence of that modified 'Huttonianism' which expresses the geological creed of a great majority of the cosmogonists of the present day, one condition has been held as incontrovertible, namely—that the ancient world was *hotter* than the modern one; that tropical animals inhabited the temperate and even the polar regions of the globe ; and that the palm and tree fern clothed the shores where now flourish only the dwarf birch and the Norwegian pine. The fossil plants of the carboniferous period, and the shells of all but the most recent of the tertiary formations, point alike to a great but indeterminate excess of warmth in those times above the present.* But the generalization so long accepted, is now assailed by a weight and combination of evidence which demands the fullest investigation. An agent, which may be termed *new* in the application which has been made of it, is now to be pressed into the service of geology ; and the 'Plutonism' of the old theorists, and the 'Neptunism' of their successors, are about to be succeeded, in the history of hypotheses, by the universal ICE FLOOD with which the modern school of Swiss Naturalists would invest our globe, from the tropics to the poles.

It is to explain the more recent and superficial changes of the earth's surface that the mechanical agency of permanent ice, or Glaciers, is proposed to be introduced. Even the fundamental questions of the aqueous or igneous origin of Granite and Trap rocks, and the doctrine of Universal Formations, have not been more keenly

contested by geologists than the nature and duration of those processes by which the *most recent* geological changes have been effected, the final *contour* given to the soil, and large masses of rock detached from their natural position, and transported, whether to form gravel beds of enormous thickness or solid angular fragments, to surprising distances from their origin. Such phenomena are the accumulations called the *drift* in the south-east of England, the gravel beds of the Great Glen of Scotland, and the beaches of Glen Roy ; the occurrence of fragments of granite, native only in the Scandinavian peninsula, dispersed along the southern shores of the Baltic, and the plains of Russia, Estonia, and Denmark ; or lastly, the deposition, on the calcareous chain of the Jura, of angular masses of rock, which are only found *in situ* at distances of eighty and one hundred miles amongst the highest Alps. These and similar phenomena have been explained by some geologists by the energy of the moving power of a great flood, which swept over the earth's surface previous to the commencement of the present age of the world ; whilst others have been found bold enough to maintain, that we see in action around us, even at this day, causes sufficiently energetic, if continued for an indefinite time, to have produced these apparently violent effects. The objections to both of these opinions will be stated in the course of this article. Suffice it to say, that assent to one or the other was rather extorted by the method of proof called a *reductio ad absurdum*— that is, by proving the difficulty or impossibility of the contrary hypothesis—than by convincing the reason that one or the other was in itself probable. The new Swiss School of Geologists have proposed to themselves to maintain that both these theories are incorrect, and that the mechanical changes which the earth's surface has undergone, in that important and interesting period which seems to connect the actual era with the earlier epochs of geological history, were due to a great extension which the glaciers of the mountainous regions of the earth then experienced, constituting agents of transport and abrasion similar in kind to those which still exist, but exaggerated in their dimensions and energy.

Guided by the experience of past times in the reception or modification of geological hypotheses, we feel ourselves called upon, in the first place, to admit with cau-

---

* Lyell's *Elements of Geology*, 1841, i. 285, ii. 125.

tion the extensive operation of an agent which, though known, has not hitherto been admitted to play any great part in the modifications of the earth's surface. But more especially do we feel the necessity of not losing sight of anything approaching to demonstrated truth in the science of geology as it stands, in our haste to adopt and appreciate what really is valuable in the novel theory. The rage for immature generalisation, which is dangerous in all sciences, is especially so in that of geology, beset as it is in almost all its parts with conflicting evidence; evidence often the more conflicting in proportion as it is more detailed. The rejection of superfluous causes from science is, indeed, one of the first rules of philosophizing; but the danger in geology, we are persuaded, lies in the opposite direction—in the tendency to mutilate the evidence in order to fit the Procrustean bed of one great fundamental assumption. At all events, let Newton's rule be practically applied, by admitting with caution *new* general causes, not by attempting to subject to these every effect which admits of a different explanation.

The Memoirs and Works specified at the head of this article, all bear upon this recent geological innovation; for we consider as properly belonging to Geology whatever has reference to conditions of the earth's surface different from the present, although such modifications have occurred within historic times. It will be seen by the dates that the inquiry or suggestion is not altogether a new one. Twenty years ago the question of the ancient extension of glaciers was already agitated; and indeed we might have carried our citation of authors much further back, only that with the Memoir of Venetz dates the origin of the phase of geological speculation to which we have alluded. The authors (all living) have brought the subject, in a strictly geological point of view, from its fundamental facts (many of which had of course been admitted and reasoned upon by others) to its present bearing, and therefore to their writings we shall chiefly confine our attention; although, to be historically exact, we must, from time to time, recall the meritorious labours of their no less eminent predecessors.

It is plain, that an attempt to prove the vastly greater energy with which glaciers formerly acted in effecting geological changes, must be grounded on a study of those glaciers which now exist. Naturally, therefore, the rise of the theory in question occurred in Switzerland, and amongst persons whose attention had been forcibly called by local and other circumstances to the conditions of gla-

cial action as exhibited in the Alps. Unless we have rigorously determined what are the effects produced by existing glaciers, it is vain to argue about the proofs of their traces in positions where they are no longer found; and unless we have advanced so far as to analyze the origin of glaciers, the causes of their subsistence, and the conditions of their internal economy, we shall want positive arguments in support of their having existed. in other places or under other circumstances. The study of glaciers, as forming a portion of physical geography, is very old indeed; and when we consider the eminence of the authors who have described them, and the infinite number of men of science who have visited them, we wonder perhaps that more should still be found to be said. The mechanism of a glacier is a problem of natural philosophy, and one much more difficult and embarrassing than it has commonly been supposed; and as the second question—namely, the efficiency of compact moving ice in modifying the earth's surface—is a strictly geological problem, and of comparatively recent date, geologists have begun, and very properly, by assuming, or establishing the laws of glacier-motion rather as the substratum of their speculations than as a distinct application of physical laws to a special case.

The ECONOMY OF GLACIERS, and the HYPOTHESIS OF THEIR FORMER MUCH GREATER EXTENSION, are therefore two very distinct questions; both of which are treated of at some length in several of the works before us. We propose to consider these points separately; but first it may be well that we endeavour to present to the reader a picture of what a glacier is, and of the curious and beautiful appearances and transformations which it exhibits.

When we approach to examine a chain of mountains whose tops are constantly covered with snow, their acclivities green, and their bases clothed with wood—we should naturally expect to find a tolerably well marked line fixed by the level at which the snow never melts. Now this is very rarely, if ever, the case. The zones marked out by the limits of growth of particular plants—the superior limit, for instance, of the chestnut, the beech, or the pine—are generally more clearly defined than the level of perpetual snow. This is soon found to be due, in a great measure, to the forms of the mountain sides in whose hollows the snow of winter, by accumulating, resists the summer's heat, which, had it lain only to its mean depth, must infallibly have caused it to disappear.

Such cases occur even in climates where glaciers, properly speaking, are never found. The highest mountains in Britain, for instance those on the boundaries of Aberdeenshire and Inverness-shire, occasionally retain a portion of the winter's snow on their shady sides during the entire summer, without exhibiting any approach to the structure of a glacier.

A glacier, in the customary meaning of the term, is a mass of ice, which descending below the usual snow line, prolongs its course down the cavity of one of those vast gorges which furrow the sides of most mountain ranges. It is better represented by a frozen torrent than by a frozen ocean. Any one placed so as to see a glacier in connection with the range from which it has its origin, at once infers that it is, in some sense or other, the outlet of the vast snow fields which occupy the higher regions. It is impossible to doubt that it results from, and is renewed by the eternal ice-springs of those riverless wilds. None who has ever seen or even clearly conceived a lava-stream, can fail to find in it the nearest analogy of a glacier. Stiff and rigid as it appears, no one can doubt that it either flows, or once has flowed. Were the glacier, like the flood of molten stone, the result of one great eruptive action, then its existence beneath the limits of the general snow line would be inexplicable. It melts—it must melt; it lies on warm ground yielding crops perhaps within a hundred yards of its lower extremity; the sun beats perpetually upon its icy pinnacles, which, though they reflect much, must retain some of the incident heat; and we see, accordingly, in a summer's day the glacier oozing out its substance from every pore—above, beneath, within. And yet, with all this the glacier wastes not; always consuming, it is never destroyed. Evident therefore it must be, upon this ground alone, that a glacier glides imperceptibly down its valley, and this independent of all direct measurements of its motion. These, as we shall presently show, fully corroborate the inference.

The glacier therefore moves progressively, or, if the reader pleases—it *flows.* The flood of water of the arrowy Rhone passes so swiftly, that the passenger almost giddily follows with his eye the bubbles which mark its flight ;—the lava stream must be watched for some seconds or minutes, perhaps hours, to mark its progress ;—the stately march of the glacier is yet a stage more slow ; months and even years are but the units of division of its dial.

But what is its dial? To answer that question we must describe the configuration of the ice which differs considerably from that of ice under most other circumstances. The lower extremity of a glacier, where it terminates in the valley, is almost always abrupt: sometimes so steep as to be nearly inaccessible, presenting a continuous rampart, from the base of which, through a vault deep in the mass of ice which hangs in half fallen fragments from the green roof, issues a turbid river, partly the produce of the melting ice, and partly, no doubt, of the springs which rise under the glacier as elsewhere, and which give a certain volume to this stream even in the depth of winter. At other times the glacier rises from its very base in isolated jagged pinnacles, fissured in every direction, and absolutely inaccessible. This is commonly the case where the glacier terminates at the *embouchure* of a ravine where it is very steeply inclined; the former character prevails more where the limit of the glacier is determined by its gradual descent into the warmer regions of a very gently sloping valley. There is yet another distinction between the terminal appearances of glaciers; and it is one of the most striking to the eye of the intelligent traveller. If the ground beneath the precipice of ice be covered with the *débris* of rocks discharged from the upper and lower surfaces of the glacier ; if the vegetation be scanty and feeble, and great surfaces of rock lie exposed without a trace of soil or even lichen, as if some crushing mass had lately ground down its naturally uneven surface—then is the glacier in a diminishing or retreating state: the waste of ice below is not compensated by the supply above, and the retreat will continue until the diminished waste corresponds to the actual supply, by the progressive movement of the ice. If, on the other hand, the termination of the glacier touches the grass or cultivated land without much intervention of scattered blocks —if we see lying by its edge the trees which have been torn up or cut over in its former progress—if the greensward is not only torn by the insinuation of the icy ploughshare, which is kept by its enormous weight in contact with the subjacent rock, but is likewise wrinkled into ponderous folds far in advance of the glacier front—there we have plainly proof of the excess of the supply above the waste— the glacier is in progress.*

* In the year 1818, the front of the glacier of the Rhone advanced 150 feet,—Charpentier, *Essai,* p. 302.

Now, suppose the first difficulty of ascent overcome, and that whether by choosing the less steep parts of the abrupt face, or by following the line of rocky masses which the glacier rolls down, and of which it forms a girdle, extending from side to side—or lastly, by climbing the walls of the valley itself in which the glacier lies, we have reached the upper surface of the ice. We then see, what so many have seen from the Montanvert at Chamouni—a gently sloping icy torrent, from half a mile to three miles wide, more or less undulating on its surface, and this undulating surface more or less broken up by *crevasses*,* which, generally nearly vertical in their direction, have a width of from a few inches to many feet; and a length which sometimes extends almost from side to side of the glacier. In all this, there is little or no resemblance to water tranquilly frozen. The surface is not only uneven, but rough; and the texture of the ice wants the homogeneity of that formed on the surface of lakes. The hollows, which appear but trifling when viewed from a height and compared with the expanse of ice, are individually so great as to render the passage amongst them toilsome in the extreme, even independent of the *crevasses;* and the traveller who has to walk for several hours along a glacier, will often prefer scrambling over stones or rocks on the side, to the harassing inequalities which appeared at first so trivial. In a day of hot sunshine or of mild rain the origin of the hummocky ridges is apparent: the intervening hollows have every one of them their rill, which, by a complicated system of surface draining, discharge the water copiously melted by the solar influence, the contact of warm air, and the washing of the rain. These rills combine and unite into larger streams, which assume sometimes the velocity and volume of a common millrace. They run in icy channels excavated by themselves, and unlike the water escaping from *beneath* the glacier, being of exquisite purity, they are both beautiful and refreshing. They seldom, however, pursue their uninterrupted course very far, but reaching some *crevasse* or cavity in the glacier mechanically formed during its motion, they are precipitated in bold cascades into its icy bowels; there, in all probability, to augment the flood which issues from its lower termination. Nothing is more striking than the contrast which day and night produce in the superficial drainage of the glacier. No sooner is the sun set, than the rapid chill of evening reducing the temperature of the air to the freezing point or lower—the nocturnal radiation at the same time violently cooling the surface—the glacier life seems to lie torpid; the sparkling rills shrink and come to nothing; their gushing murmurs and the roar of their waterfalls gradually subside; and by the time that the ruddy tints have quitted the higher hill-tops, a death-like silence reigns amidst these untenanted wilds.

Winter is a long night amongst the glaciers. The sun's rays have scarcely power to melt a little of the snowy coating which defends the proper surface of the ice;—the superficial waste is next to nothing; and the glacier torrent is reduced to its narrowest dimensions.

Pursuing our survey, we next notice the bands of fragmentary rocks which traverse the glacier in nearly parallel lines—sometimes confined to its edges, sometimes dividing its breadth into two compartments so distinct, that we can hardly help fancying that we see two glaciers separated by a vast mound of blocks, which rise from the bottom of the valley. This last appearance is admirably illustrated by the view of the lower glacier of the Aar, in the 14th plate of M. Agassiz' work. The slightest examination shows that these accumulations of *débris* (to which the name of MORAINES has been given) are perfectly superficial, and conform themselves so entirely to the configuration of the ice-surface, that on many glaciers scarcely one stone lies upon another, every one covers the ice immediately. Thus, on the Aar glacier just mentioned, where the ridge of stones seems to form a heap, or rather two parallel heaps upon the level ice, it is found that the ice itself is heaped up under the stones, and gives the entire form to this sort of backbone, which divides the surface into two nearly equal parts, rising in some places to a height of eighty feet above its general level. So irreconcilable are the facts with the theory formerly adopted of these moraines—that they were stones which, having fallen on the

---

* The translation of the French word *crevasse* into the English *crevice*, is so evidently inapplicable to these vast fissured chasms, that we shall constantly adopt the French spelling.

sides of the glacier, settled gradually
down upon the centre as being its lowest
part.*

As a general fact it may be stated, that
every glacier has two moraines at least, composed of the masses which, detached by gravity aiding the effect of moisture and the
freezing of water in the cracks of the neighbouring rocky heights, fall on the edges of
the glacier, and form two borders or *selvages*,
which accompany it, generally speaking,
throughout its entire length. These are
called *Lateral Moraines*. Besides these,
there are the parallel bands of *débris* which
divide the glacier in the direction of its length,
and of which we have just spoken. There
can be no question that the origin of these
has been, for the first time, correctly stated in
the works of Charpentier and Agassiz, mentioned at the head of this article. But this
brings us back again to the movements of
the glacier; for these moraines are the divisions on the dial of which we have above
spoken, and upon which we read the chronology of glacier history. A simple statement
of facts will at once illustrate and prove this.

The higher parts of glaciers are always
contained in valleys extending above the
limits of vegetation, and indeed, from causes
which we shall afterwards explain, the walls
or sides of these ravines are extremely precipitous in most cases, so that even the snow
covers them imperfectly. The exposed rocks
are subject to great changes of temperature,
owing to the intense effect of solar radiation
at these heights. The snow in contact with
their surfaces is melted almost every summer's day, and the moisture is absorbed into
the minute fissures of the stone. The nocturnal frosts congeal this water, and the powerful expansion thus occasioned, has the effect
of loosening and disintegrating the hardest
rocks, in a manner which has no parallel
under other circumstances. Atmospheric
causes therefore produce their maximum of
destructive effects in the neighbourhood of
glaciers; and, as a matter of course, the detached fragments, descending by their weight,
often rebound from cliff to cliff, until they
fall shivered into smaller morsels upon the
surface of the ice. Such an *eboulement*
leaves a distinct proof of its occurrence, by
the heap of rubbish resting on the glacier.
If *this* had no progressive motion the fragments would remain piled under the rock
whence they fell; until, perhaps in the succeeding spring, being joined by another group,
they would accumulate at those points where

the bounding rocks were, by their nature or
position, most liable to the recurrence of these
events. If, however, the glacier flows on in
the interval, the previous mass of *débris* has
been carried some distance downwards on the
surface before the second fall took place; and
thus, supposing only one discharge of fragments annually, the movement of the glacier
for each year would be marked by the spaces
intervening between the successive heaps.

There is an instrument, invented in France,
for the measurement of minute intervals of
time, in which, instead of a hand revolving
upon a dial or ring, the dial itselves revolves
and the hand remains fixed; this fixed hand
is provided with a minute dotting apparatus,
by means of which the slightest pressure of
the finger leaves imprinted on the white surface of the dial a small black point; thus
marking and permanently registering the instant of the occurrence of the pressure by the
position of the dial relatively to the fixed
hand; and as this operation may be repeated
any number of times during the revolution of
the dial, there are as many marks as we please,
whose intervals indicate the periods of their
occurrence. Just so we find on the surface
of the glacier a dial divided unequally by the
fallen blocks, which, detached from one promontory of rock, or descending down one
water-course, bear testimony to the intermediate motion of the surface on which they fall.
It is evident then how a moraine is formed:
it is the scattered accumulation of *débris* along
a line, whose length, reckoned from a fixed
point, may be roughly considered as proportional to the time elapsed since their fall.
To produce such a continuous mound of
stones as we often see bordering a glacier in
its whole extent, it is therefore not necessary
(as we might at first sight suppose) that they
should have fallen from every part of its walls;
a single rock near its upper extremity may be
the source of the entire lateral moraine or
mass of fragments—lying partly upon the
edges of the ice, partly on the slope or shore
which bounds the glacier, and partly wedged
between the ice and the soil.

Whenever the confluence of two glacier-
branches occurs, there must be an union of
the moraines which bordered the sides of the
respective ice-flows. These moraines, carried
forward by the progressive motion of the surface on which they repose, cannot stop short
by their union with one another. They cannot be buried in the confusion which sometimes occurs at the confluence of the two glaciers, because (as we shall afterwards attempt
to explain) the glacier throws to the surface
any extraneous bodies enveloped in its mass:
therefore the two moraines must unite and

---

* Saussure, *Voyages dans les Alpes*, § 537.

advance in the centre of the now united glacier stream. This united stream of superficial fragments is called a *medial moraine ;* and is to be seen in greater perfection on the glacier of the Aar than perhaps anywhere else in the Alps. `The two streams of blocks are never quite confounded, and for many miles along the united glacier, may be traced the characteristic colours of the stones derived from one and the other parent branch. As a general rule, wherever a tributary ice-stream joins the main glacier, (suppose on the *left* bank), it brings also its tributary moraines ; its *right* moraine joins the lateral moraine of the glacier, and forms a medial moraine, its left moraine being now the lateral one of the united glacier. The circumstances of the formation of these multiple moraines are perfectly illustrated, and in fact proved by the inspection of the first and second plates of Agassiz' Atlas; in which the numerous tributaries of the great northern glacier of Monte Rosa each produce their distinct parallel band of fragments, which only become confounded on the lower part of the glacier by the united effects of its dislocation and steepness.

From what has been said it follows, that the *direct* proofs of the movement of a glacier must be sufficiently numerous upon its surface. Any well-marked block, having its position ascertained by a reference to a fixed object on the slope of the valley, will be found in the course of a year to have passed onwards. Saussure's ladder, left on the glacier du Géant in 1788, was recognized (we believe) by its fragments not many years ago on the lower part of the same glacier, not far above the Montanvert ; having traversed in the interval a space of several leagues. But the most interesting observation on the *rate* of motion we will quote from Professor Agassiz.

'The most incontestable proof of the descending march of glaciers, is afforded by the observations which I made last year (1839) on the lower glacier of the Aar. My intention was to visit the point of junction of the glaciers of the Finster Aar and Lauter Aar, where M. Hugi had constructed a cabin in 1827 for passing the night. We had walked for nearly four hours on the great medial moraine, when we discovered all at once a cabin, very solidly built. We did not think that this could be Hugi's cabin, for we knew that it had been constructed at the foot of the rock *im Abschwung*, which forms the angle of the mountain separating the two glaciers, and we were yet a great way from this rock. It also seemed that the walls were too well preserved, to have resisted for twelve years the hurricanes of these elevated regions. It was, however, the very cabin of M. Hugi which we thus recognized. We found a broken bottle

under a little heap of stones, which served to fix a long pole on an immense block situated at one side of the cabin. This bottle contained several papers, which informed us that M. Hugi had constructed this cabin in 1827, at the foot of the *Abschwung*. Another paper in the handwriting of M. Hugi, bore that in 1830 he had returned to his cabin, and found it several hundred feet below its first position ; that six years afterwards (in 1836) he found it 2200 feet from the foot of the rock.* . . . We hastened to measure with a long cord, which we had provided, the distance from the cabin to the rock, and found it 4400 feet. . . . This year (1840) I have found it much injured, and 200 feet lower than last year.'—*Études sur les Glaciers*, p. 149-51.

It is plain from this extract that the rate of movement has been far from uniform ; since, during the nine years from 1827 to 1836, it could not have exceeded 250 feet *per annum ;* but from 1836 to 1839, it advanced in three years as far, at least, as it had done in the previous nine years, or with a mean annual velocity of above 730 feet. The velocity of a glacier at different epochs, in different seasons of the year, and at different parts of its mass, are data of the utmost importance for science, as yet but little attended to.

What a curious internal historical evidence, then, does a glacier bear to the progress of events which have modified its surface ! It is an endless scroll, a stream of time, upon whose stainless ground is engraven the succession of events, whose dates far transcend the memory of living man. Assuming, roughly, the length of a glacier to be twenty miles, (no uncommon case,) and the velocity of its progression (assumed uniform) one-tenth of a mile, or 500 feet, the block which is *now* being discharged from its inferior surface on the terminal moraine, may have started from its rocky origin *two centuries* ago! The glacier history of 200 years is revealed in the interval, and a block ten times the volume of the greatest of the Egyptian Monoliths, which has just commenced its march, will see out the course of six generations of men ere its pilgrimage too be accomplished, and it is laid low and motionless in the common grave of its predecessors.

When we come to study more carefully the arrangement of the rocky fragments and earthy matter upon the surface of the glacier, we find a multitude of curious details. One of the most striking is the occurrence of what are called Glacier Tables. These consist of masses of rock, usually connected with one of the moraines, lying on their flat

* Judging from the plan of the glacier given in Hugi's work, the cabin was never close to the foot of the rock.

side, and supported above the general level of the glacier by an icy pedestal—a 'pillar and claw' foundation. Now, this is not only a picturesque accident, but recalls our attention to a most important circumstance of the glacier economy—that there is a perpetual waste at its surface; and that the stone, by preventing this waste, remains an index of the former level of the whole mass, like the earth pillars left by workmen in the course of excavation. Though some authors have attempted to make the glacier tables on their stalks sprout like mushrooms from the surface of the ice, there cannot be a doubt that this is their real origin. A very simple experiment, which has actually been made, gives the direct proof. If a hole be made vertically in the ice, and a stick sunk into it so as to rest upon the bottom at a depth of ten or twenty feet, it will be found that during summer weather the upper part of the stick becomes gradually bared by the dissolution and evaporation of the surface of the ice. A glacier has thus been found to lose a thickness of more than three feet in as many weeks. The action of the stone is very evident. The whole of its lower part is maintained, by contact with ice, at a freezing temperature; if the thickness be considerable, it forms a pretty complete shelter against the direct action of the sun's rays, as well as against the contact of warm rains and wind.[*] Thus the ice immediately beneath it is comparatively preserved. It is a clumsy but effectual parasol.

But yet we often find precisely the contrary effect wherever the ice is pretty consistent, so as to admit of pools of water being formed: *there* we have innumerable cup-shaped cavities, each containing a bit of slate, a dead insect, or not unfrequently a *leaf*—a leaf which assuredly could not have fallen from the sides of the glacier, which have not a single tree; but leaves even of the beach and chestnut are wafted by the tremendous violence of the winds from immense distances, and across elevated chains covered with perpetual snow.[†] Here, then, the presence of a foreign body has wasted, instead of protecting, the ice. The difference lies merely in the thickness. The dark surface of the chip of stone or organized matter absorbs the solar heat, and transmitting it quickly to the ice, by being completely warmed through, excavates for itself a cavity. It is in these cavities, too, that living animals are often found—small

black insects which inhabit the snow or ice-cold water, and there propagate their species.

Sometimes the ice is completely honey-combed with these cups, which often break into one another, and unite their contents; at other times, the passage of the rills already mentioned, accumulates sand and gravel derived from the moraine; and so soon as this accumulation reaches a certain thickness, a surprising change takes place. The solar heat enters, but no longer freely penetrates the mass—the action of the extraneous matter becomes conservative, the ice melts more rapidly all round than under it; and, after a while, the face of the glacier *becomes precisely reversed*, the mould of what it was before. The heights take the shapes of corresponding hollows—a *crevasse* filled with sand becomes in time a ridge of ice, coated with the sand which formed it: we have negative water-courses, negative *crevasses*, negative holes. From what we have already said of the magnitude of the superficial water-courses, it will be conceived that the *detritus* which they bear with them may be abundant, and that it may be deposited in considerable quantity in the deeper excavations. But the result would hardly be anticipated, and indeed must be seen and watched in its various stages to be well understood. As the protected surface rises higher and higher relatively to the general level, the sand which composes it falls, or is washed gradually down, protecting the sides of the icy cone which has been formed beneath it, to which (though continually streaming with moisture) it contrives to adhere with a tenacity not easy to explain. A glacier which, by the evenness of its surface and numerous water-runs, is adapted for the production of this phenomenon, is thus covered with a number of gravel cones, whose regularity and magnitude astonish and perplex the observer. They may be seen from fifteen to twenty feet high, and seventy or eighty in circumference. It is hardly possible to doubt at first sight that these cones (which are like enormous ant-hills) are composed, to the centre, of gravel; but we invariably find, as already stated, that it is a mere covering—the heart of the cone is *pure solid ice*, which, if its apex be removed with a hatchet, appears quite black and glassy, from the obstruction of the light by the sides of the cone. This very singular phenomenon has been perfectly described and explained by M. Agassiz in the tenth chapter of his work.

These phenomena are important as explaining how it is next to impossible that extraneous matter can become imbedded in the glacier. By retarding the superficial melting as soon as its mass has become at all consider-

---

* The phenomenon of glacier tables was perfectly well explained by Saussure.—*Voyages*, § 630.
† Such have been found on the upper glacier of the Aar, which must have been transported from the lower valley of the Rhone.

able, such an accumulation of *débris* must sooner or later find its way to the surface—not by pushing through the matter of the ice, which some writers seem to suppose (as many of the peasants do) to be endowed with a sort of organic faculty of rejecting impurities —but because these impurities retain their place in the ice, which is continually thawing and evaporating by the surface; and once arrived there, they can never, for the reasons already explained, again penetrate the mass, but will in general attain a level above it.

The appearances we are describing are not to be found upon all glaciers: the gravel cones especially are rare productions, and depend probably, in a great measure, upon two circumstances—a moderate slope of ice, which, not being greatly *crevassed*, permits considerable water-courses to be formed, and abundant *moraines* affording disintegrated materials for the accumulations in question. Such a glacier is that of the Lower Aar. The glacier of Aletsch, (Agassiz, plate xii.,) though abundantly flat, is destitute of considerable medial moraines; the glaciers of Chamouni are, for the most part, too precipitous.

When a glacier descends a steep mountain ravine like those of the Allée Blanche, which pour their majestic frozen torrents down the tremendous gorges which the chain of Mount Blanc presents on its southern side—or like the lower part of the glacier of Viesch (Agassiz, plate x.,) in the Upper Vallais—or like the glacier of Rosenlaui, and that of Upper Grindenwald in the Canton of Berne—the condition of the ice differs considerably from that which we have described. Urged onwards in its flow upon the immense bed of rocks on which it reposes—forced sometimes to discharge itself over the banks of a precipice—the rigid mass is fissured in all directions. Swayed hither and thither by the unevenness of its base, the fissures maintain no constant direction; but subdivide the ponderous mass into rude prismatic fragments, whose height is the thickness of the ice, and the form of their bases is determined by the meeting of the fissures which form them. These prisms become transformed into pyramids, more or less rude, by the action of atmospheric water, the contact of air, and evaporation, which speedily sharpen their summits, rising in a thousand fantastic forms; whilst their bases, here and there irregularly cut through by the escape of glacier torrents, become excavated into not less fantastic labyrinths in the deep blue depths of the ice, which often preserves here its most characteristic purity. As the excavation proceeds, these pyramids, doubly acuminated above and below, topple over, and increase the ap-

parent confusion by mingling their ruins. The moraines with which the surface has been charged, are, as a matter of necessity, dispersed into every fissure by the discontinuity; and the masses thus fallen, and ground by the pressure of the ice, are from time to time rolled down the rocky steep, and finally are borne to a certain distance by the impetuous torrent which flows from its base. To make much way along such glaciers as these, is evidently next to impossible. The experienced guide will either cross the glacier as directly as possible, if his course requires him to do so—(as in crossing the glacier of Bossons on the ascent of Mont Blanc[*])—or scale the rocky walls of the ravine, in preference to attempting to follow the course of the glacier. Such excursions, even when not dangerous, are the most fatiguing of all sorts of climbing;—the traveller now leaping from point to point along the jagged edges of the ice which bound the fissures; now making long zig-zags to get round the *crevasses* which cannot possibly be traversed; at other times descending the walls of those less steep and profound, and laboriously climbing the opposite face. Or if he prefers the moraine (where it exists) to the ice, he must step from top to top of the curiously-piled stones which rest upon the ice, propped in the most fantastic positions, and on account of the perpetual changes of their bed not firmly jostled as on solid ground into positions of stable equilibrium; but often resting on such ticklish balance that his weight is sure to precipitate a host of them, and himself above all, down one of those treacherous slopes. Driven sometimes from all these modes of progression, there is no alternative but to scale the rocks which confine the glacier; which are generally so rugged and intersected by water-courses, that a summit or elbow has no sooner with infinite toil been gained, than the traveller finds himself compelled to make a descent to his old

---

[*] Thus described by Mr. Auldjo:—' We were surrounded by ice piled up in mountains, crevices presenting themselves at every step, and masses half sunk in some deep gulf; the remainder, raised above us, seemed to put insurmountable barriers to our proceeding, yet some part was found where steps could be cut with the hatchet; and we passed over these bridges, often grasping the ice with one hand, while the other, bearing the pole, balanced the body, hanging over some abyss into which the eye penetrated and searched in vain for the extremity. Sometimes we were obliged to climb up from one crag of ice to another, sometimes to scramble along a ledge on our hands and knees, often descending into a deep chasm on the one side and scaling the slippery precipice on the other.'—*Narrative of an Ascent of Mont Blanc*, 1827, p. 15.

level, still more difficult and alarming. Such are the alternatives which not unfrequently present themselves to the glacier tourist—alternatives which Milton, in his enumeration of the difficulties which beset the Satanic voyage to earth, has failed to particularize, doubtless (shall we say) from being unacquainted with them. Often is even the skilful mountaineer

'—— harder beset
And more endanger'd, than when Argo pass'd
Through Bosporus betwixt the justling rocks:
Or when Ulysses on the larboard shunn'd
Charybdis, and by the other whirlpool steer'd,
So he with difficulty and labour hard
Moved on, with difficulty and labour he—'

There are, however, many glaciers whose ascent is attended with no such inconveniences and perils, although generally with some labour, whether along the moraine or on the ice ; the cool footing and the exhilarating mountain air give, however, an elasticity and confidence to the tread unknown below—the eye, familiarized with precipices, forgets their terrors, and those who at home would hesitate to walk along the top of a narrow wall, can look with unblenching gaze into the fathomless depth of the glacier *crevasses*. But whether the inferior part of the glacier has been steep and dislocated, or even and gently inclined, the higher portion of the ravine or basin in which it takes its origin is very generally, for some space at least, moderately flat. The glacier here bounds with the region of perpetual snows, from which (on every theory) it depends in some way or other for its sustenance and increase; and consequently this portion of the ice-field peculiarly demands our attention, for it presents important modifications, and in fact has received from mountaineers a peculiar name—in French it is called *névé*, and in German *firn*.

The névé or firn is the unconsolidated glacier. As we approach it the fissures of the glacier become generally rarer, and always narrower. The elevation above the sea being already very considerable, perhaps 8000 or 9000 English feet, the winter's snow lies all summer on the surface of the ice, conceals the *crevasses*, and partly also the structure of the matter of the glacier itself; to discern which the snow must be carefully removed. It is a frequent, perhaps a general characteristic of the transition from the glacier proper to the névé, that whilst the former presents a *convex* surface, the latter is *concave*, and inosculates insensibly into the snowy steeps which clothe the sides of the upper glacier-basins, at these great heights. Magnificent is the prospect which these firns

sometimes present. The surface is smooth and almost level, like an artificial floor stretched across a valley, whose sides evidently descend to a great depth beneath. It is a real platform—to compare great things with small, it is a theatre with the pit boarded over; and what a theatre! From that even snowy carpet of dazzling white rise hundreds of nameless peaks on either hand, seeming to pierce a sky whose azure hue is so intense, as to find no match in nature save the gentian, which expands its lovely flowers close to the glacier. The sides, scathed by lightning, and torn by the avalanche, scarcely permit a resting-place for the snow, which accumulates in dazzling wreaths only in its sheltered nooks. Each of these pinnacles transported to an ordinary scene would seem one of nature's grandest objects, whilst here it is lost amidst the crowd of its fellows. But a very few have any specific name, and still fewer are found indicated on the best maps.[*] Sometimes the ice-field abuts abruptly against precipices which rise nearly vertically from out of it, as does the Finster Aar Horn from the névé of the Aar glacier—a splendid surface, almost flat, and of many square miles in extent, in the midst of the very highest group of mountains in Switzerland proper.

The structure and consistence of this unconsolidated glacier is extremely remarkable, and, as we have said, it is important for the theory of glacier motion. It is evidently snow in a transition state into ice, having a granular structure, resulting from the partial thaw to which it has been subjected, in consequence of the water, which the heat of the sun produces, percolating pretty freely through the mass. The *crevasses* in the névé differ from those in the glacier by their greater width and irregularity, by their beautiful green colour, and by the horizontal stratification of the material forming their sides, which is divided by bands of more or less perfectly formed ice, corresponding, perhaps, to annual periods, or to extraordinary falls of snow.[†] It is hardly necessary to say, that the passage from the glacier proper to

[*] A popular error prevails, that Switzerland is provided with better maps than any other country in Europe. This has some colour of truth with respect to a mere road map, such as the traveller on beaten paths requires. Bring any map, however, to the test of comparison with real landmarks and the natural features of mountainous tracks, and Keller's and every map now existing are found grievously wanting. There is but faint hope that this material deficiency will be effectually supplied within many years, notwithstanding the professed interest taken by the Swiss government in its fulfilment.

[†] This structure, which may be observed up even to extreme heights, and is too remarkable to be overlooked, has been mentioned by De Saussure;

the névé is graduated, not abrupt. It appears to have an intimate connection with the permanence of the winter falls of snow, which entirely vanish during summer, upon the surface of the ordinary glacier, with which they never enter into intimate combination, but are melted by degrees; excepting here and there a mass which, falling into a *crevasse*, is there consolidated by successive thaws and congelations.* The region of the névé, or firn, is one of intense and unmitigated desolation. Even where a rock appears, no plant more developed than a lichen or moss flourishes upon it; a stray insect is generally the only trace of animal life; even the chamois avoids these wilds, unless pursued: no animal, indeed, can be more sensitively afraid of the *crevasses* and chasms which, thinly covered by treacherous snow, often reveal to the amazed traveller the awfully precarious footing upon which he has just heedlessly passed.

This portion of the glacier, occupying, as we have said, the upland basins or hollows which stretch far into the mass of compound mountain systems, is succeeded by the last member of the glacier series; which occupies the sides and summits of the mountain ranges themselves, and their innumerable offshoots. The névé, whose gently swelling concave form we have attempted to describe, generally terminates tolerably abruptly against some rocky or very steep icy boundary, by which the highest mountain summits or ridges are to be scaled. There is a chasm of separation, so well marked and so general, as to be considered as forming part of the characteristic glacier type; and which is called in the German part of Switzerland the *Berg-schrund.* The passing of this forms a very frequent and notable difficulty in the way of Alpine travellers, who attempt to attain the highest regions. Once passed, the glacier features are resumed. On the flanks of the mountains, and even on their summits, the snow is consolidated into a compact icy structure, alternating, however, in the more sheltered places with crisp snow, which separates the icy layers, characteristic also of the proper névé. That true ice should be found on the highest summits, is not a matter of the

least surprise to those who reflect that the sun acts at these elevations with an intensity unknown below; and though the continued accumulation of snow is no doubt mainly prevented by the action of wind, (which may often be seen driving to leeward a delicate cloud of dry snowy particles, having all the appearance of the finest vapour), and likewise by the *immediate* evaporation of the snow without passing into the liquid form; yet there can be no question that every hot summer's day proper fusion goes forward, and a corresponding congelation during the night—forming a true icy casing of the most insulated summits where snow can rest at all. Saussure, indeed, was not convinced of this fact until he actually ascended Mont Blanc,* whose top surveyed with the greatest care from the Cramont, he had previously† supposed to be merely snow. There are other mountains, however, which bear direct testimony to the fact, even from a distance. Some of the magnificent icy pyramids in the neighbourhood of the Ortler Spitz in the Tyrol are evidently composed in their upper parts of pure ice, which, in certain positions of the sun, transmits its characteristic greenish light in a manner truly magical. ‡ A great number of mountains too, above 10,000 feet high, and having precipices on their northern or eastern sides, present the following remarkable appearance:—Icy crusts, possessing great consistency, project *many feet* over the precipices, and when the sun shines favourably upon them, exhibit their peculiar colour with extreme delicacy. These projections are formed by the tufted accumulation of gently drifted snow, which, thawing at intervals, becomes invested with a crisp coating. This crust, if pierced inadvertently, may bring a traveller into the most perilous situations, or sacrifice his life. Hugi picturesquely describes one of the most awful positions of this kind in which a human being was ever placed. Whilst attempting the ascent of the Finster Aar Horn, he broke, by his weight, through a cornice of ice such as we have described, only two feet thick, and projecting five or six feet over a sheer precipice of 4000 feet. Fortunately, one of his companions had, for security, a hold of the other extremity of a long staff which he carried, who, applying his whole weight at the opposite end, the two were held suspended in awful equilibrium, as at the arms of a balance, until help

---

Zumstein, and other Alpine travellers. Charpentier says—'La fonte incomplète des neiges annuelles des hauts névés est la cause de la stratification qu'ils présentent, mais qui s'efface et finit par disparaître entièrement, à mesure qu'ils se changent en glaciers.'—*Essai*, p. 3.

* 'Les *firns* ou *hauts névés* se trouvent à une hauteur où les neiges tombées dans le courant d'une année, ne disparaissent pas entièrement l'année suivante. En revanche les neiges qui tombent sur les glaciers se fondent complètement presque tous les étés.'—Charpentier. p. 3.

* *Voyages dans les Alpes*, § 1981. See also Auldjo's *Mont Blanc.*   † Ibid. 530 and 940.

‡ It is probably, for this reason, that the Ortler obtains on the Italian side the name of Monte Cristallo. Captain Gerard mentions, that on the Himalaya the snow visibly melts during summer at heights exceeding 20,000 feet.

was obtained.—(*Naturhistorische Alpen-reise*, p 193).

Having thus sketched the whole course and transitions of the glacier world from its inferior outlets to its highest summits, and explained, in passing, the origin of many of its most remarkable configurations—we proceed to consider what have been proposed as theories of the mechanical functions of the glacier—its reproductive faculty, by which its waste is continually made good, and consequently the theory of its motion ; how

> ' The glacier's cold and restless mass
> Moves onward day by day.'

To enter into detail respecting the arguments used by the advocates of the various hypotheses employed, would greatly exceed the limits of this article. We restrict ourselves, therefore, to a concise description of the two great rival theories; the main facts which appear to support each ; and to a few of the difficulties which appear to us to cause hesitation in the adoption of either. That we may not, however, seem to consider the subject hopeless, we shall suggest some experiments which may one day lead to a solution of these interesting questions.

The theory of De Saussure (which, though much older, owes its notoriety to his clear exposition of it) is simply this—that the accumulation of the snow in the higher icefields during the year, and especially in winter, forms not only the *pabulum* for the growth of the glacier, but is the glacier itself ;—the fusion of the snow, and the infiltration and congelation of the water, forming the gritty ice of which the glacier proper, and also the lower part of the névé, is composed.* The pressure of the accumulated snows (due not only to the mean fall on the area of the surface, but also to the discharge by avalanches from the steep sides) is the *moving cause* of the glacier, as the inferior extremity is melted away. According to this theory, the glacier melts, not only at its upper surface but at its lower one, owing to the contact of the ground beneath, which has a temperature above 32°. Now, this fusion beneath, evidenced by the flow of glacier streams even in winter, greatly facilitates the movement of the glacier along its inclined bed. It also accounts for the more rapid movement of the sides than the centre of the glacier; since there the detachment of the glacier from the trough in which it lies is usually more complete. The cre-

---

* *De Saussure*, § 526.

vasses are produced by the unequal velocity of the glacier in its different parts, and by the inequalities of the bottom over which it is compelled to heave its rigid and unwieldy mass.

The other theory, also very old—having been expounded by Scheuchzer above a century ago—ascribes to glaciers *the same origin*, viz.—the transformation of the névé into ice ; but to the *movement* of the glacier a very different one. The ice of glaciers not being solid but porous—or rather, according to the authors who maintain this theory, fissured by minute cracks in every direction—the water melted at the surface is drawn by capillarity into these rents; and during the immediately succeeding act of congelation, the mass of the glacier is momentarily increased by the expansion of this water in freezing. The swollen mass expands in the direction of least resistance—that is, vertically upwards or in thickness, and longitudinally forwards or in the direction of its motion. This theory, broached in later times by Toussaint de Charpentier, is maintained with much ingenuity of argument by Jean de Charpentier, Agassiz, and others.

In the course of the animated controversy still going on upon this subject, we have been struck by the occasional want of clear views as to physical principles, betrayed in the heat of argument upon the one side as upon the other. We will endeavour to state what we consider as real difficulties to each hypothesis; and leave the reader to judge, whether in the present state of the question he is prepared to give in his adhesion to either.

1. And first of the Gravitation Theory. De Saussure's views are most applicable to glaciers descending with a considerable inclination, and through valleys of nearly equal breadth, without notable promontories, and gently widening as they descend. Such are several of the glaciers of Chamouni, to which this eminent man directed his chief attention—the Glacier du Bois (in part) and Bossons, and those of Miage and Brenva on the Italian side of Mont Blanc. But the case becomes different when the inclination is very small, the mass very extended, and the valley, instead of enlarging beneath, contracted towards its inferior extremity ;—such as the remarkable glacier of Aletsch, into which fall the firns of the Jungfrau, Mönch, Eiger, and the mountains of the Upper Lötsch-thal, and which has its embouchure in a narrow ravine which joins the upper valley of the Rhone near Brieg: The upper surface of this glacier has a nearly uniform

inclination of only 30°.* It is certainly difficult to conceive that the mere effect of gravity upon a slope of this inclination, would be sufficient to overcome the *enormous* friction of ice upon such a bed. It must be remembered, however, that the inclination of the bottom probably much exceeds that of the surface at that part where the accumulation of ice is greatest, and the superficial inclination least. Thus, in the case before us, there is a difference of level of not less than 6000 or 7000 French feet between the commencement of the névé of the Aletsch glacier, on the slope of the Jungfrau, and the inferior extremity of the glacier. The distance between the two points may (by Weiss's map) be reckoned along the glacier at four Swiss leagues, or about 72,000 feet; consequently the mean slope, reckoning from rock to rock, is nearly 1 in 10—a very marked inclination, equal to the greatest degree of steepness admitted on the Simplon route, (5° 42′.) Even this, however, is a feeble inclination compared with the enormous friction and adhesion which such a mass of ice, embayed in rocks, must present; and we hold this objection to be a very serious one to the hypothesis.

The contrary objection, urged by Charpentier, (p. 32,) against the theory of Saussure, is more unfounded. He asks, 'What is the resistance which can maintain a glacier from sliding down a slope inclined 45°, in the case of the glaciers descending from the Dent du Midi?' We answer, *friction.* Where the force of friction is equal to that of gravity, (no uncommon case) 45° will be the angle of repose. Mr. G. Rennie found that the polished granite *voussoirs* of London Bridge only commenced slipping at an angle of 33° or 34°.†

Nor do we attach much importance to the objection of the same ingenious author, that the movement of glaciers is greatest in summer, and nothing in winter, though the pressure of snow is greatest at the latter time. During winter the glacier is so thoroughly frozen by its edges, that it is inconceivable that it should then make any considerable progress, even though the base should remain partly free.

It is a serious difficulty in the gravitation theory, that the movements of glaciers do not appear to take place violently *per saltum,* as we should expect to be the case if they were due to the preponderance of gravity over friction. The relations of glaciers

starting forwards several feet at a time, are generally considered apocryphal.—(Hugi, p. 368, and Agassiz.)

An objection which seems to us important against the theory of De Saussure, though we believe it has not been distinctly noticed, is the following:—If a glacier have no supply of material throughout its mass, but is exposed to all the influence of evaporations and thaw, which we know often diminish its thickness at the rate of a foot a-week, how comes the inclination of the surface to be so gentle as we generally find it, and the glacier to be so prolonged into the plains? If the glacier advance downwards, and at the same time diminish by its upper surface, it must continually tend to assume a wedge form, and to terminate by the meeting of its upper and lower surfaces. Perhaps, however, we shall not greatly err if we conceive the maximum-effect of waste, or one foot per week, to continue for four months in the year, and that, during the remaining eight, the waste is insensible. We shall have sixteen feet of thickness lost in a year. Suppose that in the same time the glacier has advanced 320 feet longitudinally, the inclination of the surface *due to waste,* and independent of the trough of the glacier, would be only 1 in 20. But to this must be added the waste at the inferior surface.

We have said that it has generally been regarded as an essential part of the theory of De Saussure, that the inferior surface of the ice being continually melted by the heat of the earth, the sliding of the glacier along its bed is thereby facilitated. Now, one of the most delicate parts of the whole inquiry is, ' What is the precise relation of the glacier to the supporting rocks?' No doubt MM. De Charpentier and Agassiz have stated several reasons for supposing that the contact surface of the ice and rock will be always at a freezing temperature, and beyond a certain elevation above the sea, that it will be below that temperature ; and they have supported their views by a citation of the respectable authority of Bischoff:—they have also thought themselves warranted to conclude that the ice is firmly frozen to its bed, which M. Agassiz (p. 161) considers necessary to explain the maintenance of a glacier in a deeply-fissured state, where the pyramids of ice are almost separated from one another ; and Charpentier (p. 95) derives it from the direct observations repeatedly made by M. Venetz on the glacier of Giètroz ; and yet it seems never distinctly to have occurred to these gentlemen, that, were the glacier *permanently* frozen to its bed, as they suppose,

---

* Elie de Beaumont, *Mémoires,* &c. Tom. IV. p. 215, 223.

† Philosophical Transactions, 1829.

it is impossible that it should have a true progressive motion from any cause whatever—a fact which yet all admit.

'Such an adhesion,' observes M. Agassiz, (p. 162,) 'excludes at once all idea of sliding; and if, notwithstanding, a glacier falls forward, it can only be when the weight of the masses lying on an inclined plane overcomes their adhesion to the base. But how comes it, I shall be asked, that all the while it adheres to the soil on which it rests, a glacier is yet capable of advancing? This is what I shall endeavour to demonstrate.'

It does not appear to us, however, that any thing like a demonstration follows. The question remains unanswered and unanswerable. There may be a force different from that of gravity which puts the glacier in motion—and that force may be the expansive action described by these authors; but come whence it will, this force succeeds in moving the glacier onwards, whilst the rock beneath it retains its place. Can this occur without the one surface becoming detached from the other? We apprehend not.

But what is most inconsistent is, that the motion of the glaciers on their rocky beds is just as distinctly insisted on and required, for the explanation of phenomena, by the disciples of Charpentier, as by those of De Saussure. Charpentier combats (p. 105) the idea, that the *friction* between the ice and the bottom should exceed the expansive force which he ascribes to the glacier: in another place he says—'the movement impressed by the dilatation of the WHOLE MASS of the glacier occasions a friction so inconsiderable against the rocks, (which form its bed and support it,) that the surface wears, is hollowed, becomes smooth, and take even a slight polish, if the rock be, by its hardness, capable of receiving it,' (p. 42.) And Agassiz speaks still more definitely of 'the bed of mud and gravel which is intermediate between the glacier and its bed,' (p. 194;) and of 'the rounded pebbles upon which the glaciers move in their lower part,' (p. 197.) We apprehend, therefore, that these advocates prove too much.

2. Let us now advert to the arguments which have been, or may be, urged against the dilatation theory of glacier motion, in which it is assumed that the structure of the ice being porous, and the superficial water being absorbed into the mass during the day, the water becomes frozen in the night, dilates, and pushes the glacier forward.

The first objection we shall mention is urged by M. Necker, in his zealous defence of the doctrine of his distinguished relative, De Saussure, in the work mentioned at the head of this article. He maintains that the supposed elongation would not be due to the *entire* expansion of the frozen infiltrated water, since the solid mass of ice would, doubtless, extend laterally and vertically, as well as longitudinally.[*] Admitting, then, that water expands one-seventh of its volume in freezing, we are not to infer that the glacier would expand one-seventh of its length by the thaw and re-congelation of its entire mass; for he says—'It would be to understand very imperfectly the nature and power of the molecular forces to suppose that the action of gravity can be an obstacle to them,' (so that the glacier should only extend itself down the declivity.) 'Limited in its action to very small spaces, expansion, like crystallization, acts without regard to gravity, and we know that expansion, particularly, exercises within small spaces a power almost irresistible.'—Necker, p. 153.

This is perfectly true; but it does not at all follow that because dilatation is irresistible, the form of the mass shall be unchanged, or that it shall pay no regard to the direction in which gravity aids its motion. No doubt, if we regard a glacier as a perfectly *rigid* body, (which is a peculiar molecular condition wholly independent of the quality of expansibility,) it must preserve symmetry of form during dilatation—each dimension of length, breadth, and thickness, acquiring a *proper linear* increase. This, however, admitting for a moment the theory in other respects, is evidently *not* the characteristic of a glacier; which is of a consistence somewhat yielding, without which its progression would be in fact impossible, owing to the irregularities and contractions of the channel in which it moves. The plasticity of the whole would, therefore, we apprehend, throw the enlargement chiefly in a downward direction. Could we, however, suppose the dilatation to take place equally in all directions, we cannot even then coincide with the conclusion of M. Necker, that the increase of the whole Glacier du Bois would be 'less than 6.83 feet in all directions.' In the first place, the augmentation in length

---

[*] M. Agassiz had put the matter thus. "Comme le glacier est contenu des deux côtés par les flancs de la vallée, et en haut par le poids des masses supérieures, toute l'action de la dilatation se porte naturellement dans le sens de la pente, qui est le seul côté qui lui offre une libre issue, et vers lequel elle doit déjà tendre, en vertu de la loi de gravitation.' —P. 165-6.

would of course, by its proportionality to the linear dimension, exceed that in breadth and thickness; and the amount would be nearly *one-third* of the cubical expansion, or more accurately one twenty-second of each dimension. Now, assuming with M. Necker the length of the Glacier du Bois to be 4000 toises, the expansion in length would be 182 toises, or 1092 French feet, by the recongelation of the whole ice in the glacier. We are unable to conjecture how the other palpably erroneous result has been obtained.

We could show, did space permit, that we do not consider the calculation by the same author, founded on the annual fall of rain and snow, conclusive against the dilatation theory; in which the water is not atmospheric water merely, but the matter of the glacier which goes again and again through the process of thawing and freezing.

The existence of vast *crevasses* dividing the ice into vertical segments, is an obvious difficulty in the theory of dilatation, being inconsistent with the general tension described (Charpentier, p. 12,) as being the immediate cause of motion. To this it may be replied with some show of reason, (Charp. p. 108,) that these *crevasses* never extend quite across and to the bottom of a glacier, but they occur partially and discontinuously, so as not to affect the rigidity of the whole glacier more than the slits do in a parchment sieve. On the other hand, on the theory of Saussure, (and from what was even said above, we suspect upon any theory,) if the glacier move over its bed, we have only to suppose the lowest stratum of ice to be continuous, which in all probability it is, in order to be shoved downwards.

But there seems to us to be more formidable objections to the dilatation theory than any of these. This theory supposes the ice to be composed of fragments nicely wedged into one another; which fragments enlarge as they proceed from the névé to the lower part of the glacier. The water produced by rain or heat is absorbed into these fissures; on the return of night or drought it freezes, and, expanding, urges the glacier bodily forward, occasioning likewise a growth in the directions of breadth and thickness. Now we find, in the *first* place, some difficulty in admitting the *universal* existence of the capillary fissures assumed. M. Agassiz, indeed, states their existence as general (p. 163); we confess, however, some scepticism on this point. The ca-

pillary fissures are only well shown where the ice surface is in contact with a mass of rock, whose varying temperature has no doubt fissured the neighbouring ice. In some glaciers, such as that of Rosenlaui, this structure is very beautifully developed—the great irregular grains of the glacier lying wedged into one another, with water between, so curiously packed, that though they may be shaken in their places, it is often difficult to dissect them. We are, therefore, far from denying the existence of this granulated structure in certain parts of glaciers. We only hesitate to admit its presence throughout their mass. There is, however, a structure which may perhaps aid the theory more than the other somewhat problematical hypothesis—a structure so remarkable, that we are surprised to find no mention of it amongst the authorities we have cited.* It is a ribboned texture of the ice, which seems in most glaciers disposed in bands nearly vertical, and throughout the greater part of the glacier very generally parallel with its length. This veined appearance, which is beautiful and striking, and which extends to a great depth, is occasioned by the alternation of compact and porous ice in vertical laminæ side by side—generally less than one inch in thickness; and so well marked, that when the surface of the glacier is cut and polished by a watercourse, it exhibits the appearance of the most delicately-veined chalcedony. In the sides of the great transverse *crevasses*, this structure is peculiarly evident from the greater or less persistence of the different veins. We hasten to add that it appears to have very little, if anything, in common with *stratification* properly so called. But however caused, since these porous and compact layers are generally vertical or highly inclined, it is not unlikely that they form a system of filters, which allows some of the water to percolate from the upper to the lower part of the ice.

Our *second* objection arises from the difficulty of conceiving capillary fissures having their walls continually maintained at, or below 0° per cent,† into which water is to be drawn by capillary action, not only at the surface, but throughout the whole thickness of the ice, without being frozen in the very act.

---

* But more recently described in the *Edinburgh New Philosophical Journal* for January, 1842.
† Agassiz, p. 203. Charpentier, p. 10.

Our *third* objection is—supposing these capillary fissures so filled during the day, —how comes it that the water they contain is frozen during the night, not merely at the surface, but to great depths, where the effect of the diurnal changes of temperature cannot possibly arrive by conduction ?* M. de Charpentier has stated this objection, (p. 104.) We own that his reply to it seems to us wholly unintelligible.†

Our *fourth* objection would be, that if congelation *could* occur, the upper strata must be by far the most affected, the lower ones not at all. The motion would therefore be confined to the superficial part of the glacier. This reasoning is so fully admitted by Agassiz, that he has endeavoured to make it a ground of proof in favour of his hypothesis, by maintaining ‡ that the glaciers are stratified horizontally ; and that these strata move with greater velocity in proportion as they are nearer the surface—each stratum having the motion proper to its own dilatation, superadded to the sum of the motions of the strata beneath. We are bound to state that the ingenious author seems to have erred in point of accuracy of observation. Such stratification does not exist, and it is accordingly denied by Charpentier, (p. 108, *note.*) If it existed, or if the upper portions moved faster than the lower, we should have phenomena wholly different from those observed. Were this true, no *crevasse* could remain vertical ; the top of its advanced wall must move more rapidly than the base, and slope forward, while the posterior wall would overhang. No trace of a *general* law of this kind is to be found amongst the glaciers : if some *crevasses* appear to lean forwards, others lean backwards, and a majority are vertical.§ We hold this fact to be a strong argument against the dilatation theory.

A *fifth* difficulty is this : why do the névés

not accumulate indefinitely ? for if the glaciers move only by the swelling of their mass, the névé cannot literally be said to be the feeder of the glacier, the movement of which must be great just in proportion to its distance from its origin, (the névé). If, then, in its upper part the glacier move little or nothing, the névé, which commences precisely where the winter snows never melt, what becomes of the accumulation of the winter snows ? They do not fall downwards to fill up the place of the progressive glacier, for the glacier at that point makes little or no progress. The glacier advances only in consequence of swelling or dilating, and consequently its movement depends at any point upon the length of the part whose dilatation produces the motion, which length is to be reckoned *from* the névé, for the dilatation vanishes where the névé begins. Instead, therefore, of the névé annually filling up the space left by the progressive glacier, there is no space to be filled up at all ; and the glacier must advance solely in consequence of the absorption of the dissolved snow, which falls upon its proper surface.

This important consideration suggests the *only* critical experiment we know of, for the discrimination of the true hypothesis. If Saussure's theory be true, the glacier moves onward without sensibly incorporating new matter into its substance—continually fed by the supplies from behind, which form a new and endless glacier. The mechanism may not inaptly be compared to that of the modern paper machine, which, from the gradually consolidated material of pulp, (representing the névé) at length discharges, in a perpetual flow, the snowy web. The theory of Charpentier, on the other hand, represents the fabrication of the glacier going on within the glacier itself, and so that each part swells, and the dilatation of each is added to that which acted upon itself, in order to shove on the section of the ice immediately in advance. *In the former case, then, the distance between two determinate points of the glacier remains the same ; in the latter, it will continually increase.* Again, *on the former hypothesis, the annual progress of any point of the glacier is independent of its position ; on the latter, it increases with the distance from the origin, (the transverse section of the ice being the same).* The solution of this important problem would be obtained by the correct measurement, at successive periods, of the spaces between points marked on insulated boulders on the glacier ; or between the heads of pegs of considerable length, stuck into the matter of the ice, and by the determination of their annual progress.

---

* In common soils the diurnal changes of temperature vanish at a depth of three or four feet.

† Feeling apparently its insufficiency, he has returned to it at page 307 of his work ; but by insisting more strongly on the capillary nature of the infiltration, and the low temperature of the interior of the glacier, he only brings out the difficulties more prominently. But we must refer to the work itself.

‡ Page 165-6.

§ M. Agassiz seems to have been partly misled by a figure of a glacier waterfall in Hugi's *Travels,* plate III. It is strange that he should have preferred the evidence of this single figure to all the direct observations which he has had such ample opportunities of making.

In endeavouring to present a statement of the two prevalent theories of glacier motion, and the formidable difficulties which may be suggested to either, we are far from asserting that both are necessarily wrong, or that the difficulties we have stated are incapable of a reply. We incline to think the objections to Saussure's hypothesis are of a more *positive* kind, because the theory is more intelligible; and that the other, which calls into play a *kind* of force (dilatation) very likely, from its great energy, to produce the effect in question, addresses itself in some degree to our ignorance, and therefore the objections to it retain a somewhat ambiguous character. This arises particularly from our ignorance of the habitudes of a fluid *about to freeze*—of the very minute circumstances which retard or accelerate congelation, and of the distances through which these causes may energetically act. Still less do we know the influence of the capillarity of the fissures under such circumstances. We are not disposed to accept as demonstrative the experiments yet made on the percolation of water in the mass of ice, or even the existence of the network of fissures, presumed to traverse the most compact glacier ice. The absorption of coloured fluids would appear to be one method of determining the amount and direction of such percolation. The experiment has not yet been made to our entire satisfaction.

We had intended to have explained the dependence of the direction of fissures upon the form and motion of the glacier, and the not less remarkable relation which appears to subsist between these and the varied structure of the ice; but our space does not admit of it. We will, therefore, conclude this part of the subject with the following very just remarks of Charpentier—

'Since the time of M. de Saussure, the knowledge of glaciers has made but little progress. The subject seemed to have been exhausted, and that there remained nothing to add—nothing to modify—nothing to correct. A great number, perhaps most, geologists, and many philosophers and men of science, have visited and still visit the glaciers; but very few amongst them have made them an object of study. The reason is simple, arising on the one hand from the remoteness of the glacier localities, and on the other from the number and variety of interesting objects there to be met with. . . . . The intelligent and observing foreigner, arriving for the first time amongst the higher Alps, finds, at every step, something which strikes and interests him, and which distracts his attention; whilst the inhabitant of the Alps, more familiarized with their sublime scenery and remarkable productions, is in a better state for directing and concentrating his attention upon a special object.'—(*Essai*, p. 352.)

We now turn to the last division of our subject—the application which has lately been made of the phenomena of glaciers to account for certain changes on the earth's surface, which have occurred even in places where glaciers now no longer exist. The great phenomenon for the explanation of which this theory of the ancient extension of glaciers has been contrived, is the distribution of erratic blocks over ranges of country where the material, or rock, of which the blocks are composed, is nowhere to be found *in situ*.

The geological divisions of the latest deposits found on the earth's surface, are not very uniform or consistent in different works. The first volume of the work of Professor Necker,[*] the amiable and accomplished geologist of Geneva, contains a clear and tolerably detailed statement of the aspect which they assume in the country of which we shall chiefly have to speak; namely, the flat or undulating tract intervening between the foot of the Alps, and that of the Jura range. The ordinary divisions of these superficial formations into two; the *alluvium*, which contains evidence, both zoological and mechanical, of having been produced in the present age of the world, whilst the same species lived, and the same abrading and depositing causes acted as now; and the *diluvium* or 'boulder formation,' 'terrainerratique' of continental geologists, 'drift' of England, and 'till' of Scotland, differing from the former in the species of contained fossils, many of which are extinct, or belong only to distant regions of the globe. The diluvium is rarely, if at all, stratified; the superposition of blocks, gravel, and mud, is without order; and the blocks are often enormous and angular. The reverse features characterize the alluvium. M. Necker divides the older or diluvial formation into two—the unstratified or cataclysmal diluvium; and one inferior to it, which is stratified and devoid of huge angular fragments; and which, by its structure, resembles the modern alluvium, from which, however, it is separated by the entire 'boulder formation:'—this he terms the 'old alluvium.'

'The ancient alluvial formation,' he says, 'is formed by rounded pebbles of gravel and sand, more or less fine. The pebbles have in general a magnitude which varies from the size of an egg to that of the fist, and which never attains the size of the head. They are perfectly smoothed, and often a little flattened, like those which are found on the shores of a lake. They form horizontal beds, sometimes of a thickness of

---

[*] *Etudes Géologiques dans les Alpes.*

several toises, now and then irregularly alternating with beds of gravel and sand, shorter and thicker, and having a lenticular form. The disposition of these beds is entirely similar, although on a greater scale, to those of the existing alluvia of the Arve and the Rhone.'— (*Etudes dans les Alpes*, p. 233.)

Hence, to explain these facts, it is supposed that no cause materially differing from those now in action requires to be invoked But with the proper diluvium it is different; no geologist has been able entirely to disguise the necessity of having recourse to an energy greater than is now to be found on the earth's surface—

' The masses are without any apparent order, in which materials of all sizes, from the most enormous blocks to the finest mud, are mixed and confounded together, so as to lead us to presume that only a terrible cataclysm could have produced a deposit so deep, and of such a structure.'—(*Ibid.* p. 232.)

And again—

' Although the great blocks form part of a mass composed chiefly of small débris, yet, as it is the mass of these blocks which determines the *minimum* intensity required for the force which has transported the whole, we may, without disadvantage, in order to have the principal data of the problem, neglect all the débris of smaller dimensions, and consider the blocks alone. In fact, the existence of these blocks commands the whole question; for had these masses been, like the ancient *alluvium*, composed of gravel and pebbles, we should naturally have sought (as for the latter) no causes differing in kind from our existing torrents and rivers, though perhaps more powerful.'—(*Ibid.* p. 351-2.)

This is a perfectly fair statement of the question, and it is scarcely possible to convey to one who has not seen the ' boulder formation' or ' cataclysmal diluvium' in its full development, (as for instance, on the flanks of the Jura range, above Neufchatel and facing the Alps) an adequate notion of the wonderful phenomenon to be explained.

A great part of the plain of Switzerland, as of many other large and nearly level tracts, is covered at intervals by fragments of travelled rocks, the greater part of which owe their origin to the higher Alpine tracts, as their mineralogical character unequivocally indicates. Amongst the rolled and rounded pebbles of smaller size, we find, indeed, many specimens whose origin may be stated to be completely unknown; further than that they have evidently been detached from one of the conglomerate formations which occur so plentifully on the northern side of the Alps. It is one of the real ' wonders of geology,' the occurrence of those pebbles derived from the trituration of rocks which can no longer be identified, which in a former age of the world yielded the boulders of the ' alluvium' of that period —became consolidated into rock—and now, by a fresh revolution, are tossed and ground by modern rivers, and mix again with our superficial deposits. The most important masses, however, are those which attain a considerable size— *metrical* blocks, as they have been termed —that is, having about a cubic yard of contents, which strew the plain, dot the sides of the Alpine ravines, and rise even to an elevation of several thousand feet above the sea upon the opposite flank of the Jura range, where not one fragment of a primitive rock is to be found *in situ*. The most concentrated distribution of erratics is to be found about Neufchatel, at a height of 800 or 900 feet above the lake of that name, and the valley of Switzerland. Similar masses are found on the summit of the Mount Salève, at a great height above the lake of Geneva, and insulated from the general group of Alps. It is perhaps difficult to convey upon paper too lively an impression of the singularity of the phenomenon—a belt of fragmentary masses lying on a steep, almost precipitous, slope of nearly bare or thinly-covered rock, of a nature wholly dissimilar; not few nor small, but countless and gigantic. The Pierre à Bot (*toad-stone*,) 850 feet above Neufchatel, has a length of between fifty and sixty feet, a breadth of twenty, and a height of above forty. It is of granite, and distant in a *right line* from its supposed origin in the Val Ferret, to the east of Mont Blanc, seventy English miles. Now, observing that this is no individual case, and that many other blocks, if not so large, yet comparable to it in size, are to be found on the Jura, and that those of one or two cubic yards and under are really innumerable, further, that between the Jura and the higher Alps, blocks still larger are in many places to be found, as at Steinhof in the Canton of Berne, (one out of a great number together measuring 61,000 cubic feet,) we perceive the vast extent and measure of the phenomenon to be explained ; enough, alone and at once, to overturn any hypothesis as to the omnipotence of causes now in action, unmodified in intensity, however long-continued.

It is quite needless to enter into a detail of all the explanations which have been proposed of these wonderful facts.

stumbling-blocks on the very threshold of the structure which geology designs to explore. A detail of them, and a clear statement of some of the many objections which may be urged against each, is to be found in Charpentier's lucid essay on glaciers. Of the former theories of transport, that of the action of prodigious ' diluvial' currents is the one supported by the greatest amount of authority ; and when we cite the names of De Saussure, Von Buch, and Sir James Hall, our readers will perceive that the authority is enforced by its weight as well as its generality. Playfair, indeed, in the very face of far abler arguments adduced by himself, asserted that the boulders on the Mount Saleve, near Geneva, might have been transported by the river Arve when it flowed at a higher level,[*]—a piece of ultra-Huttonianism which he could hardly have maintained had he visited the locality. But in the same memorable work in which he hazarded this assertion, we find an indication of a cause, far more adequate as well as more original, in the extension of glaciers as agents of transport. This indication, which forms part of the very able note on the *transportation of stones*, in the 'Illustrations of the Huttonian theory,' is neither vague nor indirect. It is put forward as the most probable explanation of all cases of transport where immense power was obviously required.

' For the moving of large masses of rock,' says Professor Playfair, ' THE MOST POWERFUL AGENTS WITHOUT DOUBT WHICH NATURE EMPLOYS ARE THE GLACIERS, those lakes or rivers of ice which are formed in the highest valleys of the Alps, and other mountains of the first order. These great masses are in perpetual motion, undermined by the influx of heat from the earth, and impelled down the declivities on which they rest by their own enormous weight, together with that of the innumerable fragments of rock with which they are loaded. These fragments they gradually transport to their utmost boundaries, where a formidable wall ascertains the magnitude, and attests the force, of the great engine by which it was erected. The immense quantity and size of the rocks thus transported, have been remarked with astonishment by every observer, and explain sufficiently how fragments of rock may be put in motion even where there is but little declivity, and where the actual surface of the ground is considerably uneven. In this manner, before the valleys were cut out in the form they now are, and where the mountains were still more elevated, huge fragments of rock may have been carried to a great distance ; and it is not wonderful if these same masses, greatly diminished in size, and

reduced to gravel or sand, have reached the shores, or even the bottom of the sea. NEXT IN FORCE TO THE GLACIERS, the torrents are the most powerful instruments employed in the transportation of stones,' &c.—(*Huttonian Theory*, Art. 349.)

Now, as the passage immediately preceding that we have quoted contains a statement of the problematical facts mentioned above, respecting the distribution of the travelled blocks in the plains of Switzerland and on the Jura, we cannot but give to Professor Playfair the credit of having clearly pointed out the probability of the former greater extension of glaciers as THE MOST POWERFUL known agents of transport. This was in the year 1802, before the author had had the opportunity of personally estimating the applicability of the theory to phenomena. The passage from the notes of his journey in 1816, quoted in this Journal (Volume LXIX.) and more lately by Charpentier, shows that his views in this respect had undergone no change in the interval, and were only confirmed by an inspection of the erratic blocks on the Jura, which he unhesitatingly ascribes to the former existence of glaciers which once *crossed* the lake of Geneva and the plain of Switzerland. Rivers like the Arve he no longer considers adequate agents, nor even currents of water, however great, as in the *debacle* of De Saussure. ' A current of water,' he says, ' however powerful, could never have carried it' (the Pierre à Bot, near Neufchatel) ' up an acclivity, but would have deposited it in the first valley it came to, and would in a much less distance have rounded its angles and given to it the shape so characteristic of stones subjected to the action of water. A glacier which fills up valleys in its course, and which conveys rocks on its surface free from attrition, is the ONLY AGENT we now see capable of transporting them to such a distance, without destroying that sharpness of the angles so distinctive of these masses.'[*]

Like many other anticipations of new theories, these pointed and just observations of Professor Playfair lay dormant until the opinion he advanced had been separately originated and discussed. M. Venetz, an intelligent engineer of the canton of Valais, speculating upon the irregular periods of increase and decrease of glaciers, collected partly from history and partly from tradition a variety of curious

---

[*] Huttonian Theory, in his Works, I. 338.

[*] Playfair's Works, I. p. xxix.

and distinct facts bearing upon these oscillations of the great glaciers of the Alps. He united them with judgment and impartiality in a Memoir which we have cited at the head of this article—which was read in 1821 to the Swiss Natural History Society, and published in the second part of the first volume of their transactions. In this paper M. Venetz classifies separately the facts which prove an increase, and those showing a decrease of glaciers in modern times. The former are certainly the most remarkable — showing that passes the most inaccessible, traversed now, perhaps, but a few times in a century, were frequently passed on foot, sometimes on horseback, between the eleventh and fifteenth centuries. Thus the Protestants of the Haut Valais took their children across what is now the Great Glacier of Aletsch to Grindelwald for baptism; and at the same period horses passed the Monte Moro from Saas into Italy; and the peasantry of Zermatt, at the foot of the Monte Rosa, went annually in procession through the Eringer Thal to Sion, by a pass which few inhabitants of either valley would now venture to attempt. We regard these facts, not as forming any proof of the former great extension which carried the glaciers even over to the Jura, but as evidencing one only of many oscillations which the glacier boundaries have undergone; and as important in showing that a *very notable* enlargement of these boundaries was consistent with the limits of atmospheric temperature, which we know the European climate has not materially overpassed within historic times. It may not, therefore, require so violent a depression of temperature as we might at first sight suppose, to account for any extension of the glaciers which the facts may require us to admit. The causes of these oscillations are yet very obscure. We have purposely refrained (for the sake of conciseness) from analyzing the theories which have been given, because we find them all unsatisfactory.

M. Venetz has further, in his Memoir, pointed out certain ancient moraines, belonging to modern glaciers, which indicate their previously greater extension; an evidence which had formerly been accepted by Saussure, especially in the case of the Glacier du Bois at Chamouni,* and that of the Rhone.† The remark is important, because it requires us to investigate

the character of a moraine, so as to recognize it wherever it may be found.

It does not appear that M. Venetz has published any other Memoir on the subject of glaciers; but it is quite certain that he was the first person publicly to maintain in Switzerland the doctrine of the former extension of the glaciers to the Jura, as the transporting agents of the erratics. The writer of this article was introduced to M. Venetz in 1832, as the man who had originated a speculation, which, though it had not, perhaps, then another advocate, was acknowledged to be novel, ingenious, and bold; and the reputation which the author of it had acquired, as the intrepid and skilful engineer of the works on the glacier of Giétroz, (the cause of inundations which threatened the town of Martigny with destruction,) gave it a consequence which might not otherwise have been conceded to it.

The first important convert to the new theory was M. de Charpentier, a mineralogist and geologist of reputation, author (among other works) of a geognostical essay on the Pyrenees, not even yet superseded. He undertook the examination of the question with the determination to disabuse his friend Venetz of the geological heresy he began to maintain, of the existence of ancient glaciers sixty leagues in length, at a period which was generally admitted to have afforded in Europe a climate adapted for the palm-tree and elephant.* The learned mineralogist, however, when he came to examine the evidence, found that he had 'caught a Tartar;' he bowed under the yoke of glaciers, and announced his conversion in an interesting article, read to the Swiss Natural History Society in 1834, published in the 8th volume of the *Annales des Mines*, and distributed to his scientific friends. In this short memoir of nineteen pages, we find the germ of almost all the arguments since employed in support of the glacier theory. The conveyance of great masses of rock to a distance from their origin, (p. 4), without any *sorting* or arrangement according to volume: the separation of deposits derived from different sources, not confusedly mingled, but deposited at certain levels, and leaving spaces wholly untouched, (pp. 6, 7, 14): the occurrence of a group of rocks together, of the same nature, derived from a single *eboulement* on the surface of the glacier, (p. 14): the elevation of the blocks

---

* *Voyages,* § 623.   † Do. § 1722.

* Charpentier, *Essai,* p. 243.

on the Jura, (p. 17): the partially rounded (*emoussé*) character of the angular blocks, showing friction, though evidently not waterworn, (p. 12): the non-occurrence of erratics in the equatorial regions of the globe, (note, p. 16): the polished surfaces of the fixed rocks, not only of the bottom of valleys, but the elevated flanks and even *cols* of mountain-chains, over which a *debacle* carrying stones and gravel could not possibly have passed, (p. 8, 9): the grooves which are met with in such surfaces, called *karren* (in German Switzerland):—all these varied facts are cited in support of the Glacier Theory. In particular, he attributes the abrasion and polish of the fixed rocks to the pressure of the enormous weight of glaciers upon their beds, in the following passage:—

‘We know that the glaciers rub, wear, and polish, the rocks with which they are in contact. Struggling to dilate, they follow all the sinuosities, and press and mould themselves into all the hollows and excavations they can reach, polishing *even overhanging* surfaces, which a current of water, hurrying stones along with it, could not effect.’—(Charpentier, *Mémoire*, p. 15.)

This is important, being, as M. Agassiz has remarked,[*] perhaps the first clear notice of this function of existing glaciers. M. de Charpentier attributes the cold of the glacier period to the greater height which the Alps then attained, on their first elevation—an opinion which he has since abandoned. Charpentier’s publication, though not unknown to geologists, was received with cold neglect. He employed none of the received methods of *agitating* a theory into vogue. The speech of the President of the Geological Society of London for 1836, contains a distinct citation of his views without a word of comment.[†]

In 1836 Professor Agassiz repeated with respect to M. de Charpentier what had passed between the latter and M. Venetz. He went to Bex to meet him on his own ground, and to convict him of his errors;[‡] but he, too, gradually yielded to the evidences before him, which he found to be so plain in the lower valley of the Rhone, that he adopted at once the theory of the ancient extension of glaciers. Returning home to Neufchatel, he examined the polished surfaces of calcareous

rock, locally termed *Laves*, which had been previously described; in which he found a new confirmation of the theory of Venetz, and he published this result, together with his adhesion to the *general* facts of the glacier theory, in a discourse read to the Swiss Society of Naturalists in 1837. In this pamphlet he discusses the objections to previous theories, and expresses an opinion that the icy slopes down which the Jura blocks come, formed part of a coating or crust of ice which covered Switzerland previous to the elevation of the Alps; and on which the rocky masses, detached during the convulsion producing the elevation, slid down by gravity. This hypothesis appears to be rather a retrograde step in the progress of a just theory, for it admits of refutation alike on geological and mechanical principles.

The lively discussion to which these opinions gave rise in Switzerland, naturally induced the promoters of them to lay the evidence for them in a more connected and demonstrative form before the scientific world, who, in uncertain sciences like geology, are slowly led to accept any opinion, unless sanctioned by the *highest* authority; so that the names of Charpentier and Agassiz could scarcely save from ridicule a theory opposed in some respects to the prejudices of mankind and the existing opinion of geologists, and which had not then, nor, we believe, even now, received the passport to public acceptance of the support of Von Buch, Von Humboldt, and De Beaumont:

Within not many months of each other, appeared the volumes of Charpentier and of Agassiz on the glacier theory, each being the extension of the previous notice or programme already referred to. The work of the latter appeared the earliest in point of time, but there can be no doubt that the two were simultaneously composed; and as Agassiz has honourably acknowledged his debt to Charpentier and Venetz, for principles which he has only followed out and endeavoured to extend more widely, a few ambiguities which occur as to originality are of the less consequence.

The *Etudes sur les Glaciers* of Agassiz, is a work written in many parts with ease and spirit—in many, it is obscurely expressed and deficient in method—and in some, betrays evident marks of haste, as well in reasoning as in composition. As a literary production, we own that, considering the celebrity of the author, and his happy talent for oral exposition, we

---

[*] *Etudes*, p. 190.

[†] See *Philosophical Magazine*, 3d series, viii. 338.

[‡] *Etudes sur les Glaciers*, p. 15.

were disappointed with it. Educated and esteemed as a pure naturalist, the very skill and force of imagination which recommended him when a very young man to the illustrious Cuvier, as fittest for the task of completing his investigation of fossil species, seem to interfere with the calmness of judgment, the severity of reasoning, and the formation of general views, which should characterize the reasoner on. physical geology. A second edition must materially improve the work, and give it more the character of a consolidated, consistently argued, analysis of facts; in which it is so far deficient, that we can hardly persuade ourselves that it is entirely the production of one hand. One of its distinctive recommendations is the Atlas of Plates, which, by their admirable execution, and ample explanatory sketches, serve to convey in a short time, to an entire strange, a fair idea of the facts to be explained, and the chief evidences of the theory. A good commentary on the plates would perhaps have made a more persuasive volume than that which has been written apparently with little or no reference to the atlas which accompanies it, and to which allusions are infrequent. In endeavouring to seize the arguments so ably conveyed to the eye, the reader's natural question would be, whether the plates may be depended upon—whether the features on which the author dwells are not exaggerated? We can assure him, that in all *essential* details they are exact, and this being admitted, the body of evidence they afford is very powerful indeed The points of view are generally well chosen, and the execution is admirable, being conducted under the author's eye in a lithographic institution, which owes its origin, we believe, to his zeal and enterprise. The letter-press is swelled by some bulky citations, as those upon red snow and the Siberian mammoths; whilst details of great importance are slightly passed over or omitted—as those which refer to the evidence of moraines and glacier polish in the lateral valleys of the Alps. These imperfections we mention, in the hope of seeing them amended in the new edition, which must soon be called for, of this popular work, which appeared simultaneously in French and German, and which has had an extensive circulation.*

The first and larger portion of the volume refers to the mechanism of existing glaciers, of which we have already given a full account: a chapter is then added on the oscillations of their dimensions in historic times, chiefly on the authority of Venetz: another on the ancient extension of glaciers on the Alps; and one more on the former existence of extensive sheets of ice over different parts of the earth's surface, marked by phenomena similar to those described by Charpentier. It is upon this last chapter the author chiefly rests his claim to originality in these investigations; and when we recollect that the phenomenon of erratics is not a local but a widely distributed one, we admit the importance of the extension of the reasoning, at the same time that we feel the necessity of proportional caution in the acceptance of the evidence. And it is certainly unfortunate that this part of the work, which Mr. Maclaren, in his neat summary of the glacier theory, has justly characterized as obscure, should be founded on an explanation of the distribution of erratics certainly erroneous, (that which supposes them due to the elevation of the Alps;) and that the author should have predicted the phenomena which he had yet to discover in northern Europe, and especially in Scotland. On the other hand, it is to be observed, that in applying Charpentier's theory of the dilatation of glaciers to extended sheets of ice, he rendered conceivable, at least, the existence and extension of glaciers in circumstances where they could not otherwise have occurred. We shall return presently to the phenomena of the Scandinavian boulder-flood.

The work of Charpentier entitled, *Essai sur les Glaciers, et sur le Terrain Erratique du Bassin du Rhone*, though the preface is dated in October, 1840, made its appearance only last summer, (1841.) It treats substantially of the same facts, and in the same order with the work of Agassiz, but it wants the fine illustrative plates. On the other hand, it is distinguished by simplicity, method, and clearness—in a word, by careful composition. The sections are short—the arguments distinctly stated, and the answer placed directly against the objection. The criticisms are usually, we think, sound, although the original speculations are not always tenable. Charpentier's book, and Agassiz' atlas, will readily initiate the reader into the past and present mysteries of glaciers. The second and larger part

---

* An excellent analysis of this work has been printed (privately, we believe) by Mr. Maclaren of Edinburgh.

of this work is occupied with the theory of erratics, in which the older hypotheses are successively discussed, the glacier theory explained, and the most probable objections answered. As might be expected, the most theoretical part we find to be the least plausible; and the author's theory of the cold of the glacial period, we think rather more objectionable than his older one, of the greater primitive elevation of the Alps. We approve of the caution which has generally confined the speculations of M. de Charpentier to the origin of those boulders with which he was best acquainted—namely, those of the valley of the Rhone and the opposed flank of the Jura; but he cannot be censured for omitting all reference to the cause of boulder formations generally. In his first publication, already analyzed, he had remarked the deficiency of erratic blocks in tropical regions; and in the volume before us he specifies the cases to which glacier action might be extended.

The interesting work of Professor Necker of Geneva, the learned and ingenious descendant of De Saussure, is the first of a series of volumes on the geology of the Alps, to the continuation of which we look with no common interest. We have cited it only because, treating as it does of superficial deposits, it refers frequently to the diluvial formations, and urges forcibly several objections to the modern theory—the author attaching himself to the hypothesis of a *debacle*. No detailed analysis can therefore here be given of the work itself. It is written in that graphic style which imparts even to the most minute details, and petty catastrophes, a real and scientific interest. The author is one of those meditative men, who, having gone through life with their eyes open, find everywhere a lesson of nature's teaching, and acquire knowledge, not so much from books as from events.

It now remains that we attempt to state some of the arguments upon which has been founded the admission of extensive glaciers, as amongst the latest agents which have modified the surface of Switzerland; we shall then state the more plausible objections which may be urged against it—some of which may be met with satisfactory answers, and others await further explanation.

I. And FIRST of the occurrence of angular boulders. The great blocks on the Jura and inferior Alps have been literally

amongst the greatest *stumbling stones* of modern geologists. We fairly own that the arguments of the glacier theorists in favour of their being nothing else than ancient moraines, have scarcely struck us so strongly as the total weakness of the arguments of their opponents and predecessors, who have striven to prove them something else. The absurdity of some of these hypotheses is scarcely credible; —the elder Deluc's, for instance, who supposed them the remains of primitive strata still resting in place, above the Jura limestone;* or that of Deluc the nephew, who supposed them the result of volcanic projection from the higher Alps; and of Dolomieu, that inclined planes of *débris* extended once from the summit of the Alps, up to a certain height on the Jura, of which not a trace now remains, but down which the blocks had rolled by gravity, (though this inclination could not have exceeded 2°.) Than came the theory of diluvial currents, which is perhaps tacitly accepted by most geologists at the present day, notwithstanding the inconceivable postulates which it requires. Saussure's idea appears to have been, that the currents which moved the rocks were occasioned by the rupture of barriers which confined the water in lakes; and which then, rushing towards its escape, carried down in the flood the masses which a simultaneous convulsion had torn from the Alpine summits. If this seems plausible on paper, we cannot conceive any one gravely maintaining it when he stands beside the *Pierre à Bot*, which is as large as an ordinary house, overhangs the valley by a declivity of 800 feet, and is seventy miles distant from its origin between Mount Blanc and the great St. Bernard. Von Buch has very well shown† that the arrival of such a block in its present position pre-supposes its being carried forward, notwithstanding its prodigious mass, by a current of water, which AT ONCE gave it a projectile velocity sufficient to cause it to make a *flying leap* across the valley of Switzerland, so that it reached Neufchatel *before it had time to fall by gravity into the lake of Geneva!*—a velocity which, he took the trouble to compute, must have carried it over this enormous space in eighteen seconds, or at the rate of more than 20,000 feet per second! He afterwards indeed managed to

---

* Cited in the *Annales de Chimie*, tom. x. (1819,) p. 242.

† Ueber die Ursache der Verbreitung grosser Alpengeschiebe.—*Berlin Memoirs*, 1811, page 183.

reduce this velocity to a comparatively small one, on taking into account the buoyancy caused by the water; but it is not worth while to stop to explain the grievous errors in mechanical reasoning, into which the great geologist has fallen in this amended calculation;—errors which in fact leave the result worse than before.* With respect to this argument (if common sense afford not a sufficient reply) we ask merely—1. where have we evidence that water ever moved a stone, large or small, with a tenth part of the required velocity? and 2. if this block, the size of a dwelling-house, rattled on the bare Jura limestone with a rapidity ten times that of a musket ball at first firing, why was it not dashed into a million of fragments? We may disguise, but nothing can elude these unanswerable objections, to which we might add many others—especially those arising from the distribution of the blocks.

The hypothesis of currents appears to have been adopted by Von Buch and M. Elie de Beaumont. The former attributes their origin, not to the rupture of lakes, but (so far as we understand his expressions) to the sudden elevation of the Alps. De Beaumont, on the other hand, finds the melting of ancient glaciers a sufficient cause: Having admitted the glaciers, we think he might have dispensed with melting them. Nor can we by any means allow the new arguments by which M. Necker maintains the theory of the *debacle*, although his treatment of the subject is well calculated to throw light upon it. He admits a period of cold and of enlarged glaciers, which he attributes to the great elevation of the Alps at that period, (*Etudes Geologiques*, p. 385.) These glaciers, forming barriers, produced lakes, which, bursting, carried down fragments of the neighbouring rocks; and, according to the author, the rocks which received the first impulse from the water, retaining it longest, moved further than those which were caught up by the stream at an inferior part of its course, (p. 356.) Hence he explains the greater abundance of the primitive rocks at the more distant points. We own it would rather seem to us that whatever tended to diminish the velocity of the stream, must, *à fortiori*, diminish that of the blocks carried along with it, and that the largest must come soonest to

rest. We have already observed that one of the most extraordinary facts about the erratic deposit is, that the blocks are in no way *sorted*; the largest lie with the smallest, at the greatest as well as at the least distances from their origin—a pretty clear proof that the cause of motion was *not one diminishing in intensity as it advanced.*

The most plausible of all the older explanations was undoubtedly that of rafts of ice, adopted by Sir James Hall,* which, detached from adhering glaciers, bore across an inland lake the fragments with which they were charged, as at present occurs in the icebergs of the Arctic Seas. The main objections lie—1. In the want of evidence of such vast inland lakes; for if anything be proved about the erratic formation, it is, that it was deposited when the surface of the soil had taken very nearly its present configuration.† 2. The climate, if capable of maintaining ice-rafts on a lake which filled the plains of Switzerland, might equally have maintained glaciers, which account directly for the phenomena. 3. The blocks are deposited in a certain orderly manner:—the shower of blocks (if we may use the phrase) being deposited on the Jura, nearly or exactly opposite to their points of origin in the Alps; whereas the icebergs must have floated hither and thither, and been wrecked indiscriminately in all directions. Also, the blocks would have been deposited in a horizontal line on the shore of the lake, which is not the fact. 4. The theory is still more incompatible with the position of enormous blocks which lie at great heights within the Alpine valleys, and generally on their slopes, and not in the river-courses. The nearer we approach the origin of the erratics, the higher, generally, is the level at which they are found. The blocks from the higher Alps usually occupy the highest positions on the Jura, whilst the limestone of the inferior Alps forms a lower band. The theory of floating ice has been adopted by many authors, amongst others by Venturi,‡ Darwin,§ and Lyell.‖

Now, if we contrast with these theories that which supposes the existence of gla-

---

* *Annales de Chimie*, x. 250. It is in the estimation of the terminal velocity that the error lies.

* *Edinburgh Transactions*, vii. 158. It was, we believe, suggested by Bergmann.
† *Necker*, p. 347.
‡ In a *Memoir* cited by Charpentier, p. 189.
§ *Voyages of the Adventure and Beagle*, iii. 288.
‖ *Principles*, 1st edition, vol. iii. p. 150, (1833.) *Elements*, vol. i. p. 250, (1841.)

ciers so extensive as to reach from the Alps to the Jura, we shall find that, startling as the proposition may at first sight appear, it is beset by fewer and less formidable difficulties than any we have mentioned; and we shall endeavour, by expressing the facts to be explained in the words of the opponents of the theory, and of those who never heard of the theory at all, to show that it possesses some remarkable features of truth.

i. It accounts for the transport of blocks of *any* size. No mass is too weighty for the strength of a glacier. A leaf or a pebble (as we have shown above) is more liable to sink into it than a block of 100,000 cubic feet. This is too notorious to require further proof. Saussure cites the glacier of Miage as presenting one mass of *débris* on its surface, and we have seen the glacier of Zmutt, beneath the Mont Cervin, in the same condition. We have likewise seen, on a modern glacier, a moving block at least eighty feet long, twenty broad, and forty high. So unfounded was the assertion of Agassiz, in 1837, that the blocks on the Jura are *larger* and more rounded than those found on the glaciers; a conclusion which led him, at that period, to deny the extension of glaciers (but admitting an inclined plane of ice) to the Jura, which he declared to contain no moraines.—(*Discourse*, 1837, p. xvii.)

ii. The appearance of the blocks, as to angularity, is exactly that of the blocks which form morains. We cannot quote a more unexceptionable authority than that of Professor Necker, an opponent of the glacier theory :—

'The form of the diluvial blocks *is the same as that of the blocks brought down by the glaciers*, and which they deposit on their moraines. Like these, without being generally quite round, they have their corners and edges so ground away, (*emoussés*,) that we cannot doubt but they have suffered a prolonged friction.'—(Necker, p. 348.)

The larger blocks, we must add, whether on the glaciers or on the Jura, have their angles best preserved.

iii. The erratic blocks found most abundantly on the Jura, are derived from that part of the Alpine chain where glaciers still act with intense force; and where the rock is so destructible, that blocks are yearly furnished by the present diminutive glaciers, undistinguishable in mass or material from those which a prolongation of the icy railroad stranded *first* on the steep sides of the winding valley of the Drance and the Rhone, and *finally* on the directly opposed surface of the Jura hills. It is from the glacier of Ornex, in the Val Ferret, to the East of Mont Blanc, that the masses appear to have been derived. This at least is the opinion of Von Buch, who has given an animated description of the scene :—

'Opposite the immense glacier of Ornex, one of the largest in the whole chain of Mont Blanc, the fallen fragments become like rocks, and the moraine lies like a little mountain across the valley. Glaciers tumble on glaciers down the valley; they have torn deep fissures in its walls, through which numberless blocks are continually thrown from the heights above, and beyond which, ever new rocky peaks seem to rise from the great ice-field.'—(Von Buch, *Berlin Mem.*, p. 173.)

iv. The blocks carried down the Alpine valleys lie, as we have observed, not on the bottoms where gravity would have placed them, but often at heights of 1000, 1500, or even 2000 feet above the level of the river—on ledges, and even projecting points of rock, surmounting precipices where it is hardly conceivable that water should have carried them. We admit that currents are very fantastic in this respect; but ice, either floating or in a glacier, could alone have perched them at these elevations. Such deposits were noticed in the valley of the Drance by De Saussure, (derived from the glacier of Ornex,) in many parts of the Rhone valley, by Von Buch; near Bex, by Charpentier; and in the valley of Hasli, near Meyringen, at a great height above the Aar, by Agassiz. Sometimes the non-appearance of blocks is as strong an evidence of the glacier theory as their occurrence. Thus, the best-characterized rock in the whole Alps is the euphotide of Saas, near Monte Rosa, which is found in many parts of the plain of Switzerland: nevertheless its fragments *do not* appear* in the great Rhone valley, which it joins at a right angle, and which must have infallibly been the case had they been brought down by currents. As they probably formed a medial moraine, they might have travelled indefinitely far on the surface of a glacier, without leaving a trace after its disappearance.

v. The actual distribution of blocks on the Jura and on the plain of Switzerland, is as yet but imperfectly known. Little, in fact, has been added to the masterly sketch of Von Buch, written thirty years ago, on this subject;—one on which his

---

* Charpentier.

profound knowledge of the mineral characters of rocks entitles his opinion to
great weight. On many points, no doubt,
his statements may require moderation ;
but, speaking broadly, the following three
great characteristics of the distribution
of the Jura blocks obtain :—(*a*)   The valleys in the Jura, screened from a view of
the Alps, do not generally contain many
erratics, which are found expended on
the face of the hills fronting the Alps.
(*b*) The rocks from the higher Alps (as
the granites of Ornex) lie on the higher
part of the Jura ; those from the inferior
chain occupy the base of the hill and the
plain, (as the pudding-stones of Valorsine.)
This is reasonably attributed, on the gla.
cier theory, to the retreating position of
the terminal moraine, which at first, when
the icy crust was thickest, was derived entirely from the highest Alps; but as the
effect of climate gradually restricted its
limits, its surface followed the windings
of the Rhone valley, and brought down the
bounding rocks. (*c*) Each of the great
valleys of the Rhone, the Aar, the Reuss,
&c., seems to have discharged from its
mouth a torrent of blocks, which spread
themselves fan-like from the embouchure
of the valley, being most thickly strewed,
and likewise attaining the greatest height,
exactly opposite to its mouth.   Now this
is precisely the effect which a glacier
would produce; and one passage of Von
Buch's paper is so strong, that we might
fancy he had a moraine in his eye when
he wrote it :—

'They (the erratics) proceed from snow-cov-
ered mountains directly in straight lines through
the valleys, and thence over the plains, and
spread themselves radially, in a heap, (or tuft—
büschelförmig), at the outgoing of the valleys.'
—Page 184.

· vi.   The larger masses are usually accompanied by small ones—they form, in fact, a
group: this is quite conformable to what we
have mentioned as occurring on glaciers. An
eboulement marks its occurrence by the group
of fragments which it leaves on the ice.

vii.   The fact that the accumulation of
blocks at the extremity of modern glaciers is
comparatively small, indicating that the actual limit of the ice has not long remained
fixed.   When we notice the ceaseless energy of glaciers and their enormous transporting power, and compare these with the length
of geological periods which we cannot, on
other grounds, avoid admitting to have elapsed since the earth assumed its present configuration, we are struck with the trifling ac-

cumulation of moraines which most glaciers
present.   This fact did not escape De Saussure, who found in it a proof that the existing system had not been of long duration : —

'The blocks of stone (he says) with which
the lower part of this glacier (Du Bois, at Chamouni) is charged, give rise to an important reflection. When we consider their number, and
when we recollect that they are deposited and
accumulated at this extremity of the glacier in
proportion as the ice melts, we are astonished
not to find the mass more considerable. This
observation leads us to think, with M. Deluc,
that the actual condition of our globe is not so
ancient as some philosophers have imagined.'—
(*Voyages*, ii. p. 18, § 625).

The real answer seems to be, that during
the present age of the world the glaciers
have been continually receding, leaving their
moraines behind them in the form of erratics.

II. Let us now turn to another and most
important evidence of glacier action, of which
we have yet scarcely spoken.   We mean
the figure, and polish, and states of surface,
which glaciers are capable of giving to mechanically fixed rocks over which they move.
The forms are, (1.) Rounded spheroidal or
cylindrical surfaces, exhibited on a great
scale, evidently due to the wear of the projecting angular parts. (2.) Undulating groves,
more or less longitudinal and parallel, not
unfrequently like the figures produced by a
carpenter's cornice-plane, and often highly
polished; and, (3.) Fine *striæ*, not always
parallel, which cut up these polished surfaces even when formed of pure quartz, and
which are evidently mechanically produced.
We know that water can remove considerable blocks of stone—the origination of moraines by torrents is at least a conceivable
speculation—but we totally deny the power
of running water to produce all of those appearances. Can ice do so ? This, we conceive, is the *experimentum crucis* amongst
the rival theories, and we believe it to be favourable to the hypothesis of glaciers.

The evidence, we must add, can hardly
be appreciated without a personal and elaborate study of the phenomena on the spot.
The best approximation to it may be made
from the examination of Agassiz' admirable
plates, which, for the first time, represent in
detail these extraordinary phenomena, destined certainly to play a conspicuous part in
the scientific history of the next few years.

The first form of smoothed rounded rocks
is beautifully exemplified in the 8th and 16th
plates of Agassiz' work—the one at Monte
Rosa, the other at the Handeck. The forms
in question, for which we have no descriptive name, and which few who have not ex-

amined the localities would believe to be faithfully represented in these views, evidently bear no reference whatever to the general structure of the rock, which in the one case is serpentine, in the other an imperfect granite. It must be owned that Saussure's reflections upon these singular polished spheroidal and conoidal surfaces are very unsatisfactory : he admits that the granite rocks are 'cut into portions of inclined cylinders, sometimes even of spherical forms, *no doubt* by the erosion of air, water, and avalanches.'— *Voyages*, iii. page 461. When we find that the gneiss has no concretionary structure here, such as is sometimes observed, and that these surfaces, far from being surfaces of natural desquamation, are frequently cut at right angles to the slaty cleavage, we are bound to look for some other explanation. In the parts of the valley of the Aar where this appearance occurs, the grinding off and smoothing of angular fragments is so universal, that the trough of the valley, to a depth of 1500 or 2000 feet, is marked by this distinctive character ; whilst the rocky summits of the very same material, which shoot up beyond that elevation, have the rugged and angular forms which gneiss rocks present under circumstances of ordinary decomposition. This peculiarity may be distinctly traced up to the part of the valley still occupied by glaciers, (the upper and lower glacier of the Aar), the sides of the valley being rounded and smoothed (*moutonnés ; —emoussés*) up to a height of 8000 feet above the sea. This interesting observation—of the truth of which we are persuaded—is due to M. Agassiz, (*Etudes*, page 254), and tends to show the enormous accumulation of ice then existing in the higher Alps, in accordance with their great extension in length into lower Switzerland, which has been maintained on distinct grounds.

The next configuration of rock, that of grooved surfaces, (*surfaces sillonnés*), is usually combined with the general external form already mentioned. An admirable exhibition of it is to be found in Agassiz' 17th plate, representing a portion of calcareous rock in the Jura, which has since been quarried away, (at Landeron, near Bienne). These furrows are like nothing else in nature with which we are acquainted. They follow the undulations of the *surfaces moutonnés*, and, as we have already said, resemble the indentations of a carpenter's ogee plane, carried along with a steady pressure for distances of several feet, yards, or fathoms. The reasoning into which we should be led might appear too technical were we to explain why water, whether by itself or carrying *débris*

along with it, can never produce similar effects. Being once seen and fully apprehended, we believe that water action would never come into the mind of an unprejudiced person ; their continuity, depth, and the circumstance of their rarely or almost never coinciding with the lines of greatest declivity of a surface, speak in language not to be mistaken. Such grooves may be seen and studied at the *Hollenplatte* near the Handeck, the rocks of the valley of Fee, near Saas, the precipitous face of rock above the Pissevache near Martigny, and the rocks of Le Mail near Neufchatel.[*] These phenomena are altogether of a peculiar species, incapable of confusion with any other. The only phenomena at all similar, are certain internal convolutions of the trap rocks (with a felspar basis) of which the origin is undoubtedly mysterious. That the configuration in the Swiss rocks is wholly external and mechanical is plain, both from such surfaces *never* being found covered by a superior layer of rock, and from its occurrence on the exposed side of promontories which have abutted into valleys, down which the glacier is supposed to have descended. A similar fact is described as characterizing the grooves (which every one admits to be also due to mechanical action) on the surface of the Scandinavian rocks described by Sefström and Bötlingk ; but whether they possess *all* the peculiar characters of the Swiss rocks are unable to say. The fact can only be pronounced upon by one who has studied both *in situ.*

The third class of superficial mechanical effects, also beautifully and accurately figured in Agassiz' Atlas, (plate 18,) consists of an infinite number of fine lines or *striæ* accompanying a general and often exquisite polish of the surface, observed on many rocks which, besides, exhibit the rounded outlines and the characteristic furrows which we have already described. The polish of the surface depends materially on the nature of the rock—where

---

[*] Very trifling circumstances often occasion a disparity in the conclusions of different observers. We will mention an apparently inconsiderable influence of this kind :—When the sun shines *directly* on a face of rock it appears nearly even, if we are not in a position to pass the hand across its surface. One person may thus see a surface delicately furrowed when the sun strikes it with the proper degree of obliquity, whilst another at a less favourable moment may impute his description to mere fancy and preconception. The grooved cliff above the Pissevache is in this case. From twelve to one o'clock is the time to see it to most advantage. The remarkable grooved surface of the trap rock in contact with sandstone, on the southern declivity of the Castle rock of Edinburgh, is best seen about eleven o'clock on the same account.

that is quartzose, as in the granites of the Grimsel, the polish is perfectly specular, or similar to that which a lapidary gives to rock crystal;—a condition which it is difficult to conceive that water could give under any circumstances, and which is indeed rare in nature. In the limestone rocks of Jura, this polish equals that of the finest slates used for drawing. In either case the surface is more or less cut up by *scratches*, sometimes as fine as if drawn with a diamond point, and requiring microscopic examination; at other times rough and jagged in their edges. These *striæ* have a general tendency to parallelism, but not unfrequently there are two sets inclined to one another, at a considerable angle. The slightest examination seems to show that these *striæ* were produced by hard fixed particles, which acted as gravers in indenting the surface. These phenomena are perfectly seen on the granites of the Grimsel, and the limestones of Le Chaumont in the Jura.

Such being the phenomena visible in many valleys of the Alps—extending from 8000 feet above the sea (as on the Siedelhorn, near the Grimsel) to the plains of Switzerland, (as on the banks of the Rhone near St. Maurice,) and even to the Jura range—the important question arises, are the glaciers capable of imitating these effects? This is the most difficult part of the evidence of the Glacier Theory satisfactorily to establish. We are bound to say, that after a long scepticism and a patient examination of facts, we consider this important link of evidence to be fairly made out. It is chiefly to M. Agassiz that this result of patient investigation is due, and he has taken great and praiseworthy pains to satisfy all who were willing to be convinced of the fact. The testimony of M. Studer, the most eminent living Swiss geologist, and long a sceptic like ourselves, is the best that we can possibly quote. Speaking of the glacier of Zermatt, near Monte Rosa, he says —'having mounted about fifty feet on the right or eastern side of the glacier, we were able to approach close to its contact with the fixed rock, and to observe the condition of the latter under the glacier itself. In spite of the mineralogical difference of the rock, which is here a compact green slate, I must state that I was struck with the perfect resemblance of the state of its surface, and that of the calcareous rocks of the lake of Bienne: there are the same smooth forms, the same grooves with rounded edges, the same fine *striæ ; the whole being occasioned, beyond any doubt, by the friction against the fixed rock of blocks and sand carried along under a strong pressure by some agent, and this*

agent appears in this case to have been THE GLACIER ITSELF.'*

The difficulty of proof of the direct abrasion of glaciers, arises from the difficulty of procuring a complete contact of a glacier and the bed of rock on which it reposes. The immediate junction is often covered by a moraine ; and it is evident that, supposing a glacier to maintain always precisely the same position, it could only be by an extensive and dangerous excavation that we could examine the state of a surface of rock over which it has recently passed. But all glaciers are subject to oscillations of various kinds, and their vast *crevasses* unfold occasionally the surface of the trough in which they move. This is the case in the glaciers of Rosenlaui, Viesch, and Zermatt ; and those glaciers which are retreating, of which we have many examples in the Alps, display the whole surface which they lately covered. There can be no doubt from observation, that a glacier carries along with its inferior surface a mass of pulverized gravel and lime, which, pressed by an enormous superincumbent weight of ice, *must* grind and smoothe the surface of its rocky bed. This fact, which seems natural enough when stated, does not appear to have been distinctly recognized by any writer before Charpentier. We do not remember to have seen it cited that the peculiar character of glacier water is itself a testimony to this fact. Its turbid appearance, constantly the same from year to year, and from age to age, is due to the impalpably fine *flour* of rocks ground in this ponderous mill betwixt rock and ice. It is so fine as to be scarcely depositable. No one who drives from Avignon to Vaucluse can fail to be struck with the contrast of the stream, artificially conveyed on one and on the other side of the road, in order to irrigate the parched plain at Provence. The one is the incomparably limpid water of Petrarch's fountain ; the other an offset from the river Durance, which has carried into the heart of this sunburnt region the unequivocal mark of its birth amidst the perpetual snows of Monte Viso. This is the pulverizing action of ice.

Most erroneously have those argued who object to this theory that ice cannot scratch quartz—ice is only the *setting* of the harder fragments, which first round, then furrow, afterwards polish, and finally scratch the surface over which it moves. It is not the wheel of a lapidary which slits a pebble, but

* *Bulletin de la Societe Géologique de France.*— Tom. xi. page 50.—*Seance,* 2d December, 1839. The italics and capitals are our own.

the emery with which it is primed. The gravel, sand, and impalpable mud are the emery of the glacier.

We venture to differ from the eminent mineralogist (Necker) who has declared that a mineral can never scratch another of the same degree of hardness.* We have no doubt whatever that quartz can scratch quartz, as much as it is true to a proverb that diamond cuts diamond. The minuter the fragments of a body which fractures angularly, the more advantage have its particles to penetrate the surface of another similar to itself; nor can we think it doubtful that, *with time and pressure* sufficient, a harder body may be worn, therefore scratched, (since wear is but an integration of infinitely small scratches), by a softer. In all this, then, we find no objection, but the contrary, to the theory of Charpentier and Agassiz; and, as we have said, facts demonstrate its truth. Agassiz' seventh plate shows the favourable circumstances under which it may be studied in the serpentine rocks beneath the glacier of Zermatt, (alluded to in the preceding extract from Studer); and although the neighbouring rocks, at some distance from the glacier, and much above it, indicate the same structure, yet it is so plain that the freshness and perfection of the surface increases with its proximity to the glacier, that we can hardly suppose that the presence of the glacier is accidental where the polish appears; but rather we are bound to conclude that the appearance of the polish indicates the former presence of the glacier.

It is to the evidence of the long continuous nearly horizontal furrows, such as those of Landeron, that we ascribe the most certain and conclusive evidence of glacier action. We do not doubt that hard pebbles included in the ice coursing along successively in a channel once formed in a comparatively soft rock, like limestone or serpentine, is a cause capable (considering the intense incumbent pressure) of producing the effect in question. *We know of no others such.* They may exist, but they have not yet been pointed out. The importance of this admission is very great. There is little reason to doubt that we shall soon have irresistible evidence presented to us of similar effects existing on many parts of the earth's surface.

A very eminent geologist, who still refuses assent to the glacier theory, has assured us that the specimens of *striæ* in his possession, from the valley of the Aar, the Jura, Fahlun in Sweden, and Boston in America, are so identical in character as to leave no

doubt in his mind that they were engraven by one and the same agent. When to this we add the identity established above, between the *striæ* of the Alps and Jura, and those *under* existing glaciers and in the process of formation, the importance of the admission will be fully appreciated; and it is not too much to affirm, that the authority of the individual who makes it would go far to settle the question with that preponderating class of the geological world who take their impressions from the authority of others. We would not, however, too rashly proclaim the explanation universal; for geology is one of those imperfect sciences, where it is impossible to carry out principles *à priori* into all their seemingly legitimate consequences; and amongst those wider speculations is the supposed extension of glaciers to all extra-tropical regions of the globe—first proposed by Charpentier, and since more especially insisted upon by Agassiz. It is well known that in northern Italy, in the Pyrenees, the Vosges, the Carpathians, the mountains of Sweden, Finland, and Scotland, and the plains of Russia, Prussia, Denmark, and England, similar phenomena of distributed blocks, and in many cases of grooved and polished surfaces, occur. Upon this wide field we cannot at present enter; but on the principle of employing the evidence of the opponents of the glacier theory, we will quote one most remarkable admission of M. Necker, with respect to the distribution of boulders derived from the Alps:—

'Wherever,' he says, 'the central chain of the Alps surpasses much the limit of perpetual snow, and, consequently, wherever it presents glaciers, we observe, at the openings of great valleys, masses of blocks and other diluvial débris.' Wherever, on the contrary, the central chain does not attain this limit, or but little exceeds it, we find diluvial blocks neither in the openings of the valleys, nor in the neighbouring plains . . . It is also a remarkable fact, that the only chain in Europe, besides the Alps, which penetrates considerably into the zone of perpetual snow, and which has great glaciers, namely, the Scandinavian chain, is also the only one from which have descended vast masses of rock and diluvial débris.'—(*Etudes Géologiques*, p. 359.)

We had intended stating the objections which have been, and may be urged against the glacier theory—which are no doubt both numerous and real—but what geological theory ever was or can be free from objections? And in this respect, without professing our unlimited conversion to it, we boldly assert, that the glacier theory, in its application to the Alps, has so abundant *primâ facie* evidence in its favour, as to be entitled to be

---

* *Etudes Géologiques.* P. 191.

placed under the category of *geological pro-babilities*. As to the *certainties* of geology, on which a work has lately been published, we apprehend that an unbiassed critic would purge the list to a diminutive bulk. We must, however, for the present conclude ; and will therefore only trespass for a moment longer on the reader's patience, by alluding to one of the objections which has been very generally felt and urged: it is the difficulty alluded to at the commencement of this article—the inconsistency of the hypothesis of an Arctic climate, with the geological evidence of fossils commonly supposed to indicate that the temperature of the earth's surface was, in all former times, *higher* than at present.

This difficulty is urgently pressed by M. Studer; but if the facts seem to prove the existence of ice over any large portion of the earth's surface, it would be vain to oppose all the little analogical information which we derive from historical data, and from physico-mathematical researches on the subject. Such *inferences* must bend before *facts*. The evidence of fossils, indeed, is of a more conclusive kind; but we must first see that that evidence is quite positive. The theories of a local and temporary nature proposed to account for the cold of Switzerland in particular, or Europe generally, are, we think, too vague and gratuitous to be worthy of much attention.

It is certainly remarkable, that the opponents of the so-called glacier theory are themselves obliged to admit *some* extension of the glaciers; and to explain this they admit a reduction of temperature. M. Elie de Beaumont and M. Necker have directly, and Mr. Lyell indirectly, admitted this. The first attributes the diluvial currents, which he supposes to have conveyed the Alpine blocks, to the *fusion of ancient glaciers*; the second applies similar reasoning to the lakes with *glacier barriers*, which furnished his *debacle*; and the last (together with Mr. Darwin and many others) must have his half-frozen lake with floating icebergs down to the level of the Jura range. Charpentier and Agassiz ask only a little more of what their opponents cannot altogether refuse—*cold*.

But more than this. Mr. Smith has shown[*] that the post-tertiary deposits of the west of Scotland, *coeval with the boulder formation and the till*, indicate, by their included shells, evidences of an approach to an ARCTIC climate at that period, being identical with the *existing* species of Newfoundland and even

of Spitzbergen ; and Mr. Lyell has deduced, from Canadian fossils, the conclusion that, ' at the period immediately antecedent to the present, the climate of Canada was even more excessive than it is now,' and that '*this extreme cold may have coincided with the era of the principal transportation of erratic blocks.*'[*] This is surely a beautiful and interesting coincidence, and one which, if fully established, as we believe it is likely to be by the further researches of M. Agassiz, must go far to remove the chief outstanding difficulty to the glacier theory ; for we cannot altogether understand the objection which Mr. Lyell seems to make to its application to Switzerland, from the *absence* of the post-pliocene fossils in that country.[†]

The same ingenious author has objected to the glacier theory,[‡] the small inclination which the glacier could have ; which he estimates at 2 degrees, and which Charpentier has reckoned still lower.[§] The objection is a natural one ; but it may be replied, that we have as yet no data for assigning the *lowest* inclination of a glacier consistent with motion ; and it is even probable that, as the glacier increases in size, this inclination may be less. We have already observed that the slope of some considerable glaciers is, in many places, less than 3 degrees. Objections which seem to us to be more difficult to reply to, arise from the obscurity of the manner in which the blocks derived from the *terminal* (?) moraines of the Alpine glaciers were deposited on the opposing flank of the Jura. If the plain of Switzerland were a vast glacier, of which those of the Arve, the Rhone, and the Aar, were but tributaries—and if this glacier had a north-easterly motion, as the grooves near Neufchatel and Bienne would seem to indicate—it is not easy to see how the Rhone blocks should have been deposited opposite to the embouchure of that valley, instead of forming a lateral moraine at the base of the Alps. The distribution of the remoter erratics in the very heart of the Jura range, and the position of many of the scratches on the fixed rocks, present difficulties which we believe to be still unexplained.

It is, however, impossible to expect that all such difficulties should at once, or even at any time, entirely vanish. It is in the explanation of these that Charpentier and Agassiz, the able champions of the glacier theory,

[*] Proceedings of the Geological Society of London, 24th April, 1839.
[†] Elements of Geology, i. 253, (1841).
[‡] Ibid, p. 250.
[§] Namely, 1 deg. 8 min. 50 sec. Essai, pp. 174 and 237.

[*] Proceedings of the Geological Society of London, 24th April, 1839, and 6th November, 1839.

founded by Venetz, are not agreed. We trust that their discussions will ever be conducted in the spirit of honourable rivalry in carrying out the arguments, of which so many are original to each. We have attempted, in seizing only the main details of this interesting epoch of scientific discussion, to assign to each author his due, without partiality or reserve. Such a course must eventually be most for the interests of all concerned. If we have passed over some subordinate writers, it is neither from ignorance nor negligence; but from want of space, and from a desire to concentrate the attention of our readers on the analysis we wished to present of the leading features of the controversy.*

We have not chosen to conceal the personal interest we feel in one of the most curious and many-sided physical questions which has been brought under discussion for many years. We willingly acknowledge our debts to the calm sagacity of Charpentier, and to the noble ardour of Agassiz. We owe, perhaps, still more to the generous friendship, the unvarying good temper, and the true hospitality of the latter. It is through the intermedium of Professor Agassiz and his work that this subject has been introduced to the British public; and we know that to them he looks anxiously for the affirmation of his opinions. The glacier theory has not, as we have already hinted, received as yet the usual passport to general acceptance. Excepting Dr. Buckland, no geologist of note in this country has fully adopted even the opinions of Charpentier respecting Alpine glaciers; much less those of Agassiz, which point to a great envelope of ice in the extra-tropical regions of the globe. Mr. Lyell has indeed said enough to testify his willingness to admit views, which, if proved, would so well accord with his fundamental theory; but he has not given in his adhesion to the details. Even in Switzerland the conversions to the glacier theory (though it may be considered a national one) are slow and partial. In France it has made very little way: MM. Elie de Beaumont and Arago, with the classes of geologists and natural philosophers whom they represent, still stand aloof. In Germany there is no hypothesis which will not find numerous support-

ers; but who shall lead, whilst Von Buch and Von Humboldt withhold their assent? To maintain the glacier theory still requires some confidence—some courage. We have not dissembled its difficulties; but by presenting it, as we have endeavoured to view it, with unprejudiced eyes, as fully entitled to rank among *geological probabilities*, we place it on its most defensible ground, and we venture to predict, at least abroad, a speedy reaction in its favour. Its evidences are such as must be *seen*, and carefully studied without prejudice, in order to be appreciated; and such evidences, though often required to be sought for, and difficultly found, are not less conclusive when attained. We have constructed a formidable panoply out of the missiles of its adversaries: will they not yield to their own weapons? If they pronounce the theory imperfect, we acknowledge it; but we may very safely challenge them to produce a better or less improbable one, from amongst those already proposed. If they have a new one, we are ready to consider it.

Art. III.—1. *Minutes of the Committee of Council on Education, with Appendices and plans of School-houses.* 8vo. London: 1839-40.

2. *Minutes of the Committee of Council on Education, with Appendices.* 8vo. London: 1840-41.

THESE volumes comprise, in a form accessible to general readers, the contents of two folio volumes, presented by her Majesty's command to both Houses of Parliament, in 1840 and 1841;—giving detailed information of the proceedings of the Committee of the Privy Council on Education, from the time of its appointment in 1839, down to the dissolution of the late Government, when a change necessarily took place in the members composing the Committee.

The form in which information is communicated through the medium of parliamentary Papers, is a point which, we think, might usefully engage the attention of our representatives. The bulky volumes in blue covers, which during each session of Parliament, and for some time after its close, accumulate on the table of every member of the House of Commons, rather repel than invite examination; and we are con-

---

* The work of the Rev. Canon Rendu, of Chamberry, on the Glaciers of Savoy, deserves to be specified as a rare instance of a really scientific work issuing from the press of Savoy. We regret to have seen it but cursorily, having in vain endeavoured to procure a copy even in Switzerland.

vinced that much interesting information contained in these documents is lost to the public, owing to the shape in which it is conveyed. Whether there are sufficient grounds for retaining the antiquated and generally obsolete form of a ponderous folio, 'for the use of members only,' is a question we will not pretend to decide; but the public are greatly indebted to any one who will enable them, as in the case of the volumes before us, to acquire, in a popular and accessible shape, information contained in Parliamentary Reports and Papers, on subjects of deep national interest.

These volumes will well repay an attentive perusal. The interest, indeed, with which we have read them, has on the whole been of a painful nature; arising, on the one hand, from the melancholy picture which they present to us of the state of elementary education in this country; and, on the other, from the conviction which is forced upon us, that no adequate means have as yet been taken for remedying this grievous deficiency.

We are not, however, on this ground, disposed to undervalue what has actually been accomplished towards the improvement of our national education. On the contrary, we regard with satisfaction any advances, however small, which have been made in the right direction; and accept with gratitude any measures, however short they may come of what we could have desired, having a tendency to diminish the aggregate of ignorance among our teeming population. We are bound, if we are to view this question practically, to look at it in connection with the discussions which have taken place with regard to it; and the formidable difficulties with which prejudice and party have unfortunately combined to surround it. In estimating at least the value of what has been done by the government of the country, in weighing the merits of the proceedings of the Committee of Council, we must keep in view not only what the zealous and enlightened advocates of national education justly consider as desirable in the abstract, but also what, under all the circumstances of the time, amidst conflicting opinions and party warfare, has actually been attainable; and if we still feel it our duty to contend for the assertion of larger views, and a more comprehensive policy, than have hitherto been adopted in dealing with this great national question, we must not on that account withhold a just tribute of appro-

bation from those who, through much evil report, and amidst obloquy and misrepresentation, undertook and persevered in, as members of the Government of the day, the task of endeavouring to raise the standard of elementary education in this country.

The formation of the 'Committee of the Privy Council on Education' was in itself, in our judgment, a most important step in the right direction. We are confirmed in this opinion by the outcry with which it was 'on its first announcement' assailed, and by the effort which was made to strangle it in its birth. It was a practical assertion, on the part of the Executive Government, of its right, and a practical recognition of its obligation, to promote and superintend the education of the people. The Government of this country had for a long time limited its views to the prevention or repression of crime, by severe laws and penal enactments. It had attacked by terror the effects of ignorance as developed in crime; but it had not attempted to remove the ignorance, the fruitful parent of crime. It had looked on, as an unconcerned spectator, at the benevolent but desultory efforts of individuals and societies, operating, with insufficient means and imperfect machinery, on detached portions of the community; but it had done absolutely nothing to extend to the mass of the population the advantages of sound and useful education.

The Government of Lord Grey was the first which took the subject in hand. Lord Althorp, as Chancellor of the Exchequer, proposed to Parliament an annual vote of money, to be distributed by the Treasury through the medium of two voluntary societies, in aid of the erection of school-houses, in connection with one or other of those societies; but with the character of the education professed to be given in such schools, the Government did not pretend to interfere. The functions of the Treasury, as indeed naturally followed from the constitution and duties of that Board, were limited to the object of securing the actual application of the money placed under their control to the purposes for which it had been appropriated by Parliament. Whether, indeed, they were able in all cases effectually to secure even this object, may be questioned; but this at least is clear, that while the Government asked for money from Parliament for purposes connected with education, and thus recognized their obligation to promote it, they merely undertook to be the channel through which, on certain specified terms, that money should find its way to its ultimate recipients, in aid of local funds for the erection of permanent school-houses.

The appointment of the Committee of Council in 1839, necessarily involved higher objects. The Government desired through its agency, not only by augmenting the number of school-houses to increase the means available for the instruction of the poor, but by other and more important measures to improve the quality of the instruction to be communicated in such school-houses, and to render it in some degree at least worthy of the name of education. This desire was sufficiently apparent from the terms of Lord John Russell's letter to the Marquis of Lansdowne, in which, after adverting to the exertions which had been made of late years by the National and British and Foreign School Societies, he enumerated, as among the chief defects which still subsisted, and for which a remedy was required, 'the insufficient number of qualified schoolmasters—the imperfect method of teaching which prevails in perhaps the greater number of schools—the absence of any sufficient inspection of the schools, and examination of the nature of the instruction given—the want of a model school, which might serve for the example of those societies and committees which anxiously seek to improve their own methods of teaching; and finally, the neglect of this great subject among the enactments of our voluminous legislation.' It is unnecessary to remind our readers of the storm which the formation of the Educational Committee of Council produced. The influence which it could not fail to exercise on the education of the people, was clearly apprehended by its opponents. The cry of 'Danger to the Church' was raised in the country, by those who had before experienced the value of that artifice for the obstruction of some measure founded on principles of religious liberty; and the opportunity was too favourable to be lost by the leaders of the Opposition of that day, of aiming a blow at the Government, by taking up that cry within the walls of Parliament. The Committee was denounced in the House of Commons by the noble lord who led the attack upon it —now himself a member of the Committee—as a body 'decidedly and exclusively political in its character, and necessarily

fluctuating and uncertain in its composition; and in which there was no element of a defined or fixed principle of action, and into which, from its constitution and composition, it was impossible that it could so happen that a single individual could be admitted of those who were by the laws of the country entitled to superintend the moral education, and to direct the spiritual instruction of the people;[*] and a right honourable gentleman, now also himself a member of the Committee as Secretary of State for the Home department, after declaring his determination not to advance one step beyond the plan sanctioned by Lord Althorp, and objecting, in the strongest manner, to the proposed measures of the Government, avowed that 'the root of all the evil in his mind consisted in the appointment of the Committee of Council for the superintendence of education;' and that, 'while any such body existed, the House should address the Crown against it, for the purpose of obtaining its removal; for it was his decided opinion that it would, if allowed to be followed up, lead to results disastrous to the state, and adverse to the temporal and eternal interests of the British people.'[†] Sir Robert Peel himself mainly objected to the Committee as being composed exclusively of members of the Executive Government, which rendered it rather a Committee of the Government than of the Privy Council; and, departing from his usual reserve, went so far as to hint—for the encouragement, no doubt, of such of his supporters as suspected the depth or the sincerity of his church principles, that the next Government, on whom, if the principle were established, would devolve the management of the general education of the country, would hasten to repair the injury done to the church, by adding the Archbishop of Canterbury and the Bishop of London to the Committee of Council.[‡] The Committee, however, survived the storm; and although an important part of the original intention of the Government was necessarily abandoned, the Committee itself, with its exclusively political character, composed of members of the Executive Government, and not comprising any of the dignitaries of the Church of England, laboured assiduously for two years in the advancement of the cause of National Education.

---

* Hansard's Debates, vol. xlviii. p. 230.
† Ibid. p. 655.
‡ Ibid. p. 670.

We have said that the mere appointment of such a body necessarily involved higher objects than those which had been contemplated by the Board of Treasury; and the influence which it could not fail to exercise over the education of the people was proportionably greater. It was to consist of men of high station in the country, holding ministerial appointments, and thus directly responsible to Parliament, who were to sit as a Board for the single purpose of promoting education; not by the mere distribution of the Parliamentary grant, but by the collection and publication of accurate facts as to the state of elementary education in various parts of the country—by the dissemination of useful practical information, derived from the experience of foreign countries, as well as of our own—by a comparison of various methods of teaching—by the encouragement of local efforts; and by the support and countenance of every judicious attempt to increase the efficiency of existing schools, by the preparation of well-qualified instructors, or the introduction of new and useful branches of instruction.

The volumes before us afford ample proof of the utility of such a Board. The promoters of schools will find in them a fund of valuable information, calculated to be of the greatest assistance in the establishment and conduct of their schools. They are here presented with forms of conveyance of school-sites, of building-contracts and specifications; together with a series of well-executed plans of school-houses of various dimensions, accompanied by an explanatory minute, containing all that can be required for their guidance as to the structure and machinery of the schools; the information being adapted to whatever method of instruction it may be their intention to follow. Besides these, the Committee has published a minute 'on constructive methods of teaching reading, writing, and vocal music,' full of interesting and valuable matter; and under their sanction and encouragement, Mr. Hullah has established his admirable singing-school for schoolmasters. The Committee, indeed, on the proposal for this school being submitted to them, did not feel themselves authorised by the terms of the Parliamentary grant to appropriate any portion of that grant to the support of this school; but they gave it their marked countenance and approval; and we find from a Paper recently circulated under the sanc-

tion of the committee, that within a very few weeks from the commencement of the school, on the 1st February, 1841, it already consisted of no less than three classes of schoolmasters and one of schoolmistresses, with one hundred members in each class, meeting twice a-week at Exeter Hall; where the gratifying spectacle was exhibited of this large assemblage of persons collected together in these classes—without any regard to distinction of religious creed or denomination—evincing a marked delight in their lessons, and each contributing a small sum towards the expense of the establishment.*

Such are some of the general advantages which have already resulted from the existence of the Committee of Council on Education, and which we think sufficient in themselves fully to vindicate its appointment. To these are to be added the impulse which it has given to the cause of education through the country; and the improvement which is perceptible in the views and objects of those who are engaged in the promotion of elementary education. But there is one branch of the proceedings of the Committee not yet adverted to, and to which we attach the greatest importance. We allude to the system of school inspection which it has established. On the transfer of the appropriation of the parliamentary grant from the Treasury to this Committee, it was laid down as an inflexible rule, that no portion of the grant should be applied for the establishment or support of Normal or any other schools, *except on the condition of the schools so aided being open to inspection.* No part of the Government proposal met with a more determined opposition than this. It was not, indeed, a topic of which much advantage could be taken by the opponents of the Government in the House of Commons; as it would have been difficult to have there obtained any considerable support to the proposition that, when the public money was dispensed by the Government, the Government should be deprived of the power of securing its due application by

---

* Since this was written, we have seen a statement from which it appears that the pupils in the Singing School now amount to 2000, and that other branches of instruction have been added.

A course of Lectures on the Chemistry of Daily Life, by Dr. Reid, has also been commenced at Exeter Hall, under the direction of the Committee of Council, to which masters and mistresses of elementary schools are gratuitously admitted.

their own inspection; but the vehemence with which the proposed inspection was opposed out of the House was extreme. Episcopal Charges and clerical pamphlets waged a fierce war of words against this intermeddling on the part of the State with sacred things.

The right of inspection of schools in which children belonging to the established church are educated, was boldly asserted to be vested exclusively in the ecclesiastical authorities of the Church; and much learning was displayed in attempting to prove that the inspection must emanate from the Bishop, and be exercised by his 'natural agent,' the Chancellor of the diocese; while the most extravagant assumptions were unblushingly put forth as to the probable character of the inspectors to be appointed by the Crown, on the recommendation of the Committee, as to their deficiency in every requisite qualification for their office, and as to the malignant influence which they would exercise on the schools which should be desecrated by their admission. Nor was coercion altogether wanting to swell the ranks of the opponents of the Committee of Council upon this point. The refusal to receive any aid from Government was made the condition of pecuniary grants from the national, and from some, at least, of the diocesan educational societies; in order to influence clergymen who, not participating in the views of their brethren, would, if left to act on their own unbiassed opinions, have willingly accepted a portion of the parliamentary grant, and opened the doors of their schools to the government inspector. Thanks to the firmness of the Committee, and to the good sense of the Archbishop of Canterbury and the Bishop of London, whom we believe to have been always desirous of moderating the violence of the extreme party in the Church upon this question, this opposition ultimately failed of attaining its object. The Committee adhered to their condition. Two inspectors—the Rev. J. Allen and Mr. Seymour Tremenheere—were appointed. Instructions were addressed to them—they entered on the discharge of their duties—the distribution of the parliamentary grant proceeded; and the National Society became deeply involved in advances or engagements far beyond their resources, made to clergymen, to enable or to induce them to dispense with the assistance proffered by the Government. An accommodation thus became indispensable. The extravagant pretensions which had been urged on behalf of the church were no longer insisted on; and an arrangement was made by the Committee with the Archbishop of Canterbury, and ratified by an Order in Council, by which the condition of inspection remains untouched, and the appointment of inspectors continues in the crown; but the concurrence of the two Archbishops in their respective provinces is required in the person to be entrusted with the authoritative inspection of schools connected with the established church.

We must do the members of the Church of Scotland the justice to remark, that, however jealous they may generally be of interference on the part of the State, they gave as a body no countenance to the pretensions which had been urged by their sister Church; and that at an early period the Education Committee of the General Assembly tendered their co-operation to the Committee of Council, on terms which were readily complied with; and these two bodies appear to have uniformly acted in cordial harmony and concert.

One great advantage immediately resulted from the arrangement between the Archbishop and the Committee. The latter, as we think erroneously, and with a vain desire to disarm opposition, had declared that the Inspectors should limit their inquiries to secular branches of instruction; and that the religious instruction imparted in the schools should constitute no part of their investigation. Such a limitation of their duties would, in our opinion, have most materially interfered with their usefulness, and diminished their efficiency. There was indeed a time when the recognized connection of a School with the Church of England might have been taken as some guarantee that the Doctrines and Principles of that Church, as established at the Reformation, would be instilled into the minds of the children; and that whatever deficiency there might be, on the part of the master, in conveying to their minds a clear apprehension of those doctrines and principles, nothing diametrically opposed to them would in any case be taught. In the present day, unhappily, no such guarantee is afforded; and no security exists, short of a vigilant and close inspection, against schools partly built by aid from Parliamentary grants, and placed under the superintendence of Clergymen professing to be of the 'Anglican Church,' being made seminaries for the inculcation of doctrines and principles directly opposed to the spirit of Protestantism; and wholly at variance with the plain letter and obvious intention of the Articles and Formularies of the Church. We have no desire, on this occasion, to enter further on a subject which is daily becoming one of more deep and painful interest to the faithful members of the Church of England; but we could not altogether pass it by, in estimating the value of a searching and impartial inspection into the nature of the religious instruction to be communicated in the numerous schools under the care of the Parochial Clergy—which have recently been erected, or are now in course of erection in England, aided by grants from the public money placed at the disposal of the Committee of Council. We think, therefore, that an important point was gained, when, in addition to, and incorporated with, the instructions addressed to their Inspectors by the Committee of Council, there were framed by the Archbishops instructions applicable to all schools connected with the Church of England, with a view to elicit full and accurate information on this important branch of education; and in which the Inspectors are directed to inquire with special care how far the 'Doctrines and Principles of the Established Church are instilled into the minds of the children.'

The duties of the Inspectors are clearly explained in the instructions addressed to them by the Committee. Although appointed for the specific purpose of visiting from time to time schools aided by grants of public money, other and more comprehensive duties were contemplated in their appointment; and it is in these that they have hitherto been chiefly employed. Comparatively few of the schools which have received assistance, subject to the condition of inspection, can as yet be in actual operation; but the Inspectors have been most usefully occupied in general inquiries, the results of which are presented in the volumes before us. Independently of an examination, conducted at the request of the Board of Admiralty, into the state of the Greenwich Hospital Schools, five reports have been made on the state of Elementary Education in several districts in England; and one on the state of Elementary Education in a district in Scotland. There are also two special Reports, one on the state of thirty-seven schools in connection with the Church of England, in the counties of Chester, Derby, and Lancaster; and the other on the state of the Normal Seminary at Glasgow.

These Reports furnish us with tolerable

means of judging of the character and qualifications of the gentlemen selected by the Committee for the duty of inspection. We have before alluded to the unworthy suspicions which were expressed as to their probable character; and to the confident predictions which were uttered of their entire unfitness for the office. After perusing their Reports, we have no hesitation in asserting that never were suspicions more destitute of foundation, nor predictions more completely falsified. The gentlemen appear to us to have brought to the discharge of their duties a comprehensive view of the subject with which they had to deal; great diligence and activity of mind; good practical sense and ready observation; united with strong Christian principle, and a deep sympathy with the wants and interests of those large classes whose welfare their labours were designed to promote. The cordial local co-operation which they met with, and the facilities which they gratefully acknowledge as having been universally afforded to them in the prosecution of their inquiries, furnish in themselves no slight evidence of their general bearing and conduct having been in strict accordance with what was judiciously pointed out in their instructions as calculated to conciliate the confidence and good-will of those with whom they were to communicate.

The great insufficiency in the amount or quantity of education provided for the children of the working classes throughout England, is, we believe, now so generally admitted—at all events, it has been so often and clearly demonstrated—that we think it unnecessary to make any observations on the abundant evidence contained in these Reports, as to the very large proportion of children who receive no education or instruction at any day school whatever. It is to the character and quality of instruction given to the children who do attend existing schools, that we are anxious to direct special attention; for although it has been often and ably exposed by the advocates of a better system of national education, we believe that it is not yet fully understood, and that the statements which have, from time to time, been made respecting it, are thought by many to be chargeable with exaggeration. The result of the inquiries of the Government Inspectors has been to collect a mass of facts bearing upon this point—not, indeed, presenting any striking features of novelty to those whose attention has been closely directed to the state of our elementary education—but not the less calculated to produce a deep and salutary impression. We have here the strongest concurrent testimony of men acting separately and without concert with each other, applicable to districts widely distinct, not only in their locality but in many essential particulars, as to the lamentably defective nature of the instruction given in the vast majority of the schools at present accessible to the children of the working classes; —demonstrating that it is to the improvement in the character of these schools, even more than to a rapid augmentation of their number, that the energies of the friends of education, and the superintending care and assistance of the Government, must be directed, if any real effect is to be produced on the principles and habits of the future population of this country. Indeed, unless this glaring defect can be remedied—unless masters and mistresses can be properly trained and thoroughly prepared for their profession, all other means for educating the people will be comparatively valueless; and the schools rapidly rising throughout the country will exhibit the same unsatisfactory spectacle of incompetent teachers, and ignorant or ill-taught scholars, of which such numerous instances are to be found in the Reports before us. It is justly observed by Mr. Gibson, in his Report on the state of education in the Presbyteries of Haddington and Dunbar, that 'it may be well to notice the influence that a really accomplished and active teacher almost invariably has in elevating and extending the educational course. It may be stated that wherever a teacher of ability and acquirement is located, and how poor soever may be the people among whom he labours, the expectation may, with a considerable degree of confidence, be entertained, that the extent of his pupils' acquirements will be found to be, in spite of every discouragement and local disadvantage, somewhat proportional to the amount of his own.' It is at least equally true, and indeed it is a self-evident proposition, that inefficient and incompetent teachers must keep down the education entrusted to their hands to the level of their own capacity; and that a good school cannot exist without a good schoolmaster. Now, what has been the training, and what are the qualifications of the far greater number of those to whom the education of the poorer classes has been hitherto, and is at present, committed? We do not hesitate to say of them, as a body, that they have received no training fit to qualify them for their profession—that the attainments of many of them are of the lowest possible order—and that the knowledge possessed by others, and their endeavour faithfully to discharge their duty, fail in the greater number of instances of producing a satisfac-

tory result, from their not having had the advantage of a special education for the profession they have undertaken.

Before we proceed to support this statement by evidence drawn from these Reports, we think it right to premise that we are far from intending to cast censure on those of whom we are compelled to speak thus disparagingly. The difficulty of obtaining a livelihood is well known, and it can be no matter of surprise that persons unable to maintain themselves in any other line of life —with the most ordinary notions of what is meant by education, but possessing the elements of the technical knowledge of reading and writing, and perhaps arithmetic—should attempt to earn a subsistence, by undertaking to teach others the little which they themselves know. Still less can it be imputed as matter of blame to the better class of schoolmasters, that they are wanting in the essential qualifications of their profession, when no opportunity has been afforded them of acquiring those qualifications; but we do feel it to be a national disgrace that this defect should have been so long tolerated; and that, after all that has been said and written on the subject, and, with the example before us of what has been done in this respect in other countries of Europe, no general and well directed effort should have been made to raise the character and improve the qualifications of those to whom the training of the youthful mind of the great bulk of our population has been professedly entrusted.

Mr. Tremenheere's first inquiry was conducted in a portion of a mining district comprising five parishes, (four in Monmouthshire and one in Glamorganshire,) which had been the focus of the insurrectionary movement that led to the attack on the town of Newport in November, 1839. The aggregate population of those parishes, according to the lowest estimate, amounts to 85,000; out of which the total number of children attending day and dame schools was found to be 3308, distributed among 47 common day schools and 33 dame schools. Of the 47 common day schools, 5 are under the care of females. Of the masters of the remaining 42:—

16 had been unsuccessful in some retail trade.

11 had been miners, or labouring men who had lost their health, or met with accidents in the works, and had subsequently 'got a little learning' to enable them to keep a school.

10 had received some instruction with a view to adopt the profession of teaching.

4 were ministers of dissenting places of worship.

1 was the clerk of a parish church.

42.—(*Min.* 1839–40, p. 178.)

The quality of the education does not belie the expectation created by this statement. In most instances indeed the accommodation was wretched, and every requisite of a really good school was wanting.

'In a few only,' says Mr. Tremenheere, 'did the size and cleanliness of the room, and the demeanour and apparent qualifications of the master, afford a probability that the instruction sought to be given would be imparted with effect. But even in those of the highest pretensions, the amount of instruction was very scanty. In 18 only were the principles of English grammar taught; in 4 only was a map of any kind used; and in 4 also there was a desire to communicate a few of the leading facts of general history. In all the rest, the aim of the master did not in general appear to extend beyond instruction in the mechanical processes of reading and writing, with a little arithmetic, together, in some instances, with such moral lessons, drawn from the Scriptures and the small school-books in common use, as he was able to impress on his pupils.   *   *   *   *   Of the dame schools visited, many were neat and in good order; but they seemed in general to be not so much places of instruction as of periodical confinement for children, whose parents were at work during the day. The only two infant schools in the district, although not satisfactory specimens of what that system is capable of effecting, are nevertheless valuable; as showing by the numbers which frequent them, and the comparative distance of the houses of some of the youngest pupils, that they are well suited to the habits and desires of the people. They are built, and are chiefly supported, by the gentlemen on whose property they stand. It is manifest that, under the most favourable circumstances, the instruction offered to the children of the labouring classes in the day schools of this district, could not be expected to have much permanent effect in disciplining the mind, raising the taste and habits, and correcting the disposition. But when it is also remembered that the small amount of instruction actually sought for is spread irregularly over a period seldom exceeding two or three years, the great and general deficiency in the extent and value of such elementary education as is obtained in these schools, will be more evident.'—(*Minutes*, 1839–40, p. 178.)

Such is the nature of the provision made for the mental and moral culture of the children of this large population—collected in dense masses about the works which furnish them with employment, and isolated from other portions of society. Can it be a matter of surprise that their general habits should be as they are described by Mr. Tre-

menheere—those of improvidence and intemperance—and that they should be a source of disquiet and anxiety to the Government, owing to their easy exposure to the arts of any rash or designing anarchist ?

Mr. Tremenheere was subsequently charged with similar inquiries in the Mining District of Cornwall. The chief distinctive feature in the character of the population of this district, is the natural intelligence for which the Cornish miners have long been remarkable. Mr. Tremenheere tells us, 'Those who have the best opportunities of observing, remark the apprehensiveness they display on all occasions requiring the exercise of that quality. Clergymen, strangers to the county, find that their addresses from the pulpit are readily understood and commented upon by the labouring classes. Men of science bear willing testimony to the skill and talent exhibited by the working miners, in relation to their various occupations. Every stranger who comes in contact with them is disposed to the conclusion, that the intellectual capacity of the class of miners in this county, reaches a standard above the average of a labouring population.'—(*Minutes*, 1840–41, p. 190.)

But to what an extent the cultivation of this favourable soil has been neglected, and how little has been done by education to improve the natural advantages they possess, appears from the fact, that 'of learning acquired from books, they have very little. A large proportion of the adult male population is unable to read, a still larger is unable to write; and very few of the females, young or old, can do either.' Out of a population of about 52,000 comprised within the district selected for inquiry, and containing most of the chief mines in the county, the whole number of children attending school in December, 1840, is stated to have been 1614, distributed among 37 common day schools ; leaving the estimated number of 6803 children, between 5 and 15, not attending any day school. And when we examine the character of the education conferred in these 37 day schools, we find the following statement :—

'If the children of the labouring classes now attending these day schools are few in proportion to the whole number of an age for education, and if the time allowed for it by the parents of these few be short and inadequate, still less are the methods pursued by 27 out of 32 masters and mistresses whose schools I visited, or the books and apparatus used, such as to afford any reasonable hope that instruction of any permanent value could be imparted to more than a small number of their pupils, even if they remained much longer at school than is now the custom. By all these 27, the old system of teaching is pursued, and the books in use are those ordinarily accompanying it. The payments are so low and irregular, that good classbooks cannot be afforded by the master. Whatever books are used are provided by the parents. Being themselves generally unable to read, the cheapest seem to be considered to have the most merit. * * * *

'Of the masters, the great majority had either been hurt or had lost their health in the mines, or had been unsuccessful in trade or other occupations; but their qualifications appeared in most instances to be respectable, and their demeanour towards their pupils mild and conciliatory. Nevertheless, it must be confessed that they cannot be regarded as possessing, either in their own resources or in the method they pursue, the capability of effecting, to any desirable extent, the mental and moral improvement of those under their charge. * * * *

'In the greatest number of these schools, comparatively few boys had advanced in arithmetic as far as the Rule of Three. Still fewer had learnt anything of grammar, English history, geography, mensuration, or linear drawing—subjects which almost all the masters professed to teach. In nineteen schools boys and girls were instructed together. In eight they had separate schools. In almost all, the amount of instruction which seemed to be thought requisite for the girls, scarcely passed the boundary of the merest elements.'—(*Minutes*, 1840–41, pp. 192—3.)

A few schools, indeed, were found in this district, forming honourable exceptions to the general description applicable to the great majority; and looking at the character and circumstances of its inhabitants—of which some interesting details are given by Mr. Tremenheere—we should say that there is probably no district where the advantages of a really good system of education would be more readily appreciated, or where its fruits would be more rapidly developed.

In Norfolk, Mr. Tremenheere's inquiries were limited to the town population of Norwich, Yarmouth, and Lynn, and to the agricultural population of fifty-one rural parishes in various parts of the country. Norwich presents the unusual case of an amount of school accommodation for a much larger number of children than are actually under instruction. This peculiarity appears to be attributable, partly to a suspicion, on the part of the working-classes, of the motives which influence the promoters of various day schools in desiring the attendance of their children, arising, in Mr. Tremenheere's opinion, from feelings of hostility and aversion towards their employers—prevalent among the great mass of the population. This suspicion has been hitherto unfortunately so strong, as to materially affect the success of a most generous

effort lately made in behalf of the improvement of the labouring population of Norwich, by a Mr. Geary, who erected at his own expense, in 1838, a handsome building with playgrounds annexed, capable of containing upwards of 500 boys, girls, and infants, in three separate school-rooms, to which he added a building for the purpose of an industrial school, capable of accommodating at least 300 children to receive instruction in the elements of common trades. In order to meet the case of parents who could not afford to pay for their children's education, the children who paid nothing were to work half the day at some trade for the benefit of the establishment. Owing apparently to the cause already mentioned, the three schools, at the period of Mr. Tremenheere's visit, contained only 275 children, of whom no more than forty were occupied in the industrial school. We fear, however, that another and a more prevailing cause for the neglect, on the part of the parents, of the opportunities afforded them of obtaining instruction for their children, is to be found in the physical condition of that portion of the population of Norwich which is dependent on manufacturing employment, especially the handloom weavers, whose condition is represented as 'one of great and grievous depression.' Mr. Tremenheere gives some painful details of their sufferings and privations; and we cannot be surprised if one result of this melancholy state of destitution is the neglect of the education of their children; arising partly from a recklessness engendered by poverty, and partly from poverty itself, and a consequent unwillingness 'to lose even a faint chance of making the smallest amount of money by their children's labour.' Of the general character of the schools in Norwich Mr. Tremenheere was unable to report very favourably; but there appears to be a sincere and intelligent desire on the part of persons of weight and influence to render them more efficient. The central boys' and girls' schools, and the St. Andrew's Infant School, visited by Mr. Tremenheere, at the request of the Dean, and which have been selected as model schools in aid of endeavours to form an establishment for training masters and mistresses for National Schools of the diocese, afford good promise of usefulness; and the St. James's Infant School, which had been aided by a public grant, and is chiefly supported by Dissenters, is highly spoken of. But much still remains to be done in order to render the Norwich schools generally fit instruments of effecting a real improvement in the mental and moral condition of the rising generation. 'If this,' Mr. Tremenheere observes, 'is to be usefully effected through the medium of schools, as auxiliaries and interpreters to higher and more sacred ministrations, wider views must be taken of what it is requisite to teach, and of the instrumentality by which it is to be communicated.' * * * * 'To inculcate the leading doctrines of our faith, and to present the main incidents of the Holy Scriptures in such manner as shall interest the affections of the young, and not alone burden the memory, and to impart some real knowledge applicable to the state of the society in which they live, and to the world around them, is the work in hand. This the ordinary master or mistress at from 6s. to 10s. a-week cannot do. I observed some teachers in Norwich, receiving much higher salaries than those, who were incapable of explaining the meaning of very ordinary words, who could not spell correctly, and whose capacity for clearing up and making interesting to a child's mind the subject of instruction where books of general reading had been introduced, was manifestly very limited. Remains also of the art of governing by force of lungs or voice were not wanting. In some schools a little geography had been recently attempted, but not extending in most instances beyond catalogues of names; the master often appearing to think that to point out the hardest names in the interior of China and Tartary was the most dexterous feat of geographical learning. In a few cases I found that the maps hung on the walls, not yet used, objects apparently still of respectful and distant wonder alike to master and pupils. I could see no signs of any capability to make geographical instruction really profitable, by connecting with the physical facts some knowledge of the several peculiarities of the condition and mode of life of the various inhabitants of the globe.'—(*Minutes*, 1840–41, p. 437.)

The rural parishes in Norfolk, visited by Mr. Tremenheere, contain a population in the most deplorable state of ignorance. Some instances of it are given by him, which, if not vouched for by testimony above suspicion, we could scarcely have credited. Nor are the great majority of the schools now in operation calculated to apply to it an effectual remedy. 'Many defects (says Mr. Tremenheere) in the mode of doing what was proposed to be done, were to a greater or less extent apparent in all the schools which I had an opportunity of seeing in action in the course of this tour.' * * * * 'In one, twenty-boys who had been two years at the school could not read words of four letters correctly; they ran one verse into the other,

disregarding stops, and without the smallest approach to an attempt 'to understand the meaning. In a second, thirty boys who had been from eighteen months to two years at the school, and were nearly old enough to be taken away to work, could not read a verse in the New Testament without hesitation and mistakes. In a third, fifteen boys from ten to twelve years of age, in the first class, read with a boldness and fluency which seemed to impose on the master, who allowed them to pass over connecting words, signs of tenses, and smaller obstacles, in their progress to the longer words, which he always repeated after them, sometimes before. When examined in Scripture history, only one boy could answer any one question, and his knowledge did not enable him to say who led the chil-' dren of Israel into the Promised Land. None of them knew the meaning of the words Bible, Genesis, Exodus, although the clergyman, who was present, and put the questions to them, stated they had often been told. They did not know what county joined their own, nor the direction of London, nor in what quarter the sun was in the middle of the day, nor the direction of east, west, north, and south. These were boys just about to leave school, and who will be said to have "received their education" at a school supported at some expense by a large resident landowner. In a fourth, the mistress confessed she "could not teach much figures," and in speaking she made frequent faults in grammar. She was the mistress of a handsome school-house built by a neighbouring proprietor. In a fifth, a girl of eleven years old could not repeat the Lord's prayer, and the answers of all the elder, to the questions put to them at my request by the mistress and monitors, were as far from correct as if they had been read at hazard from an index. The state of proficiency in the adjoining boys' school was also very low, and in both instances the excuse given was, that the monitors did not remain long enough to be of any effectual assistance. These five cases embody characteristics which I found very common in the rest, with but few exceptions.'—*Minutes*, 1840–41, p. 458–9).

But, while the actual state of most of these schools is thus inefficient, we are somewhat cheered by the fact of 'an awakening interest' being felt in this county on the neglect of education. The dense ignorance of the people is generally admitted and lamented; collective and individual efforts are making in various parts of the county for the extension and improvement of elementary education—and in some instances with a success which reflects great credit on the parties to whose zeal and energy it is to be attributed; and the want of capacity or attainments on the part of the master or mistress, has in other cases been partially supplied ' by the vigilant superintendence and active teaching of the clergymen or other individuals, whose presence, example, and instruction, impart a tone and character, and exercise an influence which no other source can so well supply.' In the last-mentioned schools, indeed, ' the intellectual attainments were yet very indifferent,' the necessary consequence of the inferior acquirements of the master; ' but it was evident that a process of religious and moral training was going on, most valuable in its effects on the character and manners of the children, and in creating a visible bond of attachment and good feeling among themselves and towards those around them.' It is also gratifying to observe, that far the greater part of the schools reported on by Mr. Tremenheere in Norfolk, were visited by him at the request of their promoters, and that in numerous instances he ' was invited to consult with the parochial clergy, the members of the committees of British schools, the trustees of endowed schools, and the leading supporters of those unconnected with any society, as to the improvement of existing schools, or as to the plans, arrangement, and method most desirable for their several neighbourhoods;'—affording at once satisfactory proof of the absence of any jealousy or suspicion of a Government Inspector, and of the value of such an officer.

Of Mr. Allen's two Reports, the first is on the state of elementary education in the mining districts of Durham and Northumberland. His inquiry was chiefly among the coal-fields lying along the Tyne and Weare. In the course of the six weeks which it occupied, he visited 150 schools in this district, of which 4 were Sunday schools, 15 infant, 37 dame, 46 common day schools, set on foot by masters on their own account, subject to no superintendence, and attended by children of both sexes: 15 were girls' schools under the parochial clergy, 14 were boys' schools, and 2 were schools for both sexes, also under the parochial clergy; 5 were Lancasterian schools, (3 for boys and two for girls), one was the school in Durham jail, and eleven were schools for children of a superior class, with payments varying from 10s. 6d. to L.1., 1s. and upwards per quarter. In addition to these, he visited 26 other schools, of which a short account is given in the appendix to his Report.

The general result of this inquiry, as it respects the quality of the education given in these schools, will appear from the following extract from his Report:—

'In seven out of the fifteen infant schools visited, the mistresses had never received any sufficient training, and, as it appeared, made very feeble attempts to draw out the faculties of the children; acting as if their chief business was to teach their scholars to repeat a few rhymes, and to go through certain manual and bodily exercises. Two of these fifteen schools were under a master, most of them were well supplied with prints, and all except one were fitted up with a gallery: none of them had gardens attached, nor were they supplied with any gymnastic apparatus. A cabinet of natural objects might be procured for all with very little exertion on the part of the superintendent, as the children would, if the matter were proposed to them, make no contemptible collection for themselves.

'The dame schools appeared to me to be divisible generally into two classes; those kept by persons fond of children, and of cleanly and orderly habits—and these, however scanty may be their means of imparting instruction, (the mistresses confining themselves almost entirely to teaching a little reading and knitting, or sewing,) cannot altogether fail of attaining some of the highest ends of education, as far as regards the formation of character—and those kept by widows and others, who are compelled by necessity to seek some employment by which they may eke out their scanty means of existence, without any real feelings of interest in their work. Many of this latter class presented a most melancholy aspect—the room commonly used as a living room, and filled with a very unwholesome atmosphere; the mistress apparently one whose kindly feelings had been long since frozen up, and who was regarded with terror by several rows of children, more than half of whom were in many cases without any means whatever of employing their time.

In nine-tenths of the common day schools visited, I found no profession made of giving any religious instruction; this, as it was said, was left to the Sunday school; but, as ordinarily, no care is taken by the masters that their pupils shall attend Sunday schools, the common day schools of which I am speaking must be considered, I fear, in the worst sense of the words, merely secular schools. The masters appeared in most cases to be very ill educated, and the schools being matters of private speculation, except in a few instances where schoolrooms were found by the owners of collieries, they are subject to no inspection, and are consequently in a great measure beyond the reach of those beneficial influences which could not fail to be produced by intercourse with persons of superior intelligence, and from the opportunities of visiting good schools, and of becoming acquainted with the most approved methods of instruction. Of education, in that sense of the word which includes the training and the endeavour to perfect the faculties of the entire man, there is none. No superintendence is exercised over the children during the hours of relaxation; and, in but too many instances, it seemed that the constant use of words of harsh reproof, and no unfrequent recurrence to the strap, was needed to preserve tolerable quiet and some slight appearance of order. The strap, the common instrument of punishment, is not indeed a very formidable weapon; but the frequent use of it, while it bears witness to the little real respect paid to the master, must lower the character of the children, teaching them to estimate actions, not by any fixed standard of right and wrong, but by the immediate sensible results produced on the caprice or bad temper of another. . . . .

'The deficiency of books was most lamentable; in the majority, some slates and copy-books, a few pages of a spelling-book, or an entire one, treatises on arithmetic and mensuration, with the Bible or Testament, were almost the only visible means of instruction. . . . .

'In not more than four out of the forty-six did I find that any of the children were taught to draw; they were not provided with maps or blackened boards; they have no drills nor manual exercises; no play-grounds, nor provision for recreation. . . . . But little attention seems to be paid to the cleanliness of the children. In very few instances did I find a window opened for ventilation; and when a large number of children were gathered into a small confined room, the atmosphere, highly offensive to a stranger, must prove most pernicious to the lungs and skin of the inmates, slowly but surely undermining their health and strength.

'The parochial schools were better ventilated, and in most instances filled with cleaner children than those assembled in the common day-schools, although the rate of payment is considerably lower. In most, the system of mutual instruction is strictly adhered to, the masters making, as far as I could learn, little attempts to teach the children to exercise their mental faculties, by requiring written answers to written questions, or by resorting to ellipsis or the suggestive method of instruction. The children were usually found to be orderly in their demeanour; and in the better schools, both parochial and those under no superintendence, writing seemed to be fairly, and arithmetic very successfully taught. Children of the age of twelve were not unfrequently to be found solving problems in mensuration, and many in both classes of schools were found learning practical land-surveying. The reading was in almost all cases indifferent; and in nearly every instance in which the experiment was tried, an attempt to get the meaning of the words read, failed. I met with only one instance of a pupil teacher. All the parochial schools were opened and closed with prayer, and the church catechism was repeated by the children with tolerable accuracy; but in schools even of the better class, little or no meaning seemed to be attached to the more difficult words. In some cases, indeed, the explanation furnished in the glossary attached to the broken catechism was readily given; but this, as far as I could judge, was as much a matter of rote as the rest. Of the books used there was seldom any deficiency. . . . . The Lord's prayer and the Collect for the week was learnt by almost all the children; but besides these the children were not commonly taught private prayers to repeat at home, nor have I reason to believe that much inquiry

is made by their teachers how they have profited. One matter for regret which was continually forced on my thoughts while visiting these church schools was, that the masters, though in many instances appearing to be serious-minded men, seemed to have no wish to do more for their scholars than help them to acquire a knowledge of reading, writing, and arithmetic, with psalmody. If these objects were attained, and the children could say the catechism and the Collect for the week, and, in one or two instances, some texts of scripture, the masters generally seemed to think their work was perfectly done. It is not meant to undervalue their acquirements—doubtless they prove often the means to good; but I never found in my conversation with the masters, that they felt it to be their duty to endeavour to form the characters of the children, or to lead them to think, or even to convey to them instruction apart from the routine noticed above. The sphere of reading and information of the masters will, I fear, be generally found to lie in a very narrow compass, and it is no wonder if, as long as they are not better educated, they show little anxiety about improvement. . . . .

'As a class, the masters of the Lancasterian schools appeared to aim at more in the instruction of their pupils than the masters of the parochial schools—they seemed more alive, more stirring: in two of these schools good maps were drawn by some of the pupils. I doubt, however, whether the education given in such schools has not rather the tendency to press some children forward to rise out of their own sphere of life, than to elevate the condition of the mass. The scriptures were read in all, and nearly all were opened with prayer and singing. They were well furnished with the sheet lessons of the British and Foreign School Society, and with Bibles. As far as regards moral training and the superintendence of the children out of school hours, they seemed equally defective with the schools I have just now noticed.'—(*Minutes*, 1840-41, p. 126.)

This district, however, on the whole presents encouraging features. Its moral condition, as compared with that of other populous districts of England, is satisfactory. The Wesleyans have been active coadjutors to the Established Church in promoting the religious interests of the people; an improvement in the character of the pitmen is said to have taken place within the last thirty years; the owners of collieries seem not insensible to the moral obligation imposed on them, to promote the education of the children of their workmen; and a strong disposition has in some instances been evinced by the workmen themselves, to make considerable pecuniary sacrifices in order to obtain a good education for their children. Mr. Allen, indeed, is of opinion that little is needed but some encouragement and direction from those above them, to make a material change for the better; and that, were proper school-rooms everywhere built, and good masters attainable, the schools would support themselves.

Mr. Allen's second tour of inspection was to fifty-two schools in Derbyshire, Cheshire, and Lancashire, all connected with the Church of England—eleven of them being formally liable to inspection, having been aided by the Committee of Council—and the remaining forty-one (of which thirty-nine had been aided by the Treasury) having invited the visits of the Inspector. Several of these schools being as yet only in operation as Sunday schools, and two or three being omitted for reasons assigned in the Report, the actual number inspected amounted only to thirty-seven. Many of the facts stated in this Report are interesting and instructive; but the one feature to which we are particularly desirous of drawing attention is to be found here as elsewhere—namely, the want of properly qualified teachers, and the consequent injury sustained by the children. We find, for instance, a school containing more than seventy girls in a building which had cost L.300, with a mistress who, though a good worker, was unable either to write or to detect the most gross errors of spelling. The consequence was, a large portion of the children were sitting wholly unemployed. As a contrast to this, we gladly refer to Mr. Allen's account of the Infant School attached to St. James's Church at Heywood, where the master, a *Scotch Episcopalian, trained under Mr. Stow at Glasgow,* aided by his sister, was more successful in bringing into action the intellectual faculties of the children, than any other paid teacher whom Mr. Allen saw in Lancashire. 'Here also (he says) I found a border of flowers round the playground, perfectly neat, and free from weeds. This, which is always an agreeable sight as connected with a school, is most precious in a town like Heywood, where the pleasurable feelings excited by flowers and other of the good gifts of the Author of Nature, have but few opportunities of being called into action —a flower garden is a place where lessons of self-denial may be very early taught. I was told that during the last year only one blossom had been picked without leave. The children, although coming from the most unpromising localities, were neat and clean.'

It would, however, be unfair to attribute the excellent state of this school entirely to the master. The district in which it is comprises a population of 8000, and the clergyman, who is stated to be not so well paid as an ordinary curate, has, within three years, in addition to this infant school, established an efficient day school, attended by a considerable number of factory children, where he ha-

bitually himself gives religious instruction, and also lessons in geography and history, besides three night schools for such as are at work during the day. A daily school, supported by a factory master, has been placed under his superintendence, and two more day schools were shortly to be opened along the line of his population. Mr. Allen adds ' on Mondays, Wednesdays, and Fridays, himself and his wife, and their two female servants, leave the house with the key in their pockets, to spend the evening in a room given up to their use in a manufactory two miles distant. Here some sixty young people who have been in the mill during the day are assembled— some of the girls are taught sewing and knitting; the rest with the boys learn writing and accounts—the evening's work is concluded with a short catechetical lecture out of the Bible, and prayer.'

But in most of the schools visited by Mr. Allen in this tour, we find their efficiency seriously impaired by the want of proper training on the part of the instructor. In the seven other infant schools which he inspected, he 'noticed a great lack of any systematic plan for calling out the intelligence of the scholars—what was done seemed chiefly routine work.' 'The lessons of Scripture were commonly appeals to the memory, in which a few of the more forward boys led the answers of the rest.' In none of these were the children exercised in writing or drawing at the blackened board or wall.' Of the sixteen masters of the national schools he inspected, 'five only could be said to have received any proper training;' and the result in each case was apparent in the superior character of the instruction given in the school; while six out of the remaining eleven 'taught on no apparent system, without any arrangement of the children into classes; and in these,' he adds, 'the results, as far even as mere instruction went, seemed to me inferior to that which is obtained in a good dame school.' With these facts before us we can hardly be surprised to find, that 'the table given in the appendix presents but an unsatisfactory view of the general amount of instruction conveyed.' Mr. Allen had here no faults to find with the buildings, which were substantial and well sized. 'What is wanted,' he says, ' is not so much school-rooms as efficient masters, and greater means for their support.'

Mr. Baptist Noel, though not one of the government Inspectors, undertook an inquiry, under the direction of the Committee of Education, in the summer of 1840, into the state of elementary education in Birmingham, Manchester, Liverpool, and several other towns in Lancashire. He visited altogether 159 schools, of which 42 were in Birmingham, 26 in Manchester and Talford, 52 in Liverpool, and the rest in Stockport, Warrington, Hyde, Ashton, Oldham, Rochdale, Bury, Bolton, Wigan, and Preston. Of these, 146 were day schools of various kinds, and 49 were Sunday schools. In all the large cotton districts he found the Sunday schools well attended, and the dame and common schools numerous; but all of them, with the exception of Boston, exceedingly deficient in public day schools. Ashton-under-Lyne enjoyed the unenviable distinction of not possessing one public infant, or day school. For the amount of elementary instruction in the five large towns of Birmingham, Manchester, Liverpool, Salford, and Bury, Mr. Noel refers to the well-known printed Reports of the Manchester and Birmingham Statistical Societies. We shall confine our observations entirely to the quality of the instruction. After adverting to the description given in those Reports of the wretched character of the dame and common schools in the five towns above mentioned, Mr. Noel says :—

'From the answers uniformly made to my inquiries on this subject among persons acquainted with the poor, I judge that the great majority, both of dame and common schools in the Lancashire towns, answer to these descriptions; and the very few which my time enabled me to visit did not contradict that conclusion. In one of these dame schools I found thirty-one children, from two to seven years of age. The room was a cellar, about ten feet square and seven feet high. The only window was less than eighteen inches square, and not made to open. Although it was a warm day towards the close of August, there was a fire burning ; and the door, through which any air could be admitted, was shut. Of course, therefore, the room was close and hot, but there was no remedy. The damp subterraneous walls required, as the old woman assured us, a fire throughout the year. If she opened the door, the children would rush out to light and liberty, while the cold blast rushing in would torment her aged bones with rheumatism. Still further to restrain their vagrant propensities, and to save them from the danger of tumbling into the fire, she had crammed the children as closely as possible into a dark corner at the foot of her bed. Here they sat in the pestiferous obscurity, totally destitute of books, and without light enough to enable them to read, had books been placed in their hands. Six children, indeed, out of the thirty, had bought some twopenny books ; but these also, having been made

to circulate through sixty little hands, were now so well soiled and tattered, as to be rather the memorials of past achievements than the means of leading the children to fresh exertion. The only remaining instruments of instruction possessed by the dame, who lamented her hard lot to be obliged at so advanced an age to tenant a damp cellar, and to raise the means of paying her rent by such scholastic toils, were a glassful of sugar-plums, near the tattered leaves on the table in the centre of the room, and a cane by its side.'

To this is added the description of a common school in the same neighbourhood :—

'It was a room on the ground-floor, up a dark and narrow entry, and about twelve feet square. Here forty-three boys and girls were assembled, of all ages, from five to fourteen. Patches of paper were pasted over the broken panes of the one small window, before which also sat the master, intercepting the few rays of light which would otherwise have crept into the gloom. Although it was in August, the window was closed, and a fire added to the animal heat which radiated from every part of the crowded chamber. In front of the fire, and as near to it as a joint on the spit, a row of children sat, with their faces towards the master and their backs to the furnace. By this living screen the master, though still perspiring copiously, was somewhat sheltered from the intolerable heat. As another measure of relief, amidst the oppression of the steaming atmosphere, he had also laid aside his coat. In this undress he was the better able to wield the three canes, two of which, like the weapons of an old soldier, hung conspicuously on the wall, while the third was on the table ready for service. When questioned as to the necessity of this triple instrumentality, he assured us that the children were "abrupt and rash in their tempers," that he generally reasoned with them respecting their indiscretion, but that, when civility failed, he had recourse to a little severity.'—(*Minutes*, 1840-41, p. 162-63.)

We remember to have read in the memoirs of Oberlin, the indefatigable pastor of the Ban de la Roche, an anecdote of his predecessor, M. Stouber, visiting a school in the parish held in a miserable cottage, where he found a set of unemployed and noisy children, with an old man stretched on a bed in a corner of the apartment, who professed to be their master. The old man frankly confessed, in answer to the pastor's inquiries, that he taught the children nothing, for the simple reason that he knew nothing himself ; and in reply to the natural question of how he came to be the schoolmaster, he said, 'Why, sir, I had been taking care of the Waldbach pigs for a great number of years, and when I got too old and infirm for that employment, they sent me to take care of the children.' That such a case should be found in the last century, in an obscure village in a remote district of France, is not surprising ; but it is astonishing and humiliating that cases so nearly parallel to it should be discovered in the present day, in the centre of civilisation and commercial enterprise, in our own country. Is it possible that they can be suffered to continue ?

Mr. Noel, after stating, with a view to a right estimate of our elementary schools, what he considers as the chief objects of the education of the people, proceeds to report how far these objects are effected for even the small fraction of the population in attendance on elementary day schools in the district which he visited ; for which purpose he examines first, the instruction given in the schools, and then the moral and religious training—in a passage which, although we fear that our extracts have already exceeded the limits ordinarily assigned to them, we cannot refrain from presenting to our readers :—

' The great majority of the patrons and conductors of the National and Lancasterian schools which I visited, only profess to teach the children reading, writing and arithmetic. The knowledge of the English language, natural history, geography, physiology, and the history of their country, are all excluded subjects. Upon none of these could I examine the children generally, because their teachers professed the total ignorance of the children respecting them. If occasionally I heard that Liverpool was an island, that Lancashire was one of the great towns of England, and that Asia and America were chief countries of Europe—I was led to expect this ; if I heard such grammatical inaccuracies as those contained in the following answers to questions put by me—" Them as is good goes to heaven,"—" The men as was gazing up into heaven,"—" He drownded the whole world,"—these were mistakes which the teacher did not undertake to correct. But, unhappily, many of the schools were very unsuccessful in teaching what they profess to teach. In several of those which I examined, many children of the highest classes were unable to read fluently, even in the New Testament ; words were often mistaken, stops were misplaced, small words were omitted so as to destroy the sense, and many of the children were unable to spell even short and common words occurring in the lesson.

' In some of the girls' schools, very few of the children could write, and the writing was very bad ; while even in the boys' schools, where more attention is paid to this important art, there were very few boys, and in very few schools, who had attained to a good running hand without the aid of lines. In several of the girls' schools, the children do not learn arithmetic at a'l. The masters of the boys' schools always profess to teach it ; but I found the boys some-

times exceedingly defective in their knowledge of even the earliest and simplest rules. In one National school in a large town, and a populous neighbourhood, I found only six boys capable of working a short sum in simple multiplication, and five out of the six returned a wrong answer. In another, where 167 persons were present, I found only twelve who professed to understand compound addition ; and when I set these a sum in simple multiplication to work separately, one of the twelve brought a right answer, seven brought wrong answers, two worked it so slowly that they could not finish it, and two could not even begin to work it.

' But it was in their understanding of the scriptures, daily read, that I regretted to find the most advanced children of the National schools so extremely defective. Not only were they often ignorant of the principal facts recorded in the Bible, but they could not answer even the simplest questions upon the chapters which they had most recently read. Nor was their religious ignorance lessened by their knowledge of the catechism. I several times examined the first classes upon a portion of the catechism, and I never once found them to comprehend it. Indeed, to those who consider how they generally read the scriptures and repeat the catechism, their ignorance appears to be a very natural result. Usually the first class reads one or two chapters of the Bible daily to the master or monitor. In the first case, they would probably have such short questions on what they read as the general superintendence of the school would allow—in the other, none.

' It is to the monitors also that the catechism is daily repeated, the class repeating it again and again till the prescribed half hour is completed. Both in reading the scriptures to the monitors, and in repeating the catechism, the children showed a marked inattention and weariness, occasionally varied, when the master's eye was not upon them, by tokens of a roguish merriment.

' With the very best intentions, those who have adopted the system of the National School Society, have in many cases admitted into their schools nothing for the elder children except the Bible, small volumes of extracts from it, and the catechism—and the effects seem to me most unfortunate. All the books on subjects with which children are most familiar being excluded from the school, that thirst for variety which, for the wisest purposes, has been implanted by the Creator in the minds of children, finding no gratification, their faculties are stunted in their growth, and they sink into an inert listlessness. Nothing can exceed the contrast between the eagerness of the children in a well-taught school, and the apathy manifested in most of these National schools. But this is not the worst effect of making the Bible the only class book. Being thus made the medium through which reading and spelling are taught, it becomes associated in their minds with all the rebukes and punishments to which bad reading or false spelling, or inattention in class, exposes them ; and it is well, if, being thus used for purposes never designed, it do not become permanently the symbol of all that is irksome and repulsive.

'On the moral and religious training in these schools, I can say very little. In almost all the schools which I examined on this point, there was scarcely any such thing. The children would be punished for breaking the school rules, or if a breach of morality was formally complained of to the master, he would probably punish the child for it; but any direct endeavours to bring the children to be moral and religious, I could scarcely find. When I asked masters what means they employed for these ends, I could find nothing except the reading of the scriptures and the repetition of the catechism in the manner which I have before described. But in scarcely any of these schools do the masters address the scholars on the subject of religion, or even read the scriptures to them. Very few masters instruct any of the children on religious subjects in the class-room, and scarcely one is in the habit of speaking to the children individually on the necessity of personal religion. Few visit the parents of the children, or know the children's character, or take any interest in them after leaving the school—indeed, that would be nearly impossible—the masters are so frequently changed, either from incapacity, from the lowness of their salary, from their restlessness, or from some other cause, that in most cases it is impossible that any lasting friendship should be formed between them and their scholars.

'On the whole I am obliged to report, that most of the day schools which I examined seemed to me exceedingly inefficient. The system on which they teach, confining the children to one class of subjects, would render the ablest master inefficient, and reduce the most intelligent children to listlessness. The masters, who seem generally respectable men, are without assistance, and overwhelmed by the multitude of children whom they have to teach—the monitors, generally boys of ten or eleven years of age, who have only been two or three years in the school, and have little separate instruction, are almost as ignorant as the classes whom they instruct—scarcely know how to read well themselves, and are utterly incapable of exercising the intellect of the children on the lesson which they read. Instead of having a plentiful supply of books on all the subjects most likely to interest them, the elder scholars are generally confined to the Bible for their common school exercise in reading, and are ill supplied even with Bibles. To masters so ill qualified, the school committees afford but small salaries, and the low salaries hinder able men from entering on the profession of schoolmaster, or starve them out of it when they make it their choice.

'The parochial and district ministers of the large towns which I visited, although the most active promoters of the education of the poor, are still so necessarily occupied with the duties of their large parishes and districts, that they can seldom inspect their schools, and few laymen enter them. The children are not visited at their homes, are not known to their ministers, and often before the age of ten, almost always before twelve, are removed from school to labour, when they have only been two years, or a year, or only six months at school. Under these circumstances, it is obvious that the schools must be inefficient. Owing to the energy of the patrons, or the advantage of better systems, some schools have arisen to an honourable superiority to the rest. King Edward's branch schools and St. Thomas's schools in Birmingham, Christ Church school at Salford, St. John's school in Manchester, the Caledonian schools, the Jordan Street school for boys, and the Christ Church school for girls at Liverpool, and the National Schools at Watrington, although considerably differing from each other, have all some features of excellence highly creditable to those gentlemen who have rendered them so efficient. But these are exceptions to the general rule.'—(*Minutes*, 1840–41, p. 173.)

We have scarcely reserved to ourselves space to notice as fully as it merits the Report made by Mr. Gibson, inspector of schools in Scotland, on the state of elementary education in the presbyteries of Haddington and Dunbar, which contains a clear and well-arranged statement of the results of his inquiry. The schools which he visited were of three classes—parochial schools, partially endowed or side schools, and adventure schools. Here, as in every other case, the value and efficiency of the school may be measured by the attainments of the teacher; and it is not without a feeling of satisfaction that we think we may fairly claim for Scotland an exemption from the same degree of reproach which unfortunately attaches to England, on the score of the qualifications of her schoolmasters.

We are, indeed, far from denying that very much still remains to be done, even among ourselves, in order to place elementary education on the footing which its vast importance to the national interests, and the well-being of the community requires; and we fully concur with Mr. Gibson in the opinion, that 'in the towns universally, and generally in large and populous parishes, the educational means for the children of the lower classes of the population are very defective, both in amount and quality.' Still, of the masters of the schools visited by Mr. Gibson, we find a larger proportion of superior and well-qualified instructors, than we have any reason to believe could be found in any given district in England. Of the twenty-seven parochial schools included in his Report, fifteen possessed teachers of very high qualifications, and whose attainments, experience, energy, and skill, entitled them, in Mr. Gibson's opinion, to be ranked in the first class; while six of the remaining teachers, though greatly inferior to the former, were, in point of acquirement, well fitted to conduct the business of instruction; leaving a third class, containing only five, whose schools furnished little evidence of their capability to discharge, with a moderate degree of efficiency, the duties of their profession.

The ten 'partially endowed or side schools' which Mr. Gibson visited, he found in a very unsatisfactory state. These schools are situated for the most part in extensive landward parishes, and at a distance from the parochial schools, and attended chiefly by the children of agricultural labourers. The annual emoluments of the teacher do not exceed L.35 ; and it is to this low scale of remuneration, which fails to secure the services of competent men, that Mr. Gibson attributes the great inferiority of the masters to the parochial teachers.

The greater part of the adventure schools are to be found in towns, or in populous county parishes, where the parochial or endowed schools are insufficient for the accommodation of all the children ; or in localities where the established teachers are inefficient and unpopular. Fifteen of these schools were visited by Mr. Gibson, and six out of the fifteen masters are placed by him on a footing fully equal to that of the first class of parochial teachers. Of the remaining nine he says, 'all of them originally followed some other calling, and with only one exception became teachers, when they had been rendered by accident or disease incapable of prosecuting the labours of their former occupation.' The necessary consequence is, that they are altogether unskilled in the practice of their profession, 'are only capable of imparting in the most inefficient manner the ordinary branches of knowledge,' and, 'however respectable in character, or otherwise exemplary, are quite unworthy of being depositories of interests so important.' —(*Minutes*, 1840-41, p. 284.)

We cannot close this imperfect sketch of the substance of these reports, so far as they relate to the state of elementary education, without adverting for a moment to the notice which they contain of the great number of Sunday schools to be found throughout the country. Although quite incapable of being considered adequate substitutes for elementary day schools, they doubtless form a most important auxiliary to them ; and it is difficult to estimate the full value of the benevolent labours of the numerous individuals, who, actuated by the purest motives of Christian charity, gratuitously devote, in many of our large towns, a considerable portion of their Sunday leisure hours (perhaps the only leisure they possess) to the religious instruction of the young.

These volumes, as we have before stated, comprise the history of the proceedings of the

Committee of Council only to the period of the dissolution of the late Government. But the Committee did not expire with the Government to which it owed its existence. Notwithstanding the objections with which it was assailed in 1839, it was reconstituted by Sir Robert Peel, in 1841, on precisely the same principle as before. The individual members who had composed it necessarily ceased to belong to it, on ceasing to form part of the executive government of the country ; but their seats at the Board were supplied exclusively by members of the new government, without the addition to their number even of a single dignitary of the Church ; and on looking at the names of greatest influence in the present composition of the Committee, we confess that we see no reason for disatisfaction or alarm. Credit is universally given to Lord Wharncliffe, the President of the Council, for liberal views on this question, and for a desire to carry out fairly and honestly the ends for which the Committee was appointed. The opinions of Sir Robert Peel on education, so far as they have hitherto been expressed, have not been marked by intolerance, or fettered by any strong predilection for what are termed high church principles ; and we entertain the hope and expectation that he will be desirous of at least equalling the zeal of his predecessors on this important subject. Lord Stanley, it is true, led, with his usual ardour, the attack of his party upon the whole scheme of the government in 1839 ; but we cannot forget that he was the author (we believe he still professes to be the supporter) of the Irish system of education ; and we may hope that, now that the motives for his former opposition have ceased to exist ; he, as a member of the Government, will support such an improvement of elementary education as its present state imperatively requires ; nor have we any apprehension that Sir James Graham will maintain his consistency, in opposition to his colleagues, by adhering to his determination of 1839, not to advance one step further than Lord Althorp had previously gone.

Neither can one significant omission fail to be remarked. The selection of the members of the present Committee has not been confined exclusively to the Cabinet ; and yet there is one member of the Government holding an office which places him in the rank of privy councillor, of high character and attainments, who has taken a warm interest in the question of education, and who might therefore reasonably have been expected to be found on the Committee, but whose name does not appear upon its list. We cannot regard the omission of Mr. Gladstone in any other light than as the indication of a desire, on the part of Sir Robert Peel, that no ground of suspicion even should exist, that any change was contemplated in the views or objects of the Committee, tending to restrict its influence, or to lessen the confidence with which it ought to be regarded by persons of various religious denominations. We have, moreover, the satisfaction of observing that the able and indefatigable Secretary to the late Board, Dr. Kay, (now Mr. Kay Shuttleworth), who was eminently qualified for that office, continues to act in the same capacity to the present.

These circumstances prevent our entertaining any fear that the Committee of Council will for the future adopt a more restricted course of proceeding than heretofore. We do not feel the slightest apprehension, that ' in administering the funds granted by Parliament to the crown, and placed by the crown in their hands,' they will hold, with a Right Rev. Prelate, that they have no right— that it is not within their legal competence— to divert in England any portion of the grant from education founded on the religion which alone the law recognizes as the religion of England;' or that they will be deterred by the perils of the law with which he has threatened them, ' if they venture to extravagate' beyond this limitation.* But we have a right to expect something more than this. The Committee ought not to be satisfied with merely treading in the footsteps of their predecessors. The circumstances under which its present members have charged themselves with its duties, are essentially different from those in which their predecessors were called upon to act. With the strong prejudices against which the members of the former Committee had to contend—with the formidable opposition which watched their proceedings, and would not have failed to take advantage of any step which could have been made use of to excite suspicion of their motives, and to throw discredit through them on the Government with which they were connected—the course imposed upon them was evidently one of caution and circumspection. The present Committee has a wider field of operation open to it. The Church, we may presume, will not look on them with aversion or distrust; and the majority which Sir Robert Peel can command in Parliament, places it in his power to take a bolder course, and to attempt larger and more comprehensive measures for the improvement of national education. Even should a section of that majority refuse to follow him on this subject, the loss would be more than compensated by the cordial support he would receive from those of his political opponents, who would willingly assist the present Government in effecting what they in vain attempted themselves, when in office, to accomplish. What, then, would we have the Committee do? We would not have them attempt to supersede the efforts which are making by the Church, or by Dissenters, for extending elementary education. Much as might be urged in favour of one general system under the superintendence of the Government, we do not believe it to be suited to the character or feelings of the people. We would not have the Government enter the field as rivals, either of societies or individuals, in carrying on the work of education; but there are essential aids which they might render to the zealous and increasing endeavours of others in this great work. It has been demonstrated that the chief defect in our elementary education is, the incompetency of the teachers to whom it is entrusted. Let the Committee apply itself to this defect, and lend its aid to remedy it. We know that Normal schools, which we trust will be superior to any which have hitherto been seen in England, are in course of being established, in connection both with the National and British and Foreign School Societies, aided by Parliamentary grants. We are also aware that Diocesan training schools are becoming general throughout the country; although we do not feel the same confidence that they will be equally efficient with the former. We think the Cathedral town is not generally the most favourable position which could be chosen for such a school; and that in many cases, at least, the materials are wanting in it for a good model school, or other large and well-conducted school, which ought always either to be attached to, or within easy access of a Normal school. We should have thought it far better, if, instead of these schools being restricted to particular Dioceses, they had been established in some of the most populous towns; such as Birmingham, Manchester, or Newcastle, and made available for the use of several neighbouring Dioceses. We believe, indeed, that the difficulty of maintaining Diocesan training schools has already been seriously felt in many instances; and has led to a departure from the primary object of the establishment of such schools. With a view to defray the expenses, they have been converted into middle schools, for the instruction of children assembled from the middle classes of society; and receiving

---

* Bishop of Exeter's charge, delivered at his triennial visitation, 1840, p. 34.

an education altogether unsuited to the training required for the master of an elementary school for the children of the working classes. The consequence is, that but a small number of candidates for the office of schoolmaster is to be found under instruction in the greater part of the Diocesan training schools; and that those who are found there receive instruction in common with the class of pupils to whom we have alluded, and must necessarily be very imperfectly prepared in them for their own specific and immediate duties. Still, we are willing to admit that some advantage may result from these schools, even on their present footing. We have also, in the appendix to the minutes of the Committee of Council, a detailed Report on the Normal seminary at Glasgow; which, notwithstanding some defects pointed out by Mr. Gibson, appears to be the best as yet in existence, and to which England is indebted for some of her most efficient teachers; and a similar establishment is in the course of formation in Edinburgh.

But these institutions do not, in our opinion, diminish the importance to be attached to a school of this kind, under the immediate superintendence and direction of the Government. We are convinced that such a school might be made a most useful instrument in improving the character of our elementary education, and of securing the efficiency of other kindred establishments. Into such a school every modern improvement in the system or mode of elementary instruction might, under the direction of the Committee of Council, be introduced; and whatever experience had there proved to be advantageous, would rapidly find its way into the systems of all the other Normal schools throughout the country. We would have it, in fact, stand in the relation of a model school to the rest; and it might perhaps be open for the gratuitous reception of teachers who had passed through other approved Normal schools, on the recommendation of the promoters of these schools; as well as for the reception and instruction, either of candidates for the office of schoolmaster, or of actual teachers of good moral character, who, conscious of their own deficiencies, might desire to take advantage of the opportunity thus afforded, of qualifying themselves for the efficient discharge of the duties of their profession. The elements for such a school already exist, or rather an excellent foundation for it has been laid, in the Training School at Battersea, established by Dr. Kay (now Mr.

Kay Shuttleworth) and Mr. Tufnell in 1840, at their own expense; of which a full account is to be found in the Appendix to the Report of the Poor Law Commissioners for 1841. This school has been visited by many of the most eminent friends to education; and we believe that, notwithstanding its recent establishment, and the circumstance of its having been entirely dependent for support on private resources, unanimous testimony has been borne to its efficiency and excellence. Even should there be any hesitation or doubt as to the establishment of such a school as we have recommended, under the immediate superintendence and direction of the Committee of Council, we are convinced that a portion of the funds voted by Parliament for education, would be most usefully applied, in aid of the increasing expenses of this school at Battersea.

Another mode in which the Committee might render essential service to the cause of education, is by granting gratuities to teachers whose qualifications shall have been favourably reported on by the Inspectors, and the state of whose schools shall have given evidence of their efficiency. We know that objections were urged against this proposal, when it was made by the late Government; but we hope that these objections will be no more heard of, or at least will no longer be suffered to prevent the adoption of a measure which we think well calculated to stimulate the energy and encourage the efforts of men who have often a thankless, generally an ill-paid office; and who, when faithfully discharging the duties of that office, amply merit all the encouragement which can fairly be afforded them. Or if any remaining jealousy of the influence of the Government should still raise an objection, surely some mode of obviating it might be devised—such, for instance, as requiring the recommendation of the superintendent or promoters of the school, in addition to that of the Government Inspector, in order to entitle the recipient to a gratuity. Any measure, in fact, which can tend to raise the position of the schoolmaster, to induce able and duly qualified men to undertake and retain the office, to increase the sense of the honourable nature of his duties, and to assign him* that 'status to which the importance

---

* Mr. Gibson's *Report on Education in the Presbyteries of Haddington and Dunbar.*

of his office, and the extensively beneficial nature of his labours, entitle him,' will be well deserving the consideration of the Committee, and will, we hope, not be overlooked by them.

Another mode in which the Committee might increase the efficiency of elementary schools, has been pointed out by Mr. Gibson, with whose suggestion we entirely concur. He recommends the compilation and publication of a complete set of cheap school-books. He thinks, indeed, that ' it would be difficult to mention anything, the accomplishment of which would have a more extensive and beneficial influence on elementary education.' We are fully aware of the delicacy of such a task ; and we have no wish that any attempt should be made to force the use of such books on any school. All that we wish is, that the Committee should avail themselves of the means which they can command for such a publication ; and should offer a really good set of school-books, at a cheap rate, to the promoters of schools. The want of such books is constantly noticed in the Reports of the Inspectors, and must to a great degree paralyse the efforts even of the best masters. The Committee have, we believe, already published manuals, or sheets of singing and writing lessons—so that the adoption of this suggestion would only be an extension, though a very important one, of what they have already undertaken.

Should the Committee thus enlarge the scope of their operations, and embrace these and similar objects in their proceedings, we need hardly suggest that application should be made to Parliament for a sum more worthy of the purpose for which it is to be appropriated, than that which has hitherto been granted ; and we are confident that there would, in that case, be no hesitation on the part of the House of Commons in complying with such a demand.

It is scarcely necessary to say, that it has been no part of our intention, in this article, to write an essay on national education. We have abstained, as far as possible, from raising questions involving the principles on which national education ought to be conducted. It has been our object to deal with the question practically, in connection with the means now in progress for extending and improving elementary education in this country— and to inquire how far the Committee of Council has hitherto proved, and is likely

hereafter to prove, a means of conducing to this important end. In what it has already accomplished we see much ground for satisfaction, and we trust we shall not be found to have indulged in too sanguine an expectation of its future usefulness.

Art. IV.—*Second Report from the Select Committee on South Australia.* Ordered by the House of Commons to be printed, 10th June, 1841.

In the discussion of the ' Wakefield Theory of Colonization,' which appeared in a former Number of this Journal, we briefly noticed the settlement of South Australia as an experiment, devised by the especial patrons of that theory, for the purpose of bringing its merits to a practical proof—an experiment of which the issue was still to be seen. We explained the circumstances out of which the scheme arose, the general principles by which it was distinguished from previous enterprises of the same kind, and its progress up to the date of the latest accounts then accessible to the public ; and without presuming to treat it as a failure, merely because the boasted evidences of success appeared to us to be fallacious, we confessed a growing anxiety to receive some indications of stable and permanent prosperity more substantial than the value of Bonds in the market ; or the number of capitalists who might be willing to stake large sums of money upon the chances of the speculation turning out well. For at that time, though we had heard much of the increasing value of land, as indicated by the enormous prices paid for lots in favourable situations—much of the unexampled ' attractiveness' of the new colony, its streets, squares, wharfs, public buildings, and club-houses—much of the rapid influx of settlers and of British capital, and something of a growing revenue derived from customs' duties upon goods imported ; we had as yet heard nothing of exports or of internal production—nothing of new sources of wealth opened in the colony itself—nothing, in short, of the creation of that promised fund from which was to be derived the interest upon all the capital permanently invested there, as well as the means of repaying all the borrowed money which had been laid out in making the colony 'attractive.' Of the creation and growth of this fund we were anxious to hear ; because, unless the bosom of the new land should prove capable of producing supplies of new wealth sufficient to remunerate the capitalist for his advances, it was plain that—how long soever the game of speculation might be carried on, how long soever the money might be shifted from hand to hand, how many fortunes soever might be made and lost before the cheat was finally detected, and upon whomsoever the loss might ultimately fall—it must end at last in failure and disaster.

Not many weeks after our remarks were written, serious apprehensions began to prevail that all was not so well in South Australia as it had been represented, and South Australian revenue Bonds were no longer negotiable; and these apprehensions were shortly confirmed by the refusal of the Commissioners to honour bills drawn upon them by their own officer resident in the colony—a virtual declaration of insolvency; and a reference of the whole matter to Government, on the ground that they could no longer carry out the provisions of the act without further powers than those with which it entrusted them. The result of this reference, as our readers are aware, was the appointment of a select Committee of the House of Commons, by whom the whole case was minutely investigated, and on whose recommendation a temporary advance of L.155,000 was made by Parliament to enable the Commissioners to meet the immediate emergency. Their second Report, containing a series of recommendations as to the future government of the colony, lies before us, (with evidence and an appendix), in one of those huge folios in which our legislators think it expedient to seclude from idle curiosity the fruits of their graver deliberations; and will, according to an intimation given by Lord Stanley in the House of Commons, speedily occupy the attention of Parliament. Had the getters up of this and similar experiments used a similar vehicle for the conveyance of their communications to the public, we might have been content to leave this history of the progress and issue of it to make its own impression. But advertisements, prospectuses, leading articles in newspapers, and even pamphlets, find their way into heads where no folios can follow them; and we hope, therefore, that in reducing to a circulable shape the more material results of this important investigation, and committing them to the wings of our lighter octavo, we shall be performing no unacceptable service to the idler public, whom it much concerns to be truly informed of the fate of such projects; inasmuch as it is to the idler public that all new projects, requiring borrowed money to set them on foot, especially address themselves. The broad fact, indeed, that up to this period the experiment has

proved a failure, is sufficiently notorious. The creation, within so short a time, of so great a financial embarrassment—the demand upon the public for L.155,000 before four years were out, to save from absolute ruin a colony in behalf of which it has been constantly promised that it would at least cost nothing to the mother country—speaks for itself in language which everybody can understand, and nobody can dispute. Which of the parties concerned has been most to blame, may admit of controversy; but the result which they have brought out amongst them, will not be popularly recognised under any better name than failure. Admitting, then, that the experiment has failed, the question is, what and how much we are to infer from the failure; what light does it really throw upon that theory of colonization which it was *meant* to bring to the test; and whether giving up as vicious the principles of the South Australian colonization act, we must give up the 'Wakefield principle' along with them? Our own opinion is, that the question as to the soundness and practical efficacy of that principle, as expounded by us on a former occasion, remains exactly where it was, and is not at all affected by the issue of this experiment; the miscarriage of which is sufficiently accounted for by other parts of the scheme quite apart and separable from it, though unfortunately placed in the same boat. The principles of navigation are not answerable for the wreck of a vessel entrusted to an ignorant pilot, or sent out without proper equipments; nor must Mr. Wakefield's theory of colonization be too hastily condemned, because it has not been able to overcome the threefold disadvantage under which he was content that it should be tried—of a territory unexplored and unfavourable, a Board of managers inexperienced and irresponsible, and a supply of money drawn from a source at once expensive and uncertain. We formerly intimated our opinion, that in expecting it to triumph over all natural disadvantages, its patrons expected too much from it. Our belief that it was sound, and our hope that results of great practical importance might be expected from its operation, we as yet see no reason to abandon. But to make our conclusions more intelligible, it will be convenient to begin with some account of the negotiations, and the abortive schemes that preceded the introduction of the measure which was specially adopted.

That Mr. Wakefield, once satisfied as to the value of his theory, should be in a hurry to see it at work, was natural and laudable; that he should be duly cautious and deliberate in maturing his plans, and surveying his ground, was hardly to be expected. How soon after the promulgation of his doctrine South Australia was fixed on as a fit field of operation, we are not informed : but the choice seems to have cost very little trouble. Of the 'huge cantle' which was to be cut out of the globe for this purpose, scarcely anything was then known—except the latitude and longitude, the general temperature of the climate, and the aspect of the land as seen from the coast. How far the fertility extended inwards, whether the appearances of fertility on the coasts were not themselves superficial, what supply there was of water, what the soil was capable of growing, whether the selected territory consisted chiefly of grass or jungle, sand or rock, mountain, plain, or swamp—all this was left to the imagination. But where nothing is known, more may be hoped—and, whatever might be the qualities of the land, at all events it was waste, and remote from other settlements. The very beauty of the thing was, that by securing the just proportion between the surface of the land and the labouring population, it would make all lands alike fertile. If the soil proved less rich more was expected, it was only to bestow more labour upon it— if more labour were wanted, it was only to pour in emigrants more rapidly—if more means of emigration were required, it was only to raise the price of land. Certainly an only child does not suffer more from the blindness of parental affection than an only theory. The territory 'lying between the 132d and 141st degrees of east longitude, and between the 20th parallel of south latitude on the north, and the Southern Pacific Ocean on the South,' was voted 'eminently fit for the reception of emigrants or settlers' —and negotiations commenced accordingly with the Colonial Office in the beginning of 1831.

Lord Howick, then Under Secretary for the Colonies, thought favourably of the principle, and was disposed, under proper cautions, to make the trial; and Lord Ripon had no objection, provided it could be done without an additional item in the estimates, and without involving the Government, should the scheme prove unsuccessful, in the discredit of the failure. To provide against this, it was proposed that the Government should have nothing to do with it; but that it should be undertaken by a Company, with a paid-up capital, upon whom, along with the management, would devolve all the risk and all the responsibility. A Company, with a capital of L.500,000, was to undertake the charge of founding, peopling, and governing the new settlement; of managing the land

sales according to certain principles to be defined in their charter; of applying the proceeds to emigration; and of advancing money to defray the preliminary outlay; and if, on trial, the plan did not succeed—*i. e.* if the population did not reach a certain amount within a certain period, it was to be given up; *i. e.* the peculiar principles on which the Colony was to be established were no longer to be insisted on : South Australia was to be as New South Wales, or as Van Diemen's Land. This sounded fairly. But if the Company were thus to undertake all the responsibilities of Government, they must, of course, be trusted with the authority of Government likewise ; and the authority which they required amounted to little less than a delegation of all the substantial powers of sovereignty. This Lord Ripon was not prepared to sanction ; and without this the project could not proceed. Accordingly, after a year and a half spent in fruitless endeavours to adjust the difficulty, the proposition was abandoned. And in truth it might as well have been given up at first ; for the condition required by Lord Ripon was obviously impracticable. Unless it could have been contrived, that in case of failure not only the pecuniary losses, but the social and political consequences also, should fall upon the projectors alone, it was plainly impossible for Government to escape responsibility for the issue of an experiment which could not be tried without its express sanction. By deputing others to conduct it, Lord Ripon might indeed throw upon them a subordinate responsibility ; but so far from absolving the Ministers of the Crown by that means of the responsibility in chief, he would rather involve them in a double responsibility—making them answerable, not only for the propriety of the experiment, but also for the fitness of the instruments.

Up to this point, it might be thought the obstacle to this undertaking lay solely with Lord Ripon, who demanded a condition from the undertakers which he refused them the means of fulfilling. But from the correspondence which took place on the revival of the project during Lord Stanley's administration of the Colonial department, it appears that this condition of the scheme—namely, that the Government should have no concern in the practical management, was one which the undertakers themselves were prepared to insist on quite as obstinately as Lord Ripon ; for Lord Stanley interposed no such stipulation, but, having made up his mind to sanction the experiment, was quite ready to take his share in the charge of it. The idea of a *Sovereign* Company being now abandoned, the following plan was next proposed :—The limits of the Colony being marked out, a guarantee was to be given by Government that no land should ever be sold within those limits below a certain price—that the whole of the sum derived from the sale of land should be employed in conveying to the Colony young pauper labourers of both sexes in equal proportions—and that the maximum price of Government land, though it was to be advanced from time to time, should never be reduced. The Governor and all the officers were to be appointed by the Crown ; and upon the Governor was to devolve the whole power and responsibility of the government, 'until the Colony should be thought sufficiently advanced to receive the grant of a Legislative Assembly.' But since the entire revenue derived from land sales was to be spent in emigration, a fund would still be wanting for the purposes of the civil government. Provision is to be made for this by a Joint Stock Company, who were to make themselves 'responsible to the Government for a paid annual income' during a certain period—the money so advanced constituting a colonial debt : in consideration of which they were to have the pre-emption of 100,000 acres, to be selected within a given time, at the *first minimum* price ; and the privilege, so long as those advances should be continued, of selecting the emigrants.

This scheme was at least intelligible or feasible. South Australia was to be a Crown colony, governed in the usual way ; only that the expenses of Government, instead of being provided by a Parliamentary grant, were to be advanced on speculation by a Joint Stock Company trading in land, and looking to the profits of that trade to pay the interest and cover the risk. To a project framed on these principles, Lord Stanley was ready to accede, subject to certain stipulations ; of which the chief was, that the security for the fixed income applicable to the civil government should be good. This was in August, 1833. But though the proposal originated with the South Australian Association, its purpose appears to have been premature. If the conditions satisfied Lord Stanley, they certainly did not satisfy the Association. Whether it was that capitalists hung back, and would not subscribe on such conditions ; or that the distrust of the colonial office had been revived by the intervening discussions ; or that the practical management had got into other hands ; or that the plans had been originally proposed in the hope that Lord Stanley would object, as Lord Ripon had done before, to risk his credit

by taking any direct path in carrying it out, and that so the demand for larger powers might seem to be forced upon the Association against their own desire ; or whatever may have been the cause, certain it is, that when the plan came to be drawn out in detail, it had assumed an aspect so different that it can hardly be recognized as the same. By the draft Charter, which was submitted to Lord Stanley in February, 1834, it was proposed to transfer to the proposed Company not merely all the requisite powers for managing the emigration and trading in the land, but the entire authority of government, checked by a veto on the part of the crown. They were to have power to make, or delegate the power of making, all laws, institutions, ordinances, &c. ; to constitute all courts ; to appoint all governors, judges, and magistrates ; and to levy all rates, taxes, and duties. To the Crown was reserved the power of disallowing any of their acts and appointments in the first instance, and of removing their officers in case of misconduct ; but it was to originate nothing ; nor could it otherwise interfere. When Lord Stanley objected to this delegation of authority, and refused to entertain the project further, unless it were agreed that 'the government of the colony should be left in the hands of the Crown and its constitutional advisers, until it should be able to govern itself,' he was informed by Mr. Grote, writing in behalf of the Association, that his objection was 'fatal to the project of a chartered colony ; for, of course, no body of persons would consent to take the trouble and responsibility of such an undertaking, without at the same time obtaining sufficient authority for carrying their objects into effect ;' and as he declared, at the same time, that to be a joint stock company for the purchase of land never was the object of the Association, and that 'for such a company to purchase land at a lower price than that which should afterwards be paid by others,' would be directly contrary to one of their first principles,[*] it was plain that that project was at an end.

* These assertions contrast so strangely, not only with the actual provisions, but with the proposed object of the original scheme, that one would almost think an entire chapter, in the course of which the views of both parties had completely changed, had dropped out of the correspondence. On the 6th July, 1833, Mr. Whitmore forwards to Lord Stanley 'a project for founding a new colony on the southern coast of Australia, by the means of the purchase of waste lands from Government, by a joint stock company and by individuals ;' and the views of this proposed company he thus explains :—'The inducement to the company to found this colony is this right of pre-emption at

It appears, however, that the difficulty was not in finding persons who would take the ' trouble and responsibility,' but who would purchase shares, ' without having sufficient authority to carry their objects into effect;' for it was not proposed to try whether the project of a colony, founded on Wakefield's principles, would not have credit enough in the money market to enable them to raise the requisite fund, by way of loan, on the security of its future revenues. The fundamental principle of selling the land at *minimum* price, and spending the entire proceeds upon immigration, was to be established by act of Parliament; the management of the land sale and the immigration to be entrusted to a Board of Commissioners, who were to be further charged with the duty of raising the loans; the powers of government to be vested in the Crown. To this proposition Lord Stanley was also ready to accede, provided he could be satisfied that the territory selected was fit for the purposes of colonization—that at least L.35,000 would be invested in the purchase of land

—that there were persons ready to embark for the colony with a capital of not less than L.50,000; and that an annual income, applicable to ' the support of such parts of the establishment of the colony as might seem to her Majesty's Government absolutely essential,' of L.5000 for the first three years, L.8000 for the next three, and L.10,000 for the four following, could be effectually guaranteed. The Committee of the Association undertook to satisfy him upon all these points; but before the negotiations were concluded, Lord Stanley resigned his office, and the final decision upon the proposition devolved upon his successor. In urging the new Secretary not to delay that decision, the Committee represented the plan as one which had been already approved—every condition required by his predecessor having been complied with; and which only waited for an official announcement of the official sanction which it had already received. How far this representation was just, we cannot tell— Lord Stanley's latest views having been explained at an interview of which there is no record in these papers. All we can say is, that if he was really prepared to sanction the measure in the shape which it ultimately assumed, he must either have misapprehended the effect of some of its provisions, or altered his mind on two important points which, once at least, he had been prepared to insist on. The question as to the fitness of the territory for colonization, was expressly waived as one on which those who proposed to emigrate must judge for themselves; and the clauses relating to the revenue fund, instead of securing *to the Crown* a fixed income for carrying on the government of the colony, left to the Commissioners (apparently, however, through some oversight) not merely the duty of raising, but the right of appropriating, the loan at their own discretion, without any check whatever; except one which made the arrangements with regard to salaries contingent upon the approbation of the Treasury. By this arrangement, whether attributed to oversight or to foresight, the clauses which reserved to the Crown all the ordinary powers of government became practically useless. The blood and sinews of the Government being under the control of the Commissioners, the Crown with all its powers had no effectual authority. The Commissioners could do many things without the consent of the Crown; but the Crown could scarcely carry a sin-

---

the first minimum price. Having the first choice of land, they will be able to select that upon which the seat of government will be placed, &c. The profit of the company will arise from the additional value which the increase of population, and the growth of capital, always confer upon land, and from the increase in the minimum price at which the Government land will be sold; while the price paid by the company for their land will be uniform at whatever period it may be taken up.' On the 21st March, 1834, Mr. Grote replying, in the absence of Mr. Whitmore, to Lord Stanley, remarks, as the draft charter says:—'It is true that at the interview to which you refer, Mr. Stanley suggested that the Association should be a joint stock company for the purchase and sale of land; *but this never was the object of the present Association;* and I may add, that the proposal at the conclusion of your letter, for bestowing land on such a company at a lower price then, than that which should afterwards be paid by others, is directly contrary to one of the chief objects of the Association; viz. that in the intended colony land should be uniformly sold upon equal terms to all applicants.' It would appear that there must have been somebody behind the curtain who understood the objects of the Association much better than its more prominent members; for we observe that in the draft charter, though it was provided that the company, instead of any right of pre-emption, should have the whole territory conveyed to them in trust, therefore, that in their separate capacity they could not trade in land; yet, by the 34th clause, they were to have the power of incorporating as many land-trading companies as they pleased, on such conditions as they pleased—a privilege much more extensive, and one which might be made much more profitable. For it does not seem that they were precluded from incorporating themselves, or any number of themselves, for these purposes.

gle point against the Commissioners. Even the power of appointing and removing at pleasure the members of the Commission, was one of which practically but little use could be made. The sole chance of getting the project started under such conditions, vested in the confidence reposed by a section of the public in the new principle ; and it was notorious that the faith of that section in the Wakefield theory of colonization was not more deeply rooted, than their faith in what we have called the Wakefield theory of the Colonial Office ;—their settled distrust of the capacity, the intentions, and the integrity of all ministers of that department. To intrust the duty of the Commissioners to any person enjoying the confidence of the Government, but not enjoying the confidence of what now began to be called 'the South Australian public,' would have been the same thing as to crush the scheme. None but the immediate disciples and known supporters of Mr. Wakefield would have had either the zeal or the influence necessary for overcoming the preliminary difficulties. Accordingly, it was left to the chairman of the Association to suggest the names of the Commissioners; and of the eight gentlemen recommended by him no objection was taken to any ; and the two others who were added as representatives of the Government, do not appear to have taken any active part in the proceedings. Under these auspices, the great experiment was at length afloat, with every prospect of success—if success were to be ensured by giving the projectors their own way ; but with many chances of failure should they prove unequal to the management of it.

It was necessary to go through these details, in order to show clearly in what relation the several parties concerned in this project really stood towards each other—a relation which the mere terms of the act, and power of the Commission, without reference to the preceding correspondence, from which are to be gathered the feelings and purposes, the understood expectations on one side, and the understood admissions on the other, and all the indirect or unexpressed obligations of the parties, would very imperfectly represent. At this point it will be convenient to examine the project more carefully, and to consider how far it can be regarded as a fair trial of the Wakefield principle, and how far we are bound to abide by the issue.

Now, in the first place, it is to be observed that this project involved not a simple but a complex experiment—not one but three principles of colonization, hitherto untried, were to be tried all at once in the case of South Australia. It was to be a 'self-supporting' Colony—that was one principle ;—and a colony governed by a few private gentlemen, without any previous experience in such a task, without any effective check upon their proceedings, without responsibility to any other department of the State, and without any direct interest in the success of their experiment—that was a second principle. And thirdly, it was to be a Colony founded on the system of selling the land, and spending the proceeds on immigration. So far as this last is concerned, we will not go so far as to say with Mr. Wakefield, that the experiment has been 'eminently successful'—but we will say that there has been no indication of failure. The rapid influx of capital and of population during the first three years, did not prove that the system was a sound one, but only that many persons believed it to be sound. The sudden check and financial embarrassment in the fourth, did not prove it to be unsound ; but only that the speculation had been carried too far, and that the finances had been mismanaged. The tree was in blossom, and has suffered a blight. We must wait for another season before we can know, by proof, what kind of fruit it will bear. Leaving, therefore, the Wakefield theory of colonization as still subject to the remarks with which we quitted it a year and a half ago, we turn to the two collateral novelties involved in the project, concerning which the issue proves much. To the 'self-supporting' system, and to the usurpation by private gentlemen of the proper functions of Government, may be distinctly traced the difficulties which have arisen ; and we believe it to be far from unfortunate that these popular parts of the scheme have been so soon and so fairly brought to the test, and illustrated by so conspicuous an example.

By the 'self-supporting system of colonization,' (the notion of which Mr. Wakefield seems to us to treat with more ridicule than it deserves), we understand that system, on the credit—that is to say, on the *supposed* merits—of which you can borrow the means of founding, settling, and peopling a colony,—supporting it on the *promise* of the future revenue, until such revenue shall be actually forthcoming. Every moneyless inventor who brings his inventions into the market, by means of capital borrowed on the faith of its future value, proceeds on the self-supporting system. The man who persuades his friend that he has discovered a secret in farming by which he can make his fortune, and so obtains a loan of money to buy land for the purpose of trying it, is a self-supporting farmer. So the South Australian Association proclaim a new mode of colonization, by which a large revenue may be raised within a short time; and, having no money of their own, persuade people to lend them money at ten per cent. to carry this scheme into execution. If they are right—if the new system prospers, and creates a revenue equal to the payment of the debt and the interest—then all is well. The colony, most strictly speaking, has supported itself. There it is; and it has cost nothing to anybody.

But though we see nothing absurd in the notion of a self-supporting colony, nor do we feel justified in calling the name, as Mr. Wakefield does, 'a kind of puff,'—(though no doubt it has been much used for puffing purposes),—yet to the manner in which South Australia has been required to support itself, we see very serious objections; nor can we perceive any corresponding advantage. By refusing to advance any public money, and throwing the Colony upon the money market for supplies, it was intended to hold the public safe, and throw the whole risk upon private speculators. And if the failure of the speculators had involved nothing more than the ruin of those private speculators, the precaution would have been effectual, and not unreasonable. But the fact is, that the insolvency of a colony, established under the sanction of Government, with thousands of people in it, is a calamity which Government can never throw aside, as the result of a private speculation with which it had nothing to do. If not bound to uphold its credit, (a point which it would not be easy to maintain), it is at least bound to save the inhabitants from destruction. If the speculation be a good one—that is, if the money be lent on good interest or good security—it is much better that the mother country should make the advance, which it can do on much better terms to both parties than private capitalists: if not, then it ought not to be sanctioned at all. For if unsafe with public money lent at four per cent., it must be many times more unsafe with private money lent at ten; and if it fail,

the failure must be a public, and not a private matter. The mother country must pay for the losses, whoever may have the benefit of the gains. But there is a more serious objection to this mode of raising supplies than either its extravagance, or its futility as a security against expense to the mother country, or the almost irresistible temptation which it offers to a system of puffing—namely, its precariousness. During its earlier years, not only the prosperity of the Colony, but the very lives of the inhabitants, depend upon the regularity of the supplies; and that regularity depends upon the facility of borrowing money from private capitalists; who, being only concerned for the security of their own speculations, will refuse to lend the moment they apprehend any difficulty about the repayment. Twenty accidents, against which no foresight can provide, may discredit the speculation in their eyes. There need not even be any just ground for alarm. A false rumour will stop the supplies for the time as effectually as a true one. The Colony may be ruined by a 'leading article,' as suddenly as it was created. A puff may *break* it, as a puff has made. In the short history of South Australia, something of this has been actually experienced, and more is suggested. We trust that the lesson has not been read in vain, and that no second experiment, resembling it in this feature, will be attempted.

Nor is this short history less valuable for the considerations it suggests with regard to the other novel feature which we have noticed—the delegation to private projectors of the duties which belong properly to the recognised and responsible authorities of the country. There is scarcely any popular prejudice more unreasonable, but there is scarcely any more prevalent, than that which leads men to place more confidence in those of whom they know nothing, than those of whom they know much. Hoping always for more than we can have, and knowing that we cannot get what we want from the one, we turn to the other, of whom, knowing nothing, we do not know even that. Thus it is in the disputes between Government and projectors. Government has existed for centuries, and has wrought no miracle; whilst every year sends forth some sanguine or interested projector, burning with anxiety to show how some miracle may be wrought. The objections which he is met with fail to convince him; the discouragement makes him fierce. The refusal to adopt his views, he attributes to secret hostility. The public take part with the untried promiser against the tried non-performer. The matter is brought before Parliament. The ignorant lookers-on (who form a considerable majority in both houses) are easily persuaded that the thing is an experiment, and ought to be tried; and that since the responsible officers of the Crown say they cannot undertake to bring it to a successful issue, the trial must be made by the projector himself, who says he can. The necessary powers are accordingly conveyed to him by act of Parliament, and the Government is only too happy to get rid of the responsibility, the trouble, the importunity, and the abuse, all at the same time.

Nor is this arrangement without its plausibilities. The presumptions against government in respect both to zeal and ability for making the best of a new thing, are not altogether unfair. To plod on in the old ruts, to be jealous of all nostrums and novel theories, will always be the tendency of the executive, constitute it as you may; because the credit of success in such cases bears no proportion to the discredit of failure. They are the trustees of the nation; and, like all trustees, are more concerned to keep things from growing worse than to make them better. Therefore, under the best constituted executive, many good things will be left for private projectors to suggest; and these projectors will have many plausible, and probably some just grounds of complaint. In the case of our own Government, their aversion from all that is unprecedented is unduly strong, and amounts to a serious defect. It is not to be denied that the inventive department, owing to the total want of any agency working in that direction, is weak and languid; and the distrust of other men's inventions proportionally active. Nor is it less true that, from want of a better supply of effective servants, and of stimulants to zeal and activity, many of its duties are neglected and mismanaged. The popular error is not in apprehending that the government will do the work ill, but in assuming that the projector will do it better; as if the censure of blunders in others offered any security that the censurer will commit no blunders himself. The delusion is a gross one, which the least reflection must dissipate; but it is wonderful how few of us are not, more or less, under its power. Let the securities for zeal, and ability, and integrity, in the discharge of their office by the ministers of the Crown be as defective as the most discontented projectors can assert; yet it is obvious that they are better than you have anywhere else. However defective the instruments they have to work with, they have at least a more extensive command than any other body, of the best instruments that are to be had. However inadequate the responsibility under which they act, they at least act under a more definite and effective responsibility than can be thrown upon any private persons, or Board of persons. However prone to avail themselves of the privilege of office for the purpose of shielding from inquiry what will not bear inspection, they are at least well known themselves—are liable to be called to a severe account in case of ultimate failure or palpable misconduct; and, conscious of living in the public eye, are deeply sensitive to public censure.

Whatever objections may be urged against their methods of transacting business, their methods are at least the gradual growth of many years of trial; they include all the improvements prompted by long experience—all the securities against irregularity, all the precautions, checks, and helps of which time has suggested the expediency. That each man, indeed, should believe of *himself* that he could arrange everything much better, (especially having never tried,) is not surprising; but why we, his neighbours, should believe it of *him*, is a matter of much wonder, though as old as the world. To any one who thinks, it must appear undeniable, that though securities for the good management of a new experiment in the hands of government are bad enough, compared with what they ought to be; yet compared with the security we have when the management of it is transferred to a Board of private gentlemen labouring under a superfluity of public spirit, it is ample, and worthy of all confidence. The case before us supplies as apt an illustration as we could wish. Nearly seven years ago the charge of colonizing South Australia, with all powers and privileges appertaining, was committed to eight gentlemen unconnected with the Colonial Office; because the Colonial Office, not having due faith in the principle, could not be trusted for carrying it out. They had every facility for conducting their own scheme in their own way. They were allowed to select their own officers; and we doubt whether they could quote a single measure which they were prevented from taking, or a single important point in which they were thwarted, from the day of their appointment to that of their dismissal. It is now notorious that. in the hands of these eight gentlemen, (for it is to be observed that the embarrassments had *risen* under their instructions, and before the news of the revocation of their commission had reached the colony, though the duty of dealing with them was inherited by their successors), this great charge has miscarried; that the result of their five years' administrations has been an advance of £155,-000 by the mother country, as the only means of avoiding immediate and extensive disasters in South Australia. How many of our readers can repeat the names of these eight gentlemen? Mr. Wakefield was not among them. He abjures all responsibility, and now declares that he always apprehended some evil results from the arrangement. Had the responsibility been laid upon any of the regular departments of state, the issue would have remained as a personal blot upon the reputation of the minister at the head of it. As it is, it rests upon who knows whom?

That it was only an *experiment,* cannot be admitted as an excuse for thus confiding the conduct of it to inexperienced hands. There is a mischievous fallacy lurking under that word *experiment.* 'If you will not try my experiment yourselves, stand 'aside and let me try it,' is the cry of the projector to a distrusting Government, and all the people think it reasonable. Go into the fever ward of an hospital, announce an improved mode of treatment, and call on the surgeon either to try it himself or to let you try it,—he will answer that he has no right to do either the one or the other—either to make experiments, or to allow them to be made upon the patients under his charge—the failure of the experiment may be the death of the patient. But let the inventor of an improved method of colonization demand of the State, that if his method be not adopted generally, he shall at least have a colony made over to him to try it on, and nobody doubts the reasonableness of the demand. It is forgotten that the trial cannot be made at the sole risk of the inventor, and that the State is fully as answerable for evils that may arise from permitting hazardous experiments to be tried by others, as for refusing to adopt wise and safe ones itself. The duty of the Government in such cases is plain—to entertain all projects for the good of the community; to take up and give effect to those of the wisdom of which it is satisfied; and resolutely to refuse its sanction to all such as it is not prepared to adopt.

We have dwelt thus long on this part of the subject, because we regard the establishment and the clear convincing illustration of these positions, (obvious as they seem), as by far the most important result of this South Australian embarrassment. It is of little consequence comparatively to trace the chain of events which led to it, or to settle who has been most in fault; provided the result itself be set up as a conspicuous and standing example to warn all Statesmen and Parliaments against giving way to these popular delusions, or indulging themselves in this indolent legislation. The remedy for the many defects of our administrative government, is to be sought in the improvement, and, if necessary, the reconstitution of the establishment itself—a work which will find all reformers enough to do—not in transferring its duties to other and untried hands.

With regard to the eight South Australian Commissioners themselves, we cannot fairly charge them either with any great negligence, or any great incapacity in the discharge of their trust. They appear to have been active and pains-taking —the immigration department seems to have been prosperously conducted—there has been no lack of exact and careful instructions; and, considering the novelty of the circumstances and their own inexperience, we do not know that it could be reasonably expected of them that they should do the work better. The thing they had to do, had never been attempted before—the means by which it was to be done, had never been employed before—they themselves had neither precedent to guide them, nor previous experience in the kind of duties which had devolved upon them. 'The act,' (says the Report of the Committee,) 'required that provision should be made for the reception, in a vast unexplored wilderness, and for the protection and good government of a population flowing in at a rate of unprecedented rapidity. The making of all necessary arrangements for that purpose was confided to a board of private gentlemen, not placed by their commissions under any adequate control in the exercise of their duties; and acting at a distance of 16,000 miles from the scene on which the experiment was to be tried. The only provision placed at their disposal for defraying the costs of the undertaking, was a power to borrow money from private capitalists on the security of the future revenues of that unexplored wilderness; a precarious provision, therefore, and subject to interruption from a variety of accidents which they could neither foresee nor control.'* We do not quarrel with them for failing in the execution of such a charge; their great error was in consenting to undertake it.

To transfer to an unwatered wilderness, root, branch, and blossom, the conceptions which flourished so fairly in Adelphi Terrace, and make them prosper there, was no easy task. Their policy, their plans, and their precautions, read smoothly enough on paper, and everything seems provided for. The design is clearly and carefully drawn. But when we turn to the impression which was actually printed off on the rugged and uneven ground of South Australia, a most distorted, blotted, and imperfect figure presents itself. The internal history of the colony exhibits a series of miscarriages, one treading upon the heels of another. First, the Governor quarrels with the Surveyor-General about the site of the capital; and the colonists split into factions before they have set up their houses. Then the Surveyor-General quarrels with his instructions, and throws up his office in disgust. Then his surveys stand still, to the great inconvenience of the purchasers of land, who have been promised immediate possession. Then, in the urgent necessity of carrying the surveys forward at any cost, vast unforeseen expenses are incurred. Then the Governor quarrels with the resident Commissioner, and must be recalled. Then the resident Commissioner with whom he quarrelled is convicted of gross irregularities in his capacity of Colonial Treasurer, and is dismissed under serious suspicion of peculation. Then this Colonial Treasurer is replaced by another, 'who appears to have been most irregular,' and who was shortly obliged to be placed in the hands of the Attorney-General for not rendering his accounts. Then the Colonial Storekeeper is found to have been guilty of great irregularity, proceeding 'partly from the confusion of the Colony,' but principally from his 'utter unacquaintance with the principles of public duty;' a deficiency for which 'several other heads of departments

had to be dismissed,' and which 'had been, and still was, a great cause of the difficulties of the colony.' Then the new Governor, in his zeal to correct all these irregularities, is obliged to treble the charges of the civil establishment; and under the inevitable necessity of providing for the stream of immigration which was poured in upon him, together with his great anxiety to prevent what he calls 'stagnation,' is involved in an expenditure not only beyond his authority, but beyond his power of calculation, and beyond the utmost means of the Commissioners to meet;—an expenditure of which he was unable to form the roughest estimate, but which was increasing quarter by quarter from a rate of L.12,000 per annum to a rate of L.140,000; and all this without even the advantage of a knowledge on the part of the Commissioners of the demands which were coming upon them. Upon a comparison of Colonel Gawler's Despatches, announcing the progress of his expenditure, (which will be found at pp. 220-266 of the appendix to the report,) with the dates of the bills drawn by him upon the Board in England, (which will be found at p. 172 of the same,) it may be distinctly shown, that before June, 1840, the Commissioners had no reason to suppose that the annual demands upon them would exceed L.42,000 per annum; that the bills presented for payment *during that month* indicated a demand of L.140,-000; and that the next month brought them, along with the first complete financial statement which they had received, a warning that for some time to come they must expect no less   This it was which brought the matter to a crisis; for it was now plain that the powers of borrowing, with which they were entrusted by the act, even if used to their fullest extent, would not enable them to satisfy all their liabilities. Accordingly, in August, they suspended all further payments, and then threw themselves upon the government. Colonel Gawler was recalled, and Captain Grey was sent out to declare a bankruptcy, and commence a system of rigorous retrenchments; and all other questions connected with the subject were to stand over until a committee of the House of Commons should have reported upon them.

The recommendations of the Committee are embodied in a series of resolutions, which are introduced by an explanatory Report, containing a statement of the grounds of them, a rapid but fair account of the origin and nature of the

---

* Report, p. 9.

embarrassment, and a judgment upon the conduct of the several parties implicated. Of the measures recommended by the Committee with a view to the better administration of the affairs of the colony in future, the most important are the dissolution of the Board of Commissioners; and the placing of South Australia, as to its general government, on the same footing with other Colonies belonging to the British Crown;—the making of provision by Parliament for such advances of money as may be necessary for maintaining its existence; the advances, with interest at not more than four per cent, to be charged to the colony as public debt;—the relaxation of the existing rule as to the disposal of land, so far as to allow *one-half* of the proceeds to form part of the general revenue, the other half being still devoted to immigration; to admit of the reservation by the Crown of any lands required for public purposes, or for the benefit of the aborigines; and to throw the cost of survey upon the purchaser, by an acreable charge in addition to the purchase money, instead of charging it as heretofore to the general revenue;—the establishment, instead of the uniform price system which has hitherto been adopted, of that of public auction at a minimum upset price, with some modifications, however, tending to combine the advantages of both;—namely, first, a provision that the sales by auction shall take place *periodically*; second, that between these periods any land which has been put up and not sold shall be purchasable by the first applicant at the minimum upset price; third, that blocks of land, containing not less than 20,000 acres each, may be sold by private contract, only not below the minimum price; and lastly, that the minimum price itself may be raised above its present amount of L. I per acre, 'with a view to the principle of maintaining such an amount as may tend to remedy the evils arising out of too great a facility of obtaining landed property, and a consequently disproportionate supply of labour, *and exorbitant rate of wages*.'

It will be seen, therefore, that if the recommendations of the Committee be adopted, the Wakefield principle will at length have a fair trial in South Australia; as soon, at least, as the arrears due to past mismanagement shall be paid off; for it will no longer be under the same gabardine with the two companion principles which we have spoken of above. The

colony will have a source of supply not liable to fail, *because* it is a case of extremity; and it will have the best security for good government during its infancy which the nation has been able to devise. At the same time the 'Wakefield principle of colonization,' properly so called, is retained entire;-excepting among those parts of it, (relating to the 'sufficient' price and the application of the *entire* proceeds to immigration, and to the *uniform* price as distinguished from the auction system,) against which we argued at length on a former occasion; and one of which at least Mr. Wakefield himself has now given up.

The only part of these recommendations to which we are disposed to demur, is that which relates to the raising of the minimum price. Not that we have any positive reason for thinking that the price of land in South Australia will not bear to be raised higher, but we do not see our way through the process by which it is proposed to determine it. It appears to us that there lie at the bottom of the reasoning on this matter, two assumptions which will not bear to bear the test of experience. The first is, that the *value* of the land may be increased to any extent by increasing the *price*. The second is, that by regulating the minimum price and the quantity of immigration, it is possible in a new country to reduce the price of labour; that is, to place the labourer so far at the mercy of his employer as to force him to be content with less than he wants. 'In a colony,' says the *Report*, 'where the extent of available land may, when compared with the population, be practically considered as unlimited, ordinary land, if all were allowed to appropriate what they pleased, would have no value whatever, and it only acquires a value from the policy of not allowing it to be appropriated, except by those who purchase it on certain terms.' All this we admit; but we are not so clear as to the inference which is drawn from it in the next sentence. 'As the value acquired by land under such circumstances is artificial, so it may be made *higher* or lower *at the discretion of the authority by which it is created.*' Now, surely there are other limits to the *value* of land besides the *price* demanded for it. By raising the price as high as you please, you may make it as difficult as you please to get; but not therefore as much worth having. You may make a thing so dear that it is not worth buying at the price.

You may make a penny roll as dear as a quartern loaf, if you have the command of the wheat market, but you cannot make it feed as many people. Make bread so dear that people cannot buy enough to live on, and they will feed on potatoes. So with land. So long as the produce of the soil will pay a reasonable interest on the price demanded, you can raise the value by creating an artificial scarcity; but as soon as the price rises above that point, the artificial scarcity will operate only as a prohibition upon the sale. The question is, how high you can price waste land in South Australia without making the purchase of it a bad investment of capital, or a worse one than can be had elsewhere?

If indeed by applying the additional price to the introduction of labour, you could be sure to cheapen labour in proportion—this artificial value might be increased definitely, until the productive powers of the land, as well as the value of its produce, reached their màximum. But this brings us to the other question: Is it practicable by *any* regulations to make a labouring population in a new colony so dependent upon the employer of labour, that the rate of wages shall sink in any thing like that proportion—or indeed that they shall sink at all? Certainly no tendency of the kind has appeared in South Australia. And we strongly suspect, that if the principle recommended by the Committee be adopted, of 'progressively increasing the price of land until the object of establishing a due proportion between the supply and demand for labour, and between the population and the extent of territory occupied by it, shall have been accomplished'—or as it is expressed in another page, until such a price be imposed 'as shall prevent a greater quantity of land from being bought than the number of inhabitants is sufficient to make use of to advantage'—one of two things must happen; either such a price must be demanded as no capitalist can afford to give; or such stringent regulations with regard to the labouring population must be adopted, as no Government will be able to enforce. Labour may be made more plentiful, we doubt not; but we doubt whether within any appropriate period it will become more cheap. The value of the land will in that case be determined by the nett profits of the produce which it can be made to yield; and the price must follow the value.

There is one other point on which the Report is not quite satisfactory to us. In their judgment upon the conduct of the several parties who have been implicated in the affairs which have led to this embarrassment, they appear to us to have extended their indulgence to Colonel Gawler too far. No doubt, a man who has not had an opportunity of making his defence is entitled to large allowances; and although it is difficult to believe that he has not done things on too grand a scale, and has been far more liberal in his expenditure for the benefit of the Colony than its pecuniary circumstances justified; we are not masters of the circumstances sufficiently to say positively, that, had he not determined to incur that expenditure, a worse result might not have happened. Bnt the charge against him is not merely that he involved his employers in a debt so far beyond his authority, and beyond even their means to pay—circumstances may be imagined in which an officer is justified in assuming such a responsibility —but that he did it without giving them any adequate warning of the extent to which he was prepared to go. He not only drew bills upon them for thousands upon thousands beyond his authority, without specifying the particular services for which they were drawn—this, in the confused state of affairs, it may have been impossible to do with exactness—but he did not furnish them with the means of conjecturing, within any reasonable limits of approximation, what amount they were to be prepared for. It is true that he kept warning them in general terms that he was forced to incur 'enormous' expenses, the responsibility for which 'filled him with anxiety;' but what did an 'enormous' expenditure mean, when the authorized expenditure was L.12,000 a year? Was it twice as much, or three times, or four times as much? The only account (previous to that upon the receipt of which his Commissioners threw up their charge) on which any definite conjecture could be built as to the total amount for which they must in future be prepared, was that which accompanied the half-year's Report dated 26th November, 1839, and which must have been received by them in February, 1840. In this despatch he recounts the causes which have made his actual expenditure so much exceed the expected estimate; gives a list of the things he has had to do; and adds, all this *has been done* (not 'has yet to be done') '*in a very expensive period.*' This account therefore did not indicate an increased, but rather a diminished expenditure thereafter. Now, the bills drawn by Colonel Gawler, in excess of the regulated estimate, for the services of this year, amounted to L.42,000 ;—an excess quite large enough to answer the general terms in which he had spoken, and to justify his anxiety. But while this account was on its way home, at what rate was Colonel Gawler actually drawing upon them? At a rate of L.50,000 per annum, or L.60,000, or L.100,000? No, but of L.140,000! Now, we contend that Colonel Gawler— however impossible it may have been for him to form an exact estimate, or even an estimate nearly approaching to accuracy, of the expenditure for the half year before him—ought to have been able to make a guess within a hundred thousand pounds. He should have been able to give his employers some idea whether, when he talked of enormous excesses above the regulated estimate, he meant twice as much, or twelve times as much. And this was the rather required of him, because the very ground on which he justifies his assumption of such responsibility, is the total incapacity of his Commissioners to form any judgment for themselves; and because he knows that their resources were not unlimited, and that his drafts must be trespassing very closely on the limits of these.

The Committee say that they ' are not' prepared to affirm the insufficiency of the grounds on which he has alleged his inability to furnish information as to the specific services for which he was about to draw, or to supply *any* estimates of the total amount he should be compelled to draw in the course of the year.' It appears to us that the Committee *ought to have been prepared* to allege the insufficiency of these grounds; and that, from the principle involved in their hesitation to do so, inferences may be drawn, of which very inconvenient and dangerous applications may be made by all officers serving the Government in distant places. If the excuse is good for the expenditure of hundreds of thousands, it is as good, or better, for the expenditure of unauthorized millions; inasmuch as the inability to ' furnish information as to the specific services, and to supply estimates of the total amount,' would be ten times as great. We regret this piece of false candour and indulgence on the part of the Committee; because it may be construed into an intimation that there were not sufficient grounds for recalling Colonel Gaw-

ler—a measure than which none was ever more imperatively called for. In other respects, the Report appears to us to contain a fair judgment upon the conduct of all parties.

The Evidence contains a good deal of interesting and conflicting testimony as to the natural productive capacities of South Australia ; of which Mr. Angus has a high opinion. But there is so little solid experience as yet to build on, that such opinions can be entertained only as conjectures; and, as we said before, we must wait to see what fruit the tree will bear, and what it will sell for, before we can form any grounded conclusions. What is certain is, that a very large proportion of this selected territory turns out to be unavailable from natural sterility—so barren that it will be worth nothing to a purchaser, however much you may make him pay for it—and so much of it, that it was at one time thought advisable to alter the boundaries of the colony, for the purpose of taking in a more fertile tract between it and Port Philip. Some considerable tracts of very good land, have, however, been discovered since ; and we hope that the barren parts will only operate as an anti-dispersive ; and that no practical evil will result from the unfortunate selection of the field of operations. With regard to this part of the question, however, pending the arrival of some more decisive indications, we must be content with quoting, in their own words, the result of the inquiries of the Committee as to the present position and prospects of the province :—

' The public debt charged on the future revenues of South Australia, including the sums raised by the Commissioners, the advance recently made by Parliament, and the proposed further advance to the Emigration Fund, will amount to L.296,000. The annual interest payable upon it will be about L.15,000. The number of inhabitants is supposed to be about 15,000. The ordinary revenue, which has been progressively increasing, may now be estimated at about L.30,000 per annum. The ordinary expenditure, which has been increasing still more rapidly, is now proceeding at a rate amounting, together with the interest of the loan, to about L.70,000 a-year ; and although it may be hoped that some reduction may be effected by the present Governor, your Committee are unable, from want of detailed evidence in this country, to speak with any confidence on the subject.

' With regard to the natural resources of the colony, the value of the produce, and the amount of revenue which it may hereafter yield, your Committee have not been able to obtain sufficient data to justify them in pronouncing a decided opinion ; they would, however, refer to the evidence given by Mr. Angus, as showing the recent progress of agriculture, and the aptness of the soil for raising grain, and for pasturage; to that of Mr. Elliot in explanation of the quantity of available land still unsold; to a statistical report transmitted by Colonel Gawler, and to the general tenour of his despatches, as encouraging the hope that, after making allowance for very large tracts of wholly unavailable land, the natural capacities of the colony are considerable; and that as its tillage extends, and its stock multiplies, it may in due time yield an ample revenue, and become a valuable appendage to the British crown. For the present, however, it does not appear to your Committee that there are any certain grounds for expecting either such an increase of revenue or such a reduction of expenditure, as would obviate the necessity of making provision out of some fund, over and above the ordinary revenue, for an annual deficit of a large amount.'—(*Report*, p. x.)

Art. V.—*The Poetical Works of Thomas Moore, Esq.* Collected by Himself. 10 vols. 12mo. Longman and Company. London: 1840-42.

We are glad that Mr. Moore has thought fit to raise for himself, in his own lifetime, the Monument which has been erected for other distinguished poets after their death only, and by the hand of editors more or less qualified for the task, by publishing this edition of his complete works. We are glad also to see that his eminent publishers, at whose judicious request this Monument was undertaken, have done their part to render it worthy of the name inscribed upon it. The edition is, indeed, a very tasteful and desirable one; and, enriched as it largely is with introductory and prefatory recitals and notices, replete with interesting biographical and critical details and remarks, it cannot but be hailed as a precious addition to other similar collections of elegant literature.

But we do not regard Mr. Moore as having, by yielding to the wish for a complete edition of his published poems, in that way settled his accounts with posterity, and relinquished all further control over his poetical testament. On the contrary, we perceive intimations in some of his prefaces that there still remain additions to be made—unfinished fragments, and sketches of compositions—which only await a little resolution on his part to be moulded into shape and rendered presentable. And really, when we remember how few years have elapsed since the appearance of his last poetical work of importance—the 'Epicurean;' how thoroughly that beautiful fiction, though desti-

tute of the ornament of verse, bore witness to the undiminished vigour of the poetical faculties of the writer—we feel that the public has some further claims upon him, before he finally relinquishes the Lyre. Thus much, most assuredly, we would not say, did we feel that with him the period of excellence had past. Nothing is more painful than the exhibition of genius in decay. Nothing is more distressing than to witness those who have already won for themselves a safe and lofty eminence, descending again into the arena with decayed strength and fires, and seemingly unconscious of their own decline—making a poor profit of the popularity of their well-known names, to the utter loss of all that peculiar dignity which belongs to self-respecting retirement. But, as we have said before, this appears to us to be a destiny which Mr. Moore has no reason whatever to fear. He has rather withdrawn from the field with his powers, if we may so express ourselves, not yet fully developed; for poets of a highly imaginative order do indeed grow very prematurely old. The richest outpourings of their genius are commonly the earliest, and the decline is soon perceptible. Not so with poets of quick wit, sensibility, and graceful thought—the class in which Mr. Moore holds so very distinguished a position. With them there are generally two very distinct epochs of perfection: they ripen twice, if we may so express ourselves. The first has the character of youthful fire; the second, that of pathos and reflection. Their task has been chastised by time; the luxuriance of their imagery repressed. They have lost something, probably, in buoyancy as well as in brilliancy; but those intellectual powers which lie at the foundation of excellence of this description remain the same, or rather improved and mellowed by age; for these faculties are not of the same exhausting character as imagination, and do not react with its restless and terrible power on the mind and the body.

We cannot but think that the reader of these collected poems, now placed for the first time in the order of their production, will be able to trace in them the details of the little history which we have endeavoured to sketch out. From the youthful poems, full of fire and freshness, he passes to the author's first work of importance, and as yet his greatest, 'Lalla Rookh;' written, it should seem, about 'the mid-way of this our life's career,' although not published until later. Here he will find that brilliancy of thought and diction, which in so remarkable a degree characterize the author, carried even to excess. As we proceed onwards, we perceive his occasional poetry becoming more and more coloured with the tints of reflection and of tenderness—less exciting, and more satisfying ; until at last we find the gradual change of tone completed in the 'Epicurean'—in our view, the most perfect of all Mr. Moore's compositions as a work of art ; and which probably, if it had not wanted the ornament of verse, would have been the most popular.

On this account, we cannot avoid expressing our earnest hope that the expectations vaguely held out, as we have above observed, in some parts of the prefaces, may be fulfilled. For instance, we have no doubt that out of the rejected materials for 'Lalla Rookh,' which Mr. Moore describes as lying by him, it is in his power to produce what might not perhaps attain the almost incredible popularity reached at once by that poem, but might prove even more acceptable to genuine lovers of poetry. There is, perhaps, no other bard alive (except one) to whom we could honestly give this advice—to vanquish the temptation, whether of indolence or diffidence, and write more ; and we shall resolutely refuse to consider these ten volumes as a *fait accompli*, until the time for making 'farther observations' is hopelessly gone by.

We have said that we do not regard Mr. Moore as a poet of the high imaginative order ; nor do we suppose that this is a point which will be much contested even by his warmest admirers, amongst whom we rank ourselves ; but in adding that we cannot either attribute to him the characteristic of much fancy, in the higher and more poetical sense, we shall probably encounter more opposition. And this leads us to devote a few pages to that much-vexed question, what is really meant by the term 'Fancy' in poetical criticism ?

No point in the metaphysics of poetry appears to have given English critics so much trouble, as the establishment of the distinction between Imagination and Fancy. And this difficulty, it is to be observed, is one which perplexes English critics only ; for in no other language does the distinction in question exist. Neither the French *Fantasie*, nor Italian *Fantasia*, has any resemblance at all to our word Fancy, in the sense in which we attribute it as a quality to poetical or romantic compositions. The Germans, those learned analysts, do indeed recognize very minute and refined contrasts between their *Einbildungskraft* and *Phantasie ;* but then they appear to mean something widely different from ourselves by the attributes thus designated ;—the first being rather the power

of the mind to concentrate its attention on its own imaginary creations ; the latter, a quick and keen perception of lively images, suggesting themselves spontaneously. And this very circumstance, namely, the absence of any distinction similar to our own in foreign languages, might perhaps suggest to us a doubt whether we are not sometimes a little seduced, by an accident of the dictionary, into drawing visionary contrasts where no real difference exists—a suspicion which will be rather increased than lessened, when we observe the odd perplexities into which the endeavour to define and analyse these supposed antagonists, has led some of our chief authorities on the subject.

'The distinction between Imagination and Fancy is simply,' as one writer tells us, 'that the former altogether changes and remodels the original idea, impregnating it with something extraneous. The latter leaves it undisturbed, but associates it with things to which, *in some view or other*, it bears a resemblance.'

This distinction seems to us to represent the real difference which exists between the effects of a stroke of Imagination and a stroke of quick Thought, or wit—a *concetto*, turn, or point. When Homer terms the morn 'rosy-fingered,' we recognize at once the true poetical imagination, 'remodelling,' in our critic's language, 'the original idea, and impregnating it with something extraneous.' In Butler's well-known comparison,

'When, like a lobster boil'd, the morn
From black to red began to turn,'

we discover a clever effort of wit, 'associating the original idea with a thing to which, *in some view or another*, it bears a resemblance.' But to cite this as an instance of Fancy, and at the same time to call such creations as Titania, Ariel, Caliban, fanciful, and the mental faculty which conceived them Fancy, would be to render analysis useless, and criticism ridiculous.

Let us hear a very eminent philosopher, the late Dugald Stewart, on the same subject :—

'Fancy is Imagination *at a lower point of excitement*—not dealing with passions, or creating character ; not pouring out unconsciously, under the influence of strong feeling, images as they arise massed and clustered—but going in search of comparisons and illustrations ; and when it invests them with personality, as in metaphor, still adhering much more closely to the logical fitness and sequence which govern similar ornaments in prose. It seems to act like a colder and weaker species of imagination —furnishing the thoughts which "play round the head, but do not touch the heart;" pleasing the eye and ear; creating or heightening the idea of the beautiful much more than the sublime.'

This is indeed criticism conveyed in exquisite language; but when we come to examine the philosophy of the passage, we fear it will be found indeterminate, and inconsistent with itself. The first sentence is striking, and, whether it will bear close analysis or not, it certainly conveys to our mind something nearly resembling the popular notion of the difference between the two words. But Mr. Stewart, unfortunately, loses sight forthwith of his first distinction, and goes after another. Having defined Fancy as identical with Imagination, only 'at a lower point of excitement,' he proceeds to describe its functions as altogether inconsistent with those of the other faculty; for surely there can be no process more different from any exercise of Imagination, than that of 'going in search of comparisons and illustrations.' Here he seems to approach the notion which identifies Fancy with 'Wit,' in the older and more general sense of that word. Yet presently afterwards he returns again to something more resembling his original distinction. Fancy, he says, 'creates or heightens the idea of the beautiful much more than the sublime.' Surely the process of 'going in search of comparisons and illustrations,' is just as likely to end in producing the one as the other.

But—if the reader will forgive our presumptuous attempt at dissection—Mr. Stewart does not give us, in this passage, a much clearer notion of the functions of Imagination (which he has elsewhere beautifully defined) than of Fancy. Imagination does not 'deal with the passions,' any more than Fancy—that is, it does so only incidentally: its own empire is elsewhere. Neither can it be properly said to 'create characters:' that is the proper function of the Dramatic Faculty—a faculty constantly exhibited in the highest degree by writers who are not poets in any sense of the word. To give the same name to the distinguishing characteristic of Milton, and the distinguishing characteristics of De Foe and La Sage, could surely serve no purpose but to show how completely over-refined analysis ends in confounding objects, instead of discriminating between them.

Let us next see whether a great poet will afford us any assistance in getting out of the labyrinth in which our æsthetic philosophers have involved us.

' Fancy,' says Mr. Wordsworth, ' depends upon the rapidity and profusion with which she scatters her thoughts and images, trusting that their number, and the felicity with which they are linked together, will make amends for the want of individual value; *or*, she prides herself on the curious subtlety and the successful elaboration with which she can detect their lurking affinities. If she can win you over to her purposes, and impart to you her feelings, she cares not how mutable and transitory may be her influence, knowing that it will not be out of her power to resume it on an apt occasion. But the imagination is conscious of an indestructible dominion; the soul may fall away from it, not being able to sustain its grandeur; but if once felt and acknowledged, by no act of any other faculty of the mind can it be relaxed, impaired, or diminished. *Fancy is given to quicken and to beguile the temporal part of our nature, imagination to incite and support the eternal.* Yet it is not less true, that fancy, as she is an active, is also, under her own laws and in her own spirit, a creative faculty. In what manner fancy ambitiously aims at a rivalship with the imagination, and imagination stoops to work with the materials of fancy, might be illustrated from the compositions of all eloquent writers, whether in prose or verse, and chiefly from those of our own country. Scarcely a page of the impassioned part of Bishop Taylor's works can be opened that shall not afford examples. Referring the reader to these inestimable volumes, we will content ourselves with placing a conceit, ascribed to Lord Chesterfield, in contrast with a passage from the *Paradise Lost.*

"The dews of the evening most carefully shun :
		They are tears of the sky for the loss of the sun."

' After the transgression of Adam, Milton with other appearances of sympathizing nature, thus marks the immediate consequence :—

" Sky lowered, and, muttering thunder, some few drops
		Wept at completion of the mortal sin."

' The associating link is the very same in each instance: dew and rain, not distinguishable from the liquid substance of tears, are employed as indications of sorrow. A flash of surprise is the effect in the former case: a flash of surprise, and nothing more; for the nature of things does not sustain the combination. In the latter, the effects of the act, of which there is this in mediate consequence and visible sign, are so momentous, that the mind acknowledges the justice and reasonableness of the sympathy in nature so manifested; and the sky weeps drops of water, as if with human eyes—as if earth had before trembled from her entrails, and nature gives a second groan.'

At the first opening of this splendid passage, we perceive a mysterious light, which seems to direct us out of the paths in which we were wandering; but it vanishes again before we have finished it. Indeed—if we might say so with due reverence—the poet leaves us even more perplexed than the critics ; and we are tempted to acknowledge the justice of the profound reasonings of those supporters of the successful candidate at the late Oxford election to the Professorship of Poetry, who pronounced him better qualified for it than his antagonist—first, in respect of orthodoxy ; secondly, in that he had never been known to aberrate into verse.

For surely the distinction between Imagination and Fancy cannot lie, in the first place, in the comparative profusion and rapidity of succession of their respective imagery. Take for instances the inspired Prophets, or Æschylus, or Milton, in many parts : what can exceed the rapidity with which the images are poured forth, wheel within wheel, or as if each was pregnant with its successor ? And yet we surely, in common parlance, denominate these instances of their superlative Imagination, not of their Fancy. And Mr. Wordsworth then proceeds to ascribe to Fancy, in the alternative, a very opposite function—that of subtly detecting remote affinities :—here, again, assimilating it, as other authorities have done, to something radically different, Wit ; and making it altogether unlike that which he nevertheless with the utmost truth asserts it to be—a *creative* faculty.

May we venture on the still bolder step of quarrelling with the instance which so high an authority has selected in support of his position ? The passage from Lord Chesterfield is of course a mere conceit, passable enough for 'a person of quality.' But is not the passage of Milton in reality a conceit also, although of a far higher description ? Does it exhibit any *creative* faculty ? Does it call up any image in the mind of the reader, or suggest any as present in that of the poet ? Is it, in short, anything more than an effort of thought, 'associating the original idea with things to which, in some view or other, it bears a resemblance,' by what Aristotle would have called a metaphor κατ' ἀναλογιαν ? 'For,' as that most unpoetical philosopher would infallibly have summed up the case, ' as tears are to the human face, so are drops of water to the sky.'

Nor will another distinguished poet afford us any better guidance out of our difficulties. Lord Byron, in the course of the paradoxical warfare which it was his pleasure to wage against the poetical taste of his times, thought proper to assert, among other doctrines, that Pope was an imaginative poet ; and supported his position by example, as follows :—

'We are sneeringly told that Pope is the "poet of reason "—as if this was a reason for

his being no poet ! Taking passage for passage, I will undertake to cite more lines teeming with imagination, from Pope, than from any two living poets, be they who they may. To take an instance at random from a species of composition not very favourable to imagination —satire. Set down the character of Sporus, with all the wonderful play of *fancy* which is scattered over it, and place by its side an equal number of verses, from any two existing poets of the same power and the same variety—where will you find them ?'

Let us take a few specimens from the famous 'character of Sporus,' to which Lord Byron here refers :—

' Yes, let me flap this bug with gilded wings,
This painted child of dirt, that stinks and stings ;
Whose buz the witty and the fair annoys,
Yet wit ne'er tastes, and beauty ne'er enjoys.
Eternal smiles his emptiness betray,
As shallow streams run dimpling all the way.
Eve's tempter thus the Rabbins have express'd,
A cherub's face, a reptile all the rest ;
Beauty that shocks you, parts that none can trust,
Wit that can creep, and pride that licks the dust.'

Surely, whether we agree with the noble critic in his admiration of this passage or not, it is rhetoric, not poetry ; or poetry, at best, only of that secondary sort of which we have spoken. It is a collection of witty thoughts, poured forth no doubt with great ' profusion and variety,' fetched with some trouble from various repositories, and placed in collocation by a *tour-de-force.* The last four verses are nervous and pointed enough ; but their antithetical turn shows plainly the absence of imagination. Pope was not indeed destitute of that faculty, as modern criticasters sometimes affirm. It sparkles here and there, though intermixed with much of a polished but inferior metal, in the 'Rape of the Lock.' It colours with a deep and powerful tincture the pathos which is the predominating excellence in the ' Epistle of Heloisa,' and in the ' Ode to the Memory of an Unfortunate Lady,'—especially in the fine prediction of the decay of the house of her unnatural kindred—

' While the long funerals blacken all the way.'

But these are exceptions, and do not alter the general character of his poetry. He is but the able, dexterous, and graceful workman, who fashions the material provided by others.

These and many similar definitions suggest to us the doubt, whether, in the first place, there is any radical distinction at all between true Fancy and Imagination ; and secondly, whether we are not apt to confound two very different qualities under the same name ;—

the true Fancy of which we have spoken, and that spurious Fancy which is the offspring of a quick wit, conversant with poetical imagery, but which differs from the former in being in no degree *creative*, nor one of the higher poetical faculties.

To recur to a former instance. We are apt to term the poetry of the 'Tempest,' or of the 'Midsummer Night's Dream,' indiscriminately 'imaginative,' and 'fanciful;' and no one can fail to recognize the justice with which either epithet is applied to it. No one can fail to perceive, that the same 'creative' faculty, Imagination, peopled the isle of Prospero with delicate spirits, and the heath of Forres with ghastly sibyls;—that it is by a strictly similar exercise of genius, that disordered nature is made to sympathize with the waywardness of the fairy couple, and with the desolation of Lear. And, as we have said, all these scenes and passages are commonly, and properly, called 'imaginative.' Yet the poetry of 'Macbeth' is rarely, and that of 'Lear' never, called 'fanciful,' by correct critics. From whence does this difference arise? Merely, we suspect, from the subject-matter, and not at all from any distinction between the qualities. All poetical creations are *imaginative;* but when we want a word to distinguish those of a gayer, lighter order—more beautiful than sublime, and especially those which are fetched from a very unreal and dream-like world—we are apt to term them fanciful, in much the same sense as the Germans sometimes use the word *phantastisch.*

Spurious Fancy—that which the critics above cited have called by that name—seems to us altogether a different faculty, not in the least allied to Imagination or true Fancy, but belonging to the same category as Thought, Wit, Judgment, and many other manifestations of Intellectual Power. While the first class of faculties creates, the other remodels, compares, distinguishes; and often elaborates by effort, effects very similar to those which the former produces spontaneously. But instead of encumbering ourselves any further with definitions which, we are forced to confess it, express our meaning but inadequately, let us see whether a few instances will not assist us in conveying it, whether right or wrong, to the mind of the reader; and if we choose them from among favourite and well-known passages, it is on the principle of Dante—

> ' Che l'animo di quel, ch' ode, non posa
> Né ferma fede per esempio, ch' haja
> La sua radice incognita e nascosa.'

One of the commonest exercises of the imaginative faculty is Personification; and

we are apt to forget how much of what is now merely metaphorical language, in common use, was originally imaginative in the highest degree. 'Hope and Charity, Love and Pity,' it has been said, 'have now become common-places; but they were, notwithstanding, among the first and simpler creations of the art.'

'Pallida Mors æquo pulsat pede pauperum tabernas
Regumque turres,'

says Horace. Horace was not an imaginative writer; and probably took these phrases without attaching any distinct image to them, out of the *Gradus ad Parnassum* which he carried in his head. But the first who personified Death, and *saw* the livid spectre knocking at the doors of her destined victims —(compare the description of the plague in that work of a true poet, 'Anastasius')—possessed an imagination of no common order. Let us see what success his image meets with, when it falls into the hands of a French polisher of modern days, who works with the implements of thought or wit—Malherbe :—

'La mort a des rigueurs à nulle autre pareilles :
    Nous avons beau parler,
La cruelle qu'elle est se bouche les oreilles
    Et nous laisse crier !'

Thus far he has succeeded only in reducing the phantom of old times to the similitude of an angry schoolmistress, or obdurate landlady. But the turn which follows has been universally admired :

' Le pauvre en sa cabane, où le chaume le couvre,
    Est sujet à ses lois,
Et la garde qui veille aux barrières du Louvre
    N'en défend pas nos rois.'

And a fine thought it is, but only a thought —it adds nothing to the image; the 'regum turres' are particularized, and thus the lesson is brought home with more startling truth— but there is no creation.

In the following often-quoted lines of Dubartas—

'Loins des murs flamboyans qui renferment le monde,
Dans le centre caché d'une clarté profonde,
Dieu repose en lui-même—'

the first line presents a highly imaginative picture; but, be it observed, it belongs, not to the Frenchman, but to Lucretius :—

' Extra flammantia mœnia mundi :'

Which Moore has borrowed from one or both :—

'As far
As the universe spreads her flaming wall.'

The second is a conceit, the offspring of spurious Fancy; for it does not present a simple image, but expresses an antithetical idea—the invisibility of an object placed in an intense light. And it is still a conceit in Milton, whether borrowed or not:—

' Dark with excessive light Thy skirts appear;
Yet dazzle heaven, that brightest seraphim
Approach not, but with both wings veil their eyes.'

And still more in Dryden, who expands the thought into a fine couplet, after his own fashion:—

' Thy throne is darkness in the abyss of light—
A blaze of glory which defies the sight.'

The last two lines, in the passage from Milton, are taken from another source, as Mr. Hallam has pointed out—the following noble verses of an obscure Italian poet, Girolamo Preti:—

'Tu, per soffrir della cui luce i rai
Si fan dell' ale i serafini un velo.'

But Mr. Hallam has omitted to add, that the original of both is in the vision of Isaiah: —'Each one' of the Seraphim 'had six wings: *with twain he covered his face*, and with twain he covered his feet, and with twain he did fly.' And the effort of what the critics already quoted call Fancy, but which we term Thought, is plainly seen in these modern imitations, in assigning *a reason* for the appearance. Imagination rests contented with creating, and never condescends to explain or justify. The whole passage, as was to be expected, has given birth to a variety of pretty *concettini*. See the 'Loves of the Angels,' *passim*. For instance—

' Oft, when from Alla's lifted brow
A lustre came, too bright to bear,
And all the seraph ranks would bow,
And shade their dazzled sight, nor dare
To look upon the effulgence there,' &c.

Milton is full of such conceits as that above quoted. And it may perhaps be suggested, as the most marked of all the distinctions between very early poetry and that of modern days, that in the former the creative faculty generally appears pure and naked, and absolutely unconnected with the reflective. In all modern poets, and most, perhaps, in the greatest of all, Dante, Shakspeare, Milton, Thought seems to struggle with Imagination for the mastery; and the one and the other

produce their effects in such rapid succession, and so interchangeably, that nothing can be more difficult than to assign their respective provinces.

Very different is the fate which a fine image meets, when it passes successively through the hands of a series of poets of the imaginative order. Each impregnates it with his own peculiar colouring—each communicates to it something additional, which calls up a new vision to the mental eye, and is in truth a fresh creation.

In the venerable passage—

'Οἵη περ φυλλων γενεη, τοιηδε και ανδρων,
Φυλλα τα μεν τ' ανεμος χαμαδις χεει,' &c.—

the reader recognizes (what, as we have said, is comparatively rare in ancient poets) an effort at once of Imagination or Fancy, connecting the frail existence of humanity with that of the leaf—and of Thought, drawing out the parallel between the reproduction of the leaves and of generations of mankind. The turn, or antithesis, has been made use of by hundreds of poets of the secondary or unimaginative order, from Moschus downwards. The *image* has passed into the hands of all the greater masters of the art.

In Virgil it is associated with the idea of multitude:

' Quam multa in silvis autumni frigore primo
Lapsa cadunt folia . . . .'

So in Milton; but he immediately connects it with locality, and gives it a *picturesque* colouring:—

' Thick as autumnal leaves which strew the brooks
In Vallombrosa, where the Etrurian shades
High overarched embower . . . .'

In Dante, ever working out the minute circumstances of his pictures, and clinging closely to the 'shows of things,' the image suggested is that of the gradual fall, leaf by leaf, compared with the dropping of the melancholy ghosts, one by one, into the inevitable bark:—

' Come d'autunno si levan le foglie
L'una appresso dell' altra, infin che l' ramo
Rende alla terra tutte le sue spoglie,
Similemente il mal seme d'Adamo
Gittasi da quel lito ad una ad una.'

Spenser personifies the *agent* as well as the patients:—

'With his sword disperst the raskall flocks,
Which fled asunder, and him fell before,
As wither'd leaves drop from their dried stocks,
When the wroth western wind doth reave their locks.'

From whom, lastly, Shelley receives the treasure; and adds a peculiar circumstance, that of reversing the image, and with wonderful effect.

> ' Thou wild west wind! thou breath of autumn's being,
> Before whose unseen presence the leaves dead
> Are driven, like ghosts from an enchanter fleeing,
> Pestilence-stricken multitudes——'

It is evident that the spurious fancy of which we have spoken is an inferior quality in the scale of poetical excellences to that genuine sort which is merely imagination under another aspect. And yet it would be a most uncatholic and intolerant view of the subject to exclude it from that scale altogether. In point of fact, so accustomed are we to look on Imagination as the poetical faculty *par excellence*, as undoubtedly it is, that we are sometimes induced to regard it hastily as the only one; to consider poetry as strictly and wholly the expression of Imagination. This is not the case only with the pedantic Wordsworthian school of critics who now inundate this country, but with others of more comprehensive views. And we doubt whether many have reflected how very large a proportion of the pleasure which we derive from poetry is really drawn from the expression of Thought in its various forms—indignant, energetic, graceful, witty, fanciful—without one particle of the creative faculty being concerned in it. To this class belong almost all the satirists, from Horace and Juvenal, to Boileau, Pope, Churchill, whether severe in their indignation, or playing with the follies of mankind. It includes also the rhetorical poets—Lucan, Corneille, and the like; and the ' conceited,' commonly and mistakenly called Fanciful, Donne, Cowley, Marini, Gongora, and their respective followers. It is Thought or Reflection which gives the peculiar tinge of manly energy to the verse of Dryden—which sparkles in graceful criticism in Horace—which enlivens throughout with an indulgent philosophy and playful lessons of worldly wisdom, the charming narrative of Ariosto. And, to complete the catalogue, Thought and Passion, without one scruple of the strictly poetical Imagination, form the whole stock in trade of a nation of no mean rank in poetical literature — the French. There is no such thing as an imaginative French poet or poem—hardly a scene or a passage. But Thought, in all the various forms which we have enumerated, borrowing and turning to the best account the creations of a higher faculty, constitutes the staple commodity of the whole race of French poets; and is blended in those of a higher order with

the powerful and harmonious expression of Passion—something, again, wholly distinct from Imagination proper.

We have gone rather the more at length into this attempt to establish a distinction sometimes overlooked, from an anxiety to guard ourselves against any suspicion of unduly depreciating the poet whose works are now before us, when we rank that Fancy, which is commonly reputed to be his peculiar excellence, in the secondary class already described. He cannot be called an imaginative writer; and, therefore, not ' Fancy's child' in the truest or highest sense —in the sense in which we have termed Fancy a creative quality. Not that he is by any means destitute of the first of poetical faculties, but that it is certainly not his characteristic or distinguishing excellence. His Fancy, like that of Donne and Cowley, is Wit;—wit, not only under the control of a better taste than theirs, but likewise of a purer feeling; wit suggesting images and thoughts with wonderful profusion, and a gracefulness often scarcely less admirable ;—often too profuse, no doubt, for compactness, and too graceful for strength, but uniformly brilliant, and yet relieved from monotony by its singular buoyancy.

But rich as this Wit or Fancy is, we believe that those do Mr. Moore great injustice who assign it as the attribute through which he is principally to live. To us at least, and we suspect to the infinite majority of his readers, the real charm of his poetry lies not there. It is when he speaks to the heart, not the head, that he is in his own element. The exquisite truth of sentiment, sometimes gay and sometimes melancholy, but always refined into the most perfect keeping with the common sympathies of men—this is far more delightful to us than all the more ambitious qualities of his muse. In our opinion, he may very safely allow his critics to dispute as much as they will about the real or false brilliancy of the oriental descriptions in Lalla Rookh, or the Rabbinical prettinesses of the Loves of the Angels. Both have been translated into some dozen languages, and honoured, it appears, with all manner of royal and courtly observance ;*—nay, which

---

* ' Among the incidents connected with this work, I must not omit to notice the splendid *divertissements*, founded upon it, which were acted at the Chateau Royal of Berlin, during the visit of the Grand Duke Nicholas to that capital in the year 1822. The different stories composing the work were represented in *tableaux vivants* and songs; and, among the crowd of royal and noble persons engaged in the performances, I shall mention those only who represented the principal cha-

is more to the purpose still, both have been read, we take it, more than any other poems of our time, except Lord Byron's; and yet we would confidently wager against the existence of any man, woman, or child, who could repeat thirty lines together of either, always excepting 'Paradise and the Peri,' and the delicious songs in the 'Light of the Harem.' We admit that this is not altogether a fair test; for there are peculiarities in composition which make these poems excessively difficult to learn by heart, even for their most devoted admirers. But, on the other hand, there are thousands—tens of thousands—who have almost every line of the Irish Melodies and national songs constantly in their remembrance. And this seems to us to prove our proposition beyond all contest, that Mr. Moore's true popularity rests, and will always rest, on those delicate touches of tenderness and gaiety which captivate the sense at first hearing, and once known are never forgotten;—which make so many of those genuine gems, his smaller lyrical poems, better remembered, and more constantly travelling from the heart to the lips, than any verse of any poet of these days, however lofty his pretensions may be.

Mr. Moore himself ascribes much of the magic of these strains to music; and speaks of the 'Irish Melodies' as the only work of his pen 'whose future fame (thanks to the sweet music in which it is embalmed) may boast a chance of prolonging its existence to a day much beyond our own.' And elsewhere, in the preface to his fifth volume, he goes at some length into the debatable question of the alliance between poetry of this description and music.

. It was impossible that the example of Burns, in these his higher inspirations, should not materially contribute to elevate the character of English song-writing, and even to lead to a re-

---

racters, and whom I find there enumerated in the published account of the *divertissement.*

Fadladin, Count Haack, Marechal de Cour.
Aliris, Roi de Bucharie, S. A. I. Le Grand Duc.
Lallah Rookh, S. A. I. La Grande Duchesse.
Aurungzeb, le Grand Mogol, S. A. R. Le Prince Guillaume.
Abdallah, Père d'Aliris, Le Duc de Cumberland.
La Reine, son Epouse, S. A. R. La Princesse Louise Radzivill.'—Vol. VI. p. xxv.

'Count Haack,' if he still survives, we do not doubt is as well qualified for the part of 'Fadladin' as ever; but if the subjugator of Poland ever recollects himself mouthing out the Jacobinism of 'Hafed' in the Fire Worshippers, he must be ashamed of having lent his countenance to the dissemination of 'language and principles for which nothing short of the summary criticism of the chabuk (or knout) could be advisable.'

union of the gifts which it requires, if not, as of old, in the same individual, yet in that perfect sympathy between poet and musician which almost amounts to identity, and of which we have seen, in our own times, so interesting an example in the few songs bearing the united names of those two sister muses, Mrs. Arkwright and the late Mrs Hemans.

'Very different was the state of the song department of English poesy at the time when first I tried my novice hand at the lyre. The divorce between song and sense had then reached its utmost range, and to all uses connected with music, from a birth-day ode down to the libretto of the last new opera, might fairly be applied the solution Figaro gives of the quality of the words of songs in general: "Ce qui ne vaut pas la peine d'être dit, on le chante."

'How far my own labours in this field, if, indeed, the gathering of such idle flowers may be so designated, have helped to advance, or even kept pace with the progressive improvement I have here described, it is not for me to presume to decide. I only know, that in a strong and in-born feeling for music lies the source of whatever talent I may have shown for poetical composition; and that it was the effort to translate into language the emotions and passions which music appeared to me to express, that first led to my writing any poetry at all deserving of the name. Dryden has happily described music as being "inarticulate poetry;" and I have always felt, in adapting words to an expressive air, that I was but bestowing upon it the gift of articulation, and thus enabling it to speak to others all that was conveyed in its wordless eloquence to myself.'—(Vol. V. pp. xiii.–xv.)

We believe Mr. Moore to be very sincere in these expressions of diffidence; not because we attribute to him any greater tendency to undue self-depreciation than to his brethren in general, but because we know how completely, in spirits exquisitely sensitive to music, the charm of thought and expression becomes subordinate to that of melody; and, it is, undoubtedly, extremely difficult to 'untwist the hidden chains' which bind these two charms so strangely together. But if it could be accomplished, we suspect it would appear that, for every thousand who have been chiefly captivated by the music of his songs, there are at least a thousand more whose charm is in the poetry; and in whose memory the last sweet echoes of the strain linger almost wholly disengaged from the accompaniment, or altogether unconnected with any.

But what complicates the difficulty in the present instance is this, that Mr. Moore is, in a peculiar and emphatical sense, the poet of music—a character in which no other poet approaches him, and very few even resemble him. Every one who has any susceptibility for music at all, is aware of the readiness with which some emotions of the mind are excited by it—that there are some sentiments which seem to respond immediately to particular tones, independently of all perceived or recognized association of thought. Now, Mr. Moore's peculiar skill is in giving voice to this inarticulate language. Take, for instance, many of his old Irish airs; he found them associated with vulgar or unmeaning words; he detected the language of the air under the disguise, and expressed it in verse; insomuch that the words alone now convey precisely that class of emotions which are suggested by the music. This is quite a peculiar faculty, and extremely rare indeed. Burns had something of it, Béranger perhaps more; but Moore stands absolutely pre-eminent in it.

And we are not, therefore, surprised that the charm of poetry, and that of music, seem in his mind to be often regarded as identical. The very attributes by which he characterizes the lays at the command of his 'Spirit of Song,' in Lalla Rookh, appear to us exactly his own; and the effect of his poetry is precisely, and without exaggeration, the same which he there ascribes to music.

'For mine is the lay that lightly floats,
And mine are the murmuring, dying notes,
That fall as soft as snow on the sea,
And melt in the heart as instantly.

'Mine is the charm, whose mystic sway
The spirits of past delight obey:
Let but the tuneful talisman sound,
And they come like genii, hovering round.

'And mine is the gentle song, that bears
From soul to soul the wishes of love;
As a bird that wafts through genial airs
The cinnamon seed from grove to grove.

''Tis I that mingle in one sweet measure
The past, the present, and future of pleasure:
When Memory links the tone that is gone
With the blissful tone that's still in the ear;
And Hope from a heavenly note flies on
To a note more heavenly still that is near.'

We do not intend to dwell on these exquisite recollections. It would be mere pedantry to force them into critical discussion and comparison. No enthusiastic rhapsody of ours could heighten their charm; no analysis could detect the source of it; and the genius of Fadladeen himself could not detract from it. Still, their effect is not that of pure poetry, rigorously *so* called. All the criticism in the world will not persuade the mass of readers, that the poetry which is most popular with them, which speaks most to the heart, is not the best; nor will such cavils raise the judgment of the critic in their

estimation; for though a few, like Lalla Rookh's ladies, will still begin to suspect that they 'ought not to be pleased,' we fear that the number of such obedient subjects is considerably diminished since the craft of reviewing first rose into eminence. Still it is true, that the mere tribute which susceptibility pays to that which excites it, is not the recognition of poetical excellence; otherwise the 'Gamester' and 'Isabella' would be the finest tragedies on the English stage. In order to be thoroughly alive to the impressions of music, a gentleman, as a profound critic has remarked, must be 'in a concatenation accordingly;' and the same thing is perhaps true of poetry such as Moore's, which *is* ideal music. It is when the heart is predisposed by recent emotion, or dwelling on the remembrance of its own past emotions—when it is attuned to love, or romance, or gaiety, or the soft and dreamy sadness which past illusions leave behind them, or the deeper regrets for departed youth—that such enchantment is peculiarly felt. It does not create, but finds, sympathies; it searches the very soul, but never entrances, or carries it away into another world of visionary being. Thus far it is of the earth, and earthly—of the very finest materials, doubtless, which this earth can furnish; but not of the harmony which Dante heard only in the last circle of his Paradise.

'Qualunque melodia piu dolce suona
Quaggiù, e più a se l'anime tira,
Parebbe nube che squarciata tuona
Comparata al suonar di quella Lira.'

And thus much more we will add respecting it, that this deep charm of pathos, after all, characterizes the best-remembered and most generally appreciated portions even of Moore's more ambitious poetry. It is not the gorgeous orientalism, the gracefulness, or the brilliancy of description, in Lalla Rookh, which really abide with the reader, but those occasional touches—

'The looks and tones that dart
An instant sunshine though the heart,
As if the soul that instant caught
Some treasure it through life had sought'—

which arouse the sensibilities to which his peculiar province extends.

The most substantial passions of this earth scarcely appear to us to be within that province. The strong objections which were urged against the early poetry of our author were not without foundation, undoubtedly; and nothing can be more marked than the improvement of taste which has characterized him since. But both the sins and the improvement always appeared to us to be of taste only. It is singular enough, in so extensive a collection of love verses of every variety of colour, that there is so little of the passionate order; such as is sometimes—yet, even there, rarely—to be met with in Byron. We scarcely remember above one piece, in all Moore's poetry, which really breathes the soul of Sappho: we looked for it in this new collection, and found it reduced to 'a fragment.' Why this was necessary, we hardly know; nor do we altogether appreciate the criterion according to which some of our old acquaintances have been left out, and others left in; and we are not sorry that we possess an old 'Galignani' edition.

But, as we have said, criticism is altogether inadequate to analyse those real and unrivalled beauties which we have endeavoured to point out only. It was much more our purpose to make an essay towards appreciating our author as an artist; but we perceive, the little we had to say on this subject is already nearly anticipated. His personages, angelic or human, always produced upon us the effect of Westall's drawings, with which, we suppose, it had been our fate to see his poems first illustrated—all rounded in the same unmeaningly graceful proportions—all with the same soft languishing physiognomy—as ideal a set of brothers and sisters as were ever grouped together on the walls of the Royal Academy. After our first reading of Lalla Rookh, we well remember how utterly insipid, or rather coarse and prosaic, the men and women of Shakspeare and Scott seemed to have become. We are sorry to say that, on a second perusal, it was as impossible to take an interest in Azim and Zelica, Hafed and Hinda, as in the personages of the 'Grand Cyrus.' And, perhaps, it is rather strange—one of the anomalies which seem to belong to all genius—that a poet whose peculiar spell is over the common sympathies of men—whose unstudied tones of sentiment never fail to speak *home*—should be so utterly unable to make the creatures of his stories like human beings at all. But the dramatic faculty is a gift apart from all others. It is no doubt from a consciousness of this deficiency, in part, that the author overlays the outlines of his tales with such wonderful richness and profusion of elaborate imagery; and, as we have said, this is not the imagery of fancy, but of wit. It is difficult always to apply the test; but comparison, as we have seen, is perhaps the best. That which requires thought to please—that which raises no image to the mind's eye, but gives the judgment the satisfaction arising from a comparison exquisitely drawn, from the juxtaposition of sparkling objects unexpectedly brought together—this is conceit, and not fancy: for mind speaks to mind, and that

which the poet has imagined affects the reader very differently from that which he has thought out. Yet the results are beautifully brilliant, and take the reason prisoner, until it has no small trouble to disentangle the false from the true enchantment.

A curious characteristic of poets of this order is, that in their sweetest strains we can so frequently detect a determination throughout to bring in a conceit at the end, which generally goes far to spoil the effect of all the remainder. As soon as they have touched the reader's heart by a tone or two of simple beauty, they kindly alleviate his excited sensibility, by giving him a riddle or an epigram to think about.

The following instance of what we mean, occurs in some extremely beautiful verses:—

'Peace be around thee, wherever thou rovest;
    May life be for thee one summer's day,
And all thou wishest, and all that thou lovest,
    Come smiling around thy sunny way!

'If sorrow e'er this calm should break,
    May even thy tears pass off so lightly,
Like spring showers, they'll only make
    The smiles that follow shine more brightly.

'May Time, who sheds his blight o'er all,
    And daily dooms some joy to death,
O'er thee let years so gently fall,
    They shall not crush one gloom beneath.

'*As half in shade and half in sun
    This world along its path advances,
May that side the sun's upon
    Be all that e'er shall meet thy glances.*'

Another, equally beautiful, occurs to us at random, and we cite it the rather, because we believe it to be published now for the first time:—

'Dreaming for ever, vainly dreaming,
    Life to the last pursues its flight:
Day hath its visions fairly beaming,
    But false as those of night:

'The one illusion, the other real,
    But both the same brief dreams at last:
And when we grasp the bliss ideal,
    Soon as it shines, 'tis past.

'Here, then, by this dim lake reposing,
    Calmly I'll watch, while light and gloom
Flit o'er its face, till night is closing—
    Emblem of life's short doom!

'But though, by turns, thus dark and shining,
    'Tis still unlike man's changeful day,
*Whose light returns not, once declining,
    Whose cloud, once come, will stay.*'

The following has something of the same peculiarity: But we are almost a shamed to quote what is so familiar to the ears and hearts of all who have ever stood within the circle of the magician himself :—

'Say, what shall be our sport to-day ?
    There's nothing on earth, in sea, in air,
Too bright, too high, too wild, too gay,
    For spirits like mine to dare !

' 'Tis like the returning bloom
    Of those days, alas ! gone by,
When I loved each hour I scarce knew whom,
    And was blest I scarce knew why.

' Ay, those were days when life had wings,
    And flew, oh flew, so wild a height,
That, like the lark which sunward springs,
    'Twere giddy with too much light.

' And though of some plumes bereft
    With that sun too nearly set,
I've enough of light and wing still left
    For a few gay soarings yet.'

There is one more particular in which this edition will be welcome to numbers of readers: it contains all the satirical and humorous poetry of Mr. Moore, from the ' Fudge Family in Paris,' down to his latest political squibs. These latter are quite as unrivalled in their kind as the ' Irish Melodies,' or the other serious specimens of his sentimental muse. Of course, when collected in this fashion, it cannot be expected that they should be quite as captivating as when they first enlivened us, one by one, occurring like ' green spots' in the waste of a dreary newspaper. But then, as a collection, they have the great advantage of conjuring back upon us the successive recollections of the politics of the last thirty years, more lively and more amusing than even in the works of the masters of caricature. We will only select one, which we well remember struck us with all the force of an argument when first we read it ; and sure we are, that nothing so effective in the way of answer to it has yet appeared :—

' The longer one lives the more one learns,
    Said I, as off to sleep I went,
Bemus'd with thinking of tithe concerns,
And reading a book, by the Bishop of Ferns,
    On the Irish Church Establishment.
But lo ! in sleep not long I lay
    When fancy her usual tricks began,
And I found myself bewitch'd away
    To a goodly city in Hindostan :
A city, where he who dares to dine
    On aught but rice, is deem'd a sinner :
Where sheep and kine are held divine,
    And, accordingly, never drest for dinner.

    But how is this ? I wondering cried,
As I walked that city, fair and wide,

And saw, in every marble street,
    A row of beautiful butchers' shops—
' What means, for men who can't eat meat,
    This grand display of loins and chops ?"
In vain I asked—'twas plain to see
That nobody dared to answer me.

' So on from street to street I strode :
And you can't conceive how vastly odd
The butchers look'd : a roseate crew,
Inshrined in *stalls*, with naught to do :
While some on a *bench*, half dozing, sat,
And the sacred cows were not more fat.

' Still posed to think what all this scene
Of sinecure trade was meant to mean,
" And pray," asked I, " by whom is paid
The expense of this strange masquerade ?"
" The expense—oh, that's of course defray'd "
(Said one of these well-fed hecatombers)
" By yonder rascally rice-consumers."
" What ! they, who mustn't eat meat ? "—" No
        matter :"
(And, while he spoke, his cheeks grew fatter,)
" The rogues may munch their *Paddy* crop,
But the rogues must still support our shop :
And, depend upon it, the way to treat
    Heretical stomachs that thus dissent,
Is to burden all that won't eat meat
    With a costly meat establishment."
On hearing these words so gravely said,
    With a volley of laughter loud I shook :
And my slumber fled, and my dream was sped,
And I found myself lying snug in bed,
    With my nose in the Bishop of Ferns's book,'
                        (—Vol. IX. p. 71.)

As the political education of Ireland's national poet cannot but be a matter of interest, we subjoin a piece of his early biography, which will show in what manner

' Rebellion's springs, which through the country
    ran,'

became the sources of his youthful inspiration. It will be seen how narrowly Apollo preserved the embryo ' Irish Melodies' from a ' timeless end,' and the poet himself from being metamorphosed into one of the *black* swans of another hemisphere :—

' In the meanwhile this great conspiracy was hastening on with fearful precipitancy to its outbreak, and vague and shapeless as are now known to have been the views even of those who were engaged practically in the plot, it is not any wonder that, to the young and uninitiated like myself, it should have opened prospects partaking far more of the wild dreams of poesy than of the plain and honest prose of real life. But a crisis was then fast approaching when such self-delusions could no longer be indulged, and when the mystery which had hitherto hung over the plans of the conspirators was to be rent asunder by the stern hand of power.
' Of the horrors that foreran and followed the frightful explosion of the year 1798, I have

neither inclination, nor, luckily, occasion to speak; but among those introductory scenes, which had somewhat prepared the public mind for such a catastrophe, there was one of a painful description, which, as having been myself an actor in it, I may be allowed briefly to notice.

'It was not many weeks, I think, before this crisis, that, owing to information gained by the college authorities of the rapid spread among the students not only of the principles, but of the organization of the Irish Union, a solemn visitation was held by Lord Clare, the Vice-Chancellor of the University, with the view of inquiring into the extent of this branch of the plot, and dealing summarily with those engaged in it.

'Imperious and harsh as then seemed the policy of thus setting up a sort of inquisitorial tribunal, armed with the power of examining witnesses on oath, and in a place devoted to the instruction of youth, I cannot but confess that the facts which came out in the course of the evidence went far towards justifying even this arbitrary proceeding; and to the many who, like myself, were acquainted only with the general views of the Union leaders, without even knowing, except from conjecture, who these leaders were, or what their plans or objects, it was most startling to hear the disclosures which every succeeding witness brought forth. There were a few, and, among that number, poor Robert Emmet, John Brown, and the two ——s, whose total absence from the whole scene, as well as the dead silence that day after that followed the calling out of their names, proclaimed how deep had been their share in the unlawful proceedings inquired into by the tribunal.

"But there was one young friend of mine, ——, whose appearance among the suspected and examined as much surprised as it deeply and painfully interested me. He and Emmet had long been intimate and attached friends; their congenial fondness for mathematical studies having been, I think, a far more binding sympathy between them than any arising out of their political opinions. From his being called up, however, on this day, when, as it appeared afterwards, all the most important evidence was brought forward, there could be little doubt that, in addition to his intimacy with Emmet, the college authorities must have possessed some information which led them to suspect him of being an accomplice in the conspiracy. In the course of his examination, some questions were put to him which he refused to answer—most probably from their tendency to involve and inculpate others; and he was accordingly dismissed, with the melancholy certainty that his future prospects in life were blasted; it being already known that the punishment for such contumacy was not merely expulsion from the University, but exclusion from all the learned professions.

'The proceedings, indeed, of this whole day had been such as to send me to my home in the evening with no very agreeable feelings or prospects. I had heard evidence given affecting even the lives of three friends whom I had long regarded with admiration as well as affection, and what was still worse than even their danger—a danger ennobled, I thought, by the cause in which they suffered—was the shameful spectacle exhibited by those who had appeared in evidence against them. Of these witnesses, the greater part had been themselves involved in the plot, and now came forward either as voluntary informers, or else were driven, by the fear of the consequences of refusal, to secure their own safety at the expense of companions and friends.

'I well remember the gloom, so universal, that hung over our family circle on that evening, as, talking together over the events of the day, we discussed the likelihood of my being among those who would be called up for examination on the morrow. The deliberate conclusion to which my dear honest advisers came was, that, overwhelming as the consequences were to all their plans and hopes for me, yet, if the questions tending to criminate others, which had been put to almost all examined on that day, and which poor —— alone had refused to answer, were put to me, I must, at all risks, return a similar answer. I am not quite certain whether I received any intimation on the following morning that I was to be one of those examined in the course of the morning, but I rather think some such notice had been conveyed to me; and at last my awful turn came, and I stood in the presence of the formidable tribunal. There sat, with severe look, the Vice-Chancellor, and, by his side, the memorable Doctor Duigenan—memorable for his eternal pamphlets against the Catholics.

'The oath was proffered to me.

'"I have an objection, my lord," said I, "to taking the oath."

'"What is your objection?" he asked sternly.

'"I have no fears, my lord, that anything I might say would criminate myself; but it might tend to involve others, and I despise the character of the person who would be led, under any circumstances, to inform against his associates."

'This was aimed at some of the revelations of the preceding day, and as I learned afterwards, was so understood.

'"How old are you, sir?" he then asked.

'"Between seventeen and eighteen, my lord."

'He then turned to his assessor, Duigenan, and exchanged a few words with him in an under tone of voice.

'"We cannot," he resumed, again addressing me, "suffer any one to remain in our University who refuses to take this oath."

'"I shall then, my lord," I replied, "take the oath, reserving to myself the power of refusing to answer any such questions as I have just described."

'"We do not sit here to argue with *you*, sir," he rejoined sharply; upon which I took the oath, and seated myself in the witness's chair.

'The following are the questions and answers that then ensued. After adverting to the proved existence of United Irish societies in the University, he asked, "Have you ever belonged to any of these societies?"

'"No, my lord."

'"Have you ever known of any of the proceedings that took place in them?"

'"No, my lord."

'"Did you ever hear of a proposal at any of their meetings for the purchase of arms and ammunition?"

' "Never, my lord."

' "Did you ever hear of a proposal made in one of these societies with regard to the expediency of assassination ?"

' "Oh no, my lord."

' He then turned again to Duigenan, and, after a few words with him, said to me, "When such are the answers you are able to give, pray, what was the cause of your great repugnance to taking the oath ?"

' "I have already told your lordship my chief reason; in addition to which, it was the first oath I ever took, and the hesitation was, I think, natural."

' I was now dismissed without any further questioning, and, however trying had been this short operation, was amply repaid for it by the kind zeal with which my young friends and companions flocked to congratulate me—not so much, I was inclined to hope, on my acquittal by the court, as on the manner in which I had acquitted *myself*. Of my reception on returning home, after the fears entertained of so very different a result, I will not attempt any description; it was all that *such* a home alone could furnish.'

We might have enriched this article with many more of the biographical and other notices scattered through these volumes, and by so doing, would have rendered it undoubtedly of far higher interest than by the critical inquiries in which we have indulged; but we were anxious to pay a debt long due to one, the character and tendency of whose powers we, in common with many others, misconstrued at his outset;—one whose mode of life, and habits of mind and thinking, ever involving him actively in the vortex of the existing world, and in the controversies as well as gaieties of the day, have made many unwilling to recognize his real position in the rank of poets from hostility or prejudice, and many more from real inability to conceive the power of genius to *live* on the agitated surface of society, as well as on the most tranquil lake that ever was haunted by the Muses;—one whom many pronounced at first too trifling to succeed, and then too successful in his own day to abide the test of another; but whose position in the brilliant band of the poets of this age, (now so rapidly vanishing from us one by one, and unreplaced,) is already fixed beyond the power of criticism or of Time—unrivalled in one exquisite department of his art, delightful in many.

ART. VI.—1. *Speech of the Right Hon. Sir Robert Peel, in the House of Commons, Feb.* 9, 1842.

2. *Speech of the Right Hon. Sir Robert Peel, March* 11, 1842.

NINE months ago, we remarked that our financial difficulties, painful as they are in their causes and in their immediate effects, are not without their advantages. We rejoiced that they had forced public attention towards the barbarous Commercial Code which every day tends more and more to diminish our enjoyments, to misdirect our industry, to render our trade hazardous as well as unproductive, and to divide society into hostile sections —intent some on wringing a profit out of the calamities of the country, and others on subverting the institutions under which such an oppression can be favoured or permitted. We rejoiced that they gave to a wise and patriotic Government the means of saying to classes, and even to individuals—' Unless you will allow us to increase the revenue by diminishing duties, we must tax you. If you wish sugar to continue at 8d. a pound, or bread at 9d. a loaf, or timber at 30 per cent. beyond its natural price—if you wish our manufactures to oscillate between periods of feverish prosperity and prolonged depression—if you wish to lower the price of labour, while you raise that of subsistence—if you wish to render employment irregular, while you diminish its reward—if you wish to give a temporary stimulus to rents, by injuring the profits out of which all rent is ultimately supported—you must consent to raise as a tax the revenue which you refuse as a boon. If you resolve to prolong folly and oppression until they reach the verge of ruin or revolution, you must contribute the expense of your system by a tax on your expenditure or on your income.'

We had no hope, indeed, of the immediate success of these arguments. We knew that they would be repelled by the selfishness of many, and by the prejudices of still more; and be deadened by the ignorance and apathy of the great mass of the community. We knew how comparatively small was the number of those who could estimate the evils to be encountered, or foresee the effect of the different remedies that might be applied. We knew that the party whose unhappy fate is to depend for power on misgovernment, and therefore on error, would proclaim that ' periods of distress are necessarily incidental to the state of a manufacturing and commercial people—that our financial difficulties were the temporary result of a concession to ignorant impatience—that the welfare of the whole community may be best consulted by continuing to each class of monopolists its accustomed protection—that cheaper commodities would produce lower wages, freedom of commerce, lower profits, and extension of trade dependence on foreign nations. And that the first step towards improvement must be the refusal of plans mischievous, so far as they are not visionary ; and the second step, the expulsion of their proposers.' We knew that all this would be said, and we knew that it would be believed ; and we fully anticipated, therefore, the rejection of the Whig Budget, and the accession of a Tory Ministry.

But we then felt, and we still retain, a firm reliance on the ultimate prevalence of truth. Firmly convinced that the principles proposed and rejected in 1841, are the only principles by which the country can be restored to its former, or even be enabled to retain its present, amount of wealth and of civilisation, we then believed, and we still believe, that those principles must in time be adopted.

It is possible, indeed, that the contest between good and evil may be protracted. It is possible that a long period may elapse during which months of prosperity may alternate with years of adversity ; during which the value of our currency, the extent of our commerce, and the comfort of our population, may depend on the caprices of our variable climate ; during which the barometer may be the regulator of wages and profits, and ten days of wind in March, or of rain in August, may decide the welfare or the distress of millions. But in time the struggle must end. In time we shall discover the folly of attempting to be wiser than Nature ; and of striving to produce, by a system of alternate relaxation and prohibition—a system so complicated and so uncertain, that its inventor dares not venture a conjecture as to its operation*—the regular supply and steady price which are the spontaneous results of commercial freedom. In time we shall feel the wickedness of exposing millions to privation and want, in order to supply affluence to thousands ; and in

time the small class which governs us will discover that the permanence of its rule depends on its escaping from the charge of selfish legislation.

We have said that the intervening period may be long ; but it is possible, we think even probable, that it may be short ; and we are sure that the events of the few weeks during which Parliament has been sitting, have not tended to prolong it.

If the Melbourne administration had pursued the usual course of a declining party—if they had acted in 1841 as they did in 1839, had proposed no measures which they did not fully expect to carry, and had resigned as soon as their working majority was gone—the task of their successors would, for a time, have been comparatively easy. They would have found, indeed, a deficit ; but from the twenty-five millions worth of taxes which had been repealed since the peace, there would have been no real difficulty in re-imposing an amount sufficient to re-establish the revenue. They would have proceeded, as is the practice of that party, along the beaten road, and taxed houses, or windows, or salt, or leather ; and we should have heard of no alteration in the corn law or the timber duties. —of no importation of cattle, and unquestionably of no income tax. But the Budget of 1841 was a measure, the importance of which did not depend on its success. A plan which proposed to restore revenue by cheapening the subsistence, and increasing the comforts, and extending and steadying the trade of the country, might be defeated, but could not be disregarded. The contrast between such a measure and the coarse expedient of a mere increase of taxation, would have been too glaring. Sir Robert Peel therefore felt that he must propose a Budget possessing some resemblance, at least in form, to that of his predecessors ; and we proceed, as far as the very brief time will allow, to consider how far he has succeeded.

The most mischievous of the abuses against which the Whig Budget was directed, is the gigantic injustice of the Corn Law. But not only is that law the palladium of the Tory party—it has been, until a few weeks ago, the especial favourite of Sir Robert Peel himself. ' I should like to know,' he said, in his Reply on the want of confidence motion in last June, ' who in this House has more steadily stood forward in defence of the existing Corn Law than I have done ?'

---

* See Sir R. Peel's answer to Lord Worsley, March 18, 1842.

We are inclined to think, that at this time he intended to retain unaltered the law of which he boasted to have been the steady defender. A short time afterwards when he addressed the electors of Tamworth at the nomination, he expressly stated that he had come to the conclusion that the existing system should not be altered; and that our aim ought to be to render ourselves independent of foreign supply. Such must have been his plan, too, when he admitted the Duke of Buckingham to his Cabinet. He must have been aware that such an associate would not allow even the appearance of a breach in the walls which protect his monopoly. Even the speech of the 9th of February last, in which he brought forward the alterations, such as they are, which he now proposes, was that of a man yielding not to conviction, but to popular clamour. It contained scarcely a sentence that might not have been uttered by the fiercest and blindest champion of ' No surrender.' He began by denying the supposed amount of the existing commercial and manufacturing distress, and by maintaining that the distress, whatever it may be, had not been caused, or even promoted by the Corn Laws, and will not be removed, or even palliated by their modification. Having thus disposed of those who are supported by profits, he proceeded to those who live by wages; and after stating, what is certainly true, that the bulk of the labouring classes in Great Britain are even now in a state superior to that of the bulk of the labouring classes on the Continent, he hinted (for he is too cautious to make such a statement in express words) that their superiority arose from the circumstance, that ' in this country meat is dear, corn is dear, and most of the leading articles which constitute the means of subsistence and comfort, are dearer than in the Continental states.' He went on to repeat, that it is of the first importance to the ' permanent interests of the country, that, *as far as is possible*, we should be independent of foreign supply;' and that the foreign supply, if any, ' should be limited in quantity, and should be brought in only for the purpose of repairing an accidental and comparatively slight deficiency.' On these grounds he deprecated a fixed duty. He deprecated it because it would not go to the utmost verge of possibility in excluding foreign supply — he deprecated it because it would substitute a permanent for a casual

importation ;—in other words, he deprecated it because it would give us a steady commerce and a settled currency ;—because it would give a regular trade to the merchant, a regular demand to the manufacturer, and regular wages and regular employment to the workman.

Such premises appear to lead to no conclusion except the maintenance of the existing law, or adding to the severity of its restrictions and prohibitions. At length, however, he came to the reasons for a change. These he stated to be, first, that a general impression exists that some change is expedient; secondly, that a duty of 20s. having been found in ordinary seasons nearly prohibitory, a higher duty is a piece of useless insolence; and thirdly, that under the present law the importation of a whole year is generally concentrated within a short period, and at an inconvenient season, just before the home-grown corn is threshed. Of these arguments, we have no doubt that the first was that which most influenced Sir Robert Peel, but the last was the one on which he dwelt most. ' This consideration alone,' he remarked, ' ought to prevail with those who most approve the protection at present afforded, to listen with favour to some modifications of the existing law—modifications, in my opinion, likely to prove as advantageous to the agricultural interest as to any other class.'

These were the motives which he assigned for changing a law, in defence of which he had for fourteen years ' steadily stood forth;'—motives so narrow and inadequate, that it is painful to believe that he really obeyed them. He supported his proposed alteration by no enlarged views of national welfare—by no plans to extend the trade, or increase the comforts, or relieve the distress, or appease the discontent of the people, or to increase the revenue of the State. Such objects he passed over, not because he is indifferent to them, but because he knew, and indeed avowed, that his proposed measure would not affect them. He avowed, that in proposing merely a shadow of a fixed duty —a duty still perplexed by a sliding scale, though sliding by more regular gradations, and with two intervals of rest—he was leaving the real principle of the existing Corn Law unaltered.

But though he refused to abandon the sliding scale, he might have materially improved the law ; or, to speak more accurately, have materially diminished its mischief by an effectual reduction of duty. He stated the question for the consideration of Parliament to be, 'What was the amount of duty which would give a just and satisfactory protection to domestic agriculture ?'—a question to be determined, according to Sir Robert Peel, by two considerations ; first, the price which, on the whole, may be considered a sufficient encouragement to the grower ; and secondly, the price at which foreign corn can be introduced. On the second point he said nothing. The first he fixed for wheat at 56s. At this price, therefore, he subjected foreign wheat to a duty of 16s., rising to 20s., its maximum, when the price falls to 50s. ; and sinking to 1s., its minimum, when the price rises to 73s. Instead of the sudden jumps of the present scale, two rests are interposed, one from 66s. to 68s., both inclusive, when the duty is stationary at 6s. ; and the other at 54s. and 53s., when it is stationary at 18s. As a further protection to domestic agriculture, he proposed to increase the number of towns from whose returns of prices the averages are framed ;—an increase which, by letting in returns from cheaper markets, is expected to lower the Gazette price by between two and three shillings a-quarter. It must be recollected therefore, in considering the probable results of the proposed duties, that about two shillings a-quarter will be taken from the apparent price, and therefore added to the duty; so that when wheat, under the present system of averages, would be stated at 56s. a-quarter, it will, under the new system, be stated at 54s. ; and therefore incur an eighteen instead of a sixteen shilling duty.

But even disregarding this new element in the calculation, it is clear that the proposed scale will be, as it is avowedly intended to be, in all ordinary seasons, prohibitory. Sir Robert Peel states the average price of wheat to be 56s., and at that price imposes a duty of 16s. Now, a duty of 16s. has been found from experience to be nearly prohibitory. Out of the thirteen millions and a half of quarters which have been entered for home consumption under the existing law, not a million and a half have been entered at a duty amounting to 16s.

A further, and perhaps a still clearer evidence as to the effect of the proposed duty, may be acquired by examining the question which Sir Robert Peel, after stating its importance, did not think fit to resolve ; namely, the price at which

foreign corn may be obtained. On this subject, however, we will not trouble our readers with statements of shipping charges and consular returns. The papers on corn presented to Parliament on the 4th March, 1842, (No. 50,) contain information which appears to us to be more satisfactory.

The Island of Jersey enjoys a free corn trade. She is not forced to have recourse to the nearest market, lest a cargo from a distant port should find that a sudden rise of duty has changed profit into loss. She can import at the time and from the country which affords the cheapest supply, and her demand is too slight to affect sensibly any market. Under such circumstances, the prices at which Jersey imports may be considered as the most favourable at which corn can be obtained in the British islands. We subjoin the prices of foreign wheat in Jersey since 1828, when the present Corn Law was passed, down to 1841, inclusive, the latest period for which the returns are published ; and we have added from the same Parliamentary Paper the average price in England for the same period.

Year.	English Price.		Foreign Price.	
	s.	*d.*	*s.*	*d.*
1829	66	3	68	0
1830	64	3	54	0
1831	66	4	62	6
1832	58	8	57	0
1833	52	11	39	0
1834	46	2	40	0
1835	39	4	36	0
1836	48	6	37	0
1837	55	10	47	0
1838	64	7	55	0
1839	70	8	67	0
1840	66	4	54	9
1841	64	4	51	0
	58	9½	51	5
	(within minute fractions.)			

It will be seen, that during that period the average price of foreign wheat in Jersey, which, as we have already stated, represents the most favourable price at which it could be obtained in England, has been 51s. 5d. per quarter : and that the average price in England has been 58s. 9 1-2d. a quarter—a price which Sir Robert Peel considers excessive. At this price he imposes on foreign wheat a duty of 14s., which, added to the average price of 51s. 5d., raises the cost of importing foreign wheat to 65s. 5d., and of course prohibits it. Until British corn has risen to 62s., at which price the duty falls to 10s., and the price and duty taken together, of foreign corn, amount to 61s. 5d. importation at average foreign prices cannot take place. Indeed it cannot take place even then, since the necessary results of the attempt to import—namely, a rise of the price abroad, and a fall here—would derange so even a balance. We have not the slightest doubt, that if Sir R. Peel's proposition be adopted, it will be under the law of 1842, as it was under the law of 1828. Nine-tenths of the importation will be confined to the occasions when the English price exceeds 65s., and the remainder will be sold at a loss by the victims of our perverse ingenuity.

One of the great rules of commercial legislation, indeed of all legislation whatever, is to diminish the empire of chance, to enable men to reckon on the results of their actions, or at least not to disturb the elements of the calculation. The duties which conform best to this rule, are the ordinary *ad valorem* duties The producer, the importer, and the warehouser, who deals in articles subject to such a duty, may calculate on a steadiness of profit even greater than can always be expected under a perfect freedom of trade ; since what he gains or loses by a rise or fall in the price, is in some measure balanced by an increase or diminution of duty. A fixed duty, though it contains no such principle of compensation, has the great advantage of stability. One portion of the cost of production, often a very important one, is unalterable. One of these duties, an *ad valorem* or a fixed rate, is adopted, with one exception, in our whole fiscal code; the fixed rate being generally applied to raw produce, the *ad valorem* rate to manufactured articles. The solitary exception—the single commodity as to which the law strives to aggravate the hazards of commerce—the single commodity on which it imposes a duty not *ad valorem*, but *contra valorem*—the single commodity as to which, when the price falls, the law doubles the importer's loss by a proportionate addition to the duty, and when it rises, doubles his gain by a proportionate diminution of duty—the single commodity to which this monstrous legislation is applied, is the *food of the bulk of the inhabitants of Great Britain.* It is the commodity of which the legislating classes are the principal producers, and the labouring classes the principal consumers. It is the commodity from which the incomes of the former are derived, and on which those of the latter are spent. After this, who can wonder at Chartism ?

We have often thought it a question, whether, if we had had to choose between the system of successive, but unforeseen prohibition, and free admission, under which we have suffered ever since 1815, and a permanent prohibition, we ought not to have preferred the latter. Now, of course, with a population increased forty-four per cent, Sir Robert Peel's proposed independence of foreign supplies has become impracticable—at least if the labouring classes are to be allowed to continue the use of wheat ; but it was otherwise when the population of Great Britain did not exceed thirteen millions.

The average price of corn would have been somewhat higher—the rate of increase in the towns and manufacturing districts would have been retarded—the productiveness of industry would have been diminished—wages would therefore have been somewhat lower : we should have been a less numerous and a poorer people. But, on the other hand, we should have escaped one of the main causes of the alternations of prosperity and distress, of panic and confidence, of increased and diminished demand for labour, which, with an increased rapidity of recurrence, have been interspersed during the whole of that period. Our currency would not have been deranged by sudden demands. The specie in the vaults of the Bank of England, the narrow foundation on which our vast superstructure of credit rests, would not have been periodically threatened with exhaustion. The Bank would not have been forced, in its struggles to retain the gold which the imperious demand for food was driving out, to curtail its issues, to endanger the fortunes of the mercantile world, and to alter the standard of value by which all men's proceedings are regulated. Our trade would not have been deranged by being forcibly attracted in a certain direction at one period, and forcibly repelled at another. Our workpeople would not have suffered at one period under the demoralizing influence of a sudden rise of wages, and at another under the still more demoralizing influence of a sudden depression. We are inclined to think that we should, on the whole, have been a better and a happier people.

Of course, we do not mean to prefer the

condition of Great Britain under a supposed prohibition of the importation of corn, to its condition if importation had been subjected to a moderate fixed duty. Such a duty would, indeed, have produced the effect deprecated by Sir Robert Peel. It would have occasioned, except in the rare case of a succession of abundant harvests, a steady importation. It would have made us dependent on foreign nations for a portion of our regular supply. We should have had to endure the dependence of the rich on the poor, the dependence of England on Ireland, the dependence of Sir Robert Peel himself on his own tradesmen. But that supply would have been drawn from the whole world, instead of coming from the few ports whose proximity now enables them almost exclusively to take advantage of our unforeseen demands. If it be true, according to Sir Robert Peel, that the great corn-producing countries of Europe, lying in the same latitude with this country, are affected by the same causes, and therefore participate in our scarcity and in our abundance, what can be more insane than a policy which confines us to the least favourable markets? With the whole world competing for our custom, we should have purchased our supply at the price at which the producer could afford it; not at that which he could extort from our necessities. We should have purchased it for manufactures instead of for bullion; by extending our trade instead of by deranging it; by improving instead of deteriorating the welfare of our work-people; by augmenting the public revenue instead of diminishing it; by adding to the Customs without taking from the Excise. Such would have been the results, and such would now be the results of the substitution of a fixed duty for the sliding scale, which Sir Robert Peel has thought fit to grant to the prejudices of his supporters. We are told, however, that a fixed duty could not be maintained. Whether it could be maintained or not, would depend on its amount. A fixed duty of 20s., or even of 15s., certainly could not be supported, and ought not to be supported; but it is equally clear that a fixed duty of 8s., the amount proposed by the late Government, *could* be maintained. In the whole of the fourteen years during which the present Corn Law has existed, there has been only one (1839) in which the average price has been above 66s. 4d.; and there have been only four, 1831, 1839, 1840, and 1841, in which it has been above 66s. 3d. The

latter, therefore, must be considered as a price unusually high. Yet in 1829, at this extravagantly high price, a duty much exceeding 8s. was maintained. In that year, 1,026,803 quarters of wheat were imported, at an average duty of 9s. 3d. per quarter. In the rather dearer year of 1840, when the price was 66s. 4d., a duty of 7s. 2d. a quarter was maintained. 2,011,774 quarters in that year paid that average amount of duty. Under a regular trade, a trade in which the abundance of the West and the South were allowed to supply the scarcity of the East and the North—when America, Hungary, and the Ukraine were admitted on equal terms with the countries in our own latitude, to which Sir Robert Peel confines us—when prudent merchants and corn-dealers could again venture to equalize prices, by reserving the excess of cheap years to supply the deficiency of dear ones—we do not believe that a price of 66s. 3d. a quarter would ever be reached. But if it were reached, the experience of 1829, nearly repeated in 1840, shows that a duty of 8s. could be maintained.

One of the most remarkable features of the long debates which followed Sir Robert Peel's proposal as to corn, was the abandonment by the leaders of the Tory party of most of the old bulwarks of monopoly. We were no longer told that the manufacturers are dependent on the agricultural market; and that it was their interest to pay an extra price for their bread, in the hope that a portion of that extra price would be laid out in the purchase of cottons and woollens Sir R. Peel disclaimed all wish to prop up rents, or to defend the interests of any particular class. He left it to Sir E. Knatchbull to contend, that 'the duty of corn should be calculated in such a manner as to return to the landed interest full security for their property, and for the station in the country which they had hitherto held;' and to be rewarded by indignant cheers from one side of the House, and by shame and silence on the other. Even the old fallacy, that wages depend on the price of corn—fall as it falls, and rise as it rises—was only hinted at by Sir R. Peel. He left that *falsism*, if we may be allowed to coin a term to designate what is both trite and false, to be formally asserted only by his subordinates. He left to Lord Granby to maintain, that 'the experience of all Europe shows that the certain consequence of making food cheap is to lower wages;' to Sir Francis Burdett to affirm, that 'to the labouring classes the price of corn does not signify one straw;' to Mr. Stuart Wortley to state, that 'if the price of corn were reduced, masters would reduce wages; that if sixpence a-week were saved to the artizan in corn, the diminution of wages would amount to 2s. 6d. a-week:' to Mr. Gladstone to talk of 'the fallacy of cheap bread;' and to Lord Mahon to argue, that 'the price of wheat being at Warsaw about 22s. a quarter, the people were *therefore* miserable and uneducated; and being in Amsterdam from 58s. to 63s. a-quarter, the artizan and labourer were there, as a natural result, in a comfortable condition.'

When such an error as this is maintained by men with the knowledge and sagacity of Mr. Gladstone and Lord Mahon, and almost countenanced by Sir Robert Peel himself, it may be worth while, pressed as we are by questions equally important and still more urgent, shortly to expose it. It is easy to refute it directly. For this purpose it is necessary only to remind the reader, that wages depend on the supply, on the one hand, of labour, and, on the other hand, of the commodities intended for the use of the labourer. If the supply of the commodities intended to be used by the labourer is diminished, he is forced to work more hours for the same wages; to send his children, and perhaps his wife, to the factory; in short, to increase the supply of labour. If the supply of those commodities be increased, he can support himself by less exertion; he can keep his wife, and perhaps his eldest girl, at home; in short, he can diminish the supply of labour, and he does so. All this is clearly stated by Mr. Milne, Mr. Wood, Lord Mansfield, and Lord Lauderdale, in the evidence taken by the Committee of the House of Lords on Grain and the Corn Laws in 1814. We extract a portion of Mr. Milne's evidence—the evidence of a man of great practical experience, both in agriculture and in manufactures.

'As a proprietor of land, have not you attended to the expense of agricultural labour in Scotland? I have.

'Have you not also had large concerns as a manufacturer? I have.

'Where? At Aberdeen.

'In what line? Both in the cotton and linen manufacture.

'Can you state to the committee the effect, as far as your observation has gone, of the rise or fall of grain on the value of agricultural labour in Scotland?

'In Scotland, both agricultural labour and manufacturing labour are considerably affected by the rise and fall of grain and provisions. I have always considered, that when grain and other provisions rose, both manufacturing and agricultural labour fell; on the contrary, when provisions and grain fell, manufacturing and agricultural labour rose. The reason is obvious. Supposing there are in any one parish 100 labourers, who are able to do the work of that parish: if provisions rise, those labourers will do double work; of course, there being only a certain demand for labour, the labour falls: if provisions, on the contrary, fall, those labourers do much less work, probably not one-half: you must therefore, seek more labourers: this makes a demand for labour, and labour rises.

'When you say that the labourer will do double work, do you not mean that the rise in the price of grain, and the difficulty of obtaining the same quantity, will urge him to do such a quantity of work as will enable him to have the usual enjoyment?

'Certainly; and very often it goes further than that, that he does too much work, and works beyond his strength, when grain is very high: at other times he is idle, when grain is low.

'Can you state to the committee any particular instance of agricultural work that you may have contracted for, in a dear year and a cheap year?

'I can state a very strong instance that happened to myself last year. I wished to enclose a farm at the latter end of the year 1812 or the beginning of 1813; I sent for my bailiff, and told him that I had enclosed about five-and-twenty years ago, a good deal of land; that the enclosure at that time cost me 3s. per ell of 37 inches; that a neighbour of mine, two or three years ago, had made similar enclosures, which cost him 5s. per ell; that I thought he had paid too much, and that I ought to have it cheaper:—the answer I got from my bailiff was that provisions were very high, that the labourers were doing double work, and that of course there were less demand for labour, and that he could do those enclosures last year at a cheaper rate than I had ever done them, and he actually executed this enclosure at about half-a-crown an ell. He again came to me, and told me that I had proposed to him to do some ditching and draining upon another farm, which I did not intend to do till about a twelvemonth after, from the circumstance of not being fully in possession of the whole farm; he requested I would allow him to do it that season, as he could do it so much cheaper, and that a great many labourers were idle from having a little work in consequence of those who were employed doing double work; I desired him to go on with that labour likewise, and he actually contracted for very large ditches at sixpence an ell, which I do not think I could now do under from one shilling to eighteenpence, in consequence of the fall in provisions.

'Can you give the committee any information respecting the effect of the price of provisions on manufacturing labour?

'When provisions are likely to fall, I have always been in the habit of giving orders to look out for more hands, imagining that more hands would be wanted to do the same quantity of labour; and when provisions got high, I never had much fear of getting plenty of hands, because they did more work.'

It may be said, however, that these are only temporary and immediate results, and that ultimately the supposed accordance between corn and wages would show itself. Has it shown itself in Ireland, where wages are one-third of the English prices, and corn is cheaper only by the expense of transport? Has it shown itself in the United States, where labour is worth a dollar a day, and wheat 40s. a quarter? But it may be asked, must not the labourer live? Of course he must; but not necessarily on corn. He may rise to meat, or sink to potatoes. Increase the supply of provisions, and he will live better. Add to that increase, improved trade and more regular employment, and he will live better still. Diminish the supply of provisions, and he will live worse. Increase the evil by a diminishing trade and irregular employment, and he will live worse still. But with the example of Ireland on the one side, and of America on the other, never talk of the 'fallacy of cheap bread;' or of 'wages rising and falling with the price of corn.'

On a matter, however, of such importance, it may be proper not merely to refute the error, but to show the causes which have occasioned able men to be entangled by it. The first and great cause probably is the fact, that high wages and a high price of provisions, and low wages and a low price of provisions, are in most countries co-existent; so a man who lives in a palace is generally wealthy, and a man who lives in a cottage is generally poor. But it would be rash to infer that wealth is occasioned by inhabiting a palace, or poverty by dwelling in a cottage. A high price of corn is not the cause, but the effect of high wages, and a low price of corn is not the cause, but the effect of low wages; just as a palace is the result, not the cause of wealth, and a cottage is the result, not the cause of poverty.

No principles are better established—no principles, indeed, are more trite—than that the general price of corn must correspond with the price of that portion of the whole supply, which is regularly furnished at the greatest expense; and that the price of that portion consists entirely of the wages of the labourers who produce it, and the profits of the farmers who advance those wages. If the wages of a labouring family in one country are L.40 a-year, and profits are ten per cent, the corn raised by that family's labour during a year must sell for L.44. If in another country wages are L.20 a-year, an equal quantity of corn raised by the same labour may be sold for L.22. Halve wages in the former country, and double them in the latter, and prices will at least be reversed.

Again, in every corn-eating country, the great consumers of the corn are the labourers themselves. If wages rise, the principal commodity on which their wages are expended has a double tendency to rise; first, because it costs more to produce it; secondly, because the fund for purchasing it is increased. If wages fall, the principal commodity on which wages are expended has a double tendency to fall; first, because it costs less to produce it; and secondly, because the fund for purchasing it is diminished. As a general rule, it may be laid down, that high wages produce a high price of provisions, and low wages a low price of provisions; just as wealth is the cause of good clothes, and poverty is the cause of rags.

The principal exceptions to this rule are, the case of a fertile inadequately peopled country, in which the productiveness of agricultural labour makes up for its high price, as in the example of America; and in the case of a country in which corn is raised, not for the use of the labourer, but for that of the more opulent classes, or for exportation. Such is the state of Ireland, and of Poland, when our ports are open. In such a country as the valley of the Mississippi, though labour is dear, corn may be cheap, because little labour will produce a large quantity; in such a country as Poland, though labour is cheap, corn may be dear, because it will fetch a high price in England. A third exception might be afforded by an opulent manufacturing and commercial country, which should choose to purchase with the produce of its skill, its machinery, and its capital, the corn grown by the cheap labour of its less advanced neighbours, or from the fertile lands of less densely peopled regions.

Two accidental circumstances have concurred, the one in England, the other both in England and Scotland, to give currency to the error which we have been exposing. One was the maladministration of the unreformed English poor-law. In the pauperized districts, and there were few agricultural districts uninfected by pauperism, wages and employment were not a matter of contract, but of right, on the part of the labourer, and of duty on the part of the farmer or the overseer. The labourer was treated like a slave, paid not according to his services but his wants, and entitled not to a certain sum of money, but to the money, whatever were its amount, which would purchase a certain quantity of bread for each member of his family. Of course, under such a system the expense to the farmer of his ploughmen, and of the horses which his ploughmen drove, was governed by the same causes. The wages of one rose and fell with the price of bread; just as the keep of the other rose and fell with the price of hay. Even now, though the scale has disappeared, its traces remain. The labourer with a family accustomed to wheaten bread, when its price rises beyond his means at his usual wages, threatens to enter the workhouse unless his wages are raised. The farmer is frightened at the probable increase of rates and submits; and infers that wages depend on the price of fine wheaten bread.

The other circumstance which promoted the error in question was the depreciation of the currency during the Bank Restriction Act. While the pound sterling gradually sunk till it was worth only 14s., of course, both wages and provisions had a tendency to rise, and, so far as that common cause affected them, to rise precisely in the same proportions. They did not, indeed, rise in the same proportions; as provisions were enhanced by a series of seasons the most calamitous on record, and by the obstacles opposed by the war to importation. In any ordinary state of things, wages would therefore have had a tendency to fall; but the stimulus given to trade and manufactures, by our enjoying the monopoly of the world, prevented their fall; and the alteration of the standard in which they were estimated gave them the appearance of rising. Every rise in the price of provisions, therefore, was followed by an apparent rise of wages; and among those who were ignorant of the real circumstances of the case, that is to say, among 999 out of every 1000 persons, the two ideas became connected as cause and effect.

Notwithstanding Sir Robert Peel's refusal to offer even a conjecture as to the revenue to be obtained under his Corn Bill, we have considered that bill as a part of his financial scheme. We have done so on two grounds. First, because we cannot but believe that some revenue will be obtained, though a much smaller and more irregular one than would have been derived under a rational system. And secondly, because his management of an article which, under his predecessor's plan—the plan on the rejection of which his power is founded—would in last September have produced an additional revenue of more than L.700,000, must be considered as a financial measure. Like his alterations on the duties on coffee and on timber, it may be a measure for the diminution, not for the increase of the revenue, but still it is a measure of finance.

We now proceed to consider the remainder of his Budget, so far as he has thought fit to explain it.

We join in much of the praise which has been bestowed on his speech of the 11th of March. The arrangement is good, the statements are clear, there are many passages of powerful reasoning, and a few that rise to eloquence. We have no doubt that it will survive its occasion, and be long read as one of the best productions of a great artist. Indeed, when it shall be read merely as a study, it will appear a much better speech than it does now; for its great defect will then be unperceived. It will not be seen that it is a piece of elaborate sophistry. It will not be seen that the whole argument rests on one great palpable misrepresentation.

Sir Robert Peel first showed that, comparing the current revenue with the current expenditure, there is a deficit in the present year of rather more than two millions and a half; and that it is not an occasional but a permanent deficit, and must be remedied, therefore, not by temporary, but by permanent expedients. He then proposed to go through the possible expedients exhaustively.

Loans he of course rejected: they are mischievous palliations.

He then rejected further taxation on the articles of subsistence; believing that we have arrived at the limits of such taxation. The proof which he offered was, that the additional five per cent imposed in 1840 on the customs and excise, produced an increase of only one-half per cent. He stated that to raise the post-office duties would arrest a great experiment, which has not yet been fully tried; that to revive the taxes on salt, leather, or wool, or to impose a tax upon gas, would interfere with various compacts and commercial arrangements; and that further taxes on locomotion would prevent the labourer from carrying his only capital to the best market.

At length he came to consider the possibility of augmenting revenue by reduction of taxation; a subject which, probably because he felt it to be the portion of his premises most palpably false, he reserved to the last.

Having stated that in the cases of tobacco, hemp, sugar, malt, soap, paper, and advertisements, a reduction of duty had been followed by a diminution of revenue, he inferred that such must be the result of every reduction. And having, as he assumed, proved that every other mode of increasing the revenue is objectionable or inefficient, he proposed an Income tax.

Sir Robert Peel's proposition, that increase of revenue cannot be obtained by an alteration of duties, depends of course on the assumption, that the existing duties are in every case those by which the largest revenue can be obtained. In fact, it is only a different mode of stating the same proposition. But on looking through our existing tariff, or the tariff now proposed to Parliament, it will be seen that there is scarcely a single article of any importance on which different rates of duty are not imposed, depending on the place where it is produced, or from whence it is imported. Now it is obvious that, when different rates of duty are imposed on the same commodity, one only can be that by which the largest revenue is obtainable. Of the four rates imposed on coffee, 1s. 3d.—1s.—9d.—6d., one only can be the most productive. And when we find that the duty of 1s. 3d. produced in 1840, only L.671, and that of 9d. L.544,653, or nearly a thousand times as much; it seems strange to suppose that no revenue could be obtained by a reduction of the former. When a duty on sugar of L.3, 3s. produced a revenue of L.7647, and a duty of L.I, 4s. produced L 3,717,369, would a reduction of the former be unproductive? If a duty of L.2, 16s. 6d. per load on Baltic fir timber produced L.331,325, and a duty of 11s. 6d. on Canada fir timber L.304,540, is it not obvious that one or the other, or both must be wrong? Again, if out of 3,500,000 lbs. of silk, exported from France to England, only 1,800,000 pay duty,* so that the expense of paying duty and of smuggling appear to be nearly equal,—is it not probable that a small reduction of duty would turn the balance in favour of the fair trader, and increase both the revenue and the consumption?

But the relief wanted is, it is urged, *immediate*. Well, would not a diminution of differential duties afford immediate relief? If our warehouses are filled with commodities, excluded from our market by prohibitory duties, would no revenue be obtained by such a reduction as would admit them to be entered for home consumption, instead of being re-exported to countries enjoying a wiser financial system? It is perfectly true that when a duty imposed for the purpose of revenue is reduced, the immediate effect is loss, and the ultimate gain remote. But when a differential duty is reduced, the whole result is gain, and the gain is immediate.

The fallacy of Sir Robert Peel's argument is so gross, that it almost implied disrespect for his hearers. He affirmed that the plan proposed by the late Government would not

afford any immediate relief; and his reason was, that no immediate increase of revenue followed the reduction of duties on tobacco, hemp, sugar, malt, soap, paper, and advertisements; though the two measures had, in fact, nothing in common. The duties on tobacco, hemp, sugar, malt, soap, paper, and advertisements, were revenue duties. They had been originally imposed at the amount supposed to be most productive. The presumption therefore was, that the reduction would occasion a loss. The duties which the late Government proposed to reduce, were duties originally proposed, not for the purpose of revenue, but of exclusion. They were duties for the purpose of excluding foreign sugar, foreign timber, and foreign corn. The presumption therefore was, that their reduction would produce a gain. And experience had shown that on one article, and in one month, it would have produced a gain of more than L.700,000. To confound things not only dissimilar but opposed, simply because they bear the common name of reduction, was worthy neither of the audience, the occasion, nor the speaker. And yet it was upon this fallacy that his whole argument rested; for he admitted that the expediency of an income tax depended on its *necessity*—on its being the only resource except a loan. The truth being, that we have to choose, not between an income tax and a loan, but between an income tax and cheaper bread, cheaper sugar, and cheaper coffee; and a nearer approach to equality in the burdens imposed on Canadian and Baltic timber.

We have said that the wide and bold principles of utility on which the rejected Budget of 1841 was founded, rendered it necessary that the Budget of 1842 should bear some resemblance to it. Sir Robert Peel therefore has his amended tariff. A very few years ago, such words from a Tory minister would have been ominous. They would have portended aggravated taxation and still more rapacious monopoly. But though, at length, we have rounded the corner, though we have left behind, never we trust to return towards it, the extreme point of fiscal misgovernment, the difference between the Whig and Tory tariff is as great as the improved intelligence of the times will allow. The Whig tariff proposed great improvements with respect to a few great articles. The Tory tariff proposes small improvements in a great many small articles. The Whig tariff proposed to improve the revenue by nearly two millions. The Tory tariff proposes to reduce it by about L.1,200,000. The Whig tariff was framed on the principle of diminishing differential duties; the Tory tariff not

* See Mr. Porter's evidence, Committee on the Import Duties, 2536, export.

only perpetuates and extends them, but establishes them as the general and fundamental basis of the British customs. Whether a commodity, supposed to be capable of being exported from our colonies, have or have not been hitherto subjected to a differential duty—whether it have or have not hitherto entered into colonial trade, even if it be an article which, from its obscurity, bas been left unenumerated—the monopoly of the British market is endeavoured to be secured to it by differential duties; never less than a 100 per cent, and often amounting to 500 per cent. We must say that the mere establishment of this most mischievous principle, appears to us far to outweigh the advantages, considerable as they are, offered by other portions of the scheme.

And yet the loss which this principle will occasion is one of the pretexts for the income tax. By raising the duty on colonial timber, and lowering that on foreign timber, until the advantage given to colonial timber was only 150 per cent., the late ministry expected to *add* L.600,000 a-year to the revenue. By abolishing the duty on Canadian timber, while a duty, amounting in many instances to more than 50 per cent. on the value, is retained on foreign timber, Sir Robert Peel expects to *take* L.600,000 a-year from the revenue. This difference, L.1,200,000, is nearly half of the deficiency of the year. In the same spirit, while the duty on colonial coffee is to be reduced to 4d. a pound, that on foreign coffee is to be fixed at 8d. Sir Robert Peel estimates the consequent loss at L.170,000 a-year. Now, when we recollect that foreign coffee can be furnished so much more cheaply than colonial coffee—that in the face of a differential duty of 50 per cent., and the further expense, amounting to about one halfpenny a pound, of being sent round from the Cape of Good Hope, it supplies more than one-third of our consumption, and nearly one-half of our revenue—there can be no doubt that if, instead of increasing the differential duty from 50 to 100 per cent., we abolished it, and imposed on all coffee the duty most productive of revenue, we might substitute a gain for a loss.

The coffee of Hayti, grown by freemen, and fully equal in quality to the average of what we consume, might be obtained in this country, all expenses except duty paid, at rather less than fivepence per pound. It is sold at that price on the Continent of Europe. Our present tariff subjects it to a duty, including the expense of the voyage to the Cape, of about 190 per cent. Under Sir Robert Peel's tariff, it will remain subject to a duty of 160 per cent. For what purpose is this enormous duty retained, while that on British Colonial coffee is reduced by one half? For the purpose of revenue? No. Sir Robert Peel expects a heavy loss on the whole transaction. To repress slavery, or the slave trade? No. The bulk of the coffee excluded by our present tariff, and by our proposed differential duties, is free grown. For the benefit of the proprietors and mortgagees of coffee estates in the British West Indies? *This*, of course, is the real motive; but we do not believe that the object will be attained. The effect of the monopoly given to our colonies has been a competition for labour, which, operating on an untrained population, has produced among the negroes idleness, irregularity, carelessness;—in short, every quality that can make a labourer unprofitable; and, among the planters, a blind struggle to retain their existing cultivation—fruitless in most cases, and, where it has been effected, absolutely ruinous.* The reduction of the duty on colonial coffee by more than 33 per cent., will of course raise the price in bond—that is to say, the price extra the duty; since the dealer would be able to pay for it twopence a pound more than he now pays, if he continued to sell it at the same price; and to pay for it a penny a pound more than he now pays, if he should reduce the price to the consumer by a penny a pound.

The natural result seems to be, that the increased demand should produce increased cultivation—increased supply, a fall of price, and an increased consumption. This is the result expected by Sir Robert Peel. Paradoxical as it may appear, we believe that the result will be diminished cultivation—diminished supply—no reduction of price, and, of course, no increase of consumption. And we found our expectation on the double monopoly, which is the object of Sir Robert Peel's differential duties. The monopoly possessed by the negro against the planter, in all our principal colonies, makes increased cultivation impossible. Irregular work for a few days in the week, and a few hours in the day, gives the labourer all that he requires. His present idle and insubordinate habits are the result of a fund for the purchase of labour, larger than, with the existing habits of the labourers, can be beneficially employed. Increase that fund, as must be the necessary result of a rise in the price of coffee in bond, and the disproportion between the amount of wages offered by one party, and of labour offered by the other, will

---

* See Mr. Burney's excellent observations on the Island of Trinidad.

be aggravated. The negro will act with respect to coffee as he has acted with respect to sugar. He will do less work for the same wages. Cultivation will decrease instead of increasing; the loss to the revenue will be aggravated by the loss to the consumer; and the friends of slavery, and of the slave-trade, will triumph in an additional instance of the failure of emancipation.

Some of the other errors and abuses of the proposed tariff will have a more extensive effect; but perhaps there is none that is more glaring than the proposal as to coffee. Such a wanton destruction of revenue looks almost like a determination to render an income tax necessary.

We feel some doubt, too, as to the propriety of abandoning, without inquiry, export duties amounting to L.108,000 a-year. Sir R. Peel says that such duties are contrary to a sound principle of legislation. Of course *all* duties are mischievous, and are defensible only because a revenue is necessary; but we own that we see no reason for considering an export duty as more mischievous than an import duty. In fact, all duties on imports are also duties on exports. As all steady trade is barter, and as foreign nations can purchase only as far as they sell, every restriction on importation, is a restriction on the exportation of the British commodity, with which the foreign commodity would directly or indirectly have been purchased. The only difference is, that where a direct tax is laid on exports, the inconvenience is concentrated on the producer whose commodity is taxed. He is aware of the fact, and complains. When a tax is laid on imports, the inconvenience is diffused. The aggregate of the consequent interruption of exportation may be considerable; but the share of each producer is small, and perhaps unperceived even by himself. If the export duties in question can be shown to be specifically injurious, let them be abandoned.

But we shall feel great difficulty in believing them to be specifically injurious, until we find them specifically complained of. It is to be observed that, according to Sir Robert Peel's statement, a large part of them must fall almost entirely on the foreign consumer. He states, that they arise in part ' from the export of woollens and yarns *to countries with which we have no reciprocity treaties.*' If this were true—if these export duties on woollens and yarns were imposed only on goods exported to countries with which we have no reciprocity treaties, the purchasers in those countries would unquestionably bear the whole burden. Our manufacturers and traders could not deal with them on terms less profitable than those which they exact from others, and therefore must charge them with the duty as an addition to the price. But we believe that Sir Robert Peel, whose acquaintance with the laws of the customs is but recent, has committed an error. We believe that those duties are not affected by our reciprocity treaties, and apply as much to one foreign country as to another. If, however, he has not committed an error, he has furnished an irresistible argument against his own proposal.

On the other hand, we approve, so far as the question is merely an economical one, of the proposed export duty on coals. And when we consider that those whom it will affect are few and united—the most dangerous sort of enemies with whom a minister can have to contend—we admire the courage of the proposer. It has always appeared to us, that to export a commodity incapable of reproduction, on the *abundance,* not merely the *possession*—we repeat, on the *abundance* —of which our national existence depends, and which we are consuming at home on a rapidly increasing ratio—and to export it to our manufacturing rivals—is a preference of immediate to ultimate good, resembling that of the Dutch garrison who sold powder to their besiegers. It has been said that the principal export consists of small coals, and that if it is interrupted they will be wasted at the pit's mouth. We do not believe that this would now be the result. Small coals mixed with pitch constitute Grant's patent fuel, now extensively employed in Steam-Boats; and which, if the abundance of small coal reduce its price, must come into general use. Again, small coal, mixed with clay, forms one of the most efficient and most lasting kinds of fuel; as those who have visited Liege or Aix-la-Chapelle, where scarcely any other fuel is used, must have observed. For the last century, we have been wasting our coal with the recklessness with which our Scottish ancestors wasted their forests.

On economical grounds, therefore, we are grateful to Sir R. Peel for his interposition. But the question is not purely economical. It has its political side. Our manufactures, and with our manufactures, our wealth, our power, and probably our constitution, are dependent on the importation of raw produce. Up to the present time, duties on the exportation of raw produce have been rare. Are we wise in setting an example of them? The restrictions of our different commercial codes have generally found zealous imitators. Are we sure that what we are now proposing will not be copied? Have we ascertained how far an export duty on coals may affect our pending negotiations with France? France is our principal customer for coals, and, with her irritable suspiciousness, is not unlikely to believe that the whole object of Sir R. Peel's Budget is to deprive her factories and steam-vessels of coal. The absurdity of this suspicion would not, in such a country as France, diminish its prevalence; or prevent its exercising an unfavourable influence on our commercial treaty. We do not offer these suggestions as conclusive against the proposed duty, but as matters to be deliberately considered by the public. The Cabinet of course has already considered them.

It is a strong proof of the rashness and inconsistency with which Sir Robert Peel's tariff has been framed, that the indirect effects of many of its provisions neutralize their direct influence; and sometimes convert what is apparently beneficial into evil. The export duty on coals is perhaps an instance. The admission of cattle, sheep, and fresh provisions, is perhaps another. Taken by itself, this innovation deserves the highest praise. It overthrows at once one of the strongholds of the landed monopoly. It is beneficial to commerce, to navigation, to the revenue, and indeed to the whole community as consumers. But when we consider it, not as an insulated measure, but as connected with the proposed Corn Law, our praise must be qualified till it almost approaches to censure. At the price which he considers the average price, 56s. a quarter, he imposes on wheat a duty of 16s., or more than 27 per cent. He admits cattle, sheep, and meat, at duties not exceeding 9 per cent. As far as differential duties, amounting to 300 per cent, can effect the purpose, he encourages tillage, and discourages pasture. As manager of the affairs of the public, therefore, his conduct is precisely the reverse of that followed by every man in the management of his own affairs.

The great object of every landlord is to prevent the conversion of pasture into tillage. For this purpose, land-agents and conveyancers accumulate all the resources of their ingenuity. We have no doubt that every lease granted by Sir Robert Peel contains an express reservation of L.10 a-year of additional rent for every acre of pasture ground broken up—express clauses that this additional sum shall be considered as a rent, not as a penalty, and not be relievable against, at law or in equity; and further clauses, enabling the landlord, not merely to compel payment of the additional rent, but further, to re-enter and eject the tenant. Of all rural crimes, this seems to be the most heinous.

But the act which he forbids and punishes as an individual, as a legislator, he bribes every tenant to commit. The great fault of British agriculture, and particularly of English agriculture, is the preponderance of white crops. This error—if what is knowingly done in the hope of immediate profit at the expense of the inheritance ought to be called an error—not only retards the improvement of our secondrate soils, but is one main cause of the increasing irregularity of our harvests. Much of the land now under the plough in England is productive only in extraordinary years. Five years out of six it is cultivated at a loss. The sixth, perhaps, comes a lucky season, when the harvest is good locally, but bad generally, and a prize is drawn—but a prize, probably, which does not make up for the previous blanks. It would be much better for landlord, tenant, and consumer, if such land were employed to produce the steady, moderate return of pasture, instead of being an instrument for gambling in tillage. When we consider Sir Robert Peel's Corn Law and Cattle Law as one measure, and add to them his proposed exemption from income tax, of tenants under L.300 a-year, and the consequent temptation to subdivide farms and waste capital, we doubt whether any other modern statesman has devised a system so mischievous to the agriculture of a country.

We ought to add, that the copy of the proposed tariff which we are forced to use, is that which was first delivered. It is said to contain many typographical errors, which are to be corrected in a subsequent edition. We trust that the tripling the duty on oil-seed cakes is one of these errors. We trust that the subjecting the important articles of butter, cheese, eggs, and meat, and bark, to differential duties of 400 per cent, is another. We trust, too, that either this cause, or the commercial treaties still pending, may be the explanation of the numerous *ad valorem* duties of 30 per cent, and 25 per cent, which we see scattered through the tables. And, on the whole, although we cordially approve of many of the details, we close the schedules with deep regret, that, in the present state of political knowledge, a British Minister should believe that such a tariff is worth purchasing with an income tax.

We do not mean to express any fixed abhorrence to an income tax, or to affirm even that it ought to be confined to a period of serious European war. If a real reform of the tariff were proposed to us—a reform which should not leave out or mismanage such commodities as butter, cheese, hops, sugar, coffee, and corn—a reform which should sweep away protective and differential duties—a reform which should prefer the interests of millions to those of thousands—and if it were found that such a reform would produce a temporary loss of revenue—for such a reform we should be ready to pay the price, the heavy, but not the extravagant price, of a temporary income tax.

But the tax to which, for such a purpose, we would submit, would be a very different one from that which is now proposed.

In the first place, it would include all who could be held able to pay it. Every tax, to be just, must either be self-imposed, or be proportioned to the means of the payer. Taxes upon consumption, which do not affect the necessaries of life, conform to the first of these rules—they are self-imposed. 'In the price of threepence-halfpenny,' says Adam Smith, 'now paid for a pot of porter, the different taxes may amount to three-halfpence. If a workman can conveniently spare these three-halfpence, he buys a pot of porter. If he cannot, he contents himself with a pint; and as a penny saved is a penny got, he gains a farthing by his temperance. He pays the tax as far as he can afford to pay it, and every act of payment is perfectly voluntary—what he can avoid if he chooses to do so.' A tax deducting an equal per centage from the revenue of all permanent property, conforms to the second rule; it is proportioned to the means of the payer. But taxes on the necessaries of life are unjust, since they take as much from a family with L.30 a-year, as from a family with L.300 a-year. Taxes upon ground rents, on the devolution of personal property, on the conveyance of land, or on legal proceedings, are equally unjust. They select particular classes for taxation. Taxes imposed on persons possessing a given amount of property or income, and excluding others, except on the ground of inability to pay, are equally unjust, and far more dangerous. There are no marked divisions in society depending on the nature of property. Proprietors of ground rents, lands, or funds, are interspersed among men of every condition. But society is divided, according to the amount of property, into marked classes, —the poorer being always the more numerous. To hold out any one class as the subjects of exclusive taxation, is to hold out a minority as the objects of legal plunder. Sir Robert Peel proposes to exempt all incomes under L.150 a-year; that is to say, to exempt more than nine-tenths of the community.

The return of the number of persons receiving dividends in 1838—the last year for which we have seen it—states that out of 188,498 such persons, 172,096 received an amount not exceeding L.100 a-year; 10,001 an amount between L.100 and L.200 a-year; and only 6401 an amount exceeding L.200 a-year.* We have no doubt that the persons with incomes between L.150 or L.200 a-year, far exceed in number all whose incomes are larger. Are *they* not likely to demand exemption? When once an injustice has been committed, when once a line has been drawn, depending on the arbitrary will of the legislator, what security have we that it will be adhered to? What security have we that it will not be gradually pushed up, until the opulent become what they were in the Greek republics—mere trustees for the State? The proposed exemption may be a clever party measure; it may render the tax a favourite with the ten-pound householders, and with all who are below them; it may gratify their hatred of the middle classes, and of the aristocracy; but, in the pursuit of immediate popularity, Sir Robert Peel has entered on a course in which it will be difficult to stop, and ruinous to advance. This is his first movement towards the revolutionary party which infests both sides of the House; and ranges itself, according to each member's constituency, under the ultra Tory or ultra Radical banner. We presume that he has well weighed its consequences.

In the second place, the tax to which we would submit must be confined to that portion of income which can fairly be called revenue; that is to say, to the portion which can be spent without impairing the capital. If a man has lent L.20,000, to be repaid to him with interest by four annual payments, can he be said to have an income of L.6000 the first year, L.5750 the second, L.5500 the third, and L.5250 the fourth?† Can his real annual income be said to be more than L.1000? Yet, as far as we are at present acquainted with Sir Robert Peel's plan, he will be taxed, in the first place, as if his whole receipts were income; and secondly, the income arising from the L.5000, paid off and reinvested by him every year, will be again subject to taxation; so that, in fact, he will be taxed every year as if his income were L.6000 a-year; that is to say, six times more than if he had lent his money on mortgage at five per cent, and ten times as much as if he had purchased a landed estate with it. What can be said of the fairness of a tax which, the value of the property in each case being the same, taxes one man L.18 a-year, and the other L.180?

---

* Porter's *Tables*, Part ix., p. 5.

† See Mr. Attwood's speech, March 23, 1842, where he states this to be his own case; the very government which imposes the tax being his debtor.

Of course, we would carry our principle further. Can the merchant, who derives a profit apparently high from a hazardous business; the professional man, who, if he were to spend all that he gains during his few years of eminence and health, would leave his family beggars; the clergyman and the public officer, a third of whose income is employed in insuring his life, or in effecting an accumulation which is to serve as an insurance;—can any one of these be said to possess, as a means of expenditure, all that is called his income?

But it may be said, that to attempt to obviate all these anomalies would give a great deal of trouble, and diminish the productiveness of the tax. Suppose that it would. To refuse inquiry because it would cost trouble—to refuse redress because it would cost money—to commit blind wholesale injustice, in order to save the annoyance of having to investigate, and the expense of having to exempt; this again is a conduct to which the term revolutionary, in the most hateful sense of that word, must be applied. This is a conduct which would have been revolting if it had been suggested by a demagogue to an assembly of the people; or by a committee of public safety to a national convention. It could scarcely have been excused, if it had been offered as a sudden expedient to a struggling nation, to meet an unexpected emergency. It is now proposed to a British Parliament by a Conservative minister, after six months of deliberation, to supply a voluntary deficiency.

Nor is the excuse, so far as the difficulty of the investigation is concerned, founded on fact. The case of precarious or temporary investments seems to present no difficulty whatever. We know that money cannot, as a general rule, be safely invested so as to produce interest at more than 4 per cent. Whatever is received beyond this is a compensation, generally an inadequate compensation, for risk. Let the income derived from all money investments be calculated at 4 per cent on the sum which they cost; or, when that cannot be ascertained, at 4 per cent on their value. There can be no difficulty in this; and we cannot suppose that the most rapacious financier who has ever oppressed a nation would venture to object to it, on the mere ground that it would make the tax somewhat less productive. The case of professional men, including clergymen and public officers, is less susceptible of accurate adjustment; but the supposition that such men in general put by, and that under a sense of

obligation, one-third of their professional income, is, we believe, rather under the truth. That the amount must vary according to circumstances; that an old bachelor may venture to spend more than the man with a family; a man with an independent fortune more than one whose profession is the only fund from which a provision for ill health, or for children, is to be accumulated—all this is obvious; but the impossibility of minute discriminating justice is no excuse for universal indiscriminate injustice. What we should suggest, if we were framing an income-tax, would be, that such incomes should be rated at two-thirds of the incomes derived from investments. So that under the proposed rate they would pay L.1, 18s. 10d. and a fraction per cent, instead of L.2, 18s. 4d.

With respect to the incomes derived from trades, the data are more doubtful. We suggest, as the nearest approximation at which we have been able to arrive, that the average gross profits of successful trade may be taken at 10 per cent on the capital employed; and that of this amount 4 per cent may be considered as interest, 3 per cent as the remuneration for trouble, and 3 per cent as the compensation for occasional loss—leaving the average net profit 7 per cent, or about double what can be obtained from the funds. On large capitals the compensation for trouble may be smaller, and that for risk larger; the additional trouble taken by the smaller capitalist enabling him to diminish his risk. If we assume, as we are justified in doing, that the trader ought to lay by from the three per cent, which he is supposed to receive for his trouble, one-third—the amount supposed to be reserved by professional men—his real income, the income which he can afford to spend, will be 6 per cent on his capital. We should suggest, therefore, if we were proposing an income tax, that traders should be assessed at a supposed income of 6 per cent on their capital; or, if they did not think fit to declare their capital, then, at six-tenths of their declared incomes. The extra profit, which is a mere compensation for risk, cannot be fairly taxed, unless the State return to the trader, when he has sustained a loss, what it took from him when his speculations were successful.

The objection which has been raised by Sir Robert Peel,[*] that, if the tax is to de-

---

* See his speech, 24th March, 1842.

pend on the tenure of the income, provision must be made for the case of a jointress, or that of the tenant for life of an estate which, on his death, is to go to a distant relation, scarcely deserves an answer. The instances in which property is settled on a person for his life, without power to make a provision out of it for his children, are almost too rare for calculation; those in which it can be subjected to a jointure, and yet not charged for the benefit of children, are still rarer. And if it were thought fit to provide for them by assessing the income of such a tenant for life, or of such a jointress, as if it were a professional income, where would be the difficulty?

But modify an income tax as we will, it has this inherent vice, that it is, to a considerable extent, a tax upon the creation of capital. And yet it is remarkable that this vice has often been considered as a merit. It has been often said in its praise, that it affects the hoards of the miser. Those who use such language cannot know of what the hoards of a miser consist. They consist of ships, of docks, of canals, of railways, of farm buildings, of farm stock, of reclaimed lands, of mills, of machinery; in short, of all that produces wealth and enjoyment—of all the sources of employment to the people, rent to the landlord, and revenue to the Government. Every man must spend every shilling of his income, but he may spend it productively or unproductively. If a man with L .2000 a-year spends the whole unproductively, he gives the whole of it every year in exchange for commodities or services for his own enjoyment. If he spend half of it productively, or, in common language, if he save half of it, he employs that half, either himself, or through the agency of some person to whom he lends it, or whom he pays for managing it, in creating new sources of future revenue. Such a man, at the end of twenty years, has added L 20,000 to the capital of the country—an addition which would not have existed if, instead of paying men to drain or to plant, to erect steam-engines, or to sink mines, he had paid them to wait behind his chair, or attend to his hothouses, or his hounds. Now, if the man with L.2,000 a-year, whom we have supposed to save half his income, be subjected to a tax falling on his expenditure, the only consequence will be his personal inconvenience. He has so much less to spend, the Government so much the more. He may be

forced to discharge a footman—the Government is enabled to engage a soldier. But if the tax fall on the portion of his income which he saves, it forces him to discharge, not a footman, but a man whose services created every year a capital exceeding his wages. He is forced to withdraw a workman from a farm-yard, a railway, or a manufactory. Suppose such a man to be taxed 50 per cent on his income, and to pay the tax -one-half out of what he had been accustomed to spend, and the other half out of what he had been accustomed to save, the L.500 a-year paid out of his expenditure, if it were paid for twenty years, would not affect the capital of the country; but the L.500 paid out of his savings would take L.500 from what would have been the capital of the country the first year, L.1,000 the second, L.1,500 the third, and so on, more and more during every year that it lasted. For this reason, because they fall principally on unproductive expenditure, we prefer the assessed taxes to all other forms of direct taxation. If any other form of direct taxation be necessary, we prefer a direct tax on every man's declared expenditure.

Such a tax would have little tendency to diminish the accumulation of capital: to a certain extent, indeed, it would have a tendency to promote it, since many men would save in order to avoid the tax. It would have the further advantage of being, to a considerable extent, self-imposed. Its assessment, too, would be far less painful. Few persons would feel much objection to declare their expenditure, or to suffer it to be notorious; because its notoriety would neither affect their credit nor injure their vanity; and so far as professional men and traders are concerned, expenditure is more easily ascertained than income.

We have said nothing of the vexatious proceedure by which the proposed income tax is to be assessed or enforced; nor of the evasion, fraud, and demoralization which it will introduce; nor of its tendency to drive British property into foreign funds, and British subjects into foreign countries; nor of the danger of promoting extravagance, or even war, by a source of revenue so easy of increase. We have omitted these, and many other branches of the subject, not because we undervalue their importance, but simply because we cannot discuss them, at present, as we could wish.

The same reason prevents our adverting to the details of the debate upon the Budget so far as it had proceeded at the time of writing these pages, in the House of Commons. It is a striking exhibition of the predominance of Sir Robert Peel over his immediate associates, a predominance as distinctly marked in 1842 as it was in 1835. Whether he is equally absolute in the Cabinet is a different question—a question which a comparison of the measures which he brings forward, with those which he must be supposed to wish to bring forward, would lead us to decide negatively. But in the House it is clear, that either from choice or from necessity, (we suspect from necessity,) he represents every department, and refuses to be encumbered by assistance. Another remarkable characteristic of the debate, has been the superiority of the Opposition. Their cause, without doubt, gives them a great advantage; but it might have been expected that they would have had to buy their victories in discussion a little dearer.

Before we quit this part of the subject, we must express the regret—which we believe to be general throughout the country among all who are opposed to an income tax—that this part of the Budget was not met, by Lord John Russell, with an immediate expression of decided hostility. The vigorous supporter of the repudiated Budget of the preceding year, would have been guilty of no inconsistency, no impropriety, in opposing *in toto* the Budget of 1842. But that the income tax section of it—that a proposal calculated to startle, and to meet a hesitating and grudging acquiescence even under the pressure of an expensive war for a just cause—should not have encountered, when brought forward in peace, and under no alarming destitution of other expedients, the instant resistance of the clear-sighted and firm-minded leader of the Opposition, seems to us truly surprising. The prudence and candour of his nature may have seduced him here into a great practical error. It may be that he was unwilling, without consulting his party, to follow his own impulses, and act on his own judgment. The result has been most unfortunate. The interposition of a whole week between the announcement of the measure and of the resistance, led to a suspicion that it was possible that it might be acquiesced in. It seems to us very clear that the public ought not to have been allowed, for a single day, to contemplate such a possibility. We now know

that it was not contemplated by the leaders of the Liberal party; and we think that, in such a cause, they might have ventured to assume the responsibility of answering for the opinions and conduct of the whole body of their supporters.

It is scarcely possible that this paper should come into the hands of any one who, not having heard, has not read, Lord Brougham's very cogent speech in the House of Lords, on the 17th of March. It will be seen that we differ from his Lordship as to the necessity of an income tax; but as to the general evils of such a tax, and as to the specific mischief and injustice of the details of the present measure, we are delighted to find ourselves supported by his high authority. In one respect, indeed, he goes further than we do. We have suggested that incomes derived from personal exertion should pay two-thirds of the rate of incomes derived from property. Lord Brougham proposes that they should pay only one-third. We tax them, therefore, twice as heavily as he does. We leave the public to decide between the two plans, and should not be dissatisfied if the difference were divided. But we think that Lord Brougham's proposal, of which we were not aware until the passages containing our own had been completed, proves that we have not been too liberal in our exemption.

Before concluding, we will, in despite of the ridicule which generally follows unconsummated predictions, hazard one. We are convinced that if the income tax be persisted in, it will ultimately be fatal to the present Administration. We believe that it will be carried. We believe that a combination between the country gentlemen, who think that they are raising a bulwark around the corn-law; the planters, who think that they are securing the sugar-law; and the members whose constituencies rejoice in it as a blow to the aristocracy, will force it through the House. But when once it has come into operation—when the painful exposure and the humiliating discussion have been undergone—when men have felt what it is to tremble at the knock of a tax-gatherer, and to deprecate the suspicions of a commissioner—when the pain of loss has been embittered by that of degradation;—a detestation of the tax will arise which all the discipline of the Tory party will be unable to control. Unfortunately for that party, the eminent person who leads it is not distinguished

for political foreknowledge. He has often
yielded to circumstances, but always too
late. If he should perceive the signs of
the gathering storm in time to change his
course—if the working of his new Corn
Law should be such as to convince his
followers that an alteration productive of
a steady price, and a steady revenue, is
expedient—if a treaty with Brazil should
give him a fair pretext to add a million
and a half to the revenue from sugar—if
he can open his budget for 1843 by a promise that the income tax shall expire before 1844, and it shall be believed that he
will perform that promise;—he may be
able, to a certain degree, to skin over the
wound which its introduction has inflicted
on his influence among his real supporters. Many of them, indeed, are lost to
him irretrievably. Some detest the
injustice of his measure, others are frightened at its democratic tendency, and
all writhe under its severity. It is probable that he is not aware—no minister,
perhaps, ever is aware—of the deep and
bitter feeling of distrust and dissatisfaction which he has roused. He never will
again be popular with his own party, and
he has too much experience not to know
the value of the praise with which his
fiercest enemies have endeavoured to
blind him. He knows well with what
motives and with what sincerity he is called bold, direct, and honest. Still, however, while they believe it to be their interest, a large portion of the Tory party
may continue to serve under him against
the Whigs. But they will make no sacrifices in his defence. They will volunteer
no expensive contest for him. They will
not endanger their seats in his service.
They will refuse no pledge against an income tax. If his power imply a continuance of that tax, his majority, strong as it
may now appear, will have crumbled away
long before the period which he has ventured to assign for the duration of the tax
shall have expired.

ART. VII.—*Frederic the Great and his
Times.* Edited, with an Introduction,
by THOMAS CAMPBELL, Esq. 2 vols. 8vo.
London: 1842.

THIS work, which has the high honour of
being introduced to the world by the author of 'Lochiel' and 'Hohenlinden,' is
not wholly unworthy of so distinguished a

chaperon. It professes, indeed, to be no
more than a compilation; but it is an exceedingly amusing compilation, and we
shall be glad to have more of it. The
narrative comes down at present only to
the commencement of the Seven Years'
War, and therefore does not comprise the
most interesting portion of Frederic's reign.

It may not be unacceptable to our readers that we should take this opportunity of
presenting them with a slight sketch of
the life of the greatest king that has, in
modern times, succeeded by right of birth
to a throne. It may, we fear, be impossible
to compress so long and eventful a story
within the limits which we must prescribe
to ourselves. Should we be compelled to
break off, we shall, when the continuation
of this work appears, return to the subject.

The Prussian monarchy, the youngest
of the great European states, but in population and revenue the fifth amongst them,
and in art, science, and civilisation entitled to the third, if not to the second
place, sprang from an humble origin. About
the beginning of the fifteenth century, the
marquisate of Brandenburg was bestowed
by the Emperor Sigismund on the noble
family of Hohenzollern. In the sixteenth
century that family embraced the Lutheran doctrines. Early in the seventeenth
century it obtained from the king of
Poland the investiture of the duchy of
Prussia. Even after this accession of territory, the chiefs of the house of Hohenzollern hardly ranked with the electors of
Saxony and Bavaria. The soil of Brandenburg was for the most part sterile.
Even round Berlin, the capital of the province, and round Potsdam, the favourite
residence of the Margraves, the country
was a desert. In some tracts, the deep
sand could with difficulty be forced by as-
siduous tillage to yield thin crops of rye
and oats. In other places, the ancient
forests, from which the conquerors of the
Roman empire had descended on the
Danube, remained untouched by the hand
of man. Where the soil was rich it was
generally marshy, and its insalubrity repelled the cultivators whom its fertility
attracted. Frederic William, called the
Great Elector, was the prince to whose
policy his successors have agreed to ascribe their greatness. He acquired by
the peace of Westphalia several valuable
possessions, and among them the rich city
and district of Magdeburg; and he left
to his son Frederic a principality as considerable as any which was not called a
kingdom.

Frederic aspired to the style of royalty. Ostentatious and profuse, negligent of his true interests and of his high duties, insatiably eager for frivolous distinctions, he added nothing to the real weight of the state which he governed: perhaps he transmitted his inheritance to his children impaired rather than augmented in value, but he succeeded in gaining the great object of his life, the title of king. In the year 1700 he assumed this new dignity. He had on that occasion to undergo all the mortifications which fall to the lot of ambitious upstarts. Compared with the other crowned heads of Europe, he made a figure resembling that which a Nabob or a Commissary, who had bought a title, would make in the company of Peers whose ancestors had been attainted for treason against the Plantagenets. The envy of the class which he quitted, and the civil scorn of the class into which he intruded himself, were marked in very significant ways. The elector of Saxony at first refused to acknowledge the new Majesty. Louis the Fourteenth looked down on his brother King with an air not unlike that with which the Count in Molière's play regards Monsieur Jourdain, just fresh from the mummery of being made a gentleman. Austria exacted large sacrifices in return for her recognition, and at last gave it ungraciously.

Frederic was succeeded by his son, Frederic William, a prince who must be allowed to have possessed some talents for administration, but whose character was disfigured by the most odious vices, and whose eccentricities were such as had never been seen out of a madhouse. He was exact and diligent in the transaction of business, and he was the first who formed the design of obtaining for Prussia a place among the European powers, altogether out of proportion to her extent and population, by means of a strong military organization. Strict economy enabled him to keep up a peace establishment of sixty thousand troops. These troops were disciplined in such a manner, that placed beside them, the household regiments of Versailles and St. James's would have appeared an awkward squad. The master of such a force could not but be regarded by all his neighbours as a formidable enemy, and a valuable ally.

But the mind of Frederic William was so ill regulated, that all his inclinations became passions, and all his passions partook of the character of moral and intellectual disease. His parsimony degenerated into sordid avarice. His taste for military pomp and order became a mania, like that of a Dutch burgomaster for tulips; or that of a member of the Roxburgh club for Caxtons. While the envoys of the Court of Berlin were in a state of such squalid poverty as moved the laughter of foreign capitals; while the food placed before the princes and princesses of the blood-royal of Prussia was too scanty to appease hunger, and so bad that even hunger loathed it—no price was thought too extravagant for tall recruits. The ambition of the king was to form a brigade of giants, and every country was ransacked by his agents for men above the ordinary stature. These researches were not confined to Europe. No head that towered above the crowd in the bazaars of Aleppo, of Cairo, or of Surat, could escape the crimps of Frederic William. One Irishman more than seven feet high, who was picked up in London by the Prussian ambassador, received a bounty of near L.1300 sterling—very much more than the ambassador's salary. This extravagance was the more absurd, because a stout youth of five feet eight, who might have been procured for a few dollars, would in all probability have been a much more valuable soldier. But to Frederic William, this huge Irishman was what a brass Otho, or a Vinegar Bible, is to a collector of a different kind.

It is remarkable, that though the main end of Frederic William's administration was to have a great military force, though his reign forms an important epoch in the history of military discipline, and though his dominant passion was the love of military display, he was yet one of the most pacific of princes. We are afraid that his aversion to war was not the effect of humanity, but was merely one of his thousand whims. His feeling about his troops seems to have resembled a miser's feeling about his money. He loved to collect them, to count them, to see them increase; but he could not find it in his heart to break in upon the precious hoard. He looked forward to some future time when his Pattagonian battalions were to drive hostile infantry before them like sheep. But this future time was always receding; and it is probable that, if his life had been prolonged thirty years, his superb army would never have seen any harder service than a sham fight in the fields near Berlin. But the great military means which he had collected, were destined to be employed by a spirit far more daring and inventive than his own.

Frederic, surnamed the Great, son of Frederic William, was born in January, 1712. It may safely be pronounced that he had received from nature a strong and sharp understanding, and a rare firmness of temper and intensity of will. As to the other parts of his character, it is difficult to say whether they are to be ascribed to nature, or to the strange training which he underwent. The history of his boyhood is painfully interesting. Oliver Twist in the parish workhouse, Smike at Dotheboys Hall, were petted children when compared with this wretched heir-apparent of a crown. The nature of Frederic William was hard and bad, and the habit of exercising arbitrary power had made him frightfully savage. His rage constantly vented itself to right and left in curses and blows. When his majesty took a walk, every human being fled before him, as if a tiger had broken loose from a menagerie. If he met a lady in the street, he gave her a kick, and told her to go home and mind her brats. If he saw a clergyman staring at the soldiers, he admonished the reverend gentleman to betake himself to study and prayer, and enforced this pious advice by a sound caning, administered on the spot. But it was in his own house that he was most unreasonable and ferocious. His palace was hell, and he the most execrable of fiends—a cross between Moloch and Puck. His son Frederic and his daughter Wilhelmina, afterwards Margravine of Bareuth, were in an especial manner objects of his aversion. His own mind was uncultivated. He despised literature. He hated infidels, papists, and metaphysicians, and did not very well understand in what they differed from each other. The business of life, according to him, was to drill and to be drilled. The recreations suited to a prince, were to sit in a cloud of tobacco-smoke, to sip Swedish beer between the puffs of the pipe, to play backgammon for three-halfpence a rubber, to kill wild hogs, and to shoot partridges by the thousand. The Prince-Royal showed little inclination either for the serious employments or for the amusements of his father. He shirked the duties of the parade—he detested the fume of tobacco—he had no taste either for backgammon or for field-sports. He had received from nature an exquisite ear, and performed skilfully on the flute. His earliest instructors had been French refugees, and they had awakened in him a strong passion for French literature and French society. Frederic William regarded these tastes as effeminate and contemptible, and, by abuse and persecution, made them still stronger. Things became worse when the Prince-Royal attained that time of life at which the great revolution in the human mind and body takes place. He was guilty of some youthful indiscretions, which no good and wise parent would regard with severity. At a later period he was accused, truly or falsely, of vices, from which History averts her eyes, and which even Satire blushes to name—vices such that, to borrow the energetic language of Lord-

Keeper Coventry, 'the depraved nature of man, which of itself carrieth man to all other sin, abhorreth them.' But the offences of his youth were not characterized by any peculiar turpitude. They excited, however, transports of rage in the King, who hated all faults except those to which he was himself inclined; and who conceived that he made ample atonement to heaven for his brutality, by holding the softer passions in detestation. The Prince-Royal, too, was not one of those who are content to take their religion on trust. He asked puzzling questions, and brought forward arguments which seemed to savour of something different from pure Lutheranism. The King suspected that his son was inclined to be a heretic of some sort or other, whether Calvinist or Atheist his majesty did not very well know. The ordinary malignity of Frederic William was bad enough. He now thought malignity a part of his duty as a Christian man, and all the conscience that he had stimulated his hatred. The flute was broken—the French books were sent out of the palace—the prince was kicked, and cudgelled, and pulled by the hair. At dinner the plates were hurled at his head—sometimes he was restricted to bread and water—sometimes he was forced to swallow food so nauseous, that he could not keep it on his stomach. Once his father knocked him down, dragged him along the floor to a window, and was with difficulty prevented from strangling him with the cord of the curtain. The queen, for the crime of not wishing to see her son murdered, was subjected to the grossest indignities. The Princess Wilhelmina, who took her brother's part, was treated almost as ill as Mrs. Brownrigg's apprentices. Driven to despair, the unhappy youth tried to run away; then the fury of the old tyrant rose to madness. The prince was an officer in the army; his flight was therefore desertion, and, in the moral code of Frederic William, desertion was the highest of all crimes. 'Desertion,' says this royal theologian, in one of his half-crazy letters, 'is from hell. It is a work of the children of the devil. No child of God could possibly be guilty of it.' An accomplice of the prince, in spite of the recommendation of a court-martial, was mercilessly put to death. It seemed probable that the prince himself would suffer the same fate. It was with difficulty that the intercession of the States of Holland, of the Kings of Sweden and Poland, and of the Emperor of Germany, saved the House of Brandenburg from the stain of an unnatural murder. After months of cruel suspense, Frederic learned that his life would be spared. He remained, however, long a prisoner; but he was not on that account to be pitied. He found in his jailers a tenderness which he had never found in his father; his table was not sumptuous, but he had wholesome food in sufficient quantity to appease hunger; he could read the *Henriade* without being kicked, and play on his flute without having it broken over his head.

When his confinement terminated, he was a man. He had nearly completed his twenty-first year, and could scarcely, even by such a parent as Frederick William, be kept much longer under the restraints which had made his boyhood miserable. Suffering had matured his understanding, while it had hardened his heart and soured his temper. He had learnt self-command and dissimulation; he affected to conform to some of his father's views, and submissively accepted a wife, who was a wife only in name, from his father's hand. He also served with credit, though without any opportunity of acquiring brilliant distinction, under the command of Prince Eugene, during a campaign marked by no extraordinary events. He was now permitted to keep a separate establishment, and was therefore able to indulge with caution his own tastes. Partly in order to conciliate the king, and partly, no doubt, from inclination, he gave up a portion of his time to military and political business, and thus gradually acquired such an aptitude for affairs as his most intimate associates were not aware that he possessed.

His favourite abode was at Rheinsberg, near the frontier which separates the Prussian dominions from the duchy of Mecklenburg. Rheinsberg is a fertile and smiling spot, in the midst of the sandy waste of the Marquisate. The mansion, surrounded by woods of oak and beech, looks out upon a spacious lake. There Frederic amused himself by laying out gardens in regular alleys and intricate mazes, by building obelisks, temples, and conservatories, and by collecting rare fruits and flowers. His retirement was enlivened by a few companions, among whom he seems to have preferred those who, by birth or extraction, were French. With these inmates he dined and supped well, drank freely, and amused himself sometimes with concerts, sometimes with holding chapters of a fraternity which he called the Order of Bayard; but literature was his chief resource.

His education had been entirely French. The long ascendency which Louis XIV. had enjoyed, and the eminent merit of the tragic and comic dramatists, of the satirists, and of the preachers who had flourished under that magnificent prince, had made the French language predominant in Europe. Even in countries which had a national literature, and which could boast of names greater than those of Racine, of Molière, and of Massillon—in the country of Dante, in the country of Cervantes, in the country of Shakspeare and Milton—the intellectual fashions of Paris had been to a great extent adopted. Germany had not yet produced a single masterpiece of poetry or eloquence. In Germany, therefore, the French taste reigned without rival and without limit. Every youth of rank was taught to speak and write French. That he should speak and write his own tongue with politeness, or even with accuracy and facility, was regarded as comparatively an unimportant object. Even Frederic William, with all his rugged Saxon prejudices, thought it necessary that his children should know French, and quite unnecessary that they should be well versed in German. The Latin was positively interdicted. 'My son,' his majesty wrote, 'shall not learn Latin; and, more than that, I will not suffer anybody even to mention such a thing to me.' One of the preceptors ventured to read the Golden Bull in the original with the Prince-Royal. Frederic William entered the room, and broke out in his usual kingly style.

'Rascal, what are you at there?'

'Please your majesty,' answered the preceptor, 'I was explaining the Golden Bull to his royal highness.'

'I'll Golden Bull you, you rascal!' roared the majesty of Prussia. Up went the king's cane, away ran the terrified instructor, and Frederic's classical studies ended for ever. He now and then affected to quote Latin sentences, and produced such exquisite Ciceronian phrases as these:—'Stante pede morire,'—'De gustibus non est disputandus,'—'Tot verbas tot spondera.' Of Italian, he had not enough to read a page of Metastasio with ease; and of the Spanish and English, he did not, as far as we are aware, understand a single word.

As the highest human compositions to which he had access were those of the French writers, it is not strange that his admiration for those writers should have been unbounded. His ambitious and eager temper early prompted him to imitate what he admired. The wish, perhaps, dearest to his heart was, that he might rank among the masters of French rhetoric and poetry. He wrote prose and verse as indefatigably as if he had been a starving hack of Cave or Osborn; but Nature, which had bestowed on him, in a large measure, the talents of a captain and of an administrator, had withheld from him those higher and rarer gifts, without which industry labours in vain to produce immortal eloquence or song. And, indeed, had he been blessed with more imagination, wit, and fertility of thought, than he appears to have had, he would still have been subject to one great disadvantage, which would, in all probability, have for ever prevented him from taking a high place among men of letters. He had not the full command of any language. There was no machine of thought which he could employ with perfect ease, confidence, and freedom. He had German enough to scold his servants, or to give the word of command to his grenadiers; but his grammar and pronunciation were extremely bad. He found it difficult to make out the meaning even of the simplest German poetry. On one occasion a version of Racine's *Iphigénie* was read to him. He held the French original in his hand; but was forced to own that, even with such help, he could not understand the translation. Yet though he had neglected his mother tongue in order to bestow all his attention on French, his French was, after all, the French of a foreigner. It was necessary for him to have always at his beck some men of letters from Paris to point out the solecisms and false rhymes, of which, to the last, he was frequently guilty. Even had he possessed the poetic faculty—of which, as far as we can judge, he was utterly destitute—the want of a language would have prevented him from being a great poet. No noble work of imagination, as far as we recollect, was ever composed by any man, except in a dialect which he had learned without remembering how or when; and which he had spoken with perfect ease before he had ever analysed its structure. Romans of great talents wrote Greek verses; but how many of those verses have deserved to live? Many men of eminent genius have, in modern times, written Latin poems; but, as far as we are aware, none of those poems, not even Milton's, can be ranked in the first class of art, or even very high in the second. It is not strange, therefore, that in the French verses of Frederic, we can find nothing beyond the reach of any man of good parts and industry—nothing above the level of Newdigate and Seatonian poetry. His best pieces may perhaps rank with the worst in Dodsley's collection. In history, he succeeded better. We do not, indeed, find in any part of his voluminous Memoirs, either deep reflection or vivid painting. But the narrative is distinguished by clearness, conciseness, good sense, and a certain air of truth and simplicity, which is singularly graceful in a man who, having done great things, sits down to relate them. On the whole, however, none of his writings are so agreeable to us as his Letters; particularly those which are written with earnestness, and are not embroidered with verses.

It is not strange that a young man devoted to literature, and acquainted only with the literature of France, should have looked with profound veneration on the genius of Voltaire. Nor is it just to condemn him for this feeling. 'A man who has never seen the sun,' says Calderon in one of his charming comedies, 'cannot be blamed for thinking that no glory can exceed that of the moon. A man who has seen neither moon nor sun, cannot be blamed for talking of the unrivalled brightness of the morning star.' Had Frederic been able to read Homer and Milton, or even Virgil and Tasso, his admiration of the *Henriade* would prove that he was utterly destitute of the power of discerning what is excellent in art. Had he been familiar with Sophocles or Shakspeare, we should have expected him to appreciate *Zaire* more justly. Had he been able to study Thucydides and Tacitus in the original Greek and Latin, he would have known that there were heights in the eloquence of history far beyond the reach of the author of the *Life of Charles the Twelfth.* But the finest heroic poem, several of the most powerful tragedies, and the most brilliant and picturesque historical work that Frederic had ever read, were Voltaire's. Such high and various excellence moved the young prince almost to adoration. The opinions of Voltaire on religious and philosophical questions had not yet been fully exhibited to the public. At a later period, when an exile from his country, and at open war with the Church, he spoke out. But when Frederic was at Rheinsberg, Voltaire was still a courtier; and, though he could not always curb his petulant wit, he had as yet published nothing that could exclude him from Versailles, and little that a divine of the mild and generous school of Grotius and Tillotson might not read with pleasure. In the *Henriade*, in *Zaire*, and in *Alzire*, Christian piety is exhibited in the most amiable form; and, some years after the period of which we are writing, a Pope condescended to accept the dedication of *Mahomet.* The real sentiments of the poet, however, might be clearly perceived by a keen eye through the decent disguise with which he veiled them, and could not escape the sagacity of Frederic, who held similar opinions, and had been accustomed to practise similar dissimulation.

The prince wrote to his idol in the style of a worshipper; and Voltaire replied with exquisite grace and address. A correspondence followed, which may be studied with advantage by those who wish to become proficients in the ignoble art of flattery. No man ever paid compliments better than Voltaire. His sweetest confectionary had always a delicate, yet stimulating flavour, which was delightful to palates wearied by the coarse preparations of inferior artists. It was only from his hand that so much sugar could be swallowed without making the swallower sick. Copies of verses, writing-desks, trinkets of amber, were exchanged between the friends. Frederic confided his writings to Voltaire ; and Voltaire applauded, as if Frederic had been Racine and Bossuet in one. One of his royal highness's performances was a refutation of 'the *Principe* of Machiavelli. Voltaire undertook to convey it to the press. It was entitled the *Anti-Machiavel*, and was an edifying homily against rapacity, perfidy, arbitrary government, unjust war—in short, against almost everything for which its author is now remembered among men.

The old King uttered now and then a ferocious growl at the diversions of Rheinsberg. But his health was broken ; his end was approaching ; and his vigour was impaired. He had only one pleasure left— that of seeing tall soldiers. He could always be propitiated by a present of a grenadier of six feet eight or six feet nine ; and such presents were from time to time judiciously offered by his son.

Early in the year 1740, Frederic William met death with a firmness and dignity worthy of a better and wiser man ; and Frederic, who had just completed his twenty-eighth year, became King of Prussia. His character was little understood. That he had good abilities, indeed, no person who had talked with him, or corresponded with him, could doubt. But the easy Epicurean life which he had led, his love of good cookery and good wine, of music, of conversation, of light literature, led many to regard him as a sensual and intellectual voluptuary. His habit of canting about moderation, peace, liberty, and the happiness which a good mind derives from the happiness of others, had imposed on some who should have known better. Those who thought best of him, expected a Telemachus after Fénélon's pattern. Others predicted the approach of a Medicean age—an age propitious to learning and art, and not unpropitious to pleasure. Nobody had the least suspicion that a tyrant of extraordinary military and political talents, of industry more extraordinary still, without fear, without faith, and without mercy, had ascended the throne.

The disappointment of Falstaff at his old boon-companion's coronation, was not more bitter than that which awaited some of the inmates of Rheinsberg. They had long looked forward to the accession of their patron, as to the day from which their own prosperity and greatness was to date. They had at last reached the promised land, the land which they had figured to themselves as flowing with milk and honey ; and they found it a desert. 'No more of these fooleries,' was the short, sharp admonition given by Frederic to one of them. It soon became plain that, in the most important points, the new sovereign bore a strong family likeness to his predecessor. There was a wide difference between the father and the son as respected extent and vigour of intellect, speculative opinions, amusements, studies, outward demeanour. But the groundwork of the character was the same in both. To both were common the love of order, the love of business, the military taste, the parsimony, the imperious spirit, the temper irritable even to ferocity, the pleasure in the pain and humiliation of others. But these propensities had in Frederic William partaken of the general unsoundness of his mind, and wore a very different aspect when found in company with the strong and cultivated understanding of his successor. Thus, for example, Frederic was as anxious as any prince could be about the efficacy of his army. But this anxiety never degenerated into a monomania, like that which led his father to pay fancy-prices for giants. Frederic was as thrifty about money as any prince or any private man ought to be. But he did not conceive, like his father, that it was worth while to eat unwholesome cabbages for the sake of saving four or five rixdollars in the year. Frederic was, we fear, as malevolent as his father ; but Frederic's wit enabled him often to show his malevolence in ways more decent than those to which his father resorted, and to inflict misery and degradation by a taunt instead of a blow. Frederic, it is true, by no means relinquished his hereditary privilege of kicking and cudgelling. His practice, however, as to that matter, differed in some important respects from his father's. To Frederic William, the mere circumstance that any persons whatever, men, women, or children, Prussians or foreigners, were within reach of his toes and of his cane, appeared to be a sufficient reason for proceeding to belabour them. Frederic required provocation as well as vicinity ; nor was he ever known to inflict this paternal species of correction on any but his born subjects ; though on one occasion M. Thiébault had reason, during a few seconds, to anticipate the high honour of being an exception to this general rule.

The character of Frederic was still very imperfectly understood either by his subjects or by his neighbours, when events occurred which exhibited it in a strong light. A few months after his accession died Charles VI., Emperor of Germany, the last descendant, in the male line, of the house of Austria.

Charles left no son, and had, long before his death, relinquished all hopes of male issue. During the latter part of his life, his principal object had been to secure to his descendants in the female line the many crowns of the house of Hapsburg. With this view, he had promulgated a new law of succession, widely celebrated throughout Europe under the name of the ' Pragmatic Sanction.' By virtue of this decree, his daughter, the Archduchess Maria Theresa, wife of Francis of Lorraine, succeeded to the dominions of her ancestors.

No sovereign has ever taken possession of a throne by a clearer title. All the politics of the Austrian cabinet had, during twenty years, being directed to one single end—the settlement of the succession. From every person whose rights could be considered as injuriously affected, renunciations in the most solemn form had been obtained. The new law had been ratified by the Estates of all the kingdoms and principalities which made up the great Austrian monarchy. England, France, Spain, Russia, Poland, Prussia, Sweden, Denmark, the Germanic body, had bound themselves by treaty to maintain the ' Pragmatic Sanction.' That Instrument was placed under the protection of the public faith of the whole civilized world.

Even if no positive stipulations on this subject had existed, the arrangement was one which no good man would have been willing to disturb. It was a peaceable arrangement. It was an arrangement acceptable to the great population whose happiness was chiefly concerned. It was an arrangement which made no change in the distribution of power among the states of Christendom. It was an arrangement which could be set aside only by means of a general war ; and, if it were set aside, the effect would be, that the equilibrium of Europe would be deranged, that the loyal and patriotic feelings of millions would be cruelly outraged, and that great provinces which had been united for centuries would be torn from each other by main force.

The sovereigns of Europe were, therefore, bound by every obligation which those who are intrusted with power · over their fellow-creatures ought to hold most sacred, to respect and defend the rights of the Archduchess. Her situation and her personal qualities were such as might be expected to move the mind of any generous man to pity, admiration, and chivalrous tenderness. She was in her twenty-fourth year. Her form was majestic, her features beautiful, her countenance sweet and animated, her voice musical, her deportment gracious and dignified. In all domestic relations she was without reproach. She was married to a husband whom she loved, and was on the point of giving birth to a child when death deprived her of her father. The loss of a parent, and the new cares of empire, were too much for her in the delicate state of her health. Her spirits were depressed, and her cheek lost its bloom.

Yet it seemed that she had little cause for anxiety. It seemed that justice, humanity, and the faith of treaties would have their due weight, and that the settlement so solemnly guaranteed would be quietly carried into effect. England, Russia, Poland, and Holland, declared in form their intention to adhere to their engagements. The French ministers made a verbal declaration to the same effect. But from no quarter did the young Queen of Hungary receive stronger assurances of friendship and support than from the King of Prussia.

Yet the King of Prussia, the ' Anti-Machiavel,' had already fully determined to commit the great crime of violating his plighted faith, of robbing the ally whom he was bound to defend, and of plunging all Europe into a long, bloody, and desolating war ; and all this for no end whatever, except that he might extend his dominions, and see his name in the gazettes. He determined to assemble a great army with speed and secrecy, to invade Silesia before Maria Theresa should be apprised of his design, and to add that rich province to his kingdom.

We will not condescend to refute at length the pleas which the compiler of the Memoirs before us has copied from Doctor Preuss. They amount to this—that the house of Brandenburg had some ancient pretensions to Silesia, and had in the previous century been compelled, by hard usage on the part of the Court of Vienna, to waive those pretensions. It is certain that, whoever might originally have been in the right, Prussia had submitted. Prince after prince of the house of Brandenburg had acquiesced in the existing arrangement. Nay, the Court of Berlin had recently been allied with that of Vienna, and had guaranteed the integrity of the Austrian states. Is it not perfectly clear, that if antiquated claims are to be set up against recent treaties and long possession, the world can never be at peace for a day? The laws of all nations have wisely established a time of limitation, after which titles, however illegitimate in their origin, cannot be questioned. It is felt by everybody, that to eject a person from his estate on the ground of some injustice committed in the time of the Tudors, would produce all the evils which result from arbitrary confiscation, and would make all property insecure. It concerns the commonwealth —so runs the legal maxim—that there be an end of litigation. And surely this maxim is at least equally applicable to the great commonwealth of states; for in that commonwealth litigation means the devastation of provinces, the suspension of trade and industry, sieges like those of Badajoz and St. Sebastian, pitched fields like those of Eylau and Borodino. We hold that the transfer of Norway from Denmark to Sweden was an unjustifiable proceeding; but would the king of Denmark be therefore justified in landing, without any new provocation, in Norway, and commencing military operations there? The king of Holland thinks, no doubt, that he was unjustly deprived of the Belgian provinces. Grant that it were so. Would he, therefore, be justified in marching with an army on Brussels? The case against Frederic was still stronger, inasmuch as the injustice of which he complained had been committed more than a century before. Nor must it be forgotten that he owed the highest personal obligations to the house of Austria. It may be doubted whether his life had not been preserved by the intercession of the prince whose daughter he was about to plunder.

To do the King justice, he pretended to no more virtue than he had. In Manifes-

toes he might, for form's sake, insert some idle stories about his antiquated claim on Silesia; but in his conversations and Memoirs he took a very different tone. To quote his own words: ' Ambition, interest, the desire of making people talk about me, carried the day; and I decided for war.'

Having resolved on his course, he acted with ability and vigour. It was impossible wholly to conceal his preparations; for throughout the Prussian territories regiments, guns, and baggage, were in motion. The Austrian envoy at Berlin apprised his court of these facts, and expressed a suspicion of Frederic's designs; but the ministers of Maria Theresa refused to give credit to so black an imputation on a young prince who was known chiefly by his high professions of integrity and philanthropy. 'We will not,'—they wrote— ' we cannot believe it.'

In the mean time the Prussian forces had been assembled. Without any declaration of war, without any demand for reparation, in the very act of pouring forth compliments and assurances of good-will, Frederic commenced hostilities. Many thousands of his troops were actually in Silesia before the Queen of Hungary knew that he had set up any claim to any part of her territories. At length he sent her a message which could be regarded only as an insult. If she would but let him have Silesia, he would, he said, stand by her against any power which should try to deprive her of her other dominions: as if he was not already bound to stand by her, or as if his new promise could be of more value than the old one !

It was the depth of winter. The cold was severe, and the roads deep in mire. But the Prussians passed on Resistance was impossible. The Austrian army was then neither numerous nor efficient. The small portion of that army which lay in Silesia, was unprepared for hostilities. Glogau was blockaded; Breslau opened its gates; Ohlau was evacuated. A few scattered garrisons still held out; but the whole open country was subjugated: no enemy ventured to encounter the king in the field; and, before the end of January, 1741, he returned to receive the congratulations of his subjects at Berlin.

Had the Silesian question been merely a question between Frederic and Maria Theresa, it would be impossible to acquit the Prussian king of gross perfidy. But when we consider the effects which his policy produced, and could not fail to produce, on the whole community of civilized nations, we are compelled to pronounce a condemnation still more severe. Till he began the war, it seemed possible, even probable, that the peace of the world would be preserved. The plunder of the great Austrian heritage was indeed a strong temptation; and in more than one cabinet ambitious schemes were already meditated. But the treaties by which the 'Pragmatic Sanction' had been guaranteed, were express and recent. To throw all Europe into confusion for a purpose clearly unjust, was no light matter. England was true to her engagements. The voice of Fleury had always been for peace. He had a conscience. He was now in extreme old age, and was unwilling, after a life which, when his situation was considered, must be pronounced singularly pure, to carry the fresh stain of a great crime before the tribunal of his God. Even the vain and unprincipled Belle-Isle, whose whole life was one wild daydream of conquest and spoliation, felt that France, bound as she was by solemn stipulations, could not, without disgrace, make a direct attack on the Austrian dominions. Charles, Elector of Bavaria, pretended that he had a right to a large part of the inheritance which the 'Pragmatic Sanction' gave to the Queen of Hungary; but he was not sufficiently powerful to move without support. It might, therefore, not unreasonably be expected, that after a short period of restlessness, all the potentates of Christendom would acquiesce in the arrangements made by the late Emperor. But the selfish rapacity of the King of Prussia gave the signal to his neighbours. His example quieted their sense of shame. His success led them to underrate the difficulty of dismembering the Austrian monarchy. The whole world sprang to arms. On the head of Frederic is all the blood which was shed in a war which raged during many years and in every quarter of the globe—the blood of the column of Fontenoy, the blood of the brave mountaineers who were slaughtered at Culloden. The evils produced by this wickedness were felt in lands where the name of Prussia was unknown; and, in order that he might rob a neighbour whom he had promised to defend, black men fought on the coast of Coromandel, and red men scalped each other by the Great Lakes of North America.

Silesia had been occupied without a battle; but the Austrian troops were advancing to the relief of the fortresses which still held out. In the spring Frederic rejoined his army. He had seen little of war, and had never commanded any great body of men in the field. It is not, therefore, strange that his first military operations showed little of that skill which, at a later period, was the admiration of Europe. What connoisseurs say of some pictures painted by Raphael in his youth, may be said of this campaign. It was in Frederic's early bad manner. Fortunately for him, the generals to whom he was opposed were men of small capacity. The discipline of his own troops, particularly of the infantry, was unequalled in that age; and some able and experienced officers were at hand to assist him with their advice. Of these, the most distinguished was Field-Marshal Schwerin—a brave adventurer of Pomeranian extraction, who had served half the governments in Europe, had borne the commissions of the States-General of Holland and of the Duke of Mecklenburg, and fought under Marlborough at Blenheim, and had been with Charles the Twelfth at Bender.

Frederic's first battle was fought at Molwitz; and never did the career of a great commander open in a more inauspicious manner. His army was victorious. Not only, however, did he not establish his title to the character of an able general, but he was so unfortunate as to make it doubtful whether he possessed the vulgar courage of a soldier. The cavalry, which he commanded in person, was put to flight. Unaccustomed to the tumult and carnage of a field of battle, he lost his self-possession, and listened too readily to those who urged him to save himself. His English grey carried him many miles from the field, while Schwerin, though wounded in two places, manfully upheld the day. The skill of the old Field-Marshal and the steadiness of the Prussian battalions prevailed; and the Austrian army was driven from the field with the loss of eight thousand men.

The news was carried late at night to a mill in which the king had taken shelter. It gave him a bitter pang. He was successful; but he owed his success to dispositions which others had made, and to the valour of men who had fought while he was flying. So unpromising was the first appearance of the greatest warrior of that age!

The battle of Molwitz was the signal for a general explosion throughout Europe. Bavaria took up arms. France, not yet declaring herself a principal in the war, took part in it as an ally of Bavaria. The two great statesmen to whom mankind had owed many years of tranquillity, disappeared about this time from the scene; but not till they had both been guilty of the weakness of sacrificing their sense of justice and their love of peace in the vain hope of preserving their power. Fleury, sinking under age and infirmity, was borne down by the impetuosity of Belle-Isle. Walpole retired from the service of his ungrateful country to his woods and paintings at Houghton; and his power devolved on the daring and eccentric Carteret. As were the ministers, so were the nations. Thirty years during which Europe had, with few interruptions, enjoyed repose, had prepared the public mind for great military efforts. A new generation had grown up, which could not remember the siege of Turin or the slaughter of Malplaquet; which knew war by nothing but its trophies; and which, while it looked with pride on the tapestries at Blenheim, or the statue in the 'Place of Victories,' little thought by what privations, by what waste of private fortunes, by how many bitter tears, conquests must be purchased.

For a time fortune seemed adverse to the Queen of Hungary. Frederic invaded Moravia. The French and Bavarians penetrated into Bohemia, and were there joined by the Saxons. Prague was taken. The Elector of Bavaria was raised by the suffrages of his colleagues to the Imperial throne—a throne which the practice of centuries had almost entitled the House of Austria to regard as a hereditary possession.

Yet was the spirit of the haughty daughter of the Cæsars unbroken. Hungary was still hers by an unquestionable title; and although her ancestors had found Hungary the most mutinous of all their kingdoms, she resolved to trust herself to the fidelity of a people, rude indeed, turbulent, and impatient of oppression, but brave, generous, and simplehearted. In the midst of distress and peril she had given birth to a son, afterwards the Emperor Joseph the Second. Scarcely had she risen from her couch, when she hastened to Presburg. There, in the sight of an innumerable multitude, she was crowned with the crown and robed with the robe of St. Stephen. No spectator could restrain his tears when the beautiful young mother, still weak from child-bearing, rode, after the fashion of her fathers, up the Mount of Defiance, unsheathed the ancient sword of state, shook it towards north and south, east and west, and, with a glow on her pale face, challenged the four corners of the world to dispute her rights and those of her boy. At the first sitting of the Diet she appeared clad in deep mourning for her father, and in pathetic and dignified words implored her people to support her just cause. Magnates and deputies sprang up, half drew their sabres, and with eager voices vowed to stand by her with their lives and fortunes. Till then, her firmness had never once forsaken her before the public eye, but at that shout she sank down upon her throne, and wept aloud. Still more touching was the sight when, a few days later, she came again before the Estates of her realm, and held up before them the little Archduke in her arms. Then it was that the enthusiasm of Hungary broke forth into that war-cry which soon resounded throughout Europe, 'Let us die for our King, Maria Theresa!'

In the mean time, Frederic was meditating a change of policy. He had no wish to raise France to supreme power on the Continent, at the expense of the house of Hapsburg. His first object was, to rob the Queen of Hungary. His second was, that, if possible, nobody should rob her but himself. He had entered into engagements with the powers leagued against Austria; but these engagements were in his estimation of no more force than the guarantee formerly given to the 'Pragmatic Sanction.' His game now was to secure his share of the plunder by betraying his accomplices. Maria Theresa was little inclined to listen to any such compromise; but the English government represented to her so strongly the necessity of buying off so formidable an enemy as Frederic, that she agreed to negotiate. The negotiation would not, however, have ended in a treaty, had not the arms of Frederic been crowned with a second victory. Prince Charles of Lorraine, brother-in-law to Maria Theresa, a bold and active, though unfortunate general, gave battle to the Prussians at Chotusitz, and was defeated. The king was still only a learner of the military art. He acknowledged, at a later period, that his success on this occasion was to be attributed, not at all to his own generalship, but solely to the valour and steadiness of his troops. He completely effaced, however, by his courage and energy, the stain which Molwitz had left on his reputation.

A peace concluded under the English mediation, was the fruit of this battle. Maria Theresa ceded Silesia; Frederic abandoned his allies : Saxony followed his example ; and the Queen was left at liberty to turn her whole force against France and Bavaria. She was everywhere triumphant. The French were compelled to evacuate Bohemia, and with difficulty effected their escape. The whole line of their retreat might be tracked by the corpses of thousands who had died of cold, fatigue and hunger. Many of those who reached their country carried with them the seeds of death. Bavaria was overrun by bands of ferocious warriors from that bloody ' debatable land,' which lies on the frontier between Christendom and Islam. The terrible names of the Pandoor, the Croat, and the Hussar, then first became familiar to western Europe. The unfortunate Charles of Bavaria, vanquished by Austria, betrayed by Prussia, driven from his hereditary states, and neglected by his allies, was hurried by shame and remorse to an untimely end. An English army appeared in the heart of Germany, and defeated the French at Dettingen. The Austrian captains already began to talk of completing the work of Marlborough and Eugene, and of compelling France to relinquish Alsace and the Three Bishoprics.

The Court of Versailles, in this peril, looked to Frederic for help He had been guilty of two great treasons, perhaps he might be induced to commit a third. The Duchess of Chateauroux then held the chief influence over the feeble Louis. She determined to send an agent to Berlin, and Voltaire was selected for the mission. He eagerly undertook the task; for, while his literary fame filled all Europe, he was troubled with a childish craving for political distinction. He was vain, and not without reason, of his address, and of his insinuating eloquence ; and he flattered himself that he possessed boundless influence over the King of Prussia. The truth was, that he knew, as yet, only one corner of Frederic's character. He was well acquainted with all the petty vanities and affectations of the poetaster ; but was not aware that these foibles were united with all the talents and vices which lead to success in active life; and that the unlucky versifier who bored him with reams of middling Alexandrians, was the most vigilant, suspicious, and severe of politicians.

Voltaire was received with every mark of respect and friendship, was lodged in the palace, and had a s' at daily at the royal table. The negotiation was of an extraordinary description. Nothing can be conceived more whimsical than the conferences which took place between the first literary man and the first practical man of the age, whom a strange weakness had induced to exchange their parts. The great poet would talk of nothing but treaties and guarantees, and the great king of nothing but metaphors and rhymes. On one occasion Voltaire put into his Majesty's hand a paper on the state of Europe, and received it back with verses scrawled on the margin. In secret they both laughed at each other. Voltaire did not spare the king's poems; and the king has left on record his opinion of Voltaire's diplomacy. ' He had no credentials,' says Frederic, ' and the whole mission was a joke, a mere farce.'

But what the influence of Voltaire could not effect, the rapid progress of the Austrian arms effected. If it should be in the power of Maria Theresa and George the Second to dictate terms of peace to France, what chance was there that Prussia would long retain Silesia ? Frederic's conscience told him that he had acted perfidiously and inhumanly towards the Queen of Hungary. That her resentment was strong she had given ample proof; and of her respect for treaties he judged by his own. Guarantees, he said, were mere filigree, pretty to look at, but too brittle to bear the slightest pressure. He thought it his safest course to ally himself closely to France, and again to attack the Empress Queen. Accordingly, in the autumn of 1744, without notice, without any decent pretext, he recommenced hostilities, marched through the electorate of Saxony without troubling himself about the permission of the Elector, invaded Bohemia, took Prague, and even menaced Vienna.

It was now that, for the first time, he experienced the inconstancy of fortune. An Austrian army under Charles of Lorraine threatened his communications with Silesia. Saxony was all in arms behind him. He found it necessary to save himself by a retreat. He afterwards owned that his failure was the natural effect of his own blunders. No general, he said, had ever committed greater faults. It must be added, that to the reverses of this campaign he always ascribed his subsequent successes. It was in the midst of difficulty and disgrace that he caught the first clear glimpse of the principles of the military art.

The memorable year 1745 followed. The war raged by sea and land, in Italy, in Germany, and in Flanders; and even England, after many years of profound internal quiet, saw, for the last time, hostile armies set in battle array against each other. This year is memorable in the life of Frederic, as the date at which his noviciate in the art of war may be said to have terminated. There have been great captains whose precocious and self-taught military skill resembled intuition. Condé, Clive, and Napoleon are examples. But Frederic was not one of these brilliant portents. His proficiency in military science was simply the proficiency which a man of vigorous faculties makes in any science to which he applies his mind with earnestness and industry. It was at Hohenfreidberg that he first proved how much he had profited by his errors, and by their consequences. His victory on that day was chiefly due to his skilful dispositions, and convinced Europe that the prince who, a few years before, had stood aghast in the rout of Molwitz, had attained in the military art a mastery equalled by none of his contemporaries, or equalled by Saxe alone. The victory of Hohenfreidberg was speedily followed by that of Sorr.

In the mean time, the arms of France had been victorious in the Low Countries. Frederic had no longer reason to fear that Maria Theresa would be able to give law to Europe, and he began to meditate a fourth breach of his engagements. The court of Versailles was alarmed and mortified. A letter of earnest expostulation, in the handwriting of Louis, was sent to Berlin; but in vain. In the autumn of 1745, Frederic made peace with England, and, before the close of the year, with Austria also. The pretensions of Charles of Bavaria could present no obstacle to an accommodation. That unhappy prince was no more; and Francis of Lorraine, the husband of Maria Theresa, was raised, with the general consent of the Germanic body, to the Imperial throne.

Prussia was again at peace; but the European war lasted till, in the year 1748, it was terminated by the treaty of Aix-la-Chapelle. Of all the powers that had taken part in it, the only gainer was Frederic. Not only had he added to his patrimony the fine province of Silesia; he

had, by his unprincipled dexterity, succeeded so well in alternately depressing the scale of Austria and that of France, that he was generally regarded as holding the balance of Europe—a high dignity for one who ranked lowest among kings, and whose great-grandfather had been no more than a Margrave. By the public, the King of Prussia was considered as a politician destitute alike of morality and decency, insatiably rapacious, and shamelessly false; nor was the public much in the wrong. He was at the same time allowed to be a man of parts,—a rising general, a shrewd negotiator and administrator. Those qualities wherein he surpassed all mankind, were as yet unknown to others or to himself; for they were qualities which shine out only on a dark ground. His career had hitherto, with little interruption, been prosperous; and it was only in adversity, in adversity which seemed without hope or resource, in adversity that would have overwhelmed even men celebrated for strength of mind, that his real greatness could be shown.

He had from the commencement of his reign applied himself to public business after a fashion unknown among kings. Louis XIV., indeed, had been his own prime minister, and had exercised a general superintendence over all the departments of the government; but this was not sufficient for Frederic. He was not content with being his own prime minister—he would be his own sole minister. Under him there was no room, not merely for a Richelieu or a Mazarin, but for a Colbert, a Louvois, or a Torcy. A love of labour for its own sake, a restless and insatiable longing to dictate, to intermeddle, to make his power felt, a profound scorn and distrust of his fellow creatures, indisposed him to ask counsel, to confide important secrets, to delegate ample powers. The highest functionaries under his government were mere clerks, and were not so much trusted by him as valuable clerks are often trusted by the heads of departments. He was his own treasurer, his own commander-in-chief, his own intendant of public works; his own minister for trade and justice, for home affairs and foreign affairs; his own master of the horse, steward, and chamberlain. Matters of which no chief of an office in any other government would ever hear, were in this singular monarchy, decided by the King in person. If a traveller wished for a good place to see a review, he had to write to Frederic, and received next day, from a royal messenger, Frederic's answer signed by Frederic's own hand. This was an extravagant, a morbid activity. The public business would assuredly have been better done if each department had been put under a man of talents and integrity, and if the King had contented himself with a general control. In this manner the advantages which belong to unity of design, and the advantages which belong to the division of labour, would have been to a great extent combined But such a system would not have suited the peculiar temper of Frederic. He could tolerate no will, no reason in the state, save his own. He wished for no abler assistance than that of penmen who had just understanding enough to translate, to transcribe, to make out his scrawls, and to put his concise Yes and No into an official form. Of the higher intellectual faculties, there is as much in a copying machine, or a lithographic press, as he required from a secretary of the cabinet.

His own exertions were such as were hardly to be expected from a human body, or a human mind. At Potsdam, his ordinary residence, he rose at three in summer and four in winter. A page soon appeared, with a large basketful of all the letters which had arrived for the King by the last courier—despatches from ambassadors, reports from officers of revenue, plans of buildings, proposals for draining marshes, complaints from persons who thought themselves aggrieved, applications from persons who wanted titles, military commissions, and civil situations. He examined the seals with a keen eye; for he was never for a moment free from the suspicion that some fraud might be practised on him. Then he read the letters, divided them into several packets, and signified his pleasure, generally by a mark, often by two or three words, now and then by some cutting epigram. By eight he had generally finished this part of his task. The adjutant-general was then in attendance, and received instructions for the day as to all the military arrangements of the kingdom. Then the King went to review his guards, not as kings ordinarily review their guards, but with the minute attention and severity of an old drill-sergeant. In the mean time the four cabinet secretaries had been employed in answering the letters on which the King had that morning signified his will. These unhappy men were forced to work all the year round like negro-slaves in the time of the sugar-crop. They never had a holiday. They never knew what it was to dine. It was necessary that, before they stirred, they should finish the whole of their work. The King, always on his guard against treachery, took from the heap a handful at random, and looked into them to see whether his instructions had been exactly followed. This was no bad security against foul play on the part of the secretaries; for if one of them were detected in a trick, he might think himself fortunate if he escaped with five years of imprisonment in a dungeon. Frederic then signed the replies, and all were sent off the same evening.

The general principles on which this strange government was conducted, deserve attention. The policy of Frederic was essentially the same as his father's; but Frederic, while he carried that policy to lengths to which his father never thought of carrying it, cleared it at the same time from the absurdities with which his father had encumbered it. The King's first object was to have a great, efficient, and well-trained army. He had a kingdom which in extent and population was hardly in the second rank of European powers; and yet he aspired to a place not inferior to that of the sovereigns of England, France, and Austria. For that end it was necessary that Prussia should be all sting. Louis XV., with five times as many subjects as Frederic, and more than five times as large a revenue, had not a more formidable army. The proportion which the soldiers in Prussia bore to the people, seems hardly credible. Of the males in the vigour of life, a seventh part were probably under arms; and this great force had, by drilling, by reviewing, and by the unsparing use of cane and scourge, been taught to perform all evolutions with a rapidity and a precision which would have astonished Villars or Eugene. The elevated feelings which are necessary to the best kind of army were then wanting to the Prussian service. In those ranks were not found the religious and political enthusiasm which inspired the pikemen of Cromwell—the patriotic ardour, the thirst of glory, the devotion to a great leader, which inflamed the Old Guard of Napoleon. But in all the mechanical parts of the military calling, the Prussians were as superior to the English and French troops of that day, as the English and French troops to a rustic militia.

Though the pay of the Prussian soldier was small, though every rixdollar of ex traordinary charge was scrutinized by Frederic with a vigilance and suspicion such as Mr. Joseph Hume never brought to the examination of an army-estimate, the expense of such an establishment was, for the means of the country, enormous. In order that it might not be utterly ruinous, it was necessary that every other expense should be cut down to the lowest possible point. Accordingly Frederic, though his dominions bordered on the sea, had no navy. He neither had nor wished to have colonies. His judges, his fiscal officers, were meanly paid. His ministers at foreign courts walked on foot, or drove shabby old carriages till the axletrees gave way. Even to his highest diplomatic agents, who resided at London and Paris, he allowed less than a thousand pounds sterling a-year. The royal household was managed with a frugality unusual in the establishments of opulent subjects—unexampled in any other palace. The king loved good eating and drinking, and during great part of his life took pleasure in seeing his table surrounded by guests; yet the whole charge of his kitchen was brought within the sum of two thousand pounds sterling a-year. He examined every extraordinary item with a care which might be thought to suit the mistress of a boarding-house better than a great prince. When more than four rixdollars were asked of him for a hundred oysters, he stormed as if he had heard that one of his generals had sold a fortress to the Empress-Queen. Not a bottle of champagne was uncorked without his express order. The game of the royal parks and forests, a serious head of expenditure in most kingdoms, was to him a source of profit. The whole was farmed out; and though the farmers were almost ruined by their contract, the king would grant them no remission. His wardrobe consisted of one fine gala dress, which lasted him all his life; of two or three old coats fit for Monmouth Street, of yellow waistcoats soiled with snuff, and of huge boots embrowned by time. One taste alone sometimes allured him beyond the limits of parsimony, nay, even beyond the limits of prudence—the taste for building. In all other things his economy was such as we might call by a harsher name, if we did not reflect that his funds were drawn from a heavily taxed people, and that it was impossible for him, without excessive tyranny, to keep up at once a formidable army and a splendid court.

Considered as an administrator, Frederic had undoubtedly many titles to praise. Order was strictly maintained throughout his dominions. Property was secure. A great liberty of speaking and of writing was allowed. Confident in the irresistible strength derived from a great army, the king looked down on malecontents and libellers with a wise disdain; and gave little encouragement to spies and informers. When he was told of the disaffection of one of his subjects, he merely asked, ' How many thousand men can he bring into the field?' He once saw a crowd staring at something on a wall. He rode up, and found that the object of curiosity was a scurrilous placard against himself. The placard had been posted up so high that it was not easy to read it. Frederic ordered his attendants to take it down and put it lower. ' My people and I,' he said, ' have come to an agreement, which satisfies us both. They are to say what they please, and I am to do what I please.' No person would have dared to publish in London satires on George II. approaching to the atrocity of those satires on Frederic, which the booksellers at Berlin sold with impunity. One bookseller sent to the palace a copy of the most stinging lampoon that perhaps was ever written in the world, the ' Memoirs of Voltaire,' published by Beaumarchais, and asked for his majesty's orders. ' Do not advertise it in an offensive manner,' said the king; ' but sell it by all means. I hope it will pay you well ' Even among statesmen accustomed to the license of a free press such steadfastness of mind as this is not very common.

It is due also to the memory of Frederic to say, that he earnestly laboured to secure to his people the great blessing of cheap and speedy justice. He was one of the first rulers who abolished the cruel and absurd practice of torture. No sentence of death, pronounced by the ordinary tribunals, was executed without his sanction; and his sanction, except in cases of murder, was rarely given. Towards his troops he acted in a very different manner. Military offences were punished with such barbarous scourging, that to be shot was considered by the Prussian soldier as a secondary punishment. Indeed, the principle which pervaded Frederic's whole policy was this—that the more severely the army is governed, the safer it is to treat the rest of the community with lenity.

Religious persecution was unknown under his government—unless some foolish and unjust restrictions which lay upon the Jews may be regarded as forming an exception. His policy with respect to the Catholics of Silesia presented an honourable contrast to the policy which, under very similar circumstances, England long followed with respect to the Catholics of Ireland. Every form of religion and irreligion found an asylum in his states. The scoffer whom the parliaments of France had sentenced to a cruel death, was consoled by a commission in the Prussian service. The Jesuit who could show his face nowhere else—who in Britain was still subject to penal laws, who was prescribed by France, Spain, Portugal, and Naples, who had been given up even by the Vatican—found safety and the means of subsistence in the Prussian dominions.

Most of the vices of Frederic's administration resolve themselves into one vice —the spirit of meddling. The indefatigable activity of his intellect, his dictatorial temper, his military habits, all inclined him to this great fault. He drilled his people as he drilled his grenadiers. Capital and industry were diverted from their natural direction by a crowd of preposterous regulations. There was a monopoly of coffee, a monopoly of tobacco, a monopoly of refined sugar. The public money, of which the king was generally so sparing, was lavishly spent in ploughing bogs, in planting mulberry-trees amidst the sand, in bringing sheep from Spain to improve the Saxon wool, in bestowing prizes for fine yarn, in building manufactories of porcelain, manufactories of carpets, manufactories of hardware, manufactories of lace. Neither the experience of other rulers, nor his own, could ever teach him that something more than an edict and a grant of public money is required to create a Lyons, a Brussels, or a Birmingham.

For his commercial policy, however, there is some excuse. He had on his side illustrious examples and popular prejudice. Grievously as he erred, he erred in company with his age. In other departments his meddling was altogether without apology. He interfered with the course of justice as well as with the course of trade; and set up his own crude notions of equity against the law as expounded by the unanimous voice of the gravest magistrates. It never occurred to him that a body of men, whose lives were passed in adjudicating on questions of civil right, were more likely to form correct opinions on such questions than a prince whose attention was divided between a thousand objects, and who had probably never read a law-book through. The resistance opposed to him by the tribunals inflamed him to fury. He reviled his Chancellor. He kicked the shins of his Judges. He did not, it is true, intend to act unjustly. He firmly believed that he was doing right, and defending the cause of the poor against the wealthy. Yet this well-meant meddling probably did far more harm than all the explosions of his evil passions during the whole of his long reign. We could make shift to live under a debauchee or a tyrant; but to be ruled by a busy-body is more than human nature can bear.

The same passion for directing and regulating appeared in every part of the King's policy. Every lad of a certain station in life was forced to go to certain schools within the Prussian dominions. If a young Prussian repaired, though but for a few weeks, to Leyden or Gottingen for the purpose of study, the offence was punished with civil disabilities, and sometimes with confiscation of property. Nobody was to travel without the royal permission. If the permission were granted, the pocket-money of the tourist was fixed by royal ordinances. A merchant might take with him two hundred and fifty rixdollars in gold, a noble was allowed to take four hundred : for it may be observed, in passing, that Frederic studiously kept up the old distinction between the nobles and the community. In speculation, he was a French philosopher; but in action, a German prince. He talked and wrote about the privileges of blood in the style of Siêyes; but in practice no chapter in the empire looked with a keener eye to genealogies and quarterings.

Such was Frederic the Ruler. But there was another Frederic, the Frederic of Rheinsberg, the fiddler and flute-player, the poetaster and metaphysician. Amidst the cares of state the King had retained his passion for music, for reading, for writing, for literary society. To these amusements he devoted all the time he could snatch from the business of war and government; and perhaps more light is thrown on his character by what passed during his hours of relaxation, than by his battles or his laws.

It was the just boast of Schiller, that in his country no Augustus, no Lorenzo, had watched over the infancy of art. The rich and energetic language of Luther, driven by the Latin from the schools of pedants, and by the French from the palaces of kings, had taken refuge among the people. Of the powers of that language Frederic had no notion. He generally spoke of it, and of

those who used it, with the contempt of ignorance. His library consisted of French
books ; at his table nothing was heard but
French conversation.

The associates of his hours of relaxation
were, for the most part, foreigners. Britain
furnished to the royal circle two distinguished
men, born in the highest rank, and driven by
civil dissensions from the land to which,
under happier circumstances, their talents and
virtues might have been a source of strength
and glory. George Keith, Earl Marischal of
Scotland, had taken arms for the house of
Stuart in 1715, and his younger brother
James, then only seventeen years old, had
fought gallantly by his side. When all was
lost they retired together to the Continent,
roved from country to country, served under
many standards, and so bore themselves as to
win the respect and good-will of many who
had no love for the Jacobite cause. Their
long wanderings terminated at Potsdam ; nor
had Frederic any associates who deserved or
obtained so large a share of his esteem.
They were not only accomplished men, but
nobles and warriors, capable of serving him
in war and diplomacy, as well as of amusing
him at supper. Alone of all his companions
they appear never to have had reason to complain of his demeanour towards them. Some
of those who knew the palace best pronounced that the Lord Marischal was the only human being whom Frederic ever really loved.

Italy sent to the parties at Potsdam the ingenious and amiable Algarotti, and Bastiani,
the most crafty, cautious, and servile of Abbés. But the greater part of the society
which Frederic had assembled round him,
was drawn from France. Maupertuis had
acquired some celebrity by the journey which
he made to Lapland, for the purpose of ascertaining, by actual measurement, the shape
of our planet. He was placed in the Chair
of the Academy of Berlin, a humble imitation of the renowned academy of Paris.
Baculard D'Arnaud, a young poet, who was
thought to have given promise of great things,
had been induced to quit his country, and
to reside at the Prussian Court. The Mar-
quess D'Argens was among the King's favourite companions, on account, as it should seem,
of the strong opposition between their characters. The parts of D'Argens were good,
and his manners those of a finished French
gentleman ; but his whole soul was dissolved
in sloth, timidity, and self-indulgence. His
was one of that abject class of minds which
are superstitious without being religious.
Hating Christianity with a rancour which
made him incapable of rational inquiry : unable to see in the harmony and beauty of

the universe the traces of divine power and
wisdom, he was the slave of dreams and
omens ;—would not sit down to table with
thirteen in company ; turned pale if the salt
fell towards him ; begged his guests not to
cross their knives and forks on their plates ;
and would not for the world commence a
journey on Friday. His health was a subject
of constant anxiety to him. Whenever his
head ached, or his pulse beat quick, his dastardly fears and effeminate precautions were
the jest of all Berlin. All this suited the
King's purpose admirably. He wanted somebody by whom he might be amused, and
whom he might despise. When he wished
to pass half an hour in easy polished conversation, D'Argens was an excellent companion ; when he wanted to vent his spleen and
contempt, D'Argens was an excellent butt.

With these associates, and others of the
same class, Frederic loved to spend the time
which he could steal from public cares. He
wished his supper-parties to be gay and easy ;
and invited his guests to lay aside all restraint,
and to forget that he was at the head of a hundred and sixty thousand soldiers, and was absolute master of the life and liberty of all who
sat at meat with him. There was, therefore,
at these meetings the outward show of ease.
The wit and learning of the company were
ostentatiously displayed. The discussions on
history and literature were often highly interesting. But the absurdity of all the religions
known among men was the chief topic of conversation ; and the audacity with which doctrines and names venerated throughout Christendom were treated on these occasions,
startled even persons accustomed to the society of French and English free-thinkers. But
real liberty, or real affection, was in this brilliant society not to be found. Absolute kings
seldom have friends : and Frederic's faults
were such as, even where perfect equality
exists, make friendship exceedingly precarious. He had indeed many qualities, which,
on a first acquaintance, were captivating.
His conversation was lively ; his manners to
those whom he desired to please were even
caressing. No man could flatter with more
delicacy. No man succeeded more completely in inspiring those who approached him
with vague hopes of some great advantage
from his kindness. But under this fair exterior he was a tyrant—suspicious, disdainful,
and malevolent. He had one taste which
may be pardoned in a boy, but which, when
habitually and deliberately indulged by a man
of mature age and strong understanding, is
almost invariably the sign of a bad heart —
a taste for severe practical jokes. If a friend
of the king was fond of dress, oil was flung

over his richest suit. If he was fond of money, some prank was invented to make him disburse more than he could spare. If he was hypochondriacal, he was made to believe that he had the dropsy. If he had particularly set his heart on visiting a place, a letter was forged to frighten him from going thither. These things, it may be said, are trifles. They are so; but they are indications, not to be mistaken, of a nature to which the sight of human suffering and human degradation is an agreeable excitement.

Frederic had a keen eye for the foibles of others, and loved to communicate his discoveries. He had some talent for sarcasm, and considerable skill in detecting the sore places where sarcasm would be most acutely felt. His vanity, as well as his malignity, found gratification in the vexation and confusion of those who smarted under his caustic jests. Yet in truth his success on these occasions belonged quite as much to the king as to the wit. We read that Commodus descended, sword in hand, into the arena against a wretched gladiator, armed only with a foil of lead, and, after shedding the blood of the helpless victim, struck medals to commemorate the inglorious victory. The triumphs of Frederic in the war of repartee, were much of the same kind. How to deal with him was the most puzzling of questions To appear constrained in his presence was to disobey his commands, and to spoil his amusement. Yet if his associates were enticed by his graciousness to indulge in the familiarity of a cordial intimacy, he was certain to make them repent of their presumption by some cruel humiliation. To resent his affronts was perilous; yet not to resent them was to deserve and to invite them. In his view, those who mutinied were insolent and ungrateful; those who submitted, were curs made to receive bones and kickings with the same fawning patience. It is, indeed, difficult to conceive how anything short of the rage of hunger should have induced men to bear the misery of being the associates of the Great King. It was no lucrative post. His Majesty was as severe and economical in his friendships as in the other charges of his establishment, and as unlikely to give a rixdollar too much for his guests as for his dinners. The sum which he allowed to a poet or a philosopher, was the very smallest sum for which such poet or philosopher could be induced to sell himself into slavery; and the bondsman might think himself fortunate, if what had been so grudgingly given was not, after years of suffering, rudely and arbitrarily withdrawn.

Potsdam was, in truth, what it was called by one of its most illustrious inmates, the Palace of Alcina. At the first glance it seemed to be a delightful spot, where every intellectual and physical enjoyment awaited the happy adventurer. Every new comer was received with eager hospitality, intoxicated with flattery, encouraged to expect prosperity and greatness. It was in vain that a long succession of favourites who had entered that abode with delight and hope, and who, after a short term of delusive happiness, had been doomed to expiate their folly by years of wretchedness and degradation, raised their voices to warn the aspirant who approached the charmed threshold. Some had wisdom enough to discover the truth early, and spirit enough to fly without looking back; others lingered on to a cheerless and unhonoured old age. We have no hesitation in saying that the poorest author of that time in London, sleeping on a bulk, dining in a cellar, with a cravat of paper, and a skewer for a shirt-pin, was a happier man than any of the literary inmates of Frederic's Court.

But of all who entered the enchanted garden in the inebriation of delight, and quitted it in agonies of rage and shame, the most remarkable was Voltaire. Many circumstances had made him desirous of finding a home at a distance from his country. His fame had raised him up enemies. His sensibility gave them a formidable advantage over him. They were, indeed, contemptible assailants. Of all that they wrote against him, nothing has survived except what he has himself preserved. But the constitution of his mind resembled the constitution of those bodies in which the slightest scratch of a bramble, or the bite of a gnat, never fails to fester. Though his reputation was rather raised than lowered by the abuse of such writers as Fréron and Desfontaines—though the vengeance which he took on Fréron and Desfontaines was such, that scourging, branding, pillorying, would have been a trifle to it—there is reason to believe that they gave him far more pain than he ever gave them. Though he enjoyed during his own lifetime the reputation of a classic—though he was extolled by his contemporaries above all poets, philosophers, and historians—though his works were read with as much delight and admiration at Moscow and Westminster, at Florence and Stockholm, as at Paris itself, he was yet tormented by that restless jealousy which should seem to belong only to minds burning with the desire of fame, and yet conscious of impotence. To men of letters who could by no possibility be his rivals, he was, if they behaved well to him, not merely just, not merely courteous, but often a hearty friend and a munificent benefactor. But to every writer who rose to a celebrity approaching his own, he became either a disguised or an avowed enemy. He slyly depreciated Montesquieu and Buffon. He publicly, and with violent outrage, made war on Jean Jacques. Nor had he the art of hiding his feelings under the semblance of good-humour or of contempt. With all his great talents, and all his long experience of the world, he had no more self-command than a petted child or a hysterical woman. Whenever he was mortified, he exhausted the whole rhetoric of anger and sorrow to express his mortification. His torrents of bitter words—his stamping and cursing—his grimaces and his tears of rage—were a rich feast to those abject natures whose delight is in the agonies of powerful spirits and in the abasement of immortal names. These creatures had now found out a way of galling him to the very quick. In one walk, at least, it had been admitted by envy itself that he was without a living competitor. Since Racine had been laid among the great men whose dust made the holy precinct of Port-Royal holier, no tragic poet had appeared who could contest the palm with the author of *Zaire*, of *Alzire*, and of *Merope*. At length a rival was announced. Old Crébillon, who, many years before, had obtained some theatrical success, and who had long been forgotten, came forth from his garret in one of the meanest lanes near the Rue St. Antoine, and was welcomed by the acclamations of envious men of letters, and of a capricious populace. A thing called *Catiline*, which he had written in his retirement, was acted with boundless applause. Of this execrable piece it is sufficient to say, that the plot turns on a love affair, carried on in all the forms of Scudery, between Catiline, whose confidant is the Prætor Lentulus, and Tullia, the daughter of Cicero. The theatre resounded with acclamations. The king pensioned the successful poet; and the coffee-houses pronounced that Voltaire was a clever man, but that the real tragic inspiration, the celestial fire which glowed in Corneille and Racine, was to be found in Crébillon alone.

The blow went to Voltaire's heart. Had his wisdom and fortitude been in proportion to the fertility of his intellect, and to the brilliancy of his wit, he would have seen that it was out of the power of all the puffers and detractors in Europe to put *Catiline* above *Zaire;* but he had none of the magnanimous patience with which Milton and Bentley left their claims to the unerring judgment of time. He eagerly engaged in an undignified competition with Crébillon, and produced a series of plays on the same subjects which his rival had treated. These pieces were coolly received. Angry with the court, angry with the capital, Voltaire began to find pleasure in the prospect of exile. His attachment for Madame du Châtelet long prevented him from executing his purpose. Her death set him at liberty; and he determined to take refuge at Berlin.

To Berlin he was invited by a series of letters, couched in terms of the most enthusiastic friendship and admiration. For once the rigid parsimony of Frederic seemed to have relaxed. Orders, honourable offices, a liberal pension, a well-served table, stately apartments under a royal roof, were offered in return for the pleasure and honour which were expected from the society of the first wit of the age. A thousand louis were remitted for the charges of the journey. No ambassador setting out from Berlin for a court of the first rank, had ever been more amply supplied. But Voltaire was not satisfied. At a later period, when he possessed an ample fortune, he was one of the most liberal of men; but till his means had become equal to his wishes, his greediness for lucre was unrestrained either by justice or by shame. He had the effrontery to ask for a thousand louis more, in order to enable him to bring his niece, Madame Denis, the ugliest of coquettes, in his company. The indelicate rapacity of the poet produced its natural effect on the severe and frugal king. The answer was a dry refusal. 'I did not,' said his Majesty, 'solicit the honour of the lady's society.' On this, Voltaire went off into a paroxysm of childish rage. 'Was there ever such avarice? He has hundreds of tubs full of dollars in his vaults, and haggles with me about a poor thousand louis.' It seemed that the negotiation would be broken off; but Frederic, with great dexterity, affected indifference, and seemed inclined to transfer his idolatry to Baculard d'Arnaud. His Majesty even wrote some bad verses, of which the sense was, that Voltaire was a setting sun, and that Arnaud was rising. Good-natured friends soon carried the lines to Voltaire. He was in his bed. He jumped out in his shirt, danced about the room with rage, and sent for his passport and his post-horses. It was not difficult to foresee the end of a connection which had such a beginning.

It was in the year 1750 that Voltaire left the great capital, which he was not to see again till, after the lapse of nearly thirty years, he returned, bowed down by extreme old age, to die in the midst of a splendid and ghastly triumph. His reception in Prussia was such as might well have elated a less vain and excitable mind. He wrote to his friends at Paris, that the kindness and the attention with which he had been welcomed surpassed description—that the king was the most amiable of men—that Potsdam was the Paradise of philosophers. He was created chamberlain, and received, together with his gold key, the cross of an order, and a patent ensuring to him a pension of eight hundred pounds sterling a year for life. A hundred and sixty pounds a-year were promised to his niece if she survived him. The royal cooks and coachmen were put at his disposal. He was lodged in the same apartments in which Saxe had lived, when, at the height of power and glory, he visited Prussia. Frederic, indeed, stooped for a time even to use the language of adulation. He pressed to his lips the meagre hand of the little grinning skeleton, whom he regarded as the dispenser of immortal renown. He would add, he said, to the titles which he owed to his ancestors and his sword, another title, derived from his last and proudest acquisition. His style should run thus:—Frederic, King of Prussia, Margrave of Brandenburg, Sovereign Duke of Silesia, Possessor of Voltaire. But even amidst the delights of the honey-moon, Voltaire's sensitive vanity began to take alarm. A few days after his arrival, he could not help telling his niece, that the amiable king had a trick of giving a sly scratch with one hand while patting and stroking with the other. Soon came hints not the less alarming because mysterious. ' The supper parties are delicious. The king is the life of the company. But—I have operas and comedies, reviews and concerts, my studies and books. But—but—Berlin is fine, the princess charming, the maids of honour handsome. But '

———

This eccentric friendship was fast cooling. Never had there met two persons so exquisitely fitted to plague each other. Each of them had exactly the fault of which the other was most impatient; and they were, in different ways, the most impatient of mankind. Frederic was frugal, almost niggardly. When he had secured his plaything, he began to think that he had bought it too dear. Voltaire, on the other hand, was greedy, even to the extent of impudence and knavery; and conceived that the favourite of a monarch, who had barrels full of gold and silver laid up in cellars, ought to make a fortune which a receiver-general might envy. They soon discovered each other's feelings. Both were angry, and a war began, in which Frederic stooped to the part of Harpagon, and Voltaire to that of Scapin. It is humiliating to relate, that the great warrior and statesman gave orders that his guest's allowance of sugar

and chocolate should be curtailed. It is, if possible, a still more humiliating fact, that Voltaire indemnified himself by pocketing the wax-candles in the royal antechamber. Disputes about money, however, were not the most serious disputes of these extraordinary associates. The sarcasms of the king soon galled the sensitive temper of the poet. D'Arnaud and D'Argens, Guichard and La Métrie, might, for the sake of a morsel of bread, be willing to bear the insolence of a master; but Voltaire was of another order. He knew that he was a potentate as well as Frederic; that his European reputation, and his incomparable power of covering whatever he hated with ridicule, made him an object of dread even to the leaders of armies and the rulers of nations. In truth, of all the intellectual weapons which have ever been wielded by man, the most terrible was the mockery of Voltaire. Bigots and tyrants, who had never been moved by the wailing and cursing of millions, turned pale at his name. Principles unassailable by reason, principles which had withstood the fiercest attacks of power, the most valuable truths, the most generous sentiments, the noblest and most graceful images, the purest reputations, the most august institutions, began to look mean and loathsome as soon as that withering smile was turned upon them. To every opponent, however strong in his cause and his talents, in his station and his character, who ventured to encounter the great scoffer, might be addressed the caution which was given of old to the Archangel:—

' I forewarn thee, shun
His deadly arrow; neither vainly hope
To be invulnerable in those bright arms,
Though temper'd heavenly; for that fatal dint,
Save Him who reigns above, none can resist.'

We cannot pause to recount how often that rare talent was exercised against rivals worthy of esteem—how often it was used to crush and torture enemies worthy only of silent disdain—how often it was perverted to the more noxious purpose of destroying the last solace of earthly misery, and the last restraint on earthly power. Neither can we pause to tell how often it was used to vindicate justice, humanity, and toleration—the principles of sound philosophy, the principles of free government. This is not the place for a full character of Voltaire.

Causes of quarrel multiplied fast. Voltaire, who, partly from love of money, and partly from love of excitement, was always fond of stockjobbing, became implicated in transactions of at least a dubious character. The King was delighted at having such an opportunity to humble his guest; and bitter reproaches and complaints were exchanged. Voltaire, too, was soon at war with the other men of letters who surrounded the King; and this irritated Frederic, who, however, had himself chiefly to blame: for, from that love of tormenting which was in him a ruling passion, he perpetually lavished extravagant praises on small men and bad books, merely in order that he might enjoy the mortification and rage which on such occasions Voltaire took no pains to conceal. His majesty, however, soon had reason to regret the pains which he had taken to kindle jealousy among the members of his household. The whole palace was in a ferment with literary intrigues and cabals. It was to no purpose that the imperial voice, which kept a hundred and sixty thousand soldiers in order, was raised to quiet the contention of the exasperated wits. It was far easier to stir up such a storm than to lull it. Nor was Frederic, in his capacity of wit, by any means without his own share of vexations. He had sent a large quantity of verses to Voltaire, and requested that they might be returned, with remarks and correction. 'See,' exclaimed Voltaire, 'what a quantity of his dirty linen the King has sent me to wash!' Talebearers were not wanting to carry the sarcasm to the royal ear; and Frederic was as much incensed as a Grub Street writer who had found his name in the 'Dunciad.'

This could not last. A circumstance which, when the mutual regard of the friends was in its first glow, would merely have been matter for laughter, produced a violent explosion. Maupertuis enjoyed as much of Frederic's good-will as any man of letters. He was President of the Academy of Berlin; and stood second to Voltaire, though at an immense distance, in the literary society which had been assembled at the Prussian court. Frederic had, by playing for his own amusement on the feelings of the two jealous and vainglorious Frenchmen, succeeded in producing a bitter enmity between them. Voltaire resolved to set his mark, a mark never to be effaced, on the forehead of Maupertuis; and wrote the exquisitely ludicrous diatribe of *Doctor Akakia.* He showed this little piece to Frederic, who had too much taste and too much malice not to relish such delicious pleasantry. In truth, even at this time of day, it is not easy for any person who has the least perception of the ridiculous to read the jokes on the Latin city, the Patagonians, and the hole to the centre of the earth, without laughing till he cries. But though Frederic was diverted by this charming pasquinade, he was unwilling that it should get

abroad. His self-love was interested. He had selected Maupertuis to fill the Chair of his Academy. If all Europe were taught to laugh at Maupertuis, would not the reputation of the Academy, would not even the dignity of its royal patron, be in some degree compromised? The King, therefore, begged Voltaire to suppress his performance. Voltaire promised to do so, and broke his word. The diatribe was published, and received with shouts of merriment and applause by all who could read the French language. The King stormed. Voltaire, with his usual disregard of truth, protested his innocence, and made up some lie about a printer or an amanuensis. The King was not to be so imposed upon. He ordered the pamphlet to be burned by the common hangman, and insisted upon having an apology from Voltaire, couched in the most abject terms. Voltaire sent back to the King his cross, his key, and the patent of his pension. After this burst of rage, the strange pair began to be ashamed of their violence, and went through the forms of reconciliation. But the breach was irreparable; and Voltaire took his leave of Frederic for ever. They parted with cold civility; but their hearts were big with resentment. Voltaire had in his keeping a volume of the King's poetry, and forgot to return it. This was, we believe, merely one of the oversights which men setting out upon a journey often commit. That Voltaire could have meditated plagiarism is quite incredible. He would not, we are confident, for the half of Frederic's kingdom, have consented to father Frederic's verses. The King, however, who rated his own writings much above their value, and who was inclined to see all Voltaire's actions in the worst light, was enraged to think that his favourite compositions were in the hands of an enemy, as thievish as a daw and as mischievous as a monkey. In the anger excited by this thought, he lost sight of reason and decency, and determined on committing an outrage at once odious and ridiculous.

Voltaire had reached Frankfort. His niece, Madame Denis, came thither to meet him. He conceived himself secure from the power of his late master, when he was arrested by order of the Prussian resident. The precious volume was delivered up. But the Prussian agents had, no doubt, been instructed not to let Voltaire escape without some gross indignity. He was confined twelve days in a wretched hovel. Sentinels with fixed bayonets kept guard over him. His niece was dragged through the mire by the soldiers. Sixteen hundred dollars were extorted from him by his insolent jailers. It is absurd to say that this outrage is not to be attributed to the King. Was anybody punished for it? Was anybody called in question for it? Was it not consistent with Frederic's character? Was it not of a piece with his conduct on other similar occasions? Is it not notorious that he repeatedly gave private directions to his officers to pillage and demolish the houses of persons against whom he had a grudge—charging them at the same time to take their measures in such a way that his name might not be compromised? He acted thus towards Count Buhl in the Seven Years' War. Why should we believe that he would have been more scrupulous with regard to Voltaire?

When at length the illustrious prisoner regained his liberty, the prospect before him was but dreary. He was an exile both from the country of his birth and from the country of his adoption. The French government had taken offence at his journey to Prussia, and would not permit him to return to Paris; and in the vicinity of Prussia it was not safe for him to remain.

He took refuge on the beautiful shores of Lake Leman. There, loosed from every tie which had hitherto restrained him, and having little to hope or to fear from courts and churches, he began his long war against all that, whether for good or evil, had authority over man; for what Burke said of the Constituent Assembly, was eminently true of this its great forerunner. He could not build—he could only pull down—he was the very Vitruvius of ruin. He has bequeathed to us not a single doctrine to be called by his name—not a single addition to the stock of our positive knowledge. But no human teacher ever left behind him so vast and terrible a wreck of truths and falsehoods—of things noble and things base—of things useful and things pernicious. From the time when his sojourn beneath the Alps commenced, the dramatist, the wit, the historian, was merged in a more important character. He was now the patriarch, the founder of a sect, the chief of a conspiracy, the prince of a wide intellectual commonwealth. He often enjoyed a pleasure dear to the better part of his nature, the pleasure of vindicating innocence which had no other helper—of repairing cruel wrongs—of punishing tyranny in high places. He had also the satisfaction, not less acceptable to his ravenous vanity, of hearing terrified Capuchins call him the Antichrist. But whether employed in works of benevolence, or in works of mischief, he never forgot Potsdam and Frankfort; and he listened anxiously to every murmur which indicated that a tempest was gathering in Europe, and that his vengeance was at hand.

He soon had his wish. Maria Theresa had never for a moment forgotten the great wrong which she had received at the hand of Frederic. Young and delicate, just left an orphan, just about to be a mother, she had been compelled to fly from the ancient capital of her race; she had seen her fair inheritance dismembered by robbers, and of those robbers he had been the foremost. Without a pretext, without a provocation, in defiance of the most sacred engagements, he had attacked the helpless ally whom he was bound to defend. The Empress-Queen had the faults as well as the virtues which are connected with quick sensibility and a high spirit. There was no peril which she was not ready to brave, no calamity which she was not ready to bring on her subjects, or on the whole human race, if only she might once taste the sweetness of a complete revenge. Revenge, too, presented itself to her narrow and superstitious mind, in the guise of duty. Silesia had been wrested not only from the House of Austria, but from the Church of Rome.

The conqueror had indeed permitted his new subjects to worship God after their own fashion; but this was not enough. To bigotry it seemed an intolerable hardship that the Catholic Church, having long enjoyed ascendency, should be compelled to content itself with equality. Nor was this the only circumstance which led Maria Theresa to regard her enemy as the enemy of God. The profaneness of Frederic's writings and conversation, and the frightful rumours which were circulated respecting the immoralities of his private life, naturally shocked a woman who believed with the firmest faith all that her confessor told her; and who, though young and beautiful, though ardent in all her passions, though possessed of absolute power, had preserved her fame unsullied even by the breath of slander.

To recover Silesia, to humble the dynasty of Hohenzollern to the dust, was the great object of her life. She toiled during many years for this end, with zeal as indefatigable as that which the poet ascribes to the stately goddess who tired out her immortal horses in the work of raising the nations against Troy, and who offered to give up to destruction her darling Sparta and Mycenæ, if only she might once see the smoke going up from the palace of Priam. With even such a spirit did the proud Austrian Juno strive to array against her foe a coalition such as Europe had never seen. Nothing would content her but that the whole civilized world, from the White Sea to the Adriatic, from the Bay of Biscay to the pastures of the wild horses of Tanais, should be combined in arms against one petty state.

She early succeeded by various arts in obtaining the adhesion of Russia. An ample share of spoil was promised to the King of Poland; and that prince, governed by his favourite, Count Buhl, readily promised the assistance of the Saxon forces. The great difficulty was with France. That the Houses of Bourbon and of Hapsburg should ever cordially co-operate in any great scheme of European policy, had long been thought, to use the strong expression of Frederic, just as impossible as that fire and water should amalgamate. The whole history of the Continent, during two centuries and a half, had been the history of the mutual jealousies and enmities of France and Austria. Since the administration of Richelieu, above all, it had been considered as the plain policy of the Most Christian King to thwart on all occasions the Court of Vienna; and to protect every member of the Germanic body who stood up against the dictation of the Cæsars. Common sentiments of religion had been unable to mitigate this strong antipathy. The rulers of France, even while clothed in the Roman purple, even while persecuting the heretics of Rochelle and Auvergne, had still looked with favour on the Lutheran and Calvinistic princes who were struggling against the chief of the empire. If the French ministers paid any respect to the traditional rules handed down to them through many generations, they would have acted towards Frederic as the greatest of their predecessors acted towards Gustavus Adolphus. That there was deadly enmity between Prussia and Austria, was of itself a sufficient reason for close friendship between Prussia and France. With France, Frederic could never have any serious controversy. His territories were so situated, that his ambition, greedy and unscrupulous as it was, could never impel him to attack her of his own accord. He was more than half a Frenchman. He wrote, spoke, read nothing but French; he delighted in French society. The admiration of the French he proposed to himself as the best reward of all his exploits. It seemed incredible that any French government, however notorious for levity or stupidity, could spurn away such an ally.

The Court of Vienna, however, did not despair. The Austrian diplomatists propounded a new scheme of politics, which, it must be owned, was not altogether without plausibility. The great powers, according

to this theory, had long been under a delusion. They had looked on each other as natural enemies, while in truth they were natural allies. A succession of cruel wars had devastated Europe, had thinned the population, had exhausted the public resources, had loaded governments with an immense burden of debt; and when, after two hundred years of murderous hostility or of hollow truce, the illustrious Houses whose enmity had distracted the world sat down to count their gains, to what did the real advantage on either side amount? Simply to this, that they had kept each other from thriving. It was not the King of France, it was not the Emperor, who had reaped the fruits of the Thirty Years' War, of the War of the Grand Alliance, of the War of the Pragmatic Sanction. Those fruits had been pilfered by states of the second and third rank, which, secured against jealousy by their insignificance, had dexterously aggrandized themselves while pretending to serve the animosity of the great chiefs of Christendom. While the lion and tiger were tearing each other, the jackal had run off into the jungle with the prey. The real gainer by the Thirty Years' War had been neither France nor Austria, but Sweden. The real gainer by the War of the Grand Alliance had been neither France nor Austria, but Savoy. The real gainer by the War of the Pragmatic Sanction had been neither France nor Austria, but the upstart of Brandenburg. Of all these instances, the last was the most striking: France had made great efforts, added largely to her military glory, and largely to her public burdens; and for what end? Merely that Frederic might rule Silesia. For this and this alone one French army, wasted by sword and famine, had perished in Bohemia; and another had purchased, with floods of the noblest blood, the barren glory of Fontenoy. And this prince, for whom France had suffered so much, was he a grateful, was he even an honest ally? Had he not been as false to the Court of Versailles as to the Court of Vienna? Had he not played, on a large scale, the same part which, in private life, is played by the vile agent of chicane who sets his neighbours quarrelling, involves them in costly and interminable litigation, and betrays them to each other all round, certain that, whoever may be ruined, he shall be enriched? Surely the true wisdom of the great powers was to attack, not each other, but this common barrator, who, by inflaming the passions of both, by pretending to serve both, and by deserting both, had raised himself above the station to which he was born. The great object of

Austria was to regain Silesia; the great object of France was to obtain an accession of territory on the side of Flanders. If they took opposite sides, the result would probably be that, after a war of many years, after the slaughter of many thousands of brave men, after the waste of many millions of crowns, they would lay down their arms without having achieved either object; but, if they came to an understanding, there would be no risk, and no difficulty. Austria would willingly make in Belgium such cessions as France could not expect to obtain by ten pitched battles. Silesia would easily be annexed to the monarchy of which it had long been a part. The union of two such powerful governments would at once overawe the King of Prussia. If he resisted, one short campaign would settle his fate. France and Austria, long accustomed to rise from the game of war both losers, would, for the first time, both be gainers. There could be no room for jealousy between them. The power of both would be increased at once; the equilibrium between them would be preserved; and the only sufferer would be a mischievous and unprincipled buccanier, who deserved no tenderness from either.

These doctrines, attractive from their novelty and ingenuity, soon became fashionable at the supper-parties and in the coffee-houses of Paris, and were espoused by every gay marquis and every facetious abbé who was admitted to see Madame de Pompadour's hair curled and powdered. It was not, however, to any political theory that the strange coalition between France and Austria owed its origin. The real motive which induced the great continental powers to forget their old animosities and their old state maxims, was personal aversion to the King of Prussia. This feeling was strongest in Maria Theresa; but it was by no means confined to her. Frederic, in some respects a good master, was emphatically a bad neighbour. That he was hard in all his dealings, and quick to take all advantages, was not his most odious fault. His bitter and scoffing speech had inflicted keener wounds than his ambition. In his character of wit he was under less restraint than even in his character of ruler. Satirical verses against all the princes and ministers of Europe were ascribed to his pen. In his letters and conversation he alluded to the greatest potentates of the age in terms which would have better suited Collé, in a war of repartee with young Crébillon at Pelletier's table, than a great sovereign

speaking of great sovereigns. About women he was in the habit of expressing himself in a manner which it was impossible for the meekest of women to forgive; and, unfortunately for him, almost the whole Continent was then governed by women who were by no means conspicuous for meekness. Maria Theresa herself had not escaped his scurrilous jests; the Empress Elizabeth of Russia knew that her gallantries afforded him a favourite theme for ribaldry and invective; Madame de Pompadour, who was really the head of the French government, had been even more keenly galled. She had attempted, by the most delicate flattery, to propitiate the King of Prussia, but her messages had drawn from him only dry and sarcastic replies. The Empress-Queen took a very different course. Though the haughtiest of princesses, though the most austere of matrons, she forgot in her thirst for revenge both the dignity of her race and the purity of her character, and condescended to flatter the low-born and low-minded concubine, who, having acquired influence by prostituting herself, retained it by prostituting others. Maria Theresa actually wrote with her own hand a note, full of expressions of esteem and friendship, to her dear cousin, the daughter of the butcher Poisson, the wife of the publican D'Etioles, the kidnapper of young girls for the *Parc-aux-cerfs*—a strange cousin for the descendant of so many Emperors of the West! The mistress was completely gained over, and easily carried her point with Louis, who had, indeed, wrongs of his own to resent. His feelings were not quick; but contempt, says the eastern proverb, pierces even through the shell of the tortoise; and neither prudence nor decorum had ever restrained Frederic from expressing his measureless contempt for the sloth, the imbecility, and the baseness of Louis. France was thus induced to join the coalition; and the example of France determined the conduct of Sweden, then completely subject to French influence.

The enemies of Frederick were surely strong enough to attack him openly; but they were desirous to add to all their other advantages the advantage of a surprise. He was not, however, a man to be taken off his guard. He had tools in every court; and he now received from Vienna, from Dresden, and from Paris, accounts so circumstantial and so consistent, that he could not doubt of his danger. He learnt that he was to be assailed at once by France, Austria, Russia, Saxony, Sweden, and the Germanic body; that the greater part of his dominions was to be portioned out amongst his enemies; that France, which from her geographical position could not directly share in his spoils, was to receive an equivalent in the Netherlands; that Austria was to have Silesia, and the Czarina East Prussia; that Augustus of Saxony expected Magdeburg; and that Sweden would be rewarded with part of Pomerania. If these designs succeeded, the house of Brandenburg would at once sink in the European system to a place lower than that of the Duke of Wurtemburg or the Margrave of Baden.

And what hope was there that these designs would fail? No such union of the continental powers had been seen for ages. A less formidable confederacy had in a week conquered all the provinces of Venice, when Venice was at the height of power, wealth, and glory. A less formidable confederacy had compelled Louis the Fourteenth to bow down his haughty head to the very earth. A less formidable confederacy has, within our own memory, subjugated a still mightier empire, and abased a still prouder name. Such odds had never been heard of in war. The people whom Frederic ruled were not five millions. The population of the countries which were leagued against him amounted to a hundred millions. The disproportion in wealth was at least equally great. Small communities, actuated by strong sentiments of patriotism or loyalty, have sometimes made head against great monarchies weakened by factions and discontents. But small as was Frederic's kingdom, it probably contained a greater number of disaffected subjects than were to be found in all the states of his enemies. Silesia formed a fourth part of his dominions; and from the Silesians, born under Austrian princes, the utmost that he could expect was apathy. From the Silesian Catholics he could hardly expect anything but resistance.

Some states have been enabled, by their geographical position, to defend themselves with advantage against immense force. The sea has repeatedly protected England against the fury of the whole Continent. The Venetian government, driven from its possessions on the land, could still bid defiance to the confederates of Cambray from the Arsenal amidst the lagoons. More than one great and well-appointed army, which regarded the shepherds of Switzerland as an easy prey, has perished in the passes of the Alps. Frederic had no such advantage. The form of his states, their situation, the nature of the ground, all were against him. His long, scattered, straggling territory, seemed to have been shaped with an express view to the convenience of invaders, and was protected by no sea, by no chain of hills. Scarcely any corner of it was a week's march from the territory of the enemy. The capital itself, in the event of war, would be constantly exposed to insult. In truth, there was hardly a politician or a soldier in Europe who doubted that the conflict would be terminated in a very few days by the prostration of the house of Brandenburg.

Nor was Frederic's own opinion very different. He anticipated nothing short of his own ruin, and of the ruin of his family. Yet there was still a chance, a slender chance, of escape. His states had at least the advantage of a central position; his enemies were widely separated from each other, and could not conveniently unite their overwhelming forces on one point. They inhabited different climates, and it was probable that the season of the year which would be best suited to the military operations of one portion of the league, would be unfavourable to those of another portion. The Prussian monarchy, too, was free from some infirmities which were found in empires far more extensive and magnificent. Its effective strength for a desperate struggle was not to be measured merely by the number of square miles or the number of people. In that spare but well-knit and well-exercised body, there was nothing but sinew, and muscle, and bone. No public creditors looked for dividends. No distant colonies required defence. No court, filled with flatterers and mistresses, devoured the pay of fifty battalions. The Prussian army, though far inferior in number to the troops which were about to be opposed to it, was yet strong out of all proportion to the extent of the Prussian dominions. It was also admirably trained and admirably officered, accustomed to obey and accustomed to conquer. The revenue was not only unincumbered by debt, but exceeded the ordinary outlay in time of peace. Alone of all the European princes, Frederic had a treasure laid up for a day of difficulty. Above all, he was one, and his enemies were many. In their camps would certainly be found the jealousy, the dissension, the slackness inseparable from coalitions; on his side was the energy, the unity, the secresy of a strong dictatorship. To a certain extent the deficiency of military means might be supplied by the resources of military art. Small as the king's army was, when compared with the six hundred thousand men whom the confederates could bring into the field, celerity of movement might in some degree compensate for deficiency of bulk. It was thus just possible that genius, judgment, resolution, and good-luck united, might protract the struggle during a campaign or two; and to gain even a month was of importance. It could not be long before the vices which are found in all extensive confederacies would begin to show themselves. Every member of the league would think his own share of the war too large, and his own share of the spoils too small. Complaints and recriminations would abound. The Turk might stir on the Danube; the statesmen of France might discover the error which they had committed in abandoning the fundamental principles of their national policy. Above all, death might rid Prussia of its most formidable enemies. The war was the effect of the personal aversion with which three or four sovereigns regarded Frederic; and the decease of any of those sovereigns might produce a complete revolution in the state of Europe.

In the midst of an horizon generally dark and stormy, Frederic could discern one bright spot. The peace which had been concluded between England and France in 1748, had been in Europe no more than an armistice; and had not even been an armistice in the other quarters of the globe. In India the sovereignty of the Carnatic was disputed between two great Mussulman houses; Fort Saint George had taken the one side, Pondicherry the other; and in a series of battles and sieges the troops of Lawrence and Clive had been opposed to those of Dupleix. A struggle less important in its consequences, but not less likely to produce immediate irritation, was carried on between those French and English adventurers, who kidnapped negroes and collected gold dust on the coast of Guinea. But it was in North America that the emulation and mutual aversion of the two nations were most conspicuous. The French attempted to hem in the English

colonists by a chain of military posts, extending from the Great Lakes to the mouth of the Mississippi. The English took arms. The wild aboriginal tribes appeared on each side mingled with the 'Pale Faces.' Battles were fought; forts were stormed; and hideous stories about stakes, scalpings, and death-songs reached Europe, and inflamed that national animosity which the rivalry of ages had produced. The disputes between France and England came to a crisis at the very time when the tempest which had been gathering was about to burst on Prussia. The tastes and interests of Frederic would have led him, if he had been allowed an option, to side with the house of Bourbon. But the folly of the Court of Versailles left him no choice. France became the tool of Austria, and Frederic was forced to become the ally of England. He could not, indeed, expect, that a power which covered the sea with its fleets, and which had to make war at once on the Ohio and the Ganges, would be able to spare a large number of troops for operations in Germany. But England, though poor compared with the England of our time, was far richer than any country on the Continent. The amount of her revenue, and the resources which she found in her credit, though they may be thought small by a generation which has seen her raise a hundred and thirty millions in a single year, appeared miraculous to the politicians of that age. A very moderate portion of her wealth, expended by an able and economical prince, in a country where prices were low, would be sufficient to equip and maintain a formidable army.

Such was the situation in which Frederic found himself. He saw the whole extent of his peril. He saw that there was still a faint possibility of escape; and, with prudent temerity, he determined to strike the first blow. It was in the month of August, 1756, that the great war of the Seven Years commenced. The king demanded of the Empress-Queen a distinct explanation of her intentions, and plainly told her that he should consider a refusal as a declaration of war. 'I want,' he said, 'no answer in the style of an oracle.' He received an answer at once haughty and evasive. In an instant, the rich electorate of Saxony was overflowed by sixty thousand Prussian troops. Augustus with his army occupied a strong position at Pirna. The Queen of Poland was at Dresden. In a few days Pirna was blockaded and Dresden was taken.

The first object of Frederic was to obtain possession of the Saxon State Papers; for those papers, he well knew, contained ample proofs that though apparently an aggressor, he was really acting in self-defence. The Queen of Poland, as well acquainted as Frederic with the importance of those documents, had packed them up, had concealed them in her bedchamber, and was about to send them off to Warsaw, when a Prussian officer made his appearance. In the hope that no soldier would venture to outrage a lady, a queen, the daughter of an emperor, the mother-in-law of a dauphin, she placed herself before the trunk, and at length sat down on it. But all resistance was vain. The papers were carried to Frederic, who found in them, as he expected, abundant evidence of the designs of the coalition. The most important documents were instantly published, and the effect of the publication was great. It was clear that, of whatever sins the king of Prussia might formerly have been guilty, he was now the injured party, and had merely anticipated a blow intended to destroy him.

The Saxon camp at Pirna was in the mean time closely invested; but the besieged were not without hopes of succour. A great Austrian army under Marshal Brown was about to pour through the passes which separate Bohemia from Saxony. Frederic left at Pirna a force sufficient to deal with the Saxons, hastened into Bohemia, encountered Brown at Lowositz, and defeated him. This battle decided the fate of Saxony. Augustus and his favourite, Buhl, fled to Poland. The whole army of the electorate capitulated. From that time till the end of the war, Frederic treated Saxony as a part of his dominions, or, rather, he acted towards the Saxons in a manner which may serve to illustrate the whole meaning of that tremendous sentence—*subjectos tanquam suos, viles tanquam alienos.* Saxony was as much in his power as Brandenburg; and he had no such interest in the welfare of Saxony as he had in the welfare of Brandenburg. He accordingly levied troops and exacted contributions throughout the enslaved province, with far more rigour than in any part of his own dominions. Seventeen thousand men who had been in the camp of Pirna were half compelled, half persuaded, to enlist under their conqueror. Thus, within a few weeks from the commencement of hostilities, one of the confederates had been disarmed, and his weapons pointed against the rest.

The winter put a stop to military operations. All had hitherto gone well. But the real tug of war was still to come. It was easy to foresee that the year 1757 would be a memorable era in the history of Europe.

The scheme for the campaign was simple, bold, and judicious. The Duke of Cumberland with an English and Hanoverian army was in Western Germany, and might be able to prevent the French troops from attacking Prussia. The Russians confined by their snows, would probably not stir till the spring was far advanced. Saxony was prostrated. Sweden could do nothing very important. During a few months Frederic would have to deal with Austria alone. Even thus the odds were against him. But ability and courage have often triumphed against odds still more formidable.

Early in 1757 the Prussian army in Saxony began to move. Through four defiles in the mountains they came pouring into Bohemia. Prague was his first mark; but the ulterior object was probably Vienna. At Prague lay Marshal Brown with one great army. Daun, the most cautious and fortunate of the Austrian captains, was advancing with another. Frederic determined to overwhelm Brown before Daun should arrive. On the sixth of May was fought, under those walls which, a hundred and thirty years before, had witnessed the victory of the Catholic league and the flight of the unhappy Palatine, a battle more bloody than any which Europe saw during the long interval between Malplaquet and Eylau. The King and Prince Ferdinand of Brunswick were distinguished on that day by their valour and exertions. But the chief glory was with Schwerin. When the Prussian infantry wavered, the stout old marshal snatched the colours from an ensign, and, waving them in the air, led back his regiment to the charge. Thus at seventy-two years of age, he fell in the thickest battle, still grasping the standard which bears the black eagle on the field argent. The victory remained with the King. But it had been dearly purchased. Whole columns of his bravest warriors had fallen. He admitted that he had lost eighteen thousand men. Of the enemy, twenty-four thousand had been killed, wounded, or taken.

Part of the defeated army was shut up

in Prague. Part fled to join the troops which, under the command of Daun, were now close at hand. Frederic determined to play over the same game which had succeeded at Lowositz. He left a large force to besiege Prague, and at the head of thirty thousand men he marched against Daun. The cautious Marshal, though he had a great superiority in numbers, would risk nothing. He occupied at Kolin a position almost impregnable, and awaited the attack of the King.

It was the 18th of June—a day which, if the Greek superstition still retained its influence, would be held sacred to Nemesis—a day on which the two greatest princes and soldiers of modern times were taught, by a terrible experience, that neither skill nor valour can fix the inconstancy of fortune. The battle began before noon; and part of the Prussian army maintained the contest till after the midsummer sun had gone down. But at length the King found that his troops, having been repeatedly driven back with frightful carnage, could no longer be led to the charge. He was with difficulty persuaded to quit the field. The officers of his personal staff were under the necessity of expostulating with him, and one of them took the liberty to say, 'Does your Majesty mean to storm the batteries alone?' Thirteen thousand of his bravest followers had perished. Nothing remained for him but to retreat in good order, to raise the siege of Prague, and to hurry his army by different routes out of Bohemia.

This stroke seemed to be final. Frederic's situation had at best been such, that only an uninterrupted run of good-luck could save him, as it seemed, from ruin. And now, almost in the outset of the contest, he had met with a check which, even in a war between equal powers, would have been felt as serious. He had owed much to the opinion which all Europe entertained of his army. Since his accession, his soldiers had in many successive battles been victorious over the Austrians. But the glory had departed from his arms. All whom his malevolent sarcasms had wounded, made haste to avenge themselves by scoffing at the scoffer. His soldiers had ceased to confide in his star. In every part of his camp his dispositions were severely criticised. Even in his own family he had detractors. His next brother William, heir-presumptive, or rather, in truth, heir-apparent to the throne, and great-grand-

father of the present king, could not refrain from lamenting his own fate and that of the house of Hohenzollern, once so great and so prosperous, but now, by the rash ambition of its chief, made a byword to all nations. These complaints, and some blunders which William committed during the retreat from Bohemia, called forth the bitter displeasure of the inexorable king. The prince's heart was broken by the cutting reproaches of his brother; he quitted the army, retired to a country seat, and in a short time died of shame and vexation.

It seemed that the king's distress could hardly be increased. Yet at this moment another blow not less terrible than that of Kolin fell upon him. The French under Marshal D'Estrées had invaded Germany. The Duke of Cumberland had given them battle at Hastembeck; and had been defeated. In order to save the Electorate of Hanover from entire subjugation, he had made, at Closter Severn, an arrangement with the French Generals, which left them at liberty to turn their arms against the Prussian dominions.

That nothing might be wanting to Frederic's distress, he lost his mother just at this time; and he appears to have felt the loss more than was to be expected from the hardness and severity of his character. In truth, his misfortunes had now cut to the quick. The mocker, the tyrant, the most rigorous, the most imperious, the most cynical of men, was very unhappy. His face was so haggard and his form so thin, that when on his return from Bohemia he passed through Leipsic, the people hardly knew him again. His sleep was broken; the tears, in spite of himself, often started into his eyes; and the grave began to present itself to his agitated mind as the best refuge from misery and dishonour. His resolution was fixed never to be taken alive, and never to make peace on condition of descending from his place among the powers of Europe. He saw nothing left for him except to die; and he deliberately chose his mode of death. He always carried about with him a sure and speedy poison in a small glass case; and to the few in whom he placed confidence, he made no mystery of his resolution.

But we should very imperfectly describe the state of Frederic's mind, if we left out of view the laughable peculiarities which contrasted so singularly with the gravity, energy, and harshness of his character. It is difficult to say whether the tragic or the comic predominated in the strange scene which was then acted. In the midst of all the great king's calamities, his passion for writing indifferent poetry grew stronger and stronger. Enemies all around him, despair in his heart, pills of corrosive sublimate hidden in his clothes, he poured forth hundreds upon hundreds of lines, hateful to gods and men—the insipid dregs of Voltaire's Hippocrene—the faint echo of the lyre of Chaulieu. It is amusing to compare what he did during the last months of 1757, with what he wrote during the same time. It may be doubted whether any equal portion of the life of Hannibal, of Cæsar, or of Napoleon, will bear a comparison with that short period, the most brilliant in the history of Prussia and of Frederic. Yet at this very time the scanty leisure of the illustrious warrior was employed in producing odes and epistles, a little better than Cibber's, and a little worse than Hayley's. Here and there a manly sentiment which deserves to be in prose, makes its appearance in company with Prometheus and Orpheus, Elysium and Acheron, the plaintive Philomel, the poppies of Morpheus, and all the other frippery which, like a robe tossed by a proud beauty to her waiting-woman, has long been contemptuously abandoned by genius to mediocrity. We hardly know any instance of the strength and weakness of human nature so striking, and so grotesque, as the character of this haughty, vigilant, resolute, sagacious blue-stocking, half Mithridates and half Trissotin, bearing up against a world in arms, with an ounce of poison in one pocket and a quire of bad verses in the other!

Frederic had some time before made advances towards a reconciliation with Voltaire; and some civil letters had passed between them. After the battle of Kolin their epistolary intercourse became, at least in seeming, friendly and confidential. We do not know any collection of Letters which throw so much light on the darkest and most intricate parts of human nature, as the correspondence of these strange beings after they had exchanged forgiveness. Both felt that the quarrel had lowered them in the public estimation. They admired each other. They stood in need of each other. The great King wished to be handed down to posterity by the great Writer. The great Writer felt himself exalted by the homage of the great King. Yet the wounds which they had inflicted on each other were too deep

to be effaced, or even perfectly healed. Not only did the scars remain; the sore places often festered and bled afresh.

The letters consisted for the most part of compliments, thanks, offers of service, assurances of attachment. But if any thing brought back to Frederic's recollection the cunning and mischievous pranks by which Voltaire had provoked him, some expression of contempt and displeasure broke forth in the midst of his eulogy. It was much worse when any thing recalled to the mind of Voltaire the outrages which he and his kinswoman had suffered at Frankfort. All at once his flowing panegyric is turned into invective. 'Remember how you behaved to me. For your sake I have lost the favour of my king. For your sake I am an exile from my country. I loved you. I trusted myself to you. I had no wish but to end my life in your service. And what was my reward? Stripped of all you had bestowed on me, the key, the order, the pension, I was forced to fly from your territories. I was hunted as if I had been a deserter from your grenadiers. I was arrested, insulted, plundered. My niece was dragged in the mud of Frankfort by your soldiers, as if she had been some wretched follower of your camp. You have great talents. You have good qualities. But you have one odious vice. You delight in the abasement of your fellow creatures. You have brought disgrace on the name of philosopher. You have given some colour to the slanders of the bigots, who say that no confidence can be placed in the justice or humanity of those who reject the Christian faith.' Then the King answers with less heat, but with equal severity—'You know that you behaved shamefully in Prussia. It was well for you that you had to deal with a man so indulgent to the infirmities of genius as I am. You richly deserved to see the inside of a dungeon. Your talents are not more widely known than your faithlessness and your malevolence. The grave itself is no asylum from your spite. Maupertuis is dead; but you still go on calumniating and deriding him, as if you had not made him miserable enough while he was living. Let us have no more of this. And, above all, let me hear no more of your niece. I am sick to death of her name. I can bear with your faults for the sake of your merits; but she has not written *Mahomet* or *Merope*.'

An explosion of this kind, it might be

supposed, would necessarily put an end to all amicable communication. But it was not so. After every outbreak of ill humour this extraordinary pair became more loving than before, and exchanged compliments and assurances of mutual regard with a wonderful air of sincerity.

It may well be supposed that men who wrote thus to each other, were not very guarded in what they said of each other. The English ambassador, Mitchell, who knew that the King of Prussia was constantly writing to Voltaire, with the greatest freedom on the most important subjects, was amazed to hear his majesty designate this highly favoured correspondent as a bad-hearted fellow, the greatest rascal on the face of the earth. And the language which the poet held about the king was not much more respectful.

It would probably have puzzled Voltaire himself to say what was his real feeling towards Frederic. It was compounded of all sentiments, from enmity to friendship, and from scorn to admiration; and the proportions in which these elements were mixed, changed every moment. The old patriarch resembled the spoiled child who screams, stamps, cuffs, laughs, kisses, and cuddles within one quarter of an hour. His resentment was not extinguished; yet he was not without sympathy for his old friend. As a Frenchman, he wished success to the arms of his country. As a philosopher, he was anxious for the stability of a throne on which a philosopher sat. He longed both to save and to humble Frederic. There was one way, and only one, in which all his conflicting feelings could at once be gratified. If Frederic were preserved by the interference of France, if it were known that for that interference he was indebted to the mediation of Voltaire, this would indeed be delicious revenge; this would indeed be to heap coals of fire on that haughty head. Nor did the vain and restless poet think it impossible that he might, from his hermitage near the Alps, dictate peace to Europe. D'Estrées had quitted Hanover, and the command of the French army had been entrusted to the Duke of Richelieu, a man whose chief distinction was derived from his success in gallantry. Richelieu was in truth the most eminent of that race of seducers by profession, who furnished Crébillon the younger and La Clos with models for their heroes. In his earlier days the royal

house itself had not been secure from his presumptuous love. He was believed to have carried his conquests into the family of Orleans; and some suspected that he was not unconcerned in the mysterious remorse which embittered the last hours of the charming mother of Louis the Fifteenth. But the Duke was now fifty years old. With a heart deeply corrupted by vice, a head long accustomed to think only on trifles, an impaired constitution, an impaired fortune, and worst of all, a very red nose, he was entering on a dull, frivolous, and unrespected old age. Without one qualification for military command, except that personal courage, which was common to him and the whole nobility of France, he had been placed at the head of the army of Hanover; and in that situation he did his best to repair, by extortion and corruption, the injury which he had done to his property by a life of dissolute profusion.

The Duke of Richelieu to the end of his life hated the philosophers as a sect—not for those parts of their system which a good and wise man would have condemned—but for their virtues, for their spirit of free inquiry, and for their hatred of those social abuses of which he was himself the personification. But he, like many of those who thought with him, excepted Voltaire from the list of proscribed writers. He frequently sent flattering letters to Ferney. He did the patriarch the honour to borrow money of him, and even carried his condescending friendship so far as to forget to pay interest. Voltaire thought that it might be in his power to bring the Duke and the King of Prussia into communication with each other. He wrote earnestly to both; and he so far succeeded that a correspondence between them was commenced.

But it was to very different means that Frederic was to owe his deliverance. At the beginning of November, the net seemed to have closed completely round him. The Russians were in the field, and were spreading devastation through his eastern provinces. Silesia was overrun by the Austrians. A great French army was advancing from the west under the command of Marshal Soubise, a prince of the great Armorican house of Rohan. Berlin itself had been taken and plundered by the Croatians. Such was the situation from which Frederic extricated himself, with dazzling glory, in the short space of thirty days.

He marched first against Soubise. On the fifth of November the armies met at Rosbach. The French were two to one; but they were ill-disciplined, and their general was a dunce. The tactics of Frederic, and the well-regulated valour of the Prussian troops, obtained a complete victory. Seven thousand of the invaders were made prisoners. Their guns, their colours, their baggage, fell into the hands of the conquerors. Those who escaped fled as confusedly as a mob scattered by cavalry. Victorious in the West, the king turned his arms towards Silesia. In that quarter everything seemed to be lost. Breslau had fallen; and Charles of Lorraine, with a mighty power, held the whole province. On the fifth of December, exactly one month after the battle of Rosbach, Frederic, with forty thousand men, and Prince Charles, at the head of not less than sixty thousand, met at Leuthen, hard by Breslau. The King, who was, in general, perhaps too much inclined to consider the common soldier as a mere machine, resorted, on this great day, to means resembling those which Bonaparte afterwards employed with such signal success for the purpose of stimulating military enthusiasm. The principal officers were convoked. Frederic addressed them with great force and pathos; and directed them to speak to their men as he had spoken to them. When the armies were set in battle array, the Prussian troops were in a state of fierce excitement; but their excitement showed itself after the fashion of a grave people. The columns advanced to the attack chanting, to the sound of drums and fifes, the rude hymns of the old Saxon Herrholds. They had never fought so well; nor had the genius of their chief ever been so conspicuous. 'That battle,' said Napoleon, 'was a masterpiece. Of itself it is sufficient to entitle Frederic to a place in the first rank among generals.' The victory was complete. Twenty-seven thousand Austrians were killed, wounded, or taken; fifty stand of colours, a hundred guns, four thousand waggons, fell into the hands of the Prussians. Breslau opened its gates; Silesia was reconquered; Charles of Lorraine retired to hide his shame and sorrow at Brussels; and Frederic allowed his troops to take some repose in winter quarters, after a campaign, to the vicissitudes of which it will be difficult to find any parallel in ancient or modern history.

The King's fame filled all the world. He had, during the last year, maintained a contest, on terms of advantage, against three powers, the weakest of which had more than three times his resources. He had fought four great pitched battles against superior forces. Three of these battles he had gained; and the defeat of Kolin, repaired as it had been, rather raised than lowered his military renown. The victory of Leuthen is, to this day, the proudest on the roll of Prussian fame. Leipsic indeed, and Waterloo, produced consequences more important to mankind. But the glory of Leipsic must be shared by the Prussians with the Austrians and Russians; and at Waterloo the British infantry bore the burden and heat of the day. The victory of Rosbach was, in a military point of view, less honourable than that of Leuthen; for it was gained over an incapable general and a disorganized army. But the moral effect which it produced was immense. All the preceding triumphs of Frederic had been triumphs over Germans, and could excite no emotions of national pride among the German people. It was impossible that a Hessian or a Hanoverian could feel any patriotic exultation at hearing that Pomeranians slaughtered Moravians, or that Saxon banners had been hung in the churches of Berlin. Indeed, though the military character of the Germans justly stood high throughout the world, they could boast of no great day which belonged to them as a people;—of no Agincourt, of no Bannockburn. Most of their victories had been gained over each other; and their most splendid exploits against foreigners had been achieved under the command of Eugene, who was himself a foreigner.

The news of the battle of Rosbach stirred the blood of the whole of the mighty population from the Alps to the Baltic, and from the borders of Courland to those of Lorraine. Westphalia and Lower Saxony had been deluged by a great host of strangers, whose speech was unintelligible, and whose petulant and licentious manners had excited the strongest feelings of disgust and hatred. That great host had been put to flight by a small band of German warriors, led by a prince of German blood on the side of father and mother, and marked by the fair hair and the clear blue eye of Germany. Never since the dissolution of the empire of Charlemagne, had the Teutonic race won such a field against the French. The tidings called forth a general burst of delight and pride from the whole of the great family which spoke the various dialects of the ancient language of Arminius. The fame of Frederic began to supply, in some degree, the place of a common government and of a common capital. It became a rallying point for all true Germans—a subject of mutual congratulation to the Bavarian and the Westphalian, to the citizen of Frankfort and the citizen of Nuremberg. Then first it was manifest that the Germans were truly a nation. Then first was discernible that patriotic spirit which, in 1813, achieved the great deliverance of central Europe, and which still guards, and long will guard, against foreign ambition the old freedom of the Rhine. Nor were the effects produced by that celebrated day merely political. The greatest masters of German poetry and eloquence have admitted that, though the great King neither valued nor understood his native language, though he looked on France as the only seat of taste and philosophy ; yet, in his own despite, he did much to emancipate the genius of his countrymen from the foreign yoke ; and that, in the act of vanquishing Soubise, he was, unintentionally, rousing the spirit which soon began to question the literary precedence of Boileau and Voltaire. So strangely do events confound all the plans of man. A prince who read only French, who wrote only French, who ranked as a French classic, became, quite unconsciously, the means of liberating half the Continent from the dominion of that French criticism, of which he was himself, to the end of his life, a slave. Yet even the enthusiasm of Germany in favour of Frederic, hardly equalled the enthusiasm of England. The birth-day of our ally was celebrated with as much enthusiasm as that of our own sovereign ; and at night the streets of London were in a blaze with illuminations. Portraits of the Hero of Rosbach, with his cocked hat and long pigtail, were in every house. An attentive observer will, at this day, find in the parlours of old-fashioned inns, and in the portfolios of print-sellers, twenty portraits of Frederic for one of George II. The sign-painters were everywhere employed in touching up Admiral Vernon into the King of Prussia. Some young Englishmen of rank proposed to visit Germany as volunteers, for the purpose of learning the art of war under the greatest of commanders. This last proof of British attachment and admiration, Frederic politely but firmly declined. His camp was no place for amateur students of military science. The Prussian discipline was rigorous even to cruelty. The officers, while in the field, were expected to practice an abstemiousness and self-denial such as was hardly surpassed by the most rigid monastic orders. However noble their birth, however high their rank in the service, they were not permitted to eat from anything better than pewter. It was a high crime even in a count and fieldmarshal to have a single silver spoon among his baggage. Gay young Englishmen of twenty thousand a-year, accustomed to liberty and to luxury, would not easily submit to these Spartan restraints. The King could not venture to keep them in order as he kept his own subjects in order. Situated as he was with respect to England, he could not well imprison or shoot refractory Howards and Cavendishes. On the other hand, the example of a few fine gentlemen, attended by chariots and livery servants, eating in plate, and drinking champagne and tokay, was enough to corrupt his whole army. He thought it best to make a stand at first, and civilly refused to admit such dangerous companions among his troops.

The help of England was bestowed in a manner far more useful and more acceptable. An annual subsidy of near seven hundred thousand pounds enabled the King to add probably more than fifty thousand men to his army. Pitt, now at the height of power and popularity, undertook the task of defending Western Germany against France, and asked Frederic only for the loan of a general. The general selected was Prince Ferdinand of Brunswick who had attained high distinction in the Prussian service. He was put at the head of an army, partly English, partly Hanoverian, partly composed of mercenaries hired from the petty princes of the empire. He soon vindicated the choice of the two allied courts, and proved himself the second general of the age.

Frederic passed the winter at Breslau, in reading, writing, and preparing for the next campaign. The havoc which the war had made among his troops was rapidly repaired ; and in the spring of 1758 he was again ready for the conflict. Prince Ferdinand kept the French in check. The King in the meantime, after attempting against the Austrians some operations which led to no very important result, marched to encounter the Russians, who, slaying, burning, and wasting wherever they turned, had penetrated into the heart of his realm. He gave them battle at Zorndorf, near Frankfort on the Oder. The fight was long and bloody. Quarter was neither given nor taken ; for the Germans and Scythians regarded each other with bitter aversion, and the sight of the ravages committed by the half savage invaders had incensed the King and his army. The Russians were overthrown with great slaughter, and for a few months no further danger was to be apprehended from the east.

A day of thanksgiving was proclaimed by the King, and was celebrated with pride and delight by his people. The rejoicings in England were not less enthusiastic or less sincere. This may be selected as the point of time at which the military glory of Frederic reached the zenith. In the short space of three-quarters of a year he had won three great battles over the armies of three mighty and warlike monarchies—France, Austria, and Russia.

But it was decreed that the temper of that strong mind should be tried by both extremes of fortune in rapid succession. Close upon this bright series of triumphs came a series of disasters, such as would have blighted the fame and broken the heart of almost any other commander. Yet Frederic, in the midst of his calamities, was still an object of admiration to his subjects, his allies, and his enemies. Overwhelmed by adversity, sick of life, he still maintained the contest—greater in defeat, in flight, and in what seemed hopeless ruin, than on the fields of his proudest victories.

Having vanquished the Russians, he hastened into Saxony to oppose the troops of the Empress-Queen, commanded by Daun, the most cautious, and Laudohn, the most inventive and enterprising of her generals. These two celebrated commanders agreed on a scheme, in which the prudence of the one and the vigour of the other seem to have happily combined. At dead of night they surprised the king in his camp at Hochkirchen. His presence of mind saved his troops from destruction; but nothing could save them from defeat and severe loss. Marshal Keith was among the slain. The first roar of the guns roused the noble exile from his rest, and he was instantly in the front of the battle. He received a dangerous wound, but refused to quit the field, and was in the act of rallying his broken troops, when an Austrian bullet terminated his chequered and eventful life.

The misfortune was serious. But of all generals Frederic understood best how to repair defeat, and Daun understood least how to improve victory. In a few days the Prussian army was as formidable as before the battle. The prospect was, however, gloomy. An Austrian army under General Harsch had invaded Silesia, and invested the fortress of Neisse. Daun, after his success at Hochkirchen, had written to Harsch in very confident terms:—' Go on with your operations against Neisse. Be quite at ease as to the King. I will give you a good account of him.' In truth, the position of the Prussians was full of difficulties. Between them and Silesia lay the victorious army of Daun. It was not easy for them to reach Silesia at all. If they did reach it, they left Saxony exposed to the Austrians. But the vigour and activity of Frederic surmounted every obstacle. He made a circuitous march of extraordinary rapidity, passed Daun, hastened into Silesia, raised the siege of Neisse, and drove Harsch into Bohemia. Daun availed himself of the King's absence to attack Dresden. The Prussians defended it desperately. The inhabitants of that wealthy and polished capital begged in vain for mercy from the garrison within, and from the besiegers without. The beautiful suburbs were burned to the ground. It was clear that the town, if won at all, would be won street by street by the bayonet. At this conjuncture came news, that Frederic, having cleared Silesia of his enemies, was returning by forced marches into Saxony. Daun retired from before Dresden, and fell back into the Austrian territories. The King, over heaps of ruins, made his triumphant entry into the unhappy metropolis, which had so cruelly expiated the weak and perfidious policy of its sovereign. It was now the 20th of November. The cold weather suspended military operations; and the King again took up his winter quarters at Breslau.

The third of the seven terrible years was over; and Frederic still stood his ground. He had been recently tried by domestic as well as by military disasters. On the 14th of October, the day on which he was defeated at Hochkirchen, the day on the anniversary of which, forty-eight years later, a defeat far more tremendous laid the Prussian monarchy in the dust, died Wilhelmina, Margravine of Bareuth. From the portraits which we have of her, by her own hand, and by the hands of the most discerning of her contemporaries, we should pronounce her to have been coarse, indelicate, and a good hater, but not destitute of kind and generous feelings. Her mind, naturally strong and observant, had been highly cultivated; and she was, and deserved to be, Frederic's favourite sister. He felt the loss as much as it was in his iron nature to feel the loss of any thing but a province or a battle.

At Breslau, during the winter, he was indefatigable in his poetical labours. The most spirited lines, perhaps, that he ever wrote, are to be found in a bitter lampoon on Louis and Madame de Pompadour, which he composed at this time, and sent to Voltaire. The verses were, indeed, so good, that Voltaire was afraid that he might himself be suspected of having written them, or at least of having corrected them; and partly from fright—partly, we fear, from love of mischief—sent them to the Duke of Choiseul, then prime minister of France. Choiseul very wisely determined to encounter Frederic at Frederic's own weapons, and applied for assistance to Palissot, who had some skill as a versifier, and who, though he had not yet made himself famous by bringing Rousseau and Helvetius on the stage, was known to possess some little talent 'for satire. Palissot produced some very stinging lines on the moral and literary character of Frederic, and these lines the duke sent to Voltaire. This war of couplets, following close on the carnage of Zorndorf and 'the conflagration of Dresden, illustrates well the strangely compounded character of the King of Prussia.

At this moment he was assailed by a new enemy. Benedict XIV., the best and wisest of the two hundred and fifty successors of St. Peter, was no more. During the short interval between his reign and that of his disciple Ganganelli, the chief seat in the Church of Rome was filled by Rezzonico, who took the name of Clement XIII. This absurd priest determined to try what the weight of his authority could effect in favour of the orthodox Maria Theresa against a heretic king. At the high mass on Christmas-day, a sword with a rich belt and scabbard, a hat of crimson velvet lined with ermine, and a dove of pearls, the mystic symbol of the Divine Comforter, were solemnly blessed by the supreme pontiff, and were sent with great ceremony to Marshal Daun, the conqueror of Kolin and Hochkirchen. This mark of favour had more than once been bestowed by the Popes on the great champions of the faith. Similar honours had been paid, more than six centuries earlier, by Urban II. to Godfrey of Bouillon. Similar honours had been conferred on Alba for destroying the liberties of the Low Countries, and on John Sobiesky after the deliverance of Vienna. But the presents which were received with profound reverence by the Baron of the Holy Sepulchre in the eleventh century, and which had not wholly lost their value even in the seventeenth century, appeared inexpressibly ridiculous to a generation which read Montesquieu and Voltaire. Frederic wrote sarcastic verses on the gifts, the giver, and the receiver. But the public wanted no prompter; and an universal roar of laughter from Petersburg to Lisbon, reminded the Vatican that the age of crusades was over.

The fourth campaign, the most disastrous of all the campaigns of this fearful war, had now opened. The Austrians filled Saxony, and menaced Berlin. The Russians defeated the King's generals on the Oder, threatened Silesia, effected a junction with Laudohn, and intrenched themselves strongly at Kunersdorf. Frederic hastened to attack them. A great battle was fought. During the earlier part of the day everything yielded to the impetuosity of the Prussians, and to the skill of their chief. The lines were forced. Half the Russian guns were taken. The king sent off a courier to Berlin with two lines, announcing a complete victory. But, in the mean time, the stubborn Russians, defeated yet unbroken, had taken up their stand in an almost impregnable position, on an eminence where the Jews of Frankfort were wont to bury their dead. Here the battle recommenced. The Prussian infantry, exhausted by six hours of hard fighting under a sun which equalled the tropical heat, were yet brought up repeatedly to the attack, but in vain. The King led three charges in person. Two horses were killed under him. The officers of his staff fell all round him. His coat was pierced by several bullets. All was in vain. His infantry was driven back with frightful slaughter. Terror began to spread fast from man to man. At that moment, the fiery cavalry of Laudohn, still fresh, rushed on the wavering ranks. Then followed an universal rout. Frederic himself was on the point of falling into the hands of the conquerors, and was with difficulty saved by a gallant officer, who, at the head of a handful of Hussars, made good a diversion of a few minutes. Shattered in body, shattered in mind, the king reached that night a village which the Cossacks had plundered; and there, in a ruined and deserted farm-house, flung himself on a heap of straw. He had sent to Berlin a second despatch very different from his first:—'Let the royal family leave Berlin. Send the archives to Potsdam. The town may make terms with the enemy.'

The defeat was, in truth, overwhelming. Of fifty thousand men, who had that morning marched under the black eagles, not three thousand remained together. The king bethought him again of his corrosive sublimate, and wrote to bid adieu to his friends, and to give directions as to the measures to be taken in the event of his death:—'I have no resource left'—such is the language of one of his letters—'all is lost. I will not survive the ruin of my country. Farewell forever.'

But the mutual jealousies of the confederates prevented them from following up their victory. They lost a few days in loitering and squabbling; and a few days, improved by Frederic, were worth more than the years of other men. On the morning after the battle, he had got together eighteen thousand of his troops. Very soon his force amounted to thirty thousand. Guns were procured from the neighbouring fortresses; and there was again an army. Berlin was for the present safe; but calamities came pouring on the King in uninterrupted succession. One of his generals, with a large body of troops, was taken at Maxen; another was defeated at Meissen; and when at length the campaign of 1759 closed, in the midst of a rigorous winter, the situation of Prussia appeared desperate. The only consoling circumstance was, that, in the West, Ferdinand of Brunswick had been more fortunate than his master; and by a series of exploits, of which the battle of Minden was the most glorious, had removed all apprehension of danger on the side of France.

The fifth year was now about to commence. It seemed impossible that the Prussian territories, repeatedly devastated by hundreds of thousands of invaders, could longer support the contest. But the King carried on war as no European power has ever carried on war, except the Committee of Public Safety during the great agony of the French Revolution. He governed his kingdom as he would have governed a besieged town, not caring to what extent property was destroyed, or the pursuits of civil life suspended, so that he did but make head against the enemy. As long as there was a man left in Prussia, that man might carry a musket—as long as there was a horse left, that horse might draw artillery. The coin was debased, the civil functionaries were left unpaid; in some provinces civil government altogether ceased to exist. But there were still rye-bread and potatoes; there were still lead and gunpowder; and, while the means of sustaining and destroying life remained, Frederic was determined to fight it out to the very last.

The earlier part of the campaign of 1760 was unfavourable to him. Berlin was again occupied by the enemy. Great contributions were levied on the inhabitants, and the royal palace was plundered. But at length, after two years of calamity, victory came back to his arms. At Lignitz he gained a great battle over Laudohn; at Torgau, after a day of horrible carnage, he triumphed over Daun. The fifth year closed, and still the event was in suspense. In the countries where the war had raged, the misery and exhaustion were more appalling than ever; but still there were left men and beasts, arms and food, and still Frederic fought on. In truth he had now been baited into savageness. His heart was ulcerated with hatred. The implacable resentment with which his enemies persecuted him, though originally provoked by his own unprincipled ambition, excited in him a thirst for vengeance which he did not even attempt to conceal. 'It is hard,' he says in one of his letters, 'for man to bear what I bear. I begin to feel that, as the Italians say, revenge is a pleasure for the gods. My philosophy is worn out by suffering. I am no saint, like those of whom we read in the legends; and I will own that I should die content if only I could first inflict a portion of the misery which I endure.'

Borne up by such feelings, he struggled with various success, but constant glory, through the campaign of 1761. On the whole, the result of this campaign was disastrous to Prussia. No great battle was gained by the enemy; but, in spite of the desperate bounds of the hunted tiger, the circle of pursuers was fast closing round him. Laudohn had surprised the important fortress of Schweidnitz. With that fortress, half of Silesia, and the command of the most important defiles through the mountains, had been transferred to the Austrians. The Russians had overpowered the King's generals in Pomerania. The country was so completely desolated that he began, by his own confession, to look round him with blank despair, unable to imagine where recruits, horses, or provisions were to be found.

Just at this time two great events brought on a complete change in the relations of almost all the powers of Europe. One of those events was the retirement of Mr. Pitt from office; the other was the death of the Empress Elizabeth of Russia.

The retirement of Pitt seemed to be an omen of utter ruin to the House of Brandenburg. His proud and vehement nature was incapable of anything that looked like either fear or treachery. He had often declared that, while he was in power, England should never make a peace of Utrecht;—should never, for any selfish object, abandon an ally even in the last extremity of distress. The Continental war was his own war. He had been bold enough—he who in former times had attacked, with irresistible powers of oratory, the Hanoverian policy of Carteret, and the German subsidies of Newcastle—to declare that Hanover ought to be as dear to us as Hampshire, and that he would conquer America in Germany. He had fallen; and the power which he had exercised, not always with discretion, but always with vigour and genius, had devolved on a favourite who was the representative of the Tory party—of the party which had thwarted William, which had persecuted Marlborough, and which had given up the Catalans to the vengeance of Philip of Anjou. To make peace with France—to shake off with all, or more than all, the speed compatible with decency, every Continental connexion, these were among the chief objects of the new Minister. The policy then followed inspired Frederic with an unjust, but deep and bitter aversion to the English name ; and produced effects which are still felt throughout the civilized world. To that policy it was owing that, some years later, England could not find on the whole Continent a single ally to stand by her, in her extreme need, against the House of Bourbon. To that policy it was owing that Frederic, alienated from England, was compelled to connect himself closely, during his later years, with Russia ; and was induced reluctantly to assist in that great crime, the fruitful parent of other great crimes—the first partition of Poland.

Scarcely had the retreat of Mr. Pitt deprived Prussia of her only friend, when the death of Elizabeth produced an entire revolution in the politics of the North. The Grand Duke Peter, her nephew, who now ascended the Russian throne, was not merely free from the prejudices which his aunt had entertained against Frederic, but was a worshipper, a servile imitator, a Boswell, of the great king. The days of the new Czar's government were few and evil, but sufficient to produce a change in the whole state of Christendom. He set the Prussian prisoners at liberty, fitted them out decently, and sent them back to their master ; he withdrew his troops from the provinces which Elizabeth had decided on incorporating with her dominions, and absolved all those Prussian subjects, who had been compelled to swear fealty to Russia, from their engagements.

Not content with concluding peace on terms favourable to Prussia, he solicited rank in the Prussian service, dressed himself in a Prussian uniform, wore the Black Eagle of Prussia on his breast, made preparations for visiting Prussia, in order to have an interview with the object of his idolatry, and actually sent fifteen thousand excellent troops to reinforce the shattered army of Frederic. Thus strengthened, the King speedily repaired the losses of the preceding year, reconquered Silesia, defeated Daun at Buckersdorf, invested and retook Schweidnitz, and, at the close of the year, presented to the forces of Maria Theresa a front as formidable as before the great reverses of 1759. Before the end of the campaign, his friend the Emperor Peter having, by a series of absurd insults to the institutions, manners, and feelings of his people, united them in hostility to his person and government, was deposed and murdered. The Empress, who, under the title of Catherine the Second, now assumed the supreme power, was, at the commencement of her administration, by no means partial to Frederic, and refused to permit her troops to remain under his command. But she observed the peace made by her husband ; and Prussia was no longer threatened by danger from the East.

England and France at the same time paired off together. They concluded a treaty, by which they bound themselves to observe neutrality with respect to the German war. Thus the coalitions on both sides were dissolved ; and the original enemies, Austria and Prussia, remained alone confronting each other.

Austria had undoubtedly by far greater means than Prussia, and was less exhausted by hostilities ; yet it seemed hardly possible that Austria could effect alone what she had in vain attempted to effect when supported by France on the one side, and by Russia on the other. Danger also began to menace the Imperial house from another quarter. The Ottoman Porte held threatening language, and a hundred thousand Turks were mustered on the frontiers of Hungary. The proud and revengeful spirit of the Empress-Queen at length gave way ; and, in February, 1763, the peace of Hubertsburg put an end to the conflict which had, during seven years, devastated Germany The King ceded nothing. The whole Continent in arms had proved unable to tear Silesia from that iron grasp.

The war was over. Frederic was safe. His glory was beyond the reach of envy. If he had not made conquests as vast as those of Alexander, of Cæsar, and of Napoleon— if he had not, on field of battle, enjoyed the constant success of Marlborough and Wellington—he had yet given an example unrivalled in history of what capacity and resolution can effect against the greatest superiority of power and the utmost spite of fortune. He entered Berlin in triumph, after an absence of more than six years. The streets were brilliantly lighted up ; and, as he passed along in an open carriage, with Ferdinand of Brunswick at his side, the multitude saluted him with loud praises and blessings. He was moved by those marks of attachment, and repeatedly exclaimed—' Long live my dear people !—Long live my children !' Yet, even in the midst of that gay spectacle, he could not but perceive everywhere the traces of destruction and decay. The city had been more than once plundered. The population had considerably diminished.

Berlin, however, had suffered little when compared with most parts of the kingdom. The ruin of private fortunes, the distress of all ranks, was such as might appal the firmest mind. Almost every province had been the seat of war, and of war conducted with merciless ferocity. Clouds of Croatians had descended on Silesia. Tens of thousands of Cossacks had been let loose on Pomerania and Brandenburg. The mere contributions levied by the invaders amounted, it was said, to more than a hundred millions of dollars; and the value of what they extorted was probably much less than the value of what they destroyed. The fields lay uncultivated. The very seed-corn had been devoured in the madness of hunger. Famine, and contagious maladies the effect of famine, had swept away the herds and flocks; and there was reason to fear that a great pestilence among the human race was likely to follow in the train of that tremendous war. Near fifteen thousand houses had been burned to the ground.

The population of the kingdom had in seven years decreased to the frightful extent of ten per cent. A sixth of the males capable of bearing arms had actually perished on the field of battle. In some districts, no labourers, except women, were seen in the fields at harvest-time. In others, the traveller passed shuddering through a succession of silent villages, in which not a single inhabitant remained. The currency had been debased; the authority of laws and magistrates had been suspended; the whole social system was deranged. For, during that convulsive struggle, everything that was not military violence was anarchy. Even the army was disorganized. Some great generals, and a crowd of excellent officers, had fallen, and it had been impossible to supply their places. The difficulty of finding recruits had, towards the close of the war, been so great, that selection and rejection were impossible. Whole battalions were composed of deserters or of prisoners. It was hardly to be hoped that thirty years of repose and industry would repair the ruin produced by seven years of havoc. One consolatory circumstance, indeed, there was. No debt had been incurred. The burdens of the war had been terrible, almost insupportable; but no arrear was left to embarrass the finances in the time of peace.

Here, for the present, we must pause. We have accompanied Frederic to the close of his career as a warrior. Possibly, when these Memoirs are completed, we may resume the consideration of his character, and give some account of his domestic and foreign policy, and of his private habits, during the many years of tranquillity which followed the Seven Years' War.

NOTE to the Article on the Pictorial History of England.

In a note to our account of this work, contained in the preceding Number, we stated that it was 'set on foot by the Society for the Diffusion of Useful Knowledge;' but being since informed that we were mistaken in saying so, we think it right to acknowledge the error. Having, in alluding to that Society, taken the opportunity of announcing our intention to review the series of treatises on Monarchical Governments lately published by it—forming part of a more extended series on Governments of all denominations—we, in like manner, avail ourselves of the present occasion to express our regret at having been unable to overtake that task in this Number. We regret this the more, that it would have afforded us a better opportunity than the present, to enter our protest against a doctrine promulgated in respectable quarters, in some notices of these treatises, that all jealousy of the monarchical branch of our Government may be now laid aside; and that we may henceforward look with indifference upon those principles and safeguards which it was the grand object of the Revolution of 1688 permanently to uphold. Other dangers to liberty and good government there doubtless are, and we are very far from being insensible to them; but surely it is neither wise nor seemly that liberal-minded men should enjoin the people to view with indifference, if not with scorn, that great settlement to which they owe their continued existence as freemen. We shall resume the subject when we come to view in detail these useful treatises; and we, in the meanwhile, express the hope, that the Society will proceed steadily with the Course of instruction in Politics and Political Economy which they have so auspiciously commenced; for, if prosecuted in the same calm and dispassionate manner, with the same adherence to sound principle, the same extent of information, and the same unambitious, but clear and apt style, they will put the people in possession of a stock of knowledge that may, in the most emphatic sense, be pronounced 'useful;' because it will be knowledge employed about subjects of vital importance to their comforts, their respectability, and their prosperity—to the stability of law and government, and to the general well-being of the community.

LIST OF NEW PUBLICATIONS.

ANTIQUITIES AND ARCHITECTURE.

Barr's Anglican Church Architecture. 12mo 5s.

Gallery of Antiquities selected from the British Museum. By Arundale and Banoni. No. I. 4to 2s 6d

Rustic Architecture. By T. J. Ricauti. Royal 4to 1l 15s

Remarks on English Churches. By J. H. Markland. Foolscap 5s

Etchings of Runic Monuments in the Isle of Man, with Remarks. By W. Kinnebrook. 8vo 10s 6d

An Account of Kilpeck Church, Herefordshire. Twenty-eight Illustrations by Lewis. Royal 4to 2l 2s. Imperial 4to 3l 3s

BIOGRAPHY.

Memoir of the late James Halley. 12mo 5s

Memoir of Capt. E. P. Brenton, R. N. By his Brother, Admiral Brenton. 8vo 7s

A Family Record, or Memoirs of the late Rev. Basil Woodd. Foolscap 4s

Memoir of the Life of Rev. Lant Carpenter, LL. D. Edited by his Son, R. L. Carpenter. 8vo 12s

Memoir of the Life of Richard Phillips. 8vo 7s 6d

Memoir of the Chisholm, late M. P. By the Rev. J. S. M Anderson. 12mo 5s 6d

Diary and Letters of Madame D'Arblay. Edited by her Niece. Vol I. Post 8vo 10s 6d

Correspondence of Richard Bentley. 2 vols 8vo 2l 2s

Memoir and Remains of the Rev. C. Neall. By the Rev. W. Jowett. New Edition. Foolscap 6s

Sir S. Romilly's Life. Third Edition 2 vols 12mo 12s

Memoir of the Life and Writings of Michael T. Sadler. 8vo 14s.

Sir W. Scott's Life of Napoleon. 1 vol royal 8vo 20s

Memoirs of the late Rev. W. Nunn, (of Manchester.) By the Rev. R. Pym. 8vo 10s 6d

Journal and Correspondence of Miss Adams, daughter of John Adams. 2 vols 12mo 12s.

Colonel Turnbull's Reminiscences of his Own Times. 8vo 18s

Miss Strickland's lives of the Queens of England. Vol. IV. Post 8vo 10s 6d

Life of William of Wykeham. By the Rev. J. Chandler. 18mo 2s

CLASSICS.

Self-Instructing Latin Classic. By W. Jacobs. Vol. II. 12mo 7s

Cæsar de Bello Gallico, with a Geographical Index. Edited by Philip Smith. 12mo 3s 6d

T. Livii Historiæ, ex Recensione Drakenborchii. 3 vols 8vo 1l 11s 6d

Livy, with Notes. By Travers Twiss. 4 vols 8vo 1l 18s

Ciceronis de Officiis. Alani. 12mo 4s

Ovid's Fasti, in English Verse. By Miss Emma Garland. Post 8vo 10s

Homerus. By the Rev. John Williams. Vol. I. 8vo 10s 6d

Major's Extracts from Ovid's Fasti. Foolscap 2s 6d

Cicero de Natura Deorum, (Edinburgh.) 12mo 2s 6d

——— Translated, with Notes, by T. Francklin, D. D. New Edition. 12mo 3s 6d

Homeri Ilias Græce. By T. S. Brandreth. 2 vols 8vo 21s

EDUCATION AND SCHOOL-BOOKS.

Etymology and Syntax of Murray's English Grammar systematically arranged. By Charlotte Kenuion. 12mo 4s

Grimm's Five Tales from the Arabian Nights, in German. 12mo 3s 6d

The Anglo-German Reader. By O. Schmidt. Post 8vo 6s 6d

Greek Poetry for Schools. Edited by Philip Smith. 12mo 4s

Dr. Donnegan's Greek and English Lexicon. Fourth Edition. Royal 8vo 2l 2s

The Classical Pronunciation of Proper Names. By T. S. Carr. 12mo 5s

Rational Reading Lessons. 18mo 2s 6d

Complete Treatise on Practical Arithmetic. By T. Abram. 12mo 3s 6d

Frey's Hebrew and English Dictionary. Third Edition. 8vo 8s

The Chain Rule; a Manual of brief commer-

cial Arithmetic. By C. L. Schonberg. 18mo
1s 6d

Grotefend's Materials for translating into Latin.
By the Rev. T. K. Arnold. 8vo 7s 6d

A Grammar of the English Language. By E.
Del Mar. 12mo 3s

Bialloblotzky's German Reading Lessons. 12mo
6s

State of Education, Crime, &c., in England and
Wales. By J. Bentley. 12mo 5s

A Complete Course of German Literature for
Beginners. By C. A. Feiling. Foolscap 7s

National Proverbs in the Principal Languages
of Europe. By Caroline Ward. Foolscap
3s 6d

Miniature French Dictionary. Royal 32mo 4s

A German Grammar. By William Wittich.
12mo 6s 6d

Questions and Exercises to Hiley's English
Grammar. Third Edition. 12mo 2s

National Education; its Principles and Objects
exemplified in a proposed plan for a Normal
School. By O. De B. Priaulx. 8vo 6s

Grammar of the New Testament Dialect. By
the Rev. T. S. Green. 8vo 10s

Oram's Examples in Arithmetic. Part II.
12mo 2s

———— Master's Copy. 3s

Fractional Arithmetic Reviewed and Practically
Exemplified. By E. Clifford. 12mo 7s

Eton French and English Dialogues. By J. C.
Tarver. 12mo 3s 6d

Schiller's Song of the Bell—German and English. By T. J. Arnold. 12mo 2s

Examples in Algebra. By the Rev. W. Foster.
Second Edition. 12mo 3s 6d

FINE ARTS.

London from the Thames. From Original
Drawings. By W. Parrot. Oblong 4to
2l 12s 6d

Goldsmith's Deserted Village. Illustrated. By
the Etching Club. Imperial 8vo 5l 5s. Proofs,
Coloured, folio, 10l 10s. Reserved Proofs,
13l 13s

A Selection of Pictures by Claude, Watteau,
and Canaletto, in the National and Dulwich
Galleries. Drawn and Lithographed. By
Bendixen. Folio 4l 4s

Finden's Ports, Harbours, and Watering Places.
2 vols 4to 3l 3s

Elements of Drawing and Painting in Water-
Colours. By J. Clark. Second Edition. 8s 6d

Hand-Book of the History of Painting—Italy.
Translated from the German of Hugler, with
Notes by Eastlake. Post 8vo 12s

On the Theory of Painting. By T. H. Fielding. Third Edition. Royal 8vo 26s

Characteristics of Painters. By H. Reeve.
8vo 4s

The Cartoons of Raffaelle. Oblong folio 9s 6d

The Theory of Taste founded on Association
tested. By Sir G. S. Mackenzie. 18mo 3s

The Use of a Box of Colours. By Harry Wilson. Imperial 8vo 24s

GARDENING AND AGRICULTURE.

Mrs. Loudon's Ladies Magazine of Gardening.
8vo 18s

Treatise on Manures and Farming By J.
Donaldson. 8vo 12s

Main's Fruit, Flower, and Kitchen Garden.
18mo 5s

Treatise on Landscape Gardening and Rural
Architecture. By A. J. Downing. 8vo 21s

GEOGRAPHY.

The Bengal and Agra Guide and Gazetteer. 2
vols 8vo 2l

A System of Universal Geography, founded on
the Works of Malte Brun and Balbi. 1 vol
8vo 30s

HISTORY.

Knott's New Aid to Memory. Part III. Scripture History. 12mo 7s

The History of Egypt under the Romans. By
Samuel Sharpe. 8vo 7s

Historical Sketches, Speeches, and Characters.
By the Rev. George Croly. Post 8vo 10s 6d

General History of the World. Translated from
the German of Charles Von Rotteck, LLD.
4 vols 8vo 2l

Miss Corner's History of Italy and Switzerland.
Foolscap. 3s 6d

C. M. Davis' History of Holland. Vol 2 8vo
12s

Hallam's Constitutional History of England.
Fourth Edition. 2 vols 8vo 24s

History of the Colonization of the United States.
By G. Brancroft. Ninth Edition. 3 vols 8vo
2l 2s

Greece as a Kingdom; or a Statistical Description of that Country. By F. Strong, Esq,
8vo 15s

History of the French Revolution, with reference to the Fulfilment of Prophecy. By
the Rev. F. Fysh. 8vo 12s 6d

The Annual Register, 1840. Vol LXXXII
8vo 16s

LAW AND JURISPRUDENCE.

Walford's Treatise on the Law respecting Parties to Auctions. 2 vols 12mo 30s

The Doctrine and Practice of Equity. By G.
Goldsmith. Second Edition. 12mo 8s

Practical Treatise on the Law of Estate for Life.
By A. Bissett. 8vo 15s

Hand-Book of the Law of Legacies. 18mo 2s

Jeremy's Digest of Law Reports, 1841. Royal
8vo 9s

The Justice's Pocket Manual. By S. Stone.
Foolscap. 5s 6d

Practice of the Bristol Talzey Court. By J.
Holmes. 12mo 5s

Digest of the Law of Usage and Custom between
Great Britain and France. By C. H. Okey.
8vo 10s

Fox on Simple Contracts and the Action of As-
sumpsit. 12mo 7s 6d

Archbold's Justice of the Peace. Second Edition.
Vols I. and II. (3 vols.) 1l 18s

On the Law of Settlement and Removals. By
W. G. Lumley. 12mo 4s

Archbold's Law and Practice of Bankruptcy.
Ninth Edition. Enlarged. By J. Flather.
12mo 21s

Outlines of the Law of Real Property. By R.
Maugham. 12mo 10s

Chambers on the Law relating to Infancy.
Royal 8vo 1l 10s

Synopsis of the Law relating to Indictable Offences. By B. Boothby. 12mo 14s

The Declaration on Bills of Exchange. By E. Lawes. 12mo 14s

Judgments; as they affect Real Property. By F. Prideaux. 12mo 3s

The First Book for a Conveyancing Student. By J. Phillips. Post 8vo 4s

R. G. Welford's Practical Treatise on Equity Pleadings. 8vo 18s

MECHANICS AND ENGINEERING.

Telegraphic Railways. By W. F. Cook. Royal 8vo 3s 6d

The Award of the Dean Forest Mining Commissioners. By T. Sopwith. 8vo 5s

Crocker's Elements of Land-Surveying. New Edition. By T. G. Bunt. Post 8vo 12s

Elementary Surveying. By Major Jackson. 8vo 6s 6d

Surveying, Levelling, and Railway Engineering. By W. Galbraith. 8vo 7s 6d

A Manual of the Steam-Engine. By R. D. Hoblyn. Foolscap. 6s

Treatise on Land-Surveying and Levelling. By H. J. Castle, 8vo 14s

MEDICINE, ANATOMY, AND SURGERY.

On Rheumatism in its Various Forms. By R. Macleod, M. D. 8vo 7s

Sir A. Cooper's Lectures on Surgery. Sixth Edition. Foolscap. 7s

A Manual of Veterinary Science. By Professor Dick. Post 8vo 3s

Pilcher on the Structure and Diseases of the Ear. Second Edition. 8vo 12s

Sir A. Cooper on Dislocations and Fractures. New Edition. Enlarged. Edited by B. B. Cooper. 8vo 20s

The Cyclopædia of Popular Medicine. By K. Imray, M. D. 8vo 18s

On the Treatment of Stone in the Bladder. By R. Willis, M. D. 8vo 6s

Hydropathy; or, the Cold Water Cure. By R. T. Claridge, Esq. 8vo 5s

Essay on Diabetes. By H. Bell. Translated by Markwick. 12mo 4s

Pocket Formulary and Synopsis of the Pharmacopœias. By H. Beasley. Second Edition. 32mo 3s 6d

Ricord on Venereal Diseases. Translated by H. P. Drummond, M. D. 8vo 12s

Syme's Principles of Surgery. Third Edition. 8vo 21s

The Anatomy of the Urinary Bladder of the Male. By A. Monro, M. D. 8vo 6s

A Dispensatory, or Commentary on the Pharmacopœias of Great Britain. By R. Christison, M. D. 8vo 18s

Principles of Human Physiology. By W. B. Carpenter, M. D. 8vo 20s

Practical Essays. By Sir C. Bell. Part II. Royal 8vo. 7s 6d

Frankum's Discourse on Pendulous Abdomen, with Dissertation on Gout. Second Edition. Foolscap 5s

Sir B. Brodie's Lectures on Diseases of the Urinary Organs. Third Edition. 8vo 12s

Brown's Letters to Dr. Gregory on Vaccination. Post 8vo 4s

Practical Treatise on Auscultation. Translated by P. Newbigging, M.D. 12mo 6s 6d

METAPHYSICS AND MORAL PHILOSOPHY.

The Reciprocal Influence of Body and Mind considered. By Newnham. 8vo 14s

Elements of Mental and Moral Science. By G. Payne, LL.D. Second Edition. 8vo 8s

MISCELLANEOUS LITERATURE.

Encyclopædia Britannica. Seventh Edition. Now complete in 21 vols. Cloth and boards. 37l 16s.

Ditto, ditto, half-bound, best Russia. Extra finish, cloth sides. 42l

Index. Cloth boards. 8s

Part CXXVI. 6s

The Sporting Sketch. Edited by J. W. Carleton. Post 8vo 16s

Tables for Valuing Annuities subject to Legacy-Duty. By J. C. Hudson. 8vo. 5s bds

Hand-Book of Horsemanship. Foolscap. 2s 6d

Treasury of Wit and Anecdote. Royal 32mo 2s 6d

Lewis Pocock on Assurance upon Lives. Post 8vo 7s

Female Character. By Albert Pennington. Second Edition. Foolscap. 2s 6d

The Renfrewshire Annual, 1842. Edited by Mrs Maxwell. Foolscap. 5s

George Cruikshanks' Omnibus, with One Hundred Illustrations. Medium 8vo 10s 6d

Francis' Dictionary of the Arts and Sciences. 8vo 10s

Harrison's Freighter's Guide. Fourth Edition. 12mo 5s

The Daughters of England. By Mrs. Ellis. Post 8vo 10s

Lewis' First Series of Progressive Lessons on Chess. Third Edition. 12mo 7s

The Year-Book of Facts in Science and Art, 1842. Foolscap. 5s

Selleysell on Shoeing Horses. By Cherry. 8vo 5s

The Pocket Bill-Book. By W. H. Logan. Foolscap. 7s 6d

The Book of Thought; or, Observations Selected from Various Authors. Post 8vo 10s 6d

Time and Time-Keepers. By Adam Thomson. Foolscap. 5s

Translations from the German. Prose and Verse. By H. Reeve and J. E. Taylor. Foolscap. 2s 6d

Ruff's Guide to the Turf. 18mo 2s 6d

Park's Pantology; or, a Systematic Survey of Human Knowledge. 8vo 18s

Hand-Book of Needle-Work. By Miss Lambert. Post 8vo 10s 6d

Elements of General Pathology. By the late J. Fletcher, M.D. Post 8vo 10s 6d

NATURAL HISTORY.

The Book of Geology. By W. M. Higgins. With Coloured Plates. Foolscap. 7s 6d

Transactions of the Entomological Society of London. Vol. III. Part I. 8vo 6s

Conchologia Systematica; or, a Complete Sys-

tem of Conchology. By L. Reeve. (2 vols).
Vol. I. 4to 5*l* 10s Coloured 3*l* 5s Plain
History of British Sponges and Lithophytes.
By G. Johnston, M.D. 8vo 30s
Sketch of the Geology of Moray. By P. Duff.
Royal 8vo 8s 6d

NATURAL PHILOSOPHY.
Young's Analysis and Solution of Cubic and Bi-
quadratic Equations. 12mo 6s
Jean's Plain and Spherical Trigonometry. Part
I. 12mo 3s 6d
A Course of Mathematics. By the Rev. J. Cape.
Vol. II. 8vo 16s

NOVELS, TALES, AND ROMANCES.
Jack Tench; or, The Midshipman turned Idler.
8vo 8s
Anne Boleyn; an Historical Romance. By Mrs.
A. T. Thomson. 3 vols. Post 8vo 1*l* 11s 6d
De Montford; or, The Old English Nobleman.
3 vols. Post 8vo 1*l* 11s 6d
The School for Wives. By the Authoress of
"Temptation." 3 vols. Post 8vo 1*l* 11s 6d
Manasseh, a Tale of the Jews. Foolscap. 5s
The Price of Fame. By Miss Elizabeth Youatt.
3 vols. Post 8vo 1*l* 11s 6d
Fardorougha the Miser; or, The Convicts of
Lisnamona. Second Edition. Foolscap. 6s
Henry De Pameroy; or, The Eve of St. John.
By Mrs. Bray. 3 vols. Post 8vo 1*l* 8s 6d
Temugin, afterwards surnamed Genghiskan.
A Romance. 3 vols. Post 8vo 1*l* 11s 6d
Sir Henry Morgan, the Buccaneer. By Edward
Howard. 3 vols. Post 8vo 1*l* 11s 6d
Father John; or, Cromwell in Ireland. Post
8vo 7s 6d
Karah Kapland; or, The Koordish Chief. By
the Hon. C. S. Savile. 3 vols. Post 8vo 1*l*
8s 6d
Passages from the Diary of a late Physician.
New Edition. Complete in 2 vols. Fools-
cap. 12s
Zanoni. By Sir E. L. Bulwer, Bart. 3 vols.
Post 8vo 1*l* 11s 6d
The Collegians; a Tale of Garry Owen. By
Gerald Griffin, Esq. New Edition. Fools-
cap. 8vo 6s
Fascination, and other Tales. Edited by Mrs.
Gore. 3 vols. Post 8vo 1*l* 11s 6d
Popularity; and the Destinies of Woman. By
Mrs. C. Baron Wilson. 2 vols. Post 8vo
21s
Newstoke Priors. A Novel. By Miss Wad-
dington. 3 vols Post 8vo 1*l* 11s 6d
Cakes and Ale. By Douglas Jerrold. 2 vols
Foolscap 15s
London Legends. By Paul Pindar, Gent. 2
vols Post 8vo 21s
The Two Admirals; a Tale of the Sea. By
J. F. Cooper. 2 vols Post 8vo 1*l* 11s 6d
The Traduced, An Historical Romance. By
N. Mitchell. 3 vols Post 8vo 1*l* 11s 6d
Sayings and Doings. By T. Hook. The Three
Series in 3 vols Post 8vo 18s
Many-Coloured Life. By the Author of " The
Lollards." 8vo 7s 6d
The Expectant. By Miss Ellen Pickering. 3
vols Post 8vo 1*l* 11s 6d

Trevor Hastings; or The Battle of Tewksbury.
3 vols Post 8vo 1*l* 11s 6d
The Village Voluntary. A Tale. Foolscap
4s
Lady Anne Granard; or. Keeping up Appearances. By L. E. L. 3 vols Post 8vo 1*l*
11s 6d
The Herberts. By the Author of " Elphinstone." 3 vols Post 8vo 1*l* 11s 6d

POETRY AND THE DRAMA.
The Martyrs of Provence. By W. H. Madden,
M.D. Foolscap 5s 6d
Lays and Lyrics. By Charles Gray. Fools-
cap 6s
Goethe's Faust. Translated into English Verse
by Sir G. Lefevre, M. D. 18mo 6s
Knight's Pictorial Shakspeare.—Tragedies.
Vol II. Royal 8vo 1*l* 2s 6d
Poems. By Anne Beale. 12mo 7s 6d
Babbicombe; or Visions of Memory. By M.
Bridges. 12mo 6s
Charles Knight's Library Edition of Shakspeare.
Vol I. 8vo 10s
Shakspeare's Poems. Imperial 8vo 9s
The Vow of the Gileadite; a Lyric Narrative.
By the Rev. W. Galloway. Foolscap 5s
Collyer's Edition of Shakspeare. Vol. II. 8vo
12s
Milton's Poetical Works, with Life and Notes.
By Sir E. Brydges. 8vo 16s
Zaida, and other Poems. By Lewis Evans.
Foolscap 5s
The Drunkard. A Poem. By John O'Neill.
Foolscap 2s 6d
Luther. A Poem. By Robert Montgomery
Foolscap 10s 6d
Zachary Cobble. A Rigmarole in .Rhyme.
Post 8vo 6s.
Bubbles of the Day. By Douglas Jerrold. 8vo
2s 6d
The Prisoners of War. By Douglas Jerrold.
8vo 2s 6d
One Centenary of Sonnets. By B. Hawkins,
Esq. Square 10s 6d
Power of the Passions, and other Poems. By
Mrs. K. A. Ware. Post 8vo 6s
The Pilgrim of Glencoe, and other Poems. By
T. Campbell. Post 8vo 7s
Rogers' Poems. New Edition. 1 vol 8vo
16s
The Book of Sonnets. By A. Montague
Woodford. Post 8vo 10s 6d
I Watched the Heavens. A Poem. By V.
18mo 2s 6d
The Tomb of Bonaparte. A Poem by H. Crult-
well. Foolscap 3s
Poems from Eastern Sources, &c. By R. C.
Trench. 12mo 6s
Poetry—Instructive and Devotional. 18mo 2s
The Hebrew Boy. A Dramatic Poem. By
Mrs. Leckie. Post 8vo 1s 6d

POLITICS AND POLITICAL ECONOMY.
A Third Letter to A. L. Phillips, Esq., from
John, Earl of Shrewsbury, on the Present
Posture of Affairs. 8vo 7s 6d
Inquiry into the Right of Visitation and Search
of American Vessels. By H. Wheaton,
L.L.D. 8vo 4s 6d

Political Economy, By J. Broadhurst, Esq. 8vo 7s 6d

The Addresses and Messages of the Presidents of the United States. 8vo 17s

The Four Reformed Parliaments 1832--42. By C. E. Lewis. Foolscap 4s

Political Philosophy—Library of Useful Knowledge. 8vo 12s

The Condition of the Agricultural Classes of Great Britain and Ireland, with a Preface. By H. Drummond. 2 vols 8vo 21s

Lord Campbell's Speeches at the Bar and in the House of Commons. 8vo 12s

The True State of the National Finances. By S. Wells. 12mo 6s

The True Law of Population shown to be connected with the Food of the People. By T. Doubleday. 8vo 6s

RELIGIOUS SUBJECTS.

The Book of Isaiah. Translated from the Hebrew by the Rev. John Jones. 8vo 5s

The Holy Ordinance of Christian Baptism. Foolscap 3s

Congregationalism and Modern Society. By R. Vaughan, D.D. 8vo 5s

Hambleton's Sermons on the 53d of Isaiah, and other Subjects, Fourth Edition. 12mo 5s

The Sabbath School as it should be. By W. A. Alcott. Royal 32mo 2s 6d

Sermons on Church Building. By the Rev. J. A. Emerson. 12mo 5s

Bishop Beveridge's Sermons on the Ministry and Ordinances of the Church. Second Edition. 12mo 4s

Eighteen Short Sermons. 12mo 4s

Parochial Sermons. By the Rev. W. Gresley. 12mo 7s 6d

Lectures on Popery. First Series. By the Rev. J. W. Brooks. 12mo 2s

Essays on Socinianism. By Joseph Cottle. Part I. Post 8vo 5s

Milford Malvoisin on Pew and Pewholders. By F. E. Paget. 12mo. 4s 6d

Lectures on the Liturgy. By the Rev. J. Bentall. Post 8vo. 5s 6d

Primitive Christianity. By Bishop Mant. 8vo 12s

The Kings of the East; an Exposition of the Prophecies. Post 8vo. 8s 6d

The Conversion of the Jews. A Series of Lectures. By A. Black, D.D. 12mo 2s 6d

The Messiah as an Example. By Dr. J. Abercrombie. 18mo 8d

Complete in Christ. By the Author of a "Visit to my Birth-Place." 18mo 1s 6d

Illustrations of the Saints-Days and other Festivals of the Church. By H. C. Cherry. Vol. I. Foolscap. 4s 6d

Four Addresses to the Young. By the late R. S. M'All. 12mo. 3s

O'Keefe's Patriarchal Times. Sixth Edition. Foolscap. 6s 6d

Bishop Marsh's Lectures on the Bible. New Edition. 8vo. 12s

Who is my Neighbour? An Essay on Missions. By J. B. Melson. 8vo 6s

Ecclesiastica. The Church—Her Schools, and Her Clergy. By E. M. Roose 8vo. 10s 6d

Sermons at Cheltenham during 1840-1. By C. E. Kenneway. 8vo. 6s

Sketches of Sermons for Special Occasions. By a Dissenting Minister. 12mo. 4s 6d

Sermons. By the Rev. C. E. J. Dering. 12mo 5s

Two Hundred Hymns.—Sequel to " Melodia Sacra." 18mo. 1s

The Chamber of Affliction. By the Rev. D. Smith. 32mo. 2s 6d

Connection of Sacred and Profane History. By D. Davidson. 24mo. 4s

Bayly's Practice of Piety. New Edition. 12mo. 3s 6d

The Bishopric of Souls. By the Rev. R. W. Evans. 12mo 6s

Smith's Manual of the Rudiments of Theology. Third Edition. 12mo 8s 6d

Rev. J. H. Newman's Parochial Sermons. Vol. VI. 8vo 10s 6d

The Touchstone; or Claims and Privileges of True Religion. By Mrs. A. Grant. 18mo 2s 6d

Three Discourses on the Divine Will. By A. J. Scott. 18mo 2s

The Union between Christ and His People. Four Sermons. By the Rev. C. A. Heurtley. 8vo 5s

The Tabernacle in the Wilderness the Shadow of Heavenly Things. By W. G. Rhind. Folio. Coloured Plates. 10s 6d Cloth.

Strength in Jesus to Perform Duty. By the Rev. H. J. Prince 24mo 1s 6d

A Translation and Exposition of the Book of Psalms. By the Rev. J. Fry. Second Edition. 8vo 16s 6d

Evangelical Sermons. By the Rev. J. Bush. Foolscap 4s 6d

Rev. H. Blunt's Exposition of the Pentateuch. Vol. II. Exodus and Leviticus. 12mo 6s

Rev. J. Jones' Expository Lectures on the Acts of the Apostles. 2 vols 12mo 10s 6d

Plain and Practical View of the Liturgy. By the Rev. H. Marriott. Foolscap 4s 6d

Questiones Mosaicæ; or, The Book of Genesis compared with the Remains of Ancient Religions. By O. De Beauvoir Prialux 8vo 15s

A Facsimile Reprint of the Celebrated Geneva Testament, 1557. Foolscap. 8vo 8s

The Great Commission. A Prize Essay on Missions. By the Rev. J. Harris, D.D. Post 8vo 10s 6d

Rev. H. B. Macartney's Observations on the Book of Ruth, and on the Word Redeemer. 18mo 1s 6d

The Old Testament, with a Commentary. By the Rev. C. Girdlestone. Part VIII. 8vo 9s and Vol. IV. 8vo 18s

Rev. H. Halford's Hulsean Lectures, 1841 8vo 7s

Rev. G. W. Doane's (Bishop of New Jersey) Sermons. 8vo 18s

The Office and Work of the Holy Spirit. By the Rev. J. Buchanan. 12mo 6s 6d

Missions. By the Rev. N. W. Hamilton. (Second Prize.) 8vo 8s 6d

Moral Agency; and Man as a Moral Agent. By W. M'Combie. Foolscap 4s

The Whole Works of Archbishop Usher. (18 vols.) Vol. II. 8vo 12s

Theodoxa! a Treatise on Divine Praise. By N. Rowton. 12mo 4s

Comments on the Collects. By the Rev. J. F. Hone. 12mo 6s

Parochialia; Papers Printed for the Use of the Parish of St. George's, Bloomsbury, 1834–41 By the Rev. T. V. Short. Foolscap 4s

Dr. J. P. Smith's Four Discourses on the Sacrifice and Priesthood of Christ. Second Edition. Foolscap 6s

Thirty Sermons on Various Subjects. By Living Divines 8vo 12s 6s

Muir's Practical Sermons on the Holy Spirit. 12mo 6s

Murray's Practical Remarks on Genesis and Exodus. Third Edition. 8vo 10s 6d

Prayers for the Use of the Medical Profession. 18mo 2s 6d

The Baptistery; or, the Way of Eternal Life. By the Author of " The Cathedral." 8vo 15s

Sermons Preached in the Parish Church of Saint Pancras. By the Rev. W. Wilson. 8vo. 8s

Young Men Warned; or, Life and Sudden Death of George Gabriel. By the Rev. H. Woodward. 18mo. 1s 6d

Devotions on the Passion of Our Lord and Saviour Jesus Christ. 18mo 4s

Rev. W. Jay's Works. Vol. II. Post 8vo. 7s 6d

Bennet's Guide to the Holy Eucharist. 2 vols. 18mo. 8s.

The Clergyman's Manual. By the Rev. R. Simpson. 8vo. 10s 6d

Rev. Dr. Kenney's Comments on the Epistles and Gospels. 2 vols 12mo 16s

D'Aubigne's History of the Reformation. Translated by Scott. Vol. I. 8vo 12s 6d

The Hope of Israel; an Exposition of the Prophecies. By the Rev. H. Girdlestone. 12mo 4s

Christian Missions to Heathen Nations. By Baptist W. Noel. Post 8vo 8s.

The Rev. C Bradley's Sacramental Sermons. 8vo 10s 6d

Fragments on the Sacrament of the Lord's Supper. 32mo 1s 6d

The Second Portion of Elisha, By the Author of " Elijah the Tishbite." 12mo 6s

The Jubilee of the World. An Essay on Christian Missions to the Heathen. By the Rev. J. Macfarlane. Post 8vo 6s

Sermons in Rome during Lent, 1838. By the Rev. J. H. Gray. 12mo 7s 6d

The English Reformation. By the Rev. F. C. Massingberd. (Forming Vol. XXI. of the Englishman's Library.) Foolscap 8vo 5s

STATISTICS AND TOPOGRAPHY.

Memorials of Clutha; or, Pencillings on the Clyde. By Eliza A. Phipps. 8vo 7s 6d

Observations on the Present Condition of the Island of Trinidad. By W. H. Burnley. 8vo 5s

Spackman's Statistical Tables of Great Britain. Foolscap 5s

London. Edited by Charles Knight. Vol. II. Royal 8vo 10s 6d

The Local Historian's Table-Book. By W. A. Richardson. Vol. I. Royal 8vo 9s

Manchester; its Political, Social, and Commercial History. By James Wheeler. 12mo 4s

VOYAGES AND TRAVELS.

Mesopotamia and Assyria. By J. B. Fraser, Esq. Foolscap 5s

Rambling Recollections of a Soldier of Fortune. By W. H. Maxwell. 1 vol post 8vo 10s 6d

Wanderings and Excursions in South Wales. By T. Roscoe. 8vo 25s

Excursions in Albania. By Captain J. J. Bast. Post 8vo 10s 6d

Journal of a Tour in Greece and the Ionian Islands. By W. Mure. 2 vols post 8vo 24s

Agricultural Tour in the United States and Upper Canada. By Captain Barclay. Post 8vo 7s 6d

Visit to the United States in 1841. By Joseph Sturge. 8vo 7s

A Ride on Horseback to Florence, through France and Switzerland. By a Lady. 2 vols post 8vo 18s

Excursions along the Shores of the Mediterranean. By Lieut.-Col. Napier. 2 vols post 8vo 25s

England in 1841. By Fred. Von Raumer. 2 vols post 8vo 21s

The Slave-States of America. By J. S. Buckingham, Esq. 2 vols 8vo 1l 11s 6d

Journal of a Tour to Waterloo and Paris, in company with Sir Walter Scott. By the late John Scott. Post 8vo 9s

Valery's Travels in Italy. Translated from the Second Edition. By C. E. Clifton. 12mo 16s

Ireland; its Scenery, Character, &c. By Mr. and Mrs. S. C. Hall. Vol. II. Imperial 8vo 25s

Creoliana; or, Scenes and Incidents in Barbadoes. By J. W. Orderson. Foolscap 6s

Sights and Thoughts in Foreign Churches, and among Foreign People. By the Rev. F. W. Faber. 8vo 16s

BOOKS FOR YOUNG PERSONS.

Miss Martineau's Playfellow. Vol. IV.—The Crofton Boys. 18mo 3s 6d

The Old Basket; or, Stories for a Week. By Lady E. Courtenay. 18mo 1s 6d

The New Jack the Giant-Killer. By Mrs. Lamont. 18mo 2s 6d

Conversations on the Parables. Fifth Edition. 18mo 2s 6d

My Boy's Second Book. By M. F. Tytler. Square 3s 6d

The Comic Adventures of Beau Ogleby. Oblong 8vo 6s

Instructive Tales. By Peter Prattle. Oblong 4to 5s

The Holiday Keepsake. By Mrs. Sherwood. Square 5s

The Juvenile Forget-Me-Not. By Mrs. Sherwood. Square 5s

Sintram and his Companions; a Northern Tale. From the German of De la Motte Fouque. Foolscap 3s 6d

School Girl in France. Second Edition. 12mo 5s

Philosophy in Sport made Science in Earnest. Foolscap 8s

ART. I.—*Exercitia Spiritualia S. P. Ignatii Loyolæ, cum Versione literali ex Autographo Hispanico. Præmittuntur* R. P. JOANNIS ROOTHMEN, *Præpositi Generalis Societatis Jesu, Literæ Encyclicæ ad Patres et Fratres ejusdem Societatis, de Spiritualium Exercitiorum S. P. N. Studio et Usu.* Londini, typis C. Richards : 1837.

ON the dawn of the day on which, in the year 1534, the Church of Rome celebrated the feast of the Assumption of Our Blessed Lady, a little company of men, whose vestments bespoke their religious character, emerged in solemn procession from the deep shadows cast by the towers of Notre Dame over the silent city below them. In a silence not less profound, except when broken by the chant of the matins appropriate to that sacred season, they climbed the Hill of Martyrs, and descended into the Crypt which then ascertained the spot where the Apostle of France had won the crown of martyrdom. With a stately though halting gait, as one accustomed to military command, marched at their head a man of swarthy complexion, bald-headed and of middle stature, who had passed the meridian of life; his deep-set eyes glowing as with a perennial fire, from beneath brows which, had phrenology then been born, she might have portrayed in her loftiest style, but which, without her aid, announced a commission from on high to subjugate and to rule mankind. So majestic, indeed, was the aspect of Ignatius Loyola, that, during the sixteenth century, few if any of the books of his order appeared without the impress of that imperial countenance. Beside him in the chapel of St. Denys knelt another worshipper, whose manly bearing,

buoyant step, clear blue eye, and finely-chiselled features, contrasted strangely with the solemnities in which he was engaged. Then in early manhood, Francis Xavier united in his person the dignity befitting his birth as a grandee of Spain, and the grace which should adorn a page of the Queen of Castile and Arragon. Not less incongruous with the scene in which they bore their parts, were the slight forms of the boy Alphonso Salmeron, and of his bosom friend Jago Laynez, the destined successor of Ignatius in his spiritual dynasty. With them Nicholas Alphonso Bobadilla, and Simon Rodriguez—the first a teacher, the second a student of philosophy —prostrated themselves before the altar, where ministered Peter Faber, once a shepherd in the mountains of Savoy, but now a priest in holy orders. By his hands was distributed to his associates the seeming bread, over which he had uttered words of more than miraculous efficacy; and then were lifted up their united voices, uttering, in low but distinct articulation, an oath, at the deep significance of which the nations might have trembled or rejoiced. Never did human lips pronounce a vow more religiously observed, or pregnant with results more momentous.

Descended from an illustrious family, Ignatius had in his youth been a courtier and a cavalier, and if not a poet at least a cultivator of poetry. At the siege of Pampeluna his leg was broken, and, after the failure of mere vulgar leeches, was set by a touch from the hand of the Prince of Apostles. Yet St. Peter's therapeutic skill was less perfect than might have been expected from so exalted a chirurgeon; for a splinter still protruded through the skin, and the limb was shrunk and shortened. To regain his fair proportions, Ignatius had himself literally stretched on the rack; and expiated, by a long confinement to his couch, this singular experiment to reduce his refractory bones and sinews. Books of knight-errantry relieved the lassitude of sickness, and, when these were exhausted, he betook himself to a series of still more marvellous romances. In the legends of the Saints the disabled soldier discovered a new field of emulation and of glory. Compared with their self-conquests and their high rewards, the achievements and the renown of Roland and of Amadis waxed dim. Compared with the peerless damsels for whose smiles Paladins had fought and died, how transcendently glorious the image of feminine loveliness and angelic purity which had irradiated the hermit's cell and the path of the wayworn pilgrim! Far as the heavens are above the earth would be the plighted fealty of the knight of the Virgin Mother beyond the noblest devotion of mere human chivalry. In her service he would cast his shield over the church which ascribed to her more than celestial dignities: and bathe in the blood of her enemies the sword once desecrated to the mean ends of worldly ambition. Nor were these vows unheeded by her to whom they were addressed. Environed in light, and clasping her infant to her bosom, she revealed herself to the adoring gaze of her champion. At that heavenly vision, all fantasies of worldly and sensual delight, like exorcised demons, fled from his soul into an eternal exile. He rose, suspended at her shrine his secular weapons, performed there his nocturnal vigils, and with returning day retired to consecrate his future life to the glory of the *Virgo Deipara.*

To these erotic dreams succeeded stern realities; convulsive agonies of prayer, wailings of remorse, and self-inflicted bodily torments. Exchanging dresses with a beggar, he lined his gaberdine with prickly thorns, fasted to the verge of starvation, assumed the demeanour of an idiot, became too loathsome for human contact, and then, plunging into a gloomy cavern, surrendered himself up to such wrestlings with the Evil Spirit, and to such vicissitudes of rapture and despair, that in the storm of turbid passions his reason had nearly given way. Friendly hands dragged him from his hiding-place, and hands, in intention at least not less friendly, recorded his feverish ravings. At one time he conversed with voices audible to no ear but his; at another, he sought to propitiate Him before whom he trembled, by expiations which would have been more fitly offered to Moloch. Spiritual Doctors ministered to his relief, they prescribed in vain. Too simple for their subtilized perception was the simple truth, that in revealing himself to mankind in the character of a Father, that awful Being has claimed as peculiarly his own the gentlest, the kindest, and the most confiding affections of our nature.

At the verge of madness Ignatius paused. That noble intellect was not to be whelmed beneath the tempests in which so many have sunk, nor was his deliverance to be accomplished by any vulgar methods. Standing on the steps of a Dominican church he recited the office of our Lady, when suddenly heaven itself was laid open to the eye of the worshipper. That ineffable mystery, which the author of the Athanasian creed has laboured to enunciate in words, was disclosed to him as an object not of faith, but of actual sight. The past ages of the world were rolled back in his presence, and he beheld the material fabric of things rising into being, and perceived the motives which had prompted the exercise of the creative energy. To his spiritualized sense was disclosed the actual process by which the Host is transubstantiated; and the other Christian verities which it is permitted to common men to receive but as exercises of their belief, now became to him the objects of immediate inspection and of direct consciousness. For eight successive days his body reposed in an unbroken trance; while his spirit thus imbibed disclosures for which the tongues of men have no appropriate language. In a volume of fourscore leaves he attempted indeed to impart them; but dark with excess of light, his words held the learned and the ignorant alike in speechless wonder.

Ignatius returned to this sublunary scene with a mission not unmeet for an envoy from the empyrean world, of which he had thus become a temporary denizen He returned to establish on earth a theocracy of which he should himself be the first administrator, and to which every tribe and kindred of men should be subject. He returned no longer a sordid half-distracted anchorite, but, strange to tell, a man distinguished not more by the gigantic magnitude of his designs, than by the clear good sense, the profound sagacity, the calm perseverance, and the flexible address with which he was to pursue them. History affords no more perfect illustration how readily delirious enthusiasm and the shrewdness of the exchange may combine and harmonize in minds of the heroic order. A

Swedenborg-Franklin, reconciling in himself these antagonist propensities, is no monster of the fancy.

On his restoration to human society, Ignatius reappeared in the garb, and addressed himself to the occupations of other religious men. The first fruits of his labours was the book of which we have transcribed the title-page. It was originally written in Spanish, and appeared in an inaccurate Latin version. By the order of the present Pope, Loyola's manuscript, still remaining in the Vatican, has been again translated. In this new form the book is commended to the devout study of the faithful by a bull of Pope Paul III., and by an Encyclical Epistle from the present General of the order of Jesus. To so august a sanction, slight indeed is the aid which can be given by the suffrage of northern heretics. Yet on this subject the chair of Knox, if now filled by himself, would not be very widely at variance with the throne of St Peter The 'Spiritual Exercises' form a manual of what may be called ' the act of conversion.' It proposes a scheme of self-discipline by which, in the course of four weeks, that mighty work is to be accomplished. In the first, the penitent is conducted through a series of dark retrospects to abase, and of gloomy prospects to alarm him. These ends obtained, he is during the next seven days to enrol himself—such is the military style of the book—in the army of the faithful, studying the sacred Biography of the Divine Leader of that elect host, and choosing with extreme caution the plan of life, religious or secular, in which he may be best able to tread in his steps, and to bear the standard emblematic at once of suffering and of conquest. To sustain the soldier of the cross in this protracted warfare, his spiritual eye is, during the third of his solitary weeks, to be fixed in a reverential scrutiny into that unfathomable abyss of woe, into which a descent was once made to rescue the race of Adam from the grasp of their mortal enemies : and then seven suns are to rise and set while the still secluded but now disenthralled spirit is to chant triumphant hallelujahs, elevating her desires heavenward, contemplating glories hitherto unimaginable, and mysteries never before revealed ; till the sacred exercises close with an absolute surrender of all the joys and interests of this sublunary state, as a holocaust, to be consumed by the undying flame of divine love on the altar of the regenerate heart.

He must have been deeply read in the nature of man, who should have predicted such first fruits as these from the restored health of the distracted visionary, who had alternately sounded the base strings of humility on earth, and the living chords which vibrate with spontaneous harmonies along the seventh heavens. A closer survey of the book will but enhance the wonder. To transmute profligates into converts, by a process of which, during any one of her revolutions round our planet, the moon is to witness the commencement and the close, might perhaps seem like a plagiarism from the academies of Laputa. But in his great, and indeed his only extant work, Ignatius Loyola is no dreamer. By force of an instinct with which such minds as his alone are gifted, he could assume the character to which the shrewd, the practical, and the worldly-wise aspire, even when abandoning himself to ecstasies which they are alike unable to comprehend or to endure. His mind resembled the body of his great disciple, Francis Xavier, which, as he preached or baptised, rose majestically towards the skies, while his feet (the pious curiosity of his hearers ascertained the fact) retained their firm hold on the earth below. If the spiritual exercises were designed to excite, they were not less intended to control and to regulate, religious sensibilities. To exalt the spirit above terrestrial objects was scarcely more his aim, than to disenchant mankind of the self-deceits by which that exaltation is usually attempted. The book, it is true, indicates a tone of feeling utterly removed from that which animates the gay and the busy scenes of life : but it could not have been written except by one accustomed to observe those scenes with the keenest scrutiny, and to study the actors in them with the most profound discernment. To this commendation must be added the praise (to borrow terms but too familiar) of evangelical orthodoxy. A Protestant synod might indeed have extracted from the pages of Ignatius many propositions to anathematize ; but they could also have drawn from them much to confirm the doctrines to which their confessions had given such emphatic prominency. If he yielded to the demigods of Rome what we must regard as an idolatrous homage, it would be mere prejudice to deny that his supreme adoration was reserved for that awful Being to whom alone it was due. If he ascribed to merely ritual expiations a value of which we believe them to be altogether destitute, yet were all his mighty powers held in the most earnest and submissive affiance in the Divine Nature, as revealed under the veil of human infirmity and of more than human suffering. After the lapse of two centuries, Philip Doddridge, than whom no man ever breathed more freely on earth the atmosphere of heaven, produced a work of which the Spiritual Exercises might have afforded the model—so many are still the points of contact between those who, ranging themselves round the great object of Christianity as their common centre, occupy the most opposite positions in that expanded circle.

From the publication of the 'Spiritual Exercises' to the Vow of Montmartre, nine years elapsed. They wore away in pilgrimages, in feats of asceticism, in the working of miracles, and in escapes all but miraculous, from dangers which the martial spirit of the saint, no less than his piety, impelled him to incur. In the caverns of Monreza he had vowed to scale the heights of "*perfection*," and it therefore behoved him thus to climb that obstinate eminence, in the path already trodden by all the canonized and beatified heroes of the church. But he had also vowed to conduct his fellow-pilgrims from the city of destruction to the land of Beulah. In prison and in shipwreck, fainting with hunger or wasted with disease, his inflexible spirit still brooded over that bright, though as yet shapeless vision; until at length it assumed a coherent form as he knelt on the Mount of Olives, and traced the last indelible foot-print of the ascending Redeemer of mankind. At that hallowed spot had ended the weary way of Him who had bowed the heavens, and came down to execute on earth a mission of unutterable love and matchless self-denial; and there was revealed to the prophetic gaze of the future founder of the order of Jesus, (no seer-like genius kindled by high resolves), the long line of missionaries who, animated by his example and guided by his instructions, should proclaim that holy name from the rising to the setting sun. It was indeed a futurity perceptible only to the telescopic eye of faith. At the mature age of thirty, possessing no language but his own, no science but that of the camp, and no literature beyond the biographies of Paladins and of Saints, he became the self-destined teacher of the future teachers of the world. Hoping against hope, he returned to Barcelona and there, as the class-fellow of little children, commenced the study of the first rudiments of the Latin tongue.

Among the established *facetiæ* of the stage, are the distractions of dramatic Eloisas under the tutorship of their Abelards, in the attempt to conjugate *Amo*. Few playwrights, probably, have been aware that the jest had its type, if not its origin, in the scholastic experiences of Ignatius Loyola. At the same critical point, and in the same manner, a malignant spirit arrested his advance in the grammar. On each successive inflection of the verb, corresponding elevations heavenwards were excited in his soul by the demon, who, assuming the garb of an angel of light, thus succeeded in disturbing his memory. To baffle his insidious enemy, the harassed scholar implored the pedagogue to make liberal use of that discipline of which who can ever forget the efficacy or the pain? The exorcism was complete. *Amo*, in all her affectionate moods, and changeful tenses, became familiar as household words. Thus Thomas à Kempis was made to speak intelligibly. Erasmus also revealed his hidden treasures of learning and wit, though ultimately exiled from the future schools of the Jesuits, for the same offence of having disturbed the thoughts of his devout reader. Energy won her accustomed triumphs, and, in the year 1528, he became a student of the Humanities, and of what was then called Philosophy, at the University of Paris.

Of the seven decades of human life, the brightest and the best, in which other men achieve or contend for distinction, was devoted by Ignatius to the studies preparatory to his great undertaking. Grave professors examined him on their prælections, and, when these were over, he sought the means of subsistence by traversing the Netherlands and England as a beggar. Unheeded and despised as he sat at the feet of the learned, or solicited alms of the rich, he was still maturing in the recesses of his bosom designs more lofty than the highest to which the monarchs of the houses of Valois or of Tudor had ever dared to aspire. In the University of Paris he at length found the means of carrying into effect the cherished purposes of so many years. It was the heroic age of Spain, and the countrymen of Gonsalvo and Cortes lent a willing ear to counsels of daring on any field of adventure, whether secular or spiritual. His companions in study thus became his disciples in religion. Nor were his the common-place methods of making converts. To the contemplative and the timid, he enjoined hardy exercises of active virtue. To the gay and the ardent, he appealed in a spirit still more buoyant than their own. To a debauchee, whom nothing else could move, he presented himself neck-deep in a pool of frozen water, to teach more impressively the duty of subduing the carnal appetites. To an obdurate priest, he made a general confession of his own sins, with such agonies of remorse and shame,- as to break up, by force of sympathy, the fountains of penitence in the bosom of the confessor. Nay, he even engaged at billiards with a joyous lover of the game, on condition that the defeated player should serve his antagonist for a month; and the victorious saint enforced the penalty by consigning his adversary to a month of secluded devotion. Others yielded at once and without a struggle to the united influence of his sanctity and genius; and it is remarkable that, from these more docile converts, he selected, with but two exceptions, the original members of his infant order. Having performed the initiatory rite of the Spiritual Exercises, they all swore on the consecrated Host in the Crypt of St. Denys, to accompany their spiritual father on a mission to Palestine; or, if that should be impracticable, to submit themselves to the vicar of Christ, to be disposed of as missionaries at his pleasure.

Impetuous as had been the temper of Ignatius in early life, he had learned to be patient of the slow growth of great designs. Leaving his disciples to complete their studies at Paris under the care of Peter Faber, he returned to Spain to recruit their number, to mature his plans, and, perhaps, to escape from a too familiar intercourse with his future subjects. In the winter of 1536, they commenced their pilgrimage to the eternal city. Xavier was their leader. Accomplished in all courtly exercises, he prepared for his journey by binding tight cords round his arms and legs, in holy revenge for the pleasure which their graceful agility had once afforded him; and pursued his way with Spartan constancy, till the corroded flesh closed obstinately over the ligatures. Miracle, the prompt handmaid of energies like his, burst the bands which no surgeon could extricate; and her presence was attested by the toils which his loosened limbs immediately endured in the menial service of his fellow travellers. At Venice they rejoined their leader, and there employed themselves in ministering to the patients in the hospitals. Foremost in every act of intrepid self-mortification, Xavier here signalized his zeal by exploits, the mere recital of which would derange the stomachs of ordinary men. While courting all the physical tortures of purgatory, his soul, however, inhaled the anticipated raptures of Paradise. Twice these penances and raptures brought him to the gates of death; and, in his last extremity, he caused himself to be borne to places of public resort, that his ghastly aspect might teach the awful lessons which his tongue was no longer able to pronounce.

Such prodigies, whether enacted by the saints of Rome or by those of Benares, exhibit a sovereignty of the spiritual over the animal nature, which can hardly be contemplated without some feelings akin to reverence. But, on the whole, the hooked Faqueer spinning round his gibbet is the more respectable suicide of the two; for his homage is, at least, meet for the deity he worships. He whose name had been assumed by Ignatius and his followers, equally victorious over the stoical illusions and the lower affections of our nature, had been accustomed to seek repose among the domestic charities of life, and to accept such blameless solaces as life has to offer to the weary and the heavy-laden; nor could services less in harmony with his serene self-reverence have been presented to him, than the vehement emotions, the squalid filth, and the lacerated frames of the first members of the society of Jesus. Loyola himself tolerated, encouraged, and shared these extravagances. His countenance was as haggard, his flagellations as cruel, and his couch and diet as sordid as the rest. They who will conquer crowns, whether ghostly or secular, must needs tread in slippery places. He saw his comrades faint and die with the extremity of their sufferings, and assuming the character of an inspired prophet, promoted, by predicting, their recovery. One of the gentlest and most patient of them, Rodriguez, flying for relief to a solitary hermitage, found his retreat obstructed by a man of terrible aspect and gigantic stature, armed with a naked sword and breathing menaces. Hosez, another of his associates, happening to die at the moment when Ignatius, prostrate before the altar, was reciting from the *Confiteor* the words, " et omnibus sanctis," that countless host was revealed to the eye of the saint; and among them, resplendent in glory, appeared his deceased friend, to sustain and animate the hopes of his surviving brethren. As he journeyed with Laynez, he saw a still more awful vision. It exhibited that Being whom no eye hath seen, and whom no tongue may lightly name, and with him the Eternal Son, bearing a heavy cross, and uttering the welcome assurance, " I will be propitious to you at Rome."

These, however, were but the auxiliary and occasional arts (if so they must be termed) by which the sovereignty of Ignatius was established. It behoved him to acquire the unhesitating submission of noble minds, ignited by a zeal as intense and as enduring as his own; and it was on a far loftier basis than that of bodily penances or ecstatic dreams, that for ten successive years their initiatory discipline had been conducted. Wildly as their leader may have described his survey of the celestial regions, and of their triumphant inmates, he had anxiously weighed the state of the world in which he dwelt, and the nature of his fellow sojourners there. He was intimately aware of the effects on human character of self-acquaintance, of action, and of suffering. He therefore required his disciples to scrutinize the recesses and the workings of their own hearts, till the aching sense found relief rather than excitement, in turning from the wonders and the shame within, to the mysteries and the glories of the world of unembodied spirits. He trained them to ceaseless activity, until the transmutation of means into ends was complete; and efforts, at first the most irksome, had become spontaneous and even grateful exercises. He accustomed them to every form of privation and voluntary pain, until fortitude, matured into habit, had been the source of enjoyments, as real as to the luxurious they are incomprehensible. He rendered them stoics, mystics, enthusiasts, and then combined them all into an institute, than which no human association was ever more emphatically practical, or more to the purpose and the time.

Of all the occupations to which man can devote the earlier years of life, none probably leaves on the character an impress so deep and indelible as the profession of arms. In no other calling are the whole range of our sympathetic affections, whether kindly or the reverse, called into such habitual and active exercise; nor does any other stimulate the mere intellectual powers with a force so irresistible, when once they are effectually aroused from their accustomed torpor. Loyola was a soldier to the last breath he drew, a General whose authority none might question, a comrade on whose cordiality all might rely, sustaining all the dangers and hardships he exacted of his followers, and in his religious campaigns a Strategist of consummate skill and most comprehensive survey. It was his maxim that war ought to be aggressive, and that even an inadequate force might be wisely weakened by detachments on a distant service, if the prospect of success was such, that the vague and perhaps exaggerated rumour of it would strike terror into nearer foes, and animate the hopes of irresolute allies. To conquer Lutheranism, by converting to the faith of Rome the barba-

rous or half-civilized nations of the earth, was therefore among the earliest of his projects; and his searching eye had scanned the spirits of his lieutenants to discover which of them was best adapted for enterprises so replete with difficulty and hazard. It was necessary that he should select men superior, not only to all the allurements of appetite, and the common infirmities of our race, but superior, also, to those temptations to which an inquisitive mind and abilities of a high order expose their possessor. His missionaries must be men prepared to do and to dare, but not much disposed to speculate. They must burn with a zeal which no sufferings or disappointment could extinguish; but must not feel those impulses which might prompt men of large capacity to convert a subordinate into an independent command. Long he weighed, and most sagaciously did he decide this perplexing choice. It fell on many who well fulfilled these conditions, but on none in whom all the requisites for such a service met so marvellously as on him who had borne himself so bravely in the chapel of St. Denys, and with such strange mortifications of the flesh in the pilgrimage to Rome.

It was in the year 1506 that Francis Xavier, the youngest child of a numerous family, was born in the castle of his ancestors in the Pyrenees. Robust and active, of a gay humour and ardent spirit, the young mountaineer listened with a throbbing heart to the military legends of his House, and to the inward voice which spoke of days to come, when his illustrious lineage should derive new splendour from his own achievements. But the hearts of his parents yearned over the son of their old age; and the enthusiasm which would have borne him to the pursuit of glory in the camp, was diverted by their counsels to the less hazardous contest for literary eminence at the university of Paris. From the embrace of Aristotle and his commentators, he would, however, have been prematurely withdrawn by the failure of his resources, (for the Lords of Xavier were not wealthy,) if a domestic prophetess (his elder sister) had not been inspired to reveal his marvellous career and immortal recompense. For a child destined to have altars raised to his name throughout the Catholic Church, and masses chanted in his honour till time should be no longer, every sacrifice was wisely made; and he was thus enabled to struggle on at the College of St. Barbara, till he had become qualified to earn his own maintenance as a public teacher of Philosophy. His Chair was crowded by the studious, and his society courted by the gay, the noble, and the rich. It was courted, also, by one who stood aloof from the thronging multitude; among them, but not of them. Sordid in dress but of lofty bearing, at once unimpassioned and intensely earnest, abstemious of speech, yet occasionally uttering, in deep and most melodious tones, words of strange significance, Ignatius Loyola was gradually working over the mind of his young companion a spell which no difference of taste, of habits, or of age, was of power to subdue. Potent as it was, the charm was long resisted. Hilarity was the native and indispensable element of Francis Xavier, and in his grave monitor he found an exhaustless topic of mirth and raillery. Armed with satire, which was not always playful, the light heart of youth contended, as best it might, against the solemn impressions which he could neither welcome nor avoid. Whether he partook of the frivolities in which he delighted, or in the disquisitions in which he excelled, or traced the windings of the Seine through the forest which then lined its banks, Ignatius was still at hand to discuss with him the charms of society, of learning, or of nature; but, whatever had been the theme, it was still closed by the same awful inquiry, "What shall it profit a man if he gain the whole world and lose his own soul?" The world which Xavier had sought to gain, was indeed already exhibiting to him its accustomed treachery. It had given him amusement and applause; but with his self-government had stolen from him his pupils and his emoluments. Ignatius recruited both. He became the eulogist of the genius and the eloquence of his friend, and, as he presented to him the scholars attracted by these panegyrics, would repeat them in the presence of the delighted teacher; and then, as his kindling eye attested the sense of conscious and acknowledged merit, would check the rising exultation by the ever-recurring question, "What shall it profit?" Improvidence squandered these new resources; but nothing could damp the zeal of Ignatius. There he was again, though himself the poorest of the poor, ministering to the wants of Xavier, from a purse filled by the alms he had solicited; but there again was also the same unvarying demand, urged in the same rich though solemn cadence, "What shall it profit?" In the unrelaxing grasp of the strong man—at once forgiven and assisted, rebuked and beloved by his stern associate—Xavier gradually yielded to the fascination. He became, like his master, impassive, at least in appearance, to all sublunary pains and pleasures; and having performed the initiatory rite of the Spiritual Exercises, excelled all his brethren of the society of Jesus in the fervour of his devotion and the austerity of his self-discipline.

Whatever might have been his reward in another life, his name would have probably left no trace in this world's records, if John III. of Portugal, resolving to plant the Christian faith on the Indian territories which had become subject to the dominion or influence of his crown, had not petitioned the Pope to select some fit leader in this peaceful crusade. On the advice of Ignatius, the choice of the Holy Father fell on Francis Xavier. A happier selection could not have been made, nor was a summons to toil, to suffering, and to death, ever so joyously received. In the visions of the night he had often groaned under the incumbent weight of a wild Indian, of ebon hue and gigantic stature, seated on his shoulders; and he had often traversed tempestuous seas, enduring shipwreck and famine, persecution and danger, in all their most ghastly forms; and as each peril was encountered, his panting soul had invoked, in still greater abundance, the means of making such glorious sacrifices for the conversion of mankind. When the clearer sense and the approaching accomplishment of these dark intimations were disclosed to him, the passionate sobs attested the rapture which his tongue could not speak. Light of heart, and joyful in discourse, he conducted his fellow-pilgrims from Rome to Lisbon, across the Pyrenees. As he descended their southern slopes, there rose to his sight the towers where he had enjoyed the sports of childhood, and woven the day-dreams of youth; where still lived the mother, who for eighteen years had daily watched and blessed him, and the saintly sister whose inspired voice had foretold his high vocation. It was all too high for the momentary intrusion of the holiest of merely human feelings. He was on his way with tidings of mercy to a fallen world, and he had not one hour to waste, nor one parting tear to bestow on those whom he best loved and most revered, and whom, in this life, he could never hope to meet again.

We are not left to conjecture in what light his conduct was regarded. 'I care little, most illustrious doctor, for the judgment of men, and least of all for their judgment who decide before they hear and before they understand,' was his half-sportive, half-indignant answer to the remonstrances of a grave and well-beneficed kinsman, (a shrewd, thriving, hospitable, much-respected man, no unlikely candidate for the mitre, and a candidate, too, in his own drowsy way, for amaranthine crowns and celestial blessedness,) who very plausibly believed his nephew mad. Mad or sober, he was at least impelled by a force, at the first shock of which the united common sense and respectability of mankind must needs fall to pieces—the force of will concentrated on one great end, and elevated above the misty regions of doubt, into that unclouded atmosphere, where, attended by her handmaids, hope and courage, joy and fortitude, Faith converts the future into the present, and casts the brightest hues over objects the most repulsive to human sense, and the most painful to our feeble nature.

As the vessel in which Xavier embarked for India fell down the Tagus, and shook out her reefs to the wind, many an eye was dimmed with unwonted tears; for she bore a regiment of a thousand men to reinforce the garrison of Goa; nor could the bravest of that gallant host gaze on the receding land without foreboding that he might never see again those dark chestnut forests and rich orange groves, with the peaceful convents and the long-loved homes reposing in their bosom. The countenance of Xavier alone beamed with delight. He knew that he should never tread his native mountains more; but he was not an exile. He was to depend for food and raiment on the bounty of his fellow passengers; but no thought for the morrow troubled him He was going to convert nations, of which he knew neither the language nor even the names; but he felt no misgivings. Worn by incessant sea-sickness, with the refuse food of the lowest seamen for his diet, and the cordage of the ship for his couch, he rendered to the diseased services too revolting to be described; and lived among the dying and the profligate the unwearied minister of consolation and of peace. In the midst of that floating throng, he knew how to create for himself a sacred solitude, and how to mix in all their pursuits in the free spirit of a man of the world, a gentleman, and a scholar. With the viceroy and his officers he talked, as pleased them best, of war or trade, of politics or navigation; and to restrain the common soldiers from gambling, would invent for their amusement less dangerous pastimes, or even hold the stakes for which they played, that by his presence and his gay discourse, he might at least check the excesses which he could not prevent.

Five weary months (weary to all but him) brought the ship to Mozambique, where an endemic fever threatened a premature grave to the apostle of the Indies. But his was not a spirit to be quenched or allayed by the fiercest paroxysms of disease. At each remission of his malady, he crawled to the beds of his fellow sufferers to soothe their terrors or assuage their pains. To the eye of any casual observer the most wretched of mankind, in the esteem of his companions the happiest and the most holy, he reached Goa just thirteen months after his departure from Lisbon.

At Goa, Xavier was shocked, and had fear been an element in his nature, would have been dismayed, by the almost universal depravity of the inhabitants. It exhibited itself in those offensive forms which characterize the crimes of civilized men when settled among a feebler race, and released from even the conventional decencies of civilisation. Swinging in his hand a large bell, he traversed the streets of the city, and implored the astonished crowd to send their children to him, to be instructed in the religion which they still at least professed. Though he had never been addressed by the soul-stirring name of father, he knew that in the hardest and the most dissolute heart which had once felt the parental instinct, there is one chord which can never be wholly out of tune. A crowd of little ones were quickly placed under his charge. He lived among them as the most laborious of teachers, and the gentlest and the gayest of friends; and then returned them to their homes, that by their more hallowed example they might there impart, with all the unconscious eloquence of filial love, the lessons of wisdom and of piety they had been taught. No cry of human misery reached him in vain. He became an inmate of the hospitals, selecting that of the leprous as the object of his peculiar care. Even in the haunts of debauchery, and at the tables of the profligate, he was to be seen an honoured and a welcome guest; delighting that most unmeet audience with the vivacity of his discourse, and sparing neither pungent jests to render vice ridiculous, nor sportive flatteries to allure the fallen back to the still distasteful paths of soberness and virtue. Strong in purity of purpose, and stronger still in one sacred remembrance, he was content to be called the friend of publicans and sinners. He had in truth long since deserted the standard of prudence, the offspring of forethought, for the banners of wisdom, the child of love, and followed them through perils not to be hazarded under any less triumphant leader.

Rugged were the ways along which he was thus conducted. In those times, as in our own, there was on the Coromandel coast a pearl fishery, and then, as now, the pearl-divers formed a separate and a degraded caste. It was not till after a residence of twelve months at Goa, that Xavier heard of these people He heard that they were ignorant and miserable, and he inquired no further. On that burning shore his bell once more rang out an invitation of mercy, and again were gathered around him troops of inquisitive and docile children. For fifteen months he lived among these abject fishermen, his only food their rice and water, reposing in their huts, and allowing himself but three hours' sleep in the four-and-twenty. He became at once their physician, the arbiter in their disputes, and their advocate for the remission of their annual tribute with the government at Goa. The bishop of that city had assisted him with two interpreters; but his impassioned spirit struggled, and not in vain, for some more direct intercourse with the objects of his care. Committing to memory translations, at the time unintelligible to himself, of the creeds and other symbols of his faith, he recited them with tones and gestures, which spoke at once to the senses and to the hearts of his disciples. All obstacles yielded to his restless zeal. He soon learned to converse, to preach, and to write in their language. Many an humble cottage was surmounted by a crucifix, the mark of its consecration; and many a rude countenance reflected the sorrows and the hopes which they had been taught to associate with that sacred emblem. 'I have nothing to add,' (the quotation is from one of the letters which at this time he wrote to Loyola,) ' but that they who came forth to labour for the salvation of idolaters, receive from on high such consolations, that if there be on earth such a thing as happiness, it is theirs.'

If there be such a thing, it is but as the chequered sunshine of a vernal day A hostile inroad from Madura overwhelmed the poor fishermen who had learned to call Xavier their father, threw down their simple chapels, and drove them for refuge to the barren rocks and sand-banks which line the western shores of the strait of Manar. But their father was at hand to share their affliction, to procure for them from the viceroy at Goa relief and food, and to direct their confidence to a still more powerful Father, whose presence and goodness they might adore even amidst the wreck of all their earthly treasures.

It was a lesson not unmeet for those on whom such treasures had been bestowed in the most ample abundance; and Xavier advanced to Travancore, to teach it there to the Rajah and his courtiers. No facts

resting on remote human testimony can be more exempt from doubt than the general outline of the tale which follows. A solitary, poor, and unprotected stranger, he burst through the barriers which separate men of different tongues and races; and with an ease little less than miraculous, established for himself the means of interchanging thoughts with the people of the east. They may have ill-gathered his meaning, but by some mysterious force of sympathy they soon caught his ardour. Idol temples fell by the hands of their former worshippers. Christian churches rose at his bidding; and the kingdom of Travancore was agitated with new ideas and unwonted controversies. The Brahmins argued—as the Church by law established has not seldom argued—with fire and sword, and the interdict of earth and water to the enemies of their repose. A foreign invader threw a still heavier sword into the trembling scales. From the southward appeared on the borders of Travancore the same force which had swept away the poor fishermen of Malabar. Some embers of Spanish chivalry still glowed in the bosom of Xavier. He flew to the scene of the approaching combat, and there, placing himself in the van of the protecting army, poured forth a passionate prayer to the Lord of Hosts, raised on high his crucifix, and with kindling eyes, and far-resounding voice, delivered the behests of Heaven to the impious invaders. So runs the tale, and ends (it is almost superfluous to add) in the rout of the astounded foe. It is a matter of less animated, and perhaps of more authentic history, that for his services in this war Xavier was rewarded by the unbounded gratitude of the Rajah, was honoured with the title of his Great Father, and rescued from all further Brahminical persecution.

Power and courtly influence form an intoxicating draught even when raised to the lips of an ascetic and a saint. Holy as he was, the Great Father of the Rajah of Travancore seems not entirely to have escaped this feverish thirst. Don Alphonso de Souza, a weak though amiable man, was at that time the Viceroy of Portuguese India, and Xavier (such was now his authority) despatched a messenger to Lisbon to demand, rather than to advise his recall. Within the limits of his high commission, (and what subject is wholly foreign to it?) the ambassador of the King of Kings may owe respect, but hardly deference, to any mere earthly monarch. So argued Francis, so judged King John, and so fell Alphonso de Souza, as many a greater statesman has fallen, and may yet fall, under the weight of sacerdotal displeasure. This weakness, however, was not his only recorded fault. Towards the northern extremity of Ceylon lies the Island of Manar, a dependency, in Xavier's day, of the adjacent kingdom of Jaffna, where then reigned a sort of oriental Philip II. The islanders had become converts to the Christian faith, and expiated their apostacy by their lives. Six hundred men, women, and children, fell in one royal massacre; and the tragedy was closed by the murder of the eldest son of the King of Jaffna, by his father's orders Deposition in case of misgovernment, and the transfer to the deposing Power of the dominions of the offender, was no invention of Hastings, or of Clive. It is one of the most ancient constitutional maxims of the European dynasties in India. It may even boast the venerable suffrage of St. Francis Xavier. At his instance, De Souza equipped an armament to hurl the guilty ruler of Jaffna from his throne, and to subjugate his territories to the most faithful King. In the invading fleet the indignant saint led the way, with promises of triumphs, both temporal and eternal. But the expedition failed. Cowardice or treachery defeated the design. De Souza paid the usual penalties of ill success. Xavier sailed away to discover other fields of spiritual warfare.

On the Malabar coast, near the city of Meliapor, might be seen in those times the oratory and the tomb of St. Thomas, the first teacher of Christianity in India. It was in a cool and sequestered grotto that the apostle had been wont to pray; and there yet appeared on the living rock, in bold relief, the cross at which he knelt, with a crystal fountain of medicinal waters gushing from the base of it. On the neighbouring height, a church with a marble altar, stained, after the lapse of fifteen centuries, with the blood of the martyr, ascertained the sacred spot at which his bones had been committed to the dust. To this venerable shrine Xavier retired, to learn the will of Heaven concerning him. If we may believe the oath of one of his fellow-pilgrims, he maintained on this occasion, for seven successive days an unbroken fast and silence—no unfit preparation for his approaching conflicts. Even round the tomb of the apostle malignant demons prowl by night; and, though strong in the guidance of the Virgin, Xavier not only found himself in their obscene grasp, but received from them blows, such as no weapons in human hands could have inflicted, and which had nearly brought to a close his labours and his life. Baffled by a superior power, the fiends opposed a still more subtle hindrance to his

designs against their kingdom. In the garb, and in the outward semblance of a band of choristers, they disturbed his devotions by such soul-subduing strains, that the very harmonies of heaven might seen to have been awakened to divert the Christian warrior from his heavenward path. All in vain their fury and their guile. He found the direction he implored, and the first bark which sailed from the Coromandel shore to the city of Malacca, bore the obedient missionary to that great emporium of eastern commerce.

Thirty years before the arrival of Xavier, Malacca had been conquered by Alphonso Albuquerque. It was a place abandoned to every form of sensual and enervating indulgence. Through her crowded streets a strange and solemn visiter passed along, pealing his faithful bell, and earnestly imploring the prayers of the faithful for that guilty people. Curiosity and alarm soon gave way to ridicule; but Xavier's panoply was complete. The messenger of divine wrath judged this an unfit occasion for courting aversion or contempt. He became the gayest of the gay, and, in address at least, the very model of an accomplished cavalier. Foiled at their own weapons, his dissolute countrymen acknowledged the irresistible authority of a self-devotion so awful, relieved and embellished as it was by every social grace. Thus the work of reformation prospered, or seemed to prosper. Altars rose in the open streets, the confessional was thronged by penitents, translations of devout books were multiplied; and the saint, foremost in every toil, applied himself with all the activity of his spirit, to study the structure and the graceful pronunciation of the Malayar tongue. But the plague was not thus to be stayed. A relapse into all their former habits filled up the measure of their crimes. With prophetic voice Xavier announced the impending chastisements of Heaven; and, shaking off from his feet the dust of the obdurate city, pursued his indefatigable way to Amboyna.

That island, then a part of the vast dominions of Portugal in the east, had scarcely witnessed the commencement of Xavier's exertions, when a fleet of Spanish vessels appeared in hostile array on the shores. They were invaders and even corsairs; for their expedition had been disavowed by Charles V. Pestilence, however, was raging among them; and Xavier was equally ready to hazard his life in the cause of Portugal, or in the service of her afflicted enemies. Day and night he lived in the infected ships, soothing every spiritual distress, and exerting all the magical influence of his name to procure for the sick whatever might contribute to their recovery or soothe their pains. The coals of fire, thus heaped on the heads of the pirates, melted hearts otherwise steeled to pity; and to Xavier belonged the rare, perhaps the unrivalled, glory of repelling an invasion by no weapons but those of self-denial and love.

But glory, the praise of men or their gratitude, what were these to him? As the Spaniards retired peacefully from Amboyna, he, too, quitted the half-adoring multitude whom he had rescued from the horrors of a pirates' war, and, spurning all the timid counsel which would have stayed his course, proceeded, as the herald of good tidings, to the half barbarous islands of the neighbouring Archipelago. 'If those lands,' such was his indignant exclamation, 'had scented woods and mines of gold, Christians would find courage to go there; nor would all the perils of the world prevent them. They are dastardly and alarmed, because there is nothing to be gained there but the souls of men, and shall love be less hardy and less generous than avarice? They will destroy me, you say, by poison. It is an honour to which such a sinner as I am may not aspire; but this I dare to say, that whatever form of torture or of death awaits me, I am ready to suffer it ten thousand times for the salvation of a single soul.' Nor was this the language of a man insensible to the sorrows of life, or really unaffected by the dangers he had to incur. 'Believe me, my beloved brethren,' (we quote from a letter written by him at this time to the Secretary at Rome,) 'it is in general easy to understand the evangelical maxim, that he who will lose his life shall find it. But when the moment of action has come, and when the sacrifice of life for God is to be really made, oh then, clear as at other times the meaning is, it becomes deeply obscure! so dark, indeed, that he alone can comprehend it, to whom, in his mercy, God himself interprets it. Then it is we know how weak and frail we are.'

Weak and frail he may have been; but from the days of Paul of Tarsus to our own, the annals of mankind exhibit no other example of a soul borne onward so triumphantly through distress and danger, in all their most appalling aspects. He battled with hunger, thirst, and nakedness, and assassination, and pursued his mission of love, with even increasing ardour, amidst the wildest war of the contending elements. At the island of Moro (one of the group of the Moluccas) he took his stand at the foot of a volcano; and as the pillar of fire threw up its wreaths to heaven, and the earth tottered beneath him, and the firmament was rent by falling rocks and peals of unintermitting thunder, he pointed to the fierce lightnings, and the river of molten lava, and called on the agitated crowd which clung to him for safety, to repent, and to obey the truth; but he also taught them that the sounds which racked their ears were the groans of the infernal world, and the sights which blasted their eyes, an outbreak from the atmosphere of the place of torment. Repairing for the celebration of mass to some edifice which he had consecrated for the purpose, an earthquake shook the building to its base. The terrified worshippers fled; but Xavier, standing in meek composure before the rocking altar, deliberately completed that mysterious sacrifice, with a faith at least in this instance enviable, in the real presence; rejoicing as he states in his description of the scene, to perceive that the demons of the island thus attested their flight before the archangel's sword, from the place where they had so long exercised their foul dominion. There is no schoolboy of our days who could not teach much, unsuspected by Francis Xavier, of the laws which govern the material and the spiritual worlds; nor have we many doctors who know as much as he did of the nature of Him by whom the worlds of matter and of spirit were created; and he studied in the school of protracted martyrdom and active philanthropy, where are divulged secrets unknown and unimagined by the wisest and the most learned of ordinary men. Imparting everywhere such knowledge as he possessed, he ranged over no small part of the Indian archipelago, and at length retraced his steps to Malacca, if even yet his exhortations and his prayers might avert her threatened doom.

It appeared to be drawing nigh. Aladin, a Mohamedan chief of Sumatra, had laid siege to the place at the head of a powerful fleet and army. Ill provided for defence by land, the Portuguese garrison was still more unprepared for a naval resistance. Seven shattered barks, unfit for service, formed their whole maritime strength. Universal alarm overspread the city, and the governor himself at once partook and heightened the general panic. Already, thoughts of capitulation had become familiar to the besieged, and European chivalry had bowed in abject silence to the insulting taunts and haughty menaces of the Moslem. At this moment, in his slight and weatherbeaten pinnace, the messenger of peace on earth effected an entrance into the beleaguered harbour. But he came with a loud and indignant summons to the war; for Xavier was still a Spanish cavalier, and he 'thought it foul scorn' that gentlemen, subjects of the most faithful King, should thus be bearded by Barbaric enemies, and the worshippers of Christ defied by the disciples of the Arabian impostor. He assumed the direction of the defence. By his advice the seven dismantled ships were promptly equipped for sea. He assigned to each a commander; and having animated the crews with promises of both temporal and eternal triumphs, despatched them to meet and conquer the hostile fleet. As they sailed from the harbour the admiral's vessel ran aground and instantly became a wreck. Returning hope and exultation as promptly gave way to terror; and Xavier, the idol of the preceding hour, was now the object of popular fury. He alone retained his serenity. He upbraided the cowardice of the governor, revived the troops, and encouraged the multitude with prophecies of success. Again the flotilla sailed, and a sudden tempest drove it to sea. Day after day passed without intelligence of its safety: once more the hearts of the besieged failed them. Rumours of defeat were rife; the Mohamedans had effected a landing within six leagues of the city, and Xavier's name was repeated from mouth to mouth with cries of vengeance. He knelt before the altar, the menacing people scarcely restrained by the sanctity of the place from immolating him there as a victim to his own disastrous counsels. On a sudden his bosom was seen to heave as with some deep emotion; he raised aloft his crucifix, and with a glowing eye, and in tones like one possessed, breathed a short yet passionate prayer for victory. A solemn pause ensued; the dullest eye could see that within that now fainting, pallid, agitated frame, some power more than human was in communion with the weak spirit of man What might be the ineffable sense thus conveyed from mind to mind, without the aid of symbols or of words! One half hour of deep and agonizing silence held the awe-stricken assembly in breathless expectation—when, bounding on his feet, his countenance radiant with joy, and his voice clear and ringing as with the swelling notes of the trumpet, he exclaimed, 'Christ has conquered for us! At this very moment his soldiers are charging our defeated enemies; they have made a great slaughter—we have lost only four of our defenders. On Friday next the intelligence will be here, and we shall then see our fleet again.' The catastrophe of such a tale need not be told. Malacca followed her deliverer, and

the troops of the victorious squadron, in solemn procession to the church, where, amidst the roar of cannon, the pealing of anthems, and hymns of adoring gratitude, his inward sense heard and reverenced that inarticulate voice which still reminded him, that for him the hour of repose and triumph might never come, till he should reach that state where sin would no longer demand his rebuke, nor grief his sympathy. He turned from the half-idolatrous shouts of an admiring people, and retraced his toilsome way to the shores of Coromandel.

He returned to Goa a poor and solitary, but no longer an obscure man. From the Indus to the Yellow Sea, had gone forth a vague and marvellous rumour of him. The tale bore that a stranger had appeared in the semblance of a wayworn, abject beggar, who, by some magic influence, and for some inscrutable ends, had bowed the nations to his despotic will, while spurning the wealth, the pleasures, and the homage which they offered to their conqueror. Many were the wonders which travellers had to tell of his progress, and without number the ingenious theories afloat for the solution of them. He possessed the gift of ubiquity, could at the same moment speak in twenty different tongues on as many dissimilar subjects, was impassive to heat, cold, hunger, and fatigue, held hourly intercourse with invisible beings, the guides or ministers of his designs, raised the dead to life, and could float, when so it pleased him, across the boiling ocean on the wings of the typhoon. Among the listeners to these prodigies had been Auger, a native and inhabitant of Japan. His conscience was burdened with the memory of great crimes, and he had sought relief in vain from many an expiatory rite, and from the tumults of dissipation. In search of the peace he could not find at home, he sailed to Malacca, there to consult with the mysterious person of whose *avatur* he had heard. But Xavier was absent, and the victim of remorse was retracing his melancholy voyage to Japan, when a friendly tempest arrested his retreat, and once more brought him to Malacca. He was attended by two servants, and with them, by Xavier's directions, he proceeded to Goa. In these three Japanese, his prophetic eye had at once seen the future instruments of the conversion of their native land; and to that end he instructed them to enter on a systematic course of training in a college, which he had established for such purposes, at the seat of Portuguese empire in the east. At that place Xavier, ere long, rejoined his converts. Such had been their proficiency, that soon after his arrival they were admitted not only into the church by baptism, but into the society of Jesus, by the performance of the spiritual exercises.

The history of Xavier now reaches a not unwelcome pause. He pined for solitude and silence   He had been too long in constant intercourse with man, and found that, however high and holy may be the ends for which social life is cultivated, the habit, if unbroken, will impair that inward sense through which alone the soul can gather any true intimations of her nature and her destiny. He retired to commune with himself in a seclusion where the works of God alone were to be seen, and where no voices could be heard but those which, in each varying cadence, raise an unconscious anthem of praise and adoration to their creator. There for a while reposing from labours such as few or any other of the sons of men have undergone, he consumed days and weeks in meditating prospects beyond the reach of any vision unenlarged by the habitual exercise of beneficence and piety. There, too, it may be, (for man must still be human,) he surrendered himself to dreams as baseless, and to ecstasies as devoid of any real meaning, as those which haunt the cell of the maniac. Peace be to the hallucinations, if such they were, by which the giant refreshed his slumbering powers, and from which he roused himself to a conflict never again to be remitted till his frame, yielding to the ceaseless pressure, should sink into a premature but hallowed grave.

Scarcely four years had elapsed from the first discovery of Japan by the Portuguese, when Xavier, attended by Auger and his two servants, sailed from Goa to convert the islanders to the Christian faith. Much good advice had been, as usual, wasted on him by his friends. To Loyola alone he confided the secret of his confidence. ' I cannot express to you' (such are his words) ' the joy with which I undertake this long voyage ; for it is full of extreme perils, and we consider a fleet sailing to Japan as eminently prosperous in which one ship out of four is saved. Though the risk far exceeds any which I have hitherto encountered, I shall not decline it; for our Lord has imparted to me an interior revelation of the rich harvest which will one day be gathered from the cross when once planted there.' Whatever may be thought of these voices from within, it is at least clear, that nothing magnanimous or sublime has ever yet proceeded from those who have listened only to the voices from without. But, as if resolved to show that a man may at once

act on motives incomprehensible to his fellow mortals, and possess the deepest insight into the motives by which they are habitually governed, Xavier left behind him a code of instructions for his brother missionaries, illuminated in almost every page by that profound sagacity which results from the union of extensive knowledge with acute observation, mellowed by the intuitive wisdom of a compassionate and lowly heart. The science of self-conquest, with a view to conquer the stubborn will of others, the act of winning admission for painful truth, and the duties of fidelity and reverence in the attempt to heal the diseases of the human spirit, were never taught by uninspired man with an eloquence more gentle, or in authority more impressive. A long voyage, pursued through every disaster which the malevolence of man and demons could oppose to his progress, (for he was constrained to sail in a piratical ship, with idols on her deck, and whirlwinds in her path,) brought him, in the year 1549, to Japan, there to practise his own lessons, and to give a new example of heroic perseverance.

His arrival had been preceded by what he regarded as fortuate auguries. Certain Portuguese merchants, who had been allowed to reside at the principal seaport, inhabited there a house haunted by spectres. Their presence was usually announced by the din of discordant and agonizing screams; but when revealed to the eye, presented forms resembling those which may be seen in pictures of the infernal state. Now the merchants, secular men though they were, had exorcised these fiends by carrying the cross in solemn procession through the house ; and anxious curiosity pervaded the city for some explanation of the virtue of this new and potent charm. There were also legends current through the county which might be turned to good account. Xaca, the son of Amida, the *Virgo Deipara* of Japan, had passed a life of extreme austerity to expiate the sins of men, and had inculcated a doctrine in which even Christians must recognize a large admixture of sacred truth. Temples in honour of the mother and child overspread the land, and suicidal sacrifices were daily offered in them. The Father of Lies had further propped up his kingdom in Japan by a profane parody on the institutions of the Catholic church. Under the name of the Saco, there reigned in sacerdotal supremacy a counterpart of the holy father at Rome, who consecrated the Fundi or Bishops of this Japanese hierarchy, and regulated at his infallible will whatever related to the rites and ceremonies of public worship. Subordinate to the Fundi were the Bonzes or Priests in holy orders, who, to complete the resemblance, taught, and at least professed to practise, an ascetic discipline. But here the similitude ceases; for, adds the Chronicle, they were great knaves and sad hypocrites.

With these foundations on which to build, the ideas which Xavier had to introduce into the Japanese mind, might not very widely jar with those by which they were pre-occupied. Auger, now called Paul of the Holy Faith, was despatched to his former friend and sovereign, with a picture of the Virgin and the infant Jesus, and the monarch and his courtiers admired, kissed, and worshipped the sacred symbols. Xavier himself, (to use his own words) stood by, a mere mute statue; but there was promethean fire within, and the marble soon found a voice. Of all his philological miracles, this was the most stupendous. He who, in the decline of life, bethinks him of all that he once endured to unlock the sense of Æschylus, and is conscious how stammering has been the speech with which, in later days, he has been wont to mutilate the tongues of Pascal and of Tasso, may think it a fable that in a few brief weeks Xavier could converse and teach intelligibly in the involved and ever-shifting dialects of Japan. Perhaps, had the sceptic ever studied to converse with living men under the impulse of some passion which had absorbed every faculty of his soul, he might relax his incredulity; but, whatever be the solution, the fact is attested on evidence which it would be folly to discredit—that within a very short time Xavier began to open to the Japanese, in their own language and to their perfect understanding, the commission with which he was charged. Such, indeed, was his facility of speech, that he challenged the Bonzes to controversies on all the mysterious points of their and his conflicting creeds. The arbiters of the dispute listened as men are apt to listen to the war of words, and many a long-tailed Japanese head was shaken, as if in the hope that the jumbling thoughts within would find their level by the oft-repeated oscillation. It became necessary to resort to other means of winning their assent; and in exploits of asceticism, Xavier had nothing to fear from the rivalry of Bonzes, of Fundi, or of the great Saco himself. Cangoxima acknowledged, as most other luxurious cities would perhaps acknowledge, that he who had such a mastery of his own appetites and passions, must be animated by some power wholly exempt

from that debasing influence. To fortify this salutary though not very sound conclusion, Xavier betook himself, (if we may believe his historian,) to the working of miracles. He compelled the fish to fill the nets of the fishermen, and to frequent the bay of Cangoxima, though previously indisposed to do so. He cured the leprous, and he raised the dead. Two Bonzes became the first, and indeed the only fruits of his labours. The hearts of their brethren grew harder as the light of truth glowed with increasing but ineffectual brightness around them. The King also withdrew his favour, and Xavier, with two companions, carried the rejected messages of mercy to the neighbouring states of the Japanese empire.

Carrying on his back his only viaticum, the vessels requisite for performing the sacrifice of the mass, he advanced to Firando, at once the seaport and the capital of the kingdom of that name. Some Portuguese ships, riding at anchor there, announced his arrival in all the forms of nautical triumph—flags of every hue floating from the masts, seamen clustering on the yards, cannon roaring from beneath, and trumpets braying from above. Firando was agitated with debate and wonder; all asked, but none could afford, an explanation of the homage rendered by the wealthy traders to the meanest of their countrymen. It was given by the humble pilgrim himself, surrounded in the royal presence by all the pomp which the Europeans could display in his honour. Great was the effect of these auxiliaries to the work of an evangelist; and the modern, like the ancient Apostle, ready to become all things to all men, would no longer decline the abasement of assuming for a moment the world's grandeur, when he found that such puerile acts might allure the children of the world to listen to the voice of wisdom. At Meaco, then the seat of empire in Japan, the discovery might be reduced to practice with still more important success, and thitherwards his steps were promptly directed.

Unfamiliar to the ears of us barbarians of the North-Western Ocean are the very names of the seats of Japanese civilisation through which his journey lay. At Amanguchi, the capital of Nagoto, he found the hearts of men hardened by sensuality, and his exhortations to repentance were repaid by showers of stones and insults. ' A pleasant sort of Bonze, indeed, who would ' allow us but one God and one woman!' was the summary remark with which the luxurious Amanguchians disposed of the teacher and his doctrine. They drove him forth half-naked, with no provision but a bag of parched rice, and accompanied only by three of his converts, prepared to share his danger and his reproach.

It was in the depth of winter, dense forests, steep mountains, half frozen streams, and wastes of untrodden snow, lay in his path to Meaco. An entire month was consumed in traversing the wilderness, and the cruelty and scorn of man not seldom adding bitterness to the rigours of nature. On one occasion the wanderers were overtaken in a thick jungle by a horseman bearing a heavy package. Xavier offered to carry the load, if the rider would requite the service by pointing out his way. The offer was accepted, but hour after hour the horse was urged on at such a pace, and so rapidly sped the panting missionary after him, that his tortured feet and excoriated body sank in seeming death under the protracted effort. In the extremity of his distress no repining word was ever heard to fall from him. He performed this dreadful pilgrimage in silent communion with Him for whom he rejoiced to suffer the loss of all things; or spoke only to sustain the hope and courage of his associates. At length the walls of Meaco were seen, promising a repose not ungrateful even to his adamantine frame and fiery spirit. But repose was no more to visit him. He found the city in all the tumult and horrors of a siege. It was impossible to gain attention to his doctrines amidst the din of arms; for even the Saco or Pope of Japan could give heed to none but military topics. Chanting from the Psalmist—'When Israel went out of Egypt and the house of Jacob from a strange people,' the Saint again plunged into the desert, and retraced his steps to Amanguchi.

Xavier describes the Japanese very much as a Roman might have depicted the Greeks in the age of Augustus, as at once intellectual and sensual voluptuaries; on the best possible terms with themselves, a good-humoured but faithless race, equally acute and frivolous, talkative and disputatious—' Their inquisitiveness,' he says, ' is incredible, especially in their intercourse with strangers, for whom they have not the slightest respect, but make incessant sport of them' Surrounded at Amanguchi by a crowd of these babblers, he was plied with innumerable questions about the immortality of the soul, the movement of the planets, eclipses, the rainbow—sin, grace, paradise, and hell. He heard and answered. A single response solved all these problems. Astronomers, meteorologists, metaphysicians, and divines, all heard the same sound; but to each it came with a different and an appropriate meaning. So wrote from the very spot Father Anthony Quadros four years after the event; and so the fact may be read in the process of Xavier's canonization. Possessed of so admirable a gift, his progress in the conversion of these once contemptuous people is the less surprising. Their city became the principal seat of learning in Japan, and of course, therefore, the great theatre of controversial debate. Of these polemics there remains a record of no doubtful authenticity, from which disputants of higher name than those of Amanguchi might take some useful lessons in the dialetic act. Thrusts, better made or more skilfully parried, are seldom to be witnessed in the schools of Oxford or of Cambridge.

In the midst of controversies with men, Xavier again heard that inward voice to which he never answered but by instant and unhesitating submission. It summoned him to Fucheo, the capital of the kingdom of Bungo; a city near the sea, and having for its port a place called Figer, where a rich Portuguese merchant ship was then lying. At the approach of the Saint (for such he was now universally esteemed) the vessel thundered from all her guns such loud and repeated discharges, that the startled sovereign despatched messengers from Fucheo to ascertain the cause of so universal an uproar. Nothing could exceed the astonishment with which they received the explanation. It was impossible to convey to the monarch's ear so extravagant a tale. A royal salute for the most abject of lazars—for a man, to use their own energetic language—' so abhorred of the earth, that the very vermin which crawled over him loathed their wretched fare.' If mortal man ever rose or sunk so far as to discover, without pain, that his person was the object of disgust to others, then is there one form of self-dominion in which Francis Xavier has been surpassed. Yielding with no perceptible reluctance to the arguments of his countrymen, and availing himself of the resources at their command, he advanced to Fucheo, preceded by thirty Portuguese clad in rich stuffs, and embellished with chains of gold and precious stones. ' Next came, and next did go,' in their gayest apparel, the servants and slaves of the merchants. Then appeared the apostle of the Indies himself, resplendent in green velvet and golden brocade. Chinese tapestry, and silken flags of every brilliant colour, covered the pinnace and the boats in which they were rowed up to the city, and the oars rose and fell to the sound of trumpets, flutes, and hautboys. As the procession drew near to the royal presence, the commander of the ship marched bareheaded, and carrying a wand as the esquire or major-domo of the Father. Five others of her principal officers, each bearing some costly article, stepped along, as proud to do such service; while he, in the honour of whom it was rendered, moved onwards with the majestic gait of some feudal chieftain marshalling his retainers, with a rich umbrella held over him. He traversed a double file of six hundred men-at-arms drawn up for his reception, and interchanged complimentary harangues with his royal host, with all the grace and dignity of a man accustomed to shine in courts, and to hold intercourse with Princes.

His Majesty of Bungo seems to have borne some resemblance to our own Henry the Eighth, and to have been meditating a revolt from the Saco and his whole spiritual dynasty. Much he said at the first interview, to which no orthodox Bonze could listen with composure. It drew down even on his royal head the rebuke of the learned Faxiondono. 'How,' exclaimed that eminent divine, 'dare you undertake the decision of any article of faith without having studied at the university of Fianzima, where alone are to be learned the sacred mysteries of the gods! If you are ignorant, consult the doctors appointed to teach you. Here am I, ready to impart to you all necessary instruction.' Anticipating the slow lapse of three centuries, the very genius of an university of still higher pretensions than that of Fianzima, breathed through the lips of the sage Faxiondono. But the great 'Tractarian' of Bungo provoked replies most unlike those by which his modern successors are assailed. Never was King surrounded by a gayer circle than that which then glittered at the court of Fucheo. The more the Bonze lectured on his own sacerdotal authority, the more laughed they. The King himself condescended to aid the general merriment, and congratulated his monitor on the convincing proof he had given of his heavenly mission, by the display of an infernal temper. To Xavier he addressed himself in a far different spirit. On his head the triple crown might have lighted without allaying the thirst of his soul for the conversion of mankind; and the European pomp with which he was for the moment environed, left him still the same living martyr to the faith it was his one object to diffuse. His rich apparel, and the blandishments of the great, served only to present to him, in a new and still more impressive light, the

vanity of all sublunary things. He preached, catechised, and disputed, with an ardour and perseverance which threatened his destruction, and alarmed his affectionate followers. 'Care not for me,' was his answer to their expostulation; 'think of me as a man dead to bodily comforts. My food, my rest, my life, are to rescue from the granary of Satan, the souls for whom God has sent me hither from the ends of the earth.' To such fervour the Bonzes of Fucheo could offer no effectual resistance. One of the most eminent of their number cast away his idols and became a Christian. Five hundred of his disciples immediately followed his example. The King himself, a dissolute unbeliever, was moved so far (and the concessions of the rulers of the earth must be handsomely acknowledged) as to punish the crimes he still practised; and to confess that the very face of the Saint was as a mirror, reflecting by the force of contrast all the hideousness of his own vices. Revolting, indeed, they were, and faithful were the rebukes of the tongue, no less than the countenance of Xavier. A royal convert was about to crown his labours, and the worship of Xaca and Amida seemed waning to its close. It was an occasion which demanded every sacrifice; nor was the demand unanswered.

For thirty years the mysteries of the faith of the Bonzes had been taught in the most celebrated of their colleges, by a Doctor who had fathomed all divine and human lore; and who, except when he came forth to utter the oracular voice of more than earthly wisdom, withdrew from the sight of men into a sacred retirement, there to hold high converse with the immortals. Fucarondono, for so he was called, announced his purpose to visit the city and palace of Fucheo. As when, in the agony of Agamemnon's camp, the son of Thetis at length grasped his massive spear, and the trembling sea-shores resounded at his step—so advanced to the war of words the great chieftain of Japanese theology, and so rose the cry of anticipated triumph from the rescued Bonzes. Terror seized the licentious King himself, and all foreboded the overthrow of Xavier and Christianity. 'Do you know, or rather, do you remember me?' was the inquiry with which this momentous debate was opened. 'I never saw you till now,' answered the Saint. 'A man who has dealt with me a thousand times, and who pretends never to have seen me, will be no difficult conquest,' rejoined the most profound of the Bonzes. 'Have you left any of the goods which I bought of you at the port of Frenajona?'—'I was never a merchant,' said the missionary, ' nor was I ever at Frenajona.'—' What a wretched memory!' was the contemptuous reply; it is precisely 500 years to-day since you and I met at that celebrated mart, when, by the same token, you sold me a hundred pieces of silk, and an excellent bargain I had of it' From the transmigration of the soul the sage proceeded to unfold the other dark secrets of nature—such as the eternity of matter, the spontaneous self-formation of all organized beings, and the progressive cleansing of the human spirit in the nobler and holier, until they attain to a perfect memory of the past, and are enabled to retrace their wanderings from one body to another through all preceding ages— looking down from the pinnacles of accumulated wisdom on the grovelling multitude, whose recollections are confined within the narrow limits of their latest corporeal existence. That Xavier refuted these perplexing arguments, we are assured by a Portuguese bystander who witnessed the debate; though unhappily no record of his arguments has come down to us. ' I have,' says the historian, ' neither science nor presumption enough to detail the subtle and solid reasonings by which the Saint destroyed the vain fancies of the Bonze.'

Yet the victory was incomplete. Having recruited his shattered forces, and accompanied by no less than 3000 Bonzes, Fucarondono returned to the attack. On his side, Xavier appeared in the field of controversy attended by the Portuguese officers in their richest apparel. They stood uncovered in his presence, and knelt when they addressed him. Their dispute now turned on many a knotty point;—as for example, Why did Xavier celebrate masses for the dead, and yet condemn the orthodox Japanese custom of giving to the Bonze bills of exchange payable in their favour? So subtle and difficult were their inquiries, that Xavier and his companion, the reporter of the dispute, were compelled to believe that the spirit of evil had suggested them; and that they were successfully answered is ascribed to the incessant prayers which, during the whole contest, the Christians offered for their champion Of this second polemical campaign we have a minute and animated account. It may be sufficient to extract the conclusion of the royal Moderator. ' For my own part,' he said, ' as far as I can judge, I think that Father Xavier speaks rationally, and that the rest of you don't know what you are talking about. Men must have clear heads or less violence than you have to understand these difficult questions. If you are defi-

cient in faith, at least employ your reason, which might teach you not to deny truths so evident; and do not bark like so many dogs.' So saying the King of Fungo dissolved the assembly. Royal and judicious as his award appears to have been, our Portuguese chronicler admits that the disputants on either side returned with opinions unchanged; and that, from that day forward, the work of conversion ceased. He applies himself to find a solution of the problem, why men who had been so egregiously refuted should still cling to their errors, and why they should obstinately adhere to practices so irrefragably proved to be alike foolish and criminal The answer, let us hope, is, that the obstinacy of the people of Fungo was a kind of *lusus naturæ*, a peculiarity exclusively their own; that other religious teachers are more candid than the Bonzes of Japan, and that no Professor of Divinity could elsewhere be found so obstinately wedded to his own doctrines as was the learned Fucarondono.

In such controversies, and in doing the work of an evangelist in every other form, Xavier saw the third year of his residence at Japan gliding away, when tidings of perplexities at the mother church of Goa recalled him thither, across seas so wide and stormy, that even the sacred lust of gold hardly braved them in that infancy of the art of navigation. As his ship drove before the monsoon, dragging after her a small bark which she had taken in tow, the connecting ropes were suddenly burst asunder, and in a few minutes the two vessels were no longer in sight. Thrice the sun rose and set on their dark course, the unchained elements roaring as in revelry around them, and the ocean seething like a cauldron. Xavier's shipmates wept over the loss of friends and kindred in the foundered bark, and shuddered at their own approaching doom. He also wept; but his were grateful tears. As the screaming whirlwind swept over the abyss, the present deity was revealed to his faithful worshipper, shedding tranquillity, and peace, and joy over the sanctuary of a devout and confiding heart. ' Mourn not, my friend,' was his gay address to Edward de Gama, as he lamented the loss of his brother in the bark; ' before three days, the daughter will have returned to her mother.' They were weary and anxious days; but, as the third drew to a close, a sail appeared in the horizon. Defying the adverse winds, she made straight towards them, and at last dropped along side, as calmly as the sea-bird ends her flight, and furls her ruffled plumage on the swelling surge. The cry of miracle burst from every lip; and well it might. There was the lost bark, and not the bark only, but Xavier himself on board her. What though he had ridden out the tempest in the larger vessel, the stay of their drooping spirits, he had at the same time been in the smaller ship, performing there also the same charitable office; and yet, when the two hailed and spoke each other, there was but one Francis Xavier, and he composedly standing by the side of Edward de Gama on the deck of the ' Holy Cross.' Such was the name of the commodore's vessel. For her services on this occasion, she obtained a sacred charter of immunity from risks of every kind; and as long as her timbers continued sound, bounded merrily across seas in which no other craft could have lived.

During this wondrous voyage, her deck had often been paced in deep conference by Xavier and Jago de Pereyra, her command-er. Though he pursued the calling of a merchant, he had, says the historian, the heart of a Prince Two great objects expanded the thoughts of Pereyra, the one, the conversion of the Chinese empire; the other, his own appointment as ambassador to the celestial court at Pekin. In our puny days, the dreams of traders in the east are of smuggling opium But in the sixteenth century, no enterprise appeared to them too splendid to contemplate, or too daring to hazard. Before the "Holy Cross" had reached Goa, Pereyra had pledged his whole fortune, Xavier his influence and his life, to this gigantic adventure. In the spring of the following year, the apostle and the ambassador, (for so far the project had in a few months been accomplished,) sailed from Goa in the ' Holy Cross,' for the then unexplored coasts of China. As they passed Malacca, tidings came to Xavier of the tardy though true fulfilment of one of his predictions. Pestilence, the minister of Divine vengeance, was laying waste that stiffnecked and luxurious people; but the woe he had foretold he was the foremost to alleviate. Heedless of his own safety, he raised the sick in his arms and bore them to the hospitals. He esteemed no time, or place, or office, too sacred to give way to this work of mercy. Ships, colleges, church-es, all at his bidding became so many laz-arettos. Night and day he lived among the diseased and the dying, or quitted them only to beg food or medicine, from door to door, for their relief. For the moment, even China was forgotten; nor would he advance a step though it were to convert to Christianity a third part of the human race, so long as one victim of the plague de-

manded his sympathy, or could be directed to an ever-present and still more compas-sionate Comforter. The career of Xavier (though he knew it not) was now drawing to a close; and with him the time was ripe for practising those deeper lessons of wis-dom which he had imbibed from his long and arduous discipline.

With her cables bent lay the ' Holy Cross' in the port of Malacca, ready at length to convey the embassage to China, when a difficulty arose, which not even the prophetic spirit of Xavier had foreseen. Don Alvaro d'Alayde, the governor, a grandee of high rank, regarded the envoy and his commission with an evil eye. To represent the crown of Portugal to the greatest of earthly monarchs, was, he thought, an honour more meet for a son of the house of Alayde, than for a man who had risen from the very dregs of the people. The expected emoluments also exceeded the decencies of a cupidity less than noble. He became of opinion that it was not for the advantage of the service of King John III., that the expedition should advance. Pereyra appeared before him in the hum-ble garb of a suitor, with the offer of 30,000 crowns as a bribe. All who sighed for the conversion, or for the commerce of China, lent the aid of their intercessions. Envoys, saints, and merchants, united their prayers in vain. Brandishing his cane over their heads, Alvaro swore that, so long as he was governor of Malacca and captain-general of the seas of Portugal, the em-bassy should move no further. Week after week was thus consumed, and the season was fast wearing away, when Xavier at length resolved on a measure to be justified even in his eyes only by extreme necessity. A secret of high significance had been buried in his bosom since his departure from Europe. The time for the disclosure of it had come. He produced a Papal Brief, investing him with the dignity and the powers of apostolical nuncio in the east. One more hindrance to the conver-sion of China, and the church would clothe her neck with thunders. Alvaro was still unmoved; and sentence of excommunica-tion was solemnly pronounced against him and his abettors. Alvaro answered by se-questrating the ' Holy Cross' herself. Xa-vier wrote letters of complaint to the King. Alvaro intercepted them. One appeal was still open to the vicar of the vicar of Christ. Prostrate before the altar, he invoked the aid of heaven; and rose with purposes confirmed, and hopes re-animated. In the service of Alvaro, though no longer bear-ing the embassy to China, the ' Holy Cross ' was to be despatched to Sancian, an island near the mouth of the Canton river, to which the Portuguese were permitted to resort for trade. Xavier resolved to pursue his voyage so far, and thence proceed to Macao to preach the gospel there. Imprisonment was sure to follow. But he should have Chinese fellow prisoners. These at least he might convert; and though his life would pay the forfeit, he should leave behind him in these first Christians a band of missionaries who would propagate through their native land the faith he should only be permitted to plant.

It was a compromise as welcome to Alvaro as to Xavier himself. Again the 'Holy Cross' prepared for sea; and the apostle of the Indies, followed by a grateful and admiring people, passed through the gates of Malacca to the beach. Falling on his face on the earth, he poured forth a passionate though silent prayer. His body heaved and shook with the throes of that agonizing hour. What might be the fearful portent none might divine, and none presumed to ask. A contagious terror passed from eye to eye, but every voice was hushed. It was as the calm preceding the first thunder peal which is to rend the firmament Xavier arose, his countenance no longer beaming with its accustomed grace and tenderness, but glowing with a sacred indignation, like that of Isaiah when breathing forth his inspired menaces against the king of Babylon. Standing on a rock amidst the waters, he loosed his shoes from off his feet, smote them against each other with vehement action, and then casting them from him, as still tainted with the dust of that devoted city, he leaped barefooted into the bark, which bore him away for ever from a place from which he had so long and vainly laboured to avert her impending doom.

She bore him, as he had projected, to the island of Sancian. It was a mere commercial factory; and the merchants who passed the trading season there, vehemently opposed his design of penetrating further into China. True he had ventured into the forest, against the tigers which infested it, with no other weapon than a vase of holy water; and the savage beasts, sprinkled with that sacred element, had for ever fled the place; but the Mandarins were fiercer still than they, and would avenge the preaching of the saint on the inmates of the factory—though most guiltless of any design but that of adding to their heap of crowns and moidores. Long years had now passed away since the voice of Loyola had been heard on the banks of the Seine urging the

solemn inquiry, 'What shall it profit?' But the words still rung on the ear of Xavier, and were still repeated, though in vain, to his worldly associates at Sancian. They sailed away with their cargoes, leaving behind them only the 'Holy Cross,' in charge of the officers of Alvaro, and depriving Xavier of all means of crossing the channel to Macao. They left him destitute of shelter and of food, but not of hope. He had heard that the King of Siam meditated an embassy to China for the following year; and to Siam he resolved to return in Alvaro's vessel, to join himself, if possible, to the Siamese envoys, and so at length to force his way into the empire.

But his earthly toils and projects were now to cease for ever. The angel of death appeared with a summons, for which, since death first entered our world, no man was ever more triumphantly prepared. It found him on board the vessel on the point of departing for Siam. At his own request he was removed to the shore, that he might meet his end with the greater composure. Stretched on the naked beach, with the cold blasts of a Chinese winter aggravating his pains, he contended alone with the agonies of the fever which wasted his vital power. It was a solitude and an agony for which the happiest of the sons of men might well have exchanged the dearest society and the purest of the joys of life It was an agony in which his still-uplifted crucifix reminded him of a far more awful woe endured for his deliverance; and a solitude thronged by blessed ministers of peace and consolation, visible in all their bright and lovely aspects to the now unclouded eye of faith; and audible to the dying martyr through the yielding bars of his mortal prison-house, in strains of exulting joy till then unheard and unimagined. Tears burst from his fading eyes, tears of an emotion too big for utterance. In the cold collapse of death his features were for a few brief moments irradiated as with the first beams of approaching glory. He raised himself on his crucifix, and exclaiming, *In te, Domine, speravi—non confundar in æternum!* he bowed his head and died.

Why consume many words in delineating a character which can be disposed of in three? Xavier was a Fanatic, a Papist, and a Jesuit. Comprehensive and incontrovertible as the climax is, it yet does not exhaust the censures to which his name is obnoxious. His understanding, that is, the mere cogitative faculty, was deficient in originality, in clearness, and in force. It is difficult to imagine a religious dogma which he would not have embraced, at the command of his teachers, with the same infantine credulity with which he received the creeds and legends they actually imposed upon him. His faith was not victorious over doubt; for doubt never for one passing moment assailed it. Superstition might boast him one of the most complete as well as one of the most illustrious of her conquests. She led him through a land peopled with visionary forms, and resounding with ideal voices—a land of prodigies and portents, of ineffable discourse and unearthly melodies. She bade him look on this fair world as on some dungeon unvisited by the breath of heaven; and on the glorious face of nature, and the charms of social life, as so many snares and pit-falls for his feet. At her voice he starved and lacerated his body, and rivalled the meanest lazar in filth and wretchedness. Harder still, she sent him forth to establish among half-civilized tribes a worship which to them must have become idolatrous; and to inculcate a morality in which the holier and more arduous virtues were made to yield precedence to ritual forms and outward ceremonies. And yet, never did the polytheism of ancient or of modern Rome assign a seat among the demi-gods to a hero of nobler mould, or of more exalted magnanimity, than Francis Xavier.

He lived among men as if to show how little the grandeur of the human soul depends on mere intellectual power. His it was to demonstrate with what vivific rays a heart imbued with the love of God and man may warm and kindle the nations; dense as may be the exhalations through which the giant pursues his course from the one end of heaven to the other. Scholars criticized, wits jested, prudent men admonished, and kings opposed him; but on moved Francis Xavier, borne forward by an impulse which crushed and scattered to the winds all such puny obstacles. In ten short years, a solitary wanderer, destitute of all human aid—as if mercy had lent him wings, and faith an impenetrable armour—he traversed oceans, islands, and continents, through a track equal to more than twice the circumference of our globe; everywhere preaching, disputing, baptizing, and founding Christian churches. There is at least one well authenticated miracle in Xavier's story. It is, that any mortal man should have sustained such toils as he did; and have endured them too not merely with composure, but as if in obedience to some indestructible exigency of nature. ' The Father Master Francis,' (the words are those of his associate, Melchior Nunez,)

' when labouring for the salvation of idolaters, seemed to act, not by any acquired power, but as by some natural instinct; for he could neither take pleasure nor even exist except in such employments. They were his repose; and when he was leading men to the knowledge and the love of God, however much he exerted himself, he never appeared to be making any effort.'

Seven hundred thousand converts (for in these matters Xavier's worshippers are not parsimonious) are numbered as the fruits of his mission; nor is the extravagance so extreme if the word conversion be understood in the sense in which they used it. Kings, Rajahs, and Princes were always, when possible, the first objects of his care. Some such conquests he certainly made; and as the flocks would often follow their shepherds, and as the gate into the Christian fold was not made very strait, it may have been entered by many thousands and tens of thousands. But if Xavier taught the mighty of the earth, it was for the sake of the poor and the miserable, and with them he chiefly dwelt. He dwelt with them on terms ill enough corresponding with the vulgar notions of the saint. ' You, my friends,' said he to a band of soldiers who had hidden their cards at his approach, ' belong to no religious order, nor can you pass whole days in devotion. Amuse yourselves. To you it is not forbidden, if you neither cheat, quarrel nor swear when you play.' Then good-humouredly sitting down in the midst of them, he challenged one of the party to a game at chess; and was found at the board by Don Diego Noragua, whose curiosity had brought him from far to see so holy a man, and to catch some fragments of that solemn discourse which must ever be flowing from his lips. The grandee would have died in the belief that the saint was a hypocrite, unless by good fortune he had afterwards chanced to break in on his retirement, and to find him there suspended between earth and heaven in a rapture of devotion, with a halo of celestial glory encircling his head.

Of such miraculous visitations, nor indeed of any other of his supernatural performances, will any mention be found in the letters of Xavier. Such at least is the result of a careful examination of a considerable series of them. He was too humble a man to think it probable that he should be the depositary of so divine a gift; and too honest to advance any such claims to the admiration of mankind. Indeed he seems to have been even amused with the facility with which his friends assented to those prodigies. Two of them repeated to him the tale of his having raised a dead child to life, and pressed him to reveal the truth. 'What!' he replied, 'I raise the dead! Can you really believe such a thing of a wretch like me?' Then smiling, he added, 'They did indeed place before me a child. They said it was dead, which perhaps was not the case. I told him to get up, and he did so. Do you call that a miracle?' But in this matter Xavier was not allowed to judge for himself. He was a Thaumaturgus in his own despite; and this very denial is quoted by his admirers as a proof of his profound humility. Could he by some second sight have read the Bull of his own canonization, he would doubtless, in defiance of his senses, have believed (for belief was always at his command) that the church knew much better than he did; and that he had been reversing the laws of nature without perceiving it; for at the distance of rather more than half a century from his death, Pope Urban VIII., with the unanimous assent of all the cardinals, patriarchs, archbishops, and bishops, in sacred conclave assembled, pledged his papal infallibility to the miracles already recorded, and to many more. And who can be so sceptical as to doubt their reality, when he is informed that depositions taken in proof of them were read before that august assembly; and that the apotheosis was opposed there by a learned person, who appeared at their bar in the character and with the title of 'the Devil's advocate.' A scoffer might indeed suggest that the lawyer betrayed the cause of his client if he really laboured to dispel illusion, and that the Father of Lies may have secretly instructed his counsel to make a sham fight of it, in order that one lie the more might be acted in the form of a new idol worship. Without exploring so dark a question, it may be seriously regretted that such old wives' fables have been permitted to sully the genuine history of many a man of whom the world was not worthy, and of none more than Francis Xavier They have long obscured his real glory, and degraded him to the low level of a vulgar hero of ecclesiastical romance. Casting away these puerile embellishments, refused the homage due to genius and to learning, and excluded from the number of those who have aided the progress of speculative truth, he emerges from those lower regions, clad with the mild brilliancy, and resplendent in the matchless beauty which belong to the human nature when ripening fast into a perfect union with the divine. He had attained to that childlike affiance in the author of his being, which gives an unrestrained play to every blameless impulse, even when that awful presence is most habitually felt. His was a sanctity which, at fitting seasons, could even disport itself in jests and trifling. No man, however abject his condition, disgusting his maladies, or hateful his crimes, ever turned to Xavier without learning that there was at least one human heart on which he might repose with all the confidence of a brother's love. To his eye the meanest and the lowest reflected the image of Him whom he followed and adored; nor did he suppose that he could ever serve the Saviour of mankind so acceptably as by ministering to their sorrows, and recalling them into the way of peace. It is easy to smile at his visions, to detect his errors, to ridicule the extravagant austerities of his life; and even to show how much his misguided zeal eventually counteracted his own designs. But with our philosophy, our luxuries, and our wide experience, it is not easy for us to estimate or to comprehend the career of such a man. Between his thoughts and our thoughts there is but little in common. Of our wisdom he knew nothing, and would have despised us if he had Philanthropy was his passion, reckless daring his delight; and faith glowing in meridian splendour the sunshine in which he walked He judged or felt (and who shall say that he judged or felt erroneously?) that the church demanded an illustrious sacrifice, and that he was to be the victim; that a voice which had been dumb for fifteen centuries, must at length be raised again, and that to him that voice had been imparted; that a new Apostle must go forth to break up the incrustations of man's long-hardened heart, and that to him that apostolate had been committed. So judging, or so feeling, he obeyed the summons of him whom he esteemed Christ's vicar on earth, and the echoes from no sublunary region which that summons seemed to awaken in his bosom. In holding up to reverential admiration such self-sacrifices as his, slight, indeed, is the danger of stimulating enthusiastic imitators Enthusiasm! our pulpits distil their bland rhetoric against it; but where is it to be found? Do not our share markets, thronged even by the devout, overlay it—and our rich benefices extinguish it—and our pentecosts, in the dazzling month of May, dissipate it—and our stipendiary missions, and our mitres, decked even in heathen lands with jewels and lordly titles—do they not, as so many lightning conductors, effectually divert it ? There is indeed the lackadaisical enthusiasm of devotional experiences, and the sentimental enthusiasm of religious bazars, and the oratorical enthusiasm of charitable platforms—and the tractarian enthusiasm of well-beneficed ascetics; but in what, except the name, do they resemble ' the-God-in-us,' enthusiasm of Francis Xavier?—of Xavier the magnanimous, the holy, and the gay; the canonized saint, not of Rome only, but of universal Christendom; who, if at this hour there remained not a solitary Christian to claim and to rejoice in his spiritual ancestry, should yet live in hallowed and everlasting remembrance; as the man who has bequeathed to these later ages, at once the clearest proof and the most illustrious example, that even amidst the enervating arts of our modern civilisation, the apostolic energy may still burn with all its primeval ardour in the human soul, when animated and directed by a power more than human.

Xavier died in the year 1552, in the forty-seventh of his age, and just ten years and a half from his departure from Europe. During his residence in India, he had maintained a frequent correspondence with the General of his order. On either side their letters breathe the tenderness which is an indispensable element of the heroic character—an intense though grave affection, never degenerating into fondness; but chastened, on the side of Xavier by filial reverence, on that of Ignatius by parental authority. It was as a father, or rather as a patriarch, exercising a supreme command over his family, and making laws for their future government, that Ignatius passed the last twenty years of his life. No longer a wanderer, captivating or overawing the minds of men by marvels addressed to their imagination, he dwelt in the ecclesiastical capital of the West, giving form and substance to the visions which had fallen on him at the Mount of Ascension, and had attended him through every succeeding pilgrimage.

It proved, however, no easy task to obtain the requisite Papal sanction for the establishment of his order. In that age the regular clergy had to contend with an almost universal unpopularity. To their old enemies, the bishops and secular priests, were added the wits, the reformers, and the Vatican itself. The Papal court not unreasonably attributed to their misconduct a large share of the disasters under which the Church of Rome was suffering. On the principle of opposing new defences to new dangers, the Pope had given his con-

fidence and encouragement to the Theatins, and the other isolated preachers who were labouring at once to protect and to purify the fold, by diffusing among them their own deep and genuine spirit of devotion. It seemed bad policy at such a moment to call into existence another religious order, which must be regarded with equal disfavour by these zealous recruits, and by the ancient supporters of the Papacy. Nor did the almost morbid prescience of the Vatican fail to perceive how dangerous a rival, even to the successors of St. Peter, might become the General of a society projected on a plan of such stupendous magnitude.

Three years, therefore, were consumed by Ignatius in useless solicitations. He sought to propitiate, not mere mortal man only, but the Deity himself, by the most lavish promises; and is recorded to have pledged himself on one day to the performance of three thousand masses, if so his prayer might be granted. Earth and Heaven seemed equally deaf to his offers, when the terrors of Paul III. were effectually awakened by the progress of the Reformers in the very bosom of Italy. Ferrara seemed about to fall as Germany, England, and Switzerland, had fallen; and the Consistory became enlightened to see the divine hand in a scheme which they had till then regarded as the workmanship of man, and as wrought with no superhuman purposes. Anxiously and with undisguised reluctance, though, as the event proved, with admirable foresight, Paul III., on the 27th September, 1540, affixed the Papal seal to the Bull 'Regimini,' the Magna Charta of the order of Jesus. It affords full internal evidence of the misgivings with which it was issued. ' Quamvis Evangelio doceamur, et fide orthodoxâ cognoscamus ac firmiter profiteamur, omnes Christi fideles, Romano pontifici tanquam Capiti, ac Jesu Christi Vicario, subesse, ad majorem tamen nostræ societatis humilitatem, ac perfectam unius cujusque mortificationem, et voluntatum nostrarum abnegationem, summopere conducere judicavimus, singulos nos, ultra illud commune vinculum, speciali voto adstringi, ita ut quidquid Romani pontifices, pro tempore existentes, jusserint'—' quantum in nobis fuerit exequi teneamur.'

So wrote the Pope in the persons of his new Prætorians; and to elect a General of the band, who should guide them to the performance of this vow, was the first care of Ignatius. Twice the unanimous choice of his companions fell on himself. Twice the honour was refused. At length, yielding to the absolute commands of his confessor, he ascended the throne of which he had been so long laying the foundations. Once seated there, his coyness was at an end, and he wielded the sceptre as best becomes an absolute monarch—magnanimously, and with unfaltering decision; beloved, but permitting no rude familiarity; reverenced, but exciting no servile fear; declining no enterprise which high daring might accomplish, and attempting none which headlong ambition might suggest; self-multiplied in the ministers of his will; yielding to them a large and generous confidence, yet trusting no man whom he had not deeply studied; and assigning to none a province beyond the range of his capacity.

Though not in books, yet in the far nobler school of active, and especially of military life, Loyola had learned the great secret of government; at least of his government. It was, that the social affections, if concentrated within a well-defined circle, possess an intensity and endurance, unrivalled by those passions of which self is the immediate object. He had the sagacity to perceive, that emotions like those with which a Spartan or a Jew had yearned over the land and the institutions of their fathers—emotions stronger than appetite, vanity, ambition, avarice, or death itself—might be kindled in the members of his order; if he could detect and grasp those mainsprings of human action of which the Greek and the Hebrew legislators had obtained the mastery. Nor did he seek them in vain.

It is with an audacity approaching to the sublime that Loyola demands the obedience of his subjects—an obedience to be yielded, not in the mere outward act, but by the understanding and the will. 'Non intueamini in personâ superioris hominem obnoxium erroribus atque miseriis, *sed Christum ipsum.*' 'Superioris vocem ac jussa non secus ac *Christi* vocem excipiti.' 'Ut statuatis vobiscum quidquid superior præcipit *ipsius Dei* præceptum esse ac voluntatem.' He who wrote thus had not lightly observed how the spirit of man groans beneath the weight of its own freedom, and exults in bondage if only permitted to think that the chain has been voluntarily assumed. Nor had he less carefully examined the motives which may stimulate the most submissive to revolt, when he granted to his followers the utmost liberty in outward things which could be reconciled with this inward servitude;—no peculiar habit—no routine of prayers and canticles—no prescribed system of austerities—no monastic seclusion. The enslaved soul was not to be rudely re-

minded of her slavery. Neither must the frivolous or the feeble-minded have a place in his brotherhood; for he well knew how awful is the might of folly in all sublunary affairs. No one could be admitted who had worn, though but for one day, the habit of any other religious order; for Ignatius must be served by virgin souls and by prejudices of his own engrafting. Stern initiatory discipline must probe the spirits of the Professed; for both scandal and danger would attend the faintness of any leader in the host. Gentler probations must suffice for lay or spiritual coadjutors; for every host is incomplete without a body of irregular partizans. But the General himself—the centre and animating spirit of the whole spiritual army—he must rule for life; for ambition and cabal will fill up any short intervals of choice, and the reverence due to royalty is readily impaired by the aspect of dethroned sovereigns. He must be absolute; for human authority can on no other terms exhibit itself as the image of the divine. He must reign at a distance and in solitude; for no government is effective in which imagination has not her work to do. He must be the ultimate depositary of the secrets of the conscience of each of his subjects; for irresistible power may inspire dread but not reverence, unless guided by unlimited knowledge. No subject of his may accept any ecclesiastical or civil dignity; for he must be supreme in rank as in dominion. And the ultimate object of all this scheme of government—it must be vast enough to expand the soul of the proselyte to a full sense of her own dignity; and practical enough to provide incessant occupation for his time and thoughts; and must have enough of difficulty to bring his powers into strenuous activity, and of danger to teach the lesson of mutual dependence; and there must be conflicts for the brave, and intrigues for the subtle, and solitary labours for the studious, and offices of mercy for the compassionate; and to all must be offered rewards, both temporal and eternal —in this life, the reward of a sympathy rendered intense by confinement, and stimulating by secrecy; and in the life to come, felicities of which the anxious heart might find the assurance in the promises and in the fellowship of the holy and the wise— of men whose claims to the divine favour it would be folly and impiety to doubt.

If there be in any of our universities a professor of moral philosophy lecturing on the science of human nature, let him study the Constitutions of Ignatius Loyola. They were the fruit of the solitary meditations of many years. The lamp of the retired student threw its rays on nothing but his manuscript, his crucifix, Thomas à Kempis, *De Imitatione Christi*, and the New Testament. Any other presence would have been a profane intrusion; for the work was but a transcript of thoughts imparted to his disembodied spirit when, in early manhood, it had been caught up into the seventh heavens. As he wrote, a lambent flame, in shape like a tongue of fire, hovered about his head; and as may be read in his own hand, in a still extant paper, the hours of composition were passed in tears of devotion, in holy ardour, in raptures, and amidst celestial apparitions.

Some unconscious love of power, a mind bewildered by many gross superstitions, and theoretical errors, and perhaps some tinge of insanity, may be ascribed to Ignatius Loyola; but no dispassionate reader of his writings, or of his life, will question his integrity; or deny him the praise of a devotion at once sincere, habitual, and profound. It is not to the glory of the reformers to depreciate the name of their greatest antagonist; or to think meanly of him to whom more than any other man it is owing that the Reformation was stayed, and the Church of Rome rescued from her impending doom.

In the language now current amongst us, Ignatius might be described as the leader of the Conservative against the innovating spirit of his times. It was an age, as indeed is every era of great popular revolutions, when the impulsive or centrifugal forces which tend to isolate man, preponderating over the attractive or centripetal forces which tend to congregate him, had destroyed the balance of the social system. From amidst the controversies which then agitated the world had emerged two great truths, of which, after three hundred years' debate, we are yet to find the reconcilement. It was true that the Christian Commonwealth should be one consentient body, united under one supreme head, and bound together by a community of law, of doctrine, and of worship. It was also true that each member of that body must, for himself, on his own responsibility, and at his own peril, render that worship, ascertain that doctrine, study that law, and seek the guidance of that Supreme Ruler. Between these corporate duties, and these individual obligations, there was a seeming contrariety. And yet it must be apparent only, and not real; for all truths must be consistent with each other. Here was a problem for the learned and the wise, for

schools, and presses, and pulpits. But it is not by sages, nor in the spirit of philosophy, that such problems receive their practical solution. Wisdom may be the ultimate arbiter, but is seldom the immediate agent in human affairs. It is by antagonist passions, prejudices, and follies, that the equipoise of this most belligerent planet of ours is chiefly preserved; and so it was in the sixteenth century. If Papal Rome had her Brennus, she must also have her Camillus. From the camp of the invaders arose the war-cry of absolute mental independence; from the beleaguered host, the watch-word of absolute spiritual obedience. The German pointed the way to that sacred solitude where, besides the worshipper himself, none may enter; the Spaniard to that innumerable company which, with one accord, still chant the liturgies of remotest generations. Chieftains in the most momentous warfare of which this earth had been the theatre since the subversion of Paganism, each was a rival worthy of the other in capacity, courage, disinterestedness, and the love of truth, and yet how marvellous the contrast!

Luther took to wife a nun. For thirty years together, Loyola never once looked on the female countenance. To overthrow the houses of the order to which he belonged, was the triumph of the reformer. To establish a new order on indestructible foundations, the glory of the saint. The career of the one was opened in the cell, and concluded amidst the cares of secular government. The course of life of the other, led him from a youth of camps and palaces to an old age of religious abstraction. Demons haunted both; but to the northern visionary they appeared as foul or malignant fiends, with whom he was to agonize in spiritual strife; to the southern dreamer, as angels of light marshalling his way to celestial blessedness. As best became his Teutonic honesty and singleness of heart, Luther aimed at no perfection but such as may consist with the everyday cares, and the common duties, and the innocent delights of our social existence; at once the foremost of heroes, and a very man; now oppressed with melancholy, and defying the powers of darkness, satanic or human; then 'rejoicing in gladness and thankfulness of heart for all his abundance;' loving and beloved; communing with the wife of his bosom, prattling with his children; surrendering his overburdened mind to the charms of music, awake to every gentle voice, and to each cheerful aspect of nature or of art; responding alike to every divine impulse and to every human feeling; no chord unstrung in his spiritual or sensitive frame, but all blending together in harmonies as copious as the bounties of Providence, and as changeful as the vicissitudes of life. How remote from the 'perfection' which Loyola proposed to himself, and which (unless we presume to distrust the Bulls by which he was beatified and canonized) we must suppose him to have attained. Drawn by infallible, not less distinctly than by fallible limners, the portrait of the military priest of the Casa Professa possesses the cold dignity and the grace of sculpture; but is wholly wanting in the mellow tones, the lights and shadows, the rich colouring, and the skilful composition of the sister art. There he stands apart from us mortal men, familiar with visions which he may not communicate, and with joys which he cannot impart. Severe in the midst of raptures, composed in the very agonies of pain; a silent, austere, and solitary man; with a heart formed for tenderness, yet mortifying even his best affections; loving mankind as his brethren, and yet rejecting their sympathy; one while a squalid, care-worn, self-lacerated pauper, tormenting himself that so he might rescue others from sensuality; and then, a monarch reigning in secluded majesty, that so he might become the benefàctor of his race, or a legislator exacting, though with no selfish purposes, an obedience as submissive and as prompt as is due to the King of Kings.

Heart and soul we are for the Protestant. He who will be wiser than his Maker is but seeming wise. He who will deaden one-half of his nature to invigorate the other half, will become at best a distorted prodigy. Dark as are the pages, and mystic the character in which the truth is inscribed, he who can decipher the roll will read there, that self-adoring pride is the headspring of stoicism, whether heathen or Christian. But there is a roll neither dark nor mystic, in which the simplest and the most ignorant may learn in what the 'perfection' of our humanity really consists. Throughout the glorious profusion of didactic precepts, of pregnant apothegms, of lyric and choral songs, of institutes ecclesiastical and civil, of historical legends and biographies, of homilies and apologues, of prophetic menaces, of epistolary admonitions, and of positive laws, which crowd the inspired Canon, there is still one consentient voice pro-

claiming to man, that the world within and the world without him were created for each other; that his interior life must be sustained and nourished by intercourse with external things; and that he then most nearly approaches to the perfection of his nature, when most conversant with the joys and sorrows of life, and most affected by them, he is yet the best prepared to renounce the one or to endure the other, in cheerful submission to the will of Heaven.

Unalluring, and on the whole unlovely as it is, the image of Loyola must ever command the homage of the world. No other uninspired man, unaided by military or civil power, and making no appeal to the passions of the multitude, has had the genius to conceive, the courage to attempt, and the success to establish, a polity teeming with results at once so momentous and so distinctly foreseen. Amidst his ascetic follies, and his half crazy visions, and despite all the coarse daubing with which the miracle-mongers of his Church have defaced it, his character is destitute neither of sublimity nor of grace. They were men of no common stamp with whom he lived, and they regarded him with an unbounded reverence. On the anniversary of his death Baronius and Bellarmine met to worship at his tomb; and there, with touching and unpremeditated eloquence, joined to celebrate his virtues. His successor Laynez was so well convinced that Loyola was beloved by the Deity above all other men, as to declare it impossible that any request of his should be refused. Xavier was wont to kneel when he wrote letters to him; to implore the Divine aid through the merits of his 'holy Father Ignatius,' and to carry about his autograph as a sacred relic. In popular estimation, the very house in which he once dwelt had been so hallowed by his presence, as to shake to the foundation if thoughts unbecoming its purity found entrance into the mind of any inmate. Of his theopathy, as exhibited in his letters, in his recorded discourse, and in his 'Spiritual Exercises,' it is perhaps difficult for the colder imaginations and the Protestant reserve of the North to form a correct estimate. Measured by such a standard, it must be pronounced irreverent and erotic;—a libation on the altar at once too profuse and too little filtered from the dross of human passion. But to his fellow men he was not merely benevolent, but compassionate, tolerant, and candid. However inflexible in exacting from his chosen followers an all-enduring constancy, he was gentle to others, especially to the young and the weak; and would often make an amiable though awkward effort to promote their recreation. He was never heard to mention a fault or a crime, except to suggest an apology for the offender. 'Humbly to conceal humility, and to shun the praise of being humble,' was the maxim and the habit of his later life; and on that principle he maintained the unostentatious decencies of his rank as General of his order at the Casa Professa; a convent which had been assigned at Rome for their residence. There he dwelt, conducting a correspondence more extensive and important than any which issued from the cabinets of Paris or Madrid. In sixteen years he had established twelve Jesuit Provinces in Europe, India, Africa, and Brazil; and more than a hundred colleges or houses for the Professed and the Probationers, already amounting to many thousands. His missionaries had traversed every country, the most remote and barbarous, which the enterprise of the age had opened to the merchants of the West. The devout resorted to him for guidance, the miserable for relief, the wise for instruction, and the rulers of the earth for succour. Men felt that there had appeared among them one of those monarchs who reign in right of their own native supremacy; and to whom the feebler wills of others must yield either a ready or a reluctant allegiance. It was a conviction recorded by his disciples on his tomb, in these memorable and significant words:—'Whoever thou mayest be who hast portrayed to thine own imagination Pompey, or Cæsar, or Alexander, open thine eyes to the truth, and let this marble teach thee how much greater a conqueror than they was Ignatius.'

Whatever may have been the comparative majesty of the Cæsarian and the Ignatian conquests, it was true of either, that on the death of the conqueror the succession to his diadem hung long in anxious suspense. Our tale descends from the sublime and the heroic to the region of ordinary motives and ordinary men. According to the constitution of the order, the choice of the General was to be made in a chapter, of which the fully Professed, and they alone, were members. Of that body Jago Laynez was the eldest and most eminent, and from his dying bed (so at least it was supposed) he summoned his brethren to hold the election at the Casa Professa. The citation was unanswered. A majority of the whole electoral college were detained in Spain by Philip II., who

was then engaged in his war with the Papal court, and in this extremity Laynez was nominated to the provisional office of vicar-general. That promotion is a specific in some forms of bodily disease, is as certain as any apothegm in Galen. Full of renovated life, the vicar-general at once assumed all the powers of his great predecessor, and gave prompt evidence that they had fallen into no feeble hands. But neither was that a feeble grasp in which the keys of St. Peter were held. Hotheaded and imperious as he was, Paul IV. had quailed in the solemn presence of Loyola; but now, as he believed, had found the time for arresting the advance of a power which he had learned to regard with jealousy. He began (as an Englishman might express it) by putting the vacant generalship into Commission, and assigned to Laynez nothing more than a share in that divided rule. A voyage to Spain, where in his own country and among his own friends his election would be secure, was the next resource of the vicar-general; but a Papal mandate appeared, forbidding any Jesuit to quit the precincts of Rome. Thus thwarted, Laynez resolved on immediately elevating into the class of the Professed as many of his associates as would form a college numerous enough for the choice of a head; but the vigilant old Pontiff detected and prohibited the design. Foiled in every manœuvre, nothing remained to the aspiring vicar but to await the return of peace. It came at length, and with it came from Spain the electors so long and anxiously expected.

Lowly was the chamber in which they were convened; nor did there meet that day within the compass of the Seven Hills a company, in outward semblance less imposing; and yet, scarcely had the assembled Comitia, to whose shouts those hills had once re-echoed, ever conferred on Prætor or Proconsul a power more real or extensive than that which those homely men were now about to bestow. But Laynez seemed doomed yet to another disappointment. The chapel doors were thrown open, and the Cardinal Pacheco appearing among them, interdicted, in the name of the Pope, all further proceedings, unless they would consent to choose their General for three years only; and would engage, like other religious men, daily to chant the appointed offices of the Church. What are the limits of unlimited obedience? When, a century and a half ago, our own casuists laboured for an answer to that knotty problem, they were but unconscious

imitators of Jago Laynez and his companions. Maugre vows, and Pope, and Cardinal, they forthwith elected him General
for life ; nor was one litany the more sung
by the Jesuits for all the Papal bidding

Yet, the formal decencies of the scene,
how well were they maintained ? Joyful
thanksgivings on the side of the electors ;
an aspect eloquent with reluctance, grief,
and the painful sense of responsibility on
the part of the new General. Is it incredible that some motives nobler and more
pure than those of mere secular ambition
may have animated Laynez on this occasion ? Probably not ; for there are few of
us in whom antagonist principles do not
obtain this kind of divided triumph; and
the testimonies to his virtues are such and
so many as almost to command assent to
their substantial truth. Of the twenty-
four books of the history of Orlandinus,
eight are devoted to the administration of
the affairs of the Order. They extort a
willing acknowledgment, that he possessed extraordinary abilities; and a half-re-
luctant admission, that he may have combined with them a more than common degree of genuine piety.

Laynez would seem to have been born
to supply the intellectual deficiences of Ignatius. He was familiar with the whole
compass of the theological literature of his
age, and with all the moral sciences which
a theologian was then required to cultivate.
With these stores of knowledge he had
made himself necessary to the first General. Loyola consulted, employed, trusted,
but apparently did not like him. It is
stated by Orlandinus, that there was no
other of his eminent followers whom the
great patriarch of the society treated with
such habitual rigour, and yet none who
rendered him such important services. ' Do
you not think,' said Ignatius to him, ' that
in framing their constitutions, the founders
of the religious orders were inspired ?' ' I
do,' was the answer, ' so far as the general
scheme and outline were concerned.' The
inspired saint, therefore, took for his province the compilation of the text, the uninspired scholar, the preparation of the
authoritative comment. For himself, the
law-giver claimed the praise of having
raised an edifice, of which the plan and the
arrangement were divine. To his fellow-
labourer he assigned the merit of having
supported it by the solid foundation of a
learning, which, however excellent, was
yet entirely human. An example will best
explain this division of labour.

' In theologiâ legetur Vetus et Novum

Testamentum, et doctrina scholastica Divi
Thomæ'—is the text. ' Prælegetur etiam
magister sententiarum ; sed si videatur
temporis decursu, alius autor studentibus
utilior futurus, ut si aliqua summa, vel liber
theologiæ scholasticæ, conficeretur, qui nostris temporibus accommodatior videretur'—
' prælegi poterit'—is the comment. Ignatius was content that the Divine Thomas
should be installed among the Jesuits as
the permanent interpreter of the sacred
oracles. Laynez, with deeper foresight,
perceived that the time was coming when
they must discover a teacher ' better suited
to the times.' It was a prediction fulfilled
shortly after his death in the person of
Molina, who was himself the pupil of the
second General of the order.

To Laynez belongs the praise or the reproach of having revived, in modern times,
the Molinist or Arminian doctrine. Our
latest posterity will debate, as our remotest
ancestry have debated, the soundness of
that creed ; but that it was 'temporibus
accommodatior,' few will be inclined to
dispute. The times evidently required that
the great antagonists of Protestantism
should inculcate a belief more comprehensive, and more flexible, than that of Augustine or of St. Thomas. And if to the adoption of those opinions may be traced much
of the danger and disrepute to which the
society was afterwards exposed, to the
same cause may be ascribed much of the
secret of their vitality and their strength.

The doctrines of Molina were hazarded
by Laynez, and even in the bosom of the
Council of Trent; where, though not con-
stitutionally brave, he dared the reproach of
heresy and Pelagianism. But, in the noblest theatre for the display of eloquence
which the world had seen since the fall of
the Roman commonwealth, he exhibited all
the hardihood which a conscious superiority
in the power of speech will impart to the
least courageous. Amidst cries of indignation, he maintained the freedom of the
will, and the ultramontane doctrines, the
most unwelcome to his audience ; and vehemently opposed the demand of more than
half of Europe for the admission of the
laity to the cup. He felt that resentment
must give way to those feelings on which a
great speaker seldom relies in vain. He
spoke from a position best befitting an ostentatious humility, and therefore the most
remote from the thrones of the Papal le-
gates, and the ambassadors of Christendom.
Even those thrones were for a moment abandoned. Cardinals, Bishops, Counts, and Ab-
bots, thronged around his chair ; Generals

and Doctors obeyed the same impulse ; and for two successive hours a circle more illustrious for rank and learning than ever surrounded the tribune of an orator, rewarded his efforts by their profound and silent admiration. He spoke at Paris, and he preached at Rome, with similar applause ; and yet, on examining the only two of his speeches which have been preserved by Orlandinus, it is difficult to detect the charm which once seduced the haughtiest Prelates into a passing forgetfulness of their dignity. The eloquence of Laynez would appear to have been neither impassioned nor imaginative, nor of that intense earnestness which seems to despise the very rules by the observance of which it triumphs Luminous argumentation, clothed in transparent language, and delivered with facility and grace, was probably the praise to which he was entitled—no vulgar praise indeed ; for, amidst the triumphs of oratory, few are greater or more welcome than that of infusing order, without fatigue, into the chaotic thoughts of an inquisitive audience.

Ambition clothed in rags, subtlety under the guise of candour, are the offences which the enemies of his order have ascribed to Laynez. But a man who, in the sixteenth century, refused a Cardinal's hat, (his refusal of the Papacy is a more apocryphal story,) can hardly have been the victim of a low desire for worldly honours ; and hypocrisy is a charge which every one must bear who has to do with opponents incredulous of virtue superior to their own. For eighteen years the head of a body distrusted and unpopular from its infancy, he had neither hereditary rank to avert the envy which waits on greatness, nor the lofty daring to which the world is ever prompt to yield idolatrous homage. In his hands the weapons of Ignatius or of Xavier would have been impotent ; but he wielded his own with address and with admirable effect. To him his society was first indebted for their characteristic doctrine, for the possession and the fame of learning, for many enlargements of their privileges, for a more intimate alliance with the Papacy, and the more pronounced hostility of the Reformers. He first established for them that authority in the cabinets of Europe, on which, at no distant time, the edifice of their temporal power was to rest ; and it was his melancholy distinction to number among his disciples the infamous Catherine of Medici, and her less odious, because feebler, son. He was associated with them at the very time when they were revolving the greatest crime with which the annals of Christ-

endom have been polluted. With the guilt of that massacre his memory is, however, unstained ; except so far as the doctrines he inculcated, in his debates at Paris with Beza and Peter Martyr, may have taught the sovereigns to think lightly of any bloodshed which should rid the world of a party abhorred of God, and hateful to the enlightened eye of man.

Gifted with extraordinary talents, profound learning, flexible address, and captivating eloquence, Laynez fell short of that standard at which, alone, men may inscribe their names in the roll sacred to those who have reigned over their fellow mortals by a right divine, because a right inherent and indefeasible. Without genius to devise, or the glowing passion to achieve, great things, none may be associated with those kings of the earth on whose brows nature herself has set the diadem. Far surpassing in mere intellectual resources both Xavier and Ignatius, the fiery element native to their souls was uninhabitable to his. Laynez was the first, if not the most eminent, example of the results of Loyola's discipline ; and illustrates the effect of concentrating all the interests of life, and all the affections of the heart, within the narrow circle of one contracted fellowship. It yielded in him, as it has often produced in others, a vigorous but a stunted development of character ; a kind of social selfishness and sectional virtue ; a subordination of philanthropy to the love of caste ; a spirit irreclaimably servile, because exulting in its own servitude ; a temper consistent, indeed, with great actions and often contributing to them, but destructive (at least in ordinary minds) of that free and cordial sympathy with man as man ;—of those careless graces, and of that majestic repose, which touch and captivate the heart, and to which must, in part at least, be ascribed the sacred fascination exercised over us all by the simple records of the life of Him whose name the society of Jesus had assumed.

On the 2d of July, 1565, the Casa Professa, usually the scene of a profound stillness, was agitated by an unwonted excitement. Men of austere demeanour might be seen there clasping each other's hands, and voices habitually mute were interchanging hearty congratulations. One alone appeared to take no share in the common joy. As if overpowered by some strange and unwelcome tidings, he seemed by imploring gestures to deprecate a decision against which his paralyzed lips in vain attempted to protest. His age might be nearly fifty, his dress mean and sordid, and toil or suffering had ploughed their furrows in his pallid cheek; but he balanced his tall and still graceful figure with a soldier's freedom, and gazed on his associates with a countenance cast in that mould which ladies love and artists emulate. They called him Father Francis; and on the death of Laynez their almost unanimous suffrage had just hailed him as the third General of the Order of Jesus. The wish for rank and power was never more sincerely disclaimed, for never had they been forced on any one who had a larger experience of their vanity

In the female line Father Francis was the grandson of Ferdinand of Arragon, and therefore the near kinsman of the Emperor Charles V. Among his paternal ancestry he could boast or lament the names of Alexander VI. and Cæsar Borgia. Of that house, eminent alike for their wealth, their honours, and their crimes, he was the lineal representative; and in early manhood, inherited from his father the patrimony and the title of the Dukes of Gandia.

Don Francis Borgia, as if to rescue the name he bore from the infamy of his progenitors, exhaled, even in his childish days, the odour of sanctity. With each returning month, he cast a lot to determine which he should personate of the saints with whose names it was studded on the calendar. In his tenth year, with a virtue unsung and unconceived by the *Musæ Etonienses*, he played at saints so perfectly as to inflict a vigorous chastisement on his own naked person. It is hard to resist the wish that the scourge had been yet more resolutely wielded by the arm of his tutor. So seems to have thought his maternal uncle, Don John of Arragon, Archbishop of Saragossa. Taking the charge of his nephew, that highborn prelate compelled him to study alternately the lessons of the riding-master and those of the master of the sentences; and in his nineteenth year sent him to complete his education at the court of his imperial cousin.

Ardent as were still the aspirations of the young courtier for the monastic life, no one in that gallant circle bore himself more bravely in the *ménage*, or sheathed his sword with a steadier hand in the throat of the half-maddened bull, or more skilfully disputed with his sovereign the honours of the tournament. As the youthful knight, bowing to the saddle-tree, lowered his spear before the 'Queen of Beauty,' many a full dark eye beamed with a deeper lustre; but his triumph was incomplete and worthless unless it won the approving smile of Eleo-

nora de Castro. That smile was not often refused. But the romance of Don Francis begins where other romances terminate. Foremost in the train of Charles and Isabella, the husband of the fair Eleonora still touched his lute with unrivalled skill in the halls of the Escurial, or followed the quarry across the plains of Castille in advance of the most ardent falconer. Yet that music was universally selected from the offices of the church; and in the very agony of the chase, just as the wheeling hawk paused for his last deadly plunge, (genius of Nimrod, listen!) he would avert his eyes and ride slowly home, the inventor of a matchless effort of penitential self-denial.

With Charles himself for his pupil, Don Francis studied the arts of war and fortification under the once celebrated Sainte Croix, and practised in Africa the lessons he had been taught;—earning the double praise, that in the camp he was the most magnificent, in the field the most adventurous, of all the leaders in that vaunted expedition. At the head of a troop enlisted and maintained by himself, he attended the Emperor to the Milanese and Provence; and, in honourable acknowledgment of his services, was selected by Charles to lay a report of the campaign before the Empress in person, at Segovia. Towards her he felt an almost filial regard. She had long been the zealous patron and the cordial friend of himself and of Eleonora; and at the public festivals which celebrated the victories of Charles, and the meeting of the States of Castille at Toledo, they shone among the most brilliant of the satellites by which her throne was encircled.

At the moment of triumph the inexorable arm was unbared which so often, as in mockery of human pomp, confounds together the world's bravest pageants and the humiliations of the grave. Dust to dust and ashes to ashes, but, when the imperial fall, not without one last poor assertion of their departed dignity. Isabella might not be laid in the sepulchre of the kings of Spain, until amidst the funeral rites the soldered coffin had been opened, the cerements removed, and some grandee of the highest rank had been enabled to depose, that he had seen within them the very body of the deceased sovereign. Such, in pursuance of an ancient custom, was the duty confided to the zeal of Don Francis Borgia, nor was any one better fitted for such a trust. The eye, now for ever closed, had never turned to him but with maternal kindness, and every lineament of that serene and once eloquent countenance was indelibly engraven on his memory. Amidst the half-uttered prayers which commended her soul to the Divine mercy, and the low dirge of the organ, he advanced with streaming eyes, and reverently raised the covering which concealed the secrets of the grave, when—but why or how portray the appalling and loathsome spectacle? That gentle brow, that eloquent countenance, that form so lately raised on earth's proudest throne, and extolled with an almost adoring homage! Don Francis turned from the sight to shudder and to pray.

It was the great epoch in the life of Borgia. In the eyes of the world, indeed, he may have been unchanged; but in his eyes the whole aspect of that world was altered. Lord of a princely fortune, the heir of an illustrious house, the favourite kinsman of the Emperor of the West, renowned in the very flower of his youth as a warrior, a courtier, and a musician, his home hallowed by conjugal love, and gladdened by the sports of his children; for whom had life a deeper interest, or who could erect on a surer basis a loftier fabric of more brilliant hopes? Those interests and hopes he deliberately resigned, and, at the age of twenty-nine, bound himself by a solemn vow, that in the event of his surviving Eleonora, he would end his days as a member of some religious order. He had gazed on the hideous triumph of death and sin over prospects still more splendid than his own. For him the soothing illusions of existence were no more—earth and its inhabitants, withering under the curse of their Maker, might put on their empty gauds, and for some transient hour dream and talk of happiness. But the curse was there, and there would it lie, crushing the frivolous spirit the most when felt the least, and consigning alike to that foul debasement the lovely and the brave: the sylph now floating through the giddy dance, and the warrior now proudly treading the field of victory.

From such meditations Charles endeavoured to recall his friend to the common duties of life. He required him to assume the viceroyalty of Catalonia, and adorned him with the cross of the order of Alcantara, then of all chivalric honours the noblest and the most highly prized. His administration was firm, munificent, and just; it forms the highest era of his life, and is especially signalized by the same sedulous care for the education of the young, which afterwards formed his highest praise as General of the Order of Jesus.

Ingenious above all men in mortifying his natural affections, Don Francis could not neglect the occasion which his new dignities afforded him, of incurring much wholesome contumely. Sumptuous banquets must be given in honour of his sovereign, when he could at once fast and be despised for fasting. To exhibit himself in penitential abasement before the people under his authority, would give to penitence the appropriate accompaniment of general contempt. On the festival of 'the Invention of the Holy Cross,' mysteries not unlike those of the *Bona Dea* were to be celebrated by the ladies of Barcelona, when, to prevent the profane intrusion of any of the coarser sex, the viceroy himself undertook the office of sentinel. With a naked dagger in his hand, a young nobleman demanded entrance, addressing to the viceroy insults such as every gentleman is bound, under the heaviest penalty of the laws of chivalry, to expiate by blood. A braver man did not tread the soil of Spain than Don Francis, nor any one to whom the reproach of poltronery was more hateful. And yet his sword did not leap from his scabbard. With a calm rebuke and courteous demeanour, he allowed the bravo to enter the sacred precincts—preferring the imputation of cowardice, though stinging like an adder, to the sin of avenging himself, and, indeed, to the duty of maintaining his lawful authority. History has omitted to tell what were the weapons, or what the incantation, by which the ladies promptly ejected the insolent intruder, nor has she recorded how they afterwards received their guardian knight of Alcantara. Her only care has been to excite our admiration for this most illustrious victory in the bosom of Don Francis, of the meekness of the saint over the human passions of the soldier.

At the end of four years Don Francis was relieved by the death of his father from his viceregal office, and assumed his hereditary title of Duke of Gandia. His vassals exulted in the munificence of their new chief. The ancient retainers of his family lived on his bounty—cottages, convents, and hospitals, rose on his estates—fortresses were built to check the ravages of the Moorish corsairs, and the mansion of his ancestors reappeared in all its ancient splendour. In every work of piety and mercy the wise and gentle Eleonora was the rival of her lord. But it was the only strife which ever agitated the Castle of Gandia. Austerities were practised there, but gloom and lassitude were unknown; nor did the bright suns of Spain gild any feudal ramparts, within which love, and peace the child of love, shed their milder light with a more abiding radiance.

But on that countenance, hitherto so calm and so submissive, might at length be traced the movements of an inward tempest, with which, even when prostrate before the altar, the Duke of Gandia strove in vain. Conversant with every form of self-inflicted suffering, how should he find strength to endure the impending death of Eleonora! His was a prayer transcending the resources of language and of thought; it was the mute agony of a breaking heart. But after the whirlwind and the fire, was heard the still small voice. It said, or seemed to say, ' If it be thy will, she shall recover; but not for her real welfare nor for thine.' Adoring gratitude swept away every feebler emotion, and the suppliant's grief at length found utterance. ' Thy will be done. Thou knowest what is best for us. Whom have we in heaven but thee, and whom upon earth should we desire in comparison of thee ?' At the age of thirty-six the Duke of Gandia committed to the tomb the frame once animated by a spirit from which not death itself could separate him. In the sacred retirement to which in that event he had devoted his remaining days, Eleonora would still unite her prayers to his; and as each of those days should decline into the welcome shadows of evening, one stage the more towards his reunion with her would have been traversed.

The Castle of Gandia was still hung with the funeral draperies when a welcome though unexpected guest arrived there. It was Peter Faber, the officiating priest at the Crypt of Montmartre, charged by Ignatius with a mission to promote the cause of Christian education in Spain. Aided by his counsels, and by the letters of the patriarch, the duke erected on his estates a church, a college, and a library, and placed them under the care of teachers selected by Ignatius. The sorrows of the duke were relieved as his wealth flowed still more copiously in this new channel of beneficence; and the universities of Alcala and Seville were enlarged by his bounty with similar foundations. But, as Faber remarked, a still nobler edifice was yet to be erected on the soul of the founder himself. The first stone of it was laid in the duke's performance of the Spiritual Exercises. To the completion of this invisible but imperishable building, the remainder of his life was inflexibly devoted.

With Ignatius the duke had long main-tained a correspondence, in which the stately courtesies of Spanish noblemen not ungracefully temper the severe tones of patriarchal authority and filial reverence. Admission into the order of Jesus was an honour for which, in this case, the aspirant was humbly content, and was wisely permitted long to wait and sue. To study the biography, that he might imitate the life of Him by whose holy name the society was called; to preach in his own household, or at the wicket of the nunnery of the ladies of St. Clair; and day by day, to place in humiliating contrast some proof of the divine goodness, and some proof of his own demerit, were the first probationary steps which the duke was required to tread in the toilsome path on which he had thus entered. It was a path from which Philip, then governing Spain with the title of regent, would have willingly seduced him. He consulted him on the most critical affairs; summoned him to take a high station in the states of Castille; and pressed on his acceptance the office of grand master of the royal household. It was declined in favour of the Duke of Alva. Had Gandia preferred the duties of his secular rank to those of his religious aspirations, Spain might have had a saint the less and seven provinces the more. With the elevation of Alva, the butcheries in the Netherlands, the disgrace of Spain, and the independence of Holland might have been averted.

Warned by his escape, the duke implored with renewed earnestness his immediate admission into the order; nor was Ignatius willing that his proselyte should again incur such dangers. At the chapel of his own college he accordingly pronounced the irrevocable vows; a Papal bull having dispensed during a term of four years with any public avowal of the change. They were passed in the final adjustment of his secular affairs. He had lived in the splendour appropriate to his rank and fortune, and in the exercise of the bounty becoming his eminence in the Christian commonwealth. But now all was to be abandoned, even the means of almsgiving, for he was himself henceforth to live on the alms of others. He gave his children in marriage to the noblest houses in Spain and Portugal, transferred to his eldest son the enjoyment of the patrimonial estates of Gandia, and then, at the age of forty, meekly betook himself to the study of scholastic divinity, of the traditions of the church, and of the canons of the general councils. He even submitted to all the rules, and performed all the public exercises enforced on the youngest student. Such was his piety that the thorny fagots of the schoolmen fed instead of smothering the flame; and on the margin of his Thomas Aquinas might be seen some devout aspiration, extracted by his sacred alchemy from each subtle distinction in the text. Never before or since was the degree of Doctor in Divinity, to which he now proceeded, so hardly earned or so well deserved.

Two of the brothers of the duke had been .members of the sacred college, and his humility had refused the purple offered at the instance of the emperor to two of his sons. But how should the new doctor avert from his own head the ecclesiastical cap of maintenance with which Charles was now desirous to replace the ducal coronet? He fled the presence of his imperial patron; made and executed his own testamentary dispositions, delivered his last parental charge to his eldest son, and bade a final adieu to his weeping family. The gates of the castle of Gandia closed on their self-banished lord. He went forth, like Francis Xavier, chanting the song of David—'When Israel went out of Egypt, and the house of Jacob from a strange people,'—adding from another strain of the royal minstrel, 'Our bonds are broken and we are delivered.' He lived for more than twenty years from this time, and in his future missions into Spain often passed the gates of the castle, but never more re-entered them. He became a stranger even to his children, never again passing so much as a single day in their society, or even permitting himself to become acquainted with their offspring.

As the bird set free to her nest, so hasted the emaciated duke to take his seat at the footstool of Ignatius. Yet in his route through Ferrara and Florence, his sacred impatience was arrested, and his humility confirmed, by the unwelcome honours yielded to him by his kinsmen, the reigning sovereigns of those duchies. He would have entered Rome by night; but in the city of triumphs and ovations, the victorious Loyola must exhibit so illustrious a captive. Attended by the ambassador of Spain, by a prince of the house of Colonna, and by a long train of cardinals, priests, and nobles, the Duke of Gandia advanced in solemn procession to the Casa Professa. There, in the presence of his General, his wearied spirit found at length the repose which the most profuse liberality of fortune had been unable to bestow. With tears of joy he kissed the feet of the patriarch and of his Professed brethren, esteeming the meanest office in their household an honour too exalted for so unworthy an associate; and then, in a general confession, poured into the ear of Ignatius every secret of his conscience from the dawn of life to that long-desired hour.

Such zeal was a treasure too precious to be left without some great and definite object; and as the duke was still the steward of some of this world's treasures, which he had devoted to sacred uses, they were employed in building at Rome the church and college afterwards so famous as the College *de Propagandâ Fide.* One only secular care still awaited him. His rank as a grandee of Spain, and the cross of Alcantara, could not be laid aside without the consent of the emperor. It .was solicited with all the grace of an accomplished courtier, and all the fervour of a saint. But while he awaited at Rome the answer of Charles, a new alarm disturbed the serenity of the Casa Professa. The dreaded purple was again pressed on him with all the weight of Papal admonition. To avoid it, Gandia fled the presence of the Pope and Ignatius, returned to Spain, performed a pilgrimage to the Castle of Loyola, kissed the hallowed ground, and then burying himself in a Jesuit College at Ognato, once more awaited the decision of the emperor.

It soon arrived. He was no longer a duke, a knight of St. Iago, nor even a Spanish gentleman. Solemnly, and in due legal form, he renounced all these titles, and with them all his property and territorial rights. Even his secular dress was laid aside, and his head was prepared by the tonsure for the Episcopal touch, emblematic of the most awful mystery. The astonished spectators collected and preserved the holy relics. And now bent in lowly prostration before the altar at Ognato, the Father Francis had no further sacrifice to offer there, but the sacrifice of a heart emptied of all the interests and of all the affections of the world. Long and silent was his prayer, but it was now unattended with any trace of disorder. The tears he shed were such as might have bedewed the cheek of the First Man before he had tasted the bitterness of sin. He rose from his knees, bade a last farewell to his attendants; and Father Francis was left alone with his Creator.

It was a solitude not long to be maintained. The fame of his devotion filled the Peninsula. All who needed spiritual counsel, and who wished to indulge an idle curiosity, resorted to his cell. Kings sought his advice, wondering congregations hung on his lips, and two at least of the grandees of Spain imitated his example. His spiritual triumphs were daily more and more splendid; and, if he might escape the still threatened promotion into the college of Cardinals, might be as enduring as his life. The authority of Ignatius, not unaided by some equivocal exercise of his ingenuity, at length placed Father Francis beyond the reach of this last danger. They both went down to the grave without witnessing the debasement of their order by any ecclesiastical dignity.

But there was yet one tie to the pomp and vanity of this world, which could not be entirely broken. During his viceregal administration, Father Francis had on one occasion traversed the halls of the Castle of Barcelona in deep and secret conference with his imperial cousin. Each at that interview imparted to the other his design of devoting to religious retirement the interval which should intervene between the business and the close of life. At every season of disappointment Charles reverted to this purpose, and abandoned or postponed it with each return of success. But now, broken with sickness and sorrow, he had fixed his residence in a monastery in Estremadura, and summoned the former viceroy of Catalonia to the presence of his early friend and patron. Falling on his knees, as in times of yore, Father Francis offered to impress the kiss of homage on the hand which had so lately borne the sceptre of half the civilized world. But Charles embraced his cousin, and compelled him to sit, and to sit covered, by his side. Long and frequent were their conversations; but the record of them transmitted to us by the historians of the Order of Jesus, has but little semblance of authenticity. Charles assails, and Borgia defends the new institute, and the imperial disputant of course yields to the combined force of eloquence and truth. It seems less improbable that the publication of Memoirs of the life of the Emperor, to be written by himself, was one subject of serious debate at these interviews, and that the good father dissuaded it. If the tale be true, he has certainly one claim the less to the gratitude of later times. What seems certain is, that he undertook and executed some secret mission from Charles to the court of Portugal, that he acted as one of the executors of his will, and delivered a funeral oration in praise of the deceased emperor before the Spanish court at Valladolid.

From this point, the life of Borgia merges in the general history of the order to which he had attached himself. It is a passage of history full of the miracles of self-denial, and of miracles in the more accurate acceptation of the word. To advance the cause of education, and to place in the hands of his own society the control of that mighty engine, was the labour which Father Francis as their General chiefly proposed to himself. His success was complete, and he lived to see the establishment, in almost every state of Europe, of colleges formed on the model of that which he had himself formed in the town of Gandia.

Borgia is celebrated by his admirers as the most illustrious of all conquerors of the appetites and passions of our common nature: and the praise, such as it is, may well be conceded to him. No other saint in the calendar ever abdicated or declined so great an amount of worldly grandeur and domestic happiness. No other embraced poverty and pain in forms more squalid, or more revolting to flesh and blood. So strange and shocking are the stories of his flagellations, of the diseases contracted by them, and of the sickening practices by which he tormented his senses, that even to read them is of itself no light penance. In the same spirit, our applause is demanded for feats of humility, and prodigies of obedience, and raptures of devotion, so extravagant, that his biographers might seem to have assumed the office of penitential executors to the saint; and to challenge for his memory some of the disgust and contempt which when living he so studiously courted. And yet Borgia was no ordinary man.

He had great talents with a narrow capacity. Under the control of minds more comprehensive than his own, he could adopt and execute their wider views with admirable address and vigour. With rare powers both of endurance and of action, he was the prey of a constitutional melancholy, which made him dependent on the more sanguine spirit of his guides for all his aims and for all his hopes; but once rescued from the agony of selecting his path, he moved along it not merely with firmness but with impetuosity. All his impulses came from without; but when once given they could not readily be arrested. The very dejection and self-distrust of his nature rendered him more liable than other men to impressions at once deep and abiding. Thus he was a saint in his infancy at the bidding of his nurse—then a cavalier at the command of his uncle—an inamorato because the empress desired it—a warrior and a viceroy because such was the pleasure of Charles—a devotee from seeing a corpse in a state of decomposition—a founder of colleges on the advice of Peter Faber—a Jesuit at the will of Ignatius—and General of the order because his colleagues would have it so. Yet each of these characters when once assumed, was performed, not merely with constancy, but with high and just applause. His mind was like a sycophant plant, feeble when alone, but of admirable vigour and luxuriance when properly sustained. A whole creation of such men would have been unequal to the work of Ignatius Loyola; but, in his grasp, one such man could perform a splendid though but a secondary service. His life was more eloquent than all the homilies of Chrysostom. Descending from one of the most brilliant heights of human prosperity, he exhibited everywhere, and in aspect the most intelligible and impressive to his contemporaries, the awful power of the principles by which he was impelled. Had he lived in the times and in the society of his infamous kinsmen, Borgia would not improbably have shared their disastrous renown. But his dependent nature, moulded by a far different influence, rendered him a canonized saint; an honourable, just, and virtuous man; one of the most eminent ministers of a polity as benevolent in intention as it was gigantic in design; and the founder of a system of education pregnant with results of almost matchless importance. His miracles may be not disadvantageously compared with those of the Baron Monchausen; but it would be less easy to find a meet comparison for his genuine virtues. They triumph over all the silly legends and all the real follies which obscure his character. His whole mature life was but one protracted martyrdom, for the advancement of what he esteemed the perfection of his own nature, and the highest interests of his fellow-men. Though he maintained an intimate personal intercourse with Charles IX. and his mother, and enjoyed their highest favour, there is no reason to suppose that he was entrusted with their atrocious secret. Even in the land of the Inquisition he had firmly refused to lend the influence of his name to that sanguinary tribunal; for there was nothing morose in his fanaticism; nor mean in his subservience. Such a man as Francis Borgia could hardly become a persecutor. His own church raised altars to his name. Other churches have neglected or despised it. In that all-wise and all-compassionate judgment, which is uninvaded by our narrow prejudices and by our unhallowed feelings, his fervent love of God and of man was doubtless permitted to cover the multitude of his theoretical errors and real extravagances. Human justice is severe, not merely because man is censorious, but because he reasonably distrusts himself, and fears lest his weakness should confound the distinctions of good and evil. Divine justice is lenient, because there alone love can flow in all its unfathomable depths and boundless expansion—impeded by no dread of error, and diverted by no misplaced sympathies.

To Ignatius, the founder of the order of the Jesuits; to Xavier, the great leader in their missionary enterprises; to Laynez, the author of their peculiar system of theology; and to Borgia, the architect of their system of education, two names are to be added to complete the roll of the great men from whose hands their Institute received the form it retains to the present hour. These are Bellarmine, from whom they learned the arts and resources of controversy; and Acquaviva, the fifth in number, but in effect the fourth of their Generals—who may be described as the Numa Pompilius of the order. There is in the early life of Bellarmine a kind of pastoral beauty, and even in his later days a grace, and a simplicity so winning, that it costs some effort to leave such a theme unattempted. The character of Acquaviva, one of the most memorable rulers and lawgivers of his age, it would be a still greater effort to attempt.

'Henceforth let no man say,' (to mount on the stilts of dear old Samuel Johnson,) 'come, I will write a disquisition on the history, the doctrines, and the morality of the Jesuits—at least let no man say so who has not subdued the lust of story-telling.' Filled to their utmost limits, lie before us the sheets so recently destined to that ambitious enterprise. Perhaps it may be as well thus to have yielded to the allurement which has marred the original design. If in later days the disciples of Ignatius, obeying the laws of all human institutions, have exhibited the sure though slow development of the seeds of error and of crime, sown by the authors of their polity, it must at least be admitted that they were men of no common mould. It is something to know that an impulse, which, after three centuries is still unspent, proceeded from hands of gigantic power, and that their power was moral as much as intellectual, or much more so. In our own times much indignation and much alarm are thrown away on innovators of a very different stamp. From the ascetics of the common room, from men whose courage rises high enough only to hint at their unpopular opinions, and whose belligerent passions soar at nothing more daring than to worry some unfortunate professor, it is almost ludicrous to fear any great movement on the theatre of human affairs. When we see these dainty gentlemen in rags, and hear of them from the snows of the Himmalaya, we may begin to tremble. The slave of his own appetites, in bondage to conventional laws, his spirit emasculated by the indulgences, or corroded by the cares of life, hardly daring to act, to speak, or to think for himself, man—gregarious and idolatrous man—worships the world in which he lives, adopts its maxims, and treads its beaten paths. To rouse him from his lethargy, and to give a new current to his thoughts, heroes appear from time to time on the verge of his horizon, and hero-worship, Pagan or Christian, withdraws him for a while from still baser idolatry. To contemplate the motives and the career of such men, may teach much which well deserves the knowing; but nothing more clearly than this—that no one can have shrines erected to his memory in the hearts of men of distant generations, unless his own heart was an altar on which daily sacrifices of fervent devotion, and magnanimous self-denial, were offered to the only true object of human worship.

ART. II.—1. *Procès de Madame Lafarge,* (*Vol et Empoisonment,*) *complets et detaillés. Deuxième edition. Annales Criminelles, au Bureau Rue d'Enghien.* Paris: 1840.

2. *Procès de Madame Lafarge, etc. Deuxième edition. Pagnerre, Editeur.* Paris: 1840.*

3. *Mémoires de Marie Cappelle, Veuve Lafarge. Ecrits par elle-même.* 2 Tom. 8vo. Londres : 1841.

THE works placed at the head of this paper form together a mournful and startling history. They have indeed been but too generally perused in the careless spirit with which a novel is glanced at and forgotten ; because they have been supposed to contain merely the story of one of the common horrors of the day, sent forth to gratify the prevailing taste for excitement —to occupy for its hour the columns of a Newspaper—to be hurried over, superseded by some more terrible catastrophe,

and then forgotten for ever. To one, however, who will more carefully scan the events of this singular drama, there is offered much that should be the subject of very earnest and anxious inquiry—problems, indeed, upon the solution of which depend the security and the happiness of society. The more narrowly we investigate each fearful step in this appalling proceeding, the more profound will be our astonishment and alarm at finding that among a people who must be considered to rank among the most civilized of nations—in an age, too, boasting loudly of its many and vast improvements in scince and in art—almost every judicial safeguard which experience and forethought have discovered and suggested, for the protection as well of the accused as of the society which arraigns him, has been overthrown and trampled down ; the dictates of humanity, of common justice, violated ; and a court of justice, assembled to decide upon the life or death of a fellow-creature—where all ought to be calm, impassive, dignified—mild though firm, compassionate though severe—converted into a scene of rudeness and violence, of passionate invective, of cruel and unjust vituperation, and melodramatic display.

A scene so remarkable ought not to pass by without comment. The comity of nations should so make of Europe one family, that the errors fallen into at Corrèze should be deemed an injustice done to the whole European community. The imperfections of the French system of Judicature, should be signalized by a comparison with other and varying systems ; and thus comparison and friendly criticism be made to tend to mutual improvement.

Our language respecting this celebrated proceeding will, we fear, sound harshly in the ears of our neighbours. Nevertheless, we feel assured, that before we leave the painful subject before us, the justice of our animadversions will appear but too manifest. In many things has France improved ; in many has she set a bright example to other nations ; but the judges of Calas and La Barre have unhappily been succeeded by functionaries not wholly unlike themselves ; and her system of judicature, as exhibited on this occasion, though certainly somewhat less barbarous than the atrocious proceedings signalized by Voltaire, is still at variance with most of the principles which reason and humanity would employ as guides in judicial procedure.

A comparison of the course of conduct pursued by the French court on this occasion, with that which, under similar circumstances, would have taken place in this country, will enable us, with comparative ease, to explain to an English reader the grounds of our unfavourable opinion. From thus putting, side by side, the different steps in two very dissimilar modes of procedure, we may probably be able to discover the errors of both systems, and obtain a conception of that which an enlightened people ought to adopt. Let it not be supposed that we are about to set up our own procedure as a model, or that we intend to assume that what is English is right. The comparison we propose is intended only as a means of illustration : nothing can well be more dissimilar than the two systems of procedure ; the opposition will therefore, at every step, be singular and interesting, and may, by its very singularity, suggest the true principle which ought to guide us in every step of the process.

Before we proceed to our present attempt, in this species of comparative anatomy, we would premise a few observations, upon the *end* sought to be obtained by Judicature as a *means.*

It is usually deemed sufficient to say, that the object which should be in view in all judicial inquiries is the attainment of truth. But this general statemnt is far from being sufficient ; and the very *insufficient* conception of the ends of judicature which such an assertion evinces, has led to the greater number of the cruel and pernicious mistakes exemplified in the proceedings now under our consideration. The great purpose of that class of judicial proceedings here contemplated is to maintain a feeling of security from wrong, in the society to which the tribunal belongs. If a member of the community be wronged in his person, property, or reputation, and there be impunity for the wrongdoer, then do the rest of the community tremble lest they should also suffer the same wrong : and, if this impunity be frequent, society can hardly be said to exist, as each man endeavours to defend himself since he can no longer depend upon society for security. On the other hand, the more certain and rapid the punishment which the tribunals inflict upon wrongdoers, the more complete is the security of the community—the more completely have the ends of judicature been attained.

But before we punish, must we not learn, first, whether a wrong has been done ?— next, by whom it has been done ? And when the tribunal makes this inquiry, should not the attainment of truth be the sole object of its solicitude and consideration ? Our answer is, No. If the attainment of truth be the sole object of consideration, we must seek it, no matter at what

cost of terror and insecurity to society at large : and thus the tribunal, by its inquiry, may do a greater injury to the community than did the crime it seeks to punish. Human imperfection renders the administration of justice, of necessity, a system of averages. We cannot hope for perfect certainty, and certainty in every case. All that we can expect is, to discover the necessary facts in so large a number of cases as to render society generally secure, by rendering the perpetration of crime exceedingly dangerous to those who would commit it. This can be done, and done more efficiently, if we pursue certain predetermined and specific rules of inquiry, than if we were to give the tribunal, on every occasion, perfect and uncontrolled liberty of action. The philosopher sitting quietly in his closet, may imagine that every fact that has the slightest relation to the matter in hand ought to be known and weighed—and that the more completely the facts are known, the greater is the chance of attaining a knowledge of the truth respecting the particular inquiry instituted. But it should be remembered, that in order to get at all these facts, it may be necessary to invade the peace and security of others ; that the knowledge of a multitude of comparatively insignificant facts serves often rather to confuse than enlighten ; and that the wider is the field of inquiry, the greater is the danger of mistake, from emotions created by irrelevant evidence, from passion, from prejudice.

In every judicial inquiry, then, we may say, indeed, that the object sought to be obtained is the truth ; but that truth itself must be sought according to certain fixed and pre-established modes of inquiry— modes which experience has shown to be necessary as safeguards for the security of society generally ; and that the very form of the inquiry is of vital importance as respects this security.

Let us now endeavour, by examination, to discover whether this salutary precaution was duly considered in the remarkable instance before us.

In the following narrative, we shall, as far as we can, present the facts to the reader, in the order, form, and manner, in which they were presented to the tribunal. This mode is adopted for the purpose of being better able to show what of the multitude of facts, relevant and irrelevant, submitted to the French jury, could, by the English mode of procedure, have been brought forward in evidence ; we may thus perhaps discover to what extent, and in what manner, the forms of either nation err

—the one by admitting much that is unnecessary, the other by excluding something that is needed for the proper administration of justice.

On the 14th of January, 1840, Charles Pouch Lafarge died at Glandier, in the department of La Corrèze in France. A few days after, the widow of Lafarge was arrested upon suspicion of having poisoned him.

When the house of the deceased was searched by the officers of justice, certain diamonds were found, which were supposed to have been stolen by the widow before her marriage, from Madame la Viscomtesse de Lèautaud. Hereupon the prisoner was charged with *larceny*, or stealing—*(le délit de vol.)*

By the law of France, murder is classed as a *crime*, larceny as a *délit*. The *crime* is tried by the assize court of the department—the *délit* by the *Tribunal de police correctionnelle*.

The charge of larceny was first brought to trial. The trial commenced on the 9th of July, 1840. We may here, in passing, remark upon the delay that had taken place. The prisoner was arrested towards the latter end of January upon a charge of murder. The second charge was soon after preferred, and neither the one nor the other was tried till the 9th of July. In the proceedings before us, no application for delay on the part of the prosecution seems to have been made. The delay which occurred appears to have been according to the ordinary course of proceeding.

This delay in the case of a common larceny could not well have occurred in England. But a person charged with a murder committed out of London in the autumn, cannot be tried before the end of February in the following spring. Such delay is a gross violation of justice, and ought not to be permitted to continue.

Before the charge of stealing was gone into, the counsel for the defence moved to defer the trial; first, upon the ground that there being two charges, one of having committed a *crime*, the other of having committed a *délit*, the charge of the *crime* should be tried first. The second reason given for delay was, that Madame Lafarge had not had time sufficient for her defence.

The court, however, refused the delay asked—whereupon an appeal was entered against this judgment, and delay again demanded because of this appeal. The court again refused to delay the trial, and proceeded to investigate the charge. Madame Lafarge thereupon retired—the proceeding went on in her absence, and she was found guilty of the theft;—the trial being by a judge unassisted by a jury.

The Court of Appeal gave judgment afterwards—1. That the demand for delay was properly refused. 2. But that an appeal from that judgment having been entered, the court below was not justified in proceeding further until that appeal was decided—and therefore all the subsequent proceedings of the 'court below were quashed as irregular.[*]

On the 3d of September, and before a rehearing of the trial for stealing, the court of Assize of La Corrèze proceeded to the trial of the prisoner on the charge of murder. A preliminary inquiry had already, according to due process of law, been instituted in July, before *la chambre des mises en accusation*, and by the arrêt of this court the prisoner was sent for trial before the court of Assize.

The arrêt gave a long enumeration of facts as reasons for its decision, which decision was in these words :—

' Attendu que de ces faits résultent des charges suffisantes pour prononcer la mise en accusation :—Declare qu'il y a lieu à accusation contre Marie Fortunée Cappelle, veuve Lafarge, pour avoir dans les mois de Decembre, 1839, et de Janvier, 1840, attenté à la vie de Charles Joseph Pouch Lafarge, son mari, par l'effet de substances susceptibles de donner la mort, et qui l'ont effectivement occasioné, crime prévu et puni par les articles 301, 302, du code pénal.

' La renvoie, en consequence, devant la cour d'assises du department de la Corrèze, séant à Tulle, pour y étre jugée selon la loi.

' Maintient l'ordonnance de prise de corps decernée par la chambre de conseil.'[†]

---

[*] One of the most faulty portions of English criminal jurisprudence is that which relates to the right of appeal from decisions on criminal charges. In fact, no appeal lies from the judgment of the court or the verdict of the jury, except on the ground of error patent on the face of the indictment—and as under the present system, the greater portion of all the criminals in the country are tried by unlearned justices at the quarter sessions, constant and flagrant violations of law and justice are the necessary result.

[†] The regular steps in this procedure appear to be—

1. An ordonnance *de prise de corps decernée par la chambre de conseil.* This is similar to our warrant of commitment by the committing magistrate.

2. An arrêt by the chambre *des mises en accusation.* This is similar in some things to the finding of a true bill by our grand jury—that is, the purpose of the inquiry seems the same, though the mode be different.

3. After the arrêt of the chambre *des mises en accusation*, the prisoner was examined, (on this examination we shall hereafter remark;) and upon this examination and those of the several witnesses, the *procureur-général* frames his *acte d'accusation*, which is apparently intended to serve the purposes of our indictment. There appears in both systems much unnecessary complication.

Upon this charge, on the 3d of September, the prisoner was brought to trial. The jury being chosen by lot, and declared legally constituted by the presiding judge, the prisoner was addressed by the judge :*—

'Accusée, levez-vous.
'D. Votre nom? R. Marie Cappelle, femme Lafarge.
'D. Quel est votre age? R. Vingt-quatre ans.
'D. Votre profession? R. Je n'ai pas de profession.
'D. Quel est votre domicile? R. Au Glandier.'

The jury was then sworn, and the prisoner warned by the judge to be attentive. The '*acte d'accusation*,' answering to the English indictment, was then read.

For the purposes of justice, all that this *acte d'accusation* need contain, is a clear specific description of the charge against the prisoner—so that the prisoner may know distinctly from what he has to clear himself—and the court and jury may know what they have to try. By the law of England, moreover, in cases of felony,† only one offence can be charged in the same indictment—that is, two charges cannot be tried at one and the same time; and in a grave, nay often capital charge, it is a wise and merciful precaution. The mind of the prisoner ought not to be distracted by a multiplicity of charges—nor the minds of the jury unfairly biassed by the mention of many supposed offences. Recollecting, then, the purpose for which this *acte d'accusation* is employed, an examination of the *acte* itself will prove not wholly uninstructive. Unfortunately it is impossible, from its length, to insert the whole of this extraordinary document. It is not impossible to describe it.

The *acte* is in the name of the Procureur-Général, and is therefore to be considered, not the exposition of an accusing advocate—but an official document emanating from a great public functionary. The document first declares that it is the declaration of the Procureur-Général, and thus proceeds:—

' Charles Pouch Lafarge habitait le Glandier, départment de la Corrèze—il y exploitait des forges, et possédait une fortune immobilière considerable ; sa famille était honnête ; son père, mort depuis plusieurs années, avait rempli longtemps les fonctions de juge de paix du canton du Vigeois. Doué de qualités attachantes, susceptible de sentimens tendres et généreux, il était aimé de ceux qui l'entouraient.'*

In the same strain of sentimentality, this extraordinary judicial document proceeds to detail every fact which the accuser thinks of importance. All these statements, garnished with the most outrageous vituperation, are set forth without the safeguard of an oath, without the check of cross-examination. Every insinuation that the most artful rhetoric can supply, is without hesitation adopted—motives and intentions are without any compunction boldly imputed—characters are described—and throughout, the guilt of the prisoner is assumed as a thing not capable of being disputed. In short, this grave judicial document is a written pleading against the prisoner. Having immediately to remark upon the manner and bearing of the Avocat Général upon this occasion, we shall confine ourselves to one observation upon this document, viewed in the character of a written pleading. No Barrister conducting a prosecution for murder in England, would dare to make such a statement *viva voce*—and write it he could not. The moment that he does more than give a naked simple statement of the facts, calmly weighing their value as evidence, that moment he is considered to transgress the line of his duty, and the Judge would infallibly interrupt him. But in this proceeding, we find a document on which the whole after prosecution rests—assuming the character of furious advocacy—asserting, without compunction, relevant and irrelevant facts, and taking the most unfair advantages of the unfortunate prisoner—prejudging her case without a shadow of proof—distorting, by pretending to relate, her previous history—and thus making the

---

* The jury consists of twelve jurymen, and two supplementary jurymen ; the prosecution and the prisoner had an equal number of challenges, viz. eight each. The number of challenges seems to be determined by the number of jurymen present—in the present case thirty were present ; and, as fourteen was the number required for the full jury, the number of challenges permitted became necessarily sixteen, eight to each party. This would appear an objectionable mode, as open to fraud and influence.

† There are some cases in which, by statute, it is permitted to charge more than two felonies—viz. in embezzlement, three instances may be laid, if committed within six months—and also in an indictment for coining a double charge is allowed.

* The procureur-général published two editions of this precious piece of rhetoric. The second thus varies the sentiments: 'Marié une première fois, il avait eu le douleur de perdre sa femme. Bon, généreux, chéri de ceux que l'environnaient, susceptible lui-même de sentimens exaltés, il sentait le besoin de s'environner de nouvelles et de plus douces affections. Il désirait, aussi, trouver dans le dot d'une seconde épouse, les moyens de donner à son industrie plus de développement et activité.' Love and money are here closely conjoined. The exalted affections, and the desire of a marriage-portion, are placed in no very seemly juxtaposition.

question of her guilt or innocence to turn, not upon the evidence adduced respecting the deed, for the supposed perpetration of which she was now to be tried; but upon the notion which the jury might form as to her former life and character. Doing thus, in the grave character of a public officer, what no private English Advocate with a spark of right feeling would deign to attempt, and what, if any Counsel could be found degraded enough to essay, no English Judge would permit him to accomplish.

The indictment in this country is, by the present practice, stripped of much that formerly rendered it ridiculous. It still, however, retains some things not needed for the purposes of justice, and is construed with such technical strictness, that due punishment is at times evaded, and justice mocked at   This strictness is nevertheless, upon the whole, advantageous. Particular and striking, but rare; instances may indeed be cited of impunity obtained, through its influence, for the evil-doer. The precision, however, which is thereby rendered necessary, is a great safeguard for the innocent accused; nothing extraneous is set forth—nothing is imported into the cause which can excite or mislead the jury, or confuse or terrify the accused. The very technicality of the form and language of the indictment robs it of all appearance of passion, and prevents the possibility of employing any unfair rhetorical artifice. Thus making it present a striking contrast, indeed, to that extravagant pleading which we are now considering

After stating the desire that M. Lafarge felt for a new and tender affection, and the mercantile spirit which guided him in his search of an object of future love, the *acte* sets forth the mode which he adopted to gain the desired object; and the system which it discloses is among the most extraordinary and painful incidents of this sad drama.

M. Lafarge applied at Paris to a marriage-broker (*agent matrimoniale*) in the month of August, 1839; and from this man came the proposal that he should marry Marie Cappelle. This unfortunate young woman was an orphan; her father had been an officer in the imperial guard, and had died, leaving his children to the care of his wife, who married again. She some time after died also, and her children by M. Cappelle were left in charge of her relations. Among them was an aunt, who had married a person of the name of De Martens; and this M. de Martens, though moving in a sphere of life that might be al-

most called distinguished, was evidently the person who, through the assistance of the marriage-broker, managed the marriage of his niece with a man of whom he knew nothing, and whose face he had never seen three days before he determined to entrust to him for life the orphan child then under his charge. It is remarkable that this circumstance is passed by with indifference by all persons at the trial, and does not, as far as we learn, appear to have excited remark or astonishment in the minds of the Journalists of France. Are we, then, to assume that this *agent matrimoniale* is commonly employed in France by persons of respectability and honour?—that marriage, still a matter of *convenance*, is managed after a new fashion, in consequence of the changed habits of her people—the mercantile spirit of the time having invaded and subdued the province even of love and affection? The unfortunate Madame Lafarge herself gives a detailed account of the proceedings connected with her marriage, but makes no mention of the *agent*. As her 'Memoirs' have been written since her trial, she could not fail to know the mode in which her marriage was really contracted. Her silence, then, is not among the least significant of the circumstances connected with this strange and disgraceful transaction. She avows that she married not from affection, but necessity—a necessity which her forlorn situation imposed; and there is no reason to doubt the truth of her assertion. The *acte d'accusation* thus briefly tells the story of the marriage:—
'This idea of a second marriage led him (M. Lafarge) to Paris in the month of August, 1839. There were some difficulties in the way; but he was soon introduced to a M. Foy, (a matrimonial agent,) and this man proposed to him to marry Marie Cappelle. Some inquiries were made on the part of the accused, by her friends, respecting the situation of Lafarge, and a few days had hardly elapsed before the marriage was celebrated. The following night the new-married pair left Paris for Glandier, where they arrived on the 15th of August, 1839.' The *acte* then enters into a minute history of the life of Lafarge and his wife up to the time of his death; the object of which is to show, that there were feelings in her mind which would induce her to commit the horrible crime with which she was charged. The manner of stating these facts is studiously adapted to the end of exciting prejudice and passion against the accused.

The history of this period, as given by Madame Lafarge herself, is extraordinary, and in some parts improbable. The persons who composed her 'Memoirs,' (for we believe them not to have been written by herself, but to have been concocted for her, and from her information, by professional artists,) being desirous of exciting compassion for her unhappy condition, have described very minutely the brutal conduct of Lafarge during his journey to Glandier ; and extraordinary pains are taken to press upon the reader's belief the fact, that Madame Lafarge, spite of the pressing instances of her husband, resisted successfully all his entreaties, and lived the life of a nun with the name of a wife. For what purpose this statement is made, and made with such repetition and pertinacity, we pretend not to say. The *acte* of accusation, indeed, points to the same thing ; but the object of the Procureur-Général is plain enough. He wishes o make it appear that an unconquerabe disgust had taken possession of the young wife's mind, and from this disgust he infers the probability of her being the murderer. ' Charles Lafarge était dans la joie, e se promettait le plus heureux avenir ; mais ses illusions durèrent bien peu. Le jour même de son arrivée au Glandier éclata une scène aussi imprévue qu'affligeante. Marie Cappelle s'enferma dans sa chambre et là elle écrivit à son mari la lettre la plus étrange, où le dévergondage de la pensée ne le cède qu'au cynisme les expressions par lesquelles, se flétrissaut elle-même, elle révèle à son epoux toutes les mauvaises passions dont elle est agitée.'

After preparing the minds of the jury by this description, the *acte* goes on to explain the plan which the accused was supposed to have formed and adopted. The object she proposed to herself is broadly stated to be, to get rid of her husband. The reasons for her desiring to do so were, that she disliked his person; that she deemed herself imposed upon by his false descriptions of his property, of his house, and of the position in which he could place his wife; and lastly, by a desire to possess herself of his property. In order to obtain possession of his property, and get rid of him, it is said that she determined to persuade her husband to make his will. In order to obtain this end, she is charged with pretending to make her own in favour of her husband; and that therefore the husband, cajoled by her apparent fondness, did in reality make and deliver her a will, by which he left her all his property should she survive him. ' Dès ce moment Marie Cappelle arrêta sa pensée de recouvrer son indépendence par la mort

de son mari, dont elle recueillerait la succession.'

In the same manner the whole history of the supposed murder is set forth ; and after the reading of the *acte* was finished by the officers of the court, M. Decoux, *avocat-général,* stated the case to the jury.

M. Decoux is doubtless a distinguished member of the French bar, and we may fairly assume that. he has done nothing which the manners and the morality of that body condemn. Our remarks, therefore, are not to be considered as directed against the individual advocate, but against the *system* of which, for the moment, he is the illustration. As directed against the system, indeed, which sanctions such doings as were then witnessed, our language cannot be too strong, if it is accurately to describe our feelings upon this occasion. The fact that a prosecutor in a criminal proceeding is a public officer, and as such can have no interest in obtaining the conviction of the prisoner, never for one instant seemed present to the mind of the Avocat-Général. He brought the habits, conduct, and state of feeling, of the mere advocate in a private cause into a great public proceeding. It is the duty of a prosecutor to see that all that can legally and honestly be adduced against the accused should be fairly laid before the jury. It is his interest, as it is the interest of every just member of society, that the accused should in reality turn out to be innocent; but that if he be really guilty, that he should be legally convicted. But the question of guilt or innocence, of the truth or falsehood of the charge preferred against the prisoner, cannot depend upon the feelings of compassion or commiseration towards the unfortunate family of the murdered man ; for the verdict of the jury, if their minds be disturbed by extraneous emotions of pity or anger, may be the result, not of the evidence, but of their state of feeling. Truth and justice require that their verdict should result *wholly from the evidence,* and that the evidence should relate solely to the fact charged. Did A commit that act ? The fact of A's having or not having done the deed cannot depend upon the emotions which the jury may feel or upon the misery which resulted from the act, no matter who committed it. The family of the murdered man may be worthy, respectable, now forlorn and wretched by his death ; but that misery does not prove A the murderer—why then appeal to the passions of the jury on such an occasion ? Why play the actor throughout the spectacle, and make it appear that you are overwhelmed with sorrow at the fate of the victim, and filled with violent indignation against the supposed murderer ? Why, but to confound the jury, to disturb their judgments, and to win their verdict without the aid of evidence ? It is impossible adequately to describe the conduct of the Avocat-Général throughout the whole of the trial, without following him step by step in his conduct of it. This we cannot do, but must be content with a general description, illustrated by one or two instances of the passion and almost fury exhibited by him during the investigation. To any one accustomed to the decorous, impressive calmness of an English Court, these violent displays appear like the poor attempts of a crack-brained actor, rather than the serious pleading of a grave and dignified functionary.

The language which we shall immediately quote, will appear, when read in a just and humane spirit, in the highest degree unseemly—nay, absolutely cruel. If the Avocat-Général could adduce evidence to convict the accused of the heinous crime laid to her charge, vituperation was not required; if he had not such evidence, it was iniquitous to employ it. *After* her conviction the Judge might address the prisoner as guilty ; *before* her conviction no one had a right to treat her as anything but innocent. ' I fear,' would have been the language of an English Attorney-General, ' I fear, gentlemen, the evidence I shall adduce will prove but too clearly the guilt of the prisoner at the bar. If, however, that evidence should leave upon your minds any reasonable doubts of her guilt, you will be required, as the humanity of the law directs, to let her have the benefit of that doubt; and no one will sympathize with you more than I shall, in the grateful duty that will devolve upon you, when you declare her innocent of that dreadful charge which it has been my painful office to prefer. But, gentlemen, if there be no such doubt upon your minds, then, however painful to you and to us all, your duty to your country and your God requires that you should pronounce the verdict which the evidence sanctions, and say, with an approving conscience, though with a sorrowing heart, that she is guilty.' This is the dignified and compassionate language of an honest, firm, and upright public officer, in the performance of a painful but necessary duty. Sedate, grave, considerate, just, he hardly steps out of the province of the impassive judge ; employs no artifice, descends to no subterfuge, rouses no passion, influences no prejudice—but calmly submits the legal evidence to the consideration of the jury, and

leaves it to bear with its own intrinsic weight against the scale of the accused.

The Avocat-Général, however, began with a studied description of the affliction of the sorrowing family of Lafarge. He described the mother as borne down with grief for the loss of her generous, kind, and tender son. The sister, too, is brought forward to make part of this scene of desolation and misery—and the group of the wretched victims is studiously, and we suppose, for a French audience, artfully contrasted with the cold, malicious, cruel murderer. A gay picture of expected happiness for Lafarge is carefully and elaborately painted ; his hopes of wealth, his anticipations of connubial bliss, his filial, his paternal love, are all arranged with melodramatic effect, to contrast with the sudden horrors that obscure his horizon and that of his unfortunate family. It is necessary to give the exordium of his harangue at full length, in order that the reader may form some conception of the spirit which animated the orator throughout :—

' En prenant la parole dans cette enceinte, notre esprit est livré à une vive préoccupation, notre cœur est rempli de plus douloureuses émotions. Et comment en serait-il autrement ?—comment pourrions-nous, avec un cœur tranquille, avec une raison froide, venir vous présenter l'affligeant tableau de ce crime ? Comment votre cœur pourrait-il ne pas saigner—ne pas se déchirer, à l'aspect de toutes les infortunes qui sont entassées dans cette enceinte ? Ce n'est pas seulement l'horreur du crime que nous emeut; d'autres émotions, des émotions aussi douloureuses, plus vives, peut-être, nous assiégent. En effet, il n'a pas suffi à cette femme de précipiter dans la tombe, par des moyens affreux, l'homme auquel elle venait d'enchaîner sa destinée, cet homme qui, vous l'apprendrez dans le cours de ces longs débats, n'avait eu pour elle que de l'amour et des sympathies qui dominaient sa pensée, qui remplissaient, qui debordaient son âme. Eh bien ! non ; ce crime ne lui a pas suffi—il a fallu qu'elle le commit avec une persévérance, une audace, qui sont sans example, j'ose le dire, dans les fastes des instructions criminelles.

' Mais, Messieurs, les choses qui ont été poussées à ce point ; telle a été la colère—si j'ose m'-exprimer ainsi—la colère froide et impitoyable, avec laquelle cette femme s'est precipitée sur sa victime pour s'abreuver de son sang, que peut-être l'excès même de son audace deviendra pour elle l'un des moyens les plus touchans de sa defense.

' Messieurs, ne le perdons pas de vue, nous ne sommes pas encore sur le terrain de la discussion. Dans ce moment, nous n'avons à vous retracer que les faits ; plus tard, peut-être, n'aurons-nous pas besoin d'autre tâche, car l'affaire présente ce caractère exceptionnel qu'il suffira de vous rappeler les témoignages ; vous retracer les faits, et que nous pourrons ensuite nous en remettre avec confiance à la conscience du juri.

'Il y avait dans cette contrée au Glandier, une famille qui vivait heureuse. Elle se composait d'une vieille mère, pauvre femme! Pauvre malheureuse femme, accablée de tant de douleurs et menacée de tant d'outrages. Elle avait un fils Pouch Lafarge, qui vivait avec elle dans l'intimité la plus vraie, sous l'influence de ces sentimens si doux qui unissent un fils à une mère. Ce jeune homme était dans la force de l'âge ; la nature ne l'avait pas doué d'une intelligence superieure, il n'avait pas reçu cette éducation brillante qui aurait pu plaire, convenir aux habitudes de Marie Cappelle ; mais il était bon, génereux ; mais il était aimé—il était plein de la sensibilité la plus vraie—il était disposé à aimer, à cherir tous ceux qui l'entouraient: Et puis, s'il s'etait peu livré à la culture des lettres, s'il avait peu recherché les avantages de l'éducation du monde, il avait dirigé toutes les facultés de son esprit vers des études solides, des travaux sérieux. Maitre de forges, il avait senti le besoin d'entendre les progrès de son art ; maitre de forges, veillant et la nuit et le jour, son esprit inventif s'occupait sans cesse de donner à son industrie la plus grande activité.

'J'oubliais de vous dire qu'il avait une sœur—pauvre femme encore à laquelle les douleurs n'ont point manqué. Autour de lui vivaient des gens honnêtes qui le connaissaient, l'affectionaient —c'etaient d'excellens, de sincères amis, des serviteurs fidèles, de paysans dévoués, parceque leur maitre etait plein de bonté pour eux.'

After a full statement of everything that he deemed necessary for the proof and explanation of the charge of murder, the Avocat-Général, as a peroration to his diatribe, proceeded to give the history of the charge of larceny in these words :—' I wish, gentlemen, that I could confine myself to this exposition, already so long. I wish that it was not my duty now to call your attention to other facts—and to impress upon the forehead of this woman the stamp of another ignominy, *not resulting from the present accusation.* Why did she not herself wish to save me this painful task ? In place of striving against the evidence—in place of irritating justice, if justice can be irritated, by a system of defence which is in itself a crime—if she had confessed herself guilty of the charge of stealing the diamonds which has been preferred against her, I should, in bringing before you this evidence of her character, experience a feeling of pain.' He then further says, that he is aware that between the charge of murder and the theft there is no necessary connection ; but that his duty, as a man of honour and a magistrate, compels him to set forth her guilt in the theft, because it proves her character to be deplorably bad ! Was ever such a reason given for such a proceeding—and that, too, by one boasting himself to be a man of honour and a magistrate ? He sums up his

observations respecting this separate charge in the following strain :—' By the side of this most infamous theft, is thus placed the most hideous defamation in the world—calumny, another species of poisoning—moral poisoning, which kills not the body, but which kills honour. Do you hear, Marie Cappelle ?'

After this revolting apostrophe, he addressed himself to the jury, and finished thus :—' I conjure you to communicate with no person—subject yourselves, beyond these walls, to no impression which may do violence to your convictions, or affect the purity of your verdict. I demand this of you ; because, before all things, I demand that you should be just. You cannot be so if you permit the solicitations of those who, at any cost, would save a woman who cannot be saved.'

By the law and the practice of England, as we have already stated, two felonies cannot be proved under one Indictment ; two offences cannot be described by the Counsel in his opening speech ; because he cannot state anything of which he is not able, either in fact or by law, to give evidence. M. Decoux, therefore, had he been in an English court, would have been saved any pain he might have felt on this occasion ; as he would quickly have been told by Judge and Counsel, that he had transgressed his duty, and done a gross wrong to the prisoner, merely by alluding to a charge of theft as then hanging over her. Nothing is more common with us, than for several Indictments to be preferred against one prisoner at the same time for separate offences—all to be tried at the same sessions or assizes. But on the trial of one Indictment, any allusion to the other charges would be deemed deserving of the severest censure. If, indeed, a prisoner chooses to bring forward evidence in proof of his former good character, and thus seeks to influence the jury in his favour, then it is competent to the prosecuting Counsel to cross-examine the witnesses coming forward in support of the prisoner's character as to any former conviction, and as to his general reputation ; but until the prisoner make this attempt to weigh down the evidence by his former character, no allusion can be made on the part of the prosecutor to anything but the evidence upon the specific charge then under investigation. The salutary rule of the English law and practice, by which the evidence is confined to the issue, and the observations of Counsel to what he is permitted to prove, would have materially tended to maintain the decorum and to promote the justice of all the judicial proceedings in which M. Decoux played so prominent a part.

As we proceed we shall have yet further to comment on the bearing of the Avocat-Général towards the accused: we shall now continue our description of the trial itself.

As soon as the Avocat-Général had finished his address, the Counsel for the prisoner, M. Paillet, raised the objection which we have above discussed, and prayed the court that the evidence might be confined to the issue of guilty or not guilty of the murder; and that no witnesses might be examined as to the alleged larceny—stating, and we think accurately, such to be the humane provision of the French law. But his objection was overruled, and all the witnesses produced by the prosecution were allowed to be examined; so that in reality the prisoner was put upon her trial for two offences at the same time. A greater outrage on common sense and justice was never perpetrated.

The next step in the proceeding was one directly opposed, not only to the practice of our courts, but to the feelings of our people. The first person examined was the prisoner herself—the presiding Judge conducting the examination.

A full examination of the prisoner had already been taken by the vice-president of the Tribune de Tulle, immediately after the *Chambre des mises en accusation* had pronounced the *arrêt* declaring that she was to be tried; but whether the answers of the prisoner were to be considered as a voluntary declaration, does not appear. By the English course of proceeding, on the accusation being made before the committing magistrate, the prisoner is always asked what he desires to say; being cautioned at the same time that what he says will be taken down in writing, and produced against him at the trial. He is at perfect liberty to answer or not, just as he pleases; and the important practical consequence attending the proceeding is, that his not answering is never adverted to as a circumstance to his discredit. This is the only approach, in the English system, to anything like an examination of the prisoner; but, in the French procedure, the examination of the accused appears among the most important of those submitted to the consideration of the jury. Whether this mode is that best calculated to ascertain the guilt or innocence of the person accused, is one of the most disputed and disputable of the many vexed questions of criminal judicature; and one which, we believe, cannot be properly decided without reference to the habits of thought and feeling peculiar to every people. In England, such an open examination of the prisoner would excite very general disgust, and raise up improperly compassion for the guilty. Moreover, we feel from experience that such a process is unnecessary for security; and are, therefore, well pleased to be spared the pain of inflicting upon the wretched prisoner a species of mental torture. In France, it may be, that the habits of the people do not fit them for the practical business of judicature. With us the experience of centuries is handed down from one generation to another; the people from time immemorial have taken an important part in the administration of justice, and they and our courts have become skilled in the marshalling and appreciation of evidence. The French public, on the other hand, may deem that the mode they have adopted is necessary for the public safety: if such be the general feeling, the examination of the prisoner cannot be dispensed with; though, from the experience of the case before us, we cannot say that we are at all reconciled to the practice.[*]

The story of the unfortunate young woman, as told by herself in her various interrogatories, does not justify the terrible accusation to which she was subjected; nor do the contradictions which occur in her narrative, excite in our minds the suspicion which they created in the minds of the jury which decided her fate. Her story, previous to the illness of her husband, is briefly this:—Being left an orphan, with a moderate fortune, viz. 80,000 francs, being also, as she herself says, not greatly blessed with beauty, her family were anxious to provide for her an establishment by means of a husband. They adopted in consequence, the plan already described; though she herself, in her answers, pointedly denies that she was at all cognisant of the employ-

---

* The method of examination, as practised by the French courts, seems also open to reprehension. The Judge indeed appears, on the whole, the person least exceptionable for discharging the office of examiner; but it is a matter for grave consideration, whether it be not a great evil to subject the judge to the chance of becoming excited and prejudiced by taking upon himself this office. He is very liable to be made a partizan by the conflict that of necessity must take place between the accused and the interrogator. Moreover, it appears that the examination is not carried on and finished at once, but as every point of the evidence given by the witness tells against the accused, he is suddenly called upon by the judge to explain away the difficulty, and is thus compelled to make his defence many times over, and to discharge the most difficult duty that can be devolved even upon a skilled advocate, and through a long trial to keep in his mind the whole bearing of each separate piece of evidence.

ment of the matrimonial agent. She married for the sake of the position which a husband would give her; and she was led by the representations of her family, and of Lafarge himself, to believe that she was about to become the mistress of a comfortable and even elegant household and establishment. Married at three-and-twenty to a perfect stranger, it is not wonderful that she was startled and alarmed when she suddenly found herself separated from all whom she had known through life, and placed completely in the power, and subject to the absolute control, of her stranger husband. Scenes occurred on their journey from Paris to Glandier, not very extraordinary when viewed with reference to all the surrounding circumstances; and Madame Lafarge is not the first upon record in whom the same sort of terrors led to pursue the same sort of resistance. In the midst of these disputes, with her mind heated and her fears excited, she arrived at Glandier—her dwelling for her future life. Here she, who had been accustomed to the luxurious elegance of Paris, found a rude, dilapidated, and comfortless habitation; and a family little likely, by their education or their habits, to sympathize with her, or to diminish or alleviate her distresses. In a fit of despair she wrote to her husband a wild and passionate letter, in the foolish hope of regaining her liberty, by accusing herself of having deceived her husband. She says, ' I was in such despair at my position, I desired so much that Monsieur Lafarge would allow me to go away, that I said things the most inconceivable and false in order to obtain my wish.' She told him that she was in love with another man—that he had deserted her—and that she in spite had married; and she uses the following remarkable expression, by which she seeks to explain the cause of her terror and distress :—' Helas ! je vous vis ; j'ignorais les mystères du marriage ; j'avais tressailli de bonheur en serrant ta main; malheureuse ! je crus qu'un baiser sur le front seul te serait du—que vous seriez comme un père.' She then asserts that she had seen her former lover on the road ; that she had taken poison, and had prepared a loaded pistol to destroy herself, but had not courage to carry her purpose into effect; that she desired only to be allowed to depart, intending to go to Smyrna. All these statements, in her examination, she declares to be untrue, and told only because of her desire to get away In her answer to the judge, when pressed by him to explain why she had written these various falsehoods, she accounts for it after

this fashion : ' How can you explain this letter, and the circumstances under which it was sent to your husband ?'—Answer. ' I beg of you to have some indulgence towards me. I left my home the day after my marriage; I left my family ; I found myself isolated from all the world. At Orleans, I had with my husband an extremely disagreeable scene—in truth, I was extremely wretched during the whole journey. When I arrived at Glandier, in place of that charming country-house with which they had lured me, I found a dilapidated and ruined habitation. I found myself alone, shut up in a large chamber which was to be mine for life. I lost my reason—I had an idea of travelling to the East—I thought of all these things—the contrast—my imagination was excited—I was so wretched that I would have given the whole world to get away.' This very natural description puzzled the Judge : he could not understand, could not sympathize with it ; and after various inquiries, he says, ' So then your conduct, on your arrival at Glandier, was the result of the discontent you felt upon seeing a dwelling that, without doubt, did not answer the expectations which had been raised in you ?'—Answer. ' Yes, sir.' But then it appears a change took place in her conduct, which to the Judge appeared inexplicable; but which she explains by saying, that Lafarge, by his constant kindness, had conquered her first feeling, and won her good-will; that, therefore, she wished to make him happy, and occupied herself about her house and her husband's affairs ; and these affairs of her husband are not without their mystery: but the odium, if any, must fall not on her, but her husband.[*]

It appeared that Lafarge was in want of money. He had discovered, or fancied he had discovered, a new process for the smelting of iron, and desired to take out a patent for the invention ; and also to borrow funds to carry on his iron-works more extensively, according to his new method. He had persuaded himself, and seems to have per-

---

[*] An expression used by the prisoner in this part of her examination implies a state of things at variance with that indicated, rather than actually described, in her *Mémoires*. The words are these : we keep them in the original advisedly. ' Lafarge m'avait comblé de preuves d'affection, il était aussi bon pour moi qu'il était possible. Cela m'a touché, je n'ai pas pu faire autrement que de (l'accusée hésite quelques instans sur le mot) *que de remplir mes devoirs, de rendre la vie plus heureuse à M Lafarge.* Je me suis ensuite occupée de ma maison. Le Glandier n'a plus occupé qu'une faible part de ma vie. Peu à peu je me suis senti de l'affection, de l'estime pour M Lafarge, et j'ai désiré de le rendre heureux.'

suaded his wife, that his speculations were certain to confer on him great wealth, and they both were anxious to obtain the money requisite to carry his plans into effect. She wrote to her friends in Paris, describing her expectations in glowing colours, and begged of them to interest themselves for the purpose of obtaining the patent which Lafarge sought for his discovery, as well as of borrowing the money needed for the more extensive operations contemplated. She distinctly asserts, that 'Lafarge at this time wanted to borrow money of her family. He sent me the plan of the letters which I was to write to this effect. I copied and sent them.' And, therefore, the Judge indulged in his next question in a sort of half-aside insinuation respecting this proceeding, which at once shows the dangerous character of such an examination. It converts the Judge into an Advocate—it enlists his vanity against the prisoner, and induces him to employ his practised skill and ingenuity in distorting her answers, and drawing therefrom unjust and unfavourable inferences. The whole proceeding spoken of by the accused is in itself exceedingly simple, natural, and really deserving of no reprobation. A young girl, newly married, listens to her husband's plans, enters into his schemes with eagerness, believes his calculations, and, under his dictation, writes letters to her friends, describing her hopes, and asking their aid in realizing them; and upon this, thus remarks the Judge, who sets out with assuming her to be guilty —'So, then, these letters were not the expression of your own opinion—your calculations were then nothing more than the result of the calculations and suppositions of M. Lafarge, for the purpose of obtaining for him the money he needed. *It was a species of seduction which you desired to employ with regard to those to whom you wrote*' Can we wonder at the verdict of the jury, when, at the very commencement of the trial, the presiding Judge could hazard such a remark—one so thoroughly unjust and cruel—one so likely to prepare the minds of the jury for every future unfavourable inference regarding the prisoner? Throughout, the plan of the prosecution was to represent her as a person endowed with extraordinary ability—who, by the force of her intellect, was placed above the common follies or weakness of her age and sex; obeying steadily, indeed, the dictates of a depraved and wicked spirit, but pursuing her objects with an unerring sagacity—an untiring and remorseless perseverance. The Judge throughout his interrogatory assumes this

hypothesis; he enlarges constantly upon her intelligence, and will not allow or understand in her case the ordinary motives and feelings which would impel and guide any other young girl in her situation. The instance here set forth is but one among a thousand—the whole trial was conducted after the same fashion.

Lafarge now went to Paris in order to obtain the wished-for patent, and his wife's relatives were among the first persons to whom he applied for aid. While absent, a circumstance occurred that had a fatal influence upon the future destiny of his wretched wife. Supposing her to tell the truth, nothing could be more natural than what she apparently intended to do—supposing her guilty, nothing could be more depraved, as well as wild and extravagant, than the scheme attempted.

While Lafarge was thus at Paris, his wife had her portrait drawn by a young woman in the neighbourhood. This portrait she determined to send to her absent husband. It was put into a box, and into that box she also placed some cakes made by the mother of Lafarge, and a tender and affectionate letter. Before proceeding to the more important circumstance of this affair, let us dismiss the consideration of this letter, and the others which she addressed to her husband while at Paris; the affectionate tenour of which excited the suspicions, or rather is used to justify the already excited suspicions, of the presiding Judge. He asks her how she could conciliate this amazing tenderness (tendresse exaltée,) *this sort of mystic affection*, which she here manifested towards her husband, with that cruel letter which she had written some months before to him on her arrival at Glandier; and the scene that took place during the journey from Paris, when Lafarge wanted to break into her room while she was in a bath. 'It is difficult enough,' he says, 'to understand the metamorphosis.' The poor girl answered that she saw no relation between the scene and the letter. The Judge thereupon grew angry, and declared, with some petulance, that he would persist in his question, and insisted on having an answer; and he put his question with this unfair insinuation:—'In the first letter it is easy to see that there was nothing in common between you and the husband you had accepted, either in your intellect or in your affections. In the other letters, on the contrary, there is the expansion of a heart which gives itself with warm affection, nay even with enthusiasm, to the husband to whom it is united.' (It is difficult, if not impossible, to put into intelligible English these expressions of French sentiment; the words are, ' Dans les autres, au contraire, on voit l'expansion d'un cœur qui se donne avec effusion, et même avec enthousiasme, à l'epoux auquel il est uni ') Then he goes on to say, ' This fickleness (mobilité) could indeed be understood in persons not endowed with your intelligence; but in your case it is difficult to comprehend it.' The answer of the prisoner is perfectly sufficient. ' I have already answered that the kind offices of M. Lafarge had gained my heart   In truth I loved him—not indeed with *love*, but affection. He wrote me very passionate, tender letters, and I believed it my duty to make him happy by using the same language.' Then, again, in this unseemly fencing-match between the judge and the prisoner, comes this reply in the shape of a question:—' Thus, then, according to you, in the space of three or four months, to this antipathy which you had conceived for your husband, and which had led you to desire to escape to Smyrna to get rid of him, had succeeded sentiments of gratitude, of tenderness, of devotion ?'— ' Yes, sir. You know that when one receives a letter, very kind, very good, one always feels disposed to make happy the person who has shown you this affection; above all, when it is a husband that writes, and when you wish to make this husband happy.'

But in the fated box, besides this letter, there were certain cakes. When the box left Glandier it had four or five small cakes in it, made after the fashion of the country by the mother of Lafarge. When the box arrived in Paris, it contained only one large cake; thus it is clear that, from the time when the box was last seen by the family at Glandier and its arrival at Paris, it must have been opened, and one cake substituted for several. The cake sent by Madame Lafarge, she told her husband to eat at a certain hour, saying that she, at the same hour, would do the same—this being, it seems, an established custom among lovers. Lafarge did eat of the cake, and was soon after exceedingly ill—and the inference immediately drawn was, that the cake was poisoned by the wife.

It is to be remarked that this cake was not produced. Evidence was given to show that a cake as large as a plate, and one only, was in the box on its being opened at Paris; but it was also shown, that it had necessarily been out of the hands and power of the prisoner in its transit from Glandier to Paris. It was closed by the servant Clementine, in the presence not only of the prisoner, but of her mother-in-

law, of Le Brun, and another young woman; and then given to a servant, who took it to the coach-office. Nobody seemed to think of the impossibility for the prisoner to make a poisoned cake. With so many prying eyes about, not too favourable to the accused, the making of a cake would have been known, talked of, and afterwards remembered. Moreover, the box when it left Glandier was sealed; those seals when it reached Paris were broken—by the officers of the *octroi*, it is said—but others might have done it; and if a different cake did really find its way to Paris, they who broke the seals may have substituted one for the other. A person named Denis, a clerk, went on a mysterious voyage to Paris, saying he was going elsewhere; and there were many other suspicious circumstances which pointed him out as the criminal. We shall have hereafter to speak of this man.

Soon after the reception of this box, and the illness that followed, Lafarge left Paris and returned home. He arrived ill at Glandier on the 5th of January, and died on the 14th. His wife was charged with having caused this sudden death, by administering to him arsenic while he lay ill. The Judge proceeded to interrogate her as to the accusation.

We may here remark upon another evil that is necessarily attendant on this examination of the accused. In the present case, before the prisoner could be properly convicted of the murder, the jury should have been satisfied on two distinct inquiries; the first being, did the deceased die in consequence of being poisoned by arsenic; and if he did, then, did the prisoner knowingly administer the arsenic of which he so died.

On both of these questions the English law would have required the jury to be without any reasonable doubt before they could deliver a verdict of guilty; and the Judge would distinctly tell them, that they must be satisfied on both points, but that they must be satisfied as to the first before proceeding to discuss the second. In the present case, however, the first question was assumed during the whole examination of the prisoner; and every art was employed to make the jury believe that many motives were impelling her to wish and to contrive her husband's death. The minds of the jury being thus prejudiced, they came to the consideration of the question, Did he die by poison? fully prepared to decide it in the affirmative—willing to believe everything that strengthened their adopted conception, and very averse even to listen to any evidence that tended to prove it incorrect   The long examination of the prisoner, upon the assumed ground that her husband died by poison, powerfully contributed to this mischievous prepossession—and in every case wherein two steps of proof are required to establish guilt, the same evil effect must be produced by the preliminary examination of the accused.

The quantity of irrelevant matter introduced on this trial is absolutely marvellous, while the facts stated in evidence which really related to the issue, are in the same proportion few, and for the most part insignificant;—gathered from the voluminous passages called evidence, they may thus be shortly stated.

Lafarge arrived at Glandier on the 5th of January, exceedingly ill—he went immediately to bed, and was attended by his wife, his mother, and his sister—and various other persons, besides his medical attendants, had access to him   Great confusion reigned throughout the whole household, and the dying man's bedchamber soon became a scene of strife, and of constant and wretched disturbance. His illness was apparently inflammation of the stomach and intestines. The disease from day to day made progress, and finally terminated his existence. The charge which the prosecution sought to establish was, that she, after his arrival at Glandier, at different times administered arsenic to him in his food and medicine. To substantiate this, it was proved that the prisoner had, in December, procured arsenic from a druggist, writing to him openly for it, saying, that she desired it for the purpose of destroying rats, by which, to use her own expression, she was devoured. Again it was proved, that on the 5th of January she had procured arsenic from the same druggist, and that this time it was obtained on the prescription (*ordonnance*) of the physician attending her husband—the alleged purpose being to destroy the rats which disturbed the sick man's repose; she asserting, and without contradiction, that the physician wrote his prescription for the arsenic by desire of Lafarge himself. And lastly it was proved, that the clerk Denis had been ordered by her, through her maid-servant, to bring some more arsenic, and that he did buy and bring some from Tulle. The arsenic is thus shown to be in the house, and in her possession, and certainly in her power. The next step was to show that she administered it to the deceased.

It appeared that she had sent for powdered gum at the same time that she had ordered the arsenic; and that of this powdered gum she herself drank repeatedly, and

that she gave it to Lafarge. The direct charge was, that while pretending to give him gum, she gave him the poison. The proof of this, if we strip it of all that is irrelevant, is exceedingly uncertain, confused, and weak; but the mode in which the Avocat-Général sought to prove it—the mode which the French law permitted him to adopt—well deserves the serious attention of every one who desires to make the law a protector of the innocent. Of some of the methods employed to arouse the suspicion of the jury, we have already spoken. But not content with the history of the unfortunate girl's marriage—with the story of her disappointment, her quarrel with her husband—with the strange tale of the cake sent to Paris—not content with all these irrelevant means of exciting a prejudice against her, he allowed the wildest stories to be related about her;—the fancies that entered into the heads of her neighbours, the conjectures of gossiping crones, the malicious insinuations of guilty and unworthy servants—are adduced as grave and important pieces of evidence, that ought to weigh with rational men when called upon to discharge the awful duty of deciding upon the life or death of a fellow-creature. As specimens of this mode of proceeding, and for the purpose of continuing our comparison, we will mention two instances of evidence adduced of the sort we are here describing.

One of the witnesses examined was a M. Aimé Sirey, who came voluntarily to disclose to the court an important fact; and he was allowed, after being sworn, to proceed after the following manner. In reply to the question of the Judge—What have you to say? M. Sirey answers,

'A fact which, up to the present moment, has appeared either indifferent or to confirm the guilt of the accused, now seems to me, in the presence of the new events of the trial, to be singularly modified, and to acquire such gravity as to make it imperative on my conscience to reveal it to the jury and to the court.' '*Mouvement d'attention,* says the reporter.) 'I was at Objet during the first days of December, when I received a visit from my bailiff, who manages my estate at Comborn, near to Glandier. He breakfasted with me; and the conversation falling upon the prosperity that was likely to happen in the affairs of M. Lafarge, as well through his invention as by means of the fortune he had acquired by his marriage, my bailiff spoke the following words, which I repeat verbatim.' (At this stage of the idle story, in an English court, M. Sirey would by judge, counsel, jury, have been commanded to hold his peace, and depart about his business. To the rule of evidence which would have led to this summary dismissal of such an impertinent intruder we shall immediately advert; at present, we proceed with the testimony as received by the (French court.) "M. Lafarge will not profit by these advantages, for he will be poisoned by his wife." (General marks of surprise.) 'I did not attach much importance to these words; but the remarkable coincidence of this poisoning, foretold eight or ten days before, with the death of M. Lafarge, which fulfilled the prophecy, appears to me now, in presence of the facts which have been disclosed before the court, so important as to arrest the attention of justice, and to require that the bailiff should be examined.'

'The Judge—Are you quite sure as to the date of this conversation?' Answer—'Yes, sir.' 'What day did M Lafarge die ?' 'It was the 14th.' 'But what was the day of the week ?' The Judge—after having ascertained—it was Tuesday. M. Sirey—'Well, then, it was Sunday the 5th that my bailiff said this.' The Judge, after some further inquiry as to the date of the conversation, asked whether it was deemed necessary to hear the bailiff; and the Counsel for the prisoner insisting that it was, he was ordered to attend. One curious observation respecting the report of the bailiff was made by M. Sirey—'It appeared that he (the bailiff) related these stories (*ces bruits*) *as emanating from the relations of Lafarge.*' That is, they determined beforehand to accuse his wife of murder, and (if imputations are to be permitted) they laid their plans so as to give their predetermined accusation an air of truth. This evidence was given on the 4th of September, and not till the 12th was the bailiff found; and then his version of the affair was, 'that he was talking one day with a M. Lafaurie about the arrival of Mme Lafarge at Glandier, who said that she was very rich, but that she and her husband were not happy together. That a letter had been written by her to Lafarge, in which she declared she loved another man also called Charles, but that he was not Charles Lafarge; and that then M. Lafaurie said, "if he were in the place of Lafarge, he would let her go, for fear she should do him some ill turn."'

By the law of England, hearsay evidence is not admissible, and no conversation can be given in evidence that has not taken place in the hearing of the prisoner. M. Sirey and his bailiff would therefore have been alike excluded; the minds of the jury would not have been distracted by an accumulation of idle nonsense; or subject to the improper influence of vague and unsupported reports. Once open the door to this sort of gossip, and no man would be safe—reputation, property, life, would often

depend upon a rumour which malice might designedly invent, and a foolish, busy curiosity circulate and improve—conjecture would be converted into proof, and the whisper of every doting crone would usurp the office, or outweigh the influence of evidence given by percipient witnesses under the sanction of an oath.

Another instance of the mode in which it was sought to prejudice the unfortunate accused, in the minds of the jury, by the aid of this species of evidence, was remarkably exemplified by the testimony given by the clerk Denis. Grave suspicion rested upon this man that, if the deceased did come to his death by poison, he was the person really guilty; and yet, with all the suspicion that throughout the proceedings rested upon him, he was allowed to begin his story with this statement:—

'On the 8th of January, Madame Marie Lafarge having learned that I was going to Lubersac, had me called into her apartment. When I came, she made me go out into the garden, and there commanded me to bring her some arsenic, some black puddings, and sausages. I bought the puddings and the sausages, but I did not think it proper to buy the arsenic. On the 9th I bought some for twenty sous, at the shop of M. Lafosse. On the 11th, as I was going to Tulle, on the business of M. Lafarge, I received a note, from Madame Marie Lafarge, by her maid-servant. She told me in this note* to buy at Tulle some black puddings, sausages, some arsenic, and a mouse-trap. Fearing lest Madame might be angry, I said to my wife—[Here he would have been stopped by an English judge, because about to relate a conversation that occurred out of the hearing of the prisoner]—"I suppose I must get this arsenic, since I have been told twice to get it." I again said to my wife, "I very much fear lest this arsenic may be made to serve to procure the death of M. Lafarge.' I said that, because Madame Charles had said before M. Magneaux, that, if she wished it, her husband would not be alive in twenty-four hours. She had said also she should only wear mourning a year, as they did at Paris, if her husband happened to die.'

Another violation of our rules of evidence was permitted in this witness, as in all the others   No witness is allowed to give in evidence anything beyond what he saw done, or heard said, in those cases in which he is allowed to report conversations. His

---

* This note was not produced, nor asked for   By our practice, the witness would not have been permitted to speak of its contents, until some account had been given of the note itself. Was it in existence ? If yes, then produce it, or hold your tongue as to its contents   If destroyed, explain how, when, why—all which explanations would have cast great doubt upon the testimony.

own thoughts upon the occasion of which he is speaking, he is not permitted to disclose. Denis said, that although he had bought the arsenic at Brives, yet he did not give it to Madame Lafarge. He is then asked by the Judge, why he did not give it? This question, by our rules, would not be permitted: the answer given by Denis will at once show why. 'Because,' he says, 'M. Lafarge was ill, and I feared the use that might be made of this arsenic.' Upon this the Judge remarked, 'These fears are very grave; what circumstances created them in you?' 'Because Madame Lafarge had said to M. Magneaux, the day before she wrote the note, that if she wished, her husband would not be alive four-and-twenty hours, and that she always had arsenic by her—(sur elle.)' 'Did you hear those words from the mouth of Madame Lafarge?' 'No; M. Magneaux heard them, and told them to me.' It is remarkable that Magneaux, a clerk of Lafarge, when called, does not appear to disprove or confirm the assertions of Denis.

Now, although such were the many and extraordinary means to excite suspicion by irrelevant evidence, the direct evidence as to the fact of poisoning, is absolutely almost nothing. During the illness of Lafarge, the suspicions of his mother were aroused by Denis: she readily listened to the suggestion, and saw in every act of her daughter-in-law, whom she feared and hated, an attempt to murder her son. When asked by her daughter-in-law to retire to rest, she immediately concluded that the object in view was to get rid of her superintendence. If anything was given to her son by his wife, and, as is the common result in such a malady, it was returned from the stomach, she leaped to the conclusion that poison was the cause. At length, in her alarm, she communicated her suspicions to her unfortunate son; and thus, without doing or being able to do any good thereby, she heightened every terror, every horror that could gather around the dying man. But with all her suspicions excited—with the whole household well aware of her belief —the only facts adduced in evidence which fairly tell against the prisoner are, first, that she ordered the poison to be bought; and next, that some poison was asserted to have been found in a small box which she had in her pocket; and which, she said, contained powdered gum—and also in a packet said to have been found in her bureau; and out of which, as well as out of the box, she had been supposed to take a portion of the contents, and put it into some chicken broth given by her to her husband. These last

facts were elicited from the testimony of two young women, Le Brun and Emma Ponthieu—the first violently the enemy: the second the friend of the accused.

Le Brun tells the following story:—On the 11th of January, Lafarge heard that his wife was taking some chicken broth, and desired that some of it might be brought to him. It had, however, been all drunk by his wife, and a fresh quantity was prepared—his wife saying, that they must allow him to believe it to be hers. This broth made, by the sister of Lafarge, was left on the chimney-piece in some warm water, in the 100m of the wife, in which also was Mademoiselle Le Brun— both of them being in bed. Le Brun says, that when they were left alone, she saw Madame Lafarge put her arms out of bed, reach the broth from the chimney, and put into it a white powder, and stir it with her finger;—that she did not see whence she got the powder, but only perceived that it was in a piece of torn paper.* That she, upon this, asked Madame Lafarge what she had put into the broth— who answered, orange flowers. That she expressed her surprise openly on this, as it was plainly powder; but she had no suspicion then. This was about eight in the morning; at twelve she arose and went into the sick man's room, Madame Lafarge remaining behind in bed. That she saw the remains of the broth which had been placed on the chimney, and on the surface of it there were floating white globules. She showed them to the sister, who spoke about them to the physician, M. Bardon: he looked at the globules, and thought it to be lime from the wood ashes. The broth was then thrown away, but a thick residue remained; and as some more broth was made which did not appear like that thrown away, their suspicions were excited. The residue was locked up by the mother, and was afterwards by her given up to the offi-

---

* In summing up the evidence, the Avocat-Général stated, with great, with reprehensible inaccuracy, the evidence of this witness. She was distinctly asked by the judge—
'Où prit-elle cette poudre? Etait-ce dans le buvard?' Answer. 'Je la vis verser dans la tasse, mais je ne sais pas où elle l'avait prise Je vis seulement, que cette poudre était dans un petit morceau de papier déchiré' Question. 'Reconnûtes-vous le paquet de Denis? Etait-il de la même couleur?' Answer. 'Je n'y fis pas attention, ni à la couleur du papier.' Yet the Avocat-Général, summing up the evidence, said, 'Madlle. Brun a vu'Marie Cappelle prendre la poudre blanche dans le buvard, enveloppée *dans le même papier bleu dans lequel Denis l'avait apporté!*' Not a word of this was in evidence, and part was directly at variance with this statement

cers of justice, examined by the chemists, who first analyzed the various matters supposed to contain poison; and by them declared to contain arsenic. We shall immediately speak of this analysis.

Some time after mid-day, Le Brun again says, she saw the wife up, and in the chamber of Lafarge; and as this part of her testimony is the most important portion of the evidence, we will give it in her own words :—

'In the afternoon of the same day I was alone with Madame Marie, in the sick man's room. She took a glass of water coloured with wine, and went towards the commode. I was working near the chimney, *and I could not see what she was doing;* but I thought I heard the drawer open, and the noise of a spoon striking against the side of the glass'—'comme si on délayait quelque chose.' [By which, we suppose, the witness intended to signify, that Madame Lafarge was wetting something with the water in the glass, and mixing them together,] 'Madame then gave a spoonful to her husband, and he said, "That burns my throat." I asked what he said, and Madame repeated it.' Did this astonish you? 'No. I remarked the panada. She made it. I did not see her put anything into it; but upon the surface I saw a white powder. I went near the commode, and I saw a train of powder. As the drawer was half open, I saw in it a little pot, and the train corresponded with the position of the pot.' (The words are—'et la traînée correspondait avec le pot'—that is, reached to it.) 'I tasted the powder, and it produced a pricking sensation for nearly an hour.* I remarked also a glass upon the night-table: it contained some white powder, and some drops of water. I took it between my fingers: it was like a fine resisting sand. I compared it with the gum, and the gum glued my fingers. I remarked upon this to Madame Marie, who said it was gum. "Besides," said she, "I am going to drink it;" and she filled the glass with water, and I believed she drank it, but I will not affirm that she did.'

'Question. After having drunk, did she vomit? 'Answer. I have not spoken of her vomiting on this occasion. She did so every day : every time she ate she vomited."

She then states that the residue of the chicken broth was sent to M. Eyssartier, the chemist, at the request of Lafarge, to whom his mother communicated her suspicions; and afterwards says:

'On the 13th, Monday morning, I entered early into his (Lafarge's) chamber: he told me not to leave him. Afterwards he breathed in his hands and said, "Oh! what a smell of garlic!" When he vomited, he said the same thing.* M. L'Espinasse came in the night. . . . . . Some time later I took a little of the powder of the panada; I put it upon the coals, and smelt a smell of garlic. I had taken some of the white powder from the drawer, and gave it to M. L'Espinasse: he did the same by it, and obtained the same smell.

'On the 13th, I showed M. L'Espinasse the train of white powder in the commode: he scraped some of it together with the feathers of a pen. He took some also from the little pot, and carried it away wrapped in paper.'

M. L'Espinasse confirmed this statement; and farther declared, that he had given the paper containing the powder, with its contents, to the officers of justice. He also said, that upon his finding so strong a smell of garlic upon burning the powder, he had no longer any doubt as to Lafarge being poisoned. Nevertheless he left the sick man to his fate, and returned home.

The prisoner denied all knowledge of this little pot and its contents, saying that she never saw it—that she never put any poison into it. She was asked if she suspected anybody of putting the pot there. 'It is impossible,' she answered, 'for me to suspect anybody. Besides, the whole house came into the room, and the place was not one very propitious for the hiding of anything. My answer as to the little pot is, that I did not place it there—that I do not know who did—and that I have never seen it.'

Such was the evidence of Madlle. Brun. It will at once be seen that another step is required to make this evidence bear against the accused. It was to be proved that the bottle and the powder contained arsenic. Before we proceed to the consideration of the modes taken to ascertain that fact, and of the extraordinary circumstances which attended the inquiry, we must give the only remaining piece of direct evidence—that of Emma Ponthieu, the friend of Madame Marie Lafarge.

She said, that she arrived at Glandier on the 11th, and found Lafarge ill. She describes the distress of his wife, and evidently believed her distress real. When suspicion of the poisoning arose, she heard Madame Marie address her maid-servant with great warmth, and ask what she had done with the arsenic which she had con-

---

* This assertion shows how strongly prejudice was at work. It is the opinion of the most celebrated chemists, that arsenic has no taste. See Beck's *Med. Jur.* 737, and the opinion of Dr. Christison therein quoted.

* Here again is proof of the effect of prejudice. The smell of garlic proceeds from arsenic when thrown on a strong heat; but there is no proof of its producing such a smell upon the breath of one poisoned by it.

fided to her? To this question the answer was, that she, the maid-servant, had put it into a hat, and placed the hat in the room of M. Lafarge She adds, that on the morning of his death she saw his wife undress herself; and that while she was so doing, she saw, for the first time, a small box in the pocket of her apron. That she asked Clementine, the servant-maid, what it contained, who answered, gum. That the conversations she had heard—the suspicions of the mother of Lafarge and of Madlle. Brun—the letter written by Marie on her coming first to Glandier—all worked upon her recollection; and that, although her reason refused to believe that Marie was guilty, yet she was led to take some of the powder out of the box, and give it to her uncle. Her uncle kept the powder for some time in his pocket, and afterwards gave it to the officers of justice. She afterwards, in consequence of a vague suspicion in her own mind, asked the maid for the box which she had seen, and she after some delay brought it. The box, with its contents, was also given to the officers of justice. The conclusion sought to be established by this evidence is, that the box contained arsenic: but was this proved? We shall now proceed to consider the procedure of the courts with respect to the solution of this difficulty.

During the various proceedings of this trial, three separate sets of experiments were made, by different chemists, upon—

1. The body of the deceased; and,

2. Various substances which were suspected to contain arsenic.

The first experiments were performed by the chemists of Brives. This was on the 22d of January, 1840, a few days after the death of Lafarge.

The second experiments were made by the chemists of Limoges, at the trial—and the last were performed by Mons. Orfila, soon after the second, and before the verdict.

For the moment we will pass by the analysis of the body and its contents, and confine our attention to the other substances submitted to examination. And now, judicially, the first inquiry ought to be, in whose custody were these various substances before they came into the hands of the chemists? The answer to this question in an English court of justice would of itself have been nearly sufficient to exculpate the prisoner; for with us it is not enough to cast suspicion upon the accused. The prisoner is never required to answer till the affirmative has been distinctly proved

against him—so proved, that if he do not, cannot explain away the proofs, no doubt will remain upon the minds of reasonable men as to his guilt. But if only suspicion be raised, if any other hypothesis is as reconcilable with the facts as that of the guilt of the prisoner, then our law says he must be acquitted. An hypothesis may be suggested in the present case, far more consonant with the facts than that of the guilt of the wife of the deceased—and that hypothesis is, that Lafarge did in reality die from natural causes; but that the arsenic was put in the various places by the hands of Denis the clerk, for the purpose of ruining his master's wife. Another hypothesis may yet be suggested, and from it we should not shrink—if Lafarge did die of poison, Denis was the murderer.

If any one will, with the first hypothesis respecting this man in his mind, look carefully into the evidence given by him, he will discover how wonderfully the facts agree with this supposition. From that evidence, which we have not space to analyze, it appears that Denis lived for some time by forgery, and that Lafarge himself was guilty, with his aid, of issuing factitious bills; and further, that he, Lafarge, forged (it is useless to hesitate as to the phrase) a letter, purporting to be written by his brother-in-law, M. de Violane. On the death of Lafarge this transaction, and his own utter insolvency, came to light; but there is much still hid in darkness. Denis played an important part in the whole of it, and had evidently a violent hatred against Madame Lafarge, because of the influence which she exercised over her husband, whom evidently Denis intended to employ as a tool. But the wife was in his way, and he was heard often to vow vengeance against her; two of the servants distinctly swearing to the very words he had employed. Denis, as positively denied the charge; but there could be no doubt but that the simple peasant, Bardon, told the truth. 'The clerk Denis said to me,' says this man, 'that he wished to see Madame sawed into four pieces.' 'He said that to you?' 'Yes.' 'When did he say this?' 'In the stable, eight days after the death of M. Lafarge.' 'But had Madame done him any wrong?' 'Never: she was a most kind mistress; I never saw a better.' 'He was then persuaded that Madame was guilty?' 'Oh yes —he told me that she had poisoned him during fifteen days.' 'What more do you know?' 'When Denis came from Paris he said, I am master now; I will turn you all out of doors.' Denis being recalled, attempted by his effrontery to put this witness down, but he failed. The witness also declared that he had found a packet of white powder in a foot-warmer belonging to Madame Lafarge, (the mother.)

During the absence of Lafarge, Denis, pretending to go to Guéret, went to Paris —for what purpose none could discover. But this additional circumstance came to light without being explained. Lafarge borrowed a large sum of money, 25,000 francs : but his mother asserted, that on his return she found only 3900. 'This,' said M. Paillet, 'is again one of the mysteries of this trial; in the mean time, thanks to the signatures which Madame Lafargé gave to her husband, her patrimony has been spent.'

If, then, we follow the clue afforded by our hypothesis, everything is clear ; Denis first creates suspicion ; he tells the mother her son is poisoned ; he has access to the mother's apartment, to that of the sick man, to every part of the house, in short ; and his hand might have strewed the poison where it was afterwards found ; and one very remarkable circumstance throws a strong light upon this part of the case. The broth above mentioned, of which there was a residue, and into which Madame Marie was said to have put some white powder, was a long time in the sick man's room; the residue was then taken possession of by the mother. It was afterwards sent to M. Eyssartier—by whom does not appear But this much is certain, it was exposed during a long period ; so that any one who desired, might deal with it as he pleased. If there was any one desirous of putting poison into it, he was able with ease to do so. Now Madlle. Le Brun speaks of a small quantity of powder ; but the chemists, when they come to analyze the sediment, declare *that it contained enough arsenic to poison ten persons.* This is explicable, if we suppose that some wicked hand had put arsenic into the cup *afterwards ;* but utterly inexplicable upon the supposition that it was poisoned by the wife—the cup emptied by throwing away the broth— for that is the phrase used ; and that there remained a sediment which was twice examined, first at Brives, and next during the trial, and yet there remained enough to poison ten persons. So much then for the sediment.

All the same remarks apply to the small pot found in the commode, with this additional observation—the cup did contain powdered gum, and a small portion of arsenic—but the train of powder from the cup was pure arsenic. If into a cup containing powdered gum, any one had shaken a small quantity of arsenic, and then shook a train of it along the inside of the commode, such would be the exact state of the case—*in* the case there would be gum and arsenic—*out* of it arsenic alone.

But then comes the inquiry, did the small agate box carried by the wife in the pocket of her apron, contain arsenic ? Out of this there was a small quantity taken by Emma Ponthier, and given to her uncle ; and it is a very extraordinary circumstance, that in this powder, when first examined, no arsenic was found, and this examination was made by the chemists who found arsenic in almost everything else. When this same powder underwent a second examination at the time of the trial, then a small quantity of arsenic was found therein. The agate box given by Clementine to Emma, was from the first said to contain some arsenic. This box is proved to be at times out of the possession of Madame Lafarge ; for, Emma unseen, takes some powder out of it, and Clementine finds it on Emma's request. It is not to be supposed that Madame Lafarge, knowing it to contain arsenic, would give it to her. Afterwards, indeed, she learned that the child had the box, and bade her give it to the officers of justice—a conduct wholly at variance with the supposition that she knew it contained the poison of which there was so much discussion. How are these things to be explained ? Without any very great difficulty of keeping our hypothesis in view, we look to the mode in which the suspected substances were dealt with.

The paper given by Emma to her uncle was beyond the reach of Denis, and it was found pure ; afterwards it was sent to the office of the court, (the *greffe*), and the exposure which took place on the trial, of the mode in which these fatal substances were dealt with, created universal astonishment, even among an audience who did not seem very scrupulous in their manner of eliciting or dealing with evidence.

The officers of justice came to the house of the deceased on the 15th. Every part of the house was open to Denis. The suspected substances were taken possession of. They had been collected by the mother, and put into a wrapper. It is clear that every one of these might have been tampered with ; and, according to our hypothesis, they were utterly worthless as evidence against the accused, who was already under the surveillance of justice, and in reality a prisoner.

On the 16th the body was opened; its entrails were put into vases, ticketed, but not sealed. The whole was then placed on the back of a horse, and without further precaution taken to Brives. The officer thus describes the journey:—' We slept at Vigeors. On the 17th we arrived at Brives. *I have heard* that it was then that the stomach was put into a glass; it had before that been wrapped in a cloth. On the 18th the surgeons commenced their analysis, which lasted three days. During this time we returned to Glandier, and not till our return were there any seals placed upon the vases.' Such a declaration as this, upon the suggestion of our hypothesis, would have decided the case in an English court of justice. No human being could be safe in a society which could, on such evidence, condemn a fellow creature. The body all this time lay at Glandier, exposed to any who might desire to tamper with it; so that from it no evidence could be obtained on which the accused could be safely condemned.*

But in addition to these suspicions thus cast upon any evidence to be obtained from these various suspected substances, there occurred a circumstance which not only throws doubt on the case before us, but which unhappily goes far to destroy our faith in all medical opinions on the subject of poisoning by arsenic. The chemists of Brives declared, without hesitation, that they had found arsenic in the stomach and its contents. They also declared, that a flannel which the wife had wished to apply to the throat of the deceased also contained arsenic. But on the trial, the chemists of Limoges, among the most celebrated in France, declared as positively, that these substances did *not* contain arsenic. After describing the process they adopted, M. Dupuytren (the brother, we believe, of the celebrated surgeon of that name) went on to say,—' We then introduced this residuum into the apparatus invented by Marsh (*l'appareil* de Marsh), and after many experiments (*mainte expérience*) we obtained no arsenical spots.' Even from the countenance of the poor prisoner there suddenly glanced a gleam of joy at this happy announcement; her Advocate burst into tears; and the audience giving way to a generous feeling towards the accused, and forgetting for the moment the respect due to

a court of justice, vehemently applauded. On this the Avocat-Général rose in anger. He abused (there is no other word fit to describe. his expressions) the audience generally. He picked out one young man, commanded him to stand up, threatened to commit him, and then he finished an apostrophe to the public thus—' Since when has it happened, that the sanctuary of justice has become an arena for bad passions?' (The bad passions were evinced, not by the public who rejoiced at an acquittal, but by him who pressed a failing prosecution.) ' Do you think,' he continued, ' that there remain no further resources to the prosecution?' (*sourdes rumeurs.*) ' Do you think that there does not remain a grand and solemn mission to fulfil?' And now comes the most extraordinary denunciation made on this extraordinary trial: ' Take care, lest the accused may have perhaps to accuse you with having so acted as to prolong her anxiety, and to retard the period for the determination of this inquiry.' The Avocat-Général was plainly fighting for victory, and not truth; his anger was an outbreak of wounded vanity; and the words he uttered were not the dignified language of a judicial officer, calmly rebuking a sudden but venial forgetfulness on the part of the public of the respect due to a court of justice, but a violent explosion of passion by a baffled prosecutor.

M. Dupuytren thus concluded his Report: —' Our conclusions unanimously agreed to are, that there is no arsenic in any of the animal substances submitted to our examination.' The consequence of this opinion was the sending for M. Orfila from Paris. A mystery attaches to the whole of this proceeding. Other celebrated chemists were proposed, and among them M. Raspail. From the letter written by this latter gentleman respecting his own exclusion from the inquiry, it would appear that some feelings were at work which certainly ought not to have been exhibited or acted on; but the whole matter eludes inquiry, and we are obliged to rest contented with mere suspicion.

The proceeding, nevertheless, does raise a question entirely unconnected with party feeling or momentary considerations; and herein we again perceive a great difference in the two systems of French and English judicature. By the law of England, when the prisoner stands upon his deliverance, and the jury is charged to decide upon his fate, the case must go on to its end, without interruption or delay, beyond that which it is physically impossible to avoid. The trial

---

* A curious question might have been suggested. Suppose that some wicked person had placed arsenic within the body after the death and the examination, would not this have affected every analysis made on the exhumation of the corpse? But who can possibly say that this was not done?

is one transaction, and cannot after its commencement be adjourned, except in cases in which the evidence cannot be all brought forward in one day. Rest and food being absolutely required, the jury and all others concerned on the trial must retire, but the jury must remain under strict watch—no one is allowed to have communication with them, and the trial goes on the next day without further interruption than nature absolutely requires. But by the system of France, delay is permitted to obtain further evidence. This system seems to give a fearful power to a government over those which it desires to crush; and although, at the first announcement, it appears reasonable to wait for the requisite evidence if it be not forthcoming, yet, if we look further, we shall find much of reason and humanity in the rule which makes it imperative on the prosecution to be ready at once with the evidence needful to support it. This necessity renders it far more difficult to concoct and support a false accusation; while in reality it throws very few impediments in the way of a true one. By the English system, society can be sufficiently protected without any unfair advantage against the prisoner; by that of France, very little additional assistance is gained for the public security, while the prisoner is exposed to fearful hazard should he have to meet a powerful and vindictive accuser. This subject is one deserving of a full and complete inquiry; but that we cannot now attempt. We must be content to hope, that this cursory allusion to the matter may lead some of the jurists of France to re-consider this part of their system; and to prepare the minds of their fellow-citizens for the adoption of a more effective and equitable mode of procedure.

M. Orfila came from Paris—the trial dragged on from day to day; while the chemists, having exhumed the body, pursued their inquiries respecting it This inquiry was carried on close to the court in which the trial took place; and our neighbours, who are ever alive to the influences of dramatic display, seem to have been wonderfully struck by the horrible scene then disclosed. We, however, having no liking for such horrors, pass on rapidly to the close of this painful case.

It should be remembered that the body, from the very moment of the decease of Lafarge, was wholly beyond the control of his wife, but was exposed, without any safeguard, to the machinations of her enemies. Who, then, can say, that those enemies did not place arsenic within the corpse? and who can presume positively to assert, that the phenomena which presented themselves to M. Orfila were not the result of such machinations? The letter of M. Raspail would throw doubt indeed upon the whole analysis as carried on by M. Orfila; but we are unwilling to entertain the suspicions which he would excite. We cannot, however, refrain from observing, that in a country where a rigid morality on such questions is the morality of the people, M. Orfila, having expressed an opinion before the trial, would have been deemed by the public, and certainly by himself, a very unfit person to give a solemn opinion on the same point when the trial took place. The result of M. Orfila's inquiry was, that he found arsenic in the stomach and its contents; but his inquiry as to the muscular flesh taken from the thigh was, so he expressed it, negative. This also agrees with our hypothesis. If the arsenic was put into the body after death, it would indeed be found in the viscera upon which it was strewed, but would not have been carried into the system by the action of the blood and the absorbents, as would have been the case if the poison had been taken into the system during life. Had M. Lafarge died of arsenic, would not the poison have been found in his flesh as well as in the viscera?

Now then, we ask, who is there, who, being a juryman, would from such evidence as this come to these two distinct affirmative conclusions—

1. That Lafarge did die, poisoned by arsenic.

2. That his wife knowingly administered that arsenic?

It must be recollected, that in this rapid analysis of the voluminous evidence adduced, we have been compelled to omit many things which require consideration by any one who would fairly estimate the value of the French system of procedure. The more prominent points have alone been regarded—the more marked evils signalized; but even after this short inquiry, we cannot but think that the most cursory observer will discover much to amend in a judicature which, upon such evidence, taken in such a manner, could have arrived at the conclusion which the French court and jury adopted. They have declared the unfortunate accused guilty of the crime laid to her charge. Whether she be so, no man can determine; though any one skilled in the estimation of evidence—trained to marshal and employ it under a rigid and effective system—can easily determine whether it would be safe—whether it would conduce to the security of society at large—to deem her guilty, upon evidence which in itself is so untrustworthy, and received in a manner so well calculated to destroy what little value it might otherwise have possessed. Looking back through the whole evidence, carefully weighing each separate item adduced, trying its worth by every test which the experience of ages has suggested, we are satisfied that there was not sufficient evidence to prove that the deceased came to a violent end; still less to show that his wife was the guilty cause of his death. The rude judicial system employed served to increase, and not allay alarm : it made a criminal without proving her to be guilty ; and thus taught the people to feel, that not only were they exposed to the assaults of the wrongdoer, but also liable to incur even greater harm, from the very means intended for their protection.*

Art. III.—*Incidents of Travel in Central America, Chiapas, and Yucatan.* By John T. Stephens, Author of Incidents of Travel in Egypt. 2 vols. 8vo. London : 1841.

Mr. Stephens informs us that he was entrusted by President Van Buren 'with a special and confidential mission to Central America ;' but whatever his diplomatic duties may have been, they do not appear to have engrossed much of his time or attention. Immediately after receiving his appointment, he appears to have engaged Mr. Catherwood, ' who had passed more than ten years of his life in diligently studying the antiquities of the old world,' as one familiar with the remains of ancient architecture, to assist him in exploring the ruins of Central America. It is to that part of the work before us which regards these ruins, and which, indeed, forms its only attraction, that we mean to attend. The information that has been laid before the world respecting the antiquities in question,

is scanty and scattered ; but even with the little that exists, and is easily accessible, Mr. Stephens had not taken the trouble to make himself thoroughly acquainted. His ambition seemingly was not to know all that could be known of these crumbling monuments of a now extinct civilisation ; but, as he on one occasion somewhat curiously expresses it, to try whether ' a city might not be transported bodily and set up in New York.' And he proclaims the hope, ' that the nations of the Old World will respect the rights of discovery, and leave the field of American antiquities to the United States ; that they will not deprive a destitute country of its only chance of contributing to the cause of science, but rather encourage it in the work of bringing together, from remote and almost inaccessible places, and retaining on its own soil, the architectural remains of its aboriginal inhabitants.'

The information which Mr. Stephens supplies regarding these antiquities, is rather of a nature to stimulate than to gratify curiosity. But it is but justice to say, that this was in great part owing to the wretchedly unsettled state of the country at the time of his visit, which rendered a deliberate and complete examination of the ruins out of the question. It is, however, no more than truth to add, that it seems questionable whether he, under the most favourable circumstances, would have shown himself possessed of the necessary previous acquirements, or the necessary powers of patient investigation and clear exposition, to give an entirely satisfactory and intelligible account of them.

Of the eight ruined cities of Central America which he visited, only four—Copan, Ocosingo, the ruins near Palenque, and Uxmal—appear to have afforded much to examine ; and it was only at Palenque and Copan that circumstances admitted of his considering the remains with minute attention. The difficulties with which he had to contend, even where time was allowed him, and no disturbance occasioned by the natives, will best appear from his own account of the condition of those ruins when he first approached them. The sketch has considerable interest, though not executed in the correctest taste. ' At Copan,'says he,

' Our guide cleared the way with his machete, (cutlass), and we passed, as it lay half-buried in the earth, a large fragment of stone elaborately sculptured, and came to the angle of a structure with steps on the sides, in form and appearance, so far as the trees would enable us to make it out, like the sides of a pyramid. Diverging from the base, and working our way through the thick

---

* We purposely avoided all allusion to certain extraordinary circumstances which tend to cast great suspicion on the mother of the deceased. The one hypothesis which we have suggested, is quite sufficient to make apparent the danger of the conclusion adopted by the jury. Our chief object being in fact to point out the still greater danger resulting from the means taken to gain that verdict.

woods, we came upon a square stone column about fourteen feet high, and three feet on each side, sculptured in very bold relief, and on all four of the sides, from the base to the top. The front was the figure of a man curiously and richly dressed, and the face evidently a portrait, solemn, stern, and well fitted to excite terror. The back was of a different design, unlike anything we had ever seen before, and the sides were covered with hieroglyphics. This our guide called an "idol;" and before it, at a distance of three feet, was a large block of stone, also sculptured with figures and emblematical devices, which he called an altar. The sight of this unexpected monument put at rest, at once and for ever in our minds, all uncertainty in regard to the character of American antiquities; and gave us the assurance that the objects we were in search of were interesting not only as the remains of an unknown people, but as works of art—proving, like newly discovered historical records, that the people who once occupied the continent of America were not savages. With an interest perhaps stronger than we had ever felt in wandering among the ruins of Egypt, we followed our guide, who, sometimes missing his way, with a constant and vigorous use of his machete conducted us through the thick forest, among half-buried fragments, to fourteen monuments of the same character and appearance; some with more elegant designs, and some in workmanship equal to the finest monuments of the Egyptians; one displaced from its pedestals by enormous roots; another locked in the close embrace of branches of trees, and almost lifted out of the earth; another hurled to the ground and bound down by huge vines and creepers; and one standing with its altar before it, in a grove of trees which grew around it, seemingly to shade and shroud it as a sacred thing: in the solemn stillness of the woods it seemed a divinity mourning over a fallen people. The only sounds that disturbed the quiet of this buried city, were the noise of monkeys moving among the tops of the trees, and the cracking of dry branches broken by their weight. They moved over our heads in long and swift processions, forty or fifty at a time, some with little ones wound in their long arms, walking out to the end of boughs, and, holding on with their hind feet or a curl of the tail, sprang to a branch of the next tree, and with a noise like a current of wind, passed on into the depths of the forest. It was the first time we had seen these mockeries of humanity; and with the strange monuments around us, they seemed like wandering spirits of the departed race, guarding the ruins of their former habitations.

'We returned to the base of the pyramidical structure, and ascended by regular stone steps, in some places forced apart by bushes and saplings, and in others thrown down by the growth of large trees, while some remained entire. In parts they were ornamented with sculptured figures and rows of death's heads. Climbing over the ruined top, we reached a terrace overgrown with trees, and crossing it, descended by stone steps into an area so covered with trees that at first we could not make out its form: but which, on clearing the way with the machete, we ascertained to be a square, and with steps on all the sides, almost as perfect as those of the Roman amphitheatre. The steps were ornamented with sculpture; and on the south side, about halfway up, forced out of its place by roots, was a colossal head, evidently a portrait. We ascended these steps, and reached a broad terrace a hundred feet high, overlooking the river, and supported by the wall which we had seen from the opposite bank. The whole terrace was covered with trees, and even at this height from the ground were two gigantic ceibas, or wild cotton trees of India, above twenty feet in circumference, extending their half-naked roots fifty or a hundred feet around, binding down the ruins, and shading them with their wide-spreading branches. We sat down on the very edge of the wall, and strove in vain to penetrate the mystery by which we were surrounded. . . . . There were no associations connected with the place; . . . the city was desolate. No remnant of this race hangs round the ruins, with traditions handed down from father to son, and from generation to generation. It lay before us like a shattered bark in the midst of the ocean, her masts gone, her name effaced, her crew perished, and none to tell whence she came, how long on her voyage, or what caused her destruction; her lost people to be traced only by some fancied resemblance in the construction of the vessel, and perhaps never to be known at all.'

Palenque was equally overgrown and obscured. Yet, notwithstanding the difficulties interposed in the way of a minute examination of these two heaps of ruins, by the astonishing power of vegetation within the tropics, where ruined or deserted structures, and even cities—instead of 'dying insensibly away from human thoughts and purposes,' like Mr. Wordsworth's Westmoreland tower—have the appearance of being broken up and overwhelmed by a volcanic eruption of roots, branches, and leaves, Mr. Stephens, or more properly speaking Mr. Catherwood, his attendant artist, has contrived to present us with faithful representations of the remains of the buildings and carvings—for sculpture is almost too ambitious a word to apply to them. The accuracy of Mr Catherwood's drawings is vouched by various circumstances. In general character they correspond with the drawings made by Dupaix, (1805-7,) and are evidently copies of the same originals; although Mr. Catherwood had not seen Dupaix's work at the time he made them. The mechanical process by which the drawings of Mr. Catherwood were made, and reduced and transferred to the steel or stone from which the illustrations of Mr. Stephens' book are printed, were such as to ensure a high degree of accuracy. And, not to waste time by dwelling upon other corroborative circumstances, we have examined a beautiful set of drawings from the ruins of Palenque, by Captain Caddy of the Royal Artillery, who visited them a few weeks before the present travellers; and which correspond so exactly as to leave no doubt on our minds of the perfect fidelity of Mr. Catherwood's pencil. This relates merely to Palenque; for no other artist has visited Copan; but the presumption is, that he who has succeeded so well as to one place, cannot have erred materially as to the other.

The descriptions and drawings of Copan and Palenque challenge more attention than those of any other towns visited by our travellers; not only because they are the most complete, but because these clusters of ruins may be considered as the types of two classes into which the Indian cities they examined may be divided. Copan and Quirigua are situated in the valley of the Motagua, which falls into the bay of Honduras; Palenque, Ocosingo, Quezaltenango, stand upon tributaries of the Usumasinta, which falls into the gulf of Mexico; and Patinamit, or Tecpan Quatimala, although situated on the upper waters of the Motagua, is more accessible from the Usumasinta than from the navigable parts of the river in whose drainage basin it stands. The remains found in each of these groups differ decidedly in their character—a difference which seems to be attributable in part to the materials which offered themselves to the workmen; in part to the circumstance of the constructors of the edifices in the Palenque group having advanced further than those of the other in taste and capacity for producing works of art. The material employed in the works at Copan is a solid and massive stone; and the predominating features of the ruins are huge blocks, chiselled into something intermediate between statues and rude columns, loaded with festoons and quaint carvings. At Palenque a rock of slaty and crumbling structure denied the inhabitants the power of erecting monolithic monuments; but, on the other hand, these rocks being chiefly limestone, supplied the materials of an excellent cement, with which the buildings have been coated over; and which being from its softness easily wrought, enabled them to make more rapid progress in imitating the characteristic details and graceful forms of the objects they saw in nature, than those who had only a refractory stone to work upon. The ruins at Uxmal, near the north-western angle of Yucatan, differ in a considerable degree from those of the two groups mentioned above; but though they are more easy of access, and not so encumbered with vegetation as the others, Mr. Catherwood was prevented from doing them the same justice as the infirm state of his health, which had broken down under his labours in the interior.

The ruins of Copan stand on the east bank of a small river of that name, which, some distance below, falls into the Motagua from the south. The greater part of them are contained within a parallelogram, which does not much exceed 600 by 800 feet. Nearly in the centre of the ruins is what Mr. Stephens calls a 'court yard,'—a rectangular area, a hundred and forty feet long and ninety broad, inclosed on all sides by ranges of broad steps. The entry to this inclosure is from the north, along a passage thirty feet wide, and about three hundred feet long. On the right hand, on entering this passage, is a high range of steps rising to the terrace of the river wall, at the foot of which are circular stones from eighteen inches to three feet in diameter. On the left side is a pyramidical structure with steps six feet high, and nine feet broad, and one hundred and twenty-two feet high on the slope. The inner area is thus described by Mr. Stephens:—

'There was no idol or altar, nor were there any vestiges of them. On the left, standing alone, two-thirds of the way up the steps, is a gigantic head; it is moved a little from its place, and a portion of the ornament on one side has been thrown down some distance by the expansion of the trunk of a large tree. The head is about six feet high, and the style good. Like many of the others, with the great expansion of the eyes, it seems intended to inspire awe. On either side of it, distant about thirty or forty feet, and rather lower down, are other fragments of sculpture of colossal dimensions, and good design; and at the foot are two colossal heads, turned over and partly buried, well worthy the attention of future travellers and artists. The whole area is overgrown with trees, and encumbered with decayed vegetable matter, with fragments of curious sculpture protruding above the surface, which probably, with others completely buried, would be brought to light by digging. On the opposite side, parallel with the river, is a range of fifteen steps to a terrace twelve feet wide, and then fifteen steps more to a terrace twenty feet wide, extending to the river wall. On each side of the centre of the steps [by this expression Mr. S. appears to wish to indicate the middle of the terrace halfway up the ascent] is a mound of ruins, apparently of a circular tower. About halfway up the steps on this side [judging by the annexed plan, this seems to mean halfway up the lower flight of fifteen steps] is a pit five feet square, and seventeen feet deep, cased with stone. At the bottom is an opening two feet four inches high, with a wall one foot nine inches thick, which leads into a chamber ten feet long, five feet four inches wide, and four feet high. At each end is a niche one foot nine inches high, one foot eight inches deep, and two feet five inches long. Colonel Galindo first broke into this sepulchral vault, and found the niches and the ground full of red earthenware, dishes and pots, more than fifty of which, he says, were full of human bones, packed in lime; also several sharp-edged and pointed knives of chaya, a small death's head carved in a fine green stone, its eyes closed, the lower features distorted, and the back symmetrically perforated by holes, the whole of exquisite workmanship.'

The rest of the area is occupied by pyramidal buildings and fragments of walls. so dilapidated and masked by trees, that it is impossible to conjecture what were their forms and relative positions when entire. Near the south-east angle occurs a group of the colossal carved blocks above alluded to, as forming the distinguishing characteristic of the ruins of Copan. Mr Stephens calls them statues, and idols to all appearances they have been; but the use of the term statues, unless accompanied by some explanation, would be apt to mislead a reader who has not the drawings before him. They are, on an average, twelve or thirteen feet high, four feet in front and three feet deep, and sculptured on all sides from the base to the top. Three of the sides are elaborately carved into ornaments, which bespeak a high degree of mechanical skill and neatness. Sometimes these ornaments have the appearance of festoons of drapery, or branches of trees; sometimes they consist of groups of heads, or even human figures more or less complete. In general, their arrangement bespeaks considerable taste for symmetrical arrangement. It is impossible to avoid coming to the conclusion, that the minor groups on some of the columns are what Egyptian writers on antiquities have agreed to call "cartouches" filled with hieroglyphics. On the front is in every instance carved a representation of the human figure in high relief. It is not always easy to detect it at the first glance, overwhelmed as it is beneath a profusion of what seem intended for ornaments. But a brief examination enables us to discover, about halfway, or two-thirds up the column, a broad flat face with a particularly large pair of ears; immediately below this, a rude imitation of a pair of arms curved inwards till the hands nearly meet; and still lower down a pair of stumpy legs, clothed either in a kind of petticoat, or in what looks like a pair of loose trowsers. Before some of these fig-

ures, at the distance of about eight feet, are large blocks of sculptured stone, and probably all of them have originally been thus provided. Some of these blocks are square, others circular. A drawing of one of them is given by Mr. Catherwood ; it is flat on the top; on the four sides are carved in relief human figures, s· ated crosslegged, on what have the appearance of cushions ; one half of them facing the other, as if engaged in a conference The Indians call these blocks altars ; and it is probable that they were ; and the rude images before which they are placed, the objects of adoration to the people who reared them.

The appearance of hieroglyphics upon these monuments, (of which we shall say more when we come to speak of the remains at Palenque) would seem to indicate a greater intellectual progress, on the part of the people who reared them, than was found among the inhabitants of Mexico; but the structures and sculptures themselves are indicative of the very infancy of art. With regard to the power of expressing form alone, it is clear that the artists had not advanced beyond that stage to which even children and savages can attain—in which the delineator rests satisfied with coming so near the object of imitation, as that those who see his handiwork may know what he means to represent. The statues of Greece and Rome are exact counterparts of the human figure ; the clumsy productions of Copan only approach it near enough to enable us to conjecture what those who made them intended. Again, with regard to the power of expressing emotions—of representing forms and attitudes beautiful in themselves—of telling a story—all, in a word, that constitutes the essence of art, without which the most perfect accuracy in copying the lineaments of the human form is merely mechanical—not the slightest vestige is found in the 'graven images' of Copan. Mr. Stephens says of the face of one of the idols, that it was ' solemn, stern, and well fitted to excite terror,'—vague phrases, which sound loftily ; but he is nearer the mark, probably, when he says of another, that 'with the great expansion of the eyes, it seems intended to inspire awe ;'—an expression which may enable those who have not seen the drawings, to form the accurate notion, that as works of art the statues of Copan are much upon a level with a staring Saracen's head on an old sign-board. We lay no stress, however, on the circumstance of these images appearing to have been painted red ; seeing that a similar vestige of barbarism continued to prevail in Greece after sculpture was far advanced towards perfection On the whole, it is doing no injustice to these monuments to say, that they indicate no higher advancement in taste and intellect on the par of those who made them, than the most uncouth Fetish on the coasts of Africa On the other hand, the high finish, and even elegance of the carving on such an untractable material as stone, conveys the impression that they must have made considerable progress in the mechanical arts.

As works of art, the remains at Palenque are immeasurably superior to those of Copan. In the substructures of the buildings we find the same pyramidal form that prevails there; but on the summits are erected edifices of considerable elegance. None of the visiters to old Palenque have been able to detect more than six structures—one of considerable extent, the others small. All of them are erected on high terraces, forming the summit of a truncated pyramid. Both the substructures, and the buildings reared upon them, are built of a thin slaty stone which abounds in the district. Wherever the roofs remain, they are found to have been constructed by laying broad stones across from wall to wall. In the smaller buildings, it was easy to procure flags large enough for this purpose. It is difficult to imagine how they managed in the more extensive apartments of the larger building; of which only a double corridor and square tower, two or three stories high, retain their roofs.

The palace—so the larger building is called by the Indians—stands on an artificial elevation of an oblong form—forty feet high, three hundred feet in front and rear, and two hundred and sixty feet on each side. This superstructure appears formerly to have been faced with stones, which have been dissevered and thrown down by the growth of trees. The building faces the east, and measures two hundred and twenty-eight feet in front, by one hundred and eighty deep. The front consisted originally of fifteen piers, each from six to seven feet in breadth, the intervals between them being about nine feet. The west front consists also of piers of the same size, ranged at similar intervals. They are constructed of stone, cemented with a mortar of lime and sand, and covered with stucco, painted and ornamented with figures in bas-relief. The parallel corridors are supposed to have extended along all the four sides of the building. The wall which di-

vides them, is perforated by only one door in front, and two in the rear. That in front is immediately opposite the space between the fourth and fifth piers, (counting from the north east angle); a range of broad stone steps leads to it up the slope of the terrace. The intervals between the exterior piers bear no traces of doors; but along the cornice outside, which projects about a foot from the wall, holes were drilled at intervals through the stone; and the impression of Mr. Stephens and his companion was, ' that an immense cotton cloth, running the whole length of the building, was attached to this cornice, and raised and lowered like a curtain, according to the exigencies of sun and rain : such a curtain is used now in front of the piazzas of some verandas in Yucatan The walls of the corridors were about ten feet high, and apertures, apparently for the purpose of ventilation, in the form of a cross, or of the letter T, were opened in the separating wall. The roof was made to curve inward, by successive layers of stones, each overlapping that immediately beneath it; and plastered over so as to present a smooth curved surface.

The top of the doorway in the middle wall is, by this means, wrought into an exact resemblance of a Gothic arch. The door leads into an open court-yard, eighty feet long by seventy broad, to which there is a descent by a flight of steps. On each side of this area are apartments. At the further extremity, another flight of steps leads up to a corridor, beyond which is a descent to another court-yard, also eighty feet long, but only thirty feet across. These two court-yards, with the surrounding and intervening corridors, occupy the whole depth of the building. On the south side of this second court is a third; in which is a substantial stone tower, rising to three stories from a base of thirty feet square. Within this is a second tower, quite distinct from the outer one, and a narrow stone staircase. Mr Stephens states, that the stair terminates against a dead stone ceiling; but Captain Caddy, before mentioned, who, by the assistance of a tree, scrambled up on the outside, says, that Mr. S. had been deceived by the appearance of stones which had fallen from above. The rest of the space within the outer walls is occupied by apartments, of which it is difficult to trace the arrangement and connection. At the southern extremity of the building are several flights of stairs, leading down to passages and apartments, constructed in the artificial elevation in which it stands.

The piers left standing are covered, both externally and internally, with bas-reliefs in stucco. The faces are all in profile, which seems to indicate the want of sufficient skill to delineate the front face. But the limbs are correctly formed, and frequently even graceful. There is also some attempt to arrange the figures into groups, so as to tell a story: and a variety of expression—of the same imperfect kind as in the Egyptian paintings—can be recognized in the countenances. On one pier is represented an armed warrior, with two half-naked figures crouching submissively on either side of him. On another we see an armed warrior, brandishing his weapon over the head of a person who seems to kneel and beg for life. A third appears intended to represent a male and female figure conversing. In a fourth, a standing figure is placing an ornament upon another sitting in front of him. In the interior corridor, the middle wall is ornamented with medallions, in which the outline of busts in bas-relief can still be traced. On either side of the steps which lead down into the eastern court-yard, are figures sculptured upon upright flag-stones—uncouth and grotesque enough. In one of the apartments east of the square tower, is an elliptical stone tablet set in the wall, carved in bas-relief. The principal figure sits cross-legged on a couch, the ends of which curve upwards, and are carved in imitation of the heads of beasts. The other figure is seated on the ground, and presents to the first what appears, in the drawing of Mr. Catherwood, to be merely a head-dress. All the bas-reliefs are surrounded by neat borders, and the ornamental scrolls traced along the upper part of the walls are remarkably elegant. Before offering any remarks upon this structure, it will be advisable to give the reader a general notion of the other remains at Palenque.

Mr. Stephens mentions five smaller structures, and neither Del Rio (1786) nor Dupaix (1806) gives any distinct account of more; although the words of the former would seem to imply, that more were standing when he visited the place. Of these, only four are described in detail by Mr. Stephens; the fifth he represents as a mere mass of ruins. The general plan is in all of them much the same. A truncated pyramid is crowned by a small building, which consists internally of two corridors, with converging roofs like those of the palace In three of the four, the inner corridor is divided into three apartments, all opening into the front corridors. In only one instance do these apartments form a suite,

communicating one with another by doors. The roofs are inclined; and on the tops of two of the buildings are narrow platforms supporting small towers. 'The platform,' says Mr. Stephens, 'is but two feet ten inches wide, and the superstructure of the first story is seven feet ten inches in height; that of the second, eight feet five inches, the width of the two being the same. The ascent from the one to the other is by square projecting stones, and the covering of the upper story is laid across, and projecting over. The long sides of this narrow structure are of open stucco work, formed into curious and indescribable devices, human figures, with legs and arms spreading, and apertures between; and the whole was once loaded with rich and elegant ornaments in stucco and relief. Its appearance at a distance must have been that of a high fanciful lattice.' There is no staircase or other communication between the lower apartments and this superstructure, either in the inside or on the outside of the building. The largest of these buildings is less than eighty feet in front, and the smallest is twenty-five. In the latter, stairs conduct to an apartment constructed in the pyramid on which it stands. The piers in front, and the roof, are overlaid with human figures and other ornaments executed in stucco.

But the most striking circumstance about them is a feature of internal arrangement, in which they all agree. In the middle of the back wall of the central apartment into which the largest of these buildings is subdivided, is placed a tablet of hieroglyphics; and similar tablets are, or were, placed on either side of the door which admits into this apartment. In the corresponding apartments of the two middle-sized buildings, are tablets with borders of hieroglyphics on either side, and human figures in the centre. In both, the figures are represented as facing each other, with a device placed between them; consisting, in the one, of two spears forming a St. Andrew's Cross, with an escutcheon resting on the point where they cross; and in the other, of a dart resting on its feathered end, surrounded with ornaments which assume the form of an upright cross. In both, the figure on the right hand of the spectator is taller than the other; and the dresses of the two tall figures are the same in both, as also the dresses of the two shorter figures. The dart is surmounted by a representation of the Quezale, or royal bird of Quiché. In this sculpture the taller figure appears to be making an offering to the bird; in the other, both figures appear to be making offerings to the mask on the escutcheon rested upon the two spears.

In the former the tall figure has the appearance of standing upon the ground; the shorter, upon what Mr. Stephens calls hieroglyphics: in the latter, both stand upon human figures bending beneath their weight, and the scaffolding on which the spears rest is supported by other two human figures. The dress and countenances of these crushed figures differ from those of the other two. The tablets are found in an inner inclosure, or shrine, constructed within the apartment, The piers on each side of the doorway of the shrine containing the group surmounted by the Quizale, formerly contained two tablets, which have been removed and set up in the wall of a house in the village of Palenque. They contain each one figure in bas-relief; one of which in countenance and dress resembles the principal figures of the tablet, the other nearly a counterpart of those upon whom they are represented trampling. In the smallest of the four buildings, the back corridor of which forms only one apartment, 'fronting the door and against the back wall, was a large stucco ornament representing a figure sitting on a couch; but a great part has fallen or been taken off and carried away. The body of the couch, with tigers' feet, is all that now remains   The outline of two tigers' heads and of the sitting personage is seen on the wall   The loss or destruction of this ornament is more to be regretted, as from what remains it appears to have been superior in execution to any other stucco relief in Palenque.'

As far as we can gather from the ground-plan of Palenque, and hints in the accompanying letter-press, (for Mr. Stephens' style is, too often, the reverse of precise,) the whole of the ground examined by our travellers does not exceed 600 by 800 yards. A small stream runs about three hundred yards in the direction from west to east at the south end; and then, turning to the north, nearly bisects the parallelogram. At the south-west angle of this area, close upon the rivulet, is the smallest of the lesser buildings; where the brook issues from it on the north side, is the aqueduct leading off from the east bank; nearly south of it, on the opposite side of the stream, is the 'palace;' at its south-west angle, the largest of the small structures; and east of this, on the opposite side of the stream, are the rest of the smaller structures, forming a triangular group.   The density of the forest prevented any other remains that may exist from being discovered; but two circumstances point to the inference that these are but a small portion of what once existed. The first is, that our travellers, approaching the ruins from the north-west. encountered 'masses of stone,' 'a round sculptured stone,' and 'a sharp ascent of fragments,' a good while before they came to 'the palace,' the first of the buildings they arrived at.   The second is, that the aqueduct appears to have been constructed with a view to lead off the water of the brook in a north-east direction, away from all the structures that have yet been discovered: it does not appear to have been required for drainage, and the natural conclusion is, that there must have been inhabitants and buildings in that direction, to which it was intended to carry a supply of water.

The most striking features of the ruins of Central America are the hieroglyphics. The largest of the smaller structures at Palenque—that which is nearest to the palace —contains three rectangular tablets completely covered with them.   There is one on either side of the door opening into the central apartment of the three into which the back corridor is divided; each measuring thirteen feet in length, and eight in height, and divided into two hundred squares of characters or symbols.   In the back wall of this apartment, fronting the principal door of entrance, is another tablet of hieroglyphics, four feet six inches wide, and three feet six inches high.   The tablets containing representations of human figures, described above as found in two of these lesser buildings, have at both ends deep borders of hieroglyphics; the one has sixty-four squares in each border, the other a hundred and two. Single lines of these hieroglyphics, sometimes horizontal, sometimes perpendicular, appear on almost all the bas-reliefs, both in the large and the smaller buildings.   The regular arrangement of the squares, and the repetition of the same elements—lines, points, portions of the human figure, &c.— in different combinations, render it almost impossible to avoid the conclusion that these tablets contain specimens of a written language.   This conjecture seems to derive corroboration from the introduction of lines of these symbols into the bas-reliefs; exactly in the same manner as we find hieroglyphic scrolls introduced into Egyptian paintings.   But more conclusive still is the fact, that we find the same characters in a manuscript of Agave paper, preserved in the Dresden library.   A fac-simile of this manuscript is given in (the third volume of) the great work on Mexican Antiquities, published by Aglio under the auspices of Lord Kingsborough; and a specimen of it is also given by Humboldt in his work entitled *Monumens des Peuples Indigènes de l'Amerique.* (Plate 45.)   In these, we find pictures and lines of characters essentially the same as those which Messrs. Stephens and Catherwood found on the walls of Palenque; intermingled exactly as we find written characters and pictures of Saints alternating in illuminated Missals. It is barely conceivable that the repetition of these squares on walls might have been a mere attempt at ornament; but their transference to paper, and the repetition of them in a long MS., puts such a conjecture out of the question.

Humboldt calls the manuscript in question a *Codex Mexicanus*, and Aglio and Stephens have called it, after Humboldt, a Mexican manuscript; but the truth is, that of its origin we are entirely ignorant, and that it differs materially from all known Mexican manuscripts. Humboldt says—

' According to the information which I have received from Bottiger, this Aztec manuscript was purchased at Vienna by Gotz, during the literary tour he made into Italy in 1739. It is written on Agave paper, like those which I have brought from New Spain. It forms a *tabella plicatilis* nearly 80 yards (six mètres) long, folded into forty leaves, which are covered with paintings on both sides. Each page is about seven inches three lines in length, by three inches two lines in breadth. This form, analogous to that of the ancient *diptica*, distinguishes the MS. of Dresden from those of Vienna, Veletri, and the Vatican; but what renders it still more remarkable is, the arrangement of the simple hieroglyphics, several of which are ranged in lines, as in really symbolical writing. The *Codex Mexicanus* of Dresden bears no resemblance to those ritual calendars, in which the characters of the astrological sign presiding over every semi-lunar period of thirteen days, are surrounded by the hieroglyphics of the days of the month. Here a great number of hieroglyphic characters are placed in simple juxtaposition, as in the Egyptian hieroglyphics and the keys of the Chinese."

An examination of the Mexican manuscripts alluded to—of those which Humboldt himself brought from Mexico—of those preserved in the Bodleian library, of which fac-similes are given in Aglio's work—and of one belonging to Mr. Bullock, of which a tracing has been published at New York by Delafield, confirms the opinion expressed by Humboldt. The symbolical writing of the Dresden manuscript exhibits, to all appearance, a much more fully developed system than that contained in any of the manuscripts known with certainty to be from Mexico. Symbolical writing was with the Mexicans in its very infancy. They could express numbers, the names of the days of the month, and the names of persons- and places, by phonetic hieroglyphics; but further they do not appear to have advanced. The death of a Spanish bishop or leader—the occurrence of a show storm—the punishment of insurgent negroes—are represented by pictures of the event, with hieroglyphics of the number of the year, according to the division of the Mexican cycle, of the name of the half-month, and the number of the day on which the event occurred. The events in the history or traditions of Mexico, are represented by groups of human figures sitting in council, fighting, or leading captives, placed at intervals and connected by lines. The migrations of the tribe are represented by the hieroglyphics of places and cities arranged at intervals, with representations of human footmarks impressed on the tracts which lead from one to the other. But the characters of the Dresden Manuscripts—whether they be arbitrary characters expressive of sounds, like those of the Chinese, to which their square outlines bear some analogy—or groups of a hieroglyphic alphabet, like the *cartouches* which contain the names of the kings of Egypt—show to all appearance a system of writing, by means of which words and sentences may be expressed. Of this Manuscript nothing further is known than that Gotz picked it up at Vienna. It would be rash to pronounce dogmatically on its origin; but, on the one hand, it is highly improbable that it is Mexican, as nothing like it has yet been found among the monuments of that people ; and, on the other hand, it seems probable that it is the workmanship of the same race that reared and inhabited Palenque—seeing that similar characters abound among its ruins.

Having stated our reasons for believing that these characters form a written language, the next question in point of interest relates to their geographical distribution. Mr. Stephens appears to have found similar characters at Uxmal, near the northwest angle of Yucatan : we say appears, for his language is far from precise and clear: —' In the apartment marked B, we found what we regarded as a most interesting object. It was a beam of wood, about ten feet long, and very heavy, which had fallen from its place over the doorway, and for some purpose or other been hauled inside the chamber into a dark corner. On the face was a line of characters carved or stamped, almost obliterated, but which we made out to be hieroglyphics ; and, so far as we could *understand* them, [he means *distinguish their form*—he did not *understand* them in the least,] similar to those at Copan and Palenque.' Speaking of the tablets at Palenque, he says :—' There is one important fact to be noticed. The hieroglyphics are the same as were found at Copan and Quirigua.' The sités of the other cities visited by our travellers were either too completely covered, or the time allowed to explore them too short, to enable them to furnish us with the same minute details as they have furnished regarding Copan and Palenque. At Ocosingo they found, as at Palenque, buildings consisting of outer and inner corridors erected upon truncated pyramids, with converging ceilings and figures executed in stucco. The vicinity of the two places, and the similarity of their structures, leave little room to doubt that hieroglyphics would have been found in Ocosingo, had time allowed; or the attention of the draughtsman been awakened to the same degree that it ultimately was. At Gueguetenango and Santa Cruz de Quiché, the pyramidal structures, the cement, and the remains of colours observed at Palenque, were recognized; and at the latter Mr. Stephens procured some images in *terra cotta*, the faces of which have a strong family likeness to the bas-reliefs at Palenque. In short, from the environs of Merida, about 21°, to Santa Cruz del Quiché, in 15° N. lat., and from Ocosingo near 93°, to Copan in 89° W. lon., we find ruins characterized by different peculiarities; but all possessed of resemblances in so many points as to lead to the conclusion, that the tribes who built them, if not sprung from a common stock, had yet such frequent intercourse with each other as diffused through them all an imperfect civilisation—the same in kind, and not materially differing in degree. And it is precisely in the two cities, which in other respects least resemble each other, that we find the most abundant specimens of what has every appearance of being a written language.

We are not so sanguine as our author when he says, ' I cannot help believing that the tablets of hieroglyphics will yet be read;' and still less do we expect that, if they were deciphered, his conjecture with regard to Copan will prove true :—' one thing,' says he, ' I believe, that its history is graven on its monuments.' Lists of kings, and collections of public proclamations and edicts, are not history : the former, at least, only enable the chronologist to put together the dry bones of his skeleton; the latter are more frequently statements of what it is wished men should believe than of what really is or has been. Yet, beyond this, the records of a people possessing only the cumbrous vehicle of hieroglyphics for transmitting their thoughts —of a people among whom the possession of this engine is monopolized by a caste— have never been known to advance. Even, therefore, should some lucky chance enable us one day to decipher those strange characters, it is not likely that their contents would deserve the name applied to them by our author. But what ground of hope is there that they ever can be deciphered ?

What we know about the Egyptian hieroglyphics is not very encouraging. The absurd conjectures which abound in the writings of all who treated of them in modern times, previous to the discovery of the Rosetta stone, are matter of notoriety. Yet in the writings of Clement of Alexandria was contained a pregnant hint regarding that system of writing, such as we have no reason to believe exists to serve as a key to the hieroglyphics of Central America. And even with the assistance of the indications given by Clement, aided by bilingual inscriptions, (also non-existent, so far as we know, in America,) what progress has been made in the interpretation of Egyptian hieroglyphics ? Dr. Young proved that they were really used to record events, and explained the system by which this end was accomplished ; and beyond this the work can scarcely yet be said to have proceeded. The Grammars and Vocabularies of the language, supposed to have been expressed in hieroglyphics, have been constructed upon the assumption that it was the old Coptic. Granting the probability of this assumption—what follows? The only monuments of the Coptic language we possess, are some translations from the Bible, made subsequently to the Christian era. The Egyptians ceased to be an independent nation under Cambyses. Let any person note the changes which have taken place in all European languages in the course of the last four centuries— notwithstanding the tendency of education and our system of writing to give them fixity—and say what changes must have taken place during the course of some six or seven centuries, when one favoured caste alone was able to express its thoughts by characters, and that by such a make-shift as hieroglyphics. To enable the student to master even the elements of the old Egyptian language, a long and painful course of preliminary study would be necessary : first, by classifying all the bilingual inscriptions and papyri that have been collected according to their ages ; secondly, by instituting, in succession, an exhaustive analysis of the Coptic monuments—of the hieroglyphic writings nearest to them in point of time, and so backwards, taking those of each century or half century by itself. All this drudgery must be gone through, before there can be any possibility of extracting trustworthy information from the Egyptian hieroglyphics by a sound critical interpretation. How different from this have been the shallow and presumptuous systems of guesswork pursued by all who have succeeded Dr. Young! The first scholar who shall carry on what he began, must commence by removing all the rubbish that has been piled up upon his foundation; and even then it is not history, nor the recovery of a lost literature, that we are to look for, but authentic specimens, illustrative of the manner in which written language was gradually devised; or, we might almost say, by which it insensibly grew up among men.

Under the Greeks, and apparently also under the Persians, the Egyptian language continued to be used by the natives as the language in which public as well as private business was transacted. Hence the numerous private contracts and public edicts, in which a Greek and Egyptian version went together as surely as, in modern times, a French and English version of every treaty between these nations. It is only by means of these translations of an unknown into a known language, that we have any chance of recovering a knowledge of the Egyptian. In the case of the tribe or tribes who erected cities in Central America, their language has not been thus preserved in actual use, nor do any such translations of it exist. The records of the early Spanish conquerors show that the Caciques, and their immediate adherents, were of a different race from the body of the people in several of the States. A grandson of the last king of Quiché, who embraced the Christian religion, left manuscripts, from which it appears that the dominant caste, in that and two neighbouring states, held a constant tradition, that they had immigrated from the north and obtained their power by conquest. When the dominant tribe in Chiapas offered to submit to Cortes, it was in their own name, and in that of the Zoques, Celtales, and Quelenes, whom they had subjected by force. It appears from the narrative, prepared by order of Philip II., in 1580, that the subject tribes continued to use their own languages; and, indeed, the great number still spoken—no less than twenty-six—within the limits of the old province of Guatimala, would have led to the conclusion that such was the case. The Spaniards in Guatimala assumed the place of the dominant tribe; they did not use it as their instrument for governing the

rest; its language ceased, therefore, to be of any importance, or to be cultivated except by the comparatively small number whose mother tongue it was. These deposed rulers were naturally more inclined to rebel against the new government, than the tribes whom they had accustomed to bear a foreign yoke; and consequently suffered most in the course of the struggles which the natives continued to make for independence, so late as the beginning of the last century. In Guatimala, therefore, we find no double versions of edicts, or written contracts of sale, or testamentary deeds, prepared, one in the hieroglyphic writing of the natives, the other in Spanish.[*] The descendants of the race which reared the monuments of Palenque, have retrograded into a barbarism as deep as that of the descendants of the ruder tribes over whom

---

[*] In Mexico, however, there was something of this kind. 'The use of symbolical paintings' says Humboldt, 'as documentary evidence in law suits, was preserved in the Spanish tribunals long after the conquest. The natives being unable to address the judges through the medium of an interpreter, regarded the use of hieroglyphics as doubly necessary. They continued to present them to the different courts of justice established in New Spain (the *Real Audiencia*, the *Sala del Crimen*, and the *Juzgado de Indios*) till the beginning of the seventeenth century. When the Emperor Charles V., having entertained the project of giving an impetus to science in these distant regions, founded in 1553 the University of Mexico, three chairs were established for teaching the Aztec and Otomy languages, and explaining hieroglyphic paintings. It was long considered necessary to have advocates, procurators, and judges, who could understand the emblematic paintings, in which were expressed the claims of litigants, genealogical tables, the old Mexican laws, and the tribute which each *fief* paid to its overlord. Two professorships of languages still (1813) exist at Mexico; but the chair of Mexican antiquities has been suppressed. The use of paintings has become obsolete; not because the Spanish language has made progress among the natives, but because they have learned to retain advocates to plead their causes.' But in none of the specimens of law-books, lists of tribute paid by provinces, or legal documents, of which specimens have been published by Humboldt and Aglio, do we find, except in the case of proper names, anything approaching to an alphabet of words, (like the Chinese,) of syllables, (like that of the Mandshu and Mogols,) or letters. Such an alphabet is found in the phonetic hieroglyphics of the Egyptians; and such an alphabet, there is every appearance, exists in the characters traced on the tablets of Palenque, the altars and idols of Copan, and the MS. of the Dresden library. But in Central America, where alone we can say with certainty these characters are to be found, the native writings do not appear at any time, under the Spanish dominion, to have been used and studied as they were at Mexico. No such documents appear to have been recognized by the tribunals, and the University of Guatimala (founded 1678) had only a professorship of the Kachiquel language, which had been written in Spanish characters from the time of the conquest.

their ancestors ruled. Their arts, their laws, their written language, have perished. Materials do not exist for bridging over the gulf between their language, as spoken at the close of the fifteenth, and as spoken in the middle of the nineteenth century; even although a key could be found to the phonetic powers of the characters they used; and of finding such key there is slender hope. The accounts of the written characters of the nations of Central America, preserved by the early *Conquistadores*, and by the descendants of some of the noble aboriginal families, (at least such of them as have reached the knowledge of the public.) are too vague to serve the purpose. Many manuscripts which might have thrown light upon these topics, are understood to have been long preserved in monasteries, and in the archives of cities and the episcopal sees; but every year in that unsettled and lawless, country must diminish their number, if, indeed, they have not all already perished.

But even assuming that materials should, by some lucky chance, have escaped destruction, which may one day enable the antiquary to read the hand-writing upon these desolate walls—the chilling record of what has ceased to exist, not the scorching prophecy of impending doom—the exciting story of the struggles of ambition, or the instructive moralizings of the sage, must not be looked for. Names and dates—*formulæ* for ascertaining the dates of past events, or the recurrence of festivals, will alone be found—nails in the wall of history, upon which the traditions of a living people once perhaps hung stirring associations, but which to us are nothing more than the dull, dead indication, that something of the kind, we know not what, has been. What of interest will attach to the discovery, will be for a limited public;—for those who have the patience to follow out the minute and tedious inquiries, by which only the first steps in the progress of human knowledge and civilisation can be discovered.

Except, therefore, as affording some presumption that the ruins amid which they are found were reared by men of a common origin, or at least common civilisation, these unknown characters are not likely for a considerable time to yield us much information. We must be contented to detect signs of the intelligence and capabilities of their architects in the fragments of their works that survive—in the indications they afford of progress in the useful and ornamental arts.

It is difficult to speak of such works without unconsciously falling into the language of exaggeration, either in praising or criticising them. There are many things in the ruins of Palenque which indicate a fine and susceptible taste in those who reared them. The inclosure within the inner apartment of the building, in which was found the tablet representing two human figures in the act of making offerings, is of elegant proportions; and the ornamental stucco-work upon the cornice is delicately executed. The object of Messrs. Stephens and Catherwood was to furnish the public at a moderate price, with a work that should convey a correct notion of the general effect of the ruins; and this the engravings published by the former supply. But among the drawings of Captain Caddy are some elaborate copies of the details, executed on a pretty large scale, of the ornamental stucco-work, which suggest a high estimate of the skill and taste which produced them. With regard to the human figures, the countenances are execrable; but the outlines of the bodies and limbs are bold, graceful, and true to nature. The borders in which the figures are contained, show an eye for neatness and finish, and the scroll ornaments are varied and harmoniously arranged The curves of the seeming arches in the corridors are very graceful. Altogether, the effect of these buildings upon the eye—while free from the obscuring shadow of the forest which has crept over them, and upheaved and shattered their walls by the growth of roots—while yet undilapidated, and glaring in the rich colours, of which traces still remain, must have been gay and graceful—something midway in point of effect between the irregular grace of Saracenic, and the severe elegance of Grecian architecture.

Everything, however, about the ruins, seems to indicate a people in whom taste had far outstripped intellect. In external beauty their structures rank higher than they do in the knowledge evinced by them of what may be termed scientific architecture. At Copan there are no symptoms of the constructors of the buildings having advanced so far as to be able to erect permanent covered temples. Their pyramids and sculptured blocks are only one step in advance of cairns, circles, and ranges of stones, like those reared by the Celtic race in Europe. The elaborate carvings with which these idols are overloaded, however much of mechanical neatness they may display, are scarcely more entitled to be called works of art than the equally elaborate carving lavished by New Zealanders on their paddles and canoes. In Palenque we find ornamental interiors; but the helpless make-shifts by which they are produced, carry us back to the infancy of the mason's art. We do not find even that approach to the construction of large flat-roofed halls, by the aid of pillars, which we witness in the temples of Egypt. Graceful buildings are erected by the primitive device of piling flag-stones evenly, one upon another, till the wall has reached the height of ten feet, and then making every layer overlap that beneath it to form a converging ceiling closed by a large flag laid over all. In Palenque, the unsightly ruggedness of this rude structure is covered over by a coat of stucco. At Uxmal 'the ceiling forms a triangular arch, without the keystone as at Palenque; but instead of the rough stones overlapping or being covered with stucco, the layers of stone are bevelled as they rise, and present an even and polished surface.' Their ignorance of the laws of pressure, denied the architects the power to lend to the interiors of their buildings those beauties to which spaciousness and loftiness are requisite; and restricted them to the narrower range of proportion, and richness of detailed ornament on a small scale.

The history of Palenque—with the exception of Uxmal, the most perfect and instructive of those ruined cities which have yet been visited and described by men of European origin and knowledge—is a mere blank. The common story regarding the ruins, repeated by Mr. Stephens, is, that they were casually discovered in 1750 by a party of Spaniards travelling in the province of Chiapas, and subsequently visited and examined, by order of the Spanish government, in 1787 and 1806. There is reason, however, to believe that they were never entirely lost sight of; for Juarros and Fuentes, both of whom had access to the archives of the kingdom of Guatimala, identify the ruins near Palenque with the Culhuacan of the natives. At what time it was deserted might be difficult to determine. The native cities taken by the Spaniards, and in the vicinity of which those marauders have fixed their habitations, have, without one exception, been razed to the ground. The more perfect condition of Culhuacan or Palenque, seems to point to the inference that it was deserted when the more civilized and dominant tribe of the natives, weakened by the struggles with the European invaders, was forced to desert its old abodes; leaving the country to the savage tribes who occupied the forests and mountain recesses. These either could not rebuild the towns as they fell into decay, or not caring to relinquish their forest life, left them unoccupied. But they seem long to have retained their veneration for the fanes and sanctuaries of the deserted habitations. The owner of the ground on which the few vestiges of Gueguetenango are yet to be seen, told Mr. Stephens ' that he had bought the land from Indians, and that for some time after his purchase, he was annoyed by their periodical visits to celebrate some of their ancient rites on the top of this structure, (an ancient place of sacrifice,) and this annoyance continued until he whipped two or three of the principal men, and drove them away.' A considerable time may have elapsed from the first Spanish invasion, before the natives abandoned Culhuacan, the province in which it was situated being retained in a sort of half-independence. So late as 1712 they rose in arms, and had nearly driven the Spaniards from among them. The buildings described by Mr. Stephens were probably erected near the time of the first Spanish invasion   We are led to this conclusion by the account which Juarros has given of the dress and appearance of the natives, on the authority of the history of Guatimala prepared by order of Philip II., and other manuscript documents. It might pass for a description of the figures on the walls of Culhuacan, and shows that these images represent the generations conquered by the Spaniards:—

'The nobles wore a dress of white cotton, dyed or stained with different colours; the use of which was prohibited to the other ranks. This vestment consisted of a shirt and white breeches, decorated with fringes; over these was drawn another pair of breeches, reaching to the knees, and ornamented with a species of embroidery. The legs were bare, the feet protected by sandals, fastening over the instep and at the heel by many thongs of leather; the sleeves of the shirt were looped above the elbow, with a blue or red band; the hair was worn long, and tressed behind with a cord of the colour used upon the sleeves, and terminating in a tassel, which was a distinction peculiar to the great captains; the waist was girded with a piece of cloth of various colours, fastened in a knot before: over the shoulders was thrown a white mantle, ornamented with figures of birds, lions, and other decorations, of cord and fringe. The ears and lower lip were pierced to receive star-shaped pendants of gold or silver; the insignia of office or dignity were carried in the hand. The Indians of modern times differ from the ancients only in wearing the hair short, the sleeves loose, and by the omission of earrings and lip ornaments. The civilized natives dress with great decency. * * The habit of the Mazaguales is simple and very poor; they are not permitted the use of cotton, and substitute for it cloth made of *pita*. The dress is simply a long shirt, the flaps of which are drawn between the legs and fastened: a piece of the same stuff is tied round the waist, and a similar piece forms a covering for the head."

Throughout the provinces where the ruins examined by Mr. Stephens are found, there were a number of petty Caciques, sometimes asserting independence, sometimes reduced to a state of subjection by some more valiant and able neighbour;—a multiplicity of petty states constantly growing and declining, extending or narrowing their frontiers, shifting and changing like the little kingdoms of South Britain in the early Saxon times. The anxiety of the dominant caste or tribe to preserve itself pure was, according to Juarros, very great:—

'To the offices of lieutenants and councillors, and even down to doorkeepers of the council, none but those of noble race were admitted, and there was no instance of any person being appointed to a public office, high or low, who was not selected from the nobility; for which reason great anxiety was felt by them to keep the purity of their lineage unsullied. To preserve this rank untainted in blood, it was decreed by the law, that if any cacique or noble should marry a woman who was not of noble family, he should be degraded to the caste of mazagual or plebeian, assume the name of his wife, be subject to all the duties and services imposed upon the plebeians, and his estates be sequestered to the king, leaving him only a sufficiency for a decent maintenance in his sphere of mazagual.'

The most accurate test of the progress of any country in civilisation is to be found in its penal laws. They indicate what men deem honourable, what shameful, and the character of their punishments shows how far their feelings have been softened and humanized. Taken in this point of view, Juarros' brief recapitulation of the principal penal laws of Quiché increases materially our acquaintance with the men who reared and occupied the structures of which we have been speaking:—

'The king was liable to be tried, and if convicted of extreme cruelty and tyranny, was deposed by the Ahaguoes, who for this purpose assembled a council with great secrecy: the next in succession according to law was placed on the throne, and his ejected predecessor punished by confiscation of all his property, and, as some writers affirm, put to death by decapitation. If a queen was guilty of adultery with a noble person, both she and the accomplice were strangled; but, if, forgetting her dignity, she had criminal intercourse with a commoner, they were thrown from a very high rock. If the ahaguoes impeded the collection of the tributes, or were fomenters of any conspiracy, they were condemned to death, and all the members of their families sold as slaves. Whoever was guilty of crimes against the king or the public, or convicted of homicide, was punished by death, the sequestration of property, and the slavery of his relations. Robbers were sentenced to pay the value of the things stolen, and a fine besides; for the second offence, the fine was doubled; and for the third, they were punished with death unless the calpul would redeem them; but, if they transgressed a fourth time they were thrown from a rock. Rape was punished by death. Incendiaries were deemed enemies of their country, because, said the law, fire has no bounds, and by setting fire to a house, a whole town might be destroyed; and this would be public treason; therefore death was the punishment awarded against the perpetrator, and his family was banished from the kingdom. A simarron, or runaway from the authority of his master, paid a fine to his calpul of a certain quantity of blankets; but the second offence was punished by death. The stealing of things sacred, the profanation of the temples, and contumacy to the ministers of the idols, subjected the offender to the punishment of death, and all his family were declared infamous. They had a law which is still (1800) in use; whenever a young man wished to marry, he was bound to serve the parents of his intended wife for a certain time, and make them stipulated presents; but if they afterwards rejected his proposals, they were compelled to return the things received, and serve him an equal number of days * * The manner of bringing the accused to trial was cruel and unjust; for not having the privilege of appeal when brought before the judge, he was, if he confessed the crime, immediately taken from the tribunal to undergo the punishment awarded by the laws; and if he denied the charge, he was cruelly tortured to make him confess—he was stripped naked, suspended by the thumbs, and in that situation severely flogged and smoked with chile.'

These are the laws of a people sufficiently emerged from the mere savage state to recognize the necessity of moral discipline, but still far from being humanized in their sentiments. In their harshness, their progress in art, their powerful priesthood, their secrecy of their patrician councils—the very doors of which were kept by members of the order—their skill in some mechanical arts, we recognize a people which had attained to a degree of civilisation, parallel to what we can conceive existing in the petty states among which Rome grew up, and upon whose ruins it built its empire. It is strange, that in none of the monuments figured by Mr. Catherwood do we find any trace of the astrological hieroglyphics, of which so many specimens are preserved in the calendars of Mexico, delineated on Agave paper, or graven upon stone This is the more remarkable, because Boturini expressly states, that the calendar used by the inhabitants of the province of Chiapas, (in which the ruins near Palenque are situ-

ated, differed from that used by the Mexicans only in the names which they gave to
the twenty days of which their month consisted.

In pointing out the most important facts
elicited by the researches of Mr. Stephens,
and his predecessors, we have confined ourselves to the monuments found within the
territories of the republic of Central America and Chiapas, and the Mexican province
of Yucatan.   The study of such antiquities
is of little value, except in so far as it furnishes materials for comparing what progress has been made by different communities residing far apart, and influenced by
different economical and political relations,
with a view to throw light upon the history
of society.   Even Humboldt has not always been sufficiently careful to discrimi-
nate, in the accounts he has given of American antiquities, between what customs or
monuments appear to have been common
to the inhabitants of Mexico, Oaxaca, and
Chiapas, and what were peculiar to the
people inhabiting one or other of these districts; and where he is inaccurate, others
have fallen into utter confusion.   One branch
alone of the antiquities of the northern
continent of America, has been skilfully
and accurately examined; namely, the calendar of the fallen Mexicans, and the
knowledge and opinions upon which it was
founded.   Much rubbish must be swept
away, before we can ascertain what is really
known of American antiquities; and before this field has been cleared of the entanglements and errors which have been
allowed to accumulate upon it, it would be
in vain to think of instituting comparisons
between what the nations found by the
Spaniards had effected, with what had been
accomplished by early Asiatic or European
nations; either with a view to trace the
origin of the Americans, or to throw light
upon the natural history of society.

Apart from the interest which the student of history and human nature must take
in such investigations, everything that can
throw light upon the character of their aboriginal population, has a deep practical import for the inhabitants of the Spanish republics of North America.   The two races have
never blended ; and in many provinces the
Indians far outnumber the Creoles.   The
fact mentioned by the proprietor of the site
of Gueguetenango, shows how much of the
leaven of their old superstitions is yet left
among the natives.   Even where they have
embraced Christianity, they affect having
saints of their own, whom they prefer to
those of the whites.   The legends of the
Roman Catholic Church have assumed a

local colouring in Central America, which
to a stranger appears sufficiently startling.
They are a population if possible still more
ignorant, savage, and excitable, than the
dregs of the French population at the time
of their first revolution ; and moreover, they
are distinguished from the hitherto dominant *caste* by blood, language, features, and
colour.   The fierce struggles between the
partisans of Federal and Centralized government, had, at the time of Mr. Stephens'
visit, thrown the power into the hands of the
Indians; much in the same way that the
struggle between the adherents of the monarchy and the republicans threw it into the
hands of the *sans culottes* during the Reign of
Terror.

Mr. Stephens, we are informed, undismayed by the discomforts and dangers he
encountered in his first expedition, has returned to Guatimala. This has the appearance of being in earnest; and we are bound
to wish all success to inquiries of such an
interesting description, and from which further and more matured information may be
reasonably expected.   The work before us,
notwithstanding considerable defects and
blemishes, is by no means deficient in indications of shrewdness, literary ambition,
and perseverance.   There can be little
doubt that Mr. Stephens will find ample
materials for another ; and we shall look
forward to its appearance, in due season,
with considerable expectations.

Art. IV.— *The History of Duelling.* By
J. G. Millingen, M. D., F. R. S., 2 volumes 8vo. London : 1841.

These volumes present copious details respecting a practice altogether peculiar to
the modern world. They might, perhaps,
have been made somewhat more interesting and the epochs might have been better and
more clearly distinguished ; but very great
praise is due to the diligence with which the
materials have been collected, and to the
good sense and feeling which characterize
the author's remarks   No traces of Duelling are to be found among any of the nations of antiquity.   That one man should
endanger or lose his own life, or take
away that of another, for an offence, ninety-
nine cases out of a hundred, confessedly undeserving the punishment menaced or inflicted ; that this should be everywhere
done in defiance of law and religion ; that
the perpetrating the act should be esteem-

ed meritorious—resistance to it dishonourable ; and that this anomalous violation of humanity, law and religion, should be the claimed and exclusive privilege of the most refined and best educated portion of society, are facts for the history and exemplification of which, strange to say, we must limit our inquiries to the civilized communities of Christendom. It would be idle to refer for similar instances to the single combats that have taken place in front of hostile armies, or to the delegated contests between champions selected to settle the quarrels of nations or tribes. These had nothing in common with 'the Duel' beyond mere fighting ; the motives, the sanctions, the issues were totally different ; self-devotion and obedience distinguished the one, selfishness and insubordination characterize the other.

But we utterly repudiate any other relationship than that of co-existence between the meek and forgiving spirit of Christianity and the proud anti-social practice of duelling. It has been generally referred to the customs and superstitions of the barbarous nations by whom the Roman Empire of the west was overthrown. Trials by ordeal, that is, by appeals to the Deity, were indeed in great esteem amongst them ; but these have been more or less common to all ignorant and superstitious nations, and are in practice in many parts of the world at this day. The Hindoos have no less than nine different methods of extracting justice by the pressure of the ordeal. So also, violent and insubordinate appeals to the sword and to brute force, for the vindication of wrongs, have ever been common to all nations. These practices, therefore, although our forefathers had them in excess, they held in common with other races ; but that which, with some few and obscure exceptions, appears to have been peculiar to them, was the formal and judicial appointment of single combat for the settlement of litigation. Cæsar and Tacitus state, that the elder Germans determined disputed claims to property and even to office by the sword ; and when conquest gave greater notoriety to their customs, we find these statements verified by their laws. There is a law of Gundebald the Burgundian, (A. D. 501,) enacting, as a remedy against obstinacy and avarice, that all controversies shall be decided by the sword ; and Frothius the Dane—a worthy descendant of those heroes who, after death, according to the Edda, were rewarded at the court of Odin, 'by being indulged every morning as soon they were dressed, by going out into the court to fight with each other till the close of the day, when they returned to Valhalla to drink beer or mead'—decreed *Speciosius viribus quam verbis confligendum esse casum.* This was not mincing the matter ; and even after some little advance in the repression of disorder, we find Luitprand (701) proclaiming, 'we are not convinced of the justice of what is called the judgment of God ; since we have found that many innocent persons have perished in defending a good cause; but this custom is of such antiquity amongst the Lombards that we cannot abolish it, notwithstanding its impiety.' These laws and customs are the true sources of the duel ; and it is from this ancient practice of making the sword the scale of justice, that the modern duel, modified from time to time, has descended to us While we thus trace its source to the ignorance and ferocity of our Gothic ancestors, it is truly humiliating that it should be continued to the present day ;—that the English gentleman of the nineteenth century should join with the Lombard of the eighth century, in saying 'we cannot abolish it, notwithstanding its impiety.'

This, however, is not without its explanation. There is no such thing as a radical change in the customs of nations, seldom even of individuals ; and those who examine the peculiarities of different races, well know how long the customs and institutions of early ages survive amongst, and characterize their descendants. There are still strong resemblances in all the branches of the great Gothic stem—split and separated as they have long been, under different forms of government, belief, language, and pursuits ; so, too, among the Celts, the Jews universally, and in like manner all the other great families of the earth. Generations pass away, with their attendant convulsions, before ancient prejudices, traditions, and practices, are eradicated ; time but softens their features, and in the great chain of cause and effect they are often, when lost to sight, still felt and found operating. It is thus that the judicial combat survives in our modern duel, and that in defiance of strong opposing influences.

The judicial combat besides, was upheld, though modified, by the feudal system ;— that mixture of liberty and oppression without which Europe might have run the course of the ancient eastern monarchies, and lost, with the liberty of fighting, the development of its liberty of thinking; for the right of each individual chief to ' do what he liked with his own,' and which he exercised as well as claimed, prevented the overshadowing pretensions of him who was supreme. Anarchy mitigated monarchy; and to the thousand small despots, perched on their robber crags, defending their own peculiar town from all others, while they plundered it themselves, we owe the balance of power, and the confederate institutions of Europe. So, also, we owe the continuation of the duel; for there was no one privilege that these chiefs more zealously upheld than that of fighting their own battles, and judging in their own quarrels. But whatever may have been the ultimate happy results of this system, the immediate issue was misery. The whole of middle Europe was scourged by war and bloodshed, rapine and revenge. Urban II., when he called on the faithful at the council of Clermont to join the crusade, thus describes their conduct—'Redeem by a service so agreeable to God, your pillages, conflagrations, homicides, and other mortal crimes' The Emperor Frederic II. forbade his nobles 'from plundering travellers and circulating base coin, which had hitherto been considered their privilege' This state of things naturally produced counteracting efforts and associations. The church lent its aid in the support of order. The truce of God, promulgated in 1041, forbade fighting on all festivals, and from Wednesday night till Monday morning, monasteries and asylums were opened for the penitent and the persecuted. Burghers obtained charters of defence, neighbouring towns formed leagues, and that which more immediately regards our present subject, Societies and Holy Brotherhoods were established of persons devoted to the defence of the weak, the wayfaring, and the oppressed: hence Knighthood, to whose inheritance the judicial combat fell. Scott says, the investiture of chivalry was brought to resemble as much as possible the administration of the sacraments of the church. Certainly the chastisement of the oppressor, and the assertion of individual honour and integrity were the device, as they not unfrequently were the gallant achievement, of the devoted knight.

This was the second stage of the single combat, under which it assumed a higher and a better tone. Henceforth we may trace its course more clearly; and it may not be unamusing, if, with the assistance of Dr. Millingen's materials, we hastily run over this piece of history, and mark the successive stages of those appeals which have taken place since Queen Emma dared the red-hot ploughshares, until the day when Mirfin, the linen-draper's apprentice, killed in single combat Elliott, the innkeeper's son.

We have already alluded to authentic records of the trial by single combat so early as the sixth century. The vigour and good sense of Charlemagne checked it for a while, but it broke out afresh under his feeble successors; and Otho II. re-established it in all its early vigour;—his decree at Verona extending its obligations to the clergy and to women—allowing them, however, substitutes or champions. The Danes went beyond this; for their wives and daughters were obliged to defend their own honour personally. But, in order to give them fair play, the man whom they fought was planted in a pit up to the waist, in order that his gentle antagonist might wheel about him, and strike him on the head with a sling or leathern thong, to which a heavy stone was attached—he, meanwhile, defending himself with a club; and if he missed his assailant three times, or struck the ground instead of her, he was pronounced to be vanquished. In England, Selden tells us, the trial by single combat was unknown before the Conquest; compensation was the usual mode of satisfaction, and is especially enjoined by a law of Alfred. If we desire a precedent for our damages in actions for 'criminal conversation,' we may find it in a law of Ethelred, declaring that whoever hath committed adultery with his neighbour's wife shall be obliged to buy him a new one. But the Conqueror introduced the fiercer habits of his Normans: his first act was to challenge Harold to single combat for his kingdom; and the only restriction on the trial of battle to be found in his constitutions is, that 'no priest shall fight without leave of his bishop.' It is from this time, too, that the custom dates of the pageant of a Champion attending the coronation festival of our Kings. Rude as these judicial combats were, still there was something searching and solemn in them. The sanctions of oaths, fastings, prayers, purgations, and masses, were skilfully applied. Each combatant staked his life, his honour, and his all, upon the truth of his declaration. If he failed, he was led forth dishonoured to execution; if slain, his body was hanged or otherwise insulted. At Halle a confessor, as well as a second, was always in attendance; and a bier surrounded with torches awaited the vanquished at the ends of the lists. We can easily conceive the awe with which the guilty and superstitious combatant would approach lists thus prepared. No doubt the alarmed consciences of many bade them yield up the foul plunder, or recede from their false accusations, rather than face such a trial;

and thus far this wager of battle, much as we may ridicule it now, had its advantages in those days of ignorant violence ; and the day may come when the cobweb intricacies, the ruinous expenses, and judgment deferred for years, nay, sometimes for generations, of some of our Law Courts, shall appear scarcely less barbarous, or less a mockery of justice, than these summary proceedings of our Norman forefathers. In fact, when the judges were counts, marquesses, and rude soldiers, few of whom could either read or write, perhaps the best method of settling a question was to let the litigants fight it out.

In England the combat was allowed only in the Court of Chivalry, or in appeals, or upon issue joined in writs of right. The Court of Chivalry was restricted, so early as the time of Richard II., to only such things touching war within the realm, which could not be redressed by common law; and these respected more especially, giving relief to such of the nobility and gentry as should think themselves aggrieved in matters of honour. But being no court of record it soon fell into disuse ; and the office of High Constable, under whom it was originally held, ceased with the attainder of Stafford Duke of Buckingham. But the constitutions of Clarendon, by establishing the trial by jury and grand assize under Henry II., were the most effectual means for placing litigation and the administration of law on its proper basis. These constitutions were confirmed and extended by Edward I., who did more for settling the distributive justice of his kingdom, than has perhaps been done in all the after ages. And this country was thus, by the early substitution of wise laws, imbued with a spirit of justice which has stood it in good stead on many a passionate day.

The trial by combat flourished much more vigorously and much longer amongst our vivacious neighbours in France. So late as the time of St. Louis, not only could plaintiffs and defendants appeal to the sword, but even witnesses attested the truth of their evidence by it ; and the judge himself was subject to defend his sentence in the lists, provided he were not the liege lord of either of the litigants. No doubt, many an unseated member of the present day longs for those good old French laws, which would give him a last chance of retaining his seat, by exclaiming to the chairman of his election committee, ' Thou liest, and I am ready to defend my body against thine ; and that thou shalt either be a corpse or a recreant any hour of the day !' But Philip III. reformed these matters, by

requiring, before he would grant his license for a combat, the concurrence of the four following circumstances ; namely, that the crime had been committed, and that it could not be ascertained by whom—that the crime was of such a nature as to incur the penalty of death—that there was no other means of discovering the culprit— and lastly, that there were such strong presumptions against the accused that the duel was granted him in lieu of torture and the question. This necessarily restricted the number of cases ; but though thus cautiously granted, Voet adds, ' the method was hurtful, and contrary to canonical, divine, and natural law.'

One of the earliest English trials by combat, of which we have any record, is that of the Count d'Eu, who, accused by Godefroi Baynard of a conspiracy against William Rufus, was allowed a field at Salisbury ; where, in the presence of the king and his court, having been defeated, he was, by his order, cruelly mutilated, his eyes put out, and his esquire whipped and hanged.

A more romantic instance is recorded of a count of Modena, who, imitating the continence, met (from Maria of Aragon, the Emperor Otho's wife) the treatment of the Jewish Patriarch It was in vain that he protested his innocence ; all that he was allowed was a field, where he was conquered and beheaded His wife, nothing daunted, laid his bleeding head at the feet of the Emperor, demanding vengeance—' Of whom?' replied the Emperor ?—' Of you, Cæsar,' she replied, ' who have sanctioned an iniquity, as I am ready to prove the innocence of my husband by the ordeal of fire ' A brazier of red-hot iron decided the case; for seizing it without fear and without injury, she again demanded of the Emperor his own head for having put to death an innocent man. The chronicle adds, that the Emperor, demurring to this proposal, graciously compromised the matter, by ordering his own wife to be burned alive— and which was accordingly executed at Modena, A.D. 998.

But perhaps the most singular occurrence of the kind took place at Toledo, under the Pontificate of Gregory the Great, and in furtherance of his ambitious projects. We take the abridged account from Dr. Waddington's excellent ' History of the Church,' It seems the Gothic had gradually superseded the Roman missal in Spain. The Pope's legate and Caroline, Queen of Castile, were desirous of restoring it. The nobility, the people, and even a majority of the clergy, warmly supported their own established ritual; and, after some struggles, a day was appointed to decide on the merits of the rival missals   This was to be done by the trial of combat.   Two knights contended in the presence of a vast assembly, and the Gothic champion prevailed.   The Court, dissatisfied with the result, subjected the missals to a second proof, and which they were to sustain in their own substances—the trial by fire.   Again the Gothic missal triumphed, escaping unhurt from the flames in which its rival was consumed. The triumph now seemed complete, when it was discovered that the ashes of the Roman missal had curled to the top of the flames and leaped out of them.   By this *miracle* the scales were turned ; or, at all events, the victory of the Gothic missal sufficiently impeached to allow the establishment of both missals, whereby the Papal object was gained ; for the Roman missal, once introduced, was soon made to work on the other ; and the Spaniards by this worthy process thus lost the inestimable benefit of having the service performed in their native tongue.

But these were solutions for the darkest ages, and the glimmerings of reason even then dawning, required more fitting forms of adjudication for such questions.   The pen commenced those encroachments upon the sword which have continued to the present day : and which will last until, perhaps, national even as well as individual combats shall be viewed only as proofs of bygone barbarism.   Meanwhile personal safety, advancement, and distinction, were to be found only in the profession and expert management of arms.   There was no other amusement or occupation, save the chase or the cloister, for the gentry.   Litigation and the courts of law were for women, gownsmen, and the ignoble.   Force ruled, and combats were fought, without honour and without mercy, in defence or disproof of crimes which the judge and the headsman had more fittingly investigated, and which sowed the seeds of endless feuds. Witness the fatal Hereford and Norfolk duel, which, weakly granted and still more weakly interrupted, first gave a beginning to those wars, of which old Fuller quaintly says, ‘the red rose grew pale from the blood it lost, and the white red from shedding it.’   Queen Elizabeth’s Westminster Hall, or Star-Chamber, would have crushed the cockatrice’s egg in the nest.   But the remedy was approaching.   The consolidation of the European kingdoms, and of the monarchical power, gave effect to general law ; and single combat, as a judicial proceeding for the trial of offences against the state, or of criminal violence, did not survive

the fifteenth century.   But it took a new field, and precisely where offences abounded. and where the law was dumb ; namely, the vindication of offended honour—honour, a vague, sensitive, and pugnacious quality, which the state itself cherished and required from its nobles, but whose defence and assertion it committed to their individual care and valour.   Much of this modern honour grew out of chivalry, of its mixed monastic, warlike, and celibate state.   Its best quality was its deference to, and defence of the weaker sex.   The ancient Knight went ‘pricking’ on his way, and had his rugged hands full of business.   His successors found fewer subjects for the exhibition of their prowess.   Time, numbers, wealth, power, and distinction, exercised their influences ; and the lack of adventure was supplied by a fantastic code, which became the manual of social intercourse, and the text-book of single combat among the higher classes ; and which, more or less modified, survives to the present hour.   Rules of honour, subjects of offence, methods of reparation, modes of proceeding, privileges of challengers, duties of seconds, and other details, were laid down, subdivided, and expounded, with all the subtlety of the middle ages, and with an industry worthy of a better subject.   Puffendorf and Grotius have not more rigidly investigated the laws of nations and belligerents than Mutio, Fausto, Attendolo, and Guistinopolitano the noble science of giving and taking offence.   There were detailed no less than thirty-two different species of lies !

Italy was the first great field for this modified single combat, or more properly, the duel ; as it was also the principal parent of the most elaborate treatises respecting it, the fabricators of the best arms, and the purveyor of the ablest ‘masters of fence.’ Thence the rage spread with redoubled fury into France. Spain, and the Empire.   In England we hear little of it before the profligate days of the Stuarts.

But it is France that affords the most detailed and authorised records of duelling. The French Kings and Parliament long maintained its formal and practical legality ; and Francis the First, while he set an example to the world of a dishonourable breach of his own plighted word, did not shrink from attaching a sanguinary importance to . *the lie ;* by proclaiming ‘that it was never to be put up with without satisfaction, but by a base-born fellow.’   Henry II. presided, with his whole court—the Constable, the Admiral, and the Marshals of France—at the combat between Farnac and La Chasteneraye, on a charge of scandal, which terminated in the death of La Chasteneraye; when Farnac, his hands yet reeking with his kinsman's blood, lifted them up to heaven and exclaimed, 'Not unto me, O Lord, but unto thy name, be thanks!' Henry II. might have stopped this duel at any moment, and was entreated to do so by Farnac when his adversary's life was in his power; but the king, from a feeling of *honour*, refused; and he himself, not long afterwards, met his death in a tournament Charles IX. was the last French king who presided at one of these exhibitions; but to give him his due, so also was he the first who sought to check the practice, by naming a 'Court of Honour' for the satisfaction of offences committed against its laws. And it was indeed full time; for while France and Frenchmen were boasting of this their idol honour, their country was becoming a mere charnel-house: the wars of Italy and of the League, with the breaking-up of all moral and religious restraints, had reduced society to such a state, that, during the comparatively quiet and vigorous twenty years of Henry IV.'s reign, and in defiance of his edicts, inflicting the penalty of death on all duellists, there fell in duels, within the then comparatively small number of gentlemen bearing arms in France, no less than 4000, while upwards of 14,000 pardons were granted for fighting The king himself, despite his own laws, and humane remonstrances of the brave and wise Sully, encouraged the practice. Writing to his friend Duplessis Mornay, who had complained of having been insulted, he says:— 'I feel much hurt at hearing of the insult you have received, and in which I sympathize, both as your sovereign and your friend. In the first capacity I shall see justice done, both for your sake and for mine; and if I bore only the second, you should find me most ready to draw my sword and expose my life for you.' With such an encouragement, no wonder that the person who did not fight—who had not killed his man, at least one man—should be held scarcely worthy of the name of gentleman. Lord Herbert of Cherbury, who was in France in the following reign, testifies joyously, as was to be expected of him, to the fact. But the evil did not rest here; for, when satisfaction was not taken by what is called fair means, it was held scarcely less *honourable* to take it by foul. All France went mad upon the duel. Montaigne says, 'Put three Frenchmen on the Libyan desert, and they would not be there a month without fighting.' The Bishop of Rhodes, in his life of Henry IV., says 'The madness of duels did seize the spirits of the nobility so much, that they lost more blood by each other's hands in time of peace, than had been shed by their enemies in battle.' In one province alone, there were killed in seven months, according to Chevalier, no less than one hundred and twenty gentlemen. There is a laudatory account, in Brantôme, of a worthy noble of Franche Comté who ran his companion through the body in the very porch of a church; and of two others who fought it out before the altar, to decide which had the best right to the first use of the censer! A contemporary journal says, Aug. 6, 1606:—Last week we had in Paris four assassinations 'and three duels, but no notice was taken of them.' Whole families became exterminated. As a worthy illustration, the same authority relates how a certain Socilles seduced the wife of Devese, who, in revenge, attempts twice to assassinate him, under a pretext of calling him out; for which he is dismissed by the king, who authorizes Socilles 'to attack him in whatever manner he may think proper, and to seize upon his property.' A reconciliation is proposed by means of a family marriage, to which Socilles consents, but, instead of marrying, seduces Devese's sister; for which Devese again waylays, and at length succeeds in assassinating him; whereupon a relation of Socilles procures the assassination of Devese. Are we to wonder that the assassin's knife at length reached the heart of a king who suffered such deeds to go unpunished? The eldest son of the Duc de Guise ran the Count de St Pol through the body in the streets of Rheims: two years afterwards Henry IV. made him Governor of Provence.

And while the king thus rewarded, the ladies of France, like the Roman women, who loved the gladiators, delighted in these men of blood. Lord Herbert on one occasion says, 'All things being ready for the ball, and I being near the queen (Anne of Austria),expecting when the dancers should begin, some one knocked at the door, louder, methought, than became a civil person. When he came in there was a sudden whisper amongst the ladies, saying, "C'est Monsieur Balaguy." Whereupon I also saw the ladies, one after another, invite him to sit near them; and when one lady had his company awhile, another would say, "You have engaged him long enough—I must have him now." At which bold civility of them, though I was astonished, yet it added to my wonder that his person could not be thought handsome—his hair half grey, his doublet but of sackcloth, and his breeches of plain grey cloth. Informing myself by some standers-by who he was, I was told that he was one of the gallantest men in the world, having killed eight or nine men in single fight, and that for this reason the ladies made so much of him.'

The rage was universal, and was in no degree confined to soldiers and to France. Ignatius Loyola himself called out a Moor for denying the divinity of our Saviour. Cardinal de Retz fought two duels during the Fronde; Cardinal d'Este presided at a duel at Ferrara; and so late as 1669, it was found necessary in Spain to renew a decree of the old council of Pennafiel, forbidding challenges being sent to bishops and canons. Not content that the principals fought, their seconds, thirds, and fourths also engaged from the sheer love of fighting; without any shadow of quarrel, or even acquaintance, and all in the name of honour and chivalry! Undoubtedly a high, but, as we believe, a most mistaken sense of honour actuated some of these combatants; but its dictates came not from the sanguinary custom of duelling, to which they gave way, but from the native magnanimity of their own hearts. This it was, for instance, that made Gustavus Adolphus, when at the height of his glory, follow Colonel Seaton, (one of his Scotch officers whom he had hastily offended,) and after reproaching himself for his want of temper, overtake him and exclaim—'Dismount, sir! I acknowledge that I have injured you, and I have come to give you the satisfaction of a gentleman; for we are now without my dominions, and Gustavus and you are equal!' But examples like this were the exceptions; the prevailing characteristic was violence, fraud, and contempt of life. In order rightly to estimate this spirit, one has only to mark the cold-blooded and pleasant strain with which the light-hearted, and perhaps good-hearted, Brantôme recounts its memorable deeds. He speaks of the most savage as of the greatest exploits: he tells with delight of 'ce très-beau combat' between Quielus and D'Entragues, and their seconds and thirds; these latter fighting 'par envie de mener les mains'—for the very pleasure of the thing. He grieves that there were only three or four common people present, 'wretched witnesses of the valour of these heroes:' he is proud that four out of the six fell; and, with scarcely a comment, he relates how D'Entragues owed his success to a dagger he had secretly

provided, and with which he hacked and stabbed the unfortunate Quielus, mocking him as he exclaimed, 'You have a dagger and I have none!' But his favourite hero is a Neapolitan, who killed his three men, one after another, on the same morning, and on the same spot, leaving them there with all possible indifference—'tous trois morts à la garde de Dieu pour estre enterrez.'

Now, while these human sacrifices were thus offered up on the altar of honour, what was its real value and influence? Nothing, or worse than nothing. We dwell on this period because it has been so often bepraised or referred to as the high and glorious reign of chivalry and honour; and because later, it has been said with a taunting and eloquent lament, that the age of chivalry had passed. What was it—and what was its fruits? When Bayard, the chevalier *sans peur et sans reproche*, was, with all the ceremonies of courtesy, honour, and religion, running Don Alonzo di Soto Maior through the body, for having complained of his lack of courtesy to him while his prisoner, and while the code of honour was the text-book of civilized Europe, Macchiavelli was writing his *Prince;* the Borgias were poisoning, plundering, or committing incest; the Sforza and Medici imitating them; one Pope finding his death in the poisoned elements of the eucharist; another blessing the massacre of St. Bartholomew; and a third instigating traitors to make the elevation of the host the signal for assassination at the altar; Louis XI. was giving lessons on successful fraud and villany, which the League brought to maturity; Philip II. was writing in blood and persecution the precepts of Ferdinand; and the court of Henry VIII. was the centre of baseness, apostasy, confiscation, and murder. In fact, profligacy, licentiousness, and practical atheism reigned almost unchecked and unabashed throughout Europe, during this era of *les preux chevaliers,* whose lips loudly professed the honour their acts grossly profaned.

If such were the unrebuked practices of the leaders, the deeds of their followers and subordinates kept pace with them. It is also specially to be observed, that many of these offences were precisely those which all just notions of honour should most reprobate—want of truth, of courtesy, and of mercy—praise of fraud and violence. Every portrait that has descended to us of the heroes of those days, has his dagger at his side—the weapon or the guard of the assassin. What are we to think of the comparatively late age of Henry II., that allowed M. de Fandilles to refuse to enter the lists until there had been erected a gallows, and a fire had been prepared for him on which to hang or burn his adversary, the Baron des Guerres ; or of the spirit of fair play which supported a Monsieur Malecolom, who, having dispatched his own adversary, and finding his companion slow in doing the same by his, went to his assistance—thus making two against one ; and on his victim remonstrating against this treachery, coolly replying, 'I have killed my opponent, and if you kill my companion, there may be a chance that you may also kill me—therefore here goes ;' or of the generosity of Marshal St. André's nephew, who, while hunting with Charles IX., picked a quarrel with Matas, an ancient officer, who quickly disarmed him, and was in the act of restoring his sword with some wholesome advice, when the youthful hero, watching his opportunity, stabbed him in the back and rode off, leaving him dead on the field ? No notice, adds the chronicler of the day, was taken of this transaction ; nay, Matas was blamed for having rebuked a fiery and *honourable* youth.—It is a pity to taunt a youth in the bud, it grieves God, *Dieu s'en attriste.* Or, take as a sample, the following epistle from one of the heroes of Henry IV.'s time :—'I have reduced your home to ashes ; I have dishonoured your wife and hanged your children ; and I now have the honour to be your mortal enemy.—La Garde.' Rightly did this ruffian perish by the sword he delighted in ! Perfidy was not confined to the Continent. Creighton, Lord Sanquhar, lost his eye in practising with one Turner a fencing-master ; four years afterwards he was presented to Henry IV., who asked him, 'Does the man live who inflicted that wound ?' whereupon he thought it incumbent on his honour to return to England, and hire a couple of bravoes to assassinate the wretched fencing-master, although he had already pardoned him. In Milan, not a day passed that parties were not found fighting in the streets, and leaving the dead bodies of their adversaries on the pavement. People resorted there from all countries to learn the *noble art of fence*, and to practise secret and cunning feints and strokes. Here too were numerous bravoes, who let themselves out for hire, to fight for those who were not disposed to risk their own lives This extended to Spain ; and hence that secret stabbing, which in fact grew out of duelling, although duelling has

occasionally been defended as the safeguard and preventive of it. As a specimen of the man of honour, and of the times, we cannot do better than give an abridgement of Brantôme's account of 'the Paragon of France.'

'Duprat, Baron de Vitaux, the *Paragon of France*, was son of Chancellor Duprat, and from early life displayed symptoms of undaunted courage. He commenced his career in arms by killing the Baron de Soupez, who threw a candlestick at him at dinner and broke his head ; for which he waylaid him on the road to Toulouse, and having dispatched him, escaped (*bravement*) in a woman's clothes. His next exploit was to murder Monsieur de Gonnelieu, the master of the horse to Charles IX., in revenge for the death of one of his brothers, a lad of fifteen, whom Gonnelieu had treacherously slain. Fearing the king's resentment, he fled to Italy, but shortly returned in order to revenge the death of another brother, who had just been killed by his own near relation the Baron de Mittaud. He remained concealed in an obscure lodging on the Quai des Augustins, and allowed his beard to grow ; and disguising himself as a lawyer he watched for the baron, in company with his companions, the two Baucicauts, "brave and valiant men, and called the Lions of Vitaux." At length meeting with him, they all set on him and slew him, and again fled, and again obtained pardon. But Monsieur de Gua, a gallant and distinguished officer and a favourite of the king's, opposed the grant of Vitaux's pardon ; wherefore the Paragon stole into his house with seven or eight companions, and dispatched him in his bed. 'This act,' says Brantôme, 'was considered one of great resolution and assurance. But he was again pardoned through the interest of the Duc d'Alençon and Queen Marguerite. However, his hour at length came—the brother of the Baron de Mittaud, whom he had assassinated eight years ago, called him out, and *securing himself with a cuirass under* his clothes, and painted flesh-colour to escape detection, the sword of Vitaux bent against it ; it was in vain that he repeated his thrusts, the baron's brother quietly running him through and through without having the courtesy to offer him his life. Thus,' says Brantôme, 'died this brave baron, the Paragon of France, where he was as much esteemed as in Spain, Germany, Poland, and England, and every foreigner who came to court was most anxious to behold him : he was small in stature but lofty in courage ; and though his enemies pretended that he did not kill people fairly, but had recourse to various stratagems, still it is the opinion of great captains, even Italians, who are always the best avengers in the world, that stratagem might be encountered by stratagem without any breach of honour.'

Such were the duels, such the heroes—the men of honour—of the renowned age of chivalry. There is no cant more truly such, than that which boasts of its heroism, devotion, and virtues; which were in fact little other than gross crimes, gilded over by diseased public opinion. The real virtues of the age lay deeper in the subsoil, and ultimately, and after severe trials, brought forth their fruit in better morals, better knowledge, better feelings, and better government. These are essentially opposed to the whole theory and practice of duelling, and have from that day to this been softening, modifying, narrowing, and diminishing it. We do not mean to say that duelling may not, in those bad days, have had some uses, as the trial by combat had in darker ones; but that on which we insist is, that its abuses and evils predominated, as they ever will. The work of repression went on with the march of civilisation. The church, the first civilizer, had long since led the way, and the Council of Trent declared, that 'the detestable practice of duels, which been introduced by the artifices of the devil, in order to destroy the soul after having cruelly killed the body, should be utterly abolished among Christians:' it excommunicated ' all emperors, kings, dukes, princes, marquesses, counts, and other temporal lords, of whatever denomination, who shall assign or grant any place for a duel between Christians; and the principals and seconds are excommunicated, their persons declared infamous, their goods confiscated, and their bodies denied Christian burial:' even witnesses and spectators were excommunicated.

Such exaggerated denunciations were not even then entirely disregarded: and to avoid their penalties hostile meetings were appointed in Turkey, and out of Christendom, as, in serious cases, they now sometimes are beyond the frontiers of neighbouring countries. At all events, these decrees denounced the evil; and remedies began to be earnestly thought of and applied. Charles V. forbade duelling throughout his dominions; it was prohibited in Portugal, under penalty of confiscation of goods and transportation to Africa; in Sweden by death; and Gustavus II, once interrupting a party who were about to fight, ordered them to remain on the field until a temporary gallows had been erected, when he said, 'Now, gentlemen, if you please, proceed.'

In France, sanguinary edicts had been issued against duelling by Francis I., Charles IX., and Henry IV., but they were totally inoperative. Louis XIII. endeavoured to enforce them with an irregular severity that produced little effect; yet still, it was something to see a Montmorency formally executed on the Place de Grève for fighting a duel. Louis XIV. proceeded more wisely; he reorganized and extended the powers of the Court of Honour, originally instituted by Charles IX., and composed of all the great dignitaries of the kingdom. This Court had authority to decide on all subjects of honour, with power to fine, imprison, and arrest all who might be convicted of giving the lie, striking, or committing any of those insults, or offences, which had hitherto provoked challenges. Recourse, too, was had to honour itself as a corrective of its excesses. The Marquis de Fénélon, of whom the great Condé said, that he was equally qualified for conversation, the field, and the cabinet, headed an association of gentlemen, who bound themselves by their honour and their oaths never to send or to accept a challenge. And by a public edict, Louis XIV. awarded death, with forfeiture of rank, honour, and estate, to all concerned in duels; pledging himself in the same edict, 'on the faith and word of a king, not to exempt any person, for any consideration whatever, from the rigour of this edict.' This very rigour defeated its own object: evasions naturally took place. The *rencontre* was devised, by which that which was in reality a preconcerted duel, had the semblance of an *accidental* meeting, with a quarrel growing as accidentally out of it. Still, Louis the XIV. has the credit of having done more than any other sovereign for the effectual repression of duelling Under his feeble and reckless successors, it revived with characteristic licentiousness. Lauzun, St. Evremont, and the Duc de Richelieu, were its worthy heroes. Even Ladies followed their example; and la Marquise de Nêsle and la Contesse de Polignac actually fought with pistols for the *honour* of the possession of Richelieu! But the great heroine of the duel was Moussin, an opera singer, who, after taking lessons from one of her lovers, Serane, a celebrated fencing-master, succeeded in killing her three men, when she fled to Brussels, and became the mistress of the Elector of Bavaria.

In England, Elizabeth attacked duelling by restricting fencing schools; yet Sir Henry Upton, her ambassador at Paris, thus sturdily challenged the Duc de Guise:—

'Forasmuch as lately in the lodgings of the Lord Dumogre, and in public elsewhere, impudently, indiscreetly, and overboldly, you spoke badly of my sovereign, whose sacred person here, in this country, I represent, to maintain, both by word and weapon, her honour, (which was never called into question among persons of honesty and virtue.) I say you have wickedly and maliciously lied in speaking so basely of my sovereign, and you shall do nothing else but lie whenever you dare to tax her honour. Moreover that her sacred person (being one of the most complete and virtuous princesses that ever lived in the world) ought not to be evil spoken of by the vile tongue of such a perfidious traitor to her land and country as you are; and therefore I do defy you and challenge your person to mine, with such manner of arms as you shall like or choose, be it either on horseback or on foot; nor would I have you to think any inequality of person between us, I being issued of as great a race and noble house as yourself, in assigning me an indifferent place. I will there maintain my words, and the lie which I gave and give you. If you consent not to meet me hereon, I will hold you and cause you to be generally held, for the arrantest coward and most slanderous slave in France. I expect your immediate answer.'

Nothing came of Elizabeth's regulations; and in the following reign Bacon resolutely set his face against duelling, denouncing it ' as an affront to the law, as if there were two laws—one a kind of gown law, and the other a law of reputation, as they term it; so that Paul's and Westminster, the pulpit and the courts of justice, our year books and statute books, must give place to some French and Italian pamphlets.' He obtained a decree of the Star-Chamber against duels, and prosecuted and convicted persons concerned in them, punishing them by fine and imprisonment. The decree drawn up by himself, ' did utterly reject and condemn the opinion that the private duel, in any person whatever, had any grounds of honour; as well because nothing can be honourable that is not lawful, and that it is no magnanimity or greatness of mind, but a swelling and tumour of the mind, whenever there faileth a right and sound judgment; as also, for that it was rather justly to be esteemed a weakness, and a conscience of small value in a man's self, to be dejected so with a word of trifling disgrace as to think there is no excuse of it but by the hazard of life; whereas true honour, in persons that know their own worth, is not of any such brittle substance, but of a more strong composition.' Bacon's object was to prevent duels by the moderate punishment of all the preliminary and provocatory steps—thus nipping them in the bud; which he added, ' is fuller of clemency and providence than suffering them to go on, and hanging men, with their wounds bleeding, as they did in France.' The result was, that duelling was comparatively little practised in England. Sir

Walter Raleigh, one of the bravest of the brave, strongly condemned the practice, in a dissertation regarding it, in his ' History of the World '

The wars of the League in France teemed with duels and assassinations; but our great civil struggle was comparatively unstained by them, although Charles I. set an evil example by consenting to the revival of the judicial combat on the impeachment of Ramsay by Lord Reay, and actually named the Earl of Lindsay Constable for the occasion; but happily the Marquis of Hamilton persuaded him to stay proceedings, and accommodated the matter. The great Protector too, following the example of Bacon, passed an ordinance subjecting all persons carrying a challenge to six months' imprisonment; and imposed fines on persons using provoking words or gestures; binding them over to good behaviour, and to make reparation according to the nature and quality of the offence. Whenever death ensued, it was to be treated as murder. But, with the Restoration, duelling set in with a flood-tide. True, Charles II. issued his proclamation of 1679, which amply acknowledges ' that duels were most frequent, and that the utmost rigour of the law would be exercised against them.' But Charles's practice and his proclamations were very different things. In fact, the same mania for duelling which, with its attendant licentiousness, had visited France in the preceding age, now fell on England. Pepys calls this prevalence of duelling ' a kind of emblem of the general complexion of the whole kingdom;' and in his amusing Diary, relates the following characteristic duel between Sir Henry Bellasses and Mr. Porter, in 1667.

' They two dined together, yesterday, in Sir Robert Carr's, where it seems the people drink very high, all that come. It happened that these two, the greatest friends in the world, were talking together, and Sir H. Bellasses talked a little louder than ordinary to Tom Porter, giving him some advice. Some of the people standing by said, ' What! are they quarrelling that they talk so high?' Sir H. Bellasses hearing it, said, ' No, I would have you know that I never quarrel, *but I strike*; take that as a rule of mine.' ' How!' said Tom Porter, ' strike! I would I could see the man in England that durst give me a blow?' With that Sir H. Bellasses did give him a box on the ear; and so they were going out to fight, but were hindered. And by and by Tom Porter went out, and meeting Dryden the poet told him of the business and that he was resolved to fight Sir H. Bellasses presently; for he knew if they did not, they would be friends to-morrow, and then the blow would rest upon him; and he desires Dryden to let him have his boy to bring him notice which way Sir H. Bellasses goes. By and by he is informed that Sir H. Bellasses's coach was coming; so Tom Porter went down out of the coffee-room where he staid for the tidings and stopped the coach, and bade Sir H. Bellasses come out. " Why," said he, "you will not hurt me coming out, will you?"—" No," says Tom Porter. So out he went, and they both drew, and they fell to fight, some of their acquaintances by. They wounded one another; and Sir H. Bellasses so much that it is feared he will die. He, finding himself severely wounded, called to Tom Porter, and kissed him, and bade him shift for himself. " For," says he, "Tom, thou hast hurt me, but I will make shift to stand on my legs till thou may'st withdraw, and the world not take notice of thee; for I would not have thee troubled for what thou hast done;" and then Tom Porter showed him how he was wounded too. [Bellasses survived only a few days, on which Pepy adds,] Here is a fine example! and Sir Henry a Parliament man too; and both of them such extraordinary friends. It is pretty to hear how the world talk of them, as a couple of fools that killed one another out of love.'

Even the Lord Chancellor was not safe. Lord Ossory called out Clarendon on a tariff question—a bill for the prohibition of the importation of Irish cattle. The Duke of Buckingham did not resign on the introduction of this bill, as the present Duke has done, but entered into a scuffle in the lobby of the House of Lords with a free-trading Lord Dorchester, who pulled out a handful of his Grace's hair, while the Duke retaliated by carrying off his lordship's periwig. But a blacker and fitter illustration of the morals and manners of those days is to be found in this Duke's duel with Lord Shrewsbury, for the seduction of his wife. They were attended by Captain Holman and Sir Jones Jenkins, Lord Bernard Howard and Sir John Talbot. The parties met at Barnes Elms, and the seconds as well as the principals engaged. Buckingham ran Lord Shrewsbury through the body. Sir John Talbot was severely wounded in both arms, Sir Jones Jenkins was left dead on the field, and the other seconds with Buckingham were slightly wounded. Meanwhile Lady Shrewsbury, in a page's dress, was holding Buckingham's horse in an adjoining thicket, in order to aid his escape should he kill her husband; and, according to the reports of the day, she passed that very night with him in the shirt stained with his own and her husband's blood. It is needless to add that Charles II., by proclamation, pardoned all parties concerned. Buckingham turned his wife out of doors; and he and

Lady Shrewsbury plundered and dissipated all her son's estate. Deservedly did he end his infamous career ' in the worst inn's worst room !'

The mania spread to all ranks. Doctors met in consultation with drawn swords. Mead and Woodward fought under the gate of Gresham College. Woodward's foot slipped, and he fell. " Take your life," exclaimed Mead- " Anything but your physic," replied Woodward. Dr. Williams ran Dr Bennett through the body, after discharging a brace of pistols at his head; and the dying doctor, with the sword yet in his body, *prayed to God* for strength to avenge himself, and with one last effort stabbed his opponent to death. This was in open day, in front of their houses. Williams fell dead before he reached his own door, and Bennett survived only four hours. Ball-rooms, masquerades, the theatres, the open streets, the public walks, and the coffee-houses, became the constant scenes of strife and bloodshed. Covent-Garden and Lincoln's Inn Fields were the modern Chalk Farm and Wimbledon Common; and the streets rang all night with the clashing of swords, and the riots and outrages of drunken men of fashion—the *men of honour* of that day.

So it continued from the Restoration to the accession of George the Third. The ' Bucks,' the ' Mohawks,' the ' Hell Fires,' were the leaders of the ton. One of their favourite places of resort was a tavern near Somerset House, where they assembled on Sundays, with a loud band of music, during divine service; and their approved dish was what they blasphemously called a ' Holy Ghost pie.' Duels, affrays, bloodshed, are quite as much the natural result of such manners and morals, as tearing and killing are of the organic conformation of carnivorous animals. In 1717 the Foot-Guards were called out to put down an affray of these gentlemen at the Royal Chocolate House, growing out of a dispute at hazard, and in which three of them lost their lives. In 1720 a patrol of the Royal Horse-Guards charged a party of above a hundred of them who were rioting in Windmill Street. In 1691, Lord Mohun and Major Hill publicly waylaid and assassinated Montford, the player, in Norfolk Street; and as publicly attempted to carry off Mrs. Bracegirdle by main force. In 1699, the same worthy Lord was tried for aiding and abetting the murder of Colonel Coote, after drinking a whole day and night with him and their companions at the Greyhound in the Strand; and in 1712 he lost his own life, and murdered, rather than killed, the Duke of Hamilton in a duel. Steele, too, after having written against duelling, and rebuked Thornhill, in the 'Spectator,' for having killed Sir Cholmondeley Deering, found himself compelled to fight a brother officer, whom he narrowly escaped killing; while Thornhill, two months later, was stabbed at Turnham Green by two men, who exclaimed, as they struck him, 'Remember Sir Cholmondeley Deering!'

It would be revolting to wade through the savage and insolent duels of those and later days. We willingly pass them by, and turn to the ameliorating and restricting process which once more revived with better laws and better government. The death of the Duke of Hamilton produced a strong feeling throughout the country; a bill against duelling was brought into Parliament, thrown out on the second reading; and the following year (1713) the Queen's speech pronounced, that 'the practice of duelling requires some speedy and effectual remedy;' but the bill was again thrown out. Better help came from a better source —amending morals; and for this certainly to no one individual, and scarcely to any one class, is the praise more justly due than to John Wesley, one of the most important men of his century. His preaching, his perseverance, his purity, and the persecutions which he and his followers underwent, created a church, and reacted on that from which he was separated, and by which he was reviled. Next in importance to Wesley's reformation, was the thunderstorm of the French Revolution. The one prepared better morals, the other broke down many of the old scaffoldings of class privileges and formal honour. It was a great step even the doing away with the wearing of swords; but a greater was the frightful proof which the French enormities gave of the utter insufficiency of the restraints of mere worldly honour, and abstract principles.

Still the fierce wars of the French Revolution kept up the fiercer passions; and the coarse habits of drunkenness and rioting which continued to disgrace English gentlemen, supplied plentiful employment for the pistol. It is no later than the beginning of this century that such a pest of society as the last Lord Camelford was allowed to override it, to bully and to fight whomsoever he chose, until, having killed Mr. Patterson, he met his death from Best, whom he insisted on fighting, and whom his seconds permitted him to fight, although both he and they well knew, even avowed, that he was in the wrong. He fell, and was found weltering in the mud at the back of Little Holland House, deserted by his seconds. Best's end, too, was miserable. He died at the early age of forty-eight, completely worn out. Sorrow and remorse had done on him the work of years. In his closing hours he declared that the recollection of the duel, and its results, had embittered every moment of his life—that the whole scene was fresh in his memory as if it had happened yesterday—and that there were times when Lord Camelford seemed to stand before him, and gaze on him with an earnestness and tenacity that rendered life a burden. An Irish duel of those, or rather later days, will let us see how short a time, and what thin barriers, separate us from barbarism; and will throw some light too on old Tory notions of the right-divine of landlords, and of their methods of intimidation. In 1810, Mr. Colclough and Mr. Sheridan opposed Mr. Alcock for the representation of the county of Wexford. Several tenants of a person supporting Mr Alcock declared that they should vote for Colclough and Sheridan. This was resented, and Mr. Colclough was called upon to refuse their votes. He declared that he had in no manner canvassed them, and that he would not direct them how they should vote. He was answered, 'Receive their votes at your peril!' Before the opening of the next day's poll, the rival candidates were on the field to determine the tenant's right by the pistol. Many hundred persons assembled to witness the affair, among whom *were several magistrates.* The ground was marked, the crowd separated on either side, as their party feelings dictated—a dead silence and a pause ensued—the word was given—and Mr. Colclough fell dead, shot through the heart; and, within two hours afterwards, his opponent, Mr Alcock, was returned *duly* elected! At the next assizes he was tried for murder before Baron Smith, who openly declared against a capital conviction; and the jury, without a moment's hesitation, pronounced a verdict of Not Guilty. The parties had been intimate friends, and Alcock, though acquitted, never recovered his self-composure; his intellect faded; and his sister, doubly wounded, went mad and died!

The cause, the crowd, the return, the trial, the judge, the verdict, and the melancholy results, are all truly descriptive of Ireland in those unhappy times;—times which there are even yet found persons hardy or ignorant enough to refer to, as the

era of her peace and good government.
A better example was exhibited in Scotland, where the parties in a silly duel in
1815 were fined five-and-twenty guineas
each by the Sheriff, and the fines ordered
to be applied to the benefit of the Lunatic
Asslum, as the institution most appropriate
to their proceedings. But this was the
mere punishment of unauthorised intruders
on the honours of duelling; for there, as
elsewhere, for the privileged the law has
been muzzled or defied, and public opinion
has strongly supported the primitive wisdom of Gundebald. Few have dared to
stand out against its anathema. Moore records a melancholy letter of a wretched father, written to his family the night before he
fell in a duel; 'London, Wednesday night,
Sept 3, 1783—I commit my soul to Almighty God, in hopes of his mercy and
pardon for the irreligious step I now, in
compliance with the unwarrantable custom
of this wicked world, put myself under the
necessity of taking.' Major Hillas, in 1815,
when on the ground, to which he had been
brought for his humane efforts to protect
the shipwrecked, and on which one minute
later he was lying a corpse, declared to the
bystanders, 'I am sorry the mistaken laws
of honour oblige me to come here to defend
myself; and I declare to God I have no
animosity to man or woman on the face of
the earth.' Many, no doubt, have thought
thus and done thus – seen the right, but
dared not act up to it; and allowing for the
infirmities of our nature, for the force of
example and long-descended custom, the
terror of shame, and the strength of our
social ties and affections, we frankly own
that they who rise superior to them are no
common men—and we would be the last to
throw the stone at those who have weakly,
but, as the world thinks, honourably given
way.

Another ameliorating process arose
strange to say, from duelling itself—from
the passion for duelling which infected the
political characters of the last century.
There is scarcely a distinguished politician
of the times of George III., who did not
put his patriotism, his honour, or his truth,
to the test of the pistol. Lord Talbot and
Wilkes, Lord Shelburne and Colonel Fullarton, Lord Lauderdale and General
Arnold, Townshend, Pitt, Fox, Sheridan,
Wyndham, Canning, Tierney, Burdett,
Brougham, Castlereagh, and the Duke of
Wellington, are amongst the public men
who have not refused the sanction of their
names and example to the practice of thus
adjourning a debate. There has been

benefit as well as mischief in this. By the
necessary publicity attending all the proceedings connected with a hostile meeting
between such distinguished persons, the
duel itself has become more serious and
fair—a clear statement of the cause of
offence has come to be required; a sanction has been afforded to explanations and
apologies; and founded as these duels not
unfrequently have been on public questions, all remaining traces of malice or
revenge have been nearly obliterated.
These are all palpable advantages, which
have given a milder character to duelling;
—on no occasion more modestly, bravely,
and signally exemplified, than in the duel
which the Duke of Wellington thought
himself called upon to grant to Lord Winchilsea. But with these advantages there
has been the attendant mischief of prolonging the practice by giving to it the
sanction of such high names, and, by the
mitigation of its fierceness, rendering it
less repugnant to our better feelings. Still,
it was a great advance to enforce the sanction of previous explanation, and to encourage the retractation of hasty or improper
words. Hitherto there has been a foolish
notion, and false pride, in considering it
unbecoming to apologize or retract until
the adversary's fire was received; but
common sense and humanity are now beginning to discover that there is more of
true manliness in at once acknowledging an
error, than in waiting to admit it at the
pistol's mouth. This is a duty which cannot be too strongly impressed, and which,
if properly enforced by those who undertake the responsible duty of Seconds,
would greatly tend to the prevention of
duels. It is to the honour of the younger
public men of the day, that none of them
of any note, or with very few exceptions,
have been engaged in a duel. They have,
amidst all the heat of the last twelve years'
debates, preserved their honour, their
courage, and their consciences unsullied,
without this vulgar appeal.

Dr. Millingen has attempted to enumerate the duels which took place during the
reign of George III.; but the list is manifestly incomplete, and probably does not
embrace one-fourth part of those which
actually occurred. Yet still it is a sad
catalogue, and records the death of no less
than sixty-nine individuals. For these
flagrant offences, and this heavy loss of life,
(murder in the eye of the law,) only
eighteen trials took place, which ended in
the conviction and punishment of only ten
individuals; and of these two only were

hanged, not really for duelling, but for foul fighting—that is, strictly speaking, for *not* fighting duels; and the other eight underwent short imprisonments. There is also given an additional account of some twenty-nine other remarkable duels which have occurred since the death of George III., and in which fourteen persons have perished. Upon the trials which ensued, in five cases out of six the parties were acquitted; and when convicted, their punishment has never exceeded twelve months' imprisonment, ordinarily it has been four or five months.

Such, briefly, has been the course, and such is the present state of duelling. We have seen it in its high and palmy days, when it was in fact the supreme arbiter of justice; when women and children, monks and churchmen, burghers and nobles, all brought their causes, civil, criminal, and ecclesiastical, to be decided by it; when the sword decided even the pretensions to office, and when all regarded its decisions with reverence. One age took from it its civil authority and title-deeds, and the rights of property were transferred to courts of law; another delivered traitors and murderers to their appointed judges; a third superseded the knightly right of redressing wrongs and rescuing the innocent; a fourth forbade even the privilege of the lists; but the single combat, although no longer countenanced by kings and courts, and though subjected even to nominal penalties, still met with real applause, and many a gallant won his mistress by the slaughter of his rival. But gradually this applause lessened, and causes and accusations, which had formerly justified a challenge, came to submit themselves to the arbitration of law, or to public opinion. Explanations were admitted, and society ceased to require, as a feather in the cap of a man of honour, that he had killed his man. Duelling then subsided, to become the unwelcome resource of the good and the brave; and the prized proceeding only of the bully, the gambler, and the profligate.

These are the general phases through which this singular custom has passed, under the modifying influences of advancing intelligence; and this last is now its general state throughout Europe, subject of course to certain variations, according to the manners, morals, and institutions of different communities. In several of the European states, the laws respecting duelling have undergone revision, and, by being rendered less severe, have become more effective;

this has been the more easy, as duelling on the Continent occurs chiefly amongst military men, who are necessarily more subject to control. The only exception is France, where philosophers and journalists have, since the Restoration, sharpened their pens with their swords. In Austria, by a decree of 1803, the principals concerned in a duel are punished by imprisonment varying from one to five years; if either of the parties are wounded, the term is from five to ten years; and from ten to twenty if death ensues. The seconds also are subject to confinement, extending from one to five years. In Prussia, a like substitution of imprisonment or relegation to a fortress, has superseded the penalty of death, which is inflicted only in cases of foul fighting; or of those murderous duels in which one person necessarily must fall. The Prussian code is particularly severe with respect to the conduct of the seconds. In Belgium also, and Bavaria, reforms have taken place. But in England no effective change has been attempted, and the operation of the law has been, and continues utterly powerless: it denounces duelling as murder, and affixes the punishment of death to the principals and seconds, and subjects all persons challenging others to fight to fine and imprisonment. Within the last two hundred years, there have not been twenty convictions, nor more than three or four persons executed nominally for fighting duels, but really for *not* fighting according to the rules of duelling. A few persons have been convicted of manslaughter in duels, which have been marked by some peculiarly offensive circumstances; and some few of these have been subjected to one, two, three, and, at the utmost, twelve months' imprisonment; but the vast majority have been acquitted, or escaped untried. Practically speaking, it is not probable that the law has ever prevented a single duel from taking place; the utmost it can be supposed to have done, is to uphold *fair fighting;* and this, we think, public opinion, and the high honour of the parties generally concerned, would have secured without it.

This is a mischievous anomaly. For it cannot but injure the public estimation of justice, that any one well-known law should be openly and constantly broken without shame and without punishment, and that too by one class only; for if ploughmen and shopkeepers took to imitating gentlemen, by shooting at each other, or determining their quarrels by practices which caused death, the law would speedily interfere. But as it now stands, magistrates, judges, and juries, are placed in a false and unseemly position; being tempted, since their moral sense revolts from the severity of the punishment, to make cobweb-quibbles and evasions of the law, the evidence, and their own oaths; and, amidst the quibbling, the bully, the quarrelsome, and the vicious, escape equally with the comparatively innocent; for the blind law, denouncing all as murderers, admits of no palliation—no discrimination of guilt. Even in cases of great atrocity, where the survivor has given the offence, where he has refused all compromise or apology, and borne himself savagely and haughtily throughout—still, thanks to our rigour, there grows up before his trial a feeling in his favour: stories of his boldness, of his services, of his contrition, of the distress of his wife and family, are circulated, till witnesses get out of the way, or give palliating evidence; the prosecution is gently, *humanely*, conducted; the defence is warm and impassioned; the judge declares that the offence 'is in direct contradiction to the laws both of God and man; and, therefore, the law has justly fixed to it the crime and punishment of murder;' but he also takes care to throw out some circumstances which, if the jury can satisfy their minds as to their relevancy, will alter the case; or some extenuating circumstances are supposed, which yet, they are told, must not alter their verdict; or some imaginary misnomer is discovered or prepared; or some witness refuses to give evidence, or loses his memory;—when the jury, well understanding what is meant, return a verdict of not guilty, or manslaughter coupled with a strong recommendation to mercy; and then the judge gently admonishes and gently punishes the prisoner, telling him, perhaps, 'that his conduct in the field was such as to leave no stain on his character.' Thus the offender, who, by his violence or his obstinacy, has outraged and defied the law, and brought home death with all its attendant misery and bereavement to fathers, mothers, and children, escapes with a mock trial, or some trifling imprisonment.

This is the result of unreasoning severity; of a severity, too, great even for a heinous offender, and infinitely too great for the parties implicated in ordinary duels. Lately the law has been slightly altered. By the 1st of Victoria, murder and the punishment of death are denounced, only when death or wounds dangerous to life have been inflicted, with an intent to commit murder; and felony, liable to transportation, has been substituted for ' whoever unlawfully and maliciously shall shoot at any person, or shall, by drawing a trigger, attempt to discharge any kind of loaded arms at any person, or to do some other grievous bodily harm to such person.' This was probably meant as a sufficient relaxation; but transportation is still far too severe; and accordingly the penalty was not inflicted on the only occasion when it was attempted to be enforced.

Severity will not do. Do we therefore defend duelling? Far from it, as our observations must have shown. We do not believe that its benefits are at all comparable to its evils; society is strong enough and civilized enough to do without it now; it is no longer any safeguard to it: on the contrary, experience shows that the duel is frequently used as a means for stifling inquiry, for upholding the dissolute, and reinstating the guilty. It is a kind of moral regeneration, a white-washing, a fresh start; and so many a knave has found it. It is contrary to all experience that duels have refined manners. Whenever and wherever duelling has most prevailed, then and there manners and morals have been most rude and most lax. Compare England under Elizabeth and Cromwell, with France under the League, Henry IV., and the Fronde; or reverse the picture, and place England under the latter Stuarts beside France under Louis XIV.; or change it again to France under the Regency and Louis XV.; and we shall find that as dissoluteness, and absence of all that comely self-control and consideration for the feelings of others, of all classes, which is the essence of good manners, rose or fell, so precisely did duelling flourish or decay. Where was the softening influence of the duel, and the point of honour, when they were at their height in France? Did they prevent the great Condé from slapping the face of the Comte des Rieux?—or the Duc de Beaufort, the Duc d'Orleans, and the Comte d'Harcourt, from getting drunk and picking pockets on the Pont Neuf under the statue of Henry IV.;—or did it deter the wits of Charles II. from riots and personal conflict; the Duke of Buckingham and Lord Dorchester from descending to fisticuffs in the lobby of the House of Lords?—or later still, did the Comte d'Artois lose caste for striking the Duchesse de Bourbon at a masked ball? On the contrary, when he had gone through the mere form of a rencontre with her husband, all was forgotten, and the last of the Condés was lost in admiration of the man who had wantonly struck a woman, and his wife, because that man ' conferred on him the honour of allowing him to cross swords with him.'

Duelling did not prevent these outrages, which we have taken from the highest personages as a sample of the whole; but it did, what is infinitely mischievous—it *excused* them. It was the gate through which the offender re-entered the pale of the society he had outraged. For nine cases out of ten it is the man who has done the wrong, or who is substantially in the wrong, that seeks and profits by the duel: like the sheet of Shore's wife, it is his penance, but unlike hers it is not white, but blood-coloured. There is no people with whom duelling is so frequent, and so ferocious, as the Americans of the United States, and most especially of the southern and western States; and there is no class of a rank in life corresponding with them whose manners are so rude, and with whom the bowie-knife and Lynch law—stabbing and mob-murder—are so frequent. And is the duel their corrector? Is it not, rather, the confederate of these self-willed and anti-social atrocities? They are evidences all alike of inefficient law, moral, legal, and divine. But without going higher, we stand on the plain matter-of-fact that duelling has not softened, and will not soften, manners. Advancing civilisation has undoubtedly regulated duelling, and hence the error has arisen of substituting the effect for the cause, the softened duel for the subduing civilisation; and as civilisation spreads wider and deeper, incorporating within its influences the practical instruction of administered law, no doubt the day will come when duelling will be regarded as any other gross outrage which the law punishes, and society, the complement of law, condemns.

It is for these reasons that we desire to see an alteration and mitigation of the present law. Sully, on this very subject, speaking to Henry IV., said, ' that the excessive severity of the means of repression would be the source whence would arise the principal obstacles to their execution; for frequently the penalties which produce the greatest effect are those which do not call for remission.' He was quite right; no one now or then, however much he may deprecate duelling, can deliberately place the murderer and the duellist on the same level. Undoubtedly cases may be imagined in which very extenuating circumstances being placed to the account of the murderer, and every aggravation heaped on the duellist, the one may be made as black or blacker than the other. But this is neither a fair nor useful way of viewing the subject: substantially, and for all legal practical purposes, we may assume that the duellist, he who kills his adversary in what is called *fair fight*, is no murderer—is not guilty of murder in that sense in which public opinion and the spirit of our law now regard murder. It is most unjust, therefore, that he should be classed and tried, and it would be still more unjust that he should be punished, as a murderer; and so, thanks to this false classification and trial, he escapes altogether. So he ever will, and so he ought, until he is so classed and so tried that conviction and penalties may justly follow his offence. This point is so evident that it is idle to waste words on it.

That duelling should be checked, few we think will deny. Who is there that has fought a duel who does not regret it—repent it? Let any one ask whether it is right that he who maliciously or even wantonly provokes and triumphs in a fatal duel should escape as he now does, unpunished and almost unreproved. All our better and more sober feelings answer no; it is only legal impunity which restrains their expression and prevalence. We are no disciples of Hobbes; but it is idle to deny how much of public morals, and of just notions of right and wrong, depend on the administration of public law. How many offences are there which should touch strongly the conscience, but which public opinion still tolerates or approves, only because the law cannot or will not reach them?—and there are others which happily, since the law has reached them, have fallen into disrepute. It certainly would be infinitely better that public morals rested on higher sanctions than mere law—and to a considerable extent they do; but the penalties of the one Table are instant and obvious, those of the other remote and unseen; and therefore, too frequently, when the first fail or refuse to act, the second lose their force, and a spurious judgment, a compromise of public opinion, is formed—the conventional takes the place of the just. To remedy this is the object of all legislation, whose constant tendency should be, to bring the three great ruling influences, the civil, the social, and the divine, into harmony. This has gradually been advancing as to many things; and we think the time has come, when, with respect to duelling, the hitherto dead letter prohibition of the law might be exchanged for some *practical and approved penalty*, which would at once amend and strengthen public opinion. And certainly the time has come when a real and serious responsibility ought to be attached to the conduct of seconds; because, as most duels might be prevented by the prudence, temperance, and firmness of the seconds, they ought to suffer wherever they either obviously misuse, or heedlessly omit to use the means which their situation affords to effect an arrangement; or when they continue, by their presence, to sanction a meeting originating in unjustifiable and unwarrantable expressions or behaviour.

Beyond all doubt, fighting a duel is a breach of the peace. Let it then be so classed and so punished—each duel according to its special enormity; and let this enormity, together with the respective guilt of the several parties concerned, be tried by a jury, and decided by their verdict, as in the case of other offences. It will then be discovered how the quarrel arose out of which the duel grew; who gave the offence; what offers of apology, redress, or retraction were made; how they were met, why refused; and all those other circumstances which distinguish the case of a bully, or a professed and instructed duellist, from that of a forced defender of his honour. The result of these inquiries in presence of a judge and a jury would lead to that discrimination of guilt, and apportionment of punishment, without which no law can work well; and moreover true honour and true courage, thus sifted, would stand out in honest relief from the surreptitious qualities which too often fight under their mask. Friends and relatives also, when the punishment was no longer excessive, would come forward to assist to expose and convict those who had forced on the duel, or who had not done their utmost to prevent it.

It may be said that these are matters and questions of far too fine and delicate a texture to come before a jury, and to be duly appreciated by such a tribunal ;—that the honour and sensibility of a gentleman would shrink from so matter-of-fact and threadbare a scrutiny. There may, at first sight, appear some ground for this objection, but time would or should remove it ; for substantially it rests only on prejudice, and exclusive pretensions. In Libel this is not the case ; and in the most delicate of all inquiries—and that wherein the outraged feelings are most tender, and wherein it is most desirable to spare them, and where publicity confers questionable benefits—in the honour of the marriage bed, stern law and public advantage have overruled ; and the honour, the conduct, and domestic relations of the proudest, have been laid bare, investigated, and assessed in open court, at so many pounds, shillings, and pence; and morality has gained by it.

For the vindication of the husband's honour is now almost entirely transferred from the sword to the law; truth and equity transpire ; and the vices and neglect of the profligate are exposed and corrected by nominal damages and virtual defeat. So, too, in duels, the violent and provoking would be exposed and punished, and the placable and injured protected; and generally the advantage of bringing common sense and common justice to bear upon quarrels, would come to be felt and acknowledged. At all events, the equal administration of the law would be vindicated : we should hear no more on this subject of one law for the rich and another for the poor: we should no longer have enacted the solemn farce of ' an unfortunate gentleman' tried for murder, with the certainty of his legal escape and of his moral guilt. All other classes of the community submit their quarrels, when they issue in assault, to the arbitration of the law ; and when gentlemen choose to quarrel, and to commit breaches of the peace by fighting duels and endangering lives, they too must learn to submit to have their conduct and proceedings inquired into, and punished according to their misdeeds, and according to law. The time has gone by for Courts of Honour; they belonged to the days of exclusive privileges and exclusive classes. All who offend, must now bow their heads to one common law. Every class has naturally a self-centring aggressive principle, which aspires to override that of others, and which chafes under the restraint of general law. But it is the very object of law to bind together these discordant principles, by restraining their exclusive tendencies, and compelling each to submit its own overweening pretensions to the central intelligence which consults for the common good It is this general submission to the one abstract authority which constitutes the essence and the perfection of the social state.

Following, therefore, the recommendation of Bacon, we are desirous of seeing an end put to that ' affront,' which duelling and the proceedings connected with it ' put upon our law;' and, following also his opinion, we believe it can be done only by a great *mitigation of severity.* The enactment of the 1st of Victoria has broken down, and justice cannot well afford such another mockery as Lord Cardigan's trial. Let us therefore not wait, as we usually do in England, for some revolting catastrophe before we apply a remedy. It is neither difficult nor uncalled for : we have only to substitute, as has been done in Prussia and Austria, various degrees of imprisonment for the higher penalties of the law ; and the law will then, in all probability, vindicate its authority. But it is needless to say more; we have already said enough to prove the evils of duelling, and the mischievous inefficiency of the law with respect to it; and we have therefore made out a case for amending that law. This can be done only by reconciling public opinion with its operation. It is useless to give way, on the one hand, to a high-flown horror of all duelling ; and it would be cowardly, on the other, to yield implicity to the notions of the mere men of the sword and pistol :— we must take things as we find them, and legislate for men and manners as they are, and not as they might be. And therefore, since death by duelling is not, judging from the opinions (gathered from the conduct) of judges and the verdicts of juries, viewed as murder, it is worse than useless to continue to declare it to be so by law. And again, since duelling has descended to us from time almost immemorial, and with practical impunity, if not applause, it would be vain to attempt suddenly to uproot that which has grown so long in our customs. All, therefore, that can be fairly done as society as yet exists, is to meet it with useful palliatives instead of impracticable prohibitions ; to put it, in fact, under the eye and correction of the law ; not so much to wage war with duelling itself, as with those who provoke and compel it ; to seek out and punish the guilty, *the most guilty;* those who, by their unjustifiable words or deeds —who, by refusing all explanation or apology—or who, by dissuading others to offer or accept adjustment, evince that felonious malice which all the world would gladly see punished There would be no difficulty in obtaining verdicts against such offenders, when it was known that no punishment more severe than a regulated imprisonment would follow conviction : no mawkish pity would then follow them to their prisons— no whitewashing congratulations mark their release. The law would inflict its penalty and leave its stain, and the duel and the duellist would be thus far rebuked. Further, we think the law might be improved, by following its analogy in those cases where it awards damages as compensation for injuries. It is but just that he who has unlawfully disabled another, or taken his life—depriving him, if wounded, of many enjoyments, or, if killed, robbing a family of its support, a wife of her husband, the father of his child, and the state of his ser-

vices—should be compelled to make compensation, according to his means and according to his guilt. And lastly, in support of prevention, fines, in addition to the present binding over to keep the peace, might justly be levied on those who were detected in overt attempts to break it.

These are all the penalties we would inflict. They may be thought slight, and, by their very slightness, to encourage the offence they are meant to repress; but we doubt whether any more severe could be enforced, and if we are right in this doubt, then, practically, they become the most severe. The great object is to bring the law into operation ; and when once this has been done, when its wheels begin to move, its severity may, if necessary, be increased. At all events, the law as applied to duelling is worse than a dead letter: it is partial, blind, uncertain, revolting, inoperative; and should therefore be abrogated or amended.

———

Art. V.—*Tour in Austrian Lombardy, Northern Tyrol, and Bavaria.* By John Barrow. 8vo. London : 1841.

It may truly be said that the field of discovery, by sea and land, has nearly been exhausted by the exertions of our adventurous countrymen, who, on the former element, have scarcely left unexplored any creek, or island, or even rock in the ocean ; and, on the latter, our numerous tourists have hardly allowed a single nook of the Continent of Europe to escape their curiosity ; yet naturalists of every description, and moralists of every shade, the poet and the painter, the classical scholar and the antiquary, the mere tourist in search of health or pleasure, may each still find room and scope enough to collect something for his little sketch ; were it only to serve as a help to reminiscence, or an attempt to afford recreation to friends. Nor can few of them be accused of being niggardly in giving to the public whatever information they may have acquired, according to their several tastes and capacities. Much novelty, it is true, cannot now be expected, but objects may be seen and described in a new point of view, and correct impressions may sometimes be conveyed in the place of erroneous ones.

The little tour made by Mr. Barrow is, what the title-page announces it to be, chiefly descriptive, and will be found a suitable companion to his excursions in the north of Europe;—it reminds us of his descriptions of the romantic scenery of Norway, so well according with that of the Tyrolese Alps, and of which we had occasion to speak favourably—as we now feel disposed to do with regard to the present volume; as well for the clearness and unpretending simplicity of the language, as from a conviction of its truth. Accuracy, indeed, can scarcely be doubted, where a note is taken at the moment that objects and incidents occur, and written out fair at the close of each day, which appears to be the practice of our author : the remarks and observations, therefore, made on the present tour, must be of considerable advantage to any one proceeding on the same route.

By steam and railroad, through Belgium and up the Rhine to Frankfort, and thence through the Rhenish provinces to Zurich, he arrived at this last place at the same hour almost with his friend Mr. Frederick Graham, according to agreement made long before in London to meet there on a given day—the one from England, the other from a ramble in the Alps—a punctuality owing chiefly, as Mr. Barrow says, to a nice calculation of time and distance by reliance on steam-power. Our travellers lost no time at this place, their intention being to cross the Alps into Lombardy. We shall also merely halt to give an instance of the manner in which Mr. Barrow is in the habit of associating subjects, in themselves perhaps of minor importance. In ascending the double-turreted cathedral of Zurich, he casually observed, in the adjoining one, a crow's nest, which, he says, struck his fancy no otherwise than as connected with some vague association of church and crow, and bringing to remembrance Cowper's playful lines on the subject :—

> 'There is a bird who, by his coat,
> And by the hoarseness of his note,
>   Might be supposed a crow—
> A great frequenter of the church,
> Where, bishoplike, he finds a perch,
>   And dormitory too.'

In their passage up the Zurich-see, the sight of the Righi mountain brings to his mind the disappointment he felt on a former visit, when much younger, at not seeing that spectral appearance, or shadowy illusion, which operates so powerfully on the minds of the common people, and fills them with the same superstitious notions that are produced by the awful and portentous spectre of the Brocken, when the

> ——— 'Cloud-shapen giant
> Bestrides the Hartz mountain.'

This natural phenomenon is briefly and correctly explained by Mr. Barrow; as is also the deep-blue colour of the water of the lakes of Switzerland, from those of Constance and Geneva down to

> 'The *blue* rushing of the arrowy Rhone,'

changing that colour to a sea-green ; 'according,' he supposes, 'as the rays of light are modified by the blue sky, the clouded atmosphere, the height and slope of the surrounding mountains, and the depth of the lake, for where it is shallow, and the bottom visible, the water is colourless, when even of the deepest blue, if taken up in a glass.'

Having proceeded on the line of the lakes, and arrived at Ragatz, the travellers continued on foot to the warm-baths of Pfeffers, declared to be 'one of the most extraordinary spots in all Switzerland,' and confirmed to be so by Mr. Barrow, after having seen, as he tells us, a great portion of this country. The baths are situated at the bottom of a deep mountain-gap or chasm, with a frightful precipice on either side ; or rather an almost perpendicular wall of rock, not less than six hundred feet high, while the impetuous torrent of the Tamina river roars over its rocky channel, about thirty feet below the surface on which the baths are built. A more dreary, desolate, and undesirable place could hardly be imagined than this for the reception and abode of the sick who may be sent thither, and which were not fewer than two hundred and fifty at this time, most of them exhibiting a gloomy and woful appearance. What must be the state of this den in winter, when it is reported that, even in the midst of summer, it is only visited by the sun's rays a few hours while near the meridian ? The warm spring is higher up the chasm ; and the water is conveyed from the cistern which receives it, in pipes to the pump-room; the temperature of the spring is about 96° of Fahrenheit. The only object that afforded our travellers the least gratification, was, 'the view, on returning down this magnificent chasm, of the sharp-edged, snow-clad peaks of a bold mountain called Falknis, which, rising to the height of nearly eight thousand feet, and closing as it were the aperture, was truly grand ; and the snowy summits, as the sun shone brilliantly upon them, stood out in beautiful relief against an azure sky.'

A short journey along the banks of this branch of the Rhine brought the travellers to Chur or Coire, (the *Curia Rhetorum*,) the capital of the Grisons, a curious old city of narrow lanes, whose houses of gable-ends, and overhanging upper stories, nearly approach each other; appearing to have undergone little change since the days when the canton was held by the Romans. The language of the Grisons is still in fact a *patois* of the Latin. The principal buildings are, an old irregular Gothic church of no particular order, and one that was called the Episcopal palace. In the former, it is pretended, are deposited the bones of a Saint Lucius, King of the Britons, (the Welsh) Fox, in his 'Book of Martyrs,' has included one of that name, who made several bishops and erected many churches: one old writer mentions that of St. Peter, Cornhill, and also the cathedral of Colchester. He is supposed to have died about the time that the Roman Emperor Severus was in the possession of Great Britain. The Grisons having been a province of Rome, and Lucius being a surname of Severus, the story of the bones may have some reference to that emperor.

From Coire to the village of Reichenau is a pleasant, picturesque, and romantic drive up the valley of the Rhine; and near the spot is the confluence of the two branches, the Hinter-Rhein and the Vorder-Rhein —the former having its rise in the valley leading to the Pass of the Bernardin, the latter in a spur of the Alps near to St. Gothard. Not far from this 'meeting of the waters' stands an old chateau, which was said to have formerly belonged to the Planta family. The attendant of our travellers having pointed it out as a place of some note, told a remarkable and interesting anecdote connected with it, which is fully corroborated by Murray in one of his Hand-Books. 'At the end of last century,' he says, 'a young man calling himself Chabot arrived here on foot, with a stick in his hand and a bundle on his back. He presented a letter of introduction to M Jost, the head master of the school, in consequence of which he was appointed usher, and for eight months gave lessons in French, mathematics, and history. This forlorn stranger was no other than Louis Philippe, now King of the French, then Duc de Chartres, who had been forced, by the march of the French army, to quit Bremgarten, and seek concealment here in the performance of the humble duties of a schoolmaster, and in that capacity made himself equally beloved by masters and pupils.'

From the humble and dependent situation of an usher in a Swiss country school, to the Royal occupation of the palace of the Tuilleries, must indeed have been a severe trial of human forbearance. 'It is to be hoped,' says Mr. Barrow, 'that the change, though violent, enabled the Duc de Chartres, before he became the King of the French, to think and to say with another (imaginary) banished duke, what our great poet of nature has put into the mouth of the latter—

" —— Sweet are the uses of adversity,
Which, like the toad, ugly and venomous,
Wears yet a precious jewel in its head.'

And this jewel of adversity, thus suddenly transferred to a diadem, would appear not to have essentially changed the character of the man.

The road from Coire to Thusis is described as a charming drive. 'It led us through the valley of Hinter-Rhein, hemmed in by lofty mountains, whose summits were covered with snow. The village of Thusis, with its church, at the head of the valley, is most romantically situated, the mountains on each side, a little beyond it, coming almost in close contact with each other.

'We were, in fact, about to enter a spot that may, perhaps, be considered among the most romantic of the many that occur in Switzerland —I allude to that magnificent gap, or gorge, in the mountains, along the sides of which has been constructed, with great labour and skill, a practicable road, known by the name of the *Via Mala*—not very appropriate now—as it is in reality a most excellent road; though the appearance would lead one to conclude it had once deserved the *bad* name it acquired, and has kept. It might then have been, and probably was, left nearly in a state of nature; it is now artificial, and certainly great art has been employed to make it what it is—a road hewn out of the almost perpendicular sides of one or other of the precipices of this most extraordinary rent— which looks like the splitting of a mountain for about five miles in length, and which is, probably, the most sublime and tremendous gulf that the whole Alpine region affords.'

The foaming torrent of the Hinter-Rhein, rolling and roaring over its rocky bed, at the depth of three or four hundred feet below the road, affords both to the eye and the ear a sublime object; while, above it, a perpendicular and frequently overhanging rocky precipice, of at least as many thousand feet, rises in fearful grandeur. The road itself is a mere shelf cut out of the rock, and in several places tunnelled through the solid projections. There are three bridges, of a single arch each, thrown across this gap. 'The second bridge,' says Mr. Barrow, 'bestrides the chasm at a height not less than four hundred feet; and the position of it bears some resemblance

to the old Devil's Bridge at the pass of St.
Gothard, when I saw it before the new one
was erected, though the one in question is
five times the height of the Devil's Bridge.'

They were told by an eyewitness, that
the inundations of 1834 tore up, and swept
with the current, the remains of several
houses and large trees, in such masses as
nearly to block up the arches of the bridges,
so that the water at the second bridge rose
within a few feet of the top of the arch.
Had the bridge given way, and a mass of
water of four hundred feet in depth broken
loose at once, carrying with it the floating
debris of uprooted trees and the remnants
of houses, the calamity that befell the valley
of Martigny must have been repeated; but
fortunately it gradually subsided. These
two magnificent gorges of the Via Mala
and Pfeffers, no doubt, owe their present
existence to the gradually wearing away of
the looser parts of their enclosing sides;
and by repeated inundations, the materials of
which are deposited on the plains in a double
row of ridges, have formed those expanded
valleys which are generally found at the
mouths of such chasms.

, Our travellers had now arrived at the
magnificent mountain scenery branching
out from the great chain of the Alps,
amidst which is the secluded village of
Splugen. This name is also given to the
pass over the main chain they were about
to ascend, and has recently been made the
common route of communication between
Austria, Switzerland, and Austrian Lombardy. The village is said to be about
4500 feet above the level of the sea; and
the fir, the beech, and the larch forests,
which had clothed the valleys and the sides
of the mountains, began now to put on a
rugged and scraggy appearance, and were
soon reduced to a diminutive size. As
they advanced into the snow, these trees
wholly disappeared; but some pretty
rhododendrons, campanulas, and silenes
were in full flower, on the verge of the
snow; and these, with some tufts of grass,
supplied the place of the pines, and shortly,
in their turn, gave way to mosses and
lichens, where the snow had left any rocky
part of the ground bare. The distance, in
a direct line, from the village to the crest
of the pass is about five miles, and the ascent 2000 feet, making the whole elevation
6500 feet. What the height may be of the
two cheeks of the pass, no idea could be
formed, as the fog was too dense to see
anything. The crest is so narrow, that the
descent may be said to commence on the
other side at once. At a short distance below is situated the Austrian custom-house,

dreary in the extreme. Here the passports
were *visé'd*, and a dirty greasy mark from
the oil-pot smeared upon them.

The descent on the Italian side is precipitous; but a newly-made road along the
side of the valley now affords perfect ease
and security, by zig-zags or meanderings,
which did not exist at the time that Marshal Macdonald experienced those deplorable disasters that befell his army, when
crossing the old Cardinello pass in the
midst of winter, over frozen snow, with
frequent avalanches hurling down fragments of rock and large masses of glaciers,
which blocked up the passage, and destroyed a great number of his troops and
horses. Mr. Barrow thinks it must have
been in this part of the Rhætian Alps that
the Roman general Drusus carried over
his army and subdued the Rhætians (the
Grison,) for which he is complimented by
Horace—

> 'Videre Rhætis bella sub Alpibus,
>   Drusum gerentem Vindelici.'

The post-house is a little below the
Campo Dolcino, where four Italians were
found sitting at a table, two on each side,
with great vehemence playing at the game
of *fingers* called *morra;* that is, one on
each side throwing out simultaneously,
from a clenched fist, a certain number of
fingers, to be guessed at by his antagonist.
The Romans must have left it as a legacy
to the Italians; they called it *micare digitis;*
and Cicero, speaking of it, observes, with
much *naïveté*, that great confidence is necessary when you play at this game in the
dark. But how did the Chinese get it?
Their *Tsoi-moi* is in all respects the same.
Signor Pollicinello, a great favourite with
the Italians, is also supposed to be a gift of
the Romans; at least the commentators of
Horace consider—

> 'Nervis alienis mobile lignum,'

(which Francis translates—

'Thou thing of wood and wires by others play'd,)

to relate to their *marionettes*.

Among the blocks and boulders are seen
growing a vast abundance of Spanish chestnut trees in full vigour, entwining their
roots among the rocky fragments, clothed
with mosses and lichens, and forming a fine
contrast with the dark glossy green of the
chestnut leaves. The pretty and pleasing
village of Chiavenna is situated in a small
retired valley, where grapes and vines, figs,
pears, and cherries, were at this time fully

ripe and in abundance. The climate, of course, was wholly changed; but the dress of the inhabitants, whether male or female, was not yet Italianized. The small river meandering down the valley flows through the lake Riva into the Lago di Como. This beautiful lake, towards its southern extremity, is divided by the bold promontory of Bellagio into two branches: that on the western side having Como at its termination, and that on its eastern, Lecco.

Mr. Barrow gives a very lively picture of the enchanting shores of the western arm; the hills clothed with verdure to their very summits, among which are the spreading beech, the broad-leafed platanus, the poplar, and the cypress; and interspersed in these are convents and cottages, and handsome villas of men of rank and fortune, residents of Milan. In the town of Como there is little that is remarkable. An old Roman castle, on the crest of the hill behind it, is a prominent and picturesque object. Como is flanked on either side with woods and hills, on which the mulberry and olive prevail; and close to the town are citron-groves and myrtle hedges. The surrounding country is rich in cattle, affording abundance of butter, parmesan cheese, and flesh meat for the market. The cotton plant and the mulberry supply materials for the cotton and silk mills

The road from Como to Milan, about twenty-five miles, is level and dusty, and the incessant chirping of the cicada in the hedgerows is represented as somewhat teasing; but the country is beautiful, and well-cultivated with various kinds of grain and maize, the latter being the principal food of the common people. The hedges are chiefly composed of mulberry-trees and acacias, in full flower, among which the white convolvulus, with its multitude of blossoms, creeps up to their very summits.

Milan contains a number of public buildings, of which the splendid cathedral is the most conspicuous: there are several other churches, chapels, convents, and schools, besides various charitable institutions, hospitals, and two public libraries. Mr. Barrow gives an interesting account of the Duomo or Cathedral; but we must content ourselves with his general view of it.

'In point of magnitude and massive structure, it is not perhaps to be put in competition with St. Paul's of London, or St. Peter's of Rome; but in its florid Gothic architecture, its beautiful white marble, its multitude of pinnacles and statues, its exquisite carving and fretwork, it is, I believe, generally admitted to excel both. The grand entrance is one of the most imposing pieces of architecture to be met with anywhere.

The balustrade of the roof is crowded with pinnacles, each pinnacle having its statue, the merits of which, placed at so great a height, are not to be judged of by the eye as seen from the ground. They are said to amount to many hundreds; indeed, every prominent point rising out of the building is surmounted by a statue. When seen from the top of the building, to which we ascended, they exhibited a *forest* of statues, containing, I should suppose, the whole catalogue of saints in Christendom, and something more. They pretend to say that, within and without the cathedral, there are not less than five thousand statues, great and small.'

Mr. Eustace, who piqued himself on the accuracy of his measurement of buildings, has been found to exaggerate that of the Cathedral of Milan; but he has also been incorrect in his accusation of the French with regard to the fresco painting of the Last Supper, in the refectory of the convent of Dominicans, by Leonardo da Vinci. 'The people about,' says Mr. Barrow, 'pretend that the French having made this room a sort of barrack or store for artillerymen, and also a place of confinement for prisoners, the picture was constantly shot at, and thus destroyed. I saw no signs of such being the case; several little patches had chipped off, evidently from the effect of damp.' But what says Mr. Eustace—'The picture was used as a target for the soldiers to fire at! The heads were their favourite marks, and that of our Saviour in preference to others. Their impiety, though wanton, and to them unprofitable, was impotent, and may be passed over with contemptuous abhorrence; but their barbarism, in defacing a masterpiece which, though in decay, was still a model in the art, succeeded to the full extent even of their mischievous wishes, and has erased for ever one of the noblest specimens in the world' Believing this to be slander, Mr. Barrow applied to that excellent artist Mr. Phillips, who kindly allowed him to look over his note-book, made in a tour in the year 1825. After regretting that time and accidents, and damp and repainting, had left but little of the original, he thus proceeds: 'It is but little,' says he, 'but fortunately the head of the Saviour is the most favoured, and though greatly decayed, enough remains to show the grandeur and even sublimity of form and fulness of expression which Da Vinci seems so fully to have conceived, as becoming that divine character. The expression is dignified, with meek submission; the tranquillity of a superhuman mind when conveying intelligence of the deepest and most awful import, impressed with a consciousness of the necessity and value of the great sacrifice he was about to make, and the important object for which it was ordained.' What, then, becomes of Mr. Eustace's charge against the French ? Their generals. we know, carried off works of art wherever they could find them, but never, we believe, wantonly destroyed them. Mr. Simond says—'an old woman residing on the spot told him, that when Bonaparte came to look at this picture, and found the room used as a prison for soldiers, he shrugged his shoulders, stamped his foot, ordered them out, and that a wooden partition should be built before the picture.'

The Brera library, containing about two hundred thousand volumes, annually increasing by a grant from the Austrian government, is an excellent institution, open daily except on Sundays, free admission, and the number of readers about one hundred and twenty on an average. The building contains also a collection of coins and medals, and the upper part is appropriated as an observatory. The Ambrosian library contains about one hundred thousand printed, and four thousand six hundred manuscript volumes. It was here that Maio made his valuable discovery of ancient manuscripts In these libraries all ranks of different nations assemble; and it is so far from true that the Italians universally hate the Austrians, that the principal inhabitants of Milan send their sons to Vienna for their education; that the Catholics and Protestants mingle freely together; and that the Austrian soldiers mix with the population.

The greatest ornaments of Milan were laid out and constructed by Napoleon—the Piazza d'Armi, the forum, and the circus or amphitheatre, communicating with each other. The first is a square of about 2000 feet each side. The amphitheatre, it is said, will contain 45,000 people, in which horse races, theatrical exhibitions, and games of various kinds are performed; the grand entrance to it is called the *Pulvinare* Anciently the *pulvinarium* was a place for receiving the statues of the gods, but the Roman emperors ejected the deities to witness the Circensian games—*unde Augustus et tota Cæsarum domus ludos spectabant*—and why not Napoleon ? The three places above mentioned are supposed to occupy about a sixth part of the city and suburbs. A beautiful white marble gate, named Arco del Pace, opens into the Place of Arms, surmounted in its centre by Victory drawn in a chariot; at the four corners, by four equestrian nymphs; and on the four sides are thirty-six bas-reliefs, exquisitely executed. This noble arch was planned, but not executed, by Napoleon, as a monument to celebrate the conquest of Italy.

Our travellers returned along the eastern shore of the Lake Como, over a recently constructed road, described as 'a work of immense labour and consummate skill;' made, in fact, by cutting down and levelling the margin of the mountain, and where the masses projected into the lake, boring or blasting galleries; the whole length of which, in the distance of twenty miles, Mr. Barrow estimates at 3000 feet.

On leaving the lake, the travellers proceeded up the Valteline, a valley about fifty miles in length, bordered by two mountainous branches of the Alps, with the rapid and destructive river Adda flowing down it. Towards the upper part of the valley are the town and baths of Bormio, near the foot of the pass of the Stelvio, at an elevation of from 4000 to 5000 feet above the level of the sea; 'the highest elevation, I believe,' says Mr. Barrow, 'of any town in Europe.' The height of the pass is variously stated Mr Brokendon says it is the highest in the world traversable by carriages, being 2417 feet higher than the crest of the passage over Mount Cenis. Now as the crest of Cenis is 6773 feet, add 2417, and we have 9190 feet for the highest point of the Stelvio pass.

'The view that now bursts upon the sight on reaching the summit of the pass, is superior to that of any Alpine scenery I have witnessed— the Simplon, the St. Gothard, the Splugen, bearing no comparison with it. It is a view so vast and comprehensive, and of objects so stupendous, as to impress on the mind of the observer a feeling of reverence and awe, and perhaps of humiliation also, to find himself, a mere atom in the creation, surrounded by some of the most sublime among the varied and manifold scenes which the hand of Nature has supplied for the contemplation of man.

" All that expands the spirit, yet appals,
    Gather around these summits, as to show
 How earth may pierce to heaven, yet leave vain
            man below."

'A succession of peaked rocks, rising one above another as far as the eye can reach, whose dark masses are seen protruding from the pure white glittering snow, and the frowning glaciers suspended from their sides, the varied hues which clouds and sunshine alternately impart, the magnificent mountain of the Ortler-spitz towering above all the rest, and crowning the head of the valley with its peaked summit, rising to a height of not less than 14,400 feet above the level of the sea—all these grouped together in one cluster as it were—present to the mind of the spectator a picture of grandeur and sublimity that no time can efface, and no description, either with pen or pencil, convey.'

After a long descent, over numerous zig-zags and covered galleries, the hamlet of Trefoi, with its little church, makes its appearance, leaving the traveller in doubt whether most to admire or deplore its elevated and lonely position—embosomed, as it were, amid eternal snows, and in the never-ceasing presence of two huge glaciers sloping down the sides of the gigantic Ortler-spitz, with only a deep and narrow ravine between them and the village.

On crossing the Stelvio we enter the Northern Tyrol, and proceed to its capital, Innsbruck, over a fine road, bordered by the rapid Inn, flowing down a beautiful and fertile valley, smiling with numerous towns and villages on either side. We are now in the very heart of the great body of the Alps, rising abruptly from the skirts of the valley in sublime grandeur; their varied features of rock and forest towering up the steep ascent, even to their snowy pinnacles; while gleams and glooms from sunshine and cloud, are seen to play alternately on their chequered sides. Innsbruck is embosomed in a recess of these noble mountains, which are here flanked by rich and picturesque hills It is an ancient city, chiefly made up of one long wide street, in which are numerous churches and chapels, with other public buildings; and its population is reckoned at from twelve to thirteen thousand souls.

When a stranger enters the Franciscan church, his astonishment is extreme on beholding, in the central aisle, two rows of gigantic bronze statues, above seven feet high, and mostly in armour; and between the rows a noble sarcophagus of marble, bearing on its surface a large bronze figure kneeling. The statues consist of fourteen on each side of the tomb, and are said to have been cast by a native Tyrolese artist, of the name of Loffler, in the early part of the sixteenth century. Among them are eight females. The greater part consists of persons connected with the Maximilian family; but at the head of one of the rows stands old Clovis of France, and just below him, Arthur, called King of Britain—perhaps he of the Silures; but Addison suggests he might be meant for Arthur Prince of Wales, son of Henry the VII. Whoever he was intended for, Mr. Barrow says, like a true Englishman, he was the best *set up* and the most symmetrical figure in the whole group

But the tomb is the most attractive object. It is of white Carrara marble, thirteen feet long, and about six high. On the sides and ends are twenty-four bas-reliefs in as many compartments, of very superior workmanship—pictures possessing all the qualities of a finished painting, wanting only that of colour. They are mostly historical subjects, representing the events of the life of Maximilian.

'The skill exhibited in the composition of these medallions is admirable; the figures of men and horses are exquisitely beautiful; the latter absolutely in motion, and all their equipments minutely detailed and brought out. I was particularly struck with that which represents the procession of the Princess Margaret on her return from the Court of France to the palace of Maximilian. In this group the horses, the trappings, their riders and their dresses, had the appearance of a picture taken from the life, and all as if in motion.'

These excellent specimens of sculpture are the work of Alexander Colin, a native of Malines, whose name, says Mr. Barrow, is scarcely to be found in any of the historical or biographical accounts of painters or sculptors. Besides these, there are numerous other beautiful pieces of sculpture from the same artist in Innsbruck, and also in Vienna; yet the name of such an artist has never met a favourable notice, except, as Mr. Barrow says, 'from passing travellers like myself.'—'I have looked in vain for the name of Colin in Walpole, Bryan, Ottley, Winkleman, Fuseli. In Vasari not a word is to be found in the whole sixteen volumes; or in the Cicognara, or Lanzi, or other Italian writers that I have consulted. Even Descamps, who gives an account of the Netherland artists, and of those exquisite carvings in wood that adorn the churches, and pulpits in particular, in Belgium, is silent as to Colin.' It would appear from a German work now in progress by Dr. Nagler, that when a boy he was put out to learn the trade of a stonemason; and being in the habit of seeing works of art, he used to make models of them in wax or plaster —then to cut them in wood, to bring out the sharp points—then to paint them on canvass—and lastly, to sculpture them on stone. Mr. Barrow enumerates several of his works, and says, 'I have been thus particular in my account of this neglected artist, in the hope that, should this little book fall into the hands of some of our travelling artists in Germany and Italy, they will not overlook the Valley of the Inn, nor deem the name of Colin unworthy of a place among the lives of the artists'

There are several other interesting monuments in this church; but we shall only mention one, the statue of Hofer, which surmounts his tomb—his remains being conveyed hither, in grateful remembrance of his services, by the late Emperor of Austria, and in deference to the feelings of the whole people of the Tyrol.

Of the character of these brave mountaineers, and their undeviating devotion to their beloved country, the historical sketch which Mr. Barrow has given of the unprovoked invasion of their territory by the combined forces of France, Bavaria, and Saxony, and the repeated defeats and expulsion of the invading forces, affords a spirit-stirring picture, the remembrance of which must remain indelibly stamped on the mind of every Tyrolese now living, or yet to be born. The public testimonial given by a prisoner, a Saxon colonel, speaks of their devotion and irresistible impetuosity. He and three hundred of his men had been spared by calling out for quarter; and he says, 'when all lay dead around, and the victory was complete, the Tyrolese, as if moved by one impulse, fell upon their knees, and poured forth the emotion of their hearts in prayer, under the canopy of heaven—a scene so awfully solemn, that it will ever be present to my remembrance. I joined in the devotion, and never in my life did I pray more fervently.' Indeed, a strong religious feeling, and a sense of reverential duty to their Creator, pervade the whole Tyrolese nation. As soon as the vesper bell has tolled, every family assembles for the performance of evening prayer; and then may be heard, in passing the streets of a town or village, the chanting of sacred music, and the low murmurs of the congregated members.

The ancient and romantic city and fortress of Salzburg, the capital of a circle of Upper Austria, stands at the extreme point of the Norican Alps, and overlooks the plains of Bavaria. Eight or ten miles to the southward, along the valley and river of the Salza, is the mountain Deurenberg, in the bosom of which are worked the ancient salt-mines of Hallein, said to have been in constant operation from four to five hundred years. As might be expected, the whole interior of the mountain at this time may be said to resemble a honeycomb —a series of stages or floors, of galleries and cells, with intermediate rocky partitions, from top to bottom. The usual entrance for strangers is by a sloping shaft or adit, from the top of the mountain nearly. The visiter has to slide down this adit, in an angle of about 45°, with his thighs on two parallel poles, the rock close to his head, and on both sides of him. He comes to the first stage, where there is a long gallery; and on each side of this are cells, each just large enough to allow one man to work; and out of these, right and left, proceed others of the same kind. 'At the end of each,' says Mr. Barrow, ' was a soli-

tary miner at work, with his glimmering light and a kind of pick-axe, stripped perfectly naked as to the upper part of his body, and nothing below but his trousers.' The materials dug out are a sort of clay mixed with crystals of salt, which, when a sufficient quantity is accumulated in the cell, are closed or built up; water, which is at command throughout the mountain, is then let in upon them; and when the saline particles are dissolved, the impregnated water is let off through a pipe, and received in the lower part of the mountain, in a large reservoir or lake, from which it is conveyed along an adit to the shallow iron salt-pans, where the salt is crystallized and packed into casks for the markets of Austria and Bavaria. These receiving lakes, with their accompaniments, are curious: one of them is well described by Mr. Barrow, to whom we must refer our readers

Our limits will not allow us to dwell long on Munich, the capital of Bavaria—a city that, within the last thirty years, from being a small irregular crowded assemblage of old and indifferent buildings, with few exceptions, has risen to that point of eminence which may fairly entitle it to vie with any other of equal magnitude in Europe. It abounds with splendid institutions of every kind for the encouragement of the fine arts, of science, literature and natural history; with new and elegant buildings admirably adapted for their reception—some for pictures, some for statues—others for mathematical, astronomical, and philosophical instruments; a library that reckons about 500,000 volumes; a picture gallery, to which has been given the pedantic Greek name of *Pinakothek* (painting repository,) which might have better suited Otho's repository at Athens, if he has one. Another noble building is appropriated to the reception of statues, and various marbles of antiquity, called the *Glyptothek*, (repository of sculpture.) Both these buildings are divided into numerous chambers or compartments, for each of which is a well-arranged catalogue. The halls or rooms of the former contain 596, chiefly large, and the side cabinets 673 small, pictures—altogether, 1269—mostly of the best masters of the different schools. The twelve halls of ancient marbles have each their appropriate specimens. Those of the Egina hall, containing the marbles discovered by our countrymen Cockerell and Forster, are enough to make an Englishman blush for the manner in which they were allowed to pass out of our possession.

Nothing can excel in brilliancy and beauty

of decoration the numerous apartments, public and private, of the royal palace. The walls of the state apartments on the ground floor are painted in fresco, with a series of subjects taken from a national romance or epic. The walls and ceilings of the king's apartments contain subjects from the Greek poets, commencing with Hesiod and Homer, and ending with the last of the Greek tragedians and lyric poets. The queen's apartments are superbly elegant; and the throne-room, which is also her drawing-room, is really magnificent. In many of the windows, and in those of the churches, are subjects in painted or stained glass—the brilliancy of which is considered much superior to any of the specimens of this ancient art that have been discovered.

If it be asked what new impulse has, in so short a period, converted an old and neglected city into one of splendour and celebrity—the answer is easy :—the taste, the energy, and the liberality of the present King, Charles Augustus Lewis, has done this. As Prince-Royal, out of his private funds, he commenced these improvements; and, as King, has continued and superintended their execution with the same zeal and indefatigable perseverance as in his more youthful days; and thus Munich was rapidly becoming what Florence once was —'the seat of learning and literature, the school for the fine arts and liberal professions, the resort of the scholar, the painter, the sculptor, and the architect, from every part of the continent.' But alas! for frail human nature! Three short years are said to have produced a lamentable change in the character and conduct of King Lewis. An affectionate and paternal embrace bestowed on him by the old man of the Vatican, has, as it were, consumed his energies, and induced a paralysis of all his faculties—leaving pictures, statues, and love of the fine arts, for priestly discipline, prayers, and protestations.

We have here but slightly skimmed over a small portion of Mr. Barrow's volume; but we can safely recommend it as an useful companion to any one inclined to a summer's excursion over the same delightful and diversified ground which he has trodden, and as good light reading to those who travel not at all.

ART. VI.—1. *The Twenty-Third Report of the Society for the Suppression of Mendicity.* London : 1841.

2. *An Exposure of the various Impositions daily practised by Vagrants of every Description.* 8vo. Birmingham : 1841.

MENDICITY has become an evil of frightful magnitude in every portion of the British empire; but its increase in *England* is pregnant with mighty mischiefs and untold dangers. In this paper we intend to limit ourselves to a *descriptive* account of that evil, and its various aspects, leaving the remedies to the consideration of those whose duty it is to provide them.

Pauperism and mendicity, in ordinary times, must not, and should not be confounded. The law in England provides for pauperism, viz., for want, for sickness, for infirmity, for destitution. But inasmuch as the law of England is generous and paternal, in making such a provision for all who are *really* entitled to its protection, it visits with summary and severe punishment the systematic and persevering mendicant. Does it, however, do this effectually and permanently? Let us examine the facts of the case, and see to what is to be attributed the great increase of mendicity in England; notwithstanding the application of the work-house system on the one hand, and the provisions of the vagrant act on the other. For the information of those who may not be accurately acquainted with either 'the work-house system, or the vagrant act, we shall here briefly state their objects' The first is that system established by the English Poor Law Commissioners under the amended poor laws, of requiring all who apply for parochial relief to give the best evidence they can supply of their destitution, by leaving their cottages and houses, and becoming inmates of the workhouse, or, in other words, of *the Union.* The vagrant act was passed to prevent the existence of idle and disorderly persons, vagabonds, and incorrigible rogues. To the clauses and penalties of this act we shall refer hereafter.

Mendicity is of ancient date in England. With its history, and the history of the laws which have been passed for its repression, we are not, nor are our readers, unfamiliar. But there are two general descriptions of mendicity, besides the various sectional differences into which these general descriptions are divided   The FIRST is the mendicity which is the offspring of criminal habits, bad education, indolence and crime. The SECOND is the mendicity which is momentary, which is the accompaniment of a state of transition from one condition of life or occupation to another, or which is the result of sudden accidents, and for the time, overwhelming personal disasters.

Thus the drunkard—the offspring of mendicants taught to beg, and prohibited from labour—the man who prefers begging to digging or to spinning—he who chooses a barn for his bed-room, and the shelter of a hedge for his dwelling-place, and who will not rise up early and go late to rest, work with his hands, and support, by honesty and industry, himself and his family —all belong to those whose mendicity is an offence against morals, civilisation, the laws of man and of heaven.

But this is not the case with the *second* class; and it is to these that we must draw the attention, more especially, of those who take a lively and deep interest in the movements, progress, and decline of society. We will supply some examples of the sort of mendicity which we mean to point out by our *second* division.

First Example.—A woman whose husband was a weaver in Spitalfields, and who earned scarcely sufficient wages to provide himself, his wife, and three children, with potatoes, weak tea, and cold water, is suddenly deprived by death of him on whose labour she relied for her sustenance. She pawns all disposable articles to pay for the modest funeral of her husband, rather than that he should be buried at the parish expense. One of her children is taken ill, and she is obliged to nurse it. The other two are too young to labour. Her rent gets in arrear. Her articles of furniture are seized and sold. She is left without means of subsistence; and although the chimney-place and the emptied room are there at her service for a few days more, yet she has no fuel for the one and no bed for the other. · 'She should go to the Union,' (*i. e.* she should become an inmate of the building erected in her neighbourhood by the Poor-Law Commissioners, for the residence of all the poor in the surrounding parishes who shall apply for parochial relief,) says almost every one who hears of such a case; and there seems to be no other mode of relief for her. But she has thought of another. In the Union it is necessary for the health, happiness, and morals of the whole of its inmates, that there should be a classification; and she must share the fate of those whose destitution renders it necessary to seek a shelter in the workhouse. This does not accord with that hidden, but active principle of her nature which attaches her to her offspring; and she decides that she will beg—not habitually, not for life, not as a permanent means of existence, but to support herself and her children until she shall reach her own family and friends, perhaps some hundreds of miles removed, and where she will obtain employment in the fields, or on the roads; in houses as a servant, or at a washing tub as a laundress. The wide world is before her; and if her case could be really known, in all its humiliation, truthfulness, and sorrow, many a hand would be willingly stretched out to add to her means of support, and diminish her load of care. This woman leaves the metropolis, begs her way to some forty or fifty miles from London, asks alms in the presence of a police-officer, is conducted before a magistrate, examined, reprimanded, and allowed, however, to pursue her course on her promising she will beg no more. What a wretched sarcasm, and what deliberate and official lying! How can the woman and her children exist but by begging, until they arrive at the anticipated termination of her journey? There, something in the form of a home will once more greet her, though her lineaments, from want and fatigue, will scarcely be recognizable. But until that period she is a mendicant, and her children are beggar's children. At last she arrives at her own native place; and from that moment the greatest of her sorrows, if she had not lost her husband, would have ceased. This is no imaginary case. It is that of thousands every year in England.

Second Example.—A father, with his wife and six children, inhabits a small hovel as an agricultural labourer in Buckinghamshire. One night his cottage is burned down, and every article he has in the world is consumed. Scarcely have the sorrowing family an adequate quantity of clothes to cover their nakedness. The landlord lays all the blame to the labourer; and, as the cottage was not insured, is furious with his pauper tenant. The fact was that the roof was a thatched one, and, somehow or other, it took fire; perhaps the little chimney was foul, and lighted soot fell upon the straw. 'They should go to the Union!' every one will exclaim on hearing of their sorrows; but they think far differently. Some of their neighbours take them in for the moment; a few second-hand clothes are procured here and there; and then they set about begging from house to house for the means of purchasing furniture for another hovel, and thus continuing to be a family of independent labourers. This is a kind of case well known in the English agricultural districts; but for a certain time the sufferers live by mendicity.

Third Example.—A man and his wife are

thrown out of employment in a manufactory, by the failure of their employers. They have not long been there. They have not had time to put any money into the savings' bank, and their dwelling is as yet very imperfectly furnished. What are they to do? The failure of this manufacturer has thrown hundreds out of employment, and occupation is not to be obtained in the neighbourhood. What is to be done in such a case as this? 'Oh, that's a fit case for the Union!' most persons would answer. But the man and his wife are not of the same opinion. They sell their goods, pay their rent, discharge the little debts they owe, and have from fifteen shillings to a pound remaining. They set out to seek for work—honestly and truly to do so; and they go from village to village, and town to town, and manufactory to manufactory, to obtain work. They succeed; but before they have done so, not only have they spent their fifteen shillings or a sovereign, but have levied upon public charity. They have been mendicants. There are thousands of such cases every year; and worse than this, where the man and his wife have five and six children.

Fourth Example.—A mechanic meets with a sad accident. It lames him seriously. He has been economical; but his sickness is long, and all his savings' bank money is expended. He is not a member of a friendly society; he relied on the savings' bank. The pawnbroker is next resorted to. Every article which can be taken to that receptacle of the sad proofs of poverty and destitution, is converted into money at ruinous interest, until at last there is nothing left but—'the Union,' says almost every reader. No—but to beg; for the mechanic will not go to the Union. He will not associate with the idle, the profligate, and the profane; and he prefers asking charity, for the moment, till his health is restored, to becoming the inhabitant of the district workhouse. So his wife and his children ask for alms from house to house, and become, for the time being, mendicants.

These examples of *temporary* or *occasional* mendicancy will suffice. We have inquired much into the miseries of the English poor, and we know them well. It would have been easy to have chosen cases far more disastrous and gloomy, but these are sufficient to illustrate our meaning. There is an infinity of such cases as these.

Now, then, all these parties are mendicants, and on the high-roads of England may be met a vast number—much greater than our readers imagine—of mendicants for the moment, for the month, or for the week—who are yet included in the general sweeping anathema of beggars.

But there are other classes of occasional beggars, who are not so permanently, and do not belong to the tribes of vagrants by education and profession.

In the agricultural counties of the south there are the Irish field labourers, who emigrate from their own country for the English hay harvest, then for the pea harvest, then for the grain and hop harvests, and who, between the periods of these harvests, live principally by mendicity. Their harvest money they often save to take back with them to Ireland, when all the English harvests are over; but in the mean time they must live—and they live by begging. In fine weather they sleep in barns, or under such hedges as shelter them from the wind and rain; and sometimes, when they have been successful in their mendicant applications, they obtain an occasional night's lodgings in those public-houses and private lodgings appropriated to the reception of beggars.

There is another class also of occasional Irish beggars in England—those who have been disappointed in obtaining the employment they were assured was waiting for them in the manufacturing districts of Lancashire, Yorkshire, and generally in the north of that country. The Irish are an excitable people. They love to feast on golden visions, and are not easily to be convinced that labour is not in great demand in their sister country. So to England they repair; but thousands every year meet with vast and heartbreaking disappointments, and, in default of obtaining work, they take to begging; and of all the beggars in England, none are so resolute, so importunate, and so successful, as Irish beggars. They will weep, laugh, scold, run, jump, sing, walk without shoes, and almost without clothes, sleep anywhere, eat anything, and still neither pine nor die. They are really astonishing, and almost irresistible. They are always 'going to go back to Ireland,' whether you find them in the lovely scenery of Buckinghamshire or Berkshire, or strolling through the weald of Kent or the wilds of Sussex, or visiting the southern coast with Dover, Hythe, Rye, Hastings, St. Leonard's, Brighton, and other sea-bathing places on its shores. Go back at last they do, many of them, to winter in the Irish Unions.

Unhappily for England, a still larger class than those are now mendicants; much larger, indeed;—and these are the English *agricultural poor.*

It is a deplorable fact that the English agricultural poor, who have large families of very young children, live much better as beggars than they do as labourers. Eight or nine shillings per week, will not support a man with a wife and five children. They find, by experience, that it will not; for a woman who has five or even four children, all under six years of age, cannot, even in fine weather, leave her home; and in wet and wintry weather there is no work to be obtained When the eldest of the children of a family of that class can keep her younger sisters and brothers in tolerable order, the wages of the labourer are augmented by the earnings of his wife, and to exist is just possible. But existence is impossible in those English agricultural districts where the average rate of wages is under ten shillings; and yet there are many such districts, and multitudes of agricultural labourers are thus becoming mendicants! For there is no mystery in the poor man's housekeeping or expenditure. He may pay his rent to a very kind landlord, indeed, at harvest time This *is* just possible; and the wages of harvest, of himself and wife, may go much towards that item of his disbursements. In like manner, he may wear old, patched, and very shabby clothing, and himself and family may absolutely refuse to follow the counsels of their vicar or curate to attend at church in spite of their ragged garments; and they may all hide themselves on the only holiday in the week, ashamed of confessing their extreme poverty. This is the case, and we know it to be such, in a great majority of the purely agricultural districts in England. The poor will not attend the temple of God in tattered garments, and out of their scanty wages they cannot afford even shoes for their children. And then as to firing; the children may be put to bed early in the winter afternoons, four and five in a small bed, as soon as their stomachs have been warmed with a sort of hot slop of water and brown sugar, with the mere rinsings of a milk-pot; and may sleep from five o'clock in the afternoon till seven or eight next morning. But at last the morning comes, and craving appetites with it, and many mouths to feed, and many stomachs to be satisfied, and either the loaf, rice, or potatoes, must be provided.

In fact, the stomachs of these five children must be provided with food—and for that food there is no credit. How can there be? The butcher, the baker, the grocer, and the general dealer, must make good their payments to the grazier, the miller, and the wholesale houses; and if they gave credit to the husbandman, ruin must soon come upon themselves. Indeed, since the operation of the new poor laws in England, all credit to the working classes has been withdrawn. Under the old system, the pauperized labourer received so much relief in money, that for the purpose of securing his custom credit would be given, but at prices most exorbitant and injurious. But now, when relief is given *in kind*, and when most of those who used to lay out their parochial money at the general dealer's are subjected to the workhouse system, and receive no out-door relief at all, credit is quite out of the question. We assert this distinctly, because it is undeniable that, in most of the purely agricultural districts, the wages of the labourer are not adequate to his independent existence. The food of each day must be bought and paid for; and it is very easy to calculate that, this cannot be done, when the wages of an agricultural labourer, with a family, are under fifteen shillings per week. Yet, in nearly two-thirds of these districts, the wages average scarcely more than the moiety of that sum. A gallon of flour makes 8lbs. of bread. How many pounds of bread will a father, mother, and four children, require in a week? The gallon of flour costs one shilling and sixpence. Two grown people cannot eat less when they have no meat, no beer, no milk, and no fish—but simply bread, suet puddings, potatoes, and a small portion of bacon as a relish, from Sunday morning to Saturday night—than one pound each per diem, or 14lbs. per week. Four children will require the same quantity, making a total of 28lbs. of bread per week. To make this 28lbs. of bread, three and a half gallons of flour will be required, which, at 1s. 6d. per gallon, amounts to 5s. 3d. But then the bread must be baked—count nothing for the labour, nothing for the salt, nothing for the yeast—still the fagots *must* be paid for; and the baking in the cheapest manner, *i. e.* by two or more families joining together in the expense of the oven, will cost for three and a half gallons of bread, sixpence. Thus the bread alone for a man, his wife, and four children, for one week, will be five shillings and ninepence.

Supposing, then, that the rent of the labourer is paid with the wife's earnings in the field in fine weather; and supposing the ragged clothes of this family, and the firing in winter, to be paid with the extra wages and gleanings of harvest time; still we see, that out of the labourer's earnings he has to pay, in ready money each week for second bread, the sum of five shillings and ninepence. A little tea, sugar, butter, cheese, with salted or red herrings, consume the rest of his wages; and at length he becomes exhausted, weak, an easy prey to ague and fever, and he either rushes into the workhouse or becomes a beggar.

It is true, that others, when they find that bread runs away with so much of their money, resort to another kind of diet. They resort to gruel, to potatoes, to suet and rice puddings, and eat not more than half the quantity of bread we have just mentioned in the course of the week. But their health is soon undermined, when they labour in the fields, from the want of adequate nutriment; and the dietary of the union is found actually insufficient without its walls. Yet we affirm, and we know we are correct in our affirmation, that not one-tenth portion of the English agricultural independent labourers are able to obtain, with their wages, half the food allotted to the able-bodied paupers in the unions. A man in a union has seventy-two ounces of bread per week, ten pints and a half of gruel, fifteen ounces of cooked meat, one and a half lbs. of potatoes, four and a half pints of soup, fourteen ounces of suet or rice pudding, eight ounces of cheese, and four and a half pints of broth. Now, we say it fearlessly that there are not a thousand agricultural labourers in any one English county, who can and do obtain with their weekly wages such an amount and variety of food—substantial food—as this.

We are well aware that all the dietaries of all the unions are not the same as the one we have selected; but let us take another which has been very generally adopted. According to that dietary, able-bodied men have allowed them 125 ounces of bread per week, ten and a half pints of gruel, eight ounces of dressed meat, and five ounces of bacon, one and a half lbs. of potatoes, one and a half pints of soup, and eighteen and a half ounces of cheese. In this dietary the bread, cheese, and gruel, predominate; but it must be remembered, that of bread the pauper eats nearly eight lbs. per week, or more than one pound per diem. Again, we state, that very few of the agricultural poor in England, who labour from before sunrise, very often,'till after sunset, are able to obtain such an amount of nourishment as this! Their wages, and the prices of provisions, will not admit of their doing so.

The consequence the most striking, immediate, pressing, and increasing, of this state of things, is the conversion of the inadequately-paid labourer into a mendicant. We have counted in certain districts of England the number of vagrant poor, who, in spite of the vagrant act, still demand alms; and we have taken districts removed from each other, at the same and at different epochs. We have selected spots the most favourable for these statistics: viz., those where the roads in and about the spots in question were at last concentrated near a turnpike, and near a turnpike gate, and the results are as follows:—

						On one day.
Buckingham,	September 1841,	.	.	.	.	41
Bury St. Edmunds,	August 1841,	.	.	.	.	37
Brighton,	September 1841,	.	.	.	.	92
Dover,	October 1841,	.	.	.	.	53
Hastings,	October 1841,	.	.	.	.	60
Huntingdon,	August 1841,	.	.	.	.	42
Leicester,	September 1841,	.	.	.	.	36
Marlow,	August 1841,	.	.	.	.	33
Nottingham,	September 1841,	.	.	.	.	69
Oxford,	October 1841,	.	.	.	.	31
Portsmouth,	September 1841,	.	.	.	.	71
Reading,	August 1841,	.	.	.	.	49
Tunbridge Wells,	September 1841,	.	.	.	.	69

It will be at once perceived that the object of this table is to show the number of vagrants passing through the towns, selected as examples, in one day. Let these numbers be multiplied by 365 days, and we should have a rough estimate of the numbers passing through in the course of a year—still making deductions for bad weather and inclement seasons.

These statistics have been made most conscientiously; and, it is to be observed, include the children as well as the parents or chiefs of each band. If, however, it be borne in mind that these are only the numbers of one day's vagrants at thirteen towns in England, how frightful will the total mass of mendicity appear to those who remember the vast quantity of cities and towns in the counties of England and Wales; in two-thirds of which, at the same moment of time that these vagrants were passing through, others of an equal amount were also living on the alms-giving of others!

It must unquestionably be admitted that, from April to the commencement of December, mendicity in the rural counties is greater than from December to the end of March. Those who go about begging with their children, find it more fatiguing and unhealthy. Besides which, the by-ways, to avoid the police of the towns in the day, are often not traversable in winter; the barns, still provided by the farmers for beggars to sleep in, are too cold; the nights are long and dark, and therefore unfavourable to rural and roadside begging; and the expenses at lodging-houses and public-houses are sometimes too onerous to be sustained out of the daily receipts of the mendicants. 'We shall return to the unions,' say some, as the winter sets in and the begging trade gets bad: and now it is time we should look to the receipts of these livers upon public bounty.

Unable, we have said, to obtain adequate food and raiment from their *agricultural* wages, multitudes, nay thousands, of the agricultural poor take to begging. And how much more profitable do they find begging than digging, ploughing, or even thrashing! The following table has been drawn out from the most uncontrovertible data, which we have personally procured, or which have been supplied us by those who could not be themselves deceived, and have no interest in deceiving us. The names of the individuals are in many cases supposed or fictitious, since the vagrants would not always give their real names, and even in some cases admitted they were assumed ones. At each of the places mentioned below—Dover, Canterbury, &c — suitable persons were employed, in the autumn of last year, to watch the vagrants, and obtain on a given day, the most accurate information as to their proceedings. The rural police assisted likewise in obtaining the best and most detailed data.

Table of Receipts by families consisting of a man, his wife, and from 3 to 4 children, by Mendicity, in Agricultural Distress.

			Average receipts per diem.		
			£	s.	d.
No. 1.	William Holmes, his wife, 3 children, and an infant at the breast,	Dover and Environs.	0	3	2
2.	James Smith, his wife, 3 children,	Canterbury and Environs.	0	3	8
3.	Patrick O'Reilly, his wife, and 5 children,	Brighton and Environs.	0	4	6
4.	Henry Mercer and 3 daughters all singers,	Hastings and Environs.	0	5	6
5.	James Rowe, his wife and 3 boys, all singers and beggars,	Tunbridge and Environs.	£0	4	9
6.	Mary M'Arthur, 3 girls and 1 boy, carrying matches, singing and begging,	Chelmsford and Environs.	0	5	0
7.	Samuel Davis and his wife, with 6 children all carrying on different systems of begging,	Windsor and Environs.	0	6	0
8.	David Saunders, and his wife and 4 children, selling lucifer boxes, matches, singing and begging.	Reading and Environs.	0	5	6

In giving the places where they were begging at the time that these data were procured, it must not be supposed that they were *inhabitants* of those places and their environs, but merely vagrants there for the time being. In some districts the average receipts for an English agricultural beggar, his wife, and three or four children, are 3s. per diem, besides stale provisions and old clothes—the latter being soon convertible into money; but in districts which the gentry frequent for sea-bathing, or for the benefit of the mineral waters, they will average from 4s. to 4s. 6d. per diem. And it must not be lost sight of, that whereas the independent able-bodied agricultural labourer has his expenses much increased, but his income never augmented, by an additional number of children, the mendicant's revenue is always greatly improved by having four or five, or even a greater number of offspring. A beggar's family stopping at Windsor, for example, for a night's lodging, would arrive at night, and the next morning, by eight o'clock, his five children would be sent, in at least three different directions, to solicit alms, all with different stories of misfortune and woe; whilst the parents, to avoid the penalties of the vagrant act, would remain at the public-house, waiting the return of their children, and preparing the general breakfast.

And there is another method of checking the accuracy of the data we have procured relative to the receipts of the English agricultural beggars, now so amazingly increasing, in which we cannot err. A man, his wife, and four children, are still the family whose daily proceedings we are examining and explaining, and their average expenditure is as follows:—

		£	s.	d.
Lodging at a public-house or lodging-house for one night,		£0	0	8
Breakfast.—Tea,	. . . . .	0	0	1½
Sugar,	. . . . .	0	0	1½
Butter,	. . . , .	0	0	2
Bread,	. . . . .	0	0	4¼
Dinner.—Bread	. . . . .	0	0	4¼
Bacon or herrings, (besides the cold meat and provisions they have collected,)	. .	0	0	6
Supper.—Bread,	. . . . .	0	0	4¼
Beer,	. . . . .	0	0	2
Cheese,	. . . . .	0	0	2
Biscuits, (for the children,)	. . .	0	0	2
		£0	3	2¼

If the day has been 'a good one,' and the receipts have been considerable, the supper is improved by more beer, and sometimes by fresh meat broiled on the gridiron. These are not rough estimates, or general outlines, but the result of personal investigation and of private research. Undoubtedly, there are many thousands of beggars who are less fortunate in their applications than others; but the average receipts of an English agricultural beggar, with a wife and three or four children, are not less than 3s. per day; whilst the average receipts of an agricultural labourer, in those very districts, are not more than half that amount.

It is clear, then, that the English agricultural labourer, with the present rates of wages and provisions, finds it far more profitable, and far more easy, to earn his living by begging than by work; and this is unquestionably *one* of the reasons for the enormous increase of mendicity. If the agricultural poor in England could support existence in anything approaching to comfort with the present rates of wages and food, from an intimate acquaintance with their character and sentiments, we feel justified in saying they would shun the evils and horrors of mendicity; but when, after years of unceasing toil, they find that the fire never blazes, the smoke-jack never turns, and the beer-can never foams for them, but that squalid poverty, and then disease, are their abiding portions, unless they become dependent on *'the unions'* for support, they rush away from the scenes of their sorrow and their ruin, and become beggars.

But is there not a VAGRANT ACT in England? asks the anxious and inquiring reader. Do not the Irish poor law commissioners demand a similar act, in order to repress the mendicity of three millions of Irish beggars? How is it, then, that mendicity should increase in England in the teeth of such an act?

In order to answer this question, it may be well to look for a moment at the Vagrant Act itself.

The act now in force, which consolidates, amends, and repeals, the prior statutes relative to vagrants, points out three classes of these individuals:—1st, Idle and disorderly persons; 2d, rogues and vagabonds; and 3d, incorrigible rogues.

The idle and disorderly persons are those who will not work and maintain their families—who wander abroad and trade without a licence—who walk in the streets as prostitutes—who beg or gather alms, or cause their children so to do—or who ask alms under a certificate or other instrument prohibited by law. Such persons are subject to arrest, and to hard labour, on conviction, for any time not exceeding one calendar month.

Rogues and vagabonds are those who commit any of the before-specified offences, after having been already convicted as idle and disorderly persons. They are also those who pretend to tell fortunes, or by palmistry or otherwise to deceive any of the Queen's subjects. Also all persons living in barns, carts, and unoccupied buildings, and who cannot give any good account of themselves. Also all venders of obscene objects, or exhibitors of indecent exhibitions, (and, by the statute of 1st Victoria, who sell indecent prints in shops.) Also all persons exposing their persons; all individuals seeking to obtain alms by exposing their wounds or deformities; all persons seeking to collect alms by fraudulent representations; and persons running away from, and leaving unprovided, their wives or children; all persons gambling or betting at any table or instrument of gain by games of chance; all persons having in their possession instruments which are used for picking locks and for burglary, or having weapons with the intent of committing any felonious act; all persons found in any dwelling-house or enclosed place for an unlawful purpose; every suspected person or reputed thief frequenting any river, canal, quay, wharf, street, highway, &c., with intent to commit felony. And finally, every person apprehended as an idle and disorderly person, who resists by violence the police-officer arresting him, provided he be convicted of the offence for which the police-officer took him into custody; as well as suspected persons and reputed thieves.

The punishment for rogues and vagabonds is hard labour for any time not exceeding three months.

Incorrigible rogues are those who escape out of any place of legal confinement before the time of punishment has expired; every person who, having been convicted as a rogue and vagabond, shall again, after liberation, perpetrate the same or similar offences; and any person arrested as a rogue and vagabond, and who shall violently resist the police so arresting him.

The punishment for incorrigible rogues is imprisonment till the next quarter-sessions, hard labour for any time not exceeding a year, and, in some cases, the whipping of *male* offenders.

The lodging-houses in which vagrants may be suspected of concealing themselves are subject to be searched; the moneys and effects found upon vagrants may be applied towards the expense of apprehending and maintaining them; and the laws in force give every facility towards the arrest, conviction, and punishment of offenders. And yet, in spite of this act, England is now infested, in every part and portion of her counties, though undoubtedly more in some districts than in others, with thousands of mendicants.

Before we state the reasons generally assigned by the occasional, or rather non-hereditary and non-professional beggars, for their adoption of this mode of life, it may not be uninteresting or unimportant to look at the terms, practice, and manœuvres of the begging art.

There live, then, in the midst and about all the English population, a distinct population, fearful in numbers, constantly and rapidly increasing, having a language, manners, and customs of its own—living, in nine cases out of ten, in a course of life the most immoral and profligate; and yet so living, and so increasing, in spite of the laws, in spite of the municipal arrangements of the last few years, so favourable to their detection and punishment; in spite of the new poor-law arrangements; and in spite of the general feeling that the poor-rates and the unions ought to provide for all real cases of destitution and misery. This population has its signs, its free-masonry, its terms of art, its correspondence, its halting-houses, its barns still kept open, and even well strawed by farmers and country gentlemen; its public-houses, its well-known, and even recognized lodging-houses; and its manifold plans to extract or extort, to win or to scold, out of its reluctant but deceived victims, sums amounting, we are inclined to believe, to not less than £1,375,000; being one-third of the total amount of poor-rates! This sum may at first appear utterly extravagant; but it will not be found to be so when it is remembered, that on an average each begging family extorts £55 per annum from the public. The annual poor law expenditure for the year ending in March, 1840, in England, was, in round numbers, £4,300,000. In England, including the three ridings of Yorkshire, there are forty-two counties. The population of those counties is nearly fifteen millions. If we take at this moment a rough and general, though a tolerably correct estimate of that population, with its dense misery in towns and cities, and its diffused but not less individually intense misery in the agricultural districts, we may fairly calculate that one out of every one hundred is a beggar, or lives in a state of practical vagrancy—looking, in one form or other, to alms for support. The one-hundredth part of the population is 150,000; and if each begging family, raising £55 per annum from the public by alms, be estimated as consisting of six, we shall have 25,000 English begging families, raising £55 per annum each, or the total sum of £1,375,000. But we believe that we have underrated, instead of overstated, the facts of the case in these calculations. In London alone and its vicinity, in spite of all the efforts of the police, a very large part of that sum is extorted; and we have not taken into consideration the wholesale mendicity which is now deplorably manifest in the larger English manufacturing towns. We have also omitted all Irish mendicants; and yet they are nearly in the proportion of one to three in the English agricultural districts. Naturally anxious as we are to avoid even the appearance of exaggeration, we are still bound to state, that the estimate we have made is greatly deficient, and that we have understated the real statistics.

The begging population of England, existing and increasing in spite of municipal police, and notwithstanding the penalties of the vagrant act, is divided into several classes; and we now propose to draw upon a little pamphlet, mentioned at the head of this article, which has been recently published at Birmingham, and which contains very accurate details of the mendicant population—written by one who long frequented the haunts of the vagrant community. The portion of the community to which his details extend, belong principally to the hereditary and professional class of beggars.

The writer of this pamphlet thus proceeds with his descriptive details :—

'In order fully to explain each individual character, I shall begin with those vagrants who generally obtain the most, and are considered of the *first class*, and are by some termed "Silver Beggars," but by travellers "LURKERS."

'LURKERS are persons who go about with briefs, containing false statements of losses by fire, shipwrecks, accidents, &c. The seals and signatures of two or more magistrates are affixed to those briefs, and they are so well written, that thousands of persons are daily imposed upon by them. As there are so many different ways used by these persons, it will be necessary to explain each of them separately.'

The writer then enters into details as to ' the *Fire-Lurkers*,' or those 'who go about begging for loss by fire.' They have false briefs, pretended to be signed by two magistrates and the clergyman of the place where the fire is alleged to have taken place. The documents are accompanied by a sham subscription-book, and the brief is called, in the mendicant's parlance, ' a

sham,' whilst the subscription-book they name ' a delicate.' With this ' sham and delicate' the ' lurkers,' or beggars, proceed all over the country; and the author states that one man, with whom he was acquainted, ' had been a fire-lurker for fourteen years, and had travelled through every county in England, and the greater part of Wales.'

Then there is,

' *The Shipwrecked Sailor's Lurk.*—Persons who go on this lurk, generally represent themselves as captains or masters of merchant ships, which have been wrecked, and they have, of course, lost all their property; and their pretended loss always amounts to many hundred pounds, sometimes even to thousands. This class of impostors are very respectably dressed, having mustaches, gold chains, &c.; they have either a well-written brief, or one partly printed and filled up with writing and the seals and signatures of two or three magistrates are placed at the bottom. I have seen briefs of this description from almost every part of the kingdom.'

He goes on to say, that one named Captain Johnstone had ' followed the lurk of a shipwrecked captain for many years, had been over every county in England and Wales many times, and obtained not only hundreds, but thousands of pounds.' He relates various anecdotes of the most successful ' Lurkers' in this department.

' *The Foreigner's Lurk.*—Considerable numbers proceed on this lurk representing themselves as foreigners in distress. . . . Of late years, by far the greatest number have represented themselves as *Polish* noblemen or gentlemen, who had been driven by the tyranny of Russia from their native country to seek a refuge. . . . . . Their briefs have the names and seals of two magistrates attached, and are always well written. Whenever they present their briefs, they affect not to be able to speak a word of English, and the few words they utter are spoken in broken accent. . . . One of these lurkers, known among mendicants by the nickname of "Lord Dundas," had often got several pounds in a day. . . . There are also many females who go on the foreigner's lurk. . . . I knew a female who went on the foreigner's lurk, who dressed very well; she had a boy with her, and often succeeded in getting two or three pounds in a day. When she called on any one, she *pattered* (spoke) in French, and affected not to be able to converse in the English language.'

4. ' *The Accident Lurk.*—Lurkers of this description have a sham and delicate, (brief and book;) and the sham states, that by some dreadful accident the bearer has lost all, or at least the greater part of his property, sometimes by storm, and at other times by a flood, or in some other way: but, in whatever way the accident has happened, the bearer has always suffered a very considerable loss, and is deprived of the means of supporting himself and family. The

sums raised, vary from five shillings to a pound per day.'

5. '*The Sick Lurk.*—This is worked in so many different ways, that it will be necessary to say a little on each. It would seem, 1st, That a common method of imposing upon the public is, by applying blistering ointment to the arms, causing them to have the appearance of having been badly scalded. 2d, That others go about with hands and arms tied up, said to be injured by lightning, or by some other deplorable accident. 3d, Others affect fits. 4th, Others affect pregnancy and destitution. 5th, Others obtain alms by the husband remaining at home and affecting indisposition, in case any one should visit his lodgings to examine into the merits of the case, whilst the wife goes out begging for wine, rags, clothes, &c., for the sham invalid. 6th, Others pretend to have had wounds, and beg for linen-rags and small bottles to contain medicine necessary for their cure. I saw a man who got in one day, by this means, thirteen pounds' weight of white rags, and more than five dozen of phial bottles. Rags and bottles sell well. 7th, Others affect to have children confined with scarlet fever, &c. &c., and beg for *them*. They state that they have obtained a note to take their children to an infirmary or to an hospital, and want a few clothes and a little money.'

6. '*The Deaf and Dumb Lurk.*—I have known many persons of both sexes who have acted as if deaf and dumb, and by this means succeeded very well in obtaining money, food, &c. Many of them pretend to tell fortunes, and frequently get something considerable by such practices. They carry a slate and pencil with them, to write questions and answers.'

It would appear from the pamphlet before us, that sometimes these deaf and dumb lurkers affect even in the lodging-houses to be thus afflicted; but in such cases they are generally found out by their fellow vagrants.

7. '*The Servants' Lurk.*—There are considerable numbers who go on the servants' lurk, or as servants out of place; and both males and females frequently succeed well in imposing on servants and others by false statements and tales of distress. . . . The greater part of those who go on this lurk are neatly dressed, and have exactly the appearance of servants in gentlemen's families. . . . . Many of them have the *Court Guide*, which, as it contains a list of the nobility and gentry, enables them to do the thing completely.'

8. '*Collier's Lurk.*—This is followed by thousands who were never in a coal-pit, and numbers of such are daily imposing upon the public as colliers out of employ. They generally say they have been thrown out of work by some accident, such as the flooding of the works or the falling in of the pit. . . . . They often go in parties from two to seven or eight. . . . . Others have printed papers, which are left at each house, and called for again in a few hours . . . Others have written statements of the pretended masters of the accidents, and the supposed signatures of the works are affixed to them. . . . Some of

these obtain as much as fourteen or fifteen shillings per diem.'

9. '*The Weaver's Lurk.*—There are at the present time great numbers who go on this lurk, many of them having printed papers or small handbills, and leave one at each house, and then call again for them, and to receive what persons are disposed to give . . . . . I have seen men who represented themselves as weavers of every kind, and from all the manufacturing parts of the kingdom—men who I well knew had never been near a loom, but had been born and bred vagrants.'

10. '*The Cotton-Spinner's Lurk.*—There are many going on this lurk with printed papers or small handbills also. . . . . Some who go on this lurk carry sewing cotton for sale, alleged to be their own spinning. . . . . One man I know, who travels on this lurk, has been doing so for twelve years. He sometimes obtains as much as from twelve to fifteen shillings in one day.'

11. '*The Calenderer's Lurk.*—Those who go on this lurk represent themselves as calenderers out of employ through the depression of trade and improvement in machinery. They, like sham weavers and colliers, have false papers, which are printed, some in poetry.'

The sums raised by these descriptions of 'lurks' must be immense, especially where the individuals have a good address, and can explain and enforce the written and printed appeals they take with them.

'High-Fliers,' or begging letter-writers, are, it would seem, the next in order of importance, after the Lurkers. 'These begging letter-writers scribble false statements of their having been unfortunate in business, or suffered great losses, which have reduced them to a state of extreme distress. In London, but especially in the watering and seabathing places these letters procure as much as from five to one pound per day.'

'Shallow Coves' are 'impostors begging through the country as shipwrecked sailors. They generally choose winter, and always go nearly naked. Their object in doing so is to obtain left-off clothes. . . . . They have a long pitiful got-up tale of pretended distress, which they shout through the streets, of having been shipwrecked, &c. . . . . Shallow Coves generally go in *companies* (or, technically speaking, in *school*) of from two to ten. There is generally one selected to be the spokesman. . . . . As Shallow Coves only call at respectable houses, they often obtain a great deal of money.'

'*Shallow Motts*' are females who like the Shallow Coves, go nearly naked. They also adopt that mode of begging in order to obtain wearing apparel. . . . . They plead long and severe sickness, but only ask for *clothes*. The clothes are disposed of as soon as possible, none being ever kept for their own use. . . . . I knew one of these who in ten days obtained at Kingston-upon-Thames between seven and eight pounds' worth of clothes.'

'Cadgers' are 'those who make begging their

trade, and depend upon it for their support. *Cadgers on the downright* are those who beg from door to door, and *Cadgers on the fly* are those who beg as they pass along the tober, (road.) Cadging on the fly is a profitable occupation in the vicinity of bathing-places and large towns. A person of this description generally gets many shillings in the course of the day. Cadging on the downright (from door to door) is like all other trades, getting worse; but still thousands do very well at it, and frequently get more food than they can consume. . . . . . I have often seen food, which many working people would gladly have eaten, shamefully and wantonly wasted.

'CADGERS' CHILDREN' (kiddies) 'are so well instructed in the arts of imposition by their parents, that they frequently obtain more in money and food than grow-up cadgers.'

'*Cadgers' Screeving.*—There are many cadgers who write short sentences with chalk on the flags, and some of them can do it remarkably well; these are called *screevers*. I have seen the following sentences frequently written by them in places where there were numbers passing by, and where they thought it would be likely to get plenty of halfpence, (browns,) and now and then a *tanner* or a *bob*, (sixpence or a shilling.)

"Hunger is a sharp thorn, and biteth keen."
"I cannot get work, and to beg I am ashamed."

'I have known them by this means obtain seven shillings a day.'

'*Cadgers' sitting Pad.*—Whenever cadgers' stand or sit, either in towns or by the roadside, to beg, they call it *sitting* or *standing pad ;* and this often proves a very profitable method. Some of them affect blindness: whilst others represent themselves as unable to follow any employment, in consequence of being subject to fits. Some cadgers save very considerable sums of money; but these are very few compared with the great number who live by this trade of beggary.

'*Match-sellers* never entirely depend upon selling matches, for they cadge as well; in fact, they only carry matches as a cloak for begging, and never offer them at any house where they expect to get more without them. . . . Match-sellers, as well as all other cadgers, often get what they call "*a back-door cant*:" that is, anything they can carry off where they beg, or offer their matches for sale.'

'CROSS COVES, though they beg their bread, can tell a long story about being out of employ through the badness of trade, &c., yet get what they call *on the cross*, (by theft,) . . one of their chief modes of getting things *on the cross*, is by shoplifting. '(called grabbing,) . . . . Another method is to *star the glaze*, (i. e. break or cut the window.)

'*Prigs* (or pickpockets) are another class of vagrants, and they frequent races, fairs, and prize-fights. . . . . Like cross coves, they are generally young men who have been trained to vagrancy, and have been taught the arts of their profession in their childhood.'

'*Palmers* are another description of beggars, who visit shops under pretence of collecting *harp* halfpence; and to induce shopkeepers to search for them, they offer thirteen-pence for a shilling's worth, when many persons are silly enough to empty a large quantity of copper on their counters to search for the halfpence wanted. The *palmer* is sure to have his hand amongst it; and while he pretends to search for the harps, he contrives to conceal as many as possible in the palm of his hand, and whenever he removes his hand from the coppers on the counter, always holds his fingers out straight, so that the shopkeeper has not the least suspicion that he is being robbed. Sums varying from five to fifteen shillings per diem are frequently got in this way, by characters of that description.'

The pamphlet from which we have made these extracts, concludes with strong and cogent reasons and entreaties for not giving, and for refusing to give alms to such vagrants. It has been circulated, we believe, very extensively in the agricultural districts by the Poor Law Commissioners; and if the recommendations it contains were attended to, and followed up by those for whose benefit the pamphlet is intended, the art or mystery, trade or profession of begging, by those who are brought up to it, would be greatly diminished, if not actually put a stop to. We do not mean to say that begging on the part of the destitute poor would cease; but begging, as a *science of deception* and cajolery, would soon fail.

Here it is necessary to draw the line, which throughout the whole of our observations we have endeavoured to keep steadily in view, between beggars from education and sloth, as well as from immoral habits; and beggars from real destitution and misery. The little work from which we have extracted the preceding observations on this part of our subject, has, of course, been confined to an examination of the cases, habits, and conduct of the former class. But whilst their existence, if not their increase in England is a vast evil, it is not *the* evil which presses upon the English counties; nor *the* evil to which we look with sorrow and apprehension. Undoubtedly it is a vast evil, that in a moral, Christian, and enlightened community, there should be thousands who prefer, from generation to generation, mendicity to labour, and crime to honesty. But this is an evil which belongs to all states, and which we cannot see any possible means of entirely extinguishing. The evil which is now greatly afflicting the English counties, and especially the agricultural districts, is the increase, not so much of hereditary and permanent beggars, as of persons who are really destitute; and who, in default of sufficient food, firing, and clothing, come to the resolution to 'travel,' and to earn their bread by walking from morn to night over amazing distances, and of begging by the way.

And here it is necessary to show of what description of persons these new claimants on public compassion are composed, and what are the means they resort to in order to obtain relief.

No English agricultural labourers migrate for the purpose of begging, when they receive fifteen shillings per week for their wages. Very few migrate for begging from agricultural districts where the wages are thirteen shillings and sixpence, or even twelve shillings. But when the English labourer's wages decline from twelve shillings to ten and sixpence, and then fall to nine shillings, and even to seven, the labourer has but three courses to take; viz. to starve on his wages, to enter the union, or to beg. In five cases out of seven he prefers mendicity. The great reason, then, why mendicity on the part of the English agricultural labourers is increasing is, that wages are not high enough for the prices of provisions, or provisions not low enough for the price of labour.

The present lamentable condition of the agricultural labourer in at least nine-tenths of the English counties, cannot be put too strongly, or enforced on the attention of the public in too powerful terms. The continuance of such a state will not only lead to universal mendicity, and a vast augmentation of poor-rates, but will lead likewise to the dissolution of that bond of union which ought to subsist between the labourer and his employer.

And what is the reason that the vagrant act is, in the agricultural districts, and increasingly in towns and village districts, a dead letter? How is it that the English farmers offer, yet more frequently than ever, their barns and their stables to the mendicant poor, supplying them with clean straw or hay? How is it, that when the vagrant act declares that all who wander abroad, and beg, or gather alms, or cause their children to do so, are to be deemed i lle and disorderly persons, and may be arrested, brought before a magistrate and convicted, that in the agricultural districts such an expedient is hardly ever resorted to? How is it, that when the vagrant act declares that every person who wanders abroad, and trades without a license, is an idle and disorderly person, yet in the agricultural districts is never treated as such? How is it that gipsies, though rogues and vagabonds under the same act, as well as fortune-tellers, and persons living in barns, carts, and unoccupied buildings, without

being able to give any good account of themselves, are yet not arrested, not taken before magistrates, and not condemned?— The reason is obvious; there is such a mass of real misery and destitution in the agricultural districts, that neither the nobility, clergy, gentry, nor magistrates, will enforce the vagrant act against occasional and non-hereditary mendicants.

But besides the agricultural destitute labourers who will not enter the unions, and who, if they did enter, would render further buildings all over the land for their reception immediately necessary, the Irish emigrants, and the English manufacturing poor have to be taken into the account. They have been incorrectly told, that the agricultural poor and the agricultural districts are not so badly off as the manufacturing poor and the manufacturing districts; and so they migrate, as beggars, from the north to the south. They migrate to the north for work. Work has stopped; labour is not demanded; and now they return from the north to the south—but as beggars. The agricultural poor become beggars; because, with the wages they receive they cannot live. The manufacturing poor migrate as beggars, because they have no wages at all.

Thus the tide of mendicity and misery rolls on, and threatens a vast augmentation for the future.

Both the agricultural and the manufacturing mendicants have heard of the vagrant act. In some towns and cities its provisions are partly enforced; that is to say, the policemen are stationed at the extremes of the towns and cities, and conduct vagrants through them without allowing them to beg. To avoid this, however, beggars enter towns and cities in the night, and look about in the daytime to watch the approach of their liveried enemies. A policeman in France is dressed like an ordinary man. In England, his blue coat and plated white buttons are signals to beggars and thieves by which they profit. The vagrant act, however, has to be met; for some of its provisions are extensive and sweeping. For instance, the sellers of songs, of matches, of lucifer boxes, of lace, of little books, and of a thousand other wares, in baskets, through our towns and villages, are, according to that act, idle and disorderly persons, unless they have a license. Now, none of these have licenses—not one; and yet thousands are constantly moving about, adopting this form of begging by preference. If a beggar be reprimanded in England for begging, his answer is, ' I am not a beggar, sir, you see I have got some matches to sell ;' or, if he has not matches, he has something else. The total stock in trade is often not worth a shilling; but so long as the man carries something to sell, even the policemen will not ask him for the license. Why is this? Is it that the English think the spirit or the machinery of the vagrant act too severe? By no means. The reason is this—no magistrate would convict these people for want of hawker's licenses in the present destitute and deplorable condition of the poor.

We promised to say something respecting the plans resorted to, by the vastly-increasing numbers of English and Irish mendicants in England to obtain alms. The hereditary and the professional vagrants live as lurkers, cadgers, and so forth—*i. e.* by fraud, lying, and thieving. This is not the case with the really destitute agricultural labourers and manufacturing workmen who become beggars.

1st, They sing plaintive airs and tunes, and hymns and psalms.

2d, They walk through a town or village proclaiming aloud their wants and sufferings, but still walk on.

3d, They sing songs, and get money for singing.

4th, They play some instrument of music and solicit aid.

5th, They address you personally at your houses, and tell their real tales of grief.

6th, They apply to you, imploring and beseeching you to purchase some little articles which they have to sell. This is their favourite method. They hate to be thought beggars, though they know they are so.

7th, They apply for work for a day, or half a day, and earn a little money sometimes for a few hours by their labour.

8th, They rush to any public works which may be opening, and offer their labour at much reduced prices in order to obtain employment and wages.

Some of them, of course, become corrupted by their new associates at the houses which receive alike all classes of vagrants who can pay for their beds and their beer; and, when once corrupted, they fall into the categories foreseen and described by the vagrant act. But there is always for a long time a very marked distinction, perceptible to every one, between the hereditary and professional beggar, and the mendicants who become so from want and destitution. In too many instances, indeed, the corruption of the young, and especially of young girls, very soon follows the first step of a begging life; and those who would have shuddered a few months previously at the commission of even an offence, rush headlong into the perpetration of the worst of crimes.

The magistrates of England have been blamed for not exercising greater severity towards all vagrants. But if all the 'idle and disorderly' persons spoken of by the vagrant act were conducted, at this moment, before the English justices of the peace, they would soon be unable to provide prisons and asylums for even a tithe of their number.

It has been said, that if the ticket system carried on in some unions was adopted, with some little alteration, throughout the kingdom, ' begging would receive so great a shock, and become such a bad trade, that thousands would no longer follow it, but be driven to do what they never would do otherwise—namely, work for an honest living.'

But this supposes a state of things which does not exist in England. It supposes that there is, with provisions at their present prices, labour and wages enough for all who now beg. We know that this is very far indeed from being the case; and until it shall be so, the *ticket system* would not meet, though it might mitigate, the evil.

With reference to the *ticket system*, as some of our readers may not have examined it in its details, we supply the following explanation.

The ticket system is an expedient hit upon by the Poor Law Commissioners, as well as by other enemies to vagrancy, to relieve real want, and yet provide against imposition. Every rate-payer in a parish it has been proposed to supply with a certain number of blank tickets, to be filled up by him, or her, in favour of any vagrants demanding relief. The tickets are to be addressed to the governors of the Union House to which the poor of the parish are sent to reside, and the governors are to supply the applicant with lodging or food. Some, indeed, propose that the ticket should be valid within twenty miles' distance of the spot where it was given. The author of the pamphlet above referred to, says—

' To carry out the ticket system effectually, it would not only require the sanction of the poor law commissioners but the hearty co-operation of the guardians and rate-payers. It will be further necessary, that every workhouse be provided with apartments for the reception of tramps, and with labour for them to do; that every rate-payer be supplied with plenty of the following, or some such kind of tickets to give to persons soliciting relief, and never give money or food ; and that such a ticket be a note of admission into any workhouse to which it may be directed within twenty miles of the person's house sending it.

' To the Governors of   Union Workhouse.   Admit , who solicits relief in consequence of , and charge it to the acccount of the overseers of my parish.
                                        D. B.
                    Rate-payer of the parish of
Dated this   day of   184 .
'On the other side of the note should be printed—" The person using this note (supposing him to go into workhouse in the evening) will be allowed a supper of seven ounces of bread and two ounces of cheese, a bed ; and for breakfast, a pint of gruel and seven ounces of bread, for which he must do two hours' work before leaving in the morning. If he presents the note, or remains in during the day, he will not be allowed to go out till the morning following, and will be required to work the hours the other inmates do, and at the usual meal-times have the diet of the house. Children and the sick will be dieted at discretion." '

If the vagrant act be not enforced against the hereditary and professional mendicants of England, at least this ticket system should ; and if all classes of the English people would resolve on not relieving such mendicants by any other means, their fate would be certain—they must yield. But in the present state of the agricultural and manufacturing destitute poor, who are beggars for the time being, and who are so from a real pressure of want and misery, the English people, as a nation, will not apply the ticket system to them. It will, however, be inquired, 'what right have even the agricultural or manufacturing destitute poor to complain, when an adequate provision has been made for them by the workhouse system of the poor laws? and what right have they to refuse the relief offered them by that system, and become beggars?' We have so recently defended the workhouse system, and the conduct of the poor law commissioners in enforcing it, that there is no other answer necessary on our part, than the answer of fact; viz., that there is an immense and constantly-increasing number of destitute labourers and manufacturing poor, who will not, until they have made every other effort to prevent it, become parish paupers. They will sing, sell little wares, tell their tales of misery, and beg; and try all of these expedients, before they will consent to enter the unions. Of course, in some cases, this decision is the result of indolence, but in a multitude of others it results from a love of independence.

If those labourers and artisans who decide on rejecting parochial relief according to the workhouse system, and on taking to the life of vagrants, could but foresee the wretchedness misery, degradation, corruption, and vice, to which, in so many instances, that decision must lead them, we confess we think well enough of the English working classes to feel convinced that they would come to another decision. But with this we have at present no concern. They have wages too low, or no wages at all, or the necessaries of life too dear. Something must be done, but what that something must be, we have no intention at present to discuss; as we have already stated at the commencement of this article.

————

Art. VII.—*Journal of a Tour in Greece and the Ionian Islands.* By William Mure *of Caldwell.* 2 vols. 8vo. Edinburgh: 1842.

Tours by Englishmen in Greece have not been published in numbers so very oppressive as those which have been devoted to Italy ; but even they, we fear, have been so numerous, that the public will question strictly the author of every new Grecian tour, whether he has anything to tell which they have not long ago had an opportunity of hearing. The series of travels in Greece and the adjoining regions, given to the world by our countrymen during the recent period which began with the journeys of Dr. Clarke, embraces hardly any work that is quite worthless, and many that possess very distinguished value. A few of them have high literary merit as compositions, or as evidences of scholarship ; some have thrown much light upon the classical monuments ; and two or three have gone far towards laying the foundation for an accurate acquaintance with the ancient topography of Greece and her colonies. It can make no part of our plan, amidst an overflow of other matter, to aim at appreciating in detail the works which belong to this class. But one group of them may be fitly mentioned, both because it would be unjust to speak of investigations in Greece without naming them, and because the nature of them tends to a further remark which we are desirous of making. We allude to the topographical works of Colonel Leake. These receive but insufficient praise when it is said, not only that in all essential qualities they are models of their kind, but that his researches, prosecuted though they were under manifold disadvantages, must continue to form the basis of all that yet remains to be done, towards completing our systematic knowledge of the interesting subject which has worthily occupied so many years of the veteran scholar's life.

But after all that has been performed, there yet remains ample scope for doing more; and there are, in particular, two purposes which, jointly or separately, travellers in Greece may still warrantably pursue, and the attainment of which will fully justify them in publishing the results of their labours. First, there is abundant room for original observation, both in the departments of research which have been partly cultivated already, and in new ones which, till the recent changes in the state of Greece, it was impossible to approach. Much obscurity still hangs over many points of the classical topography, and of the history and condition of the antique monuments, both in Greece itself and in the neighbouring Hellenic countries. The richness of the vein which still remains to be worked in the Grecian colonies, is sufficiently indicated by the valuable researches of Mr. Fellows in Asia Minor; and Mr. Pashley's residence in Crete has shown how abundant the fruit is which may be gathered even in continental Greece and the islands, by a traveller who, adequately prepared, chooses a narrow range of inquiry, and devotes himself for a long period to personal investigation within its limits. The political and social condition of the Greek nation, again, constitutes a class of facts which, partially investigated before the revolution, has assumed since that event an aspect entirely new, and presents phenomena deserving and demanding close and philosophical observation.

Secondly, while there thus presents itself an abundance of unexhausted matter, the method of using both the new matter and the old, offers opportunities for not less improvement. Works possessing at once high literary merit, and great value as instruments for communicating satisfactory and systematic information to ordinary readers, might be composed by travellers who, although fully qualified for original discoveries, may not have been fortunate enough to make any. Such writers might be entitled to rank far higher than mere compilers; and they might perform for Grecian topography, antiquities, and statistics, a task which our original investigators have failed to accomplish. The most picturesque and animated of our tours by Englishmen

in those regions, convey information which is either fragmentary or deficient in solidity; those, again, which are most valuable as receptacles of knowledge, are repulsive, by reason of their form or their bulk, or both.

It is time to ask whether Mr. Mure has been justified in giving his Tour to the public, by its aptness to serve either, or both, of the purposes thus indicated as worthy of attainment. We have no hesitation in saying that he has. We will not, indeed, venture to assert that in either department he has done all which might have been done; nor that everything which he has done is performed in the very best manner; but his work possesses no inconsiderable merit, both for the novelty which belongs to a good deal of its matter, and for the manner in which his materials are treated.

His travels occupied two months in the spring of 1838, during which time he visited Corfú and Ithaca, traversed Northern Greece from the mouth of the Achelous to Sunium, and made the circuit of the Peloponnesus. The few weeks thus appropriated were of course insufficient for allowing him to observe the country at large with any great minuteness; but he appears to have apportioned his time very judiciously; and in a region like Greece, which is so small in extent, and which has been visited and reported upon so often already, previous preparation and activity on the route will enable one to effect a great deal within a very short period. The time at which Mr. Mure visited Greece, was favourable for examination both of antiquities and of the existing position of the people; although opportunities yet more auspicious will be enjoyed by future travellers, when the new kingdom shall have attained completely, both internal consolidation and settled relations with its neighbours. He has watched, sagaciously and with lively interest, several of the classes of phenomena which were presented to his view, and upon these he has communicated the results of his observations.

The original merit of his book, however, can scarcely be said to lie essentially in new elucidations, either of classical topography or of classical monuments At least, such elucidations form but a small part of the work, although several of those which occur are very interesting, and vouch not only for the author's possession of an excellent turn for observation, but for his proficiency in a sound and liberal school of archæological criticism. The facts which, in this department, Mr. Mure has been absolutely the first to impart to the English public, are, if we mistake not, just three—the site of the Heræum or Temple of the Argive Juno, near Mycenæ ; the existence of two arched gateways, unobserved by Leake, (who, however, had found in the same place another gate of that construction,) among the Cyclopian ruins of Œniadæ; and the existence of an ancient arched bridge at a spot called Xerokampo, crossing a tributary of the Laconian river Eurotas.

The site of the Heræum—an object of fruitless search to preceding travellers—is supposed by our author, and (as we think) justly, to have been identified by the late General Gordon, who after repeated excursions made in vain for the purpose of discovering the spot, came upon it by chance while out on a shooting party. The principal remains consist of a conspicuous Cyclopian wall. The eminence on which this ruin stands, and the lesser fragments which are to be seen in the same place, are described with minuteness ; yet not with more than scholars would expect to find bestowed on one of the most distinguished of the Grecian temples, now for the first time made known. Mr. Mure's observations at Œniadæ and Xerokampo bear upon the vexed ' question' of the age and manner in which the ancient Greeks became acquainted with the use of the keyed arch ; and the specimens described by him will swell usefully the list of examples which call on the antiquaries of art to revise that little section of their science.

We repeat, what we hinted a little ago, that, curious and valuable as are facts like those which are thus pointed out, the collection of two or three of them is hardly an excuse for bestowing on the public anything more than a contribution or two to some periodical work. They form an excellent basis for such papers as the author has contributed to the ' Rheinisches Museum,' and to the Annals of the Roman Archæological Institute. But they scarcely carry weight enough to ballast two octavo volumes, designed (we borrow a continuation of our metaphor from an eminent professor of the Bathos) to float through the channel of criticism into the haven of public approbation. They might have served, however, as good adjuncts or interludes in a single volume, the staple of which would have been most creditably made up of two other groups of Mr. Mure's chapters ; by far the ablest and most valuable which he has devoted to the antiquities of Greece. The one group embraces the Homeric topography of Ithaca; the other deals with the topography of Athens, and the present condition of its

classical monuments. We willingly dwell for a time upon the elucidations which the author has bestowed upon each of these interesting topics

For the details of the ' Ithacan Questions,' however, we must refer to the book itself. These classical discussions are conducted not only with great good sense and acuteness, but with much liveliness ; and the scenery is described in a clear and extremely pleasing manner. On the points directly mooted in reference to the Ithaca of Homer, and to the proper method of reconciling the poetic description with the naked reality, we unreservedly concur both in the author's general conclusions, and in most steps of the process by which he reaches them. In both respects, Sir William Gell's work on Ithaca stands immeasurably lower. But one article there is in Mr. Mure's Homeric creed, which indicates a degree of vagueness not to have been expected from one so familiar, as he evidently is, with the speculations of the best German critics. We are tempted, therefore, to state some views as to the geography of the Odyssey, which, while they may form a supplement to this part of his work, admit of being aptly illustrated from his own pages.

We would say, then, that the geography of the Odyssey cannot be understood, unless the scenes of the poem be regarded as falling into three separate classes—the scenes which the poet described from his own knowledge—the scenes which he described from report—the scenes which were quite imaginary.

To the first section of this geographical system belong those few spots of the Grecian continent, to which, for a time, the action is transferred. To it belongs also, beyond question, the rocky isle of Ithaca, the domain in which Odysseus dwelt, and bore sway as an overlord over the tributary princes. All these are scenes not only real, but directly known to the poet—scenes, however, which, as we must not fail to recollect, are treated by him in the poetical and ideal fashion. We must not, like Volcker, deny reality to Homer's Ithaca more than to his Pylus or his Sparta. But, on the other hand, we must not, with Gell, derogate from the royal prerogative of the poet's genius, by endeavouring to discover, in the reality, a counterpart to every feature of beauty with which his imagination adorned what it adventured to describe. In reference to this class of the Homeric scenery, our author's introductory remarks deal justly with both of the erroneous opinions.

' The impression which a personal visit to this

island can hardly fail to leave on the mind of the impartial student of Homer is, that so great is the general resemblance between its natural features and those of the one described in the Odyssey, the difficulty is not so much to discover in each case a bay, rock, cavern or mountain, answering to his description, as to decide among the many that present themselves, on the precise one which he may happen to have had in view. In estimating the amount or value of this correspondence, he will also bear in mind how unreasonable it were to exact from the poet of any age, although possessed of the closest personal familiarity with the district selected for his scene of action, the rigid accuracy of the land-surveyor, or to deny him the privilege of his profession, even in his description of real objects, to depart a little from the truth, where a slight variation of site or appearance was necessary to their full effect. To pronounce, therefore, as some have done, in the face of so great a mass of general evidence to the contrary, that Homer had no personal knowledge of Ithaca, because the more fastidious commentator may find difficulty in arranging on his classical atlas, consistently with existing appearances, the hut of Eumæus, the fountain of Arethusa, or the port of Phorcys, were almost as unreasonable as to deny the author of Waverly any personal knowledge of Scotland, because of an equal difficulty of identifying the bay of Ellangowan or the castle of Tillietudlem.

Equally unwarrantable, on the other side, are the attempts of the more orthodox school of Homeric interpreters, to force on existing objects or localities a closeness of harmony with his descriptions, such as was doubtless as little congenial to his own taste as conducive to the interest of his poem; and this over-subtlety, as displayed in the elegant but not very critical work of Gell, the patriarch of modern Ithacan topographers, is among the chief causes that have led some of his successors into the opposite extreme. For my own part, I confess that, while nothing can be more delightful than to recognize a strong general resemblance between the descriptions of scenery contained in any poetical work of deep interest, and real localities to which they refer, it would tend but little to enhance this pleasure, could I be convinced of the accuracy of all their minutest details, even to the back-door, kitchen, and draw-well of the hero's dwelling.'—(Vol. i., pp. 60, 61.)

Thus much for one extreme of the Homeric system of geography. Diametrically opposed to it stands the other extreme, whose distinctive character Mr. Mure seems to apprehend less clearly, if we may judge from the hesitating manner in which he mentions the claims of another of the Ionian Islands to be held as representing a prominent scene in the Odyssey. He does not indeed believe that Corfu represents Scheria, and his scepticism is assuredly well founded; but he does not make the denial with sufficient boldness, nor does he, apparently, recognize clearly the principle

upon which the denial rests In the class of Homeric scenes with which we now deal, lie names signifying spots which never existed, and which were never conceived as existing by the poet himself. To this class must be referred the greater number (and some would include in it all, without exception) of the scenes in which the wandering prince of Ithaca appears, till he is landed at the Cave of the Nymphs on the beach of his native isle. These are regions situated in a world of mere imagination—their place as unreal as their dwellers and adventures are wild and fantastical. It matters nothing to us that wrong notions have been entertained as to these poetical spots—notions nourished sometimes by national and local vanity, always by erroneous comprehension of that which is the essence of old poetical tradition. We care not though from the days of Timæus the Sicilians claimed for their own delightful island the consecrated name of Thrinacria, where pastured the sacred herds of the Sun; and though there also Thucydides, and Euripides, and Polybius, placed the Cyclopes and the blood-stained den of Polyphemus. We disregard with equal confidence the belief which (perhaps springing up early in the Post-Homeric days of Greece, caught eagerly by the Roman poets, and echoed by Strabo and the other Greek flatterers of their nation) pointed to the coasts of Southern Italy as containing the Isle of Circe, the terific ocean pass between Scylla and Charybdis, the pastoral haunts of the gigantic Læstrygones. Even less ground is there for identifying with Corcyra, or with any spot on this prosaic earth, the poetic region of Scheria, the seat of the blessed Phæacians, the fairyland of Grecian legends, the ideal of Grecian happiness, and beauty, and virtue. This Elysian picture is as unreal as that to which it is a counterpart—the dismal scene at the gloomy frontiers of the earth, where the wanderer offered sacrifice to evoke the shadows of the unhappy dead. If we look for any of these scenes on the map, it should be, as Payne Knight sarcastically advised, in the same latitude with Utopia or Brobdignag.

But lastly, (although neither Nitzsch nor the other Homeric critics, whose views we chiefly follow, have brought out this point with sufficient distinctness,) there are clearly some particulars in the geography of the Odyssey which cannot be satisfactorily explained by a reference to either of these two classes—the scenes real and known to the poet—the scenes invested, whether by himself or by the framers of the older fables.

It is easy for us to recognize a third class of cases, in which Homer describes poetically scenes regarded by him in a different light. These, if they did not really exist, were at any rate supposed by him to do so; but they were known to him only from vague rumours, such as the unexact stories of Grecian mariners, or the tales of other travellers, set forth with a rich garniture of distortion and exaggeration. In the question, how many of the scenes in the Odyssey ought to be referred to this intermediate class, lies, as we venture to think, the principal field for controversy which is still fairly open to the geographical annotators on Homer. On the one hand, we may narrow the class by including in it no more than the very first steps in the hero's journey—the Cicones and the Lotophagi; and in this view we might consider the purely fabulous part of the tale to begin with the darkness, in the midst of which the adventurers sail towards the rude haven of the Cyclopes, as it ends with the happy slumber which heralds the restoration of the chief to his native isles. Or, on the other hand, we may doubt, with some show of reason, whether, in separating thus strongly between the purely and the partially invented, we do not take things too strictly, too academically, too *Teutonically;* we may doubt whether, even in the subsequent stages of Ulysses' adventures, and even throughout the marvellous tale which he tells to his believing hosts in Scheria, there do not occur scenes which, to the poet's own mind, presented the same mixed character as the account of the Lotophagi. But, in endeavouring to systematize our notions of the literary questions to which the work before us has invited, we have already, perhaps, travelled a little out of the record. It will be necessary to return ere we altogether lose sight of our traveller and his tour.

We pass to another section of his book, being that which we have mentioned as seeming to us, not less than the chapters on Ithaca, to make good his claim to be held an imparter of original information. At Athens he finds none of those primitive fortifications, amidst which, both in other parts of Northern Greece, and in many parts of the Peloponnesus, he labours with a zeal as indefatigable as if he were himself an aboriginal Pelasgian. For more than twenty centuries the turf has grown, and the flocks have wandered, among those solitary rocks where rose the Titanic ruins of Tiryns and Mycenæ. In the heart of Attica, perhaps, where the Cephisus and

Ilissus flowed beneath the rock of Athene, no monuments had ever been reared emulating the massiveness of the stupendous piles which yet stand upon the heights of Argolis; and when more civilized generations had crowned the Cecropian Hill with its Ionian Acropolis, nothing was there left of the barbaric times, except some portions of the northern walls, said to have belonged to a fortress erected by Pelasgians; probably by some remnant of that wonderful race, later and less powerful than those who had elsewhere toiled like earth-born giants. The chief antiquities of Athens belong to the proudest and brightest times of Hellenic civilisation. They have been visited, as objects of pilgrimage, by men from the uttermost ends of the earth. They have been described and depicted times without number. But both in their state and in the opportunities for investigating their history, the late vicissitudes in the political position of Greece have brought about changes of the most remarkable kind. Of these changes, the work under our notice gives an excellent account, which to most of its readers will, we suspect, be entirely new; while there can be few who will not derive additional matter for thought, both from the facts and from the opinions expressed in regard to them.

Before the emancipation of Greece, our knowledge of Athenian topography, chiefly imparted through countrymen of our own, may be said to have reached the utmost point which it could be expected to attain, so long as the country should remain in the hands of its Turkish masters. The pen had done its best, and in some instances its worst; what remained to be done was the function of the pick-axe There had been more than enough of dissertation-writing, as well as of tourist-raptures: what was wanted was a scheme of intelligent excavations. That which the French, during their occupation of Italy, began to do for Rome, it was to be hoped that the new rulers of Greece would do for Athens—laying open to the eye the ruins of the classical times, which were built up amidst the Turkish and Frankish fortifications of the Acropolis, or buried beneath the soil and the hovels of the plain at the foot of the rock. The state of Athens was alluringly favourable for such operations; singularly so, indeed, in comparison with the ground containing the relics of Rome.

The precious opportunity was unused. It may be more just to say that, with regard to the lower parts of the city, it was deliberately annihilated. The selection of

Athens as the seat of King Otho's sovereignty, whether politically right or wrong, was extremely unfortunate for the classical monuments of the place. Indeed, it may be doubted whether it was likely to be most disadvantageous on account of the risks to which it exposed the architectural works already known, or on account of the obstacles which it threatened to interpose in the way of further investigations. But a second error was added to the first. Even if Athens must be the seat of government, the new metropolis might, it should seem, have been so placed as to interfere little, or not at all, with the buried ruins of the ancient city. This wise abstinence was not practised. The Greco-Bavarian Athens lies entirely within the Athens of Theseus, Themistocles, and Hadrian; and in that space it occupies precisely the spots where many of the finest ancient structures stood, and where many of their ruins must still lie buried. In the plain, therefore, all hope of further discoveries is at an end. Little or nothing, also, has been added to our knowledge of the lower eminences about the city, where were the Areopagus, the Pnyx, the Museum. The identification of Mount Saint George with Lycabettus, which our author rightly considers to be satisfactorily made out, was first stated, if we mistake not, by Dr. Wordsworth. In the case of the Theseion, as it would appear, the German antiquaries in Greece have indicated a tendency to that revolutionary system of archæology which, with various success, they have applied to monuments and sites in Rome. The summary with which we are favoured, of the arguments by which Dr. Ross strives to support his transformation of the Temple of Theseus into a Temple of Mars, have not as yet convinced us that there are, for this change, reasons so strong as those which justified M. Bunsen in twisting the Roman Forum back into the attitude which it occupied in the eyes of the antiquaries of the seventeenth century.

On the Acropolis much has been done. The operations have already brought to light a great deal that is both new and valuable; and nothing is wanting but the demolition of the picturesque square tower of the middle ages, which is so prominent a feature in the landscape, to put this classical rock almost beyond the recognition of those who saw it a few years ago.

'The exertions of the Greco-Bavarian government towards the discovery, maintenance, or restoration of ancient monuments, have hitherto been concentrated almost exclusively within the limits of the Acropolis, and thus far, it must be admitted, the result of its measures reflects credit on the zeal, industry, and judgment of this department of administration.

'The walls of the Propylea, with the extant columns of its portico, are in a great measure disengaged from the unseemly masses of Turkish masonry in which they were formerly imbedded; the original plan of structure, which was before matter of doubtful speculation, can now be recognized nearly in its whole extent; and the square bulwark forming its left flank, which was lately the basement of a Turkish bastion, presents at least the skeleton of the celebrated Pinacotheca or Picture-gallery, mentioned in the description of Pausanias.

'But the object which, on nearer approach, can hardly fail, by its novelty as well as beauty, most forcibly to attract the attention of the traveller familiar with the Acropolis only through the medium of the older drawings or descriptions, is the little Temple of Victory, situated on the south-west edge of the precipice, immediately below the tower. This building, which was still in existence when Wheler and Spon visited Athens in 1676, had long disappeared before the days of the present or even the last generation of travellers. Some fragments of masonry, however, supposed to belong to it, still remained visible on the ground in the neighbourhood of its former site; and four slabs of its sculptured frieze, which had been built into a neighbouring wall, found their way, in the course of Lord Elgin's operations, to the British Museum. One of the first undertakings of the Royal Conservators of Antiquities, was the excavation and recomposition of its materials. It has now, under the magic auspices of Messrs. Ross and Schubart, risen like a phœnix from its ashes; and, as seen from a little distance, has much the appearance of a new but unfinished edifice; its white marble columns and walls glittering in the sun, with a splendour little short of that which they displayed when fresh from the chisels of their original constructors. The materials were found nearly complete, buried under an upper story of rubbish, belonging to Turkish buildings on the same site, ruined posterior to itself. This temple is of very small dimensions, and of the class called by Vitruvius amphiprostyle; consisting of a cell with four Ionic columns at each front, but none at the sides. The walls of the cell, with the two porticoes, have been re-constructed in their integrity. The remains of the entablature, comprising nearly the whole frieze with the exception of the pieces in the British Museum, were lying in a neighbouring shed, preparatory to being replaced. The reliefs are of the most perfect period of art, representing Greeks triumphant over Persians or other oriental barbarians, in a style somewhat more easy and lively than that of Phidias. The epoch of the construction of this temple is doubtful: some place it earlier, but it cannot well be brought lower, than the Periclean era.

'A somewhat similar process of restoration was carrying on in the case of the Erechtheum. Many of its lost fragments had already been disinterred and replaced; and, as I understood, it was the intention of the government to make good the remaining deficiencies to the extent of a complete reconstruction of the building—walls, porticoes, and roof. In a neighbouring workshop a Swiss sculptor was engaged in the execution of a new caryatid of Pentelic marble, to supply the place of that removed by Lord Elgin. Capitals of columns and other ornamental pieces of masonry were also in progress.   *   *   *

'The only considerable relic of modern structure now in the Acropolis, besides the tower at its south-western angle, is the mosque in the centre of the Parthenon; the removal of which would not probably be detrimental to the general effect of the ruin. Upon the whole, though the summit of the Acropolis, since its area has been cleared of its other Turkish appendages, presents a somewhat bare and desolate aspect, and is probably a far less picturesque scene than it was in Turkish times, yet hitherto it may be said, that what has been done has been done well. But if the square tower be pulled down— if the Erechtheum and the Parthenon be restored and roofed in upon the new renovating principles —if the surrounding area be then levelled, paved, and appropriated, as will doubtless be the case, if the system now in vogue continue to be acted upon, to displays of modern Hellenic taste in architecture—the result will hardly be such as to afford matter of congratulation to any true lover of art or antiquity.'—(Vol. ii., pp. 65, 68, 73.)

It is time to quit the purely antiquarian section of the work, upon which, it may be, we have already bestowed what to some will appear an undue share of attention. We hasten to say, that this is by no means the only portion of the author's labours in which he is entitled to claim the praise of original observation. There has not, till now, been communicated to the British public, from any competent source, a view of those singularly interesting features which have been superinduced both upon the face of the country, and upon the character and social condition of its inhabitants, by the recognition of the national independence, and the attempt to assimilate the political state of Greece to that of the other European kingdoms. Mr. Strong's volume, recently published, treats these new relations in an aspect strictly statistical; and presents a mass of documents, and figures, and tabular results, which must prove singularly valuable as the first materials for speculation on these important topics. But upon these we have at present no fit opportunity of entering. We remark only, by way of parenthesis, that we have found the Athenian Banker's systematic survey to throw much necessary light upon Mr. Mure's travelling sketches.

We have said, then, that both in this interesting department (to which he devotes a large portion of his work) and in that of classical antiquities, Mr. Mure appears to us to have contributed not a little to the stock of real knowledge in regard to Greece. The amount of the acquisitions which, in the two branches together, he has presented to his readers, would have been amply sufficient to justify the publication of his researches; even if these had been communicated in a manner inferior to that in which he has been able to communicate them.   ,

In regard to the manner of communication, the second qualification which he laid down for intending travellers, our opinion is, upon the whole, extremely favourable. The work must be regarded as one addressing itself to an extensive circle of readers, and aiming at conveying information in a popular and agreeable form. We are justified in considering it from this point of view by several features in its plan and execution, which, if it had been designed for a very narrow and highly-instructed class of students, could not have been introduced by a writer possessing so much tact as well as knowledge. As a popular book of travels, then, it is disfigured by some serious faults. It has two in particular, which run greatly into each other; a strong tendency to diffuse description—a tendency, not less strong, to controversial digressions.

The author has an excellent eye for natural scenery and its adjuncts—a quick apprehension of those salient points of human character which strike a passing observer, and a turn for meditative, half poetic reflection, which we cannot prevail upon ourselves to think unbecoming his character, whether as an accomplished scholar or as a Colonel of Militia. But his manner of expression is equally long-drawn in description and meditation; and the picture of a group clustered round a hosterly fire, the sketch of a landscape seen from a commanding height, and the enunciation of the sentiments inspired by a celebrated ruin, are alike temptations to a fulness of petty detail, which mars severely the effect of the whole. Amusing examples of this tedious circumstantiality are furnished by passages dealing with the animal kingdom; such as the apparition of the six vultures among the Acarnanian ruins, the song of the Bœotian owl at Chæronea, and the conversation with the camel beside the Attic khan of San Vlasio.

Where the objects observed tempt to the discussion of disputed questions, the same tendency is annoyingly active; but it is not to such cases that its exercise is confined. There are repeated dissertations (such as a philosophical speculation on the effects of climate upon national character) which cannot be said to have even the excuse of arising naturally out of the matter immediately in hand. This itch for digression is common enough in unpractised writers; but it is unworthy of one who does not here make his first bow to the public. For our own part, we like to see an author ride his hobby with spirit, and can make ample allowance for vagaries which may lead him now and then aside from the proper path. But when he not only gallops down every cross-road, but incessantly indulges himself in a steeple-chase ending at the point where it began, it becomes a duty to warn him, that the reader (who may be regarded as having accepted a seat on the crupper) will, if once thrown, be hardly persuaded to mount again.

Notwithstanding all this, the book will, if we mistake not, prove agreeable to every one who can by any means be excited to take an interest in the topics of which it treats. Its defects are far more than atoned for by many good qualities.

We wish it were in our power to use fully the materials which it furnishes, for aiding us to form a conception of the present aspect and position both of the Greeks and of their country. Some we cannot leave unnoticed.

The half-ruined town of Mesolonghi, and the surrounding plain with its scarred stumps, the remains of olive groves, destroyed by the Turks during the siege, presaged in like manner the gloomy features of a picture which he was to see repeated in almost every step of his route, and which he has described with much liveliness and feeling. It is a frightfully instructive example of the calamities which attend on war, and from which the justice of the cause is no protection to the inhabitants of the land that is its scene. Some of the facts collected in Mr. Gordon's statistical work, to which we formerly referred, aptly illustrate and explain the casual observations of the traveller.

At the termination of the war, the territory erected into the kingdom of Greece, was one from which those were expelled who had previously constituted, almost exclusively, the higher classes—the Turkish landholders and the functionaries of the Turkish government. They who remained, they who had resisted for years the combined strength of the Turkish empire, and had at length compelled the powers of Europe to interfere for saving them from annihilation, were a race who had, till then, been but the slaves of barbarous masters. Of this fact—a fact indispensable to be considered by those who would fairly estimate

the difficulties of establishing order and civilisation in Greek society—we speak at present in its relation to the occupancy of the soil. The lands which had belonged, either to the Turkish government or to private persons of that race, were in the end forfeited, and became the property of the Greek nation. Accordingly, the government of King Otho, although its claims are not yet wholly adjusted, has come into possession of a vast proportion of the whole country. Not more than an eighth, perhaps not more than a ninth part of the lands, is private property. Both the government and the individuals found their domains almost utterly destroyed by the ravages of the war; and, when we have regard to the formidable difficulties against which the whole nation have had to struggle since the acquisition of their independence, and to the energy with which, in various quarters, these difficulties have been combated, we shall find cause for hope, even in the midst of the desolation which all accounts agree in representing as still paramount over the greater part of a region so highly favoured by nature

The centuries of Turkish misrule had converted a very large proportion of the country into uncultivated and uninhabited wilds. The exterminating and bitter contest which raged for years after the first rising, severely aggravated these evils; and the independent kingdom can acquire but slowly the population and the wealth which are requisite for enabling it to redeem its statistical position. A country said to be capable of supporting five millions of souls, is inhabited by less than nine hundred thousand; and the poverty of its present agricultural resources may be estimated in some measure from the fact, that there is calculated to be but one yoke of oxen for every four persons engaged in tillage.

In the rural districts, one scene of ruin presents itself after another—relieved, however, in many quarters by the cheering aspect of reviving prosperity. The olive-trees were almost everywhere cut down and burned by the Turks; the plain of Argos, and the neighbourhood of Navarin, which had been covered with groves of this useful tree, were left without a growing plant. The currant vineyards were chiefly destroyed, and those which remained had grown wild. Patras, once imbedded in orchards, stands completely bare. Birds of prey prowl everywhere; and in the defile of Tretus, and between the citadel of Corinth and the sea, the bones of an army of slain Turks still lie mouldering away. The towns of Greece, almost without any exception, were, at the close of the war, mere heaps of ruins; and upon these the new towns are gradually rising. Livadìa, as Mr. Mure approached it, seemed to him to be composed of small herb-plots or kitchen-gardens: on his arrival, these were seen to be the areas and foundations of the ruined houses. Thebes, having lost the plane-trees of its bazar, its domes and minarets, is a group of 'hovels, wooden sheds, ruins, and rubbish,' with a high square tower of the middle ages standing at one extremity of its ridge, the sole remnant of its former state. Tripolizza and Argos are rising from similar devastations; and Athens itself presents its new and handsome buildings in humiliating contiguity to hillocks of overthrown masonry. The destruction of Misitra, instead of having been followed by its re-erection on the same spot, has led to the foundation of a new Sparta, on, or close beside the site of the ancient city. The name and the act are good omens. With them we gladly close this enumeration of articles included in the price which a brave nation has been made to pay for its freedom.

To the character of the nation, Mr. Mure shows every disposition to do frank and hearty justice. The excellent spirit which pervades his work, where the Greeks themselves are the objects of remark, is one of the most agreeable of the qualities which recommend it to favour. It is a spirit of good-will and kindness towards the people, and of warm sympathy with them in their past struggles and their present condition. Their character is commented upon with an allowance, not less just than kindly, for the causes of deterioration which have so long operated upon it; and the pleasing features which came under his notice are depicted with a friendly yet discriminating hand.

Very early in the wild journey along the coast of Acarnania and Ætolia, which is the first stage of his tour on the continent of Greece, he is led to speculations of a kind which he delights greatly to institute, and which, in more than one instance, are not only interesting but new and ingenious. He compares the modern race with the corresponding class in ancient times; and, upon this analogical kind of illustration, he brings to bear very much sound and minute learning.

His first remarks of this sort are elicited by a meeting with a community of Wallachian shepherds, who lie encamped on the desert banks of the Achelöus, not far from the ruins of Œniadæ. The encounters with these wandering herdsmen, and with others of the same class who come in his way afterwards, give rise to many intimations of analogy between pastoral life in ancient Greece, and that which is still to be found in the same regions. One of the most curious of these—and to travellers the most practically interesting—is the fierceness of the native dogs, who everywhere in Greece are represented by all tourists as being in spirit genuine representatives of those Ithacan dogs, that would fain have slain Ulysses as he approached the lodge of Eumæus the swineherd. Our author brings into amusing relation with this point the χερμαδια of Homer—the rough, jagged, large stones which he sees scattered everywhere over the surface of the soil; and which are alike available for pelting off a pack of savage hounds, and, in case of need, for supplying the place of more formidable missiles in the hand of a hard-pressed warrior.

Another class of antique recollections to which, in one place, we are introduced very pleasingly, are those which regard the navigation of the Mediterranean. The voyages of Ulysses are brought strikingly, and, in some particulars, not without novelty of aspect, into juxtaposition with the modern traveller's creeping sail from the Piræus to Cape Colonna and Corinth. Elsewhere ancient and modern dwellings are compared; although on this point too much has been done by others to have left much for any new observer to accomplish. There is a whimsical liveliness in the manner which our author treats another classical topic, to which he recurs again and again. This is the prevalent Grecian filth, with its natural accompaniment of vermin, the plague of all tourists from the north; and (as we are pathetically informed) peculiarly hostile to the writer of these two volumes. He makes a half serious attempt to derive the pedigree of some of his nightly tormentors in a direct line from those poetical *reptilia* which were anathematized by the Aristophanic disciple of Socrates. There is a more real seriousness in the rational observations which are made upon the points of difference between ancient and modern Greeks in the matter of personal cleanliness generally; and much discrimination is shown in the use of the classical materials which are applied to the elucidation of the question. The present state of the Greeks at large, in respect of this quality of civilisation, is amusingly illustrated by the deliberate approval which Mr. Mure pronounces upon an apartment offered to him as a lodging in Mesolonghi. It was (comparatively) clean, *because* it had been recently inhabited by fowls *only.* These unpleasing habits—to which it is needless to say the sufferings endured by the bulk of the nation for so many years in the present generation must have added greatly—contrast singularly both with the prevalent fondness of the Greeks for showy dresses, and with the well-known picturesqueness which most of their national costumes so strikingly display.

But the 'fustanella' and the dirty bed-rugs were by no means the only modern objects which attracted the notice of our traveller. Several even of his lightest sketches of scenes and characters, lead us onward to a more intimate acquaintance with the state in which the lower orders of Grecian society have been left by the convulsions whence they have lately emerged. One of the most complete groups of personages presented to us is that by which the writer found himself surrounded in the khan of Livadia, where he was detained for several days by a characteristically Bœotian deluge of rain. The description of the khan (made to illustrate the fatal fall of Homer's Elpenor,) and that of the torrent of rain (which, in its turn, illustrates some classical superstitions,) are followed by portraits of the tourist's fellow-lodgers, from which we select a few of the most striking traits. These bear more or less directly upon several very important questions as to the present aspect of society in the country : —

'Four of the small private apartments were occupied besides my own ; one by a leech merchant from Athens, who spoke bad though intelligible Italian, and was more civilized in appearance and manner than the other guests. He complained bitterly of the wet weather, which, by raising the waters of the lake to an unusual height, prevented his fishermen from pursuing their comfortless avocation, and suspended his own business. The animals are caught by country people in his employ, who wade with bare feet and legs into the water, and seize them as they fasten on their skin. Another room was occupied by a couple of Argive cotton merchants, of rude demeanour and uncouth ponderous persons, enveloped in a vast quantity of coarse white woollen drapery. A third was the quarter of two Albanian veterans, belonging to a party of irregular light infantry stationed in the town. These troops are distributed in detachments through the different provinces, as a sort of moveable armed police, liable to be called out to pursue brigands, or otherwise support the civil authorities or the regular gendarmerie. But from anything I could learn or see, I was not led to form a high opinion of the value of their services; and their employment seemed generally to be considered as little better than an expedient to prevent them from relapsing into those habits of predatory life from which they had, most of them, been previously reclaimed. They were, like others of their cloth whom I happened to meet, wild, ferocious-looking fellows, and offensively dirty, in spite of their beautiful though soiled and greasy uniform, of native fashion but Bavarian colours, white and blue. Nicóla [the traveller's servant] was very amusing on the subject of his two countrymen, speaking of them, with a mixture of compassion and contempt, under the title of " questi poveri Chimariŏtti." Chimariote is the title they usually bear, derived from the town and district of Chimara, on the Adriatic, distinguished for this class of warriors; and which has been extended in popular use to those of the whole Acroceraunian range. He gave a moving account of the shabbiness of their pay, as well as of the filth and misery of their persons, quarters, and mode of life, which was indeed too self-evident to require any commentary. They seemed to be very much their own masters, and subjected to little either of discipline, duty, or authority, that I could perceive.

'The other pilikar, who seemed to be the man of the greatest consequence of the two, at least in his own estimation, a fine athletic fellow, with a fierce sinister countenance and a free and forward manner, paid me a visit on the second afternoon ; and after shaking me cordially by the hand, uttered, with much vehement gesture, a long and energetic harangue, scarcely one word of which I understood, but which I interpreted to convey certain anathemas against brigands and klephts, with offers of his protection and services in case of emergency, with an assurance of their value. My reason for putting this construction on his address, apart from the tenour of the few expressions I comprehended, was, that about the time of our arrival, reports had reached the place of a renewal or increase of brigandage in the neighbouring districts, especially towards Thermopylæ and the Turkish frontier, always the more especial theatre of predatory warfare, and in which direction he supposed we were bound. These reports were in so far confirmed by the arrival of the post-rider from Tálanta at the Khan that forenoon, on foot, having been plundered of his horse, and stripped of every article on his person, with the exception of a few woollen rags, scarcely sufficient to cover his nakedness. Nicóla, on communicating this piece of intelligence, observed in his sarcastic way, that the travellers across the Turkish frontier, if they wished to ride in security, had better wait until the season was a little further advanced, when the government would probably send up Generals Church or Gordon, or some other of their commanders, to enlist the bands in their own service, and bestow commissions of colonel, major, or captain of light infantry, on their chiefs. I took this for a jest at the moment: but I afterwards found, to my surprise, that there was as much truth as satire in the remark, having been informed on high authority, that this strange method of encouraging the evil it was sought to check had in fact been frequently resorted to, and to a considerable extent. As regards the proffered services of the Chimariote warrior, considering the mode in which the corps to which he belonged was habitually recruited, they did not seem calculated to afford much comfort had I really been likely to require them.

'But the most curious inmates of the establishment were my own next door neighbours, a party of students at the Academy of Livadia. They were five in number, brothers, or near relatives of each other; the eldest, a fine tall handsome youth of about seventeen, the youngest, a boy of about twelve years of age. Their room contained, as usual, no article of domestic furniture; but amends were made by four oblong wooden chests of such bulk as to cover the greater portion of its area. These were the repositories of their clothes, books, provisions, and valuables of all kinds; and also served them as desks for writing their exercises, and for pillows when asleep. On the intermediate space, they reclined, squatted, romped, and reposed, upon their shaggy goat-skin cloaks or hair capottes, which protected them from the storm by day, and formed their mattrass and bedding by night. They never undressed, much less changed their attire, during the period of my residence, nor probably in the course of the year, unless when the decay of the suit they wore, or the obligation of some great religious festival, might require its partial or complete renewal.

'In the midst of all this filth and misery there was something exceedingly engaging in their temper and demeanour. We were only separated by a thin partition of boards, full of chinks, through which each party could hear every thing, and see a good deal of what was going on on the other side; and although, from daybreak until about nine or ten o'clock at night, with a short interval of absence at school hours, they kept up a perpetual clatter, swelling every now and then into boisterous screaming and romping, I never heard a cross word, or observed a symptom of quarrel or disagreement among them. Their lessons, which were all carried on in common—*vivâ voce*—and conjointly with their chattering and merriment, comprised, in as far as languages were concerned, the Greek, ancient and modern, and the Italian, but no Latin. One of their chief exercises was repeating and learning by heart portions of an Italo-Greek vocabulary. In the performance of this task, as indeed of all others imposed on them, they had instinctively resorted to the system of mutual instruction, rehearsing to each other in turns their separate allotments, every third or fourth sentence of which gave rise to a jest and peals of laughter. The older ones acted the part of tutors or monitors to their juniors, and occasionally assumed—though throughout palpably in jest—the functions of pedagogue, even to the extent of administering chastisement with the slipper, to this day as in ancient

Greece* a common mode of infliction, accompanied with the proper amount of angry words on the part of the castigator, and of entreaties, expostulations, or lamentations, on that of the chastised. They seemed all to be gifted by nature with a quickness of capacity, in the inverse ratio fortunately of the wretched means employed for its cultivation. Half an hour was occasionally devoted to reading aloud, subject of course to the same interruptions. The works selected for this exercise were chiefly in the Romaic, the exact matter of which I could rarely follow, but they appeared almost exclusively of a religious tendency.

'It was with much regret that I was obliged to forego cultivating their closer acquaintance; but after having been at such pains to free my own quarters from filth and vermin, the terror of fresh contamination, while it effectually excluded my visits to them, rendered me little disposed to encourage any similar compliment on their part. I therefore was for confining my intercourse with them to a little conversation during our occasional walks on the portico. But the elder one of the party, observing me one day reading by the fireside, took courage, and approaching very respectfully, asked to look at the book. It was a volume of the small Leipzig stereotype edition of Pausanias. He both read and understood it tolerably, was much delighted with the topographical description of his own native district of Phocis, and seemed lost in admiration of the beauty of the volume, although of very ordinary paper and homely binding. I was sorry I could not spare him a present of a number or two of my set, which I certainly would have done, had I known, as I afterwards discovered, that I could easily have replaced them at Athens. After this first inroad he renewed his visits each successive day; but had the good taste not to make them very long, and when disposed to get rid of him, I very easily succeeded by resuming my walk in the gallery. The younger ones, emboldened by his example, also once or twice attempted to effect a lodgment; but, observing with ready tact the signs of disapprobation on my countenance, he put them to flight in an instant by emphatically pronouncing the words "Exò, tetrápoda"—"get out, you brutes!" literally, "you quadrupeds." He informed me that two of them were his brothers, the other two his cousins, also brothers of each other. His father was a Papa of Distomo, ancient Ambrysus, in Phocis. He himself had been two years at the Academy, the others a proportionally shorter time. They had hired the room in the Khan as their permanent lodging. They visited the Academy at stated hours; but in other respects they lived quite independently, subject to no apparent control except an occasional visit from an old black-bearded Papa of the town, who seemed to have, or rather to fancy he had, some charge of them, either in the capacity of private tutor or religious instructor. The only perceptible effect of his

---

* Aristoph. *Lysistr.* v. 657. Terent. *Eunuch,* v. 8, 4. Persius, v. 169. Lucian, *Dial. Deor.* xi. 1; xiii. 2. Juvenal, *Sat.* vi. v. 612.

presence was a certain addition to their habitual merriment, of which he was himself not unfrequently the butt, but always in the same spirit of good-humour that pervaded their intercourse with each other.'—(Vol. i., pp. 239-246.)

This long extract conveys no inadequate impression, both of the temper in wich Mr. Mure speaks of the Greeks, and of the comparative amount of notice bestowed by him upon the several classes which together make up the Greek nation.

To the state of the rural districts, and to some sections of the rural population, he gives, as we have already had some occasion to remark, much and repeated attention. And certainly close observation is merited by a class who constitute, according to Mr. Strong's returns, about one-half of the male adults of the nation. In regard to the state and prospects of agriculture in Greece, the general impression left upon the reader's mind by Mr. Mure's casual glimpses will not differ materially, in its results, from the more specific one conveyed by the former observer's tabular and numerical details. In regard to commerce, however, to which, even before the emancipation of Greece was attained, her most intelligent friends looked with sanguine hope as the most promising source of her future prosperity, the volumes now before us afford, it may be said, no information whatever; and an impression very far from accurate might be made by one or two incidental allusions, which alone are to be found in relation to the subject. Of the state of native manufactures in Greece, it does not indeed seem easy to speak in terms too disparaging. Everything has yet to be done: the country is but rising out of the slough of barbarism into which tyranny had plunged it. But, in regard to commerce, even at this earliest stage in the new order of things, and in spite of errors here, as elsewhere, committed by the government, there is abundant room for cheerfulness and hope The Greek mercantile navy—the school in which Canaris was trained to execute vengeance upon the Turks—continues to be a school both for sturdy independence and for steady and enterprising industry. Mr. Mure's book, however, is our text; and we must not go beyond it for the matter which would be required for illustrating this assertion.

His curiosity seems, like that of most travellers, to have been strongly attracted by the wildest portions of the nation—those who have, by a discouraging crossness of destiny, been at once the most active

instruments in working out the liberation of Greece from her Turkish despots, and the most serious hinderances in the way of establishing that good order, which is a preliminary condition towards her enjoyment of the liberty she has attained. Much interest attaches to the incidental illustrations of that system of irregular tactics, which—employed under the Turkish rule in a marauding warfare, chiefly directed against the oppressors of the race, but occasionally against fellow-countrymen—was devoted usefully to the noblest purposes during the war of liberation; but which, sullied even in that contest by abuses betokening its impure origin, has, since the recognition of Greek independence, threatened, more than once, to plunge the country into an unmitigated anarchy. In the volume under notice, however, we see the character of the irregular Greek warfare treated only in its development towards one quarter, in which it ends by producing downright robbery. We should like well to receive illustrations of it in another light. The 'Klephts,' who have professionally practised that profession since the peace, are very mean rogues indeed; but among the 'Klephts' and 'Armatoli' of the Turkish times, were bred, as we must never fail to recollect, the leaders who maintained, unflinchingly for years, the most desperate national conflict recorded in the pages of modern history. Looking back to the scenes which have been caused by the wild temper of the Colokotronis, and Mavromichalis, and others, since the expulsion of the Turks—to the misrule and rebellions of the interim republic, and the bloody act of Mainote revenge which closed the reign of its wily chief—and to the more recent ebullitions of the same spirit, since the accession of King Otho—we have felt, we must own, less interest in perusing the travelling sketches of Klephtic tactics and adventures than in glancing at those parts of the other book, which give details like those of an almanac. It is interesting in the extreme, to those who are familiar with events not many years old, to see such names as Mavromichalis, and Colokotronis, and Palamedes, and Manginas, and Mavrocordatos, and Colettis, set down together as belonging to men who are members of the same Council of State. But we must wait for another opportunity, and for a few articles of information supplementary to those which we already possess, before entering upon the field thus presented.

Nor does Mr. Mure's book either tempt or entitle us to treat the state or prospects of Greece in a political point of view. He himself carefully shuns politics—thus excluding himself, perhaps, from affording some information of a kind that might have possessed both use and interest. However, if he had dealt much in speculations of this nature. it is not impossible that we should have found it necessary to enter a pretty strong dissent to some of his conclusions At least, such is the suspicion we are tempted to entertain from the perusal of that which is almost the only passage purely political throughout his work—a passage in which he speaks of the Greek Revolution in comparison with the abortive revolutions of Italy. But, in the mean time, we will not interpret his political opinions by implication. We thank him for the good spirit in which the social relations of Greece are treated generally, and decline going out of our way to seek for themes of censure

The last quotation we made does but justice to that universal zeal for education, of which, from various sources, we receive the most cheering accounts, and which is one of the fairest auguries we could desire for the future. The past history of the struggle for independence is, in itself, an augury to the same effect; and is spoken of by Mr. Mure with much enthusiasm. We gladly quote, in conclusion, part of the animated discussion which serves as the introduction to his narrative of the fall of Mesolonghi :

· I remember at Athens to have heard a veteran Philhellene. who had borne his share in the brunt of the war, and of whose name honourable mention occurs in the narrative of its vicissitudes, maintain. that the acts of prowess by which it was distinguished fell no way short of those which shed the greatest lustre on the most brilliant period of old Hellenic history—that of the Persian invasion. The remark, though acquiesced in by some of his comrades. struck me at the moment as a paradox or an exaggeration ; but, on a fair estimate of all the specialities of the two cases, it was difficult to see how it could be controverted. Apart from individual displays of valour or patriotism, it is necessary, in order to a just balance of the merits of any such comparison. that we should consider in each case. the whole circumstances under which the struggle commenced and was carried on. In the Greeks of the present age we find a people who. after having. at a remote period of history, passed through the successive stages of decline, decay, and death. to which the body politic, like the human frame, is inevitably destined—who. after having lain for upwards of a thousand years in a state of corruption and torpor, though in the enjoyment, it is true. of a species of mock independence—had been finally reduced to little better than abject slavery. by

the most cruel race of foreign tyrants that ever planted its settlements in a conquered country. During more than four successive centuries. they had been habituated to be buffeted and spit upon, to see their laws set aside or violated. their religion trampled under foot, their industry blighted. and their substance absorbed by the most grinding system of taxation ; and, under the influence of these accumulated causes of debasement, had become, perhaps not undeservedly, a by-word among the surrounding nations for all that is contemptible and worthless in our species. That any people under such circumstances should have preserved a national character at all, is perhaps a rare phenomenon ; but that they should at this last hour suddenly shake off the spirit of tame submission which had become to them a second nature, and rise to a man against the overwhelming power of their oppressors, and with all the native energy of a young and vigorous race of fierce barbarians. is an event unexampled in the history of mankind.

'How stands the case on the other side ? The Greeks. at the period of the Persian war, were a people in the flower of youth and vigour, flushed with recollections of ancient glory. filled with the loftiest spirit of national pride and independence. The whole population was regularly trained to arms, and inured to the dangers and duties of military life. Their lower classes were practised warriors, their upper ranks skilful commanders. Their armies and fleets were in a high state of discipline and equipment. and were opposed to comparatively undisciplined and unwarlike hordes. They were invaded, it is true. by the whole force of a mighty empire, of which their native country, in point of extent, would scarcely have furnished a petty province ; but it was at that time fully peopled. and the single state of Attica probably contained a population little short of that of the whole of Greece proper at the present day. Their enemies were at a distance. and full time was given to prepare and concentrate their means of defence. In the case of the modern Greeks, all these favourable circumstances were reversed. In addition to the disadvantages already noticed, the wealthier classes were either merchants or servants of the Porte—a timid and time-serving race. Their warriors were brigands and outlaws, or raw unpractised peasantry ; their mariners, fishermen or pirates. Commanders they had none above the rank of a captain of bucaniers or of mountain banditti. Funds they could scarcely be said to possess at all. Their enemies were not only a race of approved valour and powerful resources. comparatively disciplined, experienced, and well equipped, but were cantoned in the heart of the country, and in possession of all its principal fortresses. In respect to numbers, the disproportion between the Christian population of Greece and the Turkish empire. may be considered virtually as great as that between the dominions of Xerxes and the states of the Hellenic confederacy. But besides this, during the two or three first years of the war, they had not only the force of their declared enemy to contend with, but the still more galling hostility of his European allies, many of whom, under the name of neutrality. used every means consistent with the shadow of its maintenance, to favour the Turks and browbeat the Greeks. Driven from their fields and homes to make their abode for months or years " in deserts and in mountains, in dens and caves of the earth ;" astonished and appalled to find themselves as the common enemy of civilized Europe, in those very quarters to which they had most confidently looked for sympathy and support—under all these afflicting discouragements they never lost heart; and a few raw levies of squalid mountaineers or unwarlike fishermen, by the unaided resources of their own valour or conduct, successively overpowered the garrisons, dispersed the choicest armies, and baffled or discomfited the ponderous navies, of one of the mightiest empires of modern times.'—(Vol. i., p. 145–148.)

Art. VIII.—*Das Nationale System der Politische Oekonomie*, von Dr. FRIEDRICH LIST. (*The National System of Political Economy*, by Dr. FREDERIC LIST.) 8vo. Volume I. Stuttgart and Tubingen : 1841.

BEFORE we proceed to our examination of our author's pretended system, we must state the contents and the purpose of his volume, with the motives which induce us to notice it. We must preface the statement with an explanation of the causes in which this volume has originated ; and, in order to this explanation, we must advert to the origin and the objects of the ' German Customs-Union.'

Before the continental system, established by Napoleon, closed the ports of Germany against English manufactured goods, Austria and Prussia, the principal German states, protected their own manufactures by prohibitory or restrictive tariffs. Each of the states of inferior importance, into which the rest of Germany was then divided, had its separate system of import-duties as well as Austria or Prussia. The several tariffs of these numerous inferior states opposed the most mischievous obstacles to the internal commerce of Germany; but they permitted the importation of foreign manufactured goods, including those of England. It appears, moreover, from a statement made by our author, that the Prussian government had begun to perceive the mischiefs of its prohibitory and restrictive policy. In consequence of its growing tendency to a liberal commercial policy, it had considerably reduced its duties on foreign manufactured articles ; and, in consequence of these reductions, its tariff

no longer afforded to its own manufacturing subjects a complete protection against English competition.

From 1806 to the general peace in 1814, English manufactured goods were nearly excluded from Germany; the exclusion being caused by Napoleon's continental system, and by other obstacles to commerce which arose from the general war. In consequence of this exclusion, manufactures were created in parts of Germany which had not previously manufactured for themselves ; and manufactures were extended in parts of the country in which a manufacturing industry had previously arisen.

After the general peace in 1814, English manufactured goods were again imported into Germany—the Austrian states being the only parts of the country from which they were excluded by a prohibitory tariff. As the English manufacturing capitals were larger than the German, and England was superior to Germany in the arts of manufacturing industry, this renewed importation was disastrous to the German manufactures ; and it threatened to destroy the unnatural manufacturing establishments which had been created by the war, and by Napoleon's continental system.

The manufacturing distress which generally affected Germany, in consequence of the renewed importation of English manufactured goods, fell with peculiar severity on the Rhenish provinces of Prussia. During the war, those provinces had been French departments; and, in consequence of their incorporation with that extensive country, the vast markets of France had been open to their manufactured products. Accordingly, on the transfer of the Rhenish provinces from France to Prussia, the manufacturing population of those provinces were visited with a double calamity. They were excluded from the vast markets which had lately been open to their products ; while the incompleteness of the protection afforded them by the Prussian tariff, exposed them to the crushing competition of the English manufacturers.

In consequence of the distress inflicted upon them by the renewed importation of English manufactured goods, the manufacturing subjects of the Prussian government were deeply discontented at its commercial policy; and they vehemently demanded a tariff of import duties, calculated to protect them completely against English competition. The Prussian government (if we may believe our author) was inclined to the principle of free international trade ;

but there were motives, arising from its position, which urged it to comply with the demand. In the first place, the Rhenish provinces at that time were dissatisfied with the transfer to Prussia; and the severe distress of their manufacturing population, sharpened their desire for a reunion with France. In the next place, laws had been recently passed by the English legislature for the protection of the landed interest In consequence of these laws, Prussian corn and other raw products were excluded from the English markets; and, assuming that the Prussian government (agreeably to its secret inclination) had permitted the free importation of English manufactured goods, it is manifest that this exclusion (to the extent to which it operated) would ultimately have compelled its subjects to manufacture for themselves. It appears, therefore, that the English restrictions on the importation of raw products, weakened the inducements of the Prussian government to reject the demand for a more protective tariff. By rejecting the demand, it would have inflamed the existing discontent of its distressed manufacturing subjects; and, owing to the tendency of those restrictions to force Prussia to manufacture for herself, it would not have secured to the body of its subjects the full advantages of free international trade.

Determined by the motives to which we have adverted, the Prussian government, in 1818, issued a new tariff of import duties; and this tariff (afterwards copied by the German Customs-Unions) amply protected the Prussian manufacturers against their English competitors.

But though it amply protected the Prussian manufactures, it increased the distress of the manufacturers in the inferior states of Germany. The new policy of the Prussian government excluded these manufacturers from the Prussian territories; as the prohibitory systems of the Austrian and French governments had previously excluded them from the Austrian and French dominions. The effect of these exclusions from the Prussian territories, and from the Austrian and French dominions, was aggravated by the obstacles to the internal commerce of Germany, which arose from the separate tariffs of the inferior German states; so that the manufacturers in each of those small communities were nearly confined to their narrow domestic market

The distressed manufacturers in the inferior states of Germany, naturally turned their minds to the means of curing the evil; and, in 1819, a number of manufac-

turers and traders, subjects of those states, formed themselves into an association for devising and promoting a remedy. After various consultations, they determined to direct their labours to the accomplishment of the following objects :—the establishment of a tariff common to Germany, instead of the separate tariffs of the several German states; and the complete protection of the German manufacturers against English and other foreign competitors. As this association consisted of 6000 members, and represented the manufacturing interest of a large portion of Germany, they had naturally much influence with the German public, and, through the German public, with the German governments. According to our author, Germany is indebted to them for the 'Customs-Union;' and, by their labours to diffuse their opinions, and to determine the governments to adopt their objects, they seem to have brought about the establishment of the Union, or to have contributed materially to that result. Be this as it may, their objects were ultimately accomplished. Three confederacies, tending to the promotion of those objects, were successively formed by various German states. Bavaria and Wurtemburg were parties to the first; Prussia, with certain states contiguous to the Prussian dominions, were parties to the second; and certain states in central Germany, were parties to the third. The three confederacies were subsequently united; and the 'German Customs-Union' is the confederacy which resulted from the fusion. Most of the German states are now members of this Union; the Austrian states, the Mecklenburgs, Holstein, Hanover, and the Hanse Towns, being, we believe, the only states still refusing to join it.

The several states which are members of the Union have relinquished their separate tariffs;—a tariff of import duties, common to all the states, has been established by their joint authority; revenue officers, empowered by the same authority, levy the duties which the tariff imposes; and the share of each state in the proceeds of the tariff, is proportioned to the amount of its population. These financial and commercial provisions have been followed by important effects on the internal commerce of Germany. Though the several countries which are members of the Union are sovereign and distinct states, they are, nevertheless, for the purposes of the Union, one country with one frontier. Accordingly, few of the fiscal obstacles, naturally lying in the way of international trade, obstruct the mutual commerce of these independent communities.

Important effects on the foreign commerce of Germany have resulted from the duties imposed by the Union tariff on foreign manufactured goods Generally speaking, these duties are proportioned to the weight, and not to the value of the article. Accordingly, they admit the importation of the finer and dearer commodities, which are exclusively consumed by the wealthier classes; and they prevent or impede the importation of the coarser and cheaper commodities, which are objects of general consumption Considered as duties *ad valorem*, the duties imposed by the tariff on the coarser commodities vary from 20 to 60 per cent.; so that commodities of this description, manufactured in England and other foreign countries, are nearly excluded by those duties from the states belonging to the Union. One principal object of the Union tariff is the protection and encouragement of German manufacturing industry; and in preventing the importation of the coarser, and permitting the importation of the finer commodities, the authors of the tariff adopted a measure well calculated to accomplish the purpose. As the manufacturing industry of Germany is comparatively rude, she has few or no aptitudes for producing the finer commodities; and the branches of manufacturing industry which are devoted to the production of articles generally consumed, are incomparably the most important.

It appears from the preceding statement, that the authors of the Union had two principal objects :—The removal of the obstacles to the internal commerce of Germany, which arose from the separate tariffs of her several states; and the exclusion of foreign manufactures from German markets, for the protection and encouragement of German manufacturing industry. It is manifest that the two objects have no natural connection; and accordingly the members of the association of 1819, who were not directly concerned in manufacturing enterprises, aimed exclusively at the first Indeed, the principle which prompted the exclusion of foreign manufactured goods, is not consistent with the principle which required the abolition of the separate tariffs; inasmuch as the benefits which accrue to the people of Germany from freedom of commerce between her several states, would be enhanced by freedom of commerce between Germany and foreign countries.

Dr. List, the author of the volume be-

fore us, was an active member of the association, to whose labours we have adverted. It appears, indeed, from a statement in his preface, that he started the idea of such an association, and even the idea of a 'German Customs-Union.' He was then a professor (we believe of Political Economy) in the University of Tubingen; and he has since devoted his life to economical speculations, or to practical pursuits tending to suggest them. Strong in study and experience, he contemptuously rejects the principle of free international trade; and he looks upon Turgot and Adam Smith, with the other political economists by whom the principle is maintained, as drivelling and ridiculous dreamers. He thinks that the benefits conferred on the German people by the Customs-Union, chiefly arise from its prohibitory and restrictive tariff, and not from the freedom of commerce which it gives to the interior of Germany; and he zealously maintains the expediency of protecting German manufacturers, by excluding their foreign rivals from German markets. As English manufacturing industry is superior to German, it would crush the unnatural manufactures created in Germany, if the commerce between the countries were freed from prohibitions and restrictions; and as Dr. List (like too many other zealots) loves his cause less than he hates his enemies, the vehemence of his passion for promoting German manufactures, is surpassed by the fierceness of his antipathy to the manufacturing greatness of England. It appears, from his preface, that he left Germany in 1821; that he did not return to that country till 1833; and that he resided in the United States of North America during the interval, or the greater part of it. It seems that his hostility to the manufacturing greatness of England was not softened by his absence from his country. In a series of letters published in American newspapers in 1827, he supported the cause of those American manufacturers who aimed at the exclusion of English manufactured goods. It seems that these letters did good service to the cause, and got him in the favour of its partizans; for they were published as a pamphlet, entitled ' Outlines of a New System of Political Economy,' by the Pennsylvanian Society for the Encouragement of Manufactures and Arts. Since his return to Germany in 1833, he has tried to confirm his countrymen in the false economical principles which prompted the prohibitory duties imposed by the Union tariff; and he has laboured to abase the manufacturing greatness of England, by inciting other nations to exclude her manufactures from their markets. These are the principal objects of numberless articles which he has published in Newspapers and Reviews; and they are also the principal objects of the volume before us, though it wears the name and form of a System of Political Economy.

We have stated the origin and objects of the 'German Customs Union,' and explained the origin of our author's volume. Before we proceed to our examination of his pretended system, we must offer a few remarks on the title of his volume, its contents and purpose, and its method and spirit; and we must state our reasons for our careful review of a production which intrinsically is not worthy of serious notice.

It has been discovered by our author, that the theories of political economy, which embrace the principle of free international trade, are properly theories of *cosmopolitical* economy. Overlooking the international wars and the various other causes by which international trade is actually disturbed, they suppose that nations, for commercial purposes, are practically one community; and the economical interests of nations, as forming this community of mankind, are the subject with which they are concerned. But his own system of political economy, which rejects the principle of free international trade, is a theory of *political* or *national economy*, in the proper sense of the expression. It keeps in view the various causes by which international trade is actually disturbed; and it treats of the economical interests of the separate and contending nations into which the world is actually divided.

Proud of a discovery which was reserved for his own sagacity, he is eager to distinguish his political system from all cosmopolitical conceits. Accordingly, he gives his treatise the title (somewhat tautologous, it cannot be denied) which stands at the head of the present article: namely, 'The National (or political) System of Political (or national) Economy.' His poor misconception of the doctrines which he tries to brand with the nickname of cosmopolitical economy, we cannot examine in the present place; but we shall make some remarks upon it in an after part of this article, if our limits will permit us to insert them.

Assuming that our author's treatise is entitled to the name of a system, it is not a system of political economy, but a system or theory of international trade. The present volume is limited to this subject; and

if the contents of the unpublished volume may be inferred from a sketch of them which is given in the preface to the present, they will chiefly consist of subjects special in their nature, and relating exclusively to the economical interests of Germany.

Considered as a system of international trade, his treatise is unworthy of notice; as will appear sufficiently from the following statement of its contents, and the subsequent remarks upon them. He states, in his preface, his motives to undertake his inquiry; he gives, in a subsequent introduction, the principal conclusions to which his inquiry has led him; and he then affects to consider the matter of his volume, under the four books into which he divides it. The ostensible subject of the first and second books, is his system of international trade; as that of the fourth is his system of commercial policy; the professed purpose of the third book, is a review of the systems of international trade which certain preceding economists have given to the world. Now, if the contents of his volume fulfilled the promise of its ostensible plan, its substance will consist of two parts: a system or theory of international trade, and a corresponding system of commercial policy. Whether the latter system would essentially differ from the former, is a question foreign to our purpose. Although the systems might essentially differ, it is manifest that the matter of each of them would nearly correspond to that of the other. They would mainly differ in respect of the aspects from which they severally considered their common subject. The former might consider it from a speculative point of view, or treat it as the subject of a science; the latter might survey it from a practical point of view, or treat it as the subject of an art. Now, as every speculative and every practical system is intended for general application, it consists of general principles or general rules, and is not directly concerned with particulars or singulars. Accordingly, the economical interests of nations (or nations considered generally) should form the subject of our author's treatise. If his treatise be limited to the economical interests of certain particular nations, it is neither a system of international trade, nor a system of commercial policy; but it consists of applications of principles or rules (which it expressly or tacitly borrows from such system) to the particular interests with which it is really concerned. Notwithstanding its pretension to the name of a system, such is the true character of our author's treatise. It is concerned with the particular interests of the principal nations of continental Europe, with those of the United States of North America, and, above all, with those of his own country; and it is addressed to those particular nations for a special and practical object. He labours to inculcate on them, (though he occasionally extends his arguments to all nations able to manufacture for themselves,) that they ought to adopt or adhere to that policy which he styles *the protective system;* that they ought to plant manufactures on their own territories, or foster the manufactures which they have already created, by forbidding or restricting the importation of foreign manufactured goods. To this particular and directly practical object, all the contents of his volume which partake of a general and speculative character are subservient and accommodated. It is prominent in all the departments, and in most of the sub-departments, into which he divides his treatise;—in those which he affects to devote to his system of international trade, as in those which he professes to assign to his system of commercial policy. Indeed, we cannot perceive that the divisions of his volume are distinguishable by their subjects or purposes; or that it has any divisions at all, but those which are made by the titles prefixed to his books and chapters. Nor are the spirit and the tone of his treatise more scientific than its scope and method. He regards the manufacturing and commercial greatness of England with envious and bitter hostility; he anticipates the decay of that greatness with inhuman exultation; and for the purpose of promoting the cause to which his volume is devoted, he misrepresents her commercial policy, and appeals to vulgar and malignant prejudices. In fine, though his volume pretends to the name of a system, and (including the preface) runs to the length of 660 pages, its object, manner, and spirit, are those of a popular pamphlet. It is the work of a zealous and unscrupulous advocate, striving to establish a given practical conclusion, and not the production of a dispassionate inquirer, seeking to promote the improvement of a science or an art.

Dr. List's treatise, as a theory of international trade, is, therefore, unworthy of grave criticism; but the practical purpose for which it is published, and the temper of the public which it is intended to influence, give it an importance which entitles it to serious notice. Feelings of hostility to the manufactures and commerce of England,

and opinions favourable to the protective system, are widely diffused in Germany as well as France; and they are rapidly spreading in the other nations of continental Europe, in the United States, and even in Brazil and the South American republics. The extensive prevalence of these opinions and feelings, mainly arises from the restrictive policy pursued by England herself; and unless she roots them out, or stops their rapid spread, by adopting the principle of free trade, they may lead to a conspiracy of nations against her manufactures and commerce, far more formidable than the continental system of Napoleon. Napoleon's system of exclusion was limited to a part of continental Europe; and being odious (as well as mischievous) to the generality of his subjects and vassals, was extensively evaded. But all the principal countries of continental Europe, with many of the countries of the New World, may join in the conspiracy against our manufactures and commerce, which our own suicidal policy tends to provoke; and, since the governments of those countries would exclude our commodities in compliance with the wishes of their subjects, the exclusion would probably be enforced with comparative strictness. As our author continually appeals to these prevalent opinions and feelings, and is no contemptible hand at a popular pamphlet, we fear that his volume will extend them in Germany, if not in all the countries which it is intended to influence. That it will circulate widely in Germany, and make a mischievous impression on the German public, may be presumed from the rapid sale which it has already met with—a second edition having been demanded before the end of the autumn of 1841, though the first edition was not published till the close of the summer in the same year. As articles in English journals, relating to the interests of Germany, are frequently noticed in those of that country, a dissection of his volume in this Journal may do something to counteract the impression. We have found it no easy matter to detect the drift of his system, and to give a tangible shape to his loose and desultory arguments; but if we shall attract the attention, and influence the opinions, of a small number of German readers, we shall think ourselves well rewarded for the painful and disgusting drudgery. We think that our notice of a writer so hostile to England will not be uninteresting to the English public; since his volume reflects opinions widely diffused, and is a laboured expression of the arguments by which they are commonly maintained.

In reviewing this desultory volume, we shall put the substance of such of its contents as our limits will permit us to notice, in a form and order of our own. If we attempted-to follow our author through his pretended plan, the article would run to intolerable length; and for the purpose of confuting his pretended system, to the satisfaction of such of our readers as may be acquainted with his volume, we must endeavour to extricate his arguments from the confusion in which he involves them. Though many of his arguments conflict with one another, and all are impertinent to the purpose of his treatise, the desultory manner in which he presents them tends to conceal their nothingness; but if they were arranged in a regular and perspicuous series, the bare arrangement would nearly suffice to confute them. A rabble of men is powerless or feeble, because it is undisciplined and disorderly; but a rabble of contradictory and impertinent arguments is strong in its confusion.

The following is the order which we intend to observe in our review of this volume. 1. We shall first examine our author's system of international trade. 2. Certain of our remarks on his misrepresentation of the commercial policy of England, could not be inserted in that examination without breaking its continuity; and we, therefore, shall place those remarks in a second part. In this part, we shall shortly state the causes of the prevalent hostility to her manufacturing and commercial greatness; we shall shortly state the mischiefs with which it threatens herself and other civilized nations; and we shall notice the policy which she will speedily adopt if she be anxious to avert them.

I. We introduce our examination of his system with the following statement of its general purport; dividing our statement into two parts, corresponding to the two theories of which his system is compounded:—1. The interests of the individuals who compose a nation are promoted by the perfect freedom of its internal trade. The interests of the nations which compose the community of mankind would be promoted to a still higher degree, by perfect freedom of international trade; for the division of labour is extended as the field of commerce is enlarged; and every extension of the division of labour augments the productiveness of labour and capital. As a nation is formed of individuals subject to a common government, the freedom of its internal trade is protected from interruptions; and if nations were as closely united by an uni-

versal confederacy as the members of a single nation are united by a common government, freedom of international trade would be equally secured from disturbances. At present, however, the foreign trade of every nation is exposed to disturbances, arising from international wars; and also to disturbances arising from restrictions which other nations may impose upon their own external commerce. Till nations are united by a universal confederacy, having the purpose and effect of obviating such disturbances, the freedom of their mutual commerce will remain imperfect, though the freedom of their internal trade be rendered complete. At present, therefore, it is the interest of every nation which possesses the means of manufacturing for itself, to adopt or retain the protective system. By embracing or adhering to this policy, it sacrifices some good, but it obviates more evil. Although it rejects the advantages arising from freedom of international commerce, it escapes the preponderant mischiefs arising from the causes by which that freedom is troubled and abridged.

2. The principal nations of the European continent (an expression including, for the present purpose, the nations of European origin which form the United States of North America) may be divided into two classes. Of the nations in question, some are nearly in the state of a purely agricultural country; the others are more advanced from the purely agricultural condition, but are still inferior to England in manufacturing industry. As a purely agricultural country has no manufactures of its own, it has no considerable trade, internal or foreign, no skilful and highly productive agriculture; and since the state of a nation, in respect of civilisation and power, is mainly determined by its economical condition, such a country is condemned by its poverty to semi-barbarism and political weakness. Accordingly, though perfect freedom of international trade were possible at present, the nations in question would consult their present interests by declining the proffered opportunity. Such of those nations as are nearly in the state of a purely agricultural country, would plant manufactures on their own territories by forbidding or restricting the importation of foreign manufactured goods; such as are more advanced from the purely agricultural condition, would protect their rising manufactures by a similar policy, and each would persist steadily in this system of prohibitions or restrictions, until her own manufacturers, unsupported by such factitious helps, could compete with any other manufacturers in her own and in foreign

markets. In consequence of her past protection to her own manufacturers, England is now pre-eminent in manufacturing and commercial industry. Having ascended to this pre-eminence, she would promote her present interests by adopting the principle of free trade, and by persuading the nations in question to follow the specious example. At present, however, the perfect freedom of trade which would be advantageous to her, would be ruinous to them. As she could manufacture at a cost lower than that at which they could manufacture for themselves, she would supply them with goods for their own consumption, as well as exclude their manufacturers from third countries. By deluging their markets with her cheap goods, she would prevent them from planting manufactures on their own territories, or crush the rising manufactures which they had created; and she thus would keep them in the state of a merely agricultural country, or force them to retrograde to that poor and feeble condition. In fine, England would monopolize the manufactures, and therefore the commerce, of the world; she would abase the principal countries of continental Europe, as well as the countries which are less civilized and powerful, to a state of helpless and degrading dependence on her manufacturing and commercial supremacy; by the peaceful and insinuating arts of manufactures and commerce, she would establish an empire more extensive, and more opposed to the general improvement of mankind, than that which was forced on reluctant nations by the warlike policy of Rome.

At present, therefore, the nations in question would consult their interests by adopting or retaining the protective system; though when they had risen, by means of that system, to the manufacturing and commercial prosperity which England already enjoys, they would consult their own interests, and the general interests of nations, by adopting the principle of free trade. Perfect freedom of international trade would then be advantageous to the community of mankind; for, as many nations would be nearly equal in manufacturing and commercial prosperity, it would not enable England, or any single nation, to monopolize the manufactures and commerce of the world. It appears, therefore, in the last result, that the nations in question, by adopting or retaining the protective system, would pursue a policy liberal in its tendencies, though restrictive in its immediate effects. By steadily adhering to the system until they equalled England in manufacturing and commercial prosperity,

they would gradually prepare the way for the only freedom of international trade which enlightened citizens of the world can deem desirable;—the freedom of international trade which would promote the interests of mankind, and would not exalt a single nation at the cost of all other communities.

It appears from the preceding statement, that the system is compounded of two theories which flatly contradict one another. According to the first, freedom of trade would promote the present interests of all nations, if it were secured from certain disturbing causes; according to the second, it would *not* promote the present interests of the principal nations of continental Europe, though those causes were completely obviated. If we wrote for no higher purpose than that of confuting our author, we should content ourselves with stating the contradictory theories and pointing out the contradiction; but, since the opinions of which these theories are formed are widely diffused, notwithstanding their incoherency, we shall waive this preliminary objection, and proceed to our analysis of his system. We shall begin our analysis with an examination of the *second* theory; and having completed this examination, we shall briefly consider the first. We shall try to prove, in the former part of the analysis, that freedom of trade would be useful to all nations, if it were secured from the disturbances to which we have just adverted. We shall try to prove, in the latter part of the analysis, that its liability to those disturbances does not affect the hypothetical conclusion

We commence our explanation of the second theory with a statement of certain objections to which it is liable; since this preliminary statement will shorten our dissection of the arguments by which our author supports it. These objections, which are founded on mischiefs produced by the protective system, may be conveniently stated under the three following heads:—

1st. In every nation in which this system obtains, the government gives a direction to the national labour and capital, which they would not take spontaneously. In so far as the system operates, the protected manufactures are forced into existence by the interference of the government with the economical concerns of its subjects. Public prudence is substituted for private; the wisdom of an unwieldy and badly-constituted joint stock company, for the discretion of individuals. The economical concerns of the nation are not managed by the government, as those of a joint-stock company are managed by a board of directors; but the government determines the articles which its subjects shall produce, though it leaves them to produce those articles in their own way.

Now, every interference of a government with the interests and concerns of its subjects, ought to be founded on sufficient special reasons. Of those numberless interests and concerns, there is a vast and indeterminate multitude with which the government ought not to intermeddle. There is always, therefore, a general presumption against the expediency of such an interference; and unless there be special reasons sufficiently showing the contrary, the general presumption ought to prevail. There are certain cases in which the interference of the government is necessary. It is manifest, for example, that the business of legislating, or of administering justice, or of defending the nation against foreign enemies, cannot be left to the voluntary principle. In other cases, the interference of the government, if not necessary, is expedient. It is often expedient, for example, that public roads, or other means of public transport, should be created by public resources; and it is expedient (at least in our opinion) that government should provide their subjects with secular and religious instruction. But, in the last-mentioned cases, there are good special reasons for the intervention of the state, since private individuals, from want of means or motives, would not accomplish the end for which the government interferes. Our author objects to the arguments in favour of freedom of trade, that they would prove the inexpediency of various restraints universally admitted to be useful; as, for example, the inexpediency of checking the industry of thieves. But the freedom which is advocated by the partisans of free trade, is the freedom of pursuing ends which are useful or harmless, by beneficent or innocuous means; and in all the cases produced by our author, in support of his pitiful objection, the ends or the means are so palpably pernicious, that there are good special reasons for imposing the restraints.

It appears from the preceding remarks, that we are not bound to prove, in an affirmative or direct manner, the expediency of freedom of trade, since there is a general presumption against the interference of governments with the interest and concerns of their subjects. On the other hand, our author was bound to prove, by sufficient special reasons, the expediency of the protective system; and if it appear, from our dissection of his arguments, that he has not

produced such reasons, it will follow that his arguments have not touched the presumption, nor proved the conclusion which he endeavours to establish by his treatise. That the interferences of governments with the economical interests of their subjects are commonly inexpedient, is repeatedly admitted by himself. For example, he says that there are certain countries which have no aptitude for manufacturing, or (to use his own expression) no *vocation* to manufacture. He admits that such a country misapplies its labour and capital, if it creates a manufacture by means of the protective system; and he admits that the inaptitude of the country for the protected manufacture, may be sufficiently presumed from the mere fact of the protection. He therefore admits in effect, (though he does not perceive the implied consequence,) that *every* branch of industry *which has not arisen spontaneously*, is presumptively an evil to the country which has forced it into existence.

2d. The nations of continental Europe, and the United States of North America, are the nations to which he recommends his protective system. Now, if it were adopted by these nations, and also by England, all the more civilized countries of the old and new world would be prevented from exchanging their products. The extent of this mischievous consequence, which would equally affect all of them, would be proportioned to the degree of consistency with which they adopted the foolish and malignant policy. If they adopted the system to the full extent of its logical consequences, it would nearly extinguish their mutual commerce. None of these countries could sell her manufactures to the others; inasmuch as the others would refuse to buy them; nor could she sell to the others any considerable quantity of her raw products, inasmuch as she, in her turn, would reject their manufactured goods. It is manifest that their mutual commerce would be limited to exchanges of raw products; and since their raw products are nearly similar in kind, these exchanges would not be numerous or important.

A division of labour amongst nations is one of the beneficent consequences of international trade; and the extent of the division, with the magnitude of the good which it produces, are proportioned to the freedom of their mutual commerce. If all the countries in question fully adopted the principle of free trade, each would take the part in the common business of production for which it is best qualified by its natural and acquired aptitudes. In consequence of their thus co operating to the common end, the aggregate product of their industry would be greatly augmented; and as each would have a share in the aggregate product, commensurate with its contribution to the joint result, the productiveness of its labour and capital would be greatly increased But if they fully adopted the protective system, it would nearly prevent the concert which we have just described, and each would debar itself, by its own elaborate folly, from most of the advantages of that spontaneous co-operation.

Our author perceives occasionally, that his theory is open to the objection which we have just stated. To obviate the objection, he suggests a scheme of international trade which is not less absurd than his protective system. Each of the civilized nations of the temperate zones, (*i. e.* the nations of Europe and the United States of North America,) is to carry on a direct trade with the nations of the torrid zones; directly exchanging its own manufactured products for the raw products of the torrid zones, which are styled *colonial wares.*

To show that the scheme obviates the objection, he resorts to the following argument He supposes that the mutual commerce of those civilized nations is of small account; he supposes that their trade with the torrid zones is of far greater importance; and he argues that the extinction of the former, caused by his protective system, would be amply compensated by the great extension which the scheme would give to the latter. Now, this argument conflicts with a proposition which forms an essential part of his protective system According to this proposition, it is the policy of those civilized nations to feed their manufacturing industry by encouraging the importation of agricultural products; and England is sapping her manufacturing prosperity by excluding agricultural products, for the protection of her landed interests It is manifestly assumed by this proposition, that if those civilized nations adopted his protective system, they would import one another's products to some considerable extent; and this assumption conflicts with the argument which supposes that their mutual commerce is of small account. It is true, that his protective system would nearly extinguish this commerce, as we have shown above; and that he suggests his scheme of international trade, for the the purpose of removing an objection raised upon that consequence. Accordingly, his argumentation concerning the matter in question, is a tissue of contradictions. He assumes that the mutual commerce of those civilized na-

tions would *not* be extinguished by his protective system; suspecting that the system *would* extinguish the commerce, he suggests his scheme as an answer to the objection; and the principal argument by which he maintains the scheme, supposes the consequence on which the objection is founded.

According to our author, the nations of continental Europe would enlarge their motives to industry, by enlarging their consumption of colonial wares. This assumption, which he advances as an argument in support of his scheme, is impertinent to the purpose for which he produces it. From the assumed tendency of the enlarged consumption to invite them to greater industry, it will not follow that they ought to manufacture for themselves, and carry their manufactures to the torrid zone. As their aptitudes for manufacturing are inferior to those of England, they would naturally turn their industry to the raising of raw products; and they would naturally exchange these products for colonial wares which England had purchased with her cheap manufactured goods. By this roundabout process, their consumption of colonial wares would be more enlarged then by the direct process which our author recommends; since a quantity of their labour and capital, applied to the raising of raw products, would command a larger amount of foreign commodities than the same quantity applied to manufacturing. One of his arguments in support of the protective system, admits of a similar answer. He says that the consumption of manufactures invites to industry; and he infers that the protective system stimulates the industry of a nation by which it is adopted. Now, unless the nation has aptitudes for manufacturing, (or can produce manufactures more cheaply than she can buy them) the protective system, instead of stimulating her industry, tends to discourage it. The capital and labour which she unnaturally turns to manufacturing, would be more productive if they were otherwise applied; and consequently their products would exchange for a quantity of manufactures larger than the quantity which they actually produced.

He further argues, in support of his scheme, that the international trade which he suggests is recommended by nature herself. He says that the civilized nations of the temperate zones are called to manufacturing industry by their aptitudes for it; whilst the nations of the torrid zone, as wanting the intelligence and energy which that industry requires, ought to confine themselves to the raising of raw products. Without pausing to examine his assumption concerning the natural character of the last-mentioned nations, we will notice the reasoning to which it leads him. He infers, from their assumed unfitness for manufacturing industry, that they would not consult their interests by adopting the protective system : he says that their unfitness for any manufacture which they might create by dint of protection, might be presumed from its factitious origin; and he affirms that the respective vocations of various nations are determined by their several aptitudes. Now, though he applies it partially, this reasoning will hold universally. It is not more applicable to the nations of the torrid, than to the civilized nations of the temperate zones These civilized nations have different aptitudes, calling them to different branches of productive industry; some, for example, being inland counties, or being scantily furnished with the means of manufacturing, whilst others are maritime countries, or possess those means in abundance. Our author, moreover, admits by implication, that there is always a presumption against the fitness of a country for a branch of industry which it creates by protection. Accordingly, the several branches of industry for which these civilized nations are respectively fitted, ought not to be settled by protective systems; but each should take the part in the business of production, which the principle of free trade would spontaneously determine.

Our notice of the scheme to which we have just adverted, is merely incidental to our design. We have stated the arguments by which he maintains it, for the purpose of proving, by his own admissions, that his protective system is untenable. Accordingly, we shall not prolong our examination of that project, but shall proceed with our objections to his second theory.

3d. He exhorts the nations of continental Europe, and the United States of North America, to manufacture for themselves to the utmost of their physical means. In giving them this advice, he invites them to a conspiracy against the interests of England, but is far from showing them the way to promote their own. By fully adopting his protective system, they would abridge, to a great extent, the efficient demand for her manufactures; and they would annihilate, to the same extent, the manufacturing capital and skill which she has laboriously acquired. But in doing this harm to her, they would bring down evil on themselves. Generally speaking, her manufacturing industry is more productive than theirs. Accordingly, it is generally their interest to abstain om manufacturing, and to turn themselves to other employments. By producing manufactures for themselves, when they could get them from her at a smaller cost, they would abridge the general productiverss of their labour and capital, and their general command of raw and manufactured commodities. Nor would it be then interest to manufacture for themselves, though their natural means of manufacturing were equal to hers. The acquisition of factitious means equal to hers, would cost them an enormous outlay of labour and capital; and the labour and capital applied to the purpose would be expended to mere waste. If the trade between her and them were perfectly free, the manufacturing capital and skill which she has acquired, would be (in effect) theirs as well as hers; since her instruments of production would yield them all the products which they could get by instruments of their own creation By rejecting the products of her accumulated instruments for the fancied advantage of creating instruments for themselves, they would (in effect) destroy a capital of their own for the fancied advantage of replacing it. If England and the nations in question were connected by a free trade, the capital and skill which she has accumulated would be the common property of all the parties to the commerce; so that if those nations adopted the policy which this writer inculcates, they would commit the stupid atrocity of cutting their own throats, for the diabolical satisfaction of destroying a prosperous friend.

Having stated certain objections to his second theory, we shall consider the principal arguments by which he maintains it.

1st. He asserts that a country which is purely agricultural (meaning a country which has no manufacturing industry) is necessarily poor; that the civilisation of a country in that condition is necessarily low; and that her poverty and low civilisation condemn her to political weakness. If our readers will turn to the statement in which we have given the purport of his system, they will see that the assertions to which we have just referred are the cornerstone of his second theory. Accordingly, we shall examine the principal arguments by which he endeavours to establish them, as well as our limits will permit.

He says that a country not possessed of manufactures, cannot possess a skilful and highly productive agriculture ; the demand for agicultural products, which arises from manufactures, being a necessary condition of agricultural advancement. The argument confounds ideas which are palpably different, and proceeds on an assumpton which is perfectly gratuitous. It confouds a demand arising from manufactures, wh a demand arising specifically from doms-tic manufactures; and it assumes that he necessity for the former implies a necesty for the latter. From the necessity for a e-mand arising from manufactures, it will ot follow that the country is poor because shis not possessed of manufactures of her own. If her soil be fertile, and if her capacits for agriculture be otherwise great, he quantity of her agricultural products, ad the quantity of the manufactured arties which she imports, may be proportioney large. Nor will it follow, from the sae necessity. that the country would impre her agriculture by adopting the protecte system. Unless she could manufactureo advantage, (on which supposition she woud produce manufactures spontaneously,) se would misdirect her labour and capital y forcing a manufacturing industry—se would abridge the general productivens of her labour and capital, and her genel command of raw and manufactured co modities. The demand for her agricultal products, arising from manufactures, woud therefore diminish; and since the forel manufactures would be more costly thn the articles which she imports, the value f her agricultural products, as exchanged f manufactures, would proportioually d crease. He says that the agriculture f Germany has extended and improved, i consequence of the protection afforded her manufacturing industry by the tariff f the Customs-Union. Granting that h agriculture has extended and improve since the establishment of the Union, it w not follow that the extension and improv ment are consequences of ° rced m nufactures. The freedo by th Un her internal trad ea w has enjoyed si lis me sufficiently a. fact. h her policy foreig ce were wor tually i vantages wdu have be l by a genet ment of ry. If he

fact as nt for the system, he that the improve een gre would ha had principle here we tly a and inc er in ply sys cate of n ad ag r

depends (says he) on the prosperity of domestic manufactures; by the impolitic exclusion of foreign agricultural products, domestic manufactures are crippled; and, consequently, the protection of agriculture defeats the end for which it is specifically given. Assuming that the country can manufacture to advantage, this reasoning is just. The extension of domestic manufactures, which is consequent on a free importation of agricultural products, enlarges the general demand for the products of domestic agriculture; although it may abridge the demand for the domestic agricultural products, which are identical in kind with the products principally imported. If agriculture is protected, the extension of domestic manufactures is stopped or retarded; the general productiveness of the labour and capital of the country is proportionally abridged; and, consequently, the enlargement of the general demand for domestic agricultural products is prevented to the same extent. But the protection of manufactures is liable to the same objections. Unless the country can manufacture to advantage, (on which supposition the protection is impertinent,) she misdirects her labour and capital by forcing a manufacturing industry; and, consequently, she abridges the aggregate of her productive powers, and the general demand for the products of her agriculture. Speaking of the exclusion of German cattle from the French dominions, he says, that France, by this exclusive policy, abridges the general productiveness of her agricultural labour and capital. He says, that she turns them from productive employments to an employment comparatively barren; since it must be presumed, from the protection which she affords to this branch of her industry, that she is not fitted by nature for the rearing and breeding of cattle. But the objection lies to his own system, and to all protective policy 1f agricultural labour and capital rece best direction, when their direction ined by free trade, the direction of nd capital of every description oug abandoned to the guidance of the neficent principle.

To prove th try which has no anufactures of s necessarily poor l rude, he re n induction from nces. Fro erty and rudeness rtain countr ossessed of manu-es, he con hat poverty and ss are cor of the agricultu-lition. le, he refers to opean c ich, in the mid-were cultural states; , th Russia hardly barbarism be-

concerning the natural character of the last-mentioned nations, we will notice the reasoning to which it leads him He infers, from their assumed unfitness for manufacturing industry, that they would not consult their interests by adopting the protective system : he says that their unfitness for any manufacture which they might create by dint of protection, might be presumed from its factitious origin; and he affirms that the respective vocations of various nations are determined by their several aptitudes. Now, though he applies it partially, this reasoning will hold universally. It is not more applicable to the nations of the torrid, than to the civilized nations of the temperate zones. These civilized nations have different aptitudes, calling them to different branches of productive industry; some, for example, being inland countries, or being scantily furnished with the means of manufacturing, whilst others are maritime countries, or possess those means in abundance. Our author, moreover, admits by implication, that there is always a presumption against the fitness of a country for a branch of industry which it creates by protection. Accordingly, the several branches of industry for which these civilized nations are respectively fitted, ought not to be settled by protective systems; but each should take the part in the business of production, which the principle of free trade would spontaneously determine.

Our notice of the scheme to which we have just adverted, is merely incidental to our design. We have stated the arguments by which he maintains it, for the purpose of proving, by his own admissions, that his protective system is untenable. Accordingly, we shall not prolong our examination of that project, but shall proceed with our objections to his second theory.

3d. He exhorts the nations of continental Europe, and the United States of North America, to manufacture for themselves to the utmost of their physical means. In giving them this advice, he invites them to a conspiracy against the interests of England, but is far from showing them the way to promote their own. By fully adopting his protective system, they would abridge, to a great extent, the efficient demand for her manufactures; and they would annihilate, to the same extent, the manufacturing capital and skill which she has laboriously acquired. But in doing this harm to her, they would bring down evil on themselves. Generally speaking, her manufacturing industry is more productive than theirs. Accordingly, it is generally their interest to abstain from manufacturing, and to turn themselves to other employments. By producing manufactures for themselves, when they could get them from her at a smaller cost, they would abridge the general productiveness of their labour and capital, and their general command of raw and manufactured commodities. Nor would it be their interest to manufacture for themselves, though their natural means of manufacturing were equal to hers. The acquisition of factitious means equal to hers, would cost them an enormous outlay of labour and capital; and the labour and capital applied to the purpose would be expended to mere waste. If the trade between her and them were perfectly free, the manufacturing capital and skill which she has acquired, would be (in effect) theirs as well as hers; since her instruments of production would yield them all the products which they could get by instruments of their own creation. By rejecting the products of her accumulated instruments for the fancied advantage of creating instruments for themselves, they would (in effect) destroy a capital of their own for the fancied advantage of replacing it. If England and the nations in question were connected by a free trade, the capital and skill which she has accumulated would be the common property of all the parties to the commerce; so that, if those nations adopted the policy which this writer inculcates, they would commit the stupid atrocity of cutting their own throats, for the diabolical satisfaction of destroying a prosperous friend.

Having stated certain objections to his second theory, we shall consider the principal arguments by which he maintains it.

1st. He asserts that a country which is purely agricultural (meaning a country which has no manufacturing industry) is necessarily poor ; that the civilisation of a country in that condition is necessarily low ; and that her poverty and low civilisation condemn her to political weakness. If our readers will turn to the statement in which we have given the purport of his system, they will see that the assertions to which we have just referred are the cornerstone of his second theory. Accordingly, we shall examine the principal arguments by which he endeavours to establish them, as well as our limits will permit.

He says that a country not possessed of manufactures, cannot possess a skilful and highly productive agriculture ; the demand for agricultural products, which arises from manufactures, being a necessary condition of agricultural advancement. The argument confounds ideas which are palpably different, and proceeds on an assumption which is perfectly gratuitous. It confounds a demand arising from manufactures, with a demand arising specifically from domestic manufactures; and it assumes that the necessity for the former implies a necessity for the latter From the necessity for a demand arising from manufactures, it will not follow that the country is poor because she is not possessed of manufactures of her own. If her soil be fertile, and if her capacities for agriculture be otherwise great, the quantity of her agricultural products, and the quantity of the manufactured articles which she imports, may be proportionally large. Nor will it follow, from the same necessity, that the country would improve her agriculture by adopting the protective system. Unless she could manufacture to advantage, (on which supposition she would produce manufactures spontaneously,) she would misdirect her labour and capital by forcing a manufacturing industry—she would abridge the general productiveness of her labour and capital, and her general command of raw and manufactured commodities. The demand for her agricultural products, arising from manufactures, would therefore diminish; and since the forced manufactures would be more costly than the articles which she imports, the value of her agricultural products, as exchanged for manufactures, would proportionally decrease. He says that the agriculture of Germany has extended and improved, in consequence of the protection afforded to her manufacturing industry by the tariff of the Customs-Union. Granting that her agriculture has extended and improved since the establishment of the Union, it will not follow that the extension and improvement are consequences of the forced manufactures. The freedom given by the Union to her internal trade, with the peace which she has enjoyed since the establishment, would sufficiently account for the fact. Although her policy in relation to foreign commerce were worse than it actually is, those advantages would naturally have been followed by a general improvement of her industry. If he would use the fact as an argument for the protective system, he must show that the extension and improvement have been greater than they would have been if she had adhered to the principle of free trade.

And here we may conveniently advert to the partial and inconsistent manner in which he would apply his protective system. Though he advocates the protection of manufactures, he condemns the protection of agriculture. The prosperity of agriculture depends (says he) on the prosperity of domestic manufactures; by the impolitic exclusion of foreign agricultural products, domestic manufactures are crippled ; and, consequently, the protection of agriculture defeats the end for which it is specifically given. Assuming that the country can manufacture to advantage, this reasoning is just. The extension of domestic manufactures, which is consequent on a free importation of agricultural products, enlarges the general demand for the products of domestic agriculture; although it may abridge the demand for the domestic agricultural products, which are identical in kind with the products principally imported. If agriculture is protected, the extension of domestic manufactures is stopped or retarded ; the general productiveness of the labour and capital of the country is proportionally abridged; and, consequently, the enlargement of the general demand for domestic agricultural products is prevented to the same extent. But the protection of manufactures is liable to the same objections. Unless the country can manufacture to advantage, (on which supposition the protection is impertinent,) she misdirects her labour and capital by forcing a manufacturing industry ; and, consequently, she abridges the aggregate of her productive powers, and the general demand for the products of her agriculture. Speaking of the exclusion of German cattle from the French dominions, he says, that France, by this exclusive policy, abridges the general productiveness of her agricultural labour and capital. He says, that she turns them from productive employments to an employment comparatively barren ; since it must be presumed, from the protection which she affords to this branch of her industry, that she is not fitted by nature for the rearing and breeding of cattle. But the objection lies to his own system, and to all protective policy. If agricultural labour and capital receive the best direction, when their direction is determined by free trade, the direction of labour and capital of every description ought to be abandoned to the guidance of the same beneficent principle.

To prove that a country which has no manufactures of its own is necessarily poor and rude, he resorts to an induction from instances. From the poverty and rudeness of certain countries not possessed of manufactures, he concludes that poverty and rudeness are consequences of the agricultural condition. For example, he refers to the European countries which, in the middle ages, were purely agricultural states; and he says, that Poland and Russia hardly began to emerge from semi-barbarism before the beginning of the last century. Now, in these instances, (and in the others which he produces,) the poverty and rudeness of the country manifestly arose from causes which had no necessary connection with her purely agricultural condition. In each of the countries particularly in question, the political and legal institutions were unfavourable to the security of property; the working people were serfs, in a state of abject dependence on their lords or owners; and there was no sufficient demand from other countries for the products of her agriculture. Owing to these causes, (and others of a similar tendency,) there were no sufficient inducements to industry and accumulation; and accordingly the nation was indolent, indigent, and barbarous. This induction proves, beyond controversy, that a poor and rude nation is necessarily poor and rude; but it does not prove (what he was bound to prove) the necessary poverty and rudeness of a purely agricultural country. To the instances which he produces in support of his conclusion, we could easily oppose instances showing its futility; and, by an induction not more absurd than his own, we could show that the *want* of domestic manufactures is a necessary condition of opulence and civilisation. The only instance which our limits will allow us to produce, is that of the United States of America. During the last fifty years their capital has accumulated with unexampled rapidity; and, if an extraordinary proficiency in the arts of productive industry suffices to constitute a high civilisation, it will not be disputed that they are highly civilized. Now, till the beginning of the present century, these states were purely agricultural countries; previously to the tariff of 1828, their domestic manufactures were of small amount; and even at present they may rank with agricultural rather than manufacturing nations. We are not bound to multiply instances for the purpose of refuting his conclusion; since it conflicts with the part of his theory which concerns the *vocation* of a country to manufacturing industry. In this part of his theory he says, that an agricultural country in a state of poverty and rudeness has not the vocation, and that she ought to confine her industry to the production of raw products, until she reaches the degree of opulence which fits countries for manufacturing to advantage. He supposes, therefore, that some agricultural countries are not poor and rude; and that an agricultural country in a state of poverty and rudeness, may advance to opulence and civilisation by mere dint of agriculture.

The *tests* of a vocation to manufacture, as they are determined by our author, are nearly related to the subject which we have just considered; and we, therefore, may notice them conveniently here. No country (says he) has a true call to manufactures, unless she is gifted with the following capacities for manufacturing to advantage :— A large and well rounded territory; a large and manifold provision of the natural means of manufacturing; an agriculture pretty far advanced, (*ziemlich weit vorgericht;*) a general diffusion of mental cultivation amongst the individuals composing the community; political and legal institutions, which afford security for person and property, and allow a free use of bodily and mental faculties. It appears sufficiently from the bare statement, that his tests are too indeterminate to admit of application in practice. Indeed, the various applications of them, which are made in various parts of his chaotic theory, are inconsistent and contradictory. Occasionally, some of the principal nations of continental Europe are excluded from the class of *called* countries; as, for example, Spain and Russia. But, in a chapter specially given to Russia, the monstrously foolish policy which has led her to force manufactures, is mentioned with decided approbation; and it is supposed, therefore, that Russia has a true call. It sems to be assumed, in most parts of his treatise, that most of the principal nations of continental Europe are fitted for manufacturing; and, accordingly, we have supposed that his system is generally recommended to those nations, and the United States of North America. We will remark in conclusion, that the necessary vagueness of his tests proves the absurdity of his system. Whether a country be fitted for manufacturing, is a question of infinite extent and invincible difficulty. In pretending to resolve the question, and in giving a forced direction to the national labour and capital, a government falls inevitably into great and pernicious blunders If the direction be left to the determination of the principle of free trade, the question is settled with comparative certainty, and a comparatively small amount of loss and suffering. This is sufficiently shown by the close approach to precision with which the principle (where it is allowed to operate) proportions the supply of commodities to the efficient demand.

2*d*. To prove the expediency of his protective system, he produces a theory of his own invention, which he styles *the theory of productive powers*. Wealth, says he, is distinguishable from its causes; the possession of wealth, from the powers of producing it. Accordingly, the opulence of a nation is not proportioned to her wealth; *i. e.*, to the quantity of objects having a value in exchange, which the nation actually possesses. Her opulence is proportioned to her powers of production; and she is rich, though her wealth be small, if her productive powers are numerous and extensive. But, according to the economists of the cosmopolitical school, the opulence of a nation is proportioned to her wealth, and not to her means of creating it. According to the theory of production advanced by the same economists, her productive powers consist of the wealth which she has reserved as *capital ;* and this theory of theirs, which is a main source of their numerous errors, may be styled *the theory of exchangeable values.*

Now the capital of a nation is the part of her wealth which is destined to the production of further wealth; and it includes those talents of her members which are subservient to that purpose, and which have been acquired and accumulated by an expenditure of capital and labour. Accordingly, her capital consists of productive powers which she has acquired or made. Besides these, she has powers of production which are gifts of nature. Such, for example, are the natural powers of her soil; and such are the powers bodily and mental, with which her members are naturally endowed It is manifest, therefore, that her powers are partly factitious and partly natural; nor was it ever maintained (to our knowledge) that her means of creating wealth lie entirely in her capital. But, though her productive powers are larger than her capital, those powers would be merely latent unless her capital called them into action. For example, the powers of body and mind which her members have received from nature, would not be productive to any considerable extent unless they were trained to the business of production; and they cannot be trained to the business of production without an expenditure of capital. When trained, they could not be applied to the business with any considerable effect, unless they were supported and aided by further capital; as, for example, by capital extended in the payment of wages, and by machinery and other adminicles of labour. Accordingly, the productive powers of a nation, *which are active and applicable*, are nearly coextensive with her capital; and when it is said by the economists in question, that the productive powers of a nation lie in her capital, that is their manifest meaning. The theory produced by our author, with a ludi-

crous air of originality and depth, is absolutely futile ; or, at the best, it is nothing more than a captious correction of a hasty and loose expression.

To show that his protective system would promote the interests of the nations to which he recommends it, is the object of his theory of productive powers; but, granting that the theory (if such it can be called) is just as pregnant as it is shallow and futile, it is impertinent to the purpose for which he produces it.

If a country (says he) is purely agricultural, many of her natural powers are latent and useless; those especially applicable to manufacturing are not applied to the production of manufactures; and if she would avail herself of all the powers with which she is endowed by the bounty of nature, she must create a manufacturing industry by means of the protective system.

The argument which we have just stated amounts to this : that a country which does not manufacture, does not manufacture. Such, however, is the importance which he attaches to the argument, that he regards it as the corner-stone of his protective system. To the tendency of the system to turn to account latent powers, he chiefly ascribes its marvellous efficacy in raising nations from poverty to opulence.

It is clear that a country which does not manufacture, does not manufacture ; or (as our author hath it) that her natural powers specially applicable to manufacturing, are latent and idle. Whether the country, by allowing them to lie idle, does or does not promote her true economical interests, depends on the extent of her aptitudes for manufacturing industry. If she can produce manufactures more cheaply than she can import them, she does not promote her interest by neglecting her manufacturing powers. If she can import manufactures more cheaply than she can produce them, she does promote her interests by neglecting her latent capacities. If she called them into action, she would acquire *manufacturing* power which she had not virtually possessed; but, since she would make the acquisition by a misdirection of her capital and labour, she would abridge the aggregate of her productive powers and her general command of commodities. A similar answer may be given to an allegation which is made by our author for a special purpose. In defending the protective tariff of the German Customs-Union, he alleges that German manufactures have flourished under the protection. If he means that they have extended in consequence of the protection, he virtually condemns the tariff, although he intends to praise it. From the forced creation of the manufactures which have arisen under the protection, it may be presumed (according to his own admission) that Germany wants aptitudes for those branches of industry. The high protective duties by which they are saved from destruction, with our author's importunate clamour for further protection, turns the violent presumption into perfect and satisfactory proof. The unnatural manufactures in which our author exults, are, therefore, an evil to Germany. The labour and capital which she has expended upon them, have been forced from more profitable employments. In acquiring manufacturing powers by dint of protection, she has abridged the aggregate of her productive means.

In dismissing his theory of productive powers, we will notice a theory, also of his own invention, to which it is closely related. Besides the productive powers (natural and factitious) to which we have already adverted, there are various remoter causes (not within the purview of political enonomy) by which production is stimulated and increased. Such, for example, are political institutions favourable to the security of property; an intimate union between the districts into which the country is divided; political power sufficient for its effective defence against its external enemies; and the diffusion of sound knowledge and sound morality amongst the individuals and bodies of which the community is composed. By securing the fruits of industry and frugality to those who work and save, the remoter causes in question incite to labour and accumulation; and by quickening and enlarging the intelligence of the productive classes, they augment the productiveness of labour and capital. These stimulants to labour and accumulation occupy a large portion of our author's treatise. He dwells again and again on their great productive effects, though those effects (we may safely assert) were never disputed or doubted. On account of their productive effects, he insists that they ought to be ranked with the productive powers which fall within the purview of political economy; and he censures the incidental and slighting manner in which they are noticed by Dr. Adam Smith. Now, assuming their productive effects, (which nobody ever doubted), they are foreign to the purpose of his treatise. From the tendency of the causes in question to promote the wealth of nations, he cannot infer that his own protective system has a similar tendency; and this is the thing (we are compelled to

repeat) which he undertook to prove. In ranking the causes in question with those productive powers which fall within the purview of political economy, he betrays his small knowledge of this particular science, and his small acquaintance with the nature of science in general. Every science has its own subject; though such is the tendency of every subject to branch out into infinity, that every science touches occasionally on the subjects of other sciences. If every subject to which a science adverts were properly within its purview, each of the sciences would embrace the others, and the advantage of their division would-be lost. Although political economy frequently touches upon them, the causes in question lie beyond its province. For example, good political institutions promote the wealth of nations; but they cannot be ranked with the productive powers which political economy directly contemplates. They are properly the subjects of sciences (politics and legislation) which are distinct from political economy, although they border upon it.

3*d.* To prove that the nations of continental Europe would consult their interests by adopting his protective system, he asserts that the system, by extending their manufactures, would extend their trade. It appears to us, however, that the system would abridge their trade as well as their agriculture. As we have shown by our preliminary objections, it would nearly extinguish their mutual commerce; and if it were adopted by the United States and England as well as by the nations of continental Europe, it would nearly extinguish the mutual commerce of all the most civilized countries of the Old and New World. Nor is this the only answer to his groundless assertion. If a country has no aptitudes for manufacturing to advantage, she promotes her commercial interests, as well as her interests generally, by exporting raw products and importing manufactured articles; inasmuch as the export and import, if carried on to a considerable extent, form of themselves a considerable internal trade. Nor is the possession of a large manufacturing industry a necessary condition of a large external commerce. If a country has an extensive and accessible coast, an extensive coasting trade, great facilities for building and sailing ships, and numerous raw products fitted for exportation, her foreign commerce will naturally be large, although her manufacturing industry be next to nothing. For example, the foreign commerce of the United States of America is only inferior to that of England: and yet their manufacturing industry is not considerable, and till lately was extremely small. Till the beginning of the present century, they were purely agricultural and commercial countries; and yet it is admitted by our author, (whose inconsistencies are endless,) that their shipping increased, during the interval between 1789 and 1801, from two hundred thousand to a million tons. But granting that a country, which cannot manufacture to advantage, enlarges her trade by protecting her manufacturing industry, it will not follow from this admission, that her general interests are promoted by the forced manufactures. By forcing manufactures she misdirects her labour and capital; and the addition to her trade, as being an effect of the unnatural creation, is a subtraction from the sum of her economical prosperity.

It is also asserted by our author, that a purely agricultural country must force manufactures, if she wishes for the possession of colonies; since colonies come of commerce, and commerce comes of manufacturing. Without disputing this very disputable reasoning, we will remark that the possession of colonies would be useless to the country possessing them, if freedom of trade were universal and perfect. Dependent colonies are useful to the dominant country, as affording a vent for her products, and giving her products in return; and if freedom of trade were universal and perfect, the colonial markets would be open to all nations. Accordingly, other nations would share with the dominant country in all the advantages arising from the colonial trade; whilst the expense and trouble of governing the colonies would fall exclusively upon her.

4th. A purely agricultural country, by adopting the protective system, turns to use her natural powers specially applicable to manufacturing; and in consequence of the manufacturing industry which she thus forces into existence, her commerce is enlarged, and her agriculture is extended and improved. Such are the advantages which she obtains by the system, according to the arguments which we have stated and dissected. Nor are these specific advantages the only fruits of her policy. If we may trust our author, they are followed by another advantage of a general description. By the creation of the forced manufactures, by the consequent enlargement of her commerce, and by the consequent extension and improvement of her agriculture, *her productive powers are balanced or harmonized.*

He may possibly mean, by this somewhat metaphorical argument, that her labour and capital are duly distributed amongst the several branches of her productive industry; and consequently, that their general productiveness is enlarged by the distribution, to the utmost extent of her capacities for production. If this be his meaning, we have answered the argument already; having shown that the creation of the forced manufactures abridges the aggregate of her productive powers.

He may mean that the country, previously to her adoption of the system, is merely agricultural; but that she becomes, by means of the system, a manufacturing and commercial as well as an agricultural state. If this be his meaning, he supposes that the country would gain by the transition, although she had no aptitudes for manufactures or commerce—although she abridged the aggregate of her productive powers, by turning her labour and capital to those branches of industry. He supposes, therefore, that manufactures and commerce are invaluable.

Indeed, most of his arguments in support of the protective system are tacitly founded on two fallacious suppositions. According to the first, manufactures and commerce are not means to ulterior economical objects. They are not means of augmenting to the utmost the productive powers of the country, or of enlarging to the utmost its general command of commodities. They are in themselves ends; and they possess an inestimable utility, or an absolute and transcendent worth. Accordingly, a purely agricultural country, which consults its own interests, will strive with all its might to acquire manufactures and commerce; regardless of the extent of its aptitudes for these branches of industry, and of the quantity of labour and capital which the acquisition may cost. According to the second supposition, the poorest country may become, by means of the protective system, as rich as the richest. This illusion is not confined to Dr. List. It is widely spread in the countries to which his system is recommended. It has chiefly arisen from the protective system so long pursued by England;—the matchless prosperity of her manufactures, and of her commerce and agriculture, having naturally made her an authority on questions of economical policy. In these countries they naturally reason thus:—'England has protected her manufactures—England is rich; if we protect ours, we shall be as rich as she.' They forget that England has unrivalled natural capacities for manufacturing and commercial industry; that these capacities might possibly have produced her prosperity, although she had adhered to the principle of free trade; and that no country with capacities decidedly inferior, can ascend to an equal prosperity by any policy whatever. Such a country, if she were reasonable, would try to make the most of her natural aptitudes; and would not waste her resources, and vex her spirit, by vainly grasping at an opulence which nature has denied her. Whether the protective system, or the principle of free trade, would turn her natural aptitudes to the best account, may possibly admit of a doubt; but she certainly would not ascend, by means of the protective system, to the opulence of the richest nation.

5th. We close our examination of Dr. List's second theory, with a few remarks on his crowning absurdity. If freedom of trade were universal and perfect, England (says he) would monopolize the manufactures, and, therefore, the commerce of the world; she would conquer a manufacturing and commercial empire more extensive and pernicious than the military empire of Rome.

Now, granting that England would exclusively supply the manufactures consumed by all other nations, her exclusive power of supply would not resemble a *monopoly.* She would have an exclusive power of supplying all other nations with the manufactured articles which they need; as a monopolist has an exclusive right of selling his article to all who are bound by his monopoly. So far the cases are analogous; but in every other respect they are directly opposed. *He* is protected by a law from the intrusion of competitors. *She* would be liable to the competition of every nation which could produce manufactures as cheaply as herself. *His* exclusive right is commonly hurtful to the consumers; for, in consequence of his security against competition, he can raise the price of his article above its natural value. *Her* exclusive power would be advantageous to her customers; since it would arise entirely from her matchless capacities for manufacturing, and the matchless cheapness of her manufactured products.

If her power of supply would have little analogy to a monopoly, the acquisition of the power would have no analogy whatever to the conquest of an empire by force of arms. The military conqueror thrusts his dominion on the conquered, and (commonly) to their great detriment; but England would acquire her power with the free consent of her customers, and to their great advantage. It would not be her interest (as our author supposes) to crush or depress their industry;

inasmuch as the Fifth Monarchy, which haunts his imagination, would rest on no other basis than their ability to purchase her goods. In fearing that England, by force of manufactures and commerce, would erect a tyranny in the other nations of the earth, he betrays a confusion of ideas which may pass for a psychological curiosity. He fears that England, in selling them cheap goods, would inflict a benefit upon them with their own unconstrained consent.

We have tried to prove, in our examination of his second theory, that freedom of trade would be useful to all nations, if certain disturbing causes were completely obviated. We shall try to prove, in our examination of his first theory, that those causes will not affect the conclusion which we have endeavoured to establish by arguing on that hypothesis. By the theory in question, he admits that the conclusion would hold if the hypothesis were true; and his arguments for the protective system, and against the principle of freedom of trade, are exclusively drawn from the causes by which that freedom is disturbed. Of those arguments, the following are the principal.

1st. If a country imports manufactures, her intercourse with the countries from which she is supplied may be stopped by international war. In this event, she is forced to manufacture for herself during the continuance of the stoppage, although she may want capacities for manufacturing to advantage. If she adheres to the principle of free trade, her markets are deluged, after the restoration of peace, with the cheap products of the countries which are fitted for manufacturing industry; and the domestic manufactures which the war had compelled her to create, are crushed by the renewed importation. These derangements of her economical condition may arise from every war in which she is engaged or implicated. She, therefore, consults her interests by adopting the protective system, if she possesses the means of manufacturing for herself; the good which she gains by avoiding the derangements, far surpassing the good which freedom of trade could afford her.

We answer, in the first place, that the argument exaggerates the derangements arising from war. No ordinary war would prevent the importing country from obtaining manufactured articles from other countries; although the supply might be narrowed, and the prices of the articles might be raised, in consequence of the obstacles which the war would oppose to her commerce. Assuming that an ordinary war would force her to manufacture for herself, the destruction of the forced manufactures, consequent on the restoration of peace, would not be the terrible disaster which the argument supposes; since the evil might be much mitigated by a temporary protective system, calculated to let them down by gentle degrees. It appears to us, therefore, that she would suffer incomparably less from these contingent and passing derangements, than from the certain and permanent mischiefs of a restrictive commercial policy.

In the next place, freedom of trade tends to prevent war, and, therefore, to prevent the derangements on which the argument is founded. If the interests of nations were thoroughly interlaced by perfect freedom of trade, disturbances of their mutual commerce would be followed by intolerable evils; and, as being the most pernicious of all the disturbing causes, war would be feared and detested by the productive population of the world. The commerce of civilized countries is limited at present by numberless prohibitions and restraints; and the derangements which war creates, with the consequent fear which it inspires, are, therefore, comparatively slight. But if our limits would allow us to produce the proofs, we could show that the prospect of the wars with which these countries have recently been threatened, filled their industrious classes with anxiety and alarm: and that the rage for fighting which had seized on a part of their population, was opposed and subdued by those pacific dispositions. If freedom of commerce would tend to extinguish war, a restrictive commercial policy tends to perpetuate the evil. The policy is founded on pernicious misconceptions of the economical interests of nations; and having been sanctioned by the example and authority of the most thriving and influential state, the misapprehensions are widely diffused. According to these conceptions of national interests, the interests of different nations are distinct and opposed; one nation's gain is another nation's loss; and the nations which have risen to prosperity, by means of manufactures and commerce, have built their opulence and power on the poverty and depression of the rest. These misconceptions of nations, concerning their economical interests, inflame the hatred with which they regard one another, in consequence of their childish longings for military conquest and glory; and they aggravate the stupid antipathies springing from differences of races, or from differences of religions, institutions, or manners. And whilst the restrictive policy strengthens their mo-

tives to quarrel, it weakens the motives to amity and co-operation which are presented by their economical interests, as rightly understood. This malignant policy tends to sever their interests and to extinguish the pacific dispositions which arise from international commerce; and if it were adopted by all nations to the full extent of its logical consequences, the world would be plagued with universal and incessant war.

Before we dismiss the argument now in question, we must notice the form in which it is commonly put by the advocates of a restrictive policy;—by those who (like our author) advocate the exclusion of manufactured articles, and by those who (like the partisans of our own corn laws) advocate the exclusion of raw products. In consequence of war, (and the other disturbing cause which we shall consider presently,) every nation which adheres to the principle of free trade, is liable to derangements of her economical condition, like those which are described above. It is argued, therefore, that every nation should make herself independent of others, by preventing the importation of manufactured or raw products, and by producing the former or the latter on her own territory.

If human malignity and folly were as active and irremediable as the argument supposes, it might be the interest of a nation to make herself independent of others, by surrounding her territory with a brazen wall of prohibitions; since safe mediocrity, or even secure poverty, is better than opulence constantly liable to reverses. Whether it would or would not be her interest to make herself independent of others, is, however, an idle question; inasmuch as the independence is not to be attained to, by any policy which any nation will adopt. All men see or feel, distinctly or obscurely, that the good which they get by international trade far surpasses the evil which it occasionally brings upon them; and they are not to be coaxed or frightened into a total relinquishment of the good, by any fallacy or bugbear. A nation may be led, by false conceptions of her interests, to adopt a prohibitive policy to some extent; but so glaring would be the evil of a complete system of prohibition, that the governing classes would never seek to establish it, nor could they ever force it on the rest of the community. For example, the importation of raw products of some descriptions is prevented by the English landlords; but there are raw products of many other descriptions, (as sugar, coffee, tea, tobacco, wine, cotton), which they would never desire, nor ever be able to exclude. Nor is our author consistent in the scheme of prohibitions which he designs for the protection of German manufactures. Not to mention that he would permit the importation of raw products, he sees the necessity of permitting the importation of certain manufactured articles; as, for example, machines and other articles used in manufacturing, and not producible in Germany. Now, where the prohibitive policy is adopted partially, (and that is the only way in which it can be adopted), the nation is liable to the derangements which the policy pretends to obviate. For example, a war between England and America, by hindering the supply of American cotton, might hinder the manufacturing of cotton in the former country. It, therefore, might lead by consequence to a general derangement of her manufacturing industry; and it might also lead, by further consequence, to a similar derangement of her commerce and agriculture. It is manifest, therefore, that the argument in question is untenable. By adopting a restrictive policy, a nation does not avoid the economical derangements which the policy pretends to obviate; whilst she narrows her productive powers and her command of commodities, by the vain endeavour to attain to an impossible independence. If they would avoid the derangements arising from war, nations will not aim at independence of one another; but they will fully adopt the principle of free trade, and extend their mutual *dependence* to the very utmost. If it were adopted universally and completely, that principle would extinguish war; and it, therefore, could extinguish the economical evils in question, with the numberless other evils which war inflicts upon mankind.

2d. A nation which imports manufactures is liable to similar derangements, on account of the possible exclusion of her raw products by the country (or countries) from which she is supplied. In the event of that country excluding her raw products, she loses her power of purchasing manufactures, and is forced to manufacture for herself. In the event of that country abandoning the exclusive policy, she suffers from another and a greater evil. If she adheres to the p n l of free trade, that country deluges her market with cheap manufactured goods; and the domestic manufactures which the exclusion has forced her to create, are destroyed by the renewed importation. Rather than submit to the hazard of these repeated derangements, she ought to elect the smaller evil of adopting the protective system.

This argument of our author's is advanced in Germany and America, to show the expediency of the protection which they give to their domestic manufactures; England (as it is pretended) having driven them to that policy, by her previous exclusion of their raw products. The first half of the argument is manifestly fallacious. The necessity of manufacturing to a disadvantage, which is forced on the importing country by the exclusive policy of the other, is a miserable reason for her adopting the protective system. By rejecting the manufactures of the excluding country, she probably aggravates the evil which provokes her to retaliate the exclusion. If the exclusion of her raw products has not been complete, she has partly preserved her power of purchasing foreign manufactures. By adopting a system which entirely prevents their importation, she foolishly completes the necessity of manufacturing to a disadvantage, which the folly of the excluding country has partially imposed upon her. It may happen that the necessity which she lays upon herself does not aggravate the necessity proceeding from the excluding country; and in this event her retaliating policy is harmless in fact. Its tendency, however, is mischievous, although it is harmless by accident; and, consequently, it is not even entitled to the negative commendation of being an innocent absurdity. At the best, her policy is superfluous and impertinent, since her manufactures are protected, in substance and effect, by the exclusion which she idly retorts.

With regard to the destruction of the forced manufactures, consequent on the renewed importation, the evil might be much mitigated by a temporary protective system calculated to let them down by gentle degrees.

And here we must advert to a fallacy which Dr. List often insinuates, though we cannot affirm that he anywhere puts it expressly. He often confounds the protection which is granted to an unprofitable manufacture for the purpose of breaking its fall, with that which is granted to a similar manufacture for the purpose of creating it, or perpetuating its existence—leading his careless readers to infer the expediency of the latter from the obvious utility of the former.

II. We shall briefly consider the subjects of the second part of this article under the following heads:—1st. The misrepresentations of the commercial policy of England which frequently occur in the volume before us. 2d. The causes of the prevalent hostility to her manufacturing and commercial pre-eminence, with the mischiefs which the spirit has produced and threatens to produce. 3d. The nature of the commercial policy which (in our opinion) she must speedily adopt, if she would obviate the present, or avert the contingent evils.

1st He says that England preaches to other nations the principles of free trade, without any serious purpose of abandoning her restrictive policy. Now the policy pursued by her legislature, and the opinions held (till lately) by the majority of her people, have conflicted with the opinions of Dr. Adam Smith and her other eminent writers on political economy; and consequently, the majority of her legislature, and (till lately) the majority of her people, have opposed the policy recommended by her enlightened statesmen. On this inconsistency he raises a fallacy which appears again and again in the course of his volume. The enlightened minority which has contended for a liberal policy, and the majority which has stuck steadily to the wisdom of our ancestors, are, according to him, one party; and out of the one party formed by the confusion of the two contending parties, he makes a fictitious personage whom he calls England. Accordingly, England is playing the part of a double dealer. She preaches the principle of free trade to the other nations of the world, and would fain persuade them to take her manufactures; but she sticks and means to stick to her own restrictive policy, and has not the smallest wish for their raw products. Now he knows, as well as we do, that this representation is false and absurd. Whenever another representation is demanded by the purpose of his volume, he says, that the great majority of our manufacturers and traders are opposed to the laws for the protection of the landed interest; that they are willing to relinquish the prohibitions and restrictions intended for the protection of their own branches of industry; and that all enlightened Englishmen are partisans of free trade, as knowing that the principle would promote the interests of their country. He imputes the exclusion of foreign raw products to the blundering selfishness of the landlords. He says, that they are ruining the manufactures, and, therefore, the agriculture of the nation; thus killing the hen which yielded them the golden eggs. He rejoices at the blind obstinacy with which they have persisted in their suicidal policy; since the policy has created, and is cherishing, the manufactures which have sprung up in other civilized countries. The purpose of his fallacy is plain. He fears that just opinions concerning commercial policy are rapidly spreading in England; that the wiser portion of the landed class are getting correct notions of their own interests; that the demand for freedom of trade will become general and resistless before the lapse of many years; and that this demand will force the majority of the class to relinquish the laws designed for its protection. He, therefore, labours to persuade his countrymen, that England is invincibly attached to her restrictive policy; and that even the Englishmen who talk against it have no intention of giving it up. If this notion should get possession of the German people, it may confirm them in their attachment to the protective system; and if the protective system were firmly rooted in Germany, she would find it no easy matter to return to free trade, in the event of England reverting to that principle. The absurdity of his fallacy is as plain as its purpose. Suppose that England were preaching free trade, with the intention of keeping to her restrictive policy, what could she gain by her double dealing? Could she hope that her praises of free trade would persuade other nations to adopt the principle, when her own adherence to her own prohibitions and restrictions betrayed her conviction of its inexpediency? Assuming that she did persuade them, what would she get by her success? She would induce them to open their ports to her manufactured goods. That is true; but since she would exclude their products from her own markets, she would send them none of her goods, or give them her goods for nothing. She, therefore, would labour, by her deep dissembling, to get the precious privilege of working for others gratuitously; a project (it must be owned) truly Machiavelian, and worthy of the grasping and perfidious Albion.

He says that England abolished slavery in her own colonies, for the purpose of crushing the industry of other slaveholding countries. She hoped that the abolition would provoke a rebellion in those countries, resembling the servile insurrection in St. Domingo; or that their fear of the terrible consequences would compel them to follow her example. She hoped that their industry would perish or decay in either of the two events; since, in the last event, the emancipated slaves would probably be unfit for their suddenly acquired freedom, and would refuse to work for their former owners in the capacity of free labourers. Though varnished over with the cant of philanthropy, and the cant of Christian benevolence, the abolition was suggested by calculating selfishness. She thought that the measure, by destroying the productive powers of the slaveholding countries, would confine the production of colonial products to her own possessions in India; thus helping her to the acquisition of the commercial monopoly and tyranny at which she grasps with insatiable avarice and ambition.

We cannot stay to examine the construction which he here puts upon her motives; since a statement of the gratuitous assumptions and the extravagant absurdities which it implies would occupy a considerable portion of our limited space. We, therefore, must confine ourselves to a passing remark. If the destruction of the other slaveholding countries was the object of the measure, she contemplated the destruction of her own slaveholding colonies as an incidental consequence of her policy; and as some of the countries whose ruin she designed are her best markets for her manufactured products, she also designed the ruin of her own manufacturing industry. The mental state which his construction betrays, is so poor and pitiable, that our resentment merges in compassion. By doubting the benevolence which manifestly determined her to the measure, and by his blindness to her generosity in making the sacrifices which it required, he shows that his moral perceptions are as confused and obtuse as his understanding.

In thus misrepresenting her motives, he is doing his best to invite the slaveholding countries to hatred of England; hoping (like other partisans of the German protective system) that their resentment may get the better of their pecuniary interests, and may lead them to transfer their custom from England to Germany.

And here we must express our deep regret at the course which has been taken by some of the English abolitionists. In seeking to perpetuate the exclusion of foreign slave-raised products from the markets of England, they are postponing superior to inferior interests; for we do not hesitate to affirm, (though we admit the importance of their object, and respect the zeal and ability with which they have pursued it,) that the interests of humanity would be more promoted by general freedom of commerce, than by a speedy extinction of slavery. Nor would the exclusion of those products from the markets of England have any considerable tendency to advance their particular purpose; since it must be plain to all who have observed the opinions and feelings prevalent on the continent of Europe, that other countries would not abstain from the use of them, in consequence of her example. If the digression were permissible, we could show that the exclusion would rather retard than promote the accomplishment of their object; since it would retard the operation of the economical laws by which slavery must be ultimately extinguished.

2d. The misrepresentations which we have just stated, (and which are a few of those occurring in Dr. List's volume,) sufficiently show his hostility to the manufacturers and commerce of England. The hostility (we are sorry to say) is not limited to him, or the German manufacturers, whose representative and organ he may be deemed. Some of the German States have deliberative chambers, whose debates are occasionally reported; and in all the German States, (excepting the Austrian) the Newspapers and other Journals, though subject to a Censorship, enjoy, in fact, a certain freedom of discussion. Those debates, and the discussions in these Journals, are a good index to the opinions and feelings of Germany; and they will (we think) convince any one who may read them regularly and attentively, that the hostility is widely diffused amongst Germans of most classes. Indeed, the popularity of the volume before us would suffice to establish the fact; since such a tissue of absurdities would not have been received with favour by the German public, unless it had reflected prejudices which they already entertained.

The misapprehensions of national interests which lie at the bottom of the restrictive commercial policy, are undoubtedly one cause of this hostile feeling. It is commonly believed in Germany, (even by men who are otherwise instructed and unprejudiced,) that England has acquired her manufacturing pre-eminence at the cost of her foreign customers; and that Germany must persist in the protective system which she has recently adopted, in order to avoid the evils formerly inflicted upon her by English monopoly and oppression. The German manufacturers, who have been led by the system to risk their capitals in unnatural manufacturing enterprises, have appealed to these mischievous prejudices, and laboured to strengthen and extend them;—the Newspapers and other Journals, which are apparently organs of the manufacturing party, being filled with declamations against England, and misrepresentations of her conduct and motives. But in spite of the prevalence of these prejudices, and the efforts of the manufacturers to strengthen and extend them, the body of the German people would have resisted the protective system, if England had admitted the raw products of Germany. The system is mischievous to the body of the German people, and to the German agriculturists; and if their hostility to England had not been confirmed by her own policy, it would have yielded to their pecuniary interests. But in consequence of this policy, the motives which would naturally have led them to resist the protective system were extinguished or weakened. Seeing that German products were excluded from English markets, and that the exclusion imposed upon Germany the necessity of manufacturing for herself, they listened to their prejudices against England, and to the fallacies of the German manufacturers. They were persuaded by the partisans of the protective system, that forced manufactures would promote the interests of Germany; and that these manufactures would create a demand for the raw products of the country, greater than the foreign demand arising from freedom of trade. We have been assured by many Germans, well acquainted with the state of the country, that this is the course which has been taken by the public mind in most parts of Germany; and the fact might be fairly inferred from its intrinsic probability, independently of testimony or other extrinsic evidence. We believe that a similar course has been taken by the public mind in all the other countries which would naturally import manufactures; as, for example, Russia and the United States. In these countries, hostility to English manufactures, springing from misapprehensions of national interests, is more or less prevalent; but if England had opened her ports to their raw products, the interests of the public, with those of the agricultural classes, would have got the better of the senseless antipathy.

The mischief done by their own protective system to the countries of continental Europe and the United States of America, has been described in preceding parts of this article. It has abridged the natural productiveness of their labour and capital; and if the prejudices on which it is founded should acquire additional strength, the stringency of the system, with the mischief consequent upon it, will be proportionally aggravated. The same mischief has been done to England by her own restrictive policy. It has counteracted the tendency of her matchless facilities for manufacturing and commercial industry; and it, therefore, has retarded the rate at which her capital would naturally have accumulated. If she persist in the policy, she will probably be visited with the terrible evils which afflict a country whose economical condition is declining. She may provoke the countries of continental Europe to increase the severity of their protective system; and she may provoke her best customers, the United States and Brazil, to exclude her manufactures by prohibitory tariffs. If the nations of continental Europe, with the United States and Brazil, should adopt a protective system altogether or nearly prohibitory, the present demand for her manufactures will be greatly reduced; and the reduction will be followed by the destruction or exportation of a large portion of her manufacturing capital. As a further consequence, her commerce will proportionally decline, and a large portion of her commercial capital will be destroyed or exported. As an ulterior consequence, her agriculture will proportionally recede, and a large portion of her agricultural capital will be annihilated; since the extension of her agriculture (with the consequent rise of rents) has arisen from the demand for her agricultural products, created by the extension of her manufactures and commerce. The distress of the capitalists and landlords will be accompanied by a calamity which it is impossible to contemplate without dismay. A large portion of the working people will be thrown out of employment, and the wages of the rest will be greatly reduced; the evil being aggravated by the rate at which their numbers increase, in consequence of the past increase in the demand for their labour.

3d. The remedy for the evils which she has brought upon herself, and the preventive of the evils with which she is threatened, is an absolute abandonment of the prohibitory and restrictive policy. She must abolish all the laws by which importation is directly prohibited or restrained, with all the import duties which are calculated for that purpose, and not for the legitimate purpose of raising a public revenue. Though we cannot notice the provisions which the measure would require, we will advert to two of the principles by which it ought to be guided. A protected branch of industry might suffer permanently or for a time, in consequence of the transition to freedom of trade; and in every case of this description, the protection ought to be prolonged for the purpose of softening the evil, in so far as the prolongation would consist with the end of the measure. But a protection granted to a domestic product, for that temporary and limited purpose, ought not to be granted to an extent or in a manner which would prevent a regular importation of the corresponding foreign commodity.

A vent for our manufactured products in

the countries which now exclude them, would be the end of the measure; and protections granted to domestic products would manifestly defeat the end, if they prevented a regular importation of foreign commodities. For example, by the present English corn laws, foreign corn is excluded from England in ordinary seasons; and so long as the English demand for foreign corn shall be exceptional and capricious, there can be no considerable demand for English manufactures in foreign corn-growing countries. Compared with this obvious objection to the present corn laws, the other objections to which they are liable are nearly insignificant.

Temporary protections, intended to soften the transition, and not inconsistent with the end of the measure, would clearly be expedient; for, though the good of the public demands the abolition of mischievous laws, it demands that every regard, compatible with the abatement of the nuisance, should be shown to the interests which they have called into being. In reference to the interests which have been created by the corn laws, we may remark, that there are natural causes which would mitigate the evil of the transition. Though many of the countries which exclude our manufactures are fitted by nature for the growth and exportation of corn, they could hardly export a considerable quantity without a previous extension and improvement of their agriculture. As this extension and improvement (with the increase of capital and population which they suppose) would not be the work of a moment, none of those countries could supply us with a considerable quantity for some considerable time after the opening of our ports. To this it may be added, that the extension and improvement would enhance the cost of production; and owing to this cause, and to the cost of transport, the price of foreign corn in English markets would be necessarily much higher than is commonly imagined. If these natural causes were aided by a temporary protection, the evil of the transition would be unimportant, as compared with the probable mischief of persisting in the restrictive policy; and it would be amply compensated, at the long run, by the increase in the general demand for domestic agricultural products which freedom of trade would create.

The end of the measure would be very imperfectly accomplished, unless the nations of continental Europe and the United States of America followed the example given them by England. We believe, however, that these countries would relinquish their protective system, if England abandoned

her restrictive policy; and we will shortly assign the reasons on which our conviction is founded.

In the first place, we believe that the governments of these countries are inclined to the principle of free trade. We presume that most of the men by whom these governments are conducted, are men of superior abilities and superior acquirements; and we infer from this reasonable presumption, that they see the mischiefs and absurdities of the opposite policy. With regard to the German (and especially the Prussian) statesmen, our conviction is confirmed by incidental admissions occurring in the volume before us. It is manifestly the opinion of Dr. List, that they are infected, to a lamentable extent, with cosmopolitical errors; and he manifestly fears that they would abandon the protective system, unless the country compelled them to adhere to it. Although the governments in question thought the protective system advantageous to their subjects, the financial difficulties by which they are generally embarrassed, would incline them to the principle of free trade; for, if their import duties on foreign manufactured articles were considerably reduced, the reduction would be followed by an importation which would yield them a considerable revenue.

Nor would the inclination of the government be thwarted by the dispositions of their subjects, if England were wise enough to abandon her restrictive policy. If she offered a steady demand for the raw products of the countries in question, the people generally, and the agricultural classes in particular, would soon perceive the inexpediency of their protective system. Their misapprehensions of national interests, their resentment at her exclusion of their raw products, and the errors instilled into them by their own manufacturers, would speedily yield to their pecuniary interests. They would soon tire of a system which deprived them of cheap manufactures, and excluded them from the best market for the products of their agriculture. With regard to Germany, our conviction (we are happy to say) coincides with the opinion which is visibly entertained by our author. To prove that Germany should adhere to her protective system, though England relinquished her restrictive policy, is one of his principal objects; and we fairly presume, from the desperate energy with which he labours the topic, that he thinks the German agriculturists would sicken of the system if the markets of England were constantly open to their products.

If England adopted the principle of free

trade, her mere example would determine the countries in question to relinquish their protective system. The misapprehensions of national interests which lie at the bottom of the system, have been propagated or strengthened in those countries by her authority; since it is commonly imagined by the majority of their people, that she owes her economical prosperity to her prohibitory and restrictive policy. If she abandoned the policy, her authority would extinguish the errors which it has propagated or confirmed. Disabused by her wisdom of the mischievous illusions into which they have been led by her folly, the majority of the people in those countries would arrive at just apprehensions of their own interests; and having lost the support which it finds in their present misconceptions, the protective system would rest upon nothing but the sinister interests of the manufacturing classes.

We have been provoked by its pernicious tendency, and still more by its malevolent spirit, to do unsparing justice on this incendiary volume. It may possibly be supposed by our general readers, that the unceremonious manner in which we have handled the author, evinces a want of that respect which is due to his country. We should merit the contempt with which we have treated this book, if we were capable of retorting upon Germany the slightest of the insults which he has heaped upon England; and we therefore beg leave to assure them, that the possible supposition would be groundless. Germany is one of the countries which we respect the most, and to which we are the most attached; having found in the works of her philosophers, her historians, and her scholars, exhaustless mines of knowledge and instruction, and exhaustless sources of pleasure or consolation. Above all, we admire the spirit of comprehensive humanity which generally runs through the writings of her classical authors; and it is one of our causes of quarrel with Dr. List, that he labours to diffuse a spirit of exclusive and barbarous nationality in the country of Leibnitz, Kant, and Lessing.

OR

CRITICAL JOURNAL,

FOR

OCTOBER, 1842, AND JANUARY, 1843.

—

JUDEX DAMNATUR CUM NOCENS ABSOLVITUR.
PUBLIUS SYRUS.

—

VOLUME LXXVI.

AMERICAN EDITION.

NEW YORK:

PUBLISHED BY JOSEPH MASON,

102 BROADWAY, BETWEEN WALL AND PINE STREETS.

—

1843.

THE

EDINBURGH REVIEW.

No. CLIII.

FOR OCTOBER, 1842.

ART. I.—*History of Europe, from the Commencement of the French Revolution in 1789, to the Restoration of the Bourbons in 1815.* By ARCHIBALD ALISON, Esq., F. R. S. E., Advocate. 10 vols. 8vo. Edinburgh and London: 1839–1842.

THERE is much in Mr. Alison's History of the French Revolution against which we intend to record our decided protest; and there are some parts of it which we shall feel compelled to notice with strong disapprobation. We therefore hasten to preface our less favourable remarks by freely acknowledging that the present work is, upon the whole, a valuable addition to European literature, that it is evidently compiled with the utmost care, and that its narration, so far as we can judge, is not perverted by the slightest partiality.

A complete history, by an English author, of all the great events which took place in Europe from 1789 to 1815, has long been a *desideratum;* and whatever may be the imperfections of Mr. Alison's work, we cannot say that it does not supply the vacancy. Its defects, or what we deem such, are matter partly of taste, and partly of political opinion. Some readers may consider them as beauties —many will overlook them ; and even the most fastidious must acknowledge that they are not such as materially to interfere with the great plan of the work. Its merits are minuteness and honesty—qualities which may well excuse a faulty style, gross political prejudices, and a fondness for exaggerated and frothy declamation.

We cannot better illustrate the fulness and authenticity of Mr. Alison's history, than by quoting his own statement of the admirable plan on which he has selected and applied his authorities. His invariable rule, we are informed by his Preface, has been ' to give on every occasion, the authorities by volume and page from which the statement in the text was taken. . . . Not only are the authorities for every paragraph invariably given, but in many instances also those for every sentence have been accumulated in the margin. . .' . . Care has been taken to quote a preponderance of authority, in every instance where it was possible, from writers on the opposite side to that which an English historian may be supposed to adopt ; and the reader will find almost every fact in the internal history of the Revolution, supported by two Republican and one Royalist authority ; and every event in the military narrative drawn from at least two writers on the part of the French, and one on that of their opponents.' We feel convinced that Mr. Alison has acted up to the spirit of this candid and judicious system throughout his whole work. We cannot, of course, pretend to have verified his statements by constant reference to the writers from whom he has drawn his information. The events which he records are of such recent occurrence, and such deep interest, that the enormous mass of details published respecting them may well defy the curiosity of an ordinary reader. But we are bound to remark, that whenever we have been led to compare the conflicting accounts of any important event in Mr. Alison's history, we have almost invariably found that his narrative steers judiciously between them, and combines the most probable and consistent particulars contained in each. We apply this remark more especially to his narration of the intestine commotions of the French Revolution, and of the military conflicts of the Empire—particularly those which occurred in Spain. No one, we think, can read the various accounts of the troubles which led to the Reign of Terror, as collected in the able work of Professor Smyth, or the histories of the Peninsular war by Napier, Foy, and others, without feeling satisfied of the care and judgment which Mr. Alison has shown in constantly selecting, where authorities differ, the most probable and most authoritative statements.

We have already hinted our opinion, that Mr. Alison's general style is not attractive. It is not, however, at least in the narrative part of his work, either feeble or displeasing. Its principal defect is the cumbrous and unwieldy construction of its sentences, which frequently cause them to appear slovenly and obscure, and sometimes render their precise meaning doubtful. We quote, almost at random, a single passage by way of specimen :—
' Mortier, following the orders which he had received to keep nearly abreast of, though a little behind the columns on the right bank, and intent only upon inflicting loss upon the Russian troops which he knew had passed the river, and conceived to be flying across his line of march from the Danube towards Moravia, was eagerly emerging from the defiles of Diernstein, beneath the Danube, and the rocky hills beneath the towers of the castle where Richard Cœur de Lion was once immured, when he came upon the Russian rearguard, under Milaradowitch, posted in front of Stein, on heights commanding the only road by which he could advance, and supported by a powerful artillery.'—(v. 444.)

We have purposely selected a sentence obscure merely by its length and involution, and not disfigured by any tangible solecism; and we believe we speak within compass when we say, that it would be difficult to select half-a-dozen consecutive pages from any part of Mr. Alison's work, in which one or more passages of at least equally faulty construction might not be found. But there are not wanting offences of a still less excusable nature. Whenever the historian warms with his subject, he is constantly hurried into the most singular verbal blunders—some puzzling, some ludicrous—but all of a kind which a careful reperusal could scarcely have failed to discover. We quote three or four instances, not for the sake of ridiculing a few slight oversights in a long and laborious work, but in order to draw Mr. Alison's attention to a defect which, comparatively trivial as it is, might give great and unjust advantage to critics

less disposed than we are to treat him kindly. Thus he speaks of the ' *vast* and varied inhabitants' of the French empire—a phrase which can scarcely be actually misunderstood, but which sounds ludicrously inapplicable, considering that the average size of the French conscripts is stated, a few pages before, at only five feet English.—(ix. 105.) In 1800 the French armies appear to have unjustly seized some English vessels at Leghorn, an ' acquisition which,' in the singular phraseology of Mr. Alison, ' speedily *recoiled upon the heads* of those who acquired them.'—(iv. 381.) In the campaign of Austerlitz we find the Austrians defeated by Murat, ' who made 1800 of their wearied *columns* prisoners,' (v. 406.)— a capture which, supposing the statement to be literally true, and the columns of average size, must have embraced nearly the whole male population of the empire. And shortly after, we are informed, that the French army celebrated the anniversary of Napoleon's coronation by the ' *spontaneous combustion*' of their huts,—(v. 474.) We will not go farther with examples of this sort, but we cannot forbear soliciting Mr. Alison's attention to two crying defects ;—his profuse and unscrupulous use of the most barbarous Scotticisms, and the confused and even ambiguous arrangement of his antecedents and relatives. With all these imperfections, Mr. Alison's history has merits sufficient to atone, even to those readers who consider only their own amusement, for the want of an easy and polished style. The stirring interest of the events which he relates, his judgment in selecting striking traits of character for preservation, his earnest seriousness of manner, and his obvious honesty of purpose—all combine to make his narrative on the whole both interesting and impressive.

We cannot speak so favourably of the disquisitions on political events and characters, which abound throughout his work. With all our respect for his merits as a historian, we are bound to declare our honest opinion, that the attempts displayed in them at impassioned and declamatory eloquence, are generally very far below mediocrity. We have already noticed some of the blunders into which he has been betrayed in the course of his ordinary narrative. Few writers soar more easily or more securely than they walk ; and Mr. Alison's oratorical digressions abound in examples of pointless anti-climax, of quaint and ungrammatical inversion, of the carefully balanced antithesis of synonymous ideas, of periods rounded with sonorous pomp, yet constructed with slovenly obscurity. But we are in haste to dismiss this ungracious part of our task, and we shall therefore content ourselves with pointing out a few individual blemishes, the removal of which we are particularly anxious to effect.

Figurative illustrations are as fatal to Mr. Alison as they are, indeed, to most writers who are at once careless and ambitious. His opinion of the age of George III. is expressed by an astronomical metaphor, which he has contrived to distort with a perverse ingenuity rarely surpassed. 'Bright,' he says, 'as were the *stars* of its *morning* light, more brilliant still was the *constellation* which shone forth in its *meridian* splendour, or cast a glow over the twilight of its evening shades.'—(vii. 3.) The simile would have been perfect of its kind, if Mr. Alison had but added that his constellation had disappeared, as constellations are wont to do, in the darkness of the ensuing night. In the same manner, he speaks of a narrative as 'tinged with undue bias,' (Pref. xxxi.)—of a historical work as 'closed with a ray of glory,' (Pref. xxxviii.)—of a truth as 'proclaimed in characters of fire to mankind,' (vii. 7.) We cannot omit the two following sentences, which we consider to be almost unique. The first contains a simile which to us is utterly unintelligible—the other an elaborate confusion of metaphor, which nothing but the most patient ingenuity can unravel. 'In 1787,' says Mr. Alison, 'Goethe, profound and imaginative, was reflecting on the destiny of man on earth, *like a cloud which "turns up its silver lining to the moon."*'—(vii. 103.) 'In Linnæus she (Sweden) has for ever unfolded the hidden key by which the endless variety of floral beauty is to be classified, and the mysterious link is preserved between vegetable and animal life.'—(viii. 612 *)

Mr. Alison does not wear his borrowed plumes with a better grace than his original ornaments. The following is an instance of a fine thought carelessly appropriated and thoroughly spoiled. The British Bard in Gray's famous ode speaks of the banners of his victorious enemy as 'fanned by conquest's crimson wing.' Mr. Alison has adorned a passage of his history with this easy and spirited metaphor ; but he has most unskilfully transferred the ventilation from the banners to the minds of the conquerors, and assures us, that 'it is not while "fanned by conquest's crimson wing," that the *real motives* of human conduct can be made apparent.'—(ix. 104.) A similar and still more painful example of bad taste is to be found in the very next page. 'All the *springs*,' says he, "which the world can furnish to sustain the fortunes of an empire, were in full activity, and worked with consummate ability ; but *one* (query *three?*) was wanting, without which,

in the hour of trial, all the others are but as *tinkling brass*—a belief in God, a sense of duty, and a faith in immortality.' The celebrated passage from which Mr. Alison has here borrowed an illustration, is familiar to all our readers. It is that in which St. Paul compares the eloquence of an idle declaimer to the tinkling of a cymbal. The original phrase is one of such admirable point and force as to have become almost proverbial. But how has its merit survived Mr. Alison's appropriation ? He seizes on one half of the simile, severs it from the other, and tacks it to a new object with which it has no natural connection whatever. Nothing can be more apt and lively than the comparison of unmeaning verbosity to the empty ringing of metal, as every one who studies Mr. Alison's specimens of declamation will allow. But how does such a comparison express the inefficiency of a mechanical force ? For aught we know, a spring may be of brass, and of tinkling brass too, and yet be sufficiently strong and elastic. A better illustration, or a worse adaptation, to the apostle's forcible image, than the passage just quoted, we do not expect again to see.

Tedious self-repetition, the most inveterate fault of careless and declamatory writers, has been carried by Mr. Alison to an almost unprecedented extent. We have neither space nor time to extract some of his digressions, in which the self-same current of ideas is run through twice or thrice in various language. But the mere recurrence of favourite phrases cannot fail to strike and displease the most careless reader. The bow of Esop, the small black cloud of Elijah, the boon of Polypheme to Ulysses, together with numberless less remarkable allusions and expressions, are applied three or four times each, precisely under the same circumstances, and almost in the same words. Winds, waves, meteors, thunderbolts, earthquakes, and similar phenomena of all sorts, are constantly ready to be let loose upon the reader ; nor, however frequently he may have sustained them, is he ever, for a single page, secure against their recurrence. As a proof that we have not exaggerated the frequency of this unpleasing practice, we must, in justice to ourselves, refer our readers to the first fifteen pages of Mr. Alison's *eighth* volume ; within which short space they will find no less than thirteen similes and illustrations drawn from light and colour, of which nearly one half are crowded into twenty-five consecutive lines, and no less than four are expressed in the same identical phrase.

We do not think it necessary to apologise for having dwelt so long upon a subject which we have already admitted to be of secondary importance. If we believed that Mr. Alison had failed in one branch of history from real want of ability, we should have thought it ungenerous to mortify the author of a valuable and laborious work, by cavilling at the false taste of its embellishments. But we cannot imagine that this is the case. It is impossible that a man of Mr. Alison's talents and knowledge should be deliberately blind to the defects and the nonsense we have been quoting. Most of these blemishes are such as a little reflection would induce a sensible schoolboy to strike out of his theme. We are apt to think that Mr. Alison has neglected these parts of his work; that he has sketched them when fatigued and excited by his labours; and that he has left the first rough draught unaltered for publication. We are unwilling to deal harshly with such errors. There is something both striking and gratifying in the spectacle of a writer who is scrupulous of historical truth and justice, but negligent of his own literary fame—who lavishes that time and trouble in ascertaining his own facts which he omits to employ in polishing his style. We are confident that Mr. Alison might, with a little care and patience, correct more serious faults than those we have noticed; and should this prove to be the case, we shall not be sorry if we have made him feel a certain degree of regret for their commission.

As a military historian, Mr. Alison has received general and merited applause. His narratives of warlike operations are well arranged, minute, and spirited: and display considerable scientific knowledge. He is particularly remarkable for the clear and accurate descriptions which he never fails to give of the situations in which the most important manœuvres of the war took place. His sketches are written with as much spirit as topographical knowledge; and he not only impresses on the memory the principal features of the scene of action, but generally succeeds in conveying a vivid picture of them to the imagination. He appears, indeed, to have been induced, by his strong interest in the subject, to visit most of Napoleon's fields of battle in person; and it is but just to say, that he has surveyed them with the feeling of an artist and the precision of a tactician.

The lively colouring of Mr. Alison's descriptions of battles is, in general, as pleasing as the accuracy of the outline is praiseworthy. He has a strong and manly sympathy with military daring and devotion, which never blinds him to the sufferings inflicted by war, but which leads him to give warm and impartial praise to every brave action, by whichever party achieved. We might easily fill our pages with interesting extracts of this nature; but we must content ourselves with referring our readers to the work itself. There is scarcely an important victory of the war which Mr. Alison has not related in the fullest detail, and with the strictest impartiality. We may also remark the successful art with which he occasionally pauses, in the most critical moment of a great battle, to remind his readers, by a word dexterously thrown in, of the mighty interests at stake. It is an artifice to which he has perhaps too freely resorted, but which he occasionally employs with marked effect.

Still, Mr. Alison's finest descriptions are occasionally marred by the same faults which we have remarked in his political dissertations; by the same tendency to flights of poetical extravagance; the same wearisome repetitions; the same flow of sonorous verbosity. We forbear to recommence our reluctant strictures upon these faults of style; but there is a single error which we are unwilling to pass over, because we believe it to be peculiar to this branch of the narrative. We allude to the occasional substitution of the present for the past tense in the relation of events. It is one of the most unimpressive and unpleasing artifices which a writer can employ—rarely admissible in narrative poetry, scarcely ever in prose romance, and utterly inconsistent with the sober dignity of the historical style. Much of all this is, no doubt, to be attributed to the incorrectness of taste indisputably displayed by Mr. Alison in many of the most impassioned passages of his work; but much, we suspect, is owing to an injudicious and indiscriminate, though just and laudable, admiration for the genius of a rival historian.

Mr. Alison frequently speaks with warm and generous applause of the ardent military eloquence which distinguishes the style of Colonel Napier. Nothing can be more handsomely expressed than this feeling; but we suspect that it has occasionally betrayed Mr. Alison into unconscious, and not always happy, imitation. We appreciate as highly as any one the force and originality of the language employed by this great military historian. Among all his high qualities none is more conspicuous than the warmth and vigour of his narration. It is impossible not to feel animated by the fiery energy, and the graphic minuteness of his descriptions. But his most partial admirers will allow, that the more fanciful and brilliant peculiarities of his style, are such as must make all attempts at imitation difficult and dangerous to an unusual degree. Its fervent impetuosity occasionally overpowers even its master, and it is unlikely to prove more docile in less familiar hands. Colonel Napier's genius, if we may be pardoned the comparison, resembles those Indian *figurantes* described by Captain Mundy in his amusing sketches, whose chief difficulty is to restrain within graceful limits the superabundant suppleness and agility of their limbs. It is the luxuriant vivacity of the writer's imagination, and his unlimited command of pointed and original language, that occasion the principal blemishes in his style. And it is impossible to deny, that when he gives the rein to his fancy, it occasionally hurries him across the fatal step which separates the sublime, we will not say from the ridiculous, but assuredly from the quaint and grotesque.

We are far from accusing Mr. Alison of caricaturing Colonel Napier's manner. We think his descriptions a softened, and in some respects an improved copy of those of his great original. But Colonel Napier's battle-pieces are in a style which will not bear softening—we had almost said, in a style which will not bear improvement. We know no description so appropriate to it as the quaint expression applied by Henry Grattan to Lord Chatham's oratory—that 'it was very great, and very odd.' Its eccentricity cannot be corrected without weakening its energy; it is either strikingly yet irregularly lofty, or it becomes tame, hollow, and exaggerated. With Colonel Napier himself the last is never the case. His faults are as racy and as characteristic as his beauties; and in his boldest offences against taste, his originality and vigour are conspicuous.

Still, this lively melodramatic style, even when most successful, is not that which we prefer for historical narrative. We are no very rigid advocates for what is called the *dignity* of history. We have no doubt that thousands of interesting facts have perished, never to be recovered, by the supercilious neglect of over formal historians. We would have all circumstances preserved which can add the least effect to the narrative, however trivial they may appear. But we do not see the advantage of ornamental descriptions, however striking in themselves, which comprise merely general and common-place particulars, such as could not but accompany the main facts related. There is, surely, something unpleasing in seeing a historian, while recounting events which shook and terrified all Europe, glance aside to notice the trembling of the earth under a heavy cannonade, or the glittering of helmets in a charge of cavalry. We object to such flights, not because they are beneath the *dignity* of the narrative, but because they diminish the simplicity to which it must owe much of its

awful effect; and because they can be far more imposingly supplied by the imagination of the reader. It is not by such rhetorical arts as these, that the great masters of history have produced their most successful effects. Thucydides has never once throughout his work departed from the grave and simple dignity of his habitual style. Yet what classical scholar will ever forget the condensed pathos and energy with which he has described the desolation of Athens, during the pestilence, or the overthrow of the Syracusan expedition? Froissart is a still more extraordinary instance. Without for a moment suffering himself to be raised above his ordinary tone of easy and almost childish garrulity, he has yet attained that chivalrous ardour of expression, which, to borrow the emphatic words of Sidney, 'stirs the heart like the sound of a trumpet.' What soldier ever read without enthusiasm his account of the battle of Crecy? Not, we are confident, Colonel Napier, whose warm and ready sympathy with the brave is one of his noblest qualities as a historian. The brilliant array of the French chivalry—the fierce gestures and 'fell cry' of the undisciplined Genoese—the motionless silence of the English archery—the sudden and deadly flight of arrows—the mad confusion of the routed army;—all are painted with the life and vigour of Homer himself. And yet the chronicler has not employed a shade of fanciful colouring or poetical ornament—his whole narrative is full of the same simple and delightful *naiveté* with which he commends the innocence of the Black Prince's oaths; or celebrates the 'small hat of beaver' which became Edward III. so marvellously at the battle of Sluys. In reading such passages as these, we feel the same admiration as in seeing an athletic perform some feat of surpassing strength, without the distortion of a feature or a muscle. They are, in comparison with the florid and highly wrought style on which we have been remarking, what the Belvedere Apollo is in comparison with the beautiful statue of the Attacking Gladiator. Both figures are admirable works of art, and both are represented in the act of vehement and victorious exertion. But how striking is the contrast between the desperate energy of the mortal, and the serene indifference of the divinity.

During the twenty-five years included in Mr. Alison's History, Europe was so perpetually involved in war, that in giving our opinion of his merits as a military historian, we may be said to have pronounced upon those of the whole narrative part of his work. But he has taken great pains to give his readers the most complete information of all the internal transactions of the chief European nations during that period. He has, as he informs us, made it his rule 'to give the arguments for and against any public measures in the words of those who originally brought them forward, without any attempt at paraphrase or abridgment. This is more particularly the case in the debates of the National Assembly of France, the parliament of England, and the Council of State under Napoleon. . . . . It is,' as he justly remarks, 'the only mode by which the spirit and feelings of the moment could be faithfully transmitted to posterity, or justice done to the motives on either side, which influenced mankind.'—(Pref. xliv.) 'Providence,' says Mr. Alison, 'has so interwoven human affairs, that when we wish to retrace the revolutions of a people, and to investigate the causes of their grandeur or misfortune, we are insensibly conducted step by step to their cradle.'—(ii. 536.) The historian has accordingly interwoven with his narrative several very interesting and comprehensive sketches of the previous history and political state of those nations who took the most prominent share in events. We may particularize those of France, England, Russia, Turkey, and Poland, as the most complete and elaborate. They include a general description of the population, of the nature and capabilities of the countries in question, and contain much valuable statistical information. We think Mr. Alison mistaken in some of the maxims and theories which he draws from these views of European history; but it is impossible to refuse him the merit of much accurate knowledge, and much patient and ingenious reflection.

Mr. Alison's principal and fatal error is one which we can only lament; for we can neither blame him for its existence, nor wonder at its effects—he is a rigid, a sincere, and an intolerant Tory. This is the whole extent of his offence. His opinions are displayed with sufficient fairness, if not always with perfect taste and modesty;—he does not permit them to pervert his statement of facts, though he seldom loses an opportunity of asserting them in all their uncharitable austerity. To this practice every liberal-minded reader, of however opposite principles, will easily reconcile himself. He will, it is true, have to travel through an interesting tract of history, in company with an honourable opponent, instead of a sympathizing friend. He will necessarily lose much pleasure, and some instruction ; but a few precautions will ensure him against injury or annoyance.

In common with nearly all political writers of the present day, we have had repeated occasion to pronounce our opinion both upon revolutions in general, and in particular upon that which forms the main subject of Mr. Alison's history. We shall not, of course, repeat our arguments in detail; as we see no occasion to correct the conclusions which we drew from them. We shall merely allude to them so far as may be necessary for the purpose of comparing them with the opinions of Mr. Alison respecting the causes, the character, and the consequences of the French Revolution.

We must, however, preface our observations by declaring, that we have found considerable difficulty in extracting any consistent and definite opinion, from the present work, upon the general tendency of that event. We have been wholly unable to reconcile the author's calm and just remarks upon the nature of the French government under the ancient *régime*, with his vague and incoherent bursts of invective against the spirit by which it was subverted. He speaks of violent revolutions, sometimes as the stern but beneficial punishments of tyranny and corruption — sometimes as national fits of insanity, the judgment of Providence upon moral profligacy and religious scepticism. His *logic* convinces us that what he is pleased to call the revolutionary mania is in itself a very natural feeling—the instinctive desire of the oppressed for peace and security. His *rhetoric* would persuade us that it is a mysterious epidemic, displaying itself merely by a morbid thirst for innovation, and an insane delight in crime. In his second chapter, he details nearly a dozen intolerable grievances which existed in France down to the first outbreak of popular violence; almost any one of which would appear, to a freeborn Englishman, sufficient to cause a civil war. He then proceeds to notice several circumstances which were likely to render the French nation, at that moment, peculiarly impatient of the hardships they had to endure. So far, nothing can be more satisfactory. He has clearly shown that a sudden and violent change was inevitable ; and that, without the utmost skill and firmness in the government, that change was likely to be followed by fatal excesses. But he goes on to declare, in all the emphasis of capital type, that 'the circumstances which have now been mentioned, without doubt *contributed* to the formation of that discontent which formed the predisposing cause of the Revolution. But the exciting cause, as physicians would say—the immediate source of the convulsion—was the SPIRIT OF INNOVATION, which, like a malady, overspread France at that crisis, precipitated all classes into a passion for changes, of which they were far from perceiving the ultimate effects, and in the end produced evils far greater than those they were intended to remove. . . . . It would seem,' he adds, ' as if, at particular periods, from causes inscrutable to human wisdom, an universal frenzy seizes mankind; reason, experience, prudence, are alike blinded, and the very persons who are to perish in the storm are the first to raise its fury.'—(i. 149.) This is a good specimen of the superficial verbiage which formed the chorus of the English Tory press fifty years ago. We confess that we always considered it strange language to come from shrewd, sensible men of the world—from men, who, when reasoning on the crimes and follies of social life, would have been the first to laugh such vague jargon to scorn. Still these men had at least an excuse which Mr. Alison has not. The explanation, bad as it was, was the best they had to give. They did not possess the information which we now have, respecting the system which had brutalized and enraged the French people; and if they had, they might be excused, at such a crisis, for failing to reason justly upon it. But we are at a loss to conceive how Mr. Alison can think it necessary to aid the effect of his able and conclusive details, by a solution so feeble and unmeaning as the above. We forgive the schoolmen of the middle ages for saying that the water rises in the pump because nature abhors a vacuum; for the answer was merely a pompous confession of ignorance. But what should we think of a modern philosopher who should solve the same problem by telling us—' The pressure of the external atmosphere overcomes that of the rarefied air in the cylinder; this circumstance, without doubt, contributes to the phenomenon; but its immediate cause is, that nature abhors a vacuum!' If Mr. Alison means, by the ' spirit of innovation,' that natural wish for redress which is the consequence of intolerable suffering, then the sentence we have quoted, besides being a truism in itself, is incorrect in its application; for that spirit must have been an intermediate, not a collateral cause of the Revolution. But this he does *not* mean; for it would be absurd to call so rational a desire an inscrutable frenzy. It is therefore clear that he speaks of ' a spirit of innovation,' wholly unconnected with existing inconveniences—a spirit against which the wisest institutions cannot guard, and which is almost as likely to break forth in a free, as in an oppressed nation. We shall permit ourselves a few observations upon this theory; because, briefly as it is here expressed, it appears to be the text of most of his mournful and discouraging speculations both upon the future destiny of France, and the progress of Reform throughout the world.

In the first place, the remark naturally occurs, that admitting the possibility of the explanation, we do not want its assistance. Mr. Alison has ably shown that the worst follies and excesses of the Revolution may be fully accounted for by the ordinary motives of human conduct. Why then have recourse to ' causes inscrutable to human wisdom?' Why call down a divinity, when the knot can be disentangled by mortal skill? Assume, if you will, that nations, like elephants, are subject to periodical accesses of frenzy; but why apply your theory to such a case where every provocation existed to justify an outbreak of natural resentment? Nothing can, by Mr. Alison's account, be more evident, than that the political privileges of the noblesse, the oppressions of the feudal law, and the ruinous state of the finances, must have been in 1789 sources of daily and hourly annoyance to the great majority of the French nation. Most of them, even in the plebeian class, must, in the existing state of intelligence, have felt that their property had been injured, and their prospects in life disappointed, by the accident of their birth. And surely they must have been the meekest race in existence, if the severity of their sufferings, and the consciousness of their strength, and the knowledge of the impotence of their oppressors, would all have been insufficient to urge them to violence, without the assistance of this casual fit of unaccountable insanity.

In speaking thus, we fully bear in mind the wild and visionary speculations which were so common in France at the time of the Revolution. But we cannot see the necessity of referring these delusions to inscrutable causes. No one will deny that a frantic spirit of innovation *did* exist in France at that period;—the question is, whether it originated in natural resentment or spontaneous frenzy—whether, in short, the nation was driven mad, or went mad of its own accord. The latter, as we have seen, is Mr. Alison's opinion; and this opinion induces him, as well it may, to fear that the feelings which convulsed France half a century since, may be awakened in free and well-governed countries by the progress of constitutional reform. To us nothing can seem more natural than that men, who knew no more of political liberty than a blind man knows of light, should form an extravagant notion of its blessings. All our ideas of human nature would have been confounded, if we had found the French Jacobins recommending the constitution of 1789 in the calm and rational language in which Hampden might have spoken for the abolition of the

Star-Chamber, or Lord Somers for the Bill of
Rights. It is certain that nations, like individuals, are sometimes captivated by delusive
theories. But we appeal to the common
sense of our readers whether any reasonable
being ever abandoned substantial comforts, or
confronted real dangers, with no better motives. Can it be conceived that empty dreams
about universal equality, and an age of innocence, would have nerved peaceable men to
defy the cannon of the Bastile? Would the
mob have massacred good and popular rulers
for the sake of resembling Brutus and Timo-
leon? When a *homme-de-lettres* risked his
life as a demagogue, was it to realize his
fancies of republics and democracies, or to
escape from hopeless poverty and obscurity?
When a peasant set fire to the chateau of
Monseigneur, was it because he admired the
eloquence of Danton or Desmoulins, or because he found it easier to revolt at once, than
to stay at home and be ruined by *corvées* and
feudal services?

At the conclusion of his first chapter, Mr.
Alison has explained, with admirable sense
and moderation, the causes of the sanguinary
violence which distinguished the French Revolution. We are not sure that his remarks
upon the various crimes which he has to relate, are always characterized by the same
rational calmness; but he has here at least
recorded his deliberate opinion, that the atrocities of the French populace were the natural
and inevitable fruit of the oppression which
they had suffered. We have long ago expressed our belief, that the excesses of every
popular convulsion will generally be proportioned to the misgovernment which occasioned
it. We are aware that this has been eagerly
disputed; but, without pausing to discuss particular examples, we submit that the general
rule approaches very nearly to a truism.
Will not the violence of the popular party in
a revolution be in proportion to their exasperation and their political ignorance? And
will not their exasperation be in proportion to
their sufferings, and their political ignorance
to their inexperience in the use of political
power?

Of course, no one will deny that the exactness of the proportion may be disturbed by
various causes. The influence of accidental
circumstances, the authority of particular
classes, even the personal character of individuals, may have the greatest effect in exciting or restraining popular revenge. We
need not remind our readers of the various
unhappy coincidences which combined to increase the natural resentment of the French
nation;—of the foolish weakness, and more
foolish insolence of the court, the unprincipled

character of the popular leaders, the want of
moral and religious feeling among the lower
classes. Still, we do not comprehend the argument which attributes the crimes and im-
pieties of that unhappy time to the demoralizing effects of the Revolution itself. Sudden
anarchy may bring evil passions and infidel
opinions to light; but we do not understand
how it can bring them into existence. Men
do not insult their religion and massacre their
fellow-creatures, simply because it is in their
power. The desire to do so must previously
exist, and in France we have every proof that
it did exist. We might give innumerable
instances of the cruel and vindictive temper
displayed from the most ancient times by the
lower classes in France. In the *Jacquerie*, in
the civil wars of the *Bourguignons* and *Ar-
magnacs*, and in the seditions of the *League*
and the *Fronde*, they constantly displayed
the ferocity naturally excited by slavery and
oppression. Their scorn for Christianity,
though more recently acquired, had become,
long before the Revolution of 1789, as inveterate as their desire for revenge. We shall
give, in Mr. Alison's own words, one very
singular proof of the extent to which it prevailed. In speaking of the Egyptian expedition, he says—'They' (the French soldiers)
'not only considered the Christian faith as an
entire fabrication, but were for the most
part ignorant of its very elements. Lavalette
has recorded that hardly one of them had
ever been in a church, and that in Palestine
they were ignorant even of the names of the
holiest places in sacred history.'—(iii. 419.)

This was in 1799, only ten years after the
first symptoms of popular innovation. Here,
then, were 30,000 full-grown men, collected
promiscuously from all parts of France—
many of them well educated, and all of sound
mind and body—who appear to have felt
about as much interest in the religion of their
ancestors as in that of Brahma or Confucius.
And yet the great majority of this army must
have been born fifteen or twenty years before the first outbreak of the Revolution; and
the very youngest of them must have passed
their childhood entirely under the ancient
régime. There cannot, surely, be a stronger
proof that, long before the royal authority
was shaken, the great mass of the French nation had become such thorough infidels as to
be almost ignorant of the very existence of
Christianity.

Our limits will not permit us to discuss
with Mr. Alison the great question, whether
the French Revolution was on the whole a
benefit, or a disaster to mankind. Though
some passages in the earlier part of his History seem to bear a more hopeful interpreta-

tion, it is clear that upon the whole he considers it an event most fatal to France, and most menacing to the rest of Europe. The following are, in his opinion, the most pernicious consequences, as regards France alone —' The national morality has been destroyed in the citizens of towns, in whose hands alone political power is vested. There is no moral strength or political energy in the country. . . . France has fallen into a subjection to Paris, to which there is nothing comparable in European history. The Prætorian guards of the capital rule the state. . . . . Commercial opulence and habits of sober judgment have been destroyed, never to revive. A thirst for excitement everywhere prevails, and general selfishness disgraces the nation. Religion has never resumed its sway over the influential classes. . . . And the general depravity renders indispensable a powerful centralized and military government. In what respect,' he asks, ' does this state of things differ from the institutions of China or the Byzantine empire ?'—(x. 548.) In what respect, we prefer to inquire, does it differ from the institutions of France *before* the Revolution? We are no implicit admirers of the present French government; but we appeal to Mr. Alison's own statements, whether it is not infinitely preferable to that of Louis XVI.? Still less are we blind to the many and serious faults of the present generation of Frenchmen; but we are at a loss to conceive how any reasonable being, who compares the second revolution with the first, can deny the superiority of the Frenchman of 1830 to the Frenchman of 1793—that is, to the Frenchman of the ancient *régime*, when seen in his true colours. But, without stopping to argue so extensive a question in detail, we must confess that we should be glad to hear from Mr. Alison a distinct answer to a few such plain questions as the following:—Would Louis-Philippe, though he were the most depraved and violent man in Europe, dare to imitate the orgies of the regency, or the tyranny of Louis XV.? Are life, property, and honour, less safe than in the time of the Bastile, and the *Parc aux Cerfs?* Is the present condition of the peasantry worse than it was under the feudal law? Have the middle classes less political power than in 1742? Is France less prosperous at home, or less respected abroad, than in 1763 or 1783? However common infidelity may unhappily be, is religion less respected than in the days of Voltaire? However low the national standard of morality, was it higher when Madame de Parabére, or Madame du Barri, was the virtual ruler of France? All the declamation in the world

about Oriental tyrannies, and centralized despotisms, will not get rid of these simple tests; and we are at a loss to imagine how even Mr. Alison could reply to one of them in the affirmative.

If we are right on this important point, we shall not allow the crimes of the Revolution, or the sufferings which it caused, to prevent us from considering it a beneficial change. In saying this we trust that we shall not be understood as wishing to palliate the excesses of the popular party, or to undervalue the evils inseparable from all popular convulsions. A revolution, at its best, is a painful and perilous remedy; at its worst, it is the severest trial which a nation can undergo. If we are inclined, notwithstanding, to consider such trials as benefits, it is because we believe that they seldom occur, except in cases where hopeless slavery and irreparable decay are the only alternatives. There is no doubt that the French Revolution was an instance of the worst kind;—perhaps it was the very worst that ever occurred. Not only did the popular movement result in atrocities, but the exhaustion which followed led to the usurpation of Napoleon and the wars of the empire. Three millions and a half of Frenchmen,[*] and a prodigious number of foreigners, perished, who but for the Revolution and its consequences might have ended their days in peace. Human ingenuity, in short, can scarcely imagine means by which a greater amount of violence and bloodshed could have been crowded into a quarter of a century. Still we are persuaded that an escape from this fiery trial would have been dearly purchased by the continuance of the ancient *régime* for another century. The evils of violence and bloodshed, dreadful as they are, cannot be compared to those of oppressive institutions. Violence and bloodshed are necessarily partial, but oppressive institutions are universal. It is impossible to guillotine a whole nation; it is impossible to enrol a whole nation as conscripts; but it is easy to make a whole nation miserable by disabilities and exactions. Even under the Reign of Terror, each individual citizen must have felt that there were many hundred chances to one in favour of his escape from denunciation; but no peasant had a hope of escaping the tyranny of the feudal customs. Violence and bloodshed are in their nature transitory; but oppressive institutions may be

* Mr. Alison enumerates the victims of the Revolution, including those of the civil war in La Vendée, at 1,022,351 souls; and the soldiers who perished in the wars of the empire, at 2,200,400.—(See vi. 410, ii. 400). This does not include those who fell at Waterloo, in the battles of the revolutionary contest, and in the various naval actions of the war.

perpetual. Crimes which spring from passion soon exhaust themselves; but crimes which spring from habit may continue for ever. The Reign of Terror was over in fourteen months; but the ancient *régime* might have subsisted until its effects had reduced France to the decrepitude of China or Constantinople. Violence and bloodshed produce merely suffering; but oppressive institutions produce degradation also. A French peasant might retain the pride and spirit of a free man, though he knew that the next day he might be dragged before a revolutionary tribunal, or hurried off to join the army in Spain or Russia. But a French peasant who had been placed in the stocks for want of due servility to his *seigneur*, who had seen his son sent to the galleys for destroying a partridge's eggs, who knew that the honour of his family had been outraged by some licentious noble, such a man could not but feel himself a debased and unhappy slave. The sufferings of the Revolution, in short, were to the sufferings of the ancient *régime* as the plague of London to the *malaria* of a tropical climate. The one was a temporary though overwhelming blow, the other a wasting pestilence—the perpetual source of terror and misery to every successive generation existing within its influence.

Mr. Alison's opinions upon the French Revolution induce him to speak with triumphant admiration of the foresight shown by Mr. Pitt and Mr. Burke upon that subject, and with condescending compassion of the blindness of Mr. Fox. 'Posterity,' he assures us, ' will not search the speeches of Mr. Fox for historic truth, nor pronounce him gifted with any extraordinary political penetration. On the contrary, it must record with regret that the light which broke upon Mr. Burke at the outset of the Revolution, and on Mr. Pitt before its principal atrocities began, only shone on his fervent mind when descending to the grave.'— (v. 720.) That, we presume, will depend upon the view taken by posterity of the events in question. It is impossible to deny that Mr. Burke appreciated the character of the then existing generation of Frenchmen more truly than Mr. Fox. But if future ages see in the French Revolution a shock which, dreadful as it was, saved France from hopeless and lingering decay, they will scarcely deny their admiration to the statesman who discerned its true character; merely because his sanguine and generous nature led him to think too favourably of the individuals who conducted it. The physical evils inflicted by the French Revolution are already almost effaced, and their last traces will vanish with the present generation. But its moral consequences may

endure for ages, and it is by their ultimate character that the comparative wisdom of the rival statesmen must be tried.

It may be true that Mr. Fox was induced, late and reluctantly, to despair of French liberty. But it was not the turbulence of the Revolution which changed his opinions. It was the forcible interruption, not the natural tendency, of its progress, which caused his despondency. He had foreseen that the excesses of the French people were incapable of being a permanent evil; but no human skill could enable him to foresee the downfall of Napoleon. It would be unfair to blame a physician for ignorance in recommending sea-bathing, because his patient happened to be carried off by a shark; and it is equally unjust to assert that Mr. Fox was originally wrong in his opinion of the French Revolution, because he lived to see its benefits destroyed for a time by the unexpected interference of a powerful usurper.

We are at a loss to comprehend the precise moral lesson which Mr. Alison would lead his readers to draw from the French Revolution. Nor, to say the truth, is it easy to conceive how he can find any instruction at all in an event which he believes to have originated in mysterious insanity, and to have terminated in hopeless slavery. It is true that we find in his work plenty of sonorous declamation about the fatal career of guilt, the short-lived triumphs of wickedness, and the inevitable laws of retribution. But we know nothing more annoying to the reader than this sort of rhetorical amplification, upon subjects which require to be discussed with the most rigid precision of which language is capable. No doubt Robespierre was a wicked man, and was as miserable as wicked men generally are. No doubt Napoleon was rash and ambitious, and owed his downfall to his own pride and recklessness. No doubt the French populace were madmen and ruffians, and made themselves as wretched by their crimes as they deserved to be. But all this is not the sort of instruction which we expect from an elaborate history of the Revolution. We have searched Mr. Alison's work for a calm dispassionate discussion of the means by which the evils of the ancient government might have been removed, and yet the excesses of the Revolution prevented; and we have found ourselves again and again baffled and bewildered by a mazy tissue of words. No reasonable being who reads Mr. Alison's narrative requires to be lectured about the horrors of anarchy. Everybody knows that anarchy is a tremendous evil; but was it an avoidable evil? was it a greater evil than continued subjection? was there no middle course by which the dangers of both might have been avoided? These are questions which we cannot discover any direct attempt to resolve. If Mr. Alison were to see a drover trampled to death by an ox, would not his first reflection naturally be upon the danger of over-driving oxen, and the best means of keeping them in order? And would he not think that the bystanders had lost their senses if they began to dilate upon the shocking nature of the accident, as a proof that it is the duty of over-driven oxen to keep their temper?

Men are wisely forbidden to do evil that good may ensue; but they are not forbidden to admire the merciful arrangements of Providence, by which the sin and folly of individuals are so often made the source of blessings to mankind. We feel as much aversion as Mr. Alison for the cruelty and injustice of the French Revolutionists; but we do not pronounce, as he does, that their crimes must bring ruin upon their innocent posterity. We see neither sense, nor justice, nor Christian principle, in his theory of a law of retribution not confined to the guilty parties. Let Mr. Alison, if he will, regard the French Revolution as 'the second revolt of Lucifer, the prince of the morning.'—(x. 18). We prefer to recognize in its vicissitudes the same severe but merciful hand which employs earthquakes and tornadoes to dispel the pestilential stagnation of the physical atmosphere.

However vague Mr. Alison's digressions may occasionally appear, there is one feeling, in the expression of which he is uniformly clear and consistent. This is his dread and detestation of democratic institutions. So far as these sentiments are called forth by the facts of his narrative, we admit them to be perfectly reasonable. Whatever benefits we may hope from the consequences of the French Revolution, we acknowledge that the democracy which it established was in itself the worst of all possible governments. What we doubt is the intrinsic evil of a democracy in a community prepared for its reception Still, as we admit that no such community now exists, or is likely to exist for many ages, it may be thought that the subject of our dissent from Mr. Alison's opinion is merely theoretical, and therefore scarcely worth discussion. But this is far from being the case. If Mr. Alison is right, every political innovation, in every country, is necessarily absurd and mischievous in proportion as it increases the influence of the lower classes. If we are right, such innovations are only dangerous when they give influence to a class unfit to exercise it. The question therefore is, whether the great body of a nation is necessarily

and intrinsically unfit to exercise political power.

Mr. Alison's first argument, if we rightly understand it, is the utter inutility of such an experiment, whether successful or not. He draws, or attempts to draw, a distinction between social freedom and political power, and contends that one may exist in perfect security without the protection of the other. 'There is, in the first place,' he says, 'the love of freedom; that is, immunity from personal restriction, oppression, or injury. This principle is perfectly innocent, and never exists without producing the happiest effects. Every concession which is calculated to increase this species of liberty, is comparatively safe in all ages and in all places. But there is another principle, strong at all times, but especially to be dreaded in moments of excitement. This is the principle of democratic ambition;—the desire of exercising the powers of sovereignty, and of sharing in the government of the state. This is the dangerous principle;—the desire, not of exercising industry without molestation, but of exerting power without control.'—(i. 174). The principles may certainly be said to be distinct; but they are so closely connected that we scarcely see how one can exist without the other. They are equally natural, and in themselves equally harmless. The one is the wish for present relief—the other the desire of future security. The former, we suppose, is felt by every human being; the latter by every human being possessed of the commonest sense and foresight. What security, we would ask Mr. Alison, can a man have that he will continue to exercise industry without molestation, except the possession, by the class to which he belongs, of a share in the government of the state? The present existence of just and equal laws is not such a security. Who is to guard our guardians? Who is to assure us that those laws will not be repealed, if our rulers can repeal them at any moment without our consent? Suppose that they enact a new law to-morrow, declaring us all slaves and bondmen, what resource have we against it but civil war?

This, it is true, is an extreme case. When the subjects are men of spirit, and the rulers men of sense, there is no fear of such open tyranny as this. But there is fear of insensible encroachment on the national liberties—of that encroachment which has sapped the constitution and undermined the national spirit of so many continental nations—of that encroachment whose progress in England, two centuries ago, was only arrested by seven years of desperate war. Even when the popular rights are so clearly defined as to make this impracticable, there is fear that the class which is passive in the administration of affairs will suffer much unnecessary hardship. There is scarcely any conceivable political measure, which is not certain, sooner or later, directly or indirectly, more or less, to affect the personal happiness of the poorest citizen of the commonwealth. And it is in vain to hope that the best absolute government will consult the happiness of such a citizen as impartially as it would if he had the power to interfere; and the wisdom to interfere with effect.

No man of sense will consider political power as an end; but it is surely a means. It is not happiness; but Mr. Alison will scarcely dispute that, properly used, it is a powerful instrument for securing happiness. We admit that, like other useful things, it may be desired with reckless eagerness or with pernicious designs; but we say that it is in itself a legitimate object of desire. We admit that the exclusion of the great body of the community from all share in the government, is at present, in almost all European states, a necessary evil. But we say that it *is* an evil; and that, if it ever shall become unnecessary, its continued existence will become a practical as well as a theoretical injustice.

Mr. Alison's next objection is the abstract injustice of a democracy. Admitting political power to be a great benefit, he still argues that its extension to the poorer classes is necessarily an unfair and unequal measure; even though 'every man, in whatever rank, were equally capable of judging on political subjects.' His reasoning on this point is more plausible than on the preceding, but, we think, equally fallacious. 'In private life,' he says, 'men are never deceived on this subject. In the administration of any common fund, or the disposal of common property, it never was for a moment proposed to give the smallest shareholder an equal right with the greatest; to give a creditor holding a claim for 20s., for example, on a bankrupt estate, the same vote as one possessed of a bond for L.10,000. The injustice of such a proceeding is quite apparent.'—(i. 351). This analogy is far from satisfactory. There are several circumstances which make the exclusion of a citizen from the management of the state a greater hardship, than the exclusion of a shareholder from the management of the common fund. In the first place, the shareholder may withdraw his stake if he considers it insecurely deposited. Mr. Alison's twenty-shilling creditor may sell his dividend at a fair discount, if he thinks that the assignees are mismanaging the estate. In a common-

wealth it is different. Every English citizen must share the fate of his country, or become a homeless emigrant. Secondly, the amount of a shareholder's *pecuniary* interest in the joint stock, is generally a tolerably fair representation of his *moral* interest in the prosperity of the speculation. It is certainly possible that a poor man, with a small venture, may be more deeply involved than a rich man with a much larger one; but this is not likely to be a common case. There is certainly every reasonable probability that the small creditor cares comparatively little for the loss of his twenty shillings, and that the large creditor will be ruined by the loss of his L.10,000. And therefore, if we distribute authority among the shareholders in proportion to each man's pecuniary risk, we shall probably distribute it, in most cases, in proportion to each man's actual chance of enjoyment or suffering. Here again the analogy fails. The whole property of the lower classes in a commonwealth, is almost invariably staked upon that commonwealth's existence. An English peasant, who possesses nothing but a cottage and a garden, would dread the loss of his property by foreign conquest or domestic anarchy, as much as if he were Duke of Sutherland or Marquis of Westminster. Lastly, in the disposal of a joint fund, each shareholder incurs a pecuniary hazard, and nothing more. In the management of a commonwealth, the personal safety of its citizens is risked. A mechanic, living solely by his daily labour, cannot strictly be said to have any property to lose by the ruin of the state; but he may lose his life, his liberty, his means of future subsistence. A Reign of Terror, or a French invasion, could not deprive him of a fortune, but they might cause him to be murdered, or enslaved, or starved in the streets. These are our reasons for thinking that, if no other obstacles existed, it would be unjust to deprive the poorer classes of all political influence; merely on the ground that their interest in the welfare of the state is insufficient to withhold them from wanton misgovernment.

Mr. Alison repeatedly enlarges, with great justice, upon the practical evils which have hitherto been found to accompany democratic institutions. But we think that he does not sufficiently distinguish between necessary and accidental disadvantages—between the dangers inseparable from popular power, and the dangers arising from its abuse. He does not sufficiently consider that in no state which has yet existed have the poorer classes been equal, or nearly equal, to the rich in civilisation and intelligence; and that consequently in no state which has yet existed, could any form of government, at all approaching to what can be properly called a democracy, have any chance of fair trial. In ancient Athens and modern France, that constitution was adopted by men utterly unfit for its exercise. The consequences were perfectly natural—in the one case, perpetual turbulence and speedy decay—in the other, rapine, bloodshed, and anarchy. In the United States of America, the experiment is now in progress on a far wiser plan, and under far more favourable circumstances. But even here we admit that Mr. Alison is justified in regarding the result as more than doubtful. Popular power, perhaps from unavoidable causes, has even here outrun popular sense and knowledge; and the consequences have been seen in frequent outbreaks of democratic tyranny, which have created serious alarm for the security of the state. Upon the whole, the British constitution, as established in 1688, may perhaps be considered the most democratic form of government ever yet exercised with continued and undisputed success. And, therefore, the world has yet to behold the full effect which would be produced by the insensible progress of popular influence in a nation enlightened, religious, and confirmed in sober wisdom by centuries of advancing freedom and civilisation.

Mr. Alison, in his concluding chapter, points out several important advantages possessed by the aristocratic over the democratic form of government. They may generally be included under two heads: superior security to private property, and superior prudence in public measures. 'It has uniformly been found,' says Mr. Alison, 'that the holders of property advocate measures to protect that property, while the destitute masses are perpetually impelled to those likely to induce revolutionary spoliation.'—(x. 965). 'Agrarian laws,' he elsewhere asserts, 'and the equal division of property, or measures tending indirectly to that effect, will in every age be the wish of the unthinking multitude, who have nothing apparently to lose, and everything to gain, by such convulsions. Their real ultimate interests, indeed, will in the end inevitably suffer from such changes; but this is a remote consequence, which never will become obvious to the great body of mankind.' —(i. 352). That is assuming the question. If the great body of mankind are really so obtuse as to be incapable, with every advantage of instruction, of comprehending that a state where the poor unite to rob the rich will inevitably be ruined, then we acknowledge their natural unfitness for political power. But Mr. Alison forgets that in the passage we have quoted he is arguing on the supposition

of 'every man, in whatever rank, being equally capable of judging on political subjects.' Surely, if this were the case, no reasonable being would be found to advocate an agrarian law. It is precisely when the multitude cease to be unthinking—when they become competent to judge of their own real and ultimate interests—that we assert, and Mr. Alison denies, the necessity of allowing them a share of political power.

Mr. Alison's first argument for the superior political skill of aristocratic governments appears to us singular, if not incomprehensible. 'Those classes,' he says, 'who from their affluence possess leisure, and from their station have received the education requisite for acquiring extensive information, are more likely, in the long run, to acquire and exhibit the powers necessary for beneficial legislation, than those who, from the necessities of their situation, are chained to daily toil, and from the limited extent of their funds have been disabled from acquiring a thorough education. . . . No person of a different profession would think of competing with a physician in the treatment of a person afflicted with a dangerous disease, or with a lawyer in the management of an intricate or difficult lawsuit. . . . And it would be surprising indeed if the science of government could be as successfully pursued by those classes whose time is almost wholly absorbed by other pursuits, as by those who have made it the undivided object and study of their life.'—(i. 966). All this is perfectly true; but what conclusion does Mr. Alison draw from it? What is to prevent a democratic state from making proper use of the superior intelligence of any class of its citizens? Does Mr. Alison suppose that, if a democracy were established in England, the whole nation would assemble on Salisbury Plain to pass laws and transact business? Or does he think that the representative assembly and the public offices would be filled with labourers and mechanics? Every state where the supreme power is placed in the hands of the numerical majority is a democracy; just as every state where it is held by an individual is a despotism. The people, like the king, may exercise their power by any machinery that may appear convenient; they may delegate it to presidents, senators, ambassadors, and secretaries of state; and they may entrust these offices to the most deserving persons to be found in the community. Why, then, is the science of government likely to be less successfully cultivated in a democratic state? Or why have the statesmen and legislators of such a state less encouragement to make that science the object and study of their lives? History does not convince us that the fact is so. Faulty as popular governments generally are, their fault has seldom been a want of able and experienced servants. Neither America, nor Athens, nor even revolutionary France, found reason to complain of the mediocrity of their statesmen. Such ministers as Pericles, Washington, and Carnot, were surely worthy of the confidence of any aristocratic government on earth.

But, however able might be the rulers of a democratic state, Mr. Alison thinks that their policy would be constantly baffled by the thoughtless impatience of the supreme multitude. 'Whoever,' he says, 'has closely observed the dispositions of large bodies of men, whether in social or political life, must have become sensible that the most uniform and lasting feature by which they are distinguished, is that of insensibility to the future.' —(x. 969). Undoubtedly this is the great defect of all popular governments. They are machines of prodigious power; but it is difficult to set them in motion with quickness, or to direct them with precision. In persevering policy, in cautious secrecy, in unwearying vigilance, a democracy is far inferior to an aristocracy, as an aristocracy is far inferior to a despotism. Nor do we deny that this is in some measure an intrinsic disadvantage, which no degree of national intelligence could entirely eradicate. Still Mr. Alison will scarcely contend that it is a disadvantage which all democracies possess in an equal degree. He will allow that the Athenian democracy was less infatuated than the French; and that the American democracy is less thoughtless than the Athenian. He will allow, in short, that the insensibility to the future of which he speaks, varies inversely as the average intellect of the people. If this is the case, the question is, whether the great body of mankind are capable of such a degree of improvement as to diminish the want of foresight peculiar to popular governments, until it is more than balanced by their peculiar advantages.

Mr. Alison replies decidedly in the negative; but we do not think that he has fairly stated the point in dispute. He says that 'the doctrine of human *perfectibility* is so agreeable to the human heart, so flattering to human vanity, and withal so nearly allied to the generous affections, that it will in all probability, to the end of the world, constitute the basis on which all the efforts of the popular party will be rested, and all the visions of social amelioration justified.'—(x. 938). He cites as examples the visions of Rousseau and Condorcet, and proceeds of course, with perfect success, to show that such theories

have always been disappointed; and that they are wholly inconsistent with the revealed doctrine of human corruption. We perfectly agree in all this. No Christian, no philosopher, no experienced man of the world, can reasonably believe in human perfectibility, in the sense in which that term is commonly understood. But will Mr. Alison allow no schemes of social amelioration short of angelic purity?—no popular government except by impeccable beings? Does he confound all hopes of human improvement with the dreams of the enthusiasts who predicted that crime, war, disease, and death itself, would shortly yield to the advance of science and virtue? We entertain no such visionary ideas; the only means by which we look for improvement, are the natural progress of reason and religion; and the only result which we expect, is the communication of those qualities to the many, which our own observation has shown us in the few. Mr. Alison tells us that a good democracy is a dream, because men can never become angels. We reply that we shall be perfectly contented to try the experiment, when they all become Washingtons and Wilberforces.

Surely we shall not be told that this too is an idle vision. If experience, reason, and revelation deny that man is perfectible, do they not combine to assert that he is *improvable*—improvable to a degree which those who have only known him in his lowest state can scarcely imagine? All we venture to hope is, that a certain degree of this improvement will, in course of time, become general. We do not believe in human perfectibility, because we never saw or heard of a perfect man. But we are so fortunate as to have known many wise and good men; many men to whose integrity we would cheerfully entrust our dearest interests. What presumption is there in believing that the advance of knowledge and of Christianity may hereafter multiply their number? We can conceive that a savage, whose highest ideas of human excellence are drawn from the barbarians of his tribe, might ridicule such a hope. But why an Englishman, who perhaps is aware of the actual existence of many excellent men, should deny the possible existence of thousands, is to us incomprehensible.

There is one great difference between aristocratic and democratic constitutions, which Mr. Alison does not appear to notice. He constantly speaks as if wisdom and foresight were as inseparable from aristocracy, as he pronounces rashness and indolence to be from democracy. Whether he is right or wrong in the latter opinion, in the former he is assuredly mistaken. The truth appears to be, that a bad democracy displays great faults and great powers, while a bad aristocracy, with faults nearly as great, displays no power at all. The defects of an aristocracy are intrinsic, but its merits are variable; there are certain faults which it must possess, and certain advantages which it may possess. The best aristocracy cannot call forth democratic enthusiasm; but a bad aristocracy may rival democratic recklessness. The aristocracy of Austria was no match for the French republic in its moments of awakened energy; the aristocracy of Venice was as supine as the same republic in its feeblest intervals of exhaustion. The reverse of this will apply to a democracy. Its merits are intrinsic; for the worst democracies, such as Athens or revolutionary France, have surpassed, when aroused by imminent danger, the vigour of the best aristocratic governments. Its defects, on the contrary, are variable. They depend upon the average sense and principle of its citizens. When that average is low, the anarchy which ensues is worse than the severest despotism; but when it is raised as high as the imperfection of human nature will permit, it might enable a popular government to exert the self-denying vigilance of the wisest aristocracy.

We have been induced by Mr. Alison's undistinguishing abhorrence to say so much more than we had intended in favour of democratic institutions, that we feel ourselves compelled to add a few words in explanation. We are as adverse, then, as the most rigid Conservative to sudden or violent political changes. It is to avoid the necessity of any such change, whether it assumes its sternest or its mildest form—whether it appear as a Revolution or a Reform Bill—that we think the institutions of every state should be gradually modified in proportion to the intellectual progress of its subjects. Whether that progress will ever attain such a height, as to make unrestrained self-government practicable in any community of human beings, we greatly doubt. Such a change may be an idle, though surely not an ignoble or unimproving hope. But the principle for which we contend is simply this, that the fitness of the people for the exercise of political power, is the sole criterion by which political power can be safely or justly granted or denied them.

Mr. Alison, as might be expected, applies his whole theory upon popular government to the reforms in the last reign in this country; and most dismal are the forebodings with which it inspires him. We have said that we cannot condemn his devotion to his po-

litical creed; but we think we have a right to complain of it as sometimes betraying him into a tone of arrogant assumption. We have been frequently amused, and occasionally, for a moment, provoked, by the cool dogmatical decision with which he finally settles, by a passing remark, the great public controversies of the age, and then proceeds to reason upon his own opinion as upon an indisputable foundation. Thus, he alludes to Catholic Emancipation as 'that loosening of the constitution in Church and State under which the nation has so grievously laboured,' (viii. 20),—'that momentous change in our religious institutions which first loosened the solid fabric of the British empire,' (viii. 43); —and he pronounces upon the Reform Bill, and the abolition of Slavery, in the same peremptory language. If he would condescend to overthrow our political tenets by deliberate argument, we might endeavour to own his superiority with a good grace; but it is too much for human patience to find them dismissed in a parenthesis, as unworthy serious discussion. Mr. Alison must surely be aware, that many of the best and wisest of his countrymen approved of the changes which we have mentioned, and still expect them to prove fully successful. Are they at once to be condemned, because an overweening and pompous historian chooses to shake his head, with a compassionate sneer, at their 'well-meaning but injudicious philanthropy?' Or is Mr. Alison so much their superior, that he has a right to assume, on his own authority, that they are mistaken, and to draw matter of argument and rebuke from that assumption. If the measures in question were the subject of his narrative—if any part of his work were devoted to their details, and to proof of their pernicious tendency—we should not object to his delivering his opinion, however we might disapprove the self-sufficiency of his language. But we must protest against his practice of interweaving with a history of past events, what lawyers call *obiter dicta* upon the politics of the day. The writer of such a work as the present ought to imitate the dignity and self-restraint of a judge on the bench, and carefully to abstain from throwing out imputations and assertions not strictly warranted by the evidence before the court.

We have no intention, as may be supposed, of discussing with Mr. Alison the merits of the individual changes which have lately caused so much anxiety in the British nation. Those who hold what are called reforming opinions, may possibly have been wrong in the precise measure of the particular innovations which they proposed; but we certainly apprehend no danger to the British constitution from their general tendency. It is unnecessary to recapitulate the general arguments upon the progress of popular influence which we have already advanced; but we think there are many reasons for hoping that its late advance in this country will be as peaceful in its immediate effects, as beneficial in its final result.

Our chief ground for this hope is the high character, moral influence, and peculiar constitution, of the British aristocracy. That body, splendid and powerful as it is, has for ages been so intimately blended with the middle classes, and so frequently recruited from their ranks, that it is now almost impossible to draw the precise line which separates the gentleman from the *roturier.* The social rank of an Englishman depends upon his wealth, his political influence, and his personal character—not upon arbitrary heraldic distinctions. We do not see, as in Vienna, accomplished families excluded from society because their ancestors were enriched by commerce. We do not see, as in Hungary, ignorant menials assuming ridiculous airs of superiority because they trace their pedigree to some obscure baronial family.

Mr. Alison, devoted as he is to the aristocratic form of government, speaks with strong and just detestation of those odious oligarchies, in which an impassable barrier is placed between the nobility and the people, and all political power is treated as the hereditary privilege of a certain number of families. It is this tyrannical system which has so often converted the progress of liberty into a servile war—a struggle between anarchy on the one hand, and slavery on the other. It is this which causes so many rulers to resent every effort for political emancipation as a conspiracy to rob them of their private property; and which so often excites, with the first ray of popular intelligence, the deadly jealousy of the government, and the vindictive discontent of the subject. In France we have seen one dreadful instance of the consequences which an obstinate adherence to such institutions may produce. There are still European states in which the nobility, though mild and just in the exercise of their power, cling to their exclusive privileges with a tenacity which is beginning to be bitterly resented by the more aspiring of the middle classes. There may be persons to whom an aristocracy constituted upon this system of haughty superiority may appear a singularly chivalrous and interesting race. There may be persons who consider nobility as the ornament of the state —the Corinthian capital of the column—made to be looked at, boasted of, and paid for. We

know that there are tourists who judge of the most important institutions of foreign states, according to their own ideas—not always the most tasteful or refined—of the picturesque; —who detest democracy because the ladies of Cincinnati are cold and repulsive; who adore despotism because the countesses of Vienna are graceful and polite; and who forget the cowardly cruelty of a cold-blooded tyrant, in their admiration of his simple habits and familiar manners. To such judges an English gentleman may appear a far less romantic personage than the imbecile Spaniard, in whose veins stagnates the *blue blood* of Guzman or Mendoza; or than the servile and frivolous Austrian, whose worst fear is a frown from Prince Metternich; whose noblest ambition is to be *crême de la crême,* and whose proudest boast is his descent from a long succession of titled Teutonic boors. To us, and, we have no doubt, to Mr. Alison, the popular constitution of the British aristocracy appears, not merely a ground of pride and pleasure, but a blessing.

It is certain that the higher classes in England are generally opposed to all political reform. But the existence of a strong minority who hold the contrary opinion, is a sufficient proof that their opposition is that of men acting on conviction, not from sordid *esprit de corps.* They would not risk the peace of the country rather than sacrifice their prejudices; and if they had the wish of doing so, they have no longer the power. The time is past when their influence was able to provoke the collision of physical force. The people, when thoroughly roused, can now find legal and constitutional means of redress, which, slow, toilsome, and painful as they may be, are irresistible when perseveringly used. This state of things is not perfect, but it is tolerable and hopeful. We no doubt believe that it would be best for the country if all Englishmen approved of the gradual progress of reform. But as that cannot be, it is well that there should be a strong party whose error is an over cautious wish to retard it. It is well, while there is such an endless variety of opinions, that there should be every security against their result being wrong on the more dangerous side.

If the character of the British aristocracy is favourable to the temperate progress of reform, that of the popular party, generally speaking, is, in our opinion, scarcely less so. This is an assertion which we are aware will find many opponents, and none more strenuous than Mr. Alison. But it must be recollected that the Englishmen of the present generation have passed through an ordeal of no common severity—an ordeal which would have driven most nations frantic with party animosity and triumphant exultation. We do not say that they have borne it without some degree of dangerous excitement. But if the great constitutional change of 1832 has encouraged the hopes of a few crazy demagogues—if it has fostered for a time the dreams of Chartists and Socialists—how frequently has it not led to the display of temptation manfully resisted, of distress patiently borne, of power soberly exercised, and of political contests forbearingly carried on!

Mr. Alison thinks that a most alarming symptom in the present state of the British nation is 'the constant and uninterrupted increase of crime, through all the vicissitudes of peace and war, unchecked by penal vigilance, undiminished by intellectual cultivation.'—(vii. 11). A most alarming symptom, indeed, and withal a most unaccountable one. But is the last clause of the sentence really supported by the fact? It is unfortunately true that crimes of the less atrocious kind have of late years considerably increased in this country. But among whom have they increased? Among the members of the aristocracy?—among substantial farmers and tradesmen?—among decent peasants and mechanics? Far from it. The morals of the educated ranks have indisputably improved. Generations have passed since the peerage was disgraced by a Ferrers or a Lovat. Our fathers were more scandalized by a breach of the peace, or a life of open indecorum, in a man of rank, than our great grandfathers by murder or felony. The Barrymores and Queensburys of the last generation, were but spiritless successors to such men as Mohun and Charteris, the bravos and libertines of Queen Anne's golden days. Noble lords now find it easy to acquire an unenviable notoriety by frolics which would have appeared ingloriously tame and tranquil to the Mohocks of the last century. They have the honour of a trial before the Lord Chief-Justice for breaking the head of a single constable, while their ancestors were hardly carried to Bow Street for running half a dozen through the body. Serious crime, in short, is now almost wholly confined to the lowest of the populace. Vice has spread precisely in that direction in which it was not opposed by 'intellectual cultivation.' This is a very natural effect of advancing civilisation. In a barbarous community, crime is almost universal. In a well governed community, it concentrates itself in the most ignorant and most destitute classes; but the general enmity which narrows its limits increases its intensity. In such a country as Afghanistan or Caffraria, almost every man is occasionally guilty of violence

and dishonesty; but the professed outcasts from society are comparatively few. In such a country as England, nineteen men in twenty are incapable, under any ordinary circumstances of temptation, of a criminal misdemeanour; but there is a large class who entirely subsist by the practice of petty depredation. But why should Mr. Alison pronounce this last stronghold of vice impregnable? Why are our means of improvement unequal to finish what they have so well begun? We do not, indeed, venture to hope, that our posterity will ever regard a burglar or a pickpocket with the surprise and curiosity with which we regard a riotous peer of the realm—as a curious specimen of a singular and nearly extinct species. But it will at least be admitted, that the instruction which has produced a change scarcely less striking in the higher ranks, has yet to exert its full influence upon that class of the community which stands most in need of its benefits.

Whether the advance of civilisation will necessarily draw with it an advance of political wisdom, let the experience of posterity decide. Hitherto it will scarcely be denied to have done so. We gather from various passages in Mr. Alison's history, that he considers the English constitution, until modified by the Reform Bill, to have been admirably adapted to the state of the nation. Was it equally adapted to the state of the nation three centuries before? Is it not probable, that if that constitution had practically existed in the days of Tyler or Cade, it would have led to anarchy and ruin? This is at least a proof, that at the end of the seventeenth century a degree of popular influence had become useful and necessary, which would have been highly dangerous in the fourteenth or fifteenth. May not a similar improvement have taken place between 1688 and 1842? Might not the restraints swept away by the Reform Bill have become as exasperating to our descendants, as the absolute rule of the Tudors and Stuarts to our ancestors?

It is certainly possible that the present year may be the turning point of British civilisation. It is even possible that the British constitution has reached, if it has not overshot, the utmost limit which popular power can safely be allowed to attain, in any community liable to human vice and folly. We only remind our readers that this assertion has been a hundred times made, and a hundred times refuted. In every stage of unbalanced imperfection, the constitution has been extolled as the masterpiece of human wisdom. One part of it after another has been pronounced the keystone of the fabric, and has yet been discovered to be a mere excrescence.

In all ages of British history there have been men, deficient neither in sense nor in honesty, who thought that the growth of liberty should have stopped short precisely when they first became acquainted with it. Such were the men who would have rejected the *Habeas Co pus* act because it was omitted in 1216; and who opposed the Reform Bill because it was not thought of in 1688. And we have no doubt that there were honest Conservatives in the ninth and thirteenth centuries, who dreaded King Alfred as a radical reformer, and thought *Magna Charta* a fatal innovation. We are none of those who affect contempt for the present or former state of freedom in this country. We avow our faith in British superiority, and our love for British institutions. But we think it presumption, we might almost say impiety, to speak of any system of human origin as sacred from decay and from improvement.

Supposing, however, that in England political innovation is not likely to produce the anarchy of the French Revolution, it is still, in Mr. Alison's opinion, destined to put an end to her prosperity by more lingering means. Two centuries, as nearly as we can gather, are the longest term which he assigns for her independent existence; and the principal causes from which he anticipates her ruin, are the neglect of national defence, and the existence of the national debt. His only plan of safety appears to be, to increase our present expenditure by several millions yearly; to fortify London; to enlarge our naval force; and to establish an effectual sinking fund. But he acknowledges that no government could at the present time carry through such a system as this, and therefore avowedly despairs of the republic.

It is our intention, as we have elsewhere noticed, carefully to avoid all questions relating merely to party politics. We shall therefore permit Mr. Alison to assume, that of late years the resources of the British empire have really been suffered to remain dormant to an extent which the present state of our foreign relations renders in the highest degree imprudent. But we are astonished to hear him calling this an 'extraordinary decline,' and averring that its 'immediate cause is to be found in the long-continued and undue preponderance, since the peace, of the popular part of the constitution.'—(vii. 777). When, we would ask, was it otherwise? When did the English nation, or the English government, show themselves wary in providing for remote dangers? How did our ancestors display that far-sighted prudence which Mr. Alison boasts as the characteristic merit of aristocratic governments? By leaving the Thames

exposed to the Dutch fleet in 1667? by allowing 5,000 daring Highlanders to overrun half England in 1745? by their admirable state of military preparation in 1756, in 1775, and in 1793? The truth is, that the British people have for generations been as impatient of vigilance and precaution in time of peace, as they are daring and obstinate in actual war. The present generation may have inherited the reckless imprudence of their ancestors; but we think they would find considerable difficulty in surpassing it.

Mr. Alison, however, to our utter perplexity, fixes upon the sixty years preceding the peace of 1815, as an example of the mighty effects of 'combined aristocratic direction and democratic vigour.'—(x. 981). He even maintains, that 'if to any nation were given, for a series of ages, the combined wisdom and energy of England, from the days of Chatham to those of Wellington, it would infallibly acquire the empire of the world.'—(x. 982). This, if we glance at the history of that period, will appear strange language. A court intrigue cut short the triumphs of Chatham by an abrupt and inglorious peace. Those of Wellington were achieved by the high qualities of a single individual, in spite of the obstacles thrown in his way by an imbecile government. And against these successes are to be set off the loss of the American provinces, the wilful blunders of the revolutionary war, and the Walcheren expedition. We are not insensible to the glory acquired by the national character during the interval of which Mr. Alison speaks. We are aware that neither Lord North nor Mr. Pitt could incapacitate British soldiers and sailors from doing their duty. But they could, and did, employ the national energies in such a manner as to deprive them of their reward; and it is doubly mortifying to an Englishman to find his countrymen, after a useless display of strength and courage, baffled and dishonoured by the folly or corruption of an irresponsible oligarchy.

Mr. Alison has given us a very clear and comprehensive history of the national debt. Its present state he is inclined to view in the most gloomy light; but this feeling of despondency by no means interferes with his admiration of the statesman to whose unparalleled profusion we owe its sudden and enormous increase. His principal arguments in defence of Mr. Pitt's system of finance are two; the absolute necessity of contracting immense obligations, and the effectual provision made for their speedy discharge. On the former point, we shall at present say nothing. It is, as we shall soon see, Mr. Alison's own opinion, that the loans raised during the war were both extravagantly large, and lamentably misapplied. But that war was necessary and that ample supplies were required to support it, we are not prepared to deny. Of the sinking fund Mr. Alison speaks in terms of exaggerated, and to us incomprehensible, rapture. He considers it worthy, as a scientific conception, to rank with 'the discovery of gravitation, the press, and the steam-engine.' Surely we are not to believe that Mr. Pitt was the first demonstrator of the simple theorem, that a sum of money accumulating at five per cent will quadruple itself in twenty-eight years. Nor can we imagine that the natural and obvious plan of forming a fund on this principle, for the reduction of the National debt, had failed to occur to hundreds of arithmeticians from the very first year in which that debt existed. The *expediency* of the plan is another matter. That is a question on which the best-informed financiers have differed, and still differ. If Mr. Pitt, and Mr. Pitt alone, judged rightly on this point, he undoubtedly deserves high credit, not as a discoverer in political arithmetic, but as a practical statesman. Even in this respect, indeed, we are inclined to doubt both the originality and the correctness of his opinion. But we cannot think that the mere *possibility* of his scheme could long escape the notice of any man capable of working a sum in compound interest.

This marvellous invention is sufficient, in Mr. Alison's opinion, to atone for all Mr. Pitt's financial errors: and yet, by his own showing, these were neither few nor trifling. We pass over his just and forcible remarks on the ruinous system of borrowing in the three per cents; and on the undue extents to which the funding system was carried. These faults, serious as they were, are dust in the balance, compared with the one great blunder of Mr. Pitt's financial policy. We allude to the obvious, the glaring disproportion between the sacrifices and the exertions which the nation made under his direction. He lavished the wealth of England as if he expected to finish the war by one convulsive effort, while he husbanded her other resources so as to ensure its lasting for a whole generation. He wasted the courage of his countrymen in colonial expeditions—he kept eighty thousand of the finest troops in the world in inglorious repose—and he paid Russian and German armies, incomparably inferior in the most formidable qualities of the soldier, to face the enemy on the continent. 'Here,' as Mr. Alison truly and pointedly remarks, 'lay the capital error of Mr. Pitt's financial system, considered with reference to the warlike operations it was intended to promote—that while the former was calculated for a temporary effort only, and

based on the principle of great results being obtained in a short time by an extravagant system of expenditure, the latter was arranged on the plan of the most niggardly exertion of the national strength, and the husbanding of its resources for future efforts, totally inconsistent with the lavish dissipation of its present funds.'—(v. 600). Consider for a moment to what this admission amounts. Simply to this —that Mr. Pitt expended 150 millions of the national treasure without the smallest reasonable chance of any decisive advantage in return! This he did at a moment when half the sum, judiciously applied, would have spared a subsequent expense of 500 millions to England, and twenty years of bloodshed and desolation to Europe. And all this is to be forgiven because he abhorred the French Revolution, and established the sinking fund! Mr. Alison, zealous as he is in Mr. Pitt's defence, has most satisfactorily confirmed the bitter sentence of his enemies, that his war administration, from 1793 to 1799, was at once the most reckless, and the most feeble, that ever disgraced a British cabinet.

Mr. Alison, in concluding his dissertation on the national debt, coolly states that, by the abolition of the sinking fund, 'irretrievable ultimate ruin has been brought upon the state.' —(v. 616). We would fain dissent from this startling conclusion, and we shall endeavour to state a few plain reasons which induce us to look upon the present state of our finances, not indeed without anxiety, but still with cheerfulness and hope.

Mr. Alison gives two reasons for his prediction of ruin from the national debt, one of which, at least, he makes no attempt to prove. 'Not only,' he says, 'is the burden now fixed upon our resources inconsistent with the permanent maintenance of the national independence, but the steady rule has been terminated under which alone its liquidation could have been expected.'—(v. 616). The latter of these two propositions we in substance admit, but the former we greatly doubt. We admit that there is no immediate prospect of any considerable reduction in the amount of the national debt; but we trust that there is every prospect that the resources of the nation will continue to increase so as to make that amount comparatively immaterial.

Let us look to the past history of our finances. During the American war, the mad misgovernment of the sovereign and his ministers increased the national debt by more than 100 millions in seven years. In 1783, its whole amount was 240 millions—more than three-fourths of the revenue was eaten up by its interests—and yet, since all parties agreed that the country was on the verge of bankruptcy, it is but fair to conclude that the national expenditure was as large as any reasonable scale of taxation could supply. The wisest statesmen spoke of our prospects as despondently, if not quite as poetically, as Mr. Alison does at present. And yet we know that, if our present debt were no larger than that of 1783, we could, if it were thought advisable, pay it off in ten or twelve years, merely by applying to its reduction the surplus of our present annual income. But the vast strength of the British empire was to be proved in a far more wonderful manner. In 1793 broke out the most dreadful war in modern history. With two brief intervals it lasted twenty-three years. The wealth of England, squandered as it was with wasteful prodigality, was found sufficient to nourish the contest throughout the whole of Europe. In 1815, peace returned, and the British people found themselves nearly 900 millions in debt; and yet their annual expenditure more than tripled the interest of this enormous sum—a proof that the nation, which thirty years before had been nearly ruined by a debt of 240 millions, was now able to support with safety, though not without suffering, a burden nearly four times as large! Have we since become less able to bear it ? Have our energies been paralyzed by this tremendous pressure? Let Mr. Alison himself answer the question. 'Five-and-twenty years of uninterrupted peace have increased in an extraordinary degree the wealth, population, and resources of the empire. The numbers of the people during that time have increased nearly a half; the exports and imports have more than doubled; the tonnage of the commercial navy has increased a half; and agriculture, following the wants of the increased population of the empire, has advanced in a similar proportion.'—(vii. 774). Surely if we go no further, there is even here ground for hope. It is easy to see that the increase of our national incumbrances, rapid as it has been, has been less rapid than that of our national resources; that we now bear a debt of 800 millions, with less difficulty than we bore one of 80 millions, a century ago.

Let us suppose that in 1783, some soothsayer had hazarded such a prediction as the following:—' It is at present believed, that a long interval of undisturbed peace and rigid economy will barely save the country from open bankruptcy. I aver that in ten years England shall be struggling for existence with the mightiest prince in the world. For twenty years her resources shall be lavished with a profusion never before imagined; and yet, when the trial is over, it shall be found that all her reckless extravagance has barely enabled her embarrassments to keep pace with the vigorous growth of her prosperity.' How wild would such a prophecy have appeared, even to the most penetrating statesmen! Yet we know that it would have been literally fulfilled. We have borne the debt, which sixty years ago seemed so overwhelming; we have survived a sudden addition of 650 millions to its amount; for a quarter of a century we have thriven and flourished under this monstrous load, and we can already look back with thankfulness to a time when it tasked our strength far more severely than at present. And now, it is dogmatically assumed that it must crush us after all! Surely there is no reason why the progress of British prosperity should for the first time during so many ages, be suddenly arrested. And if this does not happen, who will pronounce it impossible that our descendants may look upon the debt of 1816 as lightly as we look upon the debt of 1783?

These are the considerations which incline us to hope that the national debt has not yet outrun our ability to bear it. We will now give our reasons for thinking that it is not likely to do so, and that it may even fail to keep pace with the future progress of the national wealth, as it has hitherto done. The national debt has now existed about one hundred and fifty years; and no addition has ever been made to its amount, except in time of war. Now, during this period, there have been no less than seven important wars, all perilous and burdensome, and one in particular beyond all comparison the most expensive in which this or any other nation was ever engaged. The present is the only peace, for more than a century past, which England has enjoyed during so many as ten successive years. And, upon the whole, more than seventy of the last hundred and fifty years, or about one year in every two since the origin of the debt, have been employed in active hostilities. This proportion is remarkably, indeed almost unprecedently large. During that part of the seventeenth century which preceded the Revolution, only one year in four was occupied by war, and only one in seven by foreign war. During the sixteenth century, the proportion was about one year in five. It is therefore clear that the increase of the national debt has been hitherto promoted by an unusual succession of difficulties; and it does not seem unreasonable to think that, according to the usual course of human events, so long a period of trouble and danger may probably be succeeded by one of comparative tranquillity.

But let us suppose the worst. Let us suppose that England is next year plunged in a fresh struggle with enemies as formidable, and a war administration as imbecile, as in 1793. We have no doubt that, backed by the obstinate courage and vast resources of the British people, the most incapable ministry would sooner or later achieve a triumphant peace. But the result of a prolonged and mismanaged war would of course be a heavy addition to our present burdens. In such a case we admit that national bankruptcy might appear close at hand. But does even this imply loss of national independence? It is now only fifty years since France underwent a national bankruptcy of the most disastrous kind. Is she now less formidable or less prosperous than before that misfortune? But we should not fear even this; for we do not believe that any amount of embarrassments would compel England to so degrading an expedient. Even in so dismal an emergency as we are supposing, we will not doubt that the national spirit would be found equal to the trial. We acknowledge that fearful sacrifices might be necessary—sacrifices which would be bitterly felt by every family in the united kingdom—sacrifices which might long impede the advance of prosperity and civilisation. But that a nation containing twenty millions of the Anglo-Saxon race, crowned and strengthened by a century and a half of foreign glory and domestic freedom, could be deprived of its European rank by pecuniary embarrassments, is what we cannot bring ourselves to think possible.

We have attempted, we trust with proper courtesy and forbearance, to express our dissent from some of Mr. Alison's political opinions. But there are passages in his work which we own have made us feel some difficulty in preserving this tone of moderation. We allude to the spirit of contempt and suspicion in which he occasionally permits himself to speculate on the motives and probable conduct of the reforming party in this country. When he predicts the speedy ruin of the British empire from the progress of democratic innovation, we admit that we have no right to complain. The utmost which such a prediction imputes to the most democratic politician, is an error of judgment. But when he accuses the liberal party in England of meditating the most atrocious acts of violence and treachery, and that upon mere conjecture, we certainly find it difficult to restrain our indignation. And we think that these calumnies are rendered, if possible, more offensive by the calm affectation of historical impartiality with which they are delivered. After relating with just abhorrence the atrocities committed by the British troops, in storming some of the Spanish fortresses, he concludes his remarks with the following reflection:—' A consideration of these mournful scenes, combined with the recollection of the mutual atrocities perpetrated by both parties on each other in England during the wars of the Roses, the horrors of the Tyrone rebellion in Ireland, the cold-blooded vengeance of the Covenanters after the battle of Philiphaugh, the systematic firing and pillage of London during Lord George Gordon's riots in 1780, and the brutal violence in recent times of the Chartists in England, suggest the painful doubt whether all mankind are not at bottom the same, in point of tendency to crime, when exposed to the influence of the same temptations; and whether there do not lie, smouldering beneath the boasted glories of British civilisation, the embers of a conflagration as fierce, and a devastation as widespread, as those which followed and disgraced the French Revolution.'—(ix. 821). Taken in its literal sense, this passage is a mere truism. Not only are Englishmen capable of such atrocities as disgraced the French Revolution, but they will infallibly be guilty of them, if they are ever situated as the French were fifty years ago. Deprive the British people of their free constitution, oppress and degrade them for a century as Louis XV. oppressed and degraded the French, and you will make them what the great body of the French nation was in 1789—a mob of ignorant, degraded, vindictive serfs. But it is impossible to mistake the insinuation which Mr. Alison really intends to convey. No one can seriously suppose that he feels real surprise and alarm at finding that his countrymen are not intrinsically exempt from the ordinary vices of human nature. He clearly wishes to impress his readers with the fear, that the *present* temper of the English nation resembles that of the French in 1793; and that the progress of reform in this country is likely to terminate in a violent revolution. It is against this conjecture that we wish to protest.

Nothing can be clearer than that the virtues of our national character do not belong to us by birthright. Two thousand years ago, the inhabitants of Britain offered human sacrifices at Stonehenge. Eight hundred years after, our Saxon ancestors, in morals and humanity, were much upon a par with a modern South Sea islander. The Danes and Normans were some centuries later still in abandoning their savage habits. All this does not, of course, prevent us from claiming a place for the modern English among the most enlightened nations of the world; but it induces us to attribute their sympathy with the fallen, their aversion to blood, their generous spirit of fair play, purely to the humanizing effect of free institutions and protecting laws. For 150 years, the British constitution, however imperfect in some particulars, has been, upon the whole, one of the best that ever existed; and even for some centuries earlier, the English had enjoyed more political freedom, and personal security, than almost any nation in the world. These blessings have done much to improve our character; but they have not eradicated the innate passions and weakness of humanity. They have made us a generous and humane nation; but they have not made us incapable of ever becoming otherwise. The descendants of twenty generations of English gentlemen continue to be born with the same natural propensities as the nursling of an Indian wigwam. Send them to be educated in Australia or Sumatra, and they will grow up cannibals and barbarians like their comrades. Had Howard or Romilly been kidnapped in their infancy by a Pawnee war party, they would have undoubtedly acquired a taste for stealing horses, taking scalps, and massacring prisoners. In the same manner, had the English people been trodden down by tyrants when their liberties were insecure, they would have become cowardly, cruel, and revengeful. They may still become so, if those liberties should ever be abandoned. But whether this is probable—whether they are likely deliberately to resume the savage habits so long shaken off—this is the true question at issue.

The examples cited by Mr. Alison can mislead no one. They occurred at remote times, or under extraordinary circumstances. He might as well argue the probability of a bloody rebellion from the crimes of Good, or Greenacre, as from the sacking of San Sebastian, or the violence of the Chartist mobs. The question to which his observations point, is this:—whether there are symptoms of an approaching civil war in the British empire. He appears inclined to answer in the affirmative; but how does he support his opinion? We naturally ask whether the British are a sanguinary nation? He tells us that they were so 400 years ago. We ask whether the great body of the people are attached to the laws? He tells us that there have occurred three or four destructive riots during the last half century. We ask whether British citizens are likely to rob and murder their peaceable neighbours? He tells us that British soldiers are sometimes guilty of violence in towns taken by storm. We admit the facts, but we deny that they afford any criterion of the ordinary temper of the nation. We do not flatter ourselves that we are differently

constituted from the savage warriors of the middle ages, or the brutal rioters of the last generation. We found our hopes of avoiding their example, simply upon the obvious difference of circumstances. When the English return to the barbarism of the 15th century, or the fanaticism of the 17th, then they will treat their political opponents as the Yorkists treated the Lancastrians, or the Covenanters the Royalists. When the mass of the English nation becomes as crazy or as depraved as the madmen and ruffians of the No Popery mob, then they will imitate the plunder and violence of 1780. When English citizens engage in political contests with the excitement of soldiers in a desperate attack, then they will accompany political success with the atrocities of a victorious storming party. All this was really the case in France. In 1789, the French populace were as barbarous as the Yorkists, as fanatical as the Covenanters, as depraved as the lowest follower of Lord George Gordon, as hardened by suffering, as mad with triumph, and as thirsty for revenge, as Picton's grenadiers when they carried Badajos. But the violence of human passion is generally proportioned to the provocation received. Men do not feel the same fury at the refusal of a political privilege, as at a tyranny which makes their lives miserable. The English are on the whole a free and happy nation. They may wish to improve their condition, and the wish may be perfectly justifiable; but their present political state is at least tolerable. The progress of reform in England has long been peaceful and constitutional. The Catholic might be indignant when he was refused a fair chance of public honours and profits; the citizen of Birmingham or Manchester might complain when he was denied a representative in the legislature; but they could not feel like the French peasantry under the feudal laws. The measures which they demanded might be anxiously desired, but they were not matter of life and death. Men might dislike Mr. Perceval when he refused Catholic emancipation, or the Duke of Wellington when he opposed Parliamentary reform; but it was impossible that they should hate them as the French populace hated Foulon and Berthier. Angry partisans might be found to abuse them in the papers, or even to throw mud at their windows; but it was not in human nature that any one should wish to hang them upon a lamp-post.

Still we cannot wonder at the sombre influence which Mr. Alison's anxious and prejudiced imagination exercises upon his judgment of the future, when we see how strangely it perverts his memory of the past. Singular as it may appear, he actually discovers a resemblance between the agitation of the Reform Bill, and the excesses of the French Revolution. Now we, in common with numerous writers of the liberal persuasion, have more than once remarked, with satisfaction and triumph, the circumstances which attended the great constitutional change of 1832. A desperate struggle, a complete victory, an important transfer of political power—all took place without the loss of life, or the confiscation of an acre.

But this is not the most remarkable part of the transaction. If the moderation of the popular party had been remarked and admired at the time, we should have thought the example less striking. But it was not so. Not only did the general tranquillity pass as a thing of course, but the few and slight symptoms of insubordination which did appear, excited universal alarm and indignation. Tumultuous assemblies, seditious harangues, and menacing outcries, were deplored as amounting in themselves to unprecedented atrocities. If a rabble of thoughtless rioters cheered for a republic, or displayed a tri-colour flag, words were found wanting to characterize the portentous act. A violent party journal ventured to threaten popular violence, and received from the general resentment an opprobrious *soubriquet* which is not yet forgotten. It is well known that the Duke of Wellington was, for the moment, most unjustly indeed, but naturally and excusably, one of the least popular men in England. He was known to be the strenuous opponent of a measure which the great body of the nation sincerely believed to be indispensable; and he was reported, we believe most falsely, to have accompanied the expression of his disapprobation with a haughty and contemptuous threat. An angry mob followed his carriage with hisses, and threw stones at the windows of Apsley House; and throughout all England one party was transported with rage and dismay, and the other overwhelmed with shame and sorrow. Men of all opinions, in short, were shocked and scandalized to find, that in England the surface of society was ruffled by a movement which in most countries would have broken up its very foundations. We would not be thought to palliate the partial irregularities which did occur. Riot and insult may be almost as criminal in a free citizen, as murder and plunder in an ignorant slave. But we may be permitted to exult in a national temper which leaves those irregularities so little excuse. Nobody thought of pausing among the massacres of 1792, to complain of abusive clamours or broken windows. And surely there is a strong presump-

tion of the ordinary gentleness of an individual, when he overwhelms his friends with surprise and consternation by a slight frown or a peevish murmur.

Such is not Mr. Alison's reasoning. He remembers only the panic of the Conservative party, and forgets the insufficiency of the causes which excited it. In his fourth chapter, he has made some strong and just remarks on the infatuation of the French nobility, in deserting their country in a body, almost on the first appearance of danger. In a note to this passage, he quotes the pointedly expressed, but very feeble apology of M. de Chateaubriand, which in effect amounts to this— that the French aristocracy ought not to be blamed, because the danger was fearful and imminent, and because no one, living in a peaceful country, can tell whether he himself would have behaved better in such an emergency. The answer to all this is perfectly obvious. M. de Chateaubriand's arguments may induce us to look upon cowardice and folly as venial faults; but cannot possibly prove that the French nobility were brave or wise men. We perfectly agree with him, that it is the height of presumption to speak with violent indignation of persons who, in trying circumstances, have failed in wisdom and courage; and that no man can decide, without trial, whether he possesses such qualities himself. This is an excellent reason for pardoning and pitying those who are guilty of imprudence or pusillanimity; but none at all for permitting them to deny their guilt. M. de Chateaubriand's defence is at best merely a plea for mercy, and can never be taken as a ground for acquittal. Our author's reply is very different. He takes M. de Chateaubriand at his word, and says—We *have* been tried, and we have stood the trial; for the English aristocracy did not fly their country when the Reform Bill passed. For the benefit of the incredulous reader, we hold ourselves bound to quote this most astonishing passage entire. ' Admitting,' says Mr. Alison, ' the caustic eloquence of these remarks, the British historian cannot allow their justice. The example of the nobility of his own country, in the disastrous days which succeeded the passing of the Reform Bill, has furnished him with a decisive refutation of them. The flames of Bristol and Nottingham proved that danger had reached their dwellings as well as those of the French noblemen; and if they had, in consequence, deserted their country and leagued with the stranger, it is hardly doubtful that similar excesses would have laid waste the whole fair realm of England. They did not do so; they remained at home, braving every danger, enduring every insult; and who can over-estimate the influence of such moral courage in mitigating the evils which then so evidently threatened their country?' —i. 312). We will fairly compare the circumstances of each case, and for that purpose we will quote from Mr. Alison a few of the threatening symptoms which overcame the resolution of the French noblesse. 'Everywhere the peasants rose in arms, attacked and burnt the chateaux of the landlords, and massacred or expelled the possessors. The horrors of the insurrection of the Jacquerie, in the time of Edward III., were revived on a greater scale, and with deeper circumstances of atrocity. In their blind fury they did not even spare those seigneurs who were known to be inclined to the popular side, or had done the most to mitigate their sufferings, or support their rights. The most cruel tortures were inflicted on the victims who fell into their hands.'—(i. 228).

We gladly spare ourselves and our readers the revolting details which follow. Now, what parallel has Mr. Alison to produce from English history ten years ago? 'The flames of Bristol and Nottingham!' Two isolated riots, *occurring at an interval of several years*—each confined to a single town, and each effectually put down and signally punished by the power of the law. The disturbances of Bristol undoubtedly originated in a political cause; but it is clear that those who were guilty of the chief excesses committed there, acted merely from thirst of plunder. No vindictive feeling was displayed by the mob; no certain plan, no submission to command, was observable in their excesses,—all was indiscriminate thirst for spoil. The fact is, that the civil authorities failed to do their duty in repressing the first symptoms of tumult, and a rabble of thieves and desperadoes seized the opportunity of license and robbery. But in every large community there are numbers of indigent and depraved men, who gladly plunder their neighbours whenever they can do so with impunity. What happened in Bristol would most certainly happen to-morrow in every large city in Europe, if there were reason to suppose that the attempt would not be properly repressed. But how were the British aristocracy peculiarly menaced by a destructive riot in a great commercial town? Had Clumber or Strathfieldsay been burnt to the ground, instead of half-a-dozen streets in Bristol, the case would have been somewhat different. It was not by disturbances at Lyons or Bordeaux that the French noblesse were driven to Coblenz.

We do not know how we can better expose the injustice of Mr. Alison's comparison, than by requesting our readers to imagine what their feelings of astonishment would have been, on finding by the papers, the day after the Reform Bill passed the House of Lords, that the Conservative gentry of England had emigrated in a body! Let them imagine an English emigrant peer landing, in 1832, at Calais or New York. He is eagerly pressed to describe the horrors he has witnessed—to communicate the names of the most illustrious victims—to give the particulars of the new British republic. What is his reply? 'England is in an awful state. At Bristol, only two hundred miles from my family seat, there has been a dangerous riot and great destruction of property. I have been abused in the county newspapers. The *Times* has threatened the aristocracy with brickbats and bludgeons. The Duke of Wellington's windows have been broken.' And all this would have been addressed to men who could remember the Reign of Terror, or the forays of Brandt and Butler. The French emigration is a subject for serious blame; but that of the English aristocracy would have defied the gravity of all Europe. We pity and despise the selfish cowardice of a man who flies from a dangerous conflagration, instead of staying to rescue his family and protect his property. But our pity and contempt give way to a sense of the ludicrous, when we hear of his jumping headlong from a garret window, because a few idlers in the street have raised the cry of fire.

Not only, it seems, are the liberal party in England prepared to imitate the crimes of the French Revolution, but they are, or were, on the point of betraying their country to the actual perpetrators of those enormities. After noticing that Napoleon had intended to follow his descent upon Great Britain by a proclamation, promising 'all the objects which the revolutionary party in this country have ever had at heart,' Mr. Alison proceeds as follows: —'That the French emperor would have been defeated in his attempt, if England had remained true to herself, can be doubtful to no one. . . . . But would she have remained true to herself under the temptation to swerve produced by such means? This is a point upon which there is no Briton who would have entertained a doubt, till within these few years; but the manner in which the public mind has reeled from the application of inferior stimulants since 1830, and the strong partiality to French alliance which has grown up with the spread of democratic principles, has now suggested the painful doubt, whether Napoleon did not know us better than we knew ourselves, and whether we could have resisted those methods of seduction which had proved fatal to the patriotism of so many other people.

. . . . The warmest friend to his country will probably hesitate before he pronounces upon the stability of the English mind under the influence of the prodigious excitement likely to have arisen from the promulgation of the political innovations which Napoleon had prepared for her seduction. If he is wise, he will rejoice that in the providence of God his country was saved the trial, and acknowledge with gratitude the inestimable obligations which she owes to the illustrious men whose valour averted a danger under which her courage, indeed, would never havè sunk, but to which her wisdom might possibly have proved unequal.'—(v. 379).

We have frequently found occasion to differ from Mr. Alison, but this is one of the few passages of his work which we have read with serious regret and deep displeasure. Its meaning is simply this—that had Napoleon landed in England, those Englishmen who approved of the reforms he intended to promise, would have deserted their countrymen and joined his army. The calumny is most disingenuously enveloped in the language of pretended self-abasement; but this disguise is too slight to conceal its real nature for a moment. The suspicion expressed by Mr Alison is obviously applicable only to his political opponents. It is therefore of *their* honour alone that he feels all this timid distrust. The temptation of which he expresses so much anxious dread, is one which could not have attracted *him;* the merit which he is so modestly reluctant to vaunt, is one in which *he* could have had no share. This candid renunciation of other people's credit has a twofold advantage; for it combines the grace of humility, with the pleasure of slander.

We might easily show that the political opinions of what Mr. Alison is pleased to call the revolutionary party, are perfectly consistent with the national virtues, and even with the wholesome prejudices, of true-born Britons. We might plead, that an honest Englishman may consider the British constitution as the best in the world, without thinking it absolutely perfect; that he may religiously believe himself able to beat three Frenchmen, without longing to be perpetually employed in doing it. We might plead that it is one thing to desire the support of France abroad, and another to invoke her interference at home; one thing to wish for reform by act of parliament, and another to attempt it by high treason. But we prefer giving Mr. Alison a practical proof of the dangerous nature of such rash and odious imputations. We gather two maxims from the elaborate and insidious passage we have just quoted. Every man who wishes for any alterations in the British constitution, is willing to become a traitor to obtain them. Every man who wishes for the alliance of a foreign power is willing to be its slave. Let us see whether these rules will not cut both ways. Mr. Alison is a conscientious opponent of Parliamentary reform, and a warm admirer of Russia. Suppose a Russian Army to land at Leith, and to proclaim their intention of repealing the Act of 1832. Is Mr. Alison conscious of the slightest inward misgiving lest he should be tempted to assist the invaders? Does he not feel the same instinctive scorn of such treachery, as of theft, or forgery, or any other infamous crime? And what would be his sensations if such a suspicion were publicly expressed, and if some Whig friend of his own were to answer it by moralizing upon the frailty of human resolution, and expressing thankfulness that the test is not likely to be applied? We know and feel that in such a case we could depend upon the loyalty of every respectable Conservative as upon our own; and we are heartily sorry, for Mr. Alison's own sake, that he cannot bring himself to feel the same honest confidence in the opposite party.

British loyalty has not, in Mr. Alison's opinion, survived British honour and patriotism. 'The more advanced of the present generation,' he says, 'still look back to the manly and disinterested loyalty with which, in their youth, the 4th of June was celebrated by all classes, with a feeling of interest increased by the mournful reflection, that amidst the selfish ambition and democratic infatuation of subsequent times, such feelings, in this country at least, must be numbered among the things that have been.'—(viii. 22). We certainly shall not attempt to maintain that the same feverish and thoughtless loyalty now prevails in England, which was so common thirty or forty years ago. We acknowledge our belief that the men of the present generation would scarcely abandon an important political measure, because it was understood to be repugnant to the private opinion of a 'good old King,' or even of a good young Queen. But we do sincerely believe that there never was a period when Englishmen felt more solid, sober, trustworthy attachment to the throne than at present. No man having the slightest pretension to political importance, has, of late years, expressed dislike of the monarchical form of government. No man having the least regard for his character, has, with impunity, offered any public insult to the reigning monarch. We do not say this without warrant, for the attempt has been made. It was thought that a young and inexperienced princess might possibly be intimidated by slander and invective. We will not remind Mr. Alison with what party the design originated; but we are sure that he remembers with as much pride and pleasure as ourselves, the signal defeat which it encountered from the generous indignation of the British people. We might go much further than this. We might speak of the general respect, we might almost say the general affection, which is felt for-the present occupant of the throne. We might refer to the kindly warmth with which the name of that august lady is almost invariably mentioned in society —to the universal grief and alarm excited by the late supposed attempts upon her life—to the personal unpopularity which certain zealous Conservatives have incurred by a disrespectful mention of her name. Was the return of the fourth of June, we would ask, hailed with a more exuberant loyalty than that the expression of which made the farthest hills and mountains of Scotland echo back its heart-stirring sounds, on the late royal visit to this quarter of the Island?

We have now given a few sketches of Mr. Alison's opinions respecting his liberal countrymen. The person holding these sentiments is, we believe, a well-educated gentleman, of respectable talents, of extensive historical information, of a benevolent temper, of strong religious feelings, and of a calm and contemplative turn of mind. With all these means and capacities for forming a candid judgment, he has, as we have seen, made up his mind that in 1803 the reforming party in England were prepared to betray their country to Napoleon—that in 1831 they were bent upon imitating the worst excesses of the French Revolution—and at the present moment they would rather see the British empire perish than contribute to its aid at the risk of personal inconvenience. And yet with what contempt and indignation would the author of these imputations listen to the ravings of some poor, angry, ignorant, thick-headed Chartist, about the depraved morals and evil designs of the British aristocracy!

Mr. Alison has shown much good sense and impartiality in his remarks upon the policy of the principal European powers towards France. He speaks with just admiration of the persevering courage displayed by England and Austria; but he notices, with equally just severity, the procrastination, the timidity, the obstinate prejudices, and the unreflecting ignorance of military affairs, which deprived both nations of so many opportunities of victory, and placed such fearful advantages in the hands of their keen and wary antagonist. The errors of Prussia were of a more serious nature; and Mr. Alison has too much sense of moral rectitude not to visit them with deserved indignation. We need not retrace his account of the truly degrading policy in which, for ten years, the rulers of that state persisted. The guilty parties have been punished by the scorn of every European nation, and of none more signally than their own injured countrymen. We think, however, that Mr. Alison shows far too much lenity in his remarks, upon the personal share of Frederick-William in the disgrace of this period. It is clear, from his own statements, that the treaty by which Prussia accepted Hanover from France, as the price of her treason to the cause of Germany, originated in the unprincipled cupidity of the King himself. Such an instance of political depravity deserved far stronger censure than any which Mr. Alison has applied to its author.

The unhappy situation of Prussia from 1795 to 1806 is, in our opinion, a most striking example of what Mr. Alison denies,— the close connection between political impotence and social insecurity. The Prussians are generally considered admirable specimens of the true German character;—brave, generous, honest to a proverb, and distinguished by a simplicity of manners and a kindness of heart, which has often surprised and delighted the traveller, accustomed to the levity of the French, or the reserve of the English. The ardour which they displayed in the struggles of 1806 and 1813, proves that they had felt their disgrace as became an honourable nation. But their rulers were irresponsible, and they were without a remedy. Had Frederick-William been a limited sovereign, Napoleon would have been crushed for ever in the campaign of 1805. Even as it was, the grief and indignation of the people did, too late, what their legitimate interference would have done speedily and effectually. Frederick-William, though not a man of strong sense, was not destitute of all manly feeling. The united voice of his honest and loyal subjects, and the rash insults of the French emperor, at length roused him to a sense of his duty. An army of 120,000 men, who had lain idle in their barracks, while Napoleon was struggling for life and empire in the valley of the Danube, marched to encounter him returning in triumph from Austerlitz. A decisive battle was fought—the Duke of Brunswick completed in the field what the King had begun in the cabinet— and a campaign of six weeks left Prussia the powerless slave of France for as many years. Never, with one terrible exception, did a civilized sovereign meet with a more deserved, a more signal, or a more strictly personal chastisement, than Frederick-William. The overthrow of his brave army, the capture of his capital, the misery of his faithful subjects, the shameful defection of his most trusted lieutenants—all this was but the more ordinary part of his punishment. He was compelled to attend at Tilsit, humiliated by his political ruin, and embarrassed by his intellectual incapacity—the helpless suppliant of the triumphant Napoleon, and the acute and accomplished Alexander. He was compelled to endure in person the insulting neglect, or the supercilious condescension of his ungenerous enemy, and his faithless ally. He saw his high-minded queen throw herself in tears at the feet of the French emperor, and receive an obdurate repulse. He returned home to witness her melancholy and lingering death—the result of humbled-pride and hopeless sorrow. He survived these miserable events many years—he lived to see his country free and victorious, and he ended his life in peace and prosperity. His early want of faith had brought upon him such a prompt and overwhelming punishment as few princes have undergone in this life; and the honourable consistency of his subsequent conduct may induce us to hope that so dreadful a lesson was not inflicted in vain.

We are glad to find that Mr. Alison's strong monarchical principles have not tempted him to imitate certain historians of that persuasion, in their perverted accounts of the Peninsular war. He relates the many indelible disgraces incurred by the Spanish nation in his usual tone of calm forbearance; but he does not disguise his opinion, that Spain owed to England alone her escape—if escape it can be called, from becoming a French province. We acknowledge, however, that while we admire the steady equanimity of Mr. Alison's remarks, we have occasionally, in reading this part of his history, felt more inclination to sympathize with the scornful indignation of Colonel Napier. We cannot help thinking that the resistance of the Spanish nation, fortunate as it was for Europe, was actually more discreditable to themselves than the tamest submission. Submission would at least have enabled us to suppose that the people were not averse to the French yoke. Thus the passive conduct of the Italian states in 1796, did not destroy the military reputation of their citizens. It merely proved that their unhappy political condition had, as might be expected, extinguished public spirit among them; and, therefore, no one was surprised at the bravery afterwards displayed by the Italian corps of Napoleon's army. But the struggles of Spain were as furious as they were feeble; and their rancorous violence displayed the resentment of the nation, without disguising its weakness. They made it clear, in short,

that every Spaniard hated the French, but that very few had the courage to meet them in the field. Many of our readers will remember the enthusiastic sympathy which the Peninsular contest excited in England. Orators declaimed upon the impotence of military discipline to withstand righteous enthusiasm; as if military discipline tended to extinguish enthusiasm, or as if enthusiasm were impossible except in a righteous cause. Poets wrote sonnets about the power of armies being a visible thing, while national spirit was invisible and invincible; as if the spirit which impelled a brave German to march manfully to battle, had been less formidable, or less noble, than that which prompted a Spanish peasant to lurk in some remote *sierra*, shooting stragglers and robbing convoys. But the unsparing exposures of Colonel Napier at once and for ever fixed the opinion of the English nation upon the events of the Spanish war; the substance of his narrative is confirmed, generally speaking, by the more lenient statements of Mr. Alison; and their united testimony shows, that the Spanish nation displayed in that struggle a want of common sense, of common honesty, of veracity, of humanity, and of gratitude, scarcely to be paralleled in the history of Bengal or of China.

To some of our readers—though to none, we think, who have given much attention to the subject—these observations may appear unjust and illiberal. Their justice is soon vindicated. Every British writer has allowed that the history of the regular Spanish armies, during the Peninsular war, is a mere tissue of folly, cowardice, and disaster. The shameful names of Somosierra, Rio Seco, Belchite, and Ocana, are sufficient to recall the long succession of their miserable overthrows. Their sole achievement in the field—the surrender of the French army at Baylen—has long been attributed to its true cause—the unaccountable rashness, and more unaccountable despair, of the unhappy Dupont. A few, and but a few, of the sieges sustained by their towns, have done them more honour. The heroic defence of Gerona stands unrivalled, as an example of Spanish skill and valour. That of Zaragossa, considered merely as a military exploit, was one of far inferior brilliancy. The true glory of that celebrated city consists in the invincible patience with which its defenders endured the ravages of pestilence and famine. That is a species of courage in which the Spaniards have never been deficient. Like many unwarlike nations, they are endued by their moral or physical constitution with a passive courage, under suffering, which is rarely displayed by the bold and hardy soldiers of northern Europe. But, putting this out of the question, it was surely no unparalleled achievement for 30,000 regular troops, aided by 15,000 well-armed peasants, to defend an imperfectly fortified town for six weeks against 43,000 Frenchmen.

There are persons who think the desultory exploits of the *Partidas* sufficient to redeem the honour of Spain; and who judge of Castilian skill and prowess, not from the disgraces of Blake and Cuesta, but from the adventurous feats of Mina and the Empecinado. We own that we attach little importance to the isolated and imperfect successes of such leaders as these. We see little glory in firing from a thicket, or rolling rocks down a ravine, especially at a moment when a regular force was vainly summoning recruits for the open defence of Spanish independence. It was not so that the gallant Tyrolese defended their country. They did not desert their Emperor to ensconce themselves in the fastnesses of their mountains. While a hope remained of resisting the enemy in the open field, they were constantly foremost in the ranks of the Austrian army. The partizan warfare of the Spanish peasantry may captivate romantic imaginations; but such are not the means by which a great nation should assert its independence. The details of modern warfare may wear an aspect of formal routine; but it is in the ranks of disciplined armies, with all their unpoetical accompaniments, that the true post of honour and danger is to be found. A regiment of grenadiers, trudging along the highroad, may be a less picturesque spectacle than a party of brigands wandering among forests and precipices; but if they do their duty, they incur more risk, and perform more service, and therefore deserve more credit. Even were it otherwise, it is not the bravery of a few straggling guerillas that can efface the dishonour incurred by the regular Spanish armies. It would be a poor consolation to a Spaniard, that his country, with a population of twelve millions, and a military force of 70,000 regular soldiers under arms, found her most effectual defenders in a few thousand undisciplined sharpshooters.

The accusation of illiberality we are less careful to answer. We confess that we have no idea of complimenting away the hardly-won glory of our gallant countrymen—of displaying modesty and generosity at the expense of the heroic army which really delivered the Peninsula. Still less are we restrained by any scruple of delicacy from exposing the infamy of that unworthy ally, whose jealousy constantly thwarted our generals; whose cowardice repeatedly betrayed our soldiers; whose imbecility caused our dreadful loss at Albuera; who shamefully deserted our wounded at Talavera; and who actually assassinated our stragglers during the retreat from Burgos. The inflexible justice of Angelo is all that we can grant the Spaniards:—if in the strict letter of history they can find credit or excuse, it is well; if not, let them not seek it from us.

We now come to what we certainly consider the most incomprehensible peculiarity of Mr. Alison's work—the strong and apparently causeless interest which he seems to feel in favour of the Russian nation. If this predilection had displayed itself by misrepresentations of the real history of Russia—by the suppression, or the sophistical palliation, of her numerous political crimes—it would have called for a tone of remonstrance very different from any which Mr. Alison's work has given us occasion to employ. But we have been able to detect no such attempt. Judging solely from the account before us, we should unhesitatingly conclude that the national character of the Russians is very unamiable; that their domestic government is very corrupt; and that their foreign policy is very unprincipled. How far a hostile historian might have aggravated the picture, we shall not venture to pronounce; but certain we are that the ordinary prejudices against Russia require no stronger confirmation than the statements of Mr. Alison. If, after fairly laying the case before his readers, the historian chooses to retain his own prejudices in defiance of his own facts and arguments, we cannot see that we are called upon to interfere. The truth, we suppose, is, that the formidable power and deep policy of Russia have excited in Mr. Alison's mind that species of capricious *quasi*-admiration which good and clever men sometimes feel for certain worthless characters, so long as they are not seriously called upon to form any practical judgment respecting them. The pleasure with which the characters alluded to are contemplated, proceeds entirely from the taste and imagination; and rather resembles our admiration of a striking work of art than our love or esteem for a human being. If this is all that Mr. Alison feels toward Russia, we have little more to say. The prepossession, however, is not such as we should have expected to remark in a British historian of the nineteenth century, nor is its display always regulated by the best taste. Still it may amount to no more than this—that while Mr. Alison acknowledges the numerous faults of the Russian character, he is involuntarily dazzled and attracted by some of its peculiarities. We do not, by any means, sympathize with this feeling; but so long as it does not betray its entertainer into any serious defence of Russian policy, we are content to look upon it as a harmless though somewhat unpleasing caprice.

The most interesting subject of Mr. Alison's history, next to the great Revolution which forms the groundwork of the whole, is undoubtedly the character of the extraordinary man who made that Revolution the instrument of his power. We scarcely know any stronger illustration of the genius and influence of Napoleon Bonaparte, than the simple fact, that for twenty years his life and the history of Europe are convertible terms. During the whole of that time, the annals of the smallest European state would be absolutely unintelligible without a clear view of the policy and character of the French emperor; and, on the other hand, every change of rulers in the pettiest principality—every intrigue at Petersburg or Naples—every motion in the British Parliament—was of immediate and vital concern to Napoleon. This is more than can be said of any other conqueror or statesman in modern times. The direct influence of Louis, Frederick, and Catharine, was comparatively limited. A Russian or a Turk cared little for the invasion of Holland or the Spanish succession; and an Italian was comparatively indifferent to the conquest of Silesia or the division of Poland. But no such supineness prevailed during the wars of the French empire. Wherever the great conqueror was engaged, the breathless attention of all Europe was fixed. Every citizen of every state felt his hopes or his fortunes raised or depressed by the event. The death of an English minister was hastened by the battle of Marengo; the treaty of Tilsit was felt as an object of interest in the deserts of Central Asia; the battle of Leipsic roused or paralysed every European from Cadiz to the North Cape. The French empire, in a word, resembled the talismanic globe of the sorcerers in *Thalaba*, the slightest touch upon which caused the whole universe to tremble.

There are few subjects upon which public opinion has differed more widely than upon the moral character of Napoleon. Thirty years ago, most Englishmen believed him to be one of those wretched monomaniacs who have seemed to feel a pleasurable excitement in tormenting their fellow-creatures. Even now, he is generally considered as a man naturally cold and unfeeling, and hardened by habit into a total indifference to human suffering. But we do not think that either opinion will satisfy any person who impartially examines the present account of his actions and policy.

Mr. Alison has supplied us with a new and very plausible palliation of Napoleon's ambition. He repeatedly and very reasonably insists on the precarious foundation of the French empire, and on the irresistible necessity which compelled its chief at once to dazzle and unite his subjects, by engaging them in successful war. If, indeed, this excuse stood alone, we should think comparatively little of its force. Necessity is the tyrant's plea. No spectacle can be more painfully interesting than that of a character naturally great and noble, whose moral sense has been blunted by the influence of early habit, and the encouragement of vulgar applause. But we feel no such sympathy for the man who knowingly and wilfully prefers his interest to his duty. Many a mind, which would have defied both intimidation and seduction, has been warped and weakened by the imperceptible force of custom; but when the strong temptation is combined with the enervating influence, we may well cease to wonder at its victory. Napoleon, bred, and almost born, a soldier and a revolutionist, preferred unjust war to political extinction. How many legitimate sovereigns have preferred it to undisturbed security!

We have been much gratified by the calm and impartial spirit in which Mr. Alison discusses the general character of this extraordinary man. Indeed, we feel bound to remark, that throughout the whole of the present work, we do not recollect a single case in which the political prejudices of the author, uncharitable as they sometimes appear, have been able to hurry his calm and patient mind into a harsh or hasty condemnation of individuals. His censure of Napoleon's ambition is, as we have seen, lenient almost to excess. Of his other misdeeds, real and imputed, he speaks with equal, though we trust better merited forbearance. He is willing to acquit the First Consul of the mysterious deaths of Wright and Pichegru, which he ascribes to the apprehensive cruelty of the French police—men too well known to have been familiar with every form of violence and treachery. His narrative of the lamented fate of the Duc d'Enghien does the highest credit both to his humanity and his self-command. Nothing can be more feelingly expressed than his commiseration of the brave and innocent sufferer; but he has not permitted it to hurry him into rash or unthinking denunciations against the guilty party. He represents the crime of Napoleon in its true light—not as an act of wanton murder, but as the blind vengeance of a violent man, justly alarmed and enraged by the atrocious attempts of the French Royalists against his life. But there is one scene in Napoleon's career which no sophistry can palliate—which no imagination can elevate—which his most devoted partizans can but endeavour to forget. We allude to the treacherous detention of the

English families travelling in France in 1801. We do not say that none of Napoleon's acts were more criminal; but we think that none were so inconsistent with the character of a great man. His other crimes, heavy as they may be, were at least the crimes of a conqueror and a statesman. They were crimes such as Attila or Machiavel might have committed or approved—crimes of passion, or of deep and subtle policy. The massacre of Jaffa, and the invasion of Spain might have been forgotten by a generation which had witnessed the atrocities of Ismail and Warsaw—which had pardoned Frederick-William for his sordid occupation of Hanover—and Alexander for the vile treachery which wrested Finland from his own brave and faithful ally. The ambition which provokes unjust war—the passions which prompt a violent and bloody revenge—even the craft which suggests deep-laid schemes of political treachery—have but too often been found consistent with many brilliant and useful virtues. But the measure of which we speak displayed the spirit of a Francis or a Ferdinand—the spirit which has peopled Siberia with Polish nobles, and crowded the dungeons of Austria with Italian patriots. It displayed the cold unrelenting spite of a legitimate despot, inured from childhood to the heartless policy of what is called a *paternal* government. We are not partial to a practice in which Mr. Alison frequently indulges—that of attempting to trace the immediate interference of Providence in every remarkable coincidence of human affairs ; but we cannot avoid being struck by a melancholy resemblance between the captivity in which Napoleon ended his life, and the lingering torments which he had wantonly inflicted on ten thousand of his harmless fellow-creatures.

We are pleased to find in Mr. Alison a zealous, though discriminating admirer of the military genius of Napoleon. The contrary judgment has lately been proclaimed by a few military critics, and supported with a vehement and disdainful asperity, which strikes us, to say the least, as singularly ungraceful. This is perhaps most unsparingly and offensively exemplified in a series of essays which appeared some years since in a professional Journal, and which, if we are rightly informed, excited considerable notice among military men. They are understood to be the production of an officer in the British army, well known for his speculations in the theory of war, and possessing, we believe, much experience in actual service. They are full of ingenious reasoning, of contemptuous invective, and of ironical derision.

Now we have not the slightest wish to set up authority against argument. We shall not turn upon this critic and say, 'The oldest and bravest generals in Europe still tremble at the memory of the man whom you undertake to prove a mere fortunate fool:—is it likely that your judgment should be more correct than theirs ?' But we think that the opposition of authority is a good reason, not for suppressing a theory, but for delivering it in modest and tolerant language. We know that argument is a weapon which the weakest may successfully wield, and which the strongest cannot resist. As the Chevalier Bayard complained of the arquebuse, in the hands of a child it may strike down the most valiant knight on earth. We therefore think it no presumption in the youngest ensign in the army to plead against Napoleon's claims to military glory. Let him fairly state his opinion, and fairly endeavour to establish it. The greater the impostor, the more dazzling the illusion—the higher will be our obligation to the bold and keen-sighted advocate who brings him to justice. We do not, therefore, complain of the military critics in question for attempting to place Napoleon's military reputation a step below that of Cope or Mack. But we protest against the advocate's usurping the functions of the judge. We protest against his assuming that he has triumphed—against his referring to the question as one irrevocably settled in his favour—against his pouring upon the accused the contempt and ridicule to which posterity alone can fitly sentence him. This is worse than mere disrespect to the memory of a celebrated man; it is arrogant and ridiculous self-flattery. A century and a half ago Louis XIV. acquired a high reputation as a general. Posterity has weighed and found him wanting. But suppose that a young officer of that day had written of Louis as the critics of whom we speak write of Napoleon. We should have said that he might be a clever, clear-headed man ; but that, if he chose to deliver a paradox in the tone of an oracle, it was his own fault that nobody listened to him. But this is the most favourable point of view. What do we say of the detractors whom posterity has pronounced in the wrong ? What do we say of the slanderers of Marlborough and of Moore ? The destruction of a brilliant but unmerited reputation is the most useful, the most difficult, the most invidious, and therefore, perhaps, the noblest task of an honest investigator of historic truth. But it requires candour and delicacy no less than boldness and acumen. When it is attempted from an obvious sense of duty, we admire the unflinching sincerity of the assailant, even though we condemn his severity. But when he undertakes it in the exultation of superior discernment—when he performs it with the insolence of personal antipathy—his victory will be unhonoured and unsympathized with, and his defeat will be embittered by universal scorn and indignation.

We do not possess the technical knowledge necessary to dissect the criticisms to which we have alluded. We can only judge as unlearned mortals, let scientific tacticians say what they will, always must judge—by general results. We can only consider what Napoleon did, and whether, according to the ordinary doctrine of chances, it is conceivable that he could have done so much had he been a man of no extraordinary powers. Napoleon, then, commanded in person at fourteen of the greatest pitched battles which history has recorded. Five times—at Marengo, Austerlitz, Jena, Friedland, and Wagram—he crushed the opposing army at a blow; finished the war, in his own emphatic phrase, by a *coup-de-foudre;* and laid the vanquished power humbled and hopeless at his feet. Five times —at Borodino, Lutzen, Bautzen, Dresden, and Ligny—he was also decidedly victorious, though with less overwhelming effect. At Eylau the victory was left undecided. At Leipsic, the French were defeated, as is well known, by a force which outnumbered their own as five to three. At Waterloo, it is generally acknowledged that the overthrow of Napoleon was owing, not to any deficiency in skill on his part, but to the invincible obstinacy of the British infantry, who are admitted even by the French accounts, to have displayed a passive courage, of which the most experienced warrior might be excused for thinking human nature incapable. At Aspern alone, to judge from the able account of Mr. Alison, does the partial defeat of the French emperor appear to have been owing to any faulty arrangement of his own. Five of his ten actions were gained over equal or superior forces; and among the generals defeated by him, we find the distinguished names of Wurmser, Melas, Benningsen, Blucher, and above all, the Archduke Charles. We might produce still stronger testimonies. We might relate the glorious successes of his first Italian campaign, in which four powerful armies were successively overthrown by a force comprising, from first to last, but 60,000 men. We might notice his romantic achievements in Egypt and Syria, against a new and harassing system of hostility. We might enlarge on the most wonderful of all his exploits—the protracted struggle which he maintained in the heart of France, with a remnant of only 50,000 men, against the quadruply superior numbers of the Allies. But all this is unnecessary. If the successes to which we have alluded are insufficient to prove that Napoleon was a general of the first order, the reputation of no soldier who ever existed can be considered as established.

If such numerous and extraordinary examples are insufficient to establish a rule, then there is no such thing as reasoning by induction. It is in vain to endeavour to explain away such a succession of proofs. Technical cavils can no more prove that Napoleon was a conqueror by chance, than the two sage Sergeants mentioned by Pope could persuade the public that Lord Mansfield was a mere wit. The common sense of mankind cannot be permanently silenced by scientific jargon. Plain men, though neither lawyers nor mathematicians, see no presumption in pronouncing Alfred a great legislator, or Newton a great astronomer. It is equally in vain to attempt to neutralize the proofs of Napoleon's superiority, by balancing them with occasional examples of rash presumption; or, even did such exist, of unaccountable infatuation. No number of failures can destroy the conclusion arising from such repeated and complete victories. The instances in which fools have blundered into brilliant success are rare; but the instances in which men of genius have been betrayed into gross errors are innumerable. And, therefore, where the same man has brilliantly succeeded and lamentably failed, it is but fair to conclude. that the success is the rule, and the failure the exception. Every man constantly forms his opinions respecting the affairs of real life upon this theory. In literature, in science, in the fine arts, no man's miscarriages are allowed to diminish the credit of his successes. Nobody denies that Dryden was a true poet because he wrote *Maximin ;* for it was more likely that a true poet should write *Maximin* than that a dunce should write *Absalom and Achitophel.* Nobody denies that Bacon was a true philosopher because he believed in alchemy ; for it was more likely that a true philosopher should believe in alchemy, than that an empiric should compose the *Novum Organum.* No classical scholar denies the merit of Bentley's edition of Horace, because he failed in his edition of Milton. No man of taste refuses to enjoy the wit and humour of Falstaff, because the same author imagined the pedantic quibbles of Biron.

We shall not attempt to sketch the personal character of Napoleon. Yet it is a subject upon which, could we hope to do it justice, the ample materials supplied by the present history might well tempt us to linger. No laboured eulogium could impress us with so much admiration for his surpassing genius, as the simple details collected by Mr. Alison.

We never before so clearly appreciated the mighty powers of Napoleon—his boundless fertility of resource—his calm serenity in the most desperate emergencies—his utter ignorance of personal fear—his piercing political foresight—the vast fund of miscellaneous knowledge collected by the almost involuntary operation of his perspicacious and tenacious intellect—the rapid and vigorous reasoning faculties, which applied themselves, with the ease and precision of some exquisite machine, to every subject alike which for an instant attracted his attention.

In his seventy-second chapter Mr. Alison has collected a variety of highly interesting details, respecting the private manners and habits of Napoleon. It is scarcely possible to describe the impression which its perusal leaves on the mind. The strange contrast of warm affection and vindictive hatred, of fiery impetuosity and methodical precision, of royal luxury and indefatigable self-denial, of fascinating courtesy and despotic harshness—the indomitable pride, the vehement eloquence, the magnanimous power of self-command, the fearful bursts of passion—all combine to produce an effect by which the dullest imagination must be enchanted, but which the most versatile genius might fail in depicting. The interest of the portrait is augmented by those minute personal peculiarities on which the romantic devotion of Napoleon's followers has so often dwelt—by the classical features, the piercing glance, the manners, now stern, abrupt, and imperious, now full of princely grace—even by the small plain hat, and the *redingote grise*, which have supplanted the white plume of Henri Quatre in French song and romance. We almost sympathize with the attachment of his soldiers, wild and idolatrous as it was, when we remember Mr. Alison's simple but imposing narrative of the events of the empire—of the congress of Tilsit, the farewell of Fontainbleau, and the unparalleled—the marvellous march to Paris. It is impossible, in reading the striking details which record the personal demeanour of Napoleon, during such scenes as these, not to recall the noble lines in which Southey has described Kehama:

'Pride could not quit his eye,
Nor that remorseless nature from his front
Depart; yet whoso had beheld him then
Had felt some admiration mixed with dread,
    And might have said
That sure he seemed to be the king of men;
Less than the greatest, that he could not be,
Who carried in his port such might and majesty.'

————

Art. II.—*The Life of Augustus Keppel, Admiral of the White, and First Lord of the Admiralty in* 1782-3. By the Hon. and Rev. Thomas Keppel. 2 vols. 8vo. London: 1842.

It is not often that naval subjects are brought under our consideration;—not that we are not fully impressed with the paramount importance of all that relates to this mighty arm of our power, essential, indeed, for the safety and protection of every part of the United Kingdom at home, and of its numerous dependencies abroad, and equally so for that of our valuable and extensive commerce and mercantile shipping. In fact, it so happens that, 'during the piping times of peace,' naval events are seldom of that stirring character as to cause much excitement in the public mind; but the biography of such of our brave naval defenders, who may have had the enviable good fortune of signalizing themselves in fight with the enemy, and of being placed in situations of great trust and responsibility, must always command a prominent place in the annals of the British empire.

Already, the lives of Anson, Howe, St. Vincent, Nelson, Rodney, and Saumarez are before the public; and the wonder is, that a memoir of Keppel, the friend and associate of the first three of these, and we may also add, of Hawke, Saunders, and Duncan, should have been so long delayed. The task, however, though late, is now accomplished, and by one who has proved himself well qualified to do justice to the exploits, the character, and the memory of a meritorious and gallant naval officer; by one who, owing to his first professional choice, is not altogether unacquainted with the naval service; who is descended from the same noble family; and who had access to private as well as official documents, of which he has made a copious and judicious use. In them we find the mental qualities and disposition of Admiral Lord Keppel amply developed—replete with every amiable feature—kind, benevolent and sincere. He was a man liberal in his political opinions, which were those of his family and most intimate friends—Rockingham, Shelburne, Richmond, Burke, Fox, and many others of the Whig party. And if he was not so fortunate, in his long and successful service of more than forty years, almost wholly spent at sea, as to obtain, as commander-in-chief, any great and decisive success against the enemy, such as is usually designated by the name of 'victory,' yet he had his full share in the victories of Hawke, Anson, and Pococke; and achieved signal success in numerous enterprises entrusted to his charge. Equally successful was he in conciliating the good opinion and obtaining the applause of the public, and of his highly distinguished friends;—gaining a moral triumph over those few of his enemies who might be envious of his well-acquired reputation.

The Honourable Augustus Keppel was the second son of the second Lord Albemarle, by Lady Anne Lennox, daughter of Charles first duke of Richmond, and was born the 25th April, 1725. He entered the navy at the early age of ten years, having quitted Westminster school for the cockpit of the Oxford frigate, passed his first two years on the coast of Guinea, and three in the Mediterranean, in the Gloucester. On his return, in July, 1740, he was appointed to the Centurion, under the command of Commodore Anson, destined for a voyage round the world. 'He thus,' says his biographer, 'shared in the hardships and dangers of that celebrated voyage, which, for its inauspicious commencement, its strange and protracted disasters, and its final success, is, perhaps, without a parallel in the naval annals of any country.' In the course of this voyage he contracted a steady friendship with that distinguished band of brothers—Anson, Saunders, Brett, Saumarez, Denis, Byron, Parker, and Campbell—which terminated only with their several lives.

The incidents of this voyage are so well known that we pass over our author's summary, (of about sixty pages), interspersed with a few sentences from Keppel's own journal—noticing only one incident which, with becoming modesty, is omitted in that journal, but mentioned in 'Anson's Voyage,' and which occurred at the attack of Payta: it is, that 'one side of the peak of Keppel's jockey cap was shaved off close to his temple, by a ball.' After the action with the Spanish galleon, Anson was so pleased with the conduct of Keppel, that he immediately gave him a lieutenant's commission. On the arrival of the Centurion at Portsmouth, in June, 1744, and as soon as paid off, Keppel immediately applied for employment, and was ordered to join the Dreadnought, commanded by the Hon. Edward Boscawen,—'Old Dreadnought,' as the sailors used to call him—'the most obstinate,' as Walpole says, 'of an obstinate family.' But Pitt, who is higher authority than Walpole, said of him,

'When I apply to other officers respecting any expedition I may chance to project, they always raise difficulties—Boscawen always finds expedients.' From this ship, in November of the same year, he was promoted to the rank of commander, and appointed to the Wolf sloop; and, in the following December, was advanced to that of captain, and transferred to the Greyhound frigate. Thus, in ten years from his entering the service, that is, at the age of twenty, he obtained what was then called *post* rank. Soon after he was appointed to the Sapphire, a forty gun frigate.

From this time he was actively employed in cruising and making prizes, till the Sapphire required refitting; when, on application by letter to the Duke of Bedford, then first Lord of the Admiralty, 'that he might not lie idle while the Sapphire is laid up; and stating that his Grace must be sensible how ill it appears for young officers to remain on shore upon their pleasure, when they might be doing, perhaps, a service to their country,' he was appointed to the Maidstone, a ship of fifty guns, in the squadron under Admiral Warren, who, in writing to Anson, says, 'I think Keppel a charming little man.' In his eagerness and anxiety to cut off a large vessel running for Belleisle, and being told by an old pilot that it could be done very easily, his own ship struck upon the rocks of the Pelliers, two minutes after the man in the chains called out five fathoms;—so intent was he upon the chase, and 'so uneasy,' he says, 'lest people should have thought it was the castle (which had fired upon him) he stood in fear of.' The French behaved remarkably well; they sent him and his crew to Nantz, and at the expiration of five weeks he returned to England on his parole. In a letter to his friend Saumarez, he says, 'I had my fortune before my eyes, but eagerness and a bad pilot put an end to it.' A few days after his acquittal by court-martial, he was appointed to a new seventy-four gun ship, the Anson, destined to form one of the squadron under Sir Peter Warren. In writing to Lord Anson, from Lisbon, he says, 'I find we have lost the Duke of Bedford, who is now Secretary of State. I wish our new head may be as zealous, and support us as his Grace has done. I have not the honour of knowing my Lord Sandwich so well as the Duke of Bedford, but whilst I have the happiness to behave myself deserving your Lordship's protection, I want no other.'

From the Anson, Keppel and all his officers were turned over to his old ship, the Centurion, which, after a thorough repair, was reduced from a sixty to a fifty gun ship. Keppel was highly gratified by this appointment, made by the Duke's successor, Lord Sandwich. The Centurion had not only become celebrated from her voyage round the world, but was also considered a 'crack man-of-war.' 'Among the midshipmen who now joined the Centurion, was Adam Duncan, so distinguished in after times as the gallant Lord and Admiral of that name. Duncan may be truly said to have received his professional education in Keppel's school, having served under him in the several ranks of midshipman; third, second, and first lieutenant; flag and post captain; indeed, with the exception of a short time with Captain Barrington, he had no other commander during the Seven Years' War.

It may be noticed that Duncan was destined, in after life, to sit as one of the judges at the trial of his early friend. The Centurion having put into Plymouth, the commodore, on a visit to his friend, Lord Mount-Edgecumbe, first became acquainted with Mr. (afterwards Sir Joshua) Reynolds, and was so much pleased with the young artist, that he offered him a passage in the Centurion, on the interesting voyage she was then on her way to perform. The beautiful portrait of Keppel which he afterwards painted, and from which an engraving stands as frontispiece to this work, is supposed to have been among the first to enhance the reputation of Reynolds.

During the fourteen years that had now expired since Keppel left Westminster school, his life had almost wholly been spent in active employment at sea, capturing many of the enemy's armed ships and merchantmen. Now, however, he received a notification that he was to be entrusted with a diplomatic mission to the States of Barbary, and to be appointed to the chief command in the Mediterranean, with the rank of commodore. In writing to his friend Anson, then one of the Lords of the Admiralty, he says, 'I have wrote to my Lord Sandwich by this opportunity, whom, with your Lordship, I am greatly obliged to, for entrusting me with this command.'

One main object of it was to obtain from the Dey of Algiers satisfaction for the capture of a government packet, the treasure and effects on board which, being of very considerable value, were confiscated by the Dey. His instructions were to obtain restitution, and, if this barbarian should be refractory, to use menaces to intimidate him. On the arrival of the Centurion in the bay, with six other ships of war, a salute of twenty guns was fired from the batteries, in returning which one of the Centurion's guns, by the carelessness of the gunner, was shotted, which the Dey persisted was done purposely; and this made him not only 'refractory,' but very saucy. Mr. Keppel gives the following anecdote from Northcote's 'Life of Sir Joshua Reynolds,' which is also mentioned in other publications of the day; but as the commodore does not notice it in his journal, his biographer considers it as dubious. 'The Dey, surprised at the boldness of Keppel's remonstrances, and despising his apparent youth, he being then only four-and-twenty, exclaimed that he wondered at the insolence of the King of Great Britain in sending him an insignificant, beardless boy!' On this the spirited commodore replied, 'Had my master supposed that wisdom was measured by the length of the beard, he would have sent your Deyship a he-goat.' From the character of Keppel we think the anecdote probable enough, and that Northcote may have received it from Sir Joshua Reynolds.

The negotiation for restitution of property ended by a declaration from the Dey, that the distribution of it having been made, he had not the power of restoring it; and that 'it was as much as his head was worth to restore the effects of the Prince Frederick.' It would seem he was not unaware of the position he stood in, with regard to his subjects; for two years after this he was murdered in his own palace. Before this event, the commodore had succeeded in concluding a treaty, in which the Dey agrees to treat packets as ships of war; that merchant ships shall not be subject to ill treatment by the Algerine cruisers, on pain of the severest punishment, &c. After this, Keppel succeeded in effecting treaties with Tripoli and Tunis, and obtaining the release of captives; and, on his return to England, the Admiralty expressed satisfaction with his proceedings in these as well as on every other occasion, during his command in the Mediterranean. We here add a curious anecdote which is contained in the commodore's own journal:—

'Was informed by Mr. Owen that yesterday, John Dyer (who entered at Mahon) deserted from the long boat, and fled for sanctuary to a Marabut, and turned Moor. By further information, found that he had five years ago turned Moor, and had a wife and family here. On which I sent to the Dey to demand he might be sent on board the Centurion, to receive the punishment he had incurred as a deserter, which was death. In answer to which, the Dey said, "It was contrary to his laws to give up people who turned Moors; but as he had turned backwards and forwards so often, he was neither fish nor flesh, and fit for neither of us; therefore, as the punishment on our side was death, and that of a renegado flying from his country was death likewise, he, to split the difference, would take off his head, if I had no objection;" to which I assented.'

In 1754, hostilities having broken out between the English and French authorities in North America, Keppel was ordered to hoist a broad pendant in the Centurion, and to proceed with the Norwich to take the command of all the ships on the North American station, and to co-operate with General Braddock. He left England on the 23d December; and Mr. Keppel notices the circumstance of the unexpected death of his father, the Earl of Albemarle, at Paris, on the day of his sailing, having been suddenly seized with palsy and apoplexy, which carried him off in the course of a few hours. Our author here introduces Walpole's story of Lady Albemarle's dream, who being in London, and utterly unconscious of what had happened, said to Lord Bury, ' Your father is dead. I dreamed last night that he was dead, and came to take leave of me,'—and she immediately swooned.

The elevation of Lord Bury to the peerage left the borough of Chichester vacant, to which the commander was shortly afterwards returned without opposition. We need not here dwell on the calamitous history of the European warfare among the conflicting colonies of North America, in which the only concern that Keppel had, was the very useful and active assistance he afforded to General Braddock, in supplying both men and stores, during the short time he remained on that station—little more than six months; for in July, 1755, he received a letter from the Admiralty, apprising him, that in consequence of the French having fitted out a powerful fleet at Brest, Admiral Boscawen had been despatched with eleven sail of the line to take the chief command on the American coast; that in consequence his wearing a broad pendant, with a captain under him, could no longer be continued, since several ships of the new squadron were commanded by captains senior to himself.

As soon, therefore, as Keppel had given the necessary orders for his little squadron to join Admiral Boscawen, he shifted his broad pendant on board the Seahorse, commanded by Captain Palliser. ' It was on board this ship,' observes his biographer, ' that that friendship commenced between Keppel and the captain of the Seahorse, which was destined to be marred in so extraordinary a manner in after years.' The commodore arrived in England on the 22d of August, and four days afterwards was directed to proceed to Chatham to commission the Swiftsure, of seventy guns. In January following he was removed to the Torbay, of seventy-four guns. ' In this ship,' says our author, ' of which he had the command for upwards of five years, he was destined to have an extraordinary degree of good fortune.'

This share of ' good fortune' did not, however, immediately follow. The French publicly announced their intention not only to invade the Electorate of Hanover, but also Great Britain itself: the very act of making such a declaration was intended, obviously enough, to divert our government from their real design, which was Minorca, and it succeeded; for so great was the alarm of invasion at home, that, by proclamation, all horses and other beasts of burden were ordered to be driven at least twenty miles from the place where such attempt should be made. In the meantime, the ministers had received intelligence that a large armament was fitting out at Toulon, and that its destination was Minorca. After a lapse of several weeks, a fleet was ordered to be fitted out at Portsmouth, the command of which was given to the ill-fated Admiral Byng. Ten ships only were assigned to him, and these required upwards of seven hundred men to be complete. He was directed on no account to meddle with the Torbay, Essex, or Nassau, which he was told were required for most pressing service. A few days after, he was ordered to despatch Captain Keppel to sea with the Torbay, Essex, Iris, Antelope, and Gibraltar, and to complete them out of the Nassau. This ' most pressing service,' which occupied eight days in the execution, and might have been equally well performed by our frigates, was nothing more than to watch the motions of four French frigates, which had been chased into Cherbourg on the 9th April: Keppel returned to Spithead three days after Byng had sailed.

He was again despatched on the 16th with a small squadron, under Admiral Holborne, to cruize off Brest, which was afterwards increased to eighteen sail of the line, and the command given to Sir Edward Hawke. Keppel, however, had not the good fortune of being permanently attached to it; the Torbay, having sustained some damage, was obliged to return to port for repairs. When ready for sea he rejoined the fleet; but an epidemic breaking out in his ship, obliged him again to return to Portsmouth. On the 18th September he was ordered to take the Rochester and Harwich under his command, and to cruize in the latitude of Cape Finisterre. After a month's unsuccessful cruize, he ordered one of his ships to Lisbon, the other to Cadiz. Two days after this he captured the Diligent, a French snow; and shortly after, fell in with and captured a large French storeship from Quebec with English prisoners. Scarcely had he taken possession of this prize when he recaptured an English snow that had fallen into the hands of a French privateer. Just then he discovered a French frigate, to which he gave chase, and kept up a brisk cannonade during the night. At daylight he came up with her, and, pouring in a whole broadside, compelled her to strike. She proved to be the *Chariot Royale*, of thirty-six guns. Several of her men were killed and wounded. On the 9th December the commodore returned with his prizes to England. 'A duty,' says his biographer, 'now devolved upon Keppel, the painful nature of which was fully shown by his subsequent conduct. Admiral Byng had failed in his attempt to relieve Minorca, and had been superseded in his command. He was now brought a prisoner to Portsmouth to take his trial; Keppel was the junior member of that tribunal by whose unanimous verdict he was doomed to die.'—(Vol. i. pp. 200–30).

The trial of Byng has been so much canvassed, not only at the time, but in subsequent publications, that nothing new is likely at this day to be elicited; but Mr. Keppel could not with propriety have omitted its introduction into his pages; seeing the very prominent and painful part, and we may add, the laudable and generous part, which his namesake, the young captain, took to save the life of the unfortunate admiral. Mr. Keppel, however, says—

'After a lapse of eighty-five years, public opinion has hardly yet decided upon the case of Byng. Sir John Barrow, a writer who, from his office, is necessarily conversant with such subjects, speaks somewhat slightingly of the conduct of that Admiral; and Mr. Croker, another high authority in naval matters, goes so far as to say that Byng deserved his fate. The writer of this memoir has arrived at a different conclusion. He thinks that, in Clerk's "Naval Tactics," the failure of the action with Galissonière is satisfactorily shown to be attributable to the "Fighting Instructions" then in force, and in no degree to the commander in that disastrous engagement.'

In adverting to the 'Life of Anson,' it appears to us that there is a mistake in this passage. We find nothing in Sir John Barrow's work that can be construed as speaking *slightingly* of Byng. On the contrary, he says, 'It showed no want of nerve in Byng by detaching one of his ships from the line, because he had one more in number than the enemy; for though the old *Fighting Instructions* very cavalierly enjoin this, yet it was always on the understanding that the combatants should be pretty nearly ship for ship, or on an equality of strength, which was not the case here;' and he continues, 'it is clear that Byng, amidst that disaster which paralyzed his own ship and the efforts of three others for a time, had no other means of making his communications than by calling in and despatching a frigate with verbal orders, which, with the impediment of the flag-ship continuing to go down, caused the delay, and thereby prevented him from doing his utmost.'* If Mr. Croker has said, that Byng 'deserved his fate,' Sir John gives a very different opinion. 'Thus,' he says, 'died a martyr to public clamour, excited by a timid ministry, and to one false step taken by the party who professed to be, and actually meant to be, friendly to him;—whose death can be considered in no other light than as a judicial murder.' It certainly was not, as some have called it, a political murder. His death was in no wise owing to party feeling in either House of Parliament, or in the Judges, or in the King. It rested solely on the Board of Admiralty, who, unfortunately, instead of carrying up the recommendation of the court-martial for mercy to the King, as is the usual course, and always succeeds, they requested his Majesty would take the opinion of the twelve Judges as to the *legality* of the sentence, which was never called in question. Their answer was in the affirmative; and this prevented any further appeal to the Throne from the Admiralty, and poor Byng's fate was from that moment sealed.

---

* Barrow's *Life of Anson.*

But we must briefly advert to the generous and humane part which Keppel took in the course of this unfortunate business. Ever since the signing of the sentence he felt uneasy in his conscience, and with two or three others expressed themselves exceedingly desirous to be absolved from their oaths. This was mentioned in the House of Commons, and long debates ensued as to the necessity of a dispensing bill. Some were of opinion that the members could speak out without a bill. Keppel professed his doubts whether he could do so without a dispensing act. Pitt said he honoured Mr. Keppel for his doubt. A council was held on Mr. Keppel's demand, and the sentence was respited for a fortnight by his Majesty, who had been informed that a member had declared in his place he had something of weight to say. Fox, though friendly to Keppel, affected surprise that the King should have been informed of what had passed in parliament, and asked for precedents. Pitt replied with great indignation, 'that the time had been too pressing to consult precedents; he had not thought that the life of a man was to be trifled with while clerks were searching records.'

Fox then asked Keppel, which of his associates had empowered him to make the demand? He named Holmes, Norris, Geary, and Moore. The first and third disavowed having sanctioned the use of their names; Norris and Moore avowed their feelings to be in unison with those of Keppel, and that he was authorized to make use of their names; and it seemed to be the general opinion that the other two had done the same. Walpole says Sir R. Lyttleton told him, that he had remonstrated to Geary the injustice and dishonourableness of retracting what he had authorized Keppel to say, when his reply was—' *It will hurt my preferment to tell.*' Keppel said, he understood, and did believe, all four had commissioned him to move the House in their joint names. Fox assured Keppel that his character was not affected by what Holmes and Geary had said. An angry debate followed, in which many absurd and indecent reflections were made on the authors of the proposed dispensing bill; in the course of it Pitt said emphatically—'May I fall when I refuse pity to such a suit as Mr. Keppel's, justifying a man who lies in captivity and the shadow of death. I thank God I feel something more than popularity—I feel justice!' The bill passed the Commons by 153 to 22. It went to the Lords, who rejected it with expressions of contempt and indignation. Thus these proceedings, well-intentioned as they were, together with the opinions of the Judges of the legality of the sentence, (which had never been doubted, except by the Admiralty), released the prisoner from further suspense, and his execution speedily followed.

A few weeks after the trial, Keppel resumed the command of the Torbay; and on the 24th of June sailed in company with the Channel fleet, under the command of Admiral Boscawen; was detached on a cruize, captured a rich prize laden with stores and provisions for Louisbourg; and, on rejoining the fleet, was sent home with despatches. Having received a complete refit, the Torbay was ordered to join the expedition under Sir Edward Hawke, consisting of eighteen sail of the line, besides frigates and fire-ships, forty-four transports, with ten complete regiments, under the command of Sir John Mordaunt. The object was to attempt, as far as practicable, a descent on the French coast at or near Rochefort. Keppel was in the division under Rear-Admiral Knowles,—'a vain man,' says Walpole, ' of more parade than bravery.' The following anecdote, which is authenticated by the Admiral himself, (having published it in defence of his conduct), affords a corroboration of Walpole's character of him. On clearing for action, Keppel discovered a French seventy-four gun ship standing towards the fleet, and instantly hailed Admiral Knowles to give him the information, but of which he took no notice. His defence was, 'that he looked on a ship cleared for action, and ready for battle, as a sight so entertaining, that he had desired Major-General Conway to go down to see his ship between decks; and that while they were viewing her, one of his lieutenants came down, sent by the captain, to acquaint him Captain Keppel hailed the ship, and told them there was a French man-of-war standing in for the fleet; that for some short space of time he (the admiral) took no notice of it, thinking it impossible Sir Edward Hawke's division should not see her.' After a second message, he came up, and ordered Keppel to pursue her, who got within a mile and a half of the chase; but, to prevent capture, the Frenchman ran his ship among the rocks and shoals, with which he was acquainted, and finally escaped into the Garonne.

On the 23d September, an attack was ordered on the Isle of Aix. The fort opened fire upon the ships as they advanced. Howe was first, and anchoring his ship within forty yards of the fort, opened a tremendous fire, and in thirty-five minutes the garrison struck their colours and surrendered. The *Barfleur* was next to the *Magnanime*, and no other ships are named in the short *Gazette;* but Walpole says 'Keppel pressed forward to get between them.' Nothing more was done; the disgraceful conduct of the commander of the troops disgusted both navy and army, which ended in a court-martial on the return of the expedition, on General Mordaunt, who was acquitted.

When Sir Edward Hawke quitted Basque Roads, Keppel was detached with a squadron of seven ships, took a few prizes, heard of two French ships of war, but searched for them in vain; and, after a few weeks' cruize, returned to Spithead with his squadron and a convoy of East Indiamen. He was again sent with a squadron of three vessels, under Admiralty orders, for the annoyance of the enemy's privateers, and the security of the trade of his Majesty's subjects. He captured on this cruize a large privateer; and, on his return, he was again put under the orders of Sir Edward Hawke.

Information having been received of an expedition fitting out at Rochefort, Sir Edward Hawke was again despatched with six sail of the line, of which the Torbay was one. On arriving in Basque Roads they discovered five French ships of the line, six or seven frigates, and about forty transports at anchor off the Isle of Aix. On perceiving Hawke's squadron, they cut or slipped their cables, endeavoured to escape into the Charente, and, in doing this, several of them grounded in the mud; at daylight, they were seen still aground, some lying on their broadsides, the crews busily employed in heaving everything overboard, and the troops were disembarking in boats; in short, the same scene was now exhibited as that which took place on the same spot fifty years afterwards, when Admiral Gambier and Lord Cochrane were employed on a similar service. Both expeditions were so far successful as to destroy for a time the projected plans of the enemy.

On the return of Hawke to England, he left Keppel with a small squadron to cruize in the Bay of Biscay; on which service he intercepted and captured part of a convoy proceeding for Quebec, engaged a large privateer, the *Godichon*, against which, after a constant and galling fire, chiefly directed against the Torbay's rigging, Keppel for a time refrained from firing a shot,

well knowing that he could by a broadside send her to the bottom; at length, however, he lost his forbearance, and ordered his upper-deck guns and a battery of small arms to be fired into her, when she struck her colours and called for quarter.

'An anecdote is recorded of Keppel on this occasion:—During the chase he received a wound in the leg, which for the moment was thought to be dangerous, as it brought him on the deck. The sailors instantly came to carry him down to the cockpit; but he very calmly took his handkerchief from his pocket, and bound it round the wound, saying, "Stop, my lads, reach me a chair; as I can't stand, I must sit." "This," added he, clapping his hand to the place, "may spoil my dancing, but not my stomach for fighting."'

After this the Torbay was added to the fleet under Lord Anson, and ordered to cruize off Ushant; and soon after, with the Medway and Coventry, they chased a convoy of fifty sail under the protection of two frigates, keeping up a running cannonade, until the enemy gained shelter among the rocks and in the numerous creeks of the coast, in the darkness of the night. After rejoining the fleet, it was decided that an attack should be made on the island of Goree, which, while in the hands of the French, was a constant annoyance to our settlements on the Senegal. For this purpose a squadron of three sail of the line, three frigates and other smaller vessels, were placed under the command of Keppel, and he was ordered to hoist a broad pendant in the Torbay. It was late in December when he arrived off the island; on the 29th of which month he attacked the forts and batteries, which were soon obliged to capitulate; but the demands of the Governor being rejected, the attack was renewed, when the island, the forts, and garrison, consisting of 300 Frenchmen and a great number of blacks, surrendered at discretion. This is the whole substance of the commodore's dispatch, as published in the *Gazette.* Taking with him the three ships of the line, he returned to England, struck his broad pendant, and proceeded to London, while the Torbay underwent the necessary repairs.

Keppel was not permitted long to remain idle; and nothing can more strongly mark the estimation in which his character and talents stood in the public opinion, as well as in that of the profession, than the constant demands made on his services in the course of the last twelve years, and which continued with little intermission for four years more, till the cessation of hostilities in 1763 gave him a respite for a short time.

But we cannot pass over without briefly enumerating these four years' services, the most important in their consequences personally to Keppel. Having resumed the command of the Torbay, he was again placed under the orders of Sir Edward Hawke, who had just received intelligence of four ships of the line in Port-Louis being about to join the French fleet off Ushant. With a view of intercepting them, the Admiral despatched Keppel with the following ships: the Torbay, bearing his broad-pendant; the Magnanime, Captain Lord Howe; the Fame, Captain the Hon. John Byron; the Monmouth, Captain the Hon. Augustus Harvey, and the Southampton frigate. For such a purpose never could there have been selected a more promising little squadron; and never was disappointment more strongly felt than when it was announced, by the frigate, that the enemy had escaped. The commander-in-chief had to experience equal mortification. The weather was so tempestuous during the whole summer, that his fleet was three times blown back to the English coast; and it was not till the middle of November that he received intelligence of M. Conflans being at sea. On the morning of the 20th, one of the frigates made the signal for a fleet being in sight, and another from Lord Howe, who had been sent ahead, that the fleet was an enemy.

As M. Conflans was making off for the land, Sir Edward ordered seven or eight ships of the van to make all sail after him. 'At half-past two P. M.,' he says, 'the fire beginning a-head, I made the signal for engaging. About four o'clock the Formidable struck, and a little after the Thesée and Superbe were sunk. About five, l'Héros struck, but it blowing hard, no boat could be sent on board her.' These are the only fighting occurrences, or rather their results, on this day, as given by the Admiral, and published in the *Gazette.* He names not a single officer, nor once alludes to the share which his own ship had in the action; but Mr. Keppel in some degree supplies this defect, though without any stated authority.

'From the beginning of the action, Sir Edward Hawke had ordered his ship, the Royal George, to reserve her fire until she came alongside of the French admiral, the Soleil Royale. The pilot informed him that this could not be done without the most imminent danger of running upon a shoal. It was on this occasion he gave the well-known answer: "You have done your duty in pointing out the danger; you are now to obey my commands, and lay me alongside of the French admiral." As he advanced, he received the broadsides of six of the enemy's ships. The French admiral was one of the last to give him his fire, and, as in the case of the Torbay, he showed a great disinclination for nearer contact. As the Royal George neared the Soleil, she endeavoured to make off, in which effort she was aided by the Superbe, who, perceiving our Admiral's design, generously interposed, received the fire intended for the Soleil Royale, and soon after went to the bottom.'

All the accounts we have seen of this skirmishing action disagree; but one thing is pretty clear, that the Royal George, the Magnanime, and the Torbay, were the ships principally engaged. The log-book of the Royal George, which we have seen, is almost as laconic as the Admiral's letter :—

'At fifty-five minutes after three, the French rear-admiral struck to the Resolution,' (the Royal George, the Magnanime, and the Torbay, having already silenced her.)

'At four, the ship the Torbay was engaged with, sunk.' (This must have been the Thesée, which Howe had previously engaged).

'Thirty-five minutes after four, we got up with fourteen sail of the enemy, which all wore and gave us their broadsides. Began to engage at forty-one minutes after four. The French ship abreast us sunk.' (This must have been the Superbe).

The result was the loss to the enemy of five of their best ships, and the total breakup of their intended expedition—two burnt, two sunk, and one captured. In the attempt, however, of the Resolution and the Essex to destroy the Soleil Royale and l'Héros, that had run among the rocks, our two ships were lost, but not before they had set fire to one of the enemy, and the French had done the same to the other. Those which had run up the Villaine were shattered, run aground, and dismantled, and the rest dispersed to different parts of the coast. All this was by the eight ships which had the good fortune to come up with the enemy. 'When I consider,' says the Admiral, 'the season of the year, the hard gales on the day of action, a flying enemy, the shortness of the day, and the coast we are on, I can boldly affirm, that all that could possibly be done has been done.'

On the weather moderating, Sir Edward Hawke placed a squadron of eight sail of the line and three frigates, under the orders of Keppel, to proceed to the enemy's posts to the southward as far as Aix Road, 'to take, sink, or burn them, wherever he should think it practicable to attack them.' On the day before his arrival at Aix, the

French vice-admiral, in anticipation of such a visit, had got all his guns out of the ships, and retired with his division up the Charente. In January, 1760, Sir Edward Hawke removed his flag into Keppel's ship, and returned to Plymouth.*

Mr. Keppel mentions the curious fact, that ' on the very day that Hawke was engaged in destroying the French fleet, the mob were burning him in effigy in the streets of London, for his supposed share in the failure at Rochefort.' But now, to make amends for this ungracious proceeding, ' bonfires and illuminations were exhibited throughout the kingdom.' He received the thanks of the House of Commons, and a pension of L.2000 a-year was granted to him for his own life, and for the lives of his two sons.

Captain Keppel was next ordered to remove, with his officers and crew, from the Torbay to the Valiant, and soon joined Sir Edward Hawke in Quiberon Bay. The system of harassing the enemy on their own coasts had proved so successful, that it was determined to pursue it, and Belleisle was fixed on to be the next point of attack. As little was known of this island, Keppel was selected, under secret orders, to obtain the necessary information, to make a survey of the coast, and report thereupon. After a careful examination of its shores and defences, he gave it as his opinion that a landing was practicable. An expedition was therefore resolved on, and a squadron of twenty-one ships of war, including bombs and fire-ships, was prepared, to which Keppel was appointed, and ordered to place himself under the orders of Sir Edward Hawke. On the 28th of November all was ready, but a letter from Mr. Pitt directed its suspension till further orders. In March, 1761, after the accession of George III., preparations were renewed, and the naval part was now entrusted exclusively to Keppel, who hoisted his broad pendant in the Valiant; and, on application to Lord Anson, his

friend Adam Duncan, the subsequent hero of Camperdown, was appointed his captain.

Mr. Keppel gives a detailed account of the naval and military operations carried on against this very strongly fortified island; the siege of which required all the vigour, perseverance, and courage of both army and navy, to surmount the many difficulties opposed to the invaders, and which were unremittingly struggled against for two months; when, ' on the 7th June, after a most vigorous resistance, the French garrison capitulated, and were allowed to march through the breach with the honours of war, in favour of the gallant defence they had made under the orders of their brave commander, the Chevalier de St. Croix.'

Having landed the garrison at Port-Louis, Commodore Keppel distributed his force along the western coast of France, consisting of sixty-three men-of-war. ' The assignment of so important a command,' says Mr. Keppel, ' to a post-captain, is a proof of the high opinion that was held of his courage and abilities.' But, during the remainder of the year, the French made no movements, and their whole squadron in Brest Roads amounted only to seven sail of the line and three frigates. In January, 1762, the Valiant experienced a most tremendous storm, which compelled her with other ships to seek shelter in the nearest British port. ' With five feet water in the hold, and almost in a sinking condition, she got into Torbay.'

While France was at this time suing for peace with England, and even while negotiations were pending, she was concluding that secret alliance with the Court of Spain, so well known as the *Family Compact.* On receiving intelligence of its completion, Mr. Keppel strongly urged the expediency of an immediate commencement of hostilities against the two contracting powers; but as his colleagues were disposed to denounce such a measure as rash and unadvisable, he at once resigned. It was not long, however, before war was proclaimed against Spain, and an expedition, on a very extensive scale, prepared to act against the Havannah. The command of the land forces was given to General the Earl of Albemarle, assisted by his brother, General the Hon. William Keppel; and another brother, Captain the Hon. Augustus Keppel, was appointed, with a distinguishing pendant, as commodore and second in command of the naval forces, under the orders of Admiral Sir George Pococke. The combined forces,

* Sir Edward Hawke sent his captain, Campbell, with the intelligence of his success over Conflans. Of this honest Scotchman, who had been Keppel's messmate with Anson, Sir John Barrow gives a curious anecdote, which Mr. Keppel repeats :—' Lord Anson, when taking him in his carriage to the king, said " Campbell, the king will certainly knight you, if you think proper." " Troth, my lord," said the captain, who retained his Scotch dialect as long as he lived, " I ken nae use that it will be to me." " But your lady might like it," replied his lordship. " Well, then," rejoined Campbell, " his Majesty may knight her, if he pleases." '—(*Life of Lord Anson*).

on their arrival at Cuba, amounted as follows: the navy, to nineteen sail of the line, besides frigates, bombs, and a multitude of store-ships and transports; the army, to between eleven and twelve thousand men. Six ships of the line, and smaller vessels, were placed under the orders of Commodore Keppel, on whom devolved the important duty of landing the army.

. It would be out of our province to give even a slight sketch of the operations carried on through a long siege, in which the strong fortresses of Chorea, Cavannos, and the Moro, and lastly the Havannah itself, fell into our possession. Suffice it to say, that the sailors, as usual, had their full share of the arduous operations of the siege, and that mostly by the exertions of the seamen the strong Moro castle was taken; and that Sir George Pococke does justice to the distinguished merit of Commodore Keppel, who executed the service under his directions with the greatest spirit, activity, and diligence. But that valuable and important conquest was not achieved without dreadful sufferings and great mortality. It appears from the casualties of the army alone, that, from the 1st June to the 8th October, 560 men were killed or had died of their wounds, and that 4708 had perished from sickness; and it is stated that 'the survivors returned to their native country with constitutions so broken and decayed, that a sickliness and languor were entailed on the remainder of their lives.' As some compensation for the severe shock which was here inflicted on the constitution of Commodore Keppel, his biographer informs us that his share of the prize-money alone amounted to L.24,539, 10s. 1d.; and that the Earl of Albemarle and Sir George Pococke each received L.122,697, 10s. 6d. Our author further adds, that 'In the beginning of January (1763) Keppel received two important communications;—the one, that the preliminaries of peace had been signed; the other, that the King had included him in the promotion of flag-officers made on the conclusion of the war, the list of which had been purposely extended to include him.'

The return of peace did not altogether afford Keppel that repose which thirty years of arduous and unremitting active service are stated to have made essential for the re-establishment of his health; for, on Lord Egmont succeeding to the situation of First Lord of the Admiralty in 1765, Admiral Keppel was appointed one

of the junior lords. In 1766 he hoisted his flag in the Catharine yacht, to convey to Rotterdam the Princess Caroline Matilda, the ill-fated bride of the King of Denmark. On his return, on some changes being made in the ministry, he resigned his seat in the Admiralty. In 1768 he was returned member for Windsor; and, in the autumn of the same year, he conveyed his sister, the Marchioness of Tavistock, to Lisbon, whose mournful history was the source of deep affliction to her beloved brother the Admiral. This lady is described as one 'who, to a sweetness of disposition peculiarly her own, joined all those mild and unaffected virtues which tend to perpetuate the charm first given by personal grace and innate dignity of character.' The marquis, her husband, one of the most amiable and accomplished noblemen, met his death by a fall from his horse as he was hunting, little more than a twelvemonth after their marriage. She gave birth to a posthumous infant, the late Lord William Russell, who died by the hand of an assassin. Mr. Keppel says, 'the settled melancholy of the widowed mother's heart appears, after the birth of the child, to have given way to keen sensibility and inconsolable sorrow.' We cannot resist inserting the following affecting incident, which is said to have occurred previous to her departure with her brother for Lisbon. 'At a consultation of the faculty, held at Bedford House in August, one of the physicians, whilst he felt her pulse, requested her to open her hand. Her reluctance induced him to use a degree of gentle violence, when he perceived that she had closed it to conceal a miniature of her late husband. "Ah, madam!" he exclaimed, "all our prescriptions must be useless whilst you so fatally cherish the wasting sorrow that destroys you!"—"I have kept it," she replied, "either in my bosom or my hand ever since my lord's death; and thus I must, indeed, continue to retain it, until I drop off after him into the welcome grave."' A few weeks after her arrival at Lisbon, she found 'the welcome grave,'—having survived her husband little more than a year; and then, in the words of Rogers, 'died the victim of exceeding love.' Her sister, who had watched her with unceasing assiduity, speedily followed her; and, as if misfortune was destined to pursue this family, their brother, the subject of this article, 'by a sudden lurch of the ship, fell down one of the hatchways, and thereby injured his back so severely, as ever afterwards to occasion him the greatest pain, and at times even to deprive him of the use of his legs.'

On a brevet of flag-officers in October, 1770, Keppel was promoted to the rank of Rear-Admiral of the Red, and three days afterwards, to that of Vice-Admiral of the Blue. In 1773, the state of his health required that he should go to Bath. 'Poor Admiral Keppel,' says Captain Hood, 'is now at Bath in a very deplorable way, having lost the use of his legs.' In 1775, he sustained a heavy loss in the death of his friend Admiral Sir Charles Saunders; with whom, from the time they had served together in Anson's expedition, he had lived on terms of the strictest and most intimate friendship. Sir Charles bequeathed him a legacy of £5,000, with an annuity of £1200 a-year, and included him first in the entail of his property, if his two nieces, then unmarried, should die without issue. The one, however, married Lord Westmoreland, and the other Lord Melville. Walpole says, 'Sir Charles was a pattern of most steady bravery, united with the most unaffected modesty. No man said less, or deserved more. Simplicity in his manners, generosity and good nature, adorned his genuine love of his country.'

Lord Sandwich bestowed the rank of Lieut.-General of the Marines, vacant by the death of Sir Charles Saunders, on Sir Hugh Palliser, one of the junior admirals. It was rumoured also, that Lord Howe was to have the post of General of Marines on a contemplated vacancy. This drew from Keppel the following spirited remonstrance, which, he says, 'some combat in my mind, from a friendship to Lord Howe, made me hesitate on sending to the First Lord of the Admiralty.'

'My Lord,—It is much credited that Admiral Forbes is to retire from the post of General of Marines, and that Rear-Admiral Lord Howe is appointed his successor.

'I am not used to feel disgrace or affronts; but indeed, my Lord, I must feel cold to my own honour, and the rank in which I stand in his Majesty's service, if I remain silent, and see one of the youngest rear-admirals of the fleet promoted to the rank of Lieutenant-general of Marines, and, a few days afterwards, another rear-admiral made General of Marines. It is not for me to say who should, or should not, be appointed to those honours; but I may presume to say to your Lordship, and through you, as the head of the sea department, beg leave to have it laid before his Majesty with my humblest submission to him, that, little as I am entitled to claim merit, yet a series of long service may, I hope, permit me to observe, that such a repetition of promotion to the junior admirals of the fleet can-

not but dispirit every senior officer, jealous of his own honour, inasmuch as it tends to manifest to the whole profession the low esteem he stands in; which, allow me to say, may at one time or other have its bad effects. Juniors cannot complain, nor are they dishonoured, when their seniors are promoted. My Lord, I must hope I stand excused for writing in such plain terms; but when I am writing or speaking from facts and feelings of honour, I cannot allow myself to express those sentiments in a doubtful manner.

'I have the honour to be, your Lordship's most obedient and most humble servant,

'A. Keppel.'

To this letter no answer appears; but as Keppel was now (1776) advanced to the rank of Vice-Admiral, he received a message from Lord Sandwich, stating that his Majesty desired to know, whether, in case of a war with a foreign power, he would undertake the charge of the home fleet? He had, in consequence, an audience of the King, and gave his consent to take the command of the Channel fleet. It is stated, however, by his biographer, that he had some misgivings of trusting his hard-earned fame to ministers whom he knew to be unfriendly towards him. This feeling seems to have been encouraged by a letter from 'his friend and cousin,' the Duke of Richmond, who says, 'I cannot wish you joy of having a fleet to command, prepared by the Earl of Sandwich. No one can be surprised that you should suspect a minister whom you have constantly opposed—if he has but a bad fleet to send out, 'tis doing Lord Sandwich no injustice to suppose he would be glad to put it under the command of a man whom he does not love, and yet whose name will justify the choice to the nation.' Such an illiberal sentiment we should not have expected from the noble lord. It has been held both in the army and navy, that it is not the politics of the man, but the character and talents of the officer, that the leading power ought, and, for his own sake, does generally select for an important command; and the Duke of Richmond had no cause hitherto to suspect Lord Sandwich of treachery towards Admiral Keppel, whom he had, on all occasions, selected for services above all others of his rank, notwithstanding his opposition to ministers. We are therefore glad to find, that 'the friend and cousin's advice' was not followed. He accepted, and held himself in readiness for active employment; and in 1778, when hostilities with France and Spain were on the eve of breaking out, he was appointed to the command of the Channel fleet. It is much to his credit, that though of high rank and high political connections, with a seat in Parliament, which must, almost of necessity, have drawn him towards one or other of the great political parties—though in constant familiar intercourse and correspondence with the Portlands, Richmonds, Rockinghams, and with Fox, Burke, and other Whig leaders in the House of Commons—he had too much regard for the welfare of the country, his own honour, and his love for the service, to suffer party prejudice to interfere in any way with his professional duty.

He left England on 13th June, 1778, with a fleet of twenty-one sail of the line and three frigates, two of the line being shortly afterwards added. This fleet was placed by the commander-in-chief under three divisions—his own flag being in the Victory, of 100 guns; the second division under that of Sir R. Harland, Vice-Admiral of the Red, in the Queen, 90 guns; and the third under Sir Hugh Palliser, Vice-Admiral of the Blue, in the Ocean, (afterwards changed into the Formidable), of 90 guns.

He had scarcely arrived on his station when two French frigates and smaller vessels hove in sight. They were detained, and from papers found on board two of them, and from the prisoners, it appeared that the French had thirty-two sail of the line, and ten or twelve frigates, in Brest Roads. This intelligence was wholly unexpected; but Admiral Keppel had but one course to pursue, and that was to return to St. Helen's, according to express injunctions in his instructions. 'If the French fleet shall be manifestly superior to yours, and should come out to meet you, or if you are satisfied that they are superior to you, *though they do not come out,* you are, in either of these cases, to return with the squadron under your command to St. Helen's for a reinforcement.' With these clear, intelligible, and positive instructions, with only twenty-two ships of the line against thirty-two, 'I think myself obliged,' says the Admiral, 'unpleasant as my feelings are upon the occasion, to repair thither.'

No official notice was taken, either in the shape of approval or censure, of the course the Admiral had adopted in strict conformity with his instructions; but it is stated that certain publications, in the interest of government, ascribed his return to the most disgraceful motives; and some of them even directly threatened him with the fate of Byng. But we are assured that Admiral Keppel, on this trying occasion, observed a prudent and manly forbearance; and bore in silence the unmerited obloquy lavished upon him by his anonymous accusers, who, it is charitable to suppose, were ignorant of the secret nature of his instructions. By a rigid attention to the wants of his squadron, which, by an addition of more ships, now amounted to thirty sail of the line, he was speedily ready to resume his station. The day previous to his again putting to sea, the French fleet, of thirty sail of the line, sailed from Brest, also under three divisions, commanded by Count D'Orvilliers, and assisted by the Count Duchaffault, the Duc de Chartres, and three other flag-officers. The third in command, who was afterwards well known as the infamous D'Orleans, told Sir George Rodney in Paris, that he was about to meet his countryman Mr. Keppel, and asked him, with an insulting air, what he thought would be the result? 'That my countryman,' replied Rodney, 'will carry your Royal Highness home with him to learn English.' This royal boaster, in the action of which we are about to speak, is reported to have retired into the hold of his ship, and could not be prevailed upon to show himself on deck till the engagement had ended.

On the 23d of July the French fleet was discovered, on which Keppel immediately ordered the signal for forming the line to be made; but the French Admiral used all diligence and caution to defeat Keppel's object of commencing the engagement. For four days Keppel vainly endeavoured to bring the enemy to action, who generally had the weathergage, and whenever a shift of wind favoured him he made an effort to escape under press of sail. On the 27th July, at daybreak, the French fleet was about three miles to windward, still endeavouring to avoid a meeting; but by a change of wind, and in the course of manœuvring, the centres and rears of the two fleets were brought within musket-shot, and a very sharp cannonading took place and continued for about two hours, all the time in line of battle. Keppel is said to have received the fire of six different ships in passing, before he returned a shot; the Victory's fire being reserved for D'Orvilliers' ship, and it was so powerful that two of her port-holes were driven into one.

The British ships being now dispersed, and many of them damaged in their masts and rigging, it required the remainder of the day to put them to rights, after which the signal was made again to form the line; but Sir Hugh Palliser, for some reason never explained, obstinately kept his squadron to windward, taking no notice of the signal, nor even of the message sent and delivered to him verbally by the captain of the Fox frigate, directing him to bear down into the Admiral's wake. The Admiral was, therefore, under the necessity of making specific signals for each ship of the Vice-Admiral's division, and the delay thus occasioned put an end to any further operations on that day, except to make ready to engage at daylight. It appeared, however, that the French, under cover of the night, had made their escape. Nothing, therefore, was now left but to return to England to repair damages, the French, ludicrously enough, as Burke observes, 'having mistaken their way into their own harbour.' This was quite true; their own *Gazette* having announced that 'the astonishment was general when they discovered the Isle of Ushant itself, which the Count D'Orvilliers thought himself distant from 25 or 30 leagues; and that, seeing himself off the harbour of Brest, he determined to enter it.'

Notwithstanding the highly improper conduct of the Vice-Admiral of the Blue, the good-nature of Keppel would not allow him, in his official letter, to speak of him otherwise than with praise. 'The spirited conduct,' he says, 'of the Vice-Admiral Sir Robert Harland, Vice-Admiral Sir Hugh Palliser, and the captains of the fleet, supported by their officers and men, deserves much commendation.' Alluding to this report in his defence on the trial, Keppel says—'It is very short and very general; but it goes as far as I intended it should. It does what I meant to do. I meant to commend his bravery in the engagement. As he stood high in command, to pass over one in his station would be to mark him. It would have conveyed the censure I wished for such good reasons to avoid.' Such was the good-nature and generosity of Admiral Keppel; and we shall presently see in what manner it was repaid.

Before a month had elapsed Keppel's fleet was equipped and at sea. Information was received that the French were seen to the westward of Ushant; but Keppel having cruised in vain in that track for two months, without finding or hearing anything of them, returned with his fleet to Portsmouth. About the time of his arrival there appeared, in one of the daily papers, what was called a true recital of the conduct of Sir Hugh Palliser in the late action. No sooner had the Admiral reached London than Sir Hugh addressed him by letter, in which he claimed 'to have his conduct justified from those foul aspersions;' and desiring him to contradict those scandalous reports, by publishing, in his own name, a paper which he inclosed; to which Keppel very properly returned no answer. He was called upon next day by Sir Hugh for his signature to the paper, which Keppel immediately and disdainfully refused. Sir Hugh went therefore to the office of the *Morning Post*, and gave his own version of the engagement, under his own name, which Captain Jervis pronounced to be 'replete with vanity, art, and falsehood.'

On the 9th December, five months nearly after the action, Admiral Keppel, to his great astonishment, received from the Secretary of the Admiralty a notification, that Sir Hugh Palliser had transmitted a charge of misconduct and neglect of duty against him, on the 27th and 28th July—desiring that a Court-Martial might be held for trying him for the same; and signifying their lordships' intention of complying with the desire of Sir Hugh, (*one of their lordships*). The Admiral, in reply, expresses his utter astonishment at the countenance the Lords Commissioners of the Admiralty should so far have given to this proceeding, as to resolve, on the same day on which such a charge is exhibited, to order a Court-Martial on the Commander-in-Chief of the fleet, on an attack from an inferior officer, under all the very peculiar circumstances in which he (Sir Hugh Palliser) then stood.

This extraordinary proceeding on the part of Sir Hugh, and still more extraordinary on that of the Board of Admiralty, on the requisition of one of its members, and wholly unprecedented, from the indecent haste in which it was complied with, is difficult to explain. It can only be ascribed, either to the mortification which Keppel's refusal to sign a document in which he had no concern gave him, or to the mistaken courtesy of Keppel in suppressing the misconduct of the Vice-Admiral in his report of the action. Unhappily, it is by no means a singular instance of an act of kindness or forbearance being acknowledged by ingratitude; but, in the present case, it was followed up by a vindictive attempt to destroy the character, and even endanger the life, of the benefactor. Great indignation spread itself over the naval service; and twelve British admirals, at the head of whom was the veteran

Hawke, presented a memorial to the King, on what they designated to be ' an outrageous and unprecedented proceeding.'

How Lord ·Sandwich could have been prevailed on to give his assent to such ' an outrageous and unprecedented proceeding' is quite inexplicable. ·He was well versed in naval affairs, having, for the third time, filled the office of First Lord, and in the whole, for upwards of ten years. He was a man of considerable ability : he alone negotiated and signed the treaty of peace at Aix-la-Chapelle. Walpole hated and abused him; but the late Lord Holland, who edited his (Walpole's) *Memoirs*, says —' Our author disparages his abilities ; he was a lively, sensible man, attentive to business, and not a bad speaker in Parliament ;'—and Sir John Barrow observes, ' His lordship might have added, that his voyage round the Mediterranean proved him to be a scholar, a man of just observation, cultivated intellect, and vigorous mind.' It is equally extraordinary that such a man should have failed so miserably in his defence, in the Lords, for having brought Keppel so rashly and *outrageously* to trial. That defence was neither consistent nor true. ' He had no discretion,' Lord Sandwich said, ' with regard to refusing the order for the court-martial.' His Lordship could not have forgotten the remarkable circumstance of the House of Commons having petitioned the King to order the Admiralty to try Matthews and Lestock ; that Anson, in the absence of the Duke of Bedford and himself, waited on the Duke of Newcastle, and prevailed upon him to advise the King to rescind the order he had given, as being a violation of the jurisdiction of the Admiralty, as by law established, and by royal patent confirmed ; that he (Lord Sandwich) had highly approved of what Anson had done, observing that, ' if this opportunity to establish our jurisdiction is not· made use of, I fear it will be a long time before another will offer.' His Lordship could not, therefore, be ignorant that not only the Lord High Admiral, but every Commander-in-Chief on the foreign station, has full discretionary power to grant or refuse Courts-Martial ; and to exercise other matters, under constitutional responsibility, with which neither King nor Parliament can interfere.

The trial of Keppel went forward ; the court consisted of five flag-officers and eight captains. They sat some thirty days, and examined most of the captains of the fleet who were in the action, and brought forward by the prosecutor ; after which the court, having maturely and seriously considered the whole evidence, and the prisoner's defence, was of opinion, ' that the charge was malicious and ill-founded, and that the Admiral had behaved himself as a judicious, brave, and experienced officer ; and they, therefore, unanimously and honourably acquitted the said Admiral Augustus Keppel of every part of the charge exhibited against him.'

The sentence was pronounced amidst a general acclamation of joy from the assembled crowd ; the ships at Spithead, and the Indiamen at the Mother-Bank, fired salutes. Riots followed the rejoicings. Sir Hugh Palliser was burnt in effigy ; his house entirely gutted, and its contents burnt ; the Admiralty attacked, and its gates unhinged ; the windows of Lords North, Bute, Sandwich, Lisburne, and Mulgrave, were broken. The fury of the populace was ungovernable ; the riot act was read, and parties of the Horse Guards paraded the streets. The thanks of both Houses of Parliament were given to Keppel, and dinners from all the great bodies in the capital : in short, there never was so complete a triumph. This ebullition of the public feeling was treated with contempt, by one member in particular, in the House of Commons. ' What,' said he, ' London illuminated for three nights together, on account of the glory gained on the 27th July !' To which Burke replied, ' It was not that the trial had proved the 27th to be a day of triumph to Great Britain. No ; they rejoiced because they saw that a gallant officer, a worthy and an honest man, had escaped from the malice of his accusers ; because so excellent a public character was acquitted with honour ; and because generosity, sincerity and virtue, had gained a victory over malice, treachery and meanness ! These, and these only, were the causes of the public illuminations and rejoicings ; and what honest Englishman was there whose bosom would not expand with the highest satisfaction, and the most exalted rapture, on such an occasion ?'

On the 15th of February, four days after the trial, Keppel went on board the Victory, and rehoisted his flag amidst the cheers and salutes of all the ships assembled at Spithead and Portsmouth; and on the 18th of March received an order to strike his flag and come on shore, given in consequence of his reply to a letter from the Admiralty, asking whether he intended to continue in command of the channel fleet ? This was the last of his services at sea.

Two or three awkward circumstances came out in the course of the trial. The masters of the several ships were required to make oath that the log-book produced was the ship's original log, without alterations or additions since made, between the 23d and 30th July. The master of the Robuste declined taking this oath, alleging that both alterations and additions had been made by order of his captain, Alexander Hood, (afterwards Lord Bridport,) respecting what took place on the 27th and 28th July. Captain Hood admitted the fact, and thought himself fully authorized to do so. Keppel asked him where the original entry on those days was. Captain Hood—'Upon my word I do not know.' Then Keppel said, 'As that alteration in Captain Hood's log-book tends to affect my life, I shall ask him no more questions.'

The next circumstance is that Admiral Montagu, in looking over the Formidable's log, discovered three leaves had been cut out, from the 25th to the 28th, and one leaf put in with a fresh tacking of thread. Captain Bazely was then asked how these three leaves came to be cut out? Captain Bazely—'I do not know, so help me God.' Keppel proposed to have the master before them forthwith. Sir Hugh then said, 'I mean to call the master to-morrow morning, he is not here now,'—he was then waiting in the witness-room. The master, on being examined, admitted he had been, in the course of the night, with Sir Hugh Palliser and his two lawyers, in conversation about the log-book, for about an hour and a half. The master further stated that the altered log was approved by the Vice-Admiral; but he believed that neither he nor Captain Bazely were aware of the leaves being cut out. The evidence of Bazely was reluctantly given, and in a shuffling manner. Being asked if Keppel, on the 27th July, had been guilty of neglect in not performing his duty—Said, 'I do not hold myself a competent judge to judge the behaviour and conduct of an admiral in so high a department.' And the same question frequently repeated, procured no other answer—and this from a flag captain! Lord Mulgrave of the Courageux, a Lord of the Admiralty, and Sir Hugh Palliser's colleague, being asked as to Keppel's conduct on the 27th and 28th July, declined answering; and after several attempts of the court to elicit a definite answer, said, 'he was an injured man if he were obliged to answer the question.' The manner and language of Lord Mulgrave were such as to produce a reprimand from the court.

These three are the only hesitating, we had almost said prevaricating witnesses, out of more than twenty called for the prosecution; the rest gave a distinct and positive negative to the charges preferred against the Admiral. The whole of the proceedings must, indeed, have been extremely mortifying to the feelings of Sir Hugh Palliser; and not very agreeable to the Board of Admiralty, which unquestionably manifested an indecent and unprecedented haste in bringing the Admiral to trial, which never could have happened had Lord Sandwich been fortunate enough to have had such men as Anson or Howe for his colleagues, instead of Palliser and Mulgrave.

The failure to convict Keppel induced Palliser to ask for a Court-Martial on himself. It assembled at Portsmouth, and twenty-one days were spent in examining witnesses; after which the court took three more in debating on the sentence, which was, 'that his conduct and behaviour on the 27th and 28th July were, in many respects, highly exemplary and meritorious; they blame him for not having made known to his commander-in-chief the disabled state of the Formidable (by an explosion;) that notwithstanding this omission, he is not in any other respect chargeable with misconduct or misbehaviour, and therefore acquit him.' But he was not tried for disobedience to command.

In the twenty-five sail of the line of the fleet of Keppel, the number that were engaged, were lost, 133 men killed and 373 wounded. The action and its result were much canvassed, as all general actions are, and opinions were very different—'*laudatur ab his, culpatur ab illis*'—influenced, as it would appear, in some respect by party politics; but Englishmen, as the Duke of Richmond observed, are never satisfied if one-half, at least, of the enemy's fleet are not brought into port. Jervis, who was in the action and no mean judge, says—'I have often told you that two fleets of equal force never can produce decisive events, unless they are equally determined to fight it out, or the commander-in-chief of one of them misconducts his line.' On which our author observes, "the hero of St Vincent lived to be of a different opinion,'—alluding, no doubt, to the battle of that name, where, we would remark, his *line* was fortunately so far misconducted, as utterly to be disregarded and broken up: the result is well known.

One of those critics who passed a censure on Keppel, says—'he lost his chance of a victory by not passing through the enemy's line with his van, before the shift of wind.' This his biographer considers unfair, as blaming a man for not having adopted a system of tactics not known at the period when the action was fought. There was not, however, any novelty in Keppel's time in the occasional practice of breaking through the enemy's line, though not done systematically. Thus Blake, in 1653, cut through the fleet of De Ruyter and Van Tromp, when protecting their merchant vessels off the Isle of Wight, and captured several. In 1766, Monk bore down upon the Dutch fleet, and passed through their line. But we need not go further back than the year 1747, when Anson, in pursuit of a flying enemy attempting to escape in closely formed line, threw out a signal for his whole fleet to pursue the enemy, and attack them, without any regard to the preservation of the line of battle. The result was the capture of six ships of war and four Indiamen. In the same year Rear-Admiral Hawke, falling in with a fleet under M. Letendeur, finding that much time was likely to be lost in forming the line, while the enemy was escaping *in line*, threw out a signal for the whole squadron to chase, and come to close engagement; the result was, that six sail of the enemy struck their colours, and two escaped. The French lost above 800 men in killed and wounded; the British 154 killed, and 558 wounded: among the former was Captain Philip Saumarez, of the Nottingham, the companion of Anson in his celebrated voyage. Again, in 1759, Sir Edward Hawke, with twenty-three sail of the line, engaged the French fleet of twenty-one sail of the line, under M. Conflans. The latter were evidently retiring in compact line of battle. Hawke, therefore, made the signal for a general chase, without any regard to order, observing to his officers, 'he did not intend to trouble himself by forming lines, but to attack the enemy in the old way, and make downright work with him.' Eight of our ships were the first, and almost the only ones engaged, and of these, first and most active, was the Victory, commanded by Hawke, the *Magnanime*, by Howe, and the Torbay, by Keppel; the result we have already stated. Keppel, having borne so conspicuous a part in this action, must have been fully aware of the very great advantage over the enemy by breaking up and throwing his line into confusion; and we are persuaded that if Sir Hugh Palliser had not misconducted

himself in so unaccountable a manner, but rejoined the fleet in the evening, Keppel would have done it.

We have heard officers of high rank in the navy say, that the only advantage of forming the line in a large fleet is the knowledge it gives to the Commander-in-Chief of the position of each ship, so that he may dispose of them in coming to action, either singly or in masses, as may to him appear most advisable. Among the most intelligent and best informed writers on naval subjects, is M. Charles Dupin: this author, in his 'Comparative view of the marine forces of England and France,' ridicules what he terms 'the pious respect of his countrymen for the sacred order of the line of battle,' to which, he says, the combined fleets were sacrificed at Trafalgar, by the two wings remaining immovable; while the two columns of Nelson were employed in overwhelming the centre of this sacred line, and while the combined fleet was looking on *avec une effrayante impassibilité*, until its centre was destroyed. Nelson had no regard for his own line of battle, or that of the French. Lord Collingwood distinctly says that Nelson's plan of attack was 'to avoid the inconvenience and delay of forming a line of battle in the usual manner.' The addition of a number of powerful 68-pounder steamers to our fleets, which in future we shall have, will afford additional means, and an additional reason, for running through, and breaking up, the enemy's line of battle.

The difference in the two modes of conducting an action, by the French and English, consists chiefly in this, that the French use every endeavour to keep their line compact, and, by firing high, to cripple the English ships in their masts, sails, and rigging, so as to disable them from a pursuit. The efforts of the English, on the contrary, are directed to the means of throwing the enemy's line into disorder, that every ship may seek for an opportunity of attacking her opponent. M. Dupin, indeed, tells us there is an Ordonnance by which the French fleet is directed to keep the sea, for the longest period it can remain out, without the necessity of coming to an action; and if forced to engage, to avoid compromising the fate of their fleet by a conflict too decisive. They are therefore compelled to fight while retreating, which is always to be done *in line of battle*, just as it was done by D'Orvilliers in Keppel's action. 'Thus then,' says Dupin, 'to maintain, at a great expense, a naval armament; to forbid it from making the best use of its effective power; to send it in search of an enemy; to retreat shamefully from its presence; to receive battle instead of offering it; to commence an action only to finish it by the phantom of a defeat; to lose the moral for the sake of sparing the physical force—this was the principle which, from the reign of Louis XIV. to the mistakes of Napoleon, has guided the administration of the French marine.' Whether the same system is to continue under Louis Philippe is yet to be seen. One thing practised by them is well deserving our serious consideration. The French have adopted a system of establishing a corps of sharp-shooters, or riflemen, or musqueteers, which are intended to be stationed in the tops of ships of the line, preparatory to the event of being compelled into close action. This will make it necessary for us to train a number of marines for a similar purpose, to counteract the destructive effects of such a practice.

The English go differently to work, and under very different feelings to those described by M. Dupin: their anxiety is to get into action, to attack the enemy, as Hawke said, ' in the old way'—that is, to throw them into confusion, and, when it can be done, to engage ship to ship, not merely to cripple but to capture the enemy; the officers relying on the cool and steady conduct of the men, their obedience to command, and on that imposing silence of the crew when actually engaged, which Dupin says is characteristic of British seamen—' *c'est la calme de la force, c'est le recueillement de la sagesse ;*' and we may also add, all hands, at the same time, relying on the practical seamanship, and efficient skill in gunnery, of the officers themselves. There are, it is true, among the latter, in the present day, certain naval officers indiscreetly loud in extolling every thing belonging to the French navy, and, at the same time, disparaging their own : —let no such men be trusted. How different is the conduct of the intelligent French engineer above mentioned, who condemns alike the vicious system of instruction, and the want of skill in the practical seamanship of his own countrymen, which he pronounces as infinitely inferior, in every respect, to those of the British navy.

One or both of two results may, almost to a certainty, be reckoned on, by breaking through, or otherwise throwing into a state of disorder, the enemy's line, to which the

French in particular are so partial. The one is, that by cutting off a portion of it, the part so separated may, by a previous understood arrangement, fall into the hands of the aggressors. The other, supposing the hostile fleets pretty nearly equal, is the plan of Hawke, ' to attack the enemy in the old way, and make downright work with him ;' in other words, that when once in confusion, every ship in the attacking fleet may choose its bird, and from a multitude of examples, (some of which we shall produce), the attacking ship is almost sure of its prey. In the present action, Jervis, in a private letter, says, the Foudroyant (in parading along the line) received the fire of seventeen sail, to each of which she, no doubt, returned her share, but it was seventeen to one between the Foudroyant and seventeen of the enemy : had this fire of the *Foudroyant* been reserved and directed against a single ship, (the *Bretagne* or *Ville de Paris*, which, he says, were upon her at the same time), she would unquestionably have captured one or both. We have, indeed, a brilliant example of what this same *Foudroyant* did accomplish on another occasion : Captain Jervis, in his engagement with the *Pegase*, by his consummate skill in seamanship, kept his ship in the position known to seamen as ' the angle of impunity,' till he could fairly run the Frenchman on board, when she struck her colours, having upwards of eighty of her crew killed and wounded, while the *Foudroyant* had only four wounded, one of whom was Jervis himself. This same eighty-four gun ship had been captured from the enemy by the Monmouth, of sixty-four guns, commanded by Captain Gardiner, who fell in the action. The contest was continued by the first lieutenant, Carket, when she struck, after a dreadful slaughter of one hundred killed and ninety wounded—that of the Monmouth being twenty-eight killed and seventy-nine wounded. Such is the difference between the same ship when fought by a Frenchman and by an Englishman.*

---

* This memorable action of Jervis is ingeniously recorded by the supporters of the heraldic bearings of the St. Vincent's arms, these being the Thunderer's eagle and the winged horse of Helicon. The motto is simply, *Thus*—

     ' *Thois,* very well, *thois !*'—

the well-known direction to the helmsman.

The late Captain Brenton, in his ' Life of the Earl of St. Vincent,' tells a story concerning the captain of the Foudroyant, to which we are reluctant in giving credence, and yet he says he had it from Lord St. Vincent himself. This captain had written a

Another brilliant instance may be mentioned in the action of the Nottingham of sixty guns, commanded by Captain Saumarez, and the *Magnanime*, of seventy-four guns and six hundred and eighty-six men; when the latter, after losing forty-five men killed and one hundred and five wounded, struck to the Nottingham, having sixteen killed and eighteen wounded. A third case occurs to us, between a minor class of ships, in which the results of superior skill and seamanship were displayed in a very remarkable manner. Two thirty-six gun frigates—the Crescent, commanded by Captain Saumarez, (afterwards Lord de Saumarez), and the Reunion, with seventy more men than the Crescent—fought an action of two hours; when the Reunion struck her colours, having lost thirty-four men killed and eighty-four wounded; while the Crescent had not a man killed, and only one hurt, not by the enemy, but by having his leg fractured by the recoil of a gun.

One case, however, we cannot prevail on ourselves to omit. In the fleet under the command of Lord Howe in America, was the Isis of fifty guns, commanded by Captain Raynor. This ship was chased by a French seventy-four, carrying a flag, and, being a better sailer, soon came up with and commenced an attack upon the Isis. The action continued within pistol-shot for an hour and a half, when the Frenchman bore up and made off before the wind. The Isis having suffered so much in her masts and rigging, was unable to follow her. It was afterwards ascertained that she had left France with 900 men; that Captain Bougainville lost his arm and an eye, and since had died of his wounds—and that seventy were killed and one hundred and fifty wounded; and, extraordinary as it may appear, the Isis lost only one man killed and fifteen wounded, two of whom died of their wounds. Such was the result of the consummate skill of her commander, and the disciplined activity of her brave crew. Lord Howe, in his despatch, says he must supply the deficiency of the commander's mode of recital, by observing that the su-

periority acquired over the enemy appears to be not less the effect of Captain Raynor's skilful management of his ship, than of his distinguished resolution, and the bravery of his men and officers.

Fifty other examples might be produced to show what skill in seamanship, and steady conduct, are able to effect, and from which we may lay down as an axiom in naval warfare, That good ships, well officered and manned, and skilfully handled, cannot fail, in any contest with any power, to sustain the high character of the British navy throughout the world. With such ships and such officers, we may despise those murderous schemes of charlatans, with their catamarans, their torpedoes, and other concealed modes of attack, calculated only to alarm the weak and astonish the ignorant—and with such examples, our Commanders-in-Chief need be little solicitous about preserving their line of battle, and breaking up that of the enemy.

The same writer who blamed Keppel for not passing through the enemy's line, gives a further opinion, that he 'lost another opportunity of defeating the French fleet, by not attacking it in the night,—quoting, as his authority, an observation of Nelson, who said, 'If I fall in with the French fleet in the night, I shall engage them immediately; they do badly in the day, but much worse by night.' On which our author observes, 'that the night of the 27th July was a very dark night;' and moreover, it was remarked by one of the witnesses on Keppel's trial, 'The Admiral's signals had been so ill obeyed by the Vice Admiral of the Blue during the day, that he durst not venture to make any chasing signal in the night.' On this subject Lord Howe, when about to engage a superior fleet of French and Spanish ships in the vicinity of Gibraltar, suggested to Admiral Barrington—that as the enemy had at least fifty sail of the line, (he having thirty-four of the line and six frigates),—Whether, from the superior state of discipline and tactics in his own fleet, and in order to compensate the inequality of his force, advantage might not be gained by the inferior fleet attacking the superior in the night? Barrington proposed they should take the opinions of the senior captains. Most of these, supposing it to be Howe's plan, were inclined favourably to it; but on coming to the turn of Sir John Jervis, he said he must declare, in the most decided manner, against any such night attack, even should the Commander-

letter to the Minister of the Marine, acquainting him with the unfortunate issue of the action, which he showed to Jervis, and asked his opinion of it. 'I have but one objection,' said Jervis, 'and that is, that not one word of it is true.' '*Mais comment!* pas vrai?' 'No, sir, not one word of it is true; but you can send it if you please.' He did send it, and when he was tried for the loss of his ship, the letter was produced—he was dismissed the service, and his sword broken over his head.

in-Chief be in favour of it; for that such confusion would be created, that friends might engage with friends, instead of with enemies. Admiral Barrington concurred with Jervis, adding, that he proposed daylight, if it was for no other reason than this—' that it would then be seen who did and who did not do his duty; and that, if there happened to be a *white feather* in the fleet, it would then show itself. Give us daylight, my Lord, by all means, that we may see what we are about.'

'Give me to *see*, and Ajax asks no more.'

We have a most striking practical illustration of the opinion given by Jervis, in the action off Algeziras, by the squadron under Sir James Saumarez; in which two of the largest three-deckers, of a hundred and twelve guns each, the Hermenegilda and the Real Carlos, both blew up with a tremendous explosion, and the whole nearly of their numerous crews perished, having run on board each other; each supposing he was attacking an English seventy-four, the Superb, under Captain Keats, who, having engaged the Real Carlos till she was on fire, moved on to another, leaving the Hermenegilda, who thought her an enemy, to attack and run on board her, and thus to share her melancholy fate. On the whole, therefore, we are of opinion that, circumstanced as Keppel was with regard to one division of his fleet, the superior sailing of that of the enemy, and their determination not to engage him, after parading in their line four days without affording an opportunity of coming to close action, the gallant Admiral will stand fully acquitted by posterity —as the Court ' unanimously and honourably' acquitted him: and whatever censure the opposite party in politics may have endeavoured to fix upon him, we must absolve him from all blame in not bringing ' half the French fleet into port,' as the Duke of Richmond said our countrymen always expected.

The conduct of the government, instanced in that of the Admiralty towards Admiral Keppel, ' led,' as his biographer observes, and as might be expected, ' to many angry discussions in parliament, and, night after night, a series of charges were brought against the ministers. On a motion of Mr. Dunning, condemnatory of the Admiralty, Mr. Fox declared, ' that the man (the Earl of Sandwich) who deprived this country of two of her bravest admirals, (Keppel and Howe), was a greater traitor to the nation than the man who set fire to the dockyard;' and he moved for the removal of Lord Sandwich from the

Admiralty—but he took nothing by his motion. Lord Sandwich, in spite of the attacks made on him, maintained his ground three years after this period; when, on the formation of the Rockingham ministry in April, 1782, he resigned his place to Admiral Keppel, who on this occasion was not only appointed First Lord of the Admiralty, but promoted to the rank of Admiral of the White, at this time the highest in the service; and was, moreover, created a peer, by the title of Viscount Keppel and Baron Elden.

One of his early acts in the capacity of First Lord of the Admiralty met the general approbation of the officers in the navy—this was the appointment of Lord Howe to the chief command of a powerful fleet. His next, however, was so unfortunate as to give umbrage to the whole nation: this was the appointment of Admiral Pigot to supersede Sir George Rodney, with orders to proceed immediately to relieve him. Pigot had scarcely left the shores of England, when intelligence arrived of Rodney's glorious victory over the Count de Grasse. A fast-sailing cutter was forthwith dispatched, to stop the sailing of Pigot; and, if sailed, to endeavour to overtake him, but the pursuit was in vain. The biographer of Keppel endeavours to make it appear, and we think on strong grounds, that the recall was not Admiral Keppel's act, but that of the cabinet; and he quotes a passage from the 'Life of Rodney,' which says—There is reason to believe that Keppel remonstrated, in warm terms, against the measure, threatening, if it were persisted in, to resign his new appointment. Certain it is, the recall occasioned no breach of friendship between Keppel and Rodney.

The short space of three months, in which Keppel remained in office, afforded him but little scope for the exercise of his talents; long enough, however, to learn that a First Lord of the Admiralty may be blamed for measures over which he has no control. The death of the Marquis of Rockingham dissolved the government for the time; but in the following year, when the Coalition administration was formed, Keppel was replaced in the Admiralty. This administration, which afforded but few symptoms of a long life, was overthrown in eight months; partly by the fate of Fox's Indian bill, but chiefly by the dislike of the King to the Whig section of it. Mr. Keppel introduces an amusing anecdote, from a well-known recorder of ' reminiscences,' which happened on the same evening that the Indian bill was thrown out in the Lords :—' The same night Keppel had an audience of the King. He had previously appointed Mr. Adair to sup with him at ten o'clock. It was past twelve before Keppel returned home. "Why, Admiral," said Adair, "where have you been? Here have I been waiting for my supper these two hours." Keppel replied—"I have been with the King; I thought I should never have got away. His Majesty has been most kind to me; he inquired about our prospects and plans, and treated me with so much openness and honesty, that I entered fully into the state of affairs, with which he seemed highly pleased."—"And you believe him?" dryly asked Mr. Adair. Keppel felt hurt at the doubt. Adair contented himself with saying—"Well, we shall see." Before they parted, a note arrived from Lord Temple, to inform Lord Keppel that his Majesty had no further occasion for his services. This was one of those apparent marks of kindness which the King knew so well how to practice.'

Keppel, we believe, acted with great impartiality in the small distribution of patronage that fell to his disposal. The appointment of Howe gave universal satisfaction ; but the Admiral whom he is said to have made his third in command, affords an instance of a placable and forgiving disposition for an injury of the most serious nature, that cannot be too highly admired and extolled—' He (Keppel) had been repeatedly urged to give this post to one of his early friends, but he resisted all solicitations, and appointed Sir Alexander Hood, because he declared, "Hood was the senior admiral of the two, and one of the best officers in his Majesty's service." When Hood's conduct to Keppel, at the time of the court-martial, is remembered, this appointment must be considered as an example at once both of his zeal for the public service and his great placability of temper.'*

On the breaking up of the Coalition administration, Lord Keppel was succeeded in his office at the Admiralty by his friend and companion in arms, Lord Howe. From this period, he withdrew entirely from public life. In September, 1785, he embarked for Naples to pass the winter, on the score of his health ; the failure of it caused, or at least greatly aggravated,

by that pestilential fever caught at the Havannah, which had carried off thousands of his comrades, accelerated the death of both his brothers, and from which, it is said, not one of the survivors of that dearly purchased conquest ever ultimately recovered. Lord Keppel returned to England in the spring of 1786 ; and on the 23d October, of the same year, expired in the sixty-third year of his age.

The character of Lord Keppel, as justly observed by his biographer, ' is comprised in the pages which record his actions ;' and which, we may add, are stated therein in a manner worthy of the recorder of them, by whose talents and diligence a page has been added to the history of the distinguished naval heroes of this country, which was wanting to complete the catalogue of those of our own times. Keppel had few enemies either in the service or out of it ; and he lived long enough to conciliate the affections of all. 'I ever looked on Lord Keppel,' says Burke, ' as one of the greatest and best men of his age ; and I loved and cultivated him accordingly. He was much in my heart : and, I believe, I was in his to the very last beat.' * * * ' Lord Keppel was something high. It was a wild stock of pride, on which the tenderest of all hearts had grafted the milder virtues.'

With the following extract, descriptive of his person, qualities, and opinions, we shall conclude this article :—

' The epithet "little" fondly given by the sailors to Keppel, denotes him to have been low of stature. In his early manhood, a blow received from the butt-end of a pistol, in a scuffle with foot-pads, fractured the bridge of his nose. His face, by this accident, was seriously and permanently disfigured ; yet the fascination of his smile, and the lively and benevolent expression of his eyes, redeemed the countenance from extreme plainness. The " hereditary charm" of his demeanour has been mentioned already. It combined a professional honesty and frankness with ease and simplicity of address which, if not altogether acquired, are certainly confirmed and perfected by intercourse with the best society. His popularity with all classes appeared not only at his trial, but in the esteem with which both those under whom he served, and those whom he commanded, at all times regarded him ; in the zealous affection of his friends, and in the enforced respect of his political opponents.

' The political opinions of Keppel were inherited from ancestors who for centuries had been citizens of a free state, and whose descendants shared in our own revolution of 1688. Reason and experience confirmed these sentiments in him ; and he was, throughout his life, the steady and fearless supporter of civil and religious freedom, even when an opposite course, or neutrality alone, would have smoothed and accelerated

---

* This fact was communicated by Lord Keppel's nephew, the present Sir Robert Adair. Sir John Barrow states, though he does not mention his authority, that it was at Lord Howe's suggestion that Sir Alexander was appointed third in command. The two accounts are not inconsistent.

his professional advancement. His darling object was active employment; yet, when required to serve against his unrepresented brethren on the opposite shores of the Atlantic, Keppel courted neglect and misrepresentation rather than lend his services to a cause which his feelings and his principles equally disapproved. In his numerous encounters with the enemy, we find him, while in a subordinate station, distinguished for his gallantry and his nautical science; for sagacity in comprehending, for promptness in executing, his orders; and when in superior command, successful on every occasion except the indecisive action of the 27th of July. How far the result of that day was attributable to Keppel, as well as of the circumstances which caused the exception, the foregoing pages will, perhaps, have enabled the reader to judge. As a member of the legislature he made no pretensions to eloquence, or even to political eminence. Yet, on all subjects connected with his profession, he was listened to with attention, and distinguished for the impartiality of his representations, and the practical wisdom of his opinions. His letters exhibit similar features of character. On all public questions they display, without effort or pretence, a generous ardour, comprehensive views, and an active and temperate mind. And where they relate to his personal friendships and connections, they reflect an ingenuous and affectionate nature which neither success nor disappointment could disturb.'

ART. III.—*Edwin the Fair: an Historical Drama.* By HENRY TAYLOR, author of 'Philip Van Attevelde.' London: 12mo. 1842.

THIS is a dramatic poem full of life and beauty, thronged with picturesque groups, and with characters profoundly discriminated. They converse in language the most chaste, harmonious, and energetic. In due season fearful calamities strike down the lovely and the good. Yet 'Edwin the Fair' is not to be classed among tragedies, in the full and exact sense of the expression.

'To purge the soul by pity and terror,' it is not enough that the stage should exhibit those who tread the high places of the earth as victims either of unmerited distress, or of retributive justice. It is further necessary that their sorrows should be deviations from the usual economy of human life. They must differ in their origin, and their character, from those ills which we have learned to regard as merely the established results of familiar causes. They must be attended by the rustling of the dark wings of fate, or by the still more awful march of an all-controlling Providence. The domain of the tragic theatre lies in that dim region where the

visible and invisible worlds are brought into contact; and where the wise and the simple alike perceive and acknowledge a present deity, or demon. It is by the shocks and abrupt vicissitudes of fortune, that the dormant sense of our dependence on that inscrutable power in the grasp of which we lie, is quickened into life. It is during such transient dispersion of the clouds beneath which it is at other times concealed, that we feel the agency of heaven in the affairs of earth to be a reality and a truth. It is in such occurrences alone (distinguished in popular language from the rest, as providential) that the elements of tragedy are to be found in actual or imaginable combination. There the disclosure of the laws of the universal theocracy imparts to the scene an unrivalled interest, and to the actors in it the dignity of ministers of the will of the Supreme. There each event exhibits some new and sublime aspect of the divine energy working out the divine purposes. There the great enigmas of our existence receive at least a partial solution. There, even amidst the seeming triumph of wrong, may be traced the dispensation of justice to which the dramatist is bound; and there also extends before his view a field of meditation drawn from themes of surpassing majesty and pathos.

Such is the law to which all the great tragic writers of ancient or of modern times have submitted themselves—each in his turn assuming this high office of interpreting the movements of Providence, and reconciling man to the mysteries of his being. Thus Job is the stoic of the desert—victorious over all the persecutions of Satan, till the better sense of unjust reproach and undeserved punishment breaks forth in agonies which the descending Deity rebukes, silences, and soothes. Prometheus is the temporary triumph over beneficence, of a power at once malignant and omnipotent, which, at the command of destiny, is blindly rushing on towards the universal catastrophe which is to overwhelm and ruin all things. Agamemnon returns in triumph to a home where, during his long absence, the avenging Furies have been couching to spring at last on the unhappy son of Atreus—every hand in that fated house drooping with gore, and every voice uttering the maledictions of the infernals. Œdipus, and his sons and daughters, represent a succession of calamities and crimes which would seem to exhaust the catalogue of human wretchedness; but each in turn is made to exhibit the working of one of the most awful of the laws under which we live —the visitation of the sins of parents upon their children to the third and fourth generation. Macbeth is seduced by demoniacal predictions to accomplish the purposes, by violating the commands, of Heaven ; and so to meditate, to extenuate, and to commit, the crimes suggested by the Fiend in cruel mockery. Hamlet is at once the reluctant minister and the innocent victim of the retributive justice, to the execution of which he is goaded by a voice from the world of departed spirits. Lear is crushed amidst the ruins of his house, on which parental injustice, filial impiety, foul lusts, and treacherous murder, had combined to draw down the curse of the avenger. Faust moves on towards destruction under the guidance of the Fiend, who lures him by the pride of knowledge and the force of appetite. Wallenstein plunges into destruction, drawing down with him the faithful and the good, as a kind of bloody sacrifice, to atone for treachery to which the aspect of the stars and the predictions of the diviner had impelled him. And so, through every other tragic drama which has awakened the deeper emotions of the spectator or the reader, might be traced the operation of the law to which we have referred. How far this universal characteristic of tragedy—the perceptible intervention in human affairs of powers more than human—is to be discovered in ' Edwin the Fair,' the following brief and imperfect outline of the plot may sufficiently determine.

In the fresh and dewy dawn of life, Edwin and Elgiva had been wont to rove—

> ' O'er hill, through dale, with interlacing arms,
> And thrid the thickets where wild roses grow,
> Entangled with each other like themselves.'

But their sun had scarcely risen above the eastern horizon, when the dreams of childhood faded away before the illusions of youth. He ascended the Anglo-Saxon throne, and she plighted her troth to Earl Leolf, the commander of the English armies. The Earl was ' a man in middle age, busy and hard to please,' and not happy in the art of pleasing. Such, at least, was the more deliberate opinion or feeling of Elgiva. In a day of evil augury to herself, and to her house, the inconstant maiden crushed the hopes of her grave, though generous suitor, to share the crown of her early playmate.

It sat neither firmly nor easily on his brows. Athulf, the brother, and Leolf, the discarded suitor of his queen, were the chief opponents of the powerful body which, under the guidance of Dunstan, were rapidly extending over the monarchy, and the Church of England, the authority of the monastic orders. In the approaching alliance of Athulf's family to Edwin, the Abbot of Glastonbury foresaw the transfer, to a hostile party, of his own dominion over the mind of his young sovereign. Events had occurred to enhance and justify his solicitude. Athulf's energy had enabled Edwin to baffle the pretexts by which Dunstan had delayed his coronation. It was celebrated with becoming splendour, and was followed by a royal banquet. The moment appeared to the king propitious for avoiding the vigilant eye of his formidable minister. He escaped from the noisy revels, and flew on the wings of love to an adjacent oratory, where, before his absence had excited the notice and displeasure of his guests, he exchanged with Elgiva the vows which bound them to each other till death should break the bond. They little dreamed how soon it should thus be broken. Resenting the indignity of the king's abrupt desertion of the festive board, the assembled nobles deputed the Abbot and the Archbishop of Canterbury to solicit, and if necessary to compel his return. They found him in the society of his newly-affianced bride, and assailed them with gross imputations, which she indignantly repelled by an open avowal of her marriage. Availing himself of the disorder of the moment, and of the canonical objections to their union, founded on their too near consanguinity, Dunstan caused them to be seized and imprisoned. Elgiva was despatched to Chester, the King and Athulf being secured in the Tower of London.

Leolf, who had absented himself from the coronation, was in command of the royal forces at Tunbridge, where he was quickly joined by Athulf, who had found the means of escaping from prison. The two earls then separated—Leolf proceeding to the north, with a part of the army, to rescue Elgiva, and Athulf assuming the conduct of the power destined for the deliverance of the King.

Whatever may have been the indignation of the confederate lords, their policy dictated pacific measures ; and to these the Archbishop, offended and alarmed by the audacity of Dunstan, willingly lent himself. He convened a synod to deliberate on the validity of the royal marriage, and on the propriety of applying to Rome for a dispensation. Long and fervent debate ensued. The Church as represented in that holy conclave, had given strong indications of a conciliatory spirit, when, casting himself in vehement prayer before a crucifix, Dunstan invoked the decision of Him whose sacred image it bore. An audible voice, which seemed to proceed from the cross, (though really uttered by a minister of the Abbot's crimes, who had been concealed for the purpose within its ample cavity), forbade the ratification of the royal nuptials. Rising from the earth, the holy Abbot pronounced a solemn excommunication of Edwin, Elgivà, and their adherents, and dismissed the assembly which had so vainly attempted to defeat the will of heaven, and of heaven's chosen minister.

The triumphant Dunstan then proceeded to the Tower, to obtain from the captive and excommunicated King the abdication of his crown. He was answered by indignant reproaches, and at length withdrew, but not till he had summoned into the royal presence an assassin, prepared to bring the controversy to a decisive and bloody close. At that instant Athulf with his forces burst into the Tower. Edwin regained his freedom, and Dunstan fled in disguise into Hampshire.

But the saint of Glastonbury possessed too powerful a hold on the attachment and reverence of the multitude, to be thus defeated by any blow however severe, or by any exposure however disgraceful. A popular insurrection in his favour arrested his flight to France. He resumed his self-confidence, appeared again in his proper character, and lifted up his mitred front, with its wonted superiority, in a Wittenagemot which he convened at Malpas. There, surrounded by his adherents and his military retainers, he openly denounced war on his sovereign.

Under the guidance of Athulf, the King had moved from London towards Chester, to effect a junction with Leolf and his army. The attempt was not successful. Impatient of her prison, Elgiva had exercised over her jailer the spell of her rank and beauty, and had rendered him at once the willing instrument and the companion of her escape. Leolf was apprised of her design, and anxious for the safety of her who had so ill requited his devotion, advanced to meet her, supported only by a small party of his personal attendants. They met, and, while urging their flight to Leolf's army, were overtaken by a party attached to the cause of Dunstan, and slain.

For this catastrophe Dunstan was not, in intention at least, responsible. Alarmed by intelligence of a Danish invasion, he had become desirous of a reconciliation with Edwin, and was making overtures for that purpose. But it was now too late. The King, maddened by the loss of Elgiva, rushed forward with blind and precipitate haste to Malpas, where the body of his murdered wife awaited a royal sepulture, and where was intrenched the haughty rebel who had brought her down to a premature grave. Deaf to every voice but that which from the inmost recesses of his soul cried for revenge, Edwin plunged wildly into his fate. Covered with wounds, he fell once more into the toils of his deadly enemy. An awful sound recalled him to momentary animation and strength. It was the low dirge from the choir of the neighbouring cathedral, chanting the funeral obsequies of Elgiva. He flew from his dying couch, cast himself with delirious ravings on her cold and inanimate form, and then, invoking the vengeance of heaven on their persecutor, descended with her to the grave.

Incomplete, and therefore inaccurate, as it is, this slight abridgment of the tale will show, that the dramatic action of 'Edwin the Fair' is rather disastrous than tragical. We witness, indeed, the deadly conflict of thrones, spiritual and temporal. The Sceptre falls from a feeble grasp, and the Crozier is elevated in sanguinary triumph. But it is the triumph of power over weakness, of craft over simplicity, of mature worldly wisdom over childish inexperience. An overwhelming calamity befalls Edwin and Elgiva, but it is provoked neither by any gigantic guilt, nor by any magnanimous self-devotion. They perish, the victims of imprudence rather than of crime—of a rash marriage and a venial inconstancy. This is quite probable—quite in accordance with truths to be gathered from the experience of each passing day; but for that very reason, it is a fable which does not fulfil the laws imposed on the stage by Æschylus and Shakspeare—by their imitators and their critics—or rather by reason and nature herself. It does not break up our torpid habitual associations. It excites no intense sympathy. It gives birth to no deep emotion, except, indeed, regret that vengeance does not strike down the oppressor. There is a failure of poetical justice in the progress and in the catastrophe of the drama. If it were a passage of authentic history, the mind might repose in the conviction that the Judge of all must eventually do right. But as it is a fiction, it is impossible not to repine that right is not actually done. Such unmerited disasters and prosperous injustice are, we know, consistent with the presence of a superintending Deity. But they do not suggest it. The handwriting on the wall has no pregnant meaning, nor mythic significancy. It is not apparently traced by the Divine finger, nor has the Seer given us any inspired interpretation. It is one of those legends from which a moralist might deduce important lessons of prudence, but from which a dramatist could hardly evoke a living picture of the destiny of man;—of man opposed and aided by powers mightier than his own, engaged in an unequal though most momentous conflict, impotent even when victorious, and majestic even when subdued.

·This objection to the plot of his drama has evidently been anticipated by Mr. Taylor himself. He summons some dark clouds to gather around Dunstan at the moment of his success, and dismisses him from our view, oppressed by the only domestic sorrow to which his heart was accessible, and by omens of approaching calamity from an inroad of the Northmen. Thus the triumph of the wicked is tempered, and some endeavour is made to gratify, as well as to excite, the thirst for his punishment. It is hardly a successful attempt. The loss in mature life of an aged mother, is a sorrow too familiar and transitory to be accepted as a retribution for crimes of the deepest dye ; and war, however disastrous to others, has seldom any depressing terrors for the rulers of mankind. Besides, there are yet some fetters, however light, which chronology will throw over the volatile spirit of poetry ; and it is hard to forget the historical fact, that no Danish invasion ever disturbed the tranquillity of Dunstan ; but that he lived and died in that century of repose, for which England was indebted to the wisdom and the valour of the two great predecessors of Edwin.

Mr. Taylor has therefore employed another and·more effectual resource to relieve the inherent defects of the subject he has chosen. He avails himself of the opportunity it affords for the delineation and contrast of characters, which he throws off with a careless prodigality, attesting an almost inexhaustible affluence. In every passage where the interest of the story droops, it is sustained by the appearance of some new person of the drama, who is not a mere fiction, but a reality with a fictitious name. The stage is not possessed by its ancient tenants provided with a new set of speeches, but with recruits, who represent some of the many aspects under which man has actually presented himself to a most sagacious and diligent observer. This, however, is not true of Dunstan, the most conspicuous of all those who contribute to the action or to the dialogue. He is drawn, not from actual life, but from books. In the great drama of society, which is acted in our age on the theatre of the civilized world, no part has been, or could be, assigned to a Spiritual Despot, in which to disclose freely the propensities and the mysteries of his nature. The poet has therefore taken the outline from the Anglo-Saxon Chroniclers, and has supplied the details and the colouring from his own imagination. Hence the central figure is less congruous— less in harmony with itself—than those of the group by which it is surrounded ; but then it is more ideal, is cast in bolder relief, and is thrown off with greater force and freedom.

The real Dunstan, the Recluse, the Saint, and the Statesman of the Tenth century, had his full share of the inconsistencies which distinguish man as he is, from man as he is painted. He was endowed with all the faculties by which great actions are achieved, and with the temperament without which they are never undertaken. Conversant in his early manhood with every science by which social life had then been improved, and by every art by which it had been embellished, his soul was agitated by ambition and by love. Unprosperous in both, his wounded spirit sought relief in solitude and penitential exercises ; and an age familiar with such prodigies, regarded with astonishment and reverence the austerity of his self-discipline. When, at length, he emerged from the grave, (for in that similitude he had dug his cell), he was supposed by others, and probably by himself, to have buried there all the tastes and the passions which had once enslaved him to the world. But other spirits as secular as the first, though assuming a holier garb, had entered his bosom, and taken up their abode there. All the energies once wasted on letters, music, painting, and science, or in the vain worship of her to whom his young heart had been devoted, were henceforth consecrated to the church and to his order. He became the foremost champion of sacerdotal celibacy and monastic retirement ; assumed the conduct of the war of the regular against the secular clergy ; and was the founder of the ecclesiastical system which continued for five centuries to control all the religious, and to affect all the political institutions of his native land.

But the Severn leaping down the rocks of Plinlimmon, and the same stream when expanded into a muddy and sluggish estuary, does not differ more from itself, than St. Dunstan the Abbot of Glastonbury, from Dunstan the Metropolitan of the Church, and the Minister of the Crown of England. During five successive reigns, all the powers of the government were in his hands, but he ruled ingloriously. When his supreme power had once been firmly secured, all the fire and genius of his earlier days became extinct. With the sublime example of Alfred, and the more recent glories of Athelstan before his eyes, he accomplished nothing, and attempted nothing for the permanent welfare of his country. No one social improvement can be traced to his wisdom or munificence. He had none of the vast conceptions, and splendid aims, which have ennobled the usurpations of so many other churchmen. After an undisputed possession of power of forty years' continuance, he left the State enfeebled, and the Crown in hopeless degradation. To him, more than to any man, must be ascribed the ruin of the dynasty under which he flourished, and the invasions which desolated the kingdom during half a century from his death. He had commanding talents and dauntless courage, but a low, narrow, selfish spirit. His place in the Roman calendar was justly assigned to him in acknowledgment of his incomparable services to the Papacy; but he has no station in the calendar of the great and good men who, having consecrated the noblest gifts of nature and of fortune to their proper ends, live for the benefit of all generations, and are alike revered and celebrated by all.

The Dunstan of this tragedy is not the lordly churchman reposing in the plenitude of success, but the fanatic grasping at supreme command. He is the real hero of 'Edwin the Fair,' towering over all his associates, and distinguished from them all by a character, which, in the full and proper sense of the term, may be pronounced to be dramatic. He is at once the victim of religious misanthropy and self-adoration. He has worshipped the world, has been rejected by his idol, and has turned away mortified, but not humbled, to meditate holier joys, and to seek an eternal recompense. But, in the pursuit of these sublime objects, he is haunted by the memory of the delights he has abandoned, and of the injustice which has expelled him from the ways and the society of mankind. These thoughts distil their bitterness even into his devotions. His social affections droop and wither as their proper aliment is withdrawn. His irascible feelings deepen, and pass into habits of fixed antipathy and moroseness. To feed these gloomy passions he becomes the calumniator of his species, incredulous of human virtue, and astute in every uncharitable construction of human motives. His malignity establishes a disastrous alliance with his disordered piety. He ascribes to the Being he adores the foul passions which fester in his own bosom. His personal wrongs are no longer the insignificant ills of an individual sufferer, nor have his personal resentments the meanness of a private revenge—for his foes are antagonists of the purposes of heaven; and to crush them can be no unacceptable homage to the Supreme Arbiter of rewards and punishments. With the cold unsocial propensities of a withered heart, disguised from others and from himself by the sophistries of a palsied conscience, Dunstan finds his way back to the busy world. He lives among men to satiate an ambition such as might be indulged by an incarnation of the Evil Spirit—an ambition exulting in conscious superiority, and craving for the increase and the display of it, but spurning and

trampling in the dust the victims over whom it triumphs. Patriotism, loyalty, humility, reverence—every passion by which man is kind to his brethren—all are dead in him; and an intense selfishness, covered by holy pretexts, reigns in undisputed sovereignty in his soul. Man is but the worthless instrument of his will; and even to his Creator he addresses himself with the unawed familiarity of a favourite. Proud, icy-cold, and remorseless, he wades through guilt sneeringly and exultingly—the subject of a strange spiritual disease, compounded of a paralysis of all the natural sympathies, and a morbid vigour of all the mental energies. This portrait is terrible, impressive, and (unhappily) not improbable. It labours, however, under one inconsistency.

The fanaticism of Dunstan, as delineated in this tragedy, is wanting in one essential element. He has no profound or deeply cherished convictions. He does not believe himself to be the selected depositary of divine truth. He does not regard dissent from his own opinions as criminal; nor does he revel in any vindictive anticipations of the everlasting woe of his theological antagonists. He is not clinging to any creed which, if rejected by others, may elude his own grasp. The enemies of the Church are indeed his enemies; but they are so because they endanger his power, not because they disturb the repose or the self-complacency of his mind. He has (to borrow the distinction of a great writer) the fanaticism of the scourge, the brand, and the sword, without having the fanaticism of the creed. He is a fanatic, without being an enthusiast. His guilt is not extenuated by any passionate attachment for truth or sanctity, or for what he believes to be true and sacred. He rushes into oppression, treachery, fraud, and plunder, not at the impulse of a disordered imagination, but at the bidding of a godless, brotherless heart.

This absence of theological hatred, founded on the earnest attachment to some theological opinions, impairs both the congruity and the terror of Dunstan's dramatic character. He is actuated by no passion intense enough to provoke such enormous guilt; or familiar enough to bring him within the range of our sympathies; or natural enough to suggest, that some conceivable shifting of the currents of life might hurry us into some plunge as desperate as that which we see him making. His homicides are not bloody sacrifices, but villanous murders. His scourge is not the thong of Dominic, so much as the lash with which Sancho (the knave!) imposes on the credulity of his master. His impious frauds are not oracular deceptions, but the sleight-of-hand tricks of a juggler. He is waited on by an imp of darkness, who is neither man nor fiend ; for he perpetrates the foulest crime, without malignity or cupidity, or any other obvious motive. He slaughters Elgiva and Leolf, raises his hand to assassinate the king ; and, at Dunstan's command, climbs a tree, to howl there like the Devil; and then enters the cavity of the crucifix, to utter a solemn response in the person of the Redeemer.

The objection to this is not the improbability, but the revolting hatefulness of the guilt which Dunstan and his minister divide between them. Unhappily it is not historically improbable, but the reverse. Sanguinary and devious have been the paths along which many a canonized saint has climbed that celestial eminence. Tricks, as base and profane as that of Dunstan's crucifix, have been exhibited or encouraged, not merely by the vulgar heroes, but by some of the most illustrious fathers of the Church. But if they violated the eternal laws of God, it was to accomplish what they devoutly believed to be the divine will. Saints and sinners might agree in the means to be used, but they differed entirely as to the ends to be accomplished. Ambrose, preaching at Milan over the bleeding remains of the disenterred martyrs, lent himself to what he must have suspected or known to be a lie. But the lie was told and exhibited for the confutation of the Arians, to which holy object Ambrose would as readily have sacrificed his life. And though evil done that good may come, be evil still—nay, an evil peculiarly pestilent and hard to be forgiven—yet there is, after all, a wide difference between Bishop Bonner and Jonathan Wilde. Devout fanaticism, if it may not extenuate, does at least sublimate crime. By the intensity of his convictions, the greatness of his aims, and the energy of his motives, the genuine fanatic places himself beyond the reach of contempt, of disgust, or of unmixed abhorrence We feel that, by the force of circumstances, the noblest of men might be betrayed into such illusions, and urged into such guilt as his. We acknowledge that, under happier auspices, he might have been the benefactor, not the curse of his species. We perceive that, if his erring judgment could be corrected, he might even yet be reclaimed to philanthropy and to peace. If we desire that retributive justice should overtake him, the aspiration is, that he may fall 'a victim to the gods,' and not be hewed as 'a carcass for the hounds.' Not such is the vengeance we invoke on the dramatic Dunstan and his ministering demon. We upbraid the tardiness of human invention, which laboured a thousand years in the discovery of the treadmill. Or rather our admiration of the genius which created so noble an image of intellectual power, ruthless decision, and fearful hardihood, is alloyed by some resentment that the poet should so have marred the work of his own hands. How noble a work it is will be best understood by listening to the soliloquy in which Dunstan communes with his own heart, and with his Maker, on the commission entrusted to him, and on the spiritual temptations he has to encounter in the discharge of it :—

' Spirit of speculation, rest, oh rest !
And push not from her place the spirit of prayer!
God, thou'st given unto me a troubled being—
So move upon the face thereof, that light
May be, and be divided from the darkness!
Arm thou my soul that I may smite and chase
The spirit of that darkness, whom not I
But Thou thro' me compellest.—Mighty power,
Legions of piercing thoughts illuminate,
Hast Thou committed to my large command,
Weapons of light and radiant shafts of day,
And steeds that trample on the tumbling clouds.
But with them it hath pleased Thee to let mingle
Evil imaginations, corporal stings,
A host of Imps and Ethiops, dark doubts,
Suggestions of revolt.—Who is't that dares'—

In the same spirit, at once exulting, self-exploring, and irreverent, Dunstan bursts out in a sort of pæan on his anticipated success, as he enters the Tower to persuade the abdication of his sovereign.

' Kings shall bow down before thee, said my soul,
And it is even so. Hail, ancient Hold !
Thy chambers are most cheerful, though the light
Enter not freely ; for the eye of God
Smiles in upon them. Cherish'd by His smile
My heart is glad within me, and to Him
Shall testify in works a strenuous joy.
—Methinks that I could be myself that rock
Whereon the Church is founded,—wind and flood
Beating against me, boisterous in vain.
I thank you, Gracious Powers ! Supernal Host!
I thank you that on me, though young in years,
Ye put the glorious charge to try with fire,
To winnow and to purge. I hear you call !
A radiance and a resonance from Heaven
Surrounds me, and my soul is breaking forth
In strength, as did the new-created Sun
When Earth beheld it first on the fourth day.
God spake not then more plainly to that orb
Than to my spirit now. I hear the call.
My answer, God, and Earth, and Hell shall hear.
But I could reason with thee, Gracious Power,
For that thou givest me to perform thy work
Such sorry instruments.'

The spirit thus agitated had not always been a prey to disquieting thoughts. Dunstan had once loved as other men love, and even on his seared heart were engraven recollections which revive in all their youthful

warmth and beauty as he contemplates the
agonies of his captive king, and tempts him to
abdicate his crown by the prospect of his reunion to Elgiva.

> 'When Satan first
> Attempted me, 'twas in a woman's shape;
> Such shape as may have erst misled mankind,
> When Greece or Rome uprear'd with Pagan rites
> Temples to Venus, pictured there or carved
> With rounded, polish'd, and exuberant grace,
> And mien whose dimpled changefulness betray'd,
> Thro' jocund hues, the seriousness of passion.
> I was attempted thus, and Satan sang,   ,
> With female pipe and melodies that thrill'd
> The soften'd soul, of mild voluptuous ease,
> And tender sports that chased the kindling hours
> In odorous gardens or on terraces,
> To music of the fountains and the birds,
> Or else in skirting groves by sunshine smitten,
> Or warm winds kiss'd, whilst we from shine to
>   shade   :
> Roved unregarded. Yes, 'twas Satan sang,
> Because 'twas sung to me, whom God had call'd
> To other pastime and severer joys.
> But were it not for this, God's strict behest   -
> Enjoin'd upon me,—had I not been vow'd
> To holiest service rigorously required,
> I should have owned it for an Angel's voice,
> Nor ever could an earthly crown, or toys
> And childishness of vain ambition, gauds ·
> And tinsels of the world, have lured my heart
> Into the tangle of those mortal cares
> That gather round a throne. What call is thine
> From God or Man, what voice within bids thee
> Such pleasures to forego, such cares confront?'

Dunstan is a superb sophister. Observe
with what address he reconciles himself to
the fraud so coarse and degrading as that of
making his instrument, Gurmo, shake the
forest with dismal howlings, to intimate to the
passers-by that the hour of fierce conflict between the Saint and the Prince of Darkness
had arrived. Contempt of mankind, and of
his supposed adversary, are skilfully called
up to still the voice of honour and the remonstrances of conscience.

> 'And call'st thou this a fraud, thou secular lack-
>   brain?
> Thou loose lay-priest, I tell thee it is none.
> Do I not battle wage in very deed
> With Satan? Yea, and conquer! And who's he
> Saith falsehood is deliver'd in these howls,
> Which do but to the vulgar ear translate
> Truths else to them ineffable? Where's Satan?
> His presence, life and kingdom? Not the air
> Nor bowels of the earth, nor central fires
> His habitat exhibits; it is here,
> Here in the heart of Man. And if from hence
> I cast him with discomfiture, that truth
> Is verily of the vulgar sense conceived, ·
> By utterance symbolic, when they deem
> That, met in bodily oppugnancy,
> I tweak him by the snout. A fair belief
> Wherein the fleshy and the palpable type
> Doth of pure truth substantiate the essence.

> Enough. Come down. The screech-owl from
>   afar
> Upbraids thy usurpation. Cease, I say.'

It is with admirable truth and insight into
human character the Dunstan is made to resort to artifices, as various as the occasions
suggesting them, to evade the expostulations
with which conscience still tracks him in the
path of guilt. From scorn of man he passes
to a kind of adoration of the mystical abstract
Being, to which, in the absence of more palpable idols, it is so easy to render an extravagant homage. What a labyrinth of gigantic,
vague, half-conceived images is it into which
he plunges, in the endeavour to sustain his
own mind, by contemplating the majesty and
the holiness of the impersonation in the cause
of which he is willing to believe himself engaged.

> 'The Church is great,
> Is holy, is ineffably divine!
> Spiritually seen, and with the eye of faith,
> The body of the Church, lit from within,
> Seems but the luminous phantom of a body;
> The incorporeal spirit is all in all.
> Eternity *a parte post et ante* ·
> So drinks the refuse, thins the material fibre,
> That lost in ultimate tenuity
> The actual and the mortal lineaments,
> The Church in Time, the meagre, definite, bare,
> Ecclesiastical anatomy,
> The body of this death translates itself,   ··
> And glory upon glory swallowing all
> Makes earth a scarce distinguishable speck
> In universal heaven. Such is the Church
> As seen by faith; but otherwise regarded,
> The body of the Church is search'd in vain
> To find the seat of the soul; for it is nowhere.
> Here are two Bishops, but 'tis not in them.'

To the dramatic character of Dunstan, the
antithesis is that of Wulfstan the Wise. An
idealist arrested in the current of life by the
eddy of his own thoughts, he muses away his
existence in one long, though ever-shifting
dream of labours to be undertaken, and duties
to be performed. Studious of books, of nature,
of the heart, and of the ways of man, his intellectual wealth feeds a perennial stream of
discourse, which, meandering through every
field of speculation, and in turns enriching all,
still changes the course it ought to pursue, or
overflows the blanks by which it should be
confined, as often as any obstacle is opposed
to its continuous progress. Love, poetry,
friendship, philosophy, war, politics, morals,
and manners, each is profoundly contemplated,
eloquently discussed, and helplessly abon-
doned, by this master of ineffectual wisdom:
and yet he is an element in society which
could be worse spared than the shrewdest
practical understanding in the Camp or the
Exchange. His wide circuit of meditation

has made him catholic, charitable, and indulgent. In the large horizon which his mental eye traverses, he discerns such comprehensive analogies, such countless indications of the creative goodness, and such glorious aspects of beauty and of grace, as no narrower ken could embrace, and no busier mind combine and harmonize. To form such combinations, and to scatter prodigally around him the germs of thought, if happily they may bear fruit in intellects better disciplined, though less opulent than his own, is the delight and the real duty of Wulfstan, the colloquial. His talk, when listeners are to be had, thus becomes a ceaseless exercise of kindness; and even when there are none to heed him, an imaginary circle still enables him to soliloquize most benevolently. In this munificent diffusion of his mental treasures, the good man is not merely happy, but invulnerable. Let fortune play her antics as she will, each shall furnish him with a text; and he will embellish all with quaint conceits or diagnostic expositions. His daughter steals an unworthy match; but he rebounds from the shock to moralize on parental disappointment and conjugal constancy. He is overborne and trampled down by the energy of Dunstan, and immediately discovers in his misadventure a proof how well the events of his own age are adapted for history; and how admirably a retirement to Oxford will enable himself to become the historian. Could Samuel Taylor Coleridge have really thus blossomed in the iron age of the Anglo-Saxons? It is a hard problem. But the efflorescence of his theatrical representative is rendered probable to all who ever performed the pilgrimage to the Hierophant at Highgate, in the golden era of George IV. Never was there a group of auditors better disposed or better able to appreciate the wisdom of a sage, than those who are collected round Wulfstan. See with fine discrimination and keen relish his portrait is sketched by one of them.

'Still
This life and all that it contains, to him
Is but a tissue of illuminous dreams
Fill'd with book wisdom, pictured thought, and love
That on its own creations spends itself.
All things he understands, and nothing does.
Profusely eloquent in copious praise
Of action, he will talk to you as one
Whose wisdom lay in dealings and transactions;
Yet so much action as might tie his shoe
Cannot his will command; himself alone
By his own wisdom not a jot the gainer.
Of silence, and the hundred thousand things
'Tis better not to mention, he will speak,
And still most wisely.—But, behold! he comes.'

Leolf, who thus delineates the character of Wulfstan, is about to announce to the old man the secret marriage of his daughter; and as the Earl cautiously approaches the unwelcome topic, the philosopher finds in each turn of the discourse some theme which hurries him away to a boundless distance from the matter in hand. Obeying the law by which his own ideas are associated, but with the tendency observable in all dreamers, sleeping or waking, to reconcile the vision with any suggestion from without, he involves himself in an inquiry how a man in middle life should wed, and on that critical topic thus makes deliverance:—

'Love changes with the changing life of man:
In its first youth, sufficient to itself,
Heedless of all beside, it reigns alone,
Revels or storms, and spends itself in passion.
In middle age—a garden through whose soil
The roots of neighbouring forest-trees have crept—
It strikes on stringy customs bedded deep,
Perhaps on alien passions; still it grows
And lacks not force nor freshness: but this age
Shall aptly chuse as answering best its own,
A love that clings not, nor is exigent,
Encumbers not the active purposes,
Nor drains their source; but proffers with free grace
Pleasure at pleasure touch'd, at pleasure waved
A washing of the weary traveller's feet,
A quenching of his thirst, a sweet repose
Alternate and preparative, in groves
Where loving much the flower that loves the shade,
And loving much the shade that that flower loves,
He yet is unbewilder'd, unenslaved,
Thence starting light, and pleasantly let go,
When serious service calls.'

Mr. Shandy's expenditure of eloquence on the death of his son, was not more consolatory to the bereaved rhetorician, than are the disquisitions of Wulfstan on his daughter's undutiful marriage. She must no longer be mutable of purpose. She must study the excellent uses of constancy, and abide in quietude of mind. The fickle wind may he her teacher. Then, as if himself floating on the wings of some soft and balmy gale, the poetical sage drowns all his parental anxieties in this light and beautiful parable:—

'The wind, when first he rose and went abroad
Thro' the vast region, felt himself at fault,
Wanting a voice; and suddenly to earth
Descended with a wafture and a swoop,
Where, wandering volatile from kind to kind,
He woo'd the several trees to give him one.
First he besought the ash; the voice she lent
Fitfully with a free and lashing change
Flung here and there its sad uncertainties:
The aspen next; a flutter'd frivolous twitter

Was her sole tribute: from the willow came,
So long as dainty summer dress'd her out,
A whispering sweetness, but her winter note
Was hissing, dry, and reedy: lastly the pine
Did he solicit, and from her he drew
A voice so constant, soft, and lowly deep,
That there he rested, welcoming in her
A mild memorial of the ocean cave
Where he was born.'

The spirit of rumination possesses all the persons of this drama. No wonder, then, that Leolf feeds on his own thoughts, as best becomes a discarded lover. But of that deplorable class of mankind, he is a remarkable, if not altogether a new variety. He had climbed the central arch in the bridge of life, painfully conscious of the solitude of his heart in the midst of the busy crowd, and cherishing a vague but earnest desire for deliverance. An ideal form, lovely as the day-spring, and radiant with love to him, haunted his path, and he lived in the faith that the bright reality would at length be disclosed, when his spirit should know the blessedness of that union which mystically represents to man the design and the perfection of his being. She came, or seemed to come, in the form of Elgiva—the glorious impersonation of that dazzling fantasy—the actual fulfilment of many a dream, too fondly courted by his solemn and overburdened mind. Nature had made her beautiful, and, even when the maiden's ruby lips were closed, her beaming eye and dimpled cheek gave utterance to thoughts, now more joyous or impassioned, now more profound or holy, than any which could be imparted through the coarser vehicle of articulate speech. So judged the enamoured interpreter of that fair tablet—mistaking for emanations of her mind the glowing hues reflected by that brilliant surface from his own. He threw over the object of his homage all the most rich and graceful draperies stored in the wardrobe of his own pensive imagination; unconsciously worshipped the creature of his own fancy; and adorned her with a diadem which, though visible to him alone, had for a true heart a greater value than the proudest crown which could be shared with kings.

Such was not Elgiva's judgment. Her ear drank in the flatteries of Edwin; nor had he long to sue for the hand which had been plighted to the champion and defender of his throne. A ready vengeance was in the grasp of Leolf. One word from him would have sealed the doom of his successful rival. But no such words passed his lips. In his solitude he probes the incurable wound which had blighted all the hopes, and dispelled all the illusions of life. He broods with melancholy intentness over the bleak prospect, and drains to the dregs the bitter cup of irremediable desolation. But in his noble spirit there is no place for scorn, resentment, or reproach. His duty, though it be to protect with his life the authors of his wretchedness, is performed in the true spirit of duty;—quietly, earnestly, and without vaunt or ostentation. He has sympathy to spare for the sorrows of others, while demanding none for his own. He extenuates with judicial rectitude and calmness Elgiva's infidelity to himself, and loyally dies to restore her to the arms of her husband.

Leolf is the portrait of a man in whose mind justice, in the largest conception of the word, exercises an undisputed sway;—silencing, though it cannot assuage, the deepest sorrow, representing all the importunities of self-love, restraining every severe and uncharitable censure, and exciting the faithful, though unrequited, discharge of all the obligations of loyalty, and love, and honour. The world in which we live abounds in models, which may have suggested, by the power of contrast, this image of a statesman and a soldier. Haughty self-assertion is not merely pardoned in our public men, but takes its place among their conventional virtues. We are accustomed to extol that exquisite sensitiveness which avenges every wrong, and repels every indignity, even though the welfare of our common country be the sacrifice. To appreciate the majesty of a mind which, in the most conspicuous stations of life, surrenders itself to the guidance of perfect equity—and of humility, the offspring of equity; which has mastered resentment and pride as completely as all the baser passions—we must turn from the real to the mimetic theatre, and study man not as he actually is, in camps and parliaments, but as he is here exhibited on the stage.

Relieved from attendance on his feeble sovereign and faithless queen, Leolf (a great soliloquist) takes his stand on the sea-shore, and thus gives utterance to the thoughts which disappointment had awakened in his melancholy, though well-balanced mind :—

'Rocks that beheld my boyhood! Perilous shelf
That nursed my infant courage! Once again
I stand before you—not as in other days
In your grey faces smiling—but like you
The worse for weather. Here again I stand,
Again and on the solitary shore
Old ocean plays as on an instrument,
Making that ancient music, when not known?
That ancient music only not so old
As He who parted ocean from dry land
And saw that it was good. Upon my ear,
As in the season of susceptive youth,
The mellow murmur falls—but finds the sense
Dull'd by distemper; shall I say—by time?
Enough in action has my life been spent.

Through the past decade, to rebate the edge
Of early sensibility.   The sun
Rides high, and on the thoroughfares of life
I find myself a man in middle age,
Busy and hard to please.   The sun shall soon
Dip westerly,—but oh! how little like
Are life's two twilights!   Would the last were
   first
And the first last! that so we might be soothed
Upon the thoroughfares of busy life
Beneath the noon-day sun, with hope of joy
Fresh as the morn,—with hope of breaking lights,
Illuminated mists and spangled lawns
And woodland orisons and unfolding flowers,
As things in expectation.—Weak of faith!
Is not the course of earthly outlook, thus
Reversed from Hope, an argument to Hope
That she was licensed to the heart of man
For other than for earthly contemplations,
In that observatory domiciled
For survey of the stars ?'

It is in his last interview with Elgiva that
the character of Leolf is best exhibited.   He
has rescued her from captivity, and, during a
transient pause in her flight with him to Edwin, the inconstant Queen expresses her gratitude, and suggests her contrition.   It is a
scene of pathos and dignity which we should
rejoice to transfer into our pages, but which
would be impaired by abridgment, and is too
long for quotation as it stands.

If Leolf is the example of the magnanimous endurance of the ills of life, Athulf, his
friend and brother soldier, is the portrait of a
man born to encounter and to baffle them.
It is drawn with the elaborate care, and
touched and retouched with the parental
fondness with which authors cherish, and
sometimes enervate, their favoured progeny.
Unfortunately, Athulf is surrounded by a
throng of dramatic persons, who afford him
no sufficient space for action or for speech.
We become acquainted with him chiefly by
observing the impression he leaves on the
minds of his associates, his enemies, and his
friends.   Wulfstan the Wise is one of these ;
and he will describe Athulf with a warmth
and vigour which it is impossible to emulate,
although it must be admitted to be not incon-
siderably abstruse—an infirmity to which the
good Wulfstan is greatly addicted.

'Much mirth he hath, and yet less mirth than
   fancy.
His is that nature of humanity
Which both ways doth redound, rejoicing now
With soarings of the soul, anon brought low :
For such the law that rules the larger spirits.
This soul of man, this elemental crasis,
Completed, should present the universe
Abounding in all kinds; and unto all
One law is common,—that their act and reach
Stretch'd to the farthest is resilient ever,
And in resilience hath its plenary force.
Against the gust remitting fiercelier burns

The fire, than with the gust it burnt before.
The richest mirth, the richest sadness too,
Stands from a groundwork of its opposite ;
For these extremes upon the way to meet
Take a wide sweep of Nature, gathering in
Harvests of sundry seasons.'

With Dunstan, Leolf, Wulfstan, and Athulf,
are associated a rich variety of other characters—some elaborately, some slightly, sketched—and some exhibited in that rapid outline
which is designed to suggest, rather than to
portray the image which occupies the poet's
fancy.   There is Odo the Archbishop, the
sport of the winds and currents, into which
this victim of dignity and circumstances is
passively borne—a sort of *rouge dragon*, or
clarencieux king-at-arms, hurried by some
misadventure in feats of real chivalry, with
nothing but tabard and mantle to oppose to
the sharp sword and heavy battle-axe ;—and
Clarenbald, by office a Lord Chancellor, a
pompous patronizing appendage of royalty,
who, in an age of war and treason, and
amidst the clash of arms, is no better than a
kind of master of the ceremonies in the *Aula
Regia ;*—and Ruold, a hare-brained gallant,
whom the frown of a polished brow, or the
smile of a dimpled cheek, will mould to the
fair one's purposes, though faith, life, and
honour should be the forfeit :—and Edwin
himself, the slave in turn of every passion
which assails him, love, anger, despondency,
impatience, and revenge, ever wasting his energies to no purpose, and playing the fool
with the indefeasible dignity of him who at
once wears and worships an hereditary crown ;
and Elgiva, the storm-compelling beauty, who
sets a world in flames, and who has proceeded
from the hands of her dramatic creator with a
character entirely neutral and unformed ; in
order that all may ascribe to her such fascina-
tions as may best explain to each the mystery
of her influence over the weak and the wise,
the feeble and the resolute ;—and Emma, a
damsel whose virtue (for she is virtuous and
good, and firm of heart) is but little indebted
to her discretion ; for the maiden is possessed
by the spirit of intrigue and intermeddling,
and, at his bidding, assumes by turns the disguises of a wife, of a strolling minstrel, and
of a priest, to disentangle the webs which she
has spun ; and there are military leaders and
ecclesiastics, fortune-tellers and scholars, jest-
ers, swineherds, and foresters—to each of
whom is assigned some share in the dialogue
or in the plot—which glows like the firmament with stars of every magnitude, clustering
into constellations of endless variety.

This crowding of the scene at once con-
duces to the beauty, and impairs the interest
of this drama.   If our arithmetic fail us not,

there appear on the stage not fewer than fifty interlocutors, who jostle and cross each other —impede the development of the fable, and leave on the mind of the reader, or of the spectator, an impression at once indistinct and fatiguing. It is not till after a second or a third perusal, that the narrative or succession of events emerges distinctly from the throng of the doings and the sayings. But each successive return to this drama brings to light, with a still increasing brilliancy, the exquisite structure of the verse, the manly vigour of thought, and the deep wisdom to which it gives most musical utterance; the cordial sympathy of the poet with all that is to be loved and revered in our common nature, and his no less generous antipathy for all that debases and corrupts it; his sagacious and varied insight into the chambers of imagery in the human heart; and the all-controlling and faultless taste which makes him intuitively conscious of the limits which separate the beautiful from the false, the extravagant, and the affected.

A great writer is his own most formidable rival. If 'Edwin the Fair' shall fail of due acceptance, it will be more to 'Philip Van Artevelde' than to any other hostile critic that such ill success will be really owing. Mr. Taylor has erected a standard by which he must be measured and judged. The sect of the Takeisdown is a large and active fraternity, among whom there are never wanting some to speak of powers impaired, and of exhausted resources. Untrue, in fact, as such a censure would be, it would not be quite destitute of plausibility. 'Philip Van Artevelde' has a deeper and more concentrated interest than 'Edwin the Fair.' It approaches far more nearly to the true character of tragedy. Virtues, hazardous in their growth, majestic in their triumph, and venerable even in the fall, shed a glory round the hero, with which the guilt and the impunity of Dunstan form a painful contrast. The scene of the play, moreover, is more warm and genial, and the versification flows more easily, and in closer resemblance to the numerous prose of Massinger and of Fletcher. There is also less of the uniformity which may be observed in the style of 'Edwin,' where churchmen, laics and ladies, are all members of one family, and have all the family failing, of talking philosophy. The idle King himself moralizes not a little; and even the rough huntsman pauses to compare the fawning of his dogs with the flatteries of the court. But if the earlier work be the greater drama, the later is assuredly the greater poem. More abundant mental resources of every kind are there— knowledge more comprehensive—an imagi-

nation at once more prompt and more discursive—the ear tuned to a keener sense of harmony—the points of contact and sympathy with the world multiplied—and the visible traces of that kind influence which passing years have obviously shed on a mind always replete with energy and courage, but which had not, till now, given proof that it was informed in an equal degree by charity, benevolence, and compassion.

It is, indeed, rather as a poet than as a dramatist that Mr. Taylor claims the suffrage of those with whom it rests to confer the high reward of his labours. In a memorable essay, prefixed to his former tragedy, he explained and vindicated, not his dramatic but his poetical creed, and then, as now, proceeded to illustrate his own doctrines. To the credit of having discovered any latent truth, or of having unfolded any new theory of the sublime art he pursues, he, of course, made no pretension. It would have been utterly at variance with the robust sense which is impressed on every page he writes. His object was to refute a swarm of popular sectarians, by pro claiming anew the ancient and Catholic faith. As the first postulate of his argument, he laid it down, that if a man would write well, either with rhythm or without, it behoved him to have something to say. From this elementary truth, he proceeded to the more abstruse and questionable tenet, that 'no man can be a very great poet who is not also a great philosopher.'

To what muse the highest honour is justly due, and what exercises of the poetic faculty ought to command, in the highest degree, the reverence of mankind, are problems not to be resolved without an inquiry into various re condite principles. But it is a far less obscure question what is the poetry which men do really love, ponder, commit to memory, incorporate into the mass of their habitual thoughts, digest as texts, or cherish as anodynes. This is a matter of fact, which Paternoster Row, if endowed with speech, could best determine. It would be brought to a decision, if some literary deluge (in the shape, for example, of a prohibitory book-tax) should sweep over the land—consigning to the abyss our whole poetical patrimony, and all the treasures of verse accumulated in our own generation. In that frightful catastrophe, who are the poets whom pious hands would be stretched out to save? The philosophical? They would sink unheeded, with Lucretius at their head. Or the allegorical? The waves would close unresistingly over them, though the Faery Queen herself should be submerged. Or the descriptive? Windsor Forest and Grongar Hill would disappear, with whole galleries of inferior paintings. Or the witty? In such a tempest even Hudibras would not be rich enough to attract the zeal of the Salvors. Or the moral? Essays on man, with an infinite variety of the 'pleasures' of man's intellectual faculties, would sink unwept in the vast whirlpool. There, too, would perish, Lucan, with a long line of heroic cantos, romances in verse, and rhymes—amorous, fantastic, and bacchanalian. But, at whatever cost or hazard, leaves would be snatched, in that universal wreck, from the digressions and interstitial passages of the three great Epics of Greece, Italy, and England. The bursts of exultation and agony in the 'Agamemnon' would be rescued; with some of the Anthologies, and a few of the Odes of Anacreon and Horace. There would be a sacred emulation to save, from the all absorbing flood, 'L'Allegro' and Il Penseroso;' with the 'Odes and Fables of Dryden,' 'Henry and Emma,' the 'Rape of the Lock,' and 'the Epistle to Abelard;' Gray's 'Bard,' and 'Elegy,' Lord Lyttleton's 'Monody,' 'The Traveller,' 'The Deserted Village,' and 'The Task,' Mr. Campbell's Shorter Poems, and some of Mr. Wordsworth's Sonnets; while the very spirit of martyrdom would be roused for the preservation of Burns, and the whole Shakspearian theatre; ballads and old songs out of number; much devotional Psalmody, and, far above all the rest, the inspired songs of the sweet singers of Israel.

No man, says Johnson, is a hypocrite in his pleasures. At school we learn by heart the *De Arte Poeticâ.* At college we are lectured in the Poetics. Launched into the wide world, we criticise or write, as it may happen, essays on the sublime and beautiful. But on the lonely sea-shore, or river-bank, or in the evening circle of family faces, or when the hearth glows on the silent chamber round which a man has ranged the chosen companions of his solitary hours, with which of them does he really hold the most frequent and grateful intercourse? Is it not with those who best give utterance to his own feelings, whether gay or mournful; or who best enable him to express the otherwise undefinable emotions of the passing hour? Philosophy is the high privilege of a few, but the affections are the birthright of all. It was an old complaint, that when wisdom lifted up her voice in the streets, none would regard it; but when was the genuine voice of passion ever unheeded? It is the universal language. It is the speech intelligible to every human being, though spoken, with any approach to perfection, by that little company alone, who are from time to time inspired to reveal man to himself, and to sustain and multiply the bonds of the universal brotherhood. It is a language of such power as to reject the aid of ornament, fulfilling its object best when it least strains and taxes the merely intellectual faculties. The poets, whom men secretly worship, are distinguished from the rest, not only by the art of ennobling common subjects; but by the rarer gift of imparting beauty to common thoughts, interest to common feelings, and dignity to common speech. True genius of this order can never be vulgar, and can, therefore, afford to be homely. It can never be trite, and can, therefore, pass along the beaten paths.

What philosophy is there in the wail of Cassandra? in the last dialogue of Hector and Andromache? in Gray's 'Elegy?' or in the Address to 'Mary in Heaven?' And yet when did philosophy ever appeal to mankind in a voice equally profound. About four-and-twenty years ago Mr. Wolfe established a great and permanent reputation by half a dozen stanzas. Almost as many centuries have passed since the great poetess of Greece effected a similar triumph with as small an expenditure of words. Was Mr. Wolfe a philosopher, or was Sappho? They were simply poets, who could set the indelible impress of genius on what all the world had been feeling and saying before. They knew how to appropriate for ever to themselves a combination of thoughts and feelings, which, except in the combination, have not a trace of novelty, nor the slightest claim to be regarded as original. In shorter terms, they knew how to write heart language.

A large proportion of the material of which the poetry of David, Æschylus, Homer, and Shakspeare is composed, if presented for use to many of our greatest writers in its unwrought and unfashioned state, would infallibly be rejected as common-place, and unworthy of all regard. Our poets must now be philosophers; as Burke has taught all our prose writers and most of our prosaic speakers to be, at least in effort and desire. Hence it is that so large a part of poetry which is now published is received as worthy of all admiration, but not of much love—is praised in society, and laid aside in solitude—is rewarded by an undisputed celebrity, but not by any heartfelt homage—is heard as the discourse of a superior, but not as the voice of a brother.

The diligent students and cultivated admirers of poetry will assign to the author of 'Edwin the Fair' a rank second to none of the competitors for the laurel in his own generation. They will celebrate the rich and complex harmony of his metre, the masculine force of his understanding, the wide range of his survey of life and manners, and the profusion with which he can afford to lavish his intellectual resources. The mere lovers of his art will complain, that in the consciousness of his own mental wealth, he forgets the prevailing poverty; that he levies too severe a tribute of attention, and exacts from a thoughtless world meditations more deep, and abstractions more prolonged, than they are able or willing to command. Right or wrong, it is but as the solace of the cares, and as an escape from the lassitude of life, that most men surrender their minds to the fascination of poetry; and they are not disposed to obey the summons to arduous thinking, though proceeding from a stage resplendent with picturesque forms, and resounding with the most varied harmonies. They will admit that the author of 'Edwin the Fair' can both judge as a philosopher, and feel as a poet; but will wish that his poetry had been less philosophical, or his philosophy less poetical. It is a wish which will be seconded by those who revere his wisdom, and delight in his genius; and who, therefore, regret to anticipate that his labours will hardly be rewarded by an early or an extensive popularity.

Art. IV.—*Souvenirs de* M. Berryer. 2 vols. 8vo. Paris, 1839.

Autobiographies may be divided into two classes; those which interest principally as a history of the mind of the writer, and those which derive their chief value from the events which they relate, or the persons whom they describe. The first class require the union of several rare conditions. Few men know their own history. Few men know the fluctuating nature of their own character;—how much it has varied from ten years to ten years, or even from year to year; or what qualities it would exhibit in untried circumstances, or even on the recurrence of similar events. Few men attempt to distinguish between the original predispositions and the accidental influences which, sometimes controlling and sometimes aggravating one another, together formed at any particular epoch their character for the time being. Still fewer attempt to estimate the relative force of each; and fewer still would succeed in such an attempt. The conversations, the books, the examples, the pains and the pleasures which constitute our education, exert an influence quite disproportioned to their apparent importance at the time when they occurred. Such influences operate long after their causes have been forgotten. The effects

of early education are confounded with natural predisposition, and tendencies implanted by nature are attributed to events which were merely the occasions on which they burst forth. The bulk of men think of their minds as they think of their bodies: they enjoy their strength and regret their weakness, they dwell with pleasure on the points in which they are superior to others, and with pain on those in which they are inferior; but they cannot account for the one or for the other. They know no more of the causes of their talents or of their morals, than they do of their beauty or their vigour.

Again, among the few who have the power to relate their mental history, few indeed have the wish. Most men dread the imputation of egotism or vanity. Most men, too, are aware that a full narrative of their feelings, wishes, and habits, must frequently excite the disapprobation of a reader. 'Each mind,' says Foster, 'has an interior apartment of its own, into which none but itself and the Divinity can enter. In this retired place the passions mingle and fluctuate in unknown agitations. There, all the fantastic, and all the tragic shapes of the imagination have a haunt, where they can neither be invaded nor descried. There, the surrounding human beings, while quite unconscious of it, are made the subjects of deliberate thought, and many of the designs respecting them revolved in silence. There, projects, convictions, vows, are confusedly scattered, and the records of past life are laid. There, in solitary silence, sits conscience, surrounded by her own thunders, which sometimes sleep, and sometimes roar, while the world does not know.'[*]

Men are unwilling to reveal, even posthumously, the secret which a whole life has been employed in concealing. Even those who could bear to excite disapprobation would be afraid of ridicule, and perfect frankness is certain to be absurd. We do not believe that a really unreserved autobiography has ever been written. Rousseau's appears to approach most nearly to one. Almost every chapter tends to make the writer hateful, contemptible, or ridiculous. And yet we now know that even the 'Confessions' are not to be depended upon. We now know that much has been concealed, and that much has been positively invented.

Under these circumstances, autobiographies of the first class are almost as rare as epic poems; but those of the second class— those which amuse or instruct as pictures of the events and the people among whom the

---

* Foster's *Essays*, p. 41.

writer lived—are among the most abundant products of modern literature.

It is remarkable, however, that while soldiers, statesmen, diplomatists, men of letters, actors, artists, courtiers—in short, almost all classes who have something to tell, and who have been accustomed to notoriety—have been anxious to relate their own story to the public; one body of active men, though ready enough to talk of others, have been almost uniformly silent as to themselves. With the exception of the beautiful fragments by Sir Samuel Romilly, and they belong rather to the former class of autobiographies, and of the work the title of which we have prefixed to this article, we scarcely recollect an instance in which a Lawyer, either British or foreign, has thought fit to be his own biographer. And yet there are scarcely any persons the result of whose experience would be more instructive; since there are none who obtain so close or so undisturbed a view of human nature. In courts, in public assemblies, in business, in society, men are masked, and they generally believe that their success depends on their disguise. But few men think that anything is to be gained by deceiving their lawyer. He is not their rival, but their instrument. His skill is to extricate them from difficulties where they know neither the amount of the danger nor the means of escape. He is to be the tool of their avarice or of their revenge. They generally know that, in order to enable him to execute their purposes, they must stand naked before him; and even when they are absurd enough to attempt concealment, his experience will almost uniformly detect it.

These remarks, however, do not apply to the bar of England or of Scotland. The professional rule which excludes counsel from the real client, except in the presence of the client's solicitor, deprives our barristers of almost all these peculiar opportunities of observation. But on the Continent, not only does no such rule exist, but the counsel appear to perform almost all the duties which with us are confined to the solicitors. We shall find M. Berryer receiving his clients, calling on them, travelling with them, obtaining evidence, in short, acting always in the double capacity of counsel and attorney. This circumstance adds greatly to the interest of his memoirs, and appears also to have added greatly to the interest of his professional life. His clients, instead of being mere names to be forgotten as soon as the suit should terminate, become his friends and associates. Unhappily, indeed, the miserable period through which he lived made such intimacies often a source of pain. They naturally included the men

most eminent in commerce, manufactures, and banking; and those were precisely the persons whom the anarchists thought fit to suspect at a time when suspicion was death.

But without further anticipation, we proceed to give a general view of M. Berryer's memoirs. They belong to the second class of autobiographies—those in which the interest is fixed, not on the author, but on the objects which surround him. M. Berryer's professional life endured sixty-four years, from 1774 to 1838; the most remarkable period in the history of France, perhaps in the history of the world. It extended through the delusive calm of the unreformed royalty, the brief attempt at constitutional monarchy under the Constituent Assembly, the anarchy under the Legislative Assembly and the Convention, the tyranny of the Directory, the restorative interval of the Consulate, the glories and despotism of the Empire, the impotent reaction of the Restoration, and the intrigues and corruption of the kingdom of the French. The other institutions of the country were still more unstable than the government. M. Berryer found the Roman Catholic religion established with vast wealth and exclusive domination. It is now one among several sects acknowledged and salaried by the state. During the interval its priests have been despoiled, transported, and massacred; every form of worship has been abolished; and it depended on one man whether France should be Protestant or Catholic. All the laws regulating the nature, the enjoyment, the exchange, and the devolution of real and personal property—the laws of marriage, of divorce, of legitimacy, of adoption, and of inheritance—the franchises and privileges of individuals, and of bodies politic—in short, all the rights of persons and of things, while M. Berryer was engaged in enforcing them, were altered, abolished, restored, and amended, by a legislation so transitory as really to deserve to be called, as he has called it, ephemeral. The criminal law was equally fluctuating. New crimes, new modes of trial, new rules of evidence, new tribunals, and new punishments, were invented, repealed, renewed, and modified, as it suited the convenience of a party, a faction, or an individual. A similar fate befell the law of procedure. Within two years from the meeting of the first National Assembly, not a court in which M. Berryer had practised during the first fifteen years of his professional life, was in existence. Soon afterwards, the order of which he was a member was abolished, and the law ceased to be a profession. For some years again there was no standard of value. To use, or even to possess metallic money, was a capital crime, and the only legal tender, the assignat, sank to about one four-hundredth part of its nominal value. The seller of a commodity was no longer allowed to fix its price. The price was to be determined by a committee, with reference to the ability of purchasers, whether the dealer could afford to sell at that price or not. To discontinue, or even to diminish any accustomed trade, was to incur the crime of being 'suspected;' and to be suspected was to be imprisoned; to be imprisoned was at one period to be massacred, and at another to be guillotined.

The picture of a society subjected to such influences would be most valuable, and no one had better opportunity of drawing it than M. Berryer. He had for materials not only his own experience, but that of his clients, and of clients taken from every class of society.

His recollections, as might be expected from a writer of his advanced age, seem to be more vivid as they recede towards the past. His first consultation in the dressing-room of the Duchess of Mazarin, where the aristocratic beauty, surrounded by her maids, and going through the details of her complicated toilette, listened to the conference between the timid junior and Gerbier, the leader of the bar; his first pleading in the Grand Chamber of the Parliament of Paris, its vaulted roof dimly illuminated at a seven o'clock sitting on a winter's morning, and the profound silence of the court, which awed him until he fainted; his first negotiation in the moated chateau of a feudal magistrate, while his client was concealed in the avenue;—all these scenes are dwelt upon with a minuteness of detail, and brilliancy of colouring, which gradually disappear as he approaches the modern part of his narrative. Of this, however, we do not complain. Equality is not picturesque: a society in which it prevails may perhaps be good to live in, but can seldom be good to describe; and we shall imitate our author in drawing our materials rather from the eighteenth century, than from the nineteenth.

M. Berryer was born in the year 1757 at St. Ménéhould in Champagne, a small town of 3,000 inhabitants, which seems to have been a nest of lawyers, since it contained nine different courts, and all the accessories of *avocats, notaires, procureurs,* and *greffiers.** In September, 1774, he commenced his legal studies in the office of a solicitor to the *Parlement de Paris,* which then extended its jurisdiction over the greater part of France. The state of the law was such as might have been expected in a system created, not by statesmen, but by lawyers. 'The forms of procedure,' says M. Berryer, ' were operose and intricate, and to prolong and complicate their entanglement was the business and the pride of the practitioner. Many suits were eternal; they descended from the solicitor who commenced them to his successors, or rather to generations of successors, as the property—the patrimony of the office.'* The number of persons supported by this legal property was enormous. The Grand Châtelet, an inferior court having jurisdiction only over a part of Paris, gave occupation to nearly 300 attorneys.†

M. Berryer was admitted to the bar in 1778. One of the first transactions in which he was engaged is so striking an instance of the pride and the despotism of the aristocracy of France, as it then was, that we shall relate it at some length.

M. du B———, a man of considerable fortune, was a member of the provincial parliament of Normandy. In 1771, when the parliaments were exiled by Louis XV., he retired to Holland, leaving his affairs under the management of his wife, who, together with his son, a young man of twenty-two, resided in one of the country mansions of the family, a few leagues from Rouen. In that reign, and in that country, to be out of favour with the government was almost an exclusion from society. Neither neighbours, friends, nor even relations, visited the *château,* and the young man, solitary and unemployed, fell in love with his mother's maid. The mother's consent was obtained; her general powers of acting for her husband were supposed to enable her to give the father's assent, and the marriage took place in the chapel of the *château.* Two children were born, when, in 1774, the parliaments were recalled, and M. du B——— returned. His daughter-in-law and her children fled before him and took refuge in England. The son, now in his twenty-sixth year, remained. M. du B——— required him to take proceedings to annul the marriage; and on his refusal obtained a *lettre de cachet,* under which he was confined in the prison of Saint Yon. The father visited him in his cell on the second floor of one of the towers. What passed between them is not known; but the result of the interview was, that as the father was descending the staircase, the son threw himself from the window, and was found by the father on the pavement of the court, with a fractured limb and a concussion of the brain. It does not appear that the father was softened, but the government was induced, by the horror of the catastrophe which its interference had occasioned, to re-

* Vol. i. p. 41. M. Berryer expresses a *naïve* regret that all the work is now done by a single tribunal.

* Ibid. p. 24.   † Ibid. p. 29.

voke the *lettre de cachet.* The son, at liberty, but a cripple for life, fled to join his wife and children in England. In London, however, they must all have starved, or have had recourse to parish relief, unless a M. Tubeuf, a French jeweller established in England, had supported them. M. Tubeuf's advances for this purpose amounted during four years to about £1200. They were made at the request of the mother, and with the knowledge of the father, but without his express authority. M. Tubeuf returned to France, demanded repayment from the father, was refused, commenced a suit against him in the Parliament of Paris, and engaged M. Berryer as his counsel. The first step was to obtain an order for the examination of M. du B—— on interrogatories—an order which was made, as of course, without notice to the party to be examined. Armed with this order M. Berryer and M. Tubeuf travelled to the *château* of the magistrate. When they entered its long avenue the carriage with M. Tubeuf was left concealed by the trees, and M. Berryer proceeded on foot. The first person whom he saw was Madame du B——. But such was the awe inspired by the domestic despot, that she would not venture even to hint to her husband the object of M. Berryer's mission. He was forced, therefore, to explain it himself, and to communicate to M. du B—— the astonishing fact that MM. de Paris, his brethren, had subjected him to a public examination. The result, however, was, that the fear of an open discussion prevailed, where justice, compassion, and natural affection had all been powerless. M. Tubeuf was sent for, and before they recrossed the drawbridge all had been arranged. Sixty years afterwards M. Berryer again visited Rouen as an advocate, and the matter was again a family contest originating in aristocratic pride. The *château* and the family of B—— had long disappeared. M. Berryer interested his audience by a narrative of which he was probably the only depository; and urged them to crown his second appearance in their country with equal success.

As a further illustration of the morals of the old *régime*, we shall introduce in this place the notice of a more important cause of M. Berryer's, though it terminated at a later period of his career—that of Madame de Pestre de Seneffe. When the events which we have to relate commenced she was between fifty and sixty years old, and resided at Brussels, a widow with seven children, and a still more numerous progeny of grandchildren; enjoying a high reputation for virtue and morals, and a very large jointure derived from property in Belgium and France. At a

supper in the palace of the Prince de Soubise, a set of Parisian fashionables resolved that one of them should proceed to Brussels and marry the opulent widow. The necessary funds were supplied by a contribution, and the choice of the emissary was left to chance. The lot fell upon the Comte de Wargemont, a man of high family and of considerable property heavily encumbered. On his arrival at Brussels he introduced himself to Madame de Pestre, and secured the services of her maid and of her confessor. The maid concealed him one evening in her mistress's bed-room. In the middle of the night he showed himself. Madame de Pestre called for assistance. This was the signal for the appearance of the maid, who urged on her mistress the danger to her reputation of an *éclat*, and proposed that the advice of the confessor should be taken. The Count protested that his indiscretion had been forced on him by the violence of his passion; and the confessor recommended that all scandal should be avoided by an immediate marriage. Madame de Pestre was weak enough to consent; but as she yielded, not to love, but to fear, she insisted that the marriage should take place in Brussels, that she and all her estates should continue subject to the laws of Flanders, that her husband should have no power to require her to enter France, that she should continue absolute mistress of her property, and that the only benefit derived by the Count should be a life income of 20,000 francs, and 100,000 francs as capital. The marriage on these terms took place in February, 1776. The husband almost immediately quitted his wife, and in June wrote to ask her whether she could suppose that he had any motive for marrying an old woman except the full command of her fortune. A few days afterwards he informed her that he intended to seize all her property in France, and to force her to join him there. His attempts to execute these threats produced a compromise, in pursuance of which a divorce *a mensa et toro*, in a suit instituted by the husband, was pronounced by the ecclesiastical tribunal of Mechlin; and the Count, in exchange for all his claims under the marriage or the settlement, received 350,000 francs and an annuity of 10,000 more. The 350,000 francs, however, were soon spent, and the Count renewed his legal warfare. He attempted to set aside the divorce, succeeded in getting possession of the French estates, and kept up a never-ending litigation respecting those in Belgium. Madame de Pestre died, worn out with care and vexation. The annexation of Belgium rendered the whole property of her children subject to the jurisdiction of the

French laws, and the Count spent the remainder of his life in prosecuting them from tribunal to tribunal. M. Berryer was counsel for Madame de Pestre and for her descendants; and he dwells upon his exertions in their cause as one of the most arduous, and of the most brilliant parts of his professional career. They procured him on one occasion a curious testimony of admiration. M. de Wargemont was dead, and his sister, Madame de Querrieux, had succeeded to some of his claims, and apparently to some of his litigiousness. As her brother's representative, she prosecuted an appeal against the Pestre family. An elderly lady sat behind M. Berryer while he conducted the defence. She was observed to listen with great emotion, and as soon as he sat down, pressed him to accept, as a mark of her admiration, a ring made of the hair of her youth.

The episode of Madame de Pestre has led us to anticipate a portion of M. Berryer's history. Nature had given him the bodily qualifications most useful to an advocate, a fine voice, and health independent of exercise. In the strict discipline of a *procureur's* office, where the hours of business, with a few minutes' interval for breakfast, and an hour for dinner, lasted from between six and seven in the morning till nine at night, he acquired intrepid diligence and the love of a sedentary life. He was stimulated too, as he tells us,* by the splendid pecuniary rewards of the profession. He saw Gerbier receiving 300,000 francs for a single cause, and Duvaudier's exertions in securing a jointure, paid by an equipage and an annuity of 4,000 francs for its support. He began early to emancipate himself from the *procureur's*, by obtaining a set of clients of his own. He succeeded first in becoming counsel to the eminent merchants constituting the India Company, in a cause which lasted many years; then in obtaining the conduct of a claim depending on an ancient pedigree, which appears to have remained undisposed of for more than twenty years; and lastly, in obtaining as his clients the two great ecclesiastical chapters of Brioude and Bourges. His marriage in January, 1789, with Mademoiselle Gorneau, whose father, as *Procureur aux Conseils*, had for his clients the chief bankers and merchants of Paris, placed him at once in possession of the first mercantile practice. The heads of the great houses became his clients and his friends; and we may judge of the extent of litigation in which they were engaged, when we are told that one of them, M. Magon de la Balue, paid him a daily visit.*

It does not appear that, when he married, he was aware that a time was approaching when the bravest man might wish to have no safety to provide for but his own. He had, indeed, been somewhat surprised, but not disquieted, by the anti-monarchical spirit of the press, and had felt some alarm at the opposition of the parliaments to the court; but his fears did not exceed a vague uneasiness. He does not appear, indeed, to be more of a statesman than the Carlist deputy, his son. The extent of his political sagacity may be estimated by the three causes, to which even now, after fifty years' experience, he assigns the Revolution;—namely, financial difficulties, which he thinks might have been got out of by economy; the contest between the parliaments and the crown; and the reduction of a portion of the household troops.

His fears, however, were soon to be awakened. On the evening of Sunday, the 12th of July, he was returning with his young wife from a country holiday—that day was, in fact, the last but one of the monarchy—but so little were they aware of the real nature of the events which had disturbed the previous weeks, that they felt, as he tells us, perfect security. But at the Barrière du Trône, they heard of the sanguinary conflict between the Royal Allemande and the procession carrying the busts of Orleans and Necker; and as they passed the paper manufactory of Réveillon they saw the gates guarded by soldiery, and were told that behind them lay the bodies of those who had perished in the attack on the building. Two mornings after,* M. Berryer was roused from his bed by the tocsin; he was summoned, by what authority he does not know, to a meeting of the inhabitants of his parish, in the church of St. Méry. He found there crowds as ignorant of the cause of their assembling as himself. For hours they wandered, without an object, up and down the aisles of the church. At length some persons talked of organizing the parish as a municipal body. M. Berryer suggested the means to those about him—they carried him to the pulpit, and thence he proposed his plan, which was to divide the parish into quarters, or, as we should call them, wards; the inhabitants of each ward grouping themselves round a particular pillar; and then, that each ward should present a list of six persons, to constitute the *bureau* or common council of the parish—one being the presi-

* M. Berryer's recollection has misled him as to these dates. He supposes the storming of the Bastile to have taken place on the Monday, and therefore that Sunday was the 13th. But in fact Sunday was the 12th, and a day intervened between the riot of that day and the insurrection of the 14th.

* Vol. i. p. 87.   † Vol. ii. 325.

dent, and another the secretary. His plan was adopted by acclamation; he refused the office of president, but accepted that of secretary. The *bureau* was elected, and directed to provide for the civil and military organization of the parish.

In the evening the *bureau* assembled; M. Berryer was quietly engaged in his duties as secretary; it was hot, and the windows were open, when some pikes bearing bloody heads were thrust in, and they were told that one was that of De Launay, and that the others were those of the Swiss massacred within the Bastile. This horrible incident influenced permanently the fortunes of M. Berryer. With his talents and his advantages, it was obvious that the highest professional honours were within his grasp. His advance had been checked by no difficulties, and till then, seemed to be attended by no dangers. But the 14th of July dispelled his dream of safety. He saw the time coming when the servants of the public might have to choose between death and crime. He doubted how he might stand the trial, and he felt certain that no reward was worth the risk. He resolved therefore, and he kept his resolution, to remain for life in a private station. His companions at the bar acted differently. Some perished for their virtues, some for their crimes, and some obtained and kept the most elevated civil dignities. But it was in vain that they pressed him to accompany them in their rise. He preserved his conscience, and perhaps his life, by the sacrifice of his ambition.

He soon found, however, that the humbler path of an advocate had its difficulties and its dangers. The order to which he belonged was abolished; in its room were substituted *défenseurs officieux*—a function which every one, whatever were his previous employments or his previous ignorance, was allowed to exercise. The great objects of his veneration, the Parliaments, which, with a strange misconception of history, he describes as the supporters of pure monarchy, shared the fate of the bar. New tribunals were erected in their room, with inferior powers and a more limited jurisdiction. The greater part of the old bar refused to plead before them; and the character of the new judges, generally selected from among fierce political partizans, accounts for their refusal. As an illustration of their judicial conduct, M. Berryer relates the history of a cause tried before the *Tribunal des Minimes*, one of the new metropolitan courts, over which M. Le Roy Sermaise, a violent democrat, presided. The parties were two villagers from Montreuil; the matter in dispute a small estate. The plaintiff rested his claim on a deed of conveyance,

which appeared on inspection to have nothing to do with the property; the defendant's case depended on uninterrupted possession. 'How long,' said M. Le Roy Sermaise, 'has this possession lasted?' 'Why, citizen president,' replied the peasant, 'it must be at least eighty or ninety years, taking in my great-grandfather, my grandfather, my father, and myself.' 'Then,' replied the judge, 'you ought to be satisfied; every one in his turn—yours has lasted long enough in all conscience—now let your poor neighbour have his.'[*] It must be added that the new *défenseurs officieux*, untrained in the conventional hostility of the bar, sometimes resented opposition as a personal injury; and no one could tell, in such times, what might be the consequence of making an enemy of the most insignificant or the most worthless individual. On one occasion, M. Berryer had the misfortune of being opposed to Coffinhal, afterwards the sanguinary vice-president of the revolutionary tribunal; and he tells us that, after he had heard that Coffinhal had threatened to punish him, he shuddered with terror whenever the threat returned to his memory—and with great reason, for Coffinhal might have said with Cæsar, that it was much less trouble to him to destroy than to menace.

But these were preludes. Monarchical government was destroyed by the insurrection of the 10th August, 1792; republican government by that of the 2d June, 1793. The strange sort of rule arose, which for want of a more definite word, has been called the 'Reign of Terror;'—a mixture of anarchy and despotism, of democracy, oligarchy, and tyranny, which combined all the worst faults of all the worst institutions. Two powers strove for mastery in this chaos, the Convention, and the Commune or municipal council of Paris, and each of these was subdivided into hostile factions. In all of them the objects of the leaders were power and safety; and in all of them the object of the subordinate members was safety. All joined in the endeavour to effect their purposes by the means resorted to in what has been called the state of nature;—by the destruction or intimidation of those whose power or whose safety they thought inconsistent with their own. The ordinary instruments employed by each party were the *loi des suspects*, the revolutionary committees, and the revolutionary tribunal. The extraordinary instrument was the armed population of Paris, consisting of the National Guards, furnished by the forty-eight sections into which Paris was divided; —a force generally called, in the histories of

* Vol. i, p. 133.

the times, by the somewhat puzzling name of 'the Sections.' The whole body, if it could have been collected, amounted to above 80,000 men, some provided with guns, but many more with pikes; their principal arms consisted of some pieces of artillery attached to each section.

The forty-eight revolutionary committees of Paris were appointed by the inhabitants of the forty-eight sections, voting by universal suffrage. The duty, for which they received a regular pay, was to inquire into all conduct which might affect the public safety, to give certificates of *civisme*—that is to say, of attachment to the Revolution—and to order the arrest of all suspected persons.

The *loi de suspects* declared guilty of being suspected, and therefore subject to arrest, four principal classes;—1. All those who, by their connections, their conversation, their writings, or their conduct, appeared to be opposed to liberty. 2. All those who could not prove their means of living, and of performing their civil duties. 3. All those who had been refused certificates of *civisme*. 4. All persons of noble birth, and all relations of emigrants, unless they could prove their ardent devotion to the Revolution.

The revolutionary tribunal was a criminal court of equity; a court for the punishment of those who were unpunishable by law. It is a strong proof of the little progress which France has made towards real liberty, that M. Berryer approves of the principle of such an institution, and recommends its adoption as a restraint on the press.[*]

It consisted of a public accuser, judges and jurymen, all nominated by the Convention, restrained by no form of procedure or rules of evidence, and authorized, on an application from the Convention, or from one of its two committees of *sûreté générale* and *salut public*, to judge all conspirators and opposers of the Revolution; and all those whose conduct or whose expression of opinion had a tendency to mislead the people. At first evidence was required, and the accused were allowed defenders; but as the trials increased in number, these forms were found inconvenient; and, after all, they were mere forms, for the business of the tribunal was not to try but to condemn. They were therefore abolished, and the tribunal was required to decide without hearing any witnesses, if there were grounds, material or moral, (such were the words of the decree), for believing the accused to be an enemy to the people.

Lists were kept ready of persons accused, others of persons condemned, with the names left in blank. Every evening the list of the accused was prepared by Fouquier-Tinville, the public accuser, settled by the *comité de salut public* of the Convention, and sent round to the prisons; those named in it were taken to the Conciergerie; the next morning they were before their judges, and before the evening they had suffered. That there were grounds, material or moral, for conviction, was always assumed; no witnesses were examined, and the trial, if it could be called one, was generally merely identifying the prisoner with one of the names on the list of persons accused. Even this might be dispensed with. When, as it sometimes happened, prisoners were brought to the bar whose names, in the hurry of business, had been left out of the list, the only result was that the public accuser immediately supplied the omission; and thus, in three minutes, a man might be indicted, tried, convicted, and sentenced, and an hour after executed.

As the Convention possessed the power of appointing and removing the members of the revolutionary tribunal, and of selecting its victims, it was, while its orders were obeyed, despotic in Paris; and when two committees of the Convention, that of *salut public* and *sûreté générale*, could send before the tribunal—that is to say, could send to death—any members of the Convention, the two committees became despotic in the Convention.

The inflicting death seems, like many other acts which are at first painful, to become a passion. No other explanation can be given of the condemnation by the revolutionary tribunal of many of the humblest and obscurest persons, among the petty shopkeepers, and even workmen, of Paris. No other explanation can be given of some of the capricious murders related by M. Berryer. We give one or two examples:—In 1787, money had been borrowed in Paris on printed debentures for L.100 each, signed by the Prince of Wales, the Duke of York, and the Duke of Clarence. They went by the name of *actions du Prince de Galles.* The transaction was an unfortunate one; the debentures were refused payment, lost their value, and disappeared. Six years afterwards, all persons concerned in their introduction into the Parisian market, or in their circulation, were accused as *contre-révolutionaires*, and enemies of the people. The Duc de St. Aignan, a former client of M. Berryer, on whom a money-lender had forced some of these debentures, and who had obliged him by law to take them back, was among the accused. So was his duchess, a young woman of fashion, whom no one could suppose to have been acquainted with her husband's transactions. So

_____

[*] Vol. ii., p. 419.

were even the notaries in whose hands they were deposited, and their clerks;_and even M. Chaudot, who had merely given a notarial attestation which he could not legally refuse. All were condemned, and all were executed. Another notary, M. Martin, a friend, like M. Chaudot, of M. Berryer, met at his door, on his return from a morning's walk, a *gendarme*, who required his immediate attendance before the revolutionary tribunal. He found there three persons accused of having signed a pedigree certificate, which had been deposited in his office. There was nothing objectionable in the certificate, but it was said that some ill use might be made of it. The public accuser simply asked him if the paper had been placed with him; and on his admitting it, required the tribunal to convict and sentence him to death, together with those previously accused. The tribunal instantly complied; the four prisoners were removed from the bar; room was found for them in the carriages which were setting off for the guillotine; and within three hours M. Martin was an un-accused man, and an executed criminal!

During the 'Reign of Terror,' M. Berryer gave up the public exercise of his profession. No one could act as *défenseur officieux* without a certificate of *civisme* from the revolutionary committee of his section. But he could not rely upon obtaining one from the uneducated and violent persons—a brothel-keeper, a knife-grinder, a porter, and a shoe-cleaner—who were paid forty sous a-day to administer the affairs of the section. A person to whom such a certificate had been refused, became, as we have seen, by express enactment suspected, and certain, from the notoriety of the fact, to be arrested the next day; and equally certain to be executed, as soon as the malice of an enemy, or the caprice of the public accuser, should call him forth. He at first proposed to shut himself up in his study, and act solely as a chamber counsel; but he was soon told that seclusion would inevitably attract suspicion, and that he must find some mode of life which would not bear the interpretation of fear. Fortunately he had been counsel, in happier times, for the National Treasury, and M. Turpin, the agent, (a functionary corresponding, we believe, to our secretary), was his intimate friend. M. Turpin, indeed, was not safe; for though intrusted with matters of the utmost confidence, and daily transacting business with the heads of the department, he was an object of such jealousy, that a *gendarme* watched all his proceedings, and, in fact, never quitted him by day or night. Notwithstanding the want of a certificate of *civisme*, the previous services and

the reputation of M. Berryer, and the friendship of M. Turpin, effected his admission into the offices of the Treasury as sub-agent—a favour great, not only from its importance to the person admitted, but from the danger to which it exposed them who admitted him.

In this new post, his days were passed in the office, and his evenings in transacting the legal business of his former clients; and again he fancied himself safe. Some vexations, indeed, he was exposed to, but they were almost ludicrous annoyances. He and his wife were forced to bring their table into the street, and consume, in the presence of the passers-by, "le dîner patriotique." His wife was sometimes forced to attend at the bakers to inspect the sale of bread, to see that no one was served before his turn, and that no one was allowed to purchase beyond his strict wants. At other times she had to head an address from the women of the section to the Convention, deliver a patriotic speech, and receive the fraternal embrace of the President.

Suddenly, however, he was roused to a sense of imminent danger by an accidental visit to the Treasury offices of a M. L——, one of his former brethren of the bar, now become a member of the Convention. The visiter loudly expressed his astonishment that an aristocrat, and a counter-revolutionist, in whose house conspirators met every evening, should fill a Government employment. Such remarks were deadly. They were sure to be whispered about, and to be acted upon by some wretch anxious to pay court to the deputy. It was probable that, in twenty-four hours, M. Berryer would be in one of the dungeons of the Abbaye, and in a week afterwards in the Place de la Guillotine; and there was no knowing how many of those who had favoured his employment might accompany him. Fortunately he had two friends in the Convention, Charles Lacroix and Bourdon de l'Oise, both colleagues of M. L——, and both stanch members of the *Montagne*. He ran to the chamber, and found Bourdon de l'Oise entering it, clattering, as he went, the huge sabre which he had carried in the storm of the Bastile. What were the persuasions applied by his two friends to their colleague, M. Berryer does not tell us, but they were sufficient. M. L—— returned to the Treasury, praised loudly the patriotism of M. Berryer, informed the hearers that the nightly visiters were inoffensive clients, and ended by stating that his remarks had been quite misunderstood, and in fact were meant for a different person.

But the danger had been averted, only to reappear in a form less direct, but more painful. Among M. Berryer's most honoured clients were the great bankers of the Place Vendôme, MM. Magon de la Balue and Magon de la Blinais, MM. Laurent Le Couteulx, and Le Couteulx. Cautelen, and M. Pourrat. One Heron, a merchant of Marseilles, had become bankrupt, had fled to South America, and returned in the beginning of the Revolution with some bills of the Spanish government of considerable nominal value. He offered them to the principal banking-houses, but could not get them discounted. This rankled in his mind, and as soon as the *loi des suspects* gave arms to malignity, he denounced all those who had refused him. MM. Laurent Le Couteulx, and Le Couteulx Cautelen, were detained for eleven months in the Conciergerie; saw it weekly emptied and weekly filled, but escaped at an enormous expense, by bribing the clerks to place the papers relating to them always at the bottom of the bundles of accusations. M. Pourrat fell early a victim to his own precautions. He became a member of the Jacobin club. The singularity of a banker in such a society attracted attention, and he was arrested on the benches of the club. MM. Magon de la Balue and Magon de la Blinais, both venerable men between eighty and ninety, were confined in the *Maison de santé de Belhomme;* a place celebrated for having exhibited the last traces of the ancient aristocratic habits. There those who could afford the expense of such a prison, spent the last week of their lives among the enjoyments and the forms to which they had been accustomed. The *roturiers* and the nobles, and among the nobles, those of the sword and those of the robe, kept their distinct circles. There were ceremonious visits, and full dress evening parties, where the younger portion of this short-lived society amused themselves by rehearsing the trial and the. execution. Passports signed by Robespierre, Couthon, Carnot, and Barrère, the four principal members of the ruling committee of Public Safety, were exhibited to M. Berryer; and he was desired to offer to MM. Magon, for 300,000 francs, liberty, and an escape across the frontiers. They replied, that to fly from trial would be a confession of guilt—that their perfect innocence was a security—and refused. A week after, M. Berryer read in the papers the conviction of the conspirators, Magon de la Blinais, Magon de la Balue, the woman St. Perne, daughter, the woman Cornulier, grand-daughter of the latter, and the Sieur Coureur, his secretary. Mixed with his regrets were his fears. He was known to have been their counsel. The fierce Dubarren, a member of the formidable *Comité de Sûreté générale*, had already threatened him with the consequences of defending aris-

tocrats and conspirators, and he knew that among their papers must be found whole bundles of his letters. He does not appear to be even now able to explain his escape, unless by imputing it to gratitude in Fouquier Tinville for an early service; a solution, perhaps, as improbable as the imputation of any monstrous wickedness to a man of ordinary virtue.

These dangers, however, were at length to terminate. The party of which Robespierre and his immediate friends formed the nucleus, had risen to power by a process of constant contraction. Originally it comprised nearly the whole of the deputies of the *Tiers Etat,* for who was there that refused the oath of the Tennis Court? First it threw off and destroyed the aristocratic Royalists, then the Girondists, then the Hébertists, and at last even the Dantonists. At every change, while it destroyed a rival, it deprived itself of a supporter. At first it spoke the voice of a nation, afterwards that of an assembly; then that of a party, and at length that of a committee. But the committees of *salut public,* and *sûreté générale,* were omnipotent. Fielding has remarked, that a man with a pistol may hold at bay a multitude; for though he can shoot but one man, every one feels that the first who attacks him will be that one. Nothing in the history of the Revolution is more striking than Thibaudeau's picture of the submission of the fierce and violent Convention before the governing Committee of Public Safety:—'The object of every member, from the instant that he entered the house, was to prevent his behaviour there from being a crime. Every movement, every look, every murmur, every smile, was calculated. Those who ventured to have a place, crowded to the *Montagne,* (the high benches of the left), as the republican seats; or took refuge in the centre, (answering to our benches near the bar), as the seats which manifested no party feeling. Others wandered from bench to bench, in the hope that they might be supposed to be opposed to no party and to no opinion; but the more prudent never ventured to sit. They stood in groups at the bar, and slunk away whenever a vote was probable. The sittings, once so long and so violent, were cold and short. Trifling details were discussed until the Committee of Public Safety appeared. The Committee, headed by their *rapporteur,* (the member charged to announce their decisions), entered with the air of masters. In their progress to the tribune, they were preceded and followed by those who were striving to propitiate them by apparent devotion. There was deep silence until the *rapporteur* spoke:

every one sought to read in his countenance whether he was to announce a victory or a proscription. His proposals, whatever they were, were servilely adopted, generally in silence; but if a word were spoken, it was merely an echo.'*·

Such was the state of things when, on the 24th *Prairial* (12th June, 1794), Bourdon de l'Oise requested a visit from M. Berryer. He went, little expecting the frightful confidence that was to be reposed in him. 'Robespierre,' said Bourdon, 'has become my enemy. He intends to murder me by the guillotine. I have resolved to be beforehand, and to destroy him with my own hand.' As proofs of his courage and resolution, he displayed the dress which he had worn at the storm of the Bastile, still covered with the blood of its defenders; the plumes which had ornamented his cap in the Vendéan war, torn by balls in every feather; and the huge sword with which he had pierced many an enemy, and which was now to be plunged into the heart of Robespierre. M. Berryer listened in terror; but still more dangerous matter was to come. Bourdon added, that he had selected him as depositary not only of his secrets but of his last wishes and of his fortune, and placed in his hands a parcel containing his will, his title-deeds, and instructions to be followed in the very probable event of Bourdon's fall before he had an opportunity to execute his attempt, or in consequence of the attempt.

For forty-five† anxious days, and almost sleepless nights, M. Berryer retained this terrible deposit. He was now for the first time an actual conspirator. His connection with the chief conspirator was notorious. His safety seemed to depend on Bourdon's immediate success in destroying, by his own hand, both Robespierre and the oligarchy of which he was the president. Assassination is a desperate resource. The attempt itself rarely succeeds, and where it does succeed, rarely produces the intended result.

Happily for M. Berryer events took a different turn. We have said that the committees were omnipotent; but their power depended more obviously and immediately than that of governments in general, on opinion. They had not, like the tyrannies that succeeded them, an armed force trained to unreflecting obedience. While the Convention bent before them, they seemed to be irresistible; but the Convention was obedient, not from affection or confidence, for the committees were objects of distrust and hatred, but because they were supposed to have the support of the National Guards: how far that supposition was true, was a doubt not to be solved without extreme peril, for the fact could be ascertained only by resistance, and if they really had that support those who resisted must perish. Dissensions among themselves forced the decision of this tremendous question. Robespierre threw all his colleagues in the committees into shade. He formed, with his devoted adherents St. Just and Couthon, what began to be called the triumvirate; a sort of committee of the committees, which controlled all their operations. It was rather, however, a dictatorship than a triumvirate; for St. Just from fanaticism, and Couthon from servility, were mere instruments.

Robespierre did not owe his predominance to his talents; for his talents, though it is absurd to deny him great talents both as a writer and as a speaker, were inferior to those of several of his rivals, and even of his dependents; nor to his courage, for there he was positively deficient. But he had insatiable ambition, and insatiable vanity, and no passion that interfered with them. He had no love of money, of ostentation, of pleasure, or of ease. He had no friendship, no pity, no truth, no shame, and no remorse: he appeared, therefore, to have an inflexible will. The weakest part of his character was the combination of ambition with vanity; but during the earlier part of his career these passions acted well together. His desire of immediate applause led him to flatter the self-love of the Parisian mob, by an adulation of which no man with self-respect could have been guilty; to encourage all their most mischievous prejudices, and to stimulate all their worst passions. In any ordinary state of society such conduct would have been fatal to his prospects as a statesman; but in a revolution it gave him unbounded popularity, and popularity was power. On the other hand, his love of power impelled him to destroy those whose influence interfered with his own, and thus pleased at the same time his vanity by leaving him the only prominent figure.

But the time was come when the gratification of both these passions at once became impossible. He might, perhaps, have retained predominant power if he had been satisfied with the reality, and allowed his colleagues to appear to the world as his equals; but this was repugnant to his vanity. He might have remained the general object of admiration if he

---

* *Mémoires sur la Convention et le Directoire.* Paris, 1827. Vol. i., p. 47.

† M. Berryer says sixteen days; but the time between the 24th *Prairial* and the 9th *Thermidor,* that is, from the 12th of June to the 27th of July, was forty-five days. Perhaps the error may lie in the date of the conversation.

had allowed them to be really his associates in power; but this interfered with his ambition. He wished to absorb all power and all reputation; to be the dictator of a republic of which his will was to be the law; and to be the high priest of a religion which his recognition had established. To do this it was necessary to destroy his present associates; and as their removal would have revived the more moderate revolutionary party, of which Danton had been the head, it was also necessary to destroy the remnant of Dantonists. These objects could be effected, however, only by the aid either of the Convention, or of the Commune of Paris, and the National Guards. If he could obtain from the Convention a decree for their arrest and accusation, he would have succeeded; the remainder of the Convention, deprived of all its influential members, would have been at his feet. The Commune was already devoted to him, so was Henriot, the commander of the National Guards; and he relied on the obedience of these citizen troops to orders in which all the authorities should concur. But if the Convention took part with the committees, he still hoped, with the aid of the Commune and of Henriot, to dispose of the National Guards, and put an end, by terror or by force, to all resistance. It may appear that it would have been simpler to begin by force; but, in the first place, he expected submission from the Convention; and, in the second place, until the Convention had refused his demands, there was no pretext for rising against it, and some pretext was required even in these times, and even for an insurrection.

At the meeting of the Convention on the 8th Thermidor, An. 2, (26th July, 1794), Robespierre commenced his attack. After a long description of the general mal-administration of the country, he inferred ' that there was a conspiracy to destroy the republic and the patriots; that the members of the two committees were among the conspirators; and that it had become necessary to punish the traitors, to crush all factions under the weight of the national authority, and to raise from the ruins the supremacy of justice and freedom.'

This speech was received, as no speech of Robespierre's had ever before been received in that assembly, with dead silence. The usual motion, however, for its being printed and distributed, was made and carried, and the Convention seemed to remain in obedience. But the extremity of the peril now gave courage to the members of the two committees. Those who spoke first ventured only to defend themselves; those who followed dared to recriminate. Robespierre, unaccustomed to opposition, began to explain and

retract: the Dantonists joined his opponents, and the sitting terminated by rescinding the resolution for printing his speech.

The first attack, therefore, had been repulsed. The evening and the night were spent by each party in preparation. It was resolved on the part of Robespierre that the Commune should meet the next morning; that in the Convention a definite motion, denouncing the crimes and requiring the arrest of those whom it was intended to sacrifice, should be made by St. Just, and enforced by Robespierre; and that, if the Convention refused, the Commune should declare that the people had resumed the direct exercise of its sovereignty, should assemble the National Guards, and march to deliver the Convention from the criminals who were misleading it. In the mean time the members of the committees and the Dantonists, united into one party by their common danger, were employed in endeavouring to obtain the co-operation of the other parties in the Convention. Such was the detestation which they themselves had inspired, and such the fear of Robespierre, that it was only after many repulses that they began to make any progress. Succeed, however, they did, and the next day, the celebrated 9th *Thermidor*, when Robespierre entered the assembly, he probably had not ten adherents left in a body of which two days before he had been the dictator.

We need not do more than refer to the scene of the 9th *Thermidor*—a scene probably unequalled in any deliberative assembly; when St. Just was interrupted after his first sentence, and Robespierre had to listen hour after hour to the long-compressed hatred of his revolted subjects—his cries and screams for the right of reply, drowned by the imprecations of his accusers, and the bell of the president; until at length, as he lay on the bench, gasping with fatigue, rage, and terror, he was ordered into arrest, together with his adherents, St. Just, Couthon, Le Bas, and Robespierre the younger, and seized by the attendants of the house.

It was now five o'clock, and the House adjourned to seven, exhausted by the struggle, and scarcely venturing to believe the result. The Commune in the mean time had assembled, but had not acted. It had adjourned before the arrest of Robespierre was known. Indeed, considering the strangeness and the magnitude of that event, the news appears to have circulated very slowly. Thibaudeau tells us that, when the Convention met in the evening, the greater part of the members heard for the first time the events of the morning. It is probable that the morning attendance had been comparatively thin, and consisted chiefly of those who the night before had concerted their proceedings.

The Commune had adjourned only till six. When they re-assembled, and heard of the arrest of Robespierre and his companions, they declared that the People, and the Commune, as the organ of the People, had resumed its sovereignty; ordered the tocsin to ring in every section; despatched messengers on all sides to call out the National Guards, and in short set in motion the insurrectionary machinery which had never failed during the previous course of the Revolution. They soon collected a force sufficient to rescue the prisoners from their confinement in one of the committee rooms, and to carry them in triumph to the head-quarters of the Commune, the Hôtel de Ville. By this time it was nearly eight. The Convention reassembled, but it was only to communicate their alarms. 'A few,' says Thibaudeau, 'had gained courage by their success in the morning; others awaited the result in silence; the greater part were unable to comprehend what was going on. As it became dark the horror of our situation increased. We heard the noise of the drums and of the tocsin. A few members formed themselves into a committee to consider the course to be adopted, the others listened in the utmost anxiety to the reports brought back by those who had ventured to ascertain the state of things without. At length, about midnight, the crisis appeared to approach. Collot d'Herbois, the President, said in his sepulchral voice, 'Representatives, the time is come for us to die at our posts; I am informed that Henriot's forces surround us." Instantly all the spectators fled from the galleries, the members who had been standing together in groups, took their usual seats, and prepared to die with decency. As for myself, I had not the slightest doubt that our last moment was come.'* It was true that Henriot had led his men to the attack. His cannon even were pointed at their doors. But when he gave the word to fire, his artillerymen hesitated, and at last refused. Henriot, finding that his troops could not be depended on, thought it prudent to march them back to the Hôtel de Ville. †It was thus that, on the caprice or the irresolution of half a dozen men, the fate of the Convention, and perhaps the future history of France, and even of Europe, depended. For if the cannon had fired, and Henriot's forces, many of them the same men who three years before had stormed the Tuileries and destroyed the defenders, had rushed into the hall where the members were sitting, merely

awaiting their fate without any plan of resistance, it seems probable that the greater part of the assembly would have been massacred on their seats; and certain that all who escaped would have been treated as they themselves treated their adversaries a few hours afterwards, condemned and executed without a trial. Robespierre would have been absolute master of Paris. Whether he would or would not have been able to summon another representative assembly, or without one to retain the provinces and the armies in subjection to Paris, is more questionable. But, on any supposition, the whole subsequent course of events would have been different; there would have been different scenes and different actors. Pichegru might have imitated Monk, and royalty have been restored by a native army in 1794, instead of a foreign one in 1814; or Nantes, and Lyons, and Bordeaux, and Toulon, and La Vendée, might have successfully risen against Paris, and France have split into hostile communities. Reform would have been delayed in Germany, and accelerated in Great Britain and Ireland. The half minute during which it was undecided whether the artillery would fire or not, is the most important half minute in history.

The retreat of Henriot seems to have given to the Convention the courage necessary to active resistance. They declared Henriot, Robespierre, and his associates, and the whole Commune of Paris, *hors de la loi ;* invested Barras with the command of the National Guards, and appointed members to act under him; despatched others to the headquarters of the different sections, to announce these decrees and summon the National Guards, and resolved, as soon as a sufficient body could be collected, to march and attack the Commune at the Hôtel de Ville. The events of this night have been told in so many different ways, that some future Strauss may treat the whole as a legend. The following is M. Berryer's narrative :—

'The *corps de garde* of my section, La Réunion, was at the Hôtel d'Asnières, and I determined not to return home during the night. There was great indecision among us, until the exhortations of the messengers from the Convention, marked by their dress, and raised, from their being on horseback, above the audience, decided the wavering to side with the Convention. We resolved to march immediately to the defence of the Assembly. I was armed as usual with my pike, which was the common weapon; a very few had muskets. When we reached the Place of the Carrousel, which at that time joined the Tuileries, receiving no orders we sat down on the pavement. Between midnight and one in the morning we were order-

---

* *Mémoires,* Vol. I., p. 83.

ed to form column, and march on the Hôtel de Ville, then occupied by Robespierre and his associates. On our left was the section Marat, consisting, like ourselves, of about 200 men, about as well armed as we were. Three guns with lighted matches preceded us. By the time we had reached the Oratoire in the Rue St. Honore, our artillery, very ill commanded, was in the centre of the column. I now discovered by the cries of Bourdon de l'Oise, as he was rectifying this blunder, that we were under his command. When we reached the open space before the Hôtel de Ville, we found there were many pieces of cannon, and the troops of several other sections, apparently directed like ourselves against the Commune.* Our officers had ranged us in front of the Hôtel de Ville, with our cannon behind, so that we should have been the first objects of a discharge. While Bourdon de l'Oise was setting this right, he noticed me, and congratulated me on my display of courage.

'Suddenly a sort of commotion was heard in the great hall of the Hôtel de Ville; and immediately afterwards I saw Bourdon de l'Oise, with some determined followers, rush up the large open staircase. He held a pistol in each hand, a drawn sabre between his teeth, and with his fiery eyes and burning cheeks, looked more like a fury than a human being. In a minute or two we heard shots in the interior. Robespierre the younger jumped out of one window, Henriot was thrown out of another, Robespierre was wounded, and Le Bas killed in the struggle. Couthon, pretending to be dead, was laid at full length on the coping of the Quai Pelletier, until a prick from a bayonet made him wince, and he was removed in custody; Robespierre was carried by me on a litter to endure the utmost bitterness of death.

'The next morning I found it so difficult to believe my recollections of the night, that, notwithstanding my horror of executions, I went to the Terrace of the Tuileries, which overlooks the Place de la Revolution, to watch the cart filled with the conquered party enter the enclosure of the guillotine. The long-continued shouts and applause which soon followed, left me no doubt that the head of Robespierre had really fallen.

'The next day, however, perished some whom I could not but pity. These were the seventy-two members of the Commune of Paris, who had been all seized in their hall of assembly, kept in custody for thirty-six hours, and then, without any trial beyond a mere identification, thrown into seven or eight carts, carried to the Placé de la Revolution, and executed. The greater part of them had committed no error except that of taking office in such times as these. This punishment *en masse* of a whole body, though it may comprehend a minority who have protested against the acts of the majority, is the

* On comparing M. Berryer's statements with those of other witnesses, we are inclined to believe that the greater part of these troops consisted of the National Guards, who had originally obeyed the summons of the Commune; and whom the retreat of Henriot, the decree which outlawed the Commune, and the arguments of the members who had been sent out, had subsequently induced to support the Convention.

ne plus ultra of political iniquity. As I saw them pass by to their dreadful fate, I congratulated myself again and again on my resolution to refuse public employment.

'Heron, the murderer of the Magons, was arrested under a resolution of the Convention, and immediately executed. My formidable enemy Coffinhal, who had contrived to add to the ferocity even of judgments such as his, by the jests with which he embittered them, was destroyed by the ingratitude of a wretch like himself. He had escaped from the Hôtel de Ville in the confusion of the night of the 9th Thermidor, fled to the river side, and lay hid for two days at the bottom of a barge. At length he was forced by hunger from his retreat, and reached the house of a petty shopkeeper, who owed to him his marriage and his establishment in business. It was late, and he found the husband and wife in the back room. While the wife was providing him with food, the husband went forward under the pretence of closing his shop; but in fact it was to denounce his benefactor and call in the police. Coffinhal resisted, was tied, and thrown into a cart, and carried to instant execution, shouting and screaming in impotent rage.'*

Experience had proved the mischiefs and the dangers, both to rulers and to subjects, of what had been called revolutionary government; that is to say, government by a single assembly representing the omnipotence of the people, and exercising or delegating to its own instruments all legislative and executive powers. The surviving leaders, therefore, in the Convention, a small minority of the remarkable men whom it once contained, employed themselves in preparing, for the third time, a constitution. The constitution of 1791 had failed, partly from its intrinsic defects, partly from the disinclination of the separate authorities to acknowledge the rights which the constitution gave to others, or the restraints which it imposed on themselves; and partly from the violent and unjust aggressions of foreign powers. That of 1793 had been prepared in a week, accepted by the people in three days, and immediately suspended. It scarcely differed, in fact, from the existing revolutionary government, except by subjecting to annual re-election the single assembly which was to govern as a sort of committee of the nation. The wisdom of the constitution of 1795 has been highly praised. We have been told that it would have endured, and endured beneficially, if any government not monarchical could have supported itself in France. It was prepared at leisure, and by men of talents, knowledge, and integrity; and, as it was the result of six years' experience in revolution, it provided against the most obvious of the disor-

* Vol. i., p. 231, 237.

ders under which the previous governments had fallen. It provided against the dangers of universal suffrage by establishing indirect election; and by requiring from the first body of electors, the members of what were called the primary assemblies, a qualification depending on taxation; and from the second body, the members of the electoral assemblies, a qualification depending on property. It guarded against rash legislation, by dividing the legislative body into two chambers; one intrusted with the preparation of laws, the other with their acceptance or rejection. It created a separate executive, consisting of a Directory of five persons appointed by the Chambers, and endeavoured to prevent the union of legislative and executive powers, by prohibiting any member of either chamber from filling any other office whatever. It guarded against permanence in office, by enacting that no one should be an elector of the higher order, that is to say, a member of an electoral assembly, for two successive years, or a member of the legislative body for more than six successive years, or a director for more than five years. One director and a third of the legislature were to retire annually; the first by lot, the second according to seniority of election.

It is impossible to believe that, under any circumstances, such a constitution could have been permanent. Its fundamental principles were change and collision. Neither the electoral, the legislative, nor the executive body were to remain unaltered for more than one year. It made experience in public affairs a positive disqualification. A member of the legislature was not re-eligible till after two years' interval, nor a member of the Directory till after five. The members of the legislature, incapable of any other functions, were necessarily in opposition to the Directory. The five directors, with no head, and no common interest, whom accident had made colleagues, and accident was to separate, necessarily split into factions. All the principles of good government were sacrificed to republican jealousy of those to whom power was to be intrusted.

The fitness of this new government to withstand assaults from without, cannot be said to have been tried. Before it had lasted two years it was destroyed from within; and with it was destroyed, for many years, all hope of constitutional, or even legal, government in France. From the unhappy morning of the 18th *Fructidor*, An. 5, (Sept. 4, 1797), when a portion of the Directory used a military force to overpower their colleagues and the two representative bodies of France,

the army had become the masters of the state. Such a precedent once set was not to be recalled. For many subsequent years the drum was substituted for the tocsin, the voice of the general for that of the demagogue, and a military commission for a revolutionary tribunal. From that time the history of France loses its interest. From the history of a nation it becomes the history of an army; and soon afterwards the biography of that individual whose genius enabled him to seize that coarse but irresistible instrument. The picturesque and exciting acts of the vast drama were ended; the great actors, whose audacity of thought, language, and conduct, had crowded into six years changes that seemed to require centuries, had perished, were exiled, or were silenced. The work of destruction ended with the Convention: that of reconstruction began with the Consulate. The Directory was an interval of fraud and force applied to personal purposes—combining the insecurity of a revolution without its enthusiasm, and the oppression of a tyranny without its vigour.

The establishment, however, of something resembling regular government, restored M. Berryer to the public exercise of his profession. One of his first appearances was in defence of a member of the revolutionary committee who had been the petty despots of his section. Their acts of oppression were passed over as incidental to their office, but it was thought safe to attack their miserable peculations. Among these was the robbery of a chapel; the knife-grinder had appropriated the cloth, the president had turned the velvet of the high altar into a pair of breeches, the shoe-cleaner had taken the silk, the porter the silver fringes, and the fifth member the linen. The shoe-cleaner had been M. Berryer's patron, had obtained a passport for him at a critical time, and had given countenance and protection to some others of the inhabitants of the section, who had the merit of being the customers of his stall. These services were urged by M. Berryer, and accepted by the judges as an excuse for sacrilege.

More serious questions soon arose. In a country in which the law had been powerless for nearly two years—in which property had been a ground for proscription, and every stratagem had been used to conceal it—in which the legal currency had been in a course of daily depreciation, while death was the punishment of those who ventured to refuse it, or even to take it at less than its nominal value—where even the connection and mutual rights of husband and wife, and parent and child, had been fluctuating—the relations of individuals towards one another, and towards the property which had escaped confiscation, required to be ascertained.

M. Berryer's narratives of his contests on questions depending on marriage, divorce, and legitimacy, are interesting. They describe a community unsupported by religion, delicacy, or morality—in which virtue had so often been declared to be criminal, and crimes to be virtuous, that public opinion had been destroyed, and with it the conscience and even the self-respect of individuals. Brothers and sisters bred up together attack one another's legitimacy, women set aside their own marriages, husbands disavow their wives, and parents their children; in short, all the misery is exhibited of a society in which mere law is the only restraint. But M. Berryer's stories of this kind are too concise, and too much alike in their features, to be interesting in such an abridgment as we could give of them. We shall select, therefore, some other incidents from his parti-coloured narrative.

One of the most remarkable, and one of those which throw most light upon the internal state of France, during the interval between the Reign of Terror and the Consulate, is a trial before the tribunal of Chartres, in which M. Berryer was only a spectator. For some years previous to the trial, which appears to have taken place in the year 1795, a large tract of country, of which the forest of Orgeres, extending to within thirty miles of Chartres, is the centre, had been infested by bands of ruffians, who, from the use of fire as an instrument of torture, acquired the name of *Chauffeurs.* They were accustomed to surround lonely farm-houses in numbers too large for resistance, bind the males, and force the females, by fire applied to the feet, to discover the property of the family. From the number of their outrages, the uniformity of their proceedings, and the skill with which they were conducted, it was inferred that they formed a large confederacy, acting on system, and obeying some central authority. But this was mere suspicion: common as the crime was, not one of the criminals was identified. One day, however, two *gendarmes,* as they crossed a portion of the forest, found a child about ten years old, the singularity of whose dress excited their curiosity. He asked for food, and was persuaded to accompany them to a neighbouring town. A good breakfast and a glass of wine obtained his confidence. He told them that he lived with his father and mother, and many other families, in a vast cavern in the forest. That a great many men came there from time to time, bringing with them sometimes plate and other valu-

ables, which were afterwards taken away, and sometimes provisions and clothes for the inhabitants. It seemed probable that the head-quarters of the *Chauffeurs* was now detected; but, instead of attacking the cavern, the result of which would have been only the seizure of those who might be in it at the time, and the alarm and escape of the other members of the confederacy, it was resolved to use the child as a means of arresting the out-door brigands, one by one, and to reserve the cavern for the last. For this purpose, the child, to whom we will give, by anticipation, the name of *Finfin,* which he afterwards acquired by the dexterity with which he played his part, was disguised by good clothes, and placed, under the care of a woman who acted as his nurse, at the corners of the markets of the towns to which it was supposed that the brigands would resort to sell the plundered property. Whenever he saw a face with which he had become familiar in the cavern, he gave a sign, and the person indicated was arrested. At length the number exceeded a hundred; descriptions of the prisoners, and of the property found on them, were published; and evidence poured in from all sides. The trial lasted several days. Every morning the accused, about 112 in number, were marched in a long column, guarded by a numerous escort, through the streets of Chartres, to a church in the centre of the town, which had been fitted up on this occasion as a court, and was large enough to exhibit them all to the witnesses and the jury. M. Berryer dwells on the horrors of the evidence, particularly on that of the daughters of an opulent proprietor, three sisters, whose feet had been destroyed by fire, so that they were forced to come on crutches into the court.

It appeared that the cavern, or rather the collection of caverns, from whence *Finfin* had wandered, was situated in the least accessible portion of the forest; and formed out of the quarries which had furnished the stone for the magnificent cathedral of Chartres Here a colony of malefactors, male and female, had been founded, which recruited itself partly by immigration and partly by natural increase. Like the Indian associations of the Thugs, it had a government, laws, and police, adapted to the frightful profession of its members. It had corresponding members, who indicated the dwellings most fit for attack, and an executive, which planned expeditions, and appointed the persons who were to effect them. The whole 112 were convicted. At a subsequent period, it would have been difficult to dispose of a body of criminals for whom death was the only appropriate sentence, and who would have been thought too numerous for such a punishment ; but in 1795, and in France, men were accustomed to such scenes, and M. Berryer passes over their execution without remark.

During the six years which elapsed between M. Berryer's return to his profession and the peace of Amiens, his principal employment, as honourable as it was ineffectual, was the defence of neutral owners against French privateers. At the breaking out of the war in 1793, a decree of the Convention had given jurisdiction in all cases of capture to the local tribunals of France, and even to the French consuls in foreign ports.

'It became,' says M. Berryer, 'a presumption of law in those local prize courts, that not a vessel that traversed the ocean was really neutral; that every cargo was in fact English property; and that all the exteriors of neutrality were frauds to be exposed or eluded. The most frivolous objections were raised to the different papers by which the nationality of the ship, or the ownership of the cargo, was proved, and always with success. Every syllable in every passport was challenged, and every change that, during a long voyage, had taken place in the crew. But when the law of 1798 had declared good prize every vessel containing goods (*marchandises*) the produce of England, or of any English dependency, the robberies of the privateers were unrestrained. They seized, absolutely without exception, every vessel which they met with at sea, whatever the flag, for they were sure to find on board some English goods. It might have been supposed that the word goods (*marchandises*) meant something intended for sale, or at least something for which freight was to be paid. It was held to comprehend the mere furniture of a cabin, a bed, a chair, or a carpet, or even a knife or a razor used by the captain. The presence of any such article drew after it the confiscation of ship and cargo, valued perhaps at millions. An appeal was, indeed, given from the tribunal which sat in a French port to the tribunal of the district, and from the judgment of the French consul abroad to a court sitting in France; but the right was so given as to be beneficial only to captors. In the rare case of a judgment favourable to the neutral, the captor could appeal, and the vessel and cargo were detained till the event was known; but every sentence of an inferior court in favour of a captor was put into immediate execution. No security for costs or for restitution was required, and the neutral, supposing him to succeed on appeal, had generally a mere claim for damages; a claim which the captors rendered nugatory, by converting these undertakings into a joint stock, of which the shares passed by mere delivery, so that the persons liable were unknown, and were constantly changing.

'Such was the state of the law, or of the administration of the law, under which, in the beginning of the year 1798, I was called, for the first time, as counsel to Nantes. My clients were Messrs. Duntzfels and Co , one of the first mercantile houses in Copenhagen. They were the owners of the Bernstorf and the Norge, worth more than three millions of francs, which had been captured by Nantes privateers, and condemned by the inferior tribunal. It was admitted, indeed stated in the sentence, that they were *bonâ fide* Danish property. The only pretence for condemnation was non-compliance, on the part of the captain, with some mere formal regulations, imposed indeed by the recent municipal law of France, which could not, except in violation of the treaty made between France and Denmark in 1742, be applied to the ships of our allies the Danes. I urged the express words of the treaty. I urged its recognition in a similar case by the neighbouring tribunal of St. Brienne. Such was the influence of my arguments on public opinion, even in Nantes, that instruments, purporting to assign shares in the prizes, were not saleable except at nominal prices. By an abuse which had become habitual, the superior court of justice in Nantes applied for instructions to the Directory, then the rulers of France.

'I instantly returned to Paris, in the hope of inducing the Directory, if they interfered in a matter of law, at least to interfere in favour of the treaty. But it was in vain. I soon heard that the law of nations had been overruled, and the vessels finally condemned. The notoriety of these decisions gave a still further extension to the piracy of our privateers. They seized even the coasting traders of the Mediterranean, as they were proceeding, at a distance from any seat of war, from one port belonging to our allies to another. Hundreds of appeals were put into my hands, not from the hope of redress, but because the policies which insured against capture required that every means to ward off condemnation should have been exhausted. The neutral captains and supercargoes crowded to my office —men who had been entrusted with millions ; and now, deprived of their own little funds, and even of their baggage, had to depend on the consuls of their countries for the means of existence during the suit. In one matter, I so far shook the Court of Appeal as to delay its judgment for one day. It was the case of the Federalist, a ship belonging to citizens of the United States of America, with whom we were in strict alliance. The ground of confiscation was a strip of carpet by the captain's bedside. It was discovered, or pretended to be discovered, that this bit of carpeting was of English manufacture. On this pretence the ship and her whole cargo, worth a million and a half of francs, had been condemned. At the conclusion of my address, the court was proceeding to reverse the condemnation. One judge only suggested a doubt. The decision was adjourned to the next day, and was then given in favour of the captors. Generally, I had no clue to the proceedings of the Court of Appeal, but sometimes I could account for them. Early in the morning sittings of the Council of Five Hundred, (Lower Chamber of France), or when the attendance was thin, the pirates used to obtain from the members present resolutions of the Chamber, declaring in their favour the law on any litigated point, and these resolutions were considered decisive. One day, during the hearing of a case, I saw a man, whom I believe to be a deputy from the south, give a paper to the

Government commissioner. While they were whispering together, I rushed towards them, in order to ascertain the nature of the business which brought the deputy into court. He instantly disappeared, for his business was over. The paper contained a resolution of the house, deciding the question against my client.

'The ultimate results were, that not a vessel ventured to approach a French port; that we were cut off from the supply of indispensable commodities; that our privateers, acting without concert and without prudence, fell into the power of the English cruisers; that our maritime population was crowded into the English prisons, where many perished from ill-treatment; that our colonies were lost, for want of sailors to form a military marine; and, ultimately, when the day of retribution arrived, the state had to pay for the plunder which had been profitable only to a few individuals.'*

The revolution which placed Bonaparte on the consular throne was unquestionably beneficial. The despotism which seems to be the inevitable result of military rule, was more tolerable than that of the factions which owed to treason their rise and their fall. Even the tyranny of the Empire was as great an improvement on the intrigues and violence of the Directory, as the Directory was on the anarchy of the Convention.

We are inclined, indeed, to consider the eighteen months of the Peace of Amiens, as the most brilliant portion of the history of France since the death of Charlemagne. England was supposed to be incapable of any but maritime war, and had accepted an insecure and dishonourable peace. The force of Russia was unknown, and neither Austria nor Prussia had yet adopted the systems which, at the expense of all the other objects of government, now give them powers offensive and defensive, which their happier ancestors never contemplated. The military supremacy of France seemed established; and it was supported by a territory as extensive as can be usefully united in one empire. She had incorporated Savoy, Piedmont, the Milanese, a considerable part of Switzerland, and all the great and rich countries that lie between her present frontier and the Rhine. The portions of Holland, Switzerland, and Northern Italy which she had not made French, were her dependencies. It is true that under the Empire she acquired a still more extended territory, and a still larger body of subordinate allies; but her subsequent acquisitions were not ratified by England. They were mere incidents in a fearful game, liable to be torn away, and in fact actually torn away, as soon as her fatal system of playing double or quits

should produce its usual result. At the peace of Amiens her gains were realized. Had she remained contented with them, she would probably now form the most powerful empire that the world has seen. She would possess fifty millions of rich, warlike, and highly civilized inhabitants, with the best soil, the best climate, the best frontier, and the best position, on the Continent.

The same remark may be extended to the extraordinary man who had seized the command of her destinies. He then enjoyed more real power, more real popularity, and more real glory, than at any subsequent period of his career. As a soldier, he never repeated the miracles of his Italian victories. In his subsequent campaigns he obtained vast and decisive advantages when he had a superior force; suffered vast and decisive defeats when his force was inferior; and when the force on each side was nearly balanced, as at Eylau, Aspern, Borodino, and Ligny, so was the success. As a politician, he was known only as a Pacificator; he had had nothing to do with the origin of the three great wars in which he had been an actor; and he had concluded each of them by a glorious peace. He owed, it is true, his power to usurpation, but it was the most pardonable usurpation that history records. Those whom he deposed were themselves usurpers, and for hundreds that regretted the change, there were millions that hailed it with delight. Never was there an easier or a more popular revolution; and, up to the time of which we are speaking, the millions appeared to be right. He had given to France internal as well as external peace. He had restored the rule of law, and made it omnipotent against all except himself. He had laid the foundation of a Code which, with all its defects, is superior to that of any other Continental nation. He had restored Religion, not indeed in its purest form, but in the form most attractive to a people among whom imagination and passion predominate over reason, and who yield more readily to feeling, to authority, and to example, than to conviction. With religion he had restored decency of manners, and, in a considerable degree, decency of morals. He had effected all this under the forms of a constitution which, depending not on the balanced rights and privileges of classes, but on the simple basis of centralized power, gave to the body of the people the equality which they seem to prefer to real liberty and to real security.

One of the first acts of the Consulate was to withdraw matters of prize from the ordinary tribunals, and place them in the hands of a department of the government, denominated the *Conseil des Prises.* The unfitness of the petty local courts had been shown; but the

---

* This narrative is extracted, with some changes of arrangement, from the second volume, cap. iii., § 1, 2.

referring questions of pure law to an administrative instead of a legal body, was a strange anomaly. And when we add that the persons appointed to decide between French captors and neutral owners, were mere officers of the executive, removable at pleasure, the anomaly became an oppression. It is strange that M. Berryer, himself a lawyer, approves of this institution: he had soon a remarkable opportunity of ascertaining its impartiality and its integrity.

'Holland,' says M. Berryer, 'at that time forming the Batavian Republic, was in the year 1797 the unhappy ally of the Republic of France. The price of the alliance had been the loss of all her colonies, and of all maritime commerce under her own flag: for all Indian commodities, and particularly for tea, in Holland a necessary of life, she depended on that of Denmark, the only flag respected by England on the southern ocean. The respect paid by England to the Danish flag was, indeed, a pretence for its violation by France. The French privateers and the French tribunals affected to believe that England used Danish vessels as the means of her eastern communication. When it is recollected that the Indian trade of England was carried on in the great ships of the East India company, sailing in fleets and under convoy, the insincerity of this pretence is obvious; but it served as a convenient instrument of pillage, particularly in the case which I am about to relate.

'In the Autumn of 1797, the Batavian Republic wished to import a year's supply of green tea. The attempt to send from Amsterdam to Canton ten millions of francs of Dutch property, and to bring it back in so peculiar a form, was very difficult and very perilous; on the one hand the seas of Africa and Asia were swarming with English cruisers, which respected no flag but the Danish, and on the other hand the seas of Europe were filled with the privateers of the dear ally of Holland, which respected no flag whatever.

'To delude the English cruisers, a ship which had belonged to the English East India Company, was purchased and sent to Copenhagen. There she was named the Caninholm, and fitted for her voyage; her captain was naturalized as a Dane; she had a whole set of Danish papers, and cleared for Tranquebar, a Danish settlement; taking in at Portsmouth her outward cargo in dollars. These precautions were supposed, and indeed proved, sufficient as regarded the cruisers of her enemy, England; the real danger was from those of her ally, France. To ward off this the Batavian government took into their confidence the French government, then consisting of the Directory, and obtained their sanction to the expedition, and a license or protection against all interference by French vessels. As a further precaution, a Dutch supercargo was taken in at Tranquebar, and the Caninholm, on her return voyage, cleared out at Canton for the Texel.

'The expedition lasted more than eighteen months. The Caninholm left Copenhagen in November, 1797, and it was in June, 1799, that

she was captured as she entered the European seas, by a French privateer, and carried into Bordeaux. The captain instantly went on shore to show his license to the Bordeaux authorities; but no justice was to be expected in a privateering town, when a prize of ten millions of francs was in dispute. The ship was of course condemned. The owners appealed; but before they could be heard, the revolution of 1799 had overthrown the Directory. The consular government refused to recognize the contracts of its predecessors or the rights of its ally, and the Caninholm was definitively condemned as English property. I ascertained afterwards that Bonnet and Co., the owners of the privateer, had been obliged to scatter a little of their rich prey in order to keep the remainder. Bills accepted by them suddenly appeared in the Paris market; I myself had to advise proceedings on more than half a million's worth of them.'[*]

Some branches of the legal profession may flourish under a despot; attorneys and chamber counsel do not excite his jealousy; a d judges are the best instruments of his power. They enable him to express his will in the form of general principles, and thus to regulate the actions of millions, of whose separate existence he is not even aware. They convert resistance to his power into a breach of law, and punish it without his apparent interference. An army or a mob may give power to its chief; but that power cannot be safe until it is supported by legal forms, enforced by legal authorities. But no arbitrary ruler looks favourably on advocates. The bar is essentially an aristocracy in the noblest sense of that term; the relative position of its members depends on their merit; the smiles of the crown cannot give reputation to mediocrity, its frowns cannot depress diligence and talent. The functions of the bar are still more offensive than its independence; its business is to discuss, and an absolute government hates discussion; its business is to enforce the observance of general rules, and 'adherence to precedents: such a government, though it requires them from others, refuses itself to be bound by either. 'Every day,' said Bonaparte, and he was then only Consul, 'one must break through positive laws; there is no other mode of proceeding. The action of the government must never be impeded—there must be no opposition.'[†]

Again, a bar, though it offers its services indifferently to the government and to its subjects, is really useful only to the latter. Such a government does not require the aid of an advocate to persuade judges to be subservient to a power which appoints, promotes,

---

[*] Vol. ii., Sec. iii.
[†] Thibaudeau, *Mémoires sur le Consulat*, pp. 229, 231.

and removes them; but to those whom the government is attacking, his assistance is inestimable. He may sometimes be able to protect their lives or their fortunes, and he can almost always protect their reputation. All other appeals to public opinion may be tolerated up to a certain point, and silently prevented from passing the prescribed limit. A censorship may effectually chain the press without attracting attention to any given case of interference; but if an advocate is once allowed to speak, he cannot be stopped without an apparent denial of justice.

Bonaparte, who had all the jealousies and the instincts of ambition in their utmost intensity, must, under any circumstances, have hated the French bar; but he had also a personal quarrel with its members:—out of more than two hundred advocates, only three voted in favour of the Empire, and this was a subject on which he never forgave opposition. He restored indeed the order, but he deprived it of self-government, and laid it at the feet of the imperial authorities. The express permission of the chief judge was necessary before an advocate could plead in any court but his own; the attorney-general selected the members of the *Conseils de discipline,* which regulated the internal affairs of the order; and he also selected from them the *bâtonnier,* or president of the bar; and finally, the chief judge had an arbitrary power of suspension, and even of expulsion.

M. Berryer himself incurred Bonaparte's especial displeasure. He had been counsel against Bourrienne, before Bourrienne had lost his master's favour; he had defended Moreau and Dupont, and the family of Monnet, the unfortunate defender of Flushing. For these offences he was excluded from the Tribunate, and from the honours of the bar; but the contest which he appears to think the most dangerous, was his defence of M. the Mayor of Antwerp, in 1812 and 1813.

The Mayor, an old man of high character and great wealth, and once in high favour with Bonaparte, was married to a young wife, who quarrelled with the wife of the commissioner of police about a box in the theatre. The commissioner revenged himself by accusing the Mayor, and three other municipal officers, of embezzling the proceeds of the *Octroi* of Antwerp; and having Bonaparte's confidence, contrived to render him the determined enemy of the accused.

The indictment was an enormous instrument: the attorney-general of the imperial court of Brussels, which then included Antwerp in its jurisdiction, was said to have been killed by the labour of preparing it. The trial took place at Brussels, before a jury con-sisting of the principal persons of the country. After it had gone on for some days, it became clear that it would terminate by an acquittal. The law-officers who conducted the prosecution, therefore, interrupted its progress, by indicting for perjury two of the mayor's witnesses. As this matter was to be disposed of before the Mayor's trial could be concluded, the latter was thrown over to a subsequent session and a new jury. The indictment against the witnesses utterly failed, and the Mayor's trial was resumed. A new jury was selected solely from Frenchmen, most of them public functionaries, and all devoted to the Emperor, whose determination to destroy the Mayor was now notorious. We will pursue the narrative in M. Berryer's words:—

'On my second arrival at Brussels, I had to unveil before the jury the complicated iniquity of the prosecution. I referred to the oppressive indictment of the witnesses for the defence, and showed it to have been a trick to get rid of the first jury. I dwelt on the absence of any documentary evidence against my clients, and refuted all the verbal testimony which had been procured. The trial, after several days of hearing, ended by a general acquittal. The whole population of Brussels surrounded the mayor, and drew his carriage in triumph to his hotel. Even when I left the town late in the evening, on my return to Paris, the streets were still resounding with music and acclamations. The news reached Bonaparte at Dresden, and put him in a state of fury. He instantly sent a violent despatch to Paris, ordering the mayor and his co-defendants to be re-tried, and even the jury to be tried for having acquitted them. The minister of justice transmitted the order to M. Argenson, the prefect of Antwerp. M. Argenson replied that it was impossible to try men again on charges from which a jury had acquitted them. The Council of State was assembled, and decided that the imperial command must be obeyed. This decision was notified to M. Argenson. He merely repeated his refusal. Application was now made by the minister of justice to the Senate, as the highest body in the state. The Senate referred the matter to a committee. I flew to the Luxembourg, and obtained an interview with a member of the committee. He heard all I had to say, agreed with me that such a profanation of the forms and the substance of law would be disastrous, but ended by saying, "After all, what would you have us do?—do you not perceive that we should upset ourselves?" The committee accordingly reported as the Council of State had done before; and by virtue of a decree of the Senate, the mayor and his supposed accomplices were directed to be tried before the Court of Assizes of Douai. I heard of the decree before it was published, and had time to advise two of those who had been acquitted with the mayor, and some of the members of the jury who had fled to me in Paris for my aid in the extreme danger in which they were placed, to avoid the storm by concealing themselves. M. Argenson not only persisted in his refusal, but resigned. Other persons, however, less scrupulous were found, and the mayor was arrested and conveyed to the prison of Douai. Worn out, however, by oppression and anxiety, he died there, before the period of trial. Indeed, before that trial could have been terminated, the man who had been mad enough to order it had ceased to reign.*

Though a stanch royalist, M. Berryer does not appear to have been one of the enthusiastic welcomers of the Restoration. It was connected, indeed, with the loss of his fortune, the honourable accumulation of thirty-four years of labour. A manufacturer who had been the victim of the fraud and ingratitude of his partners, became his client. He obtained for him damages sufficient to form the nucleus of a capital, and, by becoming his guarantee to a banking company, enabled him to establish himself as a cotton-spinner at Rouen. M. Berryer's security for the sums advanced on his guarantee, was the deposit of twist of double the value. At the time of the Restoration, the amount for which M. Berryer was liable exceeded L.25,000, for which he held twist valued at L.50,000. The relaxation of prohibitory duties in the first effervescence of the Restoration, instantly reduced the value of the twist to L.8000. The bankers required a further security. M. Berryer was forced to mortgage, and ultimately to sell all his own estates, and also all those of his wife, for she generously consented to surrender them.

Soon afterwards came the most important of M. Berryer's causes—a cause in which his exertions, though unproductive to his client, and injurious to his own interests, were honourable to his talents and to his courage. This was the trial of Marshal Ney. The twenty-seven years which have elapsed since that striking event, may have effaced its details from the memories of many of our readers. We will shortly recapitulate them:

In the beginning of 1815, Marshal Ney was governor of Besançon, but residing on his estate near Châteaudun, a town between Chartres and Orleans, about eighty miles from Paris. On the 6th of March he received an order from Soult, then minister of war, to proceed to Besançon. News travels slowly in France: though Bonaparte had been five days in Provence, the fact was unknown at Châteaudun, and Ney, curious as to the motive of the order, took Paris in his road. He arrived on the 7th, and found M. Batardy, his attorney, at his house waiting for him † They arranged some private business, and Batardy,

surprised at Ney's making no allusion to what occupied every mind in Paris, ventured to remark, 'This is a strange event.' 'What event?' answered Ney. 'Don't you know,' replied Batardy, 'that Bonaparte has landed at Cannes—that Monsieur proceeded this morning to Lyons, and that you are ordered to your government?' At first Ney treated the news as incredible; but when he was told that it was officially stated in the *Moniteur*, he leant his head upon the mantelpiece and exclaimed, 'What a calamity!—what a horrible event!' What can be done?—what is there to oppose such a man as that? Would he have ventured to return unless he had relied on finding here enemies to the government?'

Ney went immediately to the minister, and was told that he would find his instructions at Besançon. He then saw the King, made his memorable promise to bring back Bonaparte in a cage, left Paris for Besançon, and appears to have arrived there during the night between the 9th and 10th. The 10th he employed in directing the forces under his control to meet at Lons le Saulnier, a small town to the south of Besançon, and to the east of the high-road from Lyons to Paris. On the 11th he set out himself for Lons le Saulnier. In the mean time, Grenoble had opened its gates to Bonaparte; he had rushed forward to Lyons, the second city in France, occupied by a considerable force under Monsieur and Marshal Macdonald. The city and the garrison had received him with enthusiasm; Monsieur and Macdonald had been forced to fly; the trifling band with which he had landed had been swelled by the garrisons of Grenoble and Lyons to more than 10,000 men, and was augmenting every day by the desertion from the royal forces of individuals, companies, and even regiments. On his road, Ney met M. de St. Amour and M. de Soran returning from Lyons, who described to him the revolutionary madness which they had witnessed in the people, and the cries of *Vive l'Empereur* which they had heard from the troops whom they had met on their march. In the morning of the 12th he reached Lons le Saulnier.

During the whole of that day, and until the night of the 13th, he appears to have been making active preparations to attack Bonaparte, or at least to resist him. The troops nominally under his order did not amount to 5000 men; they were deficient in ammunition, and scarcely provided with artillery—the artillery horses having been hired by the farmers, and not to be found when unexpectedly wanted. Bonaparte's proclamations were scattered round, and seemed everywhere to produce their in-

* Vol. i., pp. 350-354.

† See M. Batardy's deposition. *Procès du Maréchal Ney*, Michaud. No. i., p. 51.

tended effects. In the evening of the 13th, Ney's spies informed him that Bonaparte, preceding his own forces with an escort of only forty men, had entered Mâcon in triumph; that from Mâcon to Bourg (which is only seven posts from Lons le Saulnier) the whole country was in what the French call *exaltation*—that even the villagers, and the people in the fields, were crying *Vive l'Empereur.* Ney's last acts on the 13th were to make arrangements—the prudence and details of which raised the admiration of the peers at his trial,[*]—to write to Marshals Suchet and Oudinot, who were co-operating with him in support of the royal cause, to communicate his proceedings; and to require all the regimental and non-commissioned officers of his small force, separately, to swear before him to be faithful to the Bourbons. It is to be observed that on this very day, at a council held in the Tuileries, it was admitted that resistance was hopeless—that not a soldier would fire on his former Emperor—and that the only debatable question was, in what direction the King should fly.[†]

Late in the night between the 13th and 14th, Ney was guilty of his first breach of duty. He admitted messengers from Bonaparte: they brought him a letter from Bertrand, assuring him that Louis had been betrayed by his ministers; that troops devoted to Bonaparte had been posted along the road to Paris, so as to ensure his advance without opposition; and that the whole enterprise had been concerted with England and Austria. The folly of the last statements ought not to revolt us, when we remember that the successor to Napoleon was the grandson of Francis; and that M. Berryer, who has passed his life in estimating evidence, even now believes that we effected Bonaparte's escape! Absurd as they really were, they did not appear so to Ney. With Bertrand's letter came a proclamation ready prepared in the name of Ney, in which he was made to declare that the cause of the Bourbons was lost for ever, and that liberty and Napoleon were triumphant. And there came also orders from Bonaparte, expressed as if the old relations between himself and Ney had remained uninterrupted, and giving him instructions in the style which he had long been accustomed to obey.

Between three and four in the morning of the 14th, he was roused from his sleep by M. de Capelle, the prefect of Bourg, who had to tell him that one of his regiments, the 76th, stationed at Bourg, had proclaimed Bonaparte; that even the regiment at St. Amour, which

formed the advanced guard of the small force at Lons le Saulnier, was preparing to go over; and that throughout the country the higher classes were stupified, and the lower mad with revolutionary excitement. This information appears to have convinced him of the impossibility of further opposition. 'Can I stop,' he said to M. de Capelle, 'with my hand the rising of the tide?' A few hours afterwards he ordered his troops to be called together; but before he took a decisive step, summoned the two generals next him in command, De Bourmont and Lecourbe, both of them supposed to be devoted to the King, showed them the proclamation, repeated the contents of Bertrand's letter, and asked their advice. No fourth person was present. De Bourmont and Lecourbe state that they urged him to remain faithful to the King; Ney maintains that they approved of his joining Bonaparte. It is in favour of Ney's statement, that they both accompanied him to the parade where the troops were formed in square, stood on each side of him while he read the proclamation, heard it without any expression of dissent, and dined with him the same evening. The dinner was silent and melancholy. We fully believe Ney's account of the effect produced on his own mind by the irrevocable step which he had taken. 'From the time of that unhappy proclamation life was a burden to me; I wished for nothing but death, and did all I could to find it at Waterloo. A hundred times I was on the point of blowing out my brains; all that restrained me was my wish to defend my character. I knew that all honourable men must blame me—I blamed myself. I did wrong, I admit it, but I was not a traitor; I was partly deceived, and partly carried away.[*]

Ney proceeded to meet Bonaparte at Dijon, and a few days afterwards was ordered to visit the northern and eastern frontier, from Lille to Landau, to ascertain the state of the fortresses and hospitals; and to publish everywhere that Bonaparte had returned under a treaty between himself, England, and Austria—stipulating that he was never to carry on war beyond the frontier of France; that he was to give France a liberal constitution; and that his wife and child were to remain as hostages in Vienna until he had performed all the positive parts of his engagement.[†] Having executed his mission, he retired into the country, and took so little part in the transactions of April and May, that when, on the 1st of June, he appeared at the ceremony of the acceptance of the new constitution, Bonaparte told him that he thought he had emi-

---

[*] See *Procès*, No. iv., p. 14.
[†] See the details in Bourrienne, vol. x., cap. 16. Bourrienne was present.

[*] *Procès*, No. i., p. 12.   [†] Ibid., p. 27.

grated. 'I ought to have done so long ago,' answered Ney; 'now it is too late.'*

He returned after the battle of Waterloo to Paris; and by his bold exposition in the Chamber of Peers, on the 22d of June, of the real facts and consequences of the battle, materially assisted in driving Bonaparte from power. In that speech, Ney maintained that the Allies would be before Paris in a week. His prediction was accomplished; and on the morning of the 3d of July it seemed probable that, before the evening, a battle would have been fought, more disastrous to France, and particularly to Paris, than any event in the history of the French nation. Davoust, who commanded the army defending the town, had a large body of infantry, (80,000 men, according to M. Berryer,†) 25,000 cavalry, and between four and five hundred pieces of field artillery‡—a force insufficient for victory, but sufficient to maintain a contest destructive of the city in which it was to take place. Already the firing had begun, when the Provisional Government and Davoust sent to propose a negotiation; of which the bases were to be, the entry of the allied forces on the one hand, and the preservation of Paris, and the security of all who inhabited it, on the other. On these terms the convention of the 3d of July, 1815, was framed; and ratified by the Duke of Wellington and Blucher on the part of the Allies, and by Davoust on the part of the Provisional Government. The twelfth article provided that all the inhabitants, and generally all persons found in Paris, should continue to enjoy all their rights and liberty, and should not be liable to any molestation or inquiry whatsoever, with relation to their functions, to their conduct, or to their political opinions. It appears, from the evidence of General Guilleminot, one of the negotiators of the convention, that this was the clause to which the defenders of Paris attached the most importance. Had it been refused, he was to break off the discussion, and the battle would have commenced.§

Relying on the protection given to him by the convention, Ney remained in Paris till the 6th of July, and continued in France until the 3d of August; when he was arrested on a charge of treason, and ordered to be tried by a court-martial, comprising among its members four of the Marshals of France. Ney protested against the jurisdiction of such a tribunal, and the court, unfortunately, as M. Berryer thinks, for the prisoner, declared itself incompetent.

The cause, therefore, was transferred to the House of Peers; the court appointed by the Charter for the trial of treason. The object of Ney's counsel was to gain time. They knew, from the experience of thirty-five years of revolution, that political resentment is a passion as fleeting as it is fierce; and that, if a delay of a few months could be obtained, the Government would no longer have the courage to execute him, nor indeed the wish. For this purpose they endeavoured to show, that, although the Charter rendered treason cognizable by the House of Peers, yet it laid down no rules by which the house was to be governed when sitting as a court of criminal justice; and they required that the trial should be suspended, until a law regulating the procedure of the house should have been passed. M. Berryer's speech * is an admirable specimen of legal and constitutional reasoning; and indicates, with great sagacity, the errors into which such a tribunal, unless supported and directed by strict regulations, would be likely to fall. The house, however, after a secret deliberation of an hour and a half, decided that the trial should go on. Objections were then raised to the indictment, and, though they were overruled, so much time was gained, that the house, which had met for the trial on the 11th of November, did not really begin it till the 4th of December.

In the mean time, Ney had applied to the ministers of the allied powers, and required them to interfere, and prevent the convention of the 3d of July from being violated in his person. Their answer, drawn up by the Duke of Wellington, and adopted by the ministers of Austria and Prussia, stated, that 'the object of the 12th article was to prevent the adoption of any measure of severity, under the military authority of those who made it, towards any persons in Paris, on account of the offices which they had filled, or their conduct, or their political opinions; but it was not intended, and could not be intended, to prevent either the existing French government or any French government which should succeed to it, from acting in this respect as it might deem fit.'†

In this extremity Madame Ney sought the aid of Lord Holland, a name illustrious throughout Europe as the friend of the oppressed. She requested him to lay Ney's Memorial before the Prince Regent. It was done; but the only effect was a letter from Lord Liverpool, referring her to the communication already made to her husband by the Duke of Wellington.‡ Lord Holland, however, did not yet despair. He still thought

---

* *Procès,* No. i. p. 12.   † Vol. i., p. 374.
† See the evidence, *Procès,* No. iv., p. 19.
‡ *Procès,* No. iv., p. 20.

* *Procès,* No. ii., p. 32.
† British and Foreign State papers, 1815, 1816, printed by the Foreign Office.—P. 262.
‡ Ibid.—P. 272.

that the Duke of Wellington's interference might be obtained, and must be decisive ; and in that hope he addressed to their common friend, Lord Kinnaird, then at Paris, a letter which was to be shown to the Duke. What effect it might have had, cannot be told. It arrived the day after the sentence had been executed. As this admirable letter has never been published, we cannot resist the temptation of extracting some of its most material passages.

'*Middleton, Dec.* 5, 1816.

'DEAR KINNAIRD,

'What is passing at Paris annoys me more than I can describe. For La Valette, on the score of private acquaintance, though slight, I am much concerned ; but from regard to the character of our country, and to that of the Duke of Wellington, (in whom, after the great things he has done, even as decided an opponent of the war as myself must feel a national interest), I have conceived more horror at the trials and executions going on in the teeth of our capitulation than mere humanity could create.

'How can such a man as Wellington assert that the impunity for political conduct extends only to impunity from the Allies for offences committed against *them?* When ships, when garrisons surrender, do the captains or commanders stipulate that the foreign conqueror shall not molest them for their political exertions ? With or without such stipulations, what shadow of right has a foreign enemy to punish individuals for opinions held, or conduct pursued in their own country ? It is clear that the impunity promised was impunity for crimes, real or supposed, against a French government. If the French government was a party to that promise, by that promise it must abide. If not, the other Allies are bound in honour not to deliver over a town taken in virtue of it, without exacting the same terms from those to whom they deliver it. Such, perhaps, is the formal technical way of putting the argument. Practically and substantially, the case, if not more striking, is yet more conclusive to men of justice and honour. The Allies have virtually, I might say formally too, been masters of Paris, while the persons who delivered it to them on the faith of impunity for political offences, have for political offences been imprisoned, tried, condemned, and executed ! Wellington has himself precluded all doubt on the question. He maintains, in his letter to Lord Castlereagh, that there is no article in the capitulation securing to the town of Paris the pictures and statues ; and therefore he argues, and he acts on his argument, that the Allies may seize the pictures, &c., and seize them without any *fresh* or formal cession from Louis XVIII. Up to that time, then, the Allies, according to him, were in military possession of Paris, and up to that time therefore, even upon his own view of the subject, the inhabitants were entitled to claim impunity for all political opinions and conduct. Those who had the right and the power of taking forcibly from Paris, property not specified or disposed of in the capitulation, notwithstanding the nominal government of

Louis XVIII., must surely have a right to enforce on any such nominal and dependent government the observance of promises, on the faith of which the inhabitants had surrendered the town.

'Technical arguments may possibly be urged on both sides ; and, though they appear to me all in favour of Ney's claim, it is not on them I lay stress, but on the obvious and practical aspect of the transaction as it must strike impartial men and posterity. The plain relation of the events in history will be this. A promise of security was held out to the inhabitants of Paris—they surrendered the town, and while Wellington and the Allies were still really in possession of it, Labedoyere was executed, and Ney was tried for political opinions and conduct. Even of subsequent executions, and I fear there will be many, it will be said—The Allies delivered over their authority, in Paris, to a French government, without exacting an observance of the stipulations on which they had originally acquired it.

'Had we taken Martinique in 1794, on a promise of not molesting individuals for political opinions or conduct, should we have been at liberty to cede it had Louis XVIII. been then restored, without insisting on the impunity of all political offenders ; or, at the very least, on the right of leaving the country for all such as might have so offended ? In Egypt the French stipulated that no natives should be molested for their conduct or opinions during the war. We took military possession of the country on these terms, and then delivered it over to the political authority of the Ottoman Porte. When, however, the Capitan Pasha, acting under that authority, began murdering the Beys, and proceeding against the adherents of the French, we not only remonstrated and threatened, but actually protected the persecuted men within our own lines. Yet, by reference to the history of those times, we find that many blamed Lord Hutchinson for not having recourse to yet more violent methods, to enforce on the legitimate political authority the observance of engagements entered into by our military power on taking military possession of the country.

'What would Wellington himself have said, if the British troops had surrendered any town in Spain to the French with a similar stipulation, and if, on the flimsy and hypocritical subterfuge of a distinction between Joseph's government and the French military authorities, all the Spaniards who had assisted us during the siege had been prosecuted for treason against Joseph ? Yet, where is the distinction ?

'The want of principle and consistency, and the disgusting changes of the Marshals, have, I know, steeled men's minds to their sufferings. This is natural enough. But when the violence of the times is gone by, and, above all, when the tomb has closed on their offences, the transaction will be judged with reference to the nature of the promise, not to the conduct or misconduct of the sufferers. *Si ego digna in quam faceres, tu tamen indignus qui feceris, Pamphile.*

'Nor is this all. If we judge by former instances, even the crime itself will be regarded with more indulgence by posterity than any irregular mode of punishing it. Allowance for individuals is made in all great changes. It is difficult in sudden emergencies and great convulsions of state, especially for professional men whose lives have been passed in camps, to weigh maturely all the considerations by which their conduct should, in the strict line of duty, be regulated. Unforeseen cases occur, and men of good principles and understanding are hurried into acts of inconsistency and political immorality.

'In this latter view of the subject, I know I am somewhat singular. Few at present make such allowances for the political tergiversations of the Marshals; and many, more indulgent than I am in their judgment of political apostasy in England, are quite outrageous with Frenchmen for not acting with inflexible principle in the most trying and difficult circumstances. Some, however, among the most indignant at their crimes, yet doubt the justice, policy, and safety of punishing them; and more, especially among the moderate of all parties, think the claim of the capitulation conclusive; or, if not quite so, of a nature questionable enough to induce Wellington, for the preservation of his own and the national character, to give it the construction most favourable to the weaker party.

'My opinion is of no importance; but it is so strong that I could not resist expressing it to you, who have access to those whose character is most interested in forming a sound one on this important subject. I have not spoken of La Valette. All my arguments apply in his favour as strongly as in Ney's; and surely he is not, as others may be, any object of a bystander's indignation. He seems an honourable man throughout.—Yours ever truly,

'VASSALL HOLLAND.'

The progress of the trial had been comparatively rapid. In two sittings, on the 5th and 6th of December, each party proved satisfactorily their principal points; the accusers, that the treason was legally completed—the defenders, that the crime had been unpremeditated. But when M. Berryer opened the real defence, the convention of the 3d of July, he was interrupted by the counsel for the Crown. M. Bellart, their leader, protested against any allusions to a convention, the conditions of which had been demanded by rebels, and had never been accepted by the King; and he presented to the house a requisition, by which he formally opposed the reading of the convention, and any allusion to it, and required the house, by the Chancellor, its president, to order Marshal Ney and his defenders to confine their defence to the mere facts of the indictment.

The Chancellor, speaking in the name of the house, answered that, foreseeing the line of defence that would be adopted, he had already taken the opinion of the house; and that the peers had decided, by a large majority, that it would be highly improper to rely in that house on a convention to which the King was no party, and by which it was ob-

vious, from the mere fact of Ney's prosecution, that his Majesty did not consider himself bound. He therefore forbade the defenders to make any use of the convention. Ney's counsel replied, that they bowed to the will of the King, and to the decision which the court, without hearing them, had thought fit to adopt; but that they felt bound to offer a plea to the jurisdiction of the court—namely, that Sarre Louis, the birth-place of their client, having been ceded to Prussia, he was no longer a subject of France.

Here, however, the counsel were interrupted by Ney.

'"No!" he exclaimed; "I was born a Frenchman—I will die a Frenchman. Up to this time my defence has been free, but I now see that it is to be fettered. I thank my generous defenders for the exertions which they have made, and which they are ready to make; but I had rather have no defence than the mere shadow of one. If, when I am accused in the teeth of a solemn treaty, I am not allowed to appeal to it, I must appeal to Europe and to posterity."

'"Gentlemen, counsel for the prisoner," said the Chancellor, "continue your defence within the limits which I have prescribed."

'"My lord," said Ney, "I forbid my counsel to say another word. Your excellency may give to the house what orders you think fit; but as to my counsel, they may go on if they are free, but if they are to be restrained by your limits, I forbid them to speak. You see," he said, turning to M. Berryer, who was anxious to continue, "that it is a decided thing. I had rather have no defence than one chalked out by my accusers."

"Then," said M. Bellart, "we waive our right of reply; if the defence is at an end, so is the accusation. We have only to demand the judgment of the Court."

'"Have you anything to add?" said the chancellor, turning to the prisoner and his counsel.

'"Nothing whatever," replied Ney, in rather an impatient tone.'[*]

The Chamber was then cleared, and the peers alone remained in deliberation; the result of their deliberation, and of the attempts afterwards made to obtain a pardon, are too notorious to require repetition.

The execution of Ney was one of the grossest faults of the Restoration: his crime was great, but, as we have seen, it was not premeditated; only a few hours' elapsed between his active fidelity and his treason; it was the effect of the pressure of circumstances of extraordinary difficulty and perplexity on a mind unaccustomed to balance conflicting motives. If Ney had been a man of higher education, he would have felt that no motive

---

[*] *Procès*, No. iv., p. 37, 38, 39. Berryer, vol. i., p. 376.

justifies a failure in honour. But he had been trained in revolutionary camps; the only fidelity to which he had been accustomed was fidelity to France, and fidelity to the Emperor. He was now required to become an emigrant from the one and an opponent to the other; he was required to do this, though he believed the cause of the Bourbons to be irretrievably lost, and the reign of Bonaparte an inevitable calamity. No one can doubt what his conduct ought to have been; but no one can wonder at what it actually was. It must be added, that his treason was really harmless; no opposition on his part could have retarded, by a single hour, the entry of Bonaparte into Paris. If he had followed the example of Macdonald, he must have shared his fate—have seen his troops join the usurper, and then have fled across the frontier; the only consequence would have been, that Bonaparte would have had one brave man less at Quatre-Bras and Waterloo. Under such circumstances, his execution, even if it had been legal, would have been impolitic. Public opinion would have sanctioned his degradation, perhaps his banishment, but not his death.

But the judgment under which he suffered was manifestly illegal. Royalist as he is, M. Berryer is so convinced of this, that he accounts for it by the irrational supposition, that it was extorted from the King by the allied powers for the mere purpose of degrading the French army. Ney was included in the words and in the spirit of the convention. To deny validity to the convention because it was entered into with rebels, was to affirm the execrable doctrine, that faith is not to be kept in civil war. To deny its validity because it was not formally accepted by the King, was to add fraud to oppression; for what can be a baser fraud than to accept the benefits of an agreement and to refuse its obligations? There was not a human being to whom that convention was so beneficial as Louis. If it had not been effected—if, after the slaughter of 25,000 of its defenders, Paris had had to endure the horrors of a town taken by assault, could Louis have retained a crown so recovered for a longer period than while English and Austrian troops occupied his capital and his country? Louis owed to that convention his throne as an independent monarch. When we recollect this, it is unnecessary to refer to the well-known fact alluded to by M. Berryer, that Louis *did* expressly recognize the convention, by appealing to it in order to prevent Blucher from destroying the Pont de Jena.

As is usually the case with political crimes, it received its retribution. The recollection of Ney's death was one of the principal causes of the unpopularity with the army which haunted the elder Bourbons; and fifteen years afterwards, when, in their utmost need, they had to rely on the army for support, that recollection precipitated their fall.

We have said that the trial of Ney exercised an unfavourable influence on the subsequent fortunes of M. Berryer. He had obtained from the King the fullest permission to act for the prisoner—a permission which might have been supposed to be unnecessary to an advocate filling no office under the crown; but, though the permission was granted, the act was registered as an offence. It was thought too, that he had too much identified himself with his client. In his honest indignation against the restriction imposed on the defence he had ventured to call it a denial of justice; and, what was worse, in consequence of the recollections which he termed excited—a revolutionary proceeding: this seems never to have been forgiven. The result was, that he was excluded under the Restoration, as he had been under the Empire, from the *Conseil de Discipline* and the dignity of *Bâtonnier,* an exclusion to which he attaches what seems to us an undue importance.

The subsequent life of M. Berryer contains no facts sufficiently interesting to lead us to dwell on them. In 1825 he visited London, on business connected with the administration of the estate of a French subject who died in England. He was charmed, as might have been expected, with his reception by ' *Sir Coppley, (aujourd'hui Lord Linthurst), Atthorney-Général,*' (we copy literatim); gratified by the respect paid to him when he appeared in court; and amused by finding there people ' en perruque à la Louis XIV.' He ascertained, he says, that his reception was meant as a return for that with which Lord Erskine had been honoured, at a sitting of the *Cour d' Appel* of Paris. This, however, we can assure him is a mistake. It was scarcely possible that any one of those who rose in Westminster Hall to welcome a distinguished stranger, could have heard how Lord Erskine had been treated twenty years before in Paris; and it must be added, that the mere announcement of M. Berryer's name was a sufficient passport to the attention of a British bar.

Soon after his return from London M. Berryer ceased to appear regularly in court; he was entering his 69th year, and began to feel daily contests oppressive. He found, too, his eldest son, by this time a distinguished advocate, often opposed to him; he thinks that this was done by the suitors intentionally, which is not very probable, since it diminished the efficiency of the son as much as that of the father. The result has been, that for some years he has nearly confined himself to chamber business and arbitrations. He continued, indeed, up to the time of the publication of his memoirs, to plead at the bar in causes in which he possessed peculiar information, and perhaps may continue to do so up to the present time. The last circumstance of this kind which he mentions, took place at Rouen in the end of the year 1837; and he tells with pleasure his reappearance, after an interval of sixty years, at the scene of one of his earliest triumphs.

M. Berryer dwells with just pride on the extent and long continuance of his labours. When we consider that his practice embraced every branch of jurisprudence, ecclesiastical, international, civil, and criminal; that he performed the duties of a solicitor as well as those of a barrister; and that he has been engaged in these duties, with scarcely any interruption, for more than sixty years; his readiness to undergo toil, and his power of enduring it, are perhaps unparalleled. He attributes his success to his domestic happiness, and to a natural gaiety of disposition, fostered by the amenity, and, to use his own expression, the joyousness, of the manners and habits which for the first thirty-four years of his life adorned his country. But now, he says, no one smiles in France; he finds himself, between eighty and ninety, too young for his associates, and is forced to repress a thousand sallies which the gravity of the times would not tolerate. He tells us, that for the same reason he has suppressed the most amusing parts of his 'Recollections;' and defers his full revelations until a period when the public may be better prepared for them.

He has appended to the narrative portion of his work some propositions on Political Economy and Legislation, the results of his long experience and meditation. We cannot venture to call the attention of our readers to them on any other ground than as specimens of the degree of knowledge on these subjects which has been acquired by a French lawyer, far superior in intelligence to the bulk of his brethren.

He conceives it to be the duty of the government to regulate production, and promote an equivalent consumption. For the first purpose, he thinks that the minister of commerce ought to direct, by a perpetual course of regulations founded on accurate statistical facts, all the proceedings of agriculture and manufactures. For the second purpose, he proposes to check the tendency to systematic economy, which he thinks the great enemy

of consumption, by a tax on accumulated capital;—the amount to be ascertained by requiring from every capitalist a declaration of his fortune, and any concealment to be punished by confiscation. Such a tax he thinks would prevent the parsimony which dries up the channels of circulation. He further proposes to establish in every department a bank, to be managed by landholders, of which the capital should consist of land, and which should issue notes to a corresponding amount; and also insurance companies, to secure the punctual payment of rents, and relieve landholders from the temptation to provide, by annual savings, against irregularity of income —such savings being, in M. Berryer's opinion, unfavourable to circulation. He thinks that eighty-three new peers ought to be created, one for each department; that their dignity should be hereditary, and that its transmission to an unfit person should be prevented by an examination, from time to time, into the moral and intellectual qualities of each successor. He thinks that the tendency in man to better his condition and to change his residence should be repressed. He proposes that no one should be allowed to exempt himself from military service (the great oppression of France) by finding a substitute, unless he can prove that he has always resided under his father's roof, and that it is probable that he will continue to do so; and that no one shall be allowed to serve as a substitute, unless he can show that he has always resided in the parish where he was born. Further, that those who have changed their residences shall be subjected to increased taxation, and that no one shall be eligible to any local office if he have quitted his birthplace.

He ventures to insinuate a regret at the complete abolition of *lettres de cachet*, and, as a substitute, proposes to give parents and guardians power over children and wards until the age of twenty-five.

He proposes to create courts of equity, with criminal and civil jurisdiction, for the purpose of punishing offences not cognizable by the existing law, and forcing people to be liberal and grateful. 'Since religion and morality,' says he, 'have lost their power,' they must be supplied by legal coercion.'

Such views, in so eminent a member of the French bar, explain Bonaparte's contempt of advocates!

The work is written in an easy, but rather careless style; and, to the inconvenience of a foreign reader, is full of unexplained technical terms. The great fault of the short narratives of which it is composed, is a perplexed arrangement of facts. To make our extracts intelligible, we have often been forced to transpose them.

———

Art. V.—*The Laws relating to India, and the East India Company : with Notes and an Appendix.* Quarto. Third Edition, London : 1842.

In treating, on several recent occasions, of the affairs of British India—of its system of land revenue, its political relations, its commercial wrongs and claims, and its judicial administration—we have studied to divest our statements of all oriental forms and colouring not absolutely essential to their fidelity ; and to communicate the information which we desired to impart, in the shape most easily intelligible, and therefore most palatable, to the largest possible number of English readers. We have taken this course, though we knew that it would expose us to the charge of shallowness from those Anglo-Indians who could not see, or would not appreciate, our end ; because we have proposed to ourselves, as the one great object of our endeavours, to open the eyes of the people of England to the great value of their much neglected possessions in the East : and to point out to them the means by which, in our judgment, that value may be most largely enhanced, and most beneficially realized. We have not, therefore, addressed ourselves primarily to persons already conversant with Indian affairs ; but to that great body—the British public—whose enlightened convictions, and the consequent exertion of whose prevailing influence, must greatly contribute both to forward and to render effective the redress of the grievances, the improvement of the institutions, and the development of the resources, of our Indian Empire.

Still, though this has been our aim, and though we have already reaped the reward of our labours, by witnessing changes in our fiscal policy, both at home and in the colonies of the Crown, most beneficial to British India, we are not without misgivings that, in endeavouring to inform the people of England of the state and prospects of their fellow-subjects in the East, and of the ample means which each possesses of benefiting the other, we have not begun sufficiently at the beginning, but have assumed the existence of a greater degree of knowledge of the subject than

actually obtains. "*Quas aures nostræ penitus reformidant,*" said Jerom, fourteen hundred years ago—speaking of the harsh sounds of the oriental dialects ; and this horror of hearing appears to have extended itself, in modern times, from Indian words to Indian things. But we have seen, of late, quite enough of improvement in this respect to encourage us to pursue our task ; being well assured that, in the present state of public intelligence, the mischievous prejudices to which we have alluded cannot survive the spread of sound information, still less any general conviction that the interests of Great Britain are deeply involved in the good government, and consequent prosperity, of our Asiatic possessions.

We propose to supply, in this paper, a primary part of the information which we believe to be wanting to the full understanding of the present state of British India ; by explaining, in as popular a manner as the subject will permit, the constitution of the government, the organization of its several departments, and their respective bearings upon the condition of the people. These, we are quite sure, are matters as little known at present to the bulk even of intelligent Englishmen, as the corresponding concerns of "the central flowery Empire." There is not one well-informed man out of ten, who knows whether the right of nominating, and the option of accepting or rejecting, a Governor-General, be severally vested in the Court of Directors, or in her Majesty's ministers. Ignorance as to the respective powers of the Court and the Board of Control, in the event of their differing as to the nature of the orders to be sent to India, upon any occasion, is still more common. But with regard to the organization of the government abroad, to the general constitution of the civil service, to the courts of justice, with their distinctions of Queen's and Company's, to the agency by which the complicated affairs of the land revenue are administered, to the other great fiscal branches of salt, opium, and customs, and to many subjects of importance only secondary to these, the ignorance is general and profound. Yet these are matters, which, on the score alike of interest and responsibility, it behoves Englishmen to understand ; and we shall consider our labour well repaid, if we are able to place them in such a point of view as to render the principal features of the system by which British India is governed, familiar to the public mind. Distaste for the subject is fast wearing off; the mighty powers of steam are bringing the dominant and the subject people into comparatively .close connexion ; and knowledge alone is wanting to ensure the happiest issue from the union.

The last Charter act, passed in 1833, effected material changes in the instrumentality by which England rules the millions of Hindostan. The Company was not only deprived of the monopoly of the trade with China, but was absolutely debarred from engaging in any commercial transactions, and became, from the date of that act, a purely governing body ; the directors of which have a strong interest, not merely on the score of reputation, but of a pecuniary nature also, in the wise and equitable administration of the affairs of a country, upon which they and their constituents have been rendered exclusively dependent for their dividends. The making India responsible for these payments, amounting to £640,000 per annum, in return for which a considerable part of the commercial assets of the Company was applied to the liquidation of funded debts, has been strongly condemned by some, —fondly disposed to believe that it would have been right or practicable to settle ·all the difficult and delicate questions at issue between the Company and the Government, by rudely casting the sword of power into the scales in which it behoved the great council of the nation to weigh fairly and considerately the claims of the body, which, however anomalous its constitution, and whatever its sins of omission or commission, had unquestionably won and maintained for England a mighty empire ; and was ruling it, at the period when the mode of its future management came under discussion, with great and increasing vigour and success. It is very questionable whether public opinion would have permitted, or the letter of the law would have sanctioned, a measure involving so much national ingratitude as the dissolution, in 1833, of all connection between the East Indian Company and the wide regions which its military and civil servants had acquired for the Crown, and had governed so long and so ably. It is certain, in our judgment, that nothing would really have been gained by it, either for England or for India. There are obvious reasons of the highest national importance, why the enormous patronage of India should not be conferred on the ministry for the time being ; and ingenuity has not yet devised any plausible scheme by which the servants of the Crown could' be debarred from the use and abuse of this superabundant supply of the richest materials for oiling the wheels of government, otherwise than by the interposition of such a body as the Company. As regards India, no one who knows how its affairs have been administered by the servants of the Company on the one hand, and how the comparatively petty business of governing the colonies of the Crown has been executed on the other, can doubt that it would have been a grievous sufferer from a change of agency. In the one case, there has been uninterrupted and signal success, achieved by a succession of able men, with scarcely an instance, in the long course of eighty years, of even partial failure at any important crisis ; in the other, there has been almost constant weakness, inefficiency, and dissatisfaction, felt and expressed by all acquainted with the working of the system ; and not seldom serious remissness or positive misrule, issuing in more or less disastrous results. Further, it is essential to the welfare of India, that the principles on which it is governed should be fixed on a more stable and enduring basis than the contingency of the maintenance of power by any ministry could afford ; that the counsels of its rulers should be free, to the utmost possible extent, from the action of English politics ; and that the singleness of their view to its interests should not be liable to be distorted by any temptation to make this or the other measure connected with its administration the means of upholding or distressing a parliamentary party. A board chosen in any imaginable manner by the Crown or the people, could not be expected to possess these aptitudes in so great a degree as the directors of the East India Company ; and it is obvious that no mere segment of the ministry could so far abstract itself from the whirl and excitement of the home politics of the day, as to make the affairs of India its primary concern. But these affairs might most beneficially engross the attention of the ablest of our statesmen ; they cannot, without grievous mischief, be regarded as objects of secondary consideration by any individual or body responsible for their administration. Yet it is certain that they would be postponed by mere politicians to a thousand matters of transitory, but nearer and more urgent interest. As to the outcry that the Charter of 1833 threw an increased charge upon the already overburdened people of India, the application of about twelve millions sterling of the Company's commercial assets to the extinction of territorial debt constitutes a very considerable offset to this liability. And even had the difference been larger, thinking that the arrangement then made was the best suited, upon the whole, to further the true interests of our Indian fellow-subjects; and that it was especially desirable to disconnect the immediate rulers of India from all concern in trade, and to get rid at once and for ever of all the juggling, or alleged juggling, between commercial and territorial assets, we should not be disposed to stickle about any reasonable price for those objects.

What India needs is not the mere saving of this or the other item of expenditure, but the blessing of an enlightened and vigorous government, able and willing to bestow upon her a wise and consistent system of laws; an efficient administration of civil and criminal justice; entire freedom, throughout the peninsula, from all restrictions or duties upon inland commerce; and measures—such as we have pointed out in former papers—necessary to raise all classes connected with the soil into their proper position, and to secure each against the other. Were these all-important matters sufficiently cared for, (it would not be just to say that they have been neglected of late years; but war and diplomacy on the one hand, and comparative trifles on the other, have engrossed a disproportionate share of the attention of the local authorities), there would be no deficiency of means for every purpose of complete administrative efficiency. It is misgovernment, long centuries of temporal and spiritual tyranny—resulting, in the latter case, from the worst of false religions—which has made the people so wretchedly poor; and whilst we would by no means encourage or excuse extravagance, we are bound to say that it is miserable quackery to attempt to cure, or even to mitigate, such a disease by mere retrenchment of expenditure. An effectual remedy would be cheaply purchased, even in a pecuniary point of view alone, by an outlay of millions. It is in the power of the people of England to cause such a remedy to be applied; and they could not confer this mighty benefit upon their Indian fellow subjects without ensuring to themselves a large participation in it. Improvements of such magnitude cannot, of course, be effected in a day; but let India be only moderately well governed—

let all persons and all property be efficiently protected—let fair and wholesome encouragement, chiefly by the dissemination of knowledge, be given to private enterprise, directed towards the development of her vast resources—and limits are scarcely assignable to the extent of the market that would be opened for British manufactures.

The Charter of 1833 did not alter very materially the practical relations of the Court of Directors to the India Board; but it defined those relations more precisely, and laid down the course to be taken in the event of the controlling authority differing with that court, on any occasion, as to the orders proper to be sent to India. No orders 'relating to any public matter whatever,' can now be issued by the court without the previous sanction of the board: formerly the directors could correspond with any parties *in this country* without the intervention or knowledge of the controlling authority. Nor can the court now make any money grant without the permission of the board. The initiative in all cases is with the directors, except when they shall omit to prepare, and submit for the consideration of the board, orders or despatches upon any subject, within fourteen days after receiving a requisition to that effect. But the board is empowered to alter, at its discretion, the drafts of any despatches submitted by the court for its sanction; and the court are required to sign and forward the orders so remodelled by the board. The court may remonstrate against directions of this nature; but if they be reiterated, their only means of resistance are passive—namely, a refusal to sign the despatch as required; leaving the board to enforce its authority by the instrumentality of the Court of Queen's Bench. The issue of such a conflict must depend entirely upon the moral strength of the parties, as resulting from their being severally right or wrong upon some important point of principle, involving considerations higher than any of mere policy—of justice or good faith; for, of course, the court would not be justified in making a stand on any lower ground, against the power with which the Board of Control is unquestionably vested by the law. In one instance since 1833, the court did take up such a position of passive resistance, and maintained it with equal spirit and judgment; the board, which was grossly in the wrong, being obliged to recede from its requisition. Such collisions, happily, can seldom occur when both parties are ordinarily honest and sensible, and are not blinded— as can, indeed, under the existing system, rarely be the case in regard to Indian affairs—by any factious motives.

It is not surprising that there should be much misconception with respect to the right of nominating the Governor-General and the Governors of the subordinate Presidencies; for though it be vested by law, as heretofore, in the court of directors, yet the appointments being subject to the approbation of the Crown, they are virtually in its gift. Hence, whatever the politics of the majority of the court, the governor-general is always the friend and supporter of the ministers of the day; and the utmost extent of the power which the court really possess, is that of refusing to nominate an individual personally distasteful to them.

The constitution of the Court of Directors is this. The directors, thirty in number, are elected by the proprietors of East India stock, voting by ballot; L.1000 stock (worth at present about L.2500) entitling to one vote; L.10,000 stock to four votes. Six of the directors go out every year, and as regularly return to office at its close, never having to encounter even a show of opposition, except when one or more of the six happen to die, or choose to retire, during the period of exclusion. In that event only, established routine permits new candidates to offer themselves, together with the remainder of the ex-directors, who constitute what is technically called the *house list;* but though such circumstances frequently occur, only two instances have been known within the memory of man, in which an individual, out of office by rotation, has failed to recover his seat.

The directors annually choose a Chairman—or rather a Deputy-Chairman, who becomes chairman after the lapse of a year, as a matter of course—to preside over their deliberations. In the hands of these two functionaries resides the principal power of the court, deliberative as well as executive. They conduct, personally or by correspondence—official or private— all the negotiations of the Company with the Board of Control; and they, with or without one other director, constitute the 'Secret Committee;'* to whose exclusive

management, in concert with and subordination to the board, all matters 'concerning the levying war or making peace, or treating or negotiating with any of the native princes or states in India, *or with any other princes or states, or touching the policy to be observed with respect to such princes or states,*' which are conceived to be 'of a nature to require secresy,' are entrusted. The late Charter increased the powers of this committee, by adding to the previous law (33 Geo. III. cap. 52, sec. xix.) the words printed in italics in the foregoing quotation; which, of course, embrace Persia and Russia, and all the states with which British India can possibly be brought into connection or dispute. In all other respects, the law which regulates the relations of the Court of Directors to the Board of Control, and keeps the court in profound ignorance of the communications of that board with the secret committee, remains exactly as Mr. Pitt made it nearly sixty years ago. Yet one would suppose, from the vehement denunciations of the Charter of 1833, and Sir John Hobhouse, both in and out of Parliament, that the functions of the secret committee were a hideous novelty of the iron age of Whig ascendency. The truth is, that by the constitution good or bad, of the Indian administration, as framed by Mr. Pitt, the ordinary members of the Court of Directors know no more of the business which falls under the special cognizance of the secret committee than the public at large. All other affairs are conducted partly by the chairman and deputy-chairman, in what are called 'previous communications' (a device to obviate the publicity and inconvenience of collision) with the president of the India Board, and partly by the several committees—revenue, judicial, military, and the like—into which the court is divided. The system actually in operation is strange enough; seeing that every subject of any importance is considered, and, to some extent at least, decided upon by the controlling authority, before it comes even under the cognizance of the body by which, according to the theory of the constitution of the government of India, it ought to be digested and laid before the court; the results of whose deliberations thereon should then be moulded into a despatch, to be submitted, in due course, for the sanction of the board. The practice almost reverses this constitutional order of things, except in so far as the chairman and deputy-chairman, under whose immediate and exclusive orders

* The chairman and deputy-chairman are not necessarily members of the secret committee, the court being authorized to appoint any directors, not exceeding three, to that committee; but we believe that, in practice, they always form a part, or the whole of it.

the drafts of 'previous communications' are prepared, and who are members *ex-officio* of all committees, may be considered to represent the Court of Directors.

This arrangement, which was kept a profound secret until it was divulged on one occasion by Mr. Canning in the House of Commons, produces a smoothness and apparent accordance of opinion in the working of the double government, at the heavy expense of relieving both the Court of Directors and the Board of Control from the responsibility which the law imposes upon those bodies respectively. It was manifestly intended that there should be entire freedom of sentiment and action on the part of the court, up to the period of their submitting the results of their deliberations to the judgment of the board; which ought then, in the unshackled exercise of its discretion, to approve, modify, or reject the proposed orders—stating openly, in either of the latter cases, the grounds of its dissent from the court. If this constitutional course of proceeding had not been departed from, the views of each authority, upon every question of importance, would be publicly known; each would be subject to the wholesome influence and control of enlightened public opinion, and each would enjoy the credit or bear the blame of the good or evil results of the measures which it recommended or opposed. The existing plan is one of compromise and concession, resulting sometimes in middle courses, which neither party altogether approves; and, in the majority of cases, in the concoction of orders to the local governments, for which neither the court nor the board can feel themselves to be distinctly responsible. This is paying too dear for mere facility in the transaction of business; or for a fender to some little warmth of discussion between the authorities in Leadenhall Street and Cannon Row. As Englishmen, we must believe that such discussion, whatever its partial inconveniences, would lead to good upon the whole; there is nothing in the condition of India to render its case an exception to the received political axiom in its favour. Indeed, the unfitness of that country for popular institutions, renders it particularly desirable that the only tolerable substitute for free and responsible government—the open canvassing by its rulers of all public measures—should be studiously encouraged. This the law prescribes—this the practice evades; and though this practice may result in some economy of time, from obviat-

ing disputes, it is certain, if we are rightly informed, that it permits of delays such as could not take place if the law were properly acted up to. The Charter act requires that the board shall return, within two months, all orders, &c., submitted for its sanction by the court, approved or disapproved; under the system of 'previous communications,' the board enjoys the license of evading this wholesome rule, and can retain the papers which have not been formally laid before it for an indefinite period. This license, which is obviously capable of being very mischievously abused, is in itself a very strong argument against the practice which involves it :—coupled with the other considerations which we have adduced, it affords, in our judgment, abundant reason why the Court of Directors should return, without delay, to the system of official intercourse with the Board, laid down by the law.

We have drawn the best sketch which our present limits will permit, of the constitution of the East India Company as a governing body, and of the mode in which the representatives of its proprietors fulfil their functions. In both, there are palpable anomalies; so great, indeed, looking only at the theory of the system, as would seem to render it, *à priori*, certain that an organ of government so constituted, and subject to such checks, could not possibly work to any good purpose. We will point out two or three of the most glaring defects—premising that this is a much easier task than the laying down of any scheme which, even in theory, should promise to work better.

In the first place, it appears to be passing strange, now especially that the commercial privileges of the company have terminated, that the power of electing the rulers of British India should be vested in every person—man, maid, or widow—who attains by purchase, marriage or inheritance, a certain amount of stock ; which is just as much the subject of daily transfer from hand to hand, as any part of the funded debt of the government. By this scheme an individual may have been an elector yesterday, may cease to be so to-day, and be reinstated in the privilege to-morrow, if the necessary share in the Company's stock be bequeathed to him: for in the case of purchase, the buyer cannot exercise his electoral functions for a year. No sort of qualification beyond the possession of stock, is required. The peer of the realm, the intelligent merchant or tradesman, the retired Indian soldier or civil servant, and the man who has accumulated a fortune, in half-pence, by sweeping a crossing in the streets, are all upon a level as to eligibility and presumed competence. The sweeper—if he be rich enough—may have four votes; the member of the legislature, the director of the Bank of England, the ex-governor-general, or member of council, only one.

Again, custom has made a very laborious and irksome personal canvass an indispensable preliminary to attaining a seat in the direction; and the most highly qualified candidate for the office must be content to walk patiently behind several, if not most of those who have preceded him in declaring their pretensions. There is no instance, we believe, of the post being taken by a *coup-de-main*, nor of a canvass being dispensed with in favour even of the most eligible individual that ever desired the office. There is a difference, indeed, as respects the ease with which the object is attained, in favour of those candidates whose fitness for the office is most generally recognized; but none are exempted from undergoing considerable labour, to say nothing more, in canvassing the electors; and, unless there be some very marked distinction in regard to qualification, the aspirant who is most earnest and constant in personal solicitation, generally outstrips his competitors. The consequences of this system are, first, that the most distinguished of the statesmen and soldiers who have served their country in India—such men as Elphinstone, Metcalfe, Malcolm—are deterred from coming forward as candidates; and, secondly, that notwithstanding the great value of the prize, on account of the patronage that it confers, the instances are very rare in which any person possessed of a sufficient stock of patience and perseverance to bear up against a certain number of defeats, has not ultimately gained his end.

Thirdly, the rule that, after four years' tenure of office, each director shall retire for one year, cannot fail to operate most injuriously on the general efficiency of the court. It often happens that a director's turn for vacating office occurs immediately after he has devoted two years, as deputy-chairman and chairman, to the almost exclusive management of the Company's affairs; and both as respects the ordinary functions of the court, and the special duties of the secret committee, is, *cæteris paribus*, more conversant with all the important subjects under discussion, or likely to present themselves, than any other member of the body. But the inexorable rule requires that all this knowledge and experience shall lie completely fallow for a year, until, perhaps, by ceasing to be recent, it has ceased to be practically useful; and the individual whose voice has been most potent in the government of an empire up to the second Wednesday in April, often ceases on that day to possess the smallest authority in its counsels.

Yet in spite of these and other anomalies, nothing is more certain than that, from the time of Warren Hastings to the present day, the administration of India has been eminently successful. We are no blind optimists. We know well, and we have not hesitated to show, that much that might have been done has been left undone; and that in too many instances the measures of the rulers of India have been unwise in principle. But, after allowing all due weight to those drawbacks and disparagements, the broad fact remains untouched, that an empire has been won and governed, which the whole civilized world regards with admiration and envy, and which none but unwise and ungrateful Englishmen are so blind as to undervalue. Such being the case, it were absurd to doubt that the system from which such results have sprung, must combine in its constitution the elements of the highest practical efficiency. But it were equally absurd to suppose that this vigour resides in such anomalies as we have exhibited, or that it is not grievously impaired by them. It is one thing to see and acknowledge that mighty progress has been made, notwithstanding hindrances:—it is quite another thing to mistake such hindrances for the propelling power. The very remarkable state of things which undeniably exists, has led two very different classes of observers into opposite errors. The one, looking at the marvellous general effects of the Company's administration, at the wide regions which its delegates govern, at the general order and peace which they maintain, and at the great and sustained efforts which they are capable of making, will not believe that there can be anything essentially unwise or unfitted to the proposed ends, still less of a counteracting tendency, in the machinery by which such mighty results are brought to pass. The other class, of sharper eyes to discern defects, but belonging to the school of the philosopher who ' travelled from Dan to Beersheba, and found all barren,' are so inflamed with indignation at this or the other anomaly in the constitution of the Company, or defect or short-coming in the discharge of its obligations to the people of India, that they can see nothing but wrong and rapine, broken faith and denial of justice, in the whole government of our eastern empire. The truth, of course, lies between the two extremes—between the optimism that can perceive no evil in a system capable of vast improvement; and the prejudice which regards the rule of the Company as a curse to the natives of India, and looks back with fond regret to the good old times when they were robbed, tortured, and murdered by princes of their own race, or by their Mahomedan conquerors. That they were scandalously misgoverned then, does not affect, in the smallest degree, their right to the best government that we can give them now; but it is equally certain that, after the fullest admission of past errors and present imperfections, the rule of England is a mighty blessing to the people of India.

The Charter of 1833 effected great improvements in the Local administration of India. The greatest, perhaps, was the creation of a really supreme government, —in the governor-general and council of India,—vested with exclusive powers of legislation for the whole of the British dominions, and with effectual control over the public expenditure. By this wise measure, a single body was made responsible for the enactment of good laws; and the power of the purse was taken out of the hands of those who never—in the case of Bombay,—or not always—in the case of Madras,—having a local income equal to their local charges, had found it a mischievously easy process to supply the deficiency, by drawing upon the well-replenished treasury of Bengal. The power of legislation was extended with equal benefit. The royal courts of justice, established at each of the three Presidencies, had previously administered the law of England in entire independence—except when the judges thought fit to recognize and register a regulation—of the local legislature. The law of 1833 abated this gross absurdity—which had been productive of much practical mischief from the time of Warren Hastings down to recent times—of placing a court of justice, the interpreter of its own charter, and of the laws which it administered, at a distance of many thousand miles from the legislature which alone it was bound to obey; whilst the local government—to whose legislation its respect was entirely optional, and which it possessed innumerable

means of thwarting, insulting, and degrading in the eyes of its subjects—was solely responsible for the peaceful and prosperous maintenance of the wonderful sway exercised by a few thousands of Englishmen over subject millions. The relations of the royal courts to the Company's government are now very nearly what, in reason and prudence, they ought to be; supposing that it is necessary to keep up establishments so large and costly for the sake of the utterly disproportionate service which they render, directly or indirectly, to the people for whose ostensible benefit, and at whose certain expense, they are maintained. Whether there be such necessity, is quite another question.

The charge which the Queen's Courts at Calcutta, Madras, and Bombay, entail upon India, is very heavy; amounting, according to the latest returns, to L.96,253 per annum, exclusive of the salaries of the Company's law-officers and their establishments, and of the charges of the coroner's office and the police. The service rendered to the community, in return for this large outlay, is extremely small; partly because the territorial jurisdictions of the courts are very limited; but mainly, we fear, as regards the civil department, because the justice which they administer is so enormously high-priced, that none but the wealthy few possess the means of taking advantage of it. To the great bulk of the people, therefore, it is, and always has been, the same as if no such courts of justice existed; except in so far as the *prestige* that accompanies them may be presumed to protect from some of the grosser outrages or wrongs. To the wealthy, these courts have been the instruments of the most exhausting chicanery. It is said, that at Madras almost all the opulent native families have been reduced to poverty by litigation. The wealthy natives of Calcutta, after spending vast sums in the supreme court, have so far profited by experience as to decide most of their differences by private arbitration. From these concurrent causes, the time of the judges is very inadequately occupied; very little civil business is brought before them; and these highly paid functionaries are often engaged, day after day, in trying petty larcenies, compared with which the pilferings of the 'artful dodgers' of our metropolis are high crimes and misdemeanours.

If the few Englishmen settled in India are so much attached to the laws, and the mode of administering those laws, which obtain in their native country, as to require that justice should be dispensed to them in this particular manner, under circumstances which render it extremely expensive; or if their fear of the government under which they live induces them to demand special protection from it—it is surely reasonable that they, and not the people among whom they have voluntarily come to sojourn, should pay for the luxury in the one case, or for the security in the other. As regards the natives, we affirm, that whether they be wronged by their rulers or by each other, they can and do obtain at least as efficient redress—certainly much cheaper—in the courts of the Company as in those of the Queen. We may state as one proof of this position, that, as far as we have been able to watch the result, fewer decisions of the former than of the latter tribunals have been reversed upon appeal to the Privy Council. The leaning of the Company's courts is decidedly against the executive government in general, and the revenue department in particular. On the other hand, whilst many outrages upon natives have been committed by Englishmen residing in the interior of the country, there is scarcely an instance upon record in which such parties have been prosecuted to conviction in the supreme courts. Not unfrequently, English principals in such outrages have escaped with impunity, whilst their native instruments, subject to the jurisdiction of the Company's courts, have been convicted and punished. The Queen's courts are equally impotent for another principal object of their original constitution. We are not aware that any public servant—though many, in so long a course of years, have been dismissed from their employment with infamy—was ever prosecuted to conviction, in those courts, for embezzlement, corruption, or extortion. The causes of impunity are the same in both cases;—the absurd facilities which the English rules of evidence afford for the escape of the guilty; the partial favour too often shown by jurymen of British birth or blood to their own countrymen; and the little less than impossibility, that the most respectable native witness should pass satisfactorily the severe ordeal of a cross-examination by an acute English lawyer. There is no case so good and strong that a native does not think it capable of a little improvement by exaggeration or positive invention; there is no action so open and unequivocal that a native eyewitness may not be driven to hesitate, prevaricate, or contradict himself concerning it.

As at present constituted, the Queen's Courts are comparatively useless, with the additional objection of being exceedingly expensive to a country which stands in the utmost need that every rupee should be applied, with the most careful judgment, to those purposes most essential to its well-being. They ought to be abolished altogether, and a far less costly machinery supplied, for the performance of those of their present functions which are really necessary; or they should be united with the supreme courts of the Company, already established at each of the three Presidencies, and at Allahabad; under a system providing for the administration of a uniform code of laws, dealing the same measure by the same processes, and with the smallest possible number of exceptions, to men of every colour, religion, and blood throughout British India. The last course would certainly be the wisest; and we are happy to hear, upon good authority, that it has been contemplated by those who are best qualified to judge of the propriety of such a change. We should anticipate the happiest results to India from the association of enlightened and liberal English lawyers with the ablest judicial officers of the Company, in a newly constituted supreme court. Such a junction could not fail to result in the interchange of much useful knowledge, and in rubbing off many hurtful prejudices on both sides. Considerable good of this sort has already been effected by the last Charter act. An English lawyer was attached to the council of India, and another to the law commission. It is partly owing to the unhappy circumstances of the times during the last three years, and partly to the vicious system which clogs the wheels of government with endless details of comparatively unimportant business, that this judicious infusion of new blood has not been followed by a larger measure of practically beneficial results. Yet, advantage there has unquestionably been;—not the least, that the ablest and most influential members of the civil service, many of whom have passed twenty or thirty years in uninterrupted exile, have been brought into intimate communication with minds formed and exercised in the highest schools of English legislation and jurisprudence. Had the upright and public-spirited philanthropist who has just retired, with the respect of all who have observed his conduct, from the chief seat in the bench of the Queen's Court of Calcutta, occupied a corresponding position in such a supreme court as we desire to see constituted, the opportunities of public usefulness which he had so sedulously endeavoured to improve to the uttermost, would have been increased an hundredfold.

The miscellaneous character of this article, and the limits to which we must necessarily confine it, forbid us to enter on an inquiry whether the Law Commission, constituted by the Charter act, has or has not worked up to its intrinsic capabilities, or duly availed itself of the means at its command, in the fulfilment of its high functions. Certainly, its labours have hitherto met with but little encouragement from those whose duty it is to examine and give practical effect to their results. As far as our knowledge extends we must say that the records of those labours have appeared to be regarded very much as the Carthagenian General, according to the Poet, regarded the victorious Consul,—

'Quem fallere et effugere est triumphus.'

The endeavour seemingly has been to suffocate them under a mass of commentary and criticism. In after years, it will cost some trouble to dig out what is really valuable from the surrounding heap of rubbish.

The constitution of the Civil Service—of the agency by which the affairs of this mighty empire are directed, superintended, and controlled—is the grand peculiarity of the system of our Indian Government. From the commencement of the Company's marvellous career—from the time when they held, by sufferance, a few petty factories on the coast of that vast continent which they now rule as absolute sovereigns—they sent out a succession of youths, to perform in the first instance the drudgery of measuring muslin, weighing pepper, and engrossing accounts; with the privilege of rising, in an order of seniority rarely departed from, to the charge of the outposts of trade or manufacture, from which the warehouses at the ports of shipment were supplied, and eventually to the council and government; involving the sale of the goods sent out by the Company, and the preparation for the annual investment for the English market. To this class belonged Orme—whose elegant and animated, though somewhat diffuse work, narrating with remarkable fidelity

the romantic progress of British ascendency in the East, is much less known than its merits deserve; and Forbes, the amiable author of the 'Oriental Memoirs.' In this school also—apparently so ill-fitted to train the founders of empire, men greater far than these—Clive and Hastings, whose remarkable history we have lately surveyed, spent the years of their early manhood. In one respect, indeed, the service of the Company, in its subordinate stations, had at least a negative recommendation as a state of discipline and probation. It was not a service of ease and indulgence. 'At that time,' (1768), says Mr. Forbes, who was upon the Bombay establishment, 'I can safely affirm, I lived in the most sparing manner, a writer's income altogether not exceeding L.65 per annum. Indeed, 'the generality' are stated to have had but L.36 or L.40. I never drank wine at my own table, and often went supperless to bed when the day closed, because I could not afford either supper or candles: as the dinner hour was one o'clock, and a writer's age generally between sixteen and twenty-one, the abstinence was not occasioned by a want of appetite.

The effects of this parsimony in an unhealthy climate, requiring many comforts and conveniences to render it endurable by Europeans, fell only upon the servants who were thus underpaid, a very small proportion of whom lived to return to their native country;—as long as the Company was merely a commercial body, and those who managed its affairs in India had no political power, and were kept in check by the parties who possessed it. But the result was very different when ambition, or the irresistible force of circumstances, had rendered the agents of this association of merchants the sovereigns, de facto, of extensive provinces teeming with population; and which, though poor in comparison with the wealthier countries of Europe, and utterly unable to render to England the regular annual tribute which sanguine politicians expected from them, were abundantly capable of compensating the actual rulers of the land for the inadequacy of their legal salaries. And no harm would have been done, if a sufficiency for this purpose had been regularly and avowedly raised and distributed: such a step, in fact, if taken immediately on the occurrence of the entire change of circumstances to which we have adverted, would have prevented that shameless corruption and rapine from which it was eventually found necessary to relieve the people, by measures of wise liberality to the functionaries placed over them. This being neglected in the first instance, it was too much to expect that those who negotiated concerning the fate of kingdoms—who presided, with almost absolute power, over great commercial marts—or who collected, on behalf of their distant masters, the revenues of fertile provinces, should rest satisfied with the scanty salaries which the Company had doled out to mere book-keepers and factors. The 'supperless' case of Mr. Forbes and his contemporaries at Bombay, was no doubt an extreme one, though perfectly true; but it is certain that the ostensible allowances of the civil servants of the Company, for some time after that body became virtually the sovereigns of Bengal, Bahar, and the Carnatic, did not exceed, even if they amounted to, the necessary expense of the barest subsistence. Of course, under such circumstances, these functionaries did not scruple to help themselves copiously to what their inconsiderate masters withheld; and it is no marvel that they did not confine their appropriations, in all cases, within the limits of a handsome remuneration for their services. As an equally certain consequence, these illicit exactions robbed the people of ten times as much—with incalculable concomitant vexation and suffering—as found its way into the pockets of the European officers of the government. The clear intellect of Lord Clive saw this plainly, and he devised and executed—with characteristic boldness—a scheme for cutting off the sources of the unauthorized profits of the public servants, and for granting them adequate allowances, raised by a public monopoly. But the system was incomplete, and therefore the effect fell short of the object, until the time of Lord Cornwallis. That nobleman placed the establishment upon such a footing, in respect to the salary allotted to each office of trust and responsibility, as left the public servant who should thenceforward grasp at gains beyond the handsome stipend issued to him from the treasury, utterly without excuse; and from that day, amidst great and daily temptations, and far removed, in that tainted atmosphere, from all purer example, the servants of the company have preserved, as a body, the most unsullied reputation. It is right to add, that a share in the credit of a result so happy as well as honourable, is justly due to those who, exercising in this country supreme control over the administration of India, have firmly and invariably visited with the most severe punishment any offence on the part of public functionaries involving fraud, peculation, or corruption.

Notwithstanding, however, the entire change in the nature of the duties devolving on it, the constitution of the civil service remains exactly as it was in the days when the preparation and shipment of investments formed the highest functions of its highest members. Even the ancient names of its gradations were, till very recently, retained: up to August, 1841, the youth who entered the service as a writer, rose successively to the ranks of factor, junior merchant, and senior merchant. In one point of view, this rigid adherence to the old order of things has been of signal benefit to India.

The mode of recruiting the public service has remained unchanged. A number of young men are annually sent out, not to particular appointments allotted to them severally in this country, but as probationers for office generally, and to be employed in this or the other department, at the discretion of the local government. There is, therefore, no possibility of entering upon public employment otherwise than at the lowest end of the scale; and as the emoluments attached to it are not, for some years, more than sufficient to maintain the servants of the government in comfort and respectability, such a line of life in a distant land, and an unhealthy climate, has no temptations to any one who does not intend to adhere to it as his profession, until the devotion of the best years of his manhood shall have been rewarded by the gradual accumulation of the means of returning to his native land. This system is, of course, open to obvious objections. General competition, from which the community reaps such great advantage in all lands governed by their own children, is altogether precluded. The number of those eligible for office is rigidly limited; and, practically, it often happens that the strictness with which the privileges of the body of public servants is upheld, debars the authorities from giving employment to men who have proceeded to that country upon some private adventure, and whom natural abilities, or intimate acquaintance with the people, have peculiarly qualified to render the most beneficial services to the community. Yet, after making the most ample allowance for these considerations, as well as for the mischiefs resulting from the passions and prejudices of *caste*, necessarily generated by the peculiar position of the civil service, we are decidedly of opinion that, due reference being had to the evils which it precludes, the benefits of the existing system greatly preponderate over its disadvantages. We are, therefore, decidedly of opinion, that to whomsoever the patronage may be entrusted, the present system of recruiting the public service in India should be jealously maintained. But it is quite another question whether that system is followed out as effectually as it might be—whether the most is made of the materials, which, upon the whole, appear to be the best suited to answer the important ends in view. This question, we fear, must be answered in the negative.

General competition is incompatible with the constitution of the public service. To this evil we must submit; that limitation of choice of agency which it involves, appearing to be the best, if not the only, means of warding off still greater evils. But it seems at least equally certain that the too great weight allowed to the claims of mere seniority, has weakened the spring of honourable emulation within the privileged body. Only a few appointments, and those almost exclusively in the higher grades of the service, are regarded as prizes for merit. These are exceptions to the general rule, and are not made upon any avowed principle; but apparently because, as in the case of the Secretaryships to government, their being filled by able men is essential to the creditable and easy working of the administrative machinery. But the great majority of situations, ninety-five at least out of every hundred, all of them in the present day highly responsible —and all of them, especially those in the judicial department, affecting most powerfully the condition of the people, are filled up with a paramount regard for seniority. No amount of superior fitness elevates an officer to a judgeship until his turn has come, or very nearly come; no mediocrity of ability or attainments, no degree of indolence or self-indulgence, or of engrossing devotion to other pursuits— nothing, in fact, which comes short of absolute incapacity—stands in the way of the operation of the rule of promotion to the judgment-seat by seniority. It is the same in every other department of the service; and in India, under every system of managing the land revenue, the people are liable to suffer as grievously when the difficult and often discretionary duties which it involves are entrusted to incompetent hands, as when justice between man and man is denied, ill-administered, or bought

and sold by underlings. There is no kind of wrong so dreadful to the natives of British India—now that the days of open pillage and bloodshed have passed away— as the nominal management of the land revenue, by officers whose inefficiency or sloth permits the abuse of their authority by a rapacious host of subordinate and irresponsible functionaries. Under the existing system, this, as well as the elevation of incompetent persons to the judicial bench, are circumstances of inevitably frequent occurrence.

Proof of the truth of these statements is to be found on the very surface of that aspect which the public service in India presents In every walk of life, where matters are left to regulate themselves—where, consequently, high success is dependent upon eminent merit, and even moderate advancement upon competent fitness— some individuals will be found to have gained the goal in the prime of life; others will reach it with difficulty, or perhaps, rest content with coming somewhat short of it, after a longer period of toil; whilst a third class, whom nature or their own misconduct have disqualified for the race, will occupy a place in their old age but little in advance of the starting-post. In England, this state of things is common in every profession and calling, and no one wonders, or thinks it a hardship, that those whom nature has not formed to excel, should hold situations subordinate to younger men on whom she has conferred the talent, the energy, and the perseverance which command success. In India, on the other hand, the advancement of the members of the body which administers or controls every branch of the government, is regulated by a diametrically opposite principle. The man who was never intended to rise is forced up; whilst the energies of the individual whom Providence designed to distinguish from the mass are cramped and crippled—if, indeed, their development is not altogether prevented— by the absurd rule which contravenes the general law of nature, and ordains that the active and vigorous shall not outstrip the apathetic and indifferent; and that, with the exception of a very few prizes, offices of the highest practical importance—such as the dispensation of civil and criminal justice, in a district as large as an English county, including the superintendence and control of twenty or thirty subordinate courts—shall be filled with an almost exclusive reference to the age and standing of individuals in the general muster-roll of a service which all have alike entered as boys. That this is no exaggerated representation, a glance at the list of civil servants, under any one of the Presidencies, will demonstrate. Those lists will not show five instances where all the individuals of a certain standing are not judges or collectors at least; if not the supervisors and controllers of judges and collectors. They will not exhibit five cases in which the officer of fifteen or twenty years' standing is on a level, in respect to distinction and emolument, with the generality of those who have been five or six years in the service. Yet it is morally impossible that every person of a certain standing should be fit to be a judge or a collector—fitter than any one of the fifty who entered the service five or even ten years later: it is equally out of the question that of the fifty or hundred who are now placed in situations of high responsibility, merely because they have passed a given number of years in India, there should not be several, who in any state of things where they were solely dependent upon their own exertions, would have remained till old age in offices of mere mechanical drudgery. The existing system picks two or three of the best out of every hundred, in order to place them in offices, the efficiency of which is essential to the ease or character of the government, and treats all the rest exactly alike.

The consequences are mischievous in the extreme. It is the old story in the main :—'*Delirunt reges, plectuntur Achivi :*' the people are the principal sufferers; but the British Government reaps directly and largely the fruit of its own absurdities. Emulation lives only in the hearts of the few competitors for the scanty prizes to which we have alluded. Beyond them, the great body of public servants, many of whom are, of course, possessed of abilities capable of being quickened into most useful activity, regard themselves as members of a sort of professional *tontine ;* and repose in the comfortable assurance that, if they live long enough, and do not absolutely disgrace themselves, they shall grow up in the paradise of promotion, like the bean-stalk in the nursery tale, by the mere force of vegetation. This feeling, doubtless, is strongest in the least worthy; and doubtless, also—to their honour be it said—there are many in the ranks of the civil service who are stimulated to the energetic discharge of their public duties by higher and purer motives than any which mere emulation—having worldly advancement for its goal—can af-

ford. But it is undeniably a grand political blunder, that this most cogent incentive is not systematically superadded to those which are derived from other sources.

In truth, it must, we think, be self-evident, that a rule of promotion that might have been, and probably was, well enough suited to regulate the advancement of the clerks and factors of a company of merchants, is utterly inapplicable to the administrators of a vast empire. It is impossible to calculate the amount of public loss that results from it ; because it is impossible to ascertain the quantum of useful ability which the absence of stimulus permits to lie dormant. That it is very heavy, no one will doubt who knows anything of human nature, or of the difficulty of governing a hundred millions of men by the agency of a handful of foreigners; and, consequently, of the importance of eliciting from such instruments the largest possible amount of useful service.

There ought to be strong grounds for continuing a system so broadly at variance with all received principles. Yet we never heard any arguments urged in its favour, which do not appear to us absolutely futile when weighed against the opposing considerations. It is alleged that promotion by seniority is a necessary safeguard against favouritism. The answer is, that the exclusive nature of the service, the members of which are alone eligible for employment, is in itself a great protection against such abuse; and that the local governments, which are necessarily trusted so largely, may well be trusted further to select the best qualified member of that service for every appointment that falls vacant. They exercise that discretion already in regard to a few prizes—affording the greatest temptation to jobbing—and that, as all admit, with the best effect. Why should anything but good result from extending the practice of selection according to merit to all offices of responsibility ? As regards what has been said about jealousies and heartburnings, such feelings on the part of the less successful, because the less worthy, are very dearly bought off at the expense of the general abandonment of the master stimulus of emulation. Lastly, we have heard it urged, that promotion by seniority is a necessary concomitant of an exclusive service. But all schools, all colleges, all universities, all professions, are exclusive ; yet in many of them emulation works with the best effect, and no one doubts that it might be beneficially introduced in all. And though it be true, as the late excellent Lord William Bentinck remarked, in a private note now before us, that in India the ordinary state of things is sometimes reversed—there being more difficulty to find men to fill places, than places to accommodate men—it is certain, that in no case could that difficulty be increased, whilst in many it would, doubtless, be altogether removed, by making the highest degree of fitness, altogether irrespective of *standing* in the service, the strongest recommendation to a candidate for office.

· We have dwelt upon this subject at considerable length, because we have long been sensible of its extreme importance to the interests of British India. The rigid single file in which the public servants are made to advance, has assuredly dwarfed their minds ; except in those rare instances in which talent is accompanied by so much energy as to be altogether irrepressible. Everything short of extraordinary qualification is levelled, by the absence of encouragement, to the low standard of passable fitness. We know but of one reason—and that one which no honest mind, once awakened to reflect on the subject, would allow to sway it—why the system should be clung to. It *enhances the value of patronage,* as regards the least worthy recipients of it, by rendering the public service of India a *lottery without blanks,* except in cases of scandalous misbehaviour. But the opportunity of entering the lists of competition in such a service is, or ought to be, a sufficient boom to any young man ; it would be amply sufficient to tempt the *élite* of the rising generation to engage in it with hopefulness and energy ; and it is too much to add a virtual guarantee, at the expense of the people of India, that unless there be misconduct of the grossest description, there shall be regular advancement, as a matter of course, to offices which can hardly be designated as otherwise than of the highest trust and responsibility. The existence of such a guarantee reduces all but the few salient minds to the dead level of mediocrity ; whilst those whom nature, sloth, or bad habits have marked out as drudges, have a claim of right to receive, and do actually receive—if their demerits fall short of absolute incapacity—the general average of promotion.

The Charter Act made a considerable change, or rather a considerable opening for change, at the discretion of the Court of Directors, in the constitution of the Indian governments. It enacted that the executive government of each of the Presidencies shall be administered by a governor and three councillors ; but, at the same time, it empowered the Directors to revoke and suspend the appointment of councils. It also made the Governor-General of India for the time being, Governor of Bengal. Under the license given to the court, the Governor of Bengal has hitherto exercised the functions of that office without the aid of a council ; as did also the Governor of Agra, as long as that office existed.

This autocracy has been objected to by some, principally, we believe, on account of the additional power which the absence of councils is supposed to throw into the irresponsible hands of secretaries ; who, it is thought, are more likely to lead or mislead one than many masters. For our part, we have always, even irrespective of the saving of expenditure, thought the change an improvement. The subordinate governments have now no powers of legislation, and very little latitude in expenditure ; their functions may, generally speaking, be better, because more promptly, performed by one mind than by many ; the governor acts alone, under individual, and therefore more stringent, responsibility ; and as to the dangerous influence of secretaries, those functionaries, though younger men—a circumstance which is not always, by any means, an objection in India—are, commonly, at least as well selected as the members of council. It would not be difficult to devise a plan which would give them all needful and wholesome responsibility.

The Local Governments transact their business in four departments :—the political, which includes the secret, and is limited to what in England we term diplomacy ; the judicial ; the revenue ; and the general, to which all the financial business appertains. A fifth—the legislative department—is peculiar to the supreme government. At the several Presidencies, and at the same Presidencies under changes of circumstances, these departments are variously arranged as regards the manner in which they are worked. Thus the supreme government has but two secretaries, one of whom undertakes the political, legislative, judicial, and revenue departments, and the other the general department ; whilst the subordinate government of Bengal, having a vast deal more of detail on its hands—much more, indeed, than it ought, in wisdom, to meddle with—has a separate secretary for the important departments of revenue and justice. The arrangements of departments, and of the business attached to them, are generally wise and efficient—the several governments taking care not to choose secretaries for themselves, as they do judges for the people, according to *seniority* in the service;—but the division of duties is not altogether free from anomalies. In Bengal, for instance, the superintendence and control of the customs, and of the salt and opium monopolies, belong not to the revenue, but to the general, department; which manages, besides the finance, all the miscellaneous business which does not come under one or other of the more specific heads. Ecclesiastical affairs, steam-boats for sea and river navigation, the post-office, and public instruction, are only a part of its multifarious cares. The government and the people would be far better served, if separate secretaries were appointed to the revenue and judicial departments; the former relieving the secretary in the general department from the charge of the customs, the two monopolies, and post-office; and the latter conducting all correspondence connected with the education of the natives. The secretary in the general department might then discharge all the important duties of the Accountant-General. Under the existing arrangements, the Admirable Crichton himself could not fulfil efficiently all the functions of the general department.

The secretary in the political department conducts all the correspondence with the numerous officers, who, under the title of Residents at the native courts, or of Agents to the governor-general, discharge, in some cases, purely diplomatic functions; and exercise, in other instances, an ambiguous sway—alternating between command and counsel—over princes and chiefs partially independent, but looking up to the British Government, not only for protection against all external danger, but for the mediation of all matters in dispute among themselves, or with powerful tributaries, or with their subjects. The residents and agents do not submit reports merely upon all important matters, but diaries of their ordinary proceedings, showing with whom they have communicated, and the nature of the conference. Those who hold the more important trusts—and some as the agent for Rajpootana, have many officers, each residing at the court of a petty prince, subordinate to them—correspond directly with the supreme government; the others are subject to the orders of the governor,

to whose jurisdiction their respective offices are attached. The subordinate governments, again, report all matters of moment to the supreme government; so that a complete chain of communication is maintained from the lowest functionary engaged in any business of diplomacy—one of whom is stationed at every spot where his services can be useful—to the Governor-General in council. In this department, the state is, and always has been, admirably served. The chief reason is easily told. In the political line, the claims of *seniority* are far less attended to than in other departments. The Company's army contends with the civil service in furnishing the requisite amount of ability; and, what is still more important—the diplomatists of British India are not, generally speaking, so hopelessly overladen with business as the officers, who perform their duties with equal zeal and energy, though with less brilliant results, in other branches of the service. They enjoy, personally, another signal advantage. They do not labour exclusively for the good of others, and for the rewards of their own conscience—though they may well promote the one and earn the other—as those who discharge important duties on the judicial bench, or in the revenue department. The nature of their functions brings them, in frequent instances, to the notice of their countrymen at home; and they reap, though not a fair share, yet a far larger share than their brethren, of those distinctions which the grace of the Crown, or public opinion, confer on those who are felt to have rendered good service to their country. To all merit displayed on the distant and disregarded theatre of India, such rewards have been dealt with niggard hand. They have been almost absolutely denied to those whose talents and devotion have been displayed in the less shining walks of the public service. In no instance, as far as we are aware, has the highest judicial merit, manifested in the Company's Courts, received any honorary acknowledgment in this country; whilst comparatively petty services, performed in the colonies of the Crown, have been abundantly rewarded! Is this generous—is it wise? The Crown should not look coldly on the distinguished men who serve their country in India, because England chooses to rule that splendid empire through the instrumentality of the Company. It would cost her nothing, it would stimulate to still greater exertions, it would be a graceful compensation for the wealth which the improved state of public morals and feeling forbids the servants of the Government to accumulate in India, if suitable honours, such as would confer rank and distinction upon those servants in the eyes of their fellow-countrymen, were bestowed with judicious liberality upon those best deserving them.

The superintendence and control of the judicial department are exercised principally by the instrumentality of the Sudder Courts—the supreme judicatories of the Company's territories, beyond the narrow precincts of the jurisdiction of the three courts chartered by the Crown. The executive government holds little direct correspondence—and that little only on trivial subjects—with any subordinate judicial functionaries; excepting only, in the case of the government of Bengal, the superintendent of police, whose office does not exist elsewhere. Throughout Bengal, including the lieutenant-governorship of Agra, the provincial courts of appeal and circuit, which formed a material part of the scheme of judicial administration devised by Lord Cornwallis, have been abolished; the Sudder Courts now preside immediately over the civil and session judges of the several districts into which the provinces are divided; each of whom, again, supervises the proceedings, and hears appeals from the decisions, of many judges of inferior jurisdiction, proportioned in number to the amount of local business, and ranked in three gradations with respect to their powers and to their official emoluments. The judges of the several districts are invariably civil servants: the officers who preside in the subordinate courts are principally natives of India, though all properly qualified persons are eligible. Those of the highest rank are competent to decide all suits, whatever the value of the property at issue: and it has been, of late years, the wise object of the government to relieve as much as possible the highly-remunerated district judges from all primary jurisdiction, and to employ them, almost exclusively, in the far more extensively useful work of superintending the proceedings of the numerous subordinate courts, and of hearing appeals from their orders and judgments. Upon the promptitude and efficiency with which these duties are executed, the character of the administration of civil justice absolutely depends. The government has most wisely abandoned the attempt commenced by Lord Cornwallis, to administer justice to millions by the almost unassisted agency of a small body of English judges, whose necessarily high remuneration rendered it impossible to increase their numbers. Of the utter inadequacy of the salaries assigned to the lowest and most numerous class of native judges, (*moonsifs*), by whom the great majority of causes are decided, we have already spoken; but the miserable economy of dispensing justice to the bulk of the people by the agency of underpaid functionaries, cannot be too often or too strongly denounced. With a proper addition to their allowances, they might most beneficially be made the effective instruments of improving the administration of criminal as well as of civil justice.

The existing system has one glaring and most prejudicial defect. It is lamentably wanting in the vigour of an active and watchful executive superintendence and direction. Those functions are ostensibly performed—as we have stated—by the Sudder Courts; the judges of which have, therefore, double and discordant responsibilities. Besides exercising the highest appellate jurisdiction, and hearing judicially, in the last resort, all complaints against the proceedings of all subordinate courts, they ought to maintain a jealous supervision over the official conduct of every functionary attached to the judicial department; availing themselves of every legitimate means of obtaining information with respect to the efficiency of each tribunal, and to the estimation in which the several judges are held by the people. It is the more necessary that this duty should be well performed by the high officers to whom it is assigned, because, in India, there is no public to discharge it on its own behalf. The people are sunk, to a degree of which home-bred Englishmen can form no adequate conception, in sloth, apathy, and moral cowardice. They regard even the grossest judicial venality as a very light offence. No extent of fraud or wrong, committed under the shelter of the forms of justice, appears—when they are not personally the victims of it—to excite in their breasts any emotions of abhorrence or indignation. Their ignorant apprehensions often deter them from complaining of the grossest injustice. There is manifestly the greater need that they should be well protected by those whose especial duty it is to watch the working of the judicial administration. This vastly important duty the Sudder Courts are, in our judgment, from the nature of their constitution, and of their other functions and responsibilities, altogether unqualified to perform. Their obligations are almost absolutely *antagonistic.* They are judges of the last resort; they are a board of justice; they are, or ought to be, keen and jealous inspectors of the proceedings of a host of subordinate judges, scattered through a vast extent of country, and dispensing justice to millions. Being always stationary, they can superintend the proceedings and estimate the character of the many officers dependent on each district court, only through the intermediate agency of the judge of that court. Their knowledge of all those subordinate to him must be coloured, at least, by his opinions regarding them. If he be blind, it is next to impossible that they should be able to see to any good purpose; but if he be dishonest or corrupt, and in league with inferiors of a like character, they must be absolutely helpless. This last consummation of iniquity is not probable; but, under such a system of promotion of judicial office as we have already described, instances must, in the nature of things, frequently occur, where, from one cause or another, the district judge is a very bad medium of supervision. We could mention an instance in which, within a few months after an English judge, personally above all suspicion, and of considerable merit, had left a district in which he had presided for some years, two of the principal subordinate judges of that district—to whom on retiring he had given certificates of high character—were dismissed from office with infamy, on proof that they had been selling justice for years. It was proved that one of them had been pulled out of his palankin in the public bazar, and flogged by a man to whom he had denied redress, after he had been paid for it. In another case, a board of revenue was compelled to denounce to the Government the open and shameless iniquities prevalent in one of the late provincial courts, situated within two miles of the Sudder Court, of which that court had taken, and appeared disposed to take, no notice.

We have specified these two instances, because they illustrate the two distinct causes of the inefficiency which characterizes the superintendence of the Sudder Court. The first shows—if it needs showing—that a stationary body, operating through local instruments of very unequal fitness—some of whom must be expected to be unsuspicious, some indolent, some inaccessible to the people, some disposed to favour and shield parasites and flatterers

—must be very ill qualified to watch with sufficient acuteness and steadiness the proceedings of inferior courts situated at distances of from seventy to four or five hundred miles. The second exemplifies the mistake involved in entrusting the most important judicial and executive functions to the same hands; and those hands trained principally to the patient and deliberate dispensation of justice. It is next to impossible that the same man should be at once a calm and dispassionate judge, and a keen and jealous supervisor. All the qualities indispensable for the first office, are little less than disqualifications for the other. The judge is bound to keep his eyes, ears, and mind closed to all that he might see or hear out of court. The superintendent, to be efficient under the extremely difficult circumstances of the case, as respects the absence of public spirit, ought to be in a constant state of inquiry—accessible to information from every quarter, listening to and investigating every rumour which bears with it a plausible appearance of truth; and prompt to pursue any clue that may enable him to test the efficiency and soundness of the system which it is his duty to watch over. The judge should assume every one to be innocent till he is proved guilty; the superintendent, whilst he judges no one, should make it his business to possess himself of the fullest information regarding the proceedings of all.

Just in proportion as the officers who preside in the Sudder Courts with so much ability, and with so much honour to the British character, are excellent judges, they are bad superintendents of civil and criminal justice. It is unfair to impose duties so incompatible upon any men:—it is vain to expect that they should both be efficiently performed.

The remedy is obvious. The Sudder Courts should be divided, and the discordant functions imposed upon them allotted to different individuals. Such an arrangement would occasion no increase of expense, since there need be no augmentation of the number of officers. It would permit the adaptation of individual qualifications to that department of duty best suited for their useful exertion. It would result in economy of time, much of which is now wasted in passing backwards and forwards from one sort of business to another totally dissimilar. The judges would be only judges; the superintendence of the administration of civil and criminal justice would be in distinct hands; either of an individual, which we think decidedly the better plan, or of a board. The efficiency of both departments would thus be much increased. The Government would learn from the court how the judges of the various grades performed those parts of their duties, the fulfilment of which could be tried by their decisions—the grounds of which are always fully recorded in India; whilst the superintendents of justice would watch and report upon all matters of an executive nature—the relations between the institution and the decision of suits, the execution of decrees, the disposal or accumulation of interlocutory and other miscellaneous business; and, pre-eminently, upon the general efficiency and purity of the courts, and the estimation in which they are held by the people. It is not sufficient in any land, but especially not in India, that the fountains of justice should be free from actual pollution; it is essential that there should be an absolute and universal conviction that they are pure. This double obligation has not, hitherto, been sufficiently attended to in British India. The government has not unfrequently stopped short, after satisfying itself by an investigation into alleged misfeasance; leaving the minds of the people as full of distrust as before, with the additional suspicion of their rulers being cognizant of, and conniving at the iniquity.

The department of the land revenue is well attended to throughout British India, owing probably—we must confess our persuasion—to the strong and direct interest which the government has in the efficiency of the instrument by which its treasury is principally replenished. In former times, for some years following the formation of the permanent settlement of the provinces of Bengal, Behar, and Benares, and, probably, in those districts also of the Madras Presidency into which a corresponding measure was subsequently introduced, it was thought that a scheme so simple might be left to execute itself; and that those public servants who were unfit for more important and difficult employment, might be well able to act as mere receivers of the dues of the state from a body of thriving and grateful landholders. How entirely, and with what a penalty for the mistake, these expectations have been frustrated, we have before had occasion to show on more than one occasion, especially in urging the necessity of an immediate survey of the whole area of the permanently settled provinces:—but much of the mischief of past mismanagement is now irreparable. In the districts subject to periodical assessments throughout the Presidencies, we have profited by experience; and whatever other errors have been committed, the state has been effectually protected from the loss of that revenue, upon the integrity and judicious dispensation of which all reasonable hopes of the improvement of British India must be built. The people are not in a state to advance their own condition. The landholders of the provinces, to whom the permanent settlement has insured so large a proportion of the rental, have done little or nothing, in the long course of fifty years, evento benefit themselves—not one in a thousand pretends to feel any care for the interests of his country: on the other hand, the government can do nothing for the people if it have not sufficient pecuniary means for their defence, against external and internal enemies, and for complete administrative efficiency. The case is essentially different from that of a country where the people are on a level with, if not in advance of, their rulers, in respect to the knowledge of their own wants, and of the best manner of supplying them— 'where private intelligence always outstrips and prevents public wisdom.' Yet there are some sincere—but deluded— philanthropists, whose single idea of benefiting British India is centred in the abandonment of the system of land revenue;— as if sufficient means for any, the most economical, government of that country could be obtained from all other sources put together; as if some of those sources were not far worse in principle than that from which the land revenue is derived; and as if it would be practicable to make any sacrifice of revenue in favour of the landholders, without mulcting somebody else to a corresponding amount.

The land revenue is managed by the collectors and deputy collectors of the numerous districts into which the provinces of British India are divided; subject to the authority of boards of revenue stationed at Calcutta, Allahabad, and Madras, and of a revenue commission at Bombay. Throughout Bengal, Behar, Benares, and the north-western provinces, commissioners of revenue, each presiding over four or five districts, were interposed, under Lord William Bentinck's administration, between the boards and the collectors; and the powers of the boards were increased, the commissioners being invested with the authority of the former boards. This measure tended most beneficially to relieve the government from the details of the revenue administration; but it still interferes much too often and too minutely, instead of confining itself to general superintendence and control, holding the boards responsible for the efficiency of the system. But this, as we have stated, is the general vice of the Indian governments, equally prevalent, and equally mischievous in all departments, both at home and abroad. It would be easy to make out a list of matters in which the Governor-General in council, the Court of Directors, and the Board of Control, busy themselves, or profess to busy themselves, in any given month of any year, which, to use the words of Junius, 'the gravest of chaplains would not be able to read without laughing.'

Our limits compel us to state briefly, that the other great departments of the revenue of Bengal, the richest by far of the Company's possessions, are managed by the Board of Customs, salt and opium, fixed in Calcutta; by the instrumentality, in the two latter branches, of agents, members of the civil service, stationed at the principal places of manufacture or store. We cannot discuss, at the close of a long article, the principles of the great monopolies of salt and opium. As monopolies they are, of course, essentially vicious; that of salt operating as a poll-tax, almost absolutely irrespective of the means, and consequently of the obligations to the state, of the person paying it; that of opium mixing up the Christian rulers of India, in a manner the most discreditable, with the demoralizing traffic by which British merchants poison the minds and bodies of the Chinese and Malays. It is clear to us that the government should abandon all concern in the manufacture of this drug, and content itself with levying such an export duty at the port of shipment as would not afford too tempting a premium to the smuggler. There would be loss of revenue in this, no doubt; but there would be great gain of character. Were it not for the unfortunate permanent settlement of the land revenue, which so many extol as the perfection both of justice and of financial wisdom, (as if there could have been no middle course between annual assessments at rack-rents, and the limitation for ever of the supply to be derived from the best possible source of national expenditure), both these monopolies, objectionable from different but equally cogent reasons, might be altogether abandoned; and the transit duties at Madras might, at the same time, be abolished, and all the ports of India be declared absolutely free. Let those who know anything of the condition of India, and of the effects of a bad system of taxation in any land, weigh these advantages against those which the community derive from the immunities enjoyed by the Zemindars in the permanently settled provinces; for no one pretends that any other class, even of those directly connected with the soil, is a whit the better off in consequence of the limitation of the public demand. Bitter cause have the people of India to rue Lord Cornwallis' mistaken benevolence, which, whilst it shackles the hands of the government, fixes, hopelessly, unequal and mischievous taxes upon the shoulders of the people.

ART. VI.—*Madame de Sévigné and her Contemporaries.* Two vols. 8vo. London: 1842.

MADAME DE SEVIGNE, in her combined and inseparable character as writer and woman, enjoys the singular and delightful reputation of having united, beyond all others of her class, the rare with the familiar, and the lively with the correct. The moment her name is mentioned, we think of the mother who loved her daughter; of the most charming of letter-writers; of the ornament of an age of license, who incurred none of its ill-repute; of the female who has become one of the classics of her language, without effort and without intention.

The sight of a name so attractive, in the title-page of the volumes before us, has made us renew an intercourse, never entirely broken, with her own. We have lived over again with her and her friends from her first letter to her last, including the new matter in the latest Paris editions. We have seen her writing in her cabinet, dancing at court, being the life of the company in her parlour, nursing her old uncle the Abbé; bantering Mademoiselle du Plessis; lecturing and then jesting with her son; devouring the romances of Calprenede, and responding to the wit of Pascal and La Fontaine; walking in her own green alleys by moonlight, enchanting cardinals, politicians, philosophers, beauties, poets, devotees, haymakers; ready to 'die with laughter' fifty times a-day; idolizing her daughter for ever.

It is somewhat extraordinary, that of all

the admirers of a woman so interesting, not one yet has been found in these islands to give any reasonably good account of her—any regular and comprehensive information respecting her life and writings. The notices in the biographical dictionaries are meagre to the last degree; and 'sketches' of greater pretension have seldom consisted of more than loose and brief memorandums, picked out of others, their predecessors. The name which report had assigned to the compiler of the volumes before us, induced us to entertain sanguine hopes that something more satisfactory was about to be done for the queen of letter-writing; and undoubtedly the portrait which has been given of her, is, on the whole, the best hitherto to be met with. But still it is a limited, hasty, and unfinished portrait, forming but one in a gallery of others; many of which have little to do with her, and some, scarcely any connection even with her times. Now, in a work entitled 'Madame de Sévigné and her Contemporaries,' we had a right to expect a picture with the foreground occupied by herself and her friends, and the rest of the group at greater or less distances, in proportion to their reference to the main figure; something analogous to an interesting French print, which exhibits Molière reading one of his plays to an assembly of wits, at the house of Ninon de l'Enclos. The great comic writer is on his legs—the prominent object—acting as well as reading his play, in a lively and silent attitude, full of French expression; near him sits the lady of the house, as the gatherer together of the party; and round both, in characteristic postures, but all listening to the reader, sit Rochefoucauld, La Fontaine, Corneille, and one or two more. But in a picture of Madame de Sévigné, and those whom an association of ideas would draw round her, what have we to do with Cardinal Richelieu, and Père Joseph, and Boisrobert? What with the man in the 'Iron Mask,' with Lord Herbert of Cherbury, the Earls of Holland and Ossory, the Dukes of Buckingham, Shrewsbury, and St. Simon, and others who flourished before and after her day? There is, it is true, a sprinkling of extracts from Madame de Sévigné's letters through the greater part of the volumes; but even these naturally fail us in many of the sketches, and of whole letters we have but two or three; whereas, what the public looked for, was a regular and satisfactory account both of her writings and her life, a selection of specimens of her letters,

and some talk about her friends; in short, about all of whom she talks herself; not excepting Ninon, of whom there is here scarcely a word; and assuredly not omitting such a friend as Corbinelli, whose name we do not remember seeing in the book. There is very little even about her son the Marquis, and not a syllable respecting her startling 'contemporaries,' Brinvilliers and La Voisin; while, on the other hand, we have a long account of the King and Queen of Spain, and a history of the very foreign transactions of Stradella the musician. It is much as if, in the print above mentioned, Molière and his friends had been thrust into the background, and the chief part of the composition given up to a view of the courts of France and England. We need not dwell upon the contradictions between the 'advertisement' and the 'introduction' respecting the chief authorities consulted; or such as those in the opinions expressed about Louis the Fourteenth, who is at one time represented as 'the greatest monarch that had appeared in France previous to the times of Napoleon and Louis-Philippe,' and at another as a man whose talents were 'below mediocrity.' The work, in a word, is one of the jobbing, book-making expedients of the day, with a dishonest title-page; and yet there are sketches and passages in it so good, and indicative of a power to do so much better, that we speak of it thus with regret. It should have been called by some other name. At present it reminds us too much of the famous ode on Doctor Pococke, in which there was something about 'one Pococke' towards the middle of the composition.

Proceeding to sketch out, from our own acquaintance with her, what we conceive to be a better mode of supplying some account of Madame de Sévigné and her writings, we shall, in the order of time, speak of her ancestors and other kindred, her friends and her daily habits, and give a few specimens of the best of her letters; and we shall do all this with as hearty a relish of her genius as the warmest of her admirers, without thinking it necessary to blind ourselves to any weaknesses that may have accompanied it. With all her good-nature, the 'charming woman' had a sharp eye to a defect herself; and we have too great a respect for the truth that was in her, not to let her honestly suffer in its behalf, whenever that first cause of all that is great and good demands it.

Marie de Rabutin-Chantal, Baroness de Chantal and Bourbilly, afterwards Marchioness de Sévigné, was born, in all probability, in Burgundy, in the old ancestral *château* of Bourbilly, between Semur and Epoisses, on the 5th of February, 1627. Her father, Celse Benigne de Rabutin, Baron as above mentioned, was of the elder branch of his name, and cousin to the famous Count Bussy-Rabutin; her mother, Marie de Coulanges, daughter of a secretary-of-state, was also of a family whose name afterwards became celebrated for wit; and her paternal grandmother, Jeanne Françoise Fremyot, afterwards known by the title of the Blessed Mother of Chantal, was a *saint*. The nuns of the Order of the Visitation, which she founded by the help of Saint Francis de Sales, beatified her, with the subsequent approbation of Benedict XIV.; and she was canonized by Clement XIV. (Ganganelli) in 1767. There was a relationship between the families of Rabutin- and De Sales;— names which it would be still stranger than it is to see in conjunction, had not the good St. Francis been the liveliest and most tolerant of his class. We notice these matters, because it is interesting to discover links between people of celebrity; and because it would be but a sorry philosophy which should deny the probable effects produced in the minds and dispositions of a distinguished race by intermixtures of blood and associations of ideas. Madame de Sévigné's father, for instance, gave a rough foretaste of her wit and sincerity, by a raillery amounting to the *brusque*, sometimes to the insolent. He wrote the following congratulatory epistle to a minister of finance, whom the King (Louis XIII.) had transformed into a marshal:—

'My Lord,
'Birth; black beard; intimacy.
'CHANTAL.'

Meaning that his new fortune had been owing to his quality, to his position near the royal person, and to his having a black beard like his master. Both the Chantals and the Fremyots, a race remarkable for their integrity, had been amongst the warmest adherents of Henry IV.; and, indeed, the whole united stock may be said to have been distinguished equally for worth, spirit, and ability, till it took a twist of intrigue and worldliness in the solitary instance of the scapegrace Bussy. We may discern, in the wit and integrity of Madame de Sévigné—in her natural piety, in her cordial partizanship, and at the same time in that tact for universality which distinguished her in spite of it—a portion of what was best in all her kindred, not excepting a spice of the satire, but without the malignity, of her supercilious cousin. She was truly the flower of the family tree; and laughed at the top of it with a brilliancy as well as a softness, compared with which Bussy was but a thorn.

The little heiress was only a few months old when the Barón de Chantal died, bravely fighting against the English in their descent on the Isle of Rhé. It was one of the figments of Gregorio Leti, that he received his death-wound from the hand of Cromwell. The Baron's widow survived her husband only five years; and it seems to have been expected that the devout grandmother, Madame de Chantal, the elder, would have been anxious to take the orphan under her care. But whether it was that the mother had chosen to keep the child too exclusively under her own, or that the future saint was too much occupied in the concerns of the other world and the formation of religious houses, (of which she founded no less than eighty-seven); the old lady contented herself with recommending her to the consideration of an Archbishop, and left her in the hands of her maternal relations. They did their part nobly by her. She was brought up with her fellow-wit and correspondent, Philippe-Emmanuel de Coulanges; and her uncle Christophe, Abbé de Livry, became her second father, in the strictest and most enduring sense of the word. He took care that she should acquire graces at court, as well as encouragements to learning from his friends; saw her married, and helped to settle her children; extricated her affairs from disorder, and taught her to surpass himself in knowledge of business; in fine, spent a good remainder of his life with her, sometimes at his own house and sometimes at hers; and when he died, repaid the tenderness with which she had rewarded his care, by leaving her all his property. The Abbé, with some little irritable particularities, and a love of extra-comfort and his bottle, appears to have been, as she was fond of calling him, *bien bon*, a right good creature; and posterity is to be congratulated, that her faculties were allowed to expand under his honest and reasonable indulgence, instead of being cramped, and formalized, and made insincere, by the half-witted training of the convent.

Young ladies at that time were taught little more than to read, write, dance, and embroider, with greater or less attention to books of religion. If the training was conventual, religion was predominant, (unless it was rivalled by comfit and flower making, great pastimes of the good nuns); and in the devout case, the danger was, either that the pupil would be frightened into bigotry, or, what happened oftener, would be tired into a passion for pleasure and the world, and only stocked with a sufficient portion of fear and superstition to return to the bigotry in old age, when the passion was burnt out. When the education was more domestic, profane literature had its turn—the poetry of Maynard and Malherbe, and the absurd but exalting romances of Gomberville, Scudery, and Calprenede. Sometimes a little Latin was added; and other tendencies to literature were caught from abbés and confessors. In all cases, somebody was in the habit of reading aloud while the ladies worked; and a turn for politics and court-gossip was given by the wars of the *Fronde,* and by the allusions to the heroes and heroines of the reigning gallantries, in the ideal personages of the romances. The particulars of Madame de Sévigné's education have not transpired; but as she was brought up at home, and we hear something of her male teachers, and nothing of her female, (whom, nevertheless, she could not have been without), the probability is that she tasted something of all the different kinds of nurture, and helped herself with her own cleverness to the rest. She would hear of the example and reputation of her saintly grandmother, if she was not much with her; her other religious acquaintances rendered her an admirer of the worth and talents of the devotees of Port-Royal; her political ones interested her in behalf of the *Frondeurs;* but, above all, she had the wholesome run of her good uncle's books, and the society of his friends, Chapelain, Menage, and other professors of polite literature; the effect of which is to fuse particular knowledge into general, and to distil from it the spirit of a wise humanity. She seems to have been not unacquainted with Latin and Spanish; and both Chapelain and Menage were great lovers of Italian, which became part of her favourite reading.

To these fortunate accidents of birth and breeding were joined health, animal spirits, a natural flow of wit, and a face and shape which, if not perfectly handsome, were allowed by everybody to produce a most agreeable impression. Her cousin Bussy Rabutin has drawn a portrait

of her when a young woman; and though he did it half in malice and resentment, like the half-vagabond he was, he could not but make the same concession. He afterwards withdrew the worst part of his words, and heaped her with panegyric; and from a comparison of his different accounts we probably obtain a truer idea of her manners and personal appearance, than has been furnished either by the wholesale eulogist or the artist. It is, indeed, corroborated by herself in her letters. She was somewhat tall for a woman; had a good shape, a pleasing voice, a fine complexion, brilliant eyes, and a profusion of light hair; but her eyes, though brilliant, were small, and, together with the eyelashes, were of different tints; her lips, though well-coloured, were too flat; and the end of her nose too 'square.' The jawbone, according to Bussy, had the same fault. He says that she had more shape than grace, yet danced well; and she had a taste for singing. He makes the coxcombical objection to her at that time of life, that she was too playful 'for a woman of quality;' as if the liveliest genius and the staidest conventionalities could be reasonably expected to go together; or as if she could have written her unique letters, had she resembled everybody else. Let us call to mind the playfulness of those letters, which have charmed all the world;—let us add the most cordial manners, a face full of expression, in which the blood came and went, and a general sensibility, which, if too quick, perhaps, to shed tears, was no less ready to 'die with laughter' at every sally of pleasantry—and we shall see before us the not beautiful but still engaging and ever-lively creature, in whose countenance, if it contained nothing else, the power to write those letters must have been visible : for, though people do not always seem what they are, it is seldom they do not look what they can do.

The good uncle, the Abbé de Coulanges, doubtless thought he had made a happy match of it, and joined like with like, when, at the age of eighteen, his charming niece married a man of as joyous a character as herself, and of one of the first houses in Brittany. The Marquis de Sévigné, or Sevigny, (the old spelling), was related to the Duguesclins and the Rohans, and also to Cardinal de Retz. But joyousness, unfortunately, was the sum-total of his character. He had none of the reflection of his bride. He was a mere laugher and jester, fond of expense and gallantry; and, though he became the father of two children, seems to have given his wife but little of his attention. He fell in a duel about some female, seven years after his marriage. The poor man was a braggart in his amours. Bussy says, that he boasted to him of the approbation of Ninon de l'Enclos; a circumstance which, like a great number of others told in connection with the 'modern Leontium,' is by no means to be taken for granted. Ninon was a person of a singular repute, owing to as singular an education; and while, in consequence of that education, a license was given her, which, to say the truth, most people secretly took, the graces and good qualities which she retained in spite of it, ultimately rendered her house a sort of academy of good breeding, which it was thought not incompatible with sober views in life to countenance.

Now, it is probable, from the great reputation which she had for good sense, that she always possessed discernment enough to see through such a character as that of Monsieur de Sévigné. The wife, it is true, many years afterwards, accused her, to the young Marquis, of having 'spoilt (or hurt) his father,' (*gâté*,) and it may have been true to a certain extent; for a false theory of love would leave a nature like his nothing to fall back upon in regard to right feeling; but people of the Marquis's sort generally come ready spoilt into society, and it is only an indulgent motive that would palm off their faults upon the acquaintances they make there. Be this as it may, Bussy-Rabutin, who had always made love to his cousin after his fashion, and who had found it met with as constant rejection, though not perhaps till he had been imprudently suffered to go the whole length of his talk about it, avows that he took occasion from the Marquis's boast about Ninon, to make her the gross and insulting proposal, that she should take her 'revenge.' Again she repulsed him. A letter of Bussy's fell into her husband's hands, who forbade her to see him more; a prohibition, of which she doubtless gladly availed herself. The Marquis perished shortly afterwards; and again her cousin made his coxcombical and successless love, which, however, he accuses her of receiving with so much pleasure as to show herself jealous when he transferred it to another; a weakness, alas! not impossible to very respectable representatives of poor human nature. But all which he says to her disadvantage must be received with caution; for, besides his having no right

to say anything, he had the mean and uncandid effrontery to pretend that he was angry with her solely because she was not generous in money matters. He tells us, that after all he had done for her and her friends, (what his favours were, God knows), she refused him the assistance of her purse at a moment when his whole prospects in life were in danger. The real amount of this charge appears to have been that Bussy, who, besides being a man of pleasure and expense, was a distinguished cavalry officer, once needed money for a campaign; and that, applying to his cousin to help him, her uncle the Abbé, who had the charge of her affairs, thought proper to ask him for securities. The cynical and disgusting, though well-written book, in which the Count libelled his cousin, (for as somebody said of Petronius, he was an author *purissimæ impuritatis*), brought him afterwards into such trouble at court, that it cost him many years of exile to his estates, and a world of servile trouble and adulation to get back to the presence of Louis the Fourteenth, who could never heartily like him. He had ridiculed, among others, the kind-hearted La Vallière. Madame de Sévigné, in consequence of these troubles, forgave him; and their correspondence, both personally and by letter, was renewed, pleasantly enough on his part, and in a constant strain of regard and admiration. He tells her, among other pretty speeches, that she would certainly have been 'goddess of something or other,' had she lived in ancient times. But Madame de Sévigné writes to him with evident constraint, as to a sort of evil genius who is to be propitiated; and the least handsome incident in her life was the apparently warm interest she took in a scandalous process instituted by him against a gentleman whom his daughter had married, and whose crime consisted in being of inferior birth; for Count Bussy-Rabutin was as proud as he was profligate.[*] Bussy tried to sustain his cause by forged letters, and had the felicity of losing it by their assistance. It is to be hoped that his cousin had been the dupe of the forgeries; but we have no doubt that she was somewhat afraid of him. She dreaded his writing another book.

We know not whether it was during her married life, or afterwards, that Bussy re-

---

[*] See a strange, painful, and vehement letter, written by her on the subject, to the Count de Guitaut. Vol xiii. of the duodecimo Paris edition of 1823-4, p. 103.

lates a little incident of her behaviour at court, to which his malignity gives one of its most ingenious turns. They were both there together at a ball, and the King took her out to dance. On returning to her seat, according to the Count's narrative,—'It must be owned,' said she, 'that the King possesses great qualities: he will certainly obscure the lustre of all his predecessors.—I could not help laughing in her face,' observes Bussy, 'seeing what had produced this panegyric.' I replied, 'there can be no doubt of it, madam, after what he has done for yourself.' 'I really thought she was going to testify her gratitude by crying, *Vive le Roi*.'*

This is amusing enough; but the spirit which induces a man to make charges of this nature, is apt to be the one most liable to them itself. Men at the court of Louis used to weep, if he turned his face from them. The bravest behaved like little boys before him, vying for his favour as children might do for an apple. Racine is said to have died of the fear of having offended him; and Bussy, as we have before intimated, was not a whit behind the most pathetic of the servile, when he was again permitted to prostrate himself in the court circle. Madame Sévigné probably felt on this occasion as every other woman would have felt, and was candid enough not to hide her emotion; but whether, instead of pretending to feel less, she might not have pleasantly affected still more, in order to regain her self-possession, and so carry it off with a grace, Bussy was not the man to tell us, even if his wit had had good nature enough to discern it.

The young widow devoted herself to her children, and would never again hear of marriage. She had already become celebrated for her letters; continued to go occasionally to court; and frequented the reigning literary circles, then famous for their pedantry, without being carried away by it. Several wits and men of fashion made love to her, besides Bussy. Among them were the learned Menage, who courted her in madrigals compiled from the Italian; the superintendent of the finances, Fouquet, who, except in her instance and that of La Vallière, is said to have made Danaës wherever he chose to shower his gold; and the Prince of Conti, brother of the great Condé, who, with the self-sufficient airs of a royal lover, declared he found her charming, and that he had

'a word or two to say to her next winter.' Even the great Turenne is said to have loved her. On none of them did she take pity but the superintendent; and not on his heart, poor man! but on his neck; when it was threatened with the axe for doing as his predecessors had done, and squandering the public money. Fouquet was magnificent and popular in his dishonesty, and hence the envious conspired to pull him down. Some of the earliest letters of Madame de Sévigné are on the subject of his trial, and show an interest in it so genuine, that fault has been found with them for not being so witty as the rest!

It was probably from this time that she began to visit the court less frequently, and to confine herself to those domestic and accomplished circles, in which, without suspecting it, she cultivated an immortal reputation for letter-writing. Her political and religious friends, the De Retzes and the Jansenists, grew out of favour, or rather into dislike, and she perhaps suffered herself to grow out of favour with them. She always manifested, however, great respect for the King; and Louis was a man of too genuine a gallantry not to be courteous to the lady whenever they met, and address to her a few gracious words. On one occasion she gazed upon the magnificent gaming-tables at court, and curtsied to his Majesty, 'after the fashion which her daughter,' she says, 'had taught her;' upon which the monarch was pleased to bow, and looked very acknowledging. And, another time, when Madame de Maintenon, the Pamela of royalty, then queen in secret, presided over the religious amusements of the King, she went to see Racine's play of Esther performed by the young ladies of St. Cyr; when Louis politely expressed his hope that she was satisfied, and interchanged a word with her in honour of the poet and the performers. She was not, indeed, at any time an uninterested observer of what took place in the world. She has other piquant, though not always very lucid notices of the court—was deeply interested in the death of Turenne—listens with emotion to the eloquence of the favourite preachers—records the atrocities of the poisoners, and is compelled by her good sense to leave off wasting her pity on the devout dulness of King James II. But the proper idea of her, for the greater part of her life, is that of a sequestered domestic woman, the delight of her friends, the constant reader, talker, laugher, and writer, and the passionate admirer of the daugh-

* *Histoire Amoureuse des Gaules.* Tom. i., p. 158. Cologne, 1709.

ter to whom she addressed the chief part of her correspondence. Sometimes she resided in Brittany, at an estate on the sea-coast, called the Rocks, which had belonged to her husband; sometimes she was at Livry, near Paris, where the good uncle possessed his abbey; sometimes at her own estate of Bourbilly, in Burgundy; and at others in her house in town, where the Hôtel Carnavalet, (now a school) has become celebrated as her latest and best-known residence. In all these abodes, not excepting the town-house, she made a point of having the enjoyment of a garden, delighting to be as much in the open air as possible, haunting her green alleys and her orangeries with a book in her hand, or a song upon her lips (for she sung as she went about, like a child), and walking out late by moonlight in all seasons, to the hazard of colds and rheumatisms, from which she ultimately suffered severely. She was a most kind mistress to her tenants. She planted trees, made labyrinths, built chapels, (inscribing them 'to God),' watched the peasants dancing, sometimes played at chess, (she did not like cards); and at almost all other times, when not talking with her friends, she was reading or hearing others read, or writing letters.

The chief books and authors we hear of are 'Tasso,' 'Ariosto,' 'La Fontaine,' 'Pascal,' 'Nicole,' 'Tacitus,' the huge old romances, 'Rabelais, 'Rochefoucauld,' the novels of her friend Madame de la Fayette, Corneille, Bourdaloue and Bossuet, Montaigne, Lucian, Don Quixote, and Saint Augustin; a goodly collection surely, a 'circle of humanity.' She reads the romances three times over; and when she is not sure that her correspondent will approve a book, says that her son has 'brought her into it,' or that he reads out 'passages.' Sometimes her household get up a little surprise or masquerade; at others, her cousin Coulanges brings his 'song-book,' and they are 'the happiest people in the world;' that is to say, provided her daughter is with her. Otherwise, the tears rush into her eyes at the thought of her absence, and she is always making 'dragons' or 'cooking,'—viz. having the blue-devils and fretting. But, when they all are comfortable, what they are most addicted to is 'dying with laughter.' They die with laughter if seeing a grimace; if told a bon-mot; if witnessing a rustic dance; if listening to Monsieur de Pomenars, who has always 'some criminal affair on his hands;' if getting drenched with rain; if

having a sore finger pinched instead of relieved. Here lounges the young Marquis on the sofa with his book; there sits the old Abbé in his arm-chair, fed with something nice; the ladies chat, and embroider, and banter Mademoiselle du Plessis; in comes Monsieur Pomenars, with the news of some forgery that is charged against him, or livelier offence, but always so perilous to his neck that he and they 'die with laughter.' Enter, with her friend Madame de la Fayette, the celebrated Duke de la Rochefoucauld, gouty, but still graceful, and he and the lady 'die with laughter;' enter the learned Corbinelli, and he dies; enter Madame de Coulanges, the sprightly mixture of airiness and witty malice, and she dies of course; and the happy mortality is completed by her husband, the singing cousin aforesaid—'a little round fat oily man,' who was always 'in' with some duke or cardinal, admiring his fine house and feasting at his table. These were among the most prominent friends or associates of Madame de Sévigné; but there were also great lords and ladies, and neighbours in abundance, sometimes coming in when they were not wanted, but always welcomed with true French politeness, except when they had been heard to say anything against the 'daughter;' and then Madame told them roundly to their faces that she was 'not at home.' There was Segrais, and Saint Pavin, and Corneille, and Bossuet, and Treville, who talked like a book; and the great Turenne; and the Duke de Vivonne, (brother of Montespan,) who called her 'darling mamma;' and Madame Scarron till she was Maintenon; and Madame de Fiesque, who did not know how to be afflicted; and D Hacqueville, whose good offices it was impossible to tire; and fat Barillon, who said good things though he was a bad ambassador; and the Abbé Têtu, thin and lively; and Benserade, who was the life of the company wherever he went; and Brancas, who liked to choose his own rivals; and Cardinal de Retz, in retirement feeding his trout, and talking metaphysics. She had known the Cardinal for thirty years; and, during his last illness, used to get Corneille, Boileau, and Molière to come and read to him their new pieces. Perhaps there is no man of whom she speaks with such undeviating respect and regard as this once turbulent statesman, unless it be Rochefoucauld, who, to judge from most of her accounts of him, was a pattern of all that was the reverse of his 'Maxims.'

With her son the Marquis, who was 'a man of wit and pleasure about town,' till he settled into sobriety with a wife who is said to have made him devout, Madame de Sévigné lived in a state of confidence and unreserve, to an excess that would not be deemed very delicate in these days, and of which, indeed, she herself sometimes expressed her dislike. There is a well-known collection of letters, professing to have passed between him and Ninon de l'Enclos, which is spurious; but we gather some remarkable particulars of their intimacy from the letters of the mother to her daughter; and, among others, Ninon's sayings of him, that he had 'a soul of pap,' and the 'heart of a cucumber fried in snow.'

The little Marquis's friends (for he was small in his person) did not think him a man of very impassioned temperament. He was, however, very pleasant and kind, and an attentive son. He had a strong contempt, too, for 'the character of Æneas,' and the merit of never having treated Bussy Rabutin with any great civility. Rochefoucauld said of him, that his greatest ambition would have been to die for a love which he did not feel. He was at first in the army, but not being on the favourite side either in politics or religion, nor probably very active, could get no preferment worth having; so he ended in living unambitiously in a devout corner of Paris, and cultivating his taste for literature. He maintained a contest of some repute with Dacier, on the disputable meaning of the famous passage in Horace, *Difficile est propriè communia dicere.* His treatise on the subject may be found in the later Paris editions of his mother's letters; but the juxtaposition is not favourable to its perusal.

But sons, dukes, cardinals, friends, the whole universe, come to nothing in these famous letters, compared with the daughter to whom they owe their existence. She had not the good spirits of her mother, but she had wit and observation; and appears to have been so liberally brought up, that she sometimes startled her more acquiescent teacher with the hardihood of her speculations. It is supposed to have been owing to a scruple of conscience in her descendants, that her part of the correspondence was destroyed. She professed herself, partly in jest and partly in earnest, a zealous follower of Descartes. It is curious that the circumstance which gave rise to the letters, was the very one to which Madame de Sévigné had looked for saving her the necessity of correspondence. The young lady became the wife of a great lord, the Count de Grignan, who, being a man of the court, was expected to continue to reside in Paris; so that the mother trusted she should always have her daughter at hand. The Count, however, who was lieutenant-governor of Provence, received orders, shortly afterwards, to betake himself to that distant region: the continued non-residence of the Duke de Vendôme, the governor, conspired to keep him there, on and off, for the remainder of the mother's existence—a space of six-and-twenty years; and though she contrived to visit and be visited by Madame de Grignan so often that they spent nearly half the time with each other, yet the remaining years were a torment to Madame de Sévigné, which nothing could assuage but an almost incessant correspondence. One letter was no sooner received than another was anxiously desired; and the daughter echoed the anxiety. Hours were counted, post-boys watched for, obstacles imagined; all the torments experienced, and not seldom manifested, of the most jealous and exacting passion, and at the same time all the delights and ecstacies vented of one the most confiding. But what we have to say of this excess of maternal love will be better kept for our concluding remarks. Suffice it to observe, in hastening to give our specimens of the letters, that these graver points of the correspondence, though numerous, occupy but a small portion of it; that the letters, generally speaking, consist of the amusing gossip and conversation which the mother *would have had* with the daughter, had the latter remained near her; and that Madame de Sévigné, after living, as it were, for no other purpose than to write them, and to straiten herself in her circumstances for both her children, died at her daughter's house in Provence, of an illness caused by the fatigue of nursing her through one of her own. Her decease took place in April, 1696, in the seventieth year of her age. Her body, it is said, long after, was found dressed in ribbons, after a Provençal fashion, at which she had expressed great disgust. Madame de Grignan did not survive many years. She died in the summer of 1705, of grief, it has been thought, for the loss of her only child, the Marquis de Grignan, in whom the male descendants of the family became extinct. It is a somewhat unpleasant evidence of the triumph of Ninon de l'Enclos over the mortality of her contemporaries, that, in one of the letters of the correspondence, this youth, the grandson of Madame de Sévigné's husband, and nephew of her son, is found studying good breeding at the table of that 'grandmother of the Loves.' The Count de Grignan, his father, does not appear to have been a very agreeable personage. Mademoiselle de Sévigné was his third wife. He was, therefore, not very young; he was pompous and fond of expense, and brought duns about her; and his face was plain, and it is said that he did not make up for his ill looks by the virtue of constancy. Madame de Sévigné seems to have been laudably anxious to make the best of her son-in-law. She accordingly compliments him on his 'fine tenor voice;' and, because he has an uncomely face, is always admiring his 'figure.' One cannot help suspecting sometimes that there is a little malice in her intimations of the contrast, and that she admires his figure most when he will not let her daughter come to see her. The Count's only surviving child, Pauline, became the wife of Louis de Simiane, Marquis d'Esparron, who seems to have been connected on the mother's side with our family of the Hays, and was lieutenant of the Scottish horse-guards in the service of the French king. Madame de Simiane inherited a portion both of the look and wit of her grandmother; but more resembled her mother in gravity of disposition. A daughter of hers married the Marquis de Vence; and of this family there are descendants now living; but the names of Grignan, Rabutin, and Sévigné, have long been extinct—in the body. In spirit they are now before us, more real than myriads of existing families; and we proceed to enjoy their deathless company.

We shall not waste the reader's time with the history of editions, and telling how the collection first partially transpired 'against the consent of friends.' Friends or families are too often afraid, or ashamed, or jealous, of what afterwards constitutes their renown; and we can only rejoice that the sweet 'winged words' of the most flowing of pens, escaped, in this instance, out of their grudging boxes. We give the letters in English instead of French, not being by any means of opinion that 'all who read and appreciate Madame de Sévigné, may be 'supposed to understand that language nearly as well as their 'own.' Undoubtedly, people of the best natural understandings are glad, when, in addition to what nature has given them, they possess, in the knowledge of a foreign language, the best means of appreciating the wit that has adorned it. But it is not impossible that some such people, nay many, in this age of 'diffusion of knowledge,' may have missed the advantages of a good education, and yet be able to appreciate the imperfectly conveyed wit of another, better than some who are acquainted with its own vehicle. Besides, we have known very distinguished people confess, that all who read, or even speak French, do not always read it with the same ready result and comfort to the eyes of their understandings as they do their own language; and as to the 'impossibility' of translating such letters as those of Madame de Sévigné, though the specimens hitherto published have not been very successful, we do not believe it. Phrases here and there may be so; difference of manners may render some few untranslatable in so many words, or even unintelligible; but for the most part the sentences will find their equivalents, if the translator is not destitute of the spirits that suggested them. We have been often given to understand, that we have been, by translation, too much in the habit, on our own part, of assuming that French, however widely known, was still more known than it is; and we shall endeavour, on the present occasion, to make an attempt to include the whole of our readers in the participation of a great intellectual pleasure.

The first letter in the Collection, written when Madame de Sévigné was a young and happy mother, gives a delightful foretaste of what its readers have to expect. She was then in her twentieth year, with a baby in her arms, and nothing but brightness in her eyes.

To the Count de Bussy-Rabutin.
'*March 15th*, (1647).*

'You are a pretty fellow, are you not? to have written me nothing for these two months. Have you forgotten who I am, and the rank I hold in the family? 'Faith, little cadet, I will make you remember it. If you put me out of sorts, I will reduce you to the ranks. You knew I was about to be confined, and yet took no more trouble to ask after my health than if I had remained a spinster. Very well: be informed to your confusion that I have got a boy, who shall suck hatred of you into his veins with his mother's milk, and that I mean to have a great many more, purely to supply you with enemies. You have not the wit to do as much, you with your feminine productions.

'After all, my dear cousin, my regard for you

---

* Madame de Sévigné never, in dating her letters, gave the *years*. They were added by one of her editors.

is not to be concealed. Nature will proclaim it in spite of art. I thought to scold you for your laziness through the whole of this letter; but I do my heart too great a violence, and must conclude with telling you that M. de Sévigné and myself love you very much, and often talk of the pleasure we should have in your company.'

Bussy writes very pleasantly in return; but it will be so impossible to make half the extracts we desire from Madame de Sévigné's own letters, that we must not be tempted to look again into those of others. The next that we shall give is the famous one on the Duke de Lauzun's intended marriage with the Princess Henrietta of Bourbon; one of the most striking, though not the most engaging, in the collection. We might have kept it for a climax, were it not desirable to preserve a chronological order. It was written nearly four-and-twenty years after the letter we have just given; which we mention to show how she had retained her animal spirits. The person to whom it is addressed is her jovial cousin De Coulanges. The apparent tautologies in the exordium are not really such. They only represent a continued astonishment, wanting words to express itself, and fetching its breath at every comma.

To Mons. de Coulanges.
'*Paris, Monday,* 15*th December,* (1670).

'I am going to tell you a thing, which of all things in the world is the most astonishing, the most surprising, the most marvellous, the most miraculous, the most triumphant, the most bewildering, the most unheard-of, the most singular, the most extraordinary, the most incredible, the most unexpected, the most exalting, the most humbling, the most rare, the most common, the most public, the most private (till this moment), the most brilliant, the most enviable—in short, a thing of which no example is to be found in past times; at least, nothing quite like it;—a thing which we know not how to believe in Paris; how then are you to believe it at Lyons? a thing which makes all the world cry out, "Lord have mercy on us!" a thing which has transported Madame de Rohan and Madame d'Hauterive; a thing which is to be done on Sunday, when those who see it will not believe their own eyes; a thing which is to be done on Sunday, and yet perhaps will not be finished till Monday. I cannot expect you to guess it at once. I give you a trial of three times; *do you give it up?* Well, then, I must tell you. M. de Lauzun is to marry, next Sunday, at the Louvre, guess whom? I give you four times to guess it in: I give you six: I give you a hundred. "Truly," cries Madame de Coulanges, "it must be a very difficult thing to guess; 'tis Madame de la Vallière." No, it isn't, Madam. "'Tis Mademoiselle de Retz, then?" No, it isn't, Madam; you are terribly provincial. "Oh, we are very stupid, no doubt!"

say you; "'tis Mademoiselle Colbert." Further off than ever. "Well, then, it must be Mademoiselle de Créqui?" You are not a bit nearer. Come, I see I must tell you at last. Well, M. de Lauzun marries, next Sunday, at the Louvre, with the king's permission, Mademoiselle, Mademoiselle de —— Mademoiselle —— guess the name;—he marries "MADEMOISELLE:"—the *great* Mademoiselle! Mademoiselle, the daughter of the late MONSIEUR; Mademoiselle, grand-daughter of Henry the Fourth; Mademoiselle d'Eu, Mademoiselle de Dombes, Mademoiselle de Montpensier, Mademoiselle d'Orleans, Mademoiselle, cousin-german of the King, Mademoiselle destined to the throne, Mademoiselle, the only woman in France fit to marry Monsieur. Here's pretty news for your coteries! Exclaim about it as much as you will;—let it turn your heads;—say we "lie," if you please; that it's a pretty joke; that it's "tiresome;" that we are a "parcel of ninnies." We give you leave: we have done just the same to others. Adieu! The letters that come by the post, will show whether we have been speaking truth or not.'

Never was French vivacity more gay, more spirited, more triumphant, than in this letter. There is a regular siege laid to the reader's astonishment; and the titles of the bride come like the pomp of victory. Or, to use a humbler image, the reader is thrown into the state of a child, who is told to open his mouth and shut his eyes, and wait for what God will send him. The holder of the secret hovers in front of the expectant, touching his lips and giving him nothing; and all is a merry flutter of laughter, guessing, and final transport. And yet this will not suit the charming misgiving that follows. Alas, for the poor subject of the wonder! The marriage was stopped; it was supposed to have taken place secretly; and Mademoiselle, who was then forty-five years of age, and had rejected kings, is said to have found her husband so brutal, that he one day called to her, 'Henrietta of Bourbon, pull off my boots.' The boots were left on, and the savage discarded.

The letter we give next—or rather, of which we give passages—is a good specimen of the way in which the writer goes from subject to subject;—from church to the fair, and from the fair to court, and mad dogs, and Ninon de l'Enclos, and sermons on death, and so round again to royalty, and 'a scene.' It is addressed to her daughter.

To Madame de Grignan.
'*Paris, Friday, March* 13, (1671).

'Behold me, to the delight of my heart, all alone in my chamber, writing to you in tranquillity. Nothing gives me comfort like being seated thus. I dined to-day at Madame de Lavardin's, after having been to hear Bourdaloue, where I saw the Mothers of the Church; for so I call the

Princesses de Conti and Longueville.* All the world was at the sermon, and the sermon was worthy of all that heard it. I thought of you twenty times, and wished you as often beside me. You would have been enchanted to be a listener, and I should have been tenfold enchanted to see you listen. `* * * *` We have been to the fair, to see a great fright of a woman, bigger than Riberpré by a whole head. She lay-in the other day of two vast infants, who came into the world abreast, with their arms a-kimbo. You never beheld such a *tout-ensemble!* `* * *` And now, if you fancy all the maids of honour run mad, you will not fancy amiss. Eight days ago, Madame de Ludre, Coetlogon, and little De Rouvroi were bitten by a puppy belonging to Théobon, and the puppy has died mad; so Ludre, Coetlogon, and De Rouvroi set off this morning for the coast, to be dipped three times in the sea. 'Tis a dismal journey: Benserade is in despair about it. Théobon does not choose to go, though she had a little bite too. The Queen, however, objects to her being in waiting till the issue of the adventure is known. Don't you think Ludre resembles Andromache? For my part, I see her fastened to the rock, and Treville coming, on a winged horse, to deliver her from the monster. "*Ah Zeesus! Madame de Grignan, vat a sing to pe trown, all naket, into te sea!*"†
`* * *` 'Your brother is under the jurisdiction of Ninon. I cannot think it will do him much good. There are people to whom it does no good at all. She hurt his father. Heaven help him, say I! It is impossible for Christian people, or at least for such as would fain be Christian, to look on such disorders without concern. Ah, Bourdaloue! what divine truths you told us to-day about death! Madame de la Fayette heard him for the first time in her life; and was transported with admiration. She is enchanted with your remembrances. `* * * *` A scene took place yesterday at Mademoiselle's, which I enjoyed extremely. In comes Madame de Gèvres, full of her airs and graces. She looked as if she expected I should give her my post; but, 'faith, I owed her an affront for her behaviour the other day, so I didn't budge. Mademoiselle was in bed: Madame de Gèvres was therefore obliged to go lower down: no very pleasant thing, that! Mademoiselle calls for drink; somebody must present the napkin; Madame de Gèvres begins to draw off the glove from her skinny hand; I give a nudge to Madame d'Arpajon, who was above me; she understands me, draws off her own glove, and advancing a step with a very good grace, cuts short the Duchess, and takes and presents the napkin. The Duchess was quite confounded; she had made her way up, and got off her gloves, and all to see the napkin presented before her by Ma-

dame d'Arpajon. My dear, I'm a wicked creature; I was in a state of delight; and indeed what could have been better done? Would any one but Madame de Gèvres have thought of depriving Madame d'Arpajon of an honour which fell so naturally to her share, standing as she did by the bedside? It was as good as a cordial to Madame de Puisieux. Mademoiselle did not dare to lift up her eyes; and, as for myself, I had the most good-for-nothing face!'

Had Madame de Gèvres seen the following passage in a letter of the 10th of June, in the same year, it might have tempted her to exclaim, 'Ah, you see what sort of people it is that treat me with malice!'— It must have found an echo in thousands of bosoms; and the conclusion of the extract is charming.

`* * *` 'My dear, I wish very much I could be religious. I plague La Mousse about it every day. I belong at present neither to God nor devil; and I find this condition very uncomfortable; though, between you and me, I think it the most natural in the world. One does not belong to the devil, because one fears God, and has at bottom a principle of religion; but then, on the other hand, one does not belong to God, because his laws appear hard, and self-denial is not pleasant. Hence the great number of the lukewarm, which does not surprise me at all; I enter perfectly into their reasons; only God, you know, hates them, and that must not be. But there lies the difficulty. Why must I torment you, however, with these endless rhapsodies? My dear child, *I ask your pardon*, as they say in these parts. I rattle on in your company, and forget everything else in the pleasure of it. Don't make me any answer. Send me only news of your health, with a spice of what you feel at Grignan, that I may know you are happy; that is all. Love me. We have turned the phrase into ridicule; but it is natural, it is good.'

The Abbé de la Mousse here mentioned was a connexion of the Coulangeses, and was on a visit to Madame de Sévigné at her house in Brittany, reading poetry and romance. The weather was so rainy and cold, that we of this island are pleased to see one of her letters dated from her 'fireside' on the 24th of June. Pomenars, the criminal gentleman who was always afraid of losing his head, was one of her neighbours; and another was the before-mentioned Mademoiselle du Plessis, whom the daughter's aversion and her own absurdities conspired to render the butt of the mother. It is said of Pomenars, who was a marquis, that having been tried for uttering false money, and cleared of the charge, he paid the expenses of the action in the same coin. It must have been some very counteracting good quality, however, in addition to his animal spirits, that kept

---

* Great sinners, who had become great saints.

† '*Ah, Zesu! Madame de Grignan, l'etrange sose l'être zeltée toute nue tans la mer.*' Madame de Ludre, by her pronunciation, was either a very affected speaker, or seems to have come from 'the borders.' Madame de Sévigné, by the tone of her narration, could hardly have believed there was anything serious in the accident.

his friends in good heart with him; for Madame de Sévigné never mentions him, but with an air of delight. He was, at this moment, under a charge of abduction; not, apparently, to any very great horror on the part of the ladies. Madame de Sévigné, however, tells her daughter that she talked to him about it very seriously, adding the jest, nevertheless, that the state of the dispute between him and his accuser was, that the latter wanted to 'have his head,' and Pomenars would not let him take it. 'The Marquis,' she says, in another letter, 'declined shaving till he knew to whom his head was to belong.' The last thing we remember of him is his undergoing a painful surgical operation; after which he rattled on as if nothing had happened. But then he had been the day before to Bourdaloue, to confess, for the first time during eight years. Here is the beginning of a letter, in which he and Du Plessis are brought delightfully together.

To Madame de Grignan.
' *The Rocks, Sunday, 26th July,* (1671).

' You must know, that as I was sitting all alone in my chamber yesterday, intent upon a book, I saw the door opened by a tall lady-like woman, who was ready to choke herself with laughing. Behind her came a man, who laughed louder still, and the man was followed by a very well-shaped woman, who laughed also. As for me, I began to laugh before I knew who they were, or what had set them a-laughing; and though I was expecting Madame de Chaulnes to spend a day or two with me here, I looked a long time before I could think it was she. She it was, however; and with her she had brought Pomenars, who had put it in her head to surprise me. The fair *Murinette** was of the party; and Pomenars was in such excessive spirits that he would have gladdened melancholy itself. They fell to playing battledoor and shuttlecock—Madame de Chaulnes plays it like you, and then came a lunch, and then we took one of our nice little walks, and the talk was of you throughout. I told Pomenars how you took all his affairs to heart, and what relief you would experience had he nothing to answer to but the matter in hand; but that such repeated attacks on his innocence quite overwhelmed you. We kept up this joke till the long walk reminded us of the fall you got there one day, the thought of which made me as red as fire. We talked a long time of that, and then of the dialogue with the gypsies, and at last of Mademoiselle du Plessis, and the nonsensical stuff she uttered; and how, one day, having treated you with some of it, and her ugly face being close to yours, you made no more ado, but gave her such a box on the ear as staggered her; upon which I, to soften matters, exclaimed, "How rudely these young people do play!" and then turning to her mother, said, "Madam, do

*Mademoiselle de Murinais.

you know they were so wild this morning, they absolutely fought! Mademoiselle du Plessis provoked my daughter, and my daughter beat her: it was one of the merriest scenes in the world;" and with this turn Madame du Plessis was so delighted, that she expressed her satisfaction at seeing the young ladies so happy together. This trait of good-fellowship between you and Mademoiselle du Plessis, whom I lumped together to make the box on the ear go down, made my visitors die with laughter. Mademoiselle du Murinais, in particular, approved your proceeding mightily, and vows that the first time Du Plessis thrusts her nose in her face, as she always does when she speaks to anybody, she will follow your example, and give her a good slap on the chaps. I expect them all to meet before long; Pomenars is to set the matter on foot; Mademoiselle is sure to fall in with it; a letter from Paris is to be produced, showing how the ladies there give boxes on the ears to one another, and this will sanction the custom in the provinces, and even make us desire them, in order to be in the fashion. In short, I never saw a man so mad as Pomenars: his spirits increase in the ratio of his criminalities; and, if he is charged with another, he will certainly die for joy.'

These practical mystifications of poor Mademoiselle du Plessis are a little strong. They would assuredly not take place now-a-days in society equal to that of Madame de Sévigné; but ages profit by their predecessors, and the highest breeding of one often becomes but second-rate in the next. If anything, however, could warrant such rough admission to the freedom of a superior circle, it was the coarse *platitudes* and affectations of an uncouth neighbour like this; probably of a family as vulgar as it was rich, and which had made its way into a society unfit for it. Mademoiselle du Plessis seems to have assumed all characters in turn, and to have suited none, except that of an avowed, yet incorrigible teller of fibs. Madame de Sévigné spoke to her plainly one day about these peccadilloes, and Mademoiselle cast down her eyes and said with an air of penitence, 'Ah, yes, Madame, it is very true; I am indeed the greatest liar in the world: I am very much obliged to you for telling me of it!' 'It was exactly,' says her reprover, 'like Tartuffe—quite in his tone; yes, brother, I am a miserable sinner, a vessel of iniquity.' Yet a week or two afterwards, giving an account of a family wedding-dinner, she said that the first course, for one day, included twelve hundred dishes. 'We all sate petrified,' says Madame de Sévigné. 'At length I took courage and said, "Consider a little, Mademoiselle, you must mean twelve, not twelve hundred. One sometimes has slips of the tongue." "Oh, no, Madam! it was twelve hundred, or eleven hundred, I am quite sure; I cannot say which, for fear of telling a falsehood, but one or the other I know it was;" and she repeated it twenty times, and would not bate us a single chicken. We found, upon calculation, that there must have been at least three hundred people to lard the fowls; that the dinner must have been served up in a great meadow, in tents pitched for the occasion; and that, supposing them only fifty, preparations must have been made a month beforehand.'

It is pleasant to bid adieu to Mademoiselle du Plessis, and breathe the air of truth, wit, and nature, in what has been justly called by the compiler of the work at the head of this article, one of ' Madame de Sévigné's most charming letters.* The crime of the fine gentleman servant who would not make hay, is set forth with admirable calmness and astonishment; and never before was the art of haymaking taught, or rather exemplified, in words so simple and so few. It is as if the pen itself had become a hay-fork, and tossed up a sample of the sweet grass. The pretended self-banter also, at the close, respecting long-winded narrations, is exquisite.

To M. de Coulanges.

' *The Rocks,* 22d *July,* (1671).

' I write, my dear cousin, over and above the stipulated fortnight communications, to advertise you that you will soon have the honour of seeing Picard; and, as he is brother to the lacquey of Madame de Coulanges, I must tell you the reason why. You know that Madame the Duchess de Chaulnes is at Vitré: she expects the duke there, in ten or twelve days, with the States of Brittany.† Well, and what then? say you. I say that the duchess is expecting the duke with all the states, and that meanwhile she is at Vitré all alone, dying with ennui. And what, return you, has this to do with Picard? Why, look;—she is dying with ennui, and I am her only consolation, and so you may readily conceive that I carry it with a high hand over Mademoiselle de Kerborgne and de Kerqueoison. A pretty roundabout way of telling my story, I must confess; but it will bring us to the point. Well then, as I am her only consolation, it follows that, after I have been to see her, she will come to see me, when of course I shall wish her to find my garden in good order, and my walks in good order—those fine walks, of which you are so fond. Still you are at a loss to conceive whither they are leading you now. Attend, then, if you please, to a little suggestion by the way. You are aware that haymaking is going forward? Well, I have no haymakers: I send into the neighbouring fields to press them into my service; there are none to be found; and so

all my own people are summoned to make hay instead. But do you know what haymaking is? I will tell you. Haymaking is the prettiest think in the world. You play at turning the grass over in a meadow; and as soon as you know how to do that, you know how to make hay. The whole house went merrily to the task, all but Picard: he said he would not go; that he was not engaged for such work; that it was none of his business; and that he would sooner betake himself to Paris. 'Faith! didn't I get angry? It was the hundredth disservice the silly fellow had done me: I saw he had neither heart nor zeal; in short, the measure of his offence was full. I took him at his word; was deaf as a rock to all entreaties in his behalf; and he has set off. It is fit that people should be treated as they deserve. If you see him, don't welcome him; don't protect him; and don't blame me. Only look upon him as, of all servants in the world, the one the least addicted to haymaking, and therefore the most unworthy of good treatment. This is the sum-total of the affair. As for me, I am fond of straight-forward histories, that contain not a word too much; that never go wandering about, and beginning again from remote points; and accordingly, I think I may say, without vanity, that I hereby present you with the model of an agreeable narration.'

In the course of the winter following this haymaking, Madame de Sévigné goes to Paris; and with the exception of an occasional visit to the house at Livry, to refresh herself with the spring blossoms and the nightingales, remains there till July, when she visits her daughter in Provence, where she stayed upwards of a year, and then returned to the metropolis. It is not our intention to notice these particulars in future; but we mention them in passing, to give the reader an idea of the round of her life between her town and country houses, and the visits to Madame de Grignan, who sometimes came from Provence to her. In the country, she does nothing but read, write, and walk, and occasionally see her neighbours. In town, she visits friends, theatres, churches, nunneries, and the court; is now at the Coulangeses, now dining with Rochefoucauld, now paying her respects to some branch of royalty; and is delighted and delighting wherever she goes, except when she is weeping for her daughter's absence, or condoling with the family disasters resulting from campaigns. In the summer of 1672 was the famous passage of the Rhine, at which Rochefoucauld lost a son, whose death he bore with affecting patience. The once intriguing but now devout princess, the Duchess de Longueville, had the like misfortune, which she could not endure so well. Her grief nevertheless was very affecting too, and Madame de Sévigné's plain and passionate account of it has been justly admired. In general, at the court of Louis XIV., all was apparent ease,

* The original appears in the ' Lettres Choisies,' edited by Girault.

† He was Governor of the province.

luxury, and delight, (with the exception of the jealousies of the courtiers and the squabbles of the mistresses), but every now and then there is a campaign—and then all is glory, and finery, and lovers' tears, when the warriors are setting out; and fright, and trepidation, and distracting suspense, when the news arrives of a bloody battle. The suspense is removed by undoubted intelligence; and then, while some are in paroxysms of pride and rapture at escapes, and exploits, and lucky wounds, others are plunged into misery by deaths.

Extract from a letter to Madame de Grignan.

'You never saw Paris in such a state as it is now; everybody is in tears, or fears to be so: poor Madame de Nogent is beside herself; Madame de Longueville, with her lamentations, cuts people to the heart. I have not seen her; but you may rely on what follows. * * * They sent to Port Royal for M. Arnauld and Mademoiselle Vertus to break the news to her. The sight of the latter was sufficient. As soon as the Duchess saw her—"Ah! Mademoiselle, how is my brother?" (the great Condé). She did not dare to ask further. "Madame, his wound is going on well; there has been a battle." "And my son?" No answer. "Ah! Mademoiselle, my son, my dear child—answer me—is he dead?" "Madame, I have not words to answer you." "Ah! my dear son; did he die instantly? had he not one little moment? Oh! great God, what a sacrifice!" And with that she fell upon her bed; and all which could express the most terrible anguish, convulsions, and faintings, *and a mortal silence*, and stifled cries, and the bitterest tears, and hands clasped towards heaven, and complaints the most tender and heart-rending—all this did she go through. She sees a few friends, and keeps herself barely alive, in submission to God's will; but has no rest; and her health, which was bad already, is visibly worse. For my part, I cannot help wishing her dead outright, not conceiving it possible that she can survive such a loss.'

We have taken no notice of the strange death of Vatel, steward to the Prince de Condé, who killed himself out of a point of honour, because a dinner had not been served up to his satisfaction. It is a very curious relation, but more characteristic of the poor man than of the writer. For a like reason, we omit the interesting though horrible accounts of Brinvilliers and La Voisin, the poisoners. But we cannot help giving a tragedy told in a few words, both because Madame de Sévigné was herself highly struck with it, and for another reason which will appear in a note.

'The other day, on his coming into a ball-room, a gentleman of Brittany was assassinated by two men in women's clothes. One held him while the other deliberately struck a poniard to his heart. Little Haronïs, who was there, was

shocked at beholding this person, whom he knew well, stretched out upon the ground, *full-dressed, bloody, and dead.* His account (adds Madame de Sévigné) forcibly struck my imagination.'*

The following letter contains a most graphic description of the French court, in all its voluptuous gaiety; and the glimpses which it furnishes of the actors on the brilliant scene, from the king and the favourite to Dangeau, the skilful gamester—cool, collected, and calculating—amidst the gallant prattle around him, give to its details a degree of life and animation not to be surpassed :—

To Madame de Grignan.

'*Paris, Wednesday, 29th July,* (1676).

'We have a change of the scene here, which will gratify you as much as it does all the world. I was at Versailles last Saturday with the Villarses. You know the Queen's toilet, the mass, and the dinner? Well, there is no need any longer of suffocating ourselves in the crowd to get a glimpse of their majesties at table. At three the King, the Queen, Monsieur, Madame, Mademoiselle, and everything else which is royal, together with Madame de Montespan and train, and all the courtiers, and all the ladies—all, in short, which constitutes the court of France—is assembled in that beautiful apartment of the king's, which you remember. All is furnished divinely, all is magnificent. Such a thing as heat is unknown; you pass from one place to another without the slightest pressure. A game at *reversis* gives the company a form and a settlement. The King and Madame de Montespan keep a bank together: different tables are occupied by Monsieur, the Queen, and Madame de Soubise, Dangeau and party, Langlée and party:—everywhere you see heaps of *louis d'ors;* they have no other counters. I saw Dangeau play, and thought what fools we all were beside him. He dreams of nothing but what concerns the game; he wins where others lose; he neglects nothing, profits by everything,

---

* We have taken the words in Italics from the version of the letters published in 1765, often a very meritorious one, probably 'by various hands,' some passages exhibiting an ignorance of the commonest terms hardly possible to be reconciled with a knowledge of the rest. The three special words above quoted are admirable, and convey a truer sense of the original than would have been attained by one more literal. The passage in Madame de Sévigné is *tout étendu, tout chaud, tout sanglant, tout habillé, tout mort.* We take the opportunity of observing that some of the directly comic as well as tragic relations in this version are rendered with great gusto; though it could not save us the necessity of attempting a new one—owing to the want of a certain life in the general tone, as well as an occasional obsoleteness of phraseology, somewhat startling to observe in so short a lapse of time as seventy-seven years. There is another version of a later date, and containing more letters; but though not destitute of pretensions of its own, it is upon the whole much inferior to the older one, of which it mainly appears to be a copy.

† The writer of the well-known Court-Diary,

never has his attention diverted; in short, his science bids defiance to chance. Two hundred thousand francs in ten days, a hundred thousand crowns in a month—these are the pretty memorandums he puts down in his pocket-book. He was kind enough to say that I was partners with him, so that I got an excellent seat. I made my obeisance to the King, as you told me; and he returned it, as if I had been young and handsome. The Queen talked as long to me about my illness, as if I had been a lying-in. The Duke said a thousand kind things without minding a word he uttered. Marshal de Lorges attacked me in the name of the Chevalier-de Grignan ; in short, *tutti quanti* (the whole company.) You know what it is to get a word from everybody you meet. Madame de Montespan talked to me of Bourbon, and asked me how I liked Vichi, and whether the place did me good. She said that Bourbon, instead of curing a pain in one of her knees, did mischief to both. Her size is reduced by a good half, and yet her complexion, her eyes, and her lips, are as fine as ever. She was dressed all in French point, her hair in a thousand ringlets, the two side ones hanging low on her cheeks, black ribbons on her head, pearls (the same that belonged to Madame de l'Hôpital), the loveliest diamond ear-rings, three or four bodkins—nothing else on the head ; in short, a triumphant beauty, worthy the admiration of all the foreign ambassadors. She was accused of preventing the whole French nation from seeing the King ; she has restored him, you see, to their eyes ; and you cannot conceive the joy it has given all the world, and the splendour it has thrown upon the court. This charming confusion, without confusion, of all which is the most select, continues from three till six. If couriers arrive, the King retires a moment to read the despatches, and returns. There is always some music going on to which he listens, and which has an excellent effect. He talks with such of the ladies as are accustomed to enjoy that honour. In short, they leave play at six; there is no trouble of counting, for there is no sort of counters; the pools consist of at least five, perhaps six or seven hundred louis ; the bigger ones of a thousand or twelve hundred. At first each person pools twenty, which is a hundred; and the dealer afterwards pools ten. The person who holds the knave is entitled to four louis ; they pass ; and when they play before the pool is taken, they forfeit sixteen, which teaches them not to play out of turn. Talking is incessantly going on, and there is no end of *hearts.* How many hearts have you ? I have two, I have three, I have one, I have four; he has only three then, he has only four;—and Dangeau is delighted with all this chatter ; he sees through the game—he draws his conclusions—he discovers which is the person he wants; truly he is your only man for holding the cards. At six, the carriages are at the door. The King is in one of them with Madame de Montespan, Monsieur and Madame de Thianges, and honest d'Heudicourt in a fool's paradise on the stool. You know how these open carriages are made; they do not sit face to face, but all looking the same way. The Queen occupies another with the Princess ; and the rest come flocking after as

it may happen. There are then gondolas on the canal, and music ! and at ten they come back, and then there is a play ; and twelve strikes, and they go to supper ; and thus rolls round the Saturday. If I were to tell you how often you are asked after—how many questions were put to me without waiting for answers—how often I neglected to answer—how little they cared, and how much less I did you would see the *iniqua corte* (wicked court) before you in all its perfection. However, it never was so pleasant before, and everybody wishes it may last.'

Not a word of the *morale* of the spectacle ! Madame de Sévigné, who had one of the correctest reputations in France, wishes even it may last. *Iniqua corte* is a mere jesting phrase, applied to any court. Montespan was a friend of the family, though it knew Maintenon also, who was then preparing the downfall of the favourite. The latter, meantime, was a sort of vice-queen, reigning over the real one. When she journeyed, it was with a train of forty people ; governors of provinces offered to meet her with addresses ; and intendants presented her with boats like those of Cleopatra, painted and gilt, luxurious with crimson damask, and streaming with the colours of France and Navarre. Louis was such a god at that time—he shook ' his ambrosial curls' over so veritable an Olympus, where his praises were hymned by loving goddesses, consenting heroes, and incense-bearing priests—that if marriage had been a less consecrated institution in the Catholic Church, and the Jesuits with their accommodating philosophy would have stood by him, one is almost tempted to believe he might have crowned half-a-dozen queens at a time, and made the French pulpits hold forth with Milton, on the merits of the patriarchal polygamies.

But, to say the truth, except when she chose to be in the humour for it, great part of Madame de Sévigné's enjoyment, wherever she was, looked as little to the *morale* of the thing as need be. It arose from her powers of discernment and description. No matter what kind of scene she beheld, whether exalted or humble, brilliant or gloomy, crowded or solitary, her sensibility turned all to account. She saw well for herself; and she knew, that what she saw she should enjoy over again, in telling it to her daughter. In the autumn of next year she is in the country, and pays a visit to an iron-foundery, where they made anchors. The scene is equally well felt with that at court. It is as good, in its way, as the blacksmith's in Spenser's 'House of Care,' where the sound was heard

" Of many iron hammers, beating rank,
    And answering their weary turns around;"

and where the visitor is so glad to get away

from the giant and his 'strong grooms,' all over smoke and horror.

Extract of a Letter to Madame de Grignan.
.' *Friday,* 1*st October,* (1677).

* * * 'Yesterday evening at Cone, we descended into a veritable hell, the true forges of Vulcan. Eight or ten cyclops were at work, forging, not arms for Æneas, but anchors for ships. You never saw strokes redoubled so justly, nor with so admirable a cadence. We stood in the middle of four furnaces, and the demons came passing about us, all melting in sweat, with pale faces, wild-staring eyes, savage mustaches, and hair long and black; a sight enough to frighten less well-bred folks than ourselves. As to me, I could not comprehend the possibility of refusing anything which these gentlemen, in their hell, might have chosen to exact. We got out at last, by the help of a shower of silver, with which we took care to refresh their souls and facilitate our exit.'

This description is immediately followed by one as lively, of another sort.

'We had a taste, the evening before, at Nevers, of the most daring race you ever beheld. Four fair ladies, in a carriage, having seen us pass them in ours, had such a desire to behold our faces a second time, that they must needs get before us again, on a causeway made only for one coach. My dear, their coachman brushed our very whiskers; it is a mercy they were not pitched into the river; we all cried out 'for God's sake;' they, for their parts, were dying with laughter; and they kept galloping on *above* us and before us, in so tremendous and unaccountable a manner, that we have not got rid of the fright to this moment.'

There is a little repetition in the following, because truth required it; otherwise it is all as good as new, fresh from the same mint that throws forth everything at a heat—whether anchors, or diamond ear-rings, or a coach in a gallop.

'*Paris,* 29*th November,* (1679.)
* * * 'I have been to the wedding of Madame de Louvois. How shall I describe it? Magnificence, illuminations, all France, dresses all gold and brocade, jewels, braziers full of fire, and stands full of flowers, confusions of carriages, cries out of doors, flambeaus, pushings back, people knocked up;—in short, a whirlwind, a distraction; questions without answers, compliments without knowing what is said, civilities without knowing who is spoken to, feet entangled in trains. From the middle of all this, issue inquiries after your health; which, not being answered as quick as lightning, the inquirers pass on, contented to remain in the state of ignorance and indifference in which they were made. O *vanity of vanities!* Pretty little De Mouchy has had the small-pox. O *vanity,* et cetera!'

In Boswell's 'Life of Johnson' is a reference by the great and gloomy moralist to a passage in Madame de Sévigné, in which she speaks of existence having been imposed upon her without her consent; but the conclusion he draws from it as to her opinion of life in general, is worthy of the critic who 'never read books through.' The momentary effusion of spleen is contradicted by the whole correspondence. She occasionally vents her dissatisfaction at a rainy day, or the perplexity produced in her mind by a sermon; and when her tears begin flowing for a pain in her daughter's little finger, it is certainly no easy matter to stop them; but there was a luxury at the heart of this woe. Her ordinary notions of life were no more like Johnson's, than rose-colour is like black, or health like disease. She repeatedly proclaims, and almost always shows, her delight in existence; and has disputes with her daughter, in which she laments that she does not possess the same turn of mind. There is a passage, we grant, on the subject of old age, which contains a reflection similar to the one alluded to by Johnson, and which has been deservedly admired for its force and honesty. But even in this passage, the germ of the thought was suggested by the melancholy of another person, not by her own. Madame de la Fayette had written her a letter urging her to retrieve her affairs, and secure her health, by accepting some money from her friends, and quitting the Rocks for Paris;—offers which, however handsomely meant, she declined with many thanks, and not a little secret indignation; for she was very jealous of her independence. In the course of this letter, Madame de la Fayette, who herself was irritable with disease, and who did not write it in a style much calculated to prevent the uneasiness it caused, made abrupt use of the words, 'You are old.' The little hard sentence came like a blow upon the lively, elderly lady. She did not like it at all; and thus wrote of it to her daughter:—

'So you were struck with the expression of Madame de la Fayette, blended with so much friendship. 'Twas a truth, I own, which I ought to have borne in mind; and yet I must confess it astonished me, for I do not yet perceive in myself any such decay. Nevertheless I cannot help making many reflections and calculations, and I find the conditions of life hard enough. It seems to me that I have been dragged, against my will, to the fatal period when old age must be endured; I see it; I have come to it; and I would fain, if I could help it, not go any further; not advance a step more in the road of infirmities, of pains, of losses of memory, of *disfigurements* ready to do me outrage; and I hear a voice which says, You must go on in spite of yourself; or, if you will not go on, you must die:—and this is another extremity, from which nature revolts. Such is the lot, however, of all who advance beyond middle life. What is their resource? To think of the will of God and of the universal law; and so restore reason to its place, and be patient. Be you then patient, accordingly, my dear child, and let not your affections often into such tears as reason must condemn.'

The whole heart and good sense of humanity seem to speak in passages like these, equally removed from the frights of the superstitious, and the flimsiness or falsehood of levity. The ordinary comfort and good prospects of Madame de Sévigné's existence, made her write with double force on these graver subjects, when they presented themselves to her mind. So, in her famous notice of the death of Louvois the minister—never, in a few words, were past ascendency and sudden nothingness more impressively contrasted.

' I am so astonished at the news of the sudden death of M. de Louvois, that I am at a loss how to speak of it. Dead, however, he is, this great minister, this potent being, who occupied so great a place; whose *me*, (*le moi*), as M. Nicole says, had so wide a dominion; who was the centre of so many orbs. What affairs had he not to manage! what designs, what projects, what secrets! what interests to unravel, what wars to undertake, what intrigues, what noble games at chess to play and to direct! Ah! my God, give me a little time; I want to give check to the Duke of Savoy—checkmate to the Prince of Orange. No, no, you shall not have a moment —not a single moment. Are events like these to be talked of? Not they. We must reflect upon them in our closets.'

This is part of a letter to her cousin Coulanges, written in the year 1691. Five years afterwards she died.

The two English writers who have shown the greatest admiration of Madame de Sévigné, are Horace Walpole and Sir James Mackintosh. The enthusiasm of Walpole, who was himself a distinguished letter-writer and wit, is mixed up with a good deal of self-love. He bows to his own image in the mirror beside her. During one of his excursions to Paris, he visits the Hôtel de Carnavalet and the house at Livry; and has thus described his impressions, after his half-good half-affected fashion:—

' Madame de Chabot I called on last night. She was not at home, but the Hôtel de Carnavalet was; and I stopped on purpose to say an Ave-Maria before it.' (This pun is suggested by one in Bussy-Rabutin). ' It is a very singular building, not at all in the French style, and looks like an *ex voto*, raised to her honour by some of her foreign votaries. I don't think her half honoured enough in her own country.'*

* *Letters, &c.* Vol. v., p. 74, Edit. 1840.

His visit to Livry is recorded in a letter to his friend Montague:—

' One must be just to all the world. Madame Roland, I find, has been in the country, and at Versailles, and was so obliging as to call on me this morning; but I was so disobliging as not to be awake. I was dreaming dreams; in short, I had dined at Livry; yes, yes, at Livry, with a Langlade and De la Rochefoucauld. The abbey is now possessed by an Abbé de Malherbe, with whom I am acquainted, and who had given me a general invitation. I put it off to the last moment, that the *bois* and *allées* might set off the scene a little, and contribute to the vision; but it did not want it. Livry is situate in the Forêt de Bondi, very agreeably on a flat, but with hills near it, and in prospect. There is a great air of simplicity and *rural* about it, more regular than our taste, but with an old-fashioned tranquillity, and nothing of *colifichet*, (frippery). Not a tree exists that remembers the charming woman, because in this country an old tree is a traitor, and forfeits his head to the crown: but the plantations are not young, and might very well be as they were in her time. The Abbé's house is decent and snug; a few paces from it is the sacred pavilion built for Madame de Sévigné by her uncle, and much as it was in her day; a small saloon below for dinner, then an arcade, but the niches now closed, and painted in fresco with medallions of her, the Grignan, the Fayette, and the Rochefoucauld. Above, a handsome large room, with a chimneypiece in the best taste of Louis the Fourteenth's time; a Holy Family in good relief over it, and the cipher of her uncle Coulanges; a neat little bedchamber within, and two or three clean little chambers over them. On one side of the garden, leading to the great road, is a little bridge of wood, on which the dear woman used to wait for the courier that brought her daughter's letters. Judge with what veneration and satisfaction I set my foot upon it! If you will come to France with me next year, we will go and sacrifice on that sacred spot together.'—*Id.* p. 142.

Sir James Mackintosh became intimate with the letters of Madame de Sévigné during his voyage from India, and has left some remarks upon them in the Diary published in his Life.

' The great charm,' he says, ' of her character seems to me a *natural* virtue. In what she does, as well as in what she says, she is unforced and unstudied; nobody, I think, had so much morality without constraint, and played so much with amiable feelings without falling into vice. Her ingenious, lively, social disposition, gave the direction to her mental power. She has so filled my heart with affectionate interest in her as a living friend, that I can scarcely bring myself to think of her as a writer, or as having a style; but she has become a celebrated, perhaps an immortal writer, without expecting it: she is the only classical writer who never conceived the possibility of acquiring fame. Without a great force of style, she could not have communicated those feelings. In what does that talent consist? It seems mainly to consist in the power of working bold metaphors, and unexpected turns of expression, out of the most familiar part of conversational language.'*

Sir James proceeds to give an interesting analysis of this kind of style, and the way in which it obtains ascendency in the most polished circles; and all that he says of it is very true. But it seems to us, that the main secret of the 'charm' of Madame de Sévigné is to be found neither in her 'natural virtue,' nor in the style in which it expressed itself, but in something which interests us still more for our own sakes than the writer's, and which instinctively compelled her to adopt that style as its natural language. We doubt extremely, in the first place, whether any great 'charm' is ever felt in her virtue, natural or otherwise, however it may be respected. Readers are glad, certainly, that the correctness of her reputation enabled her to write with so much gaiety and boldness; and perhaps (without at all taking for granted what Bussy-Rabutin intimates about secret lovers) it gives a zest to certain freedoms in her conversation, which are by no means rare; for she was anything but a prude. We are not sure that her character for personal correctness does not sometimes produce even an awkward impression, in connection with her relations to the court and the mistresses; though the manners of the day, and her superiority to sermonizing and hypocrisy, relieve it from one of a more painful nature. Certain we are, however, that we should have liked her still better, had she manifested a power to love somebody else besides her children; had she married again, for instance, instead of passing a long widowhood from her five-and-twentieth year, not, assuredly, out of devotion to her husband's memory. Such a marriage, we think, would have been quite as natural as any virtue she possessed. The only mention of her husband that we recollect in all her correspondence, with the exception of the allusion to Ninon, is in the following date of a letter:—

'Paris, Friday, Feb. 5, 1672. This day thousand years I was married.'

We do not accuse her of heartlessness. We believe she had a very good heart. Probably, she liked to be her own mistress; but this does not quite explain the matter in so loving a person. There were people in her own time who doubted the love for her daughter—surely with great want of justice. But natural as that virtue was, and delightful as it is to see it, was the *excess* of it quite so

natural? or does a thorough intimacy with the letters confirm our belief in that excess? It does not. The love was real and great; but the secret of what appears to be its extravagance is, perhaps, to be found in the love of power; or, not to speak harshly, in the inability of a fond mother to leave off her habits of guidance and dictation, and the sense of her importance to her child. Hence a fidgetiness on one side, which was too much allied to exaction and self-will, and a proportionate tendency to ill-concealed, and at last open impatience on the other. The demand for letters was not only incessant and avowed; it was to be met with as zealous a desire, on the daughter's part, to supply them. If little is written, pray write more: if much, don't write so much for fear of headaches. If the headaches are complained of, what misery! if not complained of, something worse and more cruel has taken place—it is a concealment. Friends must take care how they speak of the daughter as too well and happy. The mother then brings to our mind the Falkland of Sheridan, and expresses her disgust at these 'perfect health folks.' Even lovers tire under such *surveillance;* and as affections between mother and child, however beautiful, are not, in the nature of things, of a like measure of reciprocity, a similar result would have been looked for by the discerning eyes of Madame de Sévigné, had the case been any other than her own. But the tears of self-love mingle with those of love, and blind the kindest natures to the difference. It is too certain, or rather it is a fact which reduces the love to a good honest natural size, and therefore ought not, so far, to be lamented, that this fond mother and daughter, fond though they were, jangled sometimes, like their inferiors, both when absent and present, leaving nevertheless a large measure of affection to diffuse itself in joy and comfort over the rest of their intercourse. It is a common case, and we like neither of them a jot the less for it. We may only be allowed to repeat our wish (as Madame de Grignan must often have done) that the 'dear Marie de Rabutin,' as Sir James Mackintosh calls her, had had a second husband, to divert some of the responsibilities of affection from her daughter's head. Let us recollect, after all, that we should not have heard of the distress but for the affection; that millions who might think fit to throw stones at it, would in reality have no right to throw a pebble; and that the wit which has rendered it immortal, is beautiful for every species of truth, but this single deficiency in self-knowledge.

That is the great charm of Madame de Sévigné—*truth.* Truth, wit, and animal

---

* *Memoirs of the Life of the Right Hon. Sir James Mackintosh.* Sec. Edit., Vol. ii., p. 217.

spirits compose the secret of her delightfulness; but truth above all, for it is that which shows all the rest to be true. If she had not more natural virtues than most other good people, she had more natural *manners ;* and the universality of her taste, and the vivacity of her spirits, giving her the widest range of enjoyment, she expressed herself naturally on all subjects, and did not disdain the simplest and most familiar phraseology, when the truth required it. Familiarities of style, taken by themselves, have been common more or less to all wits, from the days of Aristophanes to those of Byron ; and, in general, so have animal spirits, Rabelais was full of both. The followers of Pulci and Berni, in Italy, abound in them. What distinguishes Madame de Sévigné is, first, that she was a woman so writing, which till her time had been a thing unknown, and has not since been witnessed in any such charming degree ; and second, and above all, that she writes ' the truth, the whole truth, and nothing but the truth ;' never giving us falsehood of any kind, not even a single false metaphor, or only half-true simile or description : nor writing for any purpose on earth, but to say what she felt, and please those who could feel with her. If we consider how few writers there are, even among the best, to whom this praise, in its integrity, can apply, we shall be struck, perhaps, with a little surprise and sorrow for the craft of authors in general ; but certainly with double admiration for Madame de Sévigné. We do not mean to say that she is always right in opinion, or that she had no party or conventional feelings. She entertained, for many years, some strong prejudices. She was bred up in so exclusive an admiration for the poetry of Corneille, that she thought Racine would go out of fashion. Her loyalty made her astonished to find that Louis was not invincible ; and her connexion with the Count de Grignan, who was employed in the *dragonades* against the Huguenots, led her but negatively to disapprove those inhuman absurdities. But these were accidents of friendship or education ; nor did they hinder her, meantime, from describing truthfully what she felt, and from being right as well as true in nine-tenths of it all. Her sincerity made even her errors a part of her truth. She never pretended to be above what she felt ; never assumed a profound knowledge ; never disguised an ignorance. Her mirth, and her descriptions, may sometimes appear exaggerated ; but the spirit of truth, not of contradiction, is in them ; and excess in such cases is not falsehood, but enjoyment—not the wine adulterated, but the cup running over. All

her wit is healthy ; all its images entire and applicable throughout—not palsy-stricken with irrelevance ; not forced in, and then found wanting, like Walpole's conceit about the trees, in the passage above quoted. Madame de Sévigné never wrote such a passage in her life. All her lightest and most fanciful images, all her most daring expressions, have the strictest propriety, the most genuine feeling, a home in the heart of truth ;—as when, for example, she says, amidst continual feasting, that she is ' famished for want of hunger;' that there were no 'interlineations' in the conversation of a lady who spoke from the heart : that she went to vespers one evening out of pure opposition, which taught her to comprehend the ' sacred obstinacy of martyrdom ;' that she did not keep a ' philosopher's shop ;' that it is difficult for people in trouble to ' bear thunder-claps of bliss in others.' It is the same from the first letter we have quoted to the last ; from the proud and merry boasting of the young mother with a boy, to the candid shudder about the approach of old age, and the refusal of death to grant a moment to the dying statesman—'no, not a single moment.' She loved nature and truth without misgiving; and nature and truth loved her in return, and have crowned her with glory and honour.

Art. VII.—*The Biographical Dictionary of the Society for the Diffusion of Useful Knowledge.* 8vo. Vol. I. Part I. London : 1842.

Although it is not our habit to notice any part of a new publication until the undertaking, if it consist of successive volumes, is completed, we think it a duty not to pass unnoticed the first step which the *Society for the Diffusion of Useful Knowledge* has taken towards adequately supplying the want long felt in English literature, of a carefully prepared Universal Biography ; because we consider this to be a work of paramount usefulness, and such as, in all probability, only an extensive Association could undertake. The design reflects the highest credit upon those who direct the concerns of the Body ; and if it is honestly completed, and in a style corresponding to the sample before us, it will carry the name of the undertakers with merited honour to every quarter of the lettered world. That it will, at any rate, be *completed*, the fact of its being set on foot by such a Society, may be taken as a sufficient guarantee ; and this is a circumstance of the utmost importance to the public, as it does away all the unpleasant apprehensions that must attend so extensive a publication, if commenced by one or a few individuals. It is on this account particularly that we now notice it, in order that it may have all the publicity, and, in as far as the design is concerned, all the recommendation that this Journal can afford it.

Down to the latter part of the seventeenth century, biographical works were confined to particular classes; the most elaborate of them relating to Ecclesiastics. Thus the *Acta Sanctorum Omnium*, written by Flemish Jesuits, and of which the first part appeared at Antwerp in 1643, extends to no less than fifty-three folio volumes; and Tillemont's *Mémoires pour servir à l'Histoire Ecclesiastique des six premiers Siècles de l'Eglise*, published at Paris in 1693, to sixteen quarto volumes.

Nor has English literature been altogether deficient in biographical works, limited to particular objects. Of these, the widest in its range is the *Biographia Britannica*, or the lives of 'the most eminent persons who have flourished in Great Britain and Ireland from the earliest ages to the present time.' The first edition was completed in five volumes folio, in 1766; and about twelve years afterwards, Dr. Andrew Kippis, with the aid of Lord Hardwicke, (the author of the *Athenian Letters*), Lord Hailes, Dr. Percy, Bishop of Dromore, Dr. Douglas, Bishop of Salisbury, Sir William Blackstone, and other eminent persons, undertook a new edition, which was carried down to the letter F, but no further. The loss, to our historical literature, by the failure of this greatly improved and extended edition, was considerable.

It was in the year 1673 that Moréri's *Grand Dictionnaire, Historique et Critique*, a work mainly biographical, appeared; and it was extended in many subsequent editions during the succeeding eighty years to ten times its original bulk. Bayle's *Dictionnaire, Historique et Critique*, so justly celebrated, was at first intended only as a supplement to Moréri: it is almost entirely biographical, and the last edition of it extends to seventeen octavo volumes. Of both Moréri and Bayle, translations or abridgments had been published in England before the middle of the last century; and both were incorporated, with many additions, in the well-known 'General Historical Dictionary,' compiled by Dr. Birch and others, and published in ten volumes folio.

At length there appeared in France, under the title of *Biographie Universelle*, a biographical Dictionary aiming at Universality, and aided by the literary contributions of the most distinguished writers in France, in fifty-two octavo volumes, completed in 1828. Since that time a supplement has been begun, of which twenty volumes have already appeared. Although unequal in the merit of its articles—an evil unavoidable in works of great extent by various authors—and although deficient in information concerning the obscurer persons whose lives one especially desires to find treated in a biographical dictionary, on account of the difficulty of finding elsewhere information concerning them, the *Biographie Universelle* is a work of which France has just reason to be proud—whether on account of the greatness of the undertaking, or the manner in which it has been executed.

We are reluctant to turn from this monument of the learning, talents, and assiduity of our neighbours, to the only corresponding publication which we can mention in our own language—namely, 'Chalmers's Biographical Dictionary,' completed in 1817, after a hurried publication of only five years, in thirty two octavo volumes—a bulk into which it had grown from its original size in 1761-7, when, under the name of the 'English General Biographical Dictionary,' it was published in twelve volumes.

Chalmers's compilation contains many lives valuable for their accuracy and their learning; but these were chiefly transferred from other works, particularly that on which his own was built; for the new contributions, though not invariably bad, are not such as can satisfy either the learned or the general reader. They often evince a narrow and intolerant spirit, and have, in a word, no authority.

Far superior, in point of ability and execution, was a work which, though by a few years earlier, we mention after that of Chalmers, because not in its plan *universal*. We here refer to the work conducted by Dr. John Aikin, and published under the title of 'General Biography, or Lives, critical and historical, of the most eminent persons of all ages, countries, conditions, and professions, arranged according to alphabetical order.' The Rev. Dr. William Enfield, the learned and skilful abridger of Brucker's 'History of Philosophy,' had been originally associated in the editorship, but he died at an early period of the progress of the work; and most and the best of the lives were written by the surviving editor. But a great many, of very considerable ability, though perhaps of less elegance, were contributed by various other writers, particularly the Rev. Thomas Morgan, Mr. Nicolson, and Mr. William Johnston. This work, which is by some thought to be a little tinged by sectarian prejudices, extended to eight quarto volumes; but these unfortunately did not complete it by exhausting the alphabet, as the volume last published closes with the life of Samuel, the Hebrew Judge and prophet. The first of these volumes appeared in the year 1799, the eighth in 1813.

These meagre notices are not introduced certainly as a completed piece of literary history, but merely as helping to show the magnitude of that *desideratum* in our literature which the *Society for the Diffusion of Useful Knowledge* (never perhaps so well deserving the title) has undertaken to supply. It may now be expected that we should say a word or two in regard to that commencing portion of the undertaking here presented to us.

It is, notwithstanding, scarcely possible, and it would, in fact, be extremely unsatisfactory, to select, in this half volume, any particular lives calculated to serve as samples of the whole. The space occupied by any one memoir, in a Biographical Dictionary which aims at universality and completeness, ought to be so small as to admit little of that discursiveness and dissertation which often destroys all proportion among the articles of the *Biographie Universelle ;* and if we here found long and elaborate lives, we should fear that they must extend the dictionary to an inconvenient bulk, or that to them must be sacrificed lives, without which it would have no claim to completeness. The lives, however, of Abelard, Pope Adrian, Sir Ralph Abercromby, the late Mr. Abernethy, and President Adams, may be mentioned, among many others, as equally interesting by their fulness and instructive by their accuracy. Among other peculiar recommendations which the practised inquirer will discover, may be mentioned the introduction of many lives, on which little or no information is to be obtained elsewhere—as the oriental, and particularly the Arabic articles, the Hebrew and the Scriptural articles. The freedom from all party and sectarian bias, is a merit of a far higher order, here easily to be discerned; thus furnishing a reasonable and strong presumption that the work will, throughout, possess this grand historical requisite.

One part of the Society's plan deserves peculiar commendation, on account both of its usefulness to the student, and of the security which it affords, that the authors have resorted to the best sources for their information—we mean the ample and exact list of authorities at the foot of each article. Although the name of the writer of a life is annexed to it, nothing can be less satisfactory to the reader than to find a number of facts related, without any means of ascertaining the truth within the author's reach; and without any indication of the sources to which an inquisitive reader may wish to resort for further knowledge. The want of this is a cardinal defect in the *Biographie Universelle,* as well as in Chalmers. Some of that extensive selection of lives contained in the new edition of the *Encyclopædia Britannica,* furnish highly commendable examples of this great recommendation ; whilst others, particularly those contributed to that work by the late Dr. Young—illustrious both as a man of Science and of Letters—may help to point out another most useful requisite, that of carefully indicating every acknowledged piece of an author, *however small,* and whether published separately, or in Transactions and Journals.

The greatest difficulty which the learned editor of this Dictionary (Professor Long) will have to encounter, is perhaps the acquiring of accurate and impartial information concerning persons who have lived in, or near our own times. In the lives of such persons, there will, too, be a perpetual tendency to give an undue extension, besides the greater danger of running into unfair censure or panegyric. On these tendencies, the eye of the Editor must be vigilantly fixed, and his authority to repress vigorously exercised. The lives of Lord Chief-Justice Abbot, of his namesake the Speaker, of the ingenious and accomplished architects Robert and James Adam, and of their amiable and venerable kinsman the Lord Chief Commissioner of the Scottish Jury Court, may be pointed out as laudably avoiding these faults.

The great importance of this undertaking we have already adverted to ; and it is one which in a peculiar manner recommends it to this Society; as there can be no more effectual means devised of diffusing knowledge, in an agreeable form, in every department of human exertion.

The expediency of a numerous Association undertaking such a work has also been already stated. Not only must it occasion a heavy temporary loss, of which no individual can be expected to run the risk; but the powers of inspection, and of correction, possessed by fifty or sixty persons, of various habits of thinking and kinds of information, give the public the best chance of truth being pursued and error avoided. Having thus hailed, with a hearty welcome, the appearance of a work which we had long wished, rather than hoped to see commenced by competent undertakers, we shall not fail to keep an eye upon its progress; and to point out any failures or backslidings that may appear to be departures from its design and spirit, and likely to interfere with the objects of its enlightened promoters.

Art. VIII.—1. *Financial Statement of Sir Robert Peel, made* 11*th March,* 1842. London, 1842.

2. *Speech of Charles Wood, Esq., M.P., on the Duty on Foreign Wool.* 1842.

3. *Speeches of Viscount Palmerston, on Wednesday,* 10*th May, and* 21*st July,* 1842. Ridgways, 1842.

Political and party triumphs differ as much in principle as in degree. By some, the mere possession of office, and the personal advantages either enjoyed or expected, are considered a party triumph. This is but low selfishness, however it may assume the disguise of public spirit. To others, party success is understood to represent the overthrow of a political opponent, and the acquisition of power by a friend. This, although raised above selfishness, is yet below true patriotism. It is the glory of the strife, and the exultation of victory :—*la gloria maggior dopo il periglio.* It resembles rather the reward ' reaped in the iron harvests of the field,' than the nobler crown which bears the inscription *ob cives servatos.* A higher and a nobler triumph is that, of which the accession of Lord Grey to power, in November, 1830, affords the most brilliant example. On that occasion the change of the government was secondary to the alteration of policy ; and the success of the Whigs was forgotten in the success of that cause which adopted as its principles Reform, Peace, and Retrenchment ;—principles carried into effect by Lord Grey in every act of his administration. In a case like this, party triumph is exalted, yet the feelings it excites are not unmixed. It is impossible to forget, that the power which is used for the benefit of others is yet possessed by ourselves. Pre-eminence, admitted superiority over the fallen enemy, are all claimed by the victorious party ; and the success of a good measure is not the less felt, when it is announced amidst the exulting cheers following a triumphant division. In each of the cases we have described, selfish feeling and personal motives may, and at times must enter ; and these, like the alloy spoken of by Lord Bacon, though making the metal of party work better, yet debase it.

To render party triumph pure, it should be separated from all these grosser substances. If reduced to a triumph of principle only—if the success attained is that of sound opinion, if the benefits we receive are gained by us as members of the community and not as members of a party, if they are shared with all our fellow-citizens, if their ultimate tendency is to benefit all our fellow-men, and if freed from all the biasses of gratified ambition—it

appears to us, that in this case political success partakes of the nature of a moral triumph ; and that it is of all triumphs the most exalted and the most enduring. Nor is it true that, in assigning this superiority to the success of party principles, as distinguished from the possession of political power, there is any over-refinement of doctrine. Our political affection is not a mere Platonism. In reality, we shall embrace the Juno, and not the cloud ; for we confidently believe that a party giving those generous impulses to their country, which practically advance the cause of liberty, knowledge, civilisation, and truth, will receive, as they deserve, from their contemporaries, and still more certainly from posterity, the reward of fame and gratitude ; whilst those who become the passive and frequently the reluctant slaves of circumstances —men who change their course while they adhere to their opinions—may, by dexterous shiftings of the sail and trimming of the ballast, keep a crazy boat afloat, or preserve a discontented crew from open mutiny ; but must lessen, if they do not forfeit, their claim on the respect and confidence of those fellowmen in whose sight they are acting, and for whose benefit they are bound to act.

The general observations we have made, apply in a most remarkable degree to the events of the Last Session. We know not whether the great victory of the Reform Bill, the success of the Municipal Act, the repeal of all laws imposing civil disqualifications for religious opinions, have been triumphs practically greater than those which may be claimed on behalf of Liberal opinions during the session of 1842. We are quite prepared for the scoffing reply of our political opponents. They will tell us, that it is to them, and to them only, that is justly due all that has been achieved. They will tell us, that as their leaders carried Catholic emancipation in 1829, so they have laid the foundation of commercial freedom in 1842. We thank them for their illustration, and we most fully admit its analogy. One which more entirely confirms our argument could not well be found. In that glorious procession which ushered in eight millions of our countrymen within the pale of the constitution, it is true that the Tory leaders were most prominent figures. But let the impartial historian decide in what character they appeared. On the car of triumph were raised the images of Fox and of Grattan, surrounded by those living statesmen who justly claimed an identity of principle, and who personified the victory which had been won. Their opponents seemed less the conquerors, than the slaves who had surrendered to force ; or they could be considered but as mercenary troops at the best, who, deserting their ancient standards, had passed over to the enemy's ranks, at the dictation of their *Condottieri.* Nor was this change of position effected without the curses loud and deep, and the bitter scoff, and the contemptuous ridicule of their former and more consistent comrades. The disgrace and ignominy were somewhat mitigated by the generous forbearance of those to whom the triumph was in reality due. Those who had made every sacrifice but that of principle for the Catholic cause, might well afford to pass over in silence the conduct of those who in 1829 were willing to sacrifice their former principle and their friends, but who declined making any other sacrifice. If the Catholic question is the precedent relied on in justification of the events of 1842, on the grounds which we have stated we fully admit its force and its applicability.

Do we then blame Sir Robert Peel's government in 1842, any more than the Duke of Wellington's cabinet of 1829? We do not blame; but neither can we commend. In both cases, the men have been compelled to yield to events. In the history of states, there are periods in which words when spoken cannot be recalled; there are measures which, however stigmatized, none but the most frantic partisans can dream of repealing. Further, these measures and declarations, if founded on just principles, become the abundant source of measures of the same character. The seed is cast into the earth—it must and will germinate—the harvest may be more or less delayed—it may be reaped by other, and by unfriendly hands; but the harvest-time will surely come, and in its abundance the labours of those who broke up what seemed, for the time, an ungrateful soil—the skill of the husbandman who first guided the plough, he who sowed the good seed, which God has blessed with the increase—will not be forgotten in acknowledgments offered to the better-paid labourer, who has gathered the sheaves into his barn, and who enjoys the produce. It is on these grounds that we thank Fox and Grattan for the Bill of 1829; and Lord J. Russell and Mr. Baring for all that is good in Sir R. Peel's Budget.

So far from exaggerating, we have greatly under-rated the events of 1842 in comparing them with the act of 1829. The last case was infinitely stronger than the former. A truer analogy would have been found if Mr. Percival, after the overthrow of the ministry of Lord Grenville, and a general election made triumphant by the cry of No Popery, had himself proposed and carried the repeal of the Catholic disqualifications. The opposing

principles of party were never so distinctly marked as at the last election. Party symbols were never so ostentatiously displayed. Elections were never made the scenes of more unscrupulous tactics, or of more deadly struggles. The last session of the last parliament had proclaimed to the world the charges brought against the Whig government, as well as their measures; these charges, collected from the debates, furnished unfailing themes at every Conservative dinner, and at the hustings of every county and borough throughout the empire. At the close of every session Toryism was made easy, and was adapted to all capacities in speeches of great point and signal disingenuousness. The astute orator, to whom the robes of the advocate are better adapted than the ermine of an impartial judge, whilst affecting to hold the balance even, never employed any other than false weights. His sarcastic and sententious accusations were repeated and multiplied by a thousand echoes. The agriculturists were taught to consider their interests to be endangered by the measures of the Whig government; they were taught to consider their existence, as a class, to be identified with the corn-laws of 1828. The new poor-law was described as being equally contrary to humanity and to religion; and the union workhouses were designated Whig Bastiles. Foreign competition, and freedom of commercial intercourse, were held up to odium, as the antagonist principles to British prosperity, and as the dreams of that reviled class, the political economists. The animosity of the manufacturing labourers was excited against their employers, by the encouragement given to the idle cry for a ten hours' bill; and by the propagation of the delusion, that the same rate of wages could be paid for a reduced period of labour. Wherever any attempt was made to introduce a police force, better adapted for the repression and punishment of crime than the inefficient Constabulary of former times, this was denounced as an invasion of the liberty of the subjects. The democratic views of the Chartists were all forgotten, and pardoned, wherever the Chartists could be used as effective adversaries to the Whig party.

The plan of the government for extending education among the poorer classes, was described as being an insult to the Church, and as leading to latitudinarianism and irreligion. Every measure of legal reform, whether it applied to the correction of that monster abuse of the Court of Chancery, or to the grand plan of Local Courts, was held up to suspicion; and opposed on the ground that it was bottomed on a love of patronage, and a desire to promote political influence and political corruption. The Irish policy of the government was denounced as being cramped and restrained by the supposed coercion exercised over the Lord-Lieutenant by Mr. O'Connell and his associates. A battery was fixed and pointed against the Irish Courts of Justice, and the guns were worked by the most violent partisans of the Orange party in parliament. The defects of the Irish acts for registering voters were exaggerated as well as exposed—the most vigorous and brilliant of the Tory debaters, taking the lead in the attack, proclaiming loudly the duty and the urgent necessity of an instant remedy, and committing himself, with characteristic impetuosity and indiscretion, to the special remedy which he and his party considered needful. Our foreign policy was made the topic of the most virulent, but, at the same time, the most contradictory attacks. The foreign secretary was alternately charged with having made this country the subservient and submissive agent of France; and with having rudely and mischievously abandoned the French alliance. At one moment was Mehemet Ali held up as the originator of all Eastern civilisation; and at another the Porte was described as the most precious and valuable of our allies. The Shah of Persia, for some short time was made the idol of the Tory skirmishers, who, however, soon transferred their allegiance to the captive courier of Sir John M'Neill. Shah Sooja, Dost Mahomed, and the Emperor of China, found their appropriate champions, who united in condemning all things done, and all persons employed by the Whig government. No passion nor prejudice was neglected that could be excited for the purpose of recruiting the Tory ranks. Some of the more violent of the anti-slavery committees were induced to raise their voices even against the party which, having first abolished the slave trade, had finally blotted out from our statute-book the name of slavery. Even the advocates of temperance were pressed into the service, and we were taught to consider hostilities in China as a war intended to compel a moral and self-denying race to consume opium against their will. It is true that the too eager hounds were now and then checked at the cover side, or stopped when in full cry, by an authoritative voice which they did not presume to disobey. And from the authority of the Duke of Wellington, as well as from the discretion and good feeling of the nobleman now at the head of the foreign office, the violence and unfairness of party attack, in the House of Lords, was mitigated, where it could not be repressed. The attacks on Lord Palmerston's measures, in the House of Lords, were generally made and supported by men who certainly did not add much of weight, either moral or intellectual, to the vehemence of assault—as ineffective as they were daring and unscrupulous. The government were also charged with weakness in being occasionally constrained, by the press of public business or by the unfair opposition they encountered, to postpone measures which had been promised and announced. Amongst these cases, the postponement of the bill for reforming the ecclesiastical courts was frequently referred to as a proof of a good measure lost, or suspended, by the incapacity or carelessness of Lord Melbourne's government. The same charges of weakness and incompetence were made whenever any government measures were curtailed or modified in deference to the judgment of their political opponents. But the best stimulated indignation was reserved for the alleged neglect of the financial interests of the country by the Whigs; for the reluctance shown by them to keep up a surplus income; for the desire practically manifested to repeal taxation; and for the augmentation, assumed to have been made, to the funded and unfunded debt. In the same category of complaint, was placed their delay in introducing measures for the regulation of banking, and of our currency. Such were a few of the grievous charges brought against Lord Melbourne's government, and its supporters; and the disunion of the liberal ranks, and the violence of many of the newspapers, were referred to as unanswerable evidence of the universal condemnation of the Whig party.

Results of the most opposite description were promised, as the immediate and inevitable consequences of a Tory advent to power. Under their Saturnian reign, all that was dark and unpropitious was to become bright and genial. Power was to be substituted for weakness; financial property for financial discredit; the influence of Britain with foreign powers was to be restored to its palmy state, as at the Congress of Vienna:—we were told that no sovereign would hereafter dare to hesitate in fulfilling his engagements; commerce was again to crowd our ports with her ships and valuable cargoes. The manufacturing population, protected from foreign competition, and from the supposed cruelty of their masters, were promised an increase in wealth, under the blessings of a ten hours' bill. Chartism and Socialism were to be extinguished; and tranquillity was to be the result of obedience to laws administered under trustworthy Tory authorities. The new poor-law bill was to be repealed, or, at least, the despots of Somerset House were to be dethroned., Ireland was to be governed on what were called Protestant principles ; the personal animosity and unmitigated railings heretofore directed against Mr. O'Connell, were to assume the shape of practical measures of repression ; and, above all, the general policy of the government was neither to be checked nor controlled by any fear of the ultra-popular party, nor interrupted or influenced from apprehensions of the Roman Catholics. The cry for repeal was to be met by unmeasured scorn and uncompromising defiance. The education of the people was to be placed in the hands of the clergy of the Established Church. The mutilated versions of the Scriptures were to be banished from the Irish national schools. Archbishop Whately and his excellent colleague, Archbishop Murray, were to be removed from their sphere of useful and honourable labour in Ireland ; and in England, a lay and political committee of the Privy Council, usurping the functions of a minister of public instruction, was to be replaced by a syndicate of bishops, assisted by the learned members for the Universities of Oxford and Cambridge. But we need not proceed with this enumeration. It is sufficient to say that in all points whatsoever, the conduct of the promised Tory ministers was described as likely to form a contrast to that pursued by their too long successful opponents ; and on every one of the questions to which we have adverted, the strongest expectations of a practical change of policy were either held out directly, or were encouraged by silent but expressive acquiescence, as the immediate results of a change in the Councils of her Majesty.

It was under the influence of these expectations that the General Election of 1842 took place. An appeal was made to the strongest and the most widely-spread prejudices. But we doubt whether this appeal would have been successful, had it not been for other contemporaneous circumstances. Unreasonable alarms had induced many very respectable but timid friends of liberal opinions to withdraw, or at least to modify, the support which they gave to the Whig government. England is never without a numerous class who are prone to be influenced by apprehension and timidity ; and in this instance the ranks of the Alarmists received many recruits. The political fallacies which have been exposed with so much humour by Bentham, were all brought into play. Those who did not, and could not, object to Lord Melbourne and his colleagues, expressed the most unbounded and unconquerable dislike to some of the members of Parliament by whom the Cabinet was supported. Where no valid

argument could be urged against the measures which the government had actually proposed, it was suggested, without a shadow of evidence, that other measures, intended to be proposed thereafter, were dangerous and revolutionary. On the other hand, while the defection took place of men over-scrupulous and apprehensive, the demands of the more eager politicians increased in number and in degree. They considered the loss of the former class of adherents, to impose upon the Government a necessity of going much beyond all their previously declared opinions. They considered the Government bound to adopt the doctrines of the Radical School, and to surrender at discretion. Nor were the attempts to accomplish this object confined to that gentle violence, which has sometimes been resorted to, even in cases of the most sincere and respectful political attachment. Threats of hostility, expressions of mistrust, and of want of confidence, were unscrupulously used in debate. The Government were called upon to confess themselves as formed of 'squeezable materials,' and as devoid of fixed opinions, and of courage to maintain them ; or they were held up to the hostility of the ultra-liberal party, as Tories in disguise. Perhaps these most unjust and impolitic attacks, which were not participated in by any great portion of the people of England, or of the liberal party in parliament, were somewhat too contumeliously repelled. But this, if it were an error, was generous and sincere ; for undoubtedly any course is more noble in public life than that of obtaining support under false pretences, or by disguising opinions—thus lowering the moral character of a statesman, in the vain expectation of increasing his political strength. We believe that it is now demonstrated that the government of Lord Melbourne did not lag behind the expectation of the great bulk of the people of England, but was rather in advance of the spirit of the times. An additional cause of weakness may be traced to the long duration of the Whig Administration itself. It had existed since November, 1830. During that period, though we are satisfied that more was done for the cause of good government, and for the liberties of mankind, than had been achieved in the whole of the preceding century, still there were men, and classes of men, whose hopes had been disappointed, and whose expectations had been frustrated. The period of ten years is a severe trial to the popularity of any party, and after so long a tenure of office, a change is sometimes sought, or submitted to, for the sake of change alone. The Roman historian, in allusion to the political claims of rival candidates for the

Consulship, gives the following as a reason why one should be preferred to his competitors:—' Accedebat quod alter decimum prope annum assiduus in oculis hominum fuerat ; quæ res minus verendos magnos homines ipsa satietate facit.' (Liv. lib. 35, c. 10).

These causes were all greatly increased in their influences at the general election, by the lavish corruption used to procure returns. Would that we could with truth and sincerity declare our conviction, that corruption, and the base acts by which low ambition purchases a degrading success, had been confined to the Tories. But though we believe that for the introduction of these vile practices that party was mainly responsible, and that corruption was much more lavishly resorted to by them, it cannot be denied that both parties entered deeply into this competition of venality ; and neither can be held free from reproach, though guilty in a far different degree. The unfortunate preservation in the Reform Bill of franchises which have fostered the most undisguised corruption ; the rapidity with which the moral contagion was allowed to spread when introduced among the new and purer constituencies ; the defence of these unconstitutional practices by those who held the poorer classes in contempt ; the example given by too many of the higher orders, showing their greedy readiness to work this iniquity, led to a wider and more intense corruption in 1842, than had ever before been exhibited to the indignation of honest men.

Such were the leading causes which, in our judgment, produced the Tory majority in 1842. That majority we believe to have greatly exceeded the expectation of the leaders of the party. Perhaps we might also surmise that it exceeded in some cases their wishes: we feel most certain that it is inconsistent with their permanent interests. When Parliament met, the majority seemed to be overwhelming. The first vote was decisive: Sir Robert Peel found himself restored to power amidst the acclamation of a very noisy, if not a well disciplined, corps of followers. This majority left him no excuse with respect to his parliamentary strength, and his ability to propound measures—unless, indeed, (as was then shrewdly suspected, and as has since been conclusively proved), the politics of the first Minister and of his supporters were not quite consistent with each other ; and thus, in proportion as his apprehensions of Whig attack were lessened, the certainty of Tory mutiny was increased. Time was demanded by the new government to prepare their measures. This, under ordinary circumstances, would not have been at all unreasonable. But when it was considered that the principles to which

the new government stood pledged, had either been openly avowed, or fully admitted, the indulgence sought for and granted was somewhat more than the occasion justified. Besides, the ' coy, reluctant, amorous delay,' which would not have been inappropriate in a young and blushing virgin, yielding her heart for the first time, seemed misplaced, if not ridiculous, when the lady at the altar was an experienced widow of maturer years, well acquainted with the world and all the ways of men.

We know not when more of curiosity and of expectation were combined, than at the real opening of the political drama in 1842. The theatre was crowded in all its parts. The applause of the Tory galleries was all prepared, and only awaited the signal. The stage lamps shone brightly. The great performers were known to be behind the scenes ; the scenery, machinery, dresses, and furnishings were all said to be new, and to be got up under the direction of the new manager. The *premier coup d'archet* was heard ; but when the curtain rose, and the performance was begun, greater astonishment and surprise could not have been created on comparing the playbill with the representation, than if the tragedy of Cato had been substituted for the Agreeable Surprise, or the dead march in Saul for the bridal chorus of the Freyschutz. It is true that all the actors whose names were announced, made their appearance ; but, alas for the lovers of the melodrama ! the actors appeared in new characters, and their dresses and machinery were those which had been so long worn and used by their rivals and predecessors. It is true that this bold confidence in the indulgence of their audience succeeded to a certain extent ; but perhaps the cause was a theatrical one. The good folks had paid their money at the door, they had secured their seats, and, if they had yielded to their discontent, they might have been left without any play at all, or have been condemned to call back her Majesty's former servants.

If this contrast between the policy professed, and the policy pursued by the government, were not of the highest importance to the public interests, as well as to the characters of public men, it would be difficult to treat the subject with any decent seriousness. But, in order to estimate fairly the conduct of our present rulers, it is necessary to scrutinize more closely their proceedings during the last session. The three great branches of policy on which they had differed with their opponents were the Corn-Bill, and all agricultural questions—the Commercial Propositions contained in Mr. Baring's and Sir Robert

Peel's Budget—and the State of the Finances. We shall advert to the proceedings of the present government in respect to each.

The Conservative party had, we may say without exception, claimed credit for being pre-eminently the friends of the Agricultural interest; and had represented the protection of that interest against foreign competition to be the public duty to which they stood especially pledged. It is quite true, that in all these proceedings the leader of the party adhered to certain words of caution, which enabled him to disclaim any specific engagement. But the spirit of all the acts, and all the declarations of the members of the Government—and still more, all the acts and declarations of their friends and supporters—tended to impress a conviction on the minds of reasonable men, of what was the fixed determination of the Tory party.

When Sir R. Peel was pressed to state his opinion on this subject, he referred, in reply, to the steady and earnest support which he had given to the existing corn-law. But he gave further and *personal* securities to the farmers of England ; he took into his Cabinet, in high office, a nobleman whose claim upon public consideration consisted in his uncompromising defence of the corn-laws; and the Paymaster of the Forces was also a man who had resisted even the most mitigated proposals for the modification of our system. These personages were his 'Johnny Nokes and Peter Styles' pledges to prosecute, on behalf of the agriculturists. If there had been any two men in the whole political world, whose names, endorsed on Sir R. Peel's political bills of exchange, would have insured their circulation amongst the country gentlemen and their dependents, he could not have offered more acceptable security than that of the Duke of Buckingham and Sir E. Knatchbull. We do not suppose that many of our readers will consider a pledge to be less binding, because it results from an honourable understanding rather than from a distinct engagement. The confidence which is accepted from a great party, becomes a consideration which ought to pledge the leader, accepting such confidence, to the most scrupulous performance of the conditions into which he has tacitly entered. It would be a new era in British politics, if the Statute of Frauds were allowed to be pleaded in politics, and if statesmen were permitted with impunity to set aside an engagement because it was not reduced to a written form. If any man thinks that we have put this argument too strongly, we are willing to bring it to a very simple but decisive test. We ask the members of the Cabinet, one and all, whether they believe that they could have obtained their parliamentary majority had their measures been announced *before* the General Election. If this question is answered in the negative, it follows that the constituencies of the country have been grossly deceived ; and it is for them to decide whether the Government, or their representatives, have been the deceivers.

But not only has the protection held out to the farmer, by the former corn-laws, been considerably relaxed ; new measures, viewed with still greater alarm by the agriculturists, have been introduced and carried. That these measures were inconsistent with the principles on which it was fully understood that Sir Robert Peel's government was founded, is sufficiently proved by the resignation of the Duke of Buckingham, and the defection of a large portion of the ministerial members on the vote for reducing the duties on foreign cattle and provisions. The latter measure was one, we admit, considerably in advance of the propositions of the Whig ministry, and the step was taken in the right direction. But the dismay it created was unparalleled. Had it been announced in the Court Circular, that huge bales of Hamburg beef blockaded the door of the Board of Trade, or that a hundred foreign oxen roared at the levee of the first minister, the astonishment would not have been greater.

If, indeed, the measure was as productive of good to the public and the consumer, as it has been of alarm to the friends of monopoly, we should have been well satisfied. But while Sir Robert Peel professed to reduce the amount of protection on British grain, and did so, to a very considerable degree, there was one principle to which he held with a ' desperate fidelity.' He might afford to disappoint the expectations of his friends—he might depart from what were considered to be his implied engagements—he might throw overboard his colleague the Duke of Buckingham, and substitute for the ties of political connection the less irksome bond of a blue ribbon ; but whilst making all these sacrifices, the Sliding-Scale was held to be a sacred principle, to be adhered to through good and evil fortune. The present will be handed down to posterity under the title of the ' Sliding-Scale Government.' A sliding-scale proper, with the motto, *hâc scalâ vinces*, may hereafter be assumed by the official chivalry of Whitehall and Downing Street as the badge of their new order. We pray these victors for one moment to suspend their triumph, and to consider the effect of their glorious success. We were told that, under this cunning device, a steady and equable supply of foreign corn would be furnished to the consumer. We were assured that foreign corn would be entered, in time of need, at a much lower rate than the eight shillings fixed duty of the Whigs; which duty, it was added, never ought to be, and could never be, enforced and collected when a state of distress prevailed. Yet what has been the operation of Sir Robert Peel's new law? The suffering people of England have known but too well how much their wretchedness has been increased, during the last spring and summer, by the high price of bread. But the effect of the present sliding-scale, as of every other modification of the same principle, has been, to check the entry of any considerable supply of foreign corn, till the price had reached its *maximum*, and the duty its *minimum*. It is obvious that, if the price of grain is steadily increasing from fifty shillings to fifty-five, to sixty, to sixty-five, and to seventy, no corn, or but a very small quantity of foreign corn, will ever be realised from bond. The tendency to hold produce back will be greatly increased, when the seller, by so doing, obtains a double advantage, in a reduced duty as well as in an advanced price. It is principally when there is a prospect of falling prices, and of rising duties, that foreign grain is largely brought into the market from the bonded warehouse. The consequence of this necessarily is, that a prospect of an abundant harvest has brought into consumption many hundred thousand quarters of wheat, which would have remained in bond had scarcity been apprehended. Thus, a prospect of scarcity excludes, and a prospect of abundance admits, foreign corn. By this double operation, prices are eventually raised and eventually depressed; and the fluctuations between the highest and lowest ranges, are greater than they could be under any other system. In other words, the sliding-scale insures the largest supply when that supply is least required by the consumer; and limits the supply, however high the prices, when that supply is most necessary. Nor is the injury confined to the consumer. The sliding-scale acts equally to the great injury of the farmer. His prospects are injured, and injured frequently for many successive years, by prices unnaturally and artificially depressed; and, to complete the blessings of the sliding-scale, the revenue is at the same time exposed to loss. All this has been exhibited in the last few months; and the demonstration is so complete, that we doubt whether there will be hereafter found any but the luckless members of the Government itself to utter one word in defence of the sliding-scale.

This result, which all reasoners on this subject, whether in or out of parliament, predicted, will be practically exemplified by the Custom-House returns of the last six months. These accounts have not been given to a late period; but from what has appeared in the public papers, as well as in parliamentary returns, it is certain that the foreign and colonial wheat imported between the close of April, and the middle of August, has exceeded 2,400,000 quarters. Of this amount, 200,000 quarters, less than one-twelfth, were imported during the nine weeks from the close of April to the middle of July, during which time the price had steadily risen, and the duty had fallen from 13s. to 8s.; whilst nearly 2,000,000 quarters were imported in the five weeks after the duty had reached its minimum—the prospects of the harvest being then known to be favourable, and there being a certainty that prices must fall. The admission of foreign corn, during four consecutive weeks in July and August, exemplifies this principle still further.

1st week,	.	62,209 quarters.
2d week,	.	71,644 ditto.
3d week,	.	364,073 ditto.
4th week,	.	1,354,797 ditto.

It was stated in the public papers that on the 11th July prices fell 2s., on the 18th 2s., and on the 25th 2s. and 3s., on August 1st 4s. and 6s., on the 25th August 2s.,—in all, a fall of 15s., which led to the introduction of 600,000 quarters in a single day.

Our readers will thus see, that in place of a steady supply of foreign wheat, as promised by Sir Robert Peel, the supply in five weeks has exceeded tenfold the supply of nine weeks preceding; that in place of duties lower than the fixed duty proposed by Lord John Russell, the duty has either been exactly the same, or it has been higher; that in place of a repeal of this duty under the pressure of distress, as was prophesied, the duty has been defended and maintained; and to complete this contrast, in place of having this supply introduced at the time it was most required, it was at the moment when the home produce was most abundant, and the prospects of a good harvest were realized, and not till then, that any very considerable amount of foreign wheat was brought into market for the benefit of the consumer.

With these observations, we think we may dismiss the Corn Bill of the last session; but in doing so, we must admit, and we do it freely, that the measure, though not in itself good, was an improvement upon the previous law; though a moderate fixed duty, as we have frequently shown, would have been infinitely preferable; and the abandonment of all protection whatever, is the ultimate object to which our future legislation should tend, not only for the benefit of the consumers, but of the agriculturists themselves. A population increased in Great Britain alone to the enormous extent of 8,000,000 during the last forty years—with this population steadily augmenting at the rate of about 1000 souls a day—with the formidable dangers which must exist, so long as discontent is enabled to attribute every scarcity to acts of the legislature—founded, as those acts are, on what are considered the selfish interests of the legislators; the sliding-scale and its advocates will be condemned, as well by common sense as by popular indignation; and Sir R. Peel is much too skilful a tactician to maintain a contest in a position which he finds to be indefensible.

Indeed, it is obvious, that in the principles he laid down, and the admissions he made, he has prepared the way, with great adroitness but with much caution, for the final abandonment of all protection whatever. His two 'rests,' at a duty of 6s. and 17s., are his preparations for a fixed duty; a fixed duty on his part will lead him further still. For this, his friends and supporters *passi graviora* must prepare themselves. They must try, if they can, to fall with dignity; or, if this is impossible, they should forget the ridicule to which '*the farmers' friends*' will be exposed by the acts of the Conservative chief, in the great benefits which his ultimate reforms will confer upon the country.

We proceed to the next of Sir Robert Peel's great measures, his Commercial Tariff; and here our approval may be more freely expressed; for the principles laid down by him, and by his distinguished coadjutor, Mr. Gladstone, were, with few exceptions, all we could wish, and all that the Masters of Economical Science could have required from public men. It was admitted unequivocally, that the aim of the legislature should be, to procure the most abundant and the cheapest supplies, and to encourage the freest and most unfettered commercial intercourse between nation and nation. We were told, and most truly, that a reduction of duty, if confined to duties paid upon home produce, would be more frequently a benefit to the monopolist than to the consumer. Sir Robert Peel most justly showed that this was the reason why the repeal of the leather-tax had not been productive of very general good. He further told us, that on the same principles a reduction of the duty on colonial sugars, if unaccompanied by a corresponding reduction on foreign sugars, would prove a failure. In all this, he laid down principles the most enlightened, in a manner the most convincing; but in so doing, it is undeniable that he *forswore the Tory faith*,

and abandoned almost all the ancient doctrines upon which home protection and our colonial system is founded. From these principles he will find that there is no retreat. When the time comes (and it approaches speedily) when Parliament will be required to reconsider the Brazilian commercial treaty, and the duties on foreign sugar, we entertain no doubt that Sir Robert Peel will be reminded of these declarations. Indeed, our hope and expectation is, that these declarations will be embodied in the new arrangements which must then be adopted; in spite of the opposition of our colonial interests, or the misapprehensions of a mistaken philanthropy;—uninstructed by experience, and relying upon remedies already shown to be inadequate either for the amelioration of the condition of the foreign slave, or for the suppression of the slave-trade.

In proportion as these measures, and more especially the reduction of the duty on foreign cattle and provisions, gratified the Political Economists, and the liberal party in parliament, in that very degree did the opposition and discontent of the Tory country gentlemen manifest themselves. 'Was it for this,' they exclaimed, ' that we fought our battles at the registration courts and on the hustings? Was it for this that we expelled the Whig government, and vindicated for ourselves the title of the farmers' friends? Not only are we called upon to bear a reduction of the existing protections upon British corn, more dangerous to us than the fixed duty of the Whigs, but we are also called on to renounce our still more valued system of entire prohibition, and to sacrifice to free-trade our flocks and herds, our firstlings and our fatlings. And we have to bear all this from our professed friends!

" Quid meruêre boves, animal sine fraude dolisque,
Innocuum. simplex, natum tolerare labores;
Quid meruistis oves, placidum pecus?" '

Nor was this discontent shown in complaints only. Indeed, if the principles of the aggrieved class had been as correct as they were sincere, they, like their oxen, might have been considered *natum tolerare labores*, had they surrendered without a struggle. They gave signs of resistance. Col. Sibthorp and Mr. George Palmer undertook the cause. Others, more able, prepared for the field; and many a ploughshare was forged into a sword, preparatory to an onslaught by the revolted agriculturists. We pray our readers to remember well the state of Parliamentary parties. Sir Robert Peel had staked the existence of his government on the success of the Tariff. If the Liberal party had hesitated in the course they ought to follow—had they joined, with the discontented agriculturists, in opposing the reduction of the duties on foreign cattle—Sir Robert Peel would have been left in a minority ; and, on his own declaration, he must have resigned. But, in acting more honourably and more justly, the Opposition acted also, more wisely. As in 1835, when, under similar circumstances, they had once before saved Sir Robert Peel from defeat on the Malt Duty, they now, for the second time, threw their weight into the scale of their political adversaries : the measure was carried, and the existence of the government was preserved, by the active support of their opponents. Most fully was Lord Palmerston justified in stating 'that the country has the satisfaction of knowing, that if the government should be deserted by any powerful body of its own friends in its attempts to carry its great principles into practice, the Opposition of the present day, unlike the Opposition of a former period, which prided itself on obstructing improvement, will cordially and honestly support the Government in its progressive course, and will assist the right honourable baronet, even when deserted by his own friends, in carrying his liberal measures into a full and complete effect.'

Still, whilst we thus are disposed to do full justice to the Government for the principles they have laid down, we must guard ourselves from the inference that these principles have either been very wisely or very justly applied in all cases. It is not just to expose the labour of the artisan to a foreign competition, while a disproportionate protection is still maintained to benefit the property of the rich. It is in vain to expect the shoemaker of Northampton, or the glover of Worcester or Yeovil, to consider that he is treated fairly, if the principles of free-trade are applied when against him, and not applied when in his favour. It is not wise to have maintained, and in some cases to have created, colonial protections by differential duties, which disfigure our commercial code, and will impede its future reform. Above all, it is contrary to sound principle, more especially at a moment like the present, to have permitted the duties upon the raw materials of Wool and Cotton to continue—increasing the difficulties of competition in foreign markets, and the distress and discontent of our manufacturing population. This subject has been most ably and conclusively argued in the speech of Mr. Charles Wood, who, having already acquired high reputation as an able servant of the Crown, has, in his argument on the Wool duties, proved his eminent qualifications as an enlightened representative of a great manufacturing community.

We proceed, next, to consider what have been the Financial Measures of the late session ; and we must here be allowed to observe, that the first acts of the government were by no means fortunate. We allude to the complicated proposition for funding and borrowing £5,000,000. Had this measure been carried, as originally proposed, it would have proved an utter failure ; and the public service would have been but inadequately provided for. It was a wise and provident suggestion made to the Chancellor of the Exchequer by his immediate predecessor, Mr. Baring, which averted this disaster. This gentleman—to whose enlightened propositions when in office may be distinctly traced all that is most useful in the budget of this year, but who was also desirous, by his measures, to have rendered the imposition of increased taxes unnecessary—perceived with great forethought, that it would be impossible, or at least highly improbable, that Mr. Goulburn's measure would yield the revenue which was anticipated. He therefore recommended that Parliament should entrust the government with a power of selling stock, within certain limits. By adopting this suggestion, the public was saved from the most serious embarrassments ; and Sir Robert Peel's government was saved from the reproach of having totally failed in their first financial operation. For this they are indebted to the disinterested suggestions of a political opponent ; and we allude to this the more freely, because it does not appear that the Opposition have condescended to claim this result as a merit for themselves ; or that they have ever pointed out the defects in Mr. Goulburn's bill as a reproach to their opponents.

This, however, was but a preliminary question, and the *novitas regni* might have been some reasonable excuse for an official mistake. It is by the merits of the Budget of the government, as deliberately brought forward by Sir Robert Peel, that the character of his policy is to be tried. Every indulgence had been shown that could have been demanded. Full time was granted to enable the minister to mature his measures. No impatient or harassing motions were made in either house. But many were the surmises of friends and foes in respect to the forthcoming budget. With these anticipations were combined a repetition of the often-refuted attacks against the Whigs. The accumulated deficiencies of four successive years were added together, and were represented as constituting one annual deficiency now to be provided for. As well might the whole national debt have been called a deficiency of the year. This inane absurdity was repeated till it found credence in a willing, because an ignorant or a malignant, audience. It was stated, with an equal want of truth, that the Duke of Wellington's government had left to Lord Grey a surplus revenue of £3,000,-000. It is true that such a surplus had existed the year before the Duke of Wellington's resignation. But Mr. Goulburn's repeal of the beer and leather taxes converted that surplus into a deficiency, amounting to nearly £700,000, in 1831. We were also told that at length we should see the public credit of England placed on a permanent and satisfactory basis. We were assured that the alarming and increasing deficiency would be amply provided for. We know not but, among the older financiers, there might have been some who contemplated the re-establishment of a permanent Sinking-Fund. But a very considerable surplus of income over expenditure was considered by all to be indispensable. The loss of revenue by the much reprobated reduction of postage duties, was now to be supplied, if not by a direct repeal of Lord Monteagle's act, at least by making provision for the income sacrificed. What had been most erroneously, as well as most mischievously, termed 'a tampering with the Savings Banks,' but which was, in fact, no tampering at all, was to be condemned and abandoned for ever. Care was to be taken that no increase of the public debt should hereafter take place; the income being to be more than equalized with the expenditure. Much of this was promised; and all that was not distinctly promised, was most confidently expected from Sir Robert Peel and his associates.

At length he made his celebrated financial propositions, in a speech of great ability and moderation, going far to satisfy the expectations of those who demanded from the Minister the enunciation of sound general principles, and extremely plausible and skilful in the manner in which his argument were marshalled.

It was on the 11th of March that he submitted to Parliament these memorable propositions. His abstract declarations were all that could have been required, however he might have failed in applying principles practically. There certainly was not much candour or fairness in his adroit and plausible statement. In order to show the necessity of extreme remedies, he, too, added together the deficiencies of six successive years, giving the Public and Parliament to understand, that a sum of L.10,720,000 was to be provided for. Had he condescended to state the whole case fairly, he would have informed the House,

that in the ten years of Whig government, from 1831 to 1840 inclusive, the surplus of income amounted to L.7,488,000, and the deficiency to L.4,803,000—showing an excess of income over expenditure of no less than L.2,101,000. Again, in referring to the charge of the debt, no reference was made either to the loan of L.20,000,000 raised for the West Indian planters; nor yet to the conversion of perpetual into terminable annuities. If an allowance is made for these operations, so far from there having been any real increase to the debt, the capital will be found to have been reduced L.22,592,000, between the years 1831 and 1841; and the annual charge to have been reduced by a sum of L.652,000 annually. We could easily point out other disingenuities and fallacies of the same kind. His statement of the resources of the present year was as follows:—

Estimated expenditure,   L.50,819,000
Estimated income,   - - 48,350,000

Deficiency, - - - L.2,469,000

In a subsequent part of the speech, he stated this deficiency to amount to L.2,570,-000. At a later period of the session, it was estimated at L.3,000,000.

The Minister greatly exaggerated the difficulties, and underrated the resources of the country. No assumption could be more groundless than that on which his entire Budget was bottomed—namely, that the power of raising revenue by indirect taxation was exhausted. But we do not, on this account, deny that a case was made out, requiring energetic and decisive remedies. Sir Robert Peel did not show any want of courage. He took a course not only bold, but wholly unprecedented in British history. He proposed to impose an income-tax in time of peace, producing, at the rate of seven-pence in the pound, L.3,700,000. From this tax he exempted Ireland, as well as all incomes below L.150 per annum. He further asked Parliament to sanction increased duties on Irish spirits, estimated at L.250,000, and on Irish stamps, estimated at L.160,000. These sums, with L.200,000 received on the export of coal, were calculated to add L.4,310,000 to the public income—converting the deficiency of L.2,469,000 into a surplus of L.1,800,000. So far the object of Sir Robert Peel would seem to have been gained, and the promises made by his party to have been fulfilled; a real and efficient surplus of income being thus provided. But he did not stop here. We remember that on the return to England of a late diplomatist, it was observed that he had earned a great character abroad: 'Wait a while,' said a cynical observer, 'for you will see that he will spend it at home like a gentleman.' So it was with Sir Robert Peel; for having obtained his surplus of L.1,800,000, he proceeded to spend it with more recklessness than the worst enemy could have attributed to any of his Whig predecessors. He sacrificed L.600,000 by reduction of the timber duties; L.170,000 by his alterations of the tariff; L.103,000 by the repeal of the export duties; and L.70,000 in stage-coach duties. These measures reduced the surplus to L.520,000. But this nominal surplus Sir Robert Peel himself admitted to be a real deficiency; for he stated, (Speech, p. 30), 'that this surplus was to meet the increased charge for the war in China,' estimated (p. 21) at L.800,000; and also to meet 'the increased expenses which the affairs in India might render necessary within the year.' It is therefore clear, that, on Sir Robert Peel's data, even after the imposition of an income-tax, he has left the country with a deficient revenue.

But this is not all. The Government was compelled to give way in their singularly absurd project of imposing a duty of four shillings on coal exported. This most unwise proposition, which would have imposed a duty of 60 per cent on large, and 120 per cent on small coal, would neither stand examination nor argument; and the intended duties were, on compulsion, reduced one-half. The supposition that L.250,000 could be raised by increasing the duties on Irish spirits, which, already too high, acted as a practical bounty on smuggling, was abundantly proved to be a delusion. In this case, the morals and peace of the country were risked for the sake of a paltry experiment. The commercial treaties with Portugal and France, which were stated to be in progress, would still more diminish the income;—the sacrifice which would be produced, in the first instance, by the French treaty, having been estimated by Mr. Baring at L.300,000. From these facts, it was evident to any one who looked below the surface of things, that the deficiency would be found infinitely greater than had ever before been voluntarily exhibited in the Budget-speech of a Chancellor of the Exchequer. This result, too, was consequent upon that strongest of all financial measures, the imposition of an Income-Tax in time of peace. Sir Robert Peel had called on Hercules for aid, but the wheel of his treasury Van was still left deep in the slough. It is thus that the Tory pledge of restoring the public credit of the country has been redeemed! The case was made still worse by explanations given on a subsequent occasion. Sir Robert Peel then stated the actual deficiency to be L.3,000,000, in addition 'to L.800,000 per

annum:' on this showing, the actual deficiency of the year could not be less than L.700,000.

But if these measures had ever appeared likely to be successful, we doubt whether they could have been viewed as expedient or justifiable. An income-tax in time of peace is a most formidable experiment. Its effect upon commercial profits, at a period when foreign competition is active in all cases, and successful in many, cannot fail to be pregnant with danger. But the *Quarterly Review*, in the Number just published, denies that the income-tax should be considered exclusively as a war-tax; and asks, somewhat imprudently and tauntingly—'Why it should be so, and in what code that dogma is written?'—(No. 140.) To this we answer, that an income-tax is a *war-tax*, by that law of common sense which forbids, in time of peace, the imposition of a tax amounting in principle to a confiscation, and which cannot be levied without an inquisition wholly unbearable. In time of war, or when contending for national existence *toto corpore regni*, every sacrifice must be submitted to, and this impost, odious as it is, may become allowable. For written authority, we can refer our contemporary to every statute which has passed on this subject anterior to 1842. In these laws the property-tax has uniformly been dealt with, when imposed or when repealed, as a *war-tax*, and as a war-tax only. We also refer to the declarations of every public man of official experience, who has argued these questions, either in or out of parliament. One quotation will here be sufficient, and we select it from the speech of a minister unswayed either by Whiggism or Political Economy. When Mr. Addington, on the 5th of April, 1802, proposed the repeal of the property-tax, he stated, 'that the burden of this tax should not be allowed to rest on the shoulders of the people in *time of peace*. It should be reserved for those *important occasions* which he trusted would not soon recur. He thought it worthy of the credit and the character of this country to look forward to such a resource in the painful event of *being obliged to struggle for our honour and independence.*' The Reviewer having failed to show that the income-tax is justifiable in time of peace, takes new ground; he discovers that we are at war, because hostilities have not ceased in China and Affghanistan. But we submit, that these contests do not amount to the state of war contemplated by Mr. Pitt, Mr. Addington, or Lord Grenville, when they proposed or augmented the income-tax. Such a construction was once attempted, it is true, when the receipt of Mr. Croker's war-salary, as Secretary to the Admiralty, was vainly attempted to be justified by reason of the expedition to Algiers. But we are sure that our contemporary cannot have forgotten the scorn with which this proposition was rejected : and yet, by a singular coincidence, we find the same argument urged in 1842.

The exemption of all incomes under L.150 a-year, whilst it operated as a bribe to secure the acquiescence of the middle and the poorer classes, introduced a principle more formidable than any in the wild dreams of the Chartists. The exemption of Ireland had been, a few years before, designated by Sir Robert Peel himself as a gross injustice to England and Scotland. This was a more important concession made to the popular party in Ireland, than had ever been made by Lord Melbourne. Within so very recent a period as on the 15th May, 1841, Sir Robert Peel himself had declared, that 'there being about L.2,500,000 about to be raised, to attempt to raise that sum by a property-tax would not be advisable;' yet, on the 11th March, 1842, to provide for a deficiency of L.2,570,000, the same Minister himself proposed the very measure against which he had advisedly protested ; and accompanied it by that very exemption of Ireland which he had declared to be unjust towards Great Britain !

If our space permitted, these arguments might be carried still further ; but unless we are entirely deceived, we think we have sufficiently proved the total inadequacy of Sir Robert Peel's measures to place the public credit on that stable footing which had been promised as the first blessing to be conferred by the Tory Government. But that we would not run the risk of wearying our readers with such dull discussions, we could show, quite as conclusively, that although a reduction of the timber duties was called for, there was no necessity sufficient to justify the *amount* of revenue sacrificed ; more especially in the total repeal of the duties on colonial produce. The new coffee duties are also far from wisely distributed. The export duties were not complained of, nor felt as a practical grievance ; and were therefore unnecessarily repealed. They amounted to no more than L.100,000 on a foreign trade exceeding L.50,000,000. The concession made to the proprietors of stage-coaches was not called for where a competition of railroads does not exist, and will be wholly ineffectual where it does. In fact—whether we consider the taxes imposed, the taxes repealed, or the balance left between the income and the expenditure—the Tory Budget will not contribute, as a revenue measure, to the reputation of Sir Robert Peel and his government.

We do not feel ourselves called upon again to argue the principles of education, as applicable either to England or to Ireland. It is sufficient for our purpose to remark that the present Government, after having opposed the system which had been so usefully carried on by their predecessors, under the able direction of Lord Lansdowne, have not only adopted it in its most minute details, but have proposed to carry it still further. The control of a Lay Board of members holding political office, had been loudly and especially condemned. This is now, most wisely and most unhesitatingly, adopted. The inspection of schools by persons named by the Crown, and responsible to Parliament, had been stigmatized as an inquisitorial exercise of authority, to which the trustees and patrons of schools never ought to submit This inspection is adhered to, and enforced. The duty of preserving a perfect equality among all classes, whether Churchmen or Dissenters, in the distribution of aid, and the public encouragement granted for schools, had been described as inconsistent with the principles of an establishment ; this reasonable and just principle was never more unequivocally affirmed than it has been by Lord Wharncliffe, the President of the Council. From the original minutes of council down to the music of Mr. Hullah, all is preserved unimpaired. For this Sir Robert Peel and his colleagues deserve thanks and praise, which should be the more liberally given, when it is considered how great are the sacrifices of former votes and declarations which have been made ; how much of self-love and of the pride of party has been necessarily abandoned ; and how much of effort must have been required to wring a reluctant assent from their colleagues and supporters, to a tribute thus offered to the merits of their Whig predecessors by the present administration. We have reason to believe, that in this, as in other questions, the measure originally intended to be adopted has not yet been fully carried out. We have reason to believe, that notwithstanding the choral meetings over which Cabinet Ministers presided, there has been some discord in the committee of council itself. What if it should be true, that the first Minister and Lord Wharncliffe were outvoted at their own council board ; and that an exception was successfully taken to the lectures in music and drawing, unless they were accompanied by more orthodox doctrine ? This attempt to unite theology to linear perspective, and to set the Thirty-nine

Articles to music, has been made; but although it has led to the abandonment of the original scheme of the government, it has not produced the adoption of the absurdities suggested by their troublesome allies and supporters. Their allies have been foiled, but not defeated; and we observe, with deep regret, the bitterness of their renewed attacks upon Mr. Kay Shuttleworth, one of the most estimable and zealous public servants; but whose merits are, we trust, too well known to Lord Wharncliffe and Sir Robert Peel, to permit them to make the secretary of the committee of council a victim to the ignorant bigotry of his detractors.

So much for education in England. In Ireland, the measures of Lord Eliot have been those bequeathed to him by his excellent predecessor, which he has adopted to the signal overthrow of the expectations of his ultra-political supporters. These misguided and ill-judging men, though they did not venture to demand that, in the case of the Roman Catholics, the use of the alphabet and primer should be made penal—the multiplication table proscribed by act of Parliament, all samplers directed to be burnt by the ordinary, unless worked in orange and purple silks, and the birch applied as a punishment for learning and not for idleness—yet have called upon the legislature to establish separate schools, founded on church principles, and under the exclusive direction of the clergy. Let them pause, and consider what would be the immediate consequence if they were 'cursed with granted prayer.' The present 2300 national schools, with their 280,000 scholars, would be at once converted into schools exclusively Roman Catholic, of which the direction would naturally, and almost justly, fall into the hands of the priesthood; and the very party who are the most jealous of the Roman Catholic clergy, would find themselves the unconscious but active agents in the erection, extension, and perpetuation of their ecclesiastical authority and dominion. In this cause, the Primate of Ireland and Archbishop Machale are fellow-labourers, but not upon equal terms; as the former, in contending for an imaginary good for the Church, is practically surrendering at discretion to the most violent of his opponents. These follies were all advocated by the zealots of the Tory party; these changes, as well as the overthrow of Maynooth, were expected from their leaders: a more bitter disappointment could not have been inflicted, than by the declarations of the government. How deeply this disappointment is felt, appears, amongst other things, in an address moved by a party of Orangemen in Dublin, praying the Queen to remove Lord Eliot from her councils for ever. It also appears in the opposition of the University of Dublin to the Irish Solicitor-General, and the pledges required from the more successful candidate, to vote against the declared wishes of Government. When, in addition to other mortifications, we consider the exclusion from political office of all the prominent members of that section in Irish politics which has furnished the most eager partisans, and the most active skirmishers in the Tory cause, we cannot imagine any line of policy so well calculated to excite discontent, and a bitter hostility, which only waits an opportunity for manifesting itself. This hostility, and the causes which produce it, must bring to the government real strength, as more than an equivalent for party support. If they lose the applause of a faction, they are laying in their claims to the gratitude of a people, who require no more than justice at their hands.

We may here be allowed to observe, that in place of the vehement declarations against the Roman Catholic priesthood, an eloquent, and, in most cases, a well-deserved panegyric upon that order has been pronounced by Lord Eliot. In place of the violent and constant abuse of Mr. O'Connell, there has been a total and prudent abstinence from attack. Repeal meetings are held; Repeal rent is collected; and yet those who were the most eager in condemning the inaction of the late Government, have discovered the prudence of a similar course. Even the rash energy of Lord Stanley has been curbed and restrained; and the insane attempt to abridge and limit the political franchises of the Irish people, under the colour of a Registration Bill, has been postponed, and we should hope, for the peace of Ireland, has been finally abandoned.

Let us next inquire how far the expectations of increased peace, good order, and obedience to the laws, have been realized since the change of Government, how lamentable is the contrast between those expectations and the event! It is, indeed, somewhat remarkable, that the closing months of Tory government in 1830, should have been made memorable by frightful agricultural riots, extending from Kent to Cornwall; and that the first year of the restoration to power of the same party should be signalized by a still more formidable movement in the manufacturing districts of Yorkshire and Lancashire. Thus, it would seem as if a Tory ministry were fated to leave us a legacy of incendiarism when they depart, and to make us a gift of insurrection when they return. We shall be asked if these acts can fairly be attributed to the measures either of the Legislature or of the Government. Without wishing to cast upon our opponents any exaggerated or undue responsibility, we cannot avoid entertaining the strongest conviction that the whole policy pursued by them, since 1835, has had a great share in producing the deplorable result which we have lately witnessed. The mode in which the new Poor-Law was opposed and discussed, diffused most widely a deep and settled, though a most unfounded conviction, that the oppression and degradation of the poorer classes was the effect, and almost the object, of the statute complained of. Those classes were taught to believe that their interests were disregarded, their feelings set at naught and outraged, and their liberties abridged. In this cry nine-tenths of the Tory party combined, and some of the demagogues disgracefully joined. At this their leaders connived, with some honourable exceptions; and of this cry the whole party took advantage. Nothing tended more than this to unsettle the minds of the people. The Poor-Law agitation prepared the way for the Chartist agitation which was sure to follow. Again, the question of the Factory Bill was used as a political instrument. The workmen were set against their employers by Tory agitators; they were taught to consider those employers as enemies and tyrants. The cry for a ten hours' bill was raised at many elections in the manufacturing districts; and riot and confusion were preached and practised in the name of religion and humanity. Further, on many occasions in which a sympathy for the cases of the felon and the convict could be turned against the government—as in the case of the Dorchester labourers—Tory sympathy was ready. The formation of a Tory democracy was proclaimed to be a necessary duty; and, under this plan, Socialists and Chartists were all cajoled and flattered, provided they but possessed the necessary qualifications of hatred to the Whigs and opposition to the Government

The effects of this alliance between Chartists and Tory Radicals were strongly felt at the general election. We witnessed with astonishment the step into which, by some unhappy mistake, the leading members of the Government were betrayed, in granting long interviews, and holding confidential communications with the least creditable members of the least creditable political societies; handying compliments and courtesies with the printer of the *Northern Star*, and with the ex-doorkeeper of the National Convention. How the zeal of the bishop of Exeter, so quick and energetic on former occasions, has been allowed to continue inactive at present, we know not; but we are certain that, with one-tenth part the provocation he has lately received, this prelate would, in 1840, have called for the impeachment of Lord Melbourne and the Marquis of Normanby. The manner in which the question of machinery was dealt with, even in the arguments of the Government—the countenance publicly given to that most dangerous of all sophisms which represents machinery as prejudicial to the artizan—added to the general irritation. The whole was brought to a head by the misfeasance and the nonfeasance of the last session. Speeches like those of Mr. Ferrand were cheered, applauded, printed, and circulated, whilst the principles of monopoly were defended as far as it was practicable; all inquiry was refused into the frightful distress so universally prevalent; the interests of the industrious classes were overlooked and undervalued in the new budget; the necessity of keeping up an artificial high price for bread was avowed, and, as far as might be, was justified; and no reduction was made in the duties levied on the raw materials of wool and cotton, by which reductions the employment of the labouring classes would have been encouraged. All these causes combined to add to the general discontent; and they were more closely connected with the late lamentable outrages than any of the absurd manifestoes of the Anti-Corn-Law League, to which they have been ascribed. Nor have these imputations been exclusively directed against the Anti-Corn-Law League; they have been extended to the whole class of mill-owners, or, in other words, to the capitalists who employ the greatest amount of labour. It is not only false, but ridiculous, to suppose that the leading manufacturers would conspire in order to arrest the progress of their own industry, to expose their own capital to certain loss, and their persons to violence and imminent danger.

It is impossible to touch upon this subject without expressing the deep sorrow and sympathy which we have felt for the sufferings of the working classes during the last twelve or eighteen months. These sufferings cannot any longer be treated as the exaggeration of interested men; they are described in the official reports made by agents employed by the Government. In all cases—whether the condition of a single town like Stockport is considered, or the interests of a whole class, like the hand-loom weavers—it is to our wretched Corn-Laws that we trace the aggravation of these calamities. Whole families are shown to have been left without fuel, furniture, with scarcely any raiment or bed-covering, and with a pittance of food inadequate to human support. In these miseries, old and young, the industrious as well as the idle, have been alike involved. The consequences have been wretchedness the most deplorable, the exhaustion of the charitable subscriptions collected, the depreciation of the property liable to assessment, the spread of contagion, and mortality frightfully increased. Under such circumstances, how strong is the appeal made to our hearts in a noble sonnet, in which Wordsworth has shown how truly the sympathies, as well as the genius, of man may be preserved and exalted in advancing years?—

' Feel for the wrongs to universal ken
Daily exposed, woe that unshrouded lies;
And seek the sufferer in his darkest den,
Whether conducted to the spot by sighs
And moanings, or he dwells (as if the wren
Taught him concealment) hidden from all eyes
In silence and the awful modesties
Of sorrow.'

That our Government and our Legislature felt deeply for these sorrows and sufferings, we are far from doubting; but let us ask, whether they have practically marked this sympathy in their acts. Perhaps it will be said, that nothing could be done in the way of relief. We are always slow in admitting this plea, the threadbare apology of indolence or ignorance. Parliament might have derived sounder instruction from a sublime exhortation which closes the poem we have quoted :

' Learn to be just; just through impartial law,
Far as ye may erect and equalize,
And what ye cannot reach by statute, draw
Each from his fountain of self-sacrifice.'

Would that this precept had, in the last session, been practically adopted! But looking through the tedious statute-book, and the debates more tedious still, we confess that we see but little evidence to prove that the condition of the suffering workmen of England has occupied a due share of the attention of our rulers.

We must, however, guard ourselves against what would be a most false inference, if it were to be deduced from these observations. Though we may admit many of the causes of complaint of the working classes to be just, we do not more strongly deplore than we condemn the late wicked outbreak. The grievances were not of a character to justify the illegal violence which has prevailed; and even if the grievances had been such, the illegal conduct of the rioters could not but aggravate them, and greatly increase the obstacles which impede the success of all remedial measures, whether political, economical, or social. Falstaff declined to give his rea-

sons upon compulsion, and John Bull is apt to refuse to do justice as long as he can, if justice is demanded in a tone of menace. All violence, by creating alarm, throws back the cause of popular reform, and increases that power of resistance on which Tory ascendency depends. But the whole movement was as absurd as it was iniquitous. Except in the ever-memorable blunder of the Irish insurgents who burned the notes of an unpopular banker, no example can be found of such signal folly as the violence which prompted men to interfere with active industry, and consequently with the remuneration of labour, at a time when the immediate cause of suffering was a want of employment. But in many cases the suffering was not the criminal class ; and even when the sufferers were led into criminal acts, they appear to have been the dupes and instruments of more guilty men. The sympathy which we feel for calamities, however deplorable, ought not to render us unwilling to repress or to condemn atrocities and violence which strike at the root of all prosperity, and whose severest and most immediate pressure falls on the poorest class of the community. Tranquillity, important as it is to all, is essential in a pre-eminent degree to those whose existence depends on their daily labour. The wages of the artizan are the first sacrifice made in times of civil confusion. The landed proprietor, and even the capitalist, may wait for better times, but the working classes perish. What to others is pain, to them is death.

We have hitherto adverted to the larger measures of policy, in which we have shown that the conduct of the present Government has been diametrically opposed to the anticipations of their friends, and to all their principles and their professions. Similar examples are to be found in almost every other act of the session, however secondary. The postponement of the Ecclesiastical Courts' Bill in former years, had been held up to reprobation as a proof of the indolence or the incapacity of the Whig Government ; yet that bill has been again postponed, as also the bill for the registration of voters. The curtailment of colonial measures in former sessions, had been relied on as conclusive evidence of the weakness of Lord Melbourne's Cabinet; yet we have seen Lord Stanley's Newfoundland Bill limited in its duration, and shorn of its fair proportions, when pertinaciously opposed by Mr. O'Connell. The alteration of financial measures had been described as an unpardonable offence in Lord Spencer and Lord Monteagle ; Sir Robert Peel not only reduced his proposed coalduties one half, but he claimed credit for the concession. A bill authorizing the importation of foreign flour into Ireland, had been rejected in 1840 by the Tories; the Tories, in 1842, have carried the same measure. A proposal to allow the grinding of foreign wheat in bond, had formerly been opposed by Sir Edward Knatchbull, as being an insult and an injury to the agriculturists; in the last session the very same proposal was made by Mr. Gladstone, and met with less opposition from the Paymaster of the Forces than he would have raised to the payment of a turnpike toll in Kent. So far from reducing the funded debt, the present Board of Treasury has increased it; and the redemption of Exchequer bills by the trustees of Savings Banks, (a measure so much misrepresented and objected to), has received a new legislative sanction under the auspices of Sir Robert Peel. In short, the fixed and definite principle on which it would appear that the Government acted throughout, has been to oppose all that they had previously supported, and to support much that they had most strenuously opposed.

We might here be taxed with disingenuousness, if we were to pass over unnoticed a remarkable defence which has been somewhat ostentatiously put forward in the last number of the *Quarterly Review.* If that defence were admitted, we confess that much of our argument would be inapplicable, and many of our inferences most uncandid and unjust. It is contended that no want of truth and candour can be attributed to the leading Conservatives, no *suppressio veri,* and no *suggestio falsi ;* because in June, 1841, before the late General Election, an article had been published in that Journal, recommending some alterations in the scale of corn and customs duties. Now, we confess that a very great bribe is held out to induce us to agree with our contemporary. We should thereby assume for ourselves, as well as grant to him, new and most extraordinary rights and functions. We should claim, for our political essays, privileges and authorities hitherto confined to speeches from the Throne, state papers, and the official declarations of responsible ministers. The present Government would rule not only by the force of a parliamentary majority, but by the grace and favour of the *Quarterly Review.*

Till a diplomatist produces his letters of credence, and his full powers, he cannot be recognized by a foreign court. We doubt whether Sir Robert Peel will sign the unlimited power of attorney under which the *Quarterly* Reviewer demands to act. Indeed, it passes all credibility, that at a moment when the secret of the minister was so very

carefully kept that the Duke of Buckingham remained his colleague, that Sir James Graham and Lord Stanley made their memorable speeches at Dorchester and in Lancashire, when all explanations were refused to Parliament, the whole future policy of the new administration should have been confided to the generous, faithful, and friendly Reviewer. The dilemma in which the over-zealous advocate has involved himself and his friends, is one of no common difficulty. If in June, 1841, Sir Robert Peel had determined on his line of policy, concealing it from his own cabinet, his friends, and the public, at a time when he confided it to any single literary and political associate, however strong his attachment and approved his fidelity, no greater deception was ever practised in the annals of our history. If, on the contrary, he only determined on his course upon subsequent deliberation, after profiting by those official counsels of which he stated himself to stand in need, the predictions of Mr. Murphy's *Weather Almanac* are entitled to as much of authority as the mere surmises of the Reviewer. As well might the glory and responsibility of the victory of Waterloo be claimed by one whose only connection with that event had been the command of a very awkward squad at Wormwood Scrubs. It also behoves us to reject this supposition, however gratifying to our own self-love as belonging to the class proposed to be exalted; because, if the supposition be founded on fact, many fatal inferences might follow. On the same principle, we might anticipate the reconstruction of the national Church of England according to Tractarian doctrines; the enactment of a new penal code in Ireland; and the excitement of hatred and all uncharitableness between the Anglo-Saxon races on each side of the Atlantic. How very indefensible must this chivalrous advocate have felt the position of his friends to be, when he thus throws himself into the breach, leads forward *les enfans perdus,* and exclaims, ' *Me, me, adsum qui feci—in me convertite ferrum !'*

There is another subject which it is impossible to overlook, and yet it is one very difficult to discuss in a sketch so rapid as the present. The anticipated foreign influences of Sir Robert Peel's government has received a most signal contradiction, in the refusal of the French cabinet to ratify the treaty not only agreed to by their minister, but in some degree negotiated at their own instance. The disgrace of this event, most fatal as it is to the character of the French government, but not very flattering to our national pride, rests, it is true, mainly with the King of the French and with M. Guizot, not with Lord Aberdeen;

but had such an event occurred to Lord Palmerston, no epithets would have been too vituperative to have been applied to his conduct. We shall not imitate this injustice. Let the disgrace rest on the foreign statesmen who are really responsible. We not only hope, but we believe, that for this event the Foreign Secretary is in no respect to blame; we have, however, some curiosity to know in what language the complaints and protests of the British Minister have been expressed.

We feel some difficulty in referring to the inexplicable policy of Lord Ellenborough in the East, and yet it cannot be entirely overlooked. In an Empire like ours in British India, which depends so peculiarly upon opinion, and upon a conviction of our moral superiority, a degrading retreat seems to have been meditated, which has only been averted or postponed in consequence of opportune orders from home, or some other happy contingency, which has saved England from unexampled ignominy. Well, indeed, was Lord Palmerston justified in saying that ' he could not conceive a fouler dishonour, or anything that would have dyed the cheek of every Englishman with a deeper blush, or that would have struck a more fatal blow at our Indian power, than a flight from Affghanistan in the circumstances in which Lord Ellenborough's order was issued.' But if this measure was disgraceful on political grounds, where shall we find words to condemn it, if English soldiers, English subjects, and English women, wives and daughters of our countrymen, were proposed to have been deserted, and left in the hands of barbarians? Our diplomatic minister had been treacherously murdered; the sacred compacts of treaty had been violated; our brave troops had been betrayed and cut to pieces; the heroic Lady Sale and her fellow-sufferers left in captivity; and yet no effort seems to have been made to avenge their wrongs, or to set them free. Scarcely less disgraceful will it be, if the safety of these unhappy persons has been made matter of low and unworthy compromise. At no former period of our history, in our most disastrous campaigns, has any event occurred which seems to us comparable to the ignominy of Lord Ellenborough's proposed retreat.

Whilst this article has been in the press, accounts have been received of the close of our diplomatic controversy with the United States, by the signature of Lord Ashburton's treaty. Considering peace between England and the United States to be important, not only to the wellbeing and happiness of both countries, but essential to the cause of liberty and good government throughout the world, we should not feel disposed to inquire curiously whether too much may not have been granted, or too little obtained, as the price of so immeasurable a benefit. Still, if the rights of British subjects, born under British allegiance, and holding their property under British grants, have been abandoned, and if new causes of dispute respecting navigation have been substituted for those which we hope are now terminated, many explanations will be required before Lord Ashburton's treaty can be admitted to be a just claim on the public for gratitude and respect. That his explanations may be satisfactory, we hope, and indeed expect; and if they are so shown, no party difference will prevent us from rendering our most sincere acknowledgments to Lord Aberdeen and his colleagues, as well as to Lord Ashburton, for having happily effected a pacification between two states of common origin, between whom no serious differences can ever arise, without consequences the most fatal to both.

We have now taken a retrospect of the measures of the last session; omitting, however, the subject of the Law Reform, including Lord Brougham's *Cessio Bonorum* Bill —one of the most benevolent results of his unwearied exertions in that great cause—for after discussion, in a separate article. We have shown, if our arguments are correct, that the corn-law of Sir R. Peel is founded upon a false principle, and that since its enactment it has worked badly for the Producer and the Consumer. We have shown that in this Tariff he has not carried out his own principles with courage and with effect. We have proved, that while the country is subjected to all the pressure and inquisitorial vexation of an Income-Tax, the Financial difficulties of the times have not been adequately met, nor has any certain surplus of revenue been secured. We have shown, that in the place of domestic tranquillity, we have had to deplore riot and insurrection; and that this has been traceable, in a considerable degree, to the exciting and exaggerated doctrines of a section of the Tories, when in opposition. We have shown that all the leading badges and symbols of party, which produced success at the late election, have been thrown aside, as being now no longer necessary. We have shown that, in as far as the measures of the Government are right, they are the very measures of their Opponents; adopted and defended with a disregard of all consistency, and in violation of all the engagements of party connexion. Yet in the adoption of these principles, *we* have our reward, and *our* justification.

Sir Robert Peel may cast his party aside at his pleasure, and they must submit; for, difficult as they find it to live with him, without him they cannot live. But Sir Robert Peel cannot arrest the great commercial movement to which, on principle, he has now given his authority. His tariff is all-important by what it promises, if not by what it has effected. It may be described in the lines which an accomplished French poet has applied to Spring—

> ' Il plait plus aux humains
> Par les plaisirs qu'il promêt, que par ceux qu'il procure.'

His measures must and will be followed up— his principles must and will be applied further: and if, in so doing, he condemns every measure adopted by his party during the last ten years; if he thus pays an unwilling, but most respectful homage to the conduct of his opponents; if he incurs the bitter hostility of his earliest friends; if he leaves himself without one single newspaper to defend his administration generally; if the keen blade of Sir Richard Vyvyan is bared against him in Cornwall; if he is called upon to plead ' Guilty or Not Guilty' at Plymouth; if in Leicestershire a cry is raised to dethrone him, in order that Lord Stanley may reign in his stead; if he makes it a punishment to any of his political supporters to meet their constituents at public meetings, there to defend the votes they have given; if a Conservative dinner would now be a grievous martyrdom, and a General Election would be all but fatal— he should be reconciled to these mortifications by the thought, that in acting on the impulses produced by the propositions of Mr. Baring, he is averting from his country dangers the most imminent, and is promoting the best interests of his fellow-subjects, and of mankind.

1 ABDY—The Water-Cure; Cases of Disease cured by Cold Water. By E. S. Abdy, M. A. 8vo. pp. 209, sewed, 4s. 6d.

2 ADDISON—The Temple Church at London; its History and Antiquities. By C. G. Addison, Esq. of the Inner Temple; Author of "The History of the Knights Templars." Square crown 8vo. *In the Press.*—This work will contain a full account of the restoration of the Temple Church—the chief ecclesiastical edifice of the Knights Templars in Great Britain, and the most beautiful and perfect memorial of the order now in existence; together with a full description of the tessellated pavement—the painted ceiling—the marble columns—the stained windows—the sacrarium—the almeries, or sacramental niches—the penitential cell—the ancient chapel of St. Anne—the monumental remains, &c.

3 ALFRED DUDLEY; or, the Australian Settlers. 2d edition, square, pp. 196, and many illustrations, cloth, 3s. 6d.

4 ALLEN—Battles of the British Navy, from A.D. 1000 to 1840. By Joseph Allen, Esq. 2 vols. 12mo. pp. 1112, cloth 21s.

4* ALLEN'S (Cardinal) Admonition to the Nobility and People, A.D. 1588. Reprinted in 12mo. pp. 60, cloth, 6s.

5 ANDERSON—The Popular Scottish Biography; being Lives of Eminent Natives of Scotland. 12mo. pp. 795, cloth, 10s.

6 ANDERSON— Guide to the Highlands and Islands of Scotland, including Orkney and Zetland; descriptive of their Scenery, Statistics, Antiquities, and Natural History: with numerous Historical and Traditional Notices, Map, Tables of Distances, Notices of Inns, and other information for the use of Tourists. By George Anderson and Peter Anderson of Inverness. New edition, 12mo. (Edinburgh), with map and index, pp. 744, cloth, 10s. 6d.

7 ANNALS OF CHYMISTRY and Practical Pharmacy. No. 1, 8vo. 8d. (To be continued Weekly.)—The aim of this work will be to afford to the English Chemist a Weekly Summary of the Discoveries of Continental Chemists, practically condensed, so that whilst thoroughly explanatory to the philosopher, it will be practically useful to the Chemist and Druggist.

8 APEL—Practical Introduction to the Study of the German Language. By Heinrich Apel. 12mo. pp. 340, cloth, 5s. 6d.

9 ARCHBOLD—The New Poor-Law Amendment Act, and the recent Rules and Orders of the Poor-Law Commissioners: with a Practical Introduction, Notes, and Forms. By John F. Archbold, Esq. Barrister-at-Law. 12mo. pp. 190, boards, 5s. 6d.

10 ARUNDALE — The Gallery of Antiquities: selected from the British Museum. By F. Arundale, Architect; and J. Bonomi, Sculptor: with Descriptions by S. Birch, Assistant to the Antiquarian Department at the British Museum. Part 1, Egyptian Art, Mythological Illustrations. 4to. pp. 60, 28 Plates, with numerous figures (many coloured), boards, 21s.

11 ATKINSON—The Recent Operations of the British Forces in Affghanistan; consisting of Views of the most beautiful Scenery through which the Army passed, with Figures illustrative of memorable Events which occurred during the Campaign, and descriptive of the Manners and Costumes of the Natives. Drawn on Stone by Louis Haghe, Esq., from the original and highly-finished drawings executed on the spot by James Atkinson, Esq., Superintending Surgeon of the Army of the Indus. 26 Plates, royal folio, 4l. 4s. half-bound; coloured and mounted as the original drawings, 10l. 10s.

12 ATKINSON—The Expedition into Affghanistan: Notes and Sketches Descriptive of the Country. By J. Atkinson, Esq., Surgeon. Post 8vo. pp. 428, cloth, 10s. 6d.

13 BARNES—The Elements of Linear Perspective, and the Projection of Shadows: adapted to the use of Mathematical and Drawing Classes and Private Students. With 61 Diagrams on Wood. By W. Barnes, of St. John's College, Cambridge. 12mo. pp. 57, cloth, 2s. 6d.

14 BARTLETT—The Scenery and Antiquities of Ireland, illustrated from Drawings by W. H. Bartlett; the literary portion of the work by N. P. Willis and J. Stirling Coyne, Esqrs. 2 vols. 4to. pp. 356, with Portrait, Map, and 120 other Illustrations, cloth lettered, gilt edges, 3l. 3s.

15 BATHURST—The Elements of Arithmetic;

expressly designed for the use of Schools. By C. Bathurst, M.A., of St. John's College, Cambridge; Second Master of Sir John Williamson's Free School, Rochester. 12mo. (Rochester), pp. 142, cloth 3s.

Key containing the Solutions of the Questions under each Rule. 12mo. (Rochester), pp. 42, cloth, 2s. 6d.

16 BEATTIE—The History of the Church of Scotland during the Commonwealth. By the Rev. James Beattie. Foolscap 8vo. (Edinburgh), pp. 372, cloth, 4s.

17 BEDFORD—Correspondence of John, Fourth Duke of Bedford, selected from the Originals at Woburn Abbey: with an Introduction by Lord John Russell, 8vo. with Portrait. *In the Press.*

18 BELL — Chambers's Educational Course: Treatise on Practical Mathematics. By A. Bell. 2 vols. 12mo. pp. 730, cloth, 8s.

19 BERNARD—The Synagogue and the Church; being an attempt to show that the Government, Ministers, and Services of the Church, were derived from those of the Synagogue. Condensed from the original Latin work of Vitringa, by I. L. Bernard, A.M. 8vo. pp. 262, cloth, 7s. 6d.

20 BIBLE—The Bible: with Notes and Reflections. By D. Davidson. With Index, &c. Foolscap folio, pp. 1423, cloth, 37s.

21 BICKERSTETH—A Companion to the Baptismal Font; being an Abridgment of "A Treatise on Baptism;" designed as a help to the due Improvement of that Holy Sacrament as administered in the Church of England. By the Rev. E. Bickersteth, Rector of Watton, Herts. 18mo. pp. 182, cloth, 2s.

22 BICKMORE—Course of Historical and Chronological Instruction. By W. E. Bickmore. Post 8vo. pp. 272, cloth lettered, 10s. 6d.

23 BINGLEY—Natural History of Animals; illustrated by Short Histories and Anecdotes. By the Rev. W. Bingley, A.M. 3d edition, 12mo. pp. 310, cloth, 7s.

24 BIOGRAPHICAL DICTIONARY of the Society for the Diffusion of Useful Knowledge; containing Memoirs of Persons from the commencement of Historical Records to the Present Time. Vol. 1, part 1, 8vo, pp. 448, cloth, 12s.

25 BLACK's Map Book and Railway Guide of England. 8vo. pp. 48, and 18 maps, cloth, 4s. 6d.

26 BLACKWOOD's Standard Novels, Vol. 9—Pen Owen. Foolscap 8vo. pp. 470, with Frontispiece, cloth, 6s.

27 BLAIR's Chronological and Historical Tables, from the Creation to the present time. New edition, carefully corrected, enlarged, and brought down to the present time. Royal 8vo. *In the Press.*

28 BONNYCASTLE—Newfoundland in 1842: a Sequel to "The Canadas in 1841." By Sir Richard Henry Bonnycastle, Knight, Lieutenant-Colonel in the Corps of Royal Engineers. 2 vols. post 8vo. with map, 3 illustrations, and portrait of the Governor, Sir John Harvey, K.C.B., pp. 734, cloth, 21s.

29 BOOK of One Syllable. With 6 plates, square, pp. 183, cloth, 3s.

30 BOSANQUET—Metallic, Paper, and Credit Currency, and the means of regulating their Quantity and Value. By J. W. Bosanquet, Esq. 8vo. pp. 156, sewed, 3s. 6d.

31 BOYS—Original Views of London as it is. Drawn from Nature, expressly for this work, and lithographed by Thomas Shotter Boys. Exhibiting its Principal Streets and Characteristic Accessories, Public Buildings in connection with the leading Thoroughfares, &c. &c. With Descriptive and Historical Notices of the Views, by Charles Ollier, in English and French. Imperial folio, printed with sepia tints, 4l. 4s. bound; a few copies, coloured by hand, and mounted, in a portfolio, 10l. 10s.

32 BRACE—Observations on Extension of Protection to Copyright of Designs, with a view to the Improvement of British Taste; including the Act passed August 10, 1842, for consolidating and amending the Laws relating thereto: to which are added Legal and Practical Notes with Instructions relative to the registering of Designs. By George Brace, Secretary to the Linen-Drapers' Association. Post 8vo. pp. 140, cloth, 5s. 6d.

33 BRITISH ARCHITECTS—Transactions of the Royal Institute of British Architects of London (Incorporated in the 7th Year of William IV.) Vol. 1, Part 2, 4to. 16 plates and numerous woodcuts, pp. 297, cloth lettered, 24s.

34 BRUFF—A Treatise on Engineering Field Work; comprising the Practice of Surveying, Levelling, and Laying-out Works: with Diagrams and Plates. By P. Bruff, C. E. Part 2—Levelling, 8vo. pp. 128, cloth, 6s. 6d.

35 BURKE—The Criminal Law, and its Sentences, in Treasons, Felonies, and Misdemeanours. By Peter Burke, Esq. of the Inner Temple, Barrister-at-Law. Square 12mo. pp. 254, bound, 5s. 6d.

36 BURNS—The Youthful Christian; containing Instructions, Counsels, Cautions, and Examples. By J. Burns, Minister of Enon Chapel, St. Marylebone, Author of "The Christian's Daily Portion," &c. 18mo. pp. 108, cloth, 2s.

37 BUSWELL—Plain Parochial Sermons on Important Subjects. By the Rev. William Buswell, B.A. 12mo. pp. 355, cloth, 6s.

38 CALCOTT—A Scripture Herbal: with upwards of One Hundred and Twenty Wood Engravings. By Lady Calcott. Square crown 8vo. This work will contain an account of all the Plants, Drugs, Perfumes, and Gums, mentioned in the Bible; with one or more woodcuts of every species, (excepting two, of which no authentic figure can be obtained). The Bible names are retained, and the modern Botanic appellations added; together with the Linnean class and order, and also the Natural orders, according to the latest authorities. The texts of Scripture in which the plants are mentioned are enumerated; and an account of the growth, native country, and uses of the plant is given, collected from ancient and modern authors. *In the Press.*

39 CATLOW—Popular Conchology; or, the Shell Cabinet arranged: being an Introduction to the Modern System of Conchology; with a Sketch of the Natural History of the Animals, an account of the Formation of the Shells, and a complete Descriptive List of the Families and Genera. By Agnes Catlow. 1 vol. foolscap 8vo. with 312 woodcuts. *In the Press.* The object of this work is to bring forward the subject of Conchology in a more popular manner than has yet been attempted. It is addressed to the young by the simplicity of its language and arrangement; and exhibits in an attractive view the system of Lamarck, with the addition of many new genera established by modern writers. By the help of the tables it contains, the student is enabled with ease to arrange, class, and name every specimen in a collection of shells.

40 CAVENDISH's (Sir H.) Debates of the House of Commons, during the Thirteenth Parliament of Great Britain, commonly called the *Unreported Parliament*, which met in May, 1768, and was dissolved in June, 1774: to which are appended Illustrations of the Parliamentary History of the Reign of George the Third. Drawn up from the Original MSS. by J. Wright, Editor of "The Parliamentary History of England," &c. To be completed in 16 Parts, price 6s. each, making 4 Volumes, royal 8vo. printed uniformly with the Parliamentary History of England, and the Parliamentary Debates. Part 5, pp. 1 to 160, vol. 2, 6s.
Vol 1 (the first Four Parts), pp. 647, cloth lettered, 25s.

41 CAWOOD—Sermons, by John Cawood, M.A., of St. Edmund Hall, Oxford, and Perpetual Curate of Bewdley, Worcestershire. 2 vols. 8vo. pp. 896, cloth, 21s.

42 CECIL—Remains of the Rev. R. Cecil, M.A., late Rector of Bisley, &c. Edited by the Rev. Josiah Pratt, B.D. F.A.S. 24mo. pp 260, cloth, 2s. 6d.

43 CHARLOTTE ELIZABETH—"Principalities and Powers in Heavenly Places." By Charlotte Elizabeth. With Introductory Remarks by the Rev. E. Bickersteth. Being Vol. 38 of the "Christian's Family Library." Foolscap, 8vo. pp. 334, cloth, 5s. This work is divided into two parts: the first treating of the Existence, Character, and Final Doom of Evil Spirits; and the second, of the Existence, Character, and Final Triumph of the Holy Angels: with concluding remarks.

44 CHESS—The Game of Chess exemplified in a concise and easy Notation, greatly facilitating Practice; being an Introduction to the Game, on a system of Progressive Instruction and Examples. By the late President of a Chess Club. *In the Press.*

45 CHILD—Tables, selected and arranged; being adapted for use in the Counting-house, the Office, and to the General Reader. By R. Child. 12mo. pp. 182; cloth, 5s. 6d. A miscellaneous collection of facts.

46 CHRISTOPHER NORTH—The Recreations of Christopher North (Prof. Wilson). Reprints from Blackwood's Magazine, in 3 vols.

crown 8vo. Vol. 2, pp. 404, cloth lettered, 10s. 6d. CONTENTS— The Moors— The Highland Snow Storm—The Holy Child— Our Parish—May Day—Sacred Poetry.

47 CLARIDGE—Hydropathy; or, the Cold Water Cure, as practised by Vincent Priessnitz, at Graefenberg, Silesia, Austria. By R. T. Claridge, Esq. Author of "Guide to the Danube." 3d edit. 8vo. pp. 318, with Frontispiece, sewed, 5s.

48 CLASSIFIED Spelling-Book, (The,) with Definitions and Explanations. 12mo. pp. 169, bound, 2s.

49 CLAVERS—Forest Life. By Mary Clavers, an Actual Settler; Author of "A New Home— Who'll Follow?" 2 vols. foolscap 8vo. pp 642, cloth, 12s

50 CLAYTON — The Drawing Book of Irish Scenery, Figures, Cattle, &c. Drawn from Nature and on Stone. By B. Clayton. Oblong, 28 plates, boards, 4s. 6d.

51 CLEMENT's Customs Guide; containing copious Extracts of the Laws, with Tables of the Duties payable upon Goods imported and exported; also, the Customs and Excise Bounties and Drawbacks, &c.: with a List of the Warehousing Ports; also, the London Waterside Practice, &c. &c. By George Clements, Custom-House, London. Seventh Annual Edition, for 1842-43. 12mo. pp. 382, cloth, 6s.

52 CLEMENTS—The Customs' Pocket Manual. By G. Clements. Foolscap pp 92, 2s.

53 COCKBURN—First Chapters on the Church of England—her Clergy, her Liturgy, her Articles, and her Temporalities, By the Rev. G. A. Cockburn, M.A. Foolscap 8vo. pp. 258, cloth, 4s.

54 COMBE—A Treatise on the Physiological and Moral Management of Infancy. By Andrew Combe, M.D. 3d edition, foolscap 8vo. pp. 404 (Edinb.,) cloth, 6s.

55 COTTAGE on the Common; and the Little Gleaners, By C. M. 16mo. pp. 105, cloth, 2s.

56 COULSON—On Diseases of the Bladder and Prostate Gland. By W. Coulson. 3d edition, revised and corrected, 8vo. pp. 302, with 4 plates, cloth, 7s.

57 COULTHARD—Rhymes for an Hour: Poems on several occasions. By Clara Coulthard. 18mo. pp. 124, cloth, 3s.

58 COWAN—A Bedside Manual of Physical Diagnosis By Charles Cowan, M.D.P. & E., Physician to the Royal Berkshire Hospital, and Reading Dispensary. 2d edition, revised and enlarged: with an Appendix, containing a Plan for the Registration of Cases in Hospital and Private Practice; also, an Abstract of Mr. Farr's Statistical Nosology. 18mo. pp. 118, cloth, 3s. 6d.

59 COWE—Parochial Sermons, on various Subjects of Doctrine and Practice. By James Cowe, M A. late Vicar of Sunbury, Middlesex. 12mo. pp. 348, boards, 6s.

60 CRICHTON—Commentaries on some Doctrines of a Dangerous Tendency in Medicine, and on the General Principles of Safe Practice. By Sir A. Crichton, M.D. F.R.S. &c. 8vo. pp. 283, cloth, 9s.

61 CROWDY—Church of England Village Dia-

logues; containing Remarks upon the Foundation, Order, Usages, Services, and Liturgy of the Church; also, answering certain Popular Objections, and showing the evil of certain Practices in religion among those who separate themselves from her. By Anthony Crowdy, A.M. Rector of Winnal, Winchester. 14th thousand, 12mo. pp. 146, sewed in cloth, 1s. 6d.

62 CRUVEILHIER—Descriptive Anatomy. By J. Cruveilhier, Professor of Anatomy to the Faculty of Medicine at Paris. (2 vols). Vol. 2, being Vol. 8 of Tweedie's Library of Practical Medicine, post 8vo. pp. 586, with numerous Illustrations on Wood, cloth, 18s.

63 CUNNINGHAM—Westminster Abbey; its Art, Architecture, and Associations: a Hand-Book for Visitors. By P. Cunningham. Foolscap, pp. 100, boards, 2s. 6d.

64 CUSTOMS—Act to Amend the Laws relating to the Customs, 5 and 6 Vict. c. 47: with an Index. 18mo. pp. 88, sewed, 1s. 6d.

65 DALLENGER's Income-Tax Tables; showing, at one view, the Amount of Duties to be paid on Property, Professions, Tithes, &c. from 1s. to L.10,000, &c. 8vo. (Woodbridge), pp. 22, sewed, 1s.

66 DALTON—An Explanatory and Practical Commentary on the New Testament of our Lord Jesus Christ: intended chiefly as a Help to Family Devotion. Edited and continued by the Rev. W. Dalton, M.A. Incumbent of St. Paul's Church, Wolverhampton. 2d edition, 2 vols. 8vo. pp. 1352, cloth, 24s.

67 D'ARBLAY—Diary and Letters of Madame D'Arblay. Edited by her Niece. Vol. 4, post 8vo. pp. 421, cloth, 10s. 6d.

68 DARWIN—The Structure and Distribution of Coral Reefs. Being the first part of the Geology of the Voyage of the Beagle, under the Command of Capt. Fitzroy, R.N. during the years 1832-36. By Charles Darwin, M.A. F.R.S. F.G.S., Naturalist to the Expedition. 8vo. pp. 226, 3 maps and woodcuts, cloth, (published in May), 15s.

69 DAUBUZ—A Symbolical Dictionary; in which, agreeably to the Nature and Principles of the Symbolical Character and Language of the Eastern Nations in the First Ages of the world, the general Signification of the Prophetic Symbols, especially of those of the Apocalypse, is laid down and proved from the most Ancient Authorities, Sacred and Profane: By Charles Daubuz, M.A. Vicar of Brotherton, Yorkshire. New and enlarged edition, with a Memoir of the Author, and Preface by Matthew Habershon. Author of "An Historical Dissertation on the Prophetic Scripture of the Old Testament," &c. Post 8vo. pp. 240, cloth, 7s.

70 DAVY—Notes and Observations on the Ionian Islands and Malta; with some Remarks on Constantinople and Turkey, and on the system of Quarantine as at present conducted. By John Davy, M.D. F.R SS. L. & E. Inspector-General of Army Hospitals, L. R. 2 vols. 8vo. pp. 948, 7 plates and a map, cloth, 1l. 12s.

71 DE FOE—The Complete Works of Daniel De Foe: with a Memoir of his Life and Writings. By William Hazlitt. 2 thick vols. royal 8vo. double columns, with Portrait, cloth, 21s.

72 DELAMOTTE—Twenty-six Views of the Colleges, Chapels, and Gardens of Oxford. From Drawings made expressly for this work, by W. A. Delamotte, corresponding in size and style with Nash's and other Works, and executed in Lithography by Guaci. Printed in tints, 4l. 4s. bound, coloured, and mounted, in portfolio, 10l. 10s.

73 DEMMLER—Exercises on the German Grammar. By Franz Demmler, Professor at the Royal Military College, Sandhurst. 12mo. pp. 84, bound, 2s. 6d.

74 DERING—Sketches of Human Life. By the Rev. C, E. J. Dering, M.A. Foolscap, pp. 130, cloth, 3s. 6d.

75 DERING—Sacred Melodies (Poems). By the Rev. C. E. J. Dering, M.A. Ch. Ch. Oxford. 32mo. (Ashford), pp. 42, cloth, 1s.

76 DE STAINS—Phonography; or, the Writing of Sounds. In two Parts, viz: Logography, or Universal Writing of Speech; and Musicography, or Symbolical Writing of Music: with a Short-Hand for both. By V. D. de Stains, Graduate of the University of Paris. 2d edition, 8vo. pp. 216, 10s.

77 DICKENSON—Rustic Figures; a Series of Sketches, in Twenty-four Lithographic Plates, 4to. cloth, 21s.

78 DICKSON—Fallacies of the Faculty: with the Principles of the Cronothermal System. In a series of Lectures. By S. Dickson, M.D. late a Medical Officer on the Staff. 2d edition, 8vo. pp. 332, (London, 1841), cloth, reduced to 5s.

79 DOCTOR HOOKWELL; or, the Anglo-Catholic Family; a Religious (Puseyite) Novel. 3 vols. post 8vo. pp. 1026, boards, 31s. 6d.

80 DOWDING—Village Lectures upon certain of the Homilies of the Church of England. By the Rev. W. C. Dowding, B.A. 12mo. pp. 96, cloth, 3s. 6d.

81 DRESDEN GALLERY—The Most Celebrated Pictures of the Royal Gallery at Dresden, drawn on stone, from the originals, by Franz Haufstaengel. With Descriptions of the plates, Biographies of the Masters, &c., in French and German, in imperial folio, Nos. to 27, (to be completed in 40 numbers,) price 20s. each, single numbers, 30s., single prints, 12s.

82 DUBLIN (The) Latin Grammar, Part First: containing an Introduction to the Eight Parts of Speech; a Vocabulary of Substantives, Adjectives, and Verbs; and an Appendix. 12mo. (Dublin,) pp. 176, bound, 2s.

83 DUNCAN—How did England become an Oligarchy? Addressed to Parliamentary Reformers: to which is added, a short Treatise on the first principles of Political Government. By J. Duncan, Esq. Author of "The History of Guernsey," &c. 12mo. pp. 110, sewed in cloth, 2s.

84 DYMOND—Essays on the Principles of Morality, and on the Private and Political Rights and Obligations of Mankind. By J. Dymond, Author of "An Inquiry into the accordance

of War with the Principles of Christianity." 4th edition, 8vo. double columns, pp. 212, sewed, 3s. 6d.

85 EAST—The Two Dangerous Diseases of England — Consumption and Apoplexy: their Nature, Causes, and Cure. By R. East, Surgeon, &c. post 8vo. pp, 129, cloth, 5s.

86 EDGEWORTH—Rosamond: a Sequel to Rosamond in Early Lessons. By Maria Edgeworth. 4th edition, 2 vols. 18mo. pp. 453, cloth, 5s.

87 EIGHT WEEKS IN GERMANY; comprising Narratives, Descriptions, and Directions for Economical Tourists. By the Pedestrian. 12mo. (Edinburgh), pp. 395, cloth, 5s. 6d.

88 ELLIOT—The Sketcher's Guide: a light and portable apparatus for Drawing Landscape and other Outlines in Perspective *without* Elementary Knowledge; to which is added, a Companion of the Rules of Perspective and Effect. By W. F. Elliot, Esq. Oblong, 16s.

89 ELLIS—Family Secrets; or, Hints to those who would make Home Happy. By Mrs. Ellis, Author of "The Women of England." Vol. 2. 8vo. 11 plates, pp, 312, cloth, gilt edges, 12s.

90 ELLIS's British Tariff for 1842-43; showing the Duties payable on Foreign Goods. 12mo. boards, 6s.

91 ENCYCLOPÆDIA BRITANNICA; or, Dictionary of Arts, Sciences, and Miscellaneous Literature. 7th edition; edited by Professor Napier, greatly improved, with the Supplements to the former editions incorporated, a General Index, and numerous illustrative Engravings, 21 vols. 4to. cloth, 37l. 16s. Half-bound russia, 42l.

92 ENGLISHMAN'S LIBRARY. Vol. 32.—Selected Letters. Edited by the Rev. T. Chamberlain. Foolscap 8vo. pp. 282, cloth, 4s.

93 ENGRAVINGS after the Best Pictures of the Great Masters, Part 4; containing Landscape with Goats, by Claude Lorraine—The Sacrifice at Lystra, by Raffaelle Sanzio—The Blind Fiddler. by Wilkie: with Descriptions in French and English. Imperial folio, 18s. sewed; or 23s. in portfolio; proofs in portfolio, 31s. 6d.; before letters 42s.

94 ERICHSEN.—A Practical Treatise on the Diseases of the Scalp. By John E. Erichsen, M.R.C.S. 8vo. pp. 192, with six coloured plates, cloth, 10s. 6d.

95 ETCHING CLUB.—Milton's L'Allegro and Il Penseroso, with Illustrations, by Members of the Etching Club. Imperial 8vo.

96 ETZLER.—The Paradise within the reach of all Men, without Labour, by Powers of Nature and Machinery: an Address to all Intelligent Men. In Two Parts. By J. A. Etzler. First Part, 2d English edition, 8vo. pp. 56, sewed, 6d.

97 SECOND PART, 8vo. pp. 40, sewed, 6d.

98 FACTS and FIGURES: a Periodical Record of Statistics applied to Current Questions. Royal 8vo. pp. 190, cloth. 6s. "To record facts, and show their use, is the object of this work."

99 FAMILY Essays on the Creation, Preservation, and Government of the Universe: intended for the Evening of every Sunday throughout the Year; each essay followed by an appropriate Prayer. 8vo. pp. 424, cloth, 10s. 6d.

100 FABER—The Primitive Doctrine of Election; or, an Historical Inquiry into the Ideality and Causation of Scriptural Election, as received and maintained in the Primitive Church of Christ. By G. S. Faber, B.D., Master of Sherburn Hospital, and Canon of Salisbury. 2d edition, 8vo. pp. 448, cloth. 14s.

101 FINDEN's Royal Gallery of British Art, Part 10; containing Rustic Hospitality, painted by W. Collins, R.A.; engraved by J. Outrim—The Lucky Escape, painted by W. F. Witherington, R.A.; engraved by S. Fisher—The Lake of Nemi, painted by J. M. W. Turner, R.A,; engraved by R. Wallis: with Critical and Descriptive Remarks. Imperial folio, in portfolio. 25s

102 FIRESIDE STORIES; or, Recollections of my Schoolfellows. 3d edition, square, pp. 220, and many illustrations, cloth. 3s, 6d.

103 FISHER—Three Poems:—1. Eleusinia; or, the Soul's Progress.—2. Nimrod, the First Tyrant.—3. Sybilla Anglica. By R. Trott Fisher, late Fellow of Pembroke College, Cambridge. 2 vols. 8vo. pp. 390, cloth. 16s.

104 FITZGERALD—Holy Scripture the Ultimate Rule of Faith to a Christian Man. By the Rev. W. Fitzgerald, B.A., Trinity College, Dublin. Foolscap 8vo. pp. 214, cloth. 4s 6d.

105 FOOT—The United Church of England and Ireland Catholic. By the Rev. S. C. Foot. 8vo. pp. 144 sewed. 2s. 6d.

106 FORD—Chorazin; or, an Appeal to the Child of many Prayers, on Questions concerning the great Salvation. By D. E. Ford. 5th thousand, 18mo. pp. 122, cloth. 1s. 6d.

107 FOSTER—Elements of Arithmetic; comprising Logarithms, and the Computations of Artificers, &c. By the Rev. W. Foster, M.A., late Head Master of St. Paul's School, Southsea. 18mo. pp. 154, bound. 2s.

108 FRANCIS—The Little English Flora; or, a Botanical and Popular Account of all our common Field Flowers. By G. W. Francis, F.L.S. 2d edition, improved and augmented, foolscap, pp. 213, cloth. 7s.

109 FRANZ—A Treatise on Mineral Waters: with particular reference to those prepared at the Royal German Spa at Brighton. By J. C. A. Franz, M.D. M.R.C.S. 12mo. pp. 169, cloth. 4s. 6d.

110 FREELING—Picturesque Excursions: with 400 Views at and near Places of Popular Resort. Edited by A. Freeling. Foolscap, pp. 332, cloth. 5s. 6d.

111 GARLANDS—A Collection of Right Merrie Garlands for North Country Anglers. Post 8vo. pp. 142. Woodcuts by Bewick, (Newcastle), cl. 10s. 6d. The following are the Contents:—The Angler's Progress, a Poem, developing the pleasures which the Angler receives from the dawn of the

propensity in infancy, till the period of his becoming a complete angler: (Newcastle, 1820.)—The Tyne Fisher's Farewell to his favourite stream on the approach of Winter: (Newcastle, 1824.)—And the Fisher's Garland: a Collection of Annual Songs, on the subject from 1821 to 1840.

112 GIBBINGS—Roman Forgeries and Falsifications: or, an Examination of Counterfeit and Corrupted Records, with especial reference to Popery. By the Rev. R. Gibbings, M.A., Rector of Ramunterdoney, Diocese of Raphoe. Part 1, 8vo. (Dublin,) pp. 172, cloth. 7s. 6d.

113 GILBERT.—Chronological Pictures of English History, from William the Conqueror to Queen Victoria; designed and drawn on Stone by John Gilbert, Esq. Each part contains five plates, accompanied with a tabular sheet of letterpress, carefully compiled. Each plate illustrates a Reign. Two parts are published. Imperial folio, each part, 7s. 6d. tinted; or beautifully coloured, 15s.

114 GODKIN.—Apostolic Christianity; or, the People's Antidote against Romanism and Puseyism. By the Rev. James Godkin, Author of "A Guide from the Church of Rome to the Church of Christ." 8vo. pp. 414, cloth. 6s.

115 GOOD.—An historical Outline of the Book of Psalms. By J. M. Good, M.D.F.R.S. Edited by the Rev. I. M. Neale. 8vo. pp. 339, cloth. 10s. 6d.

116 GRAHAM.—English; or, the Art of Composition explained in a Series of Instructions and Examples. By G. F. Graham. 12mo. pp. 347, cloth lettered. 7s.

117 GRAHAME.—Who is to blame? or, Review of American Apology for American Accession to Negro Slavery. By J. Grahame. 8vo. pp. 150, cloth. 3s. 6d.

118 GRAMMAR Lessons. By a Lady. Designed as a Supplement to "Mary's Grammar." 18mo. pp, 177, cloth. 2s. 6d.

119 GRAY.—Figures of Molluscous Animals, selected from various Authors. Etched, for the use of Students, by Maria Emma Gray. With Preface by John Edward Gray, Keeper of the Zoological Collection in the British Museum. Vol. 1. 8vo. with 88 Plates and Descriptions, cloth. 12s.

120 GREEN.—Britain; A Poem: and Miscellaneous Pieces. By James Green. 12mo. pp. 118, cloth. 3s.

121 GRIFFIN—The Works of Gerald Griffin, Esq. Vol. 6.—The Duke of Monmouth. Foolscap 8vo. pp. 423, cloth. 6s.

122 GUIDE to SERVICE.—The Cook: Plain and Practical Directions for Cooking and Housekeeping; with upwards of Seven Hundred Receipts. 18mo. pp. 336, sewed. 3s.

123 GWILT.—Sciography; or, Examples of Shadows, with Rules for their Projection; intended for the use of Architectural Draughtsmen, and other Artists. With 24 plates. By Joseph Gwilt, F.S.A. Architect; Author of "The Rudiments of Architecture," &c. New edition, with consider-

able additions and improvements, 8vo. pp. 64, cloth. 10s. 6d.

124 GWILT.—An Encyclopædia of Architecture, Historical, Theoretical, and Practical. By Joseph Gwilt. Illustrated with upwards of 1000 engravings on wood, from designs by J. S. Gwilt. In 1 thick volume, 8vo. handsomely bound in cloth. *In the press.*

125 HALDANE.—Exposition of the Epistle to the Romans: with Remarks on the Commentaries of Dr. Macknight, Professor Moses Stuart, and Professor Tholuck. By Robert Haldane, Esq. New edition, much enlarged, 3 vols. foolscap 8vo. (Edinburgh,) pp. 1428, cloth. 21s.

126 HAMILTON.—Morning and Evening Services for every day in the Week, and other Prayers; arranged for the use of the Families residing in the Parish of St. Peter in the East, Oxford. By their former Pastor, Walter Kerr Hamilton. 12mo. (Oxford,) pp. 308, cloth, 5s.

127 HANCORN.—Medical Guide for Mothers, in Pregnancy, Accouchement, Suckling, Weaning, &c.; and the most important Diseases of Children. By J. R. Hancorn, M.R.C.S. &c. 2d edition, 12mo. pp. 240, cloth. 5s.

128 HAND-BOOK (The) for Life Assurers; being a Popular Guide to the Knowledge of the System of Life Assurance: with an Exposition of its advantages, and of its useful application to the different classes of the Community; together with an explanation of the various modes of doing Business; also a General Directory of Insurance Companies. Foolscap 8vo. pp. 190, cloth. 3s. 6d.

129 HAND-BOOK for Northern Italy, the States of Sardinia, Genoa, and the Rivera, Venice, Lombardy, and Tuscany. With Map. Post 8vo. pp. 638, cloth, 12s.

130 HANKINSON's (Rev. T. E.) Lectures on Personal Religion, fcp. pp. 89, 2s. 6d.

131 HARLAN—A Memoir of India and Affghanistan: with Observations on the Present State and Future Prospects of those Countries. By J. Harlan. Post 8vo. pp. 208, cloth, 6s.

132 HARRISON—A Complete and Improved Ready Reckoner for the Coal Trade: with correct Tables of Prices, from ½d. per ton to 30s. and from 1 cwt. to 400 tons, to be used in computing the amount of cargoes of coals shipped and delivered; also the amount of freight. To which is added, a Table of Newcastle Coal Measure computed into weight, and other useful matters relative to the trade. By G. Harrison. 2d edition, 12mo. (Newcastle), pp. 51. cloth, 2s.

133 HARRISON—Deformities of the Spine and Chest successfully treated by Exercise alone. By C. H. Rogers Harrison. 8vo. pp. 164, illustrated by Drawings, 8s.

134 HARTLEY—Geography for Youth, adapted to the different classes of Learners. By the Rev. John Hartley. A new edition

containing the latest changes, 12mo. pp. 320, bound, 4s. 6d.

135 HAYDEN—Physiology for the Public; comprising Plain Principles and Rules for the Preservation of the Functions of both Body and Mind in a state of Health; in a series of Lectures. By G. T. Hayden, A. B. &c. Part 1, 8vo. pp. 324 (Dublin.) sewed, 6s.

136 HEAPHY—Narrative of a Residence in various parts of New Zealand; together with a Description of the Present State of the Company's Settlements. By C. Heaphy, Draughtsman to the New Zealand Company. Post 8vo. pp. 150, cloth, 2s. 6d.

137 HERRICK.—The Greatness of God's Mercy in Christ; or, Salvation possible to the Vilest Sinners. By J. Herrick, Minister of Stockwell Chapel, Colchester. 18mo. pp. 104, cloth, 1s. 6d.

138 HOFLAND.—The Czarina: an historical Romance of the Court of Russia. By Mrs. Hofland. 3 vols. post 8vo. pp. 944, boards, 31s. 6d.

139 HOMEWARD BOUND; or, the Chase: a Tale of the Sea. By J. Fennimore Cooper. New edition, foolscap 8vo. pp. 404, cloth, 6s.

140 HOOKER.—Icones Plantarum; or, Figures, with brief descriptive Characters and Remarks, of New or Rare Plants, selected from the author's Herbarium. By Sir W. J. Hooker, K.H.LL.D. &c. Vol. 1, new series, or vol. 5 of the entire work, 100 plates, and descriptions, cloth 28s.

141 HOOKER.—The British Flora; comprising the Flowering Plants and the Ferns. By Sir W. J. Hooker, K.H.LL.D, &c. New edition (the fifth), greatly improved in the arrangement, and accompanied by 12 plates, comprising an immense number of figures illustrative of the Genera in the difficult orders of Umbelliferous Plants, Composite Plants, Grasses, Ferns, &c. 8vo.—*Just Ready.*

142 HOPE.—My working Friend; being plain Directions for the various Stitches in Fancy Needlework, with Hints on their Employployment. By C. Curling Hope, 32mo. (Ramsgate), pp. 78, cloth, 2s.

143 HOWE.—Lessons on the Globes, on a plan entirely new. By T. H. Howe. 12mo. pp. 436, bound, 7s.

144. HOWITT.—Little Coin much Care; or, How Poor Men Live; a Tale for Young Persons. By Mary Howitt. 18mo. pp. 171, cloth, 2s. 6d.

145 HUDSON.—The Parent's Hand-Book; or, Guide to the Choice of Professions, Employments, and Situations; containing useful and practical Information on the subject of placing out Young Men, and of obtaining their Education with a view to particular occupations. By J. C. Hudson, Esq., Author of "Plain Directions for making Wills."—*In the press.*—The object of this work is to inform a Parent concerning all the different employments for which he may destine his son, the prospects of emolument, &c., in each, the manner of

obtaining them, and the best course of education for each.

146 HUGHES.—Esther and her People: Ten Sermons. By the Rev. John Hughes. 18mo. pp. 218, cloth 2s. 6d.

147 HUNT.—The Palfrey, a Love Story of Old Times. By Leigh Hunt. 8vo. pp. 80, sewed, 5s.

148 INCOME (The) and Property-Tax Act: with an Explanatory Introduction, a Table for Calculating the Payments, the Official Regulations, and a copious Index. By a Barrister. 9th thousand, 8vo. with Table of Calculations, pp. 62, sewed 1s.

149 INCOME TAX.—The Act for levying a Tax on Property and Income, (5 and 6 Vict. c. 35), with Introduction, Notes, and Index. By M. L. Wells. 12mo. pp. 223, sewed, 3s.

150 INCOME-TAX ACT (The) Epitomized and Simplified. By W. Nicholson, Esq., Clerk to the Commissioners of the Leeds District. 19th thousand, 8vo. pp. 24, sewed, 1s.

151 INCOME-TAX.—The Property-Tax Act (5 and 6 Vict. cap. 35); with a full Analysis of its Provisions, Explanatory Notes, Forms of Proceeding, Cases of Illustration, a copious Index, and Tables of Calculation. By John Tidd Pratt, of the Inner Temple, Esq., Barrister-at-Law. 12mo. pp. 360, bds., 7s. 6d.

152 INCOME-TAX Act, 5 and 6 Vict. c. 35, with a Practical and Explanatory Introduction and Index. By J. Paget. 12mo. pp. 178, sewed, 4s.

153 Ivo and Verena; or, The Snowdrop: a Tale for Children. 18mo. pp. 163, cloth, 2s.

154 JARMAN.—A Selection of Precedents, from Modern Manuscript Collections, and Drafts of Actual Practice; forming a System of Conveyancing; with Dissertations and Practical Notes. By Thomas Jarman, Esq., of the Middle Temple, Barrister-at-Law. 3d edition, by George Sweet, Esq., of the Inner Temple, Barrister-at-Law. Vol. 7, royal 8vo. pp. 752, bds. 25s.

155 JONES.—Details and Ornaments from the Alhambra. Drawn from Casts in his possession, one-half, quarter, and full size, by Owen Jones, Architect. Forming the second volume to the "Plans of the Alhambra." In 2 parts, 25 plates each, printed in colours and gold, price, each, folio, grand eagle, 5l. 5s.; colombier, 4l. 4s.; imperial (for manufacturers), 3l. 3s.

156 KELTY—Fireside Philosophy; or, Glimpses at Truth. By Mary A. Kelty, 12mo. pp. 104, cloth, 2s.

157 KENNAWAY—The Churchman's Brief Manual of Baptism. By the Rev. C. E. Kennaway, A. M. 2d edition, foolscap, pp. 266, cloth, 4s. 6d.

158 KIRBY AND SPENCE—An Introduction to Entomology; or, Elements of the Natural History of Insects: comprising an Account of noxious and useful Insects, of their Met-

amorphoses, Food, Stratagems, Habitations, Societies, Motions, Noises, Hybernation, Instinct, &c. By W. Kirby, M.A.F. R.S. and L.S., Rector of Barham; and William Spence, Esq. F.R.S. and L.S. 6th edition, corrected and considerably enlarged, in 2 vols. *In the Press.* It is intended to publish the two first volumes of the "Introduction to Entomology" as a separate work, distinct from the third and fourth volumes, and, though much enlarged, at a considerable reduction of price, in order that the numerous class of readers who confine their study of insects to that of their manners and economy, need not be burdened with the cost of the technical portion of the work, relating to their anatomy, physiology, &c.

159 KNAPP—Gramina Britannica; or, Representations of the British Grasses: with Remarks and occasional Descriptions. By I. L. Knapp, Esq., F.L.S. and A.S. 2d edition, 4to. with 118 plates, beautifully coloured, bds. 3*l*. 16s.

160 KNIGHT's Pictorial History of England—Reign of George III. Vol. 2 (1785—1791). Royal 8vo. pp. 729, cloth, 20s.

161 KOHL—Russia and the Russians in 1842. By J. G. Kohl, Esq. Vol. 1: Petersburg. Post 8vo. six plates, pp. 392, cloth, 10s. 6d. A translation from the German.

162 LADIES' (The) Hand-Book of Fancy Needlework and Embroidery; containing plain and ample directions whereby to become a perfect mistress of those delightful arts. 18mo. pp. 62, cloth, gilt edges, 1s.

163 LAING—Notes of a Traveller on the Social and Political state of France, Prussia, Switzerland, Italy, and other parts of Europe, during the present century. By Samuel Laing, Esq., Author of "A Journal of a Residence in Norway," &c. 2d edition, 8vo. pp. 536, cloth, 16s.

164 LIVY—Titi Livii Historiæ Libri Quinque priores: cum annotationibus, probatissimis et utilissimis, ex omnibus prioribus commentatoriis accurate selectis et Anglice redditis; quibus et nonnullæ suæ sunt adjecta. A Jacobo Prendeville, Univ. Dublin Schol. Loci omnes difficiles explicantur; et textus maxime emendatus datur. Editio nova, 12mo. (Dublini), pp. 586, bound, 5s.

165 LONDON—Edited by Charles Knight. Vol. 3, with numerous engravings on wood, royal 8vo. pp. 420, cloth, 10s. 6d.

166 LONDONDERRY—A Steam Voyage to Constantinople, by the Rhine and the Danube, in 1840–41; and to Portugal, Spain, &c., in 1839. By C. W. Vane, Marquis of Londonderry. To which is annexed, the Author's Correspondence with Prince Metternich, Lords Ponsonby, Palmerston, &c. 2 vols. 8vo. pp. 708, cloth, 28s.

167 M'CULLOCH—A Dictionary, Geographical, Statistical, and Historical, of the various Countries, Places, and principal Natural Objects in the World. By J. R. M'Cul-

loch, Esq. (2 vols,) Vol. 2, 8vo. pp. 948, 2 maps, cloth, 2*l*.

168 MACHALE—The Evidences and Doctrines of the Catholic Church: showing that the former are no less convincing than the latter are propitious to the Happiness of Society. By the most Rev. John Machale, D.D., Archbishop of Tuam. 2d edition, revised, with additional Notes, 8vo. pp. 542, cloth, 12s.

169 MARRYAT's (Capt.) Masterman Ready, Part Third, will be published at Christmas.

170 MARTIN—Pounds, Shillings, and Pence: a series of Money Calculations. By T. Martin. 12mo. pp. 60, 3s.

171 MASSANIELLO: an Historical Romance. Edited by Horace Smith, Esq., Author of "Brambletye House," &c. 3 vols. post 8vo. pp. 932, boards, 31s. 6d.

172 MASSON—Narrative of various Journeys in Balochistan, Affghanistan, and the Panjab; including a residence in those Countries from 1826 to 1838. By Charles Masson, Esq. 3 vols. 8vo. pp. 1494, 5 lithographic plates, and 14 woodcuts, cloth, 2*l*. 2s.

173 MAUNDER—The Treasury of History and Geography; comprising a general Introductory Outline of Universal History, Ancient and Modern, and a complete series of separate Histories of every Nation that exists or has existed in the world. By Samuel Maunder, Author of "The Treasury of Knowledge," "The Biographical Treasury," and "The Scientific and Literary Treasury." Foolscap 8vo. *In the Press.*

174 MAURICE—The Kingdom of Christ; or Hints to a Quaker, respecting the Principles, Constitution, and Ordinances of the Catholic Church. By the Rev. F. D. Maurice, M. A. 2d edition, 2 vols. post 8vo. pp. 1016, cloth, 21s.

175 MAXFIELD—Observations on Ulcers of the Legs and other Parts, showing that the most obstinate and intractable cases may be speedily cured by mild methods of treatment; to which are appended, some Remarks on Scrofulous Disorders. By A. Maxfield, Surgeon. 8vo. pp. 80, cloth, 5s.

176 MEDICO-CHIRURGICAL TRANSACTIONS, published by the Royal Medical and Chirurgical Society of London. Volume 25th. Second Series, Volume 7th, 8vo., containing Twenty Papers, illustrated by Eight Plates, boards, 14s.

177 MELVILL—Sermons, by Henry Melvill, B.D., Minister of Camden Chapel, Camberwell, and Late Fellow and Tutor of St. Peter's College, Cambridge. Vol. 2, 3d edition, 8vo. pp. 400, boards, 10s. 6d.

178 MILFORD—Norway and her Laplanders in 1841: with a few Hints to the Salmon-Fisher. By John Milford, St. John's College, Cambridge; Author of "Observations on Italy," "Peninsular Sketches," &c. 8vo. pp. 334, cloth, 10s. 6d.

179 MILLENIUM (The): a Poem; with copious Notes, proving, from Scripture Authority, the Doctrine of the Personal Reign of God-

Man Jesus Christ, during a Thousand Years of Blessedness on the Earth. By a Millennarian. Crown 4to., pp. 76, sewed 5s.

180 MILTON.—The Poetical Works of John Milton; with Notes of various Authors, and with some account of the Life and Writings of Milton, derived principally from Original Documents in Her Majesty's State-Paper Office. By the Rev. Henry John Todd, M.A., Chaplain in Ordinary to Her Majesty, and Archdeacon of Cleveland. 4th edition, 4 vols. 8vo., pp. 2103, cloth, 50s.

181 MOILE—State Trials: a Series of Poems, comprising the Trial of Anne Ayliffe for Heresy, Sir William Stanley for High Treason, and Mary Queen of Scots. By N. T. Moile. 2d edition, 12mo., pp. 268, cloth, 10s. 6d.

182 MOSELY.—A Treatise on the Mechanical Principles of Engineering. By the Rev. Henry Mosely, M.A., Professor of Natural Philosophy and Astronomy in King's College, London; Author of "Illustrations of Practical Mechanics," "A Treatise on Hydrostatics," &c. 1 vol. 8vo., with illustrations on wood. *In the Press,*

183 MOTT.—Travels in Europe and the East. By Valentine Mott, M.D., President of the Medical Faculty of the University of New York. Royal 8vo., pp. 452, cloth, 15s.

184 NARRIEN.—Elements of Geometry; consisting of the first Four and the Sixth Books of Euclid, chiefly from the Text of Dr. Robert Simson: with the principal Theorems in Proportion, and a Course of Practical Geometry on the Ground; also, Four Tracts relating to Circles, Planes, and Solids, with one on Spherical Geometry. For the use of the Royal Military College. By John Narrien, F.R.S. and R.A.S., Professor of Mathematics, &c., in the Institution. 8vo., pp. 288, numerous diagrams, bound in roan, 10s. 6d.

185 NEWTON.—The Gems of Stuart Newton, R.A.: with a brief Memoir and Descriptive Illustrations. By H. Murray. Imp. 4to., with Plates, 42s. *In the Press.*

186 OGILVY.—Popular Objections to the Study of the Prophetic Scriptures. By G. Ogilvy, Esq. 12mo., pp. 239, cloth, 4s.

187 OLIVER's Picturesque Scenery of the French Pyrenees. In 26 Plates, royal folio, lithographed by Haghe, Boys, Bourne, Allom, Dodgson, Barnard, and Walton, from the original drawings by M. Oliver, 4l. 4s., coloured and mounted, to represent original drawings, 10l. 10s. *In the press.*

188 OXENHAM.—English Notes for Latin Elegiacs, designed for early proficients in the art of Latin Versification: with Prefatory Rules. By the Rev. W. Oxenham. 12mo., pp. 186, cloth, 4s.

189 PARIS.—The Paris Estafette; or, Pilferings from the Paris and Dover Post-bag. Post 8vo., pp. 430, cloth, 6s.

190 PARNELL.—Elements of Chemical Analysis, Inorganic and Organic. By E. A. Parnell, Chemical Assistant in University College, London. 8vo., pp. 320, with diagrams, cloth, 10s. 6d.

191 PAYNE & FOSS.—Bibliotheca Grenvilliana; or, Bibliographical Notices of Rare and Curious Books, forming part of the Library of the Right Hon. Thomas Grenville. By John Thomas Payne and Henry Foss. 2 vols. 8vo., pp. 1232, cloth, 3l. 3s.

192 PEEL (Sir R.)—Memoirs of the Right Hon. Sir Robert Peel, Bart., First Lord of Her Majesty's Treasury. By the Author of "The Life of the Duke of Wellington." 2 vols. post 8vo., pp. 749, cloth, 21s.

193 PEEL (E.)—The Christian Pilgrim, a Poem of Palestine. By Edmund Peel. 12mo., cloth, 7s. 6d.

194 PERCIVAL KEENE—By Capt. Marryat, Author of "Peter Simple," &c. 3 vols. post 8vo., pp. 888, boards, 31s. 6d.

195 PEREGRINE BUNCE; or, Settled at Last. By Theodore E. Hook, Esq., Author of "Sayings and Doings." 3 vols. post 8vo., pp. 935, boards, 31s. 6d.

196 PHILPOT.—Anne Sayle: a Simple Narrative of her Illness, Conversion, and Death, A. D. 1835. By Charlotte Philpot. 24mo., (Leamington,) pp. 68, with Woodcuts, cloth, 1s.

197 RANKE's History of the Popes: their Church and State in the Sixteenth and Seventeenth Centuries. Translated from the last edition of the German, by Walter K. Kelly, Esq., B.A. of Trinity College, Dublin. Part 1, containing the first volume of the original, royal 8vo., double columns, pp. 174, sewed, 4s. Forms a portion of the "Popular Library of Modern Authors, Copyright Editions."

198 REEVE.—Conchologia Systematica; or, a complete System of Conchology. By L. Reeve. Part 10, 4to., coloured, 21s., plain, 12s.

199 REID (Dr. D. B).—The Study of Chemistry considered as a branch of Elementary Education; to which is appended, a short Statement as to the Lectures on the Chemistry of Daily Life, now in progress at Exeter Hall, under the sanction of the Committee of the Privy Council on Education. By D. B. Reid, M.D. F.R.S.E. M.R.C.S., &c. &c. Second Edition, 8vo. pp. 16, 2d.; taken in numbers exceeding twelve, for distribution, 1d.

200 REYNOLDS.—The Discourses (on Painting) of Joshua Reynolds. Illustrated by Explanatory Notes and Plates. By John Burnet, F.R.S. 4to. pp. 284, 12 plates, cloth, 2l. 2s.

201 SHAKSPEARE.—The Works of Wm. Shakspeare: the Text formed from an entirely new collection of the old editions; with the various Readings, Notes, a Life of the Poet, and a History of the Early English Stage. By J. P. Collier, Esq. F.S.A. (8 vols.) Vol. 5, 8vo. pp. 610, cloth, 12s.

202 SHAKSPEARE—The Comedies, Histories, Tragedies, and Poems of William Shakspeare. Edited by Charles Knight. 2d edition. (12 vols.) Vol. 4, 8vo. pp. 515, cloth, 10s. Vol. 5, 8vo. pp. 554, with illustrations on wood. cloth 10s.

203 SMITH—Dictionary of Greek and Roman Antiquities. Edited by William Smith, Ph. D. Illustrated by numerous engravings on wood. 8vo. pp. 1132, cloth lettered, 36s.

204 SMITH—Elementary View of the Proceedings in an Action at Law. By J. W. Smith, Esq. Barrister-at-Law. 2d edition, 12mo. pp. 242, boards, 6s.

205 SMITH—A few Arguments against Phrenology. By A. R. Smith. 18mo. pp. 30, cloth, 1s.

206 SMITH—A Diagram to define the Lives of the Patriarchs, and the Early History of the Seed of the Serpent, and the Seed of the Woman, particularly in reference to the Origin of Disease and the Danger of Unsanctified Knowledge; with an Appendix, containing Suggestions and Reports on the Pursuits of Life most acceptable to God and Man. By H. L. Smith, M. R. C. d 12mo. (Cheltenham), pp. 142, cloth 5s. S.

207 SMITH—Admonitory Epistles from a Governess to her late Pupils; comprising a brief view of those Duties, the performance of which is most likely to promote their Happiness in this Life, and through a Saviour's Merits, insure to them the Joys of Eternity. By Jane Smith. 12mo. pp. 140, cloth, 5s.

208 SOBER INQUIRY (A); or, Christ's Reign with his Saints a Thousand Years modestly asserted from Scripture: together with the Answer of most of those ordinary objections which are urged to the contrary. 2d edition, first printed in the year 1660, now reprinted, with an Advertisement by Rev. E. Bickersteth, Rector of Wotton, Herts. 18mo. pp. 148, cloth, 2s. 6d.

209 SOMERSET, (DUKE OF).—A Treatise in which the Elementary Properties of the Ellipse are deduced from the Properties of the Circle, and Geometrically demonstrated. By the Duke of Somerset. 8vo. pp. 174, 9s. 6d. cloth.

210 SOUTH INDIAN SKETCHES; containing a short Account of some of the Missionary Stations connected with the Church Missionary Society in Southern India. In Letters to a Young Friend. By S. T. Part 1, Madras and Mayaveram. 2d edition, foolscap, 8vo. pp. 153, with woodcuts, cloth, 3s. 6d.

211 SOWERBY.—A Conchological Manual. By G. C. Sowerby, Jun. Illustrated by upwards of 650 figures on copper and wood. 2d edition, considerably enlarged and improved, 8vo. pp. 320, cloth, 25s.—This edition contains additional plates, and a new introduction, illustrated by 100 woodcuts.

212 STRICKLAND.—Lives of the Queens of England, from the Norman Conquest; with anecdotes of their Courts, now first published from Official Documents and other Authentic Documents, private as well as public. By Agnes Strickland. Vol. 5, containing Katharine Parr and Mary, the first Queen-regnant of England and Ireland. Post 8vo. pp. 450, cloth, 10s. 6d.

213 SULLIVAN.—An Outline of the General Regulations and Methods of Teaching in the Male National Model Schools. For the use of Teachers in Training. By Professor Sullivan. (Dublin), 12mo. pp. 48, sewed, 6d.

214 SULLIVAN.—An Introduction to Geography, Ancient, Modern, and Sacred: with an Outline of Ancient History. By Robert Sullivan, A.M.T.C.D. 18mo. (Dublin), pp. 120, cloth, 1s.

215 SULLIVAN.—Geography Generalized; or, an Introduction to the Study of Geography on the Principles of Classification and Comparison. By Robert Sullivan, A.M.T.C.D. 12mo. (Dublin), pp. 164, cloth, 2s.

216 SULLIVAN.—Lectures and Letters on Popular Education, including a Translation of M. Guizot's celebrated Letter to the Primary Teachers of France. By Robert Sullivan, A.M.T.C.D. 12mo. (Dublin), pp. 163, cloth, 2s. 6d.

217 SUMNER.—The Evidence of Christianity derived from its Nature and Reception. By John Bird Sumner, D.D, Lord Bishop of Chester. 7th edition, 8vo. pp. 446, cloth, 10s. 6d.

218 SWITZERLAND. A Hand-Book for Travellers in Switzerland, and the Alps of Savoy and Piedmont. A new edition, revised and corrected. 12mo. with Map, Index, &c., pp. 397, cloth, lettered, 10s.

219 SYNOPSIS (A) of the Various Administrations for the Government of England from the year 1756 to 1842. Imperial 4to. pp. 7, in tabular form, sewed, 3s. 6d.

220 TARIFF.—Tables of the Duties of Customs (with Amendments) payable on Goods, Wares, and Merchandize, imported into the United Kingdom from Foreign Parts, and from British Possessions: to which are prefixed the New Clauses of the Act of Parliament for Regulating the same, passed July 9th, 1842, with the Old Duties; and the nett amount received on each article in 1840; together with the New Corn Duties. Officially compiled from Authentic Documents. 6th thousand, with copious index, 8vo. pp. 46, sewed, 1s.

221 TAYLOR (A).—On the Curative Influence of the Climate of Pau, and the Mineral Waters of the Pyrenees, on Disease; with Descriptive Notices of the Geology, Botany, Natural History, Mountain Sports, Local Antiquities, and Topography of the Pyrenees, and their principal Watering-Places. By A. Taylor, M.D. Post 8vo. pp. 354, cloth, 10s. 6d.

222 TAYLOR (J).—The Bible Garden; or, a Familiar Description of the Trees, Plants, Shrubs, and Herbs, mentioned in the Holy Scriptures. By Joseph Taylor, Author of "Remarkable Providences." 2d edition, square 18mo. pp. 260, with coloured plates, cloth, 5s.

223 TAYLOR (W. C.)—Notes of a Tour in the Manufacturing Districts of Lancashire in the Spring of the present year: in a series of Letters to his Grace the Archbishop of Dublin. By W. Cooke Taylor, LL.D. &c. of Trinity College, Dublin; Author of

"The Natural History of Society." Foolscap, 8vo. pp. 304, cloth, 5s.

224 THACKER. — The Courser's Annual Remembrancer and Stud-Book ; being an Alphabetical Return of the Running at all the Public Coursing Clubs in England, Ireland, and Scotland, for the Season 1840-1 ; with the Pedigrees (as far as received) of the Dogs that won, or ran second, for each Prize ; also a Return of all Single Matches run at those Meetings, and all Mains of Greyhounds, during the Season, that have been publicly made known. By Thomas Thacker, author of "The Courser's Companion and Breeder's Guide." 8vo. pp. 252, cloth, 10s.

225 THE PICTURESQUE ANNUAL: The American in Paris ; being a picture of Parisian Life, in the Court, the Saloon, and the Family Circle : with a Graphic Description of the Public Amusements and Festivities. By M. Jules Janin. Royal 8vo. illustrated with about 18 splendidly-engraved Plates, from the Designs of the celebrated French painter, M. E. Lami. Bound in silk. *In the Press*

226 THE KEEPSAKE : a Series of beautifully-engraved Plates of Historical subjects, Portraits, and Landscapes. Edited by the Countess of Blessington. Royal 8vo. bound in silk. *In the Press.*

227 THE BOOK OF BEAUTY : a Series of Portraits of the Women of England the most distinguished for their Beauty and Rank. Edited by the Countess of Blessington. Royal 8vo. bound in silk. *In the Press.*

228 THOMSON.—Exercises, Political and others: By Lieutenant-Colonel T. Perronet Thomson. Consisting of matter previously published with and without the Author's name, and of some not published before. 6 vols. 12mo. pp. 2980, boards, 15s.

229 THOMSON.—The Seasons. By James Thomson. With about 80 engraved illustrations, from Designs drawn on wood by Eminent Artists; and with the Life of the Author, by P. Murdoch, D.D.F.R.S. Edited by Bolton Corney, Esq. Square crown 8vo. pp. 320. morocco, 36s. ; cloth, 21s.

230 TREDGOLD on the Steam Engine and Steam Navigation—Appendix C to the New Edition ; being The Gorgon Engines, as fitted on board H.M.S. Cyclops ; illustrated by Ten Plates, in large folio, and Descriptive Letter-Press, in 4to. By Samuel Clegg, Jun. C.E. pp. 24. 14s.

231 TRUFORT—A Guide to Happiness ; or, the Advantages of a Christian Education when bestowed on the Children of the Poor. By C. F. Trufort. 18mo. pp. 184, 2s. 6d.

232 TUCKFIELD — Evening Readings for Day Scholars—Natural History of the Mammalia. By Mrs. H. Tuckfield. 12mo. pp. 82, sewed. 1s. 6d.

233 TYTLER—Questions on Select Sections of Tytler's Elements of History, Ancient and Modern ; for the Use of the Junior Department of the Royal Military College. 3d edition. 8vo. pp. 100, boards. 5s.

234 USBORNE—Tales of the Braganza : with Scenes and Sketches. By T. H. Usborne, Esq. Post 8vo. pp. 277, cloth, 9s. 6d.

235 USSHER--The whole Works of the most Rev. James Ussher, D. D. Lord Archbishop of Armagh, and Primate of all Ireland. Vol. 5 (Britannicarum Ecclesiarum Antiquitates), 8vo. pp. 544, cloth, 12s.

236 VAUGHAN—The Modern Pulpit viewed in its Relation to the State of Society. By Robert Vaughan, D.D. Post 8vo. pp. 214, cloth, 5s.

237 WARDLAW.—Lectures on Female Prostitution : its Nature, Extent, Effects, Guilt, Causes, and Remedy. By Ralph Wardlaw, D.D. Delivered and published by special request. Post 8vo, (Glasgow), pp. 176, cloth, 4s. 6d.

238 WARING.—Children's Mission ; or, Great Works Wrought by Weak Hands. Illustrated by Three Tales : The Lighthouse, The Incendiary, and Margaret Seaton's Victory. By George Waring. With 6 Wood Engravings, from Designs by Gilbert. Foolscap 8vo, pp. 250, cloth, 4s. 6d.

239 WARMINGTON.—The Fall of Leicester : a Dramatic Poem. By George Warmington, Author of "Grammatical Exercises." 2d edition, 8vo, pp. 80, sewed, 3s.

240 WATHEN.—The Arts and Chronology of Ancient Egypt, from Personal Observations in 1839. By G. H. Wathen, Architect. 1 vol. 8vo, with Illustrations, from Sketches taken on the Spot. *Just ready.*

241 WERTHEIM.—A Concise German Grammar, with an entirely new arrangement of Declensions and Exercises of the most frequent occurrences in Common Life. Adapted to every class of Students, and especially useful to Travellers. By M. Wertheim, Lecturer on English at the Carlsruhe College ; formerly Tutor of the German Language at the University of Oxford. 12mo, (Carlsruhe, 1841), pp. 264, cloth, 5s.

242 WEST—Remarks on the management, or rather the *Mis*-management, of Woods, Plantations, and Hedge-row Timber. By J. West, Land Agent, &c., North Collingham, Newark, Notts. 8vo. (Newark,) pp. 136, boards, 6s.

243 WEST India Manuel (The): containing Rates of Passage, Freight, Postage, &c., by the Royal Mail Steam Packets. 18mo. pp. 164, cloth, 4s. 6d.

244 WICKSTEAD'S (Thos. M. I. C. E.)—Elaborate Drawing of the Grand Cornish Pumping Engine, with an 80-Inch Cylinder ; together with Watt's Large Pumping Engine of 65-Inch Cylinder ; both Engines amply delineated in 8 very large folio Engravings by Mr. Gladwin. *Just ready for publication.* 2l.

245 WILDE—The Medical Institutions of Austria : with an Essay on the Present State

of Science ; and a Guide to the Hospitals of Vienna. By W. R. Wilde, M.R.I.A., Licentiate of the Royal College of Surgeons in Ireland ; Honorary Member of the Imperial Society of Physicians in Vienna ; Author of " Narrative of a Voyage to Madeira," &c. &c. *In the Press.*

246 WILLIAMS—A Biographical Dictionary of Eminent Welshmen, from the Earliest Times to the Present. By the Rev. Robert Williams, M.A., Rector of Langawalader. Part 1, 8vo. pp. 48, sewed, 1s. This work will contain notices of above eighteen hundred individuals connected with the history and lirerature of Wales ; and will be published by subscription. Subscribers' names received by all Booksellers.

247 WILSON.—The Water Cure : a Practical Treatise on the Cure of Diseases by Water, Air, Exercise, and Diet : being a new mode of restoring Injured Constitutions to robust Health, for the Radical Cure of Dyspeptic, Nervous, and Liver Complaints, Tic-Doloureux, Gout and Rheumatism, Scrofula, Syphilis, and their Consequences, Diseases peculiar to Women and Children, Fevers, Inflammations, &c. By James Wilson, Physician to his Serene Highness Prince Nassau, M.R.C.S., &c. 3d edition, 8vo, pp. 232, sewed, 4s. 6d.

248 WILSON.—A Coasting Voyage Round Scotland, in the Summer and Autumn of 1841. By James Wilson, Esq., F.R.S.E.M.W.S, &c., Author of the " Treatise on Angling" in " The Rod and the Gun." In 2 vols. post 8vo. Illustrated with 20 Etchings by Charles H. Wilson, A.R.S.A., from Sketches during the Voyage by Sir Thomas Dick Lauder, Bart., and with numerous Woodcuts from the same Sketches, by Montague Stanley, Prior, and Sargeant, Engraved by Branston, Landels, and other Artists. *In the press.*

249 WITHERS.—The Acacia Tree, Robinia Pseudo Acacia ; its Growth, Quality, and Uses : with Observations on Planting, Manuring, and Pruning. By W. Withers, Holt, Norfolk ; Author of " A Memoir on the Planting and Rearing of Forest Trees," &c. 8vo, pp. 444, cloth, 20s.

250 WITTICH—A Key to German, for Beginners ; or, Progressive Exercises on the German Language. By William Wittich, Teacher of German in the University College, London. 12mo. pp. 154, cloth, 7s.

251 WORDSWORTH—A Complete Guide to the Lakes ; comprising Minute Directions for the Tourist, with a Description of the Scenery of the Country, &c. ; and Three Letters upon the Geology of the Lake District. By the Rev. Professor Sedgwick. 12mo. pp. 271, plates and maps, boards, 5s.

252 WORTHINGTON—A General Precedent for Wills, with Practical Notes. By G. Worthington, Esq. 4th edition, with considerable additions and alterations, 12mo, pp. 640, boards, 15s.

253 YEARSLEY—A Treatise on the Enlarged Tonsil and Elongated Uvula ; in connection with defects of Voice, Speech, and Hearing, Imperfect Development of Health and Strength in Youth, &c. By James Yearsley, M.R.C.S., Author of " Contributions to Aural Surgery," &c. Royal 8vo. pp. 88, with 6 coloured plates, cloth, 7s. 6d.

254 ZOOLOGICAL SOCIETY—Transactions of the Zoological Society of London. Vol 3, Part 1, 4to, with 6 plates, pp. 130, sewed, coloured, 14s. ; plain, 12s.

255 ZOOLOGICAL—Proceedings of the Zoological Society of London. Part 9. 1841. 8vo. pp. 138, cloth, 6s.

Art. I.—1. *History and Practice of Photogenic Drawing, or the true Principles of the Daguerreotype.* By the Inventor, L. J. M. Daguerre, translated by J. S. Memes, LL.D. 8vo. Lond. 1839.

2. *Some Account of the Art of Photogenic Drawing, or the Process by which Natural Objects may be made to Delineate themselves without the aid of the Artist's Pencil.* By Henry Fox Talbot, Esq., F.R.S. 8vo. Lond. 1839.

3. *Die Calotypische Portraitirkunst.* Von Dr. F. A. W. Netto. Quedlingburg und Leipzig, 1842.

4. *Ueber der Process des Sehens und die Wirkung des Lichts auf Alle Korper.* Von Ludwig Moser, Poggendorff Annalen der Physik und Chemie, Band LVI. 1842. No. 6.

In following the steps of social improvement, and tracing the rise of those great inventions which add to the happiness of our species, we can scarcely fail to recognize the law of progressive development under which the efforts of individual minds are regulated and combined, and by which reason is destined to attain its maximum of power, and knowledge to reach its limits of extension. Under the influence of a similar law, our moral and religious condition is gradually ascending to its climax; and when these grand purposes have been fulfilled—when the high commission of the Saint and the Sage has been executed—man, thus elevated to the perfection of his nature, will enter upon a new scene of activity and enjoyment.

The supreme authority which has ordained this grand movement in the living world—this double current of our moral and intellectual sympathies—has prepared the material universe as the arena of its development; and all our civil and religious institutions have been organized as instruments by which that development is to be effected. The confusion of tongues—the physical disunion of empires—the rivalries of industrious nations—are among the auxiliaries by which this triumph is to be consummated. The outbursts of the moral and the physical world form a powerful alliance in the same cause; and in the vigorous reactions which they invoke, the highest qualities of our moral and intellectual being are called into play. The war which desolates, and the fire and flood which destroy, undermine the strongholds of prejudice and corruption, and sweep away the bulwarks in which vice and error have been intrenched. Amid convulsions like these, indeed, civilisation often seems to pause, or to recede; but her pauses are only breathing stations, at which she draws a fuller inspiration, and her retrograde steps are but surer footings, from which she is to receive a fresh and onward impulse.

The powers and positions of individuals, too, are all nicely adjusted to the functions they have to discharge. Corporeal frames of every variety of strength—moral courage of every shade of intensity—and intellects of every degree of vigour—are among the cardinal elements which are to be set in action. The Sovereign who wields the sceptre, and the Serf who crouches under it, differ only in the place which they occupy in the mysterious mechanism. While one class of agents is stationed amid the heats of friction and pressure, others occupy the quiet points of stable equilibrium; and a larger class forms the inertial mass, or acts as a drag against the stupendous momentum which has been generated. But while busy man is thus labouring at the wheel, the impelling, the maintaining, and the regulating power, is not in him: by an agency unseen are all the heterogeneous elements of force harmonized, and the whole moral and intellectual dynamics of our species brought to bear upon that single point of resistance, where vice and ignorance are to be crushed for ever.

From these general views it is a corollary not to be questioned, that when great inventions and discoveries in the arts and sciences either abridge or supersede labour—when they create new products, or interfere with old ones—they are not on these accounts to be abandoned. The advance which is thus made involves not only a grand and irrevocable fact in the progress of truth, but it is a step in the social march which can never be retraced. The wants, or the cupidity of a minister, for his ignorance it cannot be, may tax inventions and knowledge—the fanaticism of a priesthood may proscribe education, and even the Scriptures of truth—and the blind fury of a mob may stop or destroy machinery—but cupidity, fanaticism, and rage, have counter-checks within themselves which re-act on the springs of truth and justice, and finally crush the conspiracy which they had themselves hatched. If, in the conflict of rival principles, the species gains, and the individual loses, redress can only be looked for in those compensatory adjustments which so often and so strangely reconcile general and individual interests. The same law which closes one channel of labour, necessarily opens up another, and that often through a richer domain, and with a wider outlet; and in every substitution of mechanical for muscular action, man rises into a higher sphere of exertion, in which the ingenuity of his mind is combined with the exercise of his body. He is no longer on a professional level with the brutes that perish, when he ceases to exercise functions which are measured only by so many horse power, and which can be better extracted from so many pounds of coal, and so many ounces of water.

Nor is it a less questionable corollary that when one of the arts is left behind in the race of improvement, and has been lingering amid the sloth and avarice of its cultivators, it can have no claim on the sympathy and protection of the community.* Were it the art of building ships, of forging anchors, or of welding cables, to form the defensive bulwarks of the nation, or were it the most trivial manipulation which administers to the personal vanity of the most frivolous, the principle would have the same foundation in truth and justice. But when it is the art of manufacturing food—when the poor and the rich are the antagonists in the combat—and when it involves the life and death of starving multitudes, the crime of protection will, in future ages, be ranked in the same category with that of burning for heresy, or drowning for witchcraft.

Although these observations apply in an especial manner to those great mechanical inventions which have in this country altered the very form and pressure of society, yet they are not less applicable to those remarkable improvements in the Fine Arts which the progress of science has so rapidly developed. The arts of painting, sculpture, and architecture, exhibit in their progress a series of anomalies which occur in the history of almost no other pursuit. Without any very adequate cause, they have alternately advanced and receded; and we can discover no leading epoch —no cardinal principle—no striking invention immortalizing the name of any of their cultivators. It would be hazardous to assert that Apelles and Zeuxis were surpassed by Reynolds and Lawrence, and still more so that Praxiteles and Phidias must have yielded the palm to Canova and Chantrey. In our own day, however, very extraordinary inventions and discoveries have already given an impulse, and will soon give a new form to the imitative arts.

The art of multiplying statues by machinery, which we owe to the celebrated James Watt, and which has since been brought to greater perfection, might have been regarded as a vast step in the fine arts, had it not been eclipsed by the splendid process of copying all sorts of sculpture, by the voltaic deposition of metals from their solutions.† But even this has

---

* We would refer the reader to an admirable letter on this subject by Professor Johnston of Durham to the Marquis of Northampton.

† The *Electrotype*, or *Galvano-plastic* art, which

been surpassed by the art of Photography, by which we obtain perfect representations of all objects, whether animate or inanimate, through the agency of the light which they emit or reflect. From being at first a simple, and not very interesting process of taking profiles of the human face, it has called to its aid the highest resources of chemistry and physics; and while it cannot fail to give a vigorous impulse to the fine arts, it has already become a powerful auxiliary in the prosecution of physical science; and holds out no slight hope of extending our knowledge of the philosophy of the senses. The art of *Photography*, or *Photogeny* as it has been called, is indeed as great a step in the fine arts, as the steam-engine was in the mechanical arts; and we have no doubt that when its materials have become more sensitive, and its processes more certain, it will take the highest rank among the inventions of the present age.*

But before we proceed to exhibit its powers, and discuss its merits, we must put our readers in possession of its history and methods. The action of light and heat upon coloured bodies has been long known, and the changes they produce have been recorded in various countries. The commonest observer, indeed, had long ago noticed that the solar rays not only weakened, but almost destroyed the colours of curtains and other articles of furniture; but it was reserved for the chemist and the natural philosopher to determine, what rays were the efficacious ones, and what were the substances most sensitive to this action of light. Scheele had long ago discovered that muriate of silver was speedily blackened by the. *blue* rays of the solar spectrum, while the red rays produced an effect scarcely appreciable; and Sennebier found that the *violet* rays darkened the muriate of silver in fifteen seconds, while the *red* rays required twenty minutes, and the other colours intermediate times.† The celebrated Ritter, in repeating these experiments, found

that the muriate of silver was most powerfully blackened by invisible rays beyond the violet, and Dr. Wollaston afterwards proved that the rays at the two extremities of the spectrum, produced opposite effects upon Gum Guiacum, the violet rays giving it a deep green colour, and the red rays reconverting the green into the original yellow colour of the gum.

These interesting facts, though well-known throughout Europe, had never been applied to the arts till 1802,* when *a method of copying paintings upon glass, and of making profiles by the agency of light upon nitrate of silver,* was first given to the world. This method was the unquestionable invention of our celebrated countryman Mr. Thomas Wedgewood, who published it in the *Journals of the Royal Institution,*† where it was accompanied with a few observations in a note by Sir H. Davy.

Having found that white paper or white leather, moistened with a solution of nitrate of silver, passes through different shades of grey and brown, and at length becomes nearly black by exposure to daylight, Mr. Wedgewood exposed papers thus moistened to light of different intensities and colours. In the direct beams of the sun, the full effect upon the paper was produced in two or three minutes. In the shade, several hours were required. The most decided and powerful effects were produced by *blue* and *violet* glasses, while very little action took place when the sun's rays passed through *red* glasses. Hence, says Mr. Wedgewood, 'when a white surface, covered with a solution of *nitrate* of silver, (one part of the nitrate to ten of water), is placed behind a painting on glass exposed to the solar light, the rays transmitted through the differently painted surfaces produce distinct tints of brown and black, sensibly differing in intensity according to the shades of the picture; and where the light is unaltered, the colour of the light becomes deepest. For copying paintings on glass the solution should be applied on leather, and in

---

was discovered by Mr. Spencer and M. Jacobi, and which is daily finding new applications to the useful arts.

* We have not here referred to the new and beautiful art of *Anaglyptography*, by which all works in relief, and even statues, may be copied on a plane surface (and even engraved) by means of parallel lines, which deviate from their parallelism in proportion as different points, in all parallel sections of the original, rise above the general plane. This art was, we believe, first invented by an American, then tried in France, but finally brought to perfection by Mr. R. Bate, the son of the well-known optician, Mr. B. Bate of London.

† *Sur La Lumière*, Tom. iii. p. 199.

* M. Arago informs us that M. Charles had, in the first year of the 19th century, used prepared paper to produce black profiles by the action of light; but he never described the preparation; and he did not claim any priority, although he lived for a long time after the publication of Mr. Wedgewood's process.

† Vol. i. p. 170, June, 1802. See also Nicholson's Journal, 8vo. series, vol. iii. p. 167, Nov. 1802. An Account of a Method of Copying Paintings upon Glass, and of Making profiles by the Agency of Light upon Nitrate of Silver. Invented by T. Wedgewood, Esq., with Observations by H. Davy, Journals of the Royal Institution, Vol. i. p. 170. 1802.

this case, it is more readily acted upon than when paper is used.'

Mr. Wedgewood made various attempts to *fix* these copies, that is, to prevent the uncoloured parts of the copy from being acted upon by light. He tried repeated washings, and thin coatings of fine varnish; but all his trials were unsuccessful; and hence he was obliged to preserve his copies in an obscure place—to take a glimpse of them only in the shade or to view them by candle light. He applied this method to take profiles or shadows of figures by throwing the shadows on the nitrated surface, the part concealed by the shadows remaining white, and the other parts speedily becoming black. He applied it also to make delineations of the woody fibres of leaves, and the wings of insects, and likewise to the copying of prints; but in this last case the results were very unsatisfactory. But the primary object of all Mr. Wedgewood's experiments was to copy the images formed by means of a *camera obscura.* 'His numerous experiments, however, proved unsuccessful,' and the images were 'found to be too faint to produce, in any moderate time, an effect upon the nitrate of silver.' 'In following these processes,' he adds, 'I have found that the images of small objects, produced by means of the solar microscope, may be copied without difficulty on prepared paper;' but in this case, 'it is necessary that the paper be placed at but a small distance from the lens.'

Mr. Wedgewood proved that the muriate of silver was much more sensitive than the nitrate, and that the sensitiveness of both was increased when the paper was moist. In order to obtain the muriate, he immerses the paper moistened with the nitrate solution in very dilute muriatic acid. He promised to publish any additional results which he might obtain, and concluded his paper thus,—'Nothing but a method of preventing the unshaded parts of the delineation from being coloured by exposure to the day, is wanting to render the process as useful as it is elegant.'

So long ago as 1803, a Notice of Mr. Wedgewood's interesting process was published in an Edinburgh Journal, but the subject does not seem to have excited any attention either in Britain or on the continent. A friend of Mr. Talbot's, indeed, who had entertained the idea of fixing the images of the camera obscura, was discouraged from the attempt by the recorded failure of Mr. Wedgewood. Mr. Talbot himself, however, without any knowledge of Mr. Wedgewood's previous invention, had, some time previous to 1834, been led to the same process, of taking pictures by the agency of light upon

nitrate of silver; and, in the spring of that year, he had actually applied it to several useful purposes, and had even overcome the difficulty of fixing the images of the camera obscura, before he knew that that difficulty had stopped the progress of Mr. Wedgewood and his own friend. Mr. Talbot continued to improve his new art, to which he gave the name of *Calotype*, for it had now become entirely his; and, by the aid of his intimate knowledge of chemistry and physics, he has succeeded in bringing it to a very high degree of perfection.

But before we proceed to give an account of his labours, we must return to a period prior to their commencement, when a similar art—the splendid art of the *Daguerreotype* —took its rise in France. So early as 1814, M. Niepce, a private gentleman, who resided on his estate near Chalons, on the Saone, had turned his attention to the subject of Photography. His object was to fix the images of the camera, but more especially to perfect his methods of copying engravings when laid upon substances sensible to the action of light. In 1824, M. Daguerre had begun a series of experiments for the purpose of fixing the images in the camera. He had made some progress in 1826; and in that year a Parisian optician had indiscreetly disclosed to M. Nlepce some of the results at which Daguerre had arrived. In 1827, M. Niepce made a journey to England, and, in December of that year, he communicated an account of his photographic experiments to the Royal Society of London, accompanying his memoirs with several sketches on metal, in the state of advanced etchings, which proved that he had a method of making the shadows correspond to shadows, and of preventing his copies from being injured by the light of the sun. The Royal Society appears to have attached no value to the discovery of Niepce, though they had ocular demonstration of its reality. His Paper does not even seem to have been read, and the plates which accompanied it appear to have passed into the repositories of some of its members. One would have expected that a picture, painted or copied by the agency of light, would have fixed the attention of any body of men to which it was submitted; and we should have experienced some difficulty in giving credit to the statement, did we not know that the same body has refused to publish the photographic discoveries of Mr. Talbot!

Having become acquainted with each other's labours, MM. Niepce and Daguerre entered into a copartnery in 1829; the object of which was to pursue for their mutual benefit the photographic researches which they had respectively begun. The process of Niepce differed entirely from that of Daguerre. The principle on which it rests is, that light renders some substances more or less insoluble, in proportion to the duration or intensity of its action. The substance in which he found this property, was a solution of asphaltum in essential oil of lavender. A thin film of this substance spread over the clean surface of a plate of silvered copper was exposed, so as to receive the image of a landscape in the camera obscura. The parts on which no light fell were thus made more soluble than the rest; and when a solvent, consisting of one part of essential oil of lavender, and ten parts of oil of white petroleum, was made to cover the plate, the image gradually unfolded itself; and, after being washed with water, the picture was completely developed. The plate was then dried, and kept from humidity and the action of light.

Into this process, which was doubtless both troublesome in its details, and uncertain in its results, M. Daguerre introduced essential improvements; but in the course of his researches, he was lead into an entirely new field of discovery, and soon abandoned the process of his colleague. M. Niepce died in July, 1833, and a new agreement was entered into between Daguerre and his son, M. Isidore Niepce; in which it was admitted that the former had discovered an entirely new process, and it was at the same time provided, that it should bear the name of Daguerre as its sole inventor.

The following is a general description of the art of the *Daguerreotype,* as practised by its distinguished inventor: A plate of silvered copper, after having been well cleaned, and freed from any greasy substance, by polishing it with dilute nitric acid, fine Tripoli, or colcothar of vitriol, is placed in a box containing iodine, till its surface is covered with a golden yellow film of that evaporable substance. The plate being carefully kept from light, is placed in the camera obscura, so as to receive upon its surface a distinct image of the landscape, or of the single figure, or group of figures, to be painted. After remaining a number of minutes, depending on the intensity of the light, the plate is taken out of the camera, and placed in what is called a mercury box. There it is exposed to the vapour of mercury, raised by a spirit lamp; and, after a certain time, the operator, looking through a little window in front of the box, observes the landscape, or figures, gradually developing themselves on the surface of the plate, by the adhesion of the white mercurial vapour to those parts of the picture which had been acted upon by the light. When the development appears complete, the plate is placed in a vessel containing either a saturated solution of common salt, or a weak solution of the hyposulphite of pure soda. By the action of either of these fluids, the coat of iodine is dissolved, and the picture is permanently fixed. It is then simply washed in distilled water, dried, and placed in a square of strong pasteboard, covered with glass. If we now carefully examine the picture thus produced, we shall find that its shadows are nothing more than the original polished surface of the silver, reflecting a dark ground, and that the lights are the parts of the silvered surface, which have been more or less whitened by the vapour of mercury. If the plate is made to reflect a luminous surface, such as a white dress, or the sky, the shadows will appear luminous and white, and the lights dark, so as to give what may be called a *negative* picture. In this remarkable representation of nature, there is depicted, with the minutest accuracy, all her finest forms; but her gay colours are wanting; and the blue sky and the green turf are exhibited in the same monotony of light and shadow, as when we view a highly-coloured landscape, in water-colours or in oil, by the light of a monochromatic lamp.

But notwithstanding this defect, which, sanguine as we are, we can scarcely hope will ever be supplied, there is a power and truth in the delineation which almost compensates its want of colour. Self-painted by the rectilineal pencils of light, every fixed object transfers its mimic image to the silver tablet; and the only deviation from absolute truth which can intervene, is the imperfection of the lenses by which the image is formed. By an ordinary observer this defect, if it can be called one, is so inappreciable, that the perfection of the picture exceeds as it were the accuracy of the eye as its judge; and by means of a magnifying glass we can make discoveries of minute features, in the same manner as we can do in the real landscape by the application of a telescope.[*] But it is not merely the minuteness of its delineations that surprise us in the Daguerreotype. Every object is seen in true geometrical perspective; and even the aerial perspective is displayed in the diminution of sharpness which marks the outlines of all objects that recede from the eye. The combination of these two effects, the last of which is often beyond the reach of art, gives a depth—a third di-

---

[*] Every picture formed by a camera obscura, in which the focal lengths of the lens exceed the distance at which we see objects distinctly, is magnified, and on this account objects are recognized in the perfect image which the eye cannot see in the original landscape.

mension—to the picture, which it is scarcely possible to conceive without actually seeing it. In the representation, for example, of a Grecian portico with two or three columns deep, the actual depth of the recess is more distinctly seen with a magnifying glass than by the naked eye.

If any object in the picture either moves or changes its place, that object, of course, must be imperfectly delineated in the Daguerreotype. The agitated foliage, the running stream, the flying clouds, and the motions of living animals, all destroy the picture in which they occur. This great imperfection is capable of only one remedy. We must increase the sensitiveness of the ground upon which the lights act, so as to diminish the time that the plate remains in the camera. M. Daguerre saw very early the consequences of this defect in his process; and, in the course of a series of experiments on the subject, he made the important discovery, that by electrifying the plate, the action of light upon the film of iodine was so instantaneous, that the part of the plate first exposed was overdone before the action had begun on the other part of the plate.*

Two other methods have been invented for accelerating the action of light upon the plate. The first of these is founded on a beautiful optical discovery by M. Edmund Becquerel. If we conceive the solar spectrum to be divided into two halves, the *first* half containing the *violet* and *blue* rays, and the *second* the *green, yellow* and *red*, M. Becquerel found that the first half, containing the *violet* and the *blue* rays, were those which formed the picture on the plate; and hence he called them the *exciting* rays, (*rayons excitateurs*); while the other half, the *green, yellow*, and *red* rays, had no power of excitation, but *continued* the excitement when passed over the surface of the plate after it was taken out of the camera, and when the *exciting* rays no longer acted upon it. Hence he called them the *continuing* rays, (*rayons continuateurs*). The power of *exciting* was a *maximum* at the violet extremity of the spectrum, and gradually diminished towards the middle or green space; while the power of *continuing* the action was a *maximum* at the *red* extremity, and gradually diminished towards the *green* space, where a sort of neutral state existed. Hence, as the solar spectrum consists of three equal spectra, viz. violet, yellow, and red superposed, with their *maximum* illumination at different points,

we may conceive the *exciting* power to be diffused along with the *violet* rays throughout the whole spectrum; the *continuing* rays to be diffused throughout the same along with the *red*; while the neutral *yellow* possess only the powers of heat and illumination. In this way only we can account for the diminution of the exciting and continuing powers towards the middle of the spectrum; and the entire disappearance of both these actions will take place at the point where the ordinates of *excitation* and *continuation* are equal.

In applying this principle to the Daguerreotype, the plate is exposed only a short time to the action of the lights in the original picture—so short a time, indeed, that the vapour of mercury would not form a picture upon the plate. The plate being taken out of the camera, the sun's rays, passing through a red glass, are made to shine upon it for a few minutes. The action already excited is thus continued; and the plate, when exposed to the mercurial vapour, yields a picture as perfect as it would have done had it remained the proper time in the camera.

Beautiful, however, as this process is in its scientific relations, it is obviously one which is not fitted for the professional artist: for if the sun does not shine, the picture cannot be formed, and may be lost before the luminary reappears. This defect, however, we need not regret; for a practical and simple process of hastening the production of the picture has been discovered by M. Claudet, the ingenious artist who superintends the photographical department in the Adelaide Gallery. He discovered that the sensitiveness of the iodine film was singularly increased by passing it over the mouth of a bottle containing the *chloride of iodine* or of *bromine*. As soon as the vapour of either of these bodies has spread itself over the film of iodine, the plate is placed in the camera, and in a very few seconds the action of light is completed.

In consequence of these improvements, the Photographic art has assumed a new character. When the patient (for so the sitter must be described) sat for five or ten minutes in a constrained attitude, with his face exposed to a strong light, the portrait thus taken could neither be correct nor agreeable. A look of distress pervaded almost every feature; the eye, exposed to the strongest light, was half closed; the cheek was drawn up, and wrinkles, never seen in society, planted themselves upon the smooth and expanded forehead of youth and beauty. These evils are now entirely removed from the Daguerreotype. Even the momentary expression of

---

* The particulars of this process have not been published; but we have no doubt that M. Daguerre, with his usual success, will find some way of reducing the speed of this new method.

passion or feeling may be seized, and the graceful form, which never fails to accompany it, simultaneously arrested. Motion of course it is impossible to represent; but the expressions of the face, and the positions of the muscles and limbs, which precede and follow motion, and therefore necessarily indicate it, are given as they existed at the moment when the exposure of the plate took place.

Such is the invention, in its improved state, which, after fifteen years of laborious research, M. Daguerre has given to the world—an invention with which his name will be indissolubly associated. It is, more than any other art we know, peculiarly his own; for the previous labours of Wedgewood and Niepce have with it nothing in common. It belongs, therefore, to France alone; and the liberality with which she has purchased it for the benefit of universal science, will secure to her the gratitude of all nations. This wise and generous step was, we believe, the suggestion of her most eminent philosopher, M. Arago, to whom M. Daguerre had unhesitatingly confided the secrets of his art. Struck with the splendour of the discovery, and foreseeing the advantages which science and art would receive from its application, he induced the government to offer M. Daguerre an annual pension of 6000 francs, and M. Niepce a pension of 4000 francs,* for surrendering to the public the use of their inventions; and, on the 3d July, 1839, he presented to the Chamber of Deputies the report of a Commission, of which he was the chief, explaining the nature and estimating the value of the invention. Baron Gay Lussac submitted a similar report to the Chamber of Peers, breathing the same sentiments, and recommending the same national reward. The following passages from these reports, which were unanimously adopted by the Chambers, may be usefully perused in England, and show the entire unanimity of feeling which animated all parties in completing this interesting transaction:—

'The members of this Chamber, (M. Arago), to whom the Ministry gave full powers, never bargained with M. Daguerre. Their communications had no other object than to determine whether the recompense, so justly due to the accomplished artist, should be a pension or a sum of money. From the first M. Daguerre perceived, that the payment of a stipulated sum might give to the transaction the base character of a sale. The case was different with a pension. By a pension you recompense the warrior who has been wounded in the field, and the magistrate who has grown grey on the bench. It is thus that you honour the families of Cuvier

—of Jussieu, and of Champollion. Reflections like these could not fail to present themselves to a man of his exalted character, and M. Daguerre decided on a pension. He fixed the amount at 8000 francs, to be divided equally between himself and his partner, M. Niepce, junior. The proportion payable to M. Daguerre has been since raised to 6000 francs, making 10,000 in all; both on account of the condition specially imposed upon that artist of publishing *the secret of painting and illuminating the dioramic views*, and making known all future improvements with which he may enrich his photographic methods.'

'From these considerations,' says Baron Gay Lussac, 'it was thought desirable that this process should become public property. From a different motive it merited the attention of government, and ought to procure for its author a conspicuous reward. To those who are not insensible to national glory—who know that a people shine with a greater splendour among the nations of the earth, only as they have realized a higher advancement in civilisation—to those, we say, the process of M. Daguerre is a noble discovery. It is the origin of a new art in the middle of an old civilisation;—an art which will constitute an era, and be preserved as a title of glory. And shall it descend to posterity companioned with ingratitude? Let it rather stand forth a splendid evidence of the protection which the Chambers—the Government of July—the whole country—offered to great inventions.

'It is, in reality, an act of national munificence which consecrates the bill in favour of M. Daguerre. We have given it our unanimous assent, yet not without marking how elevated and honourable is a reward voted by the country. And this we have done on purpose to remind the nation, not without some sad remembrances—that France has not always shown herself so grateful; and that too many useful labours—too many works of genius, have often procured for their authors only a barren glory. These are not accusations which we urge—they are errors which we deplore, in order now to avoid a new one.'

From the homage which we have cheerfully paid to the liberality of French philosophers and legislators, we could have desired to make no deduction; but there has been an *omission* in the transaction with M. Daguerre, which affects all nations, and which we would almost venture to request M. Arago still to supply. It is evident, from the whole tenour of the two Reports to the Chambers, that France purchased Daguerre's invention *for the benefit of all nations*, and not exclusively for the French people. It would be an insult to the two distinguished Reporters, and, indeed, to all parties concerned, to suppose that they had any other object in view. M. Arago emphatically says, ' This discovery France has adopted; from the first moment she has cherished a pride in liberality, bestowing it— A GIFT TO THE WHOLE WORLD !' And M. Du-

* One half of each is settled in reversion on their widows.

chatel, the Minister of the Interior, on presenting the bill to the Chambers, distinctly declares, as an argument for a public reward, ' *that Daguerre's invention does not admit of being secured by patent.* So soon as it becomes known, every one may avail himself of its advantages. The most unskilful will produce designs with the same exactness as the most accomplished artist. Of necessity, then, this process must belong to all, or remain unknown.'

The Daguerrian Bill had scarcely passed the legislature, when ' on or about the 15th of July, 1839, *a certain foreigner residing in France,* instructed Mr. Miles Berry, patent agent in London, immediately to petition her Majesty to grant her Royal Letters Patent for the exclusive use of the same within these kingdoms ;' " and in consequence of these instructions, Mr. Miles Berry ' did apply for such letters patent, and her Majesty's solicitor-general (Sir Thomas Wilde), after hearing *all parties who opposed the same,* was pleased on or about the 2d of August, now last past, to issue his report to the Crown *in favour of the patent being granted,* and it consequently passed the great seal in the usual course, being sealed on the day above named, *which is* SOME DAYS PRIOR to the date of the exposition of the said invention or discovery to the French Government at Paris, by MM. Daguerre and Niepce, according to the terms of their agreement.'

This remarkable statement, the object of which is very palpable, is thrust into the specification of the patent, after the usual preamble to such deeds; and the patentee states with great *naiveté,* that *he believes* it to be the invention or discovery of Messrs. Louis Jacques Maude Daguerre, and Joseph Isidore Niepce, junior, both of the kingdom of France ; from whom the French Government have purchased the invention FOR THE BENEFIT OF THAT COUNTRY!

The purpose of the preceding statement is obviously to create a belief that M. Daguerre was not the foreigner who instructed the patent agent to petition her Majesty, and that he had transferred the benefit of his invention only to his own country. It is not our desire to investigate this part of the transaction any further : but we are bound to say, that the Solicitor-General of England would have done better to advise her Majesty not to withhold from *her subjects* that very invention which the King of the French had purchased for the benefit not only of *his own people,* but of *all nations.* The patent cannot stand a moment's examination, and we would exhort the interested parties to apply for a writ of *scire facias* for its immediate repeal.

It is a singular fact, though not without its parallel in the history of science, that when Daguerre in France was engaged in his beautiful experiments, another philosopher in England should have been occupied in analogous researches. Mr. Henry Fox Talbot, of Lacock Abbey, a Fellow of the Royal Society, and well known as a mathematician and natural philosopher, had, as we have seen, previous to 1834, been attempting to fix the images of the camera obscura, and to copy objects and pictures by the action of light upon nitrate of silver. The first account which he gave of his labours, was in a Paper entitled *Some Account of the art of Photogenic Drawing, or the process by which natural objects may be made to delineate themselves without the aid of the artist's pencil.* This Paper was read to the Royal Society on the 31st January, 1839, several months before the disclosure of Daguerre's invention and methods.* We mention this fact, not for the purpose of claiming for our countryman any priority in reference to Daguerre ; but merely to show that his labours, whatever analogy there may be between them, were wholly independent of those of the French philosophers. In this Paper Mr. Talbot did not give any account of his processes ; but in a subsequent letter, addressed to the Secretary of the Royal Society, and read to that body on the 21st February, 1839,† he described his method of preparing the paper, and the process by which he fixed the design.

A sheet of superfine paper, after being dipped in a weak solution of common salt, is wiped dry ; a solution of nitrate of silver, not saturated, but six or eight times diluted with water, is then spread on one surface only, and when dry the paper is fit for use. Leaves of flowers, and lace, laid upon the nitrated surface of this paper, will be self-delineated by exposure to the sun, the lights and shades being reversed. In fixing these images, Mr. Talbot at first tried ammonia and other reagents with very imperfect success. His first good result was obtained by using a weak aqueous solution of iodide of potassium. He afterwards obtained better fixation by immersing the picture in a strong solution of common salt, and then wiping off the superfluous moisture and drying it. In order to make the prepared paper sufficiently sensitive to receive the images of the camera obscura, he washed it several times, alternately, with the solutions of salt and nitrate of silver. Beautiful as some of the photographic

---

* It was printed in the *Lond. and Edin. Phil. Mag.* for March, 1839. Vol. xiv. p. 196.
† Id. Id. vol. xiv. p. 09.

drawings were, which Mr. Talbot thus produced and exhibited to the Royal Society, he felt that the art had not yet attained great perfection, and he set himself diligently to improve his processes, but particularly to obtain a paper which should be in a high degree sensitive to light. Without such a paper landscapes might be taken, and pictures of fixed natural objects copied with great accuracy; but portraits of living persons, who could not keep the same position for more than two or three minutes, at this time defied the photographic art, as practised both by Daguerre and Talbot.

In this new field of inquiry Mr. Talbot met with perfect success. He discovered a method of making the paper so sensitive, that with a camera, whose lens is one inch in diameter, and focal length fifteen inches, a picture eight or nine inches square may be taken in general in *ten seconds.* In the darkest day of winter, a sheet of this paper becomes entirely dark *in a small fraction of a second.* In five or six seconds, it will darken when held close to a wax candle; and it is even so distinctly acted upon by the light reflected from the moon, that Mr. Talbot has taken impressions of leaves on it by moonlight!

To this invention, Mr. Talbot, as already mentioned, has given the name of *Calotype,* and has secured the exclusive privilege of it for England, by a patent sealed on the 8th February, 1841.* We shall now endeavour to give our readers a popular account of the beautiful methods contained in the specification.

In order to obtain a *negative* picture, (the first and by far the most important part of the process), or one in which the lights are dark and the shades light, take paper with a smooth surface and close texture; mark one side of it with a pencil cross, and by a camel's hair brush wash the marked side with a solution of 100 grains of *nitrate of silver* in six ounces of distilled water. After having been cautiously dried it is immersed for a few minutes in a solution of *iodide of potassium,* consisting of 500 grains in one pint of distilled water. The paper when taken out is dipped in water, and dried by blotting paper and heat gently applied, or it may be dried spontaneously after it comes from the blotting-paper. This operation is carried on in candle light, and the paper thus prepared is called *iodized* paper. It is insensible to light, and will keep for any length of time without spoiling.

When this paper is required for use, a sheet is washed with a camel's-hair brush on the one side, with the following solution: To a solution of *nitrate of silver,* in *two* ounces of distilled water, add *one third* of its volume of strong *acetic acid;* then dissolve a small quantity of crystallized *gallic acid* in distilled water, and mix the two solutions together in equal proportions; but in no greater quantity than is required for immediate use, for it will not keep long. This mixture is called *gallo-nitrate of silver,* and is to be applied with the light of a candle; and after allowing the paper to remain half a minute to absorb the gallo-nitrate of silver, it should be dipped in distilled water and dried lightly; first with blotting-paper, and then by means of a fire—holding the paper at a considerable distance from it. The paper is fit for use when thus dried, and should be used within a few hours.

Mr. Talbot calls this paper *calotype* paper, and it is now placed in the camera obscura, to receive upon its surface a distinct image of the landscape or person to be drawn; no light being allowed to fall upon the paper till its surface is exposed to the image which it is to receive. The time of impressing the paper with an *invisible* image, varies from *ten seconds* to several minutes, according to the intensity of the light. In the light of a summer sun from *ten* to *fifty* seconds will be sufficient; but when the sun is not strong, *two* or *three* minutes in summer is necessary.

When the paper is removed from the camera, in candle light of course, there is generally *nothing visible upon its surface;* but by washing it all over by a camel's-hair brush, with the *gallo-nitrate of silver,* and holding it before a gentle fire, the picture will soon begin to appear, and the most luminous parts of the real object will, in its picture, be brown or black, while the other parts remain white. When the picture is sufficiently distinct, it must then be *fixed,* so that it will not be further acted upon by the strongest light. For this purpose it must be first dipped in water, then partly dried by blotting-paper, and afterwards washed with a solution of *bromide of potassium,* consisting of 100 grains of this salt, dissolved in eight or ten ounces of water; or in place of this it may be dipped in a strong solution of common salt. The picture is now fixed, and must be finally washed with water, and dried as before by blotting paper.

When a *negative* picture has been thus obtained, many *positive* ones may be taken from it in the following manner: Take a

* See Newton's London *Journal and Repertory of Patent Inventions.* Vol. xix. p. 189.

VOL. LXXVI. 22

sheet of good paper, and having dipped it for a minute or so in a solution of common salt, consisting of one part of a saturated solution to eight parts of water, dry it first in blotting paper, and then spontaneously. Wash one of its sides (having previously marked that side) with a solution of nitrate of silver, consisting of eighty grains of that salt dissolved in one ounce of distilled water. Allow this to dry, and then place the paper with its marked side upwards upon a flat surface. Above it, place the negative picture, and having put a plate of glass above, then press them together by screws or otherwise, and expose them to the light of the sun. In ten or fifteen minutes of bright sunshine, or in several hours of common daylight, a *positive* and beautiful picture will be found on the paper beneath the *negative* picture, in which the lights and shadows are now corrected. This picture, after being washed in water and then dried, is fixed by brushing it over with the solution of *bromide of potassium*, abovementioned, or by dipping it in a strong solution of *common salt*.

Mr. Talbot next proceeds to describe an entirely new method of obtaining, directly, positive pictures by a single process.* As this process is one less certain, we believe, or rather one which requires more delicate and careful manipulation than the other, we shall describe it in Mr. Talbot's own words:—

'A sheet of sensitive calotype paper is exposed to the daylight for a few seconds, or until a visible discoloration or browning of its surface takes place ; then it is to be dipped into a solution of iodide of potassium, consisting of 500 grains to one pint of water. The visible discoloration is apparently removed by this emersion ; such, however, is not the case, for if the paper were dipped into a solution of gallo-nitrate of silver it would speedily blacken all over. When the paper is removed from the iodide of potassium, it is washed with water, and then dried with blotting-paper. It is then placed in the camera obscura, and after five or ten minutes, it is removed therefrom, and washed with gallo-nitrate of silver, and warmed as before directed. An image of a positive kind is thereby produced, and represents the lights of objects by lights, and the shades by shades, as required.'

We have had an opportunity of seeing one of the pictures taken in this way, which is very good ; but the only advantage of this direct process, is, that it necessarily gives a picture with sharper lines—lines as much sharper as those in the *ordinary negative* are sharper than those in the *ordinary positive*, which must always be copied through a certain thickness of paper. This process, however, is quite inferior to the other in two essential points. It requires such a length of time that portraits could not be taken by it, and, when we do obtain good pictures, we cannot multiply them as we do in the other process. The landscape must be appealed to for every picture of it, and the sitter must sit for every portrait.*

The patent right, and the important discovery which it secures, have now been brought into actual operation and use as a branch of the fine arts. Mr. Henry Collen, a distinguished miniature painter, has quitted his own beautiful art, and devoted his whole time to the calotype process. The portraits which he has produced, one of which is now before us, are infinitely superior to the finest miniatures that have ever been painted. Devoting his chief attention to the correct and agreeable delineation of the face by the action of light alone, he corrects any imperfection in the drapery, or supplies any defect in the figure, by his professional skill ; so that his works have an entirely different aspect from those of the amateur, who must, generally speaking, be content with the result which the process gives him. In making this comparison we do not intend to convey the idea, that *perfect pictures*, both landscapes and portraits, cannot be produced without additional touches from the pencil of an artist. Without referring to the fine calotype delineations of Mr. Talbot himself, who could not be otherwise than master of his own art, we have now be-

---

* Positive photographic pictures were first obtained by a *single* process by Dr. Andrew Fyfe of Edinburgh, and M. Lassaigne of Paris, nearly about the same time ; but we have not heard that their methods have given satisfactory results. By the *double* process great advantages are obtained—the realization of the reverted pictures, and the power of multiplying copies. Mr. Talbot, Sir John Herschel and Mr. Hunt, seem to have independently discovered the property of hydriodate of potash to whiten paper darkened by exposure to light. See a ' Popular Treatise on the Art of Photography, including Daguerreotype, and all the new Methods of producing pictures by the Chemical Agency of Light. By Robert Hunt, Secretary to the Royal Cornwall Polytechnic Society. Glasgow, 1841.;' forming *Griffin's Scientific Miscellany*, No. VII. A work which we warmly recommend to the attention of photographers.

---

* Mr. Talbot's patent includes also methods of obtaining photographic images upon copper—and of obtaining coloured and otherwise diversified photogenic images upon metallic surfaces covered with a thin layer of silver, and that by means of coloured films produced from a solution of acetate of lead by a galvanic current.

fore us a collection of admirable photographs executed at St. Andrew's, by Dr. and Mr. Robert Adamson,* Major Playfair, and Captain Brewster. Several of these have all the force and beauty of the sketches of Rembrandt, and some of them have been pronounced by Mr. Talbot himself to be among the best he has seen.

Although the calotype art has attained, by Mr Talbot's labours alone, a singular degree of perfection in its ordinary results, there is yet a good deal to be done in simplifying its processes ;† in obtaining a more perfect material than common writing paper for the negative pictures ; in giving it additional sensitiveness to enable it to succeed with the light of gas ; and in rendering the result of the whole process more certain than it now is. The extension of the art, which is at this moment exciting great attention throughout the continent of Europe and also in America, will, doubtless, add to its methods and its resources ; and bring it to a degree of perfection which Mr. Talbot himself had never contemplated. In the meantime, it gives us great pleasure to learn, that though none of his photographical discoveries adorn the transactions of the Royal Society, yet the president and council have adjudged to him the Rumford Medals for the last biennial period.

Having thus given our readers a pretty ample account of the history of the Daguerreotype and Calotype, we shall now attempt to point out the advantages which these two arts, considered as the science of Photography, have conferred upon society ; and shall afterwards endeavour to form an estimate of their respective merits and applications.

It would be an idle task to eulogize the arts of painting and sculpture, whether we view their productions as works of fancy, or as correct representations of what is beautiful and grand in nature. The splendid galleries of art throughout Europe, private as well as public, form their most appropriate eulogy. Any art, therefore, which should supersede that of the painter, and deprive of employment any of its distinguished cultivators, would scarcely be hailed as a boon conferred upon society. An invention which supersedes animal, or even professional labour, must be viewed in a very different light from an invention which supersedes the efforts of genius. That the art of painting will derive incalculable advantages from Photography it is impossible to doubt. M. Delaroche, a distinguished French painter, quoted by M. Arago, considers it as 'carrying to such perfection certain of the essential principles of art, that they must become subjects of study and observation even to the most accomplished artist. * *.* The finish of inconceivable minuteness disturbs in no respect the repose of the masses, nor impairs in any manner the general effect.' 'The correctness of the lines,' he continues, ' the precision of the forms, in the designs of M. Daguerre, are as perfect as it is possible they can be, and yet at the same time we discover in them a broad and energetic manner, and a whole equally rich in tone as in effect. The painter will obtain, by this process, a quick method of making collections of studies which he could not otherwise procure without much time and labour, and in a style very far inferior, whatever might be his talents in other respects.'* The same remarks are equally applicable to the arts of sculpture and architecture.

But if the artist is thus favoured by the photographer, what must be the benefit he confers on the public—the addition which he makes to our knowledge—the direct enjoyment which he affords to our senses. How limited is our present knowledge of the architectural ornaments of other nations—of the ruined grandeur of former ages—of the gigantic ranges of the Himalaya and the Andes—and of the enchanting scenery of lakes, and rivers, and valleys, and cataracts, and volcanoes, which occur throughout the world! Excepting by the labours of some travelling artists, we know them only through the sketches of hurried visitors, tricked up with false and ridiculous illustrations, which are equal mockeries of nature and art. But when the photographer has prepared his truthful tablet, and ' held his mirror up to nature,' she is taken captive in all her sublimity and beauty ; and faithful images of her grand-

---

* All these calotypes were taken by means of excellent camera obscuras constructed by Mr. Thomas Davidson, optician, Edinburgh.

Mr. Robert Adamson, whose skill and experience in photography is very great, is about to practise the art professionally in our northern metropolis.

† Mr. William F. Channing of Boston gives a simpler process than Mr. Talbot's ; but it is only by omitting some of the steps of it. The calotype paper is therefore less sensitive. We have tried this simplified process, but without any desire to repeat it ; for a good negative picture is worth all the trouble of Mr. Talbot's process.—See the *American Journal of Science and the Arts,* July, 1842, vol. xliii. p, 73.

* *History and Practice of Photogenic Drawing,* pp. 16, 17.

est, her loveliest, and her minutest features, are transferred to her more distant worshippers, and become the objects of a new and pleasing .idolatry. The hallowed remains which . faith has consecrated in the land of Palestine, the scene of our Saviour's pilgrimage and miracles—the endeared spot where he drew his first and his latest breath—the hills and temples of the Holy City—the giant flanks of Horeb, and the awe-inspiring summits of Mount Sinai, will be displayed to the Christian's eye in the deep lines of truth, and appeal to his heart with all the powerful associations of an immortal interest. With feelings more subdued, will the antiquary and the architect study the fragments of Egyptian, Grecian, and Roman grandeur—the pyramids, the temples, the obelisks of other ages. Every inscription, every stone, will exhibit to them its outline; the grey moss will lift its hoary frond, and the fading inscription unveil its mysterious hieroglyphics. The fields of ancient and modern warfare will unfold themselves to the soldier's eye in faithful perspective and unerring outline; and reanimated squadrons will again form on the plains of Marathon, and occupy the gorge of Thermopylæ.

But it is not only the rigid forms of art and of external nature—the mere outlines and subdivisions of space—that are thus fixed and recorded. The self-delineated landscape is seized at one epoch of time, and is embalmed amid all the co-existing events of the social and physical world. If the sun shines, his rays throw their gilding upon the picture. If rain falls, the earth and the trees glisten with its reflections. If the wind blows, we see in the partially obliterated foliage the extent of its agitation. The objects of still life, too, give animation to the scene. The streets display their stationary chariots, the esplanade its military array, and the market-place its colloquial groups;—while the fields are studded with the various forms and attitudes of animal life. Thus are the incidents of time and the forms of space simultaneously recorded; and every picture becomes an authentic chapter in the history of the world.

In considering the relations of Photography to the art of portrait painting, we are disposed to give it a still higher rank. Could we now see in photogenic light and shadow Demosthenes launching his thunder against Macedon—or Brutus at Pompey's statue bending over the bleeding Cæsar—or Paul preaching at Athens—or Him whom we must not name, in godlike attitude and celestial beauty, proclaiming good-will to man, with what rapture would we gaze upon imperson.ations so exciting and divine! The heroes

and sages of ancient times, mortal though they be, would thus have been embalmed with more than Egyptian skill : and the forms of life and beauty, and the lineaments of noble affections and intellectual power, the real incarnation of living man, would have replaced the hideous fragments of princely mortality scarcely saved from corruption.

But even in the narrower, though not less hallowed, sphere of the affections, where the magic names of kindred and home are inscribed, what a deep interest do the realities of photography excite ! In the transition forms of his offspring, which link infancy with manhood, the parent will discover traces of his own mortality ; and in the successive phases which mark the sunset of life, the child, in its turn, will read the lesson that his pilgrimage, too, has a period which must close.

Nor are the delineations interesting only for their minute accuracy as works of art, or for their moral influence as incentive to virtue. They are instinct with associations equally vivid and endearing.. The picture is connected with its prototype by sensibilities peculiarly touching. It was the very light which radiated from his brow—the identical gleam which lighted up his eye—the pallid hue which hung upon his cheek—that pencilled the cherished image, and fixed themselves for ever there.

But the useful arts, too, and even the sciences themselves, have become the willing eulogists of the photographer. As the picture in the Daguerreotype is delineated by vapours of mercury, which are effaced by a touch of the finger, it became desirable to fix them upon the silvered copper by a more permanent tracery. Dr. Berres of Vienna is said to have discovered a method of doing this, in such an effective manner, that copies can.be taken from the plate as from ordinary copperplates ; and it has been asserted by Dr. Donné, that the Daguerreotype plates may be directly etched by very dilute nitric acid, which acts most powerfully upon the parts of the picture that have the least quantity of mercurial vapour. As we have not seen any of these results, and are not able to adduce the testimony of others who have seen them, we cannot form an idea of the accuracy with which they may represent the original Daguerreotype picture. We have now, however, before us *four* engravings, obtained from Daguerreotype plates by the process of Mr. Boscawen Ibbetson. *One* of these is from a Daguerreotype portrait, in which the original picture on the silvered plate is stippled by an engraver, and an impression thrown off in the usual way ; and *three* of them represent objects of natural history obtained in the following manner. The exact outline of all the parts of the picture was traced by the engraver in the Daguerreotype plate by stippling ; a print was next taken from the plate and transferred to stone ; and the lithographer then filled in the necessary shading. One of these specimens is a thin section of a madrepore, taken by the oxy-hydrogen microscope, and magnified 12½ times. The other specimens represent a silicified Pentagonaster, and a Scaphite, accompanied with other fossils ; and we venture to say, that these specimens possess every requisite that the naturalist could desire. Had the drawings been taken by the Calotype, that is, upon paper, they could have been transposed at once to stone with all their minute details, and without the intermediate step of an imperfect etching, depending on the engraver for its accuracy.

But there is still a simpler process by which the fine arts are aided by the Daguerreotype, and the results of this process are now before the world. Foreseeing the advantages of photographic pictures of the most interesting scenery in Europe, M. Lerebours, well known as one of the most distinguished opticians in Paris, has collected more than twelve hundred Daguerreotype views of the most beautiful scenery and antiquities in the world. The remarkable views from the East were taken by MM. Horace Vernet and Goupil. M. Las Cases has furnished the interesting scenery of St. Helena ; and M. Jomard has been occupied with Spanish scenery and the beauties of the Alhambra. These Daguerreotype pictures, of which it is impossible to speak too highly, are engraved in *aqua tinta*, upon steel, by the first artists ; and they actually give us the real representation of the different scenes and monuments at a particular instant of time, and under the existing lights of the sun and the atmosphere. The artists who took them, sketched separately the groups of persons, &c., that stood in the street, as the Daguerreotype process was not then sufficiently sensitive to do this of itself ; but in all the landscapes, which shall now be reproduced by this singular art, we shall possess accurate portraits of every living and moving object within the field of the picture.*

It would be almost an insult to our readers to dwell with any detail on the utility of the new art, in promoting and extending science.

We have already seen its advantages in giving the most faithful representation of objects of natural history ; and it cannot fail to be equally useful in all the sciences of observation, where visible forms are to be represented. The civil engineer and the architect have claimed it as an art incalculably useful in their profession ; and the meteorologist has seized upon it as a means of registering successive observations of the barometer, thermometer, hygrometer, and magnetometer, in the observer's absence ; and thus exhibiting to his eye, at the end of every day, accurate measures of all the atmospheric changes which have taken place.* We shall not say anything at present of the great discoveries to which it has already conducted us in physical optics, as we must devote a separate part of this article to their discussion.

In thus stating the peculiar advantages of Photography, we have supposed the Daguerreotype and Calotype to be the same art. Our readers have already seen in what the difference really consists ; but it is still necessary that we should attempt to draw a comparison between them, as sister arts, with advantages peculiar to each.

In doing this, our friends in Paris must not suppose that we have any intention of making the least deduction from the merits of M. Daguerre, or the beauty of his invention ; which cannot be affected by the subsequent discovery of the Calotype, by Mr. Talbot. While a Daguerreotype picture is much more sharp and accurate in its details than a Calotype, the latter possesses the advantage of giving a greater breadth and massiveness to its landscapes and portraits. In the one, we can detect hidden details by the application of the microscope ; in the other, every attempt to magnify its details is injurious to the general effect. In point of expense, a Daguerreotype picture vastly exceeds a Calotype one of the same size. With its silver plate and glass covering, a quarto plate must cost five or six shillings, while a Calotype one will not cost as many pence. In point of portability, permanence, and facility of examination, the Calotype picture possesses a peculiar advantage. It has been stated, but we know not the authority, that Daguerreotype pictures have been effaced before they reached the East Indies ; but if this be true, we have

---

* M. Lerebours' work is entitled *Excursions Daguerriennes, collection de 50 planches, representant les Vues et les Monumens les plus remarquables du Globe.* The views are from Paris, Milan, Venice, Florence, Rome, Naples, Switzerland, Germany, London, Malta, Egypt, Damascus, St. Jean D'Acre, Constantinople, Athens, &c.

* This application will be understood by supposing a sheet of sensitive paper to be placed *behind* the mercurial column of the barometer, and a light before the same column : the shadow of the top of the mercury will leave a white image on the paper blackened by the light, and the paper itself being moved behind the mercury by a clock, we shall thus observe the various heights of the mercury depicted at every instant of time.

no doubt that a remedy will soon be found for the defect. The great and unquestionable superiority of the Calotype pictures, however, is their power of multiplication. One Daguerreotype cannot be copied from another; and the person whose portrait is desired, must sit for every copy that he wishes. When a pleasing picture is obtained, another of the same character cannot be produced. In the Calotype, on the contrary, we can take any number of pictures, within reasonable limits, from a negative; and a whole circle of friends can procure, for a mere trifle, a copy of a successful and pleasing portrait. In the Daguerreotype the landscapes are all reverted, whereas in the Calotype the drawing is exactly conformable to nature. This objection can of course be removed, either by admitting the rays into the camera after reflection from a mirror, or by total reflection from a prism; but in both these cases, the additional reflections and refractions are accompanied with a loss of light, and also with a diminution, to a certain extent, of distinctness in the image. The Daguerreotype may be considered as having nearly attained perfection, both in the quickness of its operations and in the minute perfection of its pictures; whereas the Calotype is yet in its infancy—ready to make a new advance when a proper paper, or other ground, has been discovered, and when such a change has been made in its chemical processes as shall yield a better colour, and a softer distribution of the colouring material.

In the preceding pages we have treated of the history, the processes, the advantages, and the relative merits of the Daguerreotype and the Calotype, considered as two existing arts which we owe to M. Daguerre and Mr. Talbot; and, under this restriction, we have not felt ourselves called upon to give any particular account of the experiments and improvements of Dr. Fyfe, M. Claudet, Mr. Hunt, Mr. Ponton, M. Lassaigne, M. Netto, and many other writers. The necessary restriction of our limits, indeed, renders it impossible to enter into those minute details and discussions, which, though they might be less acceptable to a general reader, could not fail to be extremely interesting to those who may be engaged in the practice of these fascinating arts. The same cause has prevented us from describing the construction and use of the different camera obscuras, with lenses and mirrors, which have been, or which may be, successfully employed in Photography.

Extensive, however, as the subject is, and restricted as we are, there are three philosophers, Sir John Herschel, Dr. Draper, of New York, and Professor Moser, of Konigsberg, who have applied the photographic processes with such distinguished success to the advancement of optical science, that it would be unpardonable to withhold from our scientific readers an account of their discoveries; even had they been less important and of a less popular character than they are.

The researches of Sir John Herschel were both practical and theoretical.[*] In the first portion of the paper which contains them, he treats of the various parts of the photographic processes; and in the second, he treats of the chemical and calorific action of the solar rays. In the very important process of fixing photographs, whether negative or positive, Sir John gives the preference to the *hyposulphite of soda.*[†] The photograph is first well washed by soaking in water. When thoroughly dried, it is then brushed over very quickly with a flat camel-hair brush, dipped in a saturated solution of the hyposulphite, first on the face, then on the back. When the picture has been thus completely penetrated by the fluid, it must be washed repeatedly and copiously with water, until the water comes off without the slightest sweetness. Sir John recommends the repetition of this process, especially if the paper be thick. The use of common salt he has never found satisfactory; and though he regards the hydriodate of potash as good for fixation, if the right strength be hit, yet in the case of negative photographs its use would be injurious, from the yellow tint which it gives to the ground of the picture. In using a weak solution of corrosive sublimate, Sir John discovered a very singular effect of it. When the picture was washed over with this solution, and then laid for a few minutes in water, the picture was *completely obliterated.* But though invisible, it was only *dormant,* for it could easily be revived, in all its force, by merely brushing it over with a solution of a neutral hyposulphite. In this way it may be successively obliterated and revived as often as we please.

_____

* 'On the Chemical Action of the Rays of the Solar Spectrum on Preparations of Silver and other Substances, both Metallic and Non-Metallic, and on some Photographic Processes. By Sir John F. W. Herschel, Bart., K.H. V.P.R.S.,' *Phil. Trans.* 1840; pp. 1–60.

† The use of *ammonia* for fixing *positive* photographs was tried, but abandoned by Mr. Talbot. Mr. Constable of Jesus College, Cambridge, afterwards found it to be efficacious; and we have ourselves found it to be preferable to any other fixing liquid. When applied copiously and repeatedly, the photographs will resist the direct and continued light of the sun. As the ammonia always weakens the pictrue, the positive photographs should be strongly brought out by the sun. When they are weak, the bromide of potassium is preferable as the fixing material.

The 'numberless combinations' of chemical substances which were tried by Sir John Herschel, with the view of increasing the sensitiveness and facility of preparation of photographic paper, did not lead him to any very satisfactory results; and with the candour which distinguishes him, he 'most readily admits that the specimens (of photographic paper) recently placed in his hands by Mr. Talbot, far surpass, in point of sensitiveness, any that he had yet produced of a manageable kind.' Following Mr. Talbot's principle of successive alternate washes with salt and nitrate of silver, Sir John adopted the following series of washes, viz.:

1. Nitrate of silver. Spec. grav. 1.096, (say 1.1).
2. Muriate of soda. 1 salt, 19 water.
3. Nitrate of silver. Spec. grav. 1.132, (say 1.15):

saturating the muriatic solution with chloride of silver, and occasionally dividing the last, or third, application into two consecutive washes of nitrate of silver, of equal strength, by dilution. As an ordinary working paper easily prepared, Sir John considers it as having sensibility enough for most purposes. It gives, he says, good camera pictures, and when smooth demy paper is used, it retains its whiteness even in the dark. As all other papers suffered discoloration under the preceding process, and as the smooth demy might not always be obtained of the same quality, Sir John was induced to adopt, for camera pictures, a process which proved both convenient and effectual; and which he found to apply equally well to both descriptions of paper—that is, the *blue wove post* and *smooth demy*. He simply ' delays the last or efficient wash of nitrate of silver, on which the sensitive quality depends, till the moment of using it; and, in fact, using the paper actually wet with the nitrate, and applied with its sensitive face against a glass plate, whose hinder surface is in the focus of the camera. This affords other collateral advantages: 1st, That all crumpling or undulation of the paper is avoided; 2d, That being rendered in some degree transparent, the light is enabled to act deeper within its substance.'

In the practice of Photography, the artist is often disturbed with imperfections in his paper, even when it has been prepared with the utmost attention. Both Mr. Talbot and Sir John Herschel have paid particular attention to this imperfection; and have, we have no doubt, ascertained the general cause of these spots, as well as a probable means of preventing them.

' I will now add,' says Mr. Talbot, ' a few remarks concerning the very singular circumstance which I have before briefly mentioned—viz., that the paper sometimes, although intended to be prepared of the most sensitive quality, turns out on trial to be wholly insensible to light and incapable of change. The most singular part of this is the very small difference in the mode of preparation, which causes so wide a discrepancy in the result. For instance, a sheet of paper is all prepared at the same time, and with the intention of giving it as much uniformity as possible; and yet, when exposed to sunshine, this paper will exhibit large white spots of very definite outline, where the preparing process has failed; the rest of the paper, where it has succeeded, turning black as rapidly as possible. Sometimes the spots are of a pale tint of cerulean blue, and are surrounded by exceedingly definite outlines of perfect whiteness, contrasting very much with the blackness of the part immediately succeeding. With regard to the theory of this, I am only prepared to state as my opinion at present, that it is a case of what is called "unstable equilibrium." The process followed is such as to procure one of two definite chemical compounds; and when we happen to come near the limit which separates the two cases, it depends upon exceedingly small and often imperceptible circumstances, which of the two compounds shall be formed. That they are both definite compounds; is of course at present merely my conjecture; that they are signally different, is evident from their dissimilar properties.'[*]

Both Sir John Herschel and Mr. Hunt concur in the theory given of these spots by Mr. Talbot; and the former has suggested the following method of preventing their occurrence.

' It frequently happens that, however carefully the successive washes are applied, so as apparently to drench completely every part of the paper, irregular patches in the resulting sheet will be of a comparatively much lower degree of sensibility; which degree is nevertheless uniform over their whole area. These patches are always sharply defined and terminated by *rounded* outlines, indicating as their proximate cause, the spreading of the wash last applied within the pores of the paper. They have been noticed and well described by Mr. Talbot, and ascribed by him, I think justly, to the assumption of definite and different chemical states of the silver within and without their area, which it would be highly interesting to follow out. They are very troublesome in practice, but may be materially diminished in frequency, if not avoided altogether, by saturating the saline washes used, previous to their application, with chloride of silver. By attending to this precaution, and by dividing the last wash of the nitrate into two of half the strength, applied one after the other, drying the paper between them, their occurrence may be almost entirely obviated.'

The occurrence of these white spots on the

---

[*] ' Some Account of the Art of Photogenic Drawing,' &c., p. 13.

paper used for *positive* photographs, is particularly distressing. When a favourable sun and a fine *negative* drawing should have produced a powerful picture, the figures often appear without heads or hands, or with such numbers of white spots as to destroy the picture. In order to be secure against this disappointment, Sir David Brewster exposes the nitrated paper to such a degree of light as to produce a sort of neutral brownish tint over the whole.* The uniformity of this tint indicates the absence of white spots; and when the white spots do appear, we may either reject the paper or place the *negative* upon that part of it which is uniformly tinged. This tinge has another advantage. It prevents that disagreeable change of colour, which, in the course of time, comes over all photographs that have been fixed with the bromide of potassium; and it greatly adds to the effect of a picture with very deep shadows produced by an excess of light, and which has been fixed by ammonia.

Within our present limits, we cannot stop to give our reader an adequate idea of the discoveries made by Sir John Herschel during his photographic researches. We must, therefore, content ourselves with little more than an enumeration of them.

1. By concentrating the prismatic spectrum with a large lens of crown glass, and receiving it on paper prepared, as already described, the paper was tinged with colours ' imitating those of the spectrum itself.' The *red* rays give *no tint ;* the *orange yellow,* a *faint brick red ;* the *orange yellow,* a pretty strong *brick red ;* the *yellow* give a *red passing into green ;* the *yellow green* give a *dull bottle green ;* the *green* a *dull bottle green* passing into *bluish ;* the *blue green* give a *sombre blue,* almost *black ;* the *blue* give a *black,* which, by long exposure, becomes a *metallic yellow,* like imperfect gilding; the *violet* produced a *black,* passing into the same *yellow,* by long exposure in the less refrangible portions of the violet ray ; the part *beyond the violet* gave a *violet black* or *purplish black.*

2. The rays beyond the violet were found by concentration to have a decided colour, to which Sir John has given the name of *lavender grey.*

3. When hydriodate of potash, of moderate strength, is applied to darkened Photographic papers, they become susceptible of being *whitened* or *oxidized* by further exposure to light: the whitening begins in the violet

rays, but when we come to the red rays a *blackening* or *deoxidizing* effect takes place, which extends distinctly beyond the *red* extremity.

4. When the sun's rays pass through different transparent bodies before they fall upon nitrated paper, these bodies have the property, some of *exalting,* and others of *depressing* the effect of the direct light of the sun. Colourless plates of *Saxon topaz, sulphate of lime, Iceland spar, Rochelle salt, and quartz,* exalted the solar action in different degrees when the paper was in contact with them. Capricious results, however, were obtained with different kinds of glass, and different kinds of paper, differently prepared.

5. By a very interesting preparation of paper (thin post) blackened on one side with Indian ink, and washed on the other with rectified spirit of wine, and having this last side exposed to the spectrum, Sir John displayed, by means of the drying or whitening of the paper, the length and structure of the *calorific spectrum.* The chief heating power lay on that side of the yellow ray, D of Fraünhofer, and "extended as far on that side as the whole length of the ordinary luminous spectrum. He observed five nearly equidistant centres or *maxima* of action ; the first corresponding with the extreme red ray ; and the fifth, which was very faint, as far beyond the visible red extremity as the line D is from the extreme violet ray.

In pursuing these researches, this distinguished philosopher has been led to other highly interesting results. The action of light on vegetable colours, he finds to be positive ; that is, it either destroys the colour totally, or leaves a residual tint on which light has no further action.* This action is confined to the region of the spectrum occupied by the luminous rays ; and the rays which are effective in destroying any given tint, are in a great many cases ' those whose union produces a colour *complementary* to the tint destroyed.'

A still more interesting result of this inquiry has been the discovery of two new Photographic processes; to the latter of which its author has given the name of *Chrysotype,* from its being chiefly produced by a solution of *gold.* When paper has been first washed over with a solution of *ammonio-citrate* of *iron,* then dried, and afterwards washed over with a solution of *ferro-sesqui-cyanuret of potassium,* it becomes capable of receiving with great rapidity a *positive* photographic impression. When a *negative* picture has been im-

---

* Instead of using for positives the strong nitrate of 80 grains to 1 oz. of water, he uses the acetonitrate, with only 50 grains to 1 1-3 oz. of fluid, that is, of water and acetic acid. The acetic acid may be replaced by common vinegar in taking positives.

* This effect is perfectly analogous to that of the action of heat upon the colour of minerals. In Brazil topaz the residual tint is always a light pink. See *Phil. Trans.,* vol. xix. p. 25.

pressed upon paper washed with the former of the solutions, but which is originally faint and sometimes scarcely perceptible, it is immediately called forth upon being washed over with a neutral solution of GOLD. The picture does not at once acquire its full intensity, but rapidly blackens up to a certain point; when the photograph acquires a sharpness and perfection of detail which nothing can surpass. A solution of silver produces a similar effect with greater intensity, but much more slowly.*

To Professor Draper of New York, we owe many interesting facts and views connected with the photographical art. He was the first, we believe, who, under the brilliant summer sun of New York, took portraits with the Daguerreotype. This branch of Photography seems not to have been regarded as a possible application of Daguerre's invention; and no notice is taken of it in the reports made to the legislative bodies of France. We have been told that Daguerre had not at that period taken any portraits: and when we consider the period of time, twenty or twenty-five minutes, which was then deemed necessary to get a Daguerreotype landscape, we do not wonder at the observation of a French author, who describes the taking of portraits as *toujours un terrain un peu fabuleux pour la Daguerreotype.* Daguerre, however, and his countryman, M. Claudet, have nobly earned the reputation of having perfected this branch of the art.

It had been long known, that if we write upon a piece of glass with a pencil of Soapstone or Agalmatolite, the written letters, though wholly invisible, may be read by simply breathing upon the glass; and this even though the surface has been well cleaned after the letters had been written. Dr. Draper observed, that if a piece of metal, a shilling for example, or even a wafer, is laid upon a cool surface of glass or polished metal, and the glass or metal breathed upon, then, if the shilling is tossed from the surface, and the vapour dried up spontaneously, a spectral image of the shilling will be seen by breathing again upon the surface; the vapour depositing itself in a different manner upon the part previously protected by the shilling.† More recently, Professor Draper has shown, that this spectral image could be revived during a period of several months of the cold weather in the winter of 1840-1; but he has stated that he cannot find the reason of this result, though

he regards it as analogous to the deposition of mercurial vapour in the Daguerreotype.* We have often repeated this interesting experiment, by keeping the protecting body, the shilling or wafer, *at a distance* from the glass or metallic surface, or by putting it under a watch-glass; and we found that the result was always the same, (even after cleaning the surface with soft leather), so that change of temperature, or any pressure upon the glass surface, were excluded as causes of the phenomenon.

Professor Draper was led also to the interesting conclusion, 'that the chemical action produced by the rays of light, depends upon the rays being rendered latent or absorbed by sensitive bodies;' that 'by some unknown process, photographic effects on sensitive surfaces gradually disappear, and that it depends on the chemical nature of the sensitive material, which rays shall be rendered latent or absorbed.'†

During a long journey, undertaken during the last summer for the purpose of trying the photographical power of the sun's rays in lower latitudes, Professor Draper has been conducted to a very remarkable discovery. No similar result could be obtained at New York, and therefore we can have no anticipation of witnessing it in England. From photographic impressions of the solar spectrum, obtained in the South of Virginia, when the thermometer was 96° of Fahrenheit in the shade, Professor Draper found that 'under a brilliant sun, there is a class of rays commencing precisely at the termination of the *blue*, and extending beyond the extreme *red*, which totally and perfectly arrest the light of the sky. The *negative* rays seemed almost as effective in *protecting*, as the *blue* rays are in *decomposing* iodide of silver.'

'The most remarkable part of the phenomenon,' says Professor Draper, 'is, that the same class of rays makes its appearance again beyond the extreme lavender rays. Sir J Herschel has already stated, in the case of bromide of silver, that these negative rays exist low down in the spectrum. This specimen, however, proves that they exist at both ends, and do not at all depend on the refrangibility. It was obtained with yellow iodide of silver, Daguerre's preparation, the time of exposure to the sun fifteen minutes.

'In this impression, six different kinds of action may be distinctly traced, by the different effects produced on the mercurial amalgam. Those, commencing with the most refrangible rays, may be enumerated as follows:—1st, protecting rays; 2d, rays that whiten; 3d, rays that blacken; 4th, rays that whiten intensely; 5th, rays that whiten very feebly; 6th, protecting rays.

'It is obvious we could obtain negative pho-

---

* Hence Sir. J. Herschel considers the name *Siderotype*, taken from the *iron* employed in one of the solutions, as preferable to *Chrysotype*.

† *Lond. and Edin. Phil. Magazine*, vol. xviii. p. 218. Sept. 1840-41.

* *Lond. and Edin. Phil. Mag.*, v. xix. 198.

† *Id. Id.* 195-6.

tographs by the Daguerreotype process, by absorbing all the rays coming from natural objects, except the red, orange, yellow, and green, allowing at the same time diffused daylight to act on the plate.

' This constitutes a great improvement in the art of Photography, because it permits its application in a negative way to landscapes. In the original French plan, the most luminous rays are those that have least effect, whilst the sombre blue and violet rays produce all the action. Pictures produced in that way never can imitate the order of light and shadow in a coloured landscape."*

From these observations, Professor Draper considers that ' there are strong reasons for believing that the sun's light, in tropical seasons, differs intrinsically from ours.' With a French achromatic lens, which performed admirably in a camera at NewYork, the Chevalier Frederichstal, who travelled in Central America for the Prussian Government, found very long exposures in the camera necessary, to produce impressions of the ruined monuments of the deserted cities. Professor Draper says that these Daguerreotypes ' are of a very respectable aspect ; and he assures us that other competent travellers experienced similar difficulties, and even *failed to get any impressions whatever.*' These difficulties must certainly be due, as Professor Draper conjectures, to the antagonist action of the negative and positive rays.

We shall now give our readers a very condensed account of the extraordinary discoveries recently made by M. Ludwig Moser, of the University of Königsberg ; and we are fortunately able to do this with accuracy, from a detailed abstract of them communicated by Professor Moser himself to Sir David Brewster. According to his views, light produces the same general effect upon all substances, and this effect consists in its modifying their surfaces, so as to make them condense vapours differently. The quantity of vapour thus condensed, depends on the intensity of the light and the duration of its action ; and also on the elasticity of the vapour and the duration of its action. The iodide of silver is *at first* blackened by the action of light ; and this effect is produced most rapidly by the *blue* and *violet* rays, and more slowly by the other rays in the ratio of their lesser refrangibility. But when the action of light upon the iodide is prolonged, the *blackened iodide* is brought back to a *coloured iodide ;* and this restoration is produced most rapidly by the *red* and *yellow* rays, and less rapidly by the *blue* and *violet*, in the ratio of their greater refrangibility.

All bodies, according to Professor Moser,

emit light even in absolute darkness, and this light differs entirely from that which is emitted by phosphorescent bodies. It is called by Professor Moser the *proper* light of bodies. It acts upon all substances in the same manner as ordinary light ; that is, it modifies their surfaces, so as to enable them to condense vapours differently. The leading experiment from which this doctrine is deduced, consists in placing a polished surface of silver within the twentieth of an inch of a cameo of horn or agate, with white figures upon a dark ground. After remaining at that distance ten minutes, the figures engraved on the cameo have impressed themselves on the silver surface, and may be rendered visible by throwing upon that surface the vapours of mercury, water, oil, &c. If the image in a camera obscura is received upon a surface of silver, glass, wood, leather, &c., the image may, in like manner, be rendered visible. The proper light of bodies, which has a great refrangibility, is the most suitable for commencing the action upon bodies. From these results Professor Moser has drawn the important conclusion, that there exists *latent light*, analogous to *latent heat ;* and that a portion of light becomes latent when any liquor evaporates, and is again disengaged when the same vapour is condensed. The condensation of vapours, therefore, acts like light upon the condensing bodies ; particular vapours acting like particular coloured rays of the spectrum. The latent light of *mercurial* vapour is *yellow*, and their condensation produces all the effects of *yellow* light. The latent light of the vapours of *iodine* is *blue* or *violet*. The latent light of *chlorine, bromine*, and their combinations, differs a little in refrangibility from those of iodine. The latent light of the vapour of *water* is neither *green, yellow, orange*, nor *red.* The latent light of the hydro-fluoric vapours, surpasses in refrangibility that of the visible rays. Hence Professor Moser concludes, that the *iodide of silver* derives its great sensibility to ordinary light, from the circumstance that the latent light of the vapour of iodine is disengaged, and acts on the substance of the metal ; and that the iodide of silver has not a greater sensibility to the invisible rays than pure silver.*

---

* *Lond. and Edin. Phil. Mag.*, vol. xxi. p. 349.

* We have found that many of the phenomena ascribed to *latent light*, or to *heat*, are owing to the absorption of matter in the state of vapour or minute particles, passing from the object to the surface of the glass or metal upon which the image of that object is impressed ; and by this means we have obtained very fine pictures upon glass, which are *positive* when seen by reflection, and *negative* when seen by transmitted light. These pictures are rendered visible by the vapour of water, &c.

These general results are deduced from various experiments detailed in three memoirs ; only one of which is yet published in Poggendorff's *Annalen der Physik*. This *first* memoir is *On Vision, and the Action of Light upon all Bodies ;* the *second*, *On the Latent State of Light ;* and the third, *On Invisible Rays*. The published Memoir indicated at the head of this article, contains many interesting experiments connected with the Daguerreotype ; but the most important part of it is that in which its author assimilates the phenomena of vision to those of Photography. In developing his particular views on this subject, he founds them on the following experiment made by Sir David Brewster, which he regards as a complete proof of his theory :—

' If, when two candles are placed at the distance of eight or ten feet from the eye, and about a foot from each other, we view the one directly, and the other indirectly ; the indirect image will swell, as we have already mentioned, and will be succeeded with a bright ring of *yellow* light, while the bright light within the ring will have a *pale-blue* colour. If the candles are viewed through a prism, the *red* and *green* light of the *indirect* image will vanish ; and there will be left only a large mass of *yellow*, terminated with a portion of *blue* light. In making this experiment, and looking steadily and directly at one of the prismatic images of the candles, I was surprised to find that the *red* and *green* rings began to disappear, leaving only *yellow* and a small portion of *blue ;* and when the eye was kept immovably fixed on the same point of the image, the *yellow light* became almost *pure white ;* so that the prismatic image was converted into an *elongated image of white light*.'—(*Treatise on Optics*, p. 296, 297).

Professor Moser regards this experiment as inexplicable by the ordinary theory of accidental colours ; and ascribes the phenomena to a peculiar vital action not yet understood.

In the middle of this physiological difficulty, our exhausted limits compel us to stop. But we cannot allow ourselves to conclude this article without some reflections, which the preceding details must have excited in the minds of our readers, as well as in ours. Two great inventions, the produce of two of the greatest and most intellectual nations in the world, have illustrated the age in which we live. With a generous heart and open hand, France has purchased the secret of the Daguerreotype ; and while she has liberally rewarded the genius which created it, she has freely offered it as a gift to all nations—a boon to universal science—a donation to the arts—a source of amusement and instruction to every class of society. All the nations of Europe—save one—and the whole hemisphere of the New World, have welcomed the generous gift. They have received the free use of it for all their subjects ; they have improved its processes; they have applied it to the arts ; they have sent forth travellers to distant climes to employ it in delineating their beauties and their wonders. In England alone, the land of free trade—the enemy of monopoly—has the gift of her neighbour been received with contumely and dishonour. It has been treated as contraband—not at the Custom-house, but at the Patent-office. Much as we admire the principle of our Patent laws, as the only reward of mechanical genius under governments without feeling and without wisdom, we would rather see them utterly abrogated, than made, as they have in this case been made, an instrument of injustice. While every nation in the world has a staff of pilgrim philosophers, gathering on foreign shores the fragments of science and practical knowledge for the benefit of their country, England marshals only a coast-guard of patent agents, not to levy duties, but to extinguish lights ; not to seize smugglers, but to search philosophers; not to transmit their captures to the national treasury, but to retain them as fees and profits to interested individuals.

Nor does the fate of the Calotype redeem the treatment of her sister art. The Royal Society—the philosophical organ of the nation—has refused to publish its processes in their transactions. No Arago—no Gay Lussac, drew to it the notice of the Premier or his Government. No representatives of the People or the Peers unanimously recommended a national reward. No enterprising artists started for our colonies to portray their scenery, or repaired to our insular rocks and glens to delineate their beauty and their grandeur. The inventor was left to find the reward of his labours in the doubtful privileges of a patent;—and thus have these two beautiful and prolific arts been arrested on English ground, and doomed to fourteen years' imprisonment in the labyrinths of Chancery Lane.

Art. II.—*Speeches of* Lord Campbell, *at the Bar, and in the House of Commons ; with an Address to the Irish Bar as Lord Chancellor of Ireland*. 8vo. Edinburgh : 1842.

We regard the publication of this volume with interest, not derived merely from the intrinsic merit of some of the speeches which it contains, and the importance of the events with which they are associated; but from the memorials it presents of a career which it is pleasant to contemplate, and wise to hold out as an encouraging example. The professional life of its author is not illustrated by those sparkling qualities which sometimes attain a sudden triumph, and which few can emulate; nor diversified by those happy accidents which occasionally decide the fate of a bold aspirant, when trembling between obscurity and greatness; but consists of an uninterrupted course of strenuous labours, sustained with unflinching courage and unwearied patience, and, by constant and regular progress, achieving high and merited honours. From the political party to which he attached himself in youth, notwithstanding its attainment of power then beyond all expectation, he has derived no other pecuniary benefits than the office of Attorney-General conferred —the painful and ill-paid duties of which he discharged for a longer period than any of his predecessors, and with industry and care which none of his successors can ever surpass; so that of the numerous lawyers who have attained high rank, and founded noble families, he has, as much as any one within our recollection, directly worked for and earned his fortune, by that persevering toil which inferior minds may imitate with proportionate success, and which none can imitate in vain. His course has also the merit and the beauty—too often wanting, or imperfect in the history of eminent lawyers—of entire political consistency. Early in life he chose his party for better and for worse; clove to it with constancy; and now advocates in the House of Lords those principles which he embraced when their success seemed a distant hope, and which, notwithstanding the present exclusion from office of those by whom they have been supported, are, and will continue triumphant. And without imputing dishonourable motives to those successful lawyers whose career has wanted, or seemed to want, this grace—believing that the changes imputed to them have rarely been attended by feelings consciously base—we may be permitted to regard it as a ground of congratulation, when a long public career wears all the outward symbols of the integrity which has influenced its secret springs of action; when the objects of youthful and enthusiastic affection are the same with those of matured attachment; and when the whole course of active and contemplative existence is in keeping and harmony.

We should have liked this volume better if it had comprised a greater variety of speeches at the Bar, illustrating the stages of its author's progress—many of which, if we recollect rightly, were inspired by occasions of great forensic interest, and which, eminently successful with courts and juries, would have been of much value to the student of common law; and for these we could have spared the ponderous argument on the question of Parliamentary Privilege; though it is a remarkable instance of industry in searching for all possible materials, and of perfect mastery obtained over them. But perhaps the means of reviving those efforts, which were attended with the most signal success, did not remain; or the difficulty of rendering them intelligible, without a full detail of all *the surrounding incidents*, may have presented insuperable obstacles in the way of such a selection. This last difficulty considerably detracts from the effect of the first speech of this volume—the defence of the action of ' Norton v. Lord Melbourne'— which, heard in connection with the evidence which it dissects and exposes, produced entire conviction of the utter baselessness of the case which the plaintiff had been induced— we believe against his own better judgment— to bring into court, and well entitled the advocate to the cheers with which he was greeted on entering the House of Commons, after the verdict was given. Other objections have been urged to the publication of this speech, which we do not think equally valid. If, indeed, it were possible to obliterate all remembrance of an attempt—made not *by*, but *through* the ostensible plaintiff—to crush the First Minister of the Crown, by sacrificing the reputation and the peace of a beautiful and richly-gifted woman—we grant that such oblivion of the endeavour would be wisely purchased by the suppression of the effort which destroyed it. But this is surely impossible—not only because the position held by the defendant in the councils of his sovereign, from which an adverse verdict must have driven him, renders the attack part of the history of the times, but because the celebrity of the lady, exposed to double envy by the dangerous gifts of genius and beauty, imparts to her sorrows that undying interest which always attends suffering when associated with high endowments. If the splendour of hereditary association, and her own just claims to fame, deny to her the refuges of mediocrity, and preserve the memory of her trials, it is surely better that the record of the exposure of the attempt in which her character was involved should attend the recollection of the wrong, than that posterity should be left to guess at the materials of the charge, and the force of the answer. If regarded apart from the fortunes of the distinguished persons which it involved, this cause affords an egregious instance of that peculiar action which, to the disgrace of the English Law, it not only permits, but absolutely requires, before a husband, however wronged, can obtain the severance of the violated marriage-tie. It is assuredly a reproach to civilisation itself that such a remedy should be allotted to such a wrong;—that 'a man should' be compelled to seek *'compensation in damages'* for the loss of a life of affection, and the blighting of hopes which extend through human life and overstep the grave, by pouring on the greedy ears of 'his friends and the public,' all the shameful details of his wife's crime and his own dishonour.' In vain does his advocate represent his loss and his misery as beyond the power of money to compensate—it is still money that he asks; and those in whose presence that degrading appeal is made, ought to feel, not that money is inadequate in degree to the purpose for which it is sought, but wholly inapplicable in kind—that to require a jury to determine on their oaths how much in pounds, shillings, and pence the adulterer ought to pay to the friend whose wife he has seduced, is as absurd as to propound to them the child's question, *How many miles is it to Christmas-day ?*

Among the many varieties of injustice which the prosecution of such a complaint involves, perhaps the worst is that which denies to the party whose interests are most fearfully affected by its conduct and its issue —the lady whose imputed frailty is directly in question—any representative or protector; for, if she is innocent, he who should defend her is her accuser, and she has no claim on the defendant, whose relation to her is erroneously charged. In this case the injustice would have been bitterly felt, if the tissue of misapprehension and falsehood which constituted the evidence for the plaintiff had been more artfully woven; for the duty of the counsel for the defendant to their client might still have compelled them to abstain from assailing it by proof; and thus, although successful in the result, might have left the vindication of the lady imperfect. The practice of *nisi prius*, which enables a plaintiff's advisers to select fragments of the truth, and to arrange them, so as to compel or provoke their opponents to supply the deficiencies in the picture, at the peril of all those casualties which often occur in the course of evidence, and which a defendant can neither anticipate nor explain, produced on this occasion appearances essentially deceptive; which, though inadequate at the worst to influence the verdict, might have been sufficient to leave a taint on the reputation of the lady, if happy accident, wisely employed by Sir John Campbell, had not dispelled them. As the case for the plaintiff appeared in proof almost until its close, it must have been inferred that, on some discovery, a separation took place between the husband and wife, of which the action was the direct consequence; and such would have remained the conviction of the judge, jury, and spectators, if the accidental appearance in the witness-box of a female servant, to prove the handwriting of the lady to a few most innocent letters to her husband, had not enabled the counsel to elicit the important and hitherto unsuspected fact, that the unhappy difference between them arose on matter *wholly unconnected with a suspicion of her honour*—that they had, in truth, separated because he would not permit their children to accompany her on a visit to her brother, which he was not invited to share; and that weeks had elapsed before he thought of regarding the intimacy, of which he had been naturally and honourably proud, as tainted with the guilt subsequently imputed by the action. Another instance of false appearance, produced by a partial disclosure of truths, passed, in this cause, without detection. The servants of the exemplary daughter of a gallant officer were examined, to prove that they had, on two or three occasions, attended the carriage of their mistress when it conveyed Mrs. Norton to the house of the defendant; that mistress sat in a room adjoining the Court, expecting to be herself called to explain the objects of those visits to be perfectly innocent, and approved by the plaintiff; but she waited in vain;—the plaintiff left the explanation to be given by the defendant; the defendant's counsel thought the weakness of the case on other points rendered it unnecessary to answer it on this; and thus, although the witnesses on this point spoke only truth, the result of their evidence was falsehood. No one will impute to the eminent advocate who conducted the plaintiff's case, any desire to suppress or distort truth; probably the entire facts were not known to him, or some urgent reason existed for declining to present particular witnesses *as his own witnesses*, of which a stranger cannot judge: both the circumstances suggest a defect in our judicial system, which deserves serious consideration. Surely, when we expose—as we had recently occasion to expose[*]—the meretricious license of French advocacy, by which much may be asserted and insinuated which cannot be proved, we ought to allow that there is an opposite imperfection in our own practice; which, con-

---

[*] See the Article in Vol. 151, on the 'Trial of Madame Lafarge.'

fining the inquiry within narrower limits and stricter rules, and leaving to either party the option of disclosing just so many of the facts as he may think prudent, often leaves a cause to be decided while much important truth remains untold. At all events, it must be admitted that, however fair this game of *nisi prius* may be to the contending parties, its operation is most unjust when its highest stake is really the character of a woman, who has no share in its management—no power to make her own conduct clear—no organ even to express a wish on her behalf as to the production of evidence—on which her rights as a wife and a mother, and her social existence may depend. Fortunately, in this case, the truths were sufficiently developed to render a belief in the charge impossible ; and the unhesitating verdict of the jury—pronounced without the production of the proofs which might have shattered the case, if it had not fallen to pieces in its progress, and been trampled into dust by the speech for the defence—left the lady whose peace it involved, to receive all the consolation which public sympathy can minister to such trials and such sorrows.

The merits of this speech, consisting, for the most part, in masterly analysis of the evidence, and indignant exposure of the falsehood of some portions of it, and of the inferences drawn from others—does not admit of exemplification by extract ; nor, indeed, does the general style of Lord Campbell's pleading, which consists in the exact adaptation of subtle reasoning to the aim which it rarely fails to reach, afford frequent opportunities for the exhibition of passages which look remarkable even when torn asunder from the framework of the argument they illustrate. Yet the next speech—the defence of Mr. Medhurst—delivered on an occasion of deep individual interest, and applicable to a very simple state of facts, contains passages of pure diction and manly pathos, which a short statement of the circumstances attendant on its delivery will enable every reader to appreciate. The client of Sir John Campbell, a young gentleman of nineteen years of age, had the misfortune to kill a fellow-pupil of about the same age named Alsop, who, with himself, had been pursuing his studies in the interval unwisely interposed between school and the university, under the direction of a clergyman with whom they both boarded. Some alienation had occurred between the youths, which gave a fiercer character to a casual encounter, in the course of which Medhurst, under the influence of rage, and perhaps of apprehension, inflicted a wound on his adversary with a knife which he unfortunately had on his per-

son, which shortly after terminated in death. A coroner's jury—always the worst selected, and sometimes the worst directed of all English tribunals—returned a verdict of *wilful murder* against the poor lad, who was abundantly punished by the wretchedness which the issue of his sudden act entailed on him, and he was committed to take his trial for that crime. When the indictment was preferred, however, the grand jury returned a *true bill* for manslaughter ; for which offence Sir John Campbell was retained to defend him at the Central Criminal Court ; but the presiding Judges thought themselves bound to direct the trial to proceed on the inquisition, and the young prisoner stood on his deliverance for life or death—an issue which strong prejudices rendered doubtful. After describing the melancholy contest according to the truth, as forcibly elicited from the witnesses, Sir John Campbell thus alluded to the subsequent conduct of the sufferers :—

'If a desire of vengeance and not self-defence had been the motive of the prisoner, what then would have been his demeanour ? His passion would have been gratified. He would have enjoyed at least that momentary satisfaction, though to be followed by remorse, which is felt in accomplishing any object, however wicked. But he was instantly horror-struck—" O God !" he exclaimed—no other utterance could he find for grief and anguish. From that moment he could not have shown more sympathy and tenderness for his recovery, had he been a beloved brother, who, by some mischance, had met a similar fate from the hand of a stranger. Nor was this from any sordid regard to his own safety. I believe, though unconscious of ever having entertained any bad feelings towards Alsop, and certain that the offence with which he now stands charged never could be truly imputed to him, he would willingly have sacrificed his own existence to rescue his friend from the consequence of the wound of which he was the unfortunate cause. Need I remind you how kindly he conducted him to his chamber, how affectionately he hung over him in bed, trying to assuage his pain, and the earnestness he displayed that the sufferer might be surrounded by his relations ? If my client had felt any consciousness of guilt, or alarm for his own safety, he might at any time have fled to await the event. But he continued by the sick-bed to the last ; he still remained in the house when the scene had closed —and being informed of the finding of the coroner's jury accusing him of murder, he voluntarily went to a magistrate, and surrendered himself that he might be tried by God and his country.

'Is this the conduct of a murderer ?—of one who thirsted for blood ?—who planned assassination ?—who had such a wicked and depraved heart, that, without provocation or excuse, he would take the life of him who, with the exception of a boyish dispute which might have been easily appeased, had never done anything to offend him, and whom he had always loved and cherished?

'But, gentlemen, there is a witness whose evidence you must believe, and whose evidence conclusively proves the innocence of my client. That witness is the unfortunate Alsop—whose voice is heard by you from the grave. I am afraid, gentlemen, to approach the touching scenes of the reconciliation and mutual forgiveness of these two young men—whose fate, though different, is perhaps equally to be deplored—lest I should be overpowered by my feelings, and entirely disqualified for the further discharge of my duty before you. When it was announced to Alsop that his recovery was hopeless, he pressed the hand of Medhurst—embraced him—exclaimed, "We were both to blame, and I forgive you"—asked and received forgiveness. The last words he ever spoke amounted to a verdict of Not Guilty in favour of my client. When his eye was becoming dim, his hand cold, and his voice tremulous, and it was evident to himself and those around him that his earthly career was rapidly drawing to a close, the surgeon asked him if Medhurst had been actuated by malice. He answered, "Certainly not!"—and expired. That declaration of innocence was not accompanied by the form of a judicial oath to speak the truth. But is it entitled to less credit? He knew that he had nothing to hope or to fear on this side the grave; that he was speedily to appear in the immediate presence of his Maker, and that his eternal doom was to be sealed, according to the purity of his heart, and the sincerity of his parting words. Are you to suppose then, that from a false generosity, from a spurious chivalry, he wished to screen guilt from punishment; and that with this view he perverted the truth, and went out of the world pronouncing a falsehood? As a true Christian, he knew that forgiveness is the condition on which we hope to be forgiven; and, imitating the example of the Divine Founder of our religion, he would have been ready, in his last moments, to pray for mercy from above upon his murderer, if he had come to his end by the blow of premeditation and malice. But he knew that he spoke before the Searcher of all hearts—that he was forthwith to render an account of his words and of his actions to the God of truth—and that, when the commandment of God against murder has been violated, the safety of God's creatures requires that the penalty affixed to this crime should be enforced by human laws.

'He now calls upon you to acquit the prisoner. Perhaps we may, without irreverence, suppose that he is conscious of this solemn proceeding; and his gentle spirit, if it can by any mysterious means influence your minds, must inspire you with the conviction that the accused was free from malice, and that his act was unaccompanied by that criminal intention which alone constitutes guilt.

'His surviving relatives—although the prosecutors—must rejoice in his acquittal. They have done their duty to his memory, by instituting the prosecution, and laying the case fairly before you. The candour and humanity of my learned friend truly represent the spirit by which they are actuated, and show that none would more deeply regret that, from any excess of good feeling in the jury—from any preconceived opinion —from any unfounded rumour—from any desire to discountenance the practice of carrying secret weapons, my client should be in undue peril. It is impossible not to sympathize with them for the heavy loss they have sustained in the untimely death of a young man of so much promise —so likely to be a credit and a blessing to his family. It must be some consolation to them to reflect that he did not die unprepared; that repentance, there is every reason to hope, atoned for any youthful errors he might have committed; and that, for his own sake, the change is not to be deplored—as he is taken from the evil to come—withdrawn to peace and happiness— from a world beset by temptation—where the most prosperous meet with many privations, disappointments, and sorrows.

'But what must be the feelings of the relations of Medhurst—his widowed mother—his little brothers and sisters—old enough to know the nature of the charge brought against him, and its awful consequences? He, gentlemen, as you may perceive, behaves with firmness and resolution, in the consciousness of innocence—ready, with God's assistance, to meet his fate, whatever it may be. What a group would *they* now present to you! Till they suddenly heard the astounding intelligence that he was committed to prison on a charge of murder, they had ever found him quiet, mild, gentle, dutiful, and affectionate. They looked forward to an early visit from him—when, as usual, he would fly into his mother's arms—and his brothers and sisters clinging round him to kiss him, he would remark how they had increased in stature and beauty since the family was last assembled. These innocents are unacquainted with legal distinctions —they are incapable of appreciating the degree of danger to which, by law, he may be exposed; in an agony of tears they wait your verdict. But, gentlemen, their suspense and their suffering will be recompensed by the joy of that moment when you restore him to their embrace— all danger over, and his character unsullied.'— (Pp. 41-44.)

We cannot afford space to follow the advocate over the delicate ground on which he next touches—the possibility that the jury might entirely exonerate his client from guilt, by finding the wounding to have been the immediate result of mere accident; but it is glanced over with consummate skill. To have dwelt on ground so untenable might possibly have offended the jury, and would certainly have called down expressions of strong dissent from the presiding Judge; to have passed it entirely by, would have been not only to throw away a slender chance of acquittal, but to deprive the prisoner of the benefit of that sort of compromise which so often prevails in the jury-box between extremes; it was therefore suggested, and left 'with as much modesty as cunning.' The result was just—a conviction of man-slaughter, with a sentence of three years' imprisonment—leaving the fate of the two unfortunate fellow-students to answer the description given of a similar calamity by a Scottish tragedian:—

'And happy, in my mind, was he that died;
For many deaths hath the survivor suffer'd."

The speeches in Parliament are, we think, of less interest than those at the Bar; and, though distinguished for moderation and practical sense, afford little occasion for commentary. We must pass them over; and also the speeches for the 'Times,' on the trial of the criminal information obtained by Sir John Conway against the publisher of that Journal —though the suggestions of the injustice and absurdity of our libel law which the defence contains, are particularly edifying from the lips of an Attorney-General—to notice the opening speech on the prosecution of Frost for high-treason, before the Special Commission at Monmouth. This address was in happy accordance with the tone and spirit and forms of that august proceeding—which in all but forms presented a signal contrast to certain trials for treason and sedition still within the recollection of some of us—and which tended to make the administration of justice loved, even more than it caused it to be feared.

The charge of the Lord Chief-Justice Tindal, whose gentle wisdom presided over the Commission, had been delivered some time before the assembling of the parties necessary to the trial; and the effect of this grave and mild exposition of the law was felt in the profound tranquillity which reigned through the scene of the inquiry, and the confidence which the most violent partisans of the accused expressed in the impartiality of the tribunal—and never was confidence better justified and repaid! Although the little town of Monmouth lies only at the distance of about twenty miles from the wild country which had, a few weeks before, bristled with armed thousands in sanguinary revolt; and although knots of those deluded men, who rallied under the name of *Charter*, without any more knowledge of its *five points* than of those of Calvin, were sometimes seen in its streets; no tumult, no noises, not a shout or a hiss, broke the silence which prevailed during the three weeks' sitting of the court. The few Lancers who, from proper but needless precaution, had been quartered in the town, only relieved the monotony of its winter aspect by the intermixture of their dark-green uniforms with the coarse dresses of the peasantry, who silently clustered in the market-place; and when a few of them were seen following the prison Van, as it carried the leader of the insurrection between the Court and the Jail on the successive days of his trial, a spectator—who saw the little procession gleaming along the terraced road, which corresponds in beautiful curvature with the softly-swelling hills which closed and surrounded the picture—might have regarded it as some holiday pageant; instead of the guard of an alleged traitor on trial, in the midst of the multitudes whom he recently led to bloody strife. Within the court all was calm and still as if an action for a builder's bill had been languishing after vain attempts to refer it; and yet the proceedings did not want the excitement which the most ingenious defence could create; for never were the noblest qualities of the English bar more perfectly developed than in the conduct of the prisoner's counsel. Mr. Frost, the avowed leader of the Monmouthshire Chartists, with a wise reliance on these qualities, entrusted his defence to two of the most eminent Conservatives in the profession—Sir Frederick Pollock, the present Attorney-General of Sir Robert Peel, and Mr. Fitzroy Kelly; and nothing more strenuous or more fervent than their management of his cause, from first to last, can be imagined. At the earliest possible moment they took their stand, and displayed the character of their defence, by a bold and nervous opposition to the peremptory challenges of the Crown;—in the face of solemn decisions, acted on without controversy, they sustained an argument which, but for these precedents, would perhaps have succeeded, but which, against such precedents, was hopeless—in urging which they probably neither expected nor cared for direct success—but by which they manifested their resolution to cast themselves unreservedly into the struggle, and their power to dare, and persevere, in every legitimate means, however unusual, of rescuing the life committed to their protection. In arguing the subsequent objection to the list of witnesses, which they wisely reserved until the period when, if established, it could not have been obviated, they displayed even greater power—the power of investing a mere technical complaint of an informality, caused by an indulgent concession to the wish of the prisoner's attorney, with the solemnity belonging to the charge and the issue; and their splendid addresses to the Jury, at the close of the evidence for the Crown—urging that the object of the insurgents was less than traitorous—would have been triumphant but for one defect, which no ingenuity could supply, and no eloquence conceal,—the absence of any offer to explain what else that object was. The defences were also illustrated by a speech of great vigour from Mr. G. H. Rickards, a young Barrister, who was suddenly associated in the defence of Zephaniah Williams; and whose efforts were the more remarkable, as the topics had been apparently exhausted in the preceding trial; and the more pleasant, as it incidentally afforded an example of the blessings of those institutions which had been assailed, in which such ability can find its scope and its reward.

But we have been led, by the recollection of these impressive scenes, from our immediate subject—the speech of the then Attorney-General in opening the case for the prosecution of Frost. It seems to us a model for all such speeches—lucid, unimpassioned, and candid; singularly abstinent in statement when any doubt existed as to the admissibility in the import of evidence; distinct yet cautious in the annunciation of the law of treason; and no further indicating the inference to be drawn from the alleged facts than was necessary to enable the jury to apply the proofs to the charge, and the prisoner's counsel to understand the manner in which the accusation was to be sustained. Its only positive merits as a composition—all that the mild performance of his duty admitted—are the clearness of its narrative, and some touches of picturesque power, seemingly thrown in without consciousness, in mapping out before the jury the wild hill country of Monmouthshire, in which the insurrection was planned; and along the ravines of which the insurgents marched to the central point near Newport. Its details were fully sustained by the proofs, which showed that the three principal prisoners, Frost, Williams, and Jones, had assembled sturdy artisans, to the number of many thousands, in the dead of the night, many of whom were armed with formidable weapons, and conducted them along the deep valleys to the plain near Newport, in such force that, if their junction had not been prevented by rain and tempest, and the division which did arrive had not been dispersed by the troops, aided by the courage and wisdom of Sir Thomas Phillips, (who fortunately filled the office of mayor), must have caused extensive bloodshed and confusion. Many of the details were singularly instructive—manifesting the utter ignorance of the insurgents of the provisions of 'The Charter,' which they seemed to fancy was 'something to do good to the poor in workhouses;'—showing how a mere love of change and adventure could be wrought on, so as to induce thousands of men, earning excellent wages, to embrace a desperate enterprise, without knowing or caring for its purposes; how even heroic qualities, as in the case of poor George Snell, might be enlisted and urged to the death—for nothing; and all this effected

by men, two of whom were stupidly ignorant, and the third, Frost, though a man of intelligence and education, wofully deficient in constancy and every attribute of a leader! The summing up of the Lord Chief-Justice Tindal, in the case of Frost, was so studiously mild, it presented every point in favour of the prisoner with such clearness and force, that an acquittal was anticipated by many; and when the heavy tread of the Jurymen, descending the stairs from the grand jury-room, to which they had retired to deliberate, told as distinctly as words the decision of the prisoner's fate, a strange thrill for the first time became audible among the crowd of expectant spectators. The dispassionate conduct of these prosecutions by Sir John Campbell, and the solemn and gentle manner in which the Judges discharged their high functions, has probably tended more to destroy the influence of turbulent spirits among the workmen of Monmouthshire, than the terror of many executions.

One of the latest duties performed by Sir John Campbell while Attorney-General, was his address on behalf of the Bar to Mr. Justice Littledale, on the 8th of February, 1841, when that learned and excellent Judge sat in the Court of Queen's Bench for the last time; it gave universal satisfaction to the body in whose name it was delivered; and they will be glad to see it preserved in this volume, from which we will transfer it to our pages. It consists of unexaggerated truth gracefully expressed.

'Mr. Justice Littledale—It having been intimated to the Bar that we are not to have the satisfaction of again seeing you on the Bench, I am deputed by their unanimous voice to express to your Lordship the deep sorrow they feel at this separation. Notwithstanding the entire confidence they feel in the rest of the Court, they most sincerely regret that they should be deprived of a judge of such profound learning, distinguished acuteness, and spotless integrity,—who during the many years he has occupied the judgment-seat in this Court and the Circuits,—while he has ever displayed the utmost impartiality and independence, yet, from the kindness of his nature, has never given offence to a human being. Though still in the full enjoyment of the high faculties which it has pleased God to bestow upon you, they are sensible that from your eminent services to your country, you are well entitled to that dignified leisure to which you now gracefully retire. In that retirement we earnestly hope that you will long enjoy health and happiness. We rejoice to think that you will find occupation and delight in the renewed pursuit of those abstruse as well as elegant studies in which you early gained distinction, and which have been interrupted by your devotion to your professional and judicial duties. We beg leave to assure your Lordship that you carry along with you the gratitude and good wishes of every member of the profession of which you have so long been a distinguished ornament, and that we shall ever think and speak of you with feelings of respect and affection.'

Mr. Justice Littledale did not long enjoy that dignified repose which the gratitude and affection of the Bar desired for him; he has gone to his rest, full of years and honours; leaving behind him the memory of childlike simplicity of character, which has rarely indeed been preserved to old age amidst the anxieties and the labours of the profession which he adorned.

We now take leave of Lord Campbell—renewing our congratulations on the prosperity and honours which his industry has won, and our expression of regret that he has not, by the introduction of earlier speeches, enabled us to trace him through the first stages of his progress. Although his most perfect efforts—those arguments on abstruse questions of law, which for exactness of reasoning and fertility of analogical illustration have never been excelled—are too technical for general appreciation, there have been many of his speeches to Juries which, if not, in the ordinary sense of the term, eloquent, exhibit ingenuity, tact, and sense in so high a degree, as to deserve other records than the verdicts they obtained. One recollection alone is sufficient to enrich his retirement—his share in the abolition of imprisonment for debt on mesne process—with all the wretchedness which it inflicted, and all the iniquity which it fostered. If he had achieved nothing but this, he would not have lived or laboured in vain.

———

Art. III.—*Introductory Lectures on Modern History.* By Thomas Arnold, D.D., Regius Professor of Modern History in the University of Oxford, and Head Master of Rugby School. 8vo. Oxford: 1842.

Imperfectly as this volume of lectures, interrupted by the death of its lamented author, answers the promise, to the fulfilment of which we looked so eagerly, little more than a year ago, when he was appointed to the Chair of Modern History of Oxford, we should feel ourselves guilty of no common degree of neglect if we omitted to notice it; for we may perhaps find no other occasion for paying our tribute of respect to one of the noblest minds and highest characters of these days, prematurely taken from us in the middle of a

career of usefulness, which we believe we are guilty of no exaggeration in terming unparalleled in that line of life which Dr. Arnold had adopted.

As far as they throw light on the literary and intellectual attainments of their author, these lectures are undoubtedly incomplete enough; and, regarded in that point of view, they possess the positive fault of attempting too many things at once. They are impressed with the peculiarly eager temperament, the *perfervidum ingenium*, the active, but somewhat desultory range of thought which display themselves, more or less, in every production of the writer. Who that has read much, and felt strongly, on any subject, and who has not yet acquired that last and somewhat melancholy gift of experience, the art of arranging and chastening the thoughts as they arise, when favoured with some opportunity of giving vent to his accumulated ideas, has not experienced the mixture of pleasurable excitement and embarrassment produced by the throng of multitudinous topics pressing forward for utterance? This argument to be confuted, that to be urged, this long-cherished theory to be advanced, that well-remembered illustration to be furbished up for use—and all to be compressed within the narrow compass prescribed by overruling circumstances! Just so we can conceive of Dr. Arnold—from his youth an insatiable reader of history, and at the same time an active controversialist, in whose head every series of phenomena naturally crystallized into a theory—when he suddenly found himself invested with the office of an historical teacher. We perceive at once, in the odd mixture of matters huddled together in these few pages, the variety of subjects which filled his mind, and the necessity under which he lay of disburdening himself of his feelings on each, as if the retention of any part of his stores oppressed him. The province of history, the provinces of church and state, the characteristics of historical style, military ethics, military geography, national prejudices, religious and political parties in England—these are only some of the prominent topics rather glanced at than discussed in the pages before us, and put forward apparently as if for more extended consideration at some future time—topics on which he longed to speak his mind to the world, and could not abstain from a partial disclosure of it—topics, many of them, on which we shall have long to wait for an instructor as rich at once in zeal and knowledge.

But if this volume is to a certain extent disappointing, rather from the over-richness than meagreness of its contents, it will, if possible, add to the veneration with which its author's character is already regarded as a moral philosopher, and an instructor of the youth of England. It adds one more claim to those which the late head master of Rugby already possessed on public gratitude and veneration.

Every one accustomed to English society has observed the strength of that generous tie which, in after life, connects the pupil, especially when bred in our great public schools, with his former master. Even in ordinary cases, we by no means admit the truth of the ill-natured saying, that there is little of this affectionate remembrance, except where the scholar feels himself superior to his teacher. We believe it, on the contrary, to be the general rule, and that the exceptions arise only from causes discreditable either to the one party or the other. But, common as this feeling is, and derived as it is from many sources—from the instinctive attachments to old places and times—from sensibility to kindness shown and interest manifested—from real gratitude for substantial services—we are bound to add that, as far as our own observation has gone, it rarely, very rarely, has the higher tincture of reverence. The quondam schoolboy may have a host of pleasant recollections associated with the memory of his old tutor: he may regard him as the friend who directed his uniform taste—who introduced his youthful spirit into the magnificent domain of earthly knowledge — to whose counsels he may possibly be indebted for a few valuable hints in the conduct of life —more than this, who has imbued him with much of the spirit of a gentleman, and a love of fairness and honourable dealing; but in very few instances, indeed, does he remember him as his guide towards the accomplishment of the real ends of his being. We do not pause to, examine into the cause of this deficiency: much may be owing to old peculiarities in the management of great schools, something to the character of many of our most successful men in this line of life; but we think the fact will hardly be disputed. By far the most distinguished exception to the rule with whom we are acquainted, was Dr. Arnold. He possessed the art, which is perhaps not very uncommon, of winning in a peculiar manner the affections of boys, and directing their energies to whatever object he might himself hold out; but, what is much more rare, he made it the one great business of his life to give those affections and energies a religious direction. Distinguished as a schoolmaster in many respects, it was in this one that he was unrivalled. The mainspring of his success was his own deep affection for those placed under his care, which makes itself evident in every page of his sermons, chiefly addressed to the young. His was no entraining or engrossing religious eloquence, addressed as it were to minds in the mass, and carrying them away by movements of enthusiasm; but a gentle, watchful influence, directed steadily to individual temperaments; and above all, (which was partly the consequence of the thorough reality of his own religious impressions), not leaving religion to stand alone, as something to be learnt and studied apart from all things else, but connecting it with all that is most naturally attractive to the honest heart of youth — with uncompromising love of truth, with manliness and independence, with love and with gratitude.

We dare not venture further on considerations of such deep and sacred importance. It is more to our purpose, and more connected with the subject of these lectures, to trace the steps by which he was wont to lead the mind from feeling to thinking; from the formation of a religious character, his main object, to the formation of opinion on religious as well as other subjects. The first rule with him was, to follow the truth at all hazards—regardless in what apparent difficulties it may involve us—regardless into what bad company it may lead us. The absolute right and duty of the mind *to judge for itself*, the total negation of any human authority binding in matters of faith—these are points on which he insisted, in season and out of season, if we may so express ourselves, with an ardour which not only rendered him very unpopular, as well it might, with persons of different opinions, but frequently exposed him to charges of imprudence and rashness from those who in the main agreed with him. This ardour proceeded, no doubt, in part from natural impetuosity of disposition; but it also arose from a deep conviction, that the one great thing wanted, and in these times especially, is, to infuse into the mind the power and the will to rest self-balanced—to incite it to implant in itself the seeds of principles, which neither the reck-lessness of business nor pleasure, nor the thousand influences of party, might after-wards eradicate. The lines of Goethe—

‘ Denn der Mensch, der su schwankenden Zeiten
    auch Schwankend gesinnt ist,
Der vermehret das Uebel, und breitet es weiter
    und weiter ;
Aber wer fest auf dem Sinne beharrt, der bildet
    die Welt sich,’—

might almost be inscribed as the motto to the whole collection of his ethical and historical works. And his great endeavour —no one could set the example better than himself — was so to discipline the mind, as to reconcile freedom of belief with real humility of spirit; to reconcile the unqualified rejection of authority, when imposed as binding, with docility and submissiveness towards it when pro-pounded as an object of respect; a recon-cilement by no means difficult in itself, and possibly more common in practice than is generally imagined. Clear of his own way between the conflicting claims of authority and individual responsibility, he regarded with utter contempt the charges of presumption, so indiscriminately brought against all those who venture to differ from received opinions. Will-wor-ship, as he well knew, is quite as fatally manifested in wilful and passionate adhe-rence to such opinions, as in wilful and passionate rejection of them. The rule of humility does not mark out the line to be taken by the man of conscience, when au-thority and argument are in opposition; but the manner and spirit in which his choice must be made. Nor is it difficult to apply, as he would have bidden us, to the controversies of the present day, the lesson intended to be conveyed in the fol-lowing noble vindication of the Puritan character :

‘ To say that the Puritans were wanting in humility, because they did not acquiesce in the state of things which they found around them, is a mere extravagance, arising out of a total misapprehension of the nature of humility, and of the merits of the feeling of veneration. All earnestness and depth of character is incompati-ble with such a notion of humility. A man deeply penetrated with some great truth, and compelled, as it were, to obey it, cannot listen to every one who may be indifferent to it, or op-posed to it. There is a voice to which he alrea-dy owes obedience—which he serves with the humblest devotion, which he worships with the most intense veneration. It is not that such feel-ings are dead in him, but that he has bestowed them on one object and they are claimed for an-

other. To which they are most due is a ques-tion of justice : he may be wrong in his decision, and his worship may be idolatrous ; but so also may the worship which his opponents call upon him to render. If, indeed, it can be shown that a man admires and reverences nothing, he may justly be taxed with want of humility ; but this is at variance with the very notion of an earnest character, for its earnestness consists in its devo-tion to some one object, as opposed to a proud or contemptuous indifference. But if it be. meant that reverence in itself is good, so that the more objects of veneration we have the better is our character, this is to confound the essential differ-ence between veneration and love. The excel-lence of love is its universality : we are told that even the Highest Object of all cannot be loved if inferior objects are hated. And with some ex-aggeration in the expression, we may admit the truth of Coleridge’s lines—

    “ He prayeth well who loveth well
      Both man, and bird, and beast :”

Insomuch that, if we were to hear of a man sac-rificing even his life to save that of an animal, we could not help admiring him. But the excel-lence of veneration consists purely in its being fixed upon a worthy object ; when felt indiscri-minately, it is idolatry or insanity. To tax any one, therefore, with want of reverence, because he pays no respect to what we venerate, is either irrelevant or is a mere confusion. The fact, so far as it is true, is no reproach, but an honour ; because to reverence all persons and all things is absolutely wrong : reverence shown to that which does not deserve it, is no virtue—no, nor even an amiable weakness, but a plain folly and sin. But if it be meant that he is wanting in proper reverence, not respecting what is to be really respected, that is assuming the whole question at issue, because what we call divine he calls an idol ; and as, supposing that we are in the right, we are bound to fall down and wor-ship ; so, supposing him to be in the right, he is no less bound to pull it to the ground and de-stroy it.’—(p. 268.)

Those who have thus learnt the real characteristics of veneration and humility, will understand the lesson which the his-tory of the world so abundantly teaches— that self-will and pride play their vagaries quite as wantonly under the banner of au-thority as under that of private judgment ; a lesson renewed to us by the experience of every day, to the great astonishment of that part of the world which is taken in by fine professions.

It will be readily perceived, from this as well as a hundred other passages in his works, that Dr. Arnold made it a great part of his business to carry on war against prejudices; and certainly a more deter-mined, we might almost say a more indis-criminating warfare, was never waged. Those among our prejudices to which we are apt to give the tenderest names, and treat as peculiarly creditable to ourselves, met from him with no more quarter than the rest. Perhaps it may be thought, even by those who most admire the singleness of his devotion to truth, that in some instances his zeal was so unscrupulous that he ran the risk of rooting out good feelings along with mere weaknesses; but such was the character of the man. Take, for instance, the following attack on the virtue of patriotism, as vulgarly understood:—

'But here that feeling of pride and selfishness interposes, which, under the name of patriotism, has so long tried to pass itself off for a virtue. As men, in proportion to their moral advancement, learn to enlarge the circle of their regards—as men exclusive affection for our relations, our clan, or our country, is a sure mark of an unimproved mind—so is that narrow and unchristian feeling to be condemned, which regards with jealousy the progress of foreign nations, and cares for no portion of the human race but that to which itself belongs. The detestable encouragement so long given to national enmities—the low gratification felt by every people in extolling themselves above their neighbours—should not be forgotten amongst the causes which have mainly obstructed the improvement of mankind.

'Exclusive patriotism should be cast off together with the exclusive ascendency of birth, as belonging to the follies and selfishness of our uncultivated nature. Yet, strange to say, the former at least is upheld by men who not only call themselves Christians, but are apt to use the charge of irreligion as the readiest weapon against those who differ from them. So little have they learned of the spirit of that revelation, which taught emphatically the abolition of an exclusively national religion and local worship, that so men, being all born of the same blood, might make their sympathies co-extensive with their bond of universal brotherhood.'—(*Appendix to Thucydides*, Vol. i.)

This scrupulousness of conscience is carried by him into the minutest details; and we have been rather amused to observe how he labours to disabuse his class, in these lectures, of the delusive notion that one Englishman can beat three Frenchmen; assuring us that we were quite as satisfactorily beaten by them, under William the Third and the Duke of Cumberland, as they by us under Marlborough and Wellington.

It is in a similar spirit that he warns readers of history against the ordinary seduction of favourite party names and watchwords, outliving the immediate occasion which gave birth to them.

'This inattention to altered circumstances, which would make us be Guelfs in the sixteenth and seventeenth centuries, because the Guelf cause had been right in the eleventh or twelfth, is a fault of most universal application in all political questions, and is often most seriously mischievous. It is deeply seated in human nature, being in fact no other than an exemplification of the force of habit. It is like the case of a settler landing in a country overrun with wood and undrained, and visited, therefore, by excessive falls of rain. The evil of wet, and damp, and closeness, is besetting him on every side; he clears away the woods and drains his land, and by so doing mends both his climate and his own condition. Encouraged by his success, he perseveres in his system: clearing a country is with him synonymous with making it fertile and habitable; and he levels, or rather sets fire to, his forests without mercy. Meanwhile the tide has turned without his observing it; he has already cleared enough, and every additional clearance is a mischief; damp and wet are no longer the evils most to be dreaded, but excessive drought. The rains do not fall in sufficient quantity, the springs become low, the rivers become less and less fitted for navigation.* Yet habit blinds him for a long while to the real state of the case, and he continues to encourage a coming mischief in his dread of one that has become obsolete. We have long been making progress on our present tack; yet if we do not go about now, we shall run ashore. Consider the popular feeling at this moment against capital punishments; what is it but continuing to burn the woods when the country actually wants shade and moisture? Year after year men talked of the severity of the penal code, and struggled against it in vain. The feeling became stronger and stronger, and at last effected all, and more than all, which it had at first vainly demanded; yet still from mere habit it pursues its course, no longer to the restraining of legal cruelty, but to the injury of innocence and the encouragement of crime, and encouraging that worse evil, a sympathy with wickedness justly punished, rather than with the law, whether of God or man, unjustly violated. So men have continued to cry out against the power of the Crown, after the Crown had been shackled hand and foot; and to express the greatest dread of popular violence, long after that violence was exhausted, and the anti-popular party was not only rallied, but had turned the tide of battle, and was victoriously pressing upon its enemy.'— (P. 252.)

It is very unnecessary to add, after such

---

* Perhaps we may remark on this geographical illustration as suggesting some other of its author's peculiarities—his remarkable power of turning such illustrations to his purpose, and the readiness of his imagination to welcome the curious and marvellous in matters of fact. Many naturalists have thought this theory of the effect of the removal of forests on the amount of rain, carried much too far; and it would be difficult to point out an instance of a river which has become unnavigable in consequence of it. We might also refer to his strange views respecting animal magnetism and cognate matters.

comments as these, that Dr. Arnold belonged to no party in Church or State. Under
no circumstances could he have belonged
to any: his independence of spirit, his almost over-refined delicacy of conscience,
perhaps a certain restiveness of disposition
when forced to travel in company, would
alike have forbidden it. But as it was, he
detested the spirit of party with a perfect
abhorrence; he detested it as the great
rival in the minds of men with the love of
his idol, Truth. He never fails on any occasion, to impress this aversion in the
strongest language, on all whom he addresses It is a matter on which he admits of no compromise whatever; none of
that specious rhetoric by which we persuade ourselves that party is an indifferent
means of arriving at a good end—that only through becoming party men can we
hope to be useful, and so forth. His plain
language is, that all such pleas, and all
such hopes, must be abandoned by the honest man—much more by the Christian.
He had himself counted the cost, and made
the sacrifice. He had fully reconciled himself to the apparent uselessness of a life
unconnected with party in a country like
this. At one period of his career, he was
the subject of great unpopularity: his
views were misrepresented, his character
maligned, his professional success menaced; he only recovered himself, after a
long probation, by the great amiableness
of his character, and through the fame acquired by his peculiar talent for instruction; for he was of no party, and consequently had no band of brothers to back
him. Eminent in piety as in learning, he
never attained a step in the Church; for
he was of no party, and had, therefore, no
claim on any patron. Yet there is nothing
in his writings of the stoicism expressed
in the stern

  'Taci, e lascia dir le genti,'

of Dante; nothing of that querulousness
we have often remarked in excellent men
who have had the honesty to renounce
party and its advantages for themselves,
but are unreasonable enough to be disappointed that parties do not seek after and
follow them. Vehement in self-defence—
ardent in attack—fond by nature of controversial skirmishing—he is always in the
field against some class of thinkers or
other; and always seems very unaffectedly
surprised that the opposite ranks which he
alternately attacks remain alike unbroken
by his artillery; and therefore it is no
wonder that while some were abusing him

as a latitudinarian, others maintained that
he was halfway on the road to modern
'Catholicism.' But the principles of his
practical philosophy lay deep, and his
equanimity was, therefore, not to be moved
by the inevitable results of his own choice;
a choice to which he elsewhere solemnly
exhorts his young audience, in a passage
which seems to breathe the very essence
at once of his religious sincerity, and his
manly integrity of soul.

'Be of one party to the death, and that is
Christ's; but abhor every other; abhor it, that
is, as a thing to which to join yourselves;—for
every party is mixed up of good and evil, of truth
and falsehood; and in joining it, therefore, you
join with the one as well as the other. If circumstances should occur which oblige you practically to act with any one party, as the least of
two evils, then watch yourselves the more, lest
the least of two evils should, by any means,
commend itself at last to your mind as a positive
good. Join it with a sad and reluctant heart,
protesting against its evil, dreading its victory,
far more pleased to serve it by suffering than by
acting; for it is in Christ's cause only that we
can act with heart and soul, as well as patiently
and triumphantly suffer. Do this amidst reproach, and suspicion, and cold friendship, and
zealous enmity; for this is the portion of those
who seek to follow their Master, and him only.
Do it, although your foes be they of your own
household: those whom nature, or habit, or
choice, had once bound to you most closely. And
then you will understand how, even now, there
is a daily cross to be taken up by those who seek
not to please men, but God; yet you will learn
no less, how that cross, meekly and firmly borne,
whether it be the cross of men's ill opinion from
without, or of our own evil nature struggled
against within, is now, as ever, peace, and wisdom, and sanctification, and redemption, through
Him who first bore it.'—(*Sermons*, vol. iii. 263.)

But Dr. Arnold was a 'crotchety' man:
such appears to have been the general estimate of his character. It is an epithet of
many meanings; but it seems to us to be
commonly and significantly applied to
those who endeavour to ascertain the truth
on every separate subject of inquiry, instead of following the ordinary process of
taking up whole bundles of opinions as
they are commonly found connected together. Whoever does this, is very certain to agree in some points with one party, and in some with another; and equally
certain to be called crotchety by both. But
we must say in justice, that the epithet
does to a certain extent describe his character, in some of its minute peculiarities.
There was a rapidity of judgment about
him—a haste in arriving at conclusions,
which is apt to lead to the sudden forma-

tion of opinions—possibly to a little fickleness, on minor points, in adherence to them. His judgment seems to have been influenced at once by an abhorrence of dogmatism, commonly so called, and an impatience of scepticism. We do not mean in a religious sense only, but in historical and every other research. He could not, like Montaigne, *se reposer tranquillement sur l'oreiller du doute.* He had a mind averse from suspense, dissatisfied and uneasy under the pressure of doubt; and, therefore, disposed to generalize at once, where slower and more cold-blooded men would consider the process of induction hardly begun. To this was joined a strong moral perception, and a disposition particularly inclined towards ethical speculation—towards predicating moral right and wrong of every phenomenon which human history and human nature exhibit : a peculiarity which he seems to us to have caught in great measure from association with his early friend Archbishop Whately, just as he caught his style of historical research from Niebuhr;—and a deep interest in the controversies of the day, with an eagerness to liberate his own mind by expressing his sentiments upon each of them. It is no disparagement of Dr. Arnold to say, that this very eagerness sometimes appears to us to betray a secret uneasiness—a misgiving as to the results of his own conscientious inquiries. There are few, indeed, who, having deliberately rejected the idolatries of parties and systems, can rest undisturbedly on the ground they have chosen for themselves; for such thinkers have nothing of the ready support on which others so confidently lean. They would be more than men, if there were not moments when the very foundations seem to give way under them, and their own hearts to sink also—moments when they are tempted even to look with envy on those who march forward sternly or cheerfully, looking neither to the right nor the left, through regions in which they stumble and grope for light; yet their victory is not the less complete, although the enjoyment of its fruits, like all human enjoyment, is interrupted by obstinate questionings of its own reality.

It is a curious result of these tendencies, that Dr. Arnold should have gone so far out of his way as to subjoin to his Inaugural Lecture a special appendix on a subject certainly very remotely connected with the matters developed in it—namely, the refutation, by name, of the Archbishop of Dublin's views as to the separation of the duties of Church and State; and with him he has done us the honour to join ourselves, (alluding to an article in a late number of this Journal). He endeavours to unite ' one half of the Archbishop of Dublin's theory with one half of Mr. Gladstone's : agreeing cordially with Mr. Gladstone in the moral theory of the State, and agreeing as cordially with the Archbishop in the Christian theory of the Church; and deducing from the two the conclusion, that the perfect State and the perfect Church are identical.' It seems to us that there are at least four theories afloat on this much debated subject. One is, that the authorities which we commonly term ' the Church' ought to decide *circà sacra;* and that the authorities we call 'the State' have nothing to do but to enforce those decisions by civil penalties : this was the anciently received doctrine, so beautifully exemplified in the practice on the writ *de hæretico comburendo.* The next ascribes, if we may term it so, a sort of pre-existent harmony to Church and State ; allotting to the State a power *circà sacra,* on a kind of assumption that it will proceed in harmony with the ecclesiastical authorities. The third is what, in the dictionary of theological hate, is called Erastian ; namely, that the State has absolute authority *circà sacra,* to be enforced by civil penalties, irrespectively of the decisions of ecclesiastical authorities; and this is Dr. Arnold's. The fourth is, that the civil governor has no such authority whatever, either in his legislative or executive character, although he may occasionally lend his aid, with benefit, for the attainment of purely religious objects; and this appears to be the Archbishop of Dublin's. We are far from wishing to revive the controversy on our own account; least of all, in commenting on the language of an antagonist, whose pure and lofty charity of soul deprived his tenets, if erroneous they be, of all the danger which commonly attends such error ; and yet it is well to recollect that even Dr. Arnold, with a spirit to which all religious despotism was abhorrent, was driven, by the force of his theory, to refuse to all avowed ' unbelievers in Christ,' a share in the legislature of a Christian country. Our object is much more to notice the peculiarities of the man, the eager, although tolerant, spirit with which he rushed into this as into other controversies; and the tendency of his mind to rapid generalization.

Now, one fruitful parent of theories is, the use of words (to employ a trite comparison) not as current coin, but as counters, to which the reasoner may affix his own imaginary value. The word 'Church,' is a very favourite counter with theorists; the word 'State,' is another, of which the meaning is quite as arbitrary. Before we can ascertain the truth of the 'moral theory' of the State, we must understand what the State is. Now, Dr. Arnold's argument seems to rest entirely on the assumption, that Government, State, and Nation may be used as synonymous terms. Grant him this, and undoubtedly one great difficulty in the way of his theory is removed. 'When I speak of the Government,' he says, 'I am speaking of it as expressing the mind and will of the nation; and though a government may not impose its own law, human or divine, *upon an adverse people,* yet a nation, acting through its government, may certainly choose *for itself* such a law as it deems most for its good.'—'In a corrupt State, the government and people are wholly at variance; in a perfect State, they would be wholly one; in ordinary States, they are one more or less imperfectly.'—'For the right of a nation over its own territory must be at least as absolute as that of any individual over his own house and land; and it surely is not an absurdity to suppose that the voice of government can ever be the voice of the nation; although they unhappily too often differ, yet surely they may conceivably, *and very often do in practice,* completely agree.'—(p. 55). Here the right of a government to legislate *circà sacra* is rested, where all men of reasonable views must rest it, on its 'expressing the will of the nation.' Suppose the objector to take the ground, that the government, in point of fact, never does express the will of the nation except by accident; for that nine-tenths of mankind are governed by rulers who rest their authority on the principle, that they are not placed there to express, but to control, the will of the nation; while in those countries which are most democratically governed, the government can represent, at best, only the numerical majority of the nation;—a majority which may, or may not, comprehend the religious or the intelligent portion of it; how is he to be answered on these premises? If the idea of a State could be realized with any reasonable probability, we can easily understand the value of a theory founded upon it—although actual States might be but imperfect agents to carry it out; but if the idea is one which history and common sense alike show us can never be realized

at all, we do not understand how the theory can stand alone. In fact, Dr. Arnold seems elsewhere to admit that his principle goes no further than this—that 'the favourite objections against the State's concerning itself with religion, apply no less to the theory of a Church . . . . . The moral theory of a State is not open to the objection commonly brought against our actual constitution, namely, that Parliament is not a fit body to legislate on matters of religion; for the council of a *really Christian State* would consist of Christians at once good and sensible, quite as much as the council of a really Christian Church.' —(p. 63). Now, since we may very safely assume, that since Christendom began there has never been anything approaching to a 'really Christian State'—since we may safely foretell that there never will be, until the kingdoms of this world are become the kingdoms of the Lord—this comparison seems to reduce the whole to a question of expediency; whether, upon the whole, it is best that the spiritual government of mankind should be left to those authorities whom we commonly term the Church, unarmed with coercive power, or to the temporal government which possesses it. Dr. Arnold preferred the latter; and he had a perfect right to do so; but not to erect his own preference into an axiom. He considered the Church 'a society far worse governed than most States.' It may be so; but other political philosophers may think that most States are, upon the whole, worse governed than the Church; and who is to decide between them?

And some may be disposed to think, that it was the weakness of the position which he had undertaken to maintain, which drove him to put forward such paradoxes as that excommunication is a *temporal* punishment, (p. 57); or, still more unworthy of himself, such vulgar arguments as that of the 'almost unanimous consent of all writers on government, whether heathen or Christian, down to the 18th century.' Dr. Arnold, of all men, ought to have been best aware, that on the great questions which concern the government of mankind, so long as the consent of all writers is nearly unanimous, it is worthless. Consent is worthless, until people begin to think; and thought is only provoked by opposition. *Quot homines tot sententiæ,* as he elsewhere says, 'holds good only where there is any thinking at all: otherwise there may be a hundred millions of men, and only *una sententia,* if the minds of the

99,999,999 are wholly quiescent.' He might also have remembered, that if 'nearly unanimous consent' is conclusive for his views of a State, it is quite as conclusive against his views of a Church. We willingly quit so barren a subject; and could only wish that all who maintain similar views, whether on Dr. Arnold's or any other premises, would represent to themselves and their readers their main position in its literal sense; namely, that it is the chief duty of the existing governor of every existing State, whether King or Majority, to take care of the spiritual welfare of every citizen. We by no means assert that they would change their opinions, but merely that they would see the subject in a very different light, if it were once freed from the endless fallacies of general words. When it was represented to the Emperor Ferdinand II., that the course which he was pursuing towards the Protestants of Bohemia, would render that kingdom a desert, his answer was, '*malumus regnum vastatum quàm damnatum.*' All we contend is, that on Dr. Arnold's principles it is impossible to prove that the Emperor was wrong.

As a more interesting specimen of his style of writing and turn of thought, we would select his views on certain points of military morality, in which he runs as boldly into opposition to a host of commonly received and current notions, as he does, at other times, in questions of more ordinary controversy. Nothing is more customary than to speak in tones of praise of the conduct of citizens in assuming arms as volunteers, and rising *en masse*; or enrolling in guerilla-parties, to repel foreign invasion. And it seems to be rather a prevalent idea, that in proportion as nations approach more nearly to the idea of free civil government, they acquire an organization for the purpose of self-defence, which will eventually render military strength of no avail, and abolish standing armies. Not a few visionaries of our time have foretold the *euthanasia* of the modern military system, in this general arming of all classes;—the advent of the day, in the language of the clever dreamer De Vigny, when uniforms will be ridiculous, and regular war obsolete. And, whether they consider such anticipations fanciful or not, most politicians seem to assume that their realization would be a step in the social progress of the world. Dr. Arnold's views were widely different. And, as his manner was, his imagination being strongly impressed with certain evils inherent in

the system of irregular warfare, he could not stop short of wholesale and absolute condemnation of it.

'The truth is, that if war, carried on by regular armies under the strictest discipline, is yet a great evil, an irregular partizan warfare is an evil ten times more intolerable; it is in fact no other than to give a license to a whole population to commit all sorts of treachery, rapine, and cruelty, without any restraint; letting loose a multitude of armed men, with none of the obedience and none of the honourable feelings of a soldier; cowardly because they are undisciplined, and cruel because they are cowardly. It seems, then, the bounden duty of every government, not only not to encourage such irregular warfare on the part of its population, but carefully to repress it; and to oppose its enemy only with its regular troops, or with men regularly organized, and acting under authorized officers, who shall observe the ordinary humanities of civilized war. And what are called patriotic insurrections, or irregular risings of the whole population to annoy an invading army by all means, ought impartially to be condemned, by whomsoever and against whomsoever practised, as a resource of small and doubtful efficacy, but full of certain atrocity, and a most terrible aggravation of the evils of war. Of course, if an invading army sets the example of such irregular warfare; if they proceed, after the manner of the ancients, to lay waste the country in mere wantonness— to burn houses, and to be guilty of personal outrages on the inhabitants, then they themselves invite retaliation, and a guerila warfare against such an invader becomes justifiable. But our censure in all cases should have reference, not to the justice of the original war, which is a point infinitely disputable, but to the simple question —which side first set the example of departing from the laws of civilized warfare, and of beginning a system of treachery and atrocity?

'As this is a matter of some importance, I may be allowed to dwell a little longer upon a vague notion, not uncommonly, as I believe, entertained, that a people whose country is attacked, by which is meant, whose territory is the seat of war, are sustaining some intolerable wrong which they are justified in repelling by any and every means. But in the natural course of things, war must be carried on in the territory of one belligerent or of the other; it is an accident merely, if their fighting ground happen to be the country of some third party. Now, it cannot be said that the party which acts on the offensive, war having been once declared, becomes in the wrong by doing so, or that the object of all invasion is conquest; you invade your enemy in order to compel him to do you justice —that is, to force him to make peace on reasonable terms. This is your theory of the case, and it is one which must be allowed to be maintainable, just as much as that of your enemy; for all laws of war waive, and must waive, the question as to the original justice of the quarrel—they assume that both parties are equally in the right. But suppose invasion for the sake of conquest, I do not say of the whole of your enemy's country, but of that portion of it which you are invading;

as we have many times invaded French colonies with a view to their incorporation permanently with the British dominions. Conquests of such a sort are no violations necessarily of the legitimate object of war; they may be considered as a security taken for the time to come. Yet, undoubtedly, the shock to the inhabitants of the particular countries so invaded is very great; it was not a light thing for the Canadian, or the inhabitant of Trinidad, or of the Cape of Good Hope, to be severed from the people of his own blood and language, from his own mother state, and to be subjected to the dominion of foreigners —men with a strange language, strange manners, a different church, and a different law. That the inhabitants of such countries should enlist very zealously in the militia, and should place the resources of defence very readily in the hands of the government, is quite just and quite their duty. I am only deprecating the notion that they should rise in irregular warfare, each man or each village for itself, and assail the invaders as their personal enemies, killing them whenever and wherever they can find them. Or, again, suppose that the invasion is undertaken for the purpose of overthrowing the existing government of a country, as the attempted French descents to co-operate with the Jacobites, or the invasion of France by the coalescing powers in 1792 and 1793, and again in 1814 and 1815. When the English army advanced into France in 1814, respecting persons and property, and paying for every article of food which they took from the country, would it have been for the inhabitants to barricade every village, to have lurked in every thicket, and behind every wall, to shoot stragglers and sentinels, and keep up, night and day, a war of extermination? If, indeed, the avowed object of the invader be the destruction, not of any particular government, but of the national existence altogether; if he thus disclaims the usual object of legitimate war —a fair and lasting peace—and declares that he makes it a war of extermination, he doubtless cannot complain if the usual laws of war are departed from against him, when he himself sets the example. But, even then, when we consider what unspeakable atrocities a partizan warfare gives birth to, and that no nation attacked by an overwhelming force of disciplined armies was ever saved by such means, it may be doubted, even then, whether it be justifiable, unless the invader drives the inhabitants to it, by treating them from the beginning as enemies, and outraging their persons and property. If this judgment seem extreme to any one, I would only ask him to consider well, first, the cowardly, treacherous, and atrocious character of all guerilla warfare; and in the next place the certain misery which it entails on the country which practises it, and its inefficacy, as a general rule, to conquer or expel an enemy, however much it may annoy him.'—(p. 204).

This is only one instance, among many, of the tendency of which we have spoken, to deduce general lessons from every class of facts which the writer is engaged in investigating. And it appears to form, according to his view, an essential part of the duties of an historian, that he should be ready at all moments to adapt his inferences from ancient experience to the particular questions which agitate his own age—to make the present and the past mutually illustrate each other. Such, at least, is the meaning we ascribe to the following remarkable passage, in which he lays down broadly the difference between the antiquary and the historian.

'What is it that the mere antiquarian wants, and which the mere scholar wants also; so that satire, sagacious enough in detecting the weak points of every character, has often held them both up to ridicule? They have wanted what is the essential accompaniment to all our knowledge of the past, a lively and extensive knowledge of the present; they wanted the habit of continually viewing the two in combination with each other; they wanted that master-power which enables us to take a point from which to contemplate both at a distance, and so to judge of each and of both, as if we belonged to neither. For it is from the views so obtained—from the conclusions so acquired—that the wisdom is formed which may really assist in shaping and preparing the course of the future.

'Antiquarianism, then, is the knowledge of the past enjoyed by one who has no lively knowledge of the present. Thence it is, when concerned with great matters, a dull knowledge. It may be lively in little things; it may conceive vividly the shape and colour of a dress, or the style of a building, because no man can be so ignorant as not to have a distinct notion of these in his own times; he must have a full conception of the coat he wears and the house he lives in. But the past is reflected to us by the present; so far as we see and understand the present, so far we can see and understand the past; so far, but no farther. And this is the reason why scholars and antiquarians, nay, and men calling themselves historians also, have written so uninstructively of the ancient world; they could do no otherwise, for they did not understand the world around them. How can he comprehend the parties of other days who has no clear notion of those of his own? What sense can he have of the progress of the great contest of human affairs in its earlier stages, when it rages around him at this actual moment unnoticed, or felt to be no more than a mere indistinct hubbub of sounds and confusion of weapons? What cause is at issue in the combat, he knows not. Whereas, on the other hand, he who feels his own times keenly, to whom they are a positive reality, with a good and evil distinctly perceived in them, such a man will write a lively and impressive account of past times, even though his knowledge be insufficient and his prejudices strong. This, I think, is the merit of Mitford, and it is a great one. His very anti-Jacobin partialities, much as they have interfered with the fairness of his history, have yet completely saved it from being dull. He took an interest in the parties of Greece, because he was alive to the parties of his own time; he described the popular party in Athens just as he would have described the

Whigs of England; he was unjust to Demosthenes because he would have been unjust to Mr. Fox. His knowledge of the Greek language was limited, and so was his learning altogether; but because he was an English gentleman who felt and understood the state of things around him, and entered warmly into its parties, therefore he was able to write a history of Greece, which has the great charm of reality; and which, if I may judge by my own experience, is read at first with interest, and retains its hold firmly on the memory.'—(P. 108).

If the meaning of this passage only were, that the historian is better qualified for his task whose mind is rich in the knowledge of the world he lives in, (which seems to have been a part at least of Dr. Arnold's conception, from the instance he afterwards gives of Sir Walter Raleigh), no one could hesitate to admit its truth. But if it is meant that a good historian must also be interested in modern controversies, and make his history subservient to the object of influencing the convictions of his readers respecting them, it may, perhaps, be questioned whether he is not rather describing what has been called the philosophy of history, than history itself. And it would assuredly require a very severe and vigorous judgment—indeed, a greater degree of impartiality and inaccessibility to passion and prejudice than we can fairly expect from man—for a historian, who has the *present* full in sight, and strongly exciting his imagination, to be calm and just in his review of the past. Mitford's *History of Greece* may, for aught we know, be an attractive work, and so may Cobbett's *History of the Reformation;* but, after all, the interest they excite is much the same with that of a clever political pamphlet. But it could not be said of Gibbon, Hume, or Robertson, or Ranke, or even Dr. Arnold's great master Niebuhr, that they display the habit of continually viewing the past in combination with the present; and yet, who will venture to call them mere antiquarians? Histories such as theirs have all the excellence which belongs to the ablest order of conversation;—where the speaker, while he condenses the information which he has to impart, leaves, at the same time, gracefully but incidentally, the impression of the fullness of his knowledge on other subjects. History, such as Dr. Arnold would prefer it—and his own historical works afford examples of the kind—would rather resemble the brilliant talk of very clever speakers, who cannot tell us what we want to know without adorning the narration with inferences and illustrations drawn from a hundred distant sources.

We prefer, to this attempt to fix the true historical character, the following pointed sketch of the characteristics of style in different historians; and its importance as an indication of the degree of value to be reposed in them as authorities. Any reader who is conversant with this branch of literature, will readily find names to fit the following characters :—

'The main thing to look to is, of course, his work itself. Here the very style gives us an impression by no means to be dismissed. If it is very heavy and cumbrous, it indicates either a dull man or a pompous man, or at least a slow and awkward man; if it be tawdry, and full of commonplaces enunciated with great solemnity, the writer is most likely a silly man; if it be highly antithetical, and full of unusual expressions, or artificial ways of stating a plain thing, the writer is clearly an affected man. If it be plain and simple—always clear, but never eloquent—the writer may be a very sensible man, but is too hard and dry to be a very great man. If, on the other hand, it is always eloquent, rich in illustrations, full of animation, but too uniformly so, and without the relief of simple and quiet passages, we must admire the writer's genius in a very high degree; but we may fear that he is too continually excited to have attained to the highest wisdom, for that is necessarily calm. In this manner the mere language of an historian will furnish us with something of a key to his mind; and will tell us, or at least give us cause to presume, in what his main strength lies, and in what he is deficient.'—(P. 384).

We cannot place the distinction between the antiquary and historian exactly where Dr. Arnold places it; but without endeavouring at present to establish another, it is enough to say that the attempt to draw it is very characteristic of the writer. The faults of his manner (for such we would call them, if faults they are, rather than faults of style, which in all his writings is good) arise from over-eagerness in illustration and comparison. If blemishes in historical composition, they are peculiar merits in the work of education. They are among the talents by which he was so eminently successful in exciting the enthusiasm of the young, in the studies to which he directed them. What we may term the youthfulness of his manner—his luxuriant discursivenesss, when a passage in Livy invites him to a discussion of the physical geography of the Roman Campagna, or a chapter of Thucydides to speculations on the politics of modern republics;—this constituted its great charm to the temper of younger men.

And, therefore, those very qualities which possibly detracted from his excellence in the sober character of a historian, were such as to render him the most effective and useful of teachers in a lecture-room. This is one of the many respects in which his loss must be felt, and felt as at present irreparable, in that university to which he had been for so brief a space attached as a Professor. Not Oxford only, but England, has need of minds such as his, in respect of all those higher qualities which we have endeavoured faintly to delineate. Men who can follow truth with a devotion so exclusive as to leave room for no other idol—men who can enter eagerly into all the great controversies of their day, and yet allow no exclusive sect or faction the honour of counting them as adherents—men who do not shun the entanglements of party spirit from cowardice or from apathy, but who resist it as a temptation, and despise it as a weakness—men whose whole life and conversation bear testimony to the deep importance they attach to religious truth, and yet free from every taint of controversial unfairness and theological rancour;—such men are scarce and precious in all times, and the absorbing nature of party interests seems to render them scarcer every day. But at present, we are only regarding the promise which he was giving of a scarcely inferior kind of usefulness, in helping to turn, if possible, the very mischievous direction which has been given to youthful thought and enterprise of late years, and especially in his university.

Almost every one has taken an interest in the recent theological controversies which have had their birth in Oxford; few have looked to the effect which the controversial spirit has produced on the tone and character of that university as regards its primary object—education. When first the theological 'movement' began—that is to say, about ten years ago—there was excited at the same time in both universities, but especially in Oxford, a strong feeling of dissatisfaction with the existing studies and occupations of the place. It was the common language of those who deemed that the frame and temper of society needed an extensive renovation, that this renovation must begin with the young. The presumptuous turn of mind, the reliance on intellectual ability, supposed to result from instruction addressing itself to the intellect alone, were to be corrected by a strong diversion in favour of a more subjective course of study. The student was to be imbued with principles and tastes, rather than positive acquirements. The main object of the instructor was to be the formation of moral character by habit, not the imparting what is commonly called learning. Nay, much was to be unlearnt—much rubbish taken down before men could begin afresh on the old foundations—much of the *sciolism* of recent centuries removed;—natural science and literary acquirement to be brought down from that undue exaltation to which they had been raised in modern times, by generations wanting in the habits of reverence and earnestness of feeling. Catholic theology, and Moral Philosophy in accordance with Catholic doctrine, were to be the main foundations of the improved education of these newer days; science and literature were not, indeed, to be neglected, but to be cultivated as in subordination only to these great 'architectonic' sciences, and discarded wherever they could not be forced into subjection. And thus a new generation was to be trained in which inferiority in respect of mere *objective* knowledge, if such should really ensue, was to be far more than compensated by the higher cultivation of the immortal part—the nobler discipline of piety and obedience. Such aspirations may be traced in most of the many writings on the university system which the crisis of those days brought out; while those who are acquainted with the practical details of the subject, know full well how deep a tincture has been introduced into the actual studies and habits of both places, but especially of Oxford, by the prevalence of views such as these, expressed by energetic men, in language at once startling and attractive.

Nor do we imagine that those views are altered now. We have no reason to suppose that their authors would agree with us as to the consequences which we cannot but believe to have proceeded from the practical realization of their wishes. Yet that the facts themselves, of which we complain, exist, they would hardly deny. Their endeavour was undoubtedly a lofty one; and how far it may prove a vain one, must as yet be in great measure matter of conjecture. It remains to be proved, whether or not they have not proceeded on a forgetfulness of the real importance and value of mere positive knowledge in the moral education of man. Because the connection between intellectual and moral cultivation is not obvious and direct, it is easily passed over. Nor do we suppose that it can ever be fully appreciated, except by those who are prepared, with ourselves, to recognize the great principles;—that all learning is discipline—all discipline self-denial—all self-denial has the nature of virtue : and that, by consequence, however wide or strange the corollary may seem, he who knows the first propositions of Euclid, is, in so far, better than he who does not ; ay, though both may have been equally untaught to pray, and may have formed of their Creator no more than the confused terrific image entertained by the wildest of savage minds. But, even without going thus far, few can have failed to observe the importance of the acquisition of positive knowledge, in withdrawing the mind from over-contemplation of self and its attributes. It gives the faculties another world to work in, besides that microcosm within which the influences of hopes and fears, pride, ambition, vain-glory, are continually working to retain them. It corrects the passions, by substituting an excitement of a different order ; it encourages generous sentiment, because it has no immediate object but truth, irrespective of advantage ; it encourages candid and honest habits of mind, because the truth which it holds out is one which party feeling and prejudice have comparatively little interest in perverting. It has, of course, like every human pursuit, its own temptations to vanity and presumption ; but how infinitely less engrossing and dangerous than those which attend on studies which directly interest the heart, and provoke its stronger feelings !

To substitute, therefore, as the main instruments of education, for the studies of science, history, and literature, those which have for their immediate object the awakening and strengthening of the moral perceptions, is to abandon that discipline which has an indirect, but not the less powerful influence, in enlarging and strengthening the moral faculty ;—for that which has indeed for its direct object moral improvement, but is apt, by a strong and necessary under-current of action, to narrow and distort that very portion of man's nature it is intended to improve. The study of Ethical philosophy may be admirably adapted to harmonize the general education of the mind ; to recall it to itself—its own duties and constitution—from too wide a wandering over the far more attractive fields of external truth. But to have this effect it must be administered as a corrective only. To make it practically the leading discipline, and ren-

der others dependent on it, is mental ruin. It is in itself a study fraught with danger ; it throws the mind back on itself, fills it with an engrossing, and perhaps morbid, habit of self-analysis ; and eventually, and not very indirectly, of self-worship. But independently of this, teach it as you will, it must be taught on a system. That system must rest on arbitrary axioms—axioms which can neither be proved nor are self-evident—axioms in the defence of which the feelings must in the first place be enlisted. But he whose heart and faculties are wrapt up in attachment to a system—be that system truth itself—inevitably comes to love it and defend it, not because it is truth, but because it is his system. This is the danger which besets even the learner of abstract knowledge ; how infinitely more him who pursues studies in which the conclusions are practical, and in which to err is to incur moral danger! And how much the peril is increased, when philosophy is carefully enrolled in support of a theological scheme—involved, as it were, in the quarrels of dogmatic theology—in the strife which swells every heart, and lends bitterness to every tongue, in the little world which surrounds the pupil ;—when, in the language of an able Oxford writer, the Church is made to ' fix the true point of view from which all other truths may be seen in their real forms and proportions.!' But from the moment that truth, as such, and irrespectively of particular ends, ceases to be the main object proposed to the mind in tuition, farewell to honesty, openness, and independence of character. For truly, though severely, was it said, by one, too, who has had no slight share in fashioning the popular philosophy of the present day, that he who loves Christianity better than truth, will soon love his own sect better than Christianity, and end by loving himself better than either.

Again, in teaching reverence for the distant past, those whose views we are at present considering have thought themselves justified in using a tone of great bitterness—great scorn—we must add of great self-exaltation, in speaking of the present and the immediate past. They have thought it their duty to hold up the opinions and sentiments of the ages immediately preceding our own, and of by far the greater part of the world at the present day, to utter contempt : to show the futility of the objects most valued, the worthlessness of the knowledge most esteemed. This they scarcely could do, without affording infinite encouragement to that worst kind of vanity, the thinking ourselves wise above those around us ;—a far greater temptation, as Dr. Arnold himself has acutely remarked, than that of undervaluing those who have lived before us. ' Our personal superiority seems much more advanced by decrying our contemporaries, than by decrying our fathers. The dead are not our real rivals; nor is pride very much gratified by asserting a superiority over those who cannot deny it. It is far more tempting to personal vanity to think ourselves the only wise amongst a generation of fools, than to glory in belonging to a wise generation, where our personal wisdom, be it what it may, cannot at least have the distinction of singularity.' The influence of the prejudices thus excited on the moral character is bad enough; but on intellectual progress it is destruction. The fruits of the recent fashion of decrying mere scientific pursuits, or mere literary studies, as unworthy, frivolous or dangerous, are terribly apparent in the present condition of Oxford. Here, at least, we shall scarcely meet with a contradiction. The gradual desertion of the lecture rooms, in which knowledge not absolutely connected with University discipline is imparted, is notorious. The utter absence of all spirit for investigation of every sort, except in polemic theology and one or two inferior pursuits of taste, is the subject, even there, of general lamentation. Natural Philosophy, indeed, while disregarded by all, is absolutely discountenanced by many, from similar reasons to that which the late King of Naples was wont to give for refusing grants to unroll the Herculanean manuscripts ;—namely, that something might be discovered therein which would overturn the Christian religion, and then his Majesty would never get absolution. Historical study seems altogether at an end, except in the single province of ecclesiastical antiquities : indeed, as we have seen it ingeniously remarked by a writer of the Oxford school, all history is dangerous, and ought to be re-written on Church principles. Nay, the very special studies of under-graduates are no longer pursued with the spirit and zeal of former times : classical scholarship is declining. We saw it stated the other day, in a Journal favourable to the present ' movement,' that the art of prose Latin composition is absolutely lost at Oxford. To borrow again the forcible language of Dr. Arnold :—' The two great parties of the Christian world have each

their own standard of truth by which they try all things—Scripture on the one hand ; the voice of the Church on the other. To both, therefore, the pure intellectual movement is not only unwelcome, but they dislike it. It will question what they will not allow to be questioned : it may arrive at conclusions which they would regard as impious. And therefore in an age' (or seat) ' of religious movement particularly, the spirit of intellectual movement soon finds itself proscribed rather than countenanced.'

Thus much, at least, is matter of general observation—that while the loss is certain, the gain in higher respects is worse than questionable ; that much has been lost, along with knowledge itself, of the habits of mind which attend an ardent pursuit of knowledge—of manly candour, of extended sympathies, of that generous, frank enthusiasm so graceful in the young ; that a captious, close, exclusive spirit is apt to grow on the mind, under the discipline and associations now prevailing—producing in vigorous natures a concentrated heat, instead of an expansive warmth : this is complained of, we know not how justly, but seems to follow as a not unnatural consequence. For this, and much more, Oxford has to thank the peculiar exertions of the ablest and most active among her present teachers, and the success which has attended them.

It is true that they are awake now. Of course it is not to be supposed that men of really superior minds, such as many of those of whom we speak, can be content in observing the decay of knowledge around them; or the loss of interest in those pursuits to which the youthful disposition should seem adapted. It appears to be the very earnest endeavour of many of them, to keep the minds of those under actual pupilage as far as possible unpolluted by that black and bitter Styx of controversy which envelopes the region. But this is utterly impossible, unless they could influence also—which in *this* direction they cannot—the minds and studies of that body of which the condition forms by far the best test of the state of education at our universities. We mean those who have passed their short academical course, but are still detained by various duties or circumstances ; young themselves, although, for the most part, instructors of those still younger—for they form the class which gives the tone to the studious part of those under discipline. So long as theological controversy forms the great excitement and interest of their lives, so long it will exercise its miserable influence on the education in which they assist. However honestly disposed, the tutor whose head is in a whirl with the religious battles of Convocation, cannot get up among his.pupils much enthusiasm about the Punic or Peloponnesian war. Where his mind mechanically leads, theirs will follow. Nor will the tone of society, out of aeademical hours, assist in supplying the stimulus of better and more vigorous speculation; for society at Oxford—that is the society of the intelligent and active part of its denizens—is become dead and spiritless—paralyzed from the dread which prevails of mutual offence. Men stand carefully aloof from free intercourse with each other on questions which excite them, and the place supplies no topics of neutral and harmless interest. Add to this, the thousand temptations to take sides, to enlist in parties—the sad want of importance of those, old or young, who in agitated societies keep aloof from agitation. Talent, enthusiasm, self-importance, eccentricity, all take one and the same direction;—the able are easily drawn in by the desire to shine; and fools, because they have an instinctive consciousness that in no other way can a fool become a man of consequence.

It is needless to dwell on the influence which this combination of deteriorating causes may have on the prospects of the rising generation. *Væ diebus nostris,* exclaimed the old chronicler, who in his barbarous age saw and felt the moral darkness extending itself, along with the decline of that culture, of which, in these enlightened times, some men seem to fancy that we have a surfeit—*væ diebus nostris, quia periit studium litterarum a nobis!* We know full well the elements of greatness which exist at Oxford. They need no other proof than the extraordinary influence which has proceeded from thence for the last ten years for good or for evil. We know, too, that with all the degrading effect of its present condition on its usefulness as a place of instruction, the very violence of its controversies has not been without direct intellectual influence, in awakening and pointing the energies of dispositions of a peculiar order. But what the general class of minds which its present system produces need above all things, is a stimulus to a more natural and more independent action.

This is precisely what talents like those of Dr. Arnold were fitted to give; and it is in this respect that his loss is nothing less than a national calamity. Both his virtues, lofty as they were, and his talents were of an eminently practical order; nor were his very peculiarities without their usefulness. If he had been a severer analyst than he was—a man of judgment more free from the impulses of the affections—a man less solicitous about the polemics of his day—more patient in investigation, and less ready to grasp at obvious solutions of difficulties—in one word, less of a theorist; he might have been greater as a literary man; but he could scarcely have possessed, along with these faculties, his own distinctive excellence. His mode of action, in his university sphere, as his lectures prove, would have been, not to endeavour forcibly to tear away his audience from their accustomed associations, and make at once of young theologians and moralists a new race of impartial inquirers; but to bring them to the study of the past, as it were, through the present; to appeal to their acquired sympathies, to argue with their prejudices; to lead them thus gradually, and by the very means of the tendencies and propensities he found in them, into purer and freer fields of inquiry than those in which they were accustomed to expatiate. We are far from estimating his prospects of ultimate success by the popularity which attended his first appearance in his professional character. The extraordinary concourse of hearers which greeted him, was partly a homage to his high character; partly attracted by a certain fashion which his name had acquired from various incidental circumstances. Such popularity he neither coveted nor invited; for no one could be more entirely free from affectation and vanity—qualities belonging to minds of a very inferior order to his. But it afforded him an advantage at the outset, which his singular powers of illustration and discursive eloquence—his art of rendering attractive every subject he touched—would have amply qualified him to sustain. Short, indeed, was the period allotted to him, and barely sufficient even thus to indicate the road which he would have pursued. We have a high respect for the character and abilities of the gentleman who has succeeded him; and rejoice to find that Sir Robert Peel, in this instance, as in some others, has exhibited predilections in accordance with those of the liberal body of his countrymen; but all the distinguished ranks out of which the Minister had to make his selection, could not have afforded the equal of him who is departed, for the present emergency.

Art. IV.—1. *Mémoire en Faveur de la Li-berté des Cultes.* Par Alexandre Vinet. 8vo   à Paris : 1828.

2. *The Articles treated on in Tract* 90 *reconsidered, and their Interpretation vindicated ; in a Letter to the Rev. R. W. Jelf, D.D., Canon of Christ Church.* By the Rev. E. B. Pusey, D.D. 8vo. Oxford : 1841.

The metempsychosis of error is a curious phenomenon. Though not immortal, it transmigrates through many forms of being before it is finally destroyed. Apparently dead, buried, rotten—consigned to dust and darkness so long ago, that the very volumes in which it lies entombed are worm-eaten, and the controversies in which it seemingly perished no longer read, it often breathes and lives again after the lapse of centuries, and takes its place amongst 'the things that are ;'—not usually, it is true, in the very form in which it disappeared—in *that* it would not be lightly tolerated again—but in a shape adapted to new times and circumstances, with an organization, so to speak, which qualifies it to exist in a different element of thought and feeling. The chrysalis becomes a gaudy butterfly, misleading into a foolish chase thousands of those overgrown boys of the human family, who perchance would have despised it in its original deformity.

At this we are not to wonder ; for if error passes through many changes, it is because human nature is still the same. In every successive age are reproduced minds with all the tendencies which have characterized those of the past ; with the same affinities for special classes of error, or the same disposition to exaggerate and distort truth itself into substantial falsehood. Such minds may be, and usually are, modified by the age in which they live, the education to which they have been subjected, the circumstances under which they have been developed ; but they exist, and with an idiosyncrasy so marked, that even if they have never been stimulated by a knowledge of the theories of those who have erred, and been confuted before them, they often exhibit an invincible tendency to similar extravagances. What Thucydides has said of the parallelisms which we may perpetually expect in political history, is almost as applicable to the history of opinions :—γιγνόμενα μὲν καὶ ἀεὶ ἐσόμενα ἕως ἂν ἡ αὐτὴ φύσις ἀνθρώπων ᾖ, μᾶλλον δὲ, καὶ ἡσυχαίτερα, καὶ τοῖς εἴδεσι διηλλαγμένα. . . Yet have we reason to hope well of the ultimate destinies of our race ; and to believe that the progress towards the final triumph of Truth and Right is steady and certain, in spite of the alternate flux and reflux of the tide.

The remarks just made on the resuscitation of ancient error at distant intervals, and in new forms, have been signally illustrated in that great controversy, or rather complication of controversies, to which the discussion of what are called 'High Church Principles,' has recently given rise ; and to none of the antique novelties (if we may use such an expression) commended to us by the advocates of those principles, are they more applicable, than to the doctrines recently propounded by one and another of them on the subject of the 'Right of Private Judgment.' Of all the peculiarities of this modern-antique School, none, in our opinion, is of graver import or of darker omen, than its hatred, more or less disguised, of this great principle.

Few, in the present day, would seek the restoration of the brutal, or rather diabolical laws of ancient persecution, any more than they would, even if the choice were given them, breathe life into the bones of a Gardiner or a Bonner. To take those laws expressly under protection, in defiance both of reason and experience ; in defiance of the arguments of such men as Taylor, Chillingworth, Bayle, Locke, and others scarcely less illustrious ; above all, in defiance of the terrible condemnation supplied in the records of persecution itself, were the sheerest insanity. Whatever some may secretly wish, not only are hanging and burning for religious opinions abolished ; but even the more 'moderate forms' of persecution, as our ancestors facetiously called them, and which its sturdier advocates despised as poor peddling arts—the thumbscrew, branding, the pillory, incarceration, banishment—are quite out of date. Under these circumstances, we might be sure that any attempts to revive ancient error in relation to the 'Right of Private Judgment' would be very cautious ; and such, with some exceptions which have equally moved our abhorrence and indignation, we have found them to be. Not only would expediency dictate moderation, if the public is to be induced to listen at all ; but we trust that, in the vast majority of instances, even amongst men who cherish 'High Church Principles,' honour and conscience would alike recoil from the employment of the ancient methods under any modifications. How far, indeed, such men may sympathize with the views on which we shall presently animadvert—whether, though they do not at present avow it, they may not, as in other cases, have their esoteric doctrine to which the public is not yet to be admitted —whether that 'reserve' which they advocate 'in the communication of religious truth' be not operating here also—we have no means of judging. Our hope is, that the greater part of those who question, in one way or another, the 'Right of Private Judgment,' would not actually resort to any of the exploded forms of persecution. At all events, we shall not believe they would, except where they expressly tell us so. We flatter ourselves they would not find it so easy to throw off the spirit of their own age, as to apologize for the excesses of the past; or to repress the best feelings of their hearts, as to quench the light of their understandings. We shall, accordingly, bring no indefinite charges against any body of men. The particular modifications of opinion to which we object shall be referred to their proper authors; and chapter and verse duly cited for the representations we may make of them. But whether they be many or few who sympathize with the more reckless of the modern Propagandists of the doctrine of persecution, we do not anticipate that they will be actually successful. They never can be, until they can convert the present into the past, or make the wheels of time roll backward. It does not follow, however, that their attempts can be safely neglected; or that their opinions are not sufficiently dangerous to justify severe animadversion. Their intrinsic falsity, absurdity, and inconsistency, would be ample warrant for that. But when we reflect, further, on the tendency of such opinions to confound and perplex the unthinking—to foster malignity of temper—to perpetuate the remnant of intolerance which still dwells amongst us—to endear to some spiteful minds the petty forms of persecution which are still within their reach—to make them hanker after the forbidden indulgences of an obsolete cruelty—it becomes a duty to denounce them. Nor is it less incumbent to expose those more plausible, and perhaps, on that account, more dangerous, invasions of the Right of Private Judgment, which would delude multitudes into the belief that, on the authority of fallible mortals like themselves, they may repress the voice of conscience, receive as true things which they do not believe to be so, and practise as innocent rites which they deem forbidden.

One would think it very superfluous at this time of day to define what is meant by the 'Right of Private Judgment,' or to guard these terms against misapprehension. One would imagine that any mistakes about the phrase, or the mode in which it is usually understood, could not be otherwise than wilful; and, in truth, we honestly confess, it is out of our power to regard them in any other light. A recent writer, however, has attempted to show, that in the greater number of cases in which the 'Right of Private Judgment' would be usually said to be exercised, it is not in fact

exercised at all. Why? Because there is no protracted, deliberate examination as to which is the true religion, and a decision logically formed accordingly—education, feeling, prejudice, accident, having much to do with the judgment ultimately expressed! Can anything be more absurd? Does this writer imagine, that those who contend for the 'Right of Private Judgment' mean that none can actually exercise it but those who have first of all certified themselves, by actual inspection of the proofs adduced in favour of every religion that has subsisted, or still subsists, in the world, that their own is the only true one? That a man cannot be a Christian, consistently with the exercise of his 'Right of Private Judgment,' unless he has examined and decided whether Hindooism or Mahometanism may not have equal claims? Or (confining ourselves to Christianity alone) that he cannot be a Christian, in virtue of the exercise of the 'Right of Private Judgment,' if he has not profoundly examined the wide question of Christian evidences; or a Calvinist or Arminian, unless he has duly pondered the quinquarticular controversy? Could this author be so ignorant as to suppose that the advocates of the right meant this? It is notorious that writers by this phrase mean the right of *individually judging* — no matter what the *grounds* of that judgment—what is religious truth, and what not; not merely the abstract right of every man (though, it is true, each has it) deliberately to examine, if he has leisure and is so inclined, any or all systems of religion, and to make selection of that which he deems the true accordingly; but the right —in whatever way he may have arrived at his actual convictions of what is religious truth— to maintain and express that conviction, to the exclusion of all means beyond those of argument and persuasion, to make him think, or rather (for that is impossible by any except such means) to make him *say* otherwise. In a word, whether the phrase be abstractedly the best that could have been employed or not, it is chiefly designed to disallow the right of *forcing* us to believe, or profess to believe, as others bid us. This, in fact, is what is really contended for; and it implies not merely the right to judge for ourselves, but, *so far as coercion is concerned*, the right, if we please, not to judge at all; for though no man has a moral right to be in the wrong, it does not follow that another man has the right to employ force to reclaim him from his error. Much needless discussion has been wasted on this point by the adversaries of this doctrine, both ancient and modern; and yet nothing is more certain, or more a matter of daily experience, even where religion is not directly in quéstion. A man has no moral right to get drunk at his own table, and yet he has a right to deal very unceremoniously with any one who would by force prevent him. And so in a thousand other cases.

We feel almost ashamed of having been compelled, in the middle of the nineteenth century, to say anything in explanation of the meaning so generally and notoriously attached to the phrase, 'Right of Private Judgment.' Such being its meaning, however, we feel still more ashamed that there are to be found any who will deny the right itself. Yet such is the case with the writer to whom we have just referred, and who has incurred the additional odium of questioning that right, even as limited—and, one would have thought, put beyond controversy—by his own absurd interpretation of it. To one who was disposed to question the right, it might be imagined more reasonable, or rather less unreasonable, to deny it, on the supposition that it was designed to protect *all* consciences, whether the judgment formed was the result of deliberate examination or not; than on the supposition that the right was contended for *only* where such deliberate examination had been made. Yet even this limited exercise of the right, this author does not think it proper to concede to us. He thinks it reasonable to say that, if any one judges it proper to exercise this right, it is quite competent to the civil magistrate to inflict penalties on him for so doing. That any one would have been insane enough to contend for such a proposition in the present day, we could not have believed had we not read the statement with our own eyes. In order to protect ourselves from any charge of misrepresentation, and to prevent others from participating in the incredulity into which, apart from such evidence, we should undoubtedly have fallen, we shall cite the following passage:—'Now the first remark which occurs is an obvious one, which, we suppose, will be suffered to pass without opposition—that whatever be the intrinsic merits of private judgment, yet, if it at all exerts itself in the direction of proselytism and conversion, a certain *onus probandi* is upon it, and it must show cause, before it is tolerated, why it should not be convicted forthwith as a breach of the peace, and silenced *instanter* as a mere disturber of the existing constitution of things. Of course it may be safely exercised in defending what is established; and we are far indeed from saying that it is never to advance in the direction of change or revolution, else the Gospel itself could never have been introduced; but we consider that such material changes have a *primâ facie*

case against them—they have something to get over—and have to prove their admissibility, before it can reasonably be granted; and their agents may be called upon to suffer, in order to prove their earnestness, and to pay the penalty of the trouble they are causing. Considering the special countenance given in Scripture to quiet unanimity and contentedness, and the warnings directed against disorder, irregularity, a wavering temper, discord, and division; considering the emphatic words of the Apostle, laid down as a general principle, and illustrated in detail, " Let every man abide in the same calling wherein he was called;" considering, in a word, that change is really the characteristic of error, and unalterableness the attribute of truth, of holiness, of Almighty God himself, we consider that when private judgment moves in the direction of innovation, it may well be regarded with suspicion, and treated with severity. Nay, we confess even a satisfaction, when a penalty is attached to the expression of new doctrines, or to a change of communion. We repeat it, if persons have strong feelings, they should pay for them; if they think it a duty to unsettle things established, they should show their earnestness by being willing to suffer. We shall be the last to complain of this kind of persecution, even though directed against what we consider the cause of truth. Such disadvantages do no harm to that cause in the event, but they bring home to a man's mind his own responsibility; they are a memento to him of a great moral law: and warn him that his private judgment, if not a duty, is a sin.'[*]

This is, in some respects, a remarkable passage. One would almost suspect that, it must be a plagiarism from some ancient writer, were it not that people do not generally steal infected garments, nor, like old Elwes, appropriate as precious, things they have picked up out of the kennel. We almost involuntarily look for marks of quotation, or some archaisms of expression which would fix the date of the paragraph some two centuries ago. For ourselves, we peruse these arguments, thus recalled from the dead, with feelings much akin to those with which we should witness the exhumation of a mummy

---

[*] *British Critic,* July, 1841.—It is not our wont to make lengthened references to contemporary Journals. If we have departed from the usual course on the present occasion, it is assuredly, not because the Journal in question is intrinsically entitled to much notice, but because it is generally considered to be the chief organ and representative of the party who advocate the principles of the Oxford Tracts.

from the depths of the Pyramids, or the exhibition of some uncouth-looking weapons dug
out of an ancient tumulus ;--wondering the
while at the strange chance by which things
so long buried in darkness thus 'revisit the
glimpses of the moon.' We seem to be present at the awakening of some Rip Van Win-
kle, who had been sleeping, not, like him or
the *Sketch Book*, for twenty, but two hundred years. Why, these arguments are but
a feeble repetition of those which Locke so
utterly demolished in those matchless specimens of cogent and almost scornful logic—
the second and third letters on ' Toleration ;'
and which Bayle had refuted before him, in
his amusing commentary on the words ' compel them to come in.' We can hardly bring
ourselves to believe that the greater part of
those who in general agree with the Journal
from which the above passage is extracted,
can sympathise with the views of this writer.
If they do, the people of England would do
well to watch with double jealousy and suspicion the progress of 'high church principles.' If men such as he should achieve that
triumph of their principles for which they
are professedly striving, the dearest privileges
of Englishmen would no longer be safe.

There is nothing whatever to distinguish
the doctrines of this writer from those which
characterize the most barefaced, naked system
of ancient persecution ;— nothing which
might not have fallen from the lips of a
Gardiner or, a Bonner—nay, from those of a
Nero or a Dioclesian. For there is absolutely
nothing to limit the *principles* laid down ;
and those principles, thus unlimited in themselves, and pushed to their legitimate extent,
are sufficient to authorise any atrocities.
That which is established, no matter what,
has on that account presumption in its favour
of being right and true ; and therefore, wherever ' private judgment at all exerts itself in
the direction of proselytism and conversion,'
it must 'show cause,' before it is tolerated,
why it should not be 'convicted forthwith as
a breach of the peace, and silenced *instanter*
as a mere disturber of the existing constitution
of things.' It must show cause. To whom ?
Why, to the very parties, to be sure, who are
interested in suppressing it—who believe that
it has 'no cause to show ;' and until *they* are
satisfied—for the innovators are surely satisfied—that it has warrant for what it says, it
may be suppressed *instanter*, and convicted
of a breach of the peace ! A man must not
preach Christianity at Rome, till he shows
cause to the satisfaction of a Nero or a Dioclesian that there is a sufficiency of reason
on his side ; and, till then, he may be suppressed *instanter.* That our author did not

mean even to exclude this, the strongest case,
is evident by his own allusion to ' the introduction of the Gospel :' he has plainly left us
to infer from his principles, that though it was
right of the Apostles to preach, it was equally
right in the heathen to persecute them for so
doing ; they not having 'shown cause'—as
how could they to Pagans ?—that ' their case
was admissible,' and ' that there was nothing
in it which might not be got over.' The
same principles would of course justify the
Papists in persecuting the Protestants, and
Protestants in persecuting the Papists ; and
every form, either of truth or error, that happens to be established, in persecuting every
exercise of private judgment that happens to
be at variance with it. It must be confessed
that these are comprehensive principles of
persecution, but we acknowledge that we do
not like them the worse for that : they are at
all events consistent, however indescribably
absurd. The accident of previous possession
determines, it seems, the right to suppress,
and whether it be truth or error, it is all the
same : only, as truth is one, while error is
multiform, error will have the advantage of
this ruthless consistency in a hundred cases to
one. And as truth and error are armed with
equal right to employ this concise method of
' suppressing *instanter*,' so, as in the older
systems of persecution, there is here nothing
whatever to limit the degree of severity or
violence which it may be deemed necessary
to employ for that purpose. The duty is to
' suppress *instanter*,' unless sufficient cause
be shown to those who are disinclined to see
it ; and we presume, that as, when they do
not see it, they are bound to suppress *instanter*, they are at liberty to take any steps
for that purpose which may be effectual ; for
to limit them to the use only of means which
may be ineffectual, and which sturdy recu-
sants may set at defiance, would be altogether
nugatory. A right of suppressing error, provided it *can* be suppressed by the stocks or
the pillory, conjoined with a liberty to let it
run rampant if hanging or burning is necessary, would be a curious limitation ; and, as
it would be unreasonable to set any such
limits, so it would be impossible. What is
excess of severity in the code of one set of
persecutors, is childish lenience in that of
another. One man might be satisfied with
the pillory, while another might be satisfied
with nothing less than the rack. Our modern
apologist for ancient cruelty has wisely attempted no such limitation ; but, under the
general expression of 'satisfaction' at the
' infliction of penalties,' has left every variety
of persecutors to select their own. 'Help
yourselves, gentlemen,' is virtually, though

we hope not designedly, his language, 'according to your diversified tastes and appetites. The table is bountifully spread—the pillory—the rack—the scourge—the boot—the gibbet—the axe—the stake—confiscation—mutilation—expatriation—are all very much at your service, whenever those who broach novel opinions do not "show cause," to *your* satisfaction, that you would be wrong if you attempted to repress them.'*

We should consider it as a melancholy waste of time to attempt a formal proof of the wickedness and folly of persecution. Yet, as it appears that in the year of grace 1841, it was possible for one who could at least write and spell—whatever other attri-

---

* The reasoning by which this writer attempts to establish these conclusions, is as curious as are the conclusions themselves. He actually thinks that the *fact* of being *established*, is a presumption of truth in a world where there are a thousand different systems of religious opinion established; and yet it is not possible that more than one of these can be the absolute truth! He actually thinks that *fixedness* is presumption of truth in a world where the most steadfast and ancient systems of religious opinion have been, and are, notoriously, those of the worst superstition!—'Unalterableness,' a mark of truth in a world where the great innovation that is at length to remedy its miseries was reserved till four thousand years after its creation!—'.Change,' a characteristic of error in a world the great law of which is incessant change! It is true that 'unalterableness' is an attribute of truth, inasmuch as truth is always one and the same; but *he* would have us infer that what has been long 'unaltered' is 'true;' if this were so, as already shown, there would be a thousand different and conflicting systems of truth in the world. With equal logic, this writer actually imagines that the injunction, 'Let every man abide in the same calling wherein he was called,' has something to do with the determination of the present question;—that an injunction not capriciously to change our secular profession can be any warrant for inflicting penalties on those who innovate on established opinions in religion, because it is a probable case that they are actuated thereto by caprice and fickleness; or that it can justify acquiescence in opinions or practices which the conscience disapproves! Truly, this text of 'abiding in that calling wherein we are called,' is a short method of effectually settling the scruples of a restless conscience, and of insuring, to the world's end, that there shall be no further conversions from one system of opinions to another. The various *castes* are fixed, and let not any go out of them. He that is a Brahmin, let him be a Brahmin still; he that is a Mahometan, let him be a Mahometan still; he that is a Christian—Calvinist or Arminian, Episcopalian or Presbyterian—let him be such still; for, 'let every man abide in that calling wherein he is called.' One cannot wonder, after this, that Thomas Aquinas should have been able to prove that it is the duty of inferiors in the Church to submit to their superiors, from the words, 'The oxen were ploughing, and the asses were feeding beside them;' nor at the astuteness of that Papist who affirmed the propriety of worshipping the saints, *because* it is written, 'God is wonderful in all his works.'

---

butes of a rational nature he might have or want—to apologize for it, or rather to panegyrize it; it may not be uninstructive to exhibit, in one or two paragraphs, the crushing arguments by which the principles of religious freedom were first established; and the various modifications of the theory of persecution which its advocates were contented to frame, before they would wholly forego it. And most impressive it is to see how tenacious of life the monster was;—how many and oft repeated the exorcisms by which the demon was at length expelled.

We shall merely *state* the principal arguments; to state them is now enough. It was argued then—That it is not within a ruler's province to determine the religion of his subjects—he having no commission to attempt it; not from Scripture, for Peter and Paul preached Christianity in defiance of the magistrate; not from compact on the part of the people, for few would, and none could if they would, surrender to another the care of their salvation: That religion, except as intelligent and voluntary, is nothing worth: That in the very nature of things, the employment of *force* to make men believe, is a palpable absurdity: That, for example, the thumbscrew can never make a man believe the doctrine of the Trinity; and that, if it make him *say* he believes it when he does not, all that the thumbscrew does is to make the man a liar and hypocrite, in addition to being a heretic: That the unprincipled will escape by conforming, and only the conscientious be punished; so that the sole result is perjury on the one hand, and gratuitous suffering on the other: That the alleged power is as inexpedient as it is unjust; for rulers are no more likely to know the truth than private persons, nor so likely as many, as is proved by the diversity of opinions among rulers themselves: That if the rulers' religion be a false one, all the above evils are aggravated, for error has then all the advantage; those who are really converted being converted to error; those who only *say* they are converted, embracing error with a lie in their right hand; while the suffering falls solely on those who are in possession of the truth: That, supposing the right to *compel* resides in the magistrate, it must reside in every magistrate; and as truth is but one and error multiform, there will, on the whole, be a hundred-fold as much force employed against the truth as for it: That if it be said, as was often most vainly said, 'it is the duty of the magistrate to compel only to the true religion,' the question returns, 'who is to be the judge of truth?' while, as each ruler will judge *his own* religion to be true, this is but going a roundabout way to the same point : That the system, if justifiable at all, will authorize and necessitate the utmost severities; for if it be the duty of the magistrate to compel all to adopt his religion, the methods which will most surely and speedily effect this, will be the best; that therefore, burning, hanging, torture, being the most thorough and most likely to be successful, are to be preferred : lastly, That after the most remorseless and protracted application of the system, history affords the most striking proofs that it can never be successful; that the uniformity sought can never be obtained; that the conscientious are only the more fully convinced of the truth of their system, whether it be truth or error; that fortitude will be prepared to endure all that cruelty is prepared to inflict; and that not only in the history of Christianity, but in that of all religions, has it been seen that 'the blood of the Martyrs has been the seed of the Church.'

These arguments, and such as these, were, and will ever be felt to be, resistless against the ancient and only consistent scheme of persecution. No wonder, then, that men who could not gainsay, and yet would not adopt them, should seek some mitigated system which might leave them still the luxury of persecution, or secure their darling idol of uniformity with less expense to humanity and logic. It is curious to see the efforts which from time to time have been made to discover this *tertium quid*—a sort of purgatory between the heaven of perfect freedom and the hell of perfect despotism. But there is in truth no medium. The two extremes are alone consistent—and, so far as that goes, both are equally so. All intermediate systems are absurd and inconsistent; they are examples, every one of them, of unstable equilibrium—the slightest breath of wind suffices to throw them down. The old system is at least a strong-looking symmetrical fabric, cemented though it be with blood from the foundation-stone to the topmost pinnacle. The system which says, ' You shall be of my religion, or at all events *pretend* you are, whether you be or not; therefore bethink you betimes whether you love truth better than the rack, or if need be, better than burning fagots or molten lead,' is at least perfectly intelligible and consistent, however hideous. This is an iron-hearted, brazenfaced Devil enough, and one has some involuntary, shuddering awe of him. How far the petty imps who aspire to share his guilt, but dare not emulate such sublimity of wickedness, are entitled to respect of any kind, we shall presently see.

Some of the most obvious modifications by which the unqualified system of persecution might be stripped of its most revolting features, suggested themselves to the anonymous writer[*] who undertook the perilous task of answering Locke's first letter on Toleration, and were indeed anticipated by Bayle in that part of his *Philosophical Commentary* where he examines, with deliberate and minute attention, the 'objections' to his principles. First, Locke's adversary declared that it was far from his purpose to undertake the defence of the horrid cruelties by which history is disfigured. No—it was only ' moderate penalties' and ' convenient punishments' for which he pleaded ! And here—not to insist that almost all the arguments above stated against the most unqualified system, apply with unabated force to this and every modification of it—we come at once to the first of those symptoms of instability, which, as we have said, characterizes the whole. What are ' moderate penalties' and ' gentle punishments ?' Hanging is moderate compared with burning, and branding gentle compared with the rack. To some men of squeamish sensibility, even the cropping of the ears, the free use of the scourge, a few years' imprisonment or banishment, might foolishly be considered excessive. Nay, we know not whether there might not be found some who would object to ruin men even by regular process of law, by quirks and quibbles—perhaps, even to the pillory, fines, confiscation; while there might be others (as there undoubtedly have been many), who would say of all heretics, that ' hanging is too good for them ;' and who would not only show their charity by sending them, if obstinate, to perdition, but that, too, by methods which should convince them that they did not lose much by exchanging earth for hell.

As we have already remarked, our modern champion of persecution, who 'confesses a satisfaction' (we admire the felicity no less than the honesty of the phrase) 'in the infliction of penalties' for change of opinion, has left this matter equally in the dark. For this he is not to be blamed; it was impossible for him to assign limits, and he has therefore wisely refrained from attempting it. Whether a fine of a hundred pounds be thought equivalent to the luxury of a new opinion—whether such a *bonne bouche* ought to go still higher—whether it be dear at imprisonment, confiscation, banishment—whether his clemency would be ' satisfied' with the stocks, or the pillory, or branding—or whether he

---

[*] We learn from Wood's *Athenæ Oxonienses*, that the author was Jonas Proast, of Queen's College, *Oxford.*

would 'confess a satisfaction' (in very obstinate cases) at hanging or burning, is all unhappily matter of conjecture.

Locke's adversary further modified the system, by declaring that the 'moderate penalties' and the 'convenient punishments' for which he contended, were not designed to compel those on whom they were inflicted, to adopt a particular form of religion at the option of the magistrate; but to induce them to 'examine,' to 'consider,' calmly and deliberately, that they might not, as too often happens, be led by passion or caprice, or any other motive which ought to have no influence in the determination of the question! Whereupon he was asked whether he considered the *fear* of torture or banishment, and the *hope* of recompense or impunity, amongst the passions? Whether he seriously thought that the rack or the thumbscrew would *favour* that calm and equal consideration which he was so charitably desirous of promoting? Whether a man under the pangs of torture, or the dread of confiscation or banishment, is in a better condition for the exercise of his logic? Whether the mind, under such discipline, would not be as effectually under a sinister bias as if left to the dominion of any other passions whatsoever? Whether the author would have this charitable expression of concern for the souls of men fairly applied to all who, it might be deemed, had *not* given the subject of religion 'an equal and conscientious examination;' and, amongst the rest, to the multitudes of 'inconsiderate professors' of the national religion, who, as they are often more liable to take their religion on trust and in haste, than those who must suffer something for it, stand in more urgent need of such a provocative to deliberation? Whether, if he replied in the negative, 'his remedy would not resemble the helleboraster that grew in the woman's garden for the cure of worms in her neighbours' children, for that it wrought too roughly to give it to any of her own?'* Whether it could be thought that the magistrate who had established a given religion, or the clergy who preached it, would tolerate such an impartial application of the system of 'moderate and convenient penalties' to those of their own communion, however little they may have 'examined'? Whether the plan had ever been acted upon, or was ever likely to be? Whether it would not be a most curious and unprecedented act of legislation, to inflict penalties with the vague object of making people 'examine' whether they are in the right or not; or, rather, with the still more vague object of making them 'seek truth' till they find it, in the absence of a judge to determine what that truth is? Whether it would not be very much like 'whipping a scholar to make him find out the square root of a number you do not know?' Whether he who declares he has examined, and is still of the same mind, and that *not* the mind of a conformist, is to be released from all further punishment; or whether public officials are to be appointed to 'examine' whether he has 'examined' enough? Whether these are to be satisfied that he has examined enough, or are likely to be so, till he has 'examined' himself into the state of mind which will induce him to conform? and whether, if they are not to be satisfied till then, this system of 'moderate penalties' does not, after all, resolve itself into the system of compelling men to conform to the religion of the magistrate?— There are some things in the extract from that writer on whom we have been animadverting, which remind one of this system:—'Penalties bring home to a man his own responsibility'— 'they are a memento to him of a great moral law, and warn him that his private judgment, if not a duty, is a sin.'—'If persons have strong feelings, they should pay for them; if they think it a duty to unsettle things established, they should show their earnestness by being willing to suffer.' Here one would think that the charitable object, like that of Locke's antagonist, was to secure conscientiousness and deliberation on the part of the sufferers for supposed truth, or to sublime their virtues into heroism. But we have already shown, and the former part of the paragraph indeed avows it, that it is for the sake of peace and quietness—on behalf of the 'established opinions'—that he chiefly desires these penalties to be inflicted.

Locke's adversary subsequently shuffled out of his original position, and affirmed that magistrates were at liberty to persecute only for the true religion; and that it was at their peril if they indulged in any eccentricities of the kind in favour of any false religion. Locke, of course, unmercifully exposes this childish fallacy. For who is to be the judge of truth but the magistrate himself; and if it be his duty to enforce obedience to some religion, he must of course enforce obedience to that which he deems true.

Even after the general principles of toleration were established, it was long before the spirit of persecution was quite subdued; indeed, as we all know, it was only within the last few years that our statutes were purged from the last traces of it. Men found out, it seems, after the more violent forms of persecution were abandoned, that it was still very

---

* Locke's *Second Letter.* Works, vol. v., p. 99.

proper to visit those who did not conform to the religion of the magistrate, with the privation of some of their civil rights! This was no *punishment*, forsooth, it was simply a *negation*. To be kept without a thing is something very different from having something taken away from us, and what a man never had, he can never much miss; and thus, by this subtle distinction of ' negations,' men managed at the same time to gratify their bigotry and to cloak their absurdity. Happily we have got beyond this also.

The writer who has detained us so long, is, in as far as we know, the only living avower of his preference of the ancient system of persecution—the 'suppression' of the ' Right of Private Judgment' by pains and penalties. But there are not a few who ' would attempt to limit its exercise by an appeal to human authority; though they would not advocate the employment of violence for that purpose. We confess we think this system better than that of force, just upon the principle, that he who simply steals is less guilty than he who commits both theft and murder. But the system itself is far less compact and consistent. If a man be rightfully accountable to his fellows for the formation or expression of his religious opinions—if he *ought* to adopt those which he is *told* to adopt—one would imagine that it is but reasonable to arm authority with some means of enforcing its mandates. The duty of submission to any human authority, would seem to imply the correlative right of visiting disobedience with some sort of penalties. If not, it is authority only in name. What should we say to a legislator, who, enacting certain laws, should set forth in the preamble, that they were binding only on those who chose to be bound by them, and that those who did not might throw them into the' fire? It reminds us of the humorous case cited by Pelisson in his controversy with Leibnitz.* An ' inconstant lover' and his ' volatile mistress' gravely lay down the laws which are to regulate their courtship, and the last of them is, that both should break any of them they thought proper. South, consistently arguing on *his* principles, that ecclesiastical authority ought to be backed by ' temporal power,' anticipated and rebuked the inconsistency of

all half-hearted apologists for the suppression of conscience. He ridiculed the idea of authority without coercion—of laws without penalties—of obligation to obey conjoined with liberty to rebel. He consistently preferred persecution to the sanction of so singular a freedom. He exposes the fallacy in his own ludicrous manner : ' Some,' he says, ' will by no means allow the Church any further power than only to exhort and advise ; and this but with a proviso too, that it extends not to such as think themselves too wise and too great to be advised ; according to the hypothesis of which persons, the authority of the Church, and the obliging force of all Church-sanctions, can bespeak men only thus : These and these things it is your duty to do, and if you will not do them, you may as well let them alone.'*

But whether it be that the enemies of religious freedom despair of reviving the ancient opinions, or think that there is little present chance of success, or are really weary of them, it is certain that, while there is no lack of theories by which the ' Right of Private Judgment' is virtually denied, or curiously circumscribed, few, like the author on whose fanatical extravagances we have been commenting, would choose to ' confess a satisfaction, when a penalty is attached to the expression of new doctrines or to a change of communion.' Nay, as we shall shortly see, even *he*, in despair, we suppose, of getting mankind to adopt his antiquated opinions, provides, in condescension to their infirmities and ignorance, a mode of exercising the right which, as he flatters himself, will still get rid of all its principal inconveniences. This, and some other theories, we shall now briefly examine, and shall show of them all that they are absolutely nugatory, inasmuch as they still leave for the decision of ' private judgment,' questions as difficult and perplexing as those which, according to the common theory, are submitted to it ; or, what is worse, that they enjoin, in obedience to an authority neither *claiming* nor *admitted* to be infallible, a deliberate violation of the law of conscience, where the actual convictions of the individual are at variance with that authority ; or, lastly, that they are chargeable on both these counts.

Nothing, indeed, short of the Popish doctrine of the Church's infallibility, will suffice to annul or limit the ' Right of Private Judgment.' That, and that alone, will. For though we Protestants, who deny that doctrine, know very well that the ' variations of Romanism' have been nearly, if not quite, as

<hr>

* ' Je n'ose faire une comparaison trop peu sérieuse, et prise de ces lectures frivoles, qui ont amusé mon enfance; mais je ne sçaurois pourtant m'empêcher d'y penser. Dans une de nos Fables Françoises, (l'ingénieux roman de *Monsieur D'Urfé*, que tout le monde connoit), l'amant inconstant et la maitresse volage font avec grand soin les loix de leur amitié; mais la dernière de toutes est qu'on n'en observera pas une, si l'on ne veut.'—Leibnitzii *Opera*, tom. i. p. 689.

* South's *Sermons*, vol. i. p. 132.

numerous as those which Bossuet charged upon Protestantism, and many of them on points quite as important as those which the Church professes to have definitely settled; though we know that Popes have been opposed to Popes, and Councils to Councils; that Popes have contradicted Councils, and Councils contradicted Popes; though there have been infinite disputes as to where the infallibility resides; what are the doctrines it has definitively pronounced true, and who, to the *individual*, is the infallible expounder of what is thus infallibly pronounced infallible; yet he who receives this doctrine in its integrity, has nothing more to do than to eject his reason, sublime his faith into credulity, and reduce his creed to these two comprehensive articles: 'I believe whatsoever the Church believes;' 'I believe that the Church believes whatsoever my father-confessor believes that she believes.' For thus he reasons: nothing is more certain than whatsoever God says is infallibly true; it is infallibly true that the Church says just what God says; it is infallibly true that what the Church says is known; and it is also infallibly true that my father-confessor, or the parson of the next parish, is an infallible expositor, of what is thus infallibly known to be the Church's infallible belief, of what God has declared to be infallibly true. If any one of the links, even the last, in this strange *sorites*, be supposed unsound —if it be not true that the priest is an infallible expounder to the individual of the Church's infallibility—if his judgment be only his 'private judgment'—we come back at once to the perplexities of the common theory of private judgment; and the question then submitted to the individual Romanist's 'private judgment' is—whether it be reasonable in him, in a matter of which he knows nothing, but which is yet of infinite moment, to surrender *his* private judgment to that of another man? And truly, to decide a question without having any data for deciding it, appears to us quite as difficult a problem as any of those which are ordinarily submitted to 'private judgment.' The system, therefore, must be received in its integrity, and if so, the rule of conduct is very simple. If the priest tells us that bread is flesh, and wine is blood—that the sun revolves round the earth —that Gulliver's Travels, if they had not been written by a heretic,*would* have been as true as the gospel—all we have to do is to believe it, and, if need be, to believe it even for Tertullian's paradoxical reason, '*because* it is impossible.' ·　　-

Of every other mode of nullifying or circumscribing the right of judgment, and of this too, except where the claim of infallibi-lity is not merely *made* but *admitted,* it may be shown, as already said, that it is either nugatory, or flagitious, or both.

. Conscious of this, there is a small party of hybrid Protestants amongst us, who virtually claim for some Church unknown—neither the Church of Rome nor the Church of England, and yet both, but certainly *not* the Church of Scotland—some 'Visible Church,' which is not to be seen; some 'Catholic Church,' which excludes all Christians except Episcopalians; some 'Undivided Church,' which embraces the communions of the reciprocally excommunicated; some · 'Primitive Church' of uncertain date—nothing less than the infallibility, and consequent authority of the Church of Rome. But they are 'born out of due time;' their infallibility comes too late to enable them by its means to limit the 'Right of Private Judgment,' or to relieve us of our perplexities. For unhappily the Church of Rome has got the start of them; there are, therefore, *rival* claims to infallibility; and consequently, if more could be said to reconcile the manifold contradictions of the theory of these infatuated men, and to authenticate their claims to be its expositors, than ever *can* be said, 'private judgment' would still be pressed with the most transcendantly incomprehensible question ever submitted to the arbitration of ignorance—'Of two claimants to infallibility, which is the more likely to be infallible?' But to resume the modern theories.

The writer on whose appetite for persecution we have been constrained to animadvert, is not, it appears, disposed, after all, to deny the *free* exercise of 'private judgment,' but merely to limit the *range* of its inquiries; that is, the bird may *freely* range *in its cage;* nevertheless, we shall show that even there it has room to lose itself. He has discovered, it seems, that the question which 'private judgment' is called to decide is, 'Who is the teacher we are to follow? not what are the doctrines we are to believe?' The 'precedents' in Scripture, he affirms, 'sanction not an inquiry about Gospel doctrine, but about the Gospel teacher; not what has God revealed, but whom has he commissioned?' He maintains 'that the private student of Scripture would not ordinarily gain a knowledge of the Gospel from it!' Once more, he says: 'The New Testament equally with the old, as far as it speaks of examination into doctrines professedly from heaven, makes their teachers the subject of that inquiry, and not their matter.'. . .'Let it be observed how exactly this view of the province of private judgment, *where it is allowable,* as being the discovery not of doctrine, but of the teachers of doctrine, coincides both with the nature of religion and the state of human society as we find it.' We have already had a notable specimen of the exegetical talents of this writer, and need not, therefore, be surprised at his professing to find Scripture proof of this doctrine also. It must be confessed, however, that his method is somewhat novel; and would be generally imagined equally opposed to criticism and logic. He seems to think he has made out his point, if he but proves that teachers are *promised* in Scripture, and that it *is* within the province of private judgment to decide on their credentials. We deny neither. 'In remarkable coincidence,' says he, 'with this view, we find in both Testaments that teachers are promised under the dispensation of the Gospel!' Might we not just as logically say, that, 'in remarkable coincidence with *our* views,' we find it written that 'there was a man in the land of Uz, whose name was Job?' What is all this to the purpose? Who denies that religious teachers are promised? As little do we deny that it is the right of individuals to *judge* of their pretensions and credentials. But does the right terminate there? that is the question. One would imagine that the commendation bestowed on the Bereans, for searching the Scriptures to see 'whether the things told them by Paul were so,' would be alone sufficient to decide this point. But no—our author expressly says, though he attempts not to prove it, that *this*, too, is amongst the precedents which sanction not an inquiry about Gospel doctrine, but about the Gospel teacher!'

Let it be ruled so, then. And now to consider the system itself. We maintain that the question thus submitted to 'private judgment,' is as difficult as any which are ordinarily submitted to it. If a man be incompetent for the latter, he is equally incompetent for the former. The reasoning is about as good as would be that of a father who would say to his child, 'Though it is true you are not competent to say what it is fit for you to learn, and, therefore, cannot select for yourself a *school*, yet you are perfectly welcome to choose your *schoolmaster*.' We repeat, that if this exercise of judgment is to be a *bonâ fide* exercise of judgment at all, it will not be a whit less difficult to decide upon the 'teacher,' than upon the 'general doctrines to be taught.' 'It is much more easy,' says our author, 'to judge of persons than of opinions.' True—so far as regards their moral qualities; whether they be, in effect, virtuous or dissolute, benevolent or selfish, humane or cruel. But then, unhappily, if this be the criterion, it is just none at all; for men characterized by both classes of qualities are to be found in all communions. Indeed, as it is most evident from this fact that their personal qualities would be no sufficient guide, so it is by no means the criterion which our author contemplates; he would be very sorry to have it impartially applied. They are quite other qualities which are to decide the point; and the inquiry into these, we contend, is either not separable from an inquiry into the truth of the very doctrines taught, but presupposes that inquiry to have been both instituted and decided; or it is an inquiry into matters still more difficult and perplexing; for example, whether or not the clergy of a given Church possess the inestimable advantages of 'apostolical succession?' In the present divided state of Christendom, which is the more hopeful inquiry for a private individual, 'What saith the Scripture?' or, 'Which of all the religious teachers who claim my attention makes the most rightful pretensions to instruct me in the truth—I, at the same time, neither inquiring, nor being permitted to inquire, *what* that truth is?' For it must be remembered that an Episcopalian, Presbyterian, Independent, Calvinist, or Arminian, is not a trustworthy teacher, *because* he tells us he is; the awful privilege of 'apostolical succession,' is not inscribed on the bishop's forehead; no voice from heaven certifies to us that those whom he ordains are exclusively commissioned to preach the gospel. We repeat, therefore, that this liberty of 'private judgment,' if really acted upon, implies a task quite as difficult as those for which it is proposed to substitute it: in a word, either the very *same*—that of examining the pretensions of the teacher by a reference to his doctrines; or that of deciding on the historic grounds of his authority, without any investigation of his doctrine at all. This method, therefore, would not serve the purpose for which it has been invented; it would not correct the eccentricities or diminish the varieties of 'private judgment.' Nay, we have already facts in abundance to prove this. We see that there are multitudes of *all* communions who select their teacher on no wiser principles than that here advocated; without any inquiry into the truth of the doctrines taught, or the teacher's claim to the authority he assumes. It were well both for them and for truth, if they would exercise also the other and the better part of the 'Right of Private Judgment,' and diligently inquire—whether the system of doctrines taught them is in general accordance with truth, and the claims to authority, on the teacher's part, well founded. It does not appear, then, that this limitation of the 'Right of Private Judgment' would diminish the diversities of sect and party, or secure a nearer approximation to uniformity.*

---

* It is true that this writer points out some concise methods of limiting the candidates for the inquirer's suffrage. 'You may reject,' says he, 'all who do not even profess to come with authority,' To this it may be replied, first, that there are none who come to teach without professing authority to do so, and that in general the more extravagant their doctrine, the more arrogant their pretensions; and secondly, that the *absence* of those exclusive pretensions to which *he* refers—pretensions to the Apostolical Succession—would be to thousands a reason rather for admitting than rejecting the claims of a teacher who came to them with such unwonted humility. But, even according to this writer, there are at least three Churches, which, however divided on points which multitudes deem essential, possess, it seems, all that *authority* which is necessary to give validity to the claims of their teachers. These Churches—*risum teneatis?*—are the English, Romish, and Greek! But how is the perplexed inquirer to decide on their claims? Very easily, if we fairly follow out this writer's principles; for, partly by what he has said, and partly by what he has left us to infer, it does not much matter to which a man belongs; and as each are possessed of those mysterious 'gifts,' depending on the 'Succession,' which will serve to countervail any corruptions, it is difficult to say whether there are any reasons sufficient to justify a man in leaving any one of them for another. It is true, indeed, that our author disclaims all intention of discussing the question, as to whether there are reasons which can justify the Catholic in leaving his own communion; but it is plain, from what he has said, how he would decide it, and how, if consistent with his principles, he *must* decide it. Indeed, his very making it a *question* is a sufficient indication of his sentiments; for did ever *Protestant* before doubt whether it was lawful for a Catholic to leave the Church of Rome? None, assuredly, can doubt it, except those strange Protestants who deplore Protestantism itself, and who use their utmost efforts to show how much the Churches of Rome and England resemble one another! That the difference between them is not, in his estimation, very great, we may infer from such matter as this: 'We may believe that our own Church has certain imperfections; the Church of Rome certain corruptions; such a belief has no tendency to lead us to any view as to which, *on the whole*, is the better, or to induce or *warrant* us to leave the one communion for the other.' Again—'Is it not certain, even at first sight, that each of these branches (Romish, Greek, and English) has many high gifts and much grace in her communion?' Now, whether this representation be correct or not, let theologians decide; but so far from 'its being evident at first sight,' it is certain that nine-tenths in each of these communions would, in the exercise of that 'Right of Private Judgment' which even he concedes, come to a different conclusion, as to who are 'divinely appointed teachers,' from himself. Such is the very first application of this new theory of 'private judgment,' designed to limit the diversities of opinion; its very inventor manages to stumble on a 'judgment,' in which not ten out of a hundred will agree with him! On the manifold inconsistencies into which he is plunged by his attempt to show how nearly these Churches approximate, and yet to find such still subsisting differences as may justify a

But one of the most singular oversights is, that our author formally concedes the right in its full extent, for the purpose of ascertaining whether or not it is to be so conceded. 'We have arrived,' he says, with great solemnity and gravity, ' at the following conclusion, that it is our duty to betake ourselves to Scripture, and to observe how far the private search of a religion is there sanctioned, and under what circumstances!' We are, it appears, in the first instance, to make the most extensive use of our 'Right of Private Judgment' on the Scriptures; in order to ascertain whether or not we are at liberty to use our 'private judgment' in interpreting its doctrines; in other words, we are to exercise our 'private judgment' to ascertain whether or not it ought to be exercised!

Another modification of the theory of 'private judgment' is that of Mr. Gladstone. He says—'And, lastly, persons are in great alarm for their liberty of private judgment. The true doctrine of private judgment is, as has been shown by many writers, most important and most sacred; it has the direct sanction of Scripture. It teaches the duty, and, as correlative to the duty, the right of a man to assent freely and rationally to the truth. It is commonly called a right to inquire; but it is to inquire for the purpose of assenting; for he has no right (that is, none as before God) to reject the truth after his inquiry. It is a right to assent to truth—to inquire into alleged truth. Now, all that is true idea of the Church proposes to him is a probable and authorized guide. This is wholly distinct from the Romish infallibility. The Church of England holds individual freedom in things spiritual to be an essential attribute of man's true nature, and an essential condition of the right reception of the Gospel; and testifies to that sentiment in the most emphatic mode, by encouraging the fullest communication of Scripture to the people. Yet it is perfectly possible that the best use of such a freedom may often be thus exemplified; when a man having prayed for light from God, and having striven to live in the spirit of his prayer, and yet finding his own opinion upon a point of doctrine oppo-

state of separation—conceding that Rome does *not* practise idolatry, and yet discovering that there is a *note* of idolatry upon her, which may justify him who is already a Protestant in not joining her—maintaining that his own Church is *not* schismatic, and yet acknowledging that it is chargeable with something very *like* schism, and leaving us to infer that the Reformers ought never to have separated from the Church of Rome—of all this we shall say nothing, because it has nothing to do with our present subject. But as a specimen of what may be called *see-saw* argumentation, it is well worth reading.

site to that of the universal undivided Church, recognizes the answer to his prayer and the guide to his mind in the declarations of the creeds, rather than in his own single, and perhaps recent, impressions upon the subject ; not thus surrendering his own liberty of judgment, but using it in order to weigh and compare the probabilities of his or the Church's correctness respectively, and acting faithfully on the result.'

Here, first, we have the old fallacy. 'Private judgment, is, indeed a *right ;* but it is a right of assenting to the *truth.* But, then, who is to be the judge of truth? Is the individual conscience to assent to that which it honestly deems truth, or is it not? If the former, we are just in the same predicament as before. If not, what is the authority which is to justify it in setting its convictions at defiance? 'Why,' replies Mr. Gladstone, 'the voice of the undivided Church' must decide the matter. To this we might content ourselves with replying——This 'undivided Church,' amidst the ten thousand parties into which Christendom is divided, we cannot find at all ; and the search is at least as difficult as that of the truth which we are to find by its means. It is like telling us that we are to learn which of five hundred opinions is the true, by inquiring of some inhabitant of Eutopia. But the concluding sentence of this paragraph deserves more serious rebuke. Our author proposes an expedient for tranquillizing a scrupulous conscience—a conscience which finds its decisions at hopeless variance with those of the 'undivided Church'—which is, in our judgment, an outrage on morality. It is really one of the most extraordinary pieces of casuistry we have ever met with, either in ancient or modern times, and directly justifies the suppression of the voice of conscience. We are to suppose for argument's sake, that the inquirer has found that nonentity—the 'undivided Church.' Be it so; but he finds, at the same time, that this 'undivided Church' teaches a doctrine as true which he is persuaded is false ; and enjoins rites as a duty, the performance of which he believes to be sin. What is he to do? Is he at liberty to profess his acquiescence in that doctrine though he believes it false, or to perform those rites though he believes them wrong? 'Pray over the matter and inquire,' says Mr. Gladstone. 'I have done both,' replies the unhappy man. 'And you are still of the same mind?'—'Altogether.'—'But do you not think the whole undivided Church more likely to be in the right than you?—'I am not so destitute of modesty as to affirm the contrary.'—'Then you may, without further

scruple, proclaim your belief in the supposed error, and practise the forbidden rite!' So thus, it appears, the man may assent to *one* proposition which he deems *false,* because he can assent to another, altogether different, which he believes true ;—namely, that he thinks the 'undivided Church' more likely to be in the right than he. How different the decision of Mr. Gladstone from that of Saint Paul, who declares that a man who should eat meat offered to idols, with a conscience doubting its propriety, would sin ; though he at the same time declares by inspiration, that the act, in itself, is absolutely indifferent. Such a casuist as Mr. Gladstone would soon have administered relief. 'Do you not think,' he would say, 'that an inspired apostle is more likely to be in the right than you?'—'Who can doubt it?' would have been the reply. 'Then eat as soon and as much as you please,' Mr. Gladstone would have said; unless he believed the decision of an inspired apostle less likely to be the true one than that of his 'undivided Church.'

We are astonished at this doctrine we confess, and doubt whether, considering the difference of the age and circumstances, anything much more flagitious is to be found even among those Jesuitical casuists, whose extravagances Pascal so inimitably ridiculed. Mr. Gladstone's doctrine of 'probable opinions' would almost match that of the school of Loyola ; and we are half inclined to say of him, what Pascal's Jesuit Father says of Escobar : 'Truly this Escobar, said I, is a fine man.—Oh! rejoined the Father, everybody admires him ; he puts such *lovely* questions!' *

But what Mr. Gladstone, with congenial love of obscurity, has left in utter darkness, others have endeavoured to clear up. They have proceeded to furnish us with *criteria* of the undivided Church, to interpret what it has delivered, and to invest its decisions with a species of infallibility. But let it not be for one moment imagined that we are at all likely to have the exercise of the 'Right of Private Judgment' diminished by all this; on the contrary it is enlarged a thousand fold. The theory is that Scripture is incomplete ; that some things are divinely revealed which are

---

* 'Vraiment, lui dis-je, il me semble que je rêve, quand j'entends des Religieux parler de cette sorte. Et quoi, mon père, dites moi en conscience, êtes vous dans ce sentiment-là? Non vraiment, me dit le père. Vous parlez donc, continuai-je, contre votre conscience? Point de tout, dit-il. Je ne parlois pas en cela selon ma conscience, mais selon celle de Ponce et du P. Bauny; et vous pourriez les suivre en sureté, car ce sont d'habiles gens.'—*Let. Provinciales,* let. v.

not revealed *there;* that it is to be supplemented by tradition; and that whatever we find unanimously and constantly asserted by such tradition, is invested with authority coördinate with that of Scripture. Whereupon arise an infinity of questions, any one of which is as difficult as any that Private Judgment was ever called upon to decide; and which he who is no scholar has little chance of deciding except by lot, for the authorities are very numerous and diametrically contradictory on all sides. 'Nothing is more easy,' exclaims the Anglican; 'all you have to do is to adhere to the rule of Vincentius Lirinensis—*Quod semper, quod ubique, quod ab omnibus traditum est*—but, alas! on investigation, it is found that 'nobody' knows what 'everybody' has said; that what has been affirmed 'everywhere' is remembered 'no where;' and that the only thing to which all time has testified, is, *tempora mutantur, et nos mutamur in illis.* Whether a man be learned or ignorant—permitted to exercise his judgment in discovering these obscured verities of tradition for himself, or forbidden so to do—ample in either case is the scope for his private judgment. If learned, and permitted to inquire, the luckless student finds that instead of one small book he is sent to five hundred; instead of having to deal with nothing but what is *truth,* truth itself is presented to him in minute fragments, amidst mountain-loads of absurdity, ignorance and heresy. Then there are, besides, most difficult and subtle questions of criticism, to be decided, before the very materials of judgment can be laid before the mind; interpolations, erasures, forgeries to be detected—what is authentic separated from what is not—*quæstiones vexatæ* without end, in a word, to be adjusted. Again; at what point is the investigation to stop?—Is it at the end of the second, or third, or fourth, or fifth centuries? 'Stand by the first six General Councils,' exclaim Hammond and Stillingfleet; 'Stop at the end of the fifth century,' says Archbishop Bramhall; 'You must not draw bridle till the disunion of the East and West,' cries Bishop Ken; 'You are wrong,' says Archbishop Usher; 'four *or* five hundred years are sufficient;' 'Rather three *or* four,' say Waterland and Beveridge; 'The precise limit is *nowhere,*' says Mr. Newman; 'it is a question of degree and place;' 'It is everywhere,' shouts the more consistent Romanist. No wonder that, oppressed with the thought of *such* an exercise of the right of private judgment, the inquirer declares he knows not how to perform it. 'My friend,' is the reply, 'you have only to read through about a hundred and fifty folios of ecclesiastical records,

and you will find the matter is just as I tell you.' He feels that this is but meagre consolation, and, if intelligent, will declare, that rather than undergo such labour for the small *residuum* of doubtful truth which he is assured he will extract from it, he would make a voyage to the Indies to bring home a cargo of one peppercorn and two grains of rice! The right of private judgment, in such a case, he feels to be about as valuable a possession as a right to read through the statutes at large. The Puseyites may very safely grant it, for they may be assured no one will avail himself of it. If the man be ignorant, or forbidden to inquire—the other case supposed—he has only to believe. But let it not be imagined that he is not still subjected to the necessity of performing an impracticable act of private judgment. He may be told that infallible truth has been discovered, and that the priest is the infallible expounder of it. But, then, on what ground shall he believe this? 'I am commissioned,' says the priest. 'But,' (will be the reply), 'I see that there are multitudes of your *own* Church, and whom you acknowledge *equally* commissioned with yourself, who tell me that you are under an absolute delusion—that neither you nor they are commissioned to assume any such authority—that tradition is no authoritative guide, and that, if it were, what it authorizes cannot be authentically discovered. I moreover see that many of those who adopt the same general principles with yourself, differ as to *what* is primitive and catholic truth I can, therefore, regard *your* judgment only as your "private judgment;" and the knotty question which I have to decide is, whether I am to surrender *my* "private judgment," because *your* "private judgment" tells me to do so, when the "private judgment" of others equally learned, equally sincere, and equally *commissioned,* tells me that I ought not? and, as I have no data whereon to decide this question, truly I think a harder question for my private judgment, even the Scriptures of truth could scarcely have submitted to it. If I decide as you would have me, I decide absolutely without any reason whatever.' 'And is not this,' would be the *honest* reply, 'is not this the happy state of mind to which we have been endeavouring to reduce you? Have we not for years been urging you to *inquire* whether *inquiry* be not dangerous?—have we not been reasoning you (in our way) into the belief that *reasoning* on such subjects is *unreasonable?* And have we not endeavoured to illustrate precept by example, and as completely divested ourselves of all the attributes of a rational nature, as the ancient caricature of Plato's man ? Have we not shown you how much may be believed, and how little it is necessary to reason ?'*

That we are to receive with cringing acquiescence, whatever these men are pleased to say they are commissioned to teach us, will be more than doubted; till they not only lay claim to virtual infallibility, but persuade us to admit their claim. The latter they will do, when they have perfected us in the grand art of abjuring our reason; in the former, they seem ready to accommodate us at any time. But, unhappily for their pretensions, though happily for truth, their virtual claim to infallibility and unquestioning obedience is not, like that of Rome, unanimously and vigorously supported by the whole communion to which they belong. Even if it were, such unity would not (as already shown) relieve the difficulties of the inquirer; for as another Church makes the same pretensions, the knotty query would still return— 'of two Churches, both professing infallibility, which is the more likely to be infallible ?'

But such unanimity of pretensions, whether it be of any avail or not, is not to be found. *Quis custodiet ipsos custodes ?* The disease of 'Private Judgment,' has infected the shepherds as well as the flock; all the difficulties which, as we have shown, so closely beset the private student in the attempt to collect Catholic truth from the voluminous records of antiquity, have been felt by our authorized guides themselves; and have led to all those varieties of opinion which might have been expected In this point of view, the recent attempt at producing unity of opinion, and abridging the diversities of 'private judgment,' is even ludicrous. Never, since the Refor-

---

* As these remarks may appear severe, we shall justify ourselves by citing the following paragraphs from one of the most elaborate and dangerous of the *Oxford Tracts*. If the reader find it impossible to read the first without a smile, we predict that he will not be able to read the second without a sigh ;—to think that a reasonable being can talk such nonsense.—' I am not here to enter into the question of the grounds on which the duty and blessedness of believing rests; but I would observe, that nature certainly does give sentence against scepticism, against doubt, nay, against a habit (I say a *habit* of inquiry—against a critical, cold, *investigating* temper—the temper of what are called shrewd, clearheaded men; in that, by the confession of all, happiness is attached not to *their* temper, but rather to confiding, *unreasoning*, faith. I do not say that inquiry may not, under circumstances, be a duty, as going into the cold or rain may be a duty, instead of stopping at home; as serving in war may be a duty; but it does seem to me to be preposterous to confess, that free inquiry leads to scepticism, and scepticism makes one less happy than faith, and yet *that such free inquiry is right.* What is right and what is happy, cannot; in the long run and on a large scale, be disjoined. To follow truth can never be a subject of regret; *free inquiry does lead a man to regret the days of his child-like faith ;*—THEREFORE *it is not following truth.* Those who measure everything by utility, should, on their own principles, embrace the obedience of faith for its very expedience ; and they should cease this kind of seeking, that they may find.

' *I say, then, that never to have been troubled with a doubt about the truth of what has been taught us, is the happiest state of mind ;* and if any one says that to maintain this, is to admit that heretics ought to remain heretics, and Pagans Pagans, I deny it. For I have not said that it is a happy thing never to *add* to what you have learned, but not happier to *take away.* Now, true religion is the summit and perfection of false religions; it combines in one whatever there is of good and true separately remaining in each.' . . . ' So that, in matter of fact, if a religious mind were educated in, and sincerely attached to, some form of heathenism or heresy, and then were brought under the light of truth, it would be drawn off from error into the truth, not by losing what it had, but by gaining what it had not —not by being unclothed, but by being " clothed upon," " that mortality may be swallowed up of life." That same principle of faith-which attaches it to its original wrong doctrine, would attach it to the truth ; and that portion of its original doctrine which was to be cast off as absolutely false, would not be directly rejected, but indirectly rejected in the reception of the truth which is its opposite.'

The writer of this seriously believes that unthinking acquiescence in whatever we are told, is the most desirable state of mind; and that the restlessness produced by inquiry, affords a presumption, that what is offered to us is error. The Hottentot, who is contented with his brutal theology, had better, it seems, view with suspicion the *uneasiness* of mind produced by the teachers of Christianity, for they only disturb his faith and tranquillity—an ominous sign that he is 'not following the truth !' ' Where ignorance is bliss, 'tis folly to be wise.' ' Not so,' says this profound doctor, ' for I have not said that he is not to *add* to his belief, only he must be careful not to *take* away; he must become a Christian, not by *losing what he had*, but by *gaining what he had not !*' Was ever fatuity like this ? The Hottentot, when he embraces Christianity, it appears, only *adds* to his faith, but does not *take* any away! Are we to believe that if these new evangelists were to attempt the conversion of the heathen, they would act on the above maxims, and facilitate the work, as did the Romish missionaries among the Japanese, by teaching their converts to transfer their whole idolatrous stock-in-trade to Christianity—to make over to the saints the homage they once paid to idols, and baptize their wooden gods by evangelical names? What must be the desperation of a cause which stands in need of such arguments? Arguments! did we say—they do not even reach the respectability of sophistry. Are we not justified, then, in saying that these new teachers enjoin a servile and unreasoning belief—the utter prostration of the intellect? And does not such a paragraph as the above, prove that what they teach they are full willing to practise ?—The reader will find the same lesson perpetually inculcated, with various degrees of effrontery, throughout the *Oxford Tracts.* According to these men, one would think that it was so much a duty to distrust our reason, that mystery is an antecedent ground of probability, and that, if a doctrine be absolutely incomprehensible, it is almost certain to be true !

mation, has there been such a din of controversy—such a hubbub of tumultuous and discordant voices. Ill-fated project of universal concord, which terminates in the indefinite multiplication of controversies! It really reminds one of the ambitious attempt, described in the *Sketch Book*, at a new and elaborate harmony on the part of Master Simon and his village choristers. 'The usual services of the choir,' says the author, 'were managed pretty well . . . but the great trial was an anthem that had been prepared and arranged by Master Simon, and on which he had founded great expectations. Unluckily, there was a blunder at the very outset; the musicians became flurried; Master Simon was in a fever; everything went on lamely and irregularly, until they came to a chorus beginning, "Now let us sing with one accord," which seemed to be a signal for parting company, and all became discord and confusion.' Even thus is it on the present occasion; our very ears ache with the elaborate dissonance of this novel attempt at harmony.

There is one point, and but one, in which the circumstances attending this alleged attempt to restore 'primitive truth,' resemble those attending its first establishment; and in *that* we must confess the analogy to be perfect. These new teachers have come, 'not to bring peace on the earth, but à sword.'

Manifold are the arguments in favour of the Right of Private Judgment on which we have not insisted, and on which, at this period of the world's history, it would be most superfluous to dwell. Those, of course, which have been mentioned as demonstrating the wickedness and folly of persecution, are in favour of it—for whatever tends to prove the one wrong, tends to prove the other right. To these, many more might be added; some deduced from the intellectual and moral nature of man, others from the relations in which he stands to God: some from the declarations of Scripture, others from the examples it holds out to our imitation: some from abstract justice, and others from an enlarged expediency. The arguments on which we have principally insisted are, that the right must *in fact* be conceded, whether we like it or not; that the evils with which it is supposed to be connected, be they greater or less, are not likely to be remedied till we find what we shall be long in seeking—an infallible interpreter of infallible truth; and that any theory short of that, involves a flagitious tampering with the rights of conscience.

On this last argument, which we have already noticed, we should wish to add a remark or two; for this alone would be sufficient to prove the folly of attempting to circumscribe

the Right in question. If it be man's duty to embrace the truth; and if it be also his duty, which necessarily follows, to embrace that which he honestly *deems* the truth, he must follow his convictions whithersoever they lead him, in spite of any authority whatsoever not admitted by him to be infallible; in *that* case, of course, doubt or denial would imply a contradiction of his own convictions. It is not at the option of a conscientious man, we repeat —no matter how he came by his conscience— to debate whether he shall act upon its convictions. He *cannot* do otherwise. Take the case of a man who believes in his conscience that such and such doctrines are false, such and such rites sinful. Right or wrong, this is his state of mind. What is he to do? Can any authorize him to profess that these doctrines are true, or to practise those rites? If any one will answer in the affirmative, he will say more than any casuists, ancient or modern, out of the school of the Jesuits, will expressly affirm. He is bound, then, to yield obedience to the dictates of his conscience, whether his opinions be true or false: if true, even our opponent will not say that he can be authorized to profess the contrary. Nor is it otherwise, supposing them erroneous; for by the express authority of Saint Paul, who declares that 'to him who thinketh any evil' it is so, and that even a perfectly indifferent act assumes moral malignity if performed with a reluctant or accusing conscience; as well as by the decision of all the best moralists and casuists, an erroneous conscience obliges as much as a well-informed one; and by none is this more strenuously maintained than by the great Divines of the Church of England.*

* It is asserted by Jeremy Taylor in his *Ductor Dubitantium;* by Barrow in his Latin poem, entitled *Conscientia erronea obligat;* and by Archbishop Sharp, cited by Locke. Stillingfleet says, 'The plea of an erroneous conscience takes not off the obligation to follow the dictates of it; for as a man is bound to lay it down supposing it erroneous, so he is bound not to go against it while it is not laid down . . . So that let men turn and shift about which way they will, by the very same arguments that any will prove separation from the Church of Rome lawful— because she requires unlawful things as conditions of her communion—it will be proved lawful not to conform to any suspected or unlawful practice required by any Church governors upon the same terms;—if the thing so required be after serious and sober inquiry judged unwarrantable by man's own conscience.' 'If,' says Chillingworth, in his strong manner, 'they suffer themselves neither to bee betraid into their errors, not kept in them by any sin of their will; if they doe their best endeavour to free themselves from all errors, and yet faile of it through humaine frailty; so well am I perswaded of the goodnesse of God, that if in me alone should meet a confluence of all such errors of all the Protestants in the world that were thus qualified, I should not be so much afraid of them all as I should be to ask pardon for them.'

The usual evasion is, 'Let him further in-quire;' and wise counsel this may be, in the first instance. But suppose a person says he has inquired; or that he inquires again, and comes back in the same mind. What is he to do? He will say that he cannot be inquiring for ever—that religion is a practical thing, and must not be matter of investigation all his days—that he may as well embrace error as live in a state of continual pyrrhonism—and that he has no reason to expect that he will ever have a greater moral certainty than he has. Once more; what is he to do? Right or wrong he must follow the convictions of his conscience—to him the supreme law.

It is true that, after all, the individual may be much to blame; but not for thus acting in obedience to the dictates of his conscience in the last resort. There may have been haste in the inquiry—or no inquiry at all when urged to make it—or unworthy passions and prepossessions in favour of such and such conclusions. In these respects there may be much to blame, but not in the act of obedience to conscience itself. On the other hand—if, rare case! there has been nothing wanting in the process of inquiry which honesty and diligence could supply—no negligence, want of candour or patience,—the man is guiltless, even supposing the opinion erroneous, unless we suppose God to punish error absolutely and wholly involuntary. If, then, a man can truly say, 'I believe in my conscience such and such religious doctrines are God's truth, and such and such religious usages most pleasing to Him,' it is no longer at his option whether he shall profess the one or practise the other; and in like manner, if he can truly say, 'I believe in my conscience such and such doctrines are false, and such and such usages displeasing to God,' it is not in his power even to *appear* to sanction either. He must obey that which is his law—his conscience; in other words, if his private judgment be at variance with any *authority whatever*, not admitted to be infallible, he must obey the first and not the second. To this there is no exception.

It is not easy to find men who will avowedly dispute the maxim we have laid down. The opponent generally contents himself with daring those who maintain it to apply it to certain extreme cases. We should not shrink from the challenge. We believe that the general principle is universally applicable; and that the instances which seem opposed are either imaginary or irrelevant. Let us take the strongest conceivable cases, which some have been modest and reasonable enough to adduce—that, for example, of a man who is conscientiously prompted to commit mur-der or robbery. 'Is the man,' they triumphantly ask, 'to be justified, and treated as innocent?' To this, the arguments in reply are many and obvious : First, If we are to suppose that such conscientious persons are impelled by conscience to commit murder or robbery *as such*—that is, under the persuasion of their being crimes—then, 1. The notion is simply a contradiction. 2. Such a case, so far as we are aware, has never been alleged, and might safely be left to be considered when it occurs. 3. Supposing such a case to be alleged, all mankind would feel constrained. on ordinary calculations of probability, to believe either that the parties were mad, and therefore truly excused on that ground; or that they pretended to hold such opinions for an evil purpose. They would, therefore, be either confined as lunatics, or punished as knaves, according to the evidence of their being the one or the other. 4. Whether they be conscientious or not, society must protect every one against any infraction of his civil rights; and for this reason, the conscientious persons who manifest their piety by infringing them, may be very properly knocked on the head.' 'The magistrate,' says Bayle, with a gravity which is almost amusing, 'having received a power from God and man, of putting murderers to death, may justly punish him who kills a man from the instincts of conscience; for it is not his business to stand winnowing those rare and singular cases, in which conscience may happen to fall into illusions in this matter.' But, secondly, if by those who commit murder or robbery for conscience' sake, be meant those who commit acts, which, under ordinary circumstances, they themselves would consider crimes; but which, in their judgment, cease to be so when performed at the prompting of conscience—for the repression, for example, of *other people's* consciences, or for the propagation of 'the true faith'—we *might* content ourselves with replying, 1. That we never heard of such cases among those who contend that conscience is the supreme law, and that every one must obey its dictates. All who believe this necessarily learn to respect other people's rights, as well as to assert their own; it is only amongst those who deny this maxim that we find such instances as the above; and we might safely leave these men, therefore, to their own dark books of casuistry, in which the precise modes and degrees in which they may 'do evil that good may come,' are duly set forth. Assuredly, it is rather hard to adduce, against the operation of any principle, instances which, if that principle were in operation, could not even exist. Nevertheless, we are ready to affirm, 2. That if the said persecutors be truly and conscientiously convinced that it is their duty, as in the sight of God, to persecute, they are justified in so doing *while in that state of mind ;* though, in accordance with what has been laid down, they may have contracted a great amount of guilt in the process by which they have arrived at it. 3. That if they have arrived at it after having honestly investigated the subject, and without any voluntary error or self-deception—though we have our doubts whether there ever was such a case—they are wholly innocent : but, 4. that as they are infringing other people's civil rights, though *they* do not think so, it is perfectly competent to those upon whom they are exercising their freaks of eccentric piety, to deal with them as with the aforesaid *conscientious criminals ;* and punish them, (if they have the power), not for tormenting men from the best possible motives, but for *tormenting* them—those who are *de facto* ' tormented,' not being capable of understanding such refined distinctions.

Thus the principle we advocate is liable to no abuse, nor does society lose any one of its present safeguards by its universal adoption. But even were it otherwise, whether would it be preferable—that one man in a century should go unpunished, because, under a peculiar species of hallucination, he professed himself conscientiously impelled to perpetrate moral wrong ; or that we should recognize a principle which would justify the perpetual and universal oppression of conscience for speculative opinions ?

In fact, however, nothing can be more ridiculous than to profess any alarm lest mankind should plead conscience in favour of the violation of any of the great laws of morals. In these, there has ever been, and ever will be, a remarkable unanimity. As Bayle has well said—' We are all agreed about the doctrines which teach men to live soberly and righteously, to love God, to abstain from revenge, to forgive our enemies, to render good for evil, to be charitable. We are divided about points which tend not to make the yoke of Christian morality either heavier or lighter. The Papists believe transubstantiation ; the Reformed believe it not. This makes not for vice one way or other.' To the same purport, a very different writer, Robert Hall, has observed, ' The doctrines of our holy religion may be wofully curtailed and corrupted, and its profession sink into formality ; but its moral precepts are so plain and striking, and guarded by such clear and awful sanctions, as to render it impossible it can ever be converted into an active instrument of vice. Let the appeal be made to facts. Look through all the different sects

and parties into which professed Christians are unhappily divided. Where is there one to be found who has innovated the rule of life, by substituting vice in the place of virtue ?' We may safely restrict ourselves, therefore, to the case of speculative opinions ; and we will take the strongest. It may be said, ' Is a man conscientiously convinced that the Bible is false, no longer bound to believe it ?' We answer, he has a *prior duty* to perform. To believe the Bible true, in that very state of mind in which he believes it false, is a simple impossibility, and therefore not directly his duty. But it is his duty to inquire ; and we put sufficient faith in the variety and conclusiveness of the evidences of its truth, to believe that, if he inquire honestly, he will believe it true. If there be a case of one who has thus honestly inquired, and still conscientiously believes it false—if he can truly allege that he has left no means of investigation unemployed, and suffered no prejudice to interfere with his judgment—we shall rather choose to believe that he labours under some invincible obliquity of intellect, which in the eye of the Omniscient renders his error innocent, than admit the monstrous dogma, that he incurs guilt for error absolutely involuntary. But whether there be such a case is quite another question.

We maintain, then, the principle asserted by the illustrious writers we have cited—and we apply it consistently and universally.

By the assertion of this principle, we are far from justifying separation from any religious communion, merely because there are some things we disapprove, or would abstractedly wish otherwise. If this were acted upon, there would be as many sects as individuals : we merely contend, that, when such objections have assumed the form of conscientious scruples, so that he who feels them can honestly say, ' In my opinion I cannot profess such a doctrine, or practise such a rite, or appear to sanction either the one or the other, without offending God, or fearing lest I should do so'—his separation is not only justified, but *necessitated.* Be it about the most insignificant matter that ever disturbed a ' weak brother,' it matters not ; for while in that state it is not insignificant to him. If actually in the wrong, still it appears to him that he is in the right ; and while in that state he must act in harmony with his convictions.

People have not been slow to acknowledge this doctrine in words ; but they need to be reminded of it, since they will not fairly act upon it. They will still charge the Separatist, even the conscientious Separatist, with 'sin,' forgetting that, in doing so, they not only assume that they infallibly know his opinions to be erroneous, which (if their modesty be no obstacle, and it seldom is) they have a perfect right to do; but that, whether right or wrong, there has been negligence, want of candour, or some sinister bias in the process by which he has arrived at them, and this no man has a right to assume unless he has the prerogative 'of discerning spirits.' We were particularly amused with an example of this sort of inconsistency in one of the *Oxford Tracts*,* in which, while it is admitted that the conscientious Dissenter is not necessarily 'a sinner,' still it remains true that his dissent is a 'sin.' We can imagine the perplexity of one who, meditating the crime of nonconformity, comes to a clergyman professing these delightfully puzzling doctrines for solution of his doubts and difficulties. 'Can I,' he might say, 'separate from the Church of England without 'sin;' seeing that I cannot affirm what she affirms, nor practise what she enjoins, without, in my opinion, committing a sin?' 'If that be the state of your conscience,' would be the reply, 'you cannot belong to the Church of England; but remember, that neither can you secede from her without sin.' 'Why, then, I am in a hopeful case,' rejoins the miserable recusant: 'I am ruined either way; for whether I remain in the Church, or go out of it—and one of them I must do— I commit a sin.' Then how glad will his spiritual adviser be to administer that consolation, which his revered teachers of Oxford have, for this very case, made and provided. He will say, 'You must distinguish here: though you cannot secede from us without sin, yet it does not hence follow that you are a sinner.' On this his countenance brightens up, and he is most eager to learn that *supramundane* doctrine, by which it appears that a man may commit a sin and yet be no sinner. Whereupon his oracle cites the *ipsissima verba* of the 'Tracts,' and responds: 'To say that a particular thing is a sin, is a very different thing from saying that every one who does it is a sinner. . . . To kill a fellow-creature is undoubtedly a crime; but you would not say that the person who killed another by accident, or in defence of his country or his own life, or by command of lawful authorities, is a criminal?'† No, would be the easy reply; neither should we say, in *that* case, that killing was a crime. By parity of reasoning, if the conscientious

Dissenter be no sinner for dissent, it can only be because dissent, in *that* case, is no sin. You ought upon *your* principle to say, that the executioner, in hanging a man, commits a *crime*, though it is true he is no *criminal !* This distinction, therefore, will not much help him; and he is still left to decide the miserable alternative—of sinning by remaining in the Church, or sinning by going out of it.

But we must conclude; and we shall do so with a few reflections of a general nature on the advantages of the 'Right of Private Judgment;' amongst which, with some risk of being charged with paradox, we shall venture to enumerate many of its reputed 'evils.'

Whatever the evils incidental to the Right —and we by no means deny that there are evils—they are trivial compared with the advantages it secures. It frees us at once from every form and degree of persecution; it leaves inviolate the supremacy over conscience to Him who alone is its fitting and rightful Sovereign; it permits the conscience itself to move freely in obedience to its essential laws; it secures for the propagation of truth the only weapons which she can successfully employ—argument and persuasion; and it robs error of the only weapons *she* can successfully employ—penalties and violence: in a word, it prevents truth from resorting to that in which alone she is weak, and error from resorting to that in which alone she is strong. But further, to a philosophic mind, which calmly and soberly considers the subject, there will always be reason to doubt whether even what we call the *evils* incidental to the exercise of 'private judgment' are so in reality; and whether they are not connected, directly or indirectly, with more than a counterbalancing amount of good.

To confine ourselves to the common argument against the exercise of a 'Right' derived from the various interpretations of the Scriptures,—we are by no means convinced that absolute unity of opinion would be a benefit at all. If, as we devoutly believe, an honest investigation of their contents will in general secure even to the humblest a knowledge of all that is essential to salvation, the exercise of the right is vindicated; unless it be pretended that it is a general evil that men should differ on points not essential to their salvation. Now, that there has ever been a remarkable concurrence of opinion with regard to the most important doctrines, is undeniable. The only question, therefore, is, whether the remaining differences may not be connected with advantages greater than would accrue from absolute uniformi-

---

* No. 51.
† *Oxford Tracts*, No. 51, p. 3.

ty of opinion? This we do not think it difficult to prove.

That the Scriptures should be attended with difficulties, was fit in itself; that they should lead to varieties of opinion, was an incidental result of the prevailing reasons which induced the Divine Author to leave them on its pages. Such reasons we may readily discover.

With an overbalance of evidence in behalf of the authority of the Bible generally, and of its more important revelations, it was still not desirable that that evidence should be of such a nature as to *necessitate* conviction; and render the exercise of docility, candour, and faith impracticable—still less to make all diligence in its study unnecessary: it was fit that the Scriptures should contain some obscurities on minor points, to exercise patience, stimulate inquiry, teach humility, rebuke pride, exercise faith. Nor is this all. The differences of opinion thence resulting, afford the various communities of Christians, if they would but use it, the most obvious and easy method of testing and exercising the practical power of those principles of charity which they all profess. Charity towards those who think just with ourselves, is but an enlarged selfishness: we are pleased to look at the reflection of our own fair orthodoxy in the mirror of their minds. But to feel that charity, and to manifest it in defiance of the points on which we differ, requires and implies a higher principle. Charity to our own party is often but another name for party spirit: give us the charity which constrains 'Judah not to vex Ephraim, and Ephraim not to envy Judah'—the charity which induced the Samaritan to perform offices of kindness to the perishing Jew. Painful as are the disputes and controversies on non-essential points, we believe the time will come when the sublime spectacle of essential unity amidst minor differences will be fully realized; and when it will be seen how superior, after all, is such ' unity of the spirit' to any ' uniformity of the letter.'

We may add, that to demand that there should be perfect uniformity in religious opinions, is to demand a mere impossibility, so long as minds are differently constituted. This is confirmed by the general analogies observable in the constitution and development of human nature. God has so constructed us, that while there is remarkable uniformity, both in the physical and moral peculiarities on which the very existence and social well-being of the race depend, there are endless diversities on all points which do not involve them. It is much the same with

Christianity. The learned and the unlearned, if sincere, generally form a very similar notion of its fundamental doctrines. All beyond (and even the *theory* of these) is the source of interminable diversities of sentiment.

Let men say what they will, they will find it hard to discover any volume which, in all its great outlines, is plainer than the *Book of God.* It has its obscurities and its mysteries, it is true—wisely left there, as already attempted to be shown; but they trouble not the humble and docile—myriads of whom, without any teacher but itself, have learned from it enough to teach them how to live well and how to die happy. Its light has illumined the whole pathway of their present pilgrimage, and penetrated the depths of the sepulchre with the radiance of that ' hope which is full of immortality.' So far from its being true, that the indiscriminate exercise of the right of private judgment amongst the humbler classes leads to interminable diversities of interpretation and of doctrine, it is notorious that most of the profitless controversies which have obscured the Bible and cursed the world, have originated with those who have assumed to be the religious instructors of mankind. They have not sprung up amongst the poor, nor by them have they been cherished. It is, therefore, with a feeling of just indignation, that we hear professed Christians and professed Protestants—at all events those who are *not* professed Romanists —giving utterance to the sentiment, 'that the private student of Scripture would not ordinarily gain a knowledge of the gospel from it.' Such a doctrine is not merely an insult to common sense—it is a libel on the Divine Author of the Bible. Are we to believe that, ' knowing perfectly what was in man,' he has yet so constructed the volume of revelation, that even its fundamental doctrines remain an inscrutable mystery? Or did the great Teacher he sent, teach in so peculiar a manner, that even the more important truths he taught remained unintelligible? If so, we must receive in a new and monstrous sense the assurance, that 'he spake as never man spake;' that he spake not so much to reveal, as to disguise! But this record remains—that while learned ignorance cavilled and derided, ' THE COMMON PEOPLE HEARD HIM GLADLY.'

Far different from the judgment of these spurious Protestants was that of Bishop Horsley, with whose weighty words we shall now conclude. ' I will not scruple to assert, that the most illiterate Christian, if he can but read his English Bible, and will take the pains to read it in this manner, (comparing parallel passages), will not only attain all that practical knowledge which is necessary to salvation; but, by God's blessing, he will become learned in everything relating to his religion in such a degree that he will not be liable to be misled, either by the refined arguments or by the false assertions of those who endeavour to ingraft their own opinion upon the oracles of God. He may safely be ignorant of all philosophy except what is to be learned from the sacred books; which, indeed, contain the highest philosophy adapted to the lowest apprehensions. He may safely remain ignorant of all history, except so much of the history of the first ages of the Jewish and of the Christian Church, as is to be gathered from the canonical books of the Old and New Testament. Let him study these in the manner I recommend, and let him never cease to pray for the illumination of that spirit by which these books were dictated; and the whole compass of abstruse philosophy and recondite history, shall furnish no argument with which the perverse will of man shall be able to shake this learned Christian's faith. The Bible, thus studied, will indeed prove to be what we Protestants esteem it—a certain and sufficient rule of faith and practice.'

Art. V.—*The Sanative Influence of Climate: with an Account of the Best Places of Resort for Invalids.* By Sir James Clark, Bart., M.D., F.R.S. Physician in Ordinary to the Queen. 8vo. Third Edition. London: 1842.

The branch of Medical Philosophy which contemplates man as influenced in his bodily or physical condition by the medium in which he lives, and by the things with which he is perpetually in connection, is now commonly termed *Hygeiene* or *Hygiene*, from the Greek word signifying health—since it necessarily involves the consideration of everything concerned in the preservation of this invaluable blessing. This term, however, although now pretty generally employed by our more recent medical writers from the absolute want of some word of the kind, has failed to naturalize itself in England; possibly because the subject which it is intended to characterize has been singularly neglected in this country. We should not quarrel about a name, however, if we had the satisfaction of being able to state, that

the thing itself was more studied and better understood.

But we regret to say, that extremely little has been hitherto done towards the formation of even an outline of a general system of *Hygiene* applicable to the inhabitants of this country; or even towards the investigation of the more common causes of disease, as these prevail in particular towns or districts. Of the vast importance of such an inquiry, in a national point of view, no doubt can exist; since it must be admitted, in the first place, that the prevention is an object of greater consequence to the community than even the cure of disease; and secondly, that the only rational system of prevention must be founded on an accurate knowledge of the causes of our maladies. But these causes can be ascertained only by a close investigation of the circumstances under which disease occurs, in a great variety of situations; in other words, by a comprehensive system of Medical Topography.

The subject of Climate cannot be strictly classed among those belonging either to Medical Topography or *Hygiene*. Both these contemplate the object in reference to *healthy* individuals—the former being devoted to the investigation of the causes of disease; the latter teaching us the art of escaping, as much as possible, from the operation of these causes. But the labours of those who follow the track of the author of the work before us, are of a higher kind, and of much greater difficulty. They have to study the objects of Medical Topography, and to apply the doctrines of *Hygiene*, not to the state of health—that is, to a comparatively fixed state; but to that of disease—a state extremely various, and constantly varying. This application requires a degree of knowledge and experience which can fall to the lot of only few individuals. It does not by any means follow, for example, that because a certain climate or locality is innoxious in the case of a person in health, it will therefore be so in the case of one afflicted with disease; much less that it will prove beneficial to such a person. We find many instances of this important fact in the work before us.

With all his noble faculties and high aspirations, man in his present state is still of the earth, earthy, and controlled and modified throughout his whole fabric, mental as well as corporeal, by the influence of the things around him. If, by the superiority of his reasoning faculties, and the greater plasticity of his physical organization, he is, unlike other animals, enabled to pass from one end of the world to the other, and to live and multiply his kind in every climate; he is still, like the inferior creation, subject to the influence of the objects amidst which he lives, on whatever spot he may stay his foot. Every part of the surface of our globe that has been visited by man, is, no doubt, capable of sustaining human life, and is even compatible with health; but each region will present the physical and moral condition of the inhabitants under a different aspect, according to the character of the climate, and other circumstances amid which they are placed.

The difference, indeed, may be so slight, or of such a kind, as frequently to escape observation; but it is no less real on this account. And whenever there exists a considerable difference in the external circumstances, the difference in the condition of the animal will be manifest. The modification, however, even when considerable, may still be within the limits of health; this being only a relative term. What may be a state of health to one individual might be felt as disease to another. So it may be with whole classes of individuals. That condition of the physical organization which imparts to the Hottentot's mind the highest sense of healthful enjoyment, might be actual disease, or, at least, unhealthy discomfort, to the Esquimaux or Samoiede.

It is an object of the very highest interest to the medical philosopher to investigate the nature of the local circumstances which produce these important changes; and it will require centuries of patient induction to detect and expose the whole of them. At present we are probably only acquainted with a few of the more striking and obvious; but the potency of such as are known is sufficiently manifest. Without entering upon the great question how far the present varieties of the human species are attributable to the effects of climate, we need only refer to changes which have taken place almost within our own times—at least within the limits of recent history—in order to establish the vast influence of climate in modifying the physical characters of man. If we compare, for example, the present inhabitants of our West India Islands, the lineal descendants (without any admixture of foreign blood) of those who settled in them two centuries back, with the actual race of men in Great Britain, we shall find nearly as great dif-

ferences in the physical and moral characters of the two classes, as between nations which are usually considered as of distinct races.

The beneficial effects frequently produced by slight changes of situation, must have occasionally attracted the notice of even the least observant, in all ages and countries; just as it must have been observed that a removal to certain localities gave rise to formal diseases in the persons so removed. For instance, an individual migrating from an elevated and dry region to a low and marshy one, would become affected with ague; or his disease would terminate upon a second migration to the former place, or to another possessing like qualities: or a cough which had lasted for months in one place, would cease during a journey, or on the patient being removed only a few miles from his former residence; or a long series of sleepless nights would be broken and ended by a visit to a friend's house at some distance. Such results from accidental changes of residence, must have soon suggested changes with a *direct* view to procure like effects, —even if they were not naturally suggested, independently of observation, by the instinctive principle of self-preservation, common to man with the lower animals. 'We are ill here—may we not be better elsewhere?' is a most natural thought to pass through the mind of a sufferer; and if to this brief chain of reasoning could be added the link of even partial experience,—'We were well there —may we not be well if we return thither?' —the mere suggestion would rise in the untutored mind with the force of conviction, and lead to corresponding action. It need not be doubted, therefore, that an animal so fond of enjoyment, and so (laudably) averse from drugs, as man, must soon have availed himself of the highly agreeable remedy thus suggested; and that *changing the air* was a common and favourite prescription with the hoary elders and wise women of our race, long before 'physicians (by debauch) were made.' Accordingly, we find this measure strongly recommended by the very earliest medical writers, who, of course, did little more than record the popular practices most in repute, in their age and country; and it is noticed by almost every systematic writer on practical medicine, from Hippocrates downwards, as a valuable remedy in certain diseases. It may, with truth, be said to have been long received into the *matéria medica* of every practitioner, as a last resource, after the failure of every treatment of a more strictly medical kind.

But notwithstanding all this, we were, until the publication of the first edition of the work before us, ten years ago, without any very accurate ideas of the precise objects to be attained by changing the air, or climate, in diseases; and physicians were rather influenced by traditionary and empirical routine, than by any rational principles founded on a philosophical investigation of the subject; or by any accurate knowledge of the qualities of different climates, and of their effects in disease. Indeed, with the single exception of Dr. Gregory's elegant Essay, *De morbis cœli mutatione medendis,** and which can only be considered as an Academical Thesis, we are not aware of the existence, even now, of a work formally dedicated to the consideration of the influence of climate in curing diseases.

We possess, it is true, in our own language, many good works on the effects of particular climates on healthy strangers; and also some valuable memoirs on the influence of the climate of certain districts on the health of the inhabitants; but a general treatise on the effects of different climates on persons labouring under disease—in other words, a treatise on the application of climate as a general remedy in disease, was, till the period mentioned, a *desideratum* in physic.

We cannot say that the present work, however valuable, completely supplied this deficiency, as it is limited to the consideration of the effect of only one kind of climate. The avowed object of the treatise is, the consideration of the influence of a mild climate, in certain chronic diseases, on the inhabitants of colder countries. Scarcely any notice is taken in it of the effects of a removal from a temperate to a very cold or very hot climate; or the reverse. It must be admitted, however, that the branch of the subject here treated of, comprehends the majority of the diseases that are benefited by a change of climate; or, at least, the majority of the diseases of the inhabitants of the temperate and colder regions of the earth. In one chapter, the author has certainly taken notice of the beneficial effects of a mild climate upon the diseased constitutions of those who have long resided in tropical countries; but the great importance of this subject, in reference to the vast numbers that an-

---

* Edinburgh, 1774.

nually return to Europe from the colonies, entitles it to a much fuller consideration than it has here received from him; and as we are convinced that much attainable benefit is lost, and great evils incurred, by a want of proper knowledge on the part of this class of invalids, we would recommend him, in a future edition, so far to enlarge his plan as to include this subject at least.

Many causes heretofore combined to reserve the subject of the influence of climate on disease for the special investigation of our own times; but the principal of these are, unquestionably, the greatly increased desire for foreign travel, and the augmented facilities for gratifying this desire in the present age. It is indeed only since the battle of Waterloo made the path of the traveller free and safe, in every country in Europe, that the means for the composition of a work like that now before us, were accessible to any English physician.

On almost any other medical subject a book might be written by a competent person, without ever stirring beyond the bounds of his study; certainly without ever passing over the circle that encloses the field of his professional practice. But he who seeks to instruct his brethren respecting the influence of different climates on disease, must be one—

'qui multorum providus urbes
Et mores hominum inspexit:'

neither will it be sufficient for him, as is too often the case with the common traveller, to pay a brief and hurried visit to the places of which he writes. He must remain long enough at each to enable him personally to observe the influence of the climate in a sufficient number of cases; he must make himself acquainted with the nature and character of the diseases most prevalent; and he must be both willing and able to obtain and weigh the opinions of the native and resident practitioners; to test these opinions by the results of his own observations and experience; and to winnow from them all the rubbish that partiality, prejudice and self interest may have mixed with them.

To say that the author of the work before us, is in every way qualified up to the very standard of excellence in all these particulars, might possibly be too high praise; but to admit that he comes much nearer this standard than any preceding writer, seems to us only what is due to him, and to truth. Unlike one class of medical travellers, he seems not to have attempted to investigate the nature of foreign climates, and their effects on health and disease, or to judge of the merit of foreign opinions and practice, until after he had mastered the knowledge of the Schools in his own country; and had put this knowledge to the test of actual practice. Unlike another class, which may be subdivided into two orders, he seems neither to have viewed everything among our continental neighbours as greatly above or greatly below what exists at home; but to have brought to the contemplation of what was presented to him, an intellect at once sufficiently cultivated to be able to appreciate the good and the bad; and a temper sufficiently candid to permit him to adopt the former, and reject the latter, without much regard to the pride or prejudices of school or country. Unlike the most numerous class of all, he appears to have had ample time to enable him to confirm —if need were, to correct—the judgments formed on first views and impressions, or derived from inadequate authority.

The climates almost exclusively considered in his work are those which are commonly termed *the milder climates;* and on the present occasion we shall, with him, limit our observations to the milder parts of Europe, and the islands in the neighbouring seas. These climates may be arranged into four groups: Firstly, the climate of the south of England; Secondly, the climate of the south of France; Thirdly, the climate of Italy and the islands of the Mediterranean; and Fourthly, the climate of the islands in the Atlantic.

The following is a catalogue of all the places of which a particular account is given in the volume: —I. *Great Britain.*— London, Hastings, St. Leonards, Brighton, Undercliff, Salcombe, Torquay, Dawlish, Exmouth, Salterton, Sidmouth, Penzance, Falmouth, Flushing, Clifton, Bristol Hotwells, Island of Bute, Cove of Cork, Jersey. II. *France.*—Pau, Montpelier, Marseilles, Hyeres. III. *The Sardinian Territory.*—Nice, Villa Franca, San Remo.— IV. *Italy.*—Genoa, Florence, Pisa, Rome, Naples, Capo di Monte, Sorento, Castelamare, Cava, Sienna, Lucca. V. *Mediterranean and Atlantic Islands.*—Malta, Madeira, Canaries, Azores, Bermudas, Bahamas, West Indies. Of each of these places we have an account of the climate, its general influence on health, and its special effects on different diseases.

In our attempts to characterize the climates of these places respectively, as well as in reference to climate generally, viewed as a remedial agent, we must consider the *temperature* of the atmosphere breathed by the inhabitants as the principal feature. We are well aware that many other qualities, and constituents of the atmosphere, exert a powerful influence on the phenomena of animal life; but we must, in the present state of our knowledge at least, consider temperature as the most important element in climate. It is truly observed by Humboldt, that ' when we study the organic life of plants and animals, we must examine *all* the stimuli or external agents which modify their vital actions. The ratios of the mean temperatures of the months are not sufficient to characterize the climate. Its influence combines the simultaneous action of all physical causes; and it depends on heat, humidity, light, the electrical tension of vapours, and the variable pressure of the atmosphere. In making known (he adds) the empirical laws of the distribution of heat over the globe, as deducible from the thermometrical variations of the air, we are far from considering these laws as the only ones necessary to resolve all the problems of climate.'*

Next to temperature, the quantity of humidity is perhaps of the most consequence —considered as an element of climate. And in comparing the more southern climates with our own, with a view to their influence on the system of invalids, we may state their superiority to consist principally in the following particulars :—their higher temperature; the greater equability of that temperature; the greater dryness of the air; the superior serenity of the skies, and their greater freedom from rain, fogs and high winds. When we come to examine the individual climates we find particular places in each group varying very considerably from the others; but still we are justified by their general character in classing them as above.

A few remarks, of a popular kind, on the nature of diseases generally, and on the mode in which they are cured, will enable us to understand the operation of climate as a remedy. When a disease attacks a person suddenly, or with only slight warning of its approach, and comes rapidly to its acmè or height, it is called by physicians *acute.* If cured, it generally leaves the system in its pristine soundness, although for a time debilitated. This debility is soon removed by the ordinary process of nature; and the hues of health soon return to the countenance, and the wonted

---

* On Isothermal Lines.

vigour reanimates the frame. As the enemy who conquers rather by surprise and rapidity of movement than by actual superiority, and who is speedily driven from the land by the simultaneous rising of the inhabitants, leaves the institutions and the habits of the people nearly as before the invasion; so in the body natural, the brief endurance of an acute disease seems unable to impress upon the constitution any permanent changes inconsistent with health. When the weight is removed from the machine, its springs recover their wonted vigour and activity.

Sometimes, however, in place of this perfect restoration, an acute disease, although apparently subdued or expelled, leaves behind it something which, secretly preying upon the frame, not only prevents the return of perfect strength, but eventually, perhaps after a series of months or years, brings the system into greater peril than was threatened by the open violence of the primary attack. Slow diseases of this kind are called *chronic*, from the Greek word signifying time. As just stated, they are often the consequence of an acute affection, but they still more frequently arise without any evident or violent cause; and being slow in coming to their height, and in their progress afterwards, and often unattended by pain, they frequently exist for a long time before they are much noticed even by the patient. Diseases of this kind are extremely dangerous; partly because they are overlooked in their most curable stage; and partly because of their peculiar character. However local in their origin, such affections in their progress eventually involve almost every part and function of the body; and although the disorder of the individual parts may be slight, yet its universality and its duration render it of consequence. In physical, as well as in moral indispositions, it is commonly found more difficult to cure a slight affection of long standing, than a violent one of recent origin. If we compared the attack of an acute disease to the sudden inroad of an enemy, suddenly repelled, and leaving behind no permanent effects; we may liken that of the chronic disease to an invasion by a treacherous neighbour, with a view to conquest. Here the strongholds of the land are gained by stratagem—the opposition of the inhabitants is lulled by false pretences—and the country is subdued almost before the danger is perceived. If, after the lapse of years, such a country seeks to regain its freedom, it is soon found that 'the taint of the victors

is over all'—in the government and institutions of the state—in the habits and language—yea, in the very hearts of the people.

It will hardly be supposed that the same means that are calculated to expel an acute disease from an otherwise healthy body, will succeed in restoring to its pristine vigour a system that is radically diseased; nor yet that the means calculated to remedy such a disorder as the last, will be able to do so in a space of time as brief as suffices for the removal of the former. And yet we fear that this very absurd expectation is entertained, not merely by patients, but often also by their medical counsellors.

In such cases it is, to be sure, not very difficult on many occasions to give great and often immediate relief to some troublesome or distressing symptoms, by the judicious exhibition of drugs; and it is, perhaps, natural enough for a patient, so relieved, to expect that the whole of his disease is equally under the control of medicines, if only the same skill or the same good fortune might preside over their selection and administration. But nothing less than ignorance or quackery—self-deception, or the wish to deceive—can justify such an expectation on the part of the practitioner. He ought to know that a disease of the kind now under consideration—that has been silently gaining ground upon the constitution for months or years, involving in its progress one function, and structure, and organ, after another, until at last there is scarcely one solid or fluid in the body free from its contamination—is absolutely beyond the control of any one medicine, or set of medicines; and that it is only by a well-arranged and combined system of management, commensurate with the extent of the affection, and continued for a long time, that any considerable or permanent relief can be obtained. To attempt to cure so universal a disorder as this by a drug that can only act upon a part, perhaps a small and insignificant part, is only to be expected of ignorance or imposture.

It is, to be sure, the general opinion of the vulgar, that the whole art of physic consists in two things—the first, to ascertain the exact nature, or, perhaps, rather the name of the disease; and the second, to know and apply the particular remedy that has the power to cure it. That such a remedy exists for every particular disease, is not at all doubted; and the physician's skill is judged of precisely according to his success in applying the supposed specific remedy. If he is unable either to apply the true name to the malady, or the true remedy to the name, he is a bungler in his trade; and if, after what is considered a fair trial, the expected adaptation of the one to the other does not appear to have taken place, an artist of more knowledge or skill must be sought; or, if he is not sought, the continued attendance of the former practitioner is owing to other causes than confidence in his powers. A like process of reasoning, and a like practice, prevail among many who in no respect belong to the vulgar class—unless the circumstance of being uninitiated in the mysteries of medical science entitles them to be so ranked; and a consideration of this fact will, we believe, help to explain at once the fickleness of patients and the multiplicity of doctors.

The real fact, however, is, that there are hardly any *specific remedies;* that is to say, remedies possessing the power of certainly curing particular diseases. Medicine, it is true, can boast of some half dozen drugs (not more) which very frequently cure particular diseases, with a sort of specific and exclusive virtue; and with somewhat of that speedy yet invisible influence, supposed to be inherent in the obsolete race of charms. But with these few exceptions—truly insignificant when compared with the vast number of diseases and of remedies—the professors of the healing art are constrained to adopt, in their practice, a mode of cure of much humbler pretensions. Being destitute of powers to crush the invader at a single blow, they are reduced to the necessity of defeating him by indirect attacks—by cutting off his resources—by wearing him out by vigilant skirmishing—by fortifying the parts he has threatened, or is likely to attack—by repairing in detail the mischief he has done—in a word, by calling up all the natural powers of the system to exert themselves against the common enemy. We possess many means by which we can influence the functions of the living body; so as to increase, or diminish, or derange, or even to destroy them at pleasure; and it is by so acting on these functions that we are able, in many cases, to cure diseases, and that we *attempt* to do so in all cases, with the few exceptions already alluded to, in which specific remedies are admissible.

To instance the state of *local inflammation*—a state which accompanies, in one stage or other, a majority of our diseases. We have no specific remedy for inflammation—no agent which possesses a direct and immediate power to remove it. We are not, however, on this account, destitute of the means of curing inflammation. We can, for example, (by blood-letting), diminish the general mass of blood, and thus lessen it proportionably in the affected part; we can weaken the power of the heart and of the system generally, by the same means; we can in other ways diminish the quantity of fluids in the system, and determine them in a course remote from that of the affected part; we can (by abstinence from food) prevent any accession of strength to the system, and lessen that already existing; we can remove by local means a portion of the blood that distends the diseased part; and, finally, we can assist more or fewer of these intentions by the administration of certain remedies internally, which, acting on various parts and functions, co-operate in the great object of destroying the diseased action—in other words, curing the inflammation. This, it is obvious, is a very different thing from curing a disease by specific remedies. This mode of practice is one of very inferior powers to the other, but its administration requires much greater skill.

Chronic diseases are of infinitely greater importance, in a practical point of view, than acute. It is to them that far the greater part of human mortality is attributable; it is by them that much of the misery attendant on sickness is inflicted. The attack of an acute disease is rapid and brief; it may be hard to bear, and it may be hardly borne; but its pains are soon forgotten amid the enjoyment of health. It is very different with chronic diseases. They may torture through the great part of a long life, and, after all, may be only removed by death. It is in this class of cases that the physician is called upon to exert all his powers. It is here that the common or routine practitioner is sure to fail. He is constantly forgetting that, in chronic diseases, our object is almost always rather to put nature in the way of acting right, than to supersede her agency; and that our progress must, therefore, be in general guarded and slow, and the more so because we have only debilitated powers to call to our aid. It is in cases of this kind, then, that a remedy like *change of climate* is particularly indicated. This, besides acting, in many cases, directly on the principal local disease, affects the whole system at the same time, and affects it at once slowly and mildly, and for a long period. It is to this class of diseases, accordingly, that we find the recommendation of this remedy for the most part restricted by Sir James Clark.

In certain cases, a change of climate almost immediately cures a disease, by removing the cause of it—as when we remove from an unwholesome to a wholesome locality ; for example, from a low *malarious* district to an elevated and dry region : *sublatâ causâ tollitur effectus.* But although the propriety of change of climate, or perhaps we should rather here say, change of air or situation, is not, of course, overlooked by Sir James where it is so self-evident, yet it is not to cases of this kind that his observations principally apply ; nor is it as a remedy possessing such summary and direct powers that climate is contemplated in his work. In such instances as those just referred to, and in many other affections both acute and chronic, we certainly find, by experience, that a change of air and climate frequently effects a great and immediate alleviation of symptoms, or a complete cure; even when the place of residence of the patient is a very healthy one to other persons ; and when we are unable to explain, in any way, the manner in which the change of abode acts in bringing about so desirable a result. Instances of this kind must have come under the observation of most persons, and their frequency fully justifies, in many cases, the recommendation of change of air, or of climate, purely on empirical principles. But while admitting that there is much in the influence of change of climate, considered as a remedy, which we cannot at present explain, the author of the work before us wishes rather to consider this complex agent on rational principles. He rejects, wherever it is practicable, the idea of specific influence, and wishes climate to be considered, in its known qualities, as one of the agents that variously affect the body in health and disease. He submits it to the same examination, and the same tests, by which we judge of other remedies—trying it partly by studying its known qualities in reference to the known capacities of the living body ; and partly by observing the results of experience simply. In prescribing it, he, for the most part, considers it only as *one* of the many means that must co-operate towards the restoration of a constitution deranged and enfeebled by the long prevalence of a chronic disease ;—in many cases he looks upon it merely as permitting the efficient curative means to be more completely or more conveniently applied.

' The air, or climate (he says), is often regarded by patients as possessing some specific quality, by virtue of which it directly cures the disease. This erroneous view of the matter, not unfrequently proves the bane of the invalid, by leading him, in the fulness of his confidence in climate, to neglect other circumstances, an attention to which may be more essential to his recovery than that in which all his hopes are centred. . . . . If he would reap the full measure of good which his new position places within his reach, he must trust more to himself and to his own conduct than to the simple influence of any climate, however genial ; he must adhere strictly to such a mode of living as his case requires ; he must avail himself of all the advantages which the climate possesses, and eschew those disadvantages from which no climate or situation is exempt; moreover, he must exercise both resolution and patience in prosecuting all this to a successful issue. . . . . Here, as in every other department of the healing art, we must be guided by experience, and must rest satisfied with the amount of power which the remedy concedes to us. The charlatan may boast of a specific for any or for all diseases ; the man of science knows that there exists scarcely a single remedy for any disease which can warrant such a boast; and that it is only by acting on and through the numerous and complicated functions of the living body, in various ways and by various means, and by carefully adapting our agents to the circumstances of each individual case, that we can check or remove the disorders of the animal system, more especially those which have long existed. Let it not then be imagined that change of climate, however powerful as a remedy, can be considered as at all peculiar in its mode of action ; or as justifying, on the part either of the physician or patient, the neglect of those precautions which are requisite to insure the proper action of the other remedies.'

Leaving, then, on one side, the consideration of climate generally as a specific agent, let us see in what way a removal to a warmer region either obviously acts, or may rationally be presumed to act, in relieving or curing diseases.

In the first place, a warm climate is like a perpetual summer to a person accustomed to a cold one. The higher temperature of the air, and the finer weather generally, besides acting directly on the sensations, and through them on the mind—on the circulation of the blood, both general and capillary—and on the secretions—enable the invalid to do many things beneficial to his health, which he could not do in his own country. It will enable him, for instance, to be much more in the open air, and, consequently, to take much more exercise than he could do in England. Those persons, and there are many such, who languish in their chambers through the whole of the winter in this country, and only feel the pleasure of existence during the summer, will need no argument to convince them how beneficially a warm climate often acts on the enfeebled and disordered frame. An invalid of this class seems to change his very being with his climate—

'The common sun, the air, the skies,
  To him are opening paradise.'

Secondly, a removal to a mild, that is, to the natives of the north a distant, climate, effects a complete change of the air, soil, water, and other physical circumstances of a strictly local kind; one or more of which may, unknown to us, be exerting a baneful influence upon the individual, in his own place of residence. A most striking example of the effect of local circumstances upon the general health, in a place not naturally unhealthy in the common acceptation of that term, and of the influence of change of situation in removing the disorders thereby produced, is afforded us every day by the mass of human life squeezed into our large cities. This striking circumstance has not escaped the notice of Sir James Clark.

'On the Continent,' he says, 'the beneficial effects of change of air are duly estimated; and the inhabitants of this country, and more especially of this metropolis, are now becoming fully sensible of its value. The vast increase in the size of our watering-places of late years, and the deserted state of a great part of London during several months, are sufficient proofs, not to mention others, of the increasing conviction that, for the preservation of health, it is necessary to change from time to time the relaxing, I may say, deteriorating air of a large city, for the more pure and invigorating air of the country. This, indeed, is the best, if not the only cure, for that destructive malady, which may be justly termed *Cachexia Londonensis;* which preys upon the vitals, and stamps its hues upon the countenance of almost every permanent residenter in this great city. When the extent of benefit which may be derived from occasional change of air, both to the physical and moral constitution, is duly estimated, no person whose circumstances permit will neglect to avail themselves of it.'

Thirdly, a change to a new climate, in almost every case involves a great change in all the habits of life—in diet, sleep, clothing, exercise, occupations. And if all or any of these habits happens to be injurious to health, every medical man knows how difficult—often, how impossible—it is to break through them *at home*. But the chain of evil habits is frequently at once snapt asunder by a journey; and its links in many cases are prevented, by the usages of strange places, from being re-knit for so long a time that they never afterwards

coalesce. The disease, which if not produced was at least aggravated by more or fewer of these habits, either entirely and spontaneously disappears, or now yields to remedies which were previously found altogether ineffectual. Like the giant of old, it loses its power as soon as it loses hold of its native soil.

And this observation applies still better, perhaps, to moral than to physical habits; or, we should rather say to habits, whether physical or moral, which affect the mind more particularly. Not only is the merchant torn from his desk, and the student from his books, by a journey or a residence abroad, but in very many cases the wretched are torn from their cares. Most of our writers on intellectual philosophy, have shown too little regard to the influence exerted over the mind by the physical condition of the body; and it is only the physician who knows fully the immense share among the causes of unhappiness—we may say of wickedness—that bodily disorder may justly claim. In curing our corporeal disorders, the physician, in many cases, literally does 'minister to a mind diseased;' and as the disorders which most affect the mind (disorders of the digestive organs) are, of all others perhaps, most benefited by a change of climate, this remedy of course becomes entitled to a distinguished place in the *medicina mentis.*

But cares and miseries of a different kind, which have no discoverable connection with bodily disease, are no less benefited by a change of climate. It is, indeed, surprising how local many of our miseries are; but that such is the case, any one may convince himself by looking round among his friends, or by retracing his social experience. One man is happy in town, but miserable in the country; another suffers equally, but reversely; a third is only wretched in his own house, and a fourth is never happy in his neighbour's. Now, it is obvious that to this very numerous class, a journey to a distant country must be of great service; inasmuch as it must necessarily alter, at least for a time, a great number of the relations in which such persons stand to the objects, whether animate or inanimate, with which they are usually surrounded; and, therefore, we venture to assert, in despite of the satirists of all ages, that in many cases the traveller truly *does* leave his miseries behind him: *se quoque fugit.* He leaves that other gloomy self in the analogous atmosphere of the north, and assumes a new form under a more brilliant sky.

There is yet another way in which we believe change of climate often proves beneficial, and in a very considerable degree; and here, in place of a Physician, we shall quote a Poet, (Crabbe)—taking leave, however, to make a small alteration upon his lines :—

'————For change of air there's much to say,
As nature then has room to work *her* way ;—
And doing nothing often has prevail'd
When ten physicians have prescribed and fail'd.'

We are not surprised that the fact should be as here stated. Few are the Doctors, we verily believe, who can venture to put in practice all that they consider to be best in regard to the administration of medicines. Some patients will have draughts, whether the Doctor will or no; and some Doctors, perhaps, will prescribe them whether the patient will or no. Besides, it is not more strange that the professors of medicine should be fond of their instruments, than that the professors of other arts should be fond of theirs. And, may there not be something in the English character that prompts to what has been truly called the 'energetic empiricism' at present so much in fashion in this country?

A very important agent in the cure of chronic diseases, by change of climate, still remains to be mentioned; although it is rather incidental to this measure than necessarily connected with it—we mean the mere *act of travelling.* This is a remedy, to be sure, which may be as effectually enjoyed in our own country as abroad. It is nevertheless often highly proper for the physician to order his patient to a distant climate, even when all the benefit to be expected lies in the journey thither. People when sick must sometimes be cheated into health; and woe be to the Doctor who always speaks the whole truth to his patient ! Every one has heard of the cure of a chronic disease in a gentleman whom Sydenham directed to ride on horseback from London to Inverness, with the object of consulting some imaginary Doctor in that region—no longer remote in our days of steam and mail coaches. And the same pious fraud may be often pardoned in the modern physician, who sends his patient to Genoa, to Rome, or to Naples : the influence of climate may be the ostensible cause of the journey, but the journey itself may be the true source of benefit.

.' The mere act of travelling, (says Sir James Clark), over a considerable extent of country is itself a remedy of great value, and when judiciously conducted, will materially assist the beneficial action of climate. A journey may indeed be regarded as a continuous change of climate as well as of scene ; and constitutes a remedy of unequalled power in some of those morbid states of the system, in which the mind suffers as well as the body. In chronic irritation, and passive congestion of the mucous surfaces of the pulmonary and digestive organs, especially when complicated with a morbidly sensitive state of the nervous system, travelling will often effect more than any other remedy with which we are acquainted.'

In former times, indeed, if expatriation had been proposed as a common remedy for a whole host of diseases, the prescriber would assuredly have been considered as standing most in need of his own precriptions ; and *naviget Anticyram* would have occupied a prominent place in his *carte du voyage.* But in those days, steamengines and patent axles were not; neither had that organ of the Phrenologists, which gives us the inclination to change our residence, been stimulated into full activity, by universal peace abroad, and universal travelling at home. At present, we are hardly more startled at Sir James Clark's prescription of Nice, Naples, or Rome, for the cure of a cough, an attack of indigestion, or of gout, than our fathers would have been by the household words of *horehound, coltsfoot, elecampane,* or *dandelion.* At all events, such a prescription is a very agreeable one ; and, if their ailment is not very terrible, one might almost envy those patients who are obliged to use the remedy. It has been said that there is no royal road to health, any more than to learning ; but we suspect that our author has actually discovered this royal road; and, if his patients have only the means of *macadamizing* it, it is well. For our own parts, we had been led by experience, before we saw Sir James Clark's book, to think so favourably of the *Peripatetic School* of medicine, that we should be willing to submit to its severest prescriptions in the proper case, even if we were, with the heroic patients of old, to incur the risk of all the imputations and penalties attached to such a measure—

'I, demens, et sævas curre per Alpes,
    Ut pueris placeas et declamatio fias.'

The diseases in which a change from a cold to a milder climate proves beneficial, are numerous. Those more particularly noticed in the work before us, are the following :—Disorders of the digestive organs, in all their various forms; consumption ; chronic affections of the air-

passages; asthma; gout; rheumatism; diseases of the skin; scrofula; infantile disorders; diseases of *hot* climates; the climacteric disease; and broken constitutions generally. What we have already said of the nature of chronic diseases in general, and of the principles of cure in such cases, must content our readers in respect to the majority of these affections. But there are two diseases, or rather two classes of diseases, which, from their surpassing importance, ought to claim from us, as they have obtained from the author, more particular notice. These are disorders of the Digestive organs, and Consumption. In the first part of the present work we are presented with two admirable outline sketches of these affections, to which we must refer the reader; as our business in this article is not to describe diseases, or to detail their general mode of treatment, but to point out the influence of climate upon them. We must, however, take leave to say, that it has but seldom been our fortune to meet with any piece of medical writing so characteristic of the best school of physic—the school of Hippocrates and Sydenham—as these sketches present. In the chronic state, and secondary stages of dyspepsia or indigestion, and its multiform progeny, change to a mild climate is recommended by Sir James Clark as a powerful means of relief and cure. Indeed, it is in this tribe of diseases that the beneficial influence of the measure is most conspicuous. The mode of its operation is explicitly detailed in his work; and the adaptation of particular climates to the different varieties and stages of the affection, is there stated with great precision and minuteness. This seems very necessary, as the choice of a residence for this class of invalids is far from a matter of indifference. The place that is useful in one case is detrimental in another.

'The different forms of the disease require different climates. The patient with gastritic dyspepsia should not, for example, go to Nice, nor the south-east of France. In cases of this kind, the south-west of France or Devonshire are preferable, and Rome and Pisa are the best places in Italy. On the other hand, in atonic dyspepsia, in which languor and sluggishness of the system, as well as of the digestive organs, prevail, with lowness of spirits and hypochondriasis, Nice is to be preferred to all the other places mentioned; and Naples will generally agree better than Rome or Pisa; while the south-west of France and Devonshire, and all similar climates, would be injurious. In the nervous form of dyspepsia, a climate of a medium character is the best, and the choice should be regulated

according as there is a disposition to the gastritic or the atonic form. In the more complicated and protracted cases, still more discrimination is required in selecting the best climate and residence; as we must take into consideration not merely the character of the primary disorder, and the state of mind with which it is associated, but the nature of the secondary affection which may already exist, or to which the patient may be predisposed.'

But the most important of all the subjects treated of in this volume is the influence of climate in Consumption. And although, as we have already said, the beneficial effects of a mild climate is much more conspicuous in the class of disorders last noticed than in Consumption, yet the association of the latter disorder with this measure is so strongly fixed in the public mind, and such erroneous opinions prevail on the subject, that we feel it incumbent on us to notice it particularly. To establish the vast importance of the question, it suffices to state that, according to the latest and best authority, (the Registrar-General's Report), a fifth part at least of all the deaths that occur in this country is owing to Consumption! And there is too just reason for apprehending that even this tremendous mortality is on the increase.

Is a removal to a mild climate really beneficial in the cure, or even in the prevention of Consumption? If beneficial, in what way, and in what degree is it so? And what climate is the most beneficial? The work before us contains much more information relating to these important points than is to be found anywhere else; but we fear we must say that the information is satisfactory chiefly because it is extensive and accurate. It conveys to us much less hope, and opens less prospect of benefit from the change, than we could desire. But it will, no doubt, be highly valuable to the medical profession, and to the public generally?—by setting the case in a true light, and by showing what climate can do, and what it cannot do. If the effect of Sir James Clark's delineation of the true features of Consumption, and his exposition of the way in which climate influences its development and progress, were limited to the abolition or even discouragement of that insane system, so generally followed at present, and too generally countenanced by the medical profession, of sending patients abroad in a state of *confirmed* consumption—that is, in a hopeless state—his book would be of inestimable value. It would at least afford some comfort to the hearts of the hundreds of parents who are now every year compelled by this fatal custom, to see their children die under all the aggravations of evil necessarily attendant on a residence in a foreign land. But the book, we confidently predict, will do much more than this; it will be the means of saving many lives, by pointing out the way in which a mild climate can truly be made efficient in lessening the appalling fatality of this disease.

Sir James Clark coincides in opinion with all the great pathologists of the day, that consumption, when fully formed, is almost universally fatal. The essential character of this disease consists, as is well known, in the formation of numerous small masses (called *tubercles*) in the substance of the lungs, which, in their growth and progressive changes, destroy the natural structure of the organs, and fatally derange many of the functions essential to life. When once developed in the lungs, it is extremely doubtful if these bodies can ever be removed by nature or art;—when they have gone beyond their very first stage, and exist in considerable quantity, it seems nearly certain that they are utterly beyond the resources of either.* We, no doubt, every now and then, hear of this or that person cured of consumption, by a regular member of the faculty; and in the course of every half score years or so, there springs into temporary notoriety some bold pretender of the irregular order, whose confident promises (sometimes, perhaps, sincere) and loud boastings, impose upon many the belief that this hitherto intractable malady has at length been brought under the dominion of art. But the total ignorance of this class of persons respecting the real nature of the disease, and the great difficulties often experienced by the most learned in discriminating it, in its early stages, from some other diseases, sufficiently explain these occurrences. And the great teacher, Time, soon justifies the scepticism of the man of science, by covering with oblivion what, if true, could never be forgotten, nor permitted to yield its place to any novelty, however great, or any claimant, however loud. It

is, therefore, with much satisfaction that we find the present author devoting all his powers to the elucidation of the remoter causes of consumption; and of the nature and character of that morbid condition of the system to which it is found commonly to supervene. If we cannot cure consumption itself, we may possibly be enabled to obviate the circumstances that lay the first foundation of it; or we may even be enabled to remove the first changes impressed by these circumstances upon the organization.

The remote and predisposing causes of the disease are well known, and have been generally noticed by preceding writers; but Sir James Clark is the first, who, to our knowledge, has formally described the precursory disorder, or attempted (to use his own words) 'to fill up the blank which has been left in the natural history of consumption, between a state of health and of established and sensible disease of the lungs.' The precursory affection of the system is termed by him *Tubercular Cachexy;* and he looks upon it as the *nidus* or *matrix* of the subsequent disease of the lungs.*

It is a powerful adjuvant of the medical means best calculated to remove this disorder—for, unlike its progeny, it is often curable—that removal to a mild climate is strongly recommended. The same measure is likewise advised, though with much less confidence, when there are strong reasons for believing that tubercles are actually formed in the lungs. But it is denounced, as we have already stated, in the strongest terms, not only as useless but cruel in the extreme, except in a few particular cases, when the disease is *confirmed.* We will here allow Sir James Clark to speak for himself; only observing that we entirely accord with every sentiment expressed by him in the following extract:—

'Unfortunately it too often happens, that the period of constitutional disorder, which we have just been considering, is permitted to pass; and it is not until symptoms of irritation or impeded function in the lungs, such as cough, difficult breathing, or spitting of blood, appear, that the patient or relations are alarmed, and that fears are expressed that the chest is "threatened." Such symptoms are but too sure indications that tuberculous disease has already commenced in the lungs. It may, indeed, be difficult, in some cases, to ascertain the positive existence of this, although, by a careful examination of the chest, and an attentive consideration of all the circum-

---

* We are well aware of the very peculiar and extremely rare yet well authenticated case, of a cure being effected after the discharge of a tubercle or tuberculous abscess by expectoration; but this case can only be considered as a rare exception to the general rule, and ought not to be at all calculated upon in practice. See, for information on this point, the classical works of Laennec, Andral, and Louis, and especially the present author's treatise on *Consumption.*

* See also his treatise on *Consumption and Scrofulous Diseases.* London: 1835.

stances of the case, we shall seldom err in our diagnosis; and it need not, at any rate, affect our practice, as a strong suspicion of the presence of tubercles should lead us to adopt the same precautions as the certainty of their existence.

'When tuberculous matter is deposited in the lungs, the circumstances of the patient are materially changed. We have the same functional disorders which existed in the former state: and we have also pulmonary disease, predisposing to a new series of morbid actions—to bronchial affections, hæmoptysis, inflammation of the pleura and lungs, &c.—which calls for important modifications in the plan of treatment. Removal to a mild climate, especially if effected by means of a sea voyage, under favourable circumstances, may still be useful as in the former case—namely, as a means of improving the general health, of preventing inflammatory action of the lungs, and even, perhaps, arresting the progress of disease.

'When consumption is fully established—that is, when there is extensive tuberculous disease in the lungs, little benefit is to be expected from change of climate; and a long journey will almost certainly increase the sufferings of the patient, and hurry on the fatal termination. Under such circumstances, therefore, the patient will act more judiciously by contenting himself with the most favourable residence which his own country affords; or even by remaining amid the comforts of home, and the watchful care of friends. And this will be the more advisable when a disposition to sympathetic fever, to inflammation of the lungs, or to hæmoptysis, has been strongly manifested.

'It is natural for relations to cling to that which seems to afford even a ray of hope; but did they know the discomforts, the fatigue, the exposure, and irritation, necessarily attendant on a long journey in the advanced period of consumption, they would shrink from such a measure. The medical adviser, also, when he reflects upon the accidents to which such a patient is liable, should surely hesitate ere he condemns him to the additional evil of expatriation; and his motives for hesitation will be increased when he considers how often the unfortunate patient sinks under the disease before the place of destination is reached, or, at best, arrives there in a worse condition than when he left his own country, and doomed shortly to add another name to the long and melancholy list of his countrymen who have sought, with pain and suffering, a distant country, only to find in it a grave. When the patient is a female, the objections to a journey apply with increased force.'

It is not, therefore, in the hope of his patients finding something specific—some mysterious and occult virtue—in the air of a milder climate, capable of curing consumption, that our author sends them to Italy or Madeira; but it is because the climate of these countries permits the application of the means best calculated for preventing or removing those morbid actions which too often terminate in consumption. The fatal error of this country is—to wait until the lungs are obviously affected, and then to hurry the unfortunate patient at once to a mild climate; without considering, in the first place, whether the case is of such a nature as really to afford any reasonable hope of benefit from *any* climate; and, secondly, if a prospect of benefit really exists, which of the milder climates is best suited to the particular case. The plan recommended by the author is to watch the development of that train of symptoms, which, if left unchecked, too generally terminates in consumption; to institute then a comprehensive and combined system of treatment calculated to restore the disordered functions; and, as enabling some parts of this system to be carried much more effectually into operation, then to remove the invalid to the mild climate which is best suited to the peculiarities of the case. Such a climate, among other advantages, tends to produce a greater equality in the circulation, by determining the fluids to the surface and extremities; removes considerably the risk of catarrhal affections, which, in predisposed subjects, often act as exciting causes of tubercles; and—the greatest advantage of all—enables the invalid to be much more in the open air, and consequently, to take much more exercise than he could possibly do in England, during the winter. With such advantages as these, the plan of treatment calculated to restore the general health, and thereby to avert the threatened disease of the lungs, has obviously a much fairer chance of success in such a climate as Madeira, where there may be said to be a perpetual summer, than in so cold, moist, and variable a climate as that of England. We say the plan of treatment has a fairer chance of success in such a climate—not that the climate is to be considered as the sole or even principal agent in averting the impending malady; much less in curing it when it has already made good its footing. The fact is, that although a change to a mild climate may be sufficient, in some cases, to enable the natural powers of the system to restore the disordered functions without the aid of art, these powers will fail in a great majority of cases; and yet, not so much, perhaps, from their deficiency, as because they are impeded and thwarted by an injurious system of regimen or medical treatment. In the severe or more strongly marked cases, (even before the development of tubercles), it will be of little avail that the invalid changes our cold and gloomy atmosphere for the soft breezes and brilliant skies of the south; unless he changes, at the same time, the habits which have induced, or aggravated, or accelerated his present disorder; and unless he, moreover, adopts measures calculated to aid the sanative powers of nature. Nay, we will assert, however great may be the advantages of a mild climate in such cases, (and we consider them as very great), it will be much better for an invalid to remain in England under good management, than to go abroad to the best climate, under no management at all, or under bad management. *Cæteris paribus,* a mild climate is, in this case, greatly preferable to a cold one; but a good system of discipline is indispensable in both.

And here, before we conclude, and lest we should be thought desirous of having it supposed that we ourselves, or the author of this work, possesses some new and potent system of medication—calculated to avert the poisoned arrows of 'the pest,' or to stay its giant strides—we deem it necessary to state, in a very few words, the general complexion of the plan of treatment which he recommends, and in which alone we have any faith, in the case under consideration. In the first place, we utterly disclaim the possession or prescription of any specific remedy in such cases; and, in the second place, we profess to be most sparing in the use of medicines of any kind. Indeed, we are of opinion that medical science has now arrived at that stage when, in practice, it may frequently content itself by looking rather to the pathological condition of the subject, than to the efficacy of any remedial measures. At all events, we think it will generally be found, that the most scientific and skilful physicians are the most sparing in the use of drugs. The plan we advocate in the present case, consists essentially in taking a close and comprehensive view of the whole disorder under which the system labours; and in adapting our remedies (often extremely simple) to every part that is affected. What we consider as most faulty in the prevailing systems of medicine in this country is, the too great simplicity of the views of disease taken by practitioners, and the consequent too partial and exclusive system of therapeutics founded on them. We wish practitioners in their study of chronic diseases, to endeavour, like the author of the work before us, to combine the Hippocratic system of close and comprehensive observation with the more rational views of disease brought to light by modern Pathology; and in their practice

to endeavour to restore, at the same time, *all* the parts that are disordered; and to restore them by such mild and simple means as are calculated rather to solicit than to force their natural actions. In the case now more immediately under consideration—the morbid state entitled by Sir James Clark *Tubercular Cachexy*—we find almost every part of the system disordered, although some are much more so than others. There is an irregular distribution of the circulating fluids, of the nervous power, and of the animal temperature; the circulating fluids are themselves in an unhealthy state, and most of the secretions are depraved; the organs of digestion are particularly disordered; the skin and all the mucous surfaces are affected; and there exist local congestions, or irritations, or inflammations of the mucous surfaces, viscera, and internal blood-vessels. Now, is it to be supposed for a moment, that medicines, or any system of treatment that regards only one or two links of the chain, can stand any chance of removing a disorder at once so general and so deeply rooted? The experience of all the best physicians of the present day, and the results of our author's observations, recorded in the present work, and in his Treatise on Consumption, strengthen and confirm our own convictions, founded on long attention to the subject, in replying in the negative.

Art. VI.—*Lives of Eminent Foreign Statesmen.* By G. P. R. James, Esq. (Forming part of the Cabinet Cyclopædia). 5 vols. 12mo. London: 1838-40.

Mr. James, one of the most voluminous and rapid inventors of fictitious narratives, and tales of fancy, that any country or age has produced, is also known to the world, and not without some credit, as a devious labourer in the sober paths of historical inquiry—in which he has ranged over periods and reigns so widely separated, and so diverse, as those of Charlemagne and our William the Third—has, in the above work, produced a biographical collection in the loftiest walk of that department, and of such extent that years of laborious research and patient reflection might have been well employed in its composition. Yet, though neither possessing any new information, nor expressing any original or striking views regarding any of the illustrious names which it embraces, it may still be allowed to form a not unacceptable manual of the political biography of the Continent, for those who are satisfied with a tolerably agreeable and instructive account of personages frequently named, but whose lives and characters are but little known, except by the learned.

To go over so multifarious a collection, with any particularity of remark, would be altogether incompatible with our limits. Among the best of its sketches are those devoted to Barneveldt and De Witt; two statesmen who greatly adorn the annals of a country not over rich in such characters, and not so generally known as they deserve. We shall, therefore, content ourselves with a few notices and reflections regarding them—taking the latter first, as giving more effect to the observations we mean to introduce.

John De Witt, Grand Pensionary of Holland, is one of the very few unsuccessful statesmen—for such, on the whole, he must be considered—to whom merit of the highest order has been adjudged. But the wisdom of his views was so evident, and they were so ably elucidated and defended by himself, that posterity has done justice both to his abilities and his virtues, though the singular difficulties of his life prevented him from accomplishing the more important of his ends. His great anxiety was to preserve a peace which should enable Holland to rise to prosperity through the uninterrupted pursuit of commerce. Yet the whole of his official career was spent either in actual warfare, or in preparing for it. He laboured with zealous perseverance to secure the republican institutions of his country, by abolishing the anomalous office of Stadtholder; and by educating the young Prince of Orange to the moderate views and limited ambition befitting a citizen of a free state. Yet, before his death, that Prince was elected to the Stadtholderate, and his own brother was compelled to sign the ordinance for his appointment; and sixteen years afterwards, the same Prince became the sovereign of Holland's chief commercial rival, and only maritime superior.

His life extended over the most eventful portion of the seventeenth century. His birth was contemporaneous with the death of James I.; his death, with the commencement of that great reaction against royalty which drove James II. from his throne. He entered into public life soon after the accession of Louis XIV.; and resigned his official station shortly after that monarch had taken the reins of government into his own hands, and had begun to manifest that insatiable and desolating ambition, which made him, for half a century, the scourge of Europe. He lived through the most dangerous crisis of English liberty; and he died at the most flourishing period of the prosperity of France.

De Witt's father, one of the Deputies of the States of Holland, intended his son for the profession of the law; and the future statesman took his degree at the age of twenty-three. Mathematics was, however, his favourite pursuit; and, in this branch of study, he attained an eminence surpassed by few in that age. He is said to have been the author of a valuable treatise on the elements of *Curve Lines*. On his return from his travels, in the year 1650, his reputation as a student, combined with his father's influence, procured his nomination to the post of pensionary of Dort; from which, three years after, when only in his twenty-eighth year, he was promoted to the more important station of Grand Pensionary of Holland. It is not easy to ascertain the precise nature of this office, nor the powers which it conferred. It seems not improbable that its authority and importance depended, in a great measure, upon the abilities and the ambition of the individual who held it;—that he might be little more than the Secretary and official Adviser of the States;—or that he might be the soul and guide of all their deliberations. He might be the head, or he might be merely the hand. De Witt, and before him Barneveldt, seem to have had all the powers and authority of a Prime Minister. Sir William Temple thus speaks of the office in his *Account of the United Provinces:*—' The Pensioner of Holland is seated with the nobles, delivers their voice for them, and assists at all their deliberations before they come to the assembly. He is properly but the minister or servant of the province, and so his place or rank is behind all their deputies; but he has always great credit, because he is perpetual, or seldom discharged; though of right he ought to be chosen or renewed every fifth year. He has a seat in all the several assemblies of the province; and, in the States, propounds all matters, gathers the opinions, and forms or digests the resolutions; claiming, likewise, a power not to conclude any very important affair by plurality of voices, when he judges of his conscience he ought not to do it, and that it will be of ill consequence to the States."

At the time of De Witt's first accession to office, Holland was, to all appearance, both powerful and secure. Spain was governed by a weak sovereign, and had considerably impaired her strength, and wasted her resources, by a long war with France. England was just beginning to recover from the distraction of the Civil War. France was torn in pieces by the struggles of the *Fronde.* The energies of Holland had been greatly augmented by the long and successful contest she had waged for her independence. Her maritime strength had been much increased by the steady prosecution of commercial enterprise; and, from the same cause, her finances were, upon the whole, in a prosperous condition. The power of the House of Orange—the perpetual internal peril of the Republic—was centred in an infant of three years old, and thus all fear from that quarter was, for the present, at an end. The Dutch thought this a favourable moment for rebelling against those acknowledgments of her maritime superiority which England had so long and so rigorously exacted. They conceived their rival to be too much weakened by internal dissensions to offer any effectual resistance. Both the pride and the cupidity of the country were aroused; the partisans of the House of Orange spared no pains to fan the flame; and, in a short time, the passion for war with England became as general and as vehement in Holland, as the clamour for a war with Spain was, in our own country, in the time of Walpole. De Witt met the crisis with the wisdom and firmness which became a statesman. He was placed in a situation of singular difficulty, and of much temptation. He was young in office. He had yet a reputation to make. His country had, in a great measure, taken him on trust. It required no common sobriety to escape all contagion from the popular excitement, and no common fortitude to withstand the popular clamour. De Witt manfully opposed it. He felt that he was the servant of the interests, not of the passions, of his country. He urged all the considerations he could think of to turn it from its purpose. He dreaded a war for Holland on many grounds. He dreaded defeat; for he knew that England would prove a more powerful foe than his countrymen anticipated. He dreaded victory; for he knew that few circumstances have such a fatal operation in undermining republican institutions as a protracted, and especially a successful war. He grieved to see his country bent upon wasting, in fruitless quarrels, the wealth they had acquired by a long course of enterprise and labour. And he thought it a singular instance of infatuation, for the only two powerful republics then existing, to play the game of the ambitious monarchs who surrounded them, by mutually weakening each other. He pointed out all this, plainly and forcibly; and urged at the same time the signal advantages which would accrue both to commerce and freedom, from such an alliance with the Commonwealth of England as Cromwell was then

anxious to form. But his reasonings, though remembered afterwards, were unlistened to at the time. The hatred felt towards England was manifested in a variety of aggressions, which necessarily led to reprisals; and in 1652, before any declaration of war, the hostile fleets encountered in the Channel, and the Dutch were worsted in the engagement which ensued.

The councils of England were now directed, and her power wielded, by a man of very different mould from those monarchs who, for the last half century, had frittered away her energies and lowered her character. At first, success seemed pretty equally divided; but the fortunes of the war gradually inclined in favour of England; and a signal defeat sustained by their fleet, in which their admiral, Van Tromp, was slain, determined the Dutch to sue for peace. The advice and the predictions of De Witt were now remembered; and to him the negotiations were unreservedly confided. All that firmness and diplomatic skill could do, he effected; but the terms of peace were, as the fortune of the war had been, unfavourable to Holland; and the publication of them raised a storm of indignation against the Pensionary, which it required all his firmness to withstand. The wisdom of his views, however, the clearness of his arguments, and the strength of his character, had their due weight; and he persuaded the States-General to ratify the the treaty. But discontent and calumny were busy with his fame; his popularity suffered a severe check; and he early experienced how difficult it is for a man to serve his country at once faithfully and with impunity. The article of this treaty which was made the foundation of the fiercest outcry, was one suggested by Cromwell, and readily acceded to by De Witt, by which the Princes of the House of Orange were for ever excluded from the Stadtholderate. This agreement, as well as the Perpetual Edict, (a decree framed by him, and enacted in the year 1667, for abolishing for ever the office of Stadtholder), were attributed to personal enmity; and have, therefore, been regarded as blemishes upon his purity. We confess we can see no ground for this reproach.

In the first place, the office of Stadtholder was an anomaly in a Republic. He was a species of Dictator elected for life. He had a potential voice in the assemblies of the States; the power of pardoning convicted criminals; the entire command of all the forces of the confederacy by sea and land; and the virtual appointment of all naval and military officers, and of the magistrates in the principal towns. An office combining such varied and extensive powers, De Witt might justly consider to be fraught with peril to a republican government; especially when substantially a hereditary office, and held by a noble of immense possessions, and in whose single family centred all the aristocratic power of Zealand. Moreover, De Witt's distrust of that able and ambitious house was fully borne out by the experience of the past. The life and death of his predecessor Barneveldt, were fresh in his remembrance. The daring encroachments of Prince Maurice on the chartered liberties of the United Provinces were matters of recent history. The very year of De Witt's first nomination to office, had been marked by an outrage on freedom by William II. The privileges of the States had been violated in the person of his own father; whom, with five other deputies, that Prince had arrested and imprisoned, for venturing to protest against his unconstitutional aggressions. All these matters De Witt treasured in his memory; and his domestic policy was, from that time forward, directed to secure the State against any future recurrence of such perils. He was ardently attached to republican institutions, in spite of the fullest experience of their evils— or perhaps we should rather say their drawbacks; and he guarded, with a watchfulness almost amounting to jealousy, against the first approach of any danger which threatened either to undermine or overthrow them. Hence we are inclined to consider his pertinacious hostility to the power of the House of Orange, not only as unstained by any motives of personal ambition, but as entirely grounded in patriotism. A republic may, or may not, be a wise and beneficial form of government; but a republic, in which the post of military chief is held for life, and often hereditarily, by a powerful and ambitious noble, must be in hourly danger of destruction; and can only maintain its liberties by the most unwearied vigilance, and at the risk of perpetual discord.

The war with Sweden—a measure of very doubtful wisdom, but of eminent success—restored De Witt to the popularity he had lost by the peace with England; and the year 1660, which saw the restoration of Charles II. to the throne of his ancestors, the termination of hostilities between France and Spain, and the conclusion of a peace between Sweden, Holland, and Denmark, found De Witt in the zenith of his reputation; and his country respected abroad and prosperous at home.

Unhappily we have here to record an act which, though it does not appear to have called forth much disapprobation at the time, has undeniably clouded the otherwise bright fame of De Witt—an act dictated, we doubt not, by patriotic views, but which we must

think an unworthy postponement of justice to convenience—a sacrifice of honourable principle to present gain. Charles II., shortly after his restoration, brought to trial all the surviving republicans who had been concerned in the execution of his father; and inflicted the last punishment of the law on those he could seize. Three of these unhappy men had fled to Holland, to escape the fate of their comrades. Charles demanded that they should be given up. De Witt complied. They were arrested, transmitted to England, and executed. This is the single blot upon an otherwise stainless career. Holland was at that time prospering during a peace which De Witt was most anxious to preserve. He was then negotiating, with the aid of England, an advantageous commercial treaty with Portugal. Placed in a critical position between England and France, he was desirous, at almost any cost, to keep well with both. The advantages which might accrue to Holland from the friendship of Charles were numerous and palpable. If De Witt had risked a war with England by refusing the demand of Charles, thousands would have blamed his temerity— few would have appreciated his motives, or applauded his resolution. Yet, notwithstanding, we think that posterity has justly condemned his facility, as criminal and unwise; though we entirely acquit him of having been influenced by any considerations but a too exclusive regard to the material interests of his country. But we must bear in mind that patriotism is not by itself an excellence. It is an actuating motive, not a guiding principle. Like love, it is an affection, not a virtue. Like love, it may lead to base compliances, to a denial of justice, to a compromise of honour. Like love, it may manifest itself, as it did in ancient times, in a species of selfishness which, though less grovelling than that narrower affection which generally bears the name, is yet worthy of condemnation. A truly great statesman will never, though his life should be the cost, sacrifice principle to patriotic considerations. It was said of Andrew Fletcher, 'He would have died to serve his country; but he would not do a base thing to *save* it.'

Moreover, these exiles, however in some respects reprehensible, were not accused of any crime which the laws of all nations agreed in condemning. They had assisted in punishing, as they thought, a perfidious ruler. Assuredly, it was not for republicans, at any rate, to blame, or to desert them. De Witt must have looked upon the deed which they had committed only with approval. Had he been an Englishman, there can be little doubt that he would have sat with them at Whitehall on the day of retribution. The government which they had established, Holland had acknowledged. His desertion of these unhappy men we therefore think incapable of justification. History records many parallel transactions; but we know of none which has not met with reprobation.

The friendship which De Witt had stained his own and his country's reputation to preserve, proved but shortlived; and it must have been a bitter mortification to him to discover that the monarch, for whom he had sacrificed so much, was one whom no promise could bind, no principles govern, no services excite to gratitude. Between two commercial nations, like England and Holland, many points of rivalship continually subsisted; and there were not wanting individuals in either country anxious to push them to a bloody arbitrement. In spite of all De Witt's efforts, a series of reciprocal aggressions produced mutual exasperation, and in 1664 led to a declaration of war. The first great naval engagement was most disastrous to the Dutch; their fleet was almost annihilated, and their Admiral, Van Opdam, slain. The States lost no time in repairing their misfortune. De Witt was ordered to proceed to the Texel to superintend and hasten the equipment of a new fleet; and there he appears in a new character. Science has but seldom achieved so signal a triumph in public life. We will give the animating narrative in Mr. James' words:—

'He proceeded immediately to the Texel; and by immense exertions succeeded in preparing the fleet for departure, in a space of time which to others had seemed inadequate to accomplish one half of the task, and then, himself going on board, he pressed the admirals to put to sea at once.

'A new difficulty, however, now presented itself. De Witt was met by the reply, that the wind was unfavourable, and that there was no possibility of passing the difficult mouth of the Texel, unless a complete change took place. In this opinion all the Dutch seamen concurred; and showing De Witt the three passages which exist at the mouth of the Texel, called the Land's Diep, the Slenk, and the Spaniard's Gut, they informed him that it was only by the two former that vessels of any size could get to sea. Even these passages, they assured him, were only practicable when the wind blew steadily from one of ten points of the compass, while the other twenty-two points, they alleged, rendered the passage impossible. De Witt had nothing but theories to oppose to the practical knowledge of the seamen; but his mathematical skill enabled him to demonstrate, that if their charts laid down the passages correctly, any one of twenty-eight points of the compass would serve to carry the vessels out. Not satisfied with this discovery, he instantly conceived a doubt of the representations made regarding the three passages, and determined to ascertain whether

the Spaniard's Gut was not as practicable as the others. He proceeded thither in the long-boat of his vessel at the time of low water, and took the soundings along the whole of the passage with his own hand. The result fully justified his suspicions: he found that throughout its whole course the depth was at least double that which had been represented; that the banks and shallows, which the pilots had talked of, were entirely chimerical; and that it was, in fact, as safe and practicable as any of the three. The wind, according to his view, was perfectly favourable, especially for this passage; and on returning to the fleet, he announced to the officers his intention of instantly putting to sea through the very channel which they considered impassable.

'Of course he was not suffered to execute this resolution without strenuous opposition, and vehement remonstrances. All the elder seamen adhered to their opinion, and solemnly declared that the passage of the Spaniard's Gut was impracticable for large vessels; and that, even if it were not, the wind was unfavourable, and would not carry them out. De Witt took the responsibility upon himself; and to silence all further opposition, declared his purpose of leading the way in the largest vessel of the fleet. He accordingly weighed anchor on the 16th of August, 1665, and, with the wind at S.S.W., sailed without difficulty through the dreaded passage, followed in safety by the whole Dutch fleet. Though surprise might be mingled with some degree of mortification, the Dutch officers could not but respect the man they had unsuccessfully opposed; and from that day forward the passage, which he had been the first to open for the Dutch commerce, received the name of De Witt's Diep.'

After this fleet put to sea, there was a variety of indecisive expeditions and skirmishes; but it was not till June, 1666, that any important engagement took place. On the first of that month the hostile fleets encountered, and a battle, which lasted four days without intermission, terminated in favour of Holland. The following month, however, this temporary superiority was reversed; nearly the whole Dutch fleet being destroyed, and three Admirals slain. Negotiations for peace were immediately opened; and while they were proceeding, De Witt, taking advantage of the careless security into which the English had been lulled by their success, sent his brother and De Ruyter up the Thames; where they took Sheerness, burned many ships of the line, and spread such consternation through both court and country, that the Pensionary was enabled to conclude a peace on terms far more advantageous than could have been looked for, after such an unsuccessful war.

Up to this period, De Witt, though anxious to preserve peace with all his neighbours, had clung rather to the French than to the English alliance. England was a commercial and maritime rival; France was not. Moreover, the grasping and dangerous ambition of Louis XIV. had not yet fully developed itself; and the interposition of the Spanish Netherlands between Holland and France, De Witt always considered as a sufficient barrier against any attack from the latter power. But now his views were suddenly changed. With no previous notice, and in defiance of all previous engagements, Louis advanced a peremptory claim to the Spanish Netherlands; and prepared promptly to enforce it. De Witt was thunderstruck. He saw at once that, if Louis succeeded in his attempt, the independence of Holland would be placed in the most imminent and continual jeopardy. Single-handed, he had no power to prevent him; his only hopes lay in an alliance with England; and he succeeded in persuading that country that her interests, at this conjuncture, were identical with those of Holland. Many obstacles were interposed; but his frankness, earnestness, and skill removed them all; and, in a space of time almost incredibly brief, the celebrated Triple Alliance was formed between England, Holland, and Sweden. By it, the contracting powers bound themselves to mediate between France and Spain, and to compel Louis to relinquish his designs upon Flanders, on consideration of obtaining some more distant and less dangerous equivalent.

The real nature and merits of this celebrated treaty have been recently so fully discussed in this Journal, that we will not, at present, resume the question. It is certain that, at the time, the treaty was considered, on the part both of Temple and De Witt, as a masterpiece of policy. The armies of France were arrested, and the threatened danger averted for a season. Louis never forgave De Witt his share in the transaction.

It is impossible to read the details of the negotiation without entertaining the highest respect both for the sound sense and the noble character of De Witt. The effect which these qualities produced upon his fellow-diplomatist, Sir William Temple, is perhaps the strongest testimony to his merit. Not only did he speak of him at the time in terms of the sincerest esteem, but their intercourse laid the foundation of a friendship which continued till the close of De Witt's career, with as much warmth as it was in Temple's nature to feel. It is, however, by no means certain that the Triple Alliance was not more serviceable to the fame of De Witt than to the ultimate interests of his country.* We say this without

any wish to detract from the merits of this great statesman. We judge after the event. At the time when he had to make a choice, every path was fraught with danger. But the course he took resulted (though by no fault of his) in the greatest peril that Holland had ever encountered. He had to make his election between two powerful neighbours, of whose characters, ambition and faithlessness then formed, respectively, the prominent features. His decision was prompt. He chose to quarrel with an ally—a dangerous and ambitious one, it is true—but one whose friendship, though never zealous, had hitherto been tolerably steady; and he threw himself almost unreservedly into the arms of one, of whose selfishness, levity, and perfidy, he had recent and ample experience. He confided too readily in British honour and British promises. Faithful, honest, and straightforward himself, in his dealings with others he was watchful, but not suspicious. With all his experience of men and monarchs, there were depths of baseness and dishonour in the character of Charles which he had not fathomed, and could not be expected to fathom. The ink was scarcely dry in which the perpetual alliance between England and Holland had been signed, when a series of intrigues commenced—unexampled for meanness and profligacy—which ended in Charles accepting subsidies from France, which he wasted on his pleasures, and which he purchased by a secret agreement with Louis for a simultaneous attack on Holland. This De Witt had not expected. He was entitled to conceive that the Triple Alliance would insure at least a somewhat longer period of security and repose; and, though he had paid great attention to the condition of the navy, he does not appear to have acted so watchfully or energetically in the re-organization of the army, as he would have done, had he feared so speedy a renewal of the French designs upon Flanders. The storm burst upon him with a suddenness and violence for which he was not prepared. The English, not content with violating their solemn engagements, trampled upon all the principles of international law, by attacking the Dutch fleet before hostilities had been declared. Louis at the same moment issued his Manifesto, and began his march. The Hollanders were terror-stricken; and, as in the case of other panics, rage mingled with fear, and they began to look about them for a victim, whose sacrifice might allay the storm.

---

* 'It is probable,' says Sir James Mackintosh, 'that the Triple Alliance was the result of a fraudulent project, suggested originally by Gourville to ruin De Witt, by embroiling him with France beyond the probability of reconciliation.'—*History of the Revolution of* 1688.

They complained vehemently of the Pensionary, whom they accused of having first endangered the country by his measures, and then neglected its defence. In spite of his opposition, they raised William III., Prince of Orange, to the rank of Captain-General. This was in February, 1672. In July, they abolished the Perpetual Edict, and elected him to the Stadtholderate. The popular clamour, both against John de Witt and the Admiral his brother, now became loud and general. They were assailed with the most cruel calumnies. The Pensionary was attacked at night, and severely wounded. The Admiral was arrested on the accusation of a man whose infamy was notorious; and, though suffering at the time under severe illness, was put to the torture. His innocence was clearly manifested on his trial; but a corrupt Judicature, swayed by personal enmity and the public outcry, condemned him to banishment in the same sentence which acquitted him of crime. The Pensionary, indignant at the unworthy treatment his brother had met with, went in state to the prison to receive him, on his leaving it to go into exile. It was rumoured that he went to rescue him; and an infuriated crowd collected round the prison doors, calling for the two brothers to be delivered up to them. The civil and military authorities were informed of the tumult, but did nothing to allay it. The mob broke into the prison, and massacred, with every circumstance of savage barbarity, the two brothers, who, more than any men then living, had deserved well of their country.

The Prince of Orange has been sometimes charged with having been, in some measure, privy to this horrible occurrence. But stronger evidence than has ever yet been adduced, would be necessary to fix so black an accusation on so great a man. Certain it is, however, that many circumstances of his conduct in relation to the De Witts, show him forth in a most unamiable light—to use no harsher term. De Witt had, it is true, done all in his power to exclude him from the Stadtholderate. But William was, notwithstanding, under very weighty obligations to him. He had superintended his political education. He had laid the foundation of much of his future eminence as a statesman. They had long lived on terms of the strictest amity together. Yet when De Witt was assailed by two midnight assassins, one only was punished. The other was not only allowed to escape, but was suffered to retain his employments; and was even favoured by the government of which the Prince of Orange was the chief, and the right arm. When De Witt applied to the Prince to lend the weight of his voice to the contradiction of calumnies of whose falsehood no one could be more fully sensible, William coldly replied, that the Pensionary must learn to bear slander, as he himself had done. He suffered Cornelius de Witt to be imprisoned and tortured, on an accusation which he must have disbelieved; and to be banished for a crime of which he knew him to be innocent; when a word of disapproval would have prevented the perpetration of either injustice. And, without going so far as to say, (for which we assuredly should have no sufficient grounds), that he rejoiced in the death of these virtuous citizens; it is certain that he neither exerted himself to prevent the murder, nor to punish the murderers, as he must have done, had he been under the influence, at the time, of any strong feelings either of humanity or justice.

Reflections of various kinds may be supposed to arise on the contemplation of such an occurrence. 'The catastrophe of De Witt,' says Mr. Fox, ' the wisest, the best, the most truly patriotic minister that ever appeared upon the public stage—as it was an act of the most crying injustice and ingratitude, so likewise it is the most completely *discouraging example* that history affords to the lovers of liberty. If Aristides was banished, he was also recalled. If Dion was repaid for his services to the Syracusans by ingratitude, that ingratitude was more than once repented of. If Sydney and Russell died upon the scaffold, they had not the cruel mortification of falling by the hands of the people. Ample justice was done to their memory; and the very sound of their names is still animating to every Englishman attached to their glorious cause. But with De Witt fell alike his cause and his party; and, although a name respected by all who revere wisdom and virtue when employed in their noblest sphere, the political service of the people, yet I do not know that even to this day any public honours have been paid by them to his memory.' This, however, with deference be it said, is scarcely the proper light in which such facts ought to be viewed. They have a moral meaning of a loftier kind. If we deduce from the lamentable catastrophe of De Witt's career only the pusillanimous wisdom of retiring from a field where peril is to be encountered, as well as honour to be reaped, and of devoting to the enjoyment and embellishment of private life powers which, otherwise employed, might have influenced for good the destinies of thousands—assuredly we do not read aright that most instructive passage. The true lesson to be deduced from his useful life, and its melancholy close, is the almost certain disappointment of all who, in serving their country, look for their only reward in their country's gratitude. The statesman who, in treading the slippery path of politics, is sustained and guided alone by the hope of fame, or the desire of a lofty reputation, will not only find himself beset with incessant temptations to turn aside.from the line of strict integrity ; but the disappointment he is sure to meet with will probably drive him to misanthropy—perhaps even irritate him to tarnish, by vindictive treachery, a virtue founded upon no solid or enduring principle. But the statesman who looks, in the simple performance of his duty, for consolation and support amid all the toils and sufferings which that duty may call him to encounter—who aims not at popularity, because he is conscious that continued popularity rarely accompanies systematic and unyielding integrity—who, as he is urged to no questionable measures by the hope of fame, so is deterred from none that are just by the fear of censure—such a man may steer a steady course through the shoals and breakers of the stormiest sea ; and whether he meet with the hatred or the gratitude of his countrymen, is to him a consideration of minor moment, for his reward is otherwise sure. He has laboured with constancy for great objects. He has conferred signal benefits upon his fellow-men. Nobler occupation man cannot aspire to ; sublimer power no ambition need desire ; greater reward it would be very difficult to obtain.

It is impossible not to be struck with the many points of similarity between this wise and virtuous man, and and another who preceded him in the same office, pursued a nearly similar career, and whose course was terminated by an equally deplorable catastrophe.

John Van Olden Barneveldt achieved for his country that independence which John De Witt consolidated and preserved. Both held the office of Grand Pensionary for a long series of years. Both were occupied during a considerable portion of their lives in resisting the actual or expected encroachments of the House of Orange. Though bred to a peaceful profession, both were compelled by the necessities of their country to take an active part in the wars which it had perpetually to wage, in defence of its infant liberties. And, after a career of laborious and patriotic services, both suffered a violent death at the hands of those who were most indebted to their labours :—the one was massacred by the people he had saved from servitude; the other was executed on the scaffold by the sect which he had rescued from persecution—perhaps from extinction—by the oppressive bigotry of Spain.

Barneveldt was one of those fortunate individuals who may be said to have appeared at the right time. He was by character and talent peculiarly suited to the period, and to the stage on which he was called to act a part. That period was one of those that rarely fails to call into activity powers which, in more tranquil times, would have remained undeveloped or latent. His early education, his clear sense, his practical and sober turn of thought, his resolute will, his stern and energetic perseverance—all contributed to rank him with that class of men whom nature has formed for the government of free countries. And he fell upon the century of all others in modern times (save one), the most prolific of deep emotions, and the most fertile in great events ;—when the first effectual shock was given to the old system of opinions ; when religious dissension became the nurse of civil liberty ; and when statesmen were summoned to the delicate and most difficult task of constructing new formulas of faith, and new modes of government, out of the shattered relics of those which the great convulsion had destroyed. Barneveldt was early destined for the law, and he studied successively at the schools of the Hague, Louvain, and Heidelberg. In the year 1570, he began to practise as an advocate at the Hague, where his talents and connections soon procured him an ample share of professional employment. But the times were not such as to allow men of his stamp to pursue their profession in peace. The long and protracted contest between the Low Countries and Philip II., of Spain, had begun about five years before. Charles V. had always treated this portion of his dominions with peculiar favour and regard. He had respected their privileges and encouraged their commerce. Philip regarded them with very different feelings, and pursued towards them a directly opposite course. His predominant passions were, a superstitious bigotry and an insatiable thirst of power. The Low Countries offended both these ruling sentiments. The rapid spread of the Reformed doctrines in those marts of commerce and intelligence, inflamed his gloomy zeal and irritated his persecuting temper. And the constitutional rights of the Netherlands, which had been solemnly guaranteed to them by innumerable treaties, by opposing constant limitations to the exercise of his prerogative, goaded to fury his despotic disposition. He soon decided what course he should pursue. He was not of a character to shrink from any undertaking, or to scruple at any means. Disregarding alike the murmurs of the people, and the remonstrances of the nobles, he proceeded to establish the Inquisition in the Netherlands; and commenced a persecution which, both for its severity and its important consequences, is without a parallel in history. Many were imprisoned —many were tortured—numbers fled into exile—thousands were delivered over to the executioner. Still, the Duchess of Parma, to whom Philip had committed the government of the Low Countries, did not, as he conceived, execute his edicts with sufficient rigour. She was, therefore, superseded by the notorious Duke of Alva. He brought with him a considerable reinforcement, uncontrolled authority, and a character and temper cast in the mould of his master. He commenced his career of bloodshed and oppression without an hour's delay. A hundred thousand emigrants carried their skill and enterprise to foreign lands. The Prince of Orange retired into Germany. Counts Egmont and Horn were imprisoned and executed. All who were even suspected of having listened to the new opinions were seized, tortured, and burned—often without even the form of a trial. To have been once seen at a Conventicle was sufficient to insure condemnation. Philip rejoiced to hear of these proceedings. He had at length found a Deputy after his own heart. The man who had murdered his own son, could not be expected to feel compassion for the sufferings of distant heretics. He wrote to approve and encourage Alva. Then were committed oppressions too grievous to be endured—barbarities which the decorum of history refuses to describe—atrocities which the execrations of ages have left inadequately censured. Not a city throughout the Low Countries but witnessed the infliction of tortures, compared with which those of the Roman amphitheatre were merciful and gentle. The Prince of Orange and others of the exiled nobility now thought it high time to appeal to arms; and, after collecting all the forces they could draw together, invaded the Netherlands, and were for a short period signally successful. But they were ably opposed, and feebly supported; and, after a short campaign, were obliged to retire and disband their forces till a more favourable conjuncture should arise. They had not to wait long. Alva was in want of money, and, in an evil hour for his master's interests, resolved to tax the people without the consent of the States. The inhabitants of the Low Countries, who had borne everything else with comparative submission, stoutly resisted the attack upon their purses. They flew to arms, seized several of the principal towns, chose the Prince of Orange for their leader; and after a war which lasted with various fortune nearly forty years, succeeded in establishing the independence of the Northern Provinces, and the supremacy in them of the Protestant Religion.

In this great struggle it was of course impossible, and it would have been pusillanimous, for any one to remain neutral; and Barneveldt and his brethren of the Bar were called upon to make their election between unqualified submission to the iron yoke of Philip, and the chance of whatever amount of freedom a vigorous resistance might procure. They were nearly unanimous, to the lasting discredit of their profession be it recorded, in counselling submission to Spain. Three Advocates only, of whom Barneveldt was one, adhered to the Prince of Orange. So able and resolute a patriot was not likely to remain long unemployed. As a Commissary, he superintended the arming of the citizens in the revolted provinces, the levying of contributions, and the providing supplies for the troops. At the early age of twenty-nine, he was chosen Pensionary of Rotterdam; and from this time forward his services were in constant requisition, wherever activity, perseverance, and diplomatic skill were required. In the year 1586 he was promoted to the highest civil office in the United Provinces, that of Grand Pensionary—an appointment which he continued to hold till his death, a period of thirty-three years.

Barneveldt has been charged with inconsistency, by those whose only notion of consistency lies in maintaining through life the same relative position—not with regard to the object of their efforts, but with regard to the individuals with whom they have been accustomed to act. The object to which the whole of his public life was devoted, was the freedom of his country. He desired to liberate her from the yoke of Prince Maurice, as well as from the yoke of Philip. For this, up to the year 1607, he was incessantly engaged in urging his countrymen to a vigorous prosecution of the war. For this he spared no pains to negotiate a peace, as soon as it became probable that the recognition of his country's independence might be one of the articles of the treaty. For this, he persuaded the States to confer on Maurice all the authority of a military chief, as the leader most likely to offer a successful resistance to the arms of Spain. For this, he became the resolute opponent of that Prince, as soon as he discovered that he aimed at a continuance of the war as the surest means of obtaining the objects of his personal ambition; and for this he incurred that virulent and untiring hatred, which finally brought him to the scaffold. In whatever quarter might gather the dangers which successively menaced his country, he turned undismayed to meet them. When the whole power of Spain was exerted to crush the rising liberties of Holland, Barneveldt was the presiding spirit that guided and invigorated her councils. In equipping her troops, in advising her measures, in directing her campaigns, in forming her alliances, he was indefatigable. When her rights were invaded by the Earl of Leicester whom Elizabeth had sent over to command her auxiliary forces, Barneveldt withstood him, with a spirit as haughty and firmer than his own. When the ambition of Maurice, Prince of Orange, was the especial peril of the hour, the Grand Pensionary bent all his energies to defeat his schemes. And when, towards the close of his career, the Gomarites strove to establish the supremacy of the *Ecclesiastical* over the *Civil* authority, they found the aged statesman at his post, as resolute, alert, and inflexible as ever, to oppose a pretension so fatal to good government and free institutions.

After thirty-three years of indefatigable exertion, Barneveldt had the satisfaction of concluding a twelve years' truce with Spain ; by which the independence of the United Provinces was virtually, though not formally acknowledged. During the whole of this period his labours had been arduous and unremitting. He had not only to contend against foreign enemies, and to control domestic ambition, but to negotiate various alliances, and conduct an extensive and complicated correspondence ; and, what was perhaps more difficult and harassing than all the rest, to reconcile the dissensions which were continually breaking out between the various States and Cities of the Union, and to persuade each to bear with cheerfulness its fair share of the burdens of the war. It is with respect to the latter, that the peculiar difficulties of the leaders in a revolution consist. They are destitute of all usual expedients of an established government. They cannot rely upon the ordinary means of established authority. They rule over free citizens, not over subjects. They command volunteers, not regular troops. They have no power to enforce the decrees which they enact. They must temporize, cajole, persuade. They must stimulate the sluggish—rouse the ambitious—persuade the selfish—work upon the fears of the timid—excite the cupidity of the avaricious—soothe the susceptibilities of the jealous. These were the chief difficulties of Washington, as they were of Barneveldt ; and neither the Dutch nor the American patriot had characters peculiarly adapted to the task. Both were somewhat unbending and austere ; and Barneveldt, in particular, was impetuous and somewhat overbearing. Neither possessed those insinuating manners which en-

able men easily to gain the confidence, and to obtain influence over the purposes of others. But both possessed, in an eminent degree, the power to discern light through the darkest clouds, and to hope when all around despair. This is that habitude of mind to which the Roman senators paid such politic respect, when they greeted Varro, after the defeat of Cannæ, with eulogy instead of censure ; and thanked him, because even in that hour of consternation, ‘ he had not despaired of the Republic.’

It might be imagined that Barneveldt, having now attained the great object of his public exertions, and having so served his country as to entitle himself to her lasting gratitude, would have been suffered to repose upon his laurels, and to pass the remainder of his days in tranquillity—enjoying that best reward of a virtuous and enlightened statesman, the contemplation of the happiness and prosperity he has been instrumental in creating. At this period Geneva was the most celebrated theological school of the Reformers. During the revolutionary period, while Holland was struggling at once for her liberty and her religion, numbers of the Dutch clergy had fled to Geneva, partly as a place of refuge, partly as a school of learning. When peace was restored, and the Reformed faith established in their native country, these men returned, filled with a spirit the most domineering and intolerant. The peace of the country was grievously disturbed by the feuds which they created ; and the States-General were at length compelled to interfere. They acted, on the whole, with the moderation and good sense of statesmen, though certainly with little knowledge of the temper of theological disputants. By the advice of Barneveldt, they recommended a National Synod, for the purpose of devising a Confession and a Ritual that might satisfy all parties. The Church indignantly repudiated the suggestion, and the controversy was continued with as much bitterness as ever. The disputants again appealed to the States, who, being then intent upon the negotiations for independence, put them aside, and peremptorily ordered them ‘ to be quiet, and tolerate each other.’ The Calvinists insisted on the establishment of a religious creed, and the ejectment of all who refused to receive it. At length, wearied out with their importunity, the States called the two leaders of the chief opposing sects, Gomar and Arminius, before them, and desired to have an explanation of their differences. The case was argued with great vehemence, and at considerable length ; and, after both parties had been fully heard, Barneveldt rose, in the name of the States-General, and addressing the contending disputants in a tone of grave sarcasm, 'thanked God that there was no 'material difference between them;' and earnestly recommended them to seek after peace and mutual brotherhood. Both parties were somewhat disconcerted at this solemn depreciation of their grounds of quarrel; and, as divines, were but little disposed to receive the lessons of Christian charity from the lips of a civilian. They retired, as was to be expected, as little satisfied as ever.

Barneveldt, it may well be imagined, was a man but little disposed to join either party in their profitless disputes. He would have been inclined, of course, to have observed a cautious neutrality between the disputants; had he not early discovered among the Calvinistic clergy an encroaching spirit, and a disposition to raise the Ecclesiastical to a supremacy over the Civil authority in the state. The philosophic statesman could smile at the quarrels of schoolmen regarding the solution of problems too intricate for human reason, and involving no practical results; but the doctrine of Ecclesiastical Supremacy was one, he well knew, which, in the hands of such men as then filled the pulpits of the United Provinces, would lead to consequences to which no lover of his country could look with composure. He therefore threw the whole weight of his influence into the opposing scale; and besought the Stadtholder, Prince Maurice, to aid him in suppressing the existing dissensions. That Barneveldt favoured one party was, however, a sufficient motive with that wily and vindictive Prince to throw himself into the arms of its antagonists. He at once perceived the support he might secure to his own designs by espousing the Calvinistic cause; and, from this time forward, he laboured with unwearied perseverance to undermine the influence, and effect the ruin of the aged Pensionary—now the only serious obstacle between himself and the supreme power, at which he aimed. He was abetted in all his schemes by the zeal and activity of the Calvinistic clergy.

As too often happens, the greatest service which Barneveldt had ever rendered to his country, proved also the most fatal blow to his own popularity; for his conclusion of the long truce with Spain was the point from which we may date the decline of his influence in Holland. It would be to little purpose to trace the various steps by which Maurice gradually undermined the reputation, and weakened the authority of his hated opponent. The army and the populace were already devoted to him; and he at length succeeded, by dint of unwearied intrigue, in ejecting the Arminian magistrates in almost every city and province in the Union, and replacing them by ardent Gomarites; and, in spite of all the Pensionary's opposition, he procured a decree for disarming the Burgher Guards. The States of Holland were now the only support on which Barneveldt could rely, and they firmly upheld their venerable and tried servant. But Maurice contrived to procure a new election, and deputies of a very different stamp were returned—creatures of the Prince, and ready to go all lengths in pandering to his ambition. It now became evident, even to himself, that his career was fast drawing to a close. On the 29th of August, 1618, he was arrested by order of the Prince, and after an illegal delay of five months—spent in collecting charges and procuring evidence against him—he was brought to trial. The Judges were named by his great political opponent. His falsest accuser, his bitterest personal foe, sat amongst them. The trial was conducted with such secrecy, that we are left to guess at the articles of accusation. The verdict of the Judges was pronounced while the aged prisoner was engaged in preparing his defence. The result was notified to him on the evening of the 12th of May; and by a refinement of cruelty and insult, a Gomarite clergyman—a zealous enemy—was sent to embitter his last hour. He came, he said, by order of the States, to prepare and console the prisoner. Barneveldt calmly replied, that at his age he was prepared to die, and was able to console himself. Early the following morning, he was called before his Judges to hear his sentence pronounced—a sentence containing a number of charges, all vague, and all either frivolous or absurd—to which he listened with scornful but dignified composure; and then was led straight from the judgment-hall to the scaffold. His last words were—'Good people, do not believe I am a traitor!'

Thus fell, in the seventy-third year of his age, and the forty-fourth of his public services, Olden Barneveldt; not certainly a perfect man, but one who approached as near to perfection as the hard conditions of our nature will allow. He had no failings but such as naturally rose out of his excellences, or were essentially connected with them. His unwearied energy and intensity of purpose, made him somewhat impetuous, and intolerant of vexatious or interested opposition. His inflexible resolution in the pursuit of great objects, was connected with a temper unyielding even in matters of minor importance. And if he was too strongly convinced of the wisdom and integrity of his own views, to meet intrigue with patience, or to bear calumny with calmness, much must be forgiven to one endowed with no common powers—intent upon no common aims—conscious of no common rectitude. ' If,' says he, in his Apology, 'when arguments were urged irrationally, or with open and indecent falsehood, I found myself unable.to digest them, and answered such impertinence too bitterly, I beg that this may be pardoned to my great age, and to human infirmity.'

To which of the two great men, whose characters we have been considering, the crown of merit ought to be adjudged, it would be as difficult as invidious to endeavour to determine. Both were gifted with talents and virtues of no ordinary cast. Their reputation was founded, not upon one or two brilliant deeds, which might be but the happy inspirations of a moment, but upon the untiring exertions of a devoted and laborious life. On one account, however, we are disposed to estimate more highly the heroic integrity of the earlier and elder statesman. De Witt was unencumbered by any family ties. Barneveldt had a wife and children. Therefore, though not perhaps a happier man, he may reasonably be supposed to have held his life more dearly; for life is commonly valued, not in proportion to its enjoyments, but in proportion to its interests, its cares, its anxieties. Moreover, a domestic circle naturally breeds in the character a love of comfort; and the more we become accustomed to the enjoyments of life, the less disposed we are to risk them. The habitual indulgence, the constant calling forth of the gentler affections, have an irresistible tendency to relax the tone of stern and lofty, but steady and subdued enthusiasm, which alone can enable the statesman to steer his course aright in dangerous and troubled times. And when we consider how many occasions must occur, where a slight deviation from lofty principle might be the means of avoiding danger, of disarming enmity, of preserving a life dear and valuable to others, we shall look with a ready sympathy and a generous indulgence upon those who, in such trials, have been found wanting; and shall regard those who, like Barneveldt, have passed through the ordeal unfaltering and triumphant, with a proportionate veneration.* With De Witt the case was different, and the task, in consequence, incalculably easier. He had a father whom he loved, and a brother who ran

the same patriotic career with himself. But there were no helpless and confiding beings depending upon him alone for support. His line of duty, though arduous, was clear and single. There were no side influences to draw him away from that line. He had but one object of affection or desire—one faith, one aim; and to these he was faithful to the end.

———

ART. VII.—*Christian Morals.* By the Rev. W. Sewell, M.A., Fellow and Tutor of Exeter College, and Professor of Moral Philosophy in the University of Oxford. 8vo. London: 1840.

This is a book which, if we had fallen in with it at an old book stall, we might have picked up as a strange instance of the length to which the ravings and hallucinations of an individual may go. But considering it as the appointed teachings of a University Professor—and not only that, but as part of a collection which clergymen of the Church of England are engaged in circulating under the much-abused name of 'The Englishman's Library'—it has filled us with amazement. We had hoped that the University itself, or some of its members, would have put forth a disclaimer. But as this is not the case, and as the book remains before the world, with all the authority which ought to belong to the Chair of Moral Philosophy at Oxford, it is fitting that the non-academic public should be informed what sort of moral teaching an English University provides. We believe the instruction in Latin and Greek, the mere scholarship of Oxford, to be very good; but the genius of the place appears to be in irreconcilable hostility with most of the elements of modern civilisation. It looks as if a fatality hung over its walls, with regard to everything relating to real life. What Oxford loyalty would have made of the British Constitution, if it had had its way, is matter of history. The real friends of the Reformation are pretty well aware, by this time, what would have been the use of a Reformation at all, if nothing else had been to be got by it but the odds and ends which Oxford divinity would leave us now. An honest man out of Bedlam will learn, from the writings of Mr. Sewell, Tutor of Exeter College, and late Professor of Moral Philosophy to the University, the nature, means, and object of Oxford morals.

---

* Of the wife of Barneveldt only one anecdote is preserved to us; but that one indicates a character worthy of the name she bore. Some time after Barneveldt's death, his two sons were executed for a conspiracy against Prince Maurice. Their mother threw herself at the feet of Maurice to petition for their pardon. ' How is it,' asked that unfeeling enemy, ' that you will beg that mercy for your sons that you refused to solicit for your husband?' ' Because,' replied the widow, ' my husband was innocent, and my sons are guilty!'

There never was a writer less entitled to notice on his own account, except as a curiosity, than Mr. Sewell. But his connection with Oxford—the fact that the University has indorsed his bills and guaranteed his credit—makes him a person of importance on this occasion. We cannot omit the opportunity of protesting against the unprincipled way in which that learned body has compromised its reputation, and violated the trust reposed in it by so doing. The scandals of patronage, it is true, have nowhere ranged with wilder license than over every department of public education. The Church, which ought to be the great public teacher, has been jobbed, until the existence of the Church of Scotland is put in peril by the evil and the remedy ; and until the Churches of England and of Ireland can, in many quarters, no longer show the noblest title by which Christ announced that his religion* was to be known ‘ the poor have the gospel preached unto them.’ Well might Paley complain, ‘ that the converting the best share of the revenues of the church (the proper fund for maintaining those who are occupied in cultivating or communicating religious knowledge) into annuities for the gay and illiterate youth of great families, threatens to stifle the little clerical merit that is left among us.’ But if lay patrons are bad, ecclesiastical patrons are, if anything, worse. The misconduct of

---

* The Bishop of London has lately published three ‘ Sermons on the Church.’ Oxford divinity disposes us to be very thankful to him for his comparative moderation. But we must remonstrate on the part of Scotch Episcopalians, as well as of English Protestant Dissenters, against the narrowness of the test by which the Bishop tries the guilt of *schism.* ‘ No man (he says) can justify his voluntary separation from the National Church, but upon the ground that she requires of him the profession of some article of faith at variance with the fundamental truths of the Gospel, or the performance of some act of worship, forbidden, either expressly or implicitly, by the Word of God !’ There is to our minds another justification, less applicable, to be sure, on account of the class to which they respectively belong—to Episcopal seceders from the Church of Scotland—than to the great majority of Protestant seceders from the Church of England ;—we mean that they do not find the ministrations of the National Church so spiritually profitable as those of their own chapels. If Dr. Johnson could admit, with tears in his eyes, the justice of Hannah More’s defence of her dissenter-reading, the mechanic and the servant-maid, it is to be hoped, may be excused for going on a Sunday where they feel that they receive most good. The truth is, that the intellectual as well as social habits of most English clergymen have made them in many ways above their work. As to educating the poor, Dr. Arnold has said, ‘ I never knew any poor man who could properly be said to be educated.’

the Universities in this respect is so flagrant, that no man in his senses, founding a Professorship, would place it at their disposal. Private motives, good, bad, and indifferent, uniformly get the better of all public considerations. Merit is the last thing thought of. At Cambridge, for instance, a member of St. John’s College, competent or incompetent, may make sure of any University office which the votes of his college can command. At Oxford, not long ago, the newspapers were full, for weeks together, of the election of a Professor of Poetry. Not a word of the proper qualifications of the candidates. The election was turned into a trial of party strength, and nothing else, between the two religious parties which divide the University at present. Personal or party motives of this description must have the discredit of having made Mr. Sewell Professor of Morals ; a science, above all others, requiring calmness and caution, a clear comprehensive understanding, and a loving heart. Neither is arrogance the temper, nor a kind of Irish eloquence the talent, wanted. Any page of the book at which its readers may have the luck to open, will satisfy them, not only that the writer of it has a mind intellectually incapable of distinguishing truth from falsehood, but that he could never have had five minutes conversation with any body upon any serious subject, without this most striking disqualification coming out. When we give Mr. Sewell five minutes to expose himself in, we are sure that we give him time enough. For this purpose, it will be all the same whether he shall have been expounding to his friends the theories on Christian art and Christian politics, with which he encourages mankind to hope that he may live to complete his theory of Christian morals ; or whether he shall have been dilating on the only way in which, as he conceives, Natural Philosophy can be cultivated with any reasonable prospect of success. His contempt for modern science, and for the drudges digging in its mines for facts, will have prevented him from communicating with the British Association concerning the methods by which alone discoveries are to be made. But this is clear. His chapter upon the subject (ch. 22) is either greater nonsense than Swift or Munchausen durst have attributed to the academy of Laputa, or the *Novum Organum* is nothing to it. Our readers must say which.

It is declared, that Theology is the root and mother of all knowledge ; and ‘ that the sciences which relate to matter ought to be studied upon Christian principles and methods, just as much as the sciences which relate to mind.' This being assumed, the chapter consists of two propositions : First, the human mind, unless it be supported by a theological creed, is incapable of making a successful effort upon any subject. Next, from their inseparable connection with the facts with which all science has to deal, the Scriptures, duly studied and applied, are the appropriate guide to every species of scientific truth. If the first of these propositions is true, no man can trust to his understanding for any purpose—and especially no man of science can expect his understanding to stand him in any stead in scientific inquiries—unless he has first settled his religious creed to the satisfaction of Mr. Sewell. If the second proposition is true, Sir David Brewster and Dr. Whewell may save themselves the trouble of discussing whether discoverers in science can be assisted in their noble labours by any rules. They have only to read their Bibles properly, and they will find the key to the secrets of nature there. Now for the proofs of such astounding communications.

That a religious creed is necessary to preserve a man in the use of his faculties, is demonstrated as follows. Without a religious creed there can be no active moral principle ; and without an active moral principle, 'the very highest productions of the human intellect are just as much the result of circumstances, and the work of chance, (*as what?*) as a piece of cotton which comes out of a mill.' Again, 'the whole earth, every night about twelve o'clock, becomes a vast lunatic asylum,' and it is supposed, that man in his lucid intervals—that is, in his waking hours—would be precisely in the same state but for the control of the moral principle—in other words (for they are spoken of as synonymous); but for the influence of a religious creed. Our experience is appealed to for the truth of this statement. ' Scarcely anything has been done in the present day for the real advancement of science by speculative men.' A religious paralysis, it is assumed, has struck their understandings. ' Whatever discoveries have been made in that machinery which is our chief boast, have been made by common workmen by accident. It is a notorious fact.' Let the Wattses and Babbages attend. The world has been giving them credit on false pretences. Their calculations are an affair of chance.

The limits within which Mr. Sewell's disciples are allowed to look for their religious creed, are small indeed ; but stretch these limits from the east unto the west, and was there ever before printed, in any age or country, such a prodigy of falsehood as, not merely that men without religion were for the ordinary business of life no more to be depended upon than lunatics or somnambulists, but that the probabilities of a successful exercise of our intellectual powers, on whatever subject they are applied, rise or fall with the nature of our religious opinions. A moment's consideration[*] of the difference between speculative and practical reason, and of the subjects on which they are respectively exercised—and how the will, and the infirmities thereto belonging, only attach to subjects of practical as distinguished from subjects of speculative reason, would with most people have prevented all this folly. That this would not have been the case with Mr. Sewell, is but too true ; since he says, what are termed the *speculative* doctrines of the Church, are falsely termed so : and that in one instance, morals, Bishop Butler has shown ' the Athanasian Creed to be as much the basis of Christian morality, so far as morality is a part of religion, and religion a part of morality, as the Ten Commandments.'

The use to be made, in physical investigations, of the nature, attributes, and moral government of God, is illustrated more in detail.

Before we give our readers a specimen of these details, we must observe, as Pitt observed to Wilberforce on returning him Bishop Butler's celebrated treatise, that there is nothing which *Analogy* may not prove, if it is admitted as a mode of positive proof. Its proper sphere is to remove out of the way objections, whether founded on *à priori* or other reasoning, or on supposed evidence of improbability, ill applied. If this be so, what alone can be the consequence, even in the most prudent hands, of searching for similitudes between things which have nothing in common except their common author ? More especially does the folly of quoting Scriptural analogies, on the ground of the supposed connection of Scripture facts 'with every other branch of facts in every other

---

[*] Mr. Sewell likes the parade of obsolete learning. He will nowhere see this difference better put, than in the Prima Secundæ of Thomas Aquinas.— Quæst. xciv.

science,' become quite incredible, when everybody allows that much of the precise and positive language of Scripture concerning physics, as well as many of its precedents in moral and social life, are in direct contradiction with those physical truths and moral duties upon which all mankind are now agreed. The Scriptures are not the less true for their own great purpose, whatever we may think of the Astronomy and Geology which are contained in them—and whether we adopt or not Paley's explanation of the wars of Canaan, or Milton's panegyric on the polygamous marriage bed 'as Saints and Patriarchs used.'

A study of the facts with which a particular science has to deal, will be constantly suggesting to inventive minds different hypotheses or leading ideas, among which the law of their relation is likely to be found. It is part of the divination of genius, to ascertain with the least possible cost of time and labour, which of these seeds will grow. In hammering away at nature, there will be greatly too many chips in the case even of the best workmen. But the best workman will have the fewest. Mr. Sewell, we fear, is all chips. His dogmas are—first, that there can be no physical science without religion; next, that whether any kind of science can emerge under a religion, partly true and partly false, will depend on the nature of the errors; and lastly, that the leading ideas which will take philosophers by the shortest and most infallible cut to all truths, physical or metaphysical, are latent in the Scriptures, if philosophers have but religion enough to find them out. 'All the great discoveries of speculative men have been made by first taking some theory of a very high and general nature, closely connected with the nature of Almighty God.' This being the case, as it has fared with speculative men in time past, we must expect that it will fare with them in time to come. If there ever was philosopher, whose course was likely to have coincided with the above assertion, it was Kepler. But we shall see, notwithstanding, that he has declared that any religious theory would have led him, not to, but from, his discovery of the Elliptical Orbits. His great contemporary, Galileo, was the head of an opposite school. He is generally understood to have been a speculative man, and to have made some discoveries; and he has recorded his opinion not merely against religious theories, but against all suppositions of preconceived relations.

'Men ignorant of geometry might perhaps lament that the circumference of a circle does not happen to be three times the diameter, or in some other assignable proportion to it, rather than such that we have not yet been able to explain what the ratio between them is.' We are at a loss which to admire most—Mr. Sewell's recklessness in stating principles, or in stating facts.

The question, so put, resembles a question of cause and effect, more than an ordinary case of analogy. To take first the persons of no religion. From what has been said above, it would not appear to signify much on what subject they employed themselves. Being by the supposition no more rational than somnambulists, they must employ themselves equally in vain on all. In another place, however, it is suggested, that 'a separation between the Athanasian creed and the discoveries of our human philosophy' must operate much more injuriously in our researches into the mind of man, than into the world of matter. If any inconsistency in such a writer could surprise us, it would be surprising to be told, immediately after this, that the 'effect of a want of knowledge of some infinite good being' was (not the stultifying of Aristotle and Plato, or the confining their contemplations to the material world, but) that of 'compelling the highest Greek philosophy to throw all its energies into purely metaphysical speculations.'

The Hindoos seem to have been worse off with their religion than they would have been with a religion which is treated in the last paragraph as equivalent to none at all. As Mr. Sewell's style of philosophizing might lead us to expect, learned Bramins would have as much difficulty in recognizing their mythology and Avatars in the following description, as in subscribing to the supposed effects:—'The doctrine of the unity of the Divine Being, exclusive of all plurality, and of the purely spiritual nature of God, unconnected with the doctrine of the incarnation, crushed in the East all science whatever.' The reproach of the East in this place agrees but ill with the panegyric on it in another, where its learning is said to have stood like a gigantic temple on the solid foundations of antiquity—in which Plato acquired the best part of his knowledge, and in which the light of God's primitive revelations was kept alive.

But, at other times, and with other people, marvellous effects are attributed unconditionally to the simple doctrine of the unity of the Divine Being. For instance, it is said to have led to the truest ancient astronomy—and to have suggested, that the heavenly bodies were globular, and moved in circular orbits! Kepler, on the contrary, submitted his own marvellous imagination so far to facts, as to see in this proposed suggestion, the origin, not of truth but error. 'If planets were carried round by angels, (he says), their orbits would be perfectly circular; but the elliptic form, in which we find them, smacks rather of the lever and material necessity.' Mr. Sewell adds, that if the framers of this system had but believed in an author of evil, and in his final subjugation, as well as in an author of good, they might not have left it to modern astronomers to discover, that the mechanism of the heavens was full of disturbing forces, and nevertheless its regularity was faithfully maintained! In the same manner, Newton's discoveries are stated to have been owing to his belief in the unity of the Divine Being. 'The same line of thought would suggest the undulating theory of light; the whole theory of vegetable bodies as analogical to those of animals.; the identity of electricity and lightning; the application of steam to navigation; the discovery of the New World.' It is easy to assert, that the unity of the Divine Being *would* suggest all these wonders. To make out the several steps, by which the supposed suggestion would work out its way, is not merely difficult, but impossible. If all that is meant by a belief in the unity of the Divine Being, is a belief in the uniformity of the laws of matter, atheists might make experiments, and might reason (and were just as likely to do so) on that belief. But Mr. Sewell's argument requires more than a mere possibility of suggestion. It should have been shown that the doctrine of the unity of the Divine Being, or some equivalent theological tenet, *did in fact* suggest these different discoveries. If it did not, we must suppose them to have been made by accident; seeing Mr. Sewell has before informed us that all discoveries must be made by accident or by the means of a religious creed.

The discoveries of modern chemistry are mentioned as being among those lucky accidents, which modern science insists on calling discoveries by experiment. Mr. Sewell takes as an instance of this perverseness, the principle of 'definite proportions.' This, he says, is, in other words, only the Pythagorean theory, that

the world was formed by Numbers. Supposing the discovery to have been made by one of these experimental accidents, Mr. Sewell is of opinion that the more natural and simple way would have been to have had recourse to one of his theories 'of a high and general nature connected with the nature of Almighty God.' Mr. Dalton should have gone at once either with Pythagoras 'to the ancient traditions of a revelation which invested numbers with a mysterious character, and which traced up their various combinations to one primitive root—the number three: and that to a still prior root of unity, which nevertheless could not be conceived to exist without the other;' or he should have taken example from 'the ancient fathers who made use of the same mystery as enunciated in Scripture, for their interpretation of the innumerable passages in Scripture, where numbers are introduced.' Men of science, we apprehend, have shown more wisdom in taking a warning, in the opposite direction, from the seventeen years which Kepler wasted in these bewildering mazes. Mr. Sewell nevertheless expects (and his book abounds in passages, which prove how strongly the association is bound up with all his philosophical hopes), that the mysterious numbers of the Trinity in Unity, and Unity in Trinity, are incorporate with all knowledge. 'Perhaps the book of nature may be like the book of the gospel, and contain a whole world of enigmas only to be opened by this key.' With this view, Mr. Sewell notices the deficiencies of Logic and of modern Physics, as sciences of classification. He observes, that if 'the recent theory of what is called circular arrangement.—classes entering into classes, one within the other, vegetable, animal and mineral—should, as is probable, change the face of natural history, it must modify the process of syllogism also.' Now, on what is founded the probability that the new theory of circular arrangement will turn out true? On the fact, that the 'former theory did not correspond with the form of the Divine Nature as laid down by the church:' and, on the fact, that the name of 'circulation' was the name given to 'the true Catholic doctrine of the Holy Trinity, when it became necessary to state it formally, in order to contradict the very same principle of classification and subordination, which a logical Arianism endeavoured to introduce.'

Many very religious men have been materialists. They would be astounded at hearing, that the miracle of the Incarnation ('Perfect God and Perfect Man, of a reasonable soul and human flesh subsisting'), was considered to be a conclusive argument against them ; whereas, they might to the full as reasonably aver, that the distinction applied in the above passage between the Man-God and ordinary man, was a conclusive argument in favour of their opinion.

The assumption, that all creation is a shadow and revelation of God himself, is connected with the inference that, in that case, even brute matter may bear on it an inscription recording the mysteries of his nature. Dr. Buckland, accordingly, must begin the world anew. 'I believe, then, that a geologist, deeply impressed with the mystery of baptism—that mystery by which a 'new creature' is formed by means of 'water and fire'—(*how fire in baptism?*) 'would never have fallen into the absurdities of accounting for the formation of the globe solely by water, or solely by fire. He would not have maintained either a Vulcanian or a Neptunian theory. He would have suspected, as most men now suspect, that the truth lay in the union of both. And in conceiving a typical connection between the material earth and the spiritual church, he would have been justified by the whole tenour of Scripture.' Can anything be madder than this?—except what follows. For, in like manner, geologists, zoologists, and mathematicians, must take up the Cross with them in their studies. 'I believe that a spiritualized eye, seeing all the human race shut up in the person of our Lord, having before it always the figure in which it pleased Almighty God to place him before us on the Cross, might expect to find a similar figure—the figure of the Cross—placed here and there all over the work of creation ; as a religious spirit in better days than the present erected that Cross on high, wherever a human foot might be arrested by it ; and as the ancient fathers detected it in the most hidden allusions of Scripture : — Moses stretching out his hands to the Amalekites—his rod—the branch he threw into the bitter waters—the wood of the Ark— the tree of life. In every animal and material nature, he would expect to discern the figure of a cross ; and he would not be surprised to find that all mathematical figures were reducible to this element ; or, as modern anatomists have suggested, that the whole animal world is framed upon this type—a central column with lateral

processes. It is one of the grand speculations of zoological science.'

So, Oxford philologists are tutored to look on language (not merely on Greek, which, we are told, was formed for Christianity, and Latin, which was maintained by Popery, but on all language, from Sanscrit to Cherokee), with the deepest reverence. They are not to permit themselves to dream of its being an invention of man, 'weighing carefully the mysterious title of *the Word* given to our Lord.'

The application of this kind of reasoning to the affairs of civil life is as easy as putting on a glove. While we are disputing what proportion of the property of the country may be necessary to maintain the poor, the clergy, and the temples of God, 'we have forgotten the doctrine of revelation upon this subject. Would it be fanciful to suppose that a *tenth* might probably be the amount?' Does Mr. Sewell mean that he would recommend the adoption of the Jewish law of tythe throughout? Does he know what it really was? And, if the law of tythe, we should like to know, what one point our return to the Mosaic dispensation is to stop at, rather than another. The mistake of the French Revolutionists in setting apart the *tenth* day for rest, in place of the *seventh*, was set right it seems by the nature of things, as well as by the fourth commandment. 'They were compelled to return to a seventh: because (?) human nature it was found could not labour for a longer term together.'

Among our scientific desiderata, it is supposed that we are in want of a model by which we may explain the organization of the human body, and the theory of vegetation. Such a model, it is assumed, is to be found 'in a perfect ecclesiastical polity modelled after the pattern seen on the Mount.' In explanation of this, we are gravely asked, if 'we have not near us a body and a tree full formed with all its organs more perfectly developed, written in larger letters, and of which we know that man's body and the tree are but the types and symbols?' If the church be really any such tree and body, it is no wonder that Mr. Sewell and his friends attach immeasurable importance to questions of church government. In Mr. Sewell's unparalleled jargon, 'the problem of reconciling plurality with unity' is constantly recurring in all questions, ecclesiastical and temporal. It is solved in the following manner ; 'Let each insulated fact be made the type and representation of one common principle, and at once they fall into unity, however diversified in their accidental circumstances. Thus in the Scriptures, as was said before, the Cross of Christ is seen in the tree of life, in the wood of the sacrifice laid on the shoulders of Isaac, in the rod of Moses, in the pole on which the serpent hung, in the staff of David, in the wood of the ark, in the bough thrown into the bitter waters. So the mystery of Baptism is read in the deep which covered the earth, in the waters of the deluge, in the Red Sea, in Jordan; in the waters of the Nile turned into blood, in the pitcher of water changed into wine for the marriage of Cana, in the water borne by the man who prepared the room for our Lord's passover; and so of the other mysteries of Christianity. *And thus also in civil society,' &c.* God help this man's pupils! And this is the light set up by Oxford to enlighten a darkened age!

We have seen Mr. Sewell's way of treating a considerable variety of subjects. Having done so, we think that we may safely repeat the opinion, that it would have been difficult to find a subject, five minutes' conversation upon which with him would not have been sufficient to satisfy any rational being, that, whatever talents Mr. Sewell might possess, it was impossible that there should be found among them the talent of discovering, or of communicating truth.

The subject of Christian morals is certainly no exception. For, as much of the book, with this mendacious title, as has any bearing on them, is of a piece with the wild and insolent raving which Mr. Sewell pours out upon other matters. From first to last, there is not a single observation upon Morals, by which anybody can possibly be made either better, wiser, or happier; while, under the name of Christian, the subject has been undertaken with the avowed object of confounding Christianity with church government, of putting the body of the people into abject subjection to the priesthood, and of excluding almost the whole of Christendom from the benefit of the Gospel. This is done with the dashing and showy air of a most presumptuous infallibility; and with an imposing manner of familiarly appealing to one or two persons—such as Bishop Butler—whose names, we are sure, if they had but been alive, he would never have dared to utter. The atmosphere of contempt which pervades the book for all extant things and persons, except the author's

own spiritual *côterie*, must be painful to good-natured readers. But the marvel of the book is, its utter indifference to credibility in the assumptions it makes, and in the consequences it draws. If we consider the Gospel as a system of Christian morals, delivered by Christ himself, and then turn to the declamation of Mr. Sewell, it reads as though it were written under a different dispensation. Faith, hope, and charity have almost disappeared.—To make room for what, and whom?

The moral character of the supposed revelations of the Divine will, which have prevailed at different times in different countries, has been frequently analyzed and compared. There was ample choice, both metaphysical and historical, of the ways by which the relation in which Christianity stands to morals, might be expounded. But it is a scandalous misnomer to give the name to such a book as this. We will not pretend to say, that 'Church of England morals' would have been better. For we are satisfied that nine-tenths of the members of the Church of England would protest as vehemently as the rest of Christendom, against being compromised by Mr. Sewell. Among a cloud of vague and desultory words, it is often almost impossible to lay hold of the meaning of any particular page or chapter. We come out of the fog as wise as we went in. But the object of the work, as a work, is, we repeat, clear enough. Mr. Sewell describes it as being the restoration of the connection so long dissevered, between the Science of Ethics, and the Catholic Christianity of the Church. We, on the other hand, should describe it as an outrage upon all Christian freedom; and as being, to say the least of it, as dogmatical a substitution of the authority of what they call the Church, for the authority of the Bible, as was ever ventured upon by Priest or Presbyter before. If there is a word of truth in the book, the clergy ought to be looked up to as a Braminical caste, not simply entitled, but solemnly bound, to exercise a paramount influence in the state. The aggrandizement of his order may not have been among the proofs[*] by which the author of

---

[*] Bishop Philpotts, who knows man—at least controversial and sacerdotal man—as well as anybody, stirs up his clergy with the *argumentum ad hominem* upon this very point, in a recent charge. 'Until the people shall think thus of these mysteries (the sacraments) they will not think of *us* (*sic. in orig.*) as it is far more for their benefit, than for ours, that they should always think.' The real presence in the sacraments is allowed to be a difficulty; but the sacramental presence in Dr. Philpotts is a

this spider's web was guided in his researches; but it is certainly a consideration which the public will not overlook, in estimating the value of the result arrived at. The 'Christian Morals' of Mr. Sewell make the Laity absolutely and necessarily dependent upon the Clergy for all the means they can ever hope for of grace or knowledge. Upon the important point, who are the clergy, in whose keeping the benefits of Christianity are locked up, nothing positive is said, one way or another; but the reader is left with the impression, that it will not be safe for him to trust to any clergyman but a clergyman of the Church of England. We shall soon see how little the Church of England can profit by all his good intentions.

Mr. Sewell shall speak for himself. His object being to restore the connection between the Church and Morals—the first point is, to determine what Christian communities are comprehended by him under the imposing generality of the *Church.* This is soon done. According to him, Adam and the Jews had imperfect churches. But his Catholic Church, with its appropriate powers and doctrines, is another and a greater thing. It is Divine in its origin, and episcopal in its form. It has come down from the Apostles in direct succession; and can admit of no sects or schools. It is essentially independent of any human power. Its rulers are individual bishops, assisted by councils of clergy in each diocese. Its supreme authority lies in a council of these bishops.—(Pp. 29, 50.)

These being the conditions of the Catholic Church, let us see what particular church can make good its title to be a branch of it. Is the Church of Rome successful? It can comply with some of the conditions; unfortunately not with all. The Romanist has indeed received powers; but he confesses (?) to have altered the doctrines in the course of their transmission. The Pope it was who broke up the beautiful system of a federal union of independent bishops by his personal usurpations; who blotted out the catholic character of the Church and its written

word; and who left us no assurance for God's commands but the declaration of a self-chosen teacher, our choice of whom will be as erroneous as our moral character is defective.—(P. 380.) Since the Catholic Church is defined to be a church admitting neither sect nor school, the Roman Church, after this description, evidently does not belong to it. To show this must be supposed, indeed, to have been the very object with which the above description of the Roman church was inserted here. Can the Protestant Dissenter make out a better title? On the contrary, he has no case at all from the very beginning. The tyranny and usurpationt of Popery are contrasted with the still more fatal tyranny, and still more unauthorized usurpation of Dissent. It does not pretend to have received either the 'powers or the doctrines'(?)—(P. 32;) and has fallen into still worse errors even than Popery, blotting out the testimony of the Church altogether. Dissent is a vague word. Dissent from what? It would have been more in order to have stated what it was, in doctrine or discipline or institution, a dissent from which is an exclusion from the Catholic Church. It is plain, however, that the Church of England is *the church* which was present to the mind of Mr. Sewell, while inditing these damnatory clauses against dissent; as also, in a later passage, where dissenters are charitably informed what is the way in which 'an erroneous theological dogma becomes a moral crime.' But did ever monk, writing for his convent, set about his work more blindly than a self-satisfied inquirer after the Church of Christ, who, in distributing his subject, does not notice, even by name, a single national protestant communion, except the one of which he is himself a member? To be sure, the result would have been much the same; since there is not one of them —Lutheran or Calvinist, Scotch or Swiss, Dutch or German—to which any of his characteristics of the Catholic Church, whether regarding origin, government, or supreme authority, could possibly apply. It comes therefore to this. The Church of England is not only (in Oxford language) the Anglo-Catholic Church, but it is the only Catholic Church among the Western Churches. There is no *tertium quid.* Did the greatest enemies to Christianity ever say so much against it? In all the license of their irony, and satire, and malicious learning, did they ever devise so exaggerated a picture of its corruptions, of its schisms, and of the complete-

---

much greater one. The state of mind in which his Clergy must have been, when they could request their Diocesan to publish to the world at large the above singular intimation, assists us to the meaning of another passage, in which the Clergy, while restrained from meeting in Convocation, are compared to 'a maniac in a strait waistcoat.' Sir Robert Peel is a very different man from what we take him to be, if he lets them loose.—(*Charge of the Bishop of Exeter,* 1842.)

ness of its failure? .There has not been, since the days of Laud and the Nonjurors, so suicidal an attempt at cutting off the Church of England from the rest of Christendom. We do not presume to guess what is the force under which the Bishop of Exeter has been drawn into the orbit, alongst which, like an ill-omened comet, he - scorched and perplexed his Diocese in his Charge of September last. He is shrewd enough to have known, that he could not burn his neighbour's house to roast his eggs by, without running a considerable risk of setting his own on fire. Whatever may be the pleasure of saying mysterious and bitter things on the preference of unity to union; of insinuating the superiority of the corporate character of a Christian over his personal; and of telling all, who are not good churchmen, that the promises of the Gospel are not for them—the price to be paid for so. great a pleasure may, after all, be more than it is worth. What a spectacle for reasonable men, the excommunicating the greater part of Christendom, on points which it is not easy to make persons, in possession of their senses, understand! If the controversies of Christians- among themselves have done more to stop the progress of Christianity. at home and abroad,* than all other causes put together, there is nothing that we should deprecate so much, as the possibility of Mr. Sewell making out his case. Divines of common charity and common sense have been quite aware of this, from Jeremy Taylor to the Bishop of London downwards. It was for a short time, a sufficient security against any sane member of a Reformed Church—setting up extravagant pretensions in behalf of the Church in general—that it could not be done without. necessarily playing into the hands of the Church of Rome. But, more than this. Every thinking Christian could not but feel that, as far as he was successful in exposing particular

Churches, he was to a great degree weakening the foundations and the evidence of Christianity itself. Intelligent members of the Church of England had this further consciousness: whatever were the scandals of schism, heresy, idolatry, and what not, which they might object to the Church of Rome, they must stop short, in prudence, of denying her to be a Church—seeing that it was out of the bosom of the Church of Rome that the Church of England, as it was constructed and christened at the Reformation, had been itself derived.

Modern zeal or superstition was never worse employed, than in attempting to re-adapt to the curiosity or the passions of our times, high-flown theories about the Church. As every man is said to be born a Platonist, or an Aristotelian, so, we apprehend, any person with a mind capable of being misled by Mr. Sewell and the like, will have but little chance of being kept right, or of being brought back again by such books as 'the Kingdom of Christ' of Archbishop Whateley, and the Sermons of Dr. Arnold.* The Bishop of London, however, is sufficient for us on this occasion. He will be found a great deal too latitudinarian for Mr. Sewell. If the Catholic Church be a corporate community, apostolically descended, we can connect ourselves with it, whatever it may be, only by means of some particular Church. Now, the Bishop of London, we feel certain, knows as well as we do, that the Church of England cannot so connect itself, on the terms required by Mr. Sewell.

Before entering on the question of pedigree, it is right to notice that the Catholic Church of Mr. Sewell has no sects or schools. Is that the case with the Church of England? Ever since the Reformation, it has comprised, under its articles of peace, a greater variety of opinions, than would be necessary to set up a greater number of schools than heathen philosophy ever knew. We question whether there are not, at the present moment even, as many sects within, as without, its pale.

But to come to the question of pedigree: the Catholic Church of Mr. Sewell has come down from the Apostles in direct succession. In this case, the Church of England must connect itself with the Church of the Apostles, by means of the Church of Rome. For a question of succession is a question of pedigree, and noth-

---

* Hey, Norrisian Professor of Divinity at Cambridge, was a man of a very different stamp from Mr. Sewell. 'It seems likely,' he says, 'that the Christian religion would have been successfully taught in *China*, had not the different sects of Christians there got into controversy with one another, and carried it on in such a manner as to disgust the Emperor.' We once more have an opening for Christianity among those three hundred millions, who, as Hey observes, are not unimproved in that which is chiefly wanting for its reception—*morals*. Are our divines more reasonable now? What chance, to say the least, would be left for Christianity, with Oxford Missionaries, who must treat as Heathens the Missionaries of every Church, except their own?

* *Passim.*—But especially the first Appendix to the third volume, and the Introduction to his *Christian Life.*

ing else. Now, what says Mr. Sewell of the Church of Rome? He denies that, with its present constitution and doctrine, it can belong to the Catholic Church. But its constitution and doctrines at the time of the Reformation, were the same as at present. To raise a question about the Anglo-Saxon Church is beside the purpose. The only Church known in England in the reign of Henry VIII., and for many ages previous, was a local Church—a branch Church of the general Church of Rome—the same in England as the Gallican Church in France. If the Church of Rome is no part of the Catholic Church now, the English branch of it, at the time of the Reformation, could be no part of the Catholic Church then. Consequently, on the doctrine of Apostolical succession, it was incapable of transferring to itself, under the name of the Protestant Church of England, a title by descent—which title, on Mr. Sewell's supposition, it had lost already. It is one of the misfortunes of cases of pedigree, that a break in the pedigree, though but for a moment, or in a single instance, can never afterwards be repaired.

So much for the case of pedigree and descent on the part of the Church of England. There is a worse flaw, however, than this, in its title to be the Catholic Church of Mr. Sewell. For, granting the absurdity, that the Church of Rome could pass on to the Church of England a better title than it had itself,—the Church of England, from the very first, repudiated the notion of any transfer of the kind. It set up its own form of Church government, upon its own grounds, not only in independence of these suppositions, but in complete contradiction to them. The Church of England, so far from claiming any *Divine origin*, was, at its birth, emphatically designated '*the Church as by law established.*' However independent of the civil magistrate may be the truths which it professes, and the character in which it delivers them, nevertheless, in its *form and legislature*, it is a merely human institution. The legislative charter, under which this modern spiritual corporation was reformed and reconstituted, passed at a period when the English nation was more submissive to its monarchs than at any other, before or since. It owed its existence, as a church, to the humour of Henry VIII., the interests of the guardians of Edward VI., and the political necessities of Elizabeth. Parliament made it, and Parliament can unmake it. The difference between the Church of England, as it is by law, and the Church of England, which churchmen of Mr. Sewell's cast see in visions, and dream of in their dreams, cannot be better set forth than in the words of. Speaker Onslow. The passage is longer than we well have room for; but it is so complete an exposure of the ignorance by which the Church of England is represented as being, by any possibility, Mr. Sewell's church, that we could not put our answer into better form. 'By the constitution of the Church of England it is, that the supreme legislative power of the church is in King, Lords, and Commons in Parliament. And it is the same with regard to the King's supremacy, whose ecclesiastical jurisdiction and authority is an essential part of our church constitution, renewed and confirmed by Parliament, as the supreme legislature of the church, which has the same extent of true power in the Church of England as any church legislature ever had; and may therefore censure, excommunicate, deprive, degrade, &c., or may give authoritative directions to the officers of the church to perform any of them; and may also make laws and canons to bind the whole church, as they shall judge proper, not repugnant to the laws of God or nature. Nay, the laity in England cannot otherwise be bound but by Parliament, who have a right (when they think proper) to the advice and assistance of the convocations, or the true parliamentary meetings of the clergy, by the *præmunientes* clause in the parliamentary writs to the bishops, if the one or the other, or both, should be then assembled.* The legislature of the primitive church was in the whole body, and afterwards had many variations in its constituents, and may still vary with the consent of the several communities. If this distinction of legislature in the Parliament be true, (and I am not the first who has mentioned it), the Church of England is freed from the imputation of being a creature *only* of the state, which by some sects of Christians has been often and much objected to, and makes it to be agreeable to Mr. Locke's notion, indeed demonstration, "that matters of mere religion are absolutely independent of the civil magistrate, as such." Where ecclesiastical jurisdictions have cognizance of temporal matters, they are thus far civil courts; and so *vice versâ*. The King is said in our law to be *mixta persona*, as regards his supremacy in

* See the Journals of the House of Commons of the 13th and 16th of April, 1689; 1st of March, 1710, 1712, 1713.

the execution of all civil and ecclesiastical jurisdiction, and so is the Parliament a mixed legislature. As to which or what is the best church constitution, I say nothing here. But this may be said, that no church power, whatsoever or wheresoever placed, legislative or otherwise, can have any right to the sanction of civil punishments—nor ought they to be—or any temporal disadvantages. All religions ought to have their free course, where they interfere not with the peace and rights of human society; of such *the civil power is to endow one, and to protect all.*—(See Mr. Locke's "Treatise of Government and Toleration"). The convocation can by their canons bind only their own body. They are in the nature of by-laws; and that is now fully settled by a solemn determination in the King's Bench, made in my Lord Hardwicke's times there.'*

The rulers of the Catholic Church of Mr. Sewell, it must be remembered, are bishops, assisted by their clergy, and its supreme authority is in a Council of Bishops. It follows, therefore, from Speaker Onslow's statement, that the Church of England is not the Catholic Church which Mr. Sewell is in quest of. Whatever rule English bishops can legally exercise, is exercised without the assistance of their clergy. The supreme authority of the Church of England is in no Council of Bishops, but in Parliament. Ages before the Reformation this was equally the case. The canons of Popes and Councils (though they have been lately called, by way of compliment, the common law of Christendom), were admitted only partially into England; and then as *imperium sub imperio— lex sub graviore lege.* They did not become law as far as the Anglican Church was concerned, until they had received the assent of Parliament, express or implied. Witness, out of a hundred instances, the *Articuli Cleri*, and the famous answer, *Nolumus leges Angliæ mutari.* The King was even then (10, Hen. VII.) described as *persona mixta*, exercising ecclesiastical as well as temporal authority ;—an idea which was afterwards adopted and enlarged upon, in the statutes declaring the King's supremacy. (24th and 26th Henry VIII., and 1 Eliz). So complete is the royal supremacy, that the clergy cannot even pass bye-laws in their convocation, to bind merely themselves, unless these

bye-laws are confirmed afterwards by the King. Since the Reformation, the fact, that the supreme authority in legislating for the Church is Parliament, has been brought out much more clearly, as was to be expected. This is exceedingly well shown by Dr. Arnold, (*Sermons*, 3d vol. app. 431). A single paragraph from the judgment by Lord Hardwicke, referred to by Speaker Onslow, will be sufficient for our purpose. It was given more than a century ago, and has never been questioned. 'The constant uniform practice ever since the Reformation (for there is no occasion to go further back) has been, that when any material ordinances or regulations have been made to bind the laity as well as clergy, in matters merely ecclesiastical, they have been either enacted or confirmed by Parliament. Of this proposition the several acts of uniformity are so many proofs, for by those the whole doctrine and worship, the very rites and ceremonies, and the literal form of public prayers, are prescribed and established ; and it is plain from the several preambles of these acts, that though the matters were first considered and approved in convocation, yet the convocation was only looked upon as an assembly of learned men, able and proper to prepare and propound them, but not to enact and give them their force.'— (2 Atkyns, 650).

Lord Hardwicke gives it as his opinion, in the preceding page, that no notion of divine authority was attached to the legislative power under which the ancient canons were made, after the Roman Emperors became Christian. 'The binding force of these ancient canons over laymen was not derived from any particular prerogative or supremacy of the Emperor, as head of the church; but from the supreme legislative power being lodged in his person.' In the same manner, on the principles of the English constitution, the right to bind the laity, even in matters ecclesiastical, is in no apostolically descended body. Lord Hardwicke declares it cannot be anywhere but in Parliament. And why? For a common-sense English reason. In Parliament only are the laity represented. In the matter of ecclesiastical judicature and legislation, it is by no means necessary that the judge or legislator should be an ecclesiastic. We could add pages of proofs and illustrations; but the constitution of the Privy Council, and the case of lay-baptism before it, only the other day, (Martin v. Escott), being the most authoritative, solely as being the last instance,

---

* *Burnet's History of his own Times*, Vol. iv. p. 17. (Note to the last edition).

are decisive. Surely the concurring authority of Coke, Hale, Holt, and Hardwicke, upon the relation in which the Church of England stands to the State—and what is the supreme legislature therein—might satisfy even Mr. Sewell, that his general propositions are larger than they are discreet. As far as the Church of England is concerned, he is evidently falling into the folly which has become a proverb, that of reckoning without his host.

Mr. Sewell is already out of court. He is contending for a magnificent inheritance in the gifts and privileges of the church. But like an awkward advocate, in the very opening of his case, he has laid down rules of law and evidence concerning title, which are fatal to his client. On his own showing, it is highly probable that there is no ecclesiastical heir at all. At all events the inheritance does not belong to that reverend body for which Mr. Sewell is appearing. The inheritance, as described, is certainly well worth looking after. But a prior question is also worth considering. Is there really any such inheritance, except in the legendary romance of our spiritual Quixote? There is no mistaking the nature of the gifts and privileges which are supposed to be inherent in the church. They are laid down in broad and peremptory propositions. Let us hear what those are with which at present we are most concerned. Whatever moral advantages individuals are to get from Christianity, must be got through the means of membership with this unknown, or at least this unagreed upon and debated about church. These advantages consist—first, in the metaphysical change effected in our natures by the sacraments of Baptism and the Lord's Supper; next, in the help of the ecclesiastical guides, from childhood to the grave, provided for us by the Church in the persons of the clergy. Such is literally the whole of Mr. Sewell's moral commentary on the Christian Bible;—the sum total of all that he can find there, worth the teaching. These are his 'grateful but mean acknowledgments' to the university of Oxford, for all that he owes to her wise teaching and her blessed institutions—'a light in a darkened age.'

Many men have method in their madness. An instance of this is Mr. Sewell's earnestness in turning everything into revelation. Now, positive revelation is the subject of proof. Once proved, the necessity of it is of course admitted by all believing in it, to the extent to which the revelation is believed to have been made.

But with some people this is not enough. They insist further on imaginary revelations, conjectural divine commissions, and arbitrary spiritual aids. What is the reason of this? Why do persons who, after all, pretty much agree on the amount of knowledge and of virtue which men acquire, make the theory of the means by which it is supposed to be acquired, of such importance? One should have thought at first, that to persons living under positive revelation, it would be, in the way of speculation at least, a matter of indifference, whether God had given man from his birth a nature capable of acquiring knowledge and virtue, by what we call in distinction merely human means; or, whether, in the first instance, he had made man's general nature more imperfect, but had afterwards supplied the deficiency partially, and from time to time, by the means of particular revelations, and the aids provided under them. Man is equally indebted to God, his Creator and Preserver, either way. But Mr. Sewell and his school are looking to an object widely different from this. They are preparing the ground for Church Authority. By degrading man—by describing him, such as he has come out of the hands of his Maker ever since the days of Adam, as a being incapable, in his own nature, of knowledge and virtue—by representing the learning of the heathen world, as only the fragments of 'a forgotten revelation'—a foundation is in some sort of manner laid for the building up of a mighty spiritual structure, and the overshadowing of human life. In this manner it appears to follow, as a natural inference, that these latter days have probably also nothing else to look to for knowledge and virtue than to a revelation; and that they have no sense given them (for in that case there would be no use for it) but just as much as may enable them to see the testimony by which that revelation is established; which testimony, in Mr. Sewell's language, is, and only can be, the witness of the Church. So the whole argument is conveniently concluded, as a matter of course, by the testimony of Mr. Sewell's Church in its own favour. In his Cosmogony, the Church is the Elephant which supports the World.

This testimony is backed up by potent maxims. Such, for instance, as that you are to ask for no evidence—to take the Creed as it is presented to you upon trust —and, having once taken it, to make a solemn vow never to doubt its truth. The candour of the first of these maxims is exemplified by a beautiful distinction. Mr. Sewell's disciple is told: ' You must ask, not the clergyman, but all the others who come to you, to produce their credentails. *I say, not the clergyman.*' But you must be sure and ' ask the dissenter—who claims to be a minister from God, with a right to assist you in your study, and in your practice of Christian ethics,'—by whom he is appointed? The extent to which Mr. Sewell's Christians are to take their religion upon trust, is exemplified by the fact, that the first condition of entering into relation with the Church is, that the Christian learn a creed. He can believe without understanding. The transmission of a creed is indeed matter of historical evidence. But evidence will not make a Christian. It is God who gives faith. Metaphysical abstractions are, in all things, the first conveyed to the child, and must be.—(Pp. 287, 300.) The philosophy, out of which these assertions are derived, is not satisfied with the reasonable doctrine that in religion as in other subjects, there are many things which a child must receive on credit, in the hope that he may comprehend them afterwards; but it goes on to declare, even with regard to grown-up men, that '*the highest exercise of the reason or intellect*,' is the embracing as truth without evidence something that you do not understand.' Baptism is elsewhere stated to endow equally all the children of the Church with the spirit of truth and wisdom; so as to qualify all equally for appreciating the higher truths of religion, as well as its mere facts. But upon this theory of belief, where is the use of wisdom, when all appreciation is disclaimed? Suppose that a Christian has been in this manner carried blindfold within the fold, the door is locked upon him by requiring of him a vow that he will not doubt. Certain circumstances are mentioned, as ' showing the wisdom of insisting on a pledge, vow, or promise, that he will hold fast what he has been taught. It is in his power to exclude doubt as much as to exclude any evil thought. It is his moral duty to do so.' What a pleasant way Mr. Sewell has of conciliating such minds as are looking out boldly but faithfully for the truth, and of representing the service of religion to be a reasonable service !

After this, Dissenters will not wonder that the University moralist leaves them out, and passes on upon the other side. 'Does your parent take you to the church? Does he tell you that the clergyman of the parish is to be your religious instructor? If this is not the case, I have little inten-

tion of addressing myself to you.'. Yet at what peril are they omitted! For, listen to the language which he puts into the mouth of his parish clergyman:—' Look round you on this side and that, and in every part of the country you will see others like myself, each in his own district representing the same body, and ministering, like me, in an ancient holy building, especially called the Church. How came we here? Should I be permitted to preach in this pulpit as of my own will? No. We receive a special and most solemn commission from the heads and rulers of this body or society, of which I need not tell you that the name is the Church? *They delegated to us the power to which, if you would ever become good, you must have recourse at our hands.*'—(26.) We do not know whether we may test the truth of the last part of this paragraph by that of the former part. But Mr. Sewell is wofully mistaken, if he thinks his parish clergyman has any title to the parish church and parish Pulpit from bishops and councils, or otherwise than by Act of Parliament.

The University moralist proceeds in the same tone :—' Any discussion of ethics which does not include the fact of a Catholic Apostolical Church must be as faulty as a theory of astronomy which left out the sun.' . . . 'If you cannot commence any science, much less the science of morals, without learning its fundamental principles from the testimony of others, the very first thing to be done, is to show you which testimony is to be followed.' . . . ' All inquiry into ethical science is virtually a treatise on education; so every act of education throws us back upon a search for some communication from God. Without this, education is a dream.' ' And to obtain this, we must recur to Revelation ; for Revelation we must go to the Apostles; for communication with the Apostles we must go to the Catholic Church.' . . . 'I have said what many will think strange, that man by himself is *unable* to educate man. I add now what many will think stranger—that without the Church he has no right to educate him. Education without the Church is an absurdity. Therefore, a system of ethics, which is not based upon the Church, must be an absurdity likewise. Both parental and civil authority require the support and witness of the Church, or they fall to the ground. But when they thus recognize the existence of the Church as a commissioned ambassador from God, they must also recognize its full powers. Thus, if either parent or state attempt to educate man without the co-operation of the Church, without giving to it its due prominence and presidency, without allowing, nay, requiring the exercise of all the powers committed to it, they are flying in the face of their Lord and Master, and they must take the consequences.'—(40 *et passim.*)

There is a preliminary operation to be performed by the Church, the object of which is a metaphysical change in our nature, to prepare the soil for the clergyman's moral husbandry. This operation is Baptism. In consequence of the change produced by it, the Church is said to begin its education where heathen education ended. 'A system of professedly Christian education, which does not constantly bear in mind this distinction, and frame itself upon the privileges of Baptism, as on its fundamental fact, can only end in confusion and mischief.' . . . . 'Let us go back about fifteen hundred centuries, and imagine ourselves standing by the side of the cradle of an infant with a Father of the Church, and a heathen philosopher standing with us, and contemplating the condition and prospects of that little child. Before anything can be done or hoped, a ceremony must be performed over the child. What is it? We are living in an age which despises forms, and to this contempt we owe no little part of our moral evils. Without rightly appreciating them and comprehending their use, we shall not understand the most essential laws of Christian ethics. . . . The Church commences her work of education with an outward form. If you know anything of the Christianity which you possess, you will know that. . . . . The Church educates mainly and chiefly by communicating to you certain gifts of immeasurable value. These it professes to communicate through the means of certain outward acts and symbols. Its great instruments of good are the sacraments. These sacraments 1500 years ago were administered with many more symbolic forms than they are at present: especially the sacrament of Baptism, which is the beginning of your Christian education: *the act in which are condensed all the great truths of Christian ethics.*'

One of the great truths to which these symbolic forms pointed, is the fact, that Christian education must commence by literally driving out the Devil, who 'possesses' us at our births. It is represented as being a matter of the utmost consequence, that we hold, and realize, and act upon the unfigurative literal personality of a spirit of evil, going about daily, seeking whom he may devour. On this main fact must rest the foundation of all Christian ethics. . . . The ancient church first took the child and solemnly exorcised it. The origin of evil is a fundamental problem in human nature; and exorcism contains the answer to it, which was given by the Catholic Church delivering that answer from the lips of Almighty God.' By answer to the problem, Mr. Sewell, if he means anything, must mean discharge from the consequences; since, as to the *origin* of evil, exorcism leaves the problem where it found it.

What we are practically most concerned with is, with these consequences: that is, with the effect of exorcism; whether express as formerly, or implied as at present. In what state then does baptism place us by casting out the Devil? Greek sculpture had two statues: one, of man in an offensive, the other, in a defensive attitude. These statues, it is said, will serve to represent the fundamental difference between Christian and Heathen ethics. 'The perception of it is necessary to understand the ethical character of Christian doctrine; by confusing it this doctrine was corrupted; and it brings out into the fullest light the wonders, and privileges, and responsibilities of the Church. . . . . The very things which a heathen moralist would most desire—all these are described in the Bible as effected by baptism already. It is something past and done. And the subsequent struggle, for struggle there must be, is to defend what we have received, to secure ourselves from falling from the high estate in which we have been placed. I repeat the distinction again and again, because it is of vital importance. It is the grand separation between Christian and heathen ethics. It is because all modern systems of ethics, whether treated as a science, or practically applied in education, have neglected this difference, that the science has fallen into its present degraded state, and education itself has become a farce.' But in the ancient church even greater things, than the destruction of the evil power, and the removal of natural pollution, were symbolized by baptism. A want of unity is at the bottom of all human weakness; and, by the miracle of baptismal regeneration we are made members of Christ, and united with God, through the inspiration of his Holy Spirit. The union with Christianity so begun is to be continued by means of the Lord's Supper. 'Until once more the Catholic Church in this country shall restore this awful mystery to its due prominence; until it makes prayer and praise, and even right action, subservient to the reception of the Holy Communion, Christian ethics will still remain a vague, inconsistent, fluctuating chaos of contradictory principles and empty feelings. Men do not choose goodness, before it is given to them in baptism; they cannot afterwards procure it for themselves, without the ministration of the Church. The nearer you approach to the Apostolic age, the more striking is the light in which the mystery of the sacraments is placed, as if they were the great treasure committed to the keeping of the Church, not merely a metaphysical creed relating to the nature of God, but a code of laws tending to the government of man.'

Mr. Sewell has here again damaged his case by overstating it. He is aware of the vastness of the power which he is claiming for the Church—'a power which places it almost on a level with God himself.' So strongly is he aware of this, that the extravagance of the claim is made an argument in favour of it. He asks, with some simplicity, 'if any human being could dare to assume it without authority from God.'—(27). Really it is impossible to say what any Church, heathen or Christian, may not *dare*. It will be more to the purpose to ask, whether the members of a Church, really in possession of any such supernatural powers, would not be at once distinguishable from all other people by their moral excellence; and, whether a Church, thus miraculously endowed, could have ever so far lost its hold upon mankind, that not only its distinguishing characteristic, but its very identity and existence should be matter of dispute. Certain miraculous powers—as the missionary gift of tongues—may be in suspense for ages. Others may be in daily exercise, but may lie beyond the reach of human discernment—as Roman Catholics believe to be the case with transubstantiation in the mass; and as all sober-minded Christians believe to be the case with the influences of divine grace. But the miraculous transformation of man's nature, attributed to the sacraments, especially to that of baptism, is a change which takes place, if at all, in every baptised person; while, from the nature of the change described, the difference produced by it between the baptised and the unbaptised, ought to be not merely distinctly visible, but startling. If this is not the case under

the baptism of any known Christian Church, (and can anybody pretend it is so?)—there is only one alternative—either the theory is false, or not one of our Christian Churches is the Church of God.

Mr. Sewell has anticipated our doubt, and allows that though any person raising it would once have been highly criminal, yet, in the present age, such a person is more properly the object of compassion than anger. He answers, that the work of perfecting man's nature is not performed in baptism fully, finally, and unconditionally, to those who survive it long. But this is a very insufficient answer to our doubt. We complain not that the work of perfecting is not completed, but that it has not made any visible progress at all in baptism. Mr. Sewell, however, tenders us a sign of the presence of the gift, where it continues after baptism. 'There is but one infallible sign of the presence of the gift, struggles and resistance.' Was there ever such a criterion imagined? It would have been much better to have honestly spoken out with Saint Augustin, and have called the virtues of the heathens splendid sins. The behaviour of most pious Christians, after baptism, only helps to embarrass Mr. Sewell. It is admitted that they 'yet speak of their efforts to do right, as if they were endeavouring to obtain the gift of the Holy Spirit for the first time, instead of clinging to it as a treasure already within them. . . . They propose to secure to themselves the love of God and the favour of Christ, as if it had not been imparted to them while they were lying in the cradle.' Poor people! They do so from an entire unconsciousness that baptism has dispensed with these efforts and resolutions. Must they deny their own natures to make evidence for Mr. Sewell? He declares, that the moral struggles of a Christian life ought to take an entirely different character under his theory, from that which he allows they take in fact. Now, on this, we have only to observe, that man appears to have been before the Fall to a great degree the same imperfect creature as he has been since; or how came he to fall? In the same manner, whatever degree of original sin baptism may remove, it leaves enough behind, to make such representations as Mr. Sewell's, of the change wrought in our natures by it, evidently contrary to the fact. This appears two ways; first, positively, by the amount of evil remaining in us all; next, comparatively, by comparing the natures of the baptised and unbaptised; and for this purpose it is the same whether we look at unbaptised Pagans or misbaptised Presbyterians. In the true spirit of that philosophy which disposes of facts with a contemptuous sneer—so much the worse for facts—Mr. Sewell only notices the ignorance of baptised Christians by saying,' it is evident that such a mistake must introduce into all our moral acts the most startling confusion and contradictions. And such has been the case.' If morals are out of joint, Mr. Sewell has mistaken his vocation in believing that he is born to set them right. His exaggerated views of baptismal regeneration will introduce ten times more confusion than the supernatural philosophy, as he considers it, of the seventeenth article of the Church of England will remove.

In his late Charge, the Bishop of London has shown but little judgment in reviving the insoluble question of regeneration. But here again he stops short a thousand miles of Mr. Sewell. ' The plain doctrine of our church is, that baptism is instrumentally connected with justification.' . . . But our article says, 'not that we are *made* righteous, but that we are *counted* righteous before God. If, indeed, we are *made* righteous, we must of course be *accounted* righteous; but it does not follow conversely, that, if we are accounted righteous, we must be made so. The notion that God accounts us righteous by reason, and for the sake of any actual righteousness wrought in us by infused and inherent grace, seems irreconcilable with our article.' From Mr. Holloway's ' Reply' to this Charge, it is abundantly clear that the Bishop has gone further on this point than the known differences of opinion in regard to it, in the Church, authorise him to go. But the remission of sins, promised by the Bishop, is one thing, the change of nature, promised by Mr. Sewell, is another. The learned Selden, however, in Protestant practice, could scarcely perceive even the first. ' In England, of late years, I ever thought the parson baptised his own fingers rather than the child.' Oxford has Selden's books. Would to God they had the motto which he inscribed in them, and the spirit that inspired it!

Mr. Sewell talks of mistakes. The only mistake which the world will see, is in Mr. Sewell himself, and in his intrepid preference, whether the subject be morals or physics, of hypothesis to facts. Mr. Sewell casts a longing, lingering look upon the age when the rites of the Sacrament of the

Lord's Supper, and of Confirmation, were the ordinary accompaniments of the baptismal service. The practice of administering the holy Eucharist to infants is recommended to us by the following considerations:—' Our animal life is like our spiritual life; the nourishment of both is a sacrament. There is in each an outward sign and an inward power.' A sucking child clinging to the breast of its wet-nurse is compared to the condition of a young Christian with the Church for his nursing mother. The sucking child takes 'from the hand of those whom God has set to guard him, the mysterious symbols and vehicles in which the vital sustenance is embodied. He incorporates these with him in faith, for the support and development of the microcosm of the universe of his material frame, the church of his body.' Upon this we are asked, who, duly reflecting on this analogy, will dare to say that there is anything strange or incongruous in that theory of our spiritual life which the Church pronounced, when, immediately the germ of life had been imparted, she administered new sustenance and food to it through the outward emblems of bread and wine?—that theory, which the Catholic Church at this day retains, though with a dimmer apprehension and fainter belief, but which a modern ignorance has rejected. And what has it substituted instead? A speculation of spiritual vitality, without any fresh support analogous to the reception of food.' The view of Confirmation is equally new. It belongs to the branch of the subject which Mr. Sewell calls Christian Politics. Much of its significancy, it is said, depends on its close connection with baptism. 'It appears to contain in it the type and germ of the *social principle of the Church.* Baptism brings us as individuals into union with Christ; but something else is wanted to express that union with Christ can only be obtained by union with his body, the Church. * * * The forms of this ceremony imply that, besides Almighty God, the source of all wisdom and power, there is upon earth a delegated power in the person of His Church: that to this delegated minister we owe, under God, not only the beginning of the moral and spiritual blessings of Christianity, but their continuance and confirmation. * * * The rite is administered by the bishop, and the bishop only; that, as the Christian in confirmation recognizes his allegiance to the Church, he may recognize also its true monarchical constitution.' So much for the more than renewal of the old cry—No Bishop, no King.

The heathens, it is said, knew little of prayer. But its importance in a system of ethics is conveyed in the announcement, that ' all the precepts and principles of ethics are summed up in this one practice.' We will only add—Good news for monks and hermits. ' As the creed was given to the baptised person before he was baptised, so the first words to be uttered afterwards were also taught him in the Lord's Prayer. * * * If all our moral duties and moral relations, as well as our physical existence, depend on the one relation between man and God, prayer—perpetual and universal prayer—is the only form (?) in which such a relation can be acknowledged.'

After this exposition of the special powers and privileges of the Church in connection with Morals, nobody can be surprised to learn that virtue, by its very definition, is necessarily traced up to the same source. 'Virtue is obedience to external law. * * * Every thought is bad, which is erroneous, and every thought is erroneous which is not conformable to some external law or form, which you did not invent yourself, but found placed over you by a superior authority; and that authority emanating from God. Every positive institution is thus traced up to God; and those men only are to be taken as our guide, who are appointed by God, profess to deliver God's law, and found their whole authority on His commission. * * * When obedience to man, as to the appointed minister of God, is made identical with obedience to God himself, as it is in all right statements of parental, and civil, and ecclesiastical authority, the whole of man's moral duties are brought round to this one simple relation. Virtue is made intelligible to the poorest capacity.' The witnesses to this external law are Parent, King, and Church; but parent and king are only witnesses and representatives of God, as long as they act in subordination to the Church!

Peculiar rites and peculiar knowledge are thus presented to our acceptance. Both are supposed to be indispensable alike to our goodness and our salvation. For the performance of the one, and for the attainment of the other, we are further supposed to be entirely dependent on the clergy; and our state of dependence is enforced on us in a somewhat alarming tone. 'If God has been pleased to appoint that man shall be his instrument and agent in conveying his blessings to mankind, and we choose to slight and despise man, and insist on communicating with God, the sovereign of the universe, without the intervention of his ministers—to hope for blessings from other channels invented by ourselves—to intrude on Him without introduction or permission—may it not be that our very worship may become a profanation, and our prayers be turned into a curse?'

Whatever the reader may think of the spiritual powers of the Church—how far they are proved or not—and in whatever degree he may or may not shrink from the thought of taking upon himself his own responsibilities, one thing is clear, that an Englishman must be mad indeed, not to be upon his guard against Mr. Sewell and his friends. We have notice served upon us in time of the forbearance which we are to expect. 'When the Church, as it once did, stood before men in its full stature, bearing upon it all the features and insignia of a divinely constituted power and ambassador of God, and acknowledged as such by all that was wise and great among men, to dispute her word was the mark of a presuming and rebellious spirit, and deserved little more than chastisement. But in these present days, her power humbled, her body mutilated, her voice struck dumb, her history unknown, her noblest faculties torpid with disease, her name a byword among the nations, we may well pardon the man who asks for some proof of her assertions. Doubt is no longer a self-evident offence against humility and trustfulness. It is to be pitied more than punished. And until the Church has once more put forth her strength, arrayed herself in her real attributes of power, and made her claims known and felt throughout the world, she has no right whatever to complain of those who look upon her suspiciously, or even with alarm.' What should we say if we heard such language from Salamanca, or Maynooth?

We have given more space to Mr. Sewell's presumptuous hallucinations than we at first intended. But we found that, if we were to notice the book at all, this would be necessary. For the mind exhibited in it appears so marvellously strange, that we were satisfied, as we went on, that we should not be believed to be representing fairly Christian morals, as taught at Oxford, if we did not give a number of passages in the author's words. It would take up fully as much more space were we to extract an equal proportion of the hundred incidental absurdities with which the volume swarms. We will only give a specimen or two.

'The property which gives unity to plurality is the real external quality in an act to which we apply the term good. . . It is this quality, in fine, which produces in us the internal sensation of heat.' 'Every individual Christian, (perhaps it may be said that every man in the workings of his intellect), realizes in his own mind the fact of a Trinity in Unity, and an Unity in Trinity.' . . 'It seems impossible that a bad man should ever act wilfully. . . . Unless man acts as the representative and delegate of God, as doing God's will, he must act wrongly. Perhaps we may say rather, he cannot act at all : but ought rather to be considered as the unconscious minister of some other power, probably a power of evil. .. Men who are absorbed in physical or metaphysical science, or in mathematics, such men are in the sight of Scripture the most immoral. . . Are we quite aware of the real difficulty and mystery contained in the fact of a *covenant* between God and man ? . . . A covenant implies two independent agents. It implies also another fact more wonderful. These two independent agents in it must also be mutually dependent. . . . It may be that all the hierarchy of heaven are so formed that they move as a mighty machine. But the relation of man to God, even in man's corruptible and fallen state, is far higher. It is the relation of two mighty potentates, capable of making a treaty, and binding each other by mutual conditions. The language is very awful ; but it does not go beyond the truth. If I have the power of thwarting the designs of God, of marring his creation, of disobeying his laws, I am so far an independent sovereign, and a sovereign of vast power, for it is a power reaching to' the will of God himself.' Well may this misguided man say, that his language is sometimes 'very awful.'

Mr. Sewell's account of the sympathy of the Church is very different from the parable of the good Samaritan. 'None, strictly speaking, possess that spontaneity which entitles them to be considered as *persons*, except such as are acting under the inspiration of God, and as members of the body of Christ. All others we must regard as machines, which it is our duty to raise into personality, by communicating to them the spirit of God ; and which are worthless and punishable if they reject the communication, but which, simply as ma-

chines, can neither excite nor claim any moral affection or duty. Apart from the command of God, however signified, neither king, parent, friend, or fellow-creature, has a well-founded title to our respect or love.'

From the passage last cited, it will readily be believed, that Mr. Sewell has little scruple in breaking the vials of his wrath over the heads of all who differ from him. We need hardly say, that his list includes some of the most respectable names in English history, 'during the unhappy period of the last two centuries.' It is perhaps equally needless to mention, that this scorn begins with Queen Elizabeth and the Reformation, and swells and darkens, until language seems almost to refuse to do his bidding, and to choke him in the utterance of it, when he has to speak of the generation among whom he has the misfortune to be living. We will not quote any of these passages. Why need laymen know the bitterness which divines can put into Christian morals ? and what harm can come to Doddridge, Locke, and Milton, from a whole university of Sewells ? Zeal without humanity, talents without sense, thoughts connected by tricks of the imagination, instead of by the steps of reason, have never yet done much for the service of mankind.

While reviewing this book, we have more than once thrown it aside, from a feeling of humiliation in the employment. The author, in the statement of his case, had made it so absurd and offensive, that there was little left for criticism to do. But a production of this kind, proceeding from the Professor of Moral Philosophy at Oxford, is a circumstance not to be passed lightly over. Our readers will bear in mind, what is the place in education, in the Church, and in general politics, which Oxford affects to hold. When Locke (whom Mr. Sewell never mentions but to abuse him) was pressed to follow up his *Essay on the Human Understanding* with an *Essay on Morals*, he replied : 'Did the world want to rule, there would be no work so necessary nor so commendable. But the Gospel contains so perfect a body of ethics, that Reason may be excused from that inquiry, since she may find man's duty clearer and easier in Revelation than in herself.' Light and darkness certainly cannot be more opposite than the book which would have been written by Locke, and that which has been written by Mr. Sewell. What is, indeed, the element which in his life and teaching Christ has added unto morals ? What is it that the best of us aspire to learn from the ennobling precepts of Christianity, from its great encouragements, from its touching voice of patience and of charity, from its paths of pleasantness and peace? Yet, what are the elements which not only predominate, but are in truth the exclusive elements, elaborated out of it in the crucible of Mr. Sewell? The Gospel, the book of glad tidings, is turned into a Book of spiritual magic, and of ecclesiastical domination. The days, however, of the black art are over, in any form of it. Selden has quaintly said: ' There never was a merry world since the Fairies left dancing, and the Parson left conjuring. The opinion of the latter kept thieves in awe, and did as much good in a country as a justice of peace.' But the man must be more of a conjurer than Mr. Sewell, who is to persuade the English nation that Christianity and Church Government are one and the same thing. O'Connell begins his letter to the Earl of Shrewsbury with an old saying—' the greatest enemy to religion is a pious fool.' We have no means of knowing anything for or against the piety of Mr. Sewell; and he is certainly no fool, in the sense in which that uncourteous monosyllable is usually understood. But there cannot easily be a greater wrong and violence done to religion, than to tell us, that to be really Christians, we must hold our moral and intellectual natures, our hearts and consciences and understandings, upon no better title than the existence of a Church of Apostolical succession, the votes of a Council or a Convocation, and the spiritual guidance which we may happen to receive from the ministrations or the teaching of our parish priest. Men have been often told before that St. Peter kept the doors of Heaven, and that without the good word of the clergy nobody would ever get there. Terms of communion and terms of salvation, we have got accustomed to see put together; and we must bear it as best we can. Accordingly, if this had been one of the ordinary impertinences of theologians, we should have neither made nor meddled in it. But morals are another matter; and we are not as yet disposed to bear so meekly, on the mere authority of the Chair at Oxford, the imposition of a Moral Law, more oppressive than the Jewish ceremonies, and little less incredible than the Pagan superstitions, from which it is our blessing that Christianity relieved us. Mr. Sewell has fortunately defined his Church in such a manner that it is utterly impossible he ever should be able to identify its existence. But were it otherwise, and could he make out, as an historical fact, the existence of such a Church, he would be as far as ever from the possibility of proving any of the consequences, which under the fumes of a heated fancy, some ill-digested learning, and a contagious neighbourhood, he has incorporated with his imaginary fact. The Right of Private Judgment was the great prize fought for at the Reformation. It was won at the cost of many evils, but was fairly worth them all. And, at all events, Mr. Sewell may make sure of this: If Protestants are called upon to surrender it to Church authority, the bosom of the Church in which they will lie down for a false unity, and false repose, will be neither the Church of England nor that of Mr. Sewell.

ART. VIII.—*American Notes for General Circulation.* By CHARLES DICKENS. 2 vols. 8vo. London: 1842.

TRAVELLERS should be well-instructed and conscientious men, for the reputation of nations is in their hands. Lawyers, Physicians, and Clergymen, must pass their examinations, and receive their credentials, before they can give opinions which the public are authorised to confide in; but for a man who has been where no man else has been, it is enough if he can write—spelling, punctuation, and syntax, will be furnished by his publisher; and there is no Continent so large but he can pronounce upon the character of its laws, government, and manners, with an authority which few Professors enjoy. If there be any Englishman living who has smuggled himself through the interior of China, and ascertained the colour of the Emperor's eyes and beard, eluded the officers of justice, and escaped from bowstring and bastinado down the river Yang-tse-Kiang, now is his time for a book on China and the Chinese. For three months to come he will be an absolute authority on all the internal affairs of 'a third of the human race.' Everybody will read his book, and everybody will believe all he says. But he must not lose his tide; if he let anybody get the start of him, his authority will go for little more than it is worth, unless he be able, not only to write, but to write the more readable book; for it may be generally observed, that where we have conflicting accounts of a foreign country, the opinion which carries the day is not that of the person who has taken most pains, or had the best opportunities, or is best qualified, by education and natural ability, for forming a judgment, but that of the most agreeable writer.

We say this only of the 'reading public' in general. Very many, no doubt, there are amongst us of whom it is not true. Very many there are who are more particular about the formation of their opinions on such matters—who hold it to be not foolish only, but wrong, to let false impressions settle in the mind; and who, remembering that a few weeks' residence among strangers will not qualify a man to judge of the character of Nations and Governments, whose opinion nobody would ask on the working of the Poor Law or the Corporation Act in his own parish, require some better assurance of the worth of a traveller's judgment before they will take the character of a Continent from his representation. With such fastidious readers, in entering upon a book of travels, to learn something of the character and capacity of the writer is a primary object. Unfortunately, printed books having no physiognomy, but being all alike plausible, it is an object scarcely attainable; except where the writer has the rare art of impressing his character upon his composition, or where he has already written on matters which others understand. It is on this account that we have looked forward with considerable interest to a work on America by Mr. Dickens;—not as a man whose views on such a subject were likely to have any conclusive value, but as one with whom the public is personally acquainted through his former works. We all know 'Boz,' though we may not have seen his face. We know what he thinks about affairs at home, with which we are all conversant—about poor-laws and rich-laws, elections, schools, courts of justice, magistrates, police-men, cab-drivers, and housebreakers—matters which lie round about us, and which we flatter ourselves we understand as well as he. We know, therefore, what to infer from his pictures of society abroad; what weight to attribute to his representations; with what caution and allowance to entertain them. If his book abound in broad pictures of social absurdities and vulgarities, we know that his tendency in that direction is so strong, that, though possessing sources of far finer and deeper humour, he can hardly refrain from indulging it to excess. If he draw bitter pictures of harsh jailers and languishing prisoners, we know that his sympathy for human suffering sometimes betrays him into an unjust antipathy to those whose duty it is to carry into effect the severities of justice. We know, in short, where we may trust his judgment, where we must take it with caution, and where we may neglect it.

Mr. Dickens has many qualities which make his testimony, as a passing observer in a strange country, unusually valuable. A truly genial nature; an unweariable spirit of observation, quickened by continual exercise; an intimate acquaintance with the many varieties of life and character which are to be met with in large cities; a clear eye to see through the surface and false disguises of things; a desire to see things truly; a respect for the human soul, and the genuine face and voice of nature, under whatever disadvantages of person, situation, or repute in the world; a mind which, if it be too much to call it original in the highest sense of the word, yet uses always its own eyes, and applies itself to see the object before it takes the impression—to understand the case before it passes judgment; a wide range of sympathy, moreover—with sweetness, and a certain steady self-respect, which keeps the spirit clear from perturbations, and free to receive an untroubled image; a mind, in short, which moves with freedom and pleasure in a wider world than has been thrown open to the generality of men. This happy combination of rare qualities, which Mr. Dickens' previous works show that he possesses, would seem to qualify him, in some respects, beyond any English traveller that has yet written about the United States,—if not to discuss the political prospects of that country, or to draw comparisons between monarchical and republican institutions, yet to receive and reproduce, for the information of the British public, a just image of its existing social condition.

To balance these, however, it must be confessed that he labours under some considerable disadvantages. His education must have been desultory, and not of a kind likely to train him to habits of grave and solid speculation. A young man, a satirist both by profession and by humour, whose studies have lain almost exclusively among the odd characters in the odd corners of London, who does not appear to have attempted the systematic cultivation of his powers, or indeed to have been aware of them, until they were revealed to him by a sudden blaze of popularity which would have turned a weaker head—who has since been constantly occupied in his own peculiar field of fiction and humour—how can he have acquired the knowledge and the speculative powers necessary for estimating the character of a great people, placed in circumstances not only strange to him, but new in the history of mankind; or the working of institutions which are yet in their infancy, their hour of trial not yet come—in their present state resembling nothing by the analogy of which their tendency and final scope may be guessed at? Should he wander into prophecies or philosophic speculations, it is clear that such a guide must be followed with considerable distrust. How, indeed, can his opinions be taken without abatement and allowance, even in that which belongs more especially to his own province—the aspect and character of society as it exists? As a comic satirist, with a strong tendency to caricature, it has been his business to observe society in its irregularities and incongruities, not in the sum and total result of its operation; a habit which, even in scenes with which we are most familiar, can hardly be indulged without disturbing the judgment; and which, among strange men and manners, may easily mislead the fancy beyond the power of the most vigilant understanding to set it right. It is the nature of an Englishman to think everything ridiculous which contrasts with what he has been used to; and it costs some effort of his reflective and imaginative powers to make him feel that the absurdity is in himself, and not in the thing he sees. In a strange country, where the conventional manners and regulations of society are not the same as in England, every room and every street must teem with provocations to this kind of amusement, which will keep a good-humoured English traveller, of average reflective powers, in continual laughter. And though Mr. Dickens *knows* better, it is too much to expect of him that he should have always acted upon his better knowledge; especially when we consider that he had his character as an amusing writer to keep up. The obligation which he undoubtedly lies under to keep his readers well entertained, (failing which, any book by 'Boz' would be universally denounced as a catchpenny), must have involved him in many temptations quite foreign to his business as an impartial observer; for any man who would resolutely abstain from seeing things in false lights, must make up his mind to forego half his triumphs as a wit, and *vice versâ.* Even his habits as a writer of fiction must have been against him; for such a man will always be tempted to study society, with a view to gather suggestions and materials for his creative faculty to work upon, rather than simply to consider and understand it. The author of 'Pickwick' will study the present as our historical novelists study the past—to find not what it is, but what he can make of it.

It is further to be borne in mind, in estimating Mr. Dickens' claims to attention, that the study of America does not appear to have been his primary object in going, nor his main business while there. He went out, if we are rightly informed, as a kind of missionary in the cause of International Copyright; with the design of persuading the American public (for it was the public to which he seems to have addressed himself) to abandon their present privilege of enjoying the produce of all the literary industry of Great Britain without paying for it;—an excellent recommendation, the adoption of which would, no doubt, in the end prove a vast national benefit. In the mean time, however, as it cannot be carried into effect, except by taxing the very many who read for the benefit of the very few who write, and the present for the benefit of the future—to attempt to get it adopted by a legislature over which the will of the many has any paramount influence, would seem to be a very arduous, if not an altogether hopeless enterprise. In this arduous, if not hopeless enterprise, Mr. Dickens, having once engaged himself, must be presumed, during the short period of his visit, to have chiefly occupied his thoughts; therefore the gathering of materials for a book about America, must be regarded as a subordinate and incidental task—the produce of such hours as he could spare from his main employment. Nor must it be forgotten that in this, the primary object of his visit, he decidedly failed; a circumstance (not unimportant when we are considering his position and opportunities as an observer of manners in a strange country) to which we draw attention, the rather because Mr. Dickens makes no allusion to it himself. A man may read the volumes through without knowing that the question of International Copyright has ever been raised on either side of the Atlantic.

Our catalogue of cautions and drawbacks grows long; but there is yet another point to which, as it does not appear on the face of the book itself, we must advert. Though Mr. Dickens does not tell us of it, it is a notorious fact, that throughout his stay in the United States he was besieged by the whole host of lion-hunters, whose name in that land of liberty and equality is *legion.* In England, we *preserve* our lions: to be admitted to the sight of one, except on public occasions, is a privilege granted only to the select. Persons of a certain distinction in the fashionable world are alone licensed to exhibit him; and the exhibition is open to those only whom such distinguished persons may choose to honour by admission. In America, (always excepting a skin of the right colour), the pursuit of this kind of game requires no qualification whatever; for though society seems to form itself there, just as it does with us, into a series of circles, self-distinguished and excluded one from the other, yet there does not appear to be any generally acknowledged scale of social dignity. Each circle may assert its own pretensions, and act upon them; but they are not binding upon the rest. One citizen may not choose to dine with another, just as one party may refuse to act with another in politics; but they are not the less equal in the eye of the law. In the eye of the law and of the universe, a citizen is a citizen, and, as such, has a right to do the honours of his country to a stranger; and though there are, doubtless, many circles in which the stranger is pitied for having to receive such promiscuous attentions, there is none which seems to consider itself excluded from the privilege of offering them. Of the evils which necessarily beset a man whom everybody is eager to see, this is a very serious aggravation. In London his condition is bad enough; for the attentions which are prompted, not by respect, but by this prurient curiosity, must always be troublesome and thankless. But, in America, the whole population turns out, and the hunted animal has no escape. The popularity of Mr. Dickens' works is said to be even greater there than it is at home. Copies are circulated through all corners of the land at a tenth of their cost; readers, therefore, are ten times as numerous. The curiosity to see him, hear him, and touch him, was accordingly universal; and (if we may trust current report) his time must have been passed in one continual levee. It was not merely the profusion of hospitable offers—the crowd of callers that besieged his lodgings—the criticisms upon his person—and the regular announcement of his movements in the newspapers, that indicated this intense feeling. But if he walked in the street, he was followed; if he went to the play, he had to pass through a lane formed by rows of uncovered citizens; if he took his seat in the railway car a few minutes before the time of starting, the idlers in the neighbourhood came about him, and fell to discussing his personal appearance; if he sat in his room, boys from the street came in to look at him, and from the window beckoned their companions to follow, (Vol. i. p. 277); if he took the wings of the evening, and fled to the farthest limits of geography, even there his notoriety pursued him. As he lay reading in a steam-boat, between Sandusky and Buffalo, he was startled by a whisper in his ear—(which came, however, from the adjoining cabin, and was not addressed to him)—'Boz is on board still, my dear.' Again, after a pause, (complainingly), 'Boz keeps himself very close.' And once more, after a long interval of silence, 'I suppose, that Boz will be writing a book by and by, and putting all our names in it.' This is the very misery of Kings, who can enjoy no privacy, nor ever see the natural face of the world they live in, but see only their own importance reflected in the faces of the gaping crowd that surrounds them. We set down the circumstance among Mr. Dickens' most serious disadvantages—not because we suppose his judgment to have been biassed by it, for he has too much sense to be gratified by this kind of homage, and too much good-nature to take it unkindly; but because it must have prevented him from seeing society in its natural condition: it must have presented the New World to his eyes under circumstances of disturbance, which brought an undue proportion of the sediment to the surface, and thereby made his position as an observer very unfavourable. In the New World as in the Old, and in all classes, from the highest to the lowest, the curiosity which follows the steps of every much-talked-of man is essentially vulgar; and, in such a case as this, can hardly fail to leave upon the mind of the sufferer an undue impression of disgust.

Such being our opinion of Mr. Dickens' faculties and opportunities for observation, we expected from him a book, not without large defects both positive and negative, but containing some substantial and valuable addition to our stock of information with regard to this most interesting country—interesting not only for the indissoluble connection of its interests with our own, but likewise as the quarter from which we must look for light on the great question of these times.—What is to become of *Democracy*, and how is it to be dealt with? We cannot say that our expectations are justified by the result. But though the book is said to have given great offence on the other side of the Atlantic, we cannot see any sufficient reason for it.

To us it appears that Mr. Dickens deserves great praise for the care with which he has avoided all offensive topics, and abstained from amusing his readers at the expense of his entertainers; and if we had an account of the temptations in this kind which he has resisted, we do not doubt that the reserve and self-control which he has exercised, would appear scarcely less than heroical. But, on the other hand, we cannot say that his book throws any new light on his subject. He has done little more than confide to the public, what should have been a series of Letters for the entertainment of his private friends. Very agreeable and amusing letters they would have been; and as such, had they been posthumously published, would have been read with interest and pleasure. As it is, in the middle of our amusement at the graphic sketches of life and manners, the ludicrous incidents, the wayside conversations about nothing, so happily told, and the lively remarks with which these 'Notes' abound—in the middle of our respect for the tone of good sense and good humour which runs through them—and in spite of a high appreciation of the gentlemanly feeling which has induced him to refrain from all personal allusions and criticisms, and for the modesty which has kept him silent on many subjects concerning which most persons in the same situation (not being reminded of the worthlessness of their opinions by the general inattention of mankind to what they say) are betrayed into the delivery of oracles,—in the middle of all this, we cannot help feeling that we should have respected Mr. Dickens more if he had kept his book to himself; if he had been so far dissatisfied with these 'American Notes' as to shrink from the 'general circulation' of them; if he had felt unwilling to stand by and see them trumpeted to all corners of the earth, quoted and criticised in every newspaper, passing through edition after edition in England, and settling in clouds of sixpenny copies all over the United States. That he had nothing better to say, is no reproach to him. He had much to say about International Copyright; and that, we doubt not, was well worth having : we only wish it had been heard with more favour. But, having nothing better to say, why say anything. To us it seems to imply a want of respect either for himself or for his subject, that he should be thus prompt to gratify the prominent public appetite for novelty, by bringing the fruits of his mind into the market unripe. This, however, is a matter of taste. In reputation, so easy and so abundant a writer will suffer little from an occasional mistake. Though this book should only live till New-Year's day, it will have lived long enough for his fame : for on that day we observe that he is himself to come forth again in a series of Monthly Numbers—so that none but himself will be his extinguisher. In the mean time, as a candidate for 'general circulation,' it stands before us for judgment, and must be dealt with according to its deserts.

Concerning America in her graver aspects, we have already said that it does not add much to our existing stock of information. In comprehensiveness, completeness, and solidity, the fruits of a judicial temper, patient and persevering observation, and a mind accustomed to questions of politics and government, it is not to be compared to the work entitled 'Men and Manners in America,' by

the author of Cyril Thornton.* Any one who is curious about the state of things in that country, and wishes to form some idea of its real condition, should rather look there for it, than here. There he will find the matter discussed and illustrated ; here he will find little more than a loose record of the travelling impressions of Mr. Dickens. Still, even this is not without its value. To know the impression made by the first aspect of a country upon a mind like his, is to know something of the country itself. The good things he has been able to say, and the good stories he has met with in his travels, are things of less real interest, though a good deal more entertaining. Good stories grow wild in all societies ; no man who can tell one when found, had ever any difficulty in finding one to tell. Sketches of odd characters, specimens of the slang of coachmen and porters, ludicrous incidents, picturesque groups, whimsical phrases, or such as sound whimsical to strange ears— these things (though it is of such that the better part of these volumes consists) tell us nothing about a country. We want to know the total aspect, complexion, and constitution of society ; these are only its flying humours. Leaving these, therefore, to the newspapers, (which have rarely come in for such a windfall during the recess), we shall apply ourselves to discover from such hints as these volumes supply, what kind of people these transatlantic brethren of ours really are, and what kind of life they live. We shall not, indeed, inquire at what hour they dine, whether they wear their hair long or short, how they pronounce certain words, how they take their tobacco, and whether, when they wish to soften the absoluteness of their positives or negatives, they say, 'I guess,' or 'I suppose,' 'I expect,' or 'I suspect.' In these and the like matters, the natives have our good leave to please themselves. We want to know how they act and feel in the substantial relations and emergencies of life, in their marryings and givings in marriage, in their paternal, conjugal, filial duties, in the neighbourly charities, in the offices of friendship. The fireside, the market-place, the sick-room, the place of worship and the court of justice, the school, the library—it is in the management of these that the life and being of a people must be looked for, not in their dress, or dialect, or rules of etiquette.

We must confess, indeed, that to gather

---

* We are sorry to learn that the able and accomplished author of these works, (Captain Hamilton), has very lately, while in the prime of life, been called to pay the great debt of nature. He died, we believe, in Italy.

any sound knowledge, and form any just opinions on these points, is a matter of extreme difficulty; and when we say that Mr. Dickens has not given us much information about them, we are far from meaning it as a reproach. 'He that hath knowledge spareth his words'—and the stranger who thinks to understand a people in a fortnight, is not wise. In all his observations on a strange society, a man must have a reference, more or less direct, to that with which he is familiar at home. Without reference to some such standard he cannot explain his feeling to himself—much less to another. Yet to compare a familiar world with a strange one, —what is it but comparing the ore as it comes out of the smelting-house, with the ore as it comes out of the mine? In remembering his own country, a man takes no account of the dross; in observing another, he values the gross lump—dross and gold together. At home he has made himself comfortable—that is, he has gradually settled into the ways he likes, gathered about him the people he likes: of the things he did *not* like, he has got rid of when he could, reconciled himself to what he must, and forgotten all about the rest. Out of a hundred persons whose acquaintance he might have cultivated, he has cultivated ten. Out of a dozen places of resort that are open to him, he resorts to one. He has tried three or four servants, and at last found one that suits him. They gave him damp sheets and a bad breakfast at the Crown Inn: instead of making a note of the fact for general circulation, he went to the Bell, where they serve him better, and forgot it. And thus, out of the jarring elements of the world into which he was born, he has shaped out a small peculiar world expressly for himself, which fits him; and this private world it is that he boasts of to others, grumbles at to himself, and carries about in his thoughts as a standard to measure foreign pretensions by. In the foreign world, meanwhile, he can make neither selections not distinctions; he looks at everything alike, and everything he looks at he sets down as alike characteristic. Some delusion from so unequal a comparison it is impossible to avoid. But it may be partly corrected—some estimate at least may be formed of the extent of correction required—by taking any given surface of ground at home, the inhabitants of which have been drawn together, not by any common interest or pursuit, but each by his several occasion; supposing yourself suddenly set down among them without any previous knowledge of their characters; and endeavouring to imagine the impression you would take of the place and people during the first exchange of visits;

how they would figure in your Journal in that period of probation, before you had learned to treat them according to their qualities—to cultivate the esteemable, to avoid the disagreeable, and to think nothing about the greater number.

Fully aware, no doubt, of all this—desiring to be just and liberal in his observations—intending to write a book, but remembering withal, that 'in the multitude of words there wanteth not sin,' and firmly resolved to violate neither the confidence of social intercourse by revealing private conversations, nor the decency of manners by publishing criticisms upon the character and appearance of the ladies and gentlemen at whose houses he might be received—(a modern practice which, considering the activity of the press, the rapidity and regularity of communication between the two countries, and the scandalous appetite for personal sketches which afflicts both, is little better than to talk of people before their faces; and can be compared to nothing so aptly as to the conduct of the street boys in Baltimore, who came to inspect 'Boz' as he sat in the railway car[*])—he landed at Boston on the 22d of January, 1842. Having remained there about a fortnight, he proceeded towards New York, where he arrived on the 13th of February. How long he stayed we cannot learn; but in the middle of March we find him at Richmond in Virginia, having already seen all he meant to see of Philadelphia, Washington, and Baltimore, and now turning his face towards the great West. The next six or seven weeks must have been spent almost entirely in coaches and steam-boats; for we find him passing from Richmond back to Baltimore; thence up the valley of the Susquehanna to Harrisburg; across the Alleghany mountains to Pittsburg; down the whole length of the Ohio river to its junction with the Mississippi; up the Mississippi to St. Louis; back again as far as Cincinnati; thence across the state of Ohio, two or three hundred miles northward, as far as Sandusky; from Sandusky traversing the whole length of Lake Erie; and so proceeding by way of

---

* 'Being rather early, those men and boys who happened to have nothing particular to do, *and were curious in foreigners,* came (according to custom) round the carriage in which I sat; let down all the windows; thrust in their heads and shoulders; hooked themselves on conveniently by their elbows; *and fell to comparing notes on the subject of my personal appearance, with as much indifference as if I were a stuffed figure. I never gained so much uncompromising information with reference to my own nose and eyes, the various impressions wrought by my mouth and chin on different minds, and how my head looks from behind, as on these occasions.'*—(Vol. I. p. 277.) The street boys we can excuse; but our literary ladies and gentlemen should know better.

Buffalo to the falls of Niagara, which he reached about the end of April, and remained there for ten days, in a confusion of sublime emotions, upon which he has enlarged in a passage which our respect for his genius will not permit us to extract. The next three weeks were devoted to Canada; after which he had only time for a rapid journey to New York by way of Lake Champlain, and one spare day, which he devoted to the 'Shakers' at Lebanon.

If to these dates (which we have gathered with some difficulty) we could add an account of the distances between place and place, (distances of which we, who are confined within our four seas, can form no practical conception), it would be sufficiently apparent that, during the last half of Mr. Dickens's sojourn in the United States, he did not stay long enough in any one place to become even tolerably well acquainted with its society; and that his impressions of social character throughout the vast regions lying to the west of Washington, must have been drawn entirely from the company he travelled with— a class of persons whose manners must, in all countries, be far below the average. Any general judgments he may hazard must therefore be taken with the requisite allowance. A fortnight well spent in Boston, and a month between New York, Philadelphia, and Washington, may enable a wise man to say something about the people. The rest of Mr. Dickens's experience qualified him admirably well to tell us what to expect in coaches, canal boats, railway carriages, and hotels; and in these matters, if allowance be made for his habitual exaggeration—(a fault, by the way, which, we fear, increases upon him)— we dare say his authority is as good as any man's. But, as we should be sorry to have the character of England inferred from the manners of the road; or indeed to have any conclusions drawn as to our own personal proficiency in the courtesies of life, from our demeanour in the traveller's room; we shall leave his westward observations unnoticed, and endeavour to make out what kind of people he found in the drawing-rooms at Boston, Philadelphia, and Washington.

Every country—especially a new one— has a right to be judged by the best of its natural growths; for the best is that towards which the rest aspire. Of the manners and character of the best class in America, Mr. Dickens (in common, we believe, with every gentleman who has had an opportunity of judging), gives a very favourable impression. On quitting New York, after not more than a fortnight's stay there, he says:—'I never thought that going back to England, returning to all who are dear to me, and to pursuits that have insensibly grown to be a part of my nature, I could have felt so much sorrow as I endured, when I parted at last on board this ship with the friends that accompanied me from this city. I never thought the name of any place so far away, and so lately known, could ever associate itself in my mind with the crowd of affectionate remembrances that now cluster about it.' And then follows one of Mr. Dickens's fine passages, which we wish to be understood as quoting, not because we admire it, but because it shows that the last sentence was not strong enough to satisfy his feelings:—'There are those in this city who would brighten, to me, the darkest winter day that ever glimmered and went out in Lapland; and before whose presence even home grew dim, when they and I exchanged that painful word which mingles with our every thought and deed; which haunts our cradle-heads in infancy, and closes up the vista of our lives in age.'—(Vol. i., p. 230). And in his concluding remarks, he deliberately repeats the same sentiment as applicable, not to New York only, but to the nation generally:—'They are by nature frank, brave, cordial, hospitable, and affectionate. Cultivation and refinement seem but to enhance their warmth of heart and ardent enthusiasm; and it is the possession of these latter qualities in a most remarkable degree, which renders an educated American one of the most endearing and most generous of friends. I never was so won upon as by this class; never yielded up my full confidence and esteem so readily and pleasantly as to them; never can make again, in half a year, so many friends for whom I seem to entertain the regard of half a life.'—(Vol. ii., p. 288). Acknowledgments, scarcely less strong than these, of the merits of the best class of American gentry, are scattered through Captain Hamilton's book; and even Captain Basil Hall, in spite of his prejudices and conventional feelings—his horror at words wrong pronounced, and meats ungracefully swallowed, and his complacent persuasion that whatever is the fashion in England is right in the eye of universal reason—tells us, in his gossiping, good-humoured way, the very same thing of the manners and distinguishing qualities of the class to which the individuals belong who called forth the above expressions of admiration. We regret that little or nothing more of the kind can be collected from these volumes. The tone of society in Boston is only described as being 'one of perfect politeness, courtesy, and good breeding.' The ladies, we learn, are beautiful; and 'their education much as with us.' Their parties take place at more rational hours, and the conversation ' may possibly be a little louder and more cheerful' than with us In other respects, a party in Boston appeared to Mr. Dickens just like a party in London. In New York, we are only told that 'the tone of the best society is like that of Boston : here and there, it may be, with a greater infusion of the mercantile spirit, but generally polished and refined, and always most hospitable. The houses and tables are elegant; the hours later, and more rakish ; and there is perhaps a greater spirit of contention in reference to appearances, and the display of wealth and costly living :' the ladies are again described as.' singularly beautiful.' Of the society in Philadelphia, we only learn that ' what he saw of it he greatly liked'— but that it was more ' provincial' than at Boston or New York; and apparently rather *too blue* for his taste. But his stay was very short. At Washington he confines himself to legislators ; and of them he speaks only as he finds them in the arena where they exhibit. His remarks on them we shall pass over— for, being in quest of the best manners in the country, we must of course avoid all places consecrated to public debate. To learn the true character and manners of the English bar, you must look at lawyers—anywhere but in court; and before we pronounce upon the breeding of a member of Congress, we must see him in a private drawing-room. The only persons whom he speaks of as being personally known, are those whom he specially excepts from his general censures. Of these—' the foremost among those politicians who are known in Europe'—he says—' to the most favourable accounts that have been written of them, I more than fully and most heartily subscribe : and personal intercourse and free communication have bred within me, not the result predicted in the very doubtful proverb, but increased admiration and respect. They are striking men to look at, hard to deceive, prompt to act, lions in energy, Crichtons in varied accomplishment, Indians in fire of eye and gesture, Americans in strong and generous impulse ; and they as well represent the honour and wisdom of their country at home, as the distinguished gentleman who is now its minister at the ' British court sustains its highest character abroad,' (Vol. i. p. 292). This is another of those ambitious sentences, from which we can gather no distinct idea except that these gentlemen have inspired Mr. Dickens with a strong desire to pay them a splendid compliment. We cannot doubt that his admiration of them is sincere ; and we may take his known character and ability as a guarantee that it is well founded.

We do not suppose that his conversation has lain much among Professors, or that his thoughts on Universities are entitled to much authority ; but we must not omit to mention, in this place, his notice of the University of Cambridge, and its influence upon the society around. ' The resident professors at that University are gentlemen of learning and varied attainments ; and are, without one exception that I can call to mind, men who would shed a grace upon, and do honour to any society in the civilized world. Many of the resident gentry, in Boston and in its neighbourhood, and I think I am not mistaken in adding, a large majority of those who are attached to the liberal professions there, have been educated at this same school. . . . It was a source of inexpressible pleasure to me to observe the almost imperceptible, but not less certain, effect wrought by this institution among the small community at Boston ; and to note, at every turn, the humanizing tastes and desires it has engendered—the affectionate friendships to which it has given rise—the amount of, vanity and prejudice it has dispelled.'

As we are not writing an essay upon the social condition of America, but trying to collect Mr. Dickens's impressions of it, we must be content with these somewhat meagre notices of the manners and character of its best society. For further evidences as to its qualities, we must look to its fruits. And the fruits of the social character, as distinguished from the political regulations of a country, are to be looked for in those matters in which the baser appetites and worse dispositions of men having no temptation to interfere, sense, character, knowledge, and virtue have their natural influence—not, therefore, in the Legislature ; for the composition of that depends upon the law of election and the amount of qualification ; nor in the Press, for the character of that depends upon the cost of printing and paper, and the amount of taxes, direct and indirect, upon what, by courtesy, is called knowledge. The Press and the Legislature react upon the social character. but are not to be taken as representing it. The composition of the House of Representatives is not so much an index to the feelings and opinions of the American gentry, as to the number of Irish labourers who have votes. And the character of the daily and weekly Press is a measure rather of the number of uneducated persons who can read, than of the taste of the educated. But there are soedme - partments in the social establishment, which the worse half of society silently leaves to the care and taste of the better. Among these, the most conspicuous are charities of all kinds, public and private; arrangements for the education of the people; asylums for persons labouring under natural defects; provision for the relief of sick persons and young children; for the treatment of prisoners, and the like. Institutions of this kind are probably the fairest expression that can be had of the feeling and character of the people, properly considered; reckoning, that is, not by numbers but by weight—counting every man as two whose opinion carries another along with it. Now, in these matters, Mr. Dickens's testimony is not only very favourable and very strongly expressed; but is really of great value. Prisons and madhouses have always had strong attractions for him; he went out with the advantage of a very extensive acquaintance with establishments of this kind in England; and, wherever he heard of one in America, he appears to have stayed and seen it. His report leads irresistibly to the conclusion; that in this department New England has, as a people, taken the lead of the civilized world; and that Old England, though beginning to follow, is still a good way behind. And the superiority lies not merely in the practical recognition of the principle, that the care of these things belongs properly to the state; and should not be left, as with us, to the charity and judgment of individuals, however securely that charity may be relied on; but in the excellence of the institutions themselves in respect of arrangement and management. Our limits will not allow us to follow him through his observations and remarks on this subject; which are, however, upon the whole, the most valuable and interesting part of the book. He carefully inspected not less (we think) than ten institutions of this class; and of these he has given minute descriptions. Those at Boston, he believes to be 'as perfect as the most considerate wisdom, benevolence, and humanity can make them.' . . . . . 'In all of them, the unfortunate or degenerate citizens of the State are carefully instructed in their duties both to God and man; are surrounded by all reasonable means of comfort and happiness that their condition will well admit of; are appealed to as members of the great human family, however afflicted, indigent, or fallen; are ruled by the strong heart, and not by the strong (though immeasurably weaker) hand.' And the rest, (with the exception of a lunatic asylum in Long Island, and a prison nicknamed 'The Tombs' at New York), appear to deserve, so far at least as the design and the management go, the same praise. Upon one doubtful and difficult question, which has of late excited a good deal of controversy in England, Mr. Dickens's

observations will be read with great interest —we allude to the effects of the *solitary* as contrasted with the *silent* system. Against the solitary system Mr. Dickens gives his most emphatic testimony; which will, no doubt, have due weight with the department on which the consideration of this question, with reference to our own prison system, devolves. For our own part, we must confess that, highly as we esteem his opinion in such a matter, and free as we are from any prejudice in favour of the system which he condemns, we are not altogether satisfied. His manner of handling the question does not assure us that he is master of it. His facts, as stated by himself, do not appear to us to fit his theory. If not inconsistent with it, they are certainly not conclusive in favour of it. We sometimes cannot help doubting whether his *judging* faculty is strongly developed, and whether he does not sometimes mistake pictures in his mind for facts in nature. He is evidently proud of his powers of intuition—of his faculty of inferring a whole history from a passing expression. Show him any man's face, and he will immediately tell you his life and adventures. A very pretty and probable story he will make of it; and, provided we do not forget that it is all *fiction*, a very instructive one. But, in discussing disputed points in nature or policy, we cannot admit these works of his imagination as legitimate evidence. The case before us supplies a striking illustration of Mr. Dickens's power in this way; and likewise, we suspect, of his tendency to be misled by it. We shall take the opportunity of quoting a long passage, which will serve the threefold purpose of exhibiting a favourable specimen of Mr. Dickens's style, of justifying the doubts we have expressed as to his judging faculty, and of presenting the case against the solitary in a strong light.

He commences his remarks on the subject by declaring his belief 'that very few men are capable of estimating the immense amount of torture and agony which this dreadful punishment, prolonged for years, inflicts upon the sufferers,' and that, 'in guessing at it himself, and in reasoning from *what he has seen written upon their faces, and what to his certain knowledge they feel within,* he is only the more convinced that there is a depth of terrible endurance in it, which none but the sufferers themselves can fathom, and which no man has a right to inflict upon his fellow-creature.'—(Vol. i. p. 239). He then proceeds to describe the regulations of the prison, and the condition and appearance of several of the prisoners. The sight, and the feelings of awe and pity which the sight awakens, set his 'shaping spirit of imagination' at work, and he thus goes on :—

'As I walked among these solitary cells, and looked at the faces of the men within them, I tried to picture to myself the thoughts and feelings natural to their condition; I imagined the hood just taken off, and the scene of their captivity disclosed to them in all its dismal monotony.

'At first, the man is stunned. His confinement is a hideous vision; and his old life a reality. He throws himself upon his bed, and lies there abandoned to despair. By degrees the insupportable solitude and barrenness of the place rouses him from this stupor, and when the trap in his grated door is opened, he humbly begs and prays for work. "Give me some work to do, or I shall go raving mad!"

'He has it; and by fits and starts applies himself to labour; but every now and then there comes upon him a burning sense of the years that must be wasted in that stone coffin, and an agony so piercing in the recollection of those who are hidden from his view and knowledge, that he starts from his seat, and striding up and down the narrow room, with both hands clasped on his uplifted head, hears spirits tempting him to beat his brains out on the wall.

'Again he falls upon his bed, and lies there, moaning. Suddenly he starts up, wondering whether any other man is near; whether there is another cell like that on either side of him; and listens keenly.

'There is no sound: but other prisoners may be near for all that. He remembers to have heard once—when he little thought of coming there himself—that the cells were so constructed that the prisoners could not hear each other, though the officers could hear them. Where is the nearest man—upon the right, or on the left? or is there one in both directions? Where is he sitting now—with his face to the light? or is he walking to and fro? How is he dressed? Has he been there long? Is he much worn away? Is he very white and spectre like? Does *he* think of his neighbour too?

'Scarcely venturing to breathe, and listening while he thinks, he conjures up a figure with its back towards him, and imagines it moving about in this next cell. He has no idea of the face; but he is certain of the dark form of a stooping man. In the cell upon the other side, he puts another figure, whose face is hidden from him also. Day after day, and often when he wakes up in the middle of the night, he thinks of these two men until he is almost distracted. He never changes them. There they are always as he first imagined them—an old man on the right; a younger man on the left—whose hidden features torture him to death, and have a mystery that makes him tremble.

'The weary days pass on with solemn pace, like mourners at a funeral; and slowly he begins to feel that the white walls of his cell have something dreadful in them: that their colour is horrible: that their smooth surface chills his blood: that there is one hateful corner which torments him. Every morning when he wakes, he hides his head beneath the coverlet, and shudders to see the ghastly ceiling looking down upon him. The blessed light of day itself peeps in—an ugly phantom face—through the unchangeable crevice which is his prison window.

'By slow but sure degrees, the terrors of that hateful corner swell until they beset him at all times; invade his rest, make his dreams hideous, and his nights dreadful. At first, he took a strange dislike to it; feeling as though it gave birth in his brain to something of corresponding shape, which ought not to be there, and racked his head with pains. Then he began to fear it, then to dream of it; and of men whispering its name and pointing to it. Then he could not bear to look at it, nor yet to turn his back upon it. Now, it is every night the lurking place of a ghost—a shadow—a silent something, horrible to see; but whether bird or beast, or muffled human shape, he cannot tell.

'When he is in his cell by day, he fears the little yard without. When he is in the yard, he dreads to re-enter the cell. When night comes, there stands the phantom in the corner. If he have the courage to stand in its place and drive it out, (he had once, being desperate,) it broods upon his bed. In the twilight, and always at the same hour, a voice calls to him by name; as the darkness thickens, his loom begins to live; and even that, his comfort, is a hideous figure, watching him till daybreak.

'Again, by slow degrees, these horrible fancies depart from him one by one; returning sometimes unexpectedly, but at longer intervals, and in less alarming shapes. He has talked upon religious matters with the gentleman who visits him; and has read his Bible, and has written a prayer upon his slate, and has hung it up as a kind of protection, and an assurance of heavenly companionship. He dreams now sometimes of his children or his wife, but he is sure that they are dead or have deserted him. He is easily moved to tears; is gentle, submissive, and broken-spirited. Occasionally the old agony comes back; a very little thing will revive it; even a familiar sound, or the scent of summer flowers in the air; but it does not last long now; for the world without has come to be the vision, and this solitary life the sad reality.

'If his term of imprisonment be short—I mean comparatively, for short it cannot be—the last half-year is almost worse than all; for then he thinks the prison will take fire and he be burned in the ruins, or that he is doomed to die within the walls, or that he will be detained on some false charge and sentenced for another term: or that something, no matter what, must happen to prevent his going at large. And this is natural, and impossible to be reasoned against; because, after his long separation from human life, and his great suffering, any event will appear to him more probable in the contemplation than the being restored to liberty and his fellow-creatures.

'If his period of confinement have been very long, the prospect of release bewilders and confuses him. His broken heart may flutter for a moment when he thinks of the world outside, and what it might have been to him in all those lonely years; but that is all. The cell door has been closed too long on all his hopes and cares. Better to have hanged him in the beginning than bring him to this pass, and send him forth among his kind, who are his kind no more."

Now this is a most fearful sketch of a *possible* case. Had it occurred in a professed work of fiction, as a description of the actual condition of one of the characters, we should have thought it remarkable not only for force but for truth. It is terrible, but not monstrous; we can imagine a man feeling and doing all that is described. But when we are inquiring into the actual and ordinary effects of solitary confinement upon the mind of a prisoner, we are constrained to ask Mr. Dickens what authority he has for his many facts? How does he know that prisoners are affected in this manner? And, above all, how does he know that it is the general case? He will say that he saw it in their faces; they had all the same expression; and that expression told him the whole story. But he should at least show that his interpretation of the countenance was corroborated by other indications of less doubtful character.

Let us refer to the individual sufferers whom he saw and conversed with in several stages of punishment, and see whether their demeanour (as he himself describes it) accords with his supposition. There are but nine cases of which he gives any detailed report: we will take them all, placing them, however, in our own order. First, a German who had been brought in the day before—he was imploring for work. Second, an English thief, who had been in only a few days; still savage. These two cases may be set aside: the effects of the system not having had time to show itself. Third, A man convicted as a receiver of stolen goods; but who denied his guilt. He had been in for six years, and was to remain three more. 'He stopped his work when we went in, took off his spectacles, and answered freely to everything that was said to him. * * * * He wore a paper hat of his own making, and was pleased to have it noticed and commended. He had very ingeniously manufactured a sort of Dutch clock from some disregarded odds and ends; and his vinegar bottle served for the pendulum. Seeing me interested in this contrivance, he looked up at it with a great deal of pride, and said that he had been thinking of improving it, and that he hoped the hammer and a little piece of broken glass beside it would play music before long. He had extracted some colours from the yarn with which he worked, and painted a few poor figures on the wall.' Surely, this is not the demeanour, nor these the ways, of a man whose spirit is crushed and faculties destroyed—who suffers day and night from horrible fancies. Fourth, a German imprisoned for larceny; has been in for two years, and has three to come. 'With colours prepared in the same manner, he had painted every inch of the walls and ceiling quite beautifully. He had laid out the few feet of ground behind with exquisite neatness, and had made a little bed in the centre, which looked, hy the by, like a grave. The taste and ingenuity he had displayed in everything were most extraordinary.' Here again is very strange evidence of the destructive effects of solitude upon the faculties. Mr. Dickens goes on, it is true, to assure us that ' he never saw such a picture of forlorn affliction and distress of mind;' that 'his heart bled for him,' &c. And very unhappy he may well have been; people are not sent to prison to be made happy; but the question is, whether he was the worse or the better for it. Fifth, a negro burglar, notorious for his boldness and hardihood, and for the number of previous convictions—*his time nearly out.* He was at work making screws. ' He entertained us with a long account of his achievements, which he narrated with such infinite relish that he actually seemed to lick his lips as he told us racy anecdotes of stolen plate,' &c. Here, at any rate, we have a man who has not been made too miserable. Sixth, a man, of whom we are told no more than that he was allowed to keep rabbits as an indulgence; that he came out of his cell with one in his breast, and that Mr. Dickens thought it hard to say which was the nobler animal of the two. Seventh, ' a poet, who, *after doing two days' work in every four-and-twenty hours,* one for himself and one for the prison, *wrote verses* about ships, (he was by trade a mariner), and "the maddening wine-cup," and his friends at home.' Here, again, Mr. Dickens must have selected his examples very oddly—or one would think that solitary confinement called out a man's resources instead of paralyzing them. Eighth, at last we come to a case (probably *the* case) in point: a sailor who had been confined for *eleven years,* and would be free in a few months. Mr. D. does, indeed, here draw the picture of a man stupified by suffering; and we can well believe that the picture is just. But the most strenuous advocates of the solitary system will hardly maintain that there may not be too much of it. Try a man who has been in *two* years, and is going to be released next day, and see whether *his* case is hopeless. And here we have him—No. Nine, 'I have the face of this man before me now. It is almost more memorable in its happiness than the other faces in their misery. How easy and how natural was it for him to say that the system was a good one; and that the time went " pretty quick considering;" and that when a man once felt he had offended the law and must satisfy it, " he got along somehow ;" and so forth !' Upon women Mr. Dickens acknowledges that the effect of this punishment is different. He thinks it quite as wrong and cruel in their case; but admits that their faces are humanized and refined by it, and thinks it may be ' because of their *better nature* which is *elicited in solitude.*'

Upon the question at issue, we offer no opinion; but with these discrepancies between Mr. Dickens's facts and fancies, we can hardly be rash in saying that his authority, great as it is, should not be taken as decisive. Commending the matter, therefore, to the further consideration of the inspectors of prisons, we shall return to our own proper subject; which is the character of the American people as expressed in their civil institutions. In the case of this Philadelphia prison, Mr. Dickens's objections are confined to the principle. To the intentions, motives, and characters of those who are concerned in the management of it, as well as to the efficacy of the arrangements, he gives unqualified praise.

Another thing on which the true character of a people in its substantial qualities must be expected to impress itself, is the administration of Justice; and we wish that Mr. Dickens had frequented the Courts a little more. Except on extraordinary occasions, politics and party find no business there ; and where that is the case, the ablest man will naturally have the best place yielded to him, and the true interests (as distinguished from the fleeting inclinations) of the public will be consulted in all forms and proceedings; and in this, after all, consists the true health of the body politic. Let person and property be secured from violence, and let affairs be equitably adjusted between man and man, and what reasonable person would grudge his legislators their long speeches, their personal altercations, or even their *spittoons* ? From the scanty notices we have on this head scattered through these volumes, we should infer that America has no reason to shrink from this test. The high character of the Supreme Court is notorious through Europe. And Mr. Dickens tells us that in every place he visited, the Judges were men of high character and attainments; which is saying much, considering that in some of the States they are, we believe, annually elected by the people. Of their modes of proceeding he tells us nothing beyond the general picturesque effect ; and we are left to infer from his silence, that the want of wigs and gowns, and of raised platforms for witnesses and prisoners, does not obstruct the course of justice.

The condition of the Church in America is another thing which should throw great light on the character of the people ; for in this also politics does not interfere : each party can do as it pleases, and therefore no two need quarrel. Unfortunately there is a great want of sound information on this subject in England ; the popular notion of the style of religious worship in America being built, we believe, upon Mrs. Trollope's account of a *Revival.* Mr. Dickens does not tell us much : from what he does say we should imagine that the prevailing character of the Church in New England has more of old Puritanism in it than of modern Methodism. And we have heard it maintained by gentlemen who have resided in America, for months together, and visited different places of worship, that they have rarely met with any symptoms of fanaticism or sycophancy in the preacher, or of enthusiasm in the congregation ; but that the service, whatever the persuasion, was generally characterized by decency and dulness.

Of the system of Education in the United States, and the provision for it, (which should stand perhaps next in order as an illustration of the social character), Mr. Dickens says but little. We hear occasionally of a College or a School ; and we gather generally, that sufficient provision is made by each State to enable every citizen to receive some degree of education. The proportion of adults who cannot read and write is consequently extremely small ; and among these we believe there are scarcely any native Americans. Beyond this fact, which is of great importance, we can learn nothing that is much to our purpose. We could have wished to know, first, the amount of knowledge, and the kind of intellectual cultivation which a man must have, in order to take rank in general opinion as a well-educated man ; and, next, the style and amount of accomplishments which are requisite to *distinguish* him in that rank. This would show in what direction the great body of the intellect of the country is working. It would also be very interesting to know something about the composition of American Libraries, especially private ones. What kind of books do you find *permanently* established on the shelves in a gentleman's study ; and of those, which appear to have been most used ? We say permanently ; because it is of much less consequence to know which, among the publications of the day, are the most popular. These are read, as newspapers are, not because they are congenial to the taste, but because reading is fashionable, and they are of the newest fashion. Their universal popularity indicates little in the national character beyond a general appetite for light stimulants, and produces little alteration in it except perhaps some general debilitation from swallowing such a deluge of slops. But for the most part, we believe that this kind of literature passes through the mind with as little effect upon it for good or evil, as the conversation of a morning-caller. It is the favourite, not the fashionable, book that betrays the character of the man; and it is the book which works itself into public favour *against* the fashion that indicates the character of the people. That the miscellaneous writings of Mr. Carlyle had been collected and printed in America, before his name was generally known in England, is a fact which tells much more about the intellectual and spiritual capacities of the people, than we can infer from knowing that the whole brood of New-Burlington Street are circulated as fast as they come out, for an annual subscription of a few dollars. The character of the native periodical literature of the costlier class, and therefore of more limited circulation, would throw further light on the matter; for it would show not only what the more select class of readers will pay for, but what the better class of writers can produce. The North American, and the New York Reviews, for instance, will give a juster, as well as a higher idea of the tendencies and prospects of American literature, than the most ambitious and elaborate pamphlets, speeches, and state papers—all of which are addressed to a wider, but a lower, circle.

Whether Mr. Dickens has much considered the subject of American literature in its true bearings, we are not informed. From these volumes, we can only gather that he is deeply read in their Newspapers; the character of which he denounces in his bitterest, and by no means his best style. Of the justice of his censures, not having ourselves gone through the nauseous course of reading by which he has qualified himself to speak, we can form no opinion. We shall only say, that, looking at the condition of our own Daily Press, and imagining what it would be were it turned loose in a land of cheap printing and no stamp duties—where everybody could read, and everybody took a part in politics; and without any capital city in which public opinion might gather to a head and express itself with authority—we can readily believe it to be true in the full extent. Thanks to London, which concentrates and represents the feelings of the British people, the leading London Journals (and from them the provincial press throughout the country takes its tone) are held under some restraint. Gross violations of manners are not countenanced; and wanton slander of private persons would not be tolerated. Moreover, the enormous

amount of information which is demanded of an English Newspaper, cannot be supplied at first hand without a costly establishment and machinery; and this, requiring large capital to start with, excludes the worst class of adventurers from competition; and insures in the proprietor that kind and amount of respectability which in England always accompanies substance. A man with something to lose will not offend the feelings of the mass of his customers; a man with nothing, cannot get up a Paper which has any chance of general circulation. We fear, however, that it is impossible to answer for more than this. Private houses, we trust, are (from the stamped press at least) secure. But what conspicuous public man can be insured against the most malignant slander from one party, and the grossest adulation from the other—both equally unprincipled? What measure of what party was ever discussed by the Daily Press, on either side, upon its real merits, or with a desire to represent it truly? What misrepresentation is too gross for our most respectable Newspapers to take up? What rumour too injurious and too ill-founded for them to spread? What sophism so palpable, that if it can be used with effect to damage the character of a political opponent, they will not employ it? And the worst is, that in the guilt of this, the respectability of England is directly implicated. It cannot be said that the disease is incident to liberty, and must be borne with; for, strange to say, this kind of licentious writing, (known as it is, and thoroughly understood to be licentious), is what the great mass of news *readers* like. The writer has no interest in his malice; he may be a very good-humoured man, with no wish to injure anybody. But the readers must have what they call *vigour.* Their party spirit must be at once roused and gratified by powerful attacks, and powerful vindications. A leading article, written in a spirit of candour and justice, (unless it be known to proceed from some responsible quarter, in which case it has a separate and superior interest), is felt to be insipid. It is true, that the influence of these compositions is not so great as might appear at first, because they impose on nobody; everybody knows that they are full of falsehoods. Convict a newspaper of the grossest misrepresentation, and which of its 'constant readers' will be shocked?—even though the writer should not acknowledge his fault. Their influence is, however, considerable, and, so far as it goes, most pernicious. We cannot but regard the condition of our own Daily Press, as a morning and evening witness against the moral character of the people; for if this kind of scurrility were as distasteful to the public, as the grosser kinds of licentiousness are, it would at once disappear. That its condition is still worse in America, we can, for the reasons above indicated, easily believe; but we doubt whether it be fair to draw the same inference from the fact, as to the moral tastes and feelings of the people; for the respectability of America, not having the same means of expressing its will that the respectability of England has, cannot be held in the same degree answerable. In the mean time, we hope that Mr. Dickens is mistaken as to the degree in which the Press in the United States impresses and influences the general feeling. We cannot but think that, if his description of it be just, the strength of the poison must act as an antidote. Does any well-educated man in America, read these papers *with respect?*

Among other circumstances, from which something as to the social characteristics of the people may be safely inferred, certain definite, and generally established reputations of society may be mentioned;—such, for instance, as the courtesy which everybody is expected, as a matter of course, to pay to women and to strangers. And we should be inclined to draw very favourable inferences from the fact, that in all public places, including public conveyances, a woman is entitled to the best place, *occupied or unoccupied,* for possession on the part of the man goes for nothing; and also from the courtesies of the Custom-House, which, we believe, all foreigners will bear witness to. Captain Hamilton, indeed, was so possessed with the notion that this business could not be transacted without intolerable annoyance, that he kept away. But Captain Basil Hall gives a pleasant anecdote, to show in how gentlemanly a manner the thing may be done. And Mr. Dickens commends to our special consideration and imitation the 'attention, politeness, and good-humour, with which the custom-house officers at Boston discharged their duty.'

We have now nearly exhausted these volumes of the information which they supply, available for the purpose with which we set out. Of the manners of the mass of the people, Mr. Dickens gives many amusing illustrations; most of which have been already quoted in various publications, and have made us all very merry. It is but justice to him, however, to say, that he saw all these things in their true light; and that, while indulging his sense of the ludicrous by a hearty English laugh, he was not betrayed by them into any foolish conclusions, or illiberal (we wish we could add *un-English*) contempt. The following sensible remarks are worth extracting,

not because they tell us anything which is not obvious to any man who thinks; but because so few people trouble themselves with thinking about the matter. The scene is Sandusky, at the south-western extremity of Lake Erie.

'We put up at a comfortable little hotel. .... Our host, who was very attentive, and anxious to make us comfortable, was a handsome middle-aged man, who had come to this town from New England, in which part of the country he was "raised:" When I say that he constantly walked in and out of the room with his hat on, and stopped to converse in the same free-and-easy state, and lay down on our sofa, and pulled his newspaper out of his pocket and read it at his ease—I merely mention these traits as characteristic of the country; not at all as being matter of complaint, or as having been disagreeable to me. I should undoubtedly be offended by such proceedings at home, because there they are not the custom, and where they are not, they would be impertinences. But in America the only desire of a good-natured fellow of this kind is to treat his guests hospitably and well; and I had no more right, and I can truly say no more disposition, to measure his conduct by our English rule and standard, than I had to quarrel with him for not being of the exact stature which would qualify him for admission into the Queen's Grenadier Guards. As little inclination had I to find fault with a funny old lady, who was an upper domestic in this establishment, and who, when she came to wait upon us at any meal, sat herself down comfortably in the most convenient chair, and, producing a large pin to pick her teeth with, remained performing that ceremony, and steadfastly regarding us meanwhile with much gravity and composure, (now and then pressing us to eat a little more,) until it was time to clear away. It was enough for us, that whatever we wished done was done with great civility and readiness, and a desire to oblige, not only here but everywhere else; and that all our wants were in general zealously anticipated.'—Vol. ii., p. 170.

Further on in the volume, a good story about an American bootmaker, which has been quoted everywhere, is introduced by the following general remark, which has not yet, we believe, been anywhere quoted.

'The republican institutions of America undoubtedly lead the people to assert their self-respect and their equality; but a traveller is bound to bear those institutions in his mind, and not hastily to resent the near approach of a class of strangers, who at home would keep aloof. This characteristic, when it is tinctured by no foolish pride, and stops short of no honest service, never offended me; and I very seldom, if ever, experienced its rude or unbecoming display.'—Vol. ii., p. 300.

The political condition of the United States has been discussed, on various occasions, in this Journal. Mr. Dickens's *Notes* do not'throw any new light upon it; and, as ho peculiar- interest attaches to his opinions on such subjects, we do not feel called upon to criticize them. We have treated the work gravely, out of respect for its author, and the gravity of the subject; and partly because the superior attractiveness and general quotation of the lighter parts is likely, we fear, to give a false impression of the tone and spirit of the whole. In thus endeavouring to collect the substance of his more serious observations, we have no doubt, in a great measure, lost sight of the prevailing character and spirit of his book. But of this it is enough to say, that it leaves our opinion of Mr. Dickens's powers just as before.

Art. IX.—*Diary and Letters of Madame D'Arblay.* Five vols. 8vo. London: 1842.

Though the world saw and heard little of Madame D'Arblay during the last forty years of her life, and though that little did not add to her fame, there were thousands, we believe, who felt a singular emotion when they learned that she was no longer among us. The news of her death carried the minds of men back at one leap, clear over two generations, to the time when her first literary triumphs were won. All those whom we had been accustomed to revere as intellectual patriarchs, seemed children when compared with her; for Burke had sate up all night to read her writings, and Johnson had pronounced her superior [to Fielding, when Rogers was still a schoolboy, and Southey still in petticoats. Yet more strange did it seem that we should just have lost one whose name had been widely celebrated before anybody had heard of some illustrious men who, twenty, thirty, or forty years ago, were, after a long and splendid career, borne with honour to the grave. Yet so it was. Frances Burney was at the height of fame and popularity before Cowper had published his first volume, before Porson had gone up to college, before Pitt had taken his seat in the House of Commons, before the voice of Erskine had been once heard in Westminster Hall. Since the appearance of her first work, sixty-two years had passed; and this interval had been crowded, not only with political, but also with intellectual revolutions. Thousands of reputations had, during that period, sprung up, bloomed, withered, and disappeared. New kinds of composition had come into fashion, had gone out of fashion,

had been derided, had been forgotten. The fooleries of Della Crusca, and the fooleries of Kotzebue, had for a time bewitched the multitude, but had left no trace behind them; nor had misdirected genius been able to save from decay the once flourishing schools of Godwin, of Darwin, and of Radcliffe. Many books, written for temporary effect, had run through six or seven editions, and had then been gathered to the novels of Afra Behn, and the epic poems of Sir Richard Blackmore. Yet the early works of Madame D'Arblay, in spite of the lapse of years, in spite of the change of manners, in spite of the popularity deservedly obtained by some of her rivals, continued to hold a high place in the public esteem. She lived to be a classic. Time set on her fame, before she went hence, that seal which is seldom set except on the fame of the departed. Like Sir Condy Rackrent in the tale, she survived her own wake, and overheard the judgment of posterity.

Having always felt a warm and sincere, though not a blind admiration for her talents, we rejoiced to learn that her Diary was about to be made public. Our hopes, it is true, were not unmixed with fears. We could not forget the fate of the Memoirs of Dr. Burney, which were published ten years ago. That unfortunate book contained much that was curious and interesting. Yet it was received with a cry of disgust, and was speedily consigned to oblivion. The truth is, that it deserved its doom. It was written in Madame D'Arblay's later style—the worst style that has ever been known among men. No genius, no information, could save from proscription a book so written. We, therefore, opened the Diary with no small anxiety, trembling lest we should light upon some of that peculiar rhetoric which deforms almost every page of the Memoirs, and which it is impossible to read without a sensation made up of mirth, shame, and loathing. We soon, however, discovered to our great delight that this Diary was kept before Madame D'Arblay became eloquent. It is, for the most part, written in her earliest and best manner; in true woman's English, clear, natural, and lively. The two works are lying side by side before us, and we never turn from the Memoirs to the Diary without a sense of relief. The difference is as great as the difference between the atmosphere of a perfumer's shop, fetid with lavender water and jasmine soap, and the air of a heath on a fine morning in May. Both works ought to be consulted by every person who wishes to be well acquainted with the history of our literature and our manners. But to read the Diary is a pleasure; to read the Memoirs will always be a task.

We may, perhaps, afford some harmless amusement to our readers if we attempt, with the help of these two books, to give them an account of the most important years of Madame D'Arblay's life.

She was descended from a family which bore the name of Macburney, and which, though probably of Irish origin, had been long settled in Shropshire, and was possessed of considerable estates in that county. Unhappily, many years before her birth, the Macburneys began, as if of set purpose and in a spirit of determined rivalry, to expose and ruin themselves. The heir apparent, Mr. James Macburney, offended his father by making a runaway match with an actress from Goodman's Fields. The old gentleman could devise no more judicious mode of wreaking vengeance on his undutiful boy, than by marrying the cook. The cook gave birth to a son named Joseph, who succeeded to all the lands of the family, while James was cut off with a shilling. The favourite son, however, was so extravagant, that he soon became as poor as his disinherited brother. Both were forced to earn their bread by their labour. Joseph turned dancing-master, and settled in Norfolk. James struck off the Mac from the beginning of his name, and set up as a portrait-painter at Chester. Here he had a son named Charles, well known as the author of the History of Music, and as the father of two remarkable children, of a son distinguished by learning, and of a daughter still more honourably distinguished by genius.

Charles early showed a taste for that art, of which, at a later period, he became the historian. He was apprenticed to a celebrated musician in London, and applied himself to study with vigour and success. He early found a kind and munificent patron in Fulk Greville, a high-born, a high-bred man, who seems to have had in large measure all the accomplishments and all the follies, all the virtues and all the vices which, a hundred years ago, were considered as making up the character of a fine gentleman. Under such protection, the young artist had every prospect of a brilliant career in the capital. But his health failed. It became necessary for him to retreat from the smoke and river fog of London, to the pure air of the coast. He accepted the place of organist at Lynn, and settled at that town with a young lady who had recently become his wife.

At Lynn, in June, 1752, Frances Burney was born. Nothing in her childhood indicated that she would, while still a young woman, have secured for herself an honourable and permanent place among English writers. She was shy and silent. Her brothers and sisters called her a dunce, and not altogether without some show of reason; for at eight years old she did not know her letters.

In 1760, Mr. Burney quitted Lynn for London, and took a house in Poland Street; a situation which had been fashionable in the reign of Queen Anne, but which, since that time, had been deserted by most of its wealthy and noble inhabitants. He afterwards resided in St. Martin's Street, on the south side of Leicester Square. His house there is still well known, and will continue to be well known as long as our island retains any trace of civilisation; for it was the dwelling of Newton, and the square turret which distinguishes it from all the surrounding buildings was Newton's observatory.

Mr. Burney at once obtained as many pupils of the most respectable description as he had time to attend, and was thus enabled to support his family, modestly indeed, and frugally, but in comfort and independence. His professional merit obtained for him the degree of Doctor of Music from the University of Oxford; and his works on subjects connected with his art gained for him a place, respectable, though certainly not eminent, among men of letters.

The progress of the mind of Frances Burney, from her ninth to her twenty-fifth year, well deserves to be recorded. When her education had proceeded no further than the horn-book, she lost her mother, and thenceforward she educated herself. Her father appears to have been as bad a father as a very honest, affectionate, and sweet-tempered man can well be. He loved his daughter dearly; but it never seems to have occurred to him that a parent has other duties to perform to children than that of fondling them. It would indeed have been impossible for him to superintend their education himself. His professional engagements occupied him all day. At seven in the morning he began to attend his pupils, and, when London was full, was sometimes employed in teaching till eleven at night. He was often forced to carry in his pocket a tin box of sandwiches, and a bottle of wine and water, on which he dined in a hackney-coach while hurrying from one scholar to another. Two of his daughters he sent to a seminary at Paris; but he imagined that Frances would run some risk of being perverted from the Protestant faith if she were educated in a Catholic country, and he therefore kept her at home. No governess, no teacher of any art or of any language, was provided for her. But one of her sisters showed her how to write; and, before she was fourteen, she began to find pleasure in reading.

It was not, however, by reading that her

intellect was formed. Indeed, when her best novels were produced, her knowledge of books was very small. When at the height of her fame, she was unacquainted with the most celebrated works of Voltaire and Molière; and, what seems still more extraordinary, had never heard or seen a line of Churchill, who, when she was a girl, was the most popular of living poets. It is particularly deserving of observation, that she appears to have been by no means a novel reader. Her father's library was large; and he had admitted into it so many books which rigid moralists generally exclude, that he felt uneasy, as he afterwards owned, when Johnson began to examine the shelves. But in the whole collection there was only a single novel, Fielding's Amelia.

An education, however, which to most girls would have been useless, but which suited Fanny's mind better than elaborate culture, was in constant progress during her passage from childhood to womanhood. The great book of human nature was turned over before her. Her father's social position was very peculiar. He belonged in fortune and station to the middle class. His daughters seem to have been suffered to mix freely with those whom butlers and waiting-maids call vulgar. We are told that they were in the habit of playing with the children of a wig-maker who lived in the adjoining house. Yet few nobles could assemble in the most stately mansions of Grosvenor Square or St. James's Square, a society so various and so brilliant as was sometimes to be found in Dr. Burney's cabin. His mind, though not very powerful or capacious, was restlessly active; and, in the intervals of his professional pursuits, he had contrived to lay up much miscellaneous information. His attainments, the suavity of his temper, and the gentle simplicity of his manners, had obtained for him ready admission to the first literary circles. While he was still at Lynn, he had won Johnson's heart by sounding with honest zeal the praises of the English Dictionary. In London the two friends met frequently, and agreed most harmoniously. One tie, indeed, was wanting to their mutual attachment. Burney loved his own art passionately; and Johnson just knew the bell of St. Clement's church from the organ. They had, however, many topics in common; and on winter nights their conversations were sometimes prolonged till the fire had gone out, and the candles had burned away to the wicks. Burney's admiration of the powers which had produced Rasselas and the Rambler, bordered on idolatry. He gave a singular proof of this at his first visit to Johnson's ill-furnished garret. The master of the apartment was not at home. The enthusiastic visitor looked about for some relique which he might carry away; but he could see nothing lighter than the chairs and the fire-irons. At last he discovered an old broom, tore some bristles from the stump, wrapped them in silver paper, and departed as happy as Louis IX. when the holy nail of St. Denis was found. Johnson, on the other hand, condescended to growl out that Burney was an honest fellow, a man whom it was impossible not to like.

Garrick, too, was a frequent visitor in Poland Street and St. Martin's Lane. That wonderful actor loved the society of children, partly from good-nature and partly from vanity. The ecstasies of mirth and terror which his gestures and play of countenance never failed to produce in a nursery, flattered him quite as much as the applause of mature critics. He often exhibited all his powers of mimicry for the amusement of the little Burneys, awed them by shuddering and crouching as if he saw a ghost, scared them by raving like a maniac in St. Luke's, and then at once became an auctioneer, a chimney sweeper, or an old woman, and made them laugh till the tears ran down their cheeks.

But it would be tedious to recount the names of all the men of letters and artists whom Frances Burney had an opportunity of seeing and hearing. Colman, Twining, Harris, Baretti, Hawkesworth, Reynolds, Barry, were among those who occasionally surrounded the tea-table and supper-tray at her father's modest dwelling. This was not all. The distinction which Dr. Burney had acquired as a musician, and as the historian of music, attracted to his house the most eminent musical performers of that age. The greatest Italian singers who visited England regarded him as the dispenser of fame in their art, and exerted themselves to obtain his suffrage. Pachierotti became his intimate friend. The rapacious Agujari, who sang for nobody else under fifty pounds an air, sang her best for Dr Burney without a fee; and in the company of Dr. Burney even the haughty and eccentric Gabrielli constrained herself to behave with civility. It was thus in his power to give, with scarcely any expense, concerts equal to those of the aristocracy. On such occasions, the quiet street in which he lived was blocked up by coroneted chariots, and his little drawing-room was crowded with peers, peeresses, ministers, and ambassadors. On one evening, of which we happen to have a full account, there were present Lord Mulgrave, Lord Bruce, Lord and Lady Edgecumbe, Lord Barrington from the War-Office, Lord Sandwich from the Admiralty, Lord Ashburnham, with his gold key dangling from his pocket, and the French Ambassador, M.

de Guignes, renowned for his fine person and for his success in gallantry. But the great show of the night was the Russian Ambassador, Count Orloff, whose gigantic figure was all in a blaze with jewels, and in whose demeanour the untamed ferocity of the Scythian might be discerned through a thin varnish of French politeness. As he stalked about the small parlour, brushing the ceiling with his toupee, the girls whispered to each other, with mingled admiration and horror, that he was the favoured lover of his august mistress; that he had borne the chief part in the revolution to which she owed her throne; and that his huge hands, now glittering with diamond rings, had given the last squeeze to the windpipe of her unfortunate husband.

With such illustrious guests as these were mingled all the most remarkable specimens of the race of lions—a kind of game which is hunted in London every spring with more than Meltonian ardour and perseverance. Bruce, who had washed down steaks cut from living oxen with water from the fountains of the Nile, came to swagger and talk about his travels. Omai lisped broken English, and made all the assembled musicians hold their ears by howling Otaheitean love-songs, such as those with which Oberea charmed her Opano.

With the literary and fashionable society which occasionally met under Dr. Burney's roof, Frances can scarcely be said to have mingled. She was not a musician, and could therefore bear no part in the concerts. She was shy almost to awkwardness, and scarcely ever joined in the conversation. The slightest remark from a stranger disconcerted her; and even the old friends of her father who tried to draw her out could seldom extract more than a Yes or a No. Her figure was small, her face not distinguished by beauty. She was therefore suffered to withdraw quietly to the background, and, unobserved herself, to observe all that passed. Her nearest relations were aware that she had good sense, but seem not to have suspected, that under her demure and bashful deportment were concealed a fertile invention and a keen sense of the ridiculous. She had not, it is true, an eye for the fine shades of character. But every marked peculiarity instantly caught her notice and remained engraven on her imagination. Thus, while still a girl, she had laid up such a store of materials for fiction as few of those who mix much in the world are able to accumulate during a long life. She had watched and listened to people of every class, from princes and great officers of state down to artists living in garrets, and poets familiar with subterranean cook shops. Hun-

dreds of remarkable persons had passed in review before her, English, French, German, Italian, lords and fiddlers, deans of cathedrals and managers of theatres, travellers leading about newly caught savages, and singing women escorted by deputy-husbands.

So strong was the impression made on the mind of Frances by the society which she was in the habit of seeing and hearing, that she began to write little fictitious narratives as soon as she could use her pen with ease, which, as we have said, was not very early. Her sisters were amused by her stories. But Dr. Burney knew nothing of their existence; and in another quarter her literary propensities met with serious discouragement. When she was fifteen her father took a second wife. The new Mrs. Burney soon found out that her step-daughter was fond of scribbling, and delivered several good-natured lectures on the subject. The advice no doubt was well-meant, and might have been given by the most judicious friend; for at that time, from causes to which we may hereafter advert, nothing could be more disadvantageous to a young lady than to be known as a novel-writer. Frances yielded, relinquished her favourite pursuit, and made a bonfire of all her manuscripts.[*]

She now hemmed and stitched from breakfast to dinner with scrupulous regularity. But the dinners of that time were early; and the afternoon was her own. Though she had given up novel-writing, she was still fond of using her pen. She began to keep a diary, and she corresponded largely with a person who seems to have had the chief share in the formation of her mind. This was Samuel Crisp, an old friend of her father. His name, well known, near a century ago, in the most splendid circles of London, has long been forgotten. His history is, however, so interesting and instructive, that it tempts us to venture on a digression.

Long before Frances Burney was born, Mr. Crisp had made his entrance into the world, with every advantage. He was well connected and well educated. His face and figure were conspicuously handsome; his manners were polished; his fortune was easy; his character was without stain; he lived in the best society; he had read much; he

---

* There is some difficulty here as to the chronology. 'This sacrifice,' says the editor of the Diary, 'was made in the young authoress's fifteenth year.' This could not be; for the sacrifice was the effect, according to the editor's own showing, of the remonstrances of the second Mrs. Burney; and Frances was in her sixteenth year when her father's second marriage took place.

talked well; his taste in literature, music, painting, architecture, sculpture, was held in high esteem. Nothing that the world can give seemed to be wanting to his happiness and respectability, except that he should understand the limits of his powers, and should not throw away distinctions which were within his reach in the pursuit of distinctions which were unattainable.

'It is an uncontrolled truth,' says Swift, 'that no man ever made an ill figure who understood his own talents, nor a good one who mistook them.' Every day brings with it fresh illustrations of this weighty saying; but the best commentary that we remember is the history of Samuel Crisp. Men like him have their proper place, and it is a most important one, in the Commonwealth of Letters. It is by the judgment of such men that the rank of authors is finally determined. It is neither to the multitude, nor to the few who are gifted with great creative genius, that we are to look for sound critical decisions. The multitude, unacquainted with the best models, are captivated by whatever stuns and dazzles them. They deserted Mrs. Siddons to run after Master Betty; and they now prefer, we have no doubt, Jack Sheppard to Von Artevelde. A man of great original genius, on the other hand, a man who has attained to mastery in some high walk of art, is by no means to be implicitly trusted as a judge of the performances of others. The erroneous decisions pronounced by such men are without number. It is commonly supposed that jealousy makes them unjust. But a more creditable explanation may easily be given. The very excellence of a work shows that some of the faculties of the author have been developed at the expense of the rest; for it is not given to the human intellect to expand itself widely in all directions at once, and to be at the same time gigantic and well-proportioned. Whoever becomes pre-eminent in any art, nay, in any style of art, generally does so by devoting himself with intense and exclusive enthusiasm to the pursuit of one kind of excellence. His perception of other kinds of excellence is therefore too often impaired. Out of his own department he praises and blames at random, and is far less to be trusted than the mere connoisseur, who produces nothing, and whose business is only to judge and enjoy. One painter is distinguished by his exquisite finishing. He toils day after day to bring the veins of a cabbage-leaf, the folds of a lace veil, the wrinkles of an old woman's face, nearer and nearer to perfection. In the time which he employs on a square foot of canvass, a master of a different order covers the walls of a palace with gods bury-ing giants under mountains, or makes the cupola of a church alive with seraphim and martyrs. The more fervent the passion of each of these artists for his art, the higher the merit of each in his own line, the more unlikely it is that they will justly appreciate each other. Many persons who never handled a pencil, probably do far more justice to Michael Angelo than would have been done by Gerhard Douw, and far more justice to Gerhard Douw than would have been done by Michael Angelo.

It is the same with literature. Thousands who have no spark of the genius of Dryden or Wordsworth, do to Dryden the justice which has never been done by Wordsworth, and to Wordsworth the justice which, we suspect, would never have been done by Dryden. Gray, Johnson, Richardson, Fielding, are all highly esteemed by the great body of intelligent and well-informed men. But Gray could see no merit in Rasselas; and Johnson could see no merit in the Bard. Fielding thought Richardson a solemn prig; and Richardson perpetually expressed contempt and disgust for Fielding's lowness.

Mr. Crisp seems, as far as we can judge, to have been a man eminently qualified for the useful office of a connoisseur. His talents and knowledge fitted him to appreciate justly almost every species of intellectual superiority. As an adviser he was inestimable. Nay, he might probably have held a respectable rank as a writer, if he would have confined himself to some department of literature in which nothing more than sense, taste, and reading was required. Unhappily, he set his heart on being a great poet, wrote a tragedy in five acts on the death of Virginia, and offered it to Garrick, who was his personal friend. Garrick read, shook his head, and expressed a doubt whether it would be wise in Mr. Crisp to stake a reputation which stood high on the success of such a piece. But the author, blinded by self-love, set in motion a machinery such as none could long resist. His intercessors were the most eloquent man and the most lovely woman of that generation. Pitt was induced to read Virginia, and to pronounce it excellent. Lady Coventry, with fingers which might have furnished a model to sculptors, forced the manuscript into the reluctant hand of the manager; and in the year 1754, the play was brought forward.

Nothing that skill or friendship could do was omitted. Garrick wrote both prologue and epilogue. The zealous friends of the author filled every box; and, by their strenuous exertions, the life of the play was prolonged during ten nights. But, though there was no clamorous reprobation, it was universally felt that the attempt had failed. When Virginia was printed, the public disappointment was even greater than at the representation. The critics, the Monthly Reviewers in particular, fell on plot, characters, and diction without mercy, but, we fear, not without justice. We have never met with a copy of the play; but, if we may judge from the lines which are extracted in the Gentleman's Magazine, and which do not appear to have been malevolently selected, we should say that nothing but the acting of Garrick, and the partiality of the audience, could have saved so feeble and unnatural a drama from instant damnation.

The ambition of·the poet was still unsubdued. When the London season closed, he applied himself vigorously to the work of removing blemishes. He does not seem to have suspected, what we are strongly inclined to suspect, that the whole piece was one blemish, and that the passages which were meant to be fine, were, in truth, bursts of that tame extravagance into which writers fall, when they set themselves to be sublime and pathetic in spite of nature. He omitted, added, retouched, and flattered himself with hopes of a complete success in the following year; but, in the following year, Garrick showed no disposition to bring the amended tragedy on the stage. Solicitation and remonstrances were tried in vain. Lady Coventry, drooping under that malady which seems ever to select what is loveliest for its prey, could render no assistance. The manager's language was civilly evasive; but his resolution was inflexible.

Crisp had committed a great error; but he had escaped with a very slight penance His play had not been hooted from the boards. It had, on the contrary, been better received than many very estimable performances have been—than Johnson's Irene, for example—and Goldsmith's Good-Natured Man. Had Crisp been wise, he would have thought himself happy in having purchased self-knowledge so cheap. He would have relinquished without vain repinings the hope of poetical distinction, and would have turned to the many sources of happiness which he still possessed. Had he been, on the other hand, an unfeeling and unblushing dunce, he would have gone on writing scores of bad tragedies in defiance of censure and derision. But he had too much sense to risk a second defeat, yet too little to bear his first defeat like a man. The fatal delusion that he was a great dramatist, had taken firm possession of his mind. His failure he attributed to every cause except the true one. He complained of the ill-will of Garrick, who appears to have done everything that ability and zeal could

do; and who, from selfish motives, would of course, have been well pleased if Virginia had been as successful as the Beggar's Opera. Nay, Crisp complained of the languor of the friends whose partiality had given him three benefit-nights to which he had no claim. He complained of the injustice of the spectators, when, in truth, he ought to have been grateful for their unexampled patience. He lost his temper and spirits, and became a cynic and a hater of mankind. From London he retired to Hampton, and from Hampton to a solitary and long-deserted mansion, built on a common in one of the wildest tracts of Surrey. No road, not even a sheep-walk, connected his lonely dwelling with the abodes of men. The place of his retreat was strictly concealed from his old associates. In the spring he sometimes emerged, and was seen at exhibitions and concerts in London. But he soon disappeared and hid himself, with no society but his books, in his dreary hermitage. He survived his failure about thirty years. A new generation sprang up around him. No memory of his bad verses remained among men. How completely the world had lost sight of him, will appear from a single circumstance. We looked for his name in a copious Dictionary of Dramatic Authors published while he was still alive, and we found only that Mr. Samuel Crisp, of the Customhouse, had written a play called Virginia, acted in 1754. To the last, however, the unhappy man continued to brood over the injustice of the manager and the pit, and tried to convince himself and others that he had missed the highest literary honours, only because he had omitted some fine passages in compliance with Garrick's judgment. Alas, for human nature! that the wounds of vanity should smart and bleed so much longer than the wounds of affection! Few people, we believe, whose nearest friends and relations died in 1754, had any acute feeling of their loss in 1782. Dear sisters and favourite daughters, and brides snatched away before the honey-moon was passed, had been forgotten, or were remembered only with a tranquil regret. But Samuel Crisp was still mourning for his tragedy, like Rachel weeping for her children, and would not be comforted. 'Never,' such was his language twenty eight years after his disaster, 'never give up or alter a tittle unless it perfectly coincides with your own inward feelings. I can say this to my sorrow and my cost. But, mum!' Soon after these words were written, his life—a life which might have been eminently useful and happy—ended in the same gloom in which, during more than a quarter of a century, it had been passed. We have thought it worth while to rescue from oblivion this curious fragment of literary history. It seems to us at once ludicrous, melancholy, and full of instruction.

Crisp was an old and very intimate friend of the Burneys. To them alone was confided the name of the desolate old hall in which he hid himself like a wild beast in a den. For them were reserved such remains of his humanity as had survived the failure of his play. Frances Burney he regarded as his daughter. He called her his Fannikin, and she in return called him her dear Daddy. In truth, he seems to have done much more than her real father for the developement of her intellect; for though he was a bad poet, he was a scholar, a thinker, and an excellent counsellor. He was practically fond of Dr. Burney's concerts. They had, indeed, been commenced at his suggestion, and when he visited London he constantly attended them. But when he grew old, and when gout, brought on partly by mental irritation, confined him to his retreat, he was desirous of having a glimpse of that gay and brilliant world from which he was exiled, and he pressed Fannikin to send him full accounts of her father's evening parties. A few of her letters to him have been published; and it is impossible to read them without discerning in them all the powers which afterwards produced Evelina and Cecilia, the quickness in catching every odd peculiarity of character and manner, the skill in grouping, the humour, often richly comic, sometimes even farcical.

Fanny's propensity to novel-writing had for a time been kept down. It now rose up stronger than ever. The heroes and heroines of the tales which had perished in the flames, were still present to the eye of her mind. One favourite story, in particular, haunted her imagination. It was about a certain Caroline Evelyn, a beautiful damsel who made an unfortunate love-match, and died, leaving an infant daughter. Frances began to image to herself the various scenes, tragic and comic, through which the poor motherless girl, highly connected on one side, meanly connected on the other, might have to pass. A crowd of unreal beings, good and bad, grave and ludicrous, surrounded the pretty, timid, young orphan; a coarse sea-captain; an ugly insolent fop, blazing in a superb court-dress; another fop, as ugly and as insolent, but lodged on Snow-Hill, and tricked out in second-hand finery for the Hampstead ball; an old woman, all wrinkle and rouge, flirting her fan with the air of a Miss of seventeen, and screaming in a dialect made up of vulgar French and vulgar English; a poet, lean and ragged, with a broad Scotch accent. By degrees these shadows acquired stronger and stronger consistence: the impulse which urged Frances to write became irresistible; and the result was the history of Evelina.

Then came, naturally enough, a wish, mingled with many fears, to appear before the public; for, timid as Frances was, and bashful, and altogether unaccustomed to hear her own praises, it is clear that she wanted neither a strong passion for distinction, nor a just confidence in her own powers. Her scheme was to become, if possible, a candidate for fame without running any risk of disgrace. She had not money to bear the expense of printing. It was therefore necessary that some bookseller should be induced to take the risk; and such a bookseller was not readily found. Dodsley refused even to look at the manuscript unless he were trusted with the name of the author. A publisher in Fleet Street, named Lowndes, was more complaisant. Some correspondence took place between this person and Miss Burney, who took the name of Grafton, and desired that the letters addressed to her might be left at the Orange Coffee-House. But, before the bargain was finally struck, Fanny thought it her duty to obtain her father's consent. She told him that she had written a book, that she wished to have his permission to publish it anonymously, but that she hoped that he would not insist upon seeing it. What followed may serve to illustrate what we meant when we said that Dr. Burney was as bad a father as so good-hearted a man could possibly be. It never seems to have crossed his mind that Fanny was about to take a step on which the whole happiness of her life might depend—a step which might raise her to an honourable eminence, or cover her with ridicule and contempt. Several people had already been trusted, and strict concealment was therefore not to be expected. On so grave an occasion, it was surely his duty to give his best counsel to his daughter, to win her confidence, to prevent her from exposing herself if her book were a bad one, and, if it were a good one, to see that the terms which she made with the publisher were likely to be beneficial to her. Instead of this, he only stared, burst out a laughing, kissed her, gave her leave to do as she liked, and never even asked the name of her work. The contract with Lowndes was speedily concluded. Twenty pounds were given for the copyright, and were accepted by Fanny with delight. Her father's inexcusable neglect of his duty, happily caused her no worse evil than the loss of twelve or fifteen hundred pounds.

After many delays Evelina appeared in January, 1778. Poor Fanny was sick with terror, and durst hardly stir out of doors. Some days passed before anything was heard of the book. It had, indeed, nothing but its own merits to push it into public favour. Its author was unknown. The house by which it was published, was not, we believe, held in high estimation. No body of partisans had been engaged to applaud. The better class of readers expected little from a novel about a young lady's entrance into the world. There was, indeed, at that time a disposition among the most respectable people to condemn novels generally : nor was this disposition by any means without excuse ; for works of that sort were then almost always silly, and very frequently wicked.

Soon, however, the first faint accents of praise began to be heard. The keepers of the circulating libraries reported that everybody was asking for Evelina, and that some person had guessed Anstey to be the author. Then came a favourable notice in the London Review ; then another still more favourable in the Monthly. And now the book found its way to tables which had seldom been polluted by marble-covered volumes. Scholars and statesmen, who contemptuously abandoned the crowd of romances to Miss Lydia Languish and Miss Sukey Saunter, were not ashamed to own that they could not tear themselves away from Evelina. Fine carriages and rich liveries, not often seen east of Temple Bar, were attracted to the publisher's shop in Fleet Street. Lowndes was daily questioned about the author; but was himself as much in the dark as any of the questioners. The mystery, however, could not remain a mystery long. It was known to brothers and sisters, aunts and cousins : and they were far too proud and too happy to be discreet. Dr. Burney wept over the book in rapture. Daddy Crisp shook his fist at his Fannikin in affectionate anger at not having been admitted to her confidence. The truth was whispered to Mrs. Thrale ; and then it began to spread fast.

The book had been admired while it was ascribed to men of letters long conversant with the world, and accustomed to composition. But when it was known that a reserved, silent young woman had produced the best work of fiction that had appeared since the death of Smollett, the acclamations were redoubled. What she had done was, indeed, extraordinary. But, as usual, various

reports improved the story till it became miraculous. Evelina, it was said, was the work of a girl of seventeen. Incredible as this tale was, it continued to be repeated down to our own time. Frances was too honest to confirm it. Probably she was too much a woman to contradict it ; and it was long before any of her detractors thought of this mode of annoyance. Yet there was no want of low minds and bad hearts in the generation which witnessed her first appearance. There was the envious Kenrick and the savage Wolcot, the asp George Steevens and the polecat John Williams. It did not, however, occur to them to search the parish-register of Lynn, in order that they might be able to twit a lady with having concealed her age. That truly chivalrous exploit was reserved for a bad writer of our own time, whose spite she had provoked by not furnishing him with materials for a worthless edition of Boswell's life of Johnson, some sheets of which our readers have doubtless seen round parcels of better books.

But we must return to our story. The triumph was complete. The timid and obscure girl found herself on the highest pinnacle of fame. Great men, on whom she had gazed at a distance with humble reverence, addressed her with admiration, tempered by the tenderness due to her sex and age. Burke, Windham, Gibbon, Reynolds, Sheridan, were among her most ardent eulogists. Cumberland acknowledged her merit, after his fashion, by biting his lips and wriggling in his chair whenever her name was mentioned. But it was at Streatham that she tasted, in the highest perfection, the sweets of flattery, mingled with the sweets of friendship. Mrs. Thrale, at that height of prosperity and popularity—with gay spirits, quick wit, showy though superficial acquirements, pleasing though not refined manners, a singularly amiable temper, and a loving heart—felt towards Fanny as towards a younger sister. With the Thrales Johnson was domesticated. He was an old friend of Dr. Burney ; but he had probably taken little notice of Dr. Burney's daughters, and Fanny, we imagine, had never in her life dared to speak to him, unless to ask whether he wanted ed a nineteenth or a twentieth cup of tea. He was charmed by her tale, and preferred it to the novels of Fielding, to whom, indeed, he had always been grossly unjust. He did not, indeed, carry his partiality so far as to place Evelina by the side of Clarissa and Sir Charles Grandison ; yet he said that his little favourite had done enough to have made even Richardson feel uneasy. With Johnson's cordial approbation of the book was mingled a fondness, half gallant half paternal, for the writer; and this fondness his age and character entitled him to show without restraint. He began by putting her hand to his lips. But soon he clasped her in his huge arms, and implored her to be a good girl. She was his pet, his dear love, his dear little Burney, his little character-monger. At one time, he broke forth in praise of the good taste of her caps. At another time, he insisted on teaching her Latin. That, with all his coarseness and irritability, he was a man of sterling benevolence, has long been acknowledged. But how gentle and endearing his deportment could be, was not known till the Recollections of Madame D'Arblay were published.

We have mentioned a few of the most eminent of those who paid their homage to the author of Evelina. The crowd of inferior admirers would require a catalogue as long as that in the second book of the Iliad. In that catalogue would be Mrs. Cholmondeley, the sayer of odd things, and Seward, much given to yawning, and Baretti, who slew the man in the Haymarket, and Paoli, talking broken English, and Langton, taller by the head than any other member of the club, and Lady Millar, who kept a vase wherein fools were wont to put bad verses, and Jerningham, who wrote verses fit to be put into the vase of Lady Millar, and Dr. Franklin—not, as some have dreamed, the great Pennsylvanian Dr. Franklin, who could not then have paid his respects to Miss Burney without much risk of being hanged, drawn and quartered, but Dr. Franklin the less—

Αἴας
μείων, οὔτι τόσος γε ὅσος Τελαμώνιος Αἴας,
ἀλλὰ πολὺ μείων·

It would not have been surprising if such success had turned even a strong head, and corrupted even a generous and affectionate nature. But, in the Diary, we can find no trace of any feeling inconsistent with a truly modest and amiable disposition. There is, indeed, abundant proof that Frances enjoyed, with an intense, though a troubled joy, the honours which her genius had won; but it is equally clear that her happiness sprang from the happiness of her father, her sister, and her dear Daddy Crisp. While flattered by the great, the opulent, and the learned, while followed along the Steyne at Brighton and the Pantiles at Tunbridge Wells by the gaze of admiring crowds, her heart seems to have been still with the little domestic circle in St. Martin's Street. If she recorded with minute diligence all the compliments, delicate and coarse, which she heard, wherever she turned, she recorded them for the eyes of two or three persons who had loved her from her infancy, who had loved her in obscurity, and to whom her fame gave the purest and most exquisite delight. Nothing can be more unjust than to confound these outpourings of a kind heart, sure of perfect sympathy, with the egotism of a blue-stocking, who prates to all who come near her about her own novel or her own volume of sonnets.

It was natural that the triumphant issue of Miss Burney's first venture should tempt her to try a second. Evelina, though it had raised her fame, had added nothing to her fortune. Some of her friends urged her to write for the stage. Johnson promised to give her his advice as to the composition. Murphy, who was supposed to understand the temper of the pit as well as any man of his time, undertook to instruct her as to stage effect. Sheridan declared that he would accept a play from her without even reading it. Thus encouraged she wrote a comedy named The Witlings. Fortunately it was never acted or printed. We can, we think, easily perceive from the little which is said on the subject in the Diary, that The Witlings would have been damned, and that Murphy and Sheridan thought so, though they were too polite to say so. Happily Frances had a friend who was not afraid to give her pain. Crisp, wiser for her than he had been for himself, read the manuscript in his lonely retreat, and manfully told her that she had failed, that to remove blemishes here and there would be useless, that the piece had abundance of wit but no interest, that it was bad as a whole, that it would remind every reader of the *Femmes Savantes*, which, strange to say, she had never read, and that she could not sustain so close a comparison with Molière. This opinion, in which Dr. Burney concurred, was sent to Frances in what she called 'a hissing, groaning, cat-calling epistle.' But she had too much sense not to know that it was better to be hissed and cat-called by her Daddy, than by a whole sea of heads in the pit of Drury-Lane Theatre; and she had too good a heart not to be grateful for so rare an act of friendship. She returned an answer which shows how well she deserved to have a judicious, faithful, and affectionate adviser. 'I intend,' she wrote, ' to console myself for your censure, by this greatest proof I have ever received of the sincerity, candour, and, let me add, esteem, of my dear daddy. And as I happen to love myself rather more than my play, this consolation is not a very trifling one. This, however, seriously I do believe, that when my two daddies put their heads together to concert that hissing, groaning, cat-calling epistle they sent me, they felt as sorry for poor little Miss Bayes as she could possibly do for herself. You see I do not attempt to repay your frankness with the air of pretended carelessness. But, though somewhat disconcerted just now, I will promise not to let my vexation live out another day. Adieu, my dear daddy! I won't be mortified, and I won't be *downed ;* but I will be proud to find I have, out of my own family, as well as in it, a friend who loves me well enough to speak plain truth to me.'

Frances now turned from her dramatic schemes to an undertaking far better suited to her talents. She determined to write a new tale, on a plan excellently contrived for the display of the powers in which her superiority to other writers lay. It was in truth a grand and various picture-gallery, which presented to the eye a long series of men and women, each marked by some strong peculiar feature. There were avarice and prodigality, the pride of blood and the pride of money, morbid restlessness and morbid apathy, frivolous garrulity, supercilious silence, a Democritus to laugh at everything, and a Heraclitus to lament over everything. The work proceeded fast, and in twelve months was completed. It wanted something of the simplicity which had been amongst the most attractive charms of Evelina; but it furnished ample proof that the four years which had elapsed since Evelina appeared, had not been unprofitably spent. Those who saw Cecilia in manuscript pronounced it the best novel of the age. Mrs. Thrale laughed and wept over it. Crisp was even vehement in applause, and offered to insure the rapid and complete success of the book for half a crown. What Miss Burney received for the copyright is not mentioned in the Diary; but we have observed several expressions from which we infer that the sum was considerable. That the sale would be great nobody could doubt; and Frances now had shrewd and experienced advisers, who would not suffer her to wrong herself. We have been told that the publishers gave her two thousand pounds, and we have no doubt that they might have given a still larger sum without being losers.

Cecilia was published in the summer of 1782. The curiosity of the town was intense. We have been informed by persons who remember those days, that no romance of Sir Walter Scott was more impatiently awaited, or more eagerly snatched from the counters of the booksellers. High as public expectation was, it was amply satisfied; and Cecilia was placed, by general acclamation, among the classical novels of England.

Miss Burney was now thirty. Her youth had been singularly prosperous; but clouds soon began to gather over that clear and radiant dawn. Events deeply painful to a heart so kind as that of Frances, followed each other in rapid succession. She was first called upon to attend the death-bed of her best friend, Samuel Crisp. When she returned to St. Martin's Street, after performing this melancholy duty, she was appalled by hearing that Johnson had been struck with paralysis; and, not many months later, she parted from him for the last time with solemn tenderness. He wished to look on her once more; and on the day before his death she long remained in tears on the stairs leading to his bed-room, in the hope that she might be called in to receive his blessing. But he was then sinking fast, and, though he sent her an affectionate message, was unable to see her. But this was not the worst. There are separations far more cruel than those which are made by death. Frances might weep with proud affection for Crisp and Johnson. She had to blush as well as to weep for Mrs. Thrale.

Life, however, still smiled upon her. Domestic happiness, friendship, independence, leisure, letters, all these things were hers; and she flung them all away.

Among the distinguished persons to whom Miss Burney had been introduced, none appears to have stood higher in her regard than Mrs. Delany. This lady was an interesting and venerable relique of a past age. She was the niece of George Granville Lord Lansdowne, who, in his youth, exchanged verses and compliments with Edmund Waller, and who was among the first to applaud the opening talents of Pope. She had married Dr. Delany, a man known to his contemporaries as a profound scholar and an eloquent preacher, but remembered in our time chiefly as one of the small circle in which the fierce spirit of Swift, tortured by disappointed ambition, by remorse, and by the approaches of madness, sought for amusement and repose. Doctor Delany had long been dead. His widow, nobly descended, eminently accomplished, and retaining, in spite of the infirmities of advanced age, vigour of her faculties and the serenity of her temper, enjoyed and deserved the favour of the royal family. She had a pension of three hundred a-year; and a house at Windsor, belonging to the crown, had been fitted up for her accommodation. At this house the King and Queen sometimes called, and found a very natural pleasure in thus catching an occasional glimpse of the private life of English families.

In December, 1785, Miss Burney was on a visit to Mrs. Delany at Windsor. The dinner was over. The old lady was taking a nap. Her grand-niece, a little girl of seven, was playing at some Christmas game with the visitors, when the door opened, and a stout-gentleman entered unannounced, with a star on his breast, and 'What? what? what?' in his mouth. A cry of 'The King' was set up. A general scampering followed. Miss Burney owns that she could not have been more terrified if she had seen a ghost. But Mrs. Delany came forward to pay her duty to her royal friend, and the disturbance was quieted. Frances was then presented, and underwent a long examination and cross-examination about all that she had written and all that she meant to write. The Queen soon made her appearance, and his Majesty repeated, for the benefit of his consort, the information which he had extracted from Miss Burney. The good-nature of the royal pair might have softened even the authors of the Probationary Odes, and could not but be delightful to a young lady who had been brought up a Tory. In a few days the visit was repeated. Miss Burney was more at ease than before. His Majesty, instead of seeking for information, condescended to impart it, and passed sentence on many great writers, English and foreign. Voltaire he pronounced a monster. Rousseau he liked rather better. 'But was there ever,' he cried, 'such stuff as great part of Shakspeare? Only one must not say so. But what think you? What? Is there not sad stuff? What? What?'

The next day Frances enjoyed the privilege of listening to some equally valuable criticism uttered by the Queen touching Goethe and Klopstock, and might have learned an important lesson of economy from the mode in which her Majesty's library had been formed. 'I picked the book up on a stall,' said the Queen. 'Oh, it is amazing what good books there are on stalls!' Mrs. Delany, who seems to have understood from these words that her Majesty was in the habit of exploring the booths of Moorsfield and Holywell Street in person, could not suppress an exclamation of surprise. 'Why,' said the Queen, 'I don't pick them up myself. But I have a servant very clever; and, if they are not to be had at the booksellers, they are not for me more than for another.' Miss Burney describes this conversation as delightful; and indeed, we cannot wonder that, with her literary tastes, she should be delighted at hearing in how magnificent a manner the greatest lady in the land encouraged literature.

The truth is, that Frances was fascinated by the condescending kindness of the two great personages to whom she had been presented. Her father was even more infatuated than herself. The result was a step of which we cannot think with patience, but which, recorded as it is, with all its consequences, in these volumes, deserves at least this praise, that it has furnished a most impressive warning.

A German lady of the name of Haggerdorn, one of the keepers of the Queen's robes, retired about this time; and her Majesty offered the vacant post to Miss Burney. When we consider that Miss Burney was decidedly the most popular writer of fictitious narrative then living, that competence, if not opulence, was within her reach, and that she was more than usually happy in her domestic circle, and when we compare the sacrifice which she was invited to make with the remuneration which was held out to her, we are divided between laughter and indignation.

What was demanded of her was, that she should consent to be almost as completely separated from her family and friends as if she had gone to Calcutta, and almost as close a prisoner as if she had been sent to jail for a libel; that with talents which had instructed and delighted the highest living minds, she should now be employed only in mixing snuff and sticking pins; that she should be summoned by a waiting-woman's bell to a waiting-woman's duties; that she should pass her whole life under the restraints of a paltry etiquette, should sometimes fast till she was ready to swoon with hunger, should sometimes stand till her knees gave way with fatigue; that she should not dare to speak or move without considering how her mistress might like her words and gestures. Instead of those distinguished men and women, the flower of all political parties, with whom she had been in the habit of mixing on terms of equal friendship, she was to have for her perpetual companion the chief keeper of the robes, an old hag from Germany, of mean understanding, of insolent manners, and of temper which, naturally savage, had now been exasperated by disease. Now and then, indeed, poor Frances might console herself for the loss of Burke's and Windham's society, by joining in the 'celestial colloquy sublime' of his Majesty's Equerries.

And what was the consideration for which she was to sell herself into slavery? A peerage in her own right? A pension of two thousand a-year for life? A seventy-four for her brother in the navy? A deanery for her brother in the Church? Not so. The price at which she was valued was her board, her lodging, the attendance of a man-servant, and two hundred pounds a-year.

The man who, even when hard pressed by hunger, sells his birthright for a mess of pottage, is unwise. But what shall we say of him who parts with his birthright, and does not get even the pottage in return? It is not necessary to inquire whether opulence be an adequate compensation for the sacrifice of bodily and mental freedom; for Frances Burney paid for leave to be a prisoner and menial. It was evidently understood as one of the terms of her engagement, that, while she was a member of the royal household, she was not to appear before the public as an author: and, even had there been no such understanding, her avocations were such as left her no leisure for any considerable intellectual effort. That her place was incompatible with her literary pursuits, was indeed frankly acknowledged by the King when she resigned.' 'She has given up,' he said, 'five years of her pen.' That during those five years she might, without painful exertion—without any exertion that would not have been a pleasure—have earned enough to buy an annuity for life much larger than the precarious salary which she received at court, is quite certain. The same income, too, which in St. Martin's Street would afford her every comfort, must have been found scanty at St. James's. We cannot venture to speak confidently of the price of millinery and jewellery; but we are greatly deceived if a lady who had to attend Queen Charlotte on many public occasions, could possibly save a farthing out of a salary of two hundred a-year. The principle of the arrangement was, in short, simply this, that Frances Burney should become a slave, and should be rewarded by being made a beggar.

With what object their Majesties brought her to their palace, we must own ourselves unable to conceive. Their object could not be to encourage her literary exertions; for they took her from a situation in which it was almost certain she would write, and put her into a situation in which it was impossible for her to write. Their object could not be to promote her pecuniary interest; for they took her from a situation where she was likely to become rich, and put her into a situation in which she could not but continue poor. Their object could not be to obtain an eminently useful waiting-maid; for it is clear that, though Miss Burney was the only woman of her time who could have described the death of Harrel, thousands might have been found more expert in tying ribands and filling snuff-boxes. To grant her a pension on the civil list would have been an act of judicious liberality, honourable to the court. If this was impracticable, the next best thing was to let her alone. That the King and Queen meant her nothing but kindness, we do not in the least doubt. But their kindness was the kindness of persons raised high above the mass of mankind, accustomed to be addressed with profound deference, accustomed to see all who approach them modified by their coldness and elated by their smiles. They fancied that to be noticed by them, to be near them, to serve them, was in itself a kind of happiness; and that Frances Burney ought to be full of gratitude for being permitted to purchase, by the surrender of health, wealth, freedom, domestic affection, and literary fame, the privilege of standing behind a royal chair, and holding a pair of royal gloves.

And who can blame them? Who can wonder that Princes should be under such a delusion, when they are encouraged in it by the very persons who suffer from it most cruelly? Was it to be expected that George the Third and Queen Charlotte should understand the interest of Frances Burney better, or promote it with more zeal, than herself and her father? No deception was practised. The conditions of the house of bondage were set forth with all simplicity. The hook was presented without a bait; the net was spread in the sight of the bird. And the naked hook was greedily swallowed; and the silly bird made haste to entangle herself in the net.

It is not strange indeed that an invitation to court should have caused a fluttering in the bosom of an inexperienced woman. But it was the duty of the parent to watch over the child, and to show her that on the one side were only infantine vanities and chimerical hopes, on the other liberty, peace of mind, affluence, social enjoyments, honourable distinctions. Strange to say, the only hesitation was on the part of Frances. Dr. Burney was transported out of himself with delight. Not such are the raptures of a Circassian father who has sold his pretty daughter well to a Turkish slave-merchant. Yet Dr. Burney was an amiable man, a man of good abilities, a man who had seen much of the world. But he seems to have thought that going to court was like going to heaven: that to see Princes and Princesses was a kind of beatific vision; that the exquisite felicity enjoyed by royal persons was not confined to themselves, but was communicated by some mysterious efflux or reflection to all who were suffered to stand at their toilettes, or to bear their trains. He overruled all his daughter's objections, and himself escorted her to her prison. The door closed. The key was turned. She, looking back with tender regret on all that she had left, and forward with anxiety and terror to the new life on which she was entering, was unable to speak or stand; and he went on his way homeward rejoicing in her marvellous prosperity.

And now began a slavery of five years, of five years taken from the best part of life, and wasted in menial drudgery or in recreations duller than even menial drudgery, under galling restraints and amidst unfriendly or uninteresting companions. The history of an ordinary day was this: Miss Burney had to rise and dress herself early, that she might be ready to answer the royal bell, which rang at half-after seven. Till about eight she attended in the Queen's dressing-room, and had the honour of lacing her august mistress's stays, and of putting on the hoop, gown, and neck-handkerchief. The morning was chiefly spent in rummaging drawers and laying fine clothes in their proper places. Then the Queen was to be powdered and dressed for the day. Twice a week her Majesty's hair was curled and craped; and this operation appears to have added a full hour to the business of the toilette. It was generally three before Miss Burney was at liberty. Then she had two hours at her own disposal. To these hours we owe great part of her Diary. At five she had to attend her colleague, Madame Schwellenberg, a hateful old toad-eater, as illiterate as a chambermaid, as proud as a whole German Chapter, rude, peevish, unable to bear solitude, unable to conduct herself with common decency in society. With this delightful associate Frances Burney had to dine, and pass the evening. The pair generally remained together from five to eleven; and often had no other company the whole time, except during the hour from eight to nine, when the Equerries came to tea. If poor Frances attempted to escape to her own apartment, and to forget her wretchedness over a book, the execrable old woman railed and stormed, and complained that she was neglected. Yet, when Frances stayed, she was constantly assailed with insolent reproaches. Literary fame was, in the eyes of the German crone, a blemish, a proof that the person who enjoyed it was meanly born, and out of the pale of good society. All her scanty stock of broken English was employed to express the contempt with which she regarded the author of Evelina and Cecilia. Frances detested cards, and indeed knew nothing about them; but she soon found that the least miserable way of passing an evening with Madame Schwellenberg was at the card-table, and consented, with patient sadness, to give hours, which might have called forth the laughter and the tears of many generations, to the king of clubs and the knave of spades. Between eleven and twelve the bell rang again. Miss Burney had to

pass twenty minutes or half an hour in undressing the Queen, and was then at liberty to retire, and dream that she was chatting with her brother by the quiet hearth in St. Martin's Street, that she was the centre of an admiring assembly at Mrs. Crewe's, that Burke was calling her the first woman of the age, or that Dilly was giving her a cheque for two thousand guineas.

Men, we suppose, are less patient than women; for we are utterly at a loss to conceive how any human being could endure such a life, while there remained a vacant garret in Grub Street, a crossing in want of a sweeper, a parish workhouse, or a parish vault. And it was for such a life that Frances Burney had given up liberty and peace, a happy fire side, attached friends, a wide and splendid circle of acquaintance, intellectual pursuits in which she was qualified to excel, and the sure hope of what to her would have been affluence.

There is nothing new under the sun. The last great master of Attic eloquence and Attic wit, has left us a forcible and touching description of the misery of a man of letters, who, lured by hopes similar to those of Frances, had entered the service of the magnates of Rome: 'Unhappy that I am,' cries the victim of his own childish ambition, 'would nothing content me but that I must leave mine old pursuits and mine old companions, and the life which was without care, and the sleep which had no limit save mine own pleasure, and the walks which I was free to take where I listed, and fling myself into the lowest pit of a dungeon like this? And, O God! for what? Is this the bait which enticed me? Was there no way by which I might have enjoyed in freedom comforts even greater than those which I now earn by servitude? Like a lion which has been made so tame that men may lead him about with a thread, I am dragged up and down, with broken and humbled spirit, at the heels of those to whom, in mine own domain, I should have been an object of awe and wonder. And, worst of all, I feel that here I gain no credit, that here I give no pleasure. The talents and accomplishments, which charmed a far different circle, are here out of place. I am rude in the arts of palaces, and can ill bear comparison with those whose calling, from their youth up, has been to flatter and to sue. Have I then, two lives, that, after I have wasted one in the service of others, there may yet remain to me a second, which I may live unto myself?'

Now and then, indeed, events occurred which disturbed the wretched monotony of Frances Burney's life. The court moved from Kew to Windsor, and from Windsor back to Kew. One dull colonel went out of waiting, and another dull colonel came into waiting. An impertinent servant made a blunder about tea, and caused a misunderstanding between the gentlemen and the ladies. A half-witted French Protestant minister talked oddly about conjugal fidelity. An unlucky member of the household mentioned a passage in the Morning Herald reflecting on the Queen, and forthwith Madame Schwellenberg began to storm in bad English, and told him that he made her 'what you call perspire !'

A more important occurrence was the royal visit to Oxford. Miss Burney went in the Queen's train to Nuneham, was utterly neglected there in the crowd, and could with difficulty find a servant to show the way to her bed-room, or a hairdresser to arrange her curls. She had the honour of entering Oxford in the last of a long string of carriages which formed the royal procession, of walking after the Queen all day through refectories and chapels, and of standing, half-dead with fatigue and hunger, while her august mistress was seated at an excellent cold collation. At Magdalene College, Frances was left for a moment in a parlour, where she sank down on a chair. A good-natured Equerry saw that she was exhausted, and shared with her some apricots and bread, which he had wisely put into his pockets. At that moment the door opened; the Queen entered; the wearied attendants sprang up; the bread and fruit were hastily concealed. 'I found,' says poor Miss Burney, 'that our appetites were to be supposed annihilated, at the same moment that our strength was to be invincible.'

Yet Oxford, seen even under such disadvantages, 'revived in her,' to use her own words, 'a consciousness to pleasure which had long lain nearly dormant.' She forgot, during one moment, that she was a waitingmaid, and felt as a woman of true genius might be expected to feel amidst venerable remains of antiquity, beautiful works of art, vast repositories of knowledge, and memorials of the illustrious dead. Had she still been what she was before her father induced her to take the most fatal step of her life, we can easily imagine what pleasure she would have derived from a visit to the noblest of English cities. She might, indeed, have been forced to travel back in a hack-chaise, and might not have worn so fine a gown of Chambery gauze as that in which she tottered after the royal party; but with what delight would she have then paced the cloisters of Magdalene, compared the antique gloom of Merton with the splendour of Christ Church, and looked down from the dome of the Radcliffe Library on the magnificent sea of turrets and battlements below ! How gladly would learned men have laid aside for a few hours Pindar's Odes and Aristotle's Ethics, to escort the author of Cecilia from college to college ? What neat little banquets would she have found set out in their monastic cells ? With what eagerness would pictures, medals, and illuminated missals have been brought forth from the most mysterious cabinets for her amusement ? How much she would have had to hear and to tell about Johnson as she walked over Pembroke, and about Reynolds in the ante chapel of New College ! But these indulgences were not for one who had sold herself into bondage.

About eighteen months after the visit to Oxford, another event diversified the wearisome life which Frances led at court. Warren Hastings was brought to the bar of the House of Peers. The Queen and Princesses were present when the trial commenced, and Miss Burney was permitted to attend. During the subsequent proceedings a day-rule for the same purpose was occasionally granted to her ; for the Queen took the strongest interest in the trial, and, when she could not go herself to Westminster Hall, liked to receive a report of what passed from a person who had singular powers of observation, and who was, moreover, personally acquainted with some of the most distinguished managers. The portion of the Diary which relates to this celebrated proceeding is lively and picturesque. Yet we read it, we own, with pain ; for it seems to us to prove that the fine understanding of Frances Burney was beginning to feel the pernicious influence of a mode of life which is as incompatible with health of mind as the air of the Pontine marshes with health of body. From the first day she espouses the cause of Hastings with a presumptuous vehemence and acrimony, quite inconsistent with the modesty and suavity of her ordinary deportment. She shudders when Burke enters the Hall at the head of the Commons. She pronounces him the cruel oppressor of an innocent man. She is at a loss to conceive how the managers can look at the defendant, and not blush. Windham comes to her from the managers' box, to offer her refreshment. 'But,' says she, 'I could not break bread with him.' Then, again, she exclaims—'Ah, Mr. Windham, how came you ever engaged in so cruel, so unjust a cause ?' 'Mr. Burke saw me,' she says, 'and he bowed with the most marked civility of manner.' This, be it observed, was just after his opening speech, a speech which had produced a mighty effect, and which certainly no other orator that ever lived could have made. 'My curtsy,' she continues, 'was the most ungrateful, distant, and cold; I could not do otherwise; so hurt I felt to see him the head of such a cause.' Now; not only had Burke treated her with constant kindness, but the very last act which he performed on the day on which he was turned out of the Pay-Office, about four years before this trial, was to make Dr. Burney organist of Chelsea Hospital. When, at the Westminster election, Dr. Burney was divided between his gratitude for this favour and his Tory opinions, Burke in the noblest manner disclaimed all right to exact a sacrifice of principle. ' You have little or no obligations to me,' he wrote; ' but if you had as many as I really wish it were in my power, as it is certainly in my desire, to lay on you, I hope you do not think me capable of conferring them, in order to subject your mind or your affairs to a painful and mischievous servitude.' Was this a man to be uncivilly treated by a daughter of Dr. Burney, because she chose to differ from him respecting a vast and most complicated question, which he had studied deeply during many years, and which she had never studied at all? It is clear from Miss Burney's own statement, that when she behaved so unkindly to Mr. Burke, she did not even know of what Hastings was accused. One thing, however, she must have known, that Burke had been able to convince a House of Commons, bitterly prejudiced against him, that the charges were well founded; and that Pitt and Dundas had concurred, with Fox and Sheridan, in supporting the impeachment. Surely a woman of far inferior abilities to Miss Burney, might have been expected to see that this never could have happened unless there had been a strong case against the late Governor-General. And there was, as all reasonable men now admit, a strong case against him. That there were great public services to be set off against his great crimes, is perfectly true. But his services and his crimes were equally unknown to the lady who so confidently asserted his perfect innocence, and imputed to his accusers, that is to say, to all the greatest men of all parties in the state, not merely error, but gross injustice and barbarity.

She had, it is true, occasionally seen Mr. Hastings, and had found his manners and conversation agreeable. But surely she could not be so weak as to infer from the gentleness of his deportment in a drawing-room, that he was incapable of committing a great state crime, under the influence of ambition and revenge. A silly Miss, fresh from a boarding-school, might fall into such a mistake; but the woman who had drawn the character of Mr. Monckton should have known better.

The truth is, that she had been too long at Court. She was sinking into a slavery worse than that of the body. The iron was beginning to enter into the soul. Accustomed during many months to watch the eye of a mistress, to receive with boundless gratitude the slightest mark of royal condescension, to feel wretched at every symptom of royal displeasure, to associate only with spirits long tamed and broken in, she was degenerating into something fit for her place. Queen Charlotte was a violent partisan of Hastings; had received presents from him, and had so far departed from the severity of her virtue as to lend her countenance to his wife, whose conduct had certainly been as reprehensible as that of any of the frail beauties who were then rigidly excluded from the English Court. The King, it was well known, took the same side. To the King and Queen all the members of the household looked submissively for guidance. The impeachment, therefore, was an atrocious persecution; the managers were rascals; the defendant was the most deserving, and the worst used man in the kingdom. This was the cant of the whole palace, from Gold Stick in Waiting, down to the Table-Deckers and Yeomen of the Silver Scullery; and Miss Burney canted like the rest, though in livelier tones, and with less bitter feelings.

The account which she has given of the King's illness, contains much excellent narrative and description, and will, we think, be more valued by the historians of a future age than any equal portion of pepys' or Evelyn's Diaries. That account shows also, how affectionate and compassionate her nature was. But it shows also, we must say, that her way of life was rapidly impairing her powers of reasoning, and her sense of justice. We do not mean to discuss, in this place, the question, whether the views of Mr. Pitt or those of Mr. Fox respecting the Regency were the more correct. It is, indeed, quite needless to discuss that question: for the censure of Miss Burney falls alike on Pitt and Fox, on majority and minority. She is angry with the House of Commons for presuming to inquire whether the King was mad or not, and whether there was a chance of his recovering his senses. 'A melancholy day,' she writes; ' news bad both at home and abroad. At home the dear unhappy king still worse; abroad new examinations voted of the physicians. Good heavens! what an insult does this seem from Parliamentary power, to investigate and bring forth to the world every circumstance of such a malady as is ever held sacred to secrecy in the most private families! How indignant we all feel here no words can say.' It is proper to observe, that the motion which roused all this indignation at Kew was made by Mr. Pitt himself; and that if withstood by Mr. Pitt, it would certainly have been rejected. We see, therefore, that the loyalty of the minister, who was then generally regarded as the most heroic champion of his Prince, was lukewarm indeed when compared with the boiling zeal which filled the pages of the back-stairs and the women of the bed-chamber. Of the Regency bill, Pitt's own bill, Miss Burney speaks with horror. 'I shuddered,' she says, 'to hear it named.' And again—'Oh, how dreadful will be the day when that unhappy bill takes place! I cannot approve the plan of it.' The truth is, that Mr. Pitt, whether a wise and upright statesman or not, was a statesman; and whatever motives he might have for imposing restrictions on the regent, felt that in some way or other there must be some provision made for the execution of some part of the kingly office, or that no government would be left in the country. But this was a matter of which the household never thought. It never occurred, as far as we can see, to the Exons and Keepers of the Robes, that it was necessary that there should be somewhere or other a power in the state to pass laws, to preserve order, to pardon criminals, to fill up offices, to negotiate with foreign governments, to command the army and navy. Nay, these enlightened politicians, and Miss Burney among the rest, seem to have thought that any person who considered the subject with reference to the public interest, showed himself to be a bad-hearted man. Nobody wonders at this in a gentleman-usher; but it is melancholy to see genius sinking into such debasement.

During more than two years after the King's recovery, Frances dragged on a miserable existence at the palace. The consolations which had for a time mitigated the wretchedness of servitude, were one by one withdrawn. Mrs. Delany, whose society had been a great resource when the Court was at Windsor, was now dead. One of the gentlemen of the royal establishment, Colonel Digby, appears to have been a man of sense, of taste, of some reading, and of prepossessing manners. Agreeable associates were scarce in the prison-house, and he and Miss Burney were therefore naturally attached to each other. She owns that she valued him as a friend; and it would not have been strange if his attentions had led her to entertain for him a sentiment warmer than friendship. He quitted the Court, and married in a way which astonish-

ed Miss Burney greatly, and which evidently wounded her feelings, and lowered him in her esteem. The palace grew duller and duller; Madame Schwellenberg became more and more savage and insolent. And now the health of poor Frances began to give way; and all who saw her pale face, her emaciated figure, and her feeble walk, predicted that her sufferings would soon be over.

Frances uniformly speaks of her royal mistress, and of the princesses, with respect and affection. The princesses seem to have well deserved all the praise which is bestowed on them in the Diary. They were, we doubt not, most amiable women. But 'the sweet queen,' as she is constantly called in these volumes, is not by any means an object of admiration to us. She had undoubtedly sense enough to know what kind of deportment suited her high station, and self-command enough to maintain that deportment invariably. She was, in her intercourse with Miss Burney, generally gracious and affable, sometimes, when displeased, cold and reserved, but never, under any circumstances, rude, peevish or violent. She knew how to dispense, gracefully and skilfully, those little civilities which, when paid by a sovereign, are prized at many times their intrinsic value; how to pay a compliment; how to lend a book; how to ask after a relation. But she seems to have been utterly regardless of the comfort, the health, the life of her attendants, when her own convenience was concerned. Weak, feverish, hardly able to stand, Frances had still to rise before seven, in order to dress the sweet queen, and to sit up till midnight in order to undress the sweet queen. The indisposition of the handmaid could not, and did not, escape the notice of her royal mistress. But the established doctrine of the Court was, that all sickness was to be considered as a pretence until it proved fatal. The only way in which the invalid could clear herself from the suspicion of malingering, as it is called in the army, was to go on lacing and unlacing, till she dropped down dead at the royal feet. 'This,' Miss Burney wrote, when she was suffering cruelly from sickness, watching, and labour, 'is by no means from hardness of heart; far otherwise. There is no hardness of heart in any one of them; but it is prejudice, and want of personal experience.'

Many strangers sympathized with the bodily and mental sufferings of this distinguished woman. All who saw her, saw that her frame was sinking, that her heart was breaking. The last, it should seem, to observe the change was her father. At length, in spite of himself, his eyes were opened. In May,

1790, his daughter had an interview of three hours with him, the only long interview which they had had since he took her to Windsor in 1786. She told him that she was miserable, that she was worn with attendance and want of sleep, that she had no comfort in life, nothing to love, nothing to hope, that her family and friends were to her as though they were not, and were remembered by her as men remember the dead. From daybreak to midnight the same killing labour, the same recreations, more hateful than labour itself, followed each other without variety, without any interval of liberty and repose.

The Doctor was greatly dejected by this news; but was too good-natured a man not to say that, if she wished to resign, his house and arms were open to her. Still, however, he could not bear to remove her from the Court. His veneration for royalty amounted in truth to idolatry. It can be compared only to the grovelling superstition of those Syrian devotees who made their children pass through the fire to Moloch. When he induced his daughter to accept the place of Keeper of the Robes, he entertained, as she tells us, a hope that some worldly advantage or other, not set down in the contract of service, would be the result of her connection with the Court. What advantage he expected we do not know, nor did he probably know himself. But, whatever he expected, he certainly got nothing. Miss Burney had been hired for board, lodging, and two hundred a-year. Board, lodging, and two hundred a-year, she had duly received. We have looked carefully through the Diary, in the hope of finding some trace of those extraordinary benefactions on which the Doctor reckoned. But we can discover only a promise, never performed, of a gown; and for this promise Miss Burney was expected to return thanks, such as might have suited the beggar with whom St. Martin, in the legend, divided his cloak. The experience of four years was, however, insufficient to dispel the illusion which had taken possession of the Doctor's mind; and, between the dear father and the sweet queen, there seemed to be little doubt that some day or other Frances would drop down a corpse. Six months had elapsed since the interview between the parent and the daughter. The resignation was not sent in. The sufferer grew worse and worse. She took bark; but it soon ceased to produce a beneficial effect. She was stimulated with wine; she was soothed with opium; but in vain. Her breath began to fail. The whisper that she was in a decline spread through the Court. The pains in her side became so severe that

she was forced to crawl from the card-table of the old fury to whom she was tethered, three or four times in an evening, for the purpose of taking hartshorn. Had she been a negro slave, a humane planter would have excused her from work. But her Majesty showed no mercy. Thrice a day the accursed bell still rang; the Queen was still to be dressed for the morning at seven, and to be dressed for the day at noon, and to be undressed at eleven at night.

But there had arisen, in literary and fashionable society, a general feeling of compassion for Miss Burney, and of indignation against both her father and the Queen. 'Is it possible,' said a great French lady to the Doctor, 'that your daughter is in a situation where she is never allowed a holiday?' Horace Walpole wrote to Frances to express his sympathy. Boswell, boiling over with good-natured rage, almost forced an entrance into the palace to see her. 'My dear ma'am, why do you stay? It won't do, ma'am; you must resign. We can put up with it no longer. Some very violent measures, I assure you, will be taken. We shall address Dr. Burney in a body.' Burke and Reynolds, though less noisy, were zealous in the same cause. Windham spoke to Dr. Burney; but found him still irresolute. 'I will set the Literary Club upon him,' cried Windham; 'Miss Burney has some very true admirers there, and I am sure they will eagerly assist.' Indeed the Burney family seem to have been apprehensive that some public affront, such as the Doctor's unpardonable folly, to use the mildest term, had richly deserved, would be put upon him. The medical men spoke out, and plainly told him that his daughter must resign or die.

At last paternal affection, medical authority, and the voice of all London crying shame, triumphed over Dr. Burney's love of courts. He determined that Frances should write a letter of resignation. It was with difficulty that, though her life was at stake, she mustered spirit to put the paper into the Queen's hands. 'I could not,' so runs the Diary, 'summon courage to present my memorial—my heart always failed me from seeing the Queen's entire freedom from such an expectation. For, though I was frequently so ill in her presence that I could hardly stand, I saw she concluded me, while life remained, inevitably hers.'

At last with a trembling hand the paper was delivered. Then came the storm. Juno, as in the Æneid, delegated the work of vengeance to Alecto. The Queen was calm and gentle; but Madame Schwellenberg raved like a maniac in the incurable ward of Bedlam. Such insolence! Such ingratitude! Such folly! Would Miss Burney bring utter destruction on herself and her family? Would she throw away the inestimable advantage of royal protection? Would she part with the privileges which, once relinquished, could never be regained? It was idle to talk of health and life. If people could not live in the palace, the best thing that could befall them was to die in it. The resignation was not accepted. The language of the medical men became stronger and stronger. Doctor Burney's parental fears were fully roused; and he explicitly declared, in a letter meant to be shown to the Queen, that his daughter must retire. The Schwellenberg raged like a wild-cat. 'A scene almost horrible ensued,' says Miss Burney. 'She was too much enraged for disguise, and uttered the most furious expressions of indignant contempt at our proceedings. I am sure she would gladly have confined us both in the Bastile, had England such a misery, as a fit place to bring us to ourselves, from a daring so outrageous against imperial wishes.' This passage deserves notice, as being the only one in the Diary, as far as we have observed, which shows Miss Burney to have been aware that she was a native of a free country, that she could not be pressed for a waiting-maid against her will, and that she had just as good a right to live, if she chose, in St. Martin's street, as Queen Charlotte had to live at St. James'.

The Queen promised that, after the next birth-day, Miss Burney should be set at liberty. But the promise was ill kept; and her Majesty showed displeasure at being reminded of it. At length Frances was informed that in a fortnight her attendance should cease. 'I heard this,' she says, 'with a fearful presentiment I should surely never go through another fortnight, in so weak and languishing and painful a state of health. . . As the time approached, the Queen's cordiality rather diminished, and traces of internal displeasure appeared sometimes, arising from an opinion I ought rather to have struggled on, live or die, than to quit her. Yet I am sure she saw how poor was my own chance, except by a change in the mode of life, and at least ceased to wonder, though she could not approve.' Sweet Queen! What noble candour, to admit that the undutifulness of people who did not think the honour of adjusting her tuckers worth the sacrifice of their own lives, was, though highly criminal, not altogether unnatural!

We perfectly understand her Majesty's contempt for the lives of others where her own pleasure was concerned. But what pleasure she can have found in having Miss Burney about her, it is not so easy to comprehend. That Miss Burney was an eminently skilful keeper of the robes is not very probable. Few women, indeed, had paid less attention to dress. Now and then, in the course of five years, she had been asked to read aloud or to write a copy of verses. But better readers might easily have been found: and her verses were worse than even the Poet-Laureate's Birth-day Odes. Perhaps that economy which was among her Majesty's most conspicuous virtues, had something to do with her conduct on this occasion. Miss Burney had never hinted that she expected a retiring pension; and indeed would gladly have given the little that she had for freedom. But her Majesty knew what the public thought, and what became her dignity. She could not for very shame suffer a woman of distinguished genius, who had quitted a lucrative career to wait on her, who had served her faithfully for a pittance during five years, and whose constitution had been impaired by labour and watching, to leave the Court without some mark of royal liberality. George the Third, who, on all occasions where Miss Burney was concerned, seems to have behaved like an honest good-natured gentleman, felt this, and said plainly that she was entitled to a provision. At length, in return for all the misery which she had undergone, and for the health which she had sacrificed, an annuity of one hundred pounds was granted to her, dependent on the Queen's pleasure.

Then the prison was opened, and Frances was free once more. Johnson, as Burke observed, might have added a striking page to his poem on the Vanity of Human Wishes, if he had lived to see his little Burney as she went into the palace and as she came out of it.

The pleasures, so long untasted, of liberty, of friendship, of domestic affection, were almost too acute for her shattered frame. But happy days and tranquil nights soon restored the health which the Queen's toilette and Madame Schwellenberg's card-table had impaired. Kind and anxious faces surrounded the invalid. Conversation the most polished and brilliant revived her spirits. Travelling was recommended to her; and she rambled by easy journeys from cathedral to cathedral, and from watering-place to watering-place. She crossed the New Forest, and visited Stonehenge and Wilton, the cliffs of Lyme, and the beautiful valley of Sidmouth. Thence she journeyed by Powderham Castle, and by the ruins of Glastonbury Abbey, to Bath, and from Bath, when the winter was approaching, returned well and cheerful to London. There she visited her old dungeon, and found her successor already far on the way to the grave, and kept to strict duty, from morning till midnight, with a sprained ankle and a nervous fever.

At this time England swarmed with French exiles driven from their country by the Revolution. A colony of these refugees settled at Juniper Hall in Surrey, not far from Norbury Park, where Mr. Lock, an intimate friend of the Burney family, resided. Frances visited Norbury, and was introduced to the strangers. She had strong prejudices against them; for her Toryism was far beyond, we do not say that of Mr. Pitt, but that of Mr. Reeves; and the inmates of Juniper Hall were all attached to the constitution of 1791, and were therefore more detested by the Royalists of the first emigration than Petion or Marat. But such a woman as Miss Burney could not long resist the fascination of that remarkable society. She had lived with Johnson and Windham, with Mrs. Montague and Mrs. Thrale. Yet she was forced to own that she had never heard conversation before. The most animated eloquence, the keenest observation, the most sparkling wit, the most courtly grace, were united to charm her. For Madame de Staël was there, and M. de Talleyrand. There too was M. de Narbonne, a noble representative of French aristocracy; and with M. de Narbonne was his friend and follower General D'Arblay, an honourable and amiable man, with a handsome person, frank soldier-like manners, and some taste for letters.

The prejudices which Frances had conceived against the constitutional royalists of France rapidly vanished. She listened with rapture to Talleyrand and Madame de Staël, joined with M. D'Arblay in execrating the Jacobins, and in weeping for the unhappy Bourbons, took French lessons from him, fell in love with him, and married him on no better provision than a precarious annuity of one hundred pounds.

Here the Diary stops for the present. We will, therefore, bring our narrative to a speedy close, by rapidly recounting the most important events which we know to have befallen Madame D'Arblay during the latter part of her life.

M. D'Arblay's fortune had perished in the general wreck of the French Revolution; and in a foreign country his talents, whatever they may have been, could scarcely make him rich. The task of providing for the family devolved on his wife. In the year 1796, she published by subscription her third novel, Camilla. It was impatiently expected by the public; and the sum which she obtained by it was, we believe, greater than had at that time been received for a novel. We have heard that she cleared more than three thousand guineas. But we give this merely as a rumour. Camilla, however, never attained popularity like that which Evelina and Cecilia had enjoyed; and it must be allowed that there was a perceptible falling off, not indeed in humour, or in power of portraying character, but in grace and in purity of style.

We have heard that about this time, a tragedy by Madame D'Arblay was performed without success. We do not know whether it was ever printed; nor indeed have we had time to make any researches into its history or merits.

During the short time which followed the treaty of Amiens, M. D'Arblay visited France. Lauriston and La Fayette represented his claims to the French government, and obtained a promise that he should be reinstated in his military rank. M. D'Arblay, however, insisted that he should never be required to serve against the countrymen of his wife. The First Consul, of course, would not hear of such a condition; and ordered the general's commission to be instantly revoked.

Madame D'Arblay joined her husband at Paris a short time before the war of 1803 broke out; and remained in France ten years, cut off from almost all intercourse with the land of her birth. At length, when Napoleon was on his march to Moscow, she with great difficulty obtained from his ministers permission to visit her own country, in company with her son, who was a native of England. She returned in time to receive the last blessing of her father, who died in his eighty-seventh year. In 1814 she published her last novel, the Wanderer, a book which no judicious friend to her memory will attempt to draw from the oblivion into which it has justly fallen. In the same year her son Alexander was sent to Cambridge. He obtained an honourable place among the wranglers of his year, and was elected a fellow of Christ's College. But his reputation at the University was higher than might be inferred from his success in academical contests. His French education had not fitted him for the examinations of the Senate-House; but in pure mathematics, we have been assured by some of his competitors that he had very few equals. He went into the Church, and it was thought likely that he would attain high eminence as a preacher; but he died before his mother. All that we have heard of him leads us to believe, that he was such a son as such a mother deserved to have. In 1832, Madame D'Arblay published the 'Memoirs of her Father;' and, on the 6th of January, 1840, she died in her eighty-eighth year.

We now turn from the life of Madame D'Arblay to her writings. There can, we apprehend, be little difference of opinion as to the nature of her merit, whatever differences may exist as to its degree. She was emphatically what Johnson called her, a character-monger. It was in the exhibition of human passions and whims that her strength lay; and in this department of art she had, we think, very distinguished skill.

But in order that we may, according to our duty as Kings-at-Arms, versed in the laws of literary precedence, marshal her to the exact seat to which she is entitled, we must carry our examination somewhat further.

There is, in one respect, a remarkable analogy between the faces and the minds of men. No two faces are alike; and yet very few faces deviate very widely from the common standard. Among the eighteen hundred thousand human beings who inhabit London, there is not one who could be taken by his acquaintance for another; yet we may walk from Paddington to Mileend without seeing one person in whom any feature is so overcharged that we turn round to stare at it. An infinite number of varieties lies between limits which are not very far asunder. The specimens which pass those limits on either side, form a very small minority.

It is the same with the characters of men. Here, too, the variety passes all enumeration. But the cases in which the deviation from the common standard is striking and grotesque, are very few. In one mind avarice predominates; in another, pride; in a third, love of pleasure—just as in one countenance the nose is the most marked feature, while in others the chief expression lies in the brow, or in the lines of the mouth. But there are very few countenances in which nose, brow, and mouth do not contribute, though in unequal degrees, to the general effect; and so there are few characters in which one overgrown propensity makes all others utterly insignificant.

It is evident that a portrait painter, who was able only to represent faces and figures such as those which we pay money to see at fairs, would not, however spirited his execution might be, take rank among the highest artists. He must always be placed below those who have skill to seize peculiarities which do not amount to deformity. The slighter those peculiarities the greater is the merit of the limner who can catch them and transfer them to his canvass. To paint Daniel Lambert or the Living Skeleton, the Pig-faced Lady or the Siamese Twins, so that nobody can mistake them, is an exploit within the reach of a sign-painter. A third-rate artist might give us the squint of Wilkes, and the depressed nose and protuberant cheeks of Gibbon. It would require a much higher degree of skill to paint two such men as Mr. Canning and Sir Thomas Lawrence, so that nobody who had ever seen them could for a moment hesitate to assign each picture to its original. Here the mere caricaturist would be quite at fault. He would find in neither face anything on which he could lay hold for the purpose of making a distinction. Two ample bald foreheads, two regular profiles, two full faces of the same oval form, would baffle his art; and he would be reduced to the miserable shift of writing their names at the foot of his picture. Yet there was a great difference; and a person who had seen them once, would no more have mistaken one of them for the other than he would have mistaken Mr. Pitt for Mr. Fox. But the difference lay in delicate lineaments and shades, reserved for pencils of a rare order.

This distinction runs through all the imitative arts. Foote's mimicry was exquisitely ludicrous, but it was all caricature. He could take off only some strange peculiarity, a stammer or a lisp, a Northumbrian burr or an Irish brogue, a stoop or a shuffle. 'If a man,' said Johnson, 'hops on one leg, Foote can hop on one leg.' Garrick, on the other hand, could seize those differences of manner and pronunciation, which, though highly characteristic, are yet too slight to be described. Foote, we have no doubt, could have made the Haymarket Theatre shake with laughter by imitating a dialogue between a Scotchman and a Somersetshireman. But Garrick could have imitated a dialogue between two fashionable men, both models of the best breeding, Lord Chesterfield for example, and Lord Albemarle; so that no person could doubt which was which, although no person could say that, in any point, either Lord Chesterfield or Lord Albemarle spoke or moved otherwise than in conformity with the usages of the best society.

The same distinction is found in the drama and in fictitious narrative. Highest among those who have exhibited human nature by means of dialogue, stands Shakspeare. His variety is like the variety of nature, endless diversity, scarcely any monstrosity. The characters, of which he has given us an impression, as vivid as that which we receive from the characters of our own associates, are to be reckoned by scores. Yet in all these scores hardly one character is to be found which deviates widely from the common standard, and which we should call very eccentric if we met it in real life. The silly notion that every man has one ruling passion, and that this clue, once known, unravels all the mysteries of his conduct, finds no countenance in the plays of Shakspeare. There man appears as he is, made up of a crowd of passions, which contend for the mastery over him, and govern him in turn. What is Hamlet's ruling passion? Or Othello's? Or Harry the Fifth's? Or Wolsey's? Or Lear's? Or Shylock's? Or Benedick's? Or Macbeth's? Or that of Cassius? Or that of Falconbridge? But we might go on for ever. Take a single example—Shylock. Is he so eager for money as to be indifferent to revenge? Or so eager for revenge as to be indifferent to money? Or so bent on both together as to be indifferent to the honour of his nation and the law of Moses? All his propensities are mingled with each other; so that, in trying to apportion to each its proper part, we find the same difficulty which constantly meets us in real life. A superficial critic may say, that hatred is Shylock's ruling passion. But how many passions have amalgamated to form that hatred? It is partly the result of wounded pride: Antonio has called him dog. It is partly the result of covetousness: Antonio has hindered him of half a million; and, when Antonio is gone, there will be no limit to the gains of usury. It is partly the result of national and religious feeling: Antonio has spit on the Jewish gaberdine; and the oath of revenge has been sworn by the Jewish Sabbath. We might go through all the characters which we have mentioned, and through fifty more in the same way; for it is the constant manner of Shakspeare to represent the human mind as lying, not under the absolute dominion of one despotic propensity, but under a mixed government, in which a hundred powers balance each other. Admirable as he was in all parts

of his art, we most admire him for this, that, while he has left us a greater number of striking portraits than all other dramatists put together, he has scarcely left us a single caricature.

Shakspeare has had neither equal nor second. But among the writers who, in the point which we have noticed, have appeared nearest to the manner of the great master, we have no hesitation in placing Jane Austen, a woman of whom England is justly proud. She has given us a multitude of characters, all, in a certain sense, common-place, all such as we meet every day. Yet they are all as perfectly discriminated from each other as if they were the most eccentric of human beings. There are, for example, four clergymen, none of whom we should be surprised to find in any parsonage in the kingdom— Mr. Edward Ferrars, Mr. Henry Tilney, Mr. Edmund Bertram, and Mr. Elton. They are all specimens of the upper part of the middle class. They have all been liberally educated. They all lie under the restraints of the same sacred profession. They are all young. They are all in love. Not one of them has any hobbyhorse, to use the phrase of Sterne. Not one has a ruling passion, such as we read of in Pope. Who would not have expected them to be insipid likenesses of each other? No such thing. Harpagon is not more unlike to Jourdain, Joseph Surface is not more unlike to Sir Lucius O'Trigger, than every one of Miss Austen's young divines to all his reverend brethren. And almost all this is done by touches so delicate, that they elude analysis, that they defy the powers of description, and that we know them to exist only by the general effect to which they have contributed.

A line must be drawn, we conceive, between artists of this class, and those poets and novelists whose skill lies in the exhibiting of what Ben Jonson called humours. The words of Ben are so much to the purpose, that we will quote them:

'When some one peculiar quality
Doth so possess a man, that it doth draw
All his affects, his spirits, and his powers,
In their confluxions all to run one way,
This may be truly said to be a humour.'

There are undoubtedly persons, in whom humours such as Ben describes have attained a complete ascendency. The avarice of Elwes, the insane desire of Sir Egerton Brydges for a barony to which he had no more right than to the crown of Spain, the malevolence which long meditation on imaginary wrongs generated in the gloomy mind of Bellingham, are instances. The feeling which animated Clarkson and other virtuous men against the slave-trade and slavery, is an instance of a more honourable kind.

Seeing that such humours exist, we cannot deny that they are proper subjects for the imitations of art. But we conceive that the imitation of such humours, however skilful and amusing, is not an achievement of the highest order; and, as such humours are rare in real life, they ought, we conceive, to be sparingly introduced into works which profess to be pictures of real life. Nevertheless, a writer may show so much genius in the exhibition of these humours, as to be fairly entitled to a distinguished and permanent rank among classics. The chief seats, however, of all the places on the dais and under the canopy, are reserved for the few who have excelled in the difficult art of portraying characters in which no single feature is extravagantly overcharged.

If we have expounded the law soundly, we can have no difficulty in applying it to the particular case before us. Madame D'Arblay has left us scarcely anything but humours. Almost every one of her men and women has some propensity developed to a morbid degree. In Cecilia, for example, Mr. Delvile never opens his lips without some allusion to his own birth and station; or Mr. Briggs, without some allusion to the hoarding of money; or Mr. Hobson, without betraying the self-indulgence and self-importance of a purse-proud upstart; or Mr. Simpkins, without uttering some sneaking remark for the purpose of currying favour with his customers; or Mr. Meadows, without expressing apathy and weariness of life; or Mr. Albany, without declaiming about the vices of the rich and the misery of the poor; or Mrs. Belfield, without some indelicate eulogy on her son; or Lady Margaret, without indicating jealousy of her husband. Morrice is all skipping, officious impertinence, Mr. Gosport all sarcasm, Lady Honoria all lively prattle, Miss Larolles all silly prattle. If ever Madame D'Arblay aimed at more, as in the character of Monckton, we do not think that she succeeded well.

We are, therefore, forced to refuse to Madame D'Arblay a place in the highest rank of art; but we cannot deny that, in the rank to which she belonged, she had few equals, and scarcely any superior. The variety of humours which is to be found in her novels is immense; and

though the talk of each person separately is monotonous, the general effect is not monotony, but a very lively and agreeable diversity. Her plots are rudely constructed and improbable, if we consider them in themselves. But they are admirably framed for the purpose of exhibiting striking groups of eccentric characters, each governed by his own peculiar whim, each talking his own peculiar jargon, and each bringing out by opposition the oddities of all the rest. We will give one example, out of many which occur to us. All probability is violated in order to bring Mr. Delvile, Mr. Briggs, Mr. Hobson, and Mr. Albany into a room together. But when we have them there, we soon forget probability in the exquisitely ludicrous effect which is produced by the conflict of four old fools, each raging with a monomania of his own, each talking a dialect of his own, and each inflaming all the others anew every time he opens his mouth.

Madame D'Arblay was most successful in comedy, and indeed in comedy which bordered on farce. But we are inclined to infer from some passages, both in Cecilia and Camilla, that she might have attained equal distinction in the pathetic. We have formed this judgment, less from those ambitious scenes of distress which lie near the catastrophe of each of those novels, than from some exquisite strokes of natural tenderness which take us here and there by surprise. We would mention as examples, Mrs. Hill's account of her little boy's death in Cecilia, and the parting of Sir Hugh Tyrold and Camilla, when the honest baronet thinks himself dying.

It is melancholy to think that the whole fame of Madame D'Arblay rests on what she did during the earlier half of her life, and that everything which she published during the forty-three years which preceded her death, lowered her reputation. Yet we have no reason to think that at the time when her faculties ought to have been in their maturity, they were smitten with any blight. In the Wanderer, we catch now and then a gleam of her genius. Even in the Memoirs of her Father, there is no trace of dotage. They are very bad; but they are so, as it seems to us, not from a decay of power, but from a total perversion of power.

The truth is, that Madame D'Arblay's style underwent a gradual and most pernicious change,—a change which, in degree at least, we believe to be unexampled in literary history, and of which it may be useful to trace the progress.

When she wrote her letters to Mr. Crisp, her early journals, and the novel of Evelina, her style was not indeed brilliant or energetic; but it was easy, clear, and free from all offensive faults. When she wrote Cecilia she aimed higher. She had then lived much in a circle of which Johnson was the centre; and she was herself one of his most submissive worshippers. It seems never to have crossed her mind that the style even of his best writings was by no means faultless, and that even had it been faultless, it might not be wise in her to imitate it. Phraseology which is proper in a disquisition on the Unities, or in a preface to a Dictionary, may be quite out of place in a tale of fashionable life. Old gentlemen do not criticize the reigning modes, nor do young gentlemen make love, with the balanced epithets and sonorous cadences which, on occasions of great dignity, a skilful writer may use with happy effect.

In an evil hour the author of Evelina took the Rambler for her model. This would not have been wise even if she could have imitated her pattern as well as Hawkesworth did. But such imitation was beyond her power. She had her own style. It was a tolerably good one; and might, without any violent change, have been improved into a very good one. She determined to throw it away, and to adopt a style in which she could attain excellence only by achieving an almost miraculous victory over nature and over habit. She could cease to be Fanny Burney; it was not so easy to become Samuel Johnson.

In Cecilia the change of manner began to appear. But in Cecilia the imitation of Johnson, though not always in the best taste, is sometimes eminently happy; and the passages which are so verbose as to be positively offensive, are few. There were people who whispered that Johnson had assisted his young friend, and that the novel owed all its finest passages to his hand. This was merely the fabrication of envy. Miss Burney's real excellences were as much beyond the reach of Johnson, as his real excellences were beyond her reach. He could no more have written the Masquerade scene, or the Vauxhall scene, than she could have written the Life of Cowley or the Review of Soame Jenyns. But we have not the smallest doubt that he revised Cecilia, and that he retouched the style of many passages. We know that he was in the habit of giving assistance of this kind most freely. Goldsmith, Hawkesworth,

Boswell, Lord Hailes, Mrs. Williams, were among those who obtained his help. Nay, he even corrected the poetry of Mr. Crabbe, whom, we believe, he had never seen. When Miss Burney thought of writing a comedy, he promised to give her his best counsel, though he owned that he was not particularly well qualified to advise on matters relating to the stage. We therefore think it in the highest degree improbable that his little Fanny, when living in habits of the most affectionate intercourse with him, would have brought out an important work without consulting him; and, when we look into Cecilia, we see such traces of his hand in the grave and elevated passages, as it is impossible to mistake. Before we conclude this article, we will give two or three examples.

When next Madame D'Arblay appeared before the world as a writer, she was in a very different situation. She would not content herself with the simple English in which Evelina had been written. She had no longer the friend who, we are confident, had polished and strengthened the style of Cecilia. She had to write in Johnson's manner, without Johnson's aid. The consequence was, that in Camilla every passage which she meant to be fine is detestable; and that the book has been saved from condemnation only by the admirable spirit and force of those scenes in which she was content to be familiar.

But there was to be a still deeper descent. After the publication of Camilla, Madame D'Arblay resided ten years at Paris. During those years there was scarcely any intercourse between France and England. It was with difficulty that a short letter could occasionally be transmitted. All Madame D'Arblay's companions were French. She must have written, spoken, thought, in French. Ovid expressed his fear that a shorter exile might have affected the purity of his Latin. During a shorter exile, Gibbon unlearned his native English. Madame D'Arblay had carried a bad style to France. She brought back a style which we are really at a loss to describe. It is a sort of broken Johnsonese, a barbarous *patois*, bearing the same relation to the language of Rasselas, which the gibberish of the Negroes of Jamaica bears to the English of the House of Lords. Sometimes it reminds us of the finest, that is to say, the vilest parts, of Mr. Galt's novels; sometimes of the perorations of Exeter Hall; sometimes of the leading articles of the Morning Post. But it most resembles the puffs of Mr. Rowland and Dr. Goss. It matters not what ideas are clothed in such a style. The genius of Shakspeare and Bacon united, would not save a work so written from general derision.

It is only by means of specimens that we can enable our readers to judge how widely Madame D'Arblay's three styles differed from each other.

The following passage was written before she became intimate with Johnson. It is from Evelina :

'His son seems weaker in his understanding, and more gay in his temper; but his gaiety is that of a foolish overgrown schoolboy, whose mirth consists in noise and disturbance. He disdains his father for his close attention to business and love of money, though he seems himself to have no talents, spirit, or generosity to make him superior to either. His chief delight appears to be in tormenting and ridiculing his sisters, who in return most cordially despise him. Miss Branghton, the eldest daughter, is by no means ugly; but looks proud, ill-tempered, and conceited. She hates the city, though without knowing why; for it is easy to discover she has lived nowhere else. Miss Polly Branghton is rather pretty, very foolish, very ignorant, very giddy, and, I believe, very good-natured.'

This is not a fine style, but simple, perspicuous, and agreeable. We now come to Cecilia, written during Miss Burney's intimacy with Johnson; and we leave it to our readers to judge whether the following passage was not at least corrected by his hand :—

'It is rather an imaginary than an actual evil, and, though a deep wound to pride, no offence to morality. Thus have I laid open to you my whole heart, confessed my perplexities, acknowledged my vain-glory, and exposed with equal sincerity the sources of my doubts and the motives of my decision. But now, indeed, how to proceed I know not. The difficulties which are yet to encounter I fear to enumerate, and the petition I have to urge I have scarce courage to mention. My family, mistaking ambition for honour, and rank for dignity, have long planned a splendid connection for me, to which, though my invariable repugnance has stopped any advances, their wishes and their views immovably adhere. I am but too certain they will now listen to no other. I dread, therefore, to make a trial where I despair of success. I know not how to risk a prayer with those who may silence me by a command.'

Take now a specimen of Madame D'Arblay's later style. This is the way in which she tells us that her father, on his journey back from the Continent, caught the rheumatism :—

'He was assaulted, during his precipitate return, by the rudest fierceness of wintry elemental strife; through which, with bad accommodations and innumerable accidents, he became a prey to the merciless pangs of the acutest spasmodic rheumatism, which barely suffered him to reach his home, ere, long and piteously, it confined him, a tortured prisoner, to his bed. Such was the check that almost instantly curbed, though it could not subdue, the rising pleasure of his hopes of entering upon a new species of existence—that of an approved man of letters; for it was on the bed of sickness, exchanging the light wines of France, Italy and Germany, for the black and loathsome potions of the Apothecaries' Hall, writhed by darting stitches, and burning with fiery fever, that he felt the full force of that sublunary equipoise that seems evermore to hang suspended over the attainment of long-sought and uncommon felicity, just as it is ripening to burst forth with enjoyment!'

Here is a second passage from Evelina :—

'Mrs. Selwyn is very kind and attentive to me She is extremely clever. Her understanding, indeed, may be called masculine; but unfortunately her manners deserve the same epithet. For, in studying to acquire the knowledge of the other sex, she has lost all the softness of her own. In regard to myself, however, as I have neither courage nor inclination to argue with her, I have never been personally hurt at her want of gentleness—a virtue which nevertheless seems so essential a part of the female character, that I find myself more awkward and less at ease with a woman who wants it than I do with a man.'

This is a good style of its kind; and the following passage from Cecilia is also in a good style, though not in a faultless one. We say with confidence—Either Sam Johnson or the Devil :—

'Even the impervious Mr. Delvile was more supportable here than in London. Secure in his own castle, he looked around him with a pride of power and possession which softened while it swelled him. His superiority was undisputed; his will was without control. He was not, as in the great capital of the kingdom, surrounded by competitors. No rivalry disturbed his peace; no equality mortified his greatness. All he saw were either vassals of his power, or guests bending to his pleasure. He abated, therefore, considerably the stern gloom of his haughtiness, and soothed his proud mind by the courtesy of condescension.'

We will stake our reputation for critical sagacity on this, that no such paragraph as that which we have last quoted, can be found in any of Madame D'Arblay's works except Cecilia. Compare with it the following sample of her later style :—

'If beneficence be judged by the happiness which it diffuses, whose claim, by that proof, shall stand higher than that of Mrs. Montagu, from the munificence with which she celebrated her annual festival for those hapless artificers who perform the most abject offices of any authorized calling, in being the active guardians of our blazing hearths? Not to vain-glory, then, but to kindness of heart, should be adjudged the publicity of that superb charity which made its jetty objects, for one bright morning, cease to consider themselves as degraded outcasts from all society.'

We add one or two shorter samples. Sheridan refused to permit his lovely wife to sing in public, and was warmly praised on this account by Johnson.

'The last of men,' says Madame D'Arblay, 'was Doctor Johnson to have abetted squandering the delicacy of integrity by nullifying the labours of talents.'

The club, Johnson's club, did itself no no honour by rejecting on political grounds two distinguished men, the one a Tory, the other a Whig. Madame D'Arblay tells the story thus:—'A similar ebullition of political rancour with that which so difficultly had been conquered for Mr. Canning, foamed over the ballot-box to the exclusion of Mr. Rogers.'

An offence punishable with imprisonment is, in this language, an offence 'which produces incarceration.' To be starved to death is, 'to sink from inanition into nonentity.' Sir Isaac Newton is, 'the developer of the skies in their embodied movements;' and Mrs. Thrale, when a party of clever people sat silent, is said to have been 'provoked by the dulness of a taciturnity that, in the midst of such renowned interlocutors, produced as narcotic a torpor as could have been caused by a dearth the most barren of all human faculties.' In truth, it is impossible to look at any page of Madame D'Arblay's later works, without finding flowers of rhetoric like these. Nothing in the language of those jargonists at whom Mr. Gosport laughed, nothing in the language of Sir Sedley Clarendel, approaches this new Euphuism.

It is from no unfriendly feeling to Madame D'Arblay's memory that we have expressed ourselves so strongly on the subject of her style. On the contrary, we conceive that we have really rendered a service to her reputation. That her later works were complete failures, is a fact too notorious to be dissembled; and some persons, we believe, have consequently taken up a notion that she was from the first an over-rated writer, and that she had not the powers which were necessary to maintain her on the eminence on which good luck and fashion had placed her. We believe, on the contrary, that her early popularity was no more than the just reward of distinguished merit, and would

never have undergone an eclipse, if she had only been content to go on writing in her mother-tongue. If she failed when she quitted her own province; and attempted to occupy one in which she had neither part nor lot, this reproach is common to her with a crowd of distinguished men. Newton failed when he turned from the courses of the stars, and the ebb and flow of the ocean, to apocalyptic seals and vials. Bentley failed when he turned from Homer and Aristophanes to edite Paradise Lost. Inigo failed when he attempted to rival the Gothic churches of the fourteenth century. Wilkie failed when he took it into his head that the Blind Fiddler and the Rent-Day were unworthy of his powers, and challenged competition with Lawrence as a portrait-painter. Such failures should be noted for the instruction of posterity; but they detract little from the permanent reputation of those who have really done great things.

Yet one word more. It is not only on account of the intrinsic merit of Madame D'Arblay's early works that she is entitled to honourable mention. Her appearance is an important epoch in our literary history. Evelina was the first tale written by a woman, and purporting to be a picture of life and manners, that lived or deserved to live. The Female Quixotte is no exception. That work has undoubtedly great merit, when considered as a wild satirical harlequinade; but, if we consider it as a picture of life and manners, we must pronounce it more absurd than any of the romances which it was designed to ridicule.

Indeed, most of the popular novels which preceded Evelina, were such as no lady would have written; and many of them were such as no lady could without confusion own that she had read. The very name of novel was held in horror among religious people. In decent families which did not profess extraordinary sanctity, there was a strong feeling against all such works. Sir Anthony Absolute, two or three years before Evelina appeared, spoke the sense of the great body of sober fathers and husbands, when he pronounced the circulating library an ever-green tree of diabolical knowledge. This feeling, on the part of the grave and reflecting, increased the evil from which it had sprung. The novelist, having little character to lose, and having few readers among serious people, took without scruple liberties which in our generation seem almost incredible.

Miss Burney did for the English novel

what Jeremy Collier did for the English drama; and she did it in a better way. She first showed that a tale might be written in which both the fashionable and the vulgar life of London might be exhibited with great force, and with broad comic humour, and which yet should not contain a single line inconsistent with rigid morality, oreven with virgin delicacy. She took away the reproach which lay on a most useful and delightful species of composition. She vindicated the right of her sex to an equal share in a fair and noble province of letters. Several accomplished women have followed in her track. At present, the novels which we owe to English ladies form no small part of the literary glory of our country. No class of works is more honourably distinguished by fine observation, by grace, by delicate wit, by pure moral feeling. Several among the successors of Madame D'Arblay have equalled her; two, we think, have surpassed her. But the fact that she has been surpassed, gives her an additional claim to our respect and gratitude; for in truth we owe to her, not only Evelina, Cecilia, and Camilla, but also Mansfield Park and the Absentee.

NOTE to the Article, in last Number, on the *New Biographical Dictionary* of the Society for the Diffusion of Useful Knowledge.

WE have been informed that in mentioning, in the above Article, the Biographical Dictionary of the late Dr. Aikin, we committed a mistake in stating that it was not completed, which we now very willingly correct. We had said that it stopped with letter *S*, on the conclusion of its eighth volume; whereas we find that it was actually completed, and a Supplement added, by Dr. Aikin;—the whole extending to ten volumes, of which the two last were published in 1814 and 1815. But though a valuable, it is not by any means a *universal* Biography, being professedly limited to lives of 'eminent persons,'—a very different sort of undertaking from one that aspires to notice every individual who has done anything either in Letters or Art, or in any line likely to attract the curiosity of mankind, whether eminent or not. Such we understand to be the object of the New Biographical Dictionary, and this gives it a vast superiority, in respect of plan, over that of Dr. Aikin, and every other work of the kind that has been produced or attempted in this country.

LIST OF NEW PUBLICATIONS

DURING

OCTOBER, NOVEMBER, AND DECEMBER, 1842.

Abercrombie.—Essays and Tracts. By John Abercrombie, M. D. (Collected into 1 vol). 18mo. Edinburgh, pp. 306, 4s.

Addison.—The Temple Church. By C. G. Addison, Esq., author of ' The History of the Knights Templars.' Square crown 8vo. pp. 136, with 5 plates, cloth, 5s.

Addison.—A Full and Complete Guide, Historical and Descriptive, of the Temple Church. (From Mr. Addison's ' History of the Temple Church).' Square crown 8vo. pp. 48, sewed, 1s.

Aird.—The Students' Self Instructing French Grammar; consisting of Twelve Progressive Lessons. By D. M. Aird. 2d edition, revised and enlarged, square crown 8vo. pp. 76, boards, 2s.

Alexander —Letters on the Slave-Trade, Slavery, and Emancipation; with a Reply to Objections made to the Liberation of the Slaves in the Spanish Colonies. Addressed to Friends on the Continent of Europe, during a Visit to Spain and Portugal. By G. W. Alexander. Fcp. 8vo. pp. 192, cloth, 3s. 6d.

Allee Neemroo, the Buchtiaree Adventurer: a Tale of Louristan. By J. Baillie Fraser, Esq. 3 vols. post 8vo. pp. 978, boards, 31s. 6d.

Andrewes.—The Devotions of Bishop Andrewes. Translated from the Greek, and arranged anew. Fcp. (Oxford,) pp. 152, cloth, 2s. 6d.

Angas.—A Ramble in Malta and Sicily, in the Autumn of 1841. By George French Angas. Illustrated with 14 Sketches taken on the spot, and drawn on stone by the Author. Imperial 8vo. pp. 176, with illuminated title-page, cloth, 12s.

Annals of Chemistry and Practical Pharmacy. Published Weekly. 8vo. 8d.
The chief aim of this work is to afford to the English Chemist a Weekly summary of the Discoveries of Continental Chemists, practically condensed, so that, whilst thoroughly explanatory to the philosopher, it will be practically useful to the Chemist and Druggist.

Annual Register; or, a View of the History and Politics of the Year 1841. 8vo. pp. 592, boards, 16s.

Apperley.—Nimrod Abroad. By C. J. Apperley, Esq., Author of ' The Chase, the Turf, and the Road,' &c. 2 vols. post 8vo. pp. 608, cloth, 21s.

Archbold's Summary of the Law relative to Pleading and Evidence in Criminal Cases; with the Statutes, Precedents of Indictments, &c., and the Evidence necessary to support them. 9th edition, by J. Jervis, Esq. 12mo. pp. 800, boards, 21s.

Archbold.—The Poor-Law; comprising all the Authorities, to September, 1842; with Forms. 2d edition, by J. F. Archbold, Esq., Barrister at Law. Being vol. 3 of Archbold's Justice of the Peace. 12mo. pp. 678, bds. 18s.

Aristophanis Aves, ad codicum fidem recensuit, et commentario brevi critico et exegetico instruxit F. C. Blaydes, B.A. 8vo. (Oxford,) pp. 126, cloth, 5s.

Aristophanes.—A Literal Translation of the Clouds of Aristophanes, with Greek Text and English Notes. By C. P. Gerard. 8vo. pp. 116, cloth, 5s.

Arnold.—Christian Life, its Hopes, its Fears, and its Close: Sermons, preached mostly in the Chapel of Rugby School. By the late Thomas Arnold, D. D. 8vo. pp. 484, cloth, 12s.

Arnold.—Christian Life, its Course, its Hindrances, and its Helps: Sermons, preached mostly in the Chapel of Rugby School. By the late Thomas Arnold, D.D. 2d edition, 8vo. pp. 572, cloth, 12s.

Arnold.—A Practical Introduction to Latin Prose Composition. By T. K. Arnold, M. A., Rector of Lyndon. 5th edition, 8vo. pp. 232, cloth, 6s. 6d.

Bagster.—Ἡ Καινη Διαθηκη. The New Testament: consisting of the Greek Text of Scholtz, with the Readings, both Textual and Margin-